GEORGINA CAMPBELL'S GUIDES

MW01702768

GEORGINA CAMPBELL
Jameson Guide

IRELAND 2004

The Best Places to Eat, Drink and Stay

JAMESON IRISH WHISKEY

Georgina Campbell Guides

Editor: Georgina Campbell

Georgina Campbell Guides Ltd.,
PO Box 6173
Dublin 13
Ireland

website: www.ireland-guide.com
email: info@ireland-guide.com

The contents of this book are believed to be correct at time of printing. Nevertheless, the publisher can accept no responsibility for errors or omissions or changes in the details given.

Front Cover Photographs:	King Sitric Restaurant, Howth, Co. Dublin
	Wine List of the Year 2001, Award Winner (Photograph by Harry Weir)
Spine:	Coolbawn, Co. Tipperary
Back Cover from top:	Glin Castle, Co. Limerick
	Dromoland Castle, Co. Clare
	The Merrion Hotel, Dublin
	Larkins Pub, Co. Tipperary
	Farran House, Co. Cork
	Rathmullan House, Co. Donegal

Cover Design by Chaos, Dublin
Design and Artwork by The Design Station, Dublin
Printed by ColourBooks Ltd., Dublin

First published 2003 by Georgina Campbell Guides Ltd.

ISBN: 1 903164-10-9

Georgina Campbell Guides Awards

Dunraven Arms Hotel
Hotel of the Year

The Tannery
Restaurant of the Year

Neven Maguire
Chef of the Year

The Plough
Pub of the Year

Fiacrí Country House Restaurant
Féile Bia Award

Customs House Restaurant
Seafood Restaurant of the Year

The full list of awards is on page 11

How to Use the Guide

Location/Establishment name
- Cities, towns and villages arranged in alphabetical order within counties, with the exception of Dublin, Cork, Belfast, Galway and Limerick which come first within their categories
- Establishments arranged alphabetically within location
- In Dublin city, postal codes are arranged in numerical order. Even numbers are south of the River Liffey and uneven numbers on the north, with the exception of Dublin 8 which straddles the river. Dublin 1 and 2 are most central; Dublin 1 is north of the Liffey, Dublin 2 is south of it (see map). Within each district establishments are listed in alphabetical order.

Telephone Numbers
- Codes are given for use within the Republic of Ireland/Northern Ireland. To call ROI from outside the jurisdiction, the code is +353, dropping the first digit (zero) from the local code.
- To call Northern Ireland from the Republic, replace the 048 code with 028.

Category(ies) of Establishment

Address/contact details
(please phone/fax/email ahead for additional directions if required)
- includes an email address and website address if available

Rating - for outstanding cooking and accommodation

☆	- Demi-Star: restaurant approaching full star status
★	- For cooking and service well above average
★★	- Consistent excellence, one of the best restaurants in the land
★★★	- The highest restaurant grading achievable
	- Outstanding Accommodation of its type
	- De Luxe Hotel
	- Outstanding Pub - good food and atmosphere
féile bia	- Denotes establishments committed to the Féile Bia Charter
	- Denotes members of the BIM Seafood Circle
◇	- Times/prices not confirmed at time of going to press
Ⓝ	- Establishments new to this edition of the Guide

Maps are intended for reference only; Ordnance Survey maps are recommended and available from Tourist Information Offices.

PRICES & OPENING HOURS
PLEASE NOTE THAT PRICES AND OPENING HOURS MAY HAVE CHANGED SINCE THE GUIDE WENT TO PRESS. TIMES & PRICES ARE GIVEN AS A GUIDELINE ONLY AND SHOULD BE CHECKED BEFORE TRAVELLING OR WHEN MAKING A RESERVATION.

Prices in the Republic of Ireland are given in Euro and those in Northern Ireland in pounds Sterling.

Thanks and Acknowledgements
The publication of this guide would not have been possible without the support and encouragement of a large number of organisations, companies and individuals. Particular thanks must go to all the sponsors, of course, for having faith in this sixth edition which is an all-Irish project. Those who have given invaluable assistance are too numerous to mention individually but, on behalf the Guide, I would like to thank you all.

Georgina Campbell,
Editor.

GEORGINA CAMPBELL'S GUIDES

Entries are given first for **Dublin City** and **County,** then continue in county order, as follows:

A Word from the Sponsor

by Kieran Tobin
Communications and Corporate Affairs Director
Irish Distillers Wines and Spirits

Jameson is once again delighted to be associated with a Guide which will help you to sample some of the best of Ireland's hospitality, food and drink.

Jameson, and indeed Irish Whiskey in general, is an intrinsic part of the renowned welcome and hospitality to be found in Ireland. Whiskey is woven into the fabric of Irish life, whether you are enjoying the warmth of an Irish pub, relaxing in a hotel or country house, enjoying an aperitif or relaxing after a memorable meal, there is always an appropriate occasion to savour a glass of Jameson.

As with many of the best things in Ireland, the traditions of the past are combined with the expertise of the present in the crafting of Jameson Irish Whiskey. The special qualities of Jameson are achieved through distilling the whiskey three times, ensuring a product that is particularly smooth and pure. During maturation in bourbon and sherry oak casks, which are stored for many years in dark, aromatic warehouses, Jameson mellows and takes on its rich golden colour. This combination of heritage, smoothness and expertise has helped to make Jameson the World's most popular Irish Whiskey.

A culinary revolution has taken place in Ireland over the past two decades and Irish cuisine is now taking its place among the best in the world. Good food, a personal welcome and friendly pubs are amongst the most frequently cited attractions for visitors to Ireland and these can be found in establishments, both large and small, throughout the country. Irish cuisine is widely acknowledged as using natural, pure and local ingredients combined with contemporary preparation and presentation, to achieve great things. Jameson has always set itself similar standards and uses only the finest malted and unmalted barley and pure Irish water as its principal ingredients.

I hope you will enjoy using this guide to find the best that Irish hospitality, food and – of course – Whiskey, has to offer.

Kieran Tobin

Kieran Tobin
Communications and Corporate Affairs Director

Introduction

by Georgina Campbell
Editor

Hospitality has been under the microscope during the last year in Ireland - and the public debate, on whether the Irish are as good at it as traditional thinking would have us believe, has been instructive. Attitudes to tourism in Ireland tend to be ambivalent and it is sometimes portrayed as a destructive force, attracting too many people to the wrong places and causing environmental havoc. While these dangers are all too clear, tourism can also be a positive force for good if it helps us to see Ireland as others see it and value its special features more highly, thus looking after them better and working harder to ensure that necessary development is undertaken sensitively.

By the same token, if it is true that some see Ireland as an expensive, inhospitable country that gives poor value for money, we must highlight the best examples of Irish hospitality, who lead by example. This we try to do through all our recommendations in the guide, by covering every county in Ireland and seeking out those who are offering a special experience in a wide variety of categories, ranging from luxurious hotels to rural B&Bs on the accommodation side, and from the finest restaurants in the land to cheerful neighbourhood restaurants for those looking for the right place to eat. As well as the independent leisure traveller, from Ireland or abroad, we also have the business traveller in mind - and, in contrast, it's always a particular pleasure to search out those special Irish pubs that give that enjoyment out of all proportion to their (often tiny) size.

But it is particularly through the guide's Awards that we aim to highlight shining examples of genuine hospitality throughout Ireland. All year, as we travel around assessing establishments for the next edition of this guide, we take a special interest in seeking out the very best in every category - and, as the cream rises to the top, selections are made for the Awards you will find detailed in the following pages. These Awards highlight the range and variety of establishments recommended by the guide, and also reflect a wide geographical spread; they give valuable recognition to establishments doing that extra little bit to make things special - and will, hopefully, encourage others to aim for similar achievements. For users of the guide, we hope that these leading establishments will demonstrate the best that Ireland has to offer and that you will especially enjoy visiting them.

As ever, an over-riding interest which is always in our minds is to search for a sound philosophy of food, regardless of price. We seek accomplished but simple cooking that relies on quality ingredients for its success - and many of these awards reflect that philosophy. We welcome the growing commitment to quality food, demonstrated, for example, by indicating provenance on menus and by commitment to Féile Bia, and international groups like Euro-Toques and the Slow Food movement, all of which are outlined in this guide.

We hope that you will enjoy your travels with the guide, and find it a friendly and reliable companion.

Georgina Campbell

The Best of the Best

STARRED RESTAURANTS

★★ / ★ / ☆

REPUBLIC OF IRELAND

3 Star: ★★★
Dublin, Restaurant Patrick Guilbaud

2 Star: ★★
Dublin, Thornton's

1 Star: ★
Dublin, Chapter One
Dublin, Clarence Hotel, Tea Room
Dublin, L'Ecrivain
Co Cavan, MacNean Bistro, Blacklion
Co Clare, Dromoland Castle
Co Cork, Ballymaloe House, Shanagarry
Co Cork, Longueville House, Mallow
Co Kerry, Park Hotel, Kenmare
Co Kerry, Sheen Falls Lodge, Kenmare
Co Kildare, Kildare Hotel, Straffan
Co Sligo, Cromleach Lodge, Castlebaldwin
Co Waterford, Tannery, Dungarvan

Demi-Star: ☆
Dublin, Bang Café
Dublin, Mermaid Café
Dublin, One Pico Restaurant
Co Dublin, Portmarnock Hotel, Osborne Restaurant
Co. Cavan, Oakroom Restaurant, Cavan
Co. Cavan, Olde Post Inn, Cloverhill
Cork city, Café Paradiso

Demi-Star (continued): ☆
Cork city, Fleming's
Cork city, Jacob's on the Mall
Cork city, Jacques
Cork city, Lovett's
Co Cork, Blairs Cove House, Durrus
Co Cork, Casino House, Kilbrittain
Co Cork, Customs House, Baltimore
Co Cork, Good Things, Durrus
Co Cork, Grapefruit Moon, Ballycotton
Co Cork, Toddies, Kinsale
Co Kerry, Packie's, Kenmare
Co Kerry, Lime Tree, Kenmare
Co Kerry, Restaurant David Norris, Tralee
Co Limerick, Mustard Seed at Echo Lodge, Ballingarry
Co Mayo, Ashford Castle, Cong
Co Monaghan, Nuremore Hotel, Carrickmacross
Co Wexford, Dunbrody House, Arthurstown

NORTHERN IRELAND

2 Star: ★★
Belfast, Restaurant Michael Deane

1 Star: ★
Belfast, Cayenne
Belfast, Aldens

Demi-Star: ☆
Co Down, Shanks, Bangor

DELUXE HOTELS

REPUBLIC OF IRELAND

Dublin, Berkeley Court, Ballsbridge
Dublin, The Clarence, Temple Bar
Dublin, Four Seasons Hotel, Ballsbridge
Dublin, The Merrion, Merrion Street
Dublin, Morrison, Ormond Quay
Dublin, The Shelbourne, St Stephen's Green
Dublin, The Westbury, Grafton Street
Dublin, The Westin Hotel, College Green
Cork city, Hayfield Manor Hotel
Co Clare, Dromoland Castle, Newmarket-on Fergus
Co Kerry, Park Hotel, Kenmare
Co Kerry, Sheen Falls Lodge, Kenmare
Co Kildare, Kildare Hotel, Straffan
Co Kilkenny, Mount Juliet, Thomastown
Co Limerick, Adare Manor, Adare
Co Mayo, Ashford Castle, Cong
Co Wexford, Marlfield House, Gorey

NORTHERN IRELAND
Co Down, Culloden Hotel, Holywood

OUTSTANDING ACCOMMODATION

REPUBLIC OF IRELAND

Dublin, Clarion IFSC
Dublin, The Conrad, Earslfort Terrace
Dublin, The Towers, Lansdowne Road, Ballsbridge
Co Dublin, Portmarnock Hotel & Golf Links
Cork city, Kingsley Hotel
Cork city, Maryborough Hotel
Co Cork, Aherne's, Youghal
Co Cork, Assolas House, Kanturk
Co Cork, Ballymaloe House, Shanagarry
Co Cork, Ballyvolane House, Castlelyons
Co Cork, Farran House, Farran
Co Cork, Longueville House, Mallow
Co Cork, Seaview House, Ballylickey
Co Clare, Carnelly House, Clarecastle,
Co Clare, Gregans Castle Hotel, Ballyvaughan
Co Clare, Moy House, Lahinch
Co Clare, Sheedy's Hotel, Lisdoonvarna
Galway city, Killeen House, Bushypark
Galway city, SAS Radisson Hotel
Co Galway, Cashel House Hotel, Connemara
Co Galway, Dolphin Beach, Clifden
Co Galway, Fermoyle Lodge, Costello
Co Galway, The Quay House, Clifden
Co. Galway, Zetland House Hotel, Connemara
Co Kerry, Barrow House, Tralee
Co Kerry, Caragh Lodge, Caragh Lake
Co Kerry, Carrig House, Caragh Lake
Co Kerry, Emlagh Lodge, Dingle
Co Kerry, Hotel Europe, Killarney
Co Kerry, Killarney Park Hotel, Killarney
Co Kerry, Killarney Royal Hotel, Killarney
Co Kerry, Shelburne Lodge, Kenmare
Co Kildare, Barberstown Castle, Straffan
Co Kildare, Kilkea Castle, Castledermot
Co Kildare, Moyglare Manor, Maynooth
Co Laois, Ivyleigh House, Portlaoise
Co Limerick, Radisson SAS Hotel, Limerick
Co Limerick, Dunraven Arms Hotel, Adare
Co Limerick, Echo Lodge, Ballingarry
Co Limerick, Glin Castle, Glin
Co Mayo, Ardmore House, Westport
Co Mayo, Newport House, Newport
Co Monaghan, Hilton Park, Clones
Co Sligo, Coopershill House, Riverstown
Co Sligo, Cromleach Lodge, Castlebaldwin
Co Waterford, Hanora's Cottage, Nire Valley
Co Westmeath, Wineport Lodge, Glasson
Co Wexford, Dunbrody House, Arthurstown
Co Wicklow, Humewood Castle, Kiltegan
Co Wicklow, Rathsallagh House, Dunlavin
Co Wicklow, Tinakilly House, Rathnew

NORTHERN IRELAND

Belfast, TENsq Hotel
Co Antrim, Galgorm Manor, Ballymena
Co Londonderry, Ardtara House, Upperlands
Co Londonderry, Beech Hill House Hotel
Co Londonderry, Streeve Hill, Limavady
Co Tyrone, Grange Lodge, Dungannon

OUTSTANDING PUBS (for good food & atmosphere)

REPUBLIC OF IRELAND

Dublin, Café en Seine
Dublin, The Porterhouse
Co Cork, The Bosun, Monkstown
Co Cork, Bushe's, Baltimore
Co Cork, Mary Ann's, Castletownshend
Co Cork, Hayes Bar, Glandore
Co Galway, Moran's Oyster Cottage, Kilcolgan
Co Kildare, The Ballymore Inn, Ballymore Eustace
Co Kilkenny, Marble City Bar
Co Leitrim, The Oarsman, Carrick-on-Shannon
Co Mayo, Gaughan's, Ballina
Co Offaly, The Thatch, Crinkle
Co Tipperary, The Derg Inn, Terryglass
Co Waterford, Buggy's Glencairn Inn
Co Wexford, Kehoe's, Kilmore Quay
Co Wicklow, Roundwood Inn, Roundwood

NORTHERN IRELAND

Belfast, Crown Liquor Salon
Co Down, Grace Neill's, Donaghadee
Co Down, The Plough, Hillsborough

Georgina Campbell Guides
gratefully acknowledges the support of the following sponsors:

Jameson Irish Whiskey
Sponsors of:
Hotel of the Year Award
Restaurant of the Year Award
Pub of the Year Award
International Hospitality Award
Host of the Year Award
Business Hotel of the Year Award

Irish Distillers Limited
Wines and Spirits

Irish Distillers Limited Wines & Spirits
Sponsors of:
Wine Award of the Year

Kerry Foods
Sponsors of:
Denny Irish Breakfast Awards

Sharwood's

Sharwoods
Sponsors of:
Ethnic Restaurant of the Year Award

Euro-Toques, with GC Guides
Joint sponsors of:
Natural Food Award

Bord Bia
Irish Food Board

Bord Bia
Sponsors of:
Féile Bia Award

BIM Ireland

Bord Iascaigh Mhara
Sponsors of:
Seafood Restaurant of the Year Award

Bord Glas
Developing Horticulture

Bord Glas
Sponsors of:
Creative Use of Vegetables Award

RATHBORNES
ESTABLISHED 1488

Rathborne Candles
Sponsors of:
Atmospheric Restaurant
of the Year Award

IRISH
HEART
FOUNDATION

Irish Heart Foundation
Sponsors of:
Happy Heart Eat Out Award

Awards of Excellence

Annual awards for outstanding establishments and staff in a variety of categories, sponsored by leading Irish companies and organisations

2004

JAMESON IRISH WHISKEY

Hotel of the Year

Established in 1792, and set in one of Ireland's most picturesque villages, the Dunraven Arms has seen many changes over the years and is now a large hotel. Yet, under the personal management of Bryan and Louis Murphy, it somehow manages to retain the comfortable ambience of a country inn. A very luxurious inn nevertheless: the furnishing standard is superb throughout, with antiques, private dressing rooms and luxurious bathrooms, plus excellent amenities for private and business guests, all complemented by an outstanding standard of housekeeping. It's a great base for sporting activities - equestrian holidays are a speciality and both golf and fishing are available nearby - and also extremely popular for both conferences and private functions, including weddings, which are held beside the main hotel, with separate catering facilities. In recent times this family-run hotel has earned an unrivalled reputation for the value and quality of short breaks offered, something which has endeared it to many new guests who will no doubt be loyal customers for many years to come - this, and an ongoing determination to provide personal service and quality in all aspects of its operation, makes Dunraven Arms an outstanding example of contemporary Irish hospitality at its best.

GCG GEORGINA CAMPBELL'S GUIDES

Dunraven Arms Hotel
Adare, Co. Limerick

2003 WINNER

Cashel House Hotel, Co. Galway

WINNER

2004

JAMESON IRISH WHISKEY

Restaurant of the Year

Paul and Maire Flynn's stylish contemporary restaurant put Dungarvan firmly on the culinary map making it a destination for discerning diners from all over Ireland (and beyond). It is in an old leather warehouse, imaginatively converted so that Paul and his team can be seen at work in the open kitchen as guests arrive. The tannery theme is imaginatively echoed throughout the light, clean-lined interior, creating a sense of history that, along with dramatic paintings and fresh flowers, adds greatly to the atmosphere. Menus are wonderfully simple, written with a confidence that transfers to the hungry guest: you just know that every dish will be an experience. While inspired to some extent by global trends and regional cooking - particularly of the Mediterranean countries - cooking is based mainly on local ingredients, which Paul supports avidly and sources with care: local seafood stars - in Mediterranean fish soup, for example - while pork and bacon supplied by local butcher JD Power are rightly a source of pride. Equally, the Irish farmhouse cheese selection is unmissable, presented in perfect condition with oatcakes and chutney. The ambience, attentive and efficient service under Maire's direction, an interesting and kindly-priced wine list - and, above all, Paul's exceptional cooking - make for memorable meals at The Tannery: a restaurant for our times.

The Tannery
Dungarvan, Co. Waterford

2003 WINNER

Thornton's, Dublin

WINNER

2004

GEORGINA CAMPBELL'S GUIDES

Chef of the Year

Over the last decade or so, Neven Maguire's cooking has put the little border town of Blacklion firmly on the culinary map and now - in a small family restaurant, some of the best cooking in Ireland is to be found. Neven, who is a popular TV chef, shows no sign of being distracted from the restaurant and this in itself is exceptional - his cooking is better than ever: exact, perfectly judged food, based on meticulously sourced ingredients, is an experience to treasure. He has always been a staunch supporter of local and artisan produce and takes obvious delight in sharing his local riches - Eden plants, from the Organic Centre at Rossinver, Thornhill ducklings, Silke Croppe's stunning Corleggy cheeses - with a wider public. His second book, 'Neven Cooks 2', has just been published, initially to accompany a television series, but his cookery books will outlast the television interest by many a media lifetime as he has another talent which is most unusual in a chef - he relates to domestic cookery as well as to the professional kitchen, and gives sensible, down to earth recipes and advice based on personal experience as a family cook. Early influences from family members, especially his mother Vera, who started the restaurant, and encouragement from family and teachers who recognised his talent, have had a profound effect on Neven, making him the committed and wonderfully accessible chef that he is today.

Neven Maguire
MacNean Bistro, Blacklion, Co. Cavan

2003 WINNER

Maura Foley, Packies, Co. Kerry

2004

JAMESON
IRISH WHISKEY

Pub of the Year

Established in 1752, this former coaching inn enjoys a fine position at the top of the hill in the picturesque village of Hillsborough. Since 1984, it has been owned by the Patterson family, who have built up a national reputation for hospitality and good food, especially seafood. Somehow they manage to run three separate food operations each day, so pleasing customers looking for a casual daytime meal as well as more serious evening diners. A major redevelopment programme completed in 2002 has mercifully left the characterful old bar intact (fairly traditional bar food is still available there) and also the original Plough Restaurant. However the rest of the pub, including an adjacent building has been given a seriously stylish contemporary makeover - and now rejoices in the name Barretro-Café-Bar-Grill. If that sounds confusing on paper it is much the same on site; the new café has its own entrance from the street (look out for the dashing blue canopy), while the grill is above the old bar and offers bistro fare, which can be roughly translated as more substantial dishes from all over the world. Existing features like the old mahogany bar are incorporated into a design which is uncompromisingly modern; while there is obvious youth appeal, people of all ages feel comfortable here and the staff, who are clearly very proud of it, are friendly and helpful. This is a great example of a fine old family-run pub moving into the twenty-first century with style: the best from the past is still there to enjoy and the future is looking very good indeed.

The Plough
Hillsborough, Co. Down

2003 WINNER

Café en Seine, Dublin

2004

Bord Bia
Irish Food Board

Féile Bia Award

It was curiosity about their Féile Bia membership that first led the Guide to this rural restaurant, to see how Enda and Ailish Hennessy had diversified from farming into the food side of hospitality rather than the more usual B&B or farmhouse holidays. It's not the easiest place to find but, once discovered, what a welcome sight their neat pink-painted farmhouse presents. If you have ever wondered how a handsome young farmer might take to front of house work in a restaurant, it is instructive to observe the easy hospitality at work here: Enda shows guests through to a comfortable sofa in the bar, speedily offers menus and an aperitif, and then leaves you to enjoy the open fire. Excellent management, but not so surprising perhaps - after all, he's well used to running a demanding business with a special emphasis on attention to detail. Ailish, who also runs cookery classes at Fiacri, is clearly committed to using Quality Assured and local produce, through menus that offer a wide range of dishes based on the best of ingredients - always including local meats, of course, especially in fairly traditional main courses like rack of Tipperary lamb and the ever-popular sirloin steak. A dish of pan-fried medallions of pork with caramelised apple, cider & wholegrain mustard cream sauce makes a particularly welcome house speciality, given the honoured place of the pig in our culinary heritage. Flavoursome, generous country house cooking, based on the best of ingredients, and enhanced by a real sense of hospitality, make a great combination - and, at Fiacri, that's clearly a recipe for success.

Fiacri Country House Restaurant

Roscrea, Co. Tipperary

2003 WINNER

2004

BIM Ireland

Seafood Restaurant of the Year

Susan Holland and Ian Parr's uncluttered contemporary restaurant draws dedicated followers from every corner of Ireland - and beyond. Their secret is an unswerving philosophy of using only the best and freshest of local produce in season, keeping it simple - and giving real value for money. They do great daily menus - menus that highlight local seafood, especially, which is cooked by Susan with flair and served by Ian with unflappability - and are incredibly keenly priced. The couple, who are Australian, have worked in some very distinguished kitchens indeed and, between them, have over 60 years experience in hospitality, in half a dozen countries! Each summer, visitors to the little town of Baltimore are the fortunate beneficiaries of all this talent and commitment. Superb ingredients are presented with deceptive simplicity, mostly in classic French and Italian dishes served with organic salads, or simple, perfectly cooked organic side vegetables like new potatoes and spinach. You may well begin with a wonderful seafood tapas plate, typically of langoustine (Dublin Bay prawns), ceviche of john dory, peppers stuffed with brandade of salt cod and crab claws, each with its own dressing or garnish; main courses depend on the catch, but at least three of five or six main courses will probably be fish - including a classic sole meunière perhaps, and grilled monkfish with rösti potatoes and saffron & langoustine sauce. All this is complemented by an interesting, highly informative and keenly-priced wine list, and Ian Parr's efficient, refreshingly low-key service. Definitely worth a journey.

GCG GEORGINA CAMPBELL'S GUIDES

Customs House Restaurant
Baltimore, Co. Cork

2003 WINNER

Ty Ar Mor, Skibbereen, Co. Cork

2004

JAMESON IRISH WHISKEY

Business Hotel of the Year

Conveniently and attractively situated alongside the River Lee, just minutes from both Cork airport and the city centre, this modern hotel has been built and furnished to a high standard and is especially attractive for business visitors, for whom it quickly becomes a home from home - and this, even more than the excellent facilities offered to business and corporate guests, is what makes The Kingsley special. A large, comfortably furnished foyer has a luxurious yet homely feel to it - and this, as well as an adjacent informal restaurant area overlooking the weir, make good meeting places. This hospitable feeling is noticeable throughout the hotel, from the moment guests are greeted on arrival. Accommodation is personally decorated and well-planned, to make a comfortable base away from home which, together with an emphasis on service greatly enhances the hotel's appeal for business guests. These details are matched by excellent conference and business facilities - and, equally importantly, fine leisure facilities for relaxation after hours. And, of course, good food is an essential for business guests - especially those who may make the hotel their base for several days at a time - and The Kingsley looks after the inner man handsomely, both in the attractive restaurant Otters at the Kingsley, and in several private dining rooms. It seems they have thought of everything the business guest could wish for at The Kingsley.

The Kingsley Hotel
Victoria Cross, Cork

2003 WINNER

Marriott Hotel, Co. Wicklow

International Hospitality Award

The ancestral home of the O'Briens, barons of Inchiquin and direct descendants of Brian Boru, High King of Ireland, Dromoland is one of the few Irish estates tracing its history back to Gaelic royal families. Today, the visitor is keenly aware of this sense of history, but will not find it daunting: under the warm and thoughtful management of Mark Nolan, Dromoland is a very relaxing hotel, where the grandeur of the surroundings does not overpower but rather enhances the pleasure for guests. Dromoland Castle has seen momentous changes during Mark's time as General Manager - beginning, in 1989, with a kind of trial by fire as he took up the post at the onset of a five-year total refurbishment programme - and, during that period, the Brian Boru Conference and Banqueting Hall was also created. Not content with changes within the castle itself, the mid-90s saw the creation of the Golf Clubhouse - and the introduction of leisure facilities including a swimming pool. The last few years haven't been any quieter either, as the Moriarty Wing (designed to blend in with the original castle) was completed in 2001 - and, since then, there's been the minor matter of a €4 million refurbishment of the 18 hole golf course, to championship level. These are all things which key international travellers value highly when moving around the world and will bring many more to Ireland, and to Dromoland; and when they arrive, these special guests can be assured of warm hospitality from Mark Nolan and his team: International Hospitality at its best.

Mark Nolan

Dromoland Castle Hotel
Newmarket-on-Fergus, Co. Clare

2003 WINNER

Irish Distillers Limited Wines and Spirits

Wine Award of the Year

To its many visitors, a stay at Newport House symbolises all that is best about the Irish country house. Currently in the caring hands of Kieran and Thelma Thompson, Newport has been especially close to the hearts of fishing people for many years, but the comfort and warm hospitality of this wonderful house is accessible to all its guests – not least in shared enjoyment of the club-fender cosiness of the little back bar. The restaurant is all that a country house dining room should be - high-ceilinged and elegant with tall windows, mahogany furniture and fresh flowers from the garden, the perfect backdrop for "cooking which reflects the hospitable nature of the house". And then there is Kieran's renowned wine list that, for many, adds an extra magic to a meal at Newport. It includes a great collection of classic French wines – about 150 clarets from 1961-1996 vintages, a great collection of white and red burgundies, excellent Rhônes – and a good New World collection too. The foundations of this cellar go back many decades to a time when Kieran was himself a guest at Newport; great wines are a passion for him and, while acknowledging that they are irreplaceable, he offers them to guests at far less than their current retail value. Great Lists of this scale and quality are almost a thing of the past, so it is a cause for celebration that a collector such as Kieran should also be blessed with the generosity that allows others to share his passion.

Newport House
Newport, Co. Mayo

2003 WINNER

Dobbins, Dublin

2004

JAMESON IRISH WHISKEY

Host of the Year

Set in a 300-acre estate just across the river from Kenmare town, Sheen Falls Lodge made an immediate impact from the day it opened in April 1991, and it has continued to develop and mature most impressively since. The waterside location is beautiful and welcoming, fires always burn in the elegant foyer and in several of the spacious, elegantly furnished reception rooms, including a lounge bar area overlooking the tumbling waterfall. Luxurious accommodation is matched by decor that offers traditional luxury with a modern lightness of touch, and a tendency to understatement that adds up to great style. But it is the staff, under the guidance of the exceptionally warm and hospitable General Manager, Adriaan Bartels, who make this luxurious and stylish international hotel the home from home that it quickly becomes for each new guest: Adriaan seems to reflect the qualities of warmth, lightness of touch and understatement that make this hotel so special and he has a particular talent with people - nothing is ever too much trouble to ensure that guests get the best possible enjoyment and relaxation from a stay at Sheen Falls: an absolute natural for our Host of the Year Award for 2004.

Adriaan Bartels
Sheen Falls Lodge
Kenmare, Co. Kerry

2003 WINNER

Jim McCarthy, Chart House, Dingle, Co. Kerry

GEORGINA CAMPBELL'S GUIDES

Hideaway of the Year

Set in the hills just above Lough Arrow, Cromleach Lodge enjoys one of the finest views in Ireland - and, given the high priority that proprietors Moira and Christy Tighe give to pampering their guests and providing a restful retreat, this makes the perfect hideaway for a break, gloriously insulated from the 'real' world. Spacious bedrooms are thoughtfully furnished with every comfort to please the most fastidious of guests: housekeeping and attention to detail are outstanding. But, aside from that wonderful sense of being cocooned in comfort, the secret weapon at Cromleach is, of course, Moira's magnificent cooking. Dinner is the highlight of every guest's stay here, served in a series of dining rooms designed to make the most of the wonderful view. Moira and her personally trained team work superbly well together, producing memorable meals; the style is modern, without slavish attention to fashion, and, as much as the skills in the kitchen, it is Moira's pride in local produce and scrupulously careful sourcing of ingredients that makes a meal here so special. But, while Cromleach is rightly renowned for its exceptional standards of both food and accommodation, Moira and Christy have - most importantly - the magic ingredient of genuine hospitality, doing everything possible to ensure comfort and relaxation for their guests in this beautiful and unspoilt area.

GEORGINA CAMPBELL'S GUIDES

Cromleach Lodge
Castlebaldwin, Co. Sligo

2003 WINNER

Wineport Lodge, Athlone, Co. Westmeath

RATHBORNES
ESTABLISHED 1488

Atmospheric Restaurant of the Year

This unique restaurant on the square of the old village (well away from the busy main West Cork road) is just the kind of place that people visiting west Cork dream of. It has a previous commercial history that's almost tangible, yet it's not too decorated - in fact it's not 'decorated' at all. Exposed stone walls, old fishing nets and glass floats, mismatched furniture, shelves of wine bottles and candlelight all contribute to its unique atmosphere - and are well-matched by proprietor-host Sean Kearney's larger-than-life personality. But atmosphere alone is of little value in a restaurant - and this one also has substance, both in Sean's great hospitality, and the exceptional freshness and quality of Martina O'Donovan's wonderful seafood: steaks theoretically share the billing, but seafood steals the scene. Specialities to look out for include a superb Fruits de Mer platter which is available as small or large - although, in the Guide's experience, the small one is very large indeed. Ultra-freshness, attention to detail in breads and accompaniments - and, most of all, a huge dose of personality - all add up to make this place a delight.

O'Callaghan-Walshe
Rosscarbery, Co. Cork

2003 WINNER

2004

Sharwood's

Ethnic Restaurant of the Year

This smart two-storey restaurant specialising in authentic Pakistani and Northern Indian cuisine is in a scenic location overlooking Bull Island - and it is a fine example of the new wave of ethnic restaurants that is currently enlivening the Irish dining scene. There's a cosy upstairs bar with Indian cookbooks to inspire guests waiting for a table or relaxing after dinner - and a warm welcome from the Sudanese doorman, Muhammad, gets a meal off to a good start as - with a mighty grin and a swirl of the traditional costume that has become the restaurant's trademark - he sweeps arriving guests into the foyer. The menu is unusual, beginning with a useful introduction to the cuisine that explains the four fundamental flavours - tomato, garlic, ginger and onions - and their uses, then offering a series of styles to choose from: it opens with a range of traditional starters like kakeragh (local crab claws with garlic, yogurt, spices and a tandoori masala sauce) and main courses (like Shimla chicken, simmered with chopped onions & tomato, garnished with fresh coriander). There is a declared commitment to local produce - notably organic beef, lamb and chicken - and, unusually, a section of the menu is devoted to organic and 'lighter fare' main courses. Head chef Ashok Kumar and his team have over 80 years experience between them - and now Dublin has clearly taken them, and this authentic and hospitable restaurant, to her heart.

Kinara
318 Clontarf Road, Dublin 3

2004

IRISH
HEART
FOUNDATION

Happy Heart Eat Out Award

Kay Harte has a commitment to serving fresh food at Farmgate Café - and, as it is located in the gallery above the English Market, where ingredients are purchased daily, it doesn't come much fresher than this. With its classic black and white tiles, simple wooden furniture and interesting art work there's a combination of style and a comfortably down to earth atmosphere which suits the wholesome food they serve, including modern dishes as well as some famous old Cork ones with a special market connection like tripe & drisheen and corned beef & champ with green cabbage. Farmgate food is as healthy as it is delicious, meeting the Irish Heart Foundation's definition of a healthy choice, i.e. dishes with lots of fruit and vegetables that are high in fibre, low in fat, especially saturated fat. Menus depend on what is available in the English Market each day, including "the freshest of fish" - used, for example, in a chowder that market regulars love. And, however simple, everything is perfectly cooked, with careful matching of vegetables and judicious use of fresh herbs and seasonings: a delicious mushroom & Crozier Blue tart with thyme, for example, is perfectly balanced to allow the subtle mushroom flavour to come through, while traditionalists will love the classic Irish lamb stew, with its succulent chunks of lean lamb and perfectly cooked root vegetables. All this and delicious home-baked cakes, breads and desserts too... This is an interesting and lively place to enjoy good food - and it's great value for money.

Farmgate Café
English Market, Cork

2003 WINNER

Lennon's Café Bar, Carlow

2004

Bord Glas

Creative Use of Vegetables Award

Situated in what was once the stables and dairy of Kilkenny Castle - and overlooking the craft courtyard - this first floor self-service restaurant consistently provides wholesome, healthy and absolutely delicious fare at very reasonable prices. Everything is freshly prepared each day, home baking is a strong point and salads, especially, are always colourful and full of life - fresh beetroot, asparagus, spinach, red onion, coriander & crumbly Lavistown local cheese makes a salad worth travelling for, for example, and the selection changes all the time. Vegetarian dishes are invariably tempting, and contemporary cooking generally is well-represented - in, for example, a soup plate option that changes daily and offers a gourmet sandwich such as foccacia with caramelised red onion & Lavistown cheese, with the daily soup choice - an unusual carrot & mint, perhaps, served piping hot. There are also delicious old-fashioned bakes like chicken & broccoli crumble, and the humblest of vegetables are taken seriously: carrots, for example, are served seasoned with cracked pepper, cream and a little olive oil, and baby potatoes are seasoned with honey, cumin, ginger, balsamic vinegar and olive oil, while broccoli and cauliflower have a tangy dressing to give them a lift - details that make all the difference to simple foods. It is good to see local ingredients used so well in such a fresh and appetising way - if only every town could have a place like this.

Kilkenny Design Centre
Castle Yard, Kilkenny

2003 WINNER

Mermaid Café, Dublin

EURO-TOQUES

Natural Food Award

Food-lovers from all over the country make sure of building in a visit to Peter and Mary Ward's unique shop when planning a journey anywhere near Nenagh. Old hands head for the little café at the back first, fortifying themselves with the superb, simple home-cooked food that reflects a policy of seasonality – if the range is small at a particular time of year, so be it. Meats, milk, cream, eggs, butter and flour: "The economy of Tipperary is agricultural and we intend to demonstrate this with a finished product of tantalising smells and tastes." Specialities developed over the years include Cashel Blue and broccoli soup – served with their magnificent home-baked breads (made with local flours) – savoury quiches and fruit tarts, and tender, gently-cooked meat dishes like lamb ragout, and beef & Guinness casserole. The shop carries a very wide range of the finest Irish artisan produce, plus a smaller selection of specialist products from further afield, including an unusual range of quality glacé fruits that are in great demand for Christmas baking. Peter's passion for cheese is legendary - he is one of the country's best suppliers of Irish farmhouse cheeses, which he minds like babies as they ripen and, unlike most shops, only puts on display when they are mature: nobody should leave Country Choice without buying cheese. Peter Ward has been appointed Chairperson of the new TASTE Council (Traditional, Artisan, Speciality Trade Expertise in Food), to develop the potential of speciality food in Ireland, which is very good news for this country.

Peter Ward

Country Choice, Nenagh,
Co. Tipperary

2003 WINNER

BrookLodge Hotel, Co. Wicklow

2004

Newcomer of the Year

This old stone building in a neatly landscaped garden served as a post office until 1974 and, since then, has made an attractive and popular inn. In the autumn of 2002 it was taken over by the talented young chef, Gearoid Lynch, and his fiancée, Tara McCann, who have worked hard to put their stamp on it both inside and out - and they are already earning a well-deserved reputation for fine food and genuine hospitality. There's a pleasant country atmosphere about the place, which has a proper bar to enjoy your pre/post-prandial drinks and an old-world style throughout, with bare walls, dark beams and simple wooden furniture - but, comfortably rustic as it may seem, that is far from the case in the kitchen. Gearoid's route to Cloverhill has included time in some fine establishments - at least one of which lives on in Cavan, in a house speciality: 'Le Coq Hardi' chicken breast (stuffed with potato, apple, bacon & herbs, wrapped in bacon and served with an Irish whiskey sauce). A committed Euro-Toques chef, Gearoid sources ingredients with great care and his respect for regional and seasonal foods shows in many ways, notably in adaptations of traditional themes such as a speciality starter of warm bacon and cabbage terrine with a baby leek cream sauce. This is a happy ship and the talent and dedication of a good kitchen team produces excellent cooking, and there's a tangible sense of pride in the friendly, helpful service provided by local staff. It's a great asset to the area - and this level of commitment from talented young people bodes well for Ireland.

The Olde Post Inn
Cloverhill, Co. Cavan

2003 WINNER

TenSq, Belfast

2004

GEORGINA CAMPBELL'S GUIDES

Country House of the Year

Fermoyle Lodge

Costello, Co. Galway

Guesthouse of the Year

Earls Court House

Killarney, Co. Kerry

Farmhouse of the Year

Ballyknocken House

Glenealy, Ashford, Co. Wicklow

WINNER

DENNY

Breakfast Award - Ulster

Ravenhill House
Belfast

Breakfast Award - Connaught

Stella Maris Hotel
Ballycastle, Co. Mayo

Breakfast Award - Dublin

Aberdeen Lodge
Ballsbridge, Dublin 4

Breakfast Award - Munster

Sheedy's Country House Hotel
Lisdoonvarna, Co. Clare

Breakfast Award Leinster & National Winner

Dunbrody House is an elegant Georgian manor set in parkland and gardens on the Hook Peninsula, just across the estuary from Waterford city. It was the ancestral home of the Chichester family, and the long tradition of hospitality at this tranquil and luxurious retreat is very much alive and well as the present owners, Catherine and Kevin Dundon, are thoughtful and caring hosts. It's a very fine house - the tone is set in the impressive entrance hall which, like the other public rooms, is beautifully furnished and decorated with stunning flower arrangements, and the occasional unexpectedly modern piece that brings life to a fine collection of antiques. Luxurious accommodation offers all the comforts expected of such a house, with views over the gardens - or the converted outbuildings which now house Ireland's most stylish cookery school. After a good night's sleep, an exceptional breakfast awaits the lucky guests at Dunbrody. A magnificent buffet is set up in the beautiful dining room: there are fresh juices, fruit salad, fresh whole and prepared fruits of all kinds both native and exotic, a choice of fruit compôtes - made with fruit from the garden in summer - served with home-made yogurt. Then there are freshly baked breads and home-made preserves, an impressive display of Irish farmhouse cheeses, smoked salmon, and cold meats - and that's before you even think about making choices from a tempting menu of hot dishes that includes specialities like pancakes with poached fruit and crème fraîche, as well as a fine rendition of the traditional Irish breakfast... what a way to start the day!

Dunbrody House
Arthurstown, Co. Wexford

2003 WINNER

Longueville House, Mallow, Co. Cork

Getting the Flavour of Irish Whiskey

Portrait of John Jameson by Raeburn

Enjoyed by connoisseurs worldwide, Jameson enjoys universal brand awareness in Ireland. And it is a matter of national pride that this superb beverage, so much a part of Irish life, now has genuine international status.

Unlike most other whiskeys, Jameson is distilled three times, ensuring a final product that is particularly smooth and pure. During maturation in sherry and bourbon oak casks, stored in dark aromatic warehouses, the whiskey mellows over the years, and takes on its rich golden colour.

The expertise required has a long history. Irish whiskey was invented as far back as the 6th Century, when monks discovered that an apparatus called the "alembic" - originally used to distill perfume in the Middle East - could be more usefully employed to produce "Uisce Beatha", the "Water of Life". Pronounced "ishka baahaa", it was later anglicised as "whiskey".

In time, the alembic, as used for whiskey distilling, became known as the "pot still". Ireland was already rich in whiskey's essential ingredients of pure water and golden barley. But it took the particular genius of the early distillers to discover that the barley used for the malt must first be dried in closed kilns to ensure that its honeyed taste shines through in the final product, giving Irish whiskey its distinctive mellow flavour.

John Jameson founded his distillery in Dublin in 1780, at a time when quality control in the industry was often perfunctory. Jameson set out with the clearcut ambition of creating the best whiskey in the world, distilled in the finest premises under the watchful supervision of highly motivated and experienced staff.

By 1996, Jameson had become the world's fastest growing spirit brand, retaining the loyalty of traditional drinkers while reaching new consumers through its versatility with mixers. Today, the Old Jameson Distillery in Dublin, together with the Jameson Heritage Centre in Midleton, Co Cork, are ranked among the most popular visitor attractions in the country.

Jameson whiskeys - for the brand has some very special even more mature variants - can be everything from an aperitif to a digestif, and a simple celebratory drink at all appropriate times. Richly imbued with history, it lends itself well to the most famous of Irish toasts and blessings:

Health and long life to you
Land without rent to you
The woman (or man) of your choice to you
A child every year to you
and may you be in heaven before
the Devil knows you're dead!

"Blas agus sasamh go bhfaighe tu air"

Féile Bia is a year round programme that emphasizes the importance of food sourcing in hotels, restaurants, pubs and workplaces throughout the country. The programme is organised in conjunction with the Restaurants Association of Ireland and the Irish Hotels Federation, and with the support of the farming community. Féile Bia is in response to growing consumer concerns on the quality and origin of food offered when eating out.

Participants are asked to outline their commitment to the programme by providing details confirming the quality and origin of the food used in their kitchens. Féile Bia members are committed to sourcing meat, chicken and eggs from recognised Quality Assurance Schemes that can meet their customer demands for country of origin information.

Membership of Féile Bia has grown dramatically to 1,250 members since the scheme was introduced in 2001.

Consumers can identify establishments with a commitment to Quality Assured food through the display of the blue framed Feile Bia certificate. It's well worth looking out for, as a reassurance that the establishment you have selected demonstrates a commitment to sourcing their ingredients through traceable systems and providing information to the consumer.

Those establishments recommended by the Guide which have signed up to the Charter are listed below and are identified within the body of the Guide by the use of the Feile Bia logo.

Féile Bia Members

CARLOW

Ballon, The Forge
Ballon, Sherwood Park House
Carlow Town, Lennons Café Bar
Carlow Town, The Beams Restaurant
Leighlin Bridge, Mulberrys

CAVAN

Ballyconnell, The Anglers Rest
Blacklion, Mac Nean House & Bistro
Cavan Town, The Oak Room
Cavan Town, The Side Door
Cloverhill, The Olde Post Inn

CLARE

Bunratty, Fitzpatricks Hotel
Ennis, Hal Pino's Restaurant
Ennis, Temple Gate Hotel
Ennis, West County Hotel
Ennis, Woodstock Hotel
Killaloe, Cherry Tree Restaurant
Shannon, Great Southern Hotel

CORK

Baltimore, The Baltimore Harbour Hotel
Bantry, O'Connor's Seafood Restaurant
Ballylickey, Sea View House Hotel
Bantry, O'Connors Restaurant
Bantry, The Snug Bar
Blarney, Blairs Inn
Carrigaline, Carrigaline Court Hotel
Carrigaline, Gregorys Restaurant
Clonakilty, An Sugan
Clonakilty, Dunmore House Hotel
Clonakilty, Harts Coffee Shop
Clonakilty, O'Keeffes & The Emmet Hotel
Cobh, Robin Hill House
Cork City, The Douglas Hide
Cork City, Farmgate Café
Cork City, Fenns Quay Restaurant
Cork City, Hayfield Manor Hotel
Cork City, Gresham Metropole
Cork City, Idaho.Café
Cork City, Isaac's Restaurant
Cork City, The Ivory Tower
Cork City, Jacobs On The Mall
Cork City, Jurys Inn Cork
Cork City, The Kingsley Hotel
Cork City, Maryborough Hotel
Cork City, Probys Bistro
Cork City, Rochestown Park Hotel
Cork City, Silver Springs Hotel
Gougane Barra, Gougane Barra Hotel
Glanmire, The Barn Restaurant
Glengarriff, Glengarriff Eccles Hotel
Innishannon, Innishannon House Hotel
Kilbrittain, Casino House
Kinsale, Actons Hotel
Kinsale, Blue Haven

Kinsale, Crackpots Restaurant
Kinsale, Man Friday
Kinsale, Trident Hotel
Kinsale, The Old Bank House
Kinsale, The Vintage Restaurant
Macroom, The Castle Hotel
Midleton, Barnabrow Country House
Midleton, Farmgate Restaurant
Midleton, Midleton Park Hotel
Mitchelstown, O'Callaghans Delicatessen & Café
Roscarbery, Celtic Ross Hotel
Shanagarry, Ballymaloe House Hotel
Skibbereen, Ty Ar Mor Seafood Restaurant
Skibbereen, West Cork Hotel

DONEGAL

Burtonport, Skippers Tavern
Culdaff, McGrory's
Donegal Town, Weavers Loft at Magees
Fahan, St Johns Countryhouse & Restaurant
Malin, Malin Hotel

DUBLIN

Dublin 1, Chapter One Restaurant
Dublin 1, Gresham Hotel
Dublin 1, Jurys Inn Custom House
Dublin 2, Alexander Hotel
Dublin 2, Avoca Café, Suffolk Street
Dublin 2, Bang Café
Dublin 2, Bewley's Grafton St
Dublin 2, Brooks Hotel
Dublin 2, Brownes Brasserie & Townhouse
Dublin 2, Bruno's Restaurant
Dublin 2, Buswells Hotel
Dublin 2, Davenport Hotel
Dublin 2, Fitzers
Dublin 2, Jacobs Ladder
Dublin 2, Kilkenny Restaurant & Café
Dublin 2, L'Ecrivain Restaurant
Dublin 2, Mao Cafés
Dublin 2, Mont Clare Hotel

Féile Bia Members

Dublin 2, Montys Of Katmandhu
Dublin 2, One Pico Restaurant
Dublin 2, Saagar Restaurant
Dublin 2, Shalimar Indian Restaurant
Dublin 2, Shanahan's On The Green
Dublin 2, St Stephen's Green Hotel
Dublin 2, Westbury Hotel
Dublin 4, Anglesea Town House
Dublin 4, Bella Cuba
Dublin 4, Berkeley Court Hotel
Dublin 4, Burlington Hotel
Dublin 4, Ernie's Restaurant
Dublin 4, Four Seasons Hotel
Dublin 4, Herbery Park Hotel
Dublin 4, Jurys Ballsbridge Hotel
Dublin 4, Jurys Montrose Hotel
Dublin 4, Mespil Hotel
Dublin 4, O'Connells In Ballsbridge
Dublin 4, Pembroke Townhouse
Dublin 4, Rolys Bistro
Dublin 4, The Schoolhouse Hotel
Dublin 4, The Towers
Dublin 8, Jurys InnChristchurch
Dublin 9, Washerwomans Hill Restaurant
Dublin 18, Bistro One
Dublin 22, Jurys Green Isle Hotel
Dublin 22, Red Cow Moran Hotel
Dublin Airport, Great Southern Hotel
Dublin Airport, Holiday Inn
Dun Laoghaire, Brasserie Na Mara
Dun Laoghaire, Gresham Royal Marine Hotel
Glencullen, Johnnie Fox's Pub
Howth, Deerpark Hotel
Howth, King Sitric
Malahide, Bon Appetit Restaurant
Malahide, Cruzzo Restaurant
Saggart, Citywest Hotel
Skerries, Redbank House & Restaurant
Stillorgan, Stillorgan Park Hotel
Stillorgan, Radisson SAS Hotel
Swords, Old Schoolhouse Restaurant

GALWAY

Galway City, Ardilaun House Hotel
Galway City, Corrib Great Southern Hotel
Galway City, Great Southern Hotel
Galway City, Jurys Inn Galway
Galway City, Park House Hotel
Galway City, Radisson SAS Hotel
Ballinasloe, Tohers Restaurant & Bar
Clarenbridge, The Old School House Restaurant
Clifden, Ardagh Hotel
Clifden, Mitchell's Restaurant
Furbo, Connemara Coast Hotel
Moycullen, Moycullen House Restaurant
Moycullen, White Gables Restaurant
Oranmore, Galway Bay Golf & Country Club
Portmuna, Shannon Oaks Hotel & Country Club
Renvyle, Renvyle House Hotel
Roundstone, O'Dowd's
Salthill, Galway Bay Hotel
Tuam, Cre-Na-Cille Restaurant
Tuam, Finn's Restaurant

KERRY

Caherdaniel, Derrynane Hotel
Dingle, Chart House Restaurant
Dingle, Cleevaun Country House
Dingle, Dingle Skellig Hotel
Dingle, Doyles Seafood Restaurant
Dingle, Lord Bakers Restaurant
Dingle, Wild Banks Restaurant
Listowel, Allos Bistro
Listowel, Listowel Arms Hotel
Kenmare, D'Arcy's Restaurant
Kenmare, Packies
Kenmare, Sheen Falls Lodge
Killarney, The Beaufort Bar & Restaurant
Killarney, The Great Southern Hotel
Killarney, Old Presbytery Restaurant
Parknasilla, Great Southern Hotel
Tralee, Ballygarry House Hotel
Tralee, Brandon Hotel
Tralee, Meadowlands Hotel
Tralee, Val's Bar & Bistro

KILDARE

Ballymore Eustace, Ballymore Inn
Castledermot, Kilkea Castle Hotel
Naas, Killashee House Hotel
Naas, Red House Inn
Straffan, The K-Club

KILKENNY

Kilkenny City, Kilkenny Design Centre Restaurant
Kilkenny City, Kilkenny Ormonde Hotel
Kilkenny City, Lacken House
Kilkenny City, The Kilkenny Rivercourt Hotel
Kilkenny City, Marble City Bar
Thomastown, Mount Juliet Conrad Hotel

LAOIS

Abbeyleix, Preston House
Portlaoise, Kingfisher Restaurant
Portlaoise, The Kitchen & Food Hall

LEITRIM

Carrick-on-Shannon, Bush Hotel
Carrick-on-Shannon, The Oarsman

LIMERICK

Limerick City, Brulées Restaurant
Limerick City, Castletroy Park Hotel
Limerick City, Jurys Inn Limerick
Limerick City, Radisson SAS Hotel
Limerick City, South Court Hotel
Abbeyfeale, Whytes Restaurant
Adare, Adare Manor Hotel & Golf Resort
Adare, Dunraven Arms Hotel
Adare, The Wild Geese Restaurant
Adare, Woodlands House Hotel

Féile Bia Members

LOUTH

Carlingford, The Oystercatcher Bistro
Dundalk, Quaglino's Restaurant
Jenkinstown, Fitzpatricks

MAYO

Castlebar, An Carraig Restaurant
Castlebar, Breaffy House Hotel
Foxford, Healys Hotel
Westport, Ardmore House Hotel
Westport, Hotel Westport
Westport, Knockranny House Hotel
Westport, The Atlantic Coast Hotel
Westport, The Linnenmill Restaurant

MEATH

Bettystown, Bacchus At The Coastguard
Dunboyne, Caldwells Restaurant
Enfield, Johnstown House Hotel
Kells, Headford Arms Hotel (Vanilla Pod)
Kells, The Ground Floor Restaurant
Kilmessan, Station House Hotel
Navan, Ardboyne Hotel
Navan, Hudsons Bistro
Navan, The Loft Restaurant
Slane, Conyngham Arms Hotel
Trim, Franzini O'Briens

MONAGHAN

Carrickmacross, Nuremore Hotel
Glaslough, Castle Leslie
Monaghan Town, Andy's Bar & Restaurant

OFFALY

Birr, The Stables
Edenderry, Tyrrells Restaurant
Tullamore, Tullamore Court Hotel

ROSCOMMON

Roscommon Town, Abbey Hotel
Tarmonbarry, Keenan's

SLIGO

Rosses Point, Austies
Rosses Point, The Waterfront
Sligo town, Coach Lane Restaurant
Sligo town, Montmartre Restaurant

TIPPERARY

Cahir, Clifford's At The Bell
Cashel, Cashels Palace Restaurant
Cashel, Legends Townhouse & Restaurant
Clonmel, Angela's Restaurant
Clonmel, Hotel Minella
Dromineer, The Whiskey Still
Roscrea, Fiacri Country House Restaurant
Terryglass, The Derg Inn
Thurles, Inch House

WATERFORD

Waterford City, Dwyers Restaurant
Waterford City, Gatchells Restaurant
Waterford City, The Gingerman Bar
Waterford City, Granville Hotel
Waterford City, The Wine Vault
Ardmore, Whitehorses Restaurant
Cappoquin, Richmond House
Cheekpoint, McAlpin's Suir Inn
Dungarvan, Powersfield House
Tallow, Buggy's Glencairn Inn

WESTMEATH

Athlone, Hodson Bay Hotel
Athlone, Manifesto Restaurant
Athlone, Restaurant Le Chateau
Athlone, Wineport Lodge
Mullingar, Belfry Restaurant
Mullingar, Ilia
Multyfarnham, An Tintain

WEXFORD

Arthurstown, Dunbrody House
Duncannon, Sqigl Restaurant & Roche's Bar
Enniscorthy, Riverside Park Hotel
Kilmore Quay, Kehoe's Pub
New Ross, Brandon House Hotel
Rosslare, Kelly's Resort Hotel
Wexford town, Ferrycarrig Hotel
Wexford town, Forde's Restaurant
Wexford town, Heavens Above The Sky & Ground
Wexford town, La Riva Restaurant
Wexford town, Talbot Hotel

WICKLOW

Arklow, Kitty's of Arklow
Arklow, Woodenbridge Hotel
Avoca Village, Avoca Café
Blessington, Downshire House Hotel
Dunlavin, Rathsallagh House
Greystones, The Hungry Monk
Kilmacanogue, Avoca Café
Powerscourt, Avoca Café
Roundwood, The Roundwood Inn

Slow Down, Relax, & Enjoy!

Ireland today - still thriving, despite the global slowdown - is a country of surprising and vibrant contrasts. The major cities, especially Dublin, are fast paced, modern and cosmopolitan. As with other European cities, you need to know where to go to find those quiet and cherished urban oases—and they do still exist, often just around the corner from the bustling shopping streets. However, away from the cities and larger towns, there are still large tracts of unspoilt, breathtakingly beautiful scenery and picturesque towns and villages where life is lived at a gentler pace.

One thing has not changed—the Irish like the good things in life: good food, good drink, good talk. We have a real interest in other people. Genuine hospitality is ingrained in the Irish personality. It is there in high prosperity, and - if needs be - through austerity too. At all times, we are happy to share our good things with visitors, whether they are travelling from abroad or just from another part of this country.

From the discerning traveller's point of view, the most enticing aspect of modern Ireland is the coming of age of a flourishing food culture that makes this a gourmet destination of the highest order. With a large number of new hotels of international standard, and the development of many more country houses, we have the high quality accommodation to match it.

You may choose from ultra-modern hotels, or prefer the familiarity of traditional establishments, or you may opt for the luxury of a well-maintained historic country house (often sharing it with the family who have lived there for centuries). International chains are present, too, and offer a challenge to leading Irish hotels. Many of the latter have responded to this by providing stylishly up-graded facilities such as spas and state of the art leisure centres. The newcomers, however prestigious their reputations, know they face fierce competition from Irish-owned hotel groups—past masters of hospitality.

A growing number of Irish hotels now successfully operate both fine-dining and informal brasserie-style restaurants, and there's a bevy of talented and determined owner-chefs out there too—with second and even third generations coming through. So it's definitely not a walk-over for the big names, who have to find a balance between providing the services demanded by an international clientèle, and the need to give visitors a meaningful flavour of Ireland.

For generations, Irish chefs of the classical tradition have gone abroad to complete their training—the younger generation often add in a stint in the New World or Australasia. On their return, as surely as the invaders of earlier centuries, they brought back foreign culinary influences. The process continues to this day, as a glance at any popular menu shows. Fortunately this - encouraged by the expectations of discerning visitors - has created a contemporary Irish cuisine that is, at its best, quite unique.

The Food Island

Ireland is a food exporting country and Bord Bia, the Irish Food Board, is responsible for promoting Irish food at home and abroad: their slogan "Ireland the Food Island" really does means what it says. In all, they have more than 700 food and drink companies of all sizes to support, and they have become increasingly committed to the development and encouragement of speciality foods, and craft and artisan producers. Both sectors have grown in strength and variety, in particular those producers who take charge of every step in the process from farm to consumer: craft sausage-makers, organic meat and poultry farmers, fish and seafood smokers, specialists in wild game and rare breeds, producers who work with fruits, herbs, and vegetables, bakers, and farm cheesemakers, who have gained wide respect in the international food community.

In recent decades the success of niche-market foods, most notably with Irish farmhouse cheeses, has come to symbolise the hopes of food-lovers for the future of mainstream produce. It is a source of wonderment to Europeans that today's Irish farm cheeses are produced on just one farm, usually by one dedicated family. The variety and high quality is astonishing. One reason for this is the Irish climate. Our green grasslands in favoured areas are rich in wild, natural herbage and sheep, goats and cows are largely grass-fed to produce flavoursome and distinctive milk. You can experience local farmhouse cheeses and speciality foods in restaurants, or visit local food markets in Dublin, Belfast, Cork, and in dozens of towns around the country.

In the past year the growth and popularity of farmers and producers markets has been remarkable, demonstrating the increased confidence of Ireland's artisan and craft producers to meet directly with their customers - much to the benefit of all. Food markets provide a fun day out, with nourishment for body and soul. (Visit the Bord Bia website, www.bordbia.ie, for up to date information on times and places of farmers' and producers' markets all over the country). At the heart of the capital, Dublin City Fathers' investment in the traditional and brightly noisy Moore Street inner city market is especially welcome – nowadays, it provides ethnic foods from all over the world.

Féile Bia

In the current cosmopolitan atmosphere, with global cuisine the norm even in many remote rural restaurants, the best Irish chefs are increasingly aware of the need to give the Irish table "a sense of place". The Féile Bia (Celebration of Food) programme encourages chefs in every part of the country to think not so much about short-lived contemporary cooking fashions – though they certainly have their place – but to look also at all that is finest in their local neighbourhood and region. Féile Bia - which began as a week-long festival celebrating Irish food and traditional Irish cooking - has been developed as a year-round programme.

Working together, Bord Bia, the Restaurants Association of Ireland and the Irish Hotels Federation set up this scheme, with the support of the farming community. Establishments that undertake to source and use local/quality-assured products from named suppliers, and be subject to an annual audit, may display the blue-framed Féile Bia certificate. Consumer research shows that we place a high value on quality Irish food and assume when eating out that is what we are getting. At the top end of the market, especially where the chef is a member of Euro-Toques, this is generally the case; but it is not universally true.

Féile Bia aims to provide assurance for consumers that the beef, pork, bacon, lamb, chicken and eggs that are currently included in the scheme - which is under continuous development - are quality assured. Concerned consumers should look out for the certificate and talk to owners or managers about their policy on sourcing other foods - showing this interest will help the Féile Bia scheme to grow and prosper.

Avoca Cafes were the winners of the 2003 Féile Bia Award. Leylie Hayes, Executive Chef of their five cafés and food halls, has been supervising the production of Avoca's famously good home-cooked food since 1990. "Quality in, quality out" is the motto at the heart of the Avoca philosophy: they have always strived to source top quality, seasonal ingredients and the least processed, best raw materials, while developing dishes and menus that feature local ingredients. We asked why Leylie Hayes thought it helpful to join Féile Bia:

"In early 2001 we were approached about joining the new Bord Bia initiative, Féile Bia. As a working chef and executive chef of all five Avoca cafes, my first reaction was - why indeed?

"Did I really want to get us all involved in yet more form filling? Would we just be duplicating the recording we did for our own HACCP system? We already checked out our suppliers, making sure they had been passed by their local health board, and agreed with them delivery procedures and systems. For our part, we kept careful delivery records and so on. But an interesting thing, HACCP does not talk about country of origin. Féile Bia did. That set me thinking maybe Féile Bia could help us.

"At Avoca, we only serve Irish meat - end of story. We use only Irish chicken, even though we pay well over the odds. We really try to buy local, buy in season, and buy Irish. It is part of the Avoca philosophy to support the many wonderful artisan producers of Ireland. But, as we also have to bring in some artisan products that are not available here, we saw the benefit of checking out that the producers of imported products were part of a quality assurance scheme recognised by Féile Bia. So, we joined - in fact we were one of the first to sign up to the Féile Bia charter.

"Now I realise that Féile Bia helps us in many ways. It helped us fine tune our systems. Our suppliers are aware that they have to be on top of things these days, and it does help us to get even more information from them so that we can be really, really confident that everything is as we say it is.

"There are marketing benefits too. The exposure in the Georgina Campbell Jameson Guide is valuable, and the inclusion of the Féile Bia logo on guide entries is increasing consumer recognition of the emblem, and what it represents. Our customers show interest in the framed Féile Bia certificates displayed in all five of our cafés, and even more so in the plaque that shows we won the Féile Bia Award. Two years on, I think everyone at Avoca is one hundred per cent behind Féile Bia".

Euro-Toques

Thanks to the dedication of many talented Irish chefs and small producers, progress on strengthening the regional quality of Irish food is promising. A recognisably contemporary Irish cooking style is gradually emerging, producing lighter, modern food that is still based on traditional foodstuffs and themes. Chefs are encouraged to avoid the dangers of fashionable but bland internationalism, and bring a real Irish flavour back into their restaurants.

Euro-Toques, the European Community of Chefs, is an organisation with just these issues at heart, and over 200 Irish chefs are enthusiastic members. Their charter commits them to supporting the quality of natural and traditional foods, to maintaining traditional dishes and traditional ways of preparing them in order to keep regional differences alive.

Ross Lewis, chef-proprietor of Dublin's Chapter One Restaurant, is Ireland's Commissioner General, leading a strong Irish chapter whose busy members make a point of finding the time to support social activities like mushroom hunts and visits to members' restaurants, and to craft food producers. Euro-Toques believe diversity to be the future of food production and that agricultural production in Ireland can incorporate several speeds, one of them being an agriculture of specific production corresponding to local identity - more craft based, perhaps more expensive, but corresponding to the demand of a growing number of consumers.

Euro-Toques nurtures young talent through the annual Baileys/Euro-Toques Young Chef of the Year Competition, and by selecting and coaching Ireland's representative for the world's most prestigious cooking competition, the Bocuse d'Or. But in no way is this an elitist group. All chefs are encouraged to join, providing they are prepared to follow the code of honour and use fine, non-genetically engineered, quality foods, and support local craft food producers

Slow Food

The Slow Food Movement is a focal point for small craft food producers in much the same way as Euro-Toques is for chefs. This international movement was founded in 1989, and is active in 35 countries. It is dedicated to ensuring the future of small-scale, quality farm-food production. Groups of small producers have formed Convivia, (local chapters) and hold open days throughout the country. As the name suggests, the Slow Food Movement also owes much to the taste for a gentler, more thoughtful way of life

Their goal is to spread and stimulate awareness of food culture (flavours and ancient production techniques), to safeguard the food and agricultural heritage (biodiversity, artisanal techniques and traditions), to protect the heritage of traditional eating places, and resist the worldwide standardisation of tastes. Although only relatively recently activated in Ireland, it has touched a chord of resonance and is, despite the name, a fast-growing movement that promises to become highly influential.

Food for Vitality

Ireland's youthful, health-conscious population seems set to ensure that healthy fast food like juices and smoothies are more than a passing fashion, and - judging by the great variety of vegetables and side salads on restaurant tables - the Bord Glas (horticultural development board) "Four or More" slogan, urging Irish people to eat more fruit and vegetables, is proving remarkably popular. Welcome trends include the growing availability of an ever-growing range of creative vegetarian dishes (often placed top of the menu); an increased use of seasonal and named foods from local growers and producers; and the increasing availability and popularity of Irish-grown organic foods.

Most exciting of all, perhaps, is that the best vegetarian cooking is now very definitely mainstream, and much of the most innovative cooking in Ireland at the moment focuses on the creative use of Irish fruit and vegetables in season.

Happy Heart Eat Out

Most visitors lose a little bit of their heart to Ireland, and it is the Irish Heart Foundation's task to keep the hearts of natives and visitors alike physically healthy. The Irish Heart Foundation's aims coincide with those of Bord Glas and other food agencies, in that they want healthy eating to be a normal, enjoyable part of life. The Happy Heart Eat Out initiative is an imaginative (and very Irish way) of doing just that, and has been a welcome annual feature of the dining scene for some years now.

Restaurants, hotels, pubs and other eating establishments that join the programme offer healthy eating options - look out for the smiling heart-shaped face on the menu. In a country with an abundance of home-grown vegetables, fruits, herbs, seafoods, and meat, it's not difficult to offer "healthy" menu options. Increasingly, Irish restaurants recognise the need to care for their customers' health, with dishes low in fat and sodium highlighted on the menu, and a willingness to meet special dietary requirements: if you don't see what you need on the menu, "Just Ask".

Riches from Land & Sea

If you wanted to create the perfect place to catch seafood in clean Atlantic waters warmed along much of the coast by the Gulf Stream, then you'd probably invent Ireland. Bord Iascaigh Mhara, the Irish Sea Fisheries Board (BIM) is dedicated to developing the seafood industry, and encouraging everyone to cook and enjoy seafood.

A number of current developments are of special interest: in one innovative scheme, BIM and Bord Glas work together to encourage combining of fruit and vegetables with fish - a healthy idea that also makes the most of inevitably expensive seafood. The development of aquaculture and the trend towards organic fish farming is growing, with Ireland in the forefront of international research. Organic mussels, trout and salmon are already available and popular, so much so that at the pioneering Clare Island Sea Farm, the demand for organic salmon can sometimes outstrip supply.

Shellfish grown commercially include oysters, mussels, clams, and scallops; prime fish such as turbot and halibut are being successfully farmed, even in unexpected locations – clean seawater is what it's all about. An innovative, more environmentally friendly and natural way of farming salmon has been developed which reduces fat and improves texture, making it difficult to tell the difference between farmed and wild fish.

BIM's latest initiatives include a new quality seafood programme (QSP) covering trout, mussels, oysters and farmed and wild salmon: a QSP symbol on a product gives consumers an assurance that there is traceability from the hatchery to the supermarket shelf. BIM's successful bar food programme, The Seafood Circle, is also encouraging more pubs to serve seafood dishes for lunch - a meal where an increasing number of customers prefer the lighter healthier dishes. It's a practical programme involving workshops and on-going guidance on every aspect of buying, storing, and cooking seafood. There are strict criteria for entry, and there is an annual audit.

Cosmopolitan Tastes

The fashion for global cuisine quickened pace as Ireland became a net importer of people from all over the world. The influence of other food cultures (European, Asian, New World, and every possible fusion of cuisines from Cal-Ital to Pacific rim) has grown, often jostling for space on the same menu.

A significant cosmopolitan population with differing tastes and traditions has changed the way Irish people look at ethnic food, and there is a growing interest in authenticity, both in restaurants and ethnic cooking at home. It's an exciting phase which highlights the value of restaurants that are true to a particular style or cuisine, and the best are included in the Guide - all the main cultures are well-represented, with a number of Indian restaurants in their "second phase" offering refreshingly authentic regional cuisine

The internationally respected Chinese restaurant critic and cookery writer, Deh-Ta Hsiung, who re-visited Ireland recently after an absence of several years, commented that the standard of Chinese and Asian restaurants generally has improved, and there is now much more choice for consumers. However he also found that prices compare unfavourably with the UK - and, in Chinese restaurants especially, he'd like to see "imagination and daring, that would revitalise this great cuisine": now there's a challenge for Ireland's top Chinese chefs!

Value for Money or Affordable Food?

Ireland does not claim to be a low cost destination, and overhead costs in Dublin in particular are steep. However, establishments at all levels have risen to the challenge of providing value for money. The finest restaurants, especially, offer interesting keenly priced menus at lunch time - often exceptionally good value for money. Another popular option is to dine early (or late) and take advantage of value-for-money pre- and post-theatre, or early bird dinner menus.

Typically these menus are shorter, but that does not imply a compromise on food quality or service. A welcome recent innovation is that more establishments begin dinner service at six (sometimes even earlier), allowing early birds to enjoy a leisurely meal with no sense of being rushed through to make way for the second sitting.

Irish Love of Atmosphere

Assuming good food, atmosphere in restaurants is probably more important to the Irish dining public than anything else, and genuine hospitality is the main ingredient for success. Relaxing decor and sympathetic lighting are the other magic ingredients, and the Guide is privileged to have Rathborne Candles as a sponsor.

Ireland's oldest established surviving company was in existence even before Columbus reached America – Rathborne's were founded in 1488. They have been lighting churches and dining rooms in the country for almost 600 years, and are increasingly doing it again today as candles have become an essential "softening" feature in contemporary decor. So the next time you sit in a great candlelit dining-room overlooking a lake or a sunset-lit mountain, just think that for six centuries people have been enjoying something remarkably similar!

The Perfect Way to Start the Day

If enjoyment in restaurants and pubs around the country provides memorable evening entertainment, the next morning's breakfast is no small matter for visitors to Ireland - or, indeed, for the Irish on holiday, as having the leisure to indulge in a proper breakfast seems to symbolise escape from the workaday routine. The best hosts take great pride in offering guests a breakfast to remember, whether it be a meal with little choice that is cooked to perfection, or a wide-ranging breakfast menu.

In some favoured areas, the competition between neighbouring establishments to provide the supreme breakfast can be fierce, and menus occasionally run to several pages. They offer traditional country house breakfast dishes that may have fallen from favour - fresh and cured fish, European-style salami and cured meats, wonderful and varied breads, Irish farm cheeses, and vegetarian options. Not that the traditional Irish breakfast is neglected; how could it be when it remains (particularly with visitors) the most popular way to start to the day?

"The full Irish" as it is affectionately known, is not for the faint-hearted: bacon rashers, eggs, sausages, black and white puddings, tomatoes, and fried bread, once upon a time cooked on a great black cast-iron frying pan over a turf fire, but more usually grilled nowadays (or oven-baked) - except for the fried egg. The truly health-conscious will be glad to know you'll also be offered a choice of poached, scrambled, or baked eggs (which, just to confuse, are often cooked in thick Irish cream). In the north, on the other hand, the Ulster Fry can still be determinedly unreconstructed.

Its additional fried ingredients can include potato bread (boxty), soda farls (griddle bread), mushrooms, and baked beans too....Small wonder that the "all-day breakfast" is widely on offer.

You can forgive visitors for feeling slightly but happily confused sometimes: for, not only can you eat breakfast all day, but there's also a growing trend of serving Sunday lunch all afternoon - and well into the evening. You've heard of seamless hospitality? It's right here in Ireland.

Drinking a Toast

Drink is an essential element of Irish hospitality, sometimes prized above food as a way of showing our pleasure in company, our delight in entertainment, and as nourishment for mind and body. The Irish have been brewing since earliest times, and without doubt - had the climate been favourable - we would have had a thriving wine industry, too. Not that the Irish did without wine. Records show that two thousand years ago French wine was being dispatched to Ireland for "feasts in the courts of the kings". Later, early Christian monks sailed to the mouth of the Loire to fetch wine for Irish monasteries and the Vikings paid tribute to Irish kings in vats of wine. The ordinary people were content with cider, ale, and later, with porter and stout.

It is generally accepted that the craft of distillation was brought to Ireland from the Mediterranean, possibly by missionary monks around fifteen hundred years ago. It was used originally to make perfumes and medicines; and later whiskey. Much as we'd like to, no one really knows the origins of whiskey. The Celtic culture was an oral one, particularly when it came to important secrets which were never written down. Historians search ancient texts for written evidence with good reason - our reputation for having invented whiskey is at stake.

We had aqua vitae of course, distilled from wine. We do know, from a wealth of written sources, that by the mid-16th Century the making of grain aqua vitae (known to the Irish as ische beatha and to English-speakers as whiskey) was widespread. Then, on Christmas Day 1661, a tax of 4d was imposed on every gallon distilled. Folklore has it that the making of the illicit spirit poitin began on St Stephen's Day (December 26th)!

The difference between legal and illicit whiskey was small. By the 18th Century there were 2,000 stills in operation and whiskey had become the spirit of the nation, inspiring poets and musicians and promoting friendship (and frequent disputes) between native and stranger. Irish whiskey is both spelled and made differently from other whiskeys. It is made only from kiln-dried barley (both malted and unmalted), yeast and pure Irish water. It is distilled three times in a pot still, then matured in oak barrels until judged ready for drinking. Visitors can relive this history by visiting three historic distilleries: The Old Jameson Distillery in Dublin, The Bushmills Distillery in Antrim, and the Midleton Distillery in County Cork. The tours are fascinating, covering all aspects of whiskey making, and end with a whiskey tasting.

IRELAND

Tory
Rathlin
Malin
Culdaff
Tremone
Greencastle
Ballyliffen
Carndonagh
Moville
Portsalon
Portballintrae
Bushmills
Ballintoy
Ballycastle
Portstewart
Portrush
Coleraine
Dunfanaghy
Buncrana
Fahan
Cushendun
Cushendall
Gortahork
Milford
Rathmullen
Ballymoney
Aghadowey
An Bun Beag (Bunbeg)
Annagry
Gaoth Dobhair (Gweedore)
Ramelton
Limavady
Carnlough
Ailt an Chorráin (Burtonport)
An Clochán Liath (Dungloe)
Letterkenny
Derry
ANTRIM
Ballygally
Larne
DONEGAL
Feeny
Dungiven
DERRY
Ballymena
Whitehead
Glenties
Stranorlar
Lifford
Upperlands
Ballybofey
Strabane
Ballyclare
Gleann Cholm Cille (Glencolumbkille)
Ardara
Carrickfergus
Malinmore
Lough Eske
Newtownstewart
Magherafelt
Antrim
Killybegs
Donegal
TYRONE
Cookstown
Cultra
Hollywood
Bangor
Donaghadee
Bruckless
Dunkineely
Belfast
Newtownards
Rossnowlagh
Omagh
Dungannon
L. Neagh
Kesh
Comber
Ballyshannon
Irvinestown
Dromore
Lisburn
Kircubbin
Bundoran
Hillsborough
Mullaghmore
Belleek
Aughnacloy
Lurgan
Killyleagh
Portaferry
Tullaghan
Kinlough
Portadown
Grange
Tandragee
Ballynahinch
Strangford
Glencar
Enniskillen
Gilford
Banbridge
Downpatrick
Manorhamilton
Glaslough
Armagh
Béal an Mhuirthead (Belmullet)
Rosses Point
Belanaleck
DOWN
Castlewellan
Strandhill
ARMAGH
Ballycastle
Sligo
FERMANAGH
Monaghan
Keady
Dundrum
Killala
Dromahair
Blacklion
Derrylin
Newcastle
Swanlinbar
Clones
Inishcrone
Newry
Bangor Erris
SLIGO
MONAGHAN
Crossmolina
Collooney
Castleblayney
Ballina
Riverstown
Belturbet
Warrenpoint
Rostrevor
Gweesalia
Ballyconnell
Cloverhill
Kilkeel
Tubbercurry
Castlebaldwin
Butlersbridge
Cootehill
Lahardane
Ballymote
Ballinamore
Carlingford
Keel
Foxford
Keadue
Drumshanbo
Dundalk
Pontoon
Keshcarrigan
Achill Island
MAYO
Boyle
LEITRIM
Cavan
Charlestown
Arvagh
Carrickmacross
Mulrany
Swinford
Carrick-on-Shannon
Blackrock
Jamestown
Ballinagh
CAVAN
Rosturk
Newport
Rooskey
LOUTH
Castlebar
Virginia
Kingscourt
Ardee
Clare Island
ROSCOMMON
Mountnugent
Dunleer
Lecanvey
Clogherhead
Roonah Quay
Westport
Knock
Strokestown
Granard
Collon
Termonfeckin
Louisburgh
LONGFORD
Castlerea
Tarmonbarry
Kells
Slane
Drogheda
Claremorris
Ballyhaunis
Longford
Edgeworthstown
Inishbofin
Castlepollard
Navan
Bettystown
Renvyle
Leenáun
Lanesborough
Ballinrobe
Roscommon
Multifarnham
Athboy
MEATH
Balbriggan
Cleggan
Skerries
Letterfrack
Lough Inagh
Clonbur
Cong
Ballymahon
Trim
Rush
Clifden
Tuam
Kilmessan
Mullingar
Swords
Ballyconneely
Sraith Salach (Recess)
Headford
Mount Bellew
Hodson Bay
Glasson
WESTMEATH
Enfield
Dunshaughlin
Malahide

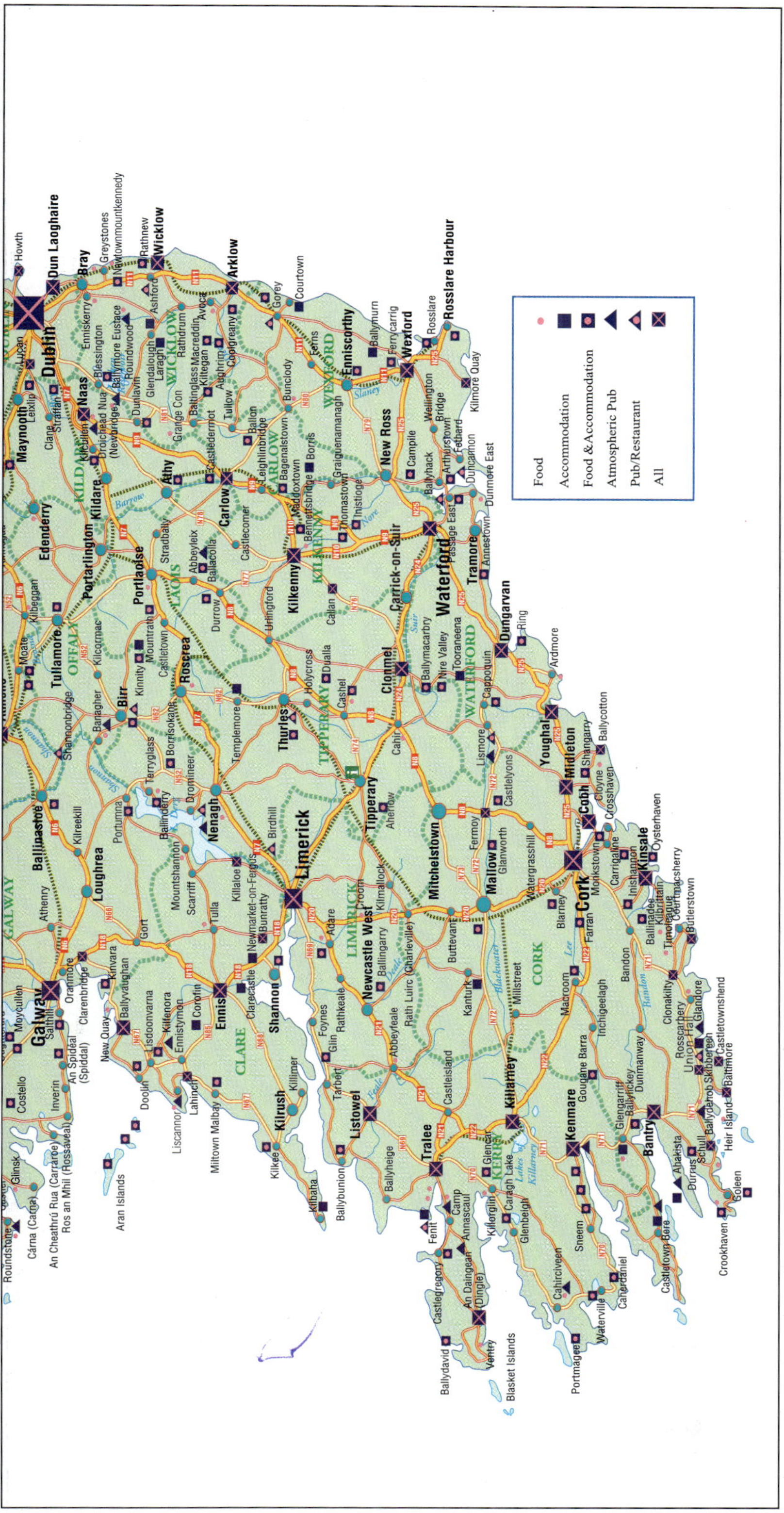
Food
Accommodation
Food & Accommodation
Atmospheric Pub
Pub/Restaurant
All
Dublin
Dun Laoghaire
Howth
Lucan
Maynooth
Leixlip
Bray
Greystones
Newtownmountkennedy
Enniskerry
Blessington
Naas
Kildare
Athy
Wicklow
Rathnew
Ashford
Roundwood
Glendalough
Laragh
Rathdrum
Avoca
Arklow
Gorey
Courtown
Enniscorthy
Ferns
Bunclody
Wexford
Rosslare
Rosslare Harbour
Kilmore Quay
New Ross
Carlow
Tullow
Kilkenny
Thomastown
Inistioge
Callan
Waterford
Tramore
Dunmore East
Passage East
Carrick-on-Suir
Clonmel
Dungarvan
Ring
Ardmore
Youghal
Ballycotton
Midleton
Cobh
Cork
Kinsale
Mallow
Fermoy
Mitchelstown
Lismore
Cappoquin
Cahir
Cashel
Tipperary
Limerick
Adare
Newcastle West
Thurles
Templemore
Roscrea
Nenagh
Birr
Portlaoise
Portarlington
Edenderry
Tullamore
Moate
Kilbeggan
Banagher
Shannonbridge
Portumna
Ballinasloe
Loughrea
Athenry
Galway
Oranmore
Kinvara
Gort
Ennis
Shannon
Bunratty
Killaloe
Kilrush
Kilkee
Lahinch
Doolin
Liscannor
Lisdoonvarna
Ballyvaughan
New Quay
Aran Islands
Costello
Inverin
Cárna (Carna)
Roundstone
An Spidéal (Spiddal)
Salthill
Moycullen
Listowel
Ballybunion
Tarbert
Glin
Foynes
Abbeyfeale
Tralee
Fenit
Castlegregory
An Daingean (Dingle)
Ventry
Ballydavid
Blasket Islands
Killorglin
Glenbeigh
Cahirciveen
Waterville
Portmagee
Caherdaniel
Sneem
Kenmare
Killarney
Glengarriff
Bantry
Castletown Bere
Durrus
Schull
Crookhaven
Goleen
Skibbereen
Baltimore
Heir Island
Castletownshend
Glandore
Rosscarbery
Clonakilty
Timoleague
Bandon
Dunmanway
Macroom
Blarney
Millstreet
Kanturk
Buttevant
Charleville
Kilmallock
Croom
CLARE
LIMERICK
CORK
KERRY
WATERFORD
TIPPERARY
KILKENNY
WEXFORD
CARLOW
WICKLOW
KILDARE
LAOIS
OFFALY
GALWAY

IONA ROAD
LINDSAY ROAD
WHITWORTH ROAD
PROSPECT ROAD
CONNAUGHT STREET
DALYMOUNT PARK
CARNLOUGH ROAD
QUARRY ROAD
DOWTH AVE
CABRA ROAD
NORTH CIRCULAR ROAD
CHARLEVILLE RD
ECCLES STREET
BLACKHORSE AVENUE
GRANGEGORMAN UPPER
RATHDOWN RD
PHIBSBOROUGH ROAD
PRUSSIA STREET
AUGHRIM STREET
OXMANTOWN ROAD
MANOR STREET
HALLIDAY RD
7
MOUNTJOY ST
DORSET ST
DOMINICK ST
CONSTITUTION HILL
KINGS INNS
BOLTON ST
Old Jameson Distillery
PHOENIX PARK
INFIRMARY ROAD
ARBOUR HILL
BRUNSWICK ST
NORTH KING ST
PARNELL ST
BLACKHALL PL
QUEEN ST
SMITHFIELD
BOW ST
CHURCH STREET
MARYS LANE
MARY ST
ABBEY ST
CAPEL STREET
PARKGATE STREET
BENBURB STREET
WOLFE TONE QUAY
ELLIS QY
ARRAN QUAY
CHANCERY STREET
VICTORIA QUAY
USHERS ISL
USHERS QUAY
INNS QY
ORMOND QY UPR
ORMOND QY LWR
WELLINGTON
MERCHANTS QUAY
TEMPLE BAR
DAME
ST JOHN'S ROAD
STEVENS LANE
WATLING ST
BRIDGEFOOT ST
BRIDGE ST
KILMAINHAM
THOMAS STREET
HIGH STREET
LORD EDWARD ST
Dublin Castle
ST JAMES'S STREET
RAINSFORD ST
MEATH ST
FRANCIS STREET
WERBURGH ST
STH GT GEORGES ST
KILMAINHAM
BROOKFIELD RD
8
MARROWBONE LANE
PIMLICO
THE COOMBE
PATRICK ST
BRIDE STREET
STEPHEN
AUNGIER STREET
YORK
SOUTH CIRCULAR ROAD
KEVIN ST
KEVIN
CUFF
ARDEE ST
NEW ST
DONORE AVENUE
CORK STREET
SUIR ROAD
MANGAN ROAD
CLANBRASSIL ST
HEYTESBURY ST
SYNGE STREET
CAMDEN STREET
DOLPHINS BARN
DOLPHIN ROAD
DUFFERIN AVE
N
W
E
S
PARNELL ROAD
RICHMOND ST
12
CRUMLIN ROAD
SUNDRIVE ROAD
RUTLAND AVE
CLOGHER ROAD
HAROLDS CROSS RD
GROVE ROAD
6W
6
RATHMINES ROAD
HAROLD'S CROSS STADIUM
0
1 MILE
1
0
1 KILOMETRE
1

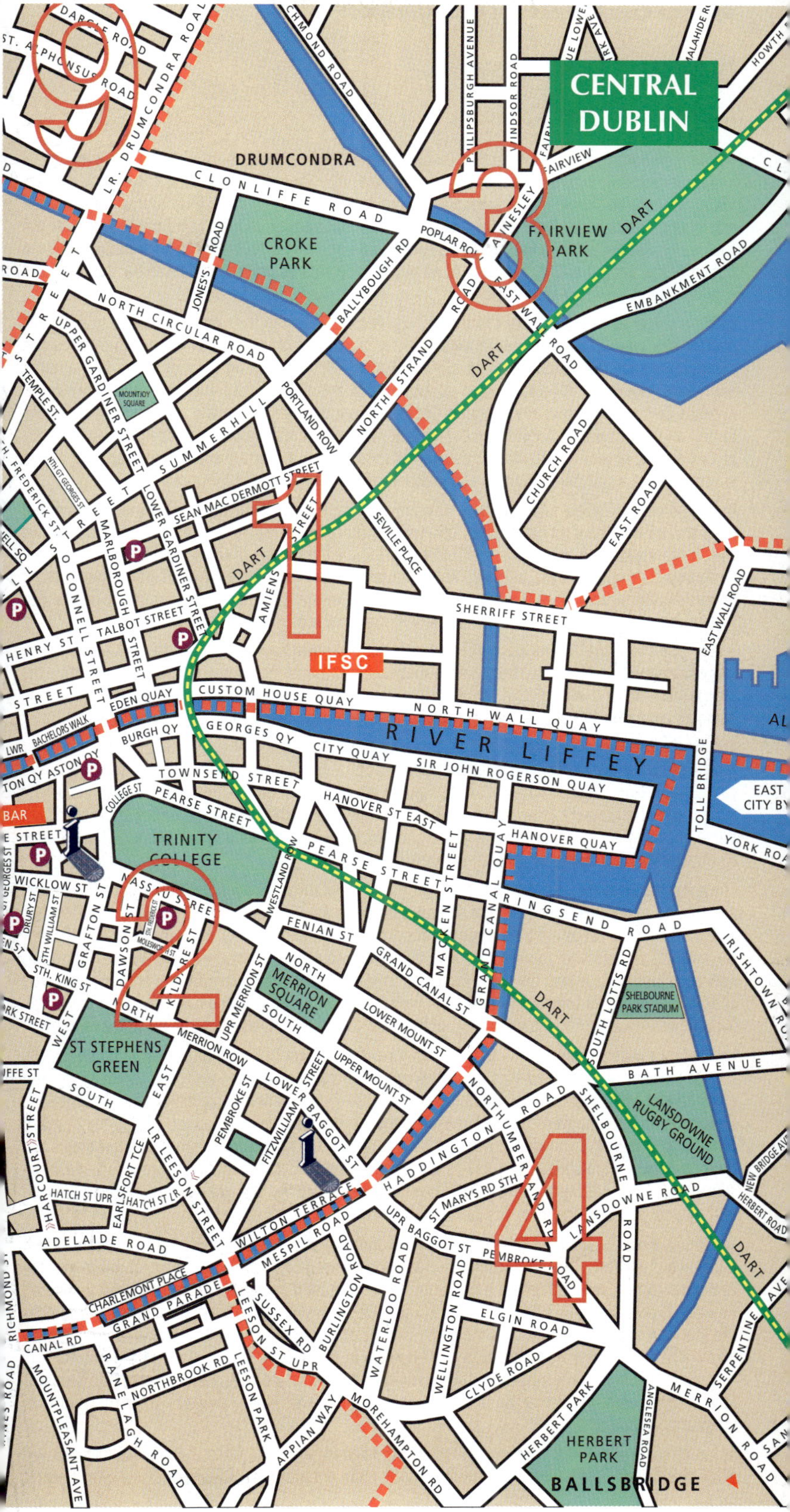
CENTRAL DUBLIN
DRUMCONDRA
DARGLE ROAD
ST. ALPHONSUS ROAD
LR. DRUMCONDRA ROAD
RICHMOND ROAD
PHILIPSBURGH AVENUE
WINDSOR ROAD
FAIRVIEW
CLONLIFFE ROAD
CROKE PARK
JONES'S ROAD
BALLYBOUGH RD
POPLAR ROW
ANNESLEY
FAIRVIEW PARK
DART
EMBANKMENT ROAD
EAST WALL ROAD
NORTH CIRCULAR ROAD
UPPER GARDINER STREET
TEMPLE ST.
MOUNTJOY SQUARE
SUMMERHILL
PORTLAND ROW
NORTH STRAND ROAD
CHURCH ROAD
EAST ROAD
SEAN MAC DERMOTT STREET
AMIENS STREET
SEVILLE PLACE
SHERRIFF STREET
EAST WALL ROAD
FREDERICK ST
NTH GT GEORGES ST
MARLBOROUGH STREET
LOWER GARDINER STREET
O'CONNELL STREET
TALBOT STREET
HENRY ST
IFSC
CUSTOM HOUSE QUAY
NORTH WALL QUAY
EDEN QUAY
BURGH QY
GEORGES QY
RIVER LIFFEY
CITY QUAY
SIR JOHN ROGERSON QUAY
TOLL BRIDGE
EAST CITY BY
YORK ROA
BACHELORS WALK
ASTON QY
TOWNSEND STREET
COLLEGE ST
PEARSE STREET
HANOVER ST EAST
HANOVER QUAY
TRINITY COLLEGE
WESTLAND ROW
MACKEN STREET
GRAND CANAL QUAY
RINGSEND ROAD
IRISHTOWN RO
WICKLOW ST
DRURY ST
STH WILLIAM ST
GRAFTON ST
DAWSON ST
KILDARE ST
NASSAU STREET
MOLESWORTH ST
FENIAN ST
GRAND CANAL ST
STH. KING ST
NORTH MERRION SQUARE SOUTH
UPR MERRION ST
LOWER MOUNT ST
UPPER MOUNT ST
SOUTH LOTTS RD
SHELBOURNE PARK STADIUM
ST STEPHENS GREEN
MERRION ROW
LOWER BAGGOT ST
PEMBROKE ST
FITZWILLIAM ST
NORTHUMBERLAND RD
BATH AVENUE
SHELBOURNE ROAD
LANSDOWNE RUGBY GROUND
HARCOURT STREET
EARLSFORT TCE
LR LEESON STREET
HATCH ST UPR
HATCH ST LR
HADDINGTON ROAD
ST MARYS RD STH
LANSDOWNE ROAD
NEW BRIDGE AV
HERBERT ROAD
ADELAIDE ROAD
WILTON TERRACE
MESPIL ROAD
UPR BAGGOT ST
PEMBROKE ROAD
CHARLEMONT PLACE
GRAND PARADE
CANAL RD
LEESON ST UPR
SUSSEX RD
BURLINGTON ROAD
WATERLOO ROAD
WELLINGTON ROAD
ELGIN ROAD
CLYDE ROAD
SERPENTINE AVE
MERRION ROAD
RANELAGH ROAD
NORTHBROOK RD
MOUNTPLEASANT AVE
LEESON PARK
APPIAN WAY
MOREHAMPTON RD
HERBERT PARK
ANGLESEA ROAD
BALLSBRIDGE
BAR
1
2
3
4
9

DUBLIN

A Town for our Times

Dublin continues to be one of Western Europe's fastest expanding economic centres, its commercial and creative energy matched by the vibrancy of its everyday life and hospitality. It's an old town where many meandering stories have interacted and combined to create today's busy riverside and coastal metropolis. Through a wide variety of circumstances, it has become an entertaining place suited to the civilised enjoyment of life in the 21st Century. That said, there's no doubting the edge there is to life in Dublin today, with the daily business news and movements in property values attracting as much popular interest as sport and politics.

Dubliners tend to wear their city's history lightly, despite having in their environment so much of the past in the way of ancient monuments, historic buildings, gracious squares and fine old urban architecture that still manages to be gloriously alive. This if anything is emphasised by the city's impressive modern architecture, seen particularly in the area around the International Financial Services Centre and across the Liffey on George's Quay, dramatically in the new Spire in O'Connell Street, and most spectacularly in the Gaelic Athletic Association's completely revamped headquarters at Croke Park, now the third largest stadium in Europe, and a masterpiece of contemporary design which provides a suitable setting for epic matches of hurling and Gaelic football.

Dubliners may not quite take their city's dynamic interaction of classic and modern for granted, but nevertheless they have to get on with life. Indeed, these days they've a vigorous appetite for it. So they'll quickly deflate any visitor's excessive enthusiasm about their city's significance with some throwaway line of Dublin wit, or sweep aside highfalutin notions of some figure of established cultural importance by recalling how their grandfathers had the measure of that same character when he was still no more than a pup making a nuisance of himself in the neighbourhood pub.

The origins of the city's name are in keeping with this downbeat approach. From the ancient Irish there came something which derived from a makeshift solution to local inconvenience. Baile Atha Cliath - the official name today - means nothing more exciting than "the townland of the hurdle ford". Ancient Ireland being an open plan sort of place without towns, the future city was no more than a river crossing.

But where the Irish saw inconvenience, the Vikings saw an opportunity. When they brought their longships up the River Liffey, they found a sheltered berth in a place which the locals of the hurdle ford called Dubh Linn - "the black pool". Although the name was to go through many mutations as the Vikings were succeeded by the Normans who in turn were in the business of becoming English, today's name of Dublin is remarkably similar to the one which the Vikings came upon, although the old Irish would have pronounced it as something more like "doo-lin".

The name makes sense, for it was thanks to the existence of the black pool that Dublin became the port and trading base which evolved as the country's natural administrative centre. Thus your Dubliner may well think that the persistent official use of Baile Atha Cliath is an absurdity. But it most empatically isn't the business of any visitor to say so, for although Dublin came into existence almost by accident, it has now been around for a long time, and Dubliners have developed their own attitudes and their own way of doing things. As for their seaport, it is still very much part of the city, and has never been busier - on September 19th 2003 it was named "Port of the Year" at the All Ireland Transport & Logistics Awards.

Located by a wide bay with some extraordinarily handsome hills and mountains near at hand, the city has long had as an important part of its makeup the dictates of stylish living, and the need to cater efficiently for individual tastes and requirements. From time to time the facade has been maintained through periods of impoverishment, but even in the earliest mediaeval period this was already a major centre of craftmanship and innovative shop-keeping. Today, the Dublin craftsmen and shop-keepers and their assistants are characterful subjects worthy of respectful academic study. And in an age when "going shopping" has become the world's favourite leisure activity, this old city has reinvented herself in the forefront of international trends.

For Dublin virtually shunned the Industrial Revolution, or at least took some care to ensure that it happened elsewhere. The city's few large enterprises tended to be aimed at personal needs and the consumer market, rather than some aspiration towards heavy industry. Typical of them was Guinness's Brewery, founded in 1759. Today, its work-force may be much slimmed in every sense, but it still creates the black nectar, and if a new mash is under way up at the brewery and the wind is coming damply across Ireland from the west, the aroma of Guinness in the making will be wafted right into the city centre, the moist evocative essence of Anna Livia herself, while the imaginatively renovated Guinness Storehouse - with its interactive museums, restaurants and bars - provides a visitor centre of international quality.

Although some of the vitality of the city faded in the periods when the focus of power had been moved elsewhere, today Dublin thrives as one of Europe's more entertaining capitals, and as a global centre of the computer, communications and financial services industries. While it may be trite to suggest that her history has been a fortuitous preparation for the needs of modern urban life in all its variety of work and relaxation, there is no denying Dublin's remarkable capacity to provide the ideal circumstances for fast-moving people-orientated modern industries, even if those same people find at times that their movement within the city is hampered by weight of traffic. Nevertheless it's a civilised city where the importance of education is a central theme of the strong family ethos, this high level of education making it a place of potent attraction in the age of information technology.

Such a city naturally has much of interest for historians of all kinds, and a vibrant cultural life is available for visitors and Dubliners alike. You can immerse yourself in it all as much or as little as you prefer, for today's Dublin is a city for all times and all tastes, and if you're someone who hopes to enjoy Dublin as we know Dubliners enjoy it, we know you'll find much of value here. And don't forget that there's enjoyment in Dublin well hidden from the familiar tourist trails.

History is well-matched by modernity, or a mixture of both. The glass palaces of the International Financial Services Centre point the way to a maturing new business district which is a pleasure to savour, particularly at the Docklands Farmers Market every Wednesday from 11.0am to 3.0pm at Excise Walk beside the Clarion Hotel.

Upriver to the westward, the award-winning transformation of the Smithfield area encompasses the popular Old Jameson Distillery Visitor Centre, another magnet for the discerning visitor - particularly someone who enjoys a sense of the past interacting with the present, not least in the age-old story of the creation of whiskey. The revitalisation of the Smithfield area has succeeded in creating its own special dynamic, and it's clearly attractive for today's new Dubliners. On Friday September 19th 2003 it was announced that the latest quality apartment development in the area had sold sixty units within 24 hours of coming on the market.

When Dublin was starting to expand to its present size during the mid-20th Century, with people flocking in from all over Ireland to work in the city, it was said that the only "real Dub" was someone who didn't go home to the country for the weekend. Today, with Dublin so popular with visitors, the more cynical citizens might well comment that the surest test of a real Dub is someone who avoids Temple Bar...

But it is rather unfair of any Dubliner to dismiss that bustling riverside hotbed of musical pubs, ethnic restaurants, cultural events and nightclubs as being no more than a tourist ghetto. After all, in addition to its many places of entertainment and hospitality, Temple Bar is also home to at least 1,300 people, their needs being served locally by useful happenings such as the Natural Food Fair, held every Saturday (10am to 6pm) in Cow's Lane, with organic foods and the freshest of produce from land and sea matching the gourmet quality of the exotic products sold through the Specialist Market in Meeting House Square.

So there's real life here too. And at the very least, it is Temple Bar which maintains the Dubliner's international reputation as a round-the-clock party animal. So now that the area has settled down and achieved a certain mellowness in its new role, you will definitely meet "real Dubs" here, though in today's very cosmopolitan city, just how we'd define a "real Dub" is a moot point.

Nevertheless, come nightfall and your discerning Dubliner is more likely to be found in a pleasant pub or restaurant in one of the city's many urban villages, delightfully named places such as Ranelagh or Rathmines or Templeogue or Stoneybatter or Phibsborough or Donnybrook or Glasnevin or Ringsend or Dundrum or Clontarf or Drumcondra or Chapelizod, to name only a few. And then there are places like Stepaside or Howth or Glasthule or Foxrock or Dalkey which are at sufficient distance as scarcely to think of themselves as being part of Dublin at all. Yet that's where you'll find today's real Dubs enjoying their fair city every bit as much as city centre folk. Happy is the visitor who is able to savour it all, in and around this town for our times.

Local Attractions & Information

Abbey & Peacock Theatres, Lower Abbey Street 01 8787222
Andrew's Lane Theatre, off Exchequer Street 01 6795720
The Ark Arts Centre, Eustace St., Temple Bar D2 .... 01 6707788
Bank of Ireland (historic), College Green 01 6615933
Botanic Gardens, Glasnevin, D 9 .... 01 8374388
Ceol - Irish Traditional Music Centre, Smithfield 01 8173820
Christchurch Cathedral, Christchurch Place, D8 .... 01 6778099
City Arts Centre, 23-25 Moss St., D2 .... 01 6770643
Croke Park, GAA Stadium and Museum D3 .... 01 8558176
Drimnagh Castle (moat, formal 17c gardens) Longmile Rd 01 4502530
Dublin Airport 01 8144222

Dublin Castle, Dame Street	01 6777129
Dublin Film Festival (April)	01 6792937
Dublin Garden Festival, RDS (June)	01 4900600
Dublin International Horse Show, RDS, (August)	01 6680866
Dublin International Organ & Choral Fest. (June)	01 6773066
Dublin Theatre Festival (October)	01 6778439
Dublin Tourism Centre (restored church), Suffolk St.	1850 230330
Dublin Writer's Museum, Parnell Square	01 8722077
Dublinia (living history), Christchurch	01 4758137
Farmleigh House, Phoenix Park	01 8155900
Farmleigh House Boathouse Restaurant	01 8157255/8157250
Gaiety Theatre, South King Street	01 6771717
Gate Theatre, Cavendish Row	01 8744045
Guinness Brewery, St Jame's Gate	01 4536700 ext 5155
Guinness Storehouse	01 4084800
Helix, DCU Performing Arts Centre, Collins Avenue, 9	01 7007000
Hugh Lane Municipal Gallery, Parnell Square	01 8741903
Irish Antique Dealers Fair, RDS (October)	01 2859294
Irish Film Centre, Eustace Street	01 6793477
IFSC Farm Market (Mayor Sq., Wed 10.30am-4pm)	087 6115016
Irish Museum of Modern Art/Royal Hospital Kilmainham	01 6718666
Irish Music Hall of Fame, Middle Abbey Street	01 8783345
Irish Tourist Board/Failte Ireland, Baggot St Bridge	01 6024000
Iveagh Gardens, Earlsfort Terrace	01 4757816
Jameson Distillery, Smithfield, Dublin 7	01 8072355
Kilmainham Gaol, Kilmainham	01 4535984
Lansdowne Road Rugby Ground, Ballsbridge	01 6684601
Mother Redcaps Market nr St Patricks/Christchurch Fri-Sun 10am-5.30pm	
National Botanic Gardens, Glasnevin	01 8377596
National Concert Hall, Earlsfort Terrace	01 6711888
National Gallery of Ireland, Merrion Square West	01 6615133
National Museum of Ireland, Kildare Street	01 6777444
National Museum of Ireland, Collins Barracks	01 6777444
Natural History Museum, Merrion Street	01 661881
Newman House, St Stephen's Green	01 4757255
Northern Ireland Tourist Board, Nassau Street	01 6791977
Number 29 (18c House), Lower Fitzwilliam Street	01 7026155
Old Jameson Distillery, Smithfield, Dublin 7	01 8072355
Olympia Theatre, Dame Street	01 6777744
Pearse St Market (St Andrew's Cntr.), Sats 9am-3pm	01 8730451
Point Depot (Concerts & Exhibitions), North Wall Quay	01 8366000
Powerscourt Townhouse, South William Street	01 6794144
Pro Cathedral, Marlborough Street	01 2874292
Project Arts Centre, 39 East Sussex St, D2	01 6796622
RDS (Royal Dublin Society), Ballsbridge	01 6680866
Royal Hospital, Kilmainham	01 6798666
St Michans Church (mummified remains), Dublin 7	01 8724154
St Patrick's Cathedral, Patrick's Close	01 4539472
Shaw birthplace, 33 Synge St., D8	01 4750854
Shelbourne Park Greyhound Stadium	01 6683502
Temple Bar Foodmarket, Sat morning	01 6772255
The Dillon Garden. 45 Sandford Rd, Ranelagh, D6	01 4971308
The Old Jameson Distillery, Smithfield, D7	01 8072355
Tivoli Theatre, Francis Street	01 4544472
Trinity College (Book of Kells & Dublin Experience)	01 6082308
Viking Adventure, Essex St W, Temple Bar,	01 6796040
Viking Splash (Amphibious Tours)	01 4539185
War Memorial Gardens (Sir Edwin Lutyens) Islandbridge	01 6770236
Zoological Gardens, Phoenix Park	01 6771425

DUBLIN 1

Dublin 1

101 Talbot Restaurant

RESTAURANT 100-102 Talbot Street Dublin 1 **Tel: 01 874 5011** Fax: 01 878 1053

Margaret Duffy and Pascal Bradley's ground breaking northside restaurant was here a decade ahead of the current gold rush to service the growing needs of the new "city" area in and around the maturing International Financial Services Centre. Its potential may be more obvious today but it is they who created the buzz here and, while the nearby Abbey and Gate Theatres and the constantly changing art exhibitions in the restaurant are partly responsible for drawing an interesting artistic/theatrical crowd, it is essentially their joyfully creative and healthy food that has earned the 101 such a fine reputation and it is heartening to see standards maintained in a busy city centre restaurant when so many around take the easier option. Mediterranean and Middle Eastern influences explain the uniquely enjoyable wholesomeness across the complete range of dishes, always including strong vegetarian options, such as baked red peppers with Moroccan style chickpeas and vegetables, served with lemon saffron sauce & cous cous - and dietary requirements are always willingly met. Children welcome. **Seats 80.** Open Tue-Sat, 5-11. A la carte. Early D €20. House Wine €16.75. No-smoking area. Closed Sun & Mon, Christmas, New Year, bank hols. Amex, MasterCard, Visa, Laser. **Directions:** 5 minutes walk between Connolly Station and O'Connell Street. Straight down from the spire.

Dublin 1

Chapter One Restaurant

★ féile bia **RESTAURANT** 18/19 Parnell Square Dublin 1 **Tel: 01 873 2266** Fax: 01 873 2330
Email: info@chapter.onerestaurant.com Web: www.chapteronerestaurant.com

Chef-proprietor Ross Lewis and his partner, restaurant manager Martin Corbett, operate this excellent restaurant in an elegantly furnished basement beneath the Dublin Writers' Museum and near The Gate Theatre - which you can visit after your main course and return later for dessert and coffee. The restaurant has great character, with understated modern decor providing a nice contrast to its underlying rusticity; arches create three main areas, of which one is an exceptionally welcoming reception/bar. Ross and Martin have built up terrific kitchen and front of house teams who work together brilliantly to ensure that a visit to Chapter One is always a special occasion: this is a place where hospitality comes first and all the little niceties of a seriously good meal are observed from the moment you taste that complimentary amuse-bouche to the last petit four. Ross, who is the current Commissioner General of Euro-Toques - the international chefs' association dedicated to defending quality produce - makes the most of impeccably sourced ingredients in classic French cooking, with some modern influences. Several menus are offered, all strongly seasonal and invariably interesting - and, whether it's a simple, deliciously dressed watercress salad starter with goats cheese, hazelnuts and apple, a magnificent main course of herb-crusted saddle of lamb with sweetbreads, kidney, minted potatoes & rosemary jus - or grande finale of classic Crêpes Suzettes flambéed at your table (very unusual these days and it is good to see it back), an exceptionally pleasing creative assurance is demonstrated in every dish. This is a restaurant which is constantly improving: specialities abound and charcuterie, for example, has always been a strength - now a charcuterie trolley is taken to your table, offering half a dozen superb dishes ranging from rillette of saddle back pork with apple & horseradish compôte to a selection of West Cork salamis. An exceptional selection of cheeses (invariably in perfect condition) is also offered and classic desserts and, unusually, savouries - such as baked Ardrahan with green tomato chutney, Crozier Blue and hot honey - round off the occasion in style. An excellent, informative (and very tempting) wine list matches menus brilliantly and offers many treats, not least of which are carefully selected house wines and wines by the glass, including a range of dessert wines. Chapter One was our Restaurant of the Year in 2001, reflecting the consistently memorable dining experience of that time - and it just goes on getting better.* Chapter One also runs the coffee shop in the Writers Museum, (10-5 pm Mon-Sat), and provides banqueting facilities for 60-80 people in the Gallery there. Small conferences. Air conditioning. Parking by arrangement with nearby carpark. Children over 6 welcome. **Seats 90** (private rooms, 14 & 20). L Tue-Fri, 12.30-2.30, D Tue-Sat, 6-10.45. Set L €27.50. Pre-theatre menu €28.50, 6-7.30; D à la carte (Tasting Menu, for entire parties, €50). House wine €20. s.c.10%. Closed L Sat, all Sun & Mon, bank hols, 24 Dec-8 Jan; 3 -19 Aug. Diners, MasterCard, Visa, Laser, Switch. **Directions:** Bottom of O'Connell Street, north side of Parnell Square, opp Garden of Remembrance.

Dublin 1

Clarion Hotel Dublin IFSC

HOTEL

Excise Walk IFSC Dublin 1
Tel: 01 433 8800 Fax: 01 433 880
Email: info@clarionhotelifsc.com Web: www.info@clarionhotelifsc.com

This dashing contemporary hotel opened on the river side of the International Financial Services Centre in March 2001. It is the first in the area to be built specifically for the mature 'city' district and is not only meeting the needs of business guests and the financial community admirably, but its high standards and central location have proved very popular with leisure guests as well, especially at weekends. Bright, airy and spacious, the style is refreshingly clean-lined yet comfortable, with lots of gentle neutrals and a somewhat eastern feel that is emphasised by the food philosophy of the hotel - a waft of lemongrass and ginger entices guests through to the Kudos Bar, where Asian wok cooking is served; the more formal restaurant, Sinergie also features world cuisine, but with more European influences. Staff show a real desire to please, the standard of cooking and service are both consistently high and the house wine selection includes 'wine geese' bottles, named after suites and bottles specially for the Clarion. Uncluttered bedrooms have many facilities to appeal to the modern traveller, especially when on business: keycard, security eye and security chain are reassuring features and there are many other conveniences, including air conditioning, 2 phone lines (with voice mail and ISDN) also a pleasing element of self-containment with tea/coffee-making, multi-channel TV, ironing facilities, power hairdryer mini-bar and safe. Generous semi-orthopaedic beds, good linen and bright bathrooms with power showers and bath heated mirror, luxurious towels and top quality toiletries all add to the sense of thoughtful planning that attaches to every aspect of the hotel. There's even a 'Sleep Programme' to help you relax before bed! Leisure facilities, in the basement, are excellent and include an 18m pool and large, well-equipped gym. (Open to membership as well as residents' use). While this is not a place for huge conferences there is a wide range of rooms for meetings of anything between 8 and 100 people, theatre style, with state-of-the art facilities. 24 hour room service. Leisure centre (indoor swimming pool, gym). Lift. Children welcome (under 12s free in parents' room, cot available free of charge, baby sitting arranged). No pets. **Rooms 162** (17 suites, 81 executive, 81 no smoking). B&B €117.50 pps. Room rate €245, no SC. Kudos Bar & Restaurant: Mon-Fri,12-8.30; **Sinergie Restaurant:** L Mon-Fri 12.15-2.30, D daily, 6-9.45. Set L €18.95; Early D €28 (6-7); D €23.50-€35, also à la carte. House wines, from €18.50. Sinergie closed L Sat & Sun. Kudos no food Sat & Sun. 24-26 Dec. [* Comfort Inn, Talbot Street (Tel: 01-874 920 is in the same group and offers budget accommodation near the IFSC.] Amex, Diners, MasterCard, Visa, Laser. **Directions:** Heading east, take the left lane on Custom House Quay. Hotel is in the 3rd block, after 2 sets of traffic lights.

Dublin 1

D.One Restaurant

RESTAURANT

North Wall Quay IFSC Dublin 1 **Tel: 01 856 162**

Proudly laying claim to be only restaurant in Dublin built right on the walls of the River Liffey, this contemporary glass cube takes full advantage of its location on the river side of the road. Although not large and often very busy (especially at lunchtime when hordes of hungry workers pour out of the nearby offices), it succeeds surprisingly well in achieving a sense of spaciousness through simple minimalist furnishing which combines comfort with eye appeal. Clean-lined surroundings seem to underline the stated aim "to offer first class food with great service and, above all, to offer outstanding value for money" which is very welcome in a part of the city where good value is not often the first concept to come to mind - starters begin at €5.25, main courses range from around €13.50 (pasta) to about €23 (fillet of beef with roast shallots & green peppercorn sauce) and the 3-course pre-theatre menu is a snip. The cooking style is contemporary, (which can be taken to mean a mixture of many styles and influences, some more successful than others) and specialities include D.One fish & chips and their variation on a modern Irish classic of roast breast of chicken stuffed with tomato & creamed cheese wrapped in bacon, served with champ mash & wholegrain mustard cream. In the Guide's experience starters tend to be a strong point and desserts a weak one, and the most successful main courses are the ones that don't attempt to marry too many flavours, so simplest choices are often the wisest. Perhaps reflecting demand from the heady world of high finance across the road, a brief wine list rather surprisingly includes four champagnes, with a top price of €196.80. Not suitable for children. **Seats 8** No smoking area. Air conditioning. Wheelchair accessible. Street parking available 7pm-7am an weekends. L Mon-Sat, 12-3; D Mon-Sat, 5-10. A la carte. House wine €14.60. Closed all Sun, bank hols, 23-30 Dec. Visa, Laser. **Directions:** On the waterside at Customs House Quay, opposite Clarion Hotel.

Dublin 1

Epicurean Food Hall

RESTAURANT

Lr Liffey Street Dublin 1

The Epicurean Food Hall brings together a wide range of gourmet foods, cooked and uncooked - and the wines to go with them. The hall is open during the day every day (opens later on Sunday, stays open later for late shoppers on Thursday); there are lots of lovely little shops and cafes in the hall, these few are just a taster:

C-Bar (01 8656663) Little sister to Dublin's most popular restaurant, L'Ecrivain, C-Bar is a tiny fish restaurant where customers perching on high stools at an aluminium counter are treated to superb restaurant-quality seafood cooking, served in classy white porcelain dishes. Try the ultra-fresh seafood platter (with modish sauces like salsa verde or aioli and a few baby potatoes). Open afternoons/early evening (later on Thu, to 9pm).

La Corte (01 873 4200) One of two north river outposts of Stefano Crescenzi and David Izzo's smart Bar Italia (see entry)

Miss Sushi (Tel 01 617 4820) Japanese food has taken great strides in Dublin over the last few years and Miss Sushi, which was opened here in 2000 by a well-travelled Laois lady, Margaret Scully, features food (mostly free range and organic) prepared by a team of professional sushi chefs at The Japanese Food Company and delivered twice daily. There's much more to sushi than raw fish, as Dublin diners are beginning to discover: sushi may have originated as a way to preserve fish in vinegared rice but it has long since taken on a wider meaning - the marriage of vinegared rice with other ingredients. There's a lunch special, changed daily, individual pieces can be selected to taste, or there are Bento (lunch) Boxes which are a good start. Soy sauce, wasabi (Japanese mustard), pickled ginger and rolling mats comes with all sushi. Part platters are available (24 hours notice) and, although Miss Sushi is mainly a gourmet take-away, plated sushi can be eaten on the premises.

Itsabagel (Tel 01 874 0486) Domini and Peaches Kemps' classy bagel bar is very popular with discerning lunchers: choose from bagels, savoury breads with fillings, juices, muffins and cookies. Just delicious. Also at The Pavilion, Dun Laoghaire.

* Although not enclosed within a mall, or indeed a formal grouping of any kind, the nearby Moore Street/Parnell Street area - well known for its street markets and the recent arrival of specialist food shops catering for a newly cosmoplitan population - has become a hothouse of international flavours and is a place to wander for authentic, keenly priced food from different cultures. **Directions:** On the corner of Liffey Street and Middle Abbey Street. ◇

Dublin 1

Expresso Bar Café I.F.S.C.

RESTAURANT

6 Custom House Square I.F.S.C. Dublin 1
Tel: 01 6721812 Fax: 01 6721813 Email: expressobar@ireland.com

Sister of the Expresso Bar Café in Ballsbridge - Anne Marie Nohl and Jane Cathcart have applied the same winning formula to this stylish little contemporary restaurant in Dublin's financial heartland. Breakfasts worth getting in early for kick off with freshly squeezed orange juice and lead on to a wonderful menu of temptations, from the best of traditional fries through the likes of pancakes with crispy bacon and syrup or pain au choc. Lunches are in a class of their own too, offering lots of lovely, colourful dishes - baked cod with a parmesan & basil crust, potato cake & garden pea purée is typical - all based on the best ingredients, impeccably sourced. Desserts are given daily on a board and there's a wide choice of coffees, minerals and a compact, well-selected wine list. **Seats 60.** Open 7-5 Mon-Fri, 10-5 Sat & Sun; L11.30-5. No-smoking area; air-conditioning. Closed 25 Dec, bank hols. Amex, MasterCard, Visa, Switch. **Directions:** On corner, left of Custom Square, IFSC.

Dublin 1

The Gresham

HOTEL / RESTAURANT

23 Upper O'Connell Street Dublin 1
Tel: 01 874 6881 Fax: 01 878 7175
Email: info@thegresham.com Web: www.gresham-hotels.com

This famous hotel has been at the centre of Dublin society since the early nineteenth century and is one of the city's best business hotels. A recent makeover has transformed the ground floor, including the lobby lounge, which is a favourite meeting place and renowned for its traditional afternoon tea, and also the Gresham and Toddy's Bars, both popular rendezvous for a pint. Business guests especially appreciate the newer air-conditioned bedrooms in the Lavery Wing and the hotel takes commendable pride in the quality of its staff. Dining options in the hotel offer a choice between the more traditional

Aberdeen Restaurant, and a smaller contemporary restaurant "23", which was opened last year. Smart and welcoming, it gives guests a change of style, although cooking (based on excellent raw materials) can be uneven and service is sometimes a bit bit haphazard; however, it is encouraging to find such an option in an old hotel, and cosmopolitan young staff know their food and wine. Conference/banqueting (350/280). Business centre; secretarial services; video conferencing. Fitness suite. Wheelchair access. Secure multi-storey parking. No pets. **Rooms 288** (4 suites, 2 junior suites, 96 executive, 60 no-smoking, 3 disabled). Lifts. B&B €160pps, ss up to €100 (Room-only rate €255). [Aberdeen Restaurant open for breakfast, lunch & dinner daily; "23" open breakfast (Tue-Fri) and dinner (Mon-Sat). SC 12.5%.] Hotel open all year.

Restaurant: Friendly staff get visitors to this new and stylish contemporary restaurant off to a good start - and, with food, service and ambience to match this should be an enjoyable, perhaps even memorable, dining experience, in which excellent raw materials are handled with respect and cooked with finesse. The menu is lucid and informative and while the wine list - which offers just 23 bottles - may seem a bit gimmicky, the selection is interesting and mark-up moderate. This is an ambitious project for an hotel and, on the whole, it works well: on the downside it feels a bit like eating in a corridor: an upstairs area feels more like a private room; service can be a bit haphazard, perhaps, but cosmopolitan young staff certainly know their food and wine. **Seats 23.** L 12-2.30 & D 5.30-10 Mon-Sat, closed Sun. A la carte; SC 12.5%. Amex, Diners, MasterCard, Visa, Laser. **Directions:** City centre, on north side of the River Liffey.

Dublin 1

The Harbourmaster Bar & Restaurant

RESTAURANT / BAR IFSC Dublin 1 **Tel: 01 670 1688** Fax: 01 670 1690

In a waterside setting at Dublin's thriving financial services centre this old Dock Offices building has genuine character and makes a fine restaurant and bar. The bar is very busy at times, but the development has been more towards the restaurant end of the business, now including an impressive contemporary upstairs restaurant, The Greenhouse, in a modern extension which has been designed in sympathy with the original building. Most tables have an interesting (and increasingly attractive) view of the development outside but, as there are now several dining areas, it is wise to ensure you get to the right one on arrival. For fine weather there's also a decked outdoor area overlooking the inner harbour and fountain, with extra seating. The Harbourmaster has that indefinable buzz that comes from being in the financial centre of a capital city and the food is appropriately international and contemporary in style. **The Greenhouse Restaurant:** L, Mon-Fri. Restaurant closed evenings and weekends (except for functions). Bar open Mon-Wed, noon-closing daily (Sun 12.30-11) Brasserie food all day, daily. Closed 25 Dec & Good Fri. Amex, Diners, MasterCard, Visa. **Directions:** In IFSC, near Connolly train station. ◇

Dublin 1

Insomnia

CAFÉ Unit 2 Lower Mayor Street Custom House Quay IFSC Dublin 1 **Tel: 01 671 8651**

This speciality coffee company has a small chain of outlets around Dublin (some under the brand Bendini & Shaw, whose complementary speciality is in sandwiches). All coffees made on the premises are based on top quality beans (Kenya, Java, Colombia and House Blend) and the range is wide. You name it, if it's quality coffee connected you can get it here: espresso-based drinks like cappuccino, caffe latte, caffe mocha and caffe americano and their cousins ('essence of coffee'), espresso, espresso con panna (with whipped cream), espresso macchiato (with foamed milk) , espresso ristretto (extra strong) and extras (espresso shot, flavoured syrup, whipped cream). Speciality teas, hot chocolates and chilled drinks like iced coffee are available too, and a selection of pastries (croissants, muffins, biscotti for dunking); Bendini & Shaw sandwiches also available. * Also at Charlotte Way, Dublin 1; Ballsbridge, Dublin 4; Main Street, Blackrock; Pavilion Shopping Centre, Swords. **Seats 45.** Open 7.30am-4pm daily. Closed 25-26 Dec. **Directions:** In IFSC. ◇

Dublin 1

Jurys Custom House Inn

féile bia **HOTEL** Custom House Quay Dublin 1
Tel: 01 607 5000 Fax: 01 829 0400

Right beside the International Financial Services Centre, overlooking the Liffey and close to train and bus stations, this hotel meets the requirements of business guests with better facilities than is usual in budget hotels. Large bedrooms have all the usual facilities, but also fax/modem lines and a higher standard of finish than earlier sister hotels; fabrics and fittings are better quality and neat bathrooms are more thoughtfully designed, with more generous shelf space. As well as a large bar, there is a full restaurant on site, plus conference facilities for up to 100 and a staffed business centre. No room service. Adjacent multi-storey car park has direct access to the hotel. **Rooms 239.** Room Rate from €92 (max 3 guests); breakfast from €9. Closed 24-26 Dec. Amex, Diners, MasterCard, Visa. **Directions:** IFSC, overlooking River Liffey.

Dublin 1

The Morrison Hotel

HOTEL / RESTAURANT

Ormond Quay Dublin 1
Tel: 01 887 2400 Fax: 01 874 4039
Email: sales@morrisonhotel.ie Web: www.morrisonhotel.ie

Located in the heart of the city close to the new Millennium Bridge over the River Liffey, this stunning contemporary hotel is within walking distance of theatres, the main shopping areas and the financial district. It was a first for Dublin, with dazzling 'east meets west' interiors created by the internationally renowned designer, John Rocha. His simple, cool bedroom design - the essence of orderly thinking - contrasts pleasingly with the dramatic, even flamboyant, style of public areas. In addition to the more usual facilities, bedrooms have CD players (CD library available), individually controlled air conditioning, safe, modem and mini-bar. Public areas include a range of stylish bars and restaurants catering to the needs of different times - the Café Bar, for example, is ideal for morning coffee or light pre-post-theatre meals, while The Morrison Bar has become the place for cocktails and Lobo is a late night bar (open to 3 am on Friday and Saturday nights). Siting this highly original hotel on the north quays underlines the recent shift of emphasis across the river - to the area which is currently seeing Dublin's most exciting developments. Conference/banqueting (90/95). Children welcome (under 12 free in parents' room, cot available without charge, babysitting arranged.) Pets permitted. **Rooms 94** (7 suites, 2 for disabled). Lift. Room service (limited hours). B&B about €153 pps; room rate from €270 (weekend breaks). Closed 24-27 Dec.

Halo: High drama comes into its own in the restaurant, which is on two levels, with angled mirrors giving a sense of unity and acres of curtains - notably a rich purple velvet - falling the full height. Having taken some time to settle in the early days, Jean-Michel Poulot's stylish French and fusion cooking at this fashionable restaurant is reliably excellent; seafood dishes are a particular strength - a fillet of turbot with organic baby vegetables, lobster ravioli and shellfish sauce is a typically luxurious example - and imaginative vegetarian dishes make attractive mainstream choices. Original desserts (Morrison Surprise...The Spike) are spectacularly presented and a choice of dessert wines is offered by the glass. In recent experience, service has left a lot to be desired - and guests are sometimes waiting too long to be seated. Value for money is good, however, especially at lunch time. **Seats 95.** No-smoking area. Air conditioning. L& D daily,12.30-2.30 & 6.30-10.15; Set L from €25, D from €35, also à la carte; house wine from €25; sc 12.5%. Amex, Diners, MasterCard, Visa, Laser, Switch. **Directions:** Located near the city centre beside the Millennium Bridge.

Dublin 1

Panem

CAFÉ

Ha'penny Bridge House 21 Lower Ormond Quay Dublin 1
Tel: 01 872 8510 Fax: 01 872 8510

Ann Murphy and Raffaele Cavallo's little bakery and café has been delighting discerning Dubliners - and providing a refuge from the thundering traffic along the quays outside - since 1996. Although tiny, it just oozes Italian chic - not surprisingly, perhaps, as Ann's Italian architect husband designed the interior - and was way ahead of its time in seeing potential north of the Liffey. Italian and French food is prepared on the premises from 3 am each day: melt-in-the-mouth croissants with savoury and sweet fillings, chocolate-filled brioches, traditional and fruit breads, filled foccacia breads are just a few of the temptations on offer. No cost is spared in sourcing the finest ingredients (Panem bread is baked freshly each day using organic flour) and special dietary needs are considered too: soups, for example, are usually suitable for vegans and handmade biscuits - almond & hazelnut perhaps - for coeliacs. They import their own 100% arabica torrisi coffee from Sicily and hot chocolate is a speciality, made with the best Belgian dark chocolate. Simply superb. Open Mon-Sat 9-5.30. Closed Sun & 24 Dec-8 Jan. **No Credit Cards. Directions:** North quays, opposite Millennium Bridge.

Dublin 1

Soup Dragon

CAFÉ

168 Capel Street Dublin 1 **Tel: 01 872 3277** Fax: 01 872 3277

This tiny place offers a stylish way to have a hot meal on a budget: a daily choice of soups and stews is available in three different sizes, with a medium portion and a selection of delicious home-made breads and a piece of fruit starting at about €5. Some change daily, while others stay on the menu for a week or a season. Choose from dahl (Indian lentil), potato & leek or carrot & coriander soup; or opt for something more substantial like beef chilli or a very fine Thai chicken curry from the blackboard menu. In keeping with their healthy philosophy, a range of wholesome and innovative breakfasts is offered, and also a range of freshly squeezed drinks (Red Dragon: strawberry, raspberry and cranberry or home-made lemon & lime lemonade) and smoothies, all made to order so they taste fresh and vibrant. Desserts include old favourites like rice pudding (served with cream) and a range of unusual home-made ice creams. Food to go is also available. **Seats 10.** Open Mon-Fri 8-5.30 & Sat 11-5. Closed Sun, bank hols, Christmas. [Opening times not confirmed at time of going to press.] **Directions:** Bridge at Capel Street. ◇

Dublin 1

The Vaults

PUB / RESTAURANT

Harbourmaster Place IFSC Dublin 1 **Tel: 01 605 4700**
Fax: 01 605 4701 Email: info@the vaults.ie Web: www.thevaults.ie

These ten soaring vaulted chambers underneath Connolly Station were built in the mid 19th century to support the railway between Amiens Street and the Royal Canal and have since found many uses, including the storage of Jameson whiskey, which used to occupy a tunnel running from Connolly to Westland Row! In 2002 this wonderful space entered a new and exciting era when Michael Martin - previously best known for his culinary expertise as head chef of the Clarence Hotel restaurant, The Tea Rooms - opened it as a multi-purpose venue. Despite the size - and a ceiling height of four metres - the atmosphere is surprisingly intimate: the Portland Stone floor is warm and welcoming and the vaults, which have been treated individually in styles ranging from sleek contemporary (brown leather booth seating) to neo-classical (salvaged lamps, aged sculptures) add up to a stylish and highly versatile space. Each has its own entrance, allowing a number of events to take place simultaneously and, in addition to high-resolution digital projectors allowing cinema quality audio-visual effects, surround sound and drop-down screens in three of the vaults, others have plasma screens - ideal for sports events (seats bookable in advance). Given Michael Martin's background, culinary expectations are high at The Vaults and Sardinian head chef Max Usai ensures that everything is made from scratch, including pasta, ice cream and breads; menus are simple - mainly grills, pizzas and pastas - but brilliantly executed and beautifully presented on plain white modern crockery. This place encapsulates the dramatic changes taking place north of the Liffey: simply stunning. **Seats 210.** Private room 120. (All spaces available to hire, for business or pleasure). Food served 12-8 daily. Various menus - lunch, afternoon/evening, Saturday brunch and Sunday roast - à la carte. Vegetarian dishes on main menu. House wine about €18. Late night bar. Closed 25-26 Dec, 1 Jan. Amex, Diners, MasterCard, Visa, Laser. **Directions:** Under Connolly station; accessible from station or IFSC. ◇

DUBLIN 2

Dublin 2

Acapulco Mexican Restaurant

RESTAURANT

7 South Great Georges St. Dublin 2 **Tel: 01 677 1085**

Reliable Tex-Mex fare at this bright, cheap and notably cheerful place on the edge of Temple Bar. Authentic Mexican - nachos with salsa & guacamole, enchiladas, burrito, sizzling fajitas - and good coffee. No smoking area. **Seats 70.** Open 7 days: L 12-3pm, D 6-10.30pm (Fri & Sat 12-4pm & 6-11pm, Sun 2-10.30pm). House wine €16.50. 10% SC on parties of 6+. Amex, MasterCard, Visa, Laser. **Directions:** Bottom of South Gt George's St (Dame Street end).

Dublin 2

Alexander Hotel

HOTEL

Merrion Square Dublin 2 **Tel: 01 607 3900** Fax: 01 661 5663
Email: alexanderres@ocallaghanhotels.ie Web: www.ocallaghanhotels.ie

Very well situated at the lower end of Merrion Square within a stone's throw of Dail Éireann (Government Buildings), the National Art Gallery and History Museum as well as the city's premier shopping area, this large new hotel is remarkable for classic design that blends into the surrounding Georgian area quite inconspicuously. In contrast to its subdued public face, the interior is strikingly modern and colourful, both in public areas and bedrooms, which are all to executive standard, spacious and unusual. Perhaps its most positive attribute, however, is the exceptionally friendly and helpful attitude of the hotel's staff, who immediately make guests feel at home and take a genuine interest in their comfort during their stay. Conference/banqueting (400/400). Business centre. Secretarial services. Video conferencing. Gym. Children welcome (Under 2s free in parents' room; cots available). No pets. **Rooms 102** (4 suites, 40 no-smoking, 2 for disabled). Lift. B&B €105. Room-only rate €295 (max. 2 guests). Open all year. Amex, Diners, MasterCard, Visa. **Directions:** Off Merrion Square.

Dublin 2

Ar Vicoletto Osteria Romana

RESTAURANT

5 Crow Street Temple Bar Dublin 2 **Tel: 01 670 8662**

Genuine little Italian restaurant, doing authentic, restorative food in a relaxing atmosphere and at very moderate prices - a set two-course lunch which includes a glass of wine and tea or coffee, is particularly good value. Very friendly helpful staff too - one of the pleasantest spots in Temple Bar. Children welcome. **Seats 35.** L &D daily. Children welcome. Air conditioning. Closed 24-25 Dec. Amex, MasterCard, Visa. ◇

Dublin 2

Avoca Café

féile bia RESTAURANT

11-13 Suffolk St. Dublin 2 **Tel: 01 672 6019**
Fax: 01 672 6021 Email: info@avoca.ie Web: www.avoca.ie

City sister to the famous craftshop and café who have their flagship store in Kilmacanogue, County Wicklow, this large centrally located shop is a favourite daytime dining venue for discerning Dubliners. The restaurant (which is up rather a lot of stairs, where queues of devotees wait patiently at lunchtime) has low-key style and an emphasis on creative, healthy cooking that is common to all the Avoca establishments recommended in the Guide. Avoca Cafés received the Happy Heart Eat Out Award in 2000 and the Féile Bia Award for 2003. The importance of using only the very best ingredients has always been recognised at Avoca: their food is based on the best available produce, as much of it as possible local and artisan and, when the Féile Bia programme was initiated, group executive chef Leylie Hayes was one of the first to recognise its benefits and sign up to the Féile Bia Charter. Avoca's chic little menus speak volumes - together with careful cooking, meticulously sourced ingredients like Woodstock tuna, Hederman mussels, Gubbeen bacon and Hicks sausages lift dishes such as smoked fish platter, organic bacon panini and bangers & mash out of the ordinary. All this sits happily alongside the home baking for which Avoca is famous - much of which (along with other specialist produce) can be bought downstairs. Meals daily 10-5, (Sunday 11-5); à la carte. Bookings accepted but not required. Amex, Diners, MasterCard, Visa. **Directions:** Turn left into Suffolk St. from the bottom of Grafton St.

Dublin 2

Aya @ Brown Thomas

RESTAURANT

49/52 Clarendon Street Dublin 2 **Tel: 01 677 1544**
Fax: 01 677 1546 Email: mail@aya.ie Web: www.aya.ie

This dashing contemporary Japanese restaurant was Dublin's first conveyor sushi bar, restaurant and food hall - it's owned by the Hoashi family, who established Dublin's first authentic Japanese restaurant, Ayumi-Ya, in 1983 - and was a runaway success from the day it opened, in 1999. As we go to press, Aya has just opened a refurbished restaurant, extended into what was the Aya Deli next door (now relocated nearby on South William Street; sells Japanese food, including sushi; also has an ice cream counter selling Tipperary Organic Ice Cream). The sushi conveyor belt has been expanded and now has 35 stools and six 8-seater booths for communal diners, as well as à la carte seating for thirty. Wall-to-wall style remains the order of the day in the - the decor is in tones of red and brown, building on the existing walnut panelled feature wall, which has been extended, and a raised seating area at the window has been floored with white oak planking, which curves up to line the wall. A new menu includes a wide range of sushi, all authentically Japanese, and also some hot food, including Asian and Japanese tapas, as well as tempura and teriyaki dishes and additions with broader Asian flavours to tempt a wider range of customers. Children welcome before 8pm. **Seats 60.** Air conditioning. Open daily: L 12-4. D 5.30-11 (Sun to 10). Set L from €10; Set D from €21 (6-7pm), €25 (7-close). Also à la carte. House wine from €21. SC 12% (at night). Closed 25-26 Dec. Also at: Aya Deli @IFSC (Custom House Square, IFSC, Dublin 1). Tel: 01 672 1852. Run on similar lines, although with less seating and greater emphasis on food to go. Amex, MasterCard, Visa, Laser. **Directions:** Directly behind Brown Thomas off Wicklow Street.

Dublin 2

The Bad Ass Café

CAFÉ / RESTAURANT

9-11 Crown Alley Temple Bar Dublin 2
Tel: 01 671 2596 Fax: 01 671 2596
Email: bad_ass_@hotmail.com Web: www.badasscafe.com

Original and still the best - the Bad Ass Café has been charming youngsters (and a good few oldsters) with its particular brand of wackiness and good, lively food since 1983, when most people running Temple Bar restaurants were still at school. Kids love the food (the Bad Ass burger is still one of the favourites, and very good too), the warehouse atmosphere, the loopy menu and the cash shuttles (from an old shop) that whizz around the ceiling. Over twenty years after opening, young people still find it cool. Children welcome. **Seats 92.** Open daily 11.30-11.30. Lunch special €7.30 (11.30-4.30); Bad Ass

Special €15.85, any time. A la carte also available. House wine from €17.50. Air conditioning. SC 10%. Closed 25-26 Dec, Good Fri. Amex, MasterCard, Visa, Laser. **Directions:** Behind the Central Bank on the way to the Ha'penny Bridge.

Dublin 2

The Bailey

ATMOSPHERIC PUB

2-3 Duke Street Dublin 2

Although it's now more of a busy lunchtime spot and after-work watering hole for local business people and shoppers, this famous Victorian pub has a special place in the history of Dublin life - literary, social, political - and attracts many a pilgrim seeking the ghosts of great personalities who have frequented this spot down through the years. Closed 25 Dec & Good Friday. ◇

Dublin 2

Bang Café

☆ féile bia **RESTAURANT**

11 Merrion Row Dublin 2 **Tel: 01 676 0898** Fax: 01 676 0899
Web: www.bangrestaurant.com

Stylishly minimalist in natural tones of dark wood and pale beige leather complement simple white linen and glassware, this smart restaurant is well-located just yards from the Shelbourne Hotel. It is on two levels with a bar in the basement; upstairs, unstressed chefs can be seen at work in one of the open kitchens: an air of calm, relaxed and friendly professionalism prevails. Head chef Lorcan Cribbin's menus offer innovative, modern food: a starter of perfectly cooked foie gras served atop a crisp onion bahji with Sauternes jus is typical and well-balanced main course options include a signature dish of bangers & mash (made with Hicks sausages) and tempting fish dishes - using fresh fish from Bantry, in West Cork. Tempting desserts include several fruity finales (Scandinavian iced berries are a speciality) as well as the ever-popular dark chocolate treats, or there's an Irish farmhouse cheese selection. Attention to detail is the keynote throughout and this, seen in carefully sourced food and skilful cooking combined with generous servings and professional service under the management of Kelvin Rynhart, ensures an enjoyable dining experience and value for money (especially at lunch time). The only downside, noted on the Guide's most recent visit, is that great popularity has resulted in some wear and tear - which is always particularly noticeable in minimalist restaurants. **Seats 90.** Private room, 35. Air conditioning. L &D Mon-Sat 12.30-3, 6-10.30 (Thu-Sat to 11). Set L €35, Set D €45. Also à la carte. House wine €20. 12.5% sc on parties of 6+. Closed Sun, bank hols, 1 week New Year. Amex, MasterCard, Visa, Laser, Switch. **Directions:** Just past Shelbourne Hotel, off St Stephen's Green.

Dublin 2

Bewley's Oriental Café

féile bia **CAFÉ**

78-79 Grafton Street Dublin 2 **Tel: 01 635 5470**
Fax: 01 679 9237 Email: manager@graftonstbewleys.ie Web: www.bewleys.com

Established in 1840, Bewley's Cafés - and especially the Grafton Street café - have a special place in the affection of Irish people. Bewleys has always been a great meeting place for everyone, whether native Dubliners or visitors to the capital 'up from the country'. Although they have changed hands and undergone renovations in recent years, they have retained a unique atmosphere and it's this - together with some outstanding architectural features, notably the Harry Clarke stained glass windows in the Grafton Street premises - which makes them special, rather than the food. It seems highly appropriate that this great Dublin institution should venture into theatre - there's a lunchtime event daily, and cabaret on Thursday, Friday and Saturday (Phone for details.) Full licence. Open daily, from 7.30 am 'until late' Branches at: Westmoreland Street, Dublin 2; Mary Street, Dublin 1. MasterCard, Visa, Laser. **Directions:** Halfway up Dublin's premier shopping street. ◇

Dublin 2

Bleu Bistro Moderne

Ⓝ **RESTAURANT / WINE BAR**

Dawson St. Dublin 2 **Tel: 01 676 7015**
Fax: 01 676 7027 Web: www.onepico.com

A younger sister to Eamonn O'Reilly's excellent flagship restaurant One Pico (see entry), this modern bistro (now known generally as simply 'Bleu' or even 'Blue') opened to some acclaim in 2003 and, at its best, can be impressive. Smartly laid tables are rather close together (paper napkins at lunch time - linen at night) and hard surfaces make for a good bit of unnecessary noise which contributes nothing to a relaxing dining ambience. That all said however, head chef Jamie Farrugia is talented and can certainly wow his customers with food which is based on quality ingredients, very well cooked and beautifully presented on plain white plates: signature dishes include salmon fish cakes with cucumber pickle & saffron aïoli and crispy baby chicken with mustard fruit & roast squash. Portions are small, which may make value on the plate seem less than it looks on the menu (vegetables, salads etc charged as extras). Good wine list, with 14 wines by the glass (from €4.50). **Seats 56** (private room

12/14). Reservations required. Air conditioning. Open all day, 12-11 (Sun to 9). L 12-3 (Sun to 4), D 6-11(Sun 5-9). "Value" D menu €30, otherwise à la carte. House wine from €18. Closed bank hols. Amex, Diners, MasterCard, Visa, Laser. **Directions:** At top of Dawson St. off St. Stephen's Green.

Dublin 2

Brooks Hotel

HOTEL / RESTAURANT

59-62 Drury Street Dublin 2
Tel: 01 670 4000 Fax: 01 670 4455
Email: reservations@brookshotel.ie Web: wwwsinnotthotels.com

A city sister for the Sinnott family's hotels in Galway (see entry for Connemara Coast), this boutique hotel is very well located, close to the Drury Street multi-storey car park and just a couple of minutes walk from Grafton Street. It has always been an attractive and discreet hotel, but recent developments have transformed it into one of Dublin's most desirable addresses, especially for business guests. An adjoining building was recently acquired, allowing the development of a wonderful new ground floor space with bar, lounge and restaurant all linking together, as well as the addition of 23 luxurious new rooms. The style is a pleasing combination of traditional with new minimalist touches, using a variety of woods, some marble, wonderful fabrics and modern paintings - and, while a grand piano adds gravitas, there's a welcome emphasis on comfort (especially in the residents' lounge). All bedrooms have exceptionally good amenities, including well-designed bathrooms with power showers as well as full baths (some also have tile screen TV), air conditioning and many other features. New boardrooms offer state-of-the-art facilities for meetings and small conferences, and a 45-seater screening room. Fitness suite. Children welcome (under 3 free in parents' room; cots available). No pets. **Rooms 98** (1 suite, 2 junior suites, 3 executive, 50 superior, 87 no-smoking, 5 for disabled). Lift. B&B from about €110pps, ss €50. Open all year.

Francescas Restaraunt: Now relocated more conveniently on the ground floor, the restaurant has a young contemporary café style look, and a welcoming ambience with wooden floors, leather seating and an open plan kitchen where head chef Patrick McLarnon and his team can be seen at work from all angles, thanks to well positioned mirrors. Tables are elegantly appointed with classic linen cloths and napkins - and waiting staff, smartly attired in black, look after customers with warmth and professionalism. Patrick sources ingredients with great care (wild salmon, organic chicken, dry aged steak, wild boar sausage), his cooking is imaginative - and there's a strong emphasis on fish: a dish attracting particular praise on a recent visit was a starter of seared scallops, served on a warm potato salad, with chive & garlic dressing. Although not quite settled down as we go to press, this is a restaurant with considerable potential. [*Bar food is served from noon-7pm daily in the Butter Lane Bar.] **Seats 60.** Air conditioning. L daily,12.30-2.30; D daily, 6.30-10 (Sun 7-9.30). Set D from €29; L&D also à la carte. Closed to non-residents at Christmas. Amex, MasterCard, Visa, Laser. **Directions:** Between Grafton and Great St. Georges Streets, 2 mins. from St. Stephen's Green.

Dublin 2

Brownes Brasserie & Townhouse

RESTAURANT / GUESTHOUSE

22 St Stephen's Green Dublin 2
Tel: 01 638 3939 Fax: 01 638 3900
Email: info@brownesdublin.com Web: www.brownesdublin.com

Stylish conversion of this fine period house on the stretch of St Stephen's Green between Grafton Street and the Shelbourne Hotel makes an impressive and exceptionally well-located restaurant and guesthouse. Up a short flight of granite steps, you pass through a reception area and small drawing room area furnished with antiques (where aperitifs and digestifs can be served) into the restaurant, which is a long well-appointed split-level room, with big mirrors and plenty of decorative interest to occupy guests between courses. Good-sized tables, comfortable chairs and fresh flowers all create a good impression and well-balanced international menus offer a wide choice - home-smoked salmon is a speciality in, for example, an unusual main course of roast fillet, served with a spring onion mash and a red wine & mustard seed sauce - also char-grilled meats. Imaginative vegetarian dishes also feature - typically a starter of deep-fried halloumi cheese, served with tzatziki & aubergine tomato salad and main courses like sesame-infused crêpes filled with wild mushrooms, leeks & blue cheese, served with a green salad. Finish with rather luscious desserts (pavlova filled with a crunchy cream, topped with summer berries, perhaps), or a cheese plate with home-made chutney. Children welcome. **Seats 70** (private room, 33). Air conditioning. L&D daily: 12.30 -2.30 (Sun to 2.45), D 6.30-10.30 (Sun to 9.30). Set L €20-37.50 (Sun €28.50), Set D €52.50. A la carte also available. House wine from €20. SC discretionary. Closed 24 Dec-3 Jan.

Accommodation: The house has something of the atmosphere of a private home about it and includes a front first floor junior suite which can be converted for meetings and private parties, as the bed swings up into the wall. The spacious bedrooms have quality reproduction furniture including generous beds (although not for the very tall, perhaps) and well-finished bathrooms, with quality toiletries and towelling robes. An ironing board is tucked neatly into the wardrobe and there's a CD player as well as TV. Browne's was the Dublin winner of the 2002 Denny Irish Breakfast Awards, in association with the Guide, and is truly a feast worth allowing plenty of time for. Small conference/banqueting (24/70). Children welcome (under 6 free in parents' room, cot available without charge). No pets. **Rooms 12** (2 suites). Lift. 24 hour room service. B&B €200 pps. Closed Christmas/New Year. Amex, MasterCard, Visa, Laser. **Directions:** Stephens Green North,between Kildare & Dawson Street.

Dublin 2

Bruno's - Kildare Street

féile bia RESTAURANT

21 Kildare Street Dublin 2 **Tel: 01 662 4724**
Fax: 01 662 3857 Web: www.brunos.ie

Bruno Berta's conversion of a characterful cellar under Mitchell's wine shop into a sleek contemporary restaurant in 2000 may have dismayed devotees of the previous establishment which highlighted its old-world charm, but even the style critics admit that the restaurant is a great success. Warm hospitality and efficient, professional service back up consistently excellent cooking by head chef Ian Connelly, who sources carefully and produces some marvellous food in the French/modern Irish genre. Imaginative, well-judged combinations, accurate cooking and pleasing presentation add up to an unusually satisfying dining experience. A typically delicious lunch, for example, offers four choices on each course and might begin with salt cod croquettes served with smoked lemon mayonnaise and contrastingly fresh-flavoured tomato, rocket & red onion salad (or there may be a seriously tempting option of baked figs stuffed with stilton and Parma ham, with a rocket salad and baked red onions); a main course of roast cod may come with a superb shrimp risotto and courgette fingers - and vegetarians always get interesting choices a gruyère potato cake, for instance, with baby leeks, onion marmalade and onion sauce. Desserts are a high point and worth leaving room for - there may be something intriguing, like cherry clafoutis with nutmeg ice cream (all the ice creams are particularly good) - but Irish cheeses supplied by Sheridans cheesemongers are also hard to resist. Not suitable for children under 12 after 7 pm. Air-conditioning. **Seats 100.** L 12.30-2.30 & D 6-10.30 Mon-Sat. Set L & early D about €18.50; L&D à la carte available. SC discretionary (10% on tables of 4+). Closed Sun, bank hol Mons, Christmas/New Year & 2 wks in Aug. [Informal sister restaurant at: East Essex Street, Temple Bar, Dublin 2. Tel: 01 670 6767] Amex, Diners, MasterCard, Visa, Laser. **Directions:** Across the road from side door of Shelbourne Hotel. ◇

Dublin 2

Buswells Hotel

féile bia HOTEL / RESTAURANT

25 Molesworth Street Dublin 2
Tel: 01 614 6500 Fax: 01 676 2090
Email: buswells@quinn-hotels.com Web: quinnhotels.com

Home from home to Ireland's politicians, this 18th century townhouse close to the Dail (parliament) has been an hotel since 1921 and is held in great affection by Dubliners. Since major refurbishment several years ago, it now offers a fine range of services for conferences, meetings and private dining. Accommodation is comfortable in the traditional style with good amenities for business guests and it's just a few yards from the city's prime shopping and cultural area, making it an ideal base for private visits. The lobby and characterful bar are handy meeting places. Conference/banqueting (85/50). Secretarial services. Video conferencing. Children welcome (Under 3s free in parents' room; cots available). No pets. **Rooms 69** (2 suites, 17 no-smoking, 1 for disabled). Lift. B&B about €110pps, ss about €33. Closed 24-26 Dec.

Trumans Restaurant: This elegant well-appointed restaurant has a separate entrance from Kildare Street or access through the hotel. Menus feature lively modern dishes and have the little touches that endear guests to an establishment, such as a tasty little amuse-bouche presented before the meal 'compliments of the chef'. Wisely, given the likely clientèle, simpler dishes are always an option - notably roast beef or steaks presented various ways - and vegetarian dishes are creative. Desserts are also interesting (eg, date-stuffed pear in a phyllo crown) or you can finish with Irish cheeses, which attract a small supplement on set menus. No children under 12 after 9pm. **Seats 45** (private room, 12). L 12:30-2 Mon - Fri. D 6-10 Mon - Sat. Set L&D; also à la carte. House wine around €16. SC discretionary. Closed lunch Sat, all Sun, 24-26. Amex, Diners, MasterCard, Visa. **Directions:** Close to Dail Eireann, 5 minutes walk from Grafton Street. ◇

Dublin 2

Café Bar Deli

RESTAURANT

12-13 Sth Great George's Street Dublin 2 **Tel: 01 677 1646**
Fax: 01 677 6044 Email: dublin@cafébardeli.ie
Web: www.cafebardelidublin@eircom.net

Despite its obvious contemporary appeal - paper place mat menus set the tone by kicking off with Tasters, the first of which is home-made breads with three dips and marinated olives - the friendly ghosts of the old Bewleys Café are still alive and well in Jay Bourke and Eoin Foyle's inspired reincarnation of one of Dublin's favourite comfort zones. Even the name is a play on what was the essence of a café in the old-fashioned sense - steaming pots of tea and milky coffee, with scones or a traditional fry; today it suggests a very different character. Tables may be old café style, with simple bentwood chairs, the original fireplace and a traditional brass railing remain but a smartly striped awning over the the large street window signals the real nature of the place from the outset. Imaginative salads are packed with colourful, flavoursome treats in the modern idiom - rocket, parmesan, anchovies, baby spinach, goat's cheese, hazelnuts, chickpeas, couscous, tapenade are the vocabulary of this menu - with pizza and pasta menus continuing in the same tone. The ten or so pizzas offered include a Café Bar Deli special, changed daily, as do the pastas - and there are also family sized bowls available. A sensibly limited wine list combines quality and style (sparkling and dessert wines included) with value; service is friendly and efficient and prices remarkably moderate - an attractive formula for a family outing. Branches at: Cork (Bodega) and Sligo (Garavogue). Children welcome. **Seats 150.** Open 12.30-11 daily. Air conditioning. A la carte. House wine €19 (litre). No reservations. Closed 25-26 Dec, 1 Jan, Good Fri. Amex, Diners, MasterCard, Visa, Laser. **Directions:** In the original Bewleys building, beside the Globe Bar.

Dublin 2

Café en Seine

Pub Star **CAFÉ / PUB**

40 Dawson Street Dublin 2 **Tel: 01 648 1200** Fax: 01 677 4488
Email: caféenseine@capitalbars.com Web: www.capitalbars.com

The first of the continental style café-bars to open in Dublin, in 1993, Café en Seine is still ahead of the fashion a decade later - after closing for complete refurbishment, it re-opened in December 2001 to reveal a stunning new interior in an opulent art deco style reminiscent of turn-of-the-century Paris. Not so much a bar as a series of bars (your mobile phone could be your most useful accessory if you arrange to meet somebody here), the soaring interior is truly awe-inspiring with a 3-sto-rey atrium culminating in beautiful glass-panelled ceilings, forty foot trees, enormous art nouveau glass lanterns, and statues and a 19th century French hotel lift among its many amazing features. No expense has been spared in ensuring the quality of design, materials and craftsmanship necessary to create this beautiful Aladdin's cave of a bar. Lush ferns create a deliciously decadent atmosphere and the judicious mixture of old and new which make it a true original - and its many 'bars within bars' create intimate spaces that are a far cry from the impersonality of the superpub. Appealing food is a major part of its appeal too - there's an informal range of contemporary dishes available over lunchtime every day, light bites all day and a popular Jazz Brunch every Sunday. Little wonder that so many people of all ages see it as the coolest place in town. Lunch daily 12-3. Sunday brunch, 1-4 pm. Wheelchair access. Bar open 10.30am-2.30am daily. Carvery lunch 12-3. Snack menu 4-10. Closed 25-26 Dec & Good Fri. Amex, MasterCard, Visa. **Directions:** Upper Dawson Street, on right walking towards St Stephen's Green. ◇

Dublin 2

Camden Court Hotel

HOTEL

Camden Street Dublin 2 **Tel: 01 475 9666** Fax: 01 478 9139
Email: sales@camdencourthotel.com Web: www.camdencourthotel.com

This stylish modern hotel, in a thriving area convenient to St Stephen's Green, has two entrances - one next to the Bleeding Horse pub, the other via an arched passageway through a courtyard. The spacious reception area leads to a smart restaurant, where an enticing breakfast buffet is laid out each morning. All bedrooms have neat bathrooms, practical fitted furniture and the usual facilities (plus satellite TV which can show your room bill, speeding check-out). Friendly staff, business and leisure facilities and reasonable rates for the location make this a good city centre base. Conference/banqueting (115/100). Leisure centre (swimming pool, gym, sauna, steam). Children (Under 2s free in parents' room; cots available without charge). No pets. **Rooms 246** (1 suite, 13 no-smoking, 13 for disabled). Lift. 24 hr room service. B&B from €92.50 pps, ss €57.50; no SC. Closed Christmas. Diners, MasterCard, Visa. **Directions:** City centre, 10 minutes walk from St.Stephen's Green.

Dublin 2

Central Hotel

HOTEL

2-5 Exchequer Street Dublin 2 **Tel: 01 679 7302** Fax: 01 679 7303
Email: reservations@centralhotel.ie Web: www.centralhotel.ie

Very conveniently located on the corner of South Great George's Street, this hotel is over a hundred years old and is a handy place to stay on business or for short breaks. Extensive renovations have recently been completed, it's quite reasonably priced for the city centre and special offers are often available, including weekends. Conference/banqueting (120/100). Children welcome (Under 5s free in parents' room; cots available without charge). Lift. No pets. **Rooms 70** (3 suites, 1 junior suite, 1 executive, 16 shower only, 14 no smoking). Lift. B&B from about €75 pps, ss €25. Closed 24-26 Dec. Amex, Diners, MasterCard, Visa, Laser. **Directions:** City centre, between Trinity College & Dublin Castle.

Dublin 2

Chili Club

RESTAURANT

1 Anne's Lane South Annes Street Dublin 2 **Tel: 01 677 3721**
Fax: 01 635 1928 Web: www.adlib.ie

This cosy restaurant, in a laneway just off Grafton Street, was Dublin's first authentic Thai restaurant and is still as popular as ever a decade later. Owned and managed by Patricia Kenna, who personally supervises a friendly and efficient staff, it is small and intimate, with beautiful crockery and genuine Thai art and furniture. Supot Boonchouy, who has been head chef since 1996, prepares a fine range of genuine Thai dishes which are not 'tamed' too much to suit Irish tastes. Children welcome. **Seats 40** (private room, 12) L Mon-Sat 12.30-2.30, D daily 6-11. Set L €15. Set D from €20 (6-7pm), later€25. A la carte L&D also available. House wine €18. SC discretionary. Closed L Sun, 25-31 Dec,1 Jan. Amex, Diners, MasterCard, Visa, Laser. **Directions:** Off Grafton Street.

Dublin 2

The Clarence Hotel

HOTEL /RESTAURANT

6-8 Wellington Quay Dublin 2
Tel: 01 407 0800 Fax: 01 407 0820
Email: reservations@theclarence.ie Web: www.theclarence.ie

Dating back to 1852, this hotel has long had a special place in the hearts of Irish people - especially the clergy and the many who regarded it as a home from home when 'up from the country' for business or shopping in Dublin - largely because of its convenience to Heuston Station. Since the early '90s, however, it has achieved cult status through its owners - Bono and The Edge of U2 - who have completely refurbished the hotel, creating the coolest of jewels in the crown of Temple Bar. No expense was spared to get the details right, reflecting the hotel's original arts and crafts style whenever possible. Accommodation offers a luxurious combination of contemporary comfort and period style, with excellent amenities including mini-bar, private safe, PC/fax connections (fax available on request), remote control satellite television and video and temperature control panels. Public areas include the clublike, oak-panelled Octagon Bar, which is a popular Temple Bar meeting place, and The Study, a quieter room with an open fire. Parking is available in several multi-storey carparks within walking distance; valet parking available for guests. Conference/banqueting (5-120); secretarial services. Beauty salon; fitness room. Children welcome (Under 12s free in parents' room, cots available without charge). No pets. **Rooms 49** (5 suites, 45 executive, 3 for disabled). Lift. Room rate from €300; no SC.

★**The Tea Room:** The restaurant, which has its own entrance on Essex Street, is a high-ceilinged room furnished in the light oak which is a feature throughout the hotel. Pristine white linen, designer cutlery and glasses, high windows softened by the filtered damson tones of pavement awnings, all combine to create an impressive dining room. Solicitous staff move quietly, quickly offering aperitifs and menus. Now in his fourth year, head chef Anthony Ely presents fashionably international seasonal menus that offer plenty of choice, including vegetarian options, but are not overlong or overpriced. Seasonal à la carte dinner menus offer around nine or ten starters and main courses in a modern European/Irish style that is bright and sassy, with strong but not overworked presentation - dishes singled out for special praise on a recent visit include a fascinating starter of deep-fried bacon & potato cakes, with a ham hock terrine & caper sauce - an imaginative modern rendition of the traditional Irish theme - and a superb navarin of lamb, served with dauphinoise potato, spring vegetables & rosemary. A wonderful 8-course Tasting Menu is also offered, at €70 per person (available for whole tables only). Lunch menus offer especially good value and an imaginative approach to the varying requirements of the clientèle": in addition to The Tea Room menu, working lunch menus for meetings provide several no-choice options and there's an "all-day" lunch in The Octagon bar offering a light à la carte and a different main course dish every day of the week. Very good wine list (and good value for the quality). Excellent ingredients, skilful cooking, thoughtful presentation that successfully balances colours and textures, attentive service by well-trained, knowledgeable staff - and very good value for money considering the high quality of everything offered. **Seats 80.** Toilets wheelchair accessible. No-smoking area. L 12.30-2.30 (Sun 12-3), D 6.30-10.30 daily. Set L from €24; Set D from €41.50. Tatsing Menu €70. A la carte L available. House wine from €24.50. No SC. Octagon Bar Menu,11-5 daily. Closed 23-27 Dec. Amex, Diners, MasterCard, Visa, Laser. **Directions:** Overlooking the River Liffey at Wellington Quay, southside.

Dublin 2

Clarion Stephen's Hall Hotel & Suites

HOTEL

14-17 Lower Leeson Street Dublin 2 **Tel: 01 638 1111** Fax: 01 638 1122
Email: stephens@premgroup.com Web: premgroup.ie

Conveniently located just off St Stephen's Green, this 'all-suite' hotel consists of units (bedroom, bathroom, living room, kitchenette) each with modem point, fax machines and CD players. **Rooms 33** (all suites, 9 no-smoking). Wheelchair access. Lift. Room rate from about €225. Free underground parking. Open all year.

Romanza: George Sabongi took over this attractive semi-basement adjacent to the hotel in 2001 and with him came the piano bar concept for which he is well-known in Dublin. An enclosed coffee terrace at the back creates a pleasantly summery 'outdoor' atmosphere and, as the restaurant is accessible directly from the hotel and nearby offices, it's a popular lunchtime venue - and very convenient to the National Concert Hall in the evening too. Moderately priced menus include informal Italian fare like quality pizzas and pastas, but there's also a range of antipasti and substantial main courses like charcoal grilled rib eye of beef and barbecue leg of lamb, and Egyptian influence showing in a vegetarian dish such as koushery, which is based on black lentils. You can also just have a drink at the bar (10am-midnight); there's quite an extensive cocktail list and a short bar food menu, 10.30-5.30. Live music at weekends. L Mon-Fri, 12.30-3; D Mon-Sat 5-12. A la carte. House wine about €16. 10% s.c. on parties of 6+. Closed L Sat, all Sun. [Times/prices not confirmed at time of going to press.] Amex, Diners, MasterCard, Visa, Laser. **Directions:** Just off St.Stephen's Green on Lower Leeson Street. ◇

Dublin 2

The Commons Café

CAFÉ

The National Concert Hall Earlsfort Terrace Dublin 2
Tel: 01 475 0060 Fax: 01 478 5037
Email: info@thecommonscafe.ie Web: www.thecommonscafe.ie

This spacious restaurant in the main Concert Hall building is operated by Philip Ryan and Michael Andrews (previously of The Commons Restaurant) and makes a good place to drop into before a concert, or just for a meal. The room is lovely - high-ceilinged, bright and airy room with a large mirrored bar area, blue banquettes and white walls setting off impressive paintings - and friendly staff under Michael Andrews' skilful direction are anxious to please. Menus are quite short and flexible, with no distinction between starters and main courses, but proceed in a fairly logical way from soup and lighter dishes like focaccia and pasta through to more substantial fare. Their Café Club Sandwich has become a signature dish or, for those with a hankering for comfort food, haddock deep-fried in beer batter and served with potato wedges and pea purée is the business. The cooking is good, the quality of carefully sourced ingredients shines through and it's also good value for money: a winning formula. Children welcome. **Seats 60.** No smoking area. Toilets wheelchair accessible. Open Mon-Sat, 9.30am-11pm (but closes at 6pm on non-concert evenings), Sun D 6 -"late" on concert evenings. A la carte. House wine from €21. No SC except 10% on groups of 6+. [*The name of this establishment may be changed.] Amex, MasterCard, Visa, Laser. **Directions:** St Stephen's Green South, oposite Conrad Hotel.

Dublin 2

Conrad Dublin

HOTEL

Earlsfort Terrace Dublin 2
Tel: 01 602 8900 Fax: 01 676 5424
Email: dublininfo@conradhotels.com Web: www.conradhotels.com

Just a stroll away from the beautiful St Stephen's Green and right in the heart of the city centre, this fine hotel celebrated its tenth anniversary in 1999; service by committed staff is excellent and facilities are constantly upgraded. Many of the bedrooms enjoy views of the piazza below and across the city, and all have recently been refurbished in a contemporary style, offering luxuriously comfortable accommodation with individual temperature control, Internet access, mini bar, trouser press, executive writing desk, safe and CD player.

Conference space is flexible, with a variety of syndicate meeting rooms, all with ISDN lines and individually temperature and light controlled. A state of the art fitness centre is reserved exclusively for the use of hotel guests. Public areas include a raised lounge, two restaurants, the Alexandra and Plurabelle Brasserie (breakfast, lunch and dinner served here), and Alfie Byrne's Pub, which is home to locals and visitors alike and opens on to a sheltered terrace. Conference/banqueting (350/260). Executive boardroom (12). Business centre; secretarial services; video conferencing. Underground carpark. Children welcome (cots available without charge, baby sitting arranged). **Rooms 192** (9 suites, 141 no-smoking, 1 for disabled). Lift. B&B €130 pps, ss €130; room-only rate €220. SC incl. Open all year. Amex, Diners, MasterCard, Visa, Laser. **Directions:** On the south-eastern corner of St Stehen's Green, opposite the National Concert Hall.

Dublin 2

Cornucopia

RESTAURANT

19 Wicklow Street Dublin 2 **Tel: 01-677 7583**
Fax: 01 6719449 Email: cornucopia@eircom.net

You don't have to be vegetarian to enjoy this long-established wholefood restaurant and it's very well located for a wholesome re-charge if you're shopping around the Grafton Street area. It was originally a wholefood store with a few tables at the back and, although it has now been a dedicated restaurant for some time, a welcoming waft of that unmistakable aroma remains. The atmosphere is informal, especially during the day (when window seats are well placed for people watching) and people like it for its simple wholesomeness, redolent of good home cooking. Vegetarian breakfasts are a speciality (lots of freshly squeezed juices to choose from) and all ingredients are organic, as far as possible. Yeast-free, dairy-free, gluten-free and wheat-free diets catered for and no processed or GM foods are used. Organic wines too. **Seats 40.** Mon-Sat 8.30am-8pm (Thu to 9pm), Sun 12-7. All à la carte (menus change daily); organic house wine about €16 (large glass about €3.95). Closed 25-27 Dec, 1 Jan, Easter Sun. MasterCard, Visa, Laser. **Directions:** Off Grafton St. turn at Brown Thomas.

Dublin 2

Da Pino

RESTAURANT

38-40 Parliament Street Dublin 2 **Tel: 01 671 9308**
Fax: 01 677 3409 Email: m.jimenez@tinet.ie

Just across the road from Dublin Castle, this busy youthful Italian/Spanish restaurant is always full - and no wonder, as they serve cheerful, informal, well cooked food that does not make too many concessions to trendiness and is sold at very reasonable prices. Paella is a speciality and the pizzas, which are especially good, are prepared in full view of customers. Children welcome. **Seats 80.** Open 12-11.30 daily. 2-course L (Mon-Fri), about €7; also à la carte. Wine from about €15. Closed Christmas & Good Fri. Amex, Diners, MasterCard, Visa, Laser. **Directions:** Opposite Dublin Castle. ◇

Dublin 2

The Davenport Hotel

féile bia **HOTEL**

Merrion Square Dublin 2 **Tel: 01 607 3900** Fax: 01 661 5663
Email: davenportres@ocallaghanhotels.ie Web: www.ocallaghenhotels.ie

On Merrion Square, close to the National Gallery, the Dail (Parliament Buildings) and Trinity College, this striking hotel is fronted by the impressive 1863 facade of the Alfred Jones designed Merrion Hall, which was restored as part of the hotel building project in the early '90s. Inside, the architectural theme is continued in the naming of rooms - Lanyon's Restaurant, for example honours the designer of Queen's University Belfast and Gandon Suite is named after the designer of some of Dublin's finest buildings, including the Custom House. The hotel, which is equally suited to leisure and business guests, has been imaginatively designed to combine interest and comfort, with warm, vibrant colour schemes and a pleasing mixture of old and new in both public areas and accommodation. Bedrooms are furnished to a high standard with orthopaedic beds, air conditioning, voicemail, modem lines, personal safes and turndown service in addition to the more usual amenities - all also have ample desk space, while the suites also have fax and laser printer. Conference/banqueting (380/400). Business centre. Gym. Children welcome (Under 2s free in parents' room; cots available, baby sitting arranged). No pets. **Rooms 115** (2 suites, 10 junior suites). Lift. 24 hr room service. B&B €105 pps. Room-only rate €295 (max. 2 guests). Open all year. Amex, Diners, MasterCard, Visa. **Directions:** just off Merrion Square.

Dublin 2

Davy Byrnes

ATMOSPHERIC PUB

21 Duke Street Dublin 2 **Tel: 01 677 5217**
Fax: 01 671 7619 Web: www.davybyrnes.com

Just off Grafton Street, Davy Byrnes is one of Dublin's most famous pubs - references in Joyce's Ulysses mean it is very much on the tourist circuit. Despite all this fame it remains a genuine, well-run place and equally popular with Dubliners, who find it a handy meeting place and also enjoy the bar food. The style is quite traditional, providing 'a good feed' at reasonable prices (most meals, with hearty vegetables, are under €15). Oysters with brown bread & butter, Irish stew, beef & Guinness pie and deep-fried plaice with tartare sauce are typical and there's always a list of daily specials like sautéed lambs liver with bacon & mushroom sauce, pheasant in season - and, in deference to the Joycean connections, there's also a Bloomsday Special (gorgonzola and burgundy). Not suitable for children under 7. Outside eating area. Bar food served daily, 12-9 (Fri to 6). Closed 25-26 Dec & Good Fri. MasterCard, Visa, Laser. **Directions:** 100 yards from Grafton Street.

Dublin 2

Diep Le Shaker

RESTAURANT

55 Pembroke Lane Dublin 2 **Tel: 01 661 1829**
Fax: 01 661 5905 Email: info@diep.net Web: www.diep.net

This fashionable two-storey restaurant is elegantly appointed with comfortable high-back chairs, good linen and fine glasses, while sunny yellow walls and a long skylight along one side of the upper floor create a bright, summery atmosphere and the ambience is always lively. The cuisine is mainly Thai, offering a wide range from a superb, intensely flavoured Tom Yum Koong soup (with prawns and aromatics) to a selection of the equally typical green and red curries - and, in between, a wide choice including many based on luxurious ingredients like fresh lobster, seabass and black sole. Head chef Taweesak Trakoolwattana, who has expereince in five star hotels in Thailand, joined the restaurant in 2002 and the cooking is excellent at its best, although it can be uneven. Some Chinese favourites are also listed, like sizzling dishes, crispy fried pork and sweet & sour king prawns; however the menu is due to be changed to Royal Thai Cuisine shortly, and Chinese dishes will be dropped. Service is charming and solicitous. Not suitable for children after 8 pm. Air conditioning. Jazz Wed night. **Seats 120.** L Mon-Fri 12.30-2.15, D Mon-Wed 6.30-10.30, Thu-Sat 6.30-11.15. Set L €28; Set D from €38.50; also à la carte. House wine from €19.50. SC 10%. Closed L Sat, all Sun, bank hols, 25 Dec. Amex, MasterCard, Visa, Laser. **Directions:** First Lane on left off Pembroke Street.

Dublin 2

Dobbins Wine Bistro

RESTAURANT

15 Stephens Lane Dublin 2 **Tel: 01 661 3321** / 676 4679
Fax: 01 661 3331 Email: dobbinswinebistro@eircom.net

This 'Nissen hut' hidden away near Merrion Square is something of a Dublin institution, having been run since 1978 by the late John O'Byrne and manager Patrick Walsh. A visit to this unique oasis is always a treat and, along with great hospitality and food which is consistently delicious in a style that demonstrates awareness of current trends without slavishly following them, they're renowned for their wines, which have always been at the centre of their philosophy: twenty five years ago people started recognising their food when coming to Dobbins for the best glass of good quality wines around at that time - and today it's not just 'the list' that is special, but a system they put in place some years ago, whereby the exclusive 'Front Page Wines' on the regular list are available for off-sales, by the bottle or case - which greatly pleases the many wine buffs who frequent the restaurant, as they are sold at half the list price. The wines selected change regularly and, as they're bought specially for Dobbins and their own Internet company, offer exceptional quality and value to customers. They also hold a wine fair every December, buying bin ends and selling them a vineyard prices; needless to say it's very popular with customers and their friends - and sorts out the Christmas shopping very pleasantly too. Dobbins may well have the most extensive - and probably the most eclectic - wine list in Ireland and their customers certainly have fun trying them. Leisurely lunches have been known to run on a bit too long, hence the warning on the menu: "Bar closes at 5.30pm and re-opens at 7.30 for dinner service." The only down side to this conviviality is that tables for two can seem a little forlorn, so it's best to make up a party. Dobbins was selected for our Wine Award in 2003. Children welcome. Air conditioning. **Seats 120** (private room, 40). L Mon-Fri12.30-2.30, D Tue-Sat 7.30-10. Set L about €23, D à la carte. House wine from about €19.50. SC discretionary. Closed L Sat, all Sun, D Mon, bank hols, Christmas week. Amex, Diners, MasterCard, Visa, Laser. **Directions:** Between Lower & Upper Mount Street. ◇

Dublin 2

Doheny & Nesbitt

PUB

5 Lower Baggot Street Dublin 2
Tel: 01 676 2945 Fax: 01 676 0655

Only a stone's throw from Toner's (see entry), Doheny & Nesbitt is another great Dublin institution, but there the similarity ends. Just around the corner from the Dail (Irish Parliament), this Victorian pub has traditionally attracted a wide spectrum of Dublin society - politicians, economists, lawyers, business names, political and financial journalists - all with a view to get across, or some new scandal to divulge, so a visit here can often be unexpectedly rewarding. Like the Horseshoe Bar at the nearby Shelbourne

Hotel which has a similar reputation and shares the clientèle, half the fun of drinking at Nesbitt's is anticipation of 'someone' arriving or 'something' happening, both more likely than not. Although it has been greatly extended recently and is now in essence a superpub, it has at its heart the original, very professionally run bar with an attractive Victorian ambience and a traditional emphasis on drinking and conversation. Closed 25 Dec & Good Fri. ◇

Dublin 2

Dunne & Crescenzi

RESTAURANT

14 South Frederick Street Dublin 2
Tel: 01 677 3815 Fax: 01 677 3815

This little Italian restaurant and deli very near the Nassau Street entrance to Trinity College delights Dubliners with its unpretentiousness and the simple good food it offers at reasonable prices. It's the perfect place to shop for genuine Italian ingredients - risotto rice, pasta, oils, vinegars, olives, cooked meats, cheeses, wines and much more - and a great example of how less can be more. Menus offer sandwiches or panini, antipasti and desserts: How good to sit down with a glass of wine (bottles on sale can be opened for a small corkage charge) and, perhaps, a plate of antipasti - with wafer-thin Parma ham, perhaps, several salamis, peppers preserved in olive oil, olives and a slice of toasted ciabatta drizzled with extra virgin olive oil... There are even a couple of little tables on the pavement, if you're lucky enough to get them on a sunny day. Indoors or out, expect to queue: this place has a loyal following. A short Italian wine list. **Seats 30.** Air conditioning. Open 9-7 Mon & Tue, to 10 pm Wed-Sat. Closed Sun. A la carte; wine from about €11. Amex, MasterCard, Visa, Laser. **Directions:** Off Nassau Street, between Kilkenny and Blarney stores. ◇

Dublin 2

Eden

RESTAURANT

Meeting House Square Temple Bar Dublin 2
Tel: 01 670 5372 Fax: 01 670 3330
Email: bookings@edenrestaurant.ie Web: www.edenrestaurant.ie

This spacious two-storey restaurant has its own outdoor terrace on the square; modern, with lots of greenery and hanging baskets, there's an open kitchen which adds to the buzz and provides entertainment if service is slow. Executive chef Eleanor Walsh has established a house style which suits the restaurant and has become very popular; her seasonal menus are quite extensive and make use of organic produce where possible, in updated classics which suit the restaurant well. A summer menu might include a tempting lobster salad (with dill potatoes, mango relish & mayonnaise) and hot specialities include smokies (smoked haddock with spring onion, crème fraîche and melted Cheddar cheese) and an organic beef and Guinness stew, which many would call a pie as it comes with a pastry lid as well as button mushrooms and mash. A well-balanced and not-too-expensive wine list offers several wines by the glass. Children welcome. **Seats 110** (private room, 14). Air conditioning. L daily, 12.30-3 (Sat & Sun from 12). D 6-10:30 daily. Set L from €18; early D from €19 (6-7pm), also à la carte. House wine €22. SC discretionary. Closed bank hols, 25-29 Dec. Amex, Diners, MasterCard, Visa, Laser. **Directions:** Next to the Irish Film Theatre, opposite Diceman's Corner.

Dublin 2

Elephant & Castle

RESTAURANT

18 Temple Bar Dublin 2 **Tel: 01 679 3121** Fax: 01 679 1399

This buzzy Temple Bar restaurant was one of the first new-wave places in the area and is still doing a good job; ingredients are carefully sourced and served in a range of big, generous and wholesome salads (their special Caesar salad is renowned), pasta dishes, home-made burgers and great big baskets of chicken wings. Service can sometimes be a problem - waiting staff are usually foreign students and, although willing and friendly, it can take longer than anticipated to finish a meal; however, atmosphere is perhaps the strongest attraction here, so the time passes agreeably. Children welcome. Air conditioning. **Seats 85.** Open Mon-Fri, 8am-11.30pm; Sat, 10.30am-11.30pm, Sun from 12. Toilets wheelchair accessible. Closed Christmas & Good Fri. Amex, Diners, MasterCard, Visa. **Directions:** Behind Central Bank, Dame Street. ◇

Dublin 2

Ely Winebar & Café

RESTAURANT / WINE BAR

22 Ely Place Dublin 2 **Tel: 01 676 8986**
Fax: 01 661 7288 Email: elywine@eircom.net

Just around the corner from The Shelbourne and a stone's throw from the Merrion Hotel, Erik and Michelle Robson's unusual wine bar and café occupies the ground floor and basement of an imaginatively renovated Georgian townhouse - polished wooden floors, brick arches and contemporary furnishings are completely at home here, a successful and refreshing blend of old and new. Ely's remarkable wine list is the main attraction, offering a huge number of carefully selected wines, with over seventy available by the glass thus providing the opportunity to taste wines which would otherwise be completely unaffordable to most people. Regular customers seem to be addicted to the system, demanding an ever-increasing selection of wines - the number offered is now running at over 300 and they're on their seventh wine list, with 80 by the glass. Although not the first restaurant to try this, it is done with great dedication and style at Ely - and the exceptional wine list is backed up by other specialities including a list of premium beers and cigars. On the food side, organic produce, notably meats from the family farm in Co. Clare, are a special feature - and not just premium cuts, but also products like black pudding and home-made sausages which make all the difference to simple dishes like sausages and mash or beefburgers. Although food was originally presented more or less as an accompaniment to the exceptional wines, quite extensive lunch and evening menus are now offered - including, many visitors will be glad to hear, Kilkee oysters with brown bread and traditional Irish stew made with Burren lamb as well as many contemporary dishes - and wine suggestions are given with each dish. Mature Irish and continental cheeses make the ideal accompaniment to a glass of wine and they also serve great coffee, a perfect accompaniment for their fine selection of hand-made Irish chocolates. **Seats 100** (due to extend to 135 in 2004). Open Mon-Sat L 12-3, D 6-10 (Bar open to midnight). Wines from €20. SC 12.5% on groups of 6+. Closed Sun, Christmas week, bank hol Mons. Amex, Diners, MasterCard, Visa, Laser. **Directions:** Junction of Baggot Street/Merrion Street off St Stephens Green.

Dublin 2

Fado Restaurant

RESTAURANT

Mansion House Dawson Street Dublin 2 **Tel: 01 676 7200**
Fax: 01 676 7530 Email: info@fado.ie Web: www.fado.ie

The Mansion House has been the official residence of the Lord Mayor of Dublin since 1715 - the only mayoral residence in Ireland, it is older than any mayoral residence in Britain. The room previously known as The Supper Room has been imaginatively renovated as a restaurant - the room itself is of sufficient interest to be worth a look even if you haven't time to eat - and the contemporary food served somehow seems very appropriate to this sparkling restoration. Since opening in 2000, Myles Tuthill's team have worked hard to achieve a well-earned reputation for hospitality and attention to detail, in both food and service. Well-balanced menus, which include a quick set lunch, an early dinner and a nice little children's menu as well as quite extensive à la carte menus, perhaps lean a little towards seafood - specialities include salmon & herb fish cakes - but meat and poultry are well-represented and there are some less usual dishes offered, such as an appealing starter - terrine of rabbit, with watercress salad, apple & Calvados; vegetarian options are imaginative too: a main course of walnut and Gorgonzola ravioli with cream and tarragon is a typically tempting example from a lunch menu. Desserts tend to be classic and there's always a cheese plate (supplied by Sheridan's cheesemongers). The wine list includes some serious bottles, and a fair choice of half bottles and wines by the glass. Open Mon-Sat, 12-10. Set L €14, early D (5.30-7pm) €20; also à la carte. House wines from €16.95. Closed Sun, 25 Dec, Good Fri. Amex, Diners, MasterCard, Visa, Laser. **Directions:** City centre, beside the Lord Mayor's residence, the Mansion House.

Dublin 2

Fitzers Restaurant

féile bia **RESTAURANT**

51 Dawson Street Dublin 2 **Tel: 01 677 1155**
Fax: 01 670 6575 Email: fitzcat@indigo.ie

Reliable Cal-Ital influenced cooking in a dashing contemporary setting with a heated al fresco dining area on the pavement. Open daily 11.30am-11pm. Closed Dec 25/26, Jan 1, Good Friday. Amex, Diners, MasterCard, Visa. Also at:

*Temple Bar Square, Tel: 01-679 0440 (12-11 daily, cl 25 Dec & Good Fri)

*National Gallery, Merrion Square Tel: 01-663 3500 (Mon-Sat 9.30-5, Sun 12-4.30, closed Gallery Opening days).

Directions: Halfway up Dawson Street, on the right heading towards St Stephen's Green. ◇

Dublin 2

The Fitzwilliam Hotel

HOTEL

St Stephens Green Dublin 2 **Tel: 01 478 7000** Fax: 01 478 7878
Email: enq@fitzwilliamhotel.com Web: www.fitzwilliamhotel.com

This stylish contemporary hotel enjoys a superb location on the north-western corner of St Stephen's Green. Behind its deceptively low-key frontage lies an impressively sleek interior created by Sir Terence Conran's design group CD Partnership. Public areas combine elegant minimalism with luxury fabrics and finishes, notably leather upholstery and a fine pewter counter in the bar, which is a chic place to meet in the Grafton Street area. In addition to the hotels' premier restaurant, Thornton's (see separate entry), breakfast, lunch and dinner are served daily in their informal restaurant Citron, on the mezzanine level. Bedrooms, while quite compact for a luxury hotel, are finished to a high standard with air-conditioning, safe, fax/modem point, stereo CD player and minibar, and care has been lavished on the bathrooms too, down to details such as high quality toiletries. Conference/banqueting (80/60). Secretarial services. Children welcome; (under12s free in parents' room; cots available free of charge). 24 hour room service. **Rooms 128** (2 suites, 128 executive, 90 no-smoking, 4 for disabled). Lift. B&B €160pps No service charge. Open all year.

Dublin 2

Good World Chinese Restaurant

RESTAURANT

18 South Great Georges Street Dublin 2
Tel: 01 677 5373 Fax: 01 677 5373

One of a cluster of interesting ethnic restaurants around Wicklow Street and South Great George's Street, this was one of the first and is popular with the local Chinese community, who appreciate the high standard of their Dim Sums - a selection of which can be had after 6pm at €5 per item. A more interesting and authentic Chinese menu is available as well as the standard one, offering unusual dishes such as 'Fish Slices Congee' - a sort of rice porridge not often seen even in London - other variations are beef, chicken, salted eggs and pickle. Another satisfying concoction consists of assorted meats (chicken, pork etc and also seafood including squid, prawns and scallops) with tofu, mushrooms and Chinese leaf - delicious and a real bargain at under €14. The restaurant prides itself on an especially full range of Chinese dishes, suitable for both Chinese and European customers, and service is both friendly and efficient. **Seats 95.** Open 12.30pm-midnight daily; Special L Mon-Fri 12.30-2.15; Set D from €25.50; also à la carte. House wine €18. Closed 25-26 Dec. Amex, Diners, MasterCard, Visa, Laser. **Directions:** Corner of Sth Gt George's St & Wicklow Street.

Dublin 2

Gotham Café

RESTAURANT

8 South Anne Street Dublin 2 **Tel: 01 679 5266** Fax: 01 679 5280

A lively, youthful café-restaurant just off Grafton Street, the Gotham does quality informal food at reasonable prices and is specially noted for its gourmet pizzas - try the Central Park, for example, a Greek style vegetarian pizza with black olives, red onion & fresh tomato on a bed of spinach with feta & mozzarella cheeses and fresh hummus, which is just one of a choice of sixteen tempting toppings. Other specialities include Caesar salad, baby calzoni (two miniatures - one with chèvre, prosciutto, basil & garlic; the other with baby potato, spinach, caramelised red onion, mozzarella & fresh pesto) and Asian chicken noodle salad (satay chicken fillets on a salad of egg noodles tossed in a light basil & crème fraîche dressing). There's a good choice of pastas too - and it's a great place for brunch on Sundays and bank holidays.[*A sister outlet, The Independent Pizza Company, is at 28 Lr Drumcondra Road, Dublin 9]. Children welcome. Air conditioning. **Seats 65** (outdoor seating, 12). Open daily: Mon-Sat 12 -12 (L 12-5, D 5-12); Sun brunch & bank hol Mondays, 12-4.30 & D 5-10.30. A la carte. House wine €15. SC discretionary (10% on parties of 6+). Closed 2 days Christmas & Good Fri. Amex, MasterCard, Visa, Laser. **Directions:** Just off Grafton Street.

Dublin 2

The Grafton Capital

HOTEL

Stephens Street Lower Dublin 2 **Tel: 01 6481100** Fax: 01 6481122
Email: info@graftoncapital-hotel.com Web: www.capital-hotels.com

In a prime city centre location just a couple of minutes walk from Grafton Street, this attractive hotel offers well furnished rooms and good amenities at prices which are not unreasonable for the area. Rooms are also available for small conferences, meetings and interviews. The popular 'Break for the Border' nightclub next door is in common ownership with the hotel. Small conferences (22). Business centre. Wheelchair access. Parking by arrangement with nearby carpark. Children welcome (Under 12s free in parents' room; cots available; baby sitting arranged). No Pets. **Rooms 75** (3 junior suites, 19 no-smoking, 4 for disabled). Lift. B&B €96, ss €40. Short breaks offered. Closed 24-26 Dec. Amex, Diners, MasterCard, Visa, Laser. **Directions:** Near St. Stephen's Green (opposite Drury Street carpark).

Dublin 2

Harrington Hall

GUESTHOUSE

69/70 Harcourt Street Dublin 2 **Tel: 01 475 3497** Fax: 01 475 4544
Email: harringtonhall@eircom.net Web: www.harringtonhall.com

Conveniently located close to St Stephen's Green and within comfortable walking distance of the city's premier shopping areas, Trinity College and the National Concert Hall, this fine family-run guesthouse was once the home of a former Lord Mayor of Dublin and has been sympathetically and elegantly refurbished, retaining many original features. Echoes of Georgian splendour remain in the ornamental ceilings and fireplaces of the well-proportioned ground and first floor rooms, which include a peaceful drawing room. Bedrooms, which are both comfortable and practical, have neat en-suite bathrooms and have recently had all the windows sound-proofed and ceiling fans installed. All round this is a welcoming alternative to a city-centre hotel, offering good value and with the huge advantage of free parking behind the building; luggage can be stored for guests arriving before check-in time (2pm). Snack menu available (with wine list). Small conferences (24). Children welcome (under 2s free in parents' room, cot available without charge). Staff are friendly and helpful. **Rooms 28** (2 junior suites, 2 shower only, 6 executive, 2 for disabled). Lift. 24 hour room service. B&B €90, ss €48. Open all year. Amex, Diners, MasterCard, Visa, Laser. **Directions:** Off southwest corner of St Stephens Green (one-way system approaches from Adelaide Road).

Dublin 2

Hilton Dublin

HOTEL

Charlemont Place Dublin 2 **Tel: 01 402 9988** Fax: 01 402 9966
Email: reservations_dublin@hilton.com Web: www.dublin.hilton.com

Overlooking the Grand Canal, this modern hotel (previously Stakis), is just a few minutes walk from the city centre and caters well for the business guest. Each double-glazed bedroom provides a worktop with modem point, swivel satellite TV and individual heater as well as the usual facilities. A buffet-style breakfast is served in the well-appointed Waterfront Restaurant. Conference/banqueting (350/270). Underground carpark. Children welcome (Under 12s free in parents' room; cots available). No pets. Lift. **Rooms 189** (78 no-smoking, 8 for disabled). Room rate from about €110 (max. 2 guests). Weekend specials from €176. Open all year. Amex, MasterCard, Visa. **Directions:** Off Fitzwilliam Square. ◇

Dublin 2

Hodges Figgis

CAFÉ

56-58 Dawson Street Dublin 2
Tel: 01 677 4754 Email: books@hodgesfiggis.ie

One of Europe's largest bookshops is also one of the oldest - they've been selling books here since 1768. Always innovative, they were also one of the first to hit on the idea of nourishing the book-hunter's body as well as the mind - their in-store café opened in 1995. As this is the kind of shop where you could easily lose a day, this was one of their best ideas. Café open 9.30-5.30, (Thursday to 7pm). **No Credit Cards. Directions:** At lower end of Dawson Street. ◇

Dublin 2

Il Primo

RESTAURANT

16 Montague Street Dublin 2 **Tel: 01 478 3373** Fax: 01 8749949
Email: alto.primo@iolfree.ie Web: www.ilprimoireland.com

Dieter Bergman's cheery little two storey restaurant and wine bar between Harcourt Street and Camden Street was way ahead of current fashions when it opened in 1991. Separate air conditioned dining rooms are simply furnished, but the essentials are right: warm hospitality and excellent, imaginative, freshly cooked modern Italian food that includes gourmet pizzas (with smoked salmon & spinach, for example), excellent pastas and lovely salads (try the insalata misto, with mixed leaves, cheese, olives & French beans). Unusual speciality dishes include Ravioli Il Primo - open ravioli filled with chicken breast, parma ham and wild mushrooms, in a cream sauce - and lasagne with crabmeat and leek. The wines are Dieter's special passion: the list is impressive and a large number are available by the millilitre - you drink as much or as little as you want and that's the amount you pay for, which is a brilliant idea. Dieter also organises regular wine tastings and dinners. Food prices are quite moderate - most main courses are under €18 - but the bill can mount alarmingly if you don't watch the wine orders closely. Separate dining/function rooms available. Children welcome. **Seats 76.** Air conditioning. L Mon-Sat, 12.30-3, D daily 6-11 (Sun to 10); à la carte. House wines €19.50. SC10%. Closed L Sun, bank hols. Amex, MasterCard, Visa, Laser. **Directions:** 5 mins from Stephens Green between Harcourt Street & Wexford Street.

Dublin 2

Imperial Chinese Restaurant

RESTAURANT

12A Wicklow Street Dublin 2 **Tel: 01 677 2580**
Fax: 01 677 9851 Email: imperial@hotmail.com

Mrs Cheung's long-established city centre restaurant has enjoyed enduring popularity with Dubliners and has also a clear vote of confidence from the local Chinese community, who flock here for the Dim Sum at lunchtime - a good selection of these delectable Cantonese specialities is available between 12.30 and 5.30 daily: prawn stuffing in bean curd rolls was disappointingly bland on a recent visit - fresh local Dublin Bay prawns would have so much more flavour than imported frozen tiger prawns - but beef tripe was really enjoyable. Fried Seafood Noodles also attracted particular praise: lots of succulent prawns, scallops and squid with Pak Choi. Crispy aromatic duck is another speciality from a wide-ranging selection of Chinese dishes. Children welcome. **Seats 180.** Private room available. Open daily 12.30-11.30 (L12.30-2.10 Mon-Sat). Set L about €11, Set D about €28. Also à la carte. House wine about €16. SC 10%. Closed 25-26 Dec. Amex, MasterCard, Visa, Laser. **Directions:** On Wicklow Street near Brown Thomas. ◇

Dublin 2

The International Bar

ATMOSPHERIC PUB

23 Wicklow Street Dublin 2

Just a minute's walk from Grafton Street, this unspoilt Victorian bar makes a great meeting place - not a food spot, but good for chat and music. Closed 25 Dec. & Good Friday. **Directions:** Corner of Wicklow Street & St Andrew Street.

Dublin 2

Jacobs Ladder

féile bia **RESTAURANT**

4 Nassau Street Dublin 2 **Tel: 01 670 3865** Fax: 01 670 3868
Email: dining@jacobsladder.ie Web: www.jacobsladder.ie

Adrian and Bernie Roche's smart contemporary restaurant is up a couple of flights of stairs and has a fine view, overlooking the playing fields of Trinity College. The decor is on the minimalist side with a wooden floor (which can make for an unwelcome noise level) and paintings for sale by new Irish artists; good-sized tables with classic white linen and comfortable high-back chairs bode well for the meal ahead. Aidan is one of Dublin's most talented younger chefs; the cooking style is modern Irish and, while there is a leaning towards fish - Dublin seafood coddle is a speciality, also scallops with roast beetroot and spiced lentils - his wide ranging seasonal menus always include some less usual meat dishes: roast loin of rabbit, perhaps, with its kidney and livers - and imaginative vegetarian dishes - which, along with 'healthy eating' dishes, are considerately highlighted. Several menus are offered including a compact à la carte selection at lunch, and a short 3-course set dinner which is very good value. An 8-course tasting menu, for complete parties, is also offered. Service can sometimes be a little slow but food is cooked to order and, on the lunch menu, there's a warning to allow 25 minutes cooking time for the main course; it's worth allowing time to finish off with a classic dessert (lemon parfait with marinated raspberries & almond sauce, perhaps) or Irish farmhouse cheeses, which are served with tomato chutney & oat biscuits. The wine selection is not overlong, but includes a fair number of half bottles and a fine wine list. Children welcome. **Seats 80** (private room, 50). L Tue-Sat 12.30-3; D Tue-Sat, 6-10; Set D €31.74; Menu Surprise €70, L à la carte. House wine €19.50. No SC. Closed Sun & Mon, 1 week Aug, 2 weeks from 25 Dec. Amex, Diners, MasterCard, Visa, Laser. **Directions:** City centre overlooking Trinity College.

Dublin 2

Jaipur

RESTAURANT

41-46 South Great Georges Street Dublin 2 **Tel: 01 207 0324**
Fax: 01 2070325 Email: dublin@jaipur.ie Web: www.jaipur.ie

This custom-built restaurant is named after the "Jewel of Rajasthan" and offers a different, more contemporary image of ethnic dining. It's a cool and spacious place, with a large modern spiral staircase leading up to an area that can be used for private parties and the main restaurant below it. Although the modern decor may seem strange in comparison with traditional Indian restaurants, warm colours send the right messages and it is a pleasing space. Kaushik Roy, who has been head chef since the restaurant opened and is highly regarded in India, is keen to make the most of Irish ingredients, notably organic lamb (Khato Ghosth - Wicklow lamb braised in yoghurt with carrom seeds & mustard oil, finished with asafoetida and dried mango powder - is a signature dish), while importing fresh and dried spices directly. Menus offer an attractive combination of traditional and more creative dishes - try Jaipur Jugalbandi, an assortment of five appetisers, to set the tone. A recent visit by the Guide did not live up to previous experiences but, at its best, Jaipur is a fine restaurant - and was the first ethnic restaurant in Ireland to devise a wine list especially suited to spicy foods. Service is attentive and discreet. **Seats 110.** D daily, 5.30-11.30. Set D from €20. A la carte. House wine from €15.

*Also at: 21 Castle Street Dalkey, Co. Dublin. Tel: 01 285 0552

5 St. James' Terrace, Malahide, Co. Dublin. Tel: 01 845 5455 Amex, MasterCard, Visa, Laser, Switch. **Directions:** At the corner of Sth Great Georges St. and Lower Stephens St.

Dublin 2

John Mulligan

ATMOSPHERIC PUB

8 Poolbeg Street Dublin 2 **Tel: 01 677 5582**

One of Dublin's oldest and best-loved pubs, Mulligan's 'wine & spirit merchant' is mercifully un-renovated and likely to stay that way - dark, with no decor (as such) and no music, it's just the way so many pubs used to be. The only difference is that it's now so fashionable that it gets very crowded (and noisy) after 6pm - better to drop in during the day and see what it's really like. Closed 25 Dec & Good Fri.

Dublin 2

The Joose Bar

CAFÉ

7a Poolbeg Street Dublin 2 **Tel: 01 679 9611**
Fax: 01 679 9642 Web: joosebar.com

Tucked away behind office blocks near Tara Street station, this cheerful café offers a wide variety of excellent drinks, all made to order: Smoothies, made with low fat frozen yoghurt, include The Grind (blueberry, raspberry, banana & apple) and The Squash (blueberry, strawberry and OJ & banana) for example, while Joose Juices include a Stressbuster (orange, lemon, apple & lettuce) and the aptly named The Hair of the Dog (pink grapefruit, lemon, lime and orange) while City Squeezes are combinations of just one or two types of fruit and/or vegetable juice. They also have a soup of the day and a chill cabinet, offering a selection of basic sandwiches, wraps and salads, along with tubs of muesli for the breakfast brigade. Open Mon to Fri, early morning to mid afternoon. Closed Sat, Sun & Bank Hols. **Directions:** Beside Mulligans Pub. ◇

Dublin 2

Kehoe's

ATMOSPHERIC PUB

9 South Anne Street Dublin 2 **Tel: 01 677 8312**

One of Dublin's best, unspoilt traditional pubs, Kehoe's changed hands recently and added another floor upstairs, but without damaging the character of th original bar. Very busy in the evening - try it for a quieter daytime pint instead. Closes 25 Dec and Good Friday.

Dublin 2

Kilkenny Restaurant & Café

RESTAURANT / CAFÉ

5-6 Nassau Street Dublin 2 **Tel: 677 7075**
Fax: 01 670 7735 Email: info@kilkennyshop.com

Situated on the first floor of the shop now known simply as Kilkenny, with a clear view into the grounds of Trinity College, the Kilkenny Restaurant is one of the pleasantest places in Dublin to have a bite to eat - and the food matches the view. It looks good and the experience lives up to anticipation: ingredients are fresh and additive-free (as are all the products on sale in the shop's Food Hall) and food has a home-cooked flavour. Salads, quiches, casseroles, home-baked breads and cakes are the specialities of the Kilkenny Restaurant and they are very good. They also do an excellent breakfast: fresh orange juice to start and then variations combinations of the traditional fare (crispy bacon, poached egg, onions, mushrooms, tomatoes, home-made Kilkenny relish) and lighter options like bagels with cream cheese & bacon, croissants with bacon, Emmental & Kilkenny relish, or toast with home-made marmalade. High quality ingredients, good cooking and appetising presentation make this a rewarding place to start the day. For quicker all-day bites the shop has a second eating place, Kilkenny Café, where Italian panini and cappuccino are served and the same principles of quality apply. A range of Kilkenny preserves and dressings - all made and labelled on the premises - is available in the shop. Children welcome. **Seats 190.** Open 8.30-5 (Thu to 7), Sat 9-5, Sun 11-3. Breakfast to 11.15, lunch 11.30-3. A la carte. Licensed. Air conditioning. Closed 25-26 Dec, 1 Jan, Easter Sun. Amex, Diners, MasterCard, Visa. **Directions:** Opposite TCD playing fields. ◇

Dublin 2

L'Ecrivain

★ **RESTAURANT**

109a Lr Baggot St Dublin 2 **Tel: 01 661 1919** Fax: 01 661 0617
Email: mary@lecrivain.com Web: www.lecrivain.com

On two levels - spacious and very dashing - Derry and Sallyanne Clarke's acclaimed city centre restaurant is light and airy, with lots of pale wood and smoky mirrors - and lovely formal table settings which promise seriously good food. Derry's cooking style - classic French with contemporary flair and a strong leaning towards modern Irish cooking - remains consistent, although new ideas are constantly incorporated and the list of specialities keeps growing. Special treats to try include a wonderful signature starter of baked rock oysters with York cabbage & crispy cured bacon, with a Guinness sabayon - perhaps followed by a main course of roast rump of lamb, with garlic & rosemary polenta, foie gras croquette and tomato & mint chutney. Thoughtful little touches abound - a fine complimentary amuse-bouche before your first course, for example - and there are some major ones too, like the policy to add the price of your wine after the 10% service charge has been added to your bill, instead of charging on the total as other restaurants do. Seafood, lamb, beef and game, in season, are all well-represented, but menus could also include neglected ingredients like rabbit, which is always appealingly served, and offal as in a main course 'Tasting of Offal': kidney, oxtail, tongue, caramelised sweetbreads and seared liver. Wonderful puddings are presented with panache and might include a hot soufflé or a classic vanilla crème brulée with lemon curd ice cream. Presentation is impressive but not ostentatious and attention to detail - garnishes designed individually to enhance each dish, careful selection of plates, delicious home-made breads and splendid farmhouse cheeses - is excellent. A fine wine list is augmented by a tempting selection of coffees and digestifs - all this, plus excellent service, adds up to a very caring approach and an exceptional restaurant. **Seats 100.** L Mon-Fri 12.30-2, D Mon-Sat 7-11, Set L €30-35. Set D €58 (Vegetarian Menu €50). Tasting Menu €85. House wine €25. 10% SC (on food only). Closed L Sat, all Sun, Christmas week, bank hols. Amex, MasterCard, Visa, Laser. **Directions:** 10 minutes walk east of St Stephens Green, opposite Bank of Ireland HQ.

Dublin 2

La Cave Wine Bar & Restaurant

RESTAURANT

28 South Anne Street Dublin 2 **Tel: 01 679 4409** Fax: 01 670 5255
Email: lacave@iol.ie Web: www.lacavewinebar.com

Wine bars were not a noticeable feature of Dublin's hospitality scene until recently, but Margaret and Akim Beskri have run this characterful place just off Grafton Street since 1989 and it's well-known for its cosmopolitan atmosphere, late night opening and lots of chat. An excellent wine list of over 350 bins includes 15 bubblies, an exceptional choice of half bottles and 30 by the glass. With its traditional bistro atmosphere, classic French cooking ("food for the gourmet at reasonable prices"), it makes a handy place to take a break from shopping, for an evening out or for a party. Classic menus with the occasional contemporary twist make a refreshing change from the ubiquitous eclectic fare that has taken over the restaurant scene in recent years: paté de campagne, goats cheese tartlet à la Provençale, rack of Wicklow lamb with a thyme jus, wild mushroom crêpe, sauce forestière and chocolate mousse au Grand Marnier all indicate the style. A private room upstairs (with bar) is ideal for parties and small functions - Christmas parties are a speciality, but it's ideal for any kind of party, family reunions or even small weddings. No children after 7pm. **Seats 25** (private room, 32). Air conditioning. Open Mon-Sat 12.30-11, Sun 5.30-11. Set L €29.50. Early D €15. Also à la carte. House wine from €16. SC discretionary. Closed L Sun, 25-26 Dec, Good Fri. Amex, Diners, MasterCard, Visa, Laser. **Directions:** Just off Grafton Street.

Dublin 2

La Maison des Gourmets

CAFÉ

15 Castle Market Dublin 2 **Tel: 01 672 7258**

In a pedestrianised area handy to car parks and away from the hustle and bustle of nearby Grafton Street, this French boulangerie has a smart little café on the first floor and also a couple of outdoor tables on the pavement for fine weather. Home-baked bread is the speciality, made to a very high standard by French bakers who work in front of customers throughout the day, creating a wonderful aroma that wafts through the entire premises. Their speciality is sourdough bread, which is used as the base for a selection of tartines - French open-style sandwiches served warm - on the lunch menu (about €10): baked ham with thyme jus and smoked bacon cream; smoked salmon with crème fraîche, lemon confit & fresh dill and vegetarian ones like roast aubergine with plum tomato, fresh parmesan & basil pesto are all typical. Add to this a couple of delicious soups (French onion with Emmental croûtons, perhaps), one or two salads, and a charcuterie selection (about €15) - and a simple dessert like strawberries with balsamic reduction and fresh cream - and the result is as tempting a little menu as any discerning luncher could wish for. Portions are on the small side, which suits most lunch time appetites, and service can be alittle slow; but everything is very appetising, the atmosphere is chic and you can stock up on bread and croissants from the shop as you leave - just don't think in terms of a quick bite. **Seats 26.** Open Mon-Sat, 8-6 (L12-4). A la carte. SC discretionary. House wine €16. Closed Sun, Bank hols. Amex, MasterCard, Visa, Laser. **Directions:** Pedestrianised area between Georges Street Arcade and Powerscourt Shopping Centre.

Dublin 2

La Mère Zou

RESTAURANT

22 St Stephen's Green Dublin 2
Tel: 01 661 6669 Fax: 01 661 6669
Email: merzou@indigo.ie

Eric Tydgadt's French/Belgian restaurant is situated in a Georgian basement on the north side of the Green. Although there are some concessions to current cuisine (especially on the lunch menu), this establishment's reputation is based on French country cooking, as in rillette of pork with toasted baguette or confit duck leg with braised lentils, mashed potato & red wine jus; specialities include steamed mussels (various ways) with French fries and prices are reasonable - a policy carried through to the wine list too. The lunch menu - which offers a choice of three dishes on each course - also suggests six or seven more luxurious seafood dishes from the à la carte, so you can make a feast of it if time allows or, at the other extreme, they offer a range of Big Plates, with a salad starter and a main course served together on a king size plate which is great value and ideal if you're in a hurry. This is one of Dublin's pleasantest and most reliable restaurants. [* The associated business, Supper's Ready - an enlightened takeaway doing real food like navarin of lamb and potée paysanne - now has three outlets: 51, Pleasant Street, Dublin, 8. (Tel: 01-475 4556); 58 Clontarf Road, Dublin 3 (Tel: 01 853 3555) and Monread Avenue, Naas, Co. Kildare (Tel: 045 889554). Check the website for further details: www.suppersready.ie] **Seats 55.** L Mon-Fri, 12-2.30. D 6-11 (Sun to 9.30). Early D €21.50 (6-7.30), Set L €18.50; also à la carte. House wine from €17.50. SC discretionary. Closed L Sat, L Sun, 24 Dec-6 Jan. Amex, Diners, MasterCard, Visa, Laser. **Directions:** Beside Shelbourne Hotel. ◇

Dublin 2

La Stampa Hotel & Restaurant

HOTEL / RESTAURANT

35 Dawson Street Dublin 2 **Tel: 01 677 4444**
Fax: 01 677 4411 Email: dine@lastampa.ie Web: www.lastampa.ie

Already well-established as a restaurant, La Stampa has also been an hotel since the summer of 2001 and development continues as we go to press: three new suites, a new reception area and lift are all due for completion shortly - and a spa should not be far behind. There's an exotic lounge bar on the ground floor - to the right of the restaurant entrance - and the reception desk is upstairs, on the first floor. Rooms are very attractive, with an abundance of sumptuous fabrics, notably velvet, in rich colours echoing the ambience of the restaurant and bar below and neat en-suite bathrooms. No pets. **Rooms 30** (6 suites). Lift. 24 hour room service. Room rate €135. Open all year.

La Stampa: Reminiscent of a grand French belle époque brasserie, this is one of Ireland's finest dining rooms - high-ceiling, with large mirrors, wooden floor, candelabra, Victorian lamps, plants, flowers and various bits of bric-a-brac, the whole noisily complemented by a constant bustle. There's a small bar with a few comfortable seats where you can sip a drink while studying menus that encompass dishes from around the world. Menus are changed fairly often and, although prices can mount rather quickly for the style and quality of food and service, this is a fun and lively place, offering international brasserie-style food in delightful surroundings. No children under 12 after 8pm. Air conditioning. **Seats 230** (private room, 70). L daily, 12-3; D daily, 6-12.30am. Early/late D €25-32 (6-7.30/11-12); Set D €55-65; also à la carte. SC10%. * Tiger Becs, a mainly Thai restaurant downstairs, is under the same management. Seats 130, D Mon-Sat 6-12.30; D from about €20 (6-7.30). *Sam Sara Bar and Café is also part of the La Stampa complex. Amex, Diners, MasterCard, Visa, Laser. **Directions:** Across Dawson Street from the Mansion House.

Dublin 2

Les Frères Jacques

RESTAURANT

74 Dame Street Dublin 2 **Tel: 01 679 4555** Fax: 01 679 4725
Email: info@lesfreresjacques.com Web: www.lesfreresjacques.com

One of the few genuinely French restaurants in Dublin, Les Frères Jacques opened beside the Olympia Theatre in 1986, well before the development of Temple Bar made the area fashionable. Most of the staff are French, the atmosphere is French - and the cooking is classic French. Seasonal menus are wide-ranging and well-balanced but - as expected when you notice the lobster tank on entering - there is a strong emphasis on fish and seafood, all of it from Irish waters; game also features in season. Lunch at Les Frères Jacques is a treat (and good value) but dinner is a feast. Lunch offers at least three choices on each course, plus a few luxurious options from the à la carte listed as extras; west coast mussel risotto with a saffron cream, roast lamb tian with aubergine, courgette & thyme juices and strawberry tiramisu with a red fruit coulis are all typical. The à la carte offers classics such as west coast oysters (native or rock) and grilled lobster, individually priced, and there may be game in season. Finish with cheeses (including some Irish ones) or a classic dessert like warm thin apple tart (baked to order), with a rum & raisin ice cream. The wine list naturally favours France and makes interesting reading, notably the two pages of "recommendations du patron" (en rouge et blanc). Children welcome. Air conditioning.* At the time of going to press the restaurant is undergoing a complete refurbishment and will re-emerge 'more luxurious and more modern'! **Seats 60** (private room, 40). L Mon-Fri, 12.30-2.30; D Mon-Sat, 7.15-10.30. Set L €22; Set D €35; D also à la carte. House wine €18.50. SC 12.5%. Closed L Sat, all Sun, 24 Dec-2 Jan. Amex, MasterCard, Visa, Laser. **Directions:** Next to Olympia Theatre.

Dublin 2

Little Caesar's Palace

RESTAURANT

Balfe Street Dublin 2 **Tel: 01 671 8714**

This genuine little pizza place is just a stone's throw from the door of the Westbury Hotel - fresh, tasty and inexpensive pizzas (with good crisp bases) cooked before your very eyes could be the perfect antidote to too much luxury, or too much shopping. Open 12 noon-midnight. Closed 25 Dec & Good Fri. *There's also a related Mediterranean food shop & café nearby on Chatham Street and Little Caesar branches at: Rathfarnham (Unit 2, Butterfield, The Orchard Inn. Tel: 01-493 4060); Blackrock, Co. Dublin (Main Street. Tel: 01 278 1533). **Directions:** Just across from entrance to Westbury Hotel. ◇

Dublin 2

The Long Hall Bar

ATMOSPHERIC PUB

51 South Great George's Dublin 2 **Tel: 01-475 1590**

A wonderful old pub with magnificent plasterwork ceilings, traditional mahogany bar and Victorian lighting. One of Dublin's finest bars and well worth a visit. Closed 25 Dec & Good Fri.

Dublin 2

Longfields Hotel

HOTEL / RESTAURANT

10 Lower Fitzwilliam Street Dublin 2
Tel: 01 676 1367 Fax: 01 676 1542
Email: info@longfields.ie Web: www.longfields.ie

Located in a Georgian terrace between Fitzwilliam and Merrion Squares, this reasonably priced hotel is more like a well proportioned private house, furnished with antiques in period style - notably in elegant public areas. Comfortable bedrooms are individually furnished, some with four-posters or half-tester beds, although they vary considerably in size as rooms are smaller on the upper floors. Staff are friendly and there is morning coffee and afternoon tea available in The Drawing Room, which can also be used for private dining or small conferences (22). 24 hour room service. Children welcome (cots available). No pets. Lift. **Rooms 26** (2 junior suites, 19 shower only). B&B €87.50pps, ss €47.50 Open all year.

Kevin Arundel @ Number 10: In the basement, with direct access from Longfields Hotel or the street, this excellent restaurant is currently one of Dublin's best-kept secrets. In 2001 Kevin Arundel, previously second chef at L'Ecrivain, took over as chef-patron, refurbished the restaurant and moved the kitchen up into a higher gear. Modern French is the style, seen in starters like a rich balottine of ham hock with with shallot compôte and herb salad and pan-fried wild sea trout, with braised fennel and cassoulet of haricot beans. Careful sourcing and excellent cooking at fair prices add up to great value - it is impressive, for example, to find wild sea trout on a set lunch menu, and the dinner menu offers some luxurious dishes without supplements. But be sure to leave room for a grand finale of wonderful desserts, such as an exemplary caramelised crème brulée with vanilla ice cream, beautifully presented. Kevin also presents an 8-course Tasting Menu which features many of his specialities, with an option of specially selected wines with each course. Impeccable service complements the fine food, making this an equally good venue for lunch or dinner. Interesting wine list. Children welcome; wheelchair accessible. **Seats 35** (private room, 20). L Mon-Fri 12.30-2.30, D Mon-Sat 6.30-10.30. Set L €28, Set D €45; Tasting Menu €65; house wine €24. SC 12.5%. Closed L Sat, all Sun & Christmas. Amex, MasterCard, Visa, Laser. **Directions:** On corner of Fitzwilliam Street & Baggot Street.

Dublin 2

Mao Café Bar

féile bia **RESTAURANT**

2-3 Chatham Row Dublin 2 **Tel: 01 670 4899** Fax: 01 670 4993
Email: info@cafemao.com Web: www.cafemao.com

In simple but stylish surroundings, Mao Café Bar brings to the Grafton Street area the cuisines of Thailand, Malaysia, Indonesia, Japan and China - about as 'Asian Fusion' as it gets. The atmosphere is bright and very buzzy, and interesting food is based on seasonal ingredients; the standard of cooking is consistently good and so is value for money, although the bill can mount up quickly if you don't watch the number of Asian beers ordered. Chilli squid, Nasi Goreng and Malaysian chicken are established favourites, also tempura sole with stir-fried vegetables in a citrus sauce; vegetarians might try a starter of Jakarta salad (crisp vegetables and fruits in a piquant chilli dressing) followed by Thai green vegetable curry, with Jasmine rice. Chilli strength is considerately indicated on the menu, also vegetarian and low fat dishes, dishes containing nuts. A compact but wide-ranging drinks menu includes cocktails, fresh juices and smoothies, a range of coffees and teas and speciality beers as well as wines. While authenticity may not always be guaranteed, the cooking is good here. No reservations. Wheelchair access. Children welcome. **Seats 120.** Air conditioning. Open daily, 12-11. Menu à la carte. House wine from about €17; Asian beers from about €4.50. SC discretionary. Closed 25-26 Dec, Good Fri. MasterCard, Visa, Laser. **Directions:** City centre - just off Grafton Street. ◇

Dublin 2

The Market Bar

Ⓝ **BAR**

Fade Street Dublin 2 **Tel: 01 613 9094**

The latest addition to the chain of bars operated by Jay Bourke and Eoin Foyle, this large bar opened just before we went to press, and is is located in the Victorian redbrick block best known for the

George's Street Market Arcade that runs through its centre. It's a very attractive space with lofty ceilings (high enough to allow the addition of a mezzanine floor) and simple, stylish furnishings - a little too simple perhaps, as the wooden floor and hard surfaces bounce noise around and there's precious little to absorb it. It's been an immediate hit with Dubliners however and the food, which is cooked in an open kitchen, is part of the attraction. The menu is loosely Spanish, offering nibbles like olives, smoked almonds and anchovies, and more substantial dishes which can be ordered as small or large portions (about €6-9 each) and include fairly faithful renditions of Spanish classics like tortilla and patatas bravas. It's early days for this new venture, but it seems to be offering good food in a fashionable space, at very reasonable prices: long may it continue to do so. Food daily: Mon-Sat 12-9.30; Sun 4-9.30. Closed 25 Dec, Good Fri. MasterCard, Visa.

Dublin 2

McDaids

ATMOSPHERIC PUB

3 Harry Street Dublin 2

Established in 1779, McDaids more recently achieved fame as one of the great literary pubs - and its association with Brendan Behan, especially, brings a steady trail of pilgrims from all over the world to this traditional premises just beside the Westbury Hotel. Dubliners, however, tend to be immune to this kind of thing and drink there because it's a good pub - and, although its character is safe, it's not a place set in aspic either, as a younger crowd has been attracted by recent changes. History and character are generally of more interest than food here, but sandwiches are available. Open Mon-Wed,10.30am-11.30pm; Thu-Sat, 10.30am-12.30am; Sun 12.30-11. Closed 25 Dec & Good Fri. ◇

Dublin 2

The Mermaid Café

☆ **RESTAURANT**

69-70 Dame Street Dublin 2 **Tel: 01 670 8236** Fax: 01 670 8205
Email: info.@mermaid.ie Web: www.mermaid.ie

Interesting decor and imaginative French and American-inspired cooking are to be found at Ben Gorman and Mark Harrell's unusual restaurant on the edge of Temple Bar. The two dining areas have recently been supplemented by a new wine lounge, which still hasn't transformed it into a big restaurant - but every inch of space has always been used with style here. Cooking at The Mermaid is among the best in the area - innovative, mid-Atlantic, seasonal and often memorable for inspired combinations of flavour, texture and colour - and service, although not always notable for swiftness, is invariably courteous and helpful. Menus change frequently but there would be public outcry if specialities like New England crab cakes with piquant mayonnaise, the Giant Seafood Casserole (which changes daily depending on availability) or pecan pie were taken off. Mermaid Café won the Bord Glas Creative Use of Irish Vegetables Award for 2003 and it's easy to see why: terrific vegetarian main courses such as steamed globe artichoke stuffed with basil pesto & niçoise salad rub shoulders with hearty meat dishes which vary with the seasons but are invariably full of interest. Vegetables, always used imaginatively, are beautifully integrated into main courses - loin of lamb with beetroot and couscous is a good, colourful example, and there are many more like it on each day's menus. Then delicious desserts, wonderful Irish cheeses (like the deeply flavoured Gabriel and Desmond from West Cork, served with celery biscuits) and coffees with crystallised pecan nuts: attention to detail right to the finish. Sunday brunch is not to be missed if you are in the area. Wines are imported privately and are exclusive to the restaurant. Children welcome. **Seats 55** (private room, 28) Air conditioning. L 12.30-3 (Sun to 3.30), D 6.30-11 (Sun to 9). Set L about €22; Set D from about €30; also à la carte. House wine from about €18. SC discretionary. Closed 24-26 Dec,31 Dec, 1 Jan, Good Fri. New Year, Good Fri. [Times & prices not confirmed at time of going to press.] * Next door, Gruel (Tel 01 670 7119), is a quality fast-food outlet under the same management; open Mon-Fri 7.30-9.30; Sat & Sun 10.30-4.30.] MasterCard, Visa, Laser. **Directions:** Next door to Olympia Theatre.

Dublin 2

HOTEL / RESTAURANT

The Merrion Hotel

Upper Merrion Street Dublin 2

Tel: 01 603 0600 Fax: 01 603 0700

Email: info@merrionhotel.com Web: www.merrionhotel.com

Right in the heart of Georgian Dublin opposite the Government Buildings, the main house of this luxurious hotel comprises four meticulously restored Grade 1 listed townhouses built in the 1760s and now restored to their former glory; behind them, a contemporary garden wing has been added, overlooking two private period and formal landscaped gardens. Inside, Irish fabrics and antiques reflect the architecture and original interiors with rococo plasterwork ceilings and classically proportioned windows - and the hotel has one of the most important private collections of 20th-century art. Public areas include three interconnecting drawing rooms (one is the cocktail bar with a log fire), with French windows giving access to the gardens. Elegant and gracious bedrooms have individually controlled air-conditioning, three telephones, personalised voice-mail with remote access, fax/modem, broadband and video conference facilities, also a mini-bar and safe (VCRs, DVDs, CD players and tea/coffee making facilities are available on request). Sumptuous Italian marble bathrooms, with a separate walk-in shower, pamper guests to the extreme. The six meeting/private dining rooms combine state-of-the-art technology and Georgian splendour, while the splendid leisure complex, The Tethra Spa, with classical mosaics, is almost Romanesque. Staff, under the excellent direction of General Manager Peter MacCann, are quite exemplary and courteous, suggesting standards of hospitality from a bygone era. Complimentary underground valet parking. Restaurant Patrick Guilbaud (see separate entry) is also on site. Conference/banqueting (50). Secretarial services. Leisure centre; swimming pool. Garden. Children welcome (under 12 free in parents' room, cots available free of charge). No pets. Lift. Valet parking. **Rooms 145** (20 suites, 10 junior suites, 1 shower only, 80 no-smoking, 5 for disabled). Room rate from €320. Open all year.

The Cellar Restaurant: This elegant vaulted dining-room has a new entrance from Merrion Street, through a pleasing corridor decorated with flower arrangements. Warm, friendly staff seat arriving guests at beautiful classically appointed tables, and explain menus - which are well-balanced and straightforward. With everything of the best quality (including the lighting and ventilation), it is a very relaxing room - and the philosophy of sourcing the best ingredients and treating them with respect in a simple style makes a refreshing change from the multi-cultural menus in so many restaurants. Cooking is careful, and also presentation - which shows the food to advantage with over-emphasis on display. Delicious flavours, excellent service and great value for the quality of food and surroundings - this fine restaurant should prove very attractive to those who value quality in a discreet atmosphere. A good wine list also offers value, including wines by the glass. Air conditioning. **Seats 60.** Reservations required. L 12.30-2 Sun-Fri, D 6-10 daily. Set L from €19.95. Early D from €22.95, (6-7pm). D also à la carte. House wine from €24. Closed L Sat. Amex, Diners, MasterCard, Visa, Laser. **Directions:** City centre, opposite Government Buildings.

Dublin 2

RESTAURANT / CAFÉ

Mimo/Ba Mizu

Powerscourt Townhouse Centre South William Street Dublin 2

Tel: Mimo: 01 679 4160 / Bá Mizu: 01 674 6712

These two attractive sister establishments are within a whisper of each other in the lovely Powerscourt Shopping Centre: Mimo, in the central focal area, is more of a café-cum-champagne bar while the younger Bá Mizu is a fully-fledged restaurant with full bar - between them, you will find just about anything you could wish for in the way of interesting, freshly-prepared food and drink throughout the day and evening. Bá Mizu offers an extensive drinks menu, including a comprehensive choice of liqueurs and cocktails, and the restaurant - which is in an atmospheric vaulted area and stylishly furnished with comfy leather chairs - offers a wide range of food from tasty bar bites to full meals, with seafood a particular strength. Children are welcome during the daytime. Mimo: Open 7 days, in shopping hours (closed bank hols); also due to open Tue-Sun nights (noodle/pasta menu). Bá Mizu: Open Sun-Wed, 12 noon-11.30pm; Thu-Sat 12 noon-12.30am. Closed 25 Dec, 1 Jan, Good Fri. Amex, MasterCard, Visa, Laser. **Directions:** In an 18th century listed building 2 minutes west of Grafton Street.

Dublin 2

Mont Clare Hotel

féile bia HOTEL

Merrion Square Dublin 2 **Tel: 01 607 3800** Fax: 01 661 5663
Email: montclareres@ocallaghanhotels.ie Web: www.ocallaghanhotels.ie

A few doors away from the National Gallery, this well-located and reasonably priced hotel is in common ownership with the nearby Davenport and Alexander Hotels. The hotel is imaginatively decorated in contemporary style - except the old stained glass and mahogany Gallery Bar, which has retained its original pubby atmosphere. Compact bedrooms are well furnished and comfortable - and executive rooms are for business guests with full marbled bathrooms and good amenities, including air conditioning, three direct line phones, a personal safe, ISDN lines and fax - and multi-channel TV with video channel. Business centre; use of gym (at Davenport Hotel). Conference/banqueting. (200). Children welcome (Under 2s free in parents' room; cots available free of charge). No pets. **Rooms 80** (40 no-smoking). Lift. Room rate €245. Open all year. Amex, Diners, MasterCard, Visa, Laser. **Directions:** Corner of Clare Street. just off Merrion Square.

Dublin 2

Montys of Kathmandu

féile bia RESTAURANT

28 Eustace Street Temple Bar Dublin 2 **Tel: 01 670 4911**
Fax: 01 494 4359 Email: montys@tinet.ie Web: www.montys.ie

At first glance this restaurant deep in the heart of Temple Bar seems ordinary enough, but the food here can have real character - and at agreeably low prices. The chefs are all from Nepal and although all the familiar dishes are represented there are definite undertones of Nepalese cooking throughout the menu. At its best, this is a really rewarding restaurant: friendly staff are more than happy to offer suggestions or choose a well balanced meal for you; sheesh kebabs , for example, and other specialities like kachela (raw minced lamb), Momo (Nepalese dumplings) and Tandoori butter chicken: moist pieces of tender tandoori chicken off the bone, cooked in a creamy masala sauce. And they even have their own beer, 'Shiva', brewed exclusively for the restaurant. The Guide's most recent visit was a less happy experience than previously, but it is to be hoped that this was just an off-night. Children welcome. **Seats 60** (private room, 30) L Mon-Sat, 12-2.15; Set L about €15, Early D about €20 (6-7pm), D daily 6-11.30, (Sun to 11), Tasting Menu about €27-40. L&D à la carte available. SC discretionary except on parties of 6+ (12.5%). House wine from about €17. Closed L Sun, 25-26 Dec & Good Fri. Amex, MasterCard, Visa, Laser. **Directions:** Opposite the Irish Film Centre (IFC). ◇

Dublin 2

Morgan Hotel

HOTEL

10 Fleet Street Temple Bar Dublin 2 **Tel: 01 679 3939** Fax: 01 679 3946
Email: sales@themorgan.com Web: www.themorgan.com

In deepest Temple Bar, this unusual boutique hotel is characterised by clean simple lines and uncluttered elegance. Bedrooms have 6' beds in light beech, with classic white cotton bed linen and natural throws, while standard bedroom facilities include satellite TV and video, CD/hi-fi system, mini-bar, safe, voicemail and Internet access. The stylish Morgan Bar is open all day and offers an oasis of comfort and relaxation amongst the hustle and bustle of Temple Bar - try an exotic Morgan Mai Tai, perhaps? Strangely, as it seems so much at odds with the cool, reserved style of the rest of the hotel, the brash All Sports Café next door is part of it. Children welcome (cots available). **Rooms 66** (1 suite, 1 junior suite, 13 executive, 30 shower only, 25 no-smoking). Lift. Room rate €215. Closed 23-28 Dec. Amex, Diners, MasterCard, Visa, Laser. **Directions:** off Westmoreland Street.

Dublin 2

Neary's

ATMOSPHERIC PUB

1 Chatham Street Dublin 2 **Tel: 01 677 8596** Fax: 01 677 7371

This unspoilt Edwardian pub off Grafton Street has been in the present ownership for over half a century and is is popular at all times of day - handy for lunch or as a meeting place in the early evening and full of buzz later when a post-theatre crowd, including actors from the nearby Gaiety Theatre, will probably be amongst the late night throng in the downstairs bar. Traditional values assert themselves through gleaming brass, well-polished mahogany and classics like smoked salmon and mixed meat salads amongst the bar fare. Open Mon-Thu 10.30-11 (to 12.30 Fr & Sat), Sun 12-11. Bar food: 10.30-2.30. Closed 25 Dec & Good Fri. MasterCard, Visa, Laser. **Directions:** Off Grafton St.

Dublin 2

Nude Restaurant

CAFÉ

21 Suffolk Street Dublin 2 **Tel: 01 672 5577**
Fax: 01 672 5773 Email: niamh@nude.ie

Nude offers fantastic very fresh food - organic whenever possible - in an ultra-cool, youthful environment. Just off Grafton Street it's a great place for a quick snack, with plenty of room to sit down at long canteen-style tables. Queue up, order and pay at the till, then collect your food if it's ready or it will be delivered to your table. If you eat with your eyes, just looking at the fresh fruit and vegetables hanging or racked up in the open kitchen should revive you while you wait! A choice of soups includes seafood chowder, chunky vegetable and Thai chicken broth, all served with freshly baked breads; there are hot wraps - chicken satay or vegetarian Jumping Bean, for example - and paninis, including one with Gubeen cheese, or try the chill cabinet for salads like Caesar or tomato & mozzarella, and cold wraps such as hummus or spinach & peppers, or soft bread rolls (e.g. smoked salmon & cream cheese). Freshly squeezed juices, smoothies and organic Fair Trade coffees, teas and herbal teas are all very popular (drinks can be made up to order) and the menu caters for vegetarians, people with nut allergies and other dietary requirements. **Seats 40.** Open Mon-Sat, 8am-9.30pm, Sun 11-7. MasterCard, Visa, Laser. **Directions:** Near Dublin Tourism office. ◇

Dublin 2

Number 31

GUESTHOUSE

31 Leeson Close Lower Leeson St. Dublin 2
Tel: 01 676 5011 Fax: 01 676 2929
Email: number31@iol.ie Web: number31.ie

Formerly the home of leading architect Sam Stephenson, Noel and Deirdre Comer's 'oasis of tranquillity and greenery' just off St Stephen's Green makes an excellent city centre base, with virtually everything within walking distance in fine weather. Warm hospitality, huge breakfasts and secure parking add greatly to the attraction and rooms have everything you could wish for, including phones, TVs and tea/coffee trays. Not suitable for children under 10. No pets. Rooms at the back are quieter. **Rooms 20** (all en-suite & no smoking). B&B about €85, ss € 19.95. Open all year. Amex, MasterCard, Visa. **Directions:** From St. Stephens Green onto Baggot St., turn right on to Pembroke St. and left on to Leeson St. ◇

Dublin 2

O'Donoghue's

ATMOSPHERIC PUB

15 Merrion Row Dublin 2 **Tel: 01 676 2807**

O'Donoghues has long been the Dublin mecca for visitors in search of a lively evening with traditional music - live music every night is a major claim to fame - but a visit to this famous pub near the Shelbourne Hotel at quieter times can be rewarding too. Closed 25 Dec & Good Fri.

Dublin 2

O'Neill's Pub & Guesthouse

PUB / GUESTHOUSE

37 Pearse Steet Dublin 2
Tel: 01 677 5213 Fax: 01 832 5218
Email: oneilpub@iol.ie Web: www.oneillsdublin.com

Established in 1885, this centrally located pub on the corner of Pearse Street and Shaw Street is easily recognised by the well-maintained floral baskets that brighten up the street outside. Inside, this cosy bar has kept its Victorian character and charm (two bars have lots of little alcoves and snugs) and serves a good range of reasonably priced home-cooked food - typically steak champignon with red wine sauce, served with French fries and an attractive salad; lamb filo parcels with mint yoghurt and chilli con carne - all good value (under €15). (Accommodation is available in en-suite rooms, with breakfast served in a pleasant room above the pub; rather expensive for simple accommodation at €45 pps midweek - €50 at weekends - but conveniently located.) Bar food: L 12.30-2.30, D 5.30-8. Closed Christmas & Good Fri. Amex, MasterCard, Visa, Laser. **Directions:** Opposite Pearse Street side of Trinity College. ◇

Dublin 2

O'Neill's Public House

PUB

2 Suffolk Street Dublin 2 **Tel: 01 679 3656** Fax: 01 679 0689
Email: mike@oneillsbar.com Web: www.oneillsbar.com

A striking pub with its own fine clock over the door and an excellent corner location, this large pub has been in the O'Neill family since 1920 and is popular with Dubliners and visitors alike. Students from Trinity and several other colleges nearby home into O'Neill's for its wide range of reasonably priced bar food, which includes a carvery with a choice of five or six roasts and an equal number of other dishes (perhaps including traditional favourites such as Irish Stew) each day; finish off with some home-made rhubarb pie, perhaps. There is also a well-presented sandwich/salad bar. Carvery 2pm - 3.30pm on Monday to Thursday, Friday 12pm - 6pm, Saturday 12pm - 8pm and Sunday 12pm - 10pm. An extensive a la carte bar menu takes over after the carvery, except on Fridays. Live traditional music every Sunday night at 8:30pm. Wheelchair access. No children after 6pm. Closed 25 & 26 Dec, Good Fri. Amex, MasterCard, Visa, Laser. **Directions:** On the corner of Suffolk St and Church Lane, opposite the DublinTourist Centre.

Dublin 2

Odessa Lounge & Grill

BAR / CAFÉ

13/14 Dame Lane Dublin 2 **Tel: 01 670 7634**

Tucked away about 5 minutes from Grafton Street this is a favourite haunt for Dublin's bright young things and was one of the first places in Dublin to do brunch. Upstairs is bright and modern but the room downstairs is the perfect place to nurse a hangover with no natural light, subdued lighting, comfy chairs with plenty of room to spread out and read the papers in peace. The food is basic brunch fare - Eggs Benedict or Florentine, huevos rancheros or a char-grilled steak sandwich (all around €10) - but the atmosphere is a major attraction. The service is relaxed and friendly even when they are very busy there's never a feeling of being rushed. At night is just right for those who want more than a fast-food burger, but who do not want to dress for dinner - and it's also perfect for large groups with something to celebrate. **Seats 100.** Air conditioning. Sat & Sun open noon-midnight, brunch 12-4. D Mon-Wed 6-11, Thu & Fri 5-12. SC discretionary (10% on parties of 6+). Amex, MasterCard, Visa. **Directions:** Left off Dame Street onto George's Street, left onto Exchequer Street, then left again. ◇

Dublin 2

The Old Mill

RESTAURANT

14 Temple Bar Dublin 2 **Tel: 01 671 9262**

Long before this area became trendy Temple Bar, Moroccan chef-patron Lahcen Iouani had a loyal following in the area - since the mid-80s, in fact, when this restaurant delighted discerning Dubliners in an earlier guise as 'Pigalle'. The name change has relevance to local history (you can read all about it on the back of the menu) but other things have thankfully remained the same and Lahcen continues to offer admirably traditional French cooking at refreshingly modest prices. The place has a homely feeling, like stepping back in time to an old French restaurant - giving good value to the customer is something he feels strongly about. A blackboard menu offers traditional starters like pate de foie de canard and salade niçoise (around €8), while classic maincourses such as boeuf Bourginonne and sole meunière are well-priced at around €18.50 each. Vegetarian dishes are under €10 and there's also an excellent value early menu. **Seats 50.** Air conditioning. Open Mon-Fri, 12.30-11.30pm; Sat-Sun, 5-11.30. Early Menu Mon-Fri, 12.30-7.30; Sat-Sun, 5-7.30. House wine from €18.50. SC discretionary except on parties of 8+ (12.5%). MasterCard, Visa, Laser, Switch. **Directions:** Above Merchants Arch on Temple Bar Square (behind Central Bank). ◇

Dublin 2

The Old Stand

ATMOSPHERIC PUB

37 Exchequer Street Dublin 2 **Tel: 01 677 7220**

This fine traditional pub, which is a sister establishment to Davy Byrnes, off Grafton Street, occupies a prominent position on the corner of Exchequer Street and St Andrew Street and lays claim to being "possibly the oldest public house in Ireland"! Named after the Old Stand at the Lansdowne Road rugby grounds, it has a loyal following amongst the local business community, notably from the 'rag trade' area around South William Street, and also attracts a good mixture of rugby fans and visitors, who enjoy the atmosphere. They offer no-nonsense traditional bar food, but its warm and friendly atmosphere is a bigger draw than the food. Not suitable for children under 7. Closed 25-26 Dec & Good Fri. Amex, MasterCard, Visa, Laser. **Directions:** Off Grafton Street.

Dublin 2

One Pico Restaurant

☆ féile bia **RESTAURANT**

5-6 Molesworth Place Schoolhouse Lane Dublin 2
Tel: 01 676 0300 Fax: 01 676 0411
Email: eamonoreilly@ireland.com Web: www.onepico.com

Eamonn O'Reilly
Proprietor/Chef

In a magical location near St Stephen's Green, nicely tucked in a laneway just a couple of minutes walk from the Dail (Parliament) and Grafton Street, Eamonn O'Reilly's One Pico is one of Dublin's most popular restaurants. The surroundings are elegant and cooking good - the style distinctly contemporary, with worldwide influences; sophisticated, technically demanding dishes are executed with confidence and flair. Eamonn has always based his menus on first class ingredients and it is their flavours that stand out, together with the precision of the cooking. Menus offered include a 2- and 3-course lunch which, as usual in restaurants of this calibre represents great value (although beware of side orders, which are charged separately at €4.50 each). An early evening menu and a 'value' dinner menu are offered as well as an à la carte, with about ten quite luxurious dishes offered on each course, plus optional side dishes which should not be necessary as each main course is individually garnished. Specialities include a small nod to our own traditions in a starter of bacon & cabbage terrine with sauce gribiche & plum chutney and a main course of seared black scallops & black pudding with pommes mousseline & horseradish foam, but dishes with Irish influences are not much in evidence, alas and, although carefully sourced, the provenance of ingredients is not highlighted. But be sure to sample an innovative and delicious cheese menu and/or beautifully presented desserts that taste as good as they look. An 8-course tasting menu is also offered, for whole tables up to a maximum of six. Service, under the direction of restaurant manager Florian Ademell, is professional and friendly and a good wine list is generally fairly priced, except for Bordeaux. This is a fine restaurant and has the potential to be outstanding. * A sister restaurant, Bleu Bistro Moderne, opened nearby in 2003 - see separate entry. **Seats 110** (private room, 45). Air conditioning. L& D Mon-Sat: L12-3, D 6-11. Set L €23-26, Early D €27 (6-7); Set D 35, Tasting Menu €70, also à la carte. House wine €25. SC 10% (on food only). Closed Sun, bank hols, 25 Dec-6 Jan. Amex, Diners, MasterCard, Visa. **Directions:** 2 mins walk off St Stephens Green/Grafton Street.

Dublin 2

The Palace Bar

ATMOSPHERIC PUB 21 Fleet Street Dublin 2 **Tel: 01 671 7388**

Just around the corner from the Irish Times offices, The Palace has had strong connections with writers and journalists for many a decade. Its unspoilt frosted glass and mahogany are impressive enough but the special feature is the famous sky-lighted snug, which is really more of a back room. Many would cite The Palace as their favourite Dublin pub. Closed 25 Dec & Good Fri.

Dublin 2

Pasta Fresca

RESTAURANT 2-4 Chatham Street Dublin 2 **Tel: 01 679 2402**
Fax: 01 668 4563 Email: info@pastafresca.ie

This long-established Italian restaurant in the Grafton Street shopping area specialises in fresh pasta. The popular all-day menu is based on good home-made pastas, thin-based crispy Neapolitan pizzas, a wide range of interesting salads with well-made dressings. There are plenty of vegetarian dishes on offer as well as Tuscan favourites like pollo all Toscana (chargrilled marinated chicken served with Tuscan white beans and salad) and a speciality pasta salad (with Tuscan beans, sweetcorn, fresh vegetables, shaved Parmesan & house dressing). Evening menus offer a wider choice and shoppers and diners alike can buy Italian groceries, fresh pasta and sauces made on the premises from their deli counter. Children welcome. **Seats 80** (outdoors, 20). Air conditioning. Open all day Mon-Sat, 11.30-11.30, Sun 12 -10. L 12-5, D 5.30-12 (Sun to10); Set L €9.95; also à la carte. House wine from €18. SC discretionary. Closed 25 Dec, 1 Jan. Amex, Diners, MasterCard, Visa, Laser. **Directions:** Off top of Grafton Street.

Dublin 2

Pearl Brasserie

RESTAURANT 20 Merrion Street Upper Dublin 2 **Tel: 01 661 3572** Fax: 01 661 3629
Email: info@pearl-brasserie.com Web: www.pearl-brasserie.com

Just a few doors away from The Merrion Hotel, this stylish basement restaurant has an open fire and colourful blue banquettes picking up tones from an aquarium that runs the length of the bar. It's run by Sebastien Masi and his partner Kirsten Batt, who is the restaurant manager, and the style is contemporary international, with a classic French base and a pleasing emphasis on clean flavours, highlighting the quality of ingredients. Menus lean towards towards fish, which Sebastien cooks with accuracy and flair - nearly half of the starters and main courses on the à la carte menu are seafood of some sort and very attractive they are too - who could resist crispy prawns with mango & black pepper dressing, or a main course of Kilkee lobster (poached in saffron bouillon & ginger confit)? But there's plenty from the land too, with specialities including luscious pan-fried foie gras with toasted brioche with strawberry compôte and a simple dish of pan-fried sirloin steak with home-made French fries & mushroom sauce. A separate wine bar area - the Oyster Bar - offers some interesting options, including some small dishes (baked fish cake with marinated tomato in balsamic dressing, for instance) and a range of platters for two; a Fish Platter, for example, comprises a selection of squid tempura, crispy prawns, crab salad, salmon gravalax & dips - the perfect complement to an expanded list of wines available by the glass. Service is charming and well informed. The wine list is a good match for the food, favouring France and offering a good few champagnes and a fair choice of half bottles. **Seats 80** (private area, 10); Air-conditioning. L Tue-Fri 12-2.30, D daily 6-10.30; L à la carte; Early D €19 (6-7.30, Mon-Fri), Set D from €28; Gourmet menu €60. House wine €19.50. SC discretionary. Closed bank hols, 1st 2 wks Jan. Amex, MasterCard, Visa, Laser. **Directions:** Opposite Government Building, near Merrion Hotel.

Dublin 2

The Pembroke

PUB

31/32 Lower Pembroke Street Dublin 2 **Tel: 01 676 2980** Fax: 01 676 6579
Email: briancrowley@hotmail.com Web: www.pembroke.ie

There was consternation amongst traditionalists when this fine old pub was given a complete makeover several years ago, creating the bright and trendy bar that it is now - it even has a cyber café in the basement. But, even if the cosiness of old has now gone for ever, the spacious new bar that has been created has character of its own and, along with some striking design features (notably lighting), the atrium/ conservatory area at the back brings the whole place to life. Meeting the needs of those who get in to work before the traffic builds up, bar food begins with breakfast. **Seats 200.** Food served Mon-Sat, 7.30am-8pm; carvery lunch, 12-2.30. Closed Sun, Christmas & Good Fri. Amex, MasterCard, Visa, Laser. **Directions:** Near St Stephen's Green - off Lr. Baggot Street.

Dublin 2

Pizza Stop

RESTAURANT

6-10 Chatham House Chatam Lane Dublin 2
Tel: 01 679 6712 Fax: 01 679 6712

This cheap and cheerful little restaurant has been doing good pizzas and pastas in style since the late '80s. If you're not in the mood for pizza or pasta try one of their other Italian specialities - diced leg of Wicklow lamb with Mediterranean sauce, perhaps. Just the place to meet up with the family for a tasty meal that won't break the bank. **Seats 70.** Air conditioning. Open Mon-Sat 12-12, Sun 3-11. A la carte. House wine about €15. SC5%. MasterCard, Visa, Laser. **Directions:** Beside Westbury Hotel, off Grafton Street. ◇

Dublin 2

The Porterhouse

PUB

16-18 Parliament Street Temple Bar Dublin 2
Tel: 01 679 8847 Fax: 01 670 9605 Email: porterh.indigo.ie

Dublin's first micro-brewery pub opened in 1996 and, although several others have since set up and are doing an excellent job, The Porterhouse was at the cutting edge. Ten different beers are brewed on the premises and beer connoisseurs can sample a special tasting tray selection of plain porter (a classic light stout), oyster stout (brewed with fresh oysters, the logical development of a perfect partnership), Wrasslers 4X (based on a West Cork recipe from the early 1900s, and said to be Michael Collins' favourite tipple), Porter House Red (an Irish Red Ale with traditional flavour), An Brain Blasta (dangerous to know) and the wittily named Temple Brau. But you don't even have to like beer to love The Porterhouse. The whole concept is an innovative move away from the constraints of the traditional Irish pub and yet it stays in tune with its origins - it is emphatically not just another theme pub. The attention to detail which has gone into the decor and design is a constant source of pleasure to visitors and the food, while definitely not gourmet, is a cut above the usual bar food and, like the pub itself, combines elements of tradition with innovation. This is a real Irish pub in the modern idiom and was a respected winner of our Jameson Pub of the Year award in 1999. No children after 7pm. Bar food served 12.30-9.30 daily. Closed 25 Dec & Good Fri. MasterCard, Visa. [* The original Porterhouse is located on Strand Road on the seafront in Bray, Co. Wicklow and, like its sister pub in Temple Bar, it offers bar food daily from 12:30-9:30. No children after 7pm. Closed 25 Dec & Good Fri. MasterCard, Visa. Tel/Fax: 01 286 1839. There is also a newer Porterhouse in London, located at Covent Garden.] ◇

Dublin 2

The Principal Hotel

HOTEL

19/20 Fleet Street Temple Bar Dublin 2 **Tel: 01 670 8122**
Fax: 01 670 8103 Email: principalhotel@eircom.net

Conveniently situated in the heart of Temple Bar, within easy walking distance of all the city's main attractions, this reasonably priced hotel is fairly small, allowing an intimate atmosphere and a welcome emphasis on service. Children welcome (under 12 free in parents' room; cots available without charge). No pets. **Rooms 71** (40 shower only, 35 no-smoking). Room rate €149. Lift. Closed 24-26 Dec. Amex, Diners, MasterCard, Visa. **Directions:** Heart of Temple Bar, near Fleet Street.

Dublin 2

Queen of Tarts

CAFÉ

4 Cork Hill Dame Street Dublin 2 **Tel: 01 670 7499**

Behind this quaint traditional shopfront near Dublin Castle lies an equally quaint traditional tea room, with warmly welcoming friendly and efficient staff and wonderful smells wafting across the room as they struggle to make space for new arrivals to the comfortable, lived-in little room. Breakfast (including a vegetarian cooked breakfast) is served from 7.30 and the lunch/afternoon menu takes over at noon. Baking is a speciality, with home-made scones, buttermilk brown bread, hot savoury tarts, roast chicken & coriander tartlets, warm plum & cinnamon tarts, warm chocolate fudge cake, orange chocolate pinwheel cookies and much else besides taking their place on a surprisingly extensive menu, which includes some seriously good sandwiches and salads - most people pop in for a snack, but you could just as easily have a 3-course lunch. Inexpensive (there's not much over €7.95), consistently excellent food and great service - what more could anyone ask? [Also at: City Hall. Open museum hours, Sat 10-5, Sun 2-5]. **Seats 20.** Air conditioning. Open daily: Mon-Fri 7.30-6; Sat 9-6; Sun 10-6. Closed 24 Dec -3 Jan. **No Credit Cards. Directions:** Opposite the gates of Dublin Castle.

Dublin 2

Rajdoot Tandoori

RESTAURANT

26 -28 Clarendon Street Dublin 2 **Tel: 01 679 4274** Fax: 01 679 4274
Email: info@rajdoottandoori.com Web: www.rajdoottandoori.com

A member of a small UK chain of restaurants specialising in subtle, aromatic North Indian cuisine, this restaurant has had a fine reputation for its food and service since it opened in 1984. Tandoori dishes are the main speciality, based on a wide range of ingredients authentically cooked - this is possibly the only restaurant in Ireland that still uses the traditional charcoal-fired clay ovens rather than gas. Speciality dishes include duck jaipur (with spring onions, green peppers, mushrooms, garlic & red wine), chicken johl (a spicy Nepalese dish with ginger, garlic, fresh coriander & fenugreek) and lamb chili garlic. There is also plenty of choice for vegetarians. Set menus include a keenly priced 3-course lunch and pre-theatre dinner. Children over 6 welcome until 7pm. **Seats 120.** No smoking area; air conditioning. L Mon-Sat 12-2.30, Sun 1.30-5.30. D 6-11 daily. Set L €11.35 Set D from €21.59. Early D €20.32 (6-7pm). House wine €14.60. Air conditioning. SC discretionary. Closed 25-26 Dec. Amex, Diners, MasterCard, Visa, Laser, Switch. **Directions:** Parallel to top of Grafton Street, behind Westbury Hotel.

Dublin 2

Relax Café @ Habitat

Ⓝ **RESTAURANT**

6-7 St Stephen's Green Dublin 2 **Tel: 01 674 6624**

Relax Café is on the first floor at Habitat, overlooking St Stephen's Green and got off to a good start when it opened in the summer of 2003. It's a useful address to bear in mind when spending a day in town, as they're open for breakfast - and throughout the day - serving just the kind of wholesome contemporary food that you'd expect of Habitat, in predictably chic surroundings. Everything is freshly prepared using locally sourced ingredients: gourmet sandwiches, salads, pastas are the style and, unlike many other comparable places offering a degree of style, it is particularly family-friendly. Licensed. Open daily: 10 am-6pm (Sat from 10.30am; Thu to 8pm).

Dublin 2

Restaurant Patrick Guilbaud

★★★ **RESTAURANT**

21 Upper Merrion Street Dublin 2
Tel: 01 676 4192 Fax: 01 661 0052
Email: restaurantpatrickguilbaud@eircom.net

The capital's premier French restaurant occupies an elegant ground-floor restaurant in the Main House of The Merrion Hotel, opening on to a terrace and landscaped garden (with al fresco eating in fine weather). Although access can also be gained via the hotel, the main entrance is through the original front door to the 1760s Georgian townhouse. Works by Irish artists are a major decorative feature, making a very fine setting for Ireland's most renowned restaurant (look out especially for Harry Kernoff's 'Jammet's Restaurant', probably Dublin's finest restaurant in the Sixties). Head chef Guillaume Lebrun has presided over this fine kitchen since the restaurant opened in its original premises in 1982 and presents wide-ranging à la carte and set menus. The table d'hôte lunch menu is changed daily - and a snip at €30 - while, at the other end of the spectrum a new 9-course Tasting Menu (€130) celebrates traditional Irish themes - Guinness &

oysters, lamb stew, Irish whiskey - with Gallic flair. Contemporary French cooking at its best, combined with the precision and talents of a team of gifted chefs, produces dishes of dexterity, appeal and flavour: consistent excellence is the order of the day. Desserts are particularly interesting, cheeses are supplied by Sheridan's cheesemongers, breads are home-made, and the mostly French wine list includes some great classics, with some reasonably-priced offerings. Service, under the supervision of Stéphane Robin, is immaculate and Patrick Guilbaud himself is almost invariably present to greet guests personally and, discreetly working the tables, he makes a point of having a chat with everyone - whether a resident at the Merrion Hotel, local business person or simply an individual bent on a gastronomic treat - and making sure that all is well. Every capital city has its great restaurant and this is Dublin's: Restaurant Patrick Guilbaud sets the standard by which all others are judged. Children welcome. **Seats 85** (private room, 25; outdoor, 12). Air conditioning. L Tue-Sat 12.30-2.15, D Tue-Sat 7.30-10.15. Set L €30. Vegetarian Menu €24 Mid-week Menu Decourverte €65. 9-course Tasting Menu €130. L&D à la carte available. House wine from €32. SC discretionary. Closed Sun & Mon, bank hols, Christmas week. Amex, Diners, MasterCard, Visa, Laser. **Directions:** Opposite Government Buildings.

Dublin 2

Saagar Indian Restaurant

féile bia RESTAURANT

16 Harcourt Street Dublin 2
Tel: 01 475 5060 / 5012 Fax: 01 475 5741
Email: info@saagarindianrestaurantscom Web: www.saagarindianrestaurants.com

Meera and Sunil Kumar's highly-respected basement restaurant just off St Stephen's Green has had a revamp, with new wooden flooring, redecoration - and a new music system featuring the latest Indian music. But the cooking will be just as good, offering a wide range of speciality dishes, all prepared from fresh ingredients and thoughtfully coded with a range of one to four stars to indicate the heat level. Thus Malai Kabab is a safe one-star dish, while traditional Lamb Balti and Lamb Aayish (marinated with exotic spices and cooked in a cognac-flavoured sauce) is a three-star and therefore pretty hot. Beef and pork are not served but this is balanced by a good vegetarian selection and the side dishes such as Naan breads, which are made to order in the tandoori oven, are excellent. Customer care is a high priority and service is knowledgeable and attentive. The Kumars also have restaurants in Athlone and Mullingar. Children welcome, but not very young babies (under 1), or after 10pm. **Seats 60.** Toilets wheelchair accessible. L Mon-Fri, 12.30-2.30; D 6-11 daily. L&D à la carte available. House wine €15. SC discretionary. Closed L Sat, L Sun & Christmas week. Amex, Diners, MasterCard, Visa, Laser, Switch. **Directions:** Opposite Children's Hospital on Harcourt Street (off Stephen's Green).

Dublin 2

Salamanca

féile bia RESTAURANT

1 St Andrew's Street Dublin 2 **Tel: 01 670 8628**

This atmospheric tapas bar and Spanish restaurant in the heart of Dublin has no waiting space for new arrivals, but the entrance is pleasant - past a bar with flowers on the counter - and welcoming staff show you straight to a simple marble-topped table. The menu - which is in Spanish with English explanations - is flexible enough to suit anything from a light lunch to a full dinner and offers an embarrassment of good choices: three tapas plates will make a generous lunch for two. Decor is warm and bright, with interesting Spanish details to enjoy in the unlikely event that service might be slow. Food is tasty and Spanish staples are well-handled - garlic roast chicken, langoustines with serrano ham, squid in chilli butter and patatas bravas are all delicious and there are no short cuts on ingredients, including the quality of olive oil used for frying; presentation is simple and traditional, oval plates and shallow casseroles are used, with nice little touches like fresh parsley and drizzles of sour cream set off the food and their lovely frothy-topped mocha served in a tall glass makes a great post-prandial reviver. Excellent food, delightful staff and very good value (individual tapas from about €3.75) make this place a sure fire winner; food is served throughout the day and they don't take bookings - so be prepared to wait at peak times. Wine list includes a range of sherries by the glass - the traditional accompaniment for tapas. Meals: Mon-Thu, 12 noon-11 pm, Fri & Sat to midnight. Closed Sun. MasterCard, Visa. **Directions:** Near Dublin Tourism. ◇

Dublin 2

Shanahan's on the Green

féile bia RESTAURANT

119 St. Stephen's Green Dublin 2 **Tel: 01 407 0939** Fax: 01 407 0940
Email: sales@shanahans.ie Web: www.shanahans.ie

Located on the west side of the Green, this opulent restaurant was Dublin's first dedicated American style steakhouse - although, as they will be quick to reassure you if required, their wide-ranging menu also offers plenty of other meats, poultry and seafood. However, the big attraction for many of the hungry diners who head for Shanahan's is their certified Irish Angus beef, which is seasoned and cooked in a special broiler, 1600-1800°F, to sear the outside and keep the inside tender and juicy. Their steaks range from a 'petit filet' at a mere 8 oz/225g right up to The Shanahan Steak (24 oz/700g), which is a sight to gladden the heart of many a traditionally-minded Irishman - and many of his trendier young friends too. Strange to think that steak was passé such a short time ago. There is much else to enjoy, of course, and the cooking style is admirably simple, but bring a good appetite - and a fat wallet. (Portions tend to be very large, so regulars often order less courses than in other restaurants, which makes for better value.) The wide-ranging wine list includes many special bottles - with, naturally, a strong presence from the best of Californian producers; no house wine and little to choose from under €30.Less formal fare is served in The Oval Office bar, from 5pm daily. Not suitable for children. **Seats 100.** Air conditioning. L Fri only (except for groups), 12.30-2.15. D daily, 6-10. Set L €45. D à la carte. (SC discretionary, but 15% on parties of 6+). Closed Christmas, Good Fri, bank hols. Amex, Diners, MasterCard, Visa, Laser. **Directions:** On the west side ofStephen's Green.

Dublin 2

Shelbourne Hotel

HOTEL / RESTAURANT

27 St Stephen's Green Dublin 2
Tel: 01 663 4500 Fax: 01 661 6006
Email: shelbourneinfo@lemeridian-hotels.com Web: www.shelbourne.ie

The Irish Constitution was drafted here and this opulent 18th-century hotel overlooking St Stephen's Green (Europe's largest garden square) is still central to Dublin life today. Major renovations haverecently taken place, confirming its ranking among the world's great hotels: it has retained all its grandeur, and the entrance creates a strong impression with its magnificent faux-marble entrance hall and Lord Mayor's Lounge, a popular meeting place for afternoon tea. The Shelbourne Bar on Kildare Street is relatively new (food served 12-8 daily - may vary on Sun - includes 'traditional daily specials', some more traditional than others) but the Horseshoe Bar, renowned as a meeting place for local politicians and theatrical society, is nothing short of a Dublin institution. The best rooms and suites are very luxurious but accommodation varies somewhat due to the age of the building; however all rooms are well-appointed, with good bathrooms, bathrobes, mini-bars and three telephones as standard. The hotel has two restaurants, No 27 The Green (see below) and **The Side Door At The Shelbourne** (12-11 daily) which has a separate entrance from Kildare Street and, with its striking minimalist decor and Cal-Ital menus, provides a complete contrast to the ultra-traditional atmosphere of the hotel. The Shelbourne Club, a fine leisure complex with 18m swimming pool, sauna, jacuzzi, steam room and much else besides is situated within the hotel complex. Conference/banqueting (400/320). Business centre. Fitness centre (indoor swimming pool); hairdressing/beauty salon. Valet Parking. 24 hour room service. Children welcome. Lift. **Rooms 190** (22 suites, 101 no smoking) B&B from about €110ps, SC 15%. Open all year.

No. 27 The Green: This elegant and lofty dining-room offers some very good cooking, combining the best of Irish produce with some traditional/continental flair and expertise. Alongside the daily-changing table d'hôte menus (five choices of starter and main course), there's an à la carte offered at lunch and dinner. Specialities, which are strongly seasonal, typically include the best Irish beef, in The Shelbourne Roast (sirloin on the trolley, with traditional garnish) and several other specialities on the evening menu: prime seafood such as No 27 Howth Seafood Caesar Salad and The Shelbourne Special (fricassée of lobster in its shell with tarragon leaves & bisque emulsion). The restaurant is a credit to the hotel, with excellent food and service to match. **Seats 60.** L Sun-Fri,12.30-2.30; D 6.30-10.30 Mon-Sat, Sun 6-10. Set menus from about €35. L A la carte. House wine from about €20. SC15%. Closed L Sat. Amex, Diners, MasterCard, Visa. **Directions:** From Trinity College take 3rd right, turn up Kildare Street, Shelbourne on left hand side. ◇

Dublin 2

Silk Road Café

CAFÉ

Chester Beatty Library Dublin Castle Dublin 2
Tel: 01 407 0770 Fax: 01 407 0788 Email: silkroadcafe@hotmail.com

In a fine location in the heart of the city centre, Dublin Castle provides wonderful gardens and historic architecture which greatly enhance the enjoyment of a visit to this unusual restaurant, which is situated in the clock tower beside the Chester Beatty Library (European Museum of the Year in 2002). Middle Eastern, Mediterranean, vegetarian and organic are the themes brought together by a dedicated small team who create inspired versions of classics like Greek moussaka, Moroccan cous cous, falafel and spinach & feta pie to the delight of their many returning customers. Fresh organic herbs are used in all dishes and, in line with halal/kosher rules, all dishes are made without the use of pork or beef. Prices are very reasonable - an average main course served with rice or salad is around €10. Children welcome. **Seats 65** (private room 25). Air conditioning. Open Mon-Fri, 10-5; à la carte. No service charge. Visa, Laser. **Directions:** Beside Chester Beatty Library in Dublin Castle.

Dublin 2

The Stag's Head

ATMOSPHERIC PUB

1 Dame Court Dublin 2 **Tel: 01 679 3701**

In Dame Court, just behind the Adams Trinity Hotel, this impressive establishment has retained its original late-Victorian decor and is one of the city's finest pubs. It can get very busy at times - sometimes dusty and sticky surfaces suggest that the volume of business makes it difficult to keep up with routine housekeeping, but this lovely pub is still worth a visit. Closed 25 Dec & Good Fri. ◇

Dublin 2

Stauntons on the Green

GUESTHOUSE

83 St Stephen's Green Dublin 2 **Tel: 01 478 2300** Fax: 01 478 2263
Email: stauntonsonthegreen@eircom.net Web: www.stauntonsonthegreen.ie

Well-located with views over St Stephen's Green at the front and its own private gardens at the back, this guesthouse - which is in an elegant Georgian terrace on the south of the Green and has fine period reception rooms - offers moderately priced accommodation of a good standard, with all the usual amenities. Maintenance could be a little sharper and front rooms would benefit from sound-proofing from traffic noise. Meeting rooms are available, with secretarial facilities on request - and there's private parking (valet parking service offered - it would be wise to phone ahead with your time of arrival to arrange this, as there is no parking at the door). Children welcome. No pets. **Rooms 38** (all en-suite, 24 shower only). B&B €76 pps, ss €20. Closed 24-27 Dec. Amex, Diners, MasterCard, Visa, Laser. **Directions:** On south side of the Green.

Dublin 2

Stephen's Green Hotel

féile bia **HOTEL**

St Stephen's Green Dublin 2 **Tel: 01 607 3600** Fax: 01 661 5663
Email: stephensgreenres@ocallaghanhotels.ie Web: www.ocallaghanhotels.ie

This striking landmark hotel on the south-western corner site overlooking St Stephen's Green is the newest of the O'Callaghan Hotels group and is a great location for business or leisure; bedrooms have exceptionally good facilities, particularly for business travellers, including air conditioning, 3 direct line telephones, voice mail and modem line, desk, mini-bar as standard. Small conference/meeting rooms. Business centre. Gym. Children welcome (Under 2s free in parents' room; cots available). No pets. **Rooms 75** (9 suites, including 2 studio terrace suites, 3 penthouse suites, junior suites; 40 no-smoking rooms, 2 for disabled). Lift. 24 hour room service. Room rate €295, max. 2 guests). Open all year. Amex, Diners, MasterCard, Visa, Switch. **Directions:** Corner of Harcourt St. and St. Stephen's Green.

Dublin 2

Steps of Rome

RESTAURANT

1 Chatham Street Dublin 2 **Tel: 01-670 5630**

For some reason good, inexpensive little Italian places specialising in pizza have clustered around Balfe and Chatham Streets. Each has its following and this authentic little one-room café just beside Neary's pub is a favourite lunch spot for many discerning Dubliners. (Branch at: Ciao Bella Roma, Parliament St.) **Seats 18.** Open 12 noon-11pm Mon-Sat, Sun 1-10pm. House wine about €14. No service charge. **No Credit Cards. Directions:** Just off top of Grafton Street. ◇

Dublin 2

Thornton's Restaurant

★★ RESTAURANT

128 St Stephen's Green Dublin 2 **Tel: 01 478 7008**
Fax: 01 478 7009 Email: thorntonsrestaurant@eircom.net

Seriously good cooking in a seriously good restaurant is to be found at this lofty city-centre restaurant on the top floor of the Fitzwilliam Hotel. It can be reached by lift from the lobby, but is best approached from its own entrance on St Stephen's Green: mounting the wide staircase, deep-carpeted in dark blue, conveys a sense of occasion. Once inside, the decor is stunningly simple and elegant: a striking flower arrangement catches the eye on arrival; a deep wine carpet and comfortable high-back chairs in green velvet paint a strong background for pastels and neutrals that leave you in no doubt that the food is to be the star here: pale walls washed with reflected colour from heavy primrose silk curtains highlight a series of wonderfully subtle oil paintings (commissioned from the talented young Monaghan artist, Siobhán McDonald) while linen-clad tables each have a silver candlestick and a simple white candle, classical modern cutlery and glasses and restrained china with just a silver rim. A superb team of

French waiting staff set the tone from the outset, providing highly professional service to complement Kevin Thornton's superb cooking; the neat reception area which divides the restaurant has room for only half a dozen or so guests to assemble, so the warmly professional maître d', Olivier Meisonnave, may show you straight to your table to consider a menu which, literally, bears the hand of the master on the cover, in another stroke of understated originality. Menus offered include a concise 2 or 3 course lunch menu (which is great value), a vegetarian menu and a table d'hôte dinner menu, in addition to a shortish à la carte offering about eight luxurious choices on each course - Kevin Thornton has a name for generosity with truffles and he will not disappoint: a vegetarian first course terrine of leek and truffle is also served with black truffle vinaigrette... a main course of poussin with polenta and aubergine with purple potato comes with a truffle ball and truffle sauce. Seafood is well-represented in, for example, a signature dish of sautéed foie gras with scallops and cep sauce, served with warm brioche, and another starter of fresh lobster with forest mushrooms, gnocchi, red chard leaves and lobster jus. Other signature dishes include braised suckling pig, and trotter served with, glazed turnip and a light poitin sauce - and variations on these creations appear throughout an 8-course Surprise Menu (€125) which is just that - there is nothing written and the menu created for each table is unique. This is creative cooking of the highest class, conceived with confidence to utilise first-rate seasonal ingredients, and beautifully (but not flamboyantly) presented with a perfectionist's eye for detail and a palate to match: this is extraordinarily intense, deeply flavoured food and - despite the occasional flash of gold leaf - it is far from the show-off creations commonly associated with top chefs: Kevin Thornton's cooking has soul. Service throughout is impeccable, from the moment a basket of breads arrive to the final presentation of assorted petits fours accompanying coffees and teas. An outstanding Irish and French cheese trolley deserves special mention (cheese supplied by Sheridan's cheesemongers) and there's also excellent wine list - and a fine sommelier, Julien Herrebert, to steer you through it, which is especially important for those who opt for the Surprise Menu. Children welcome. Air conditioning. **Seats 80** (private area, 30). L Tue-Sat, 12.30-1.45; D Tue-Sat, 7-10.30. Set L €30-40. Set D €65; Surprise Menu €125, A la carte also offered. House wine from €25. SC discretionary. Closed Sun & Mon, 2 wks Christmas & Aug. Amex, Diners, MasterCard, Visa, Laser. **Directions:** On St Stephen's Green (corner at top of Grafton Street); entrance beside Fitzwilliam Hotel.

Dublin 2

Toners

ATMOSPHERIC PUB

139 Lower Baggot Street Dublin 2
Tel: 01 676 3090 Fax: 01 676 2617

One of the few authentic old pubs left in Dublin, Toners is definitely worth a visit (or two). Among many other claims to fame, it is said to be the only pub ever frequented by the poet W.B. Yeats. Closed 25 Dec & Good Fri.

Dublin 2

Trinity Capital Hotel

HOTEL

Pearse Street Dublin 2 **Tel: 01 648 1000** Fax: 01 648 1010
Email: info@trinitycapital-hotel.com Web: www.capital-hotels.com

A stylish hotel right beside the headquarters of Dublin's city centre fire brigade (inspiring the name 'Fireworks' for its unusual club-style bar) and opposite Trinity college. Very centrally located for business and leisure, the hotel is within easy walking distance of all the main city centre attractions on both sides of the Liffey and the lobby wine and coffee bar make handy meeting places. Rooms have a safe, interactive TV, phone, data ports, hair dryer, trouser press, tea/coffee trays, comfortable beds and good bathrooms -junior suites suites have jacuzzi baths, hi-fi system and mini-bar. Guests have free admission all 11 bars and clubs in the city centre owned by Capital Bars, including the adjacent Fireworks night club. Conference/banqueting 40/80. Meeting rooms; secretarial services. Children welcome (under 12s free in parents' room; cots available without charge, baby sitting arranged). **Rooms 82** (4 suites, 4 junior suites, 24 no-smoking, 3 shower only. Lift. 24 hour room service. B&B €109.50 pps, ss €57. No SC. Amex, Diners, MasterCard, Visa, Laser. **Directions:** City centre.

Dublin 2

Trinity Lodge

GUESTHOUSE

12 South Frederick Street Dublin 2 **Tel: 01 679 5044** Fax: 01 679 5223
Email: trinitylodge@eircom.net Web: www.trinitylodge.com

As centrally located as it is possible to get, this owner-run guesthouse offers a high standard of accommodation at a reasonable price just yards away from Trinity College. Air-conditioned rooms have a safe, direct-dial phone, tea/coffee making facilities, multi-channel TV, trouser press and iron. Children welcome (under 12 free in parents' room; cots available free of charge). No pets. **Rooms 16** (3 superior, all shower only and no-smoking). Room service (limited hours). B&B €75pps, ss €20. Closed 22-29 Dec. Amex, Diners, MasterCard, Visa, Laser. **Directions:** Off Nassau Street, near Trinity College.

Dublin 2

Trocadero Restaurant

RESTAURANT

3/4 St Andrew Street Dublin 2 **Tel: 01 677 5545** Fax: 01 679 2385 Web: www.restaurants indublin.ie

The Dublin theatrical restaurant par excellence with deep blood-red walls and gold-trimmed stage curtains, black and white pictures of the celebrities who've passed through the place – dimly lit, intimate tables with individual beaded lampshades and snug, cosy seating, the 'Troc' is one of Dublin's longest-established restaurants and has presided over St. Andrew Street since 1956. It has atmosphere in spades, food and service to match. Comforting menus reminiscent of the Seventies offer starters like French onion soup, deep-fried brie, chicken liver pâté and avocado prawn Marie Rose, followed by ever-popular grills - fillet steak (with Cashel Blue cheese perhaps), Wicklow rack of lamb and sole on the bone are the mainstays of the menu, also wild Irish salmon and Dublin Bay Prawns from Clogherhead, naturally all with a sprinkling of freshly chopped parsley. Desserts include apple and cinnamon strudel and wicked chocolate and Baileys slice, and a better-value winelist will be hard to find. There's privacy too – sound-absorbing banquettes and curtains allow you to hear everything at your own table with just a pleasing murmur in the background. Lovely friendly service too: magic. **Seats 100.** Air conditioning. Children welcome (up to 9pm). D Mon-Sat, 5-12. D à la carte (pre-theatre D 5-7.30, about €18). House wine from about €18.50. Closed Sun, 25-26 Dec, 31 Dec, Good Fri. Amex, Diners, MasterCard, Visa, Laser. **Directions:** Beside Dublin Tourism Centre.

Dublin 2

Tulsi Restaurant

RESTAURANT

17a Lr Baggot Street Dublin 2 **Tel: 01 676 4578** Fax: 01 6764579 Email: sharmin@gofree.indigo.ie Web: www.tulsi-indian.com

One of a small chain of authentic Indian restaurants, this bustling place has a compact reception area leading into a pleasingly elegant restaurant with echoes of the Raj in the decor. Tables are set up with plate warmers, fresh flowers, sauces and pickles and service is brisk so you will quickly be presented with menus offering a broad range of Indian styles - there's a slight leaning towards Punjabi style cooking, with its use of nuts and fruit in sauces, but also tandoori, tikka, biryani, balti and an extensive vegetarian menu. A selection of naan breads is offered and the food quality overall is consistently high; this, together with good value, make booking at both lunch and dinner advisable. A range of special menus offers variety and value; Indian beer available. **Seats 52.** L Mon-Sat, 12-2.15; D daily, 6-11.30 (Sun to 11). Set L €10.50. Set D €20/24. Also à la carte. House wine €16.95. Closed L Sun, L bank hols; 25-26 Dec, Good Fri. * Branches at: Lr Charles St., Castlebar, Co Mayo (Tel: 094 25066); Buttermilk Way, Middle St., Galway Tel: 092-564831). Sister restaurants 'Shanai Indian' at Cornelscourt S.C. and Old Bray Road, Foxrock, Co Dublin. Amex, Diners, MasterCard, Visa, Laser. **Directions:** 2 minutes walk east from St Stephens Green (Shelbourne Hotel side). ◇

Dublin 2

Unicorn Restaurant

RESTAURANT

12B Merrion Court off Merrion Row Dublin 2 **Tel: 01 676 2182** Fax: 01 662 5485 Email: unicorn12b@eircom.net

In a lovely, secluded location just off a busy street near the Shelbourne Hotel, this informal and perennially fashionable restaurant is famous for its buffet hors d'oeuvres selection, piano bar and exceptionally friendly staff. It's particularly charming in summer, as the doors open out onto a terrace which is used for al fresco dining in fine weather - and the Number Five piano bar, which now extends to two floors, is also a great attraction for after-dinner relaxation with live music (Wed-Sat 9pm-3am). Good food (regional and modern Italian), efficient service and atmosphere all partially explain The Unicorn's enduring success - another element is the constant quest for further improvement. The "Unicorn Foodstore" Italian delicatessen on Merrion Row is a relatively recent addition to the enterprise, also the newer Unicorn Antipasto/Tapas Bar. Many of the Italian wines listed are exclusive to The Unicorn: uniquely, in Ireland, they stock the full collection of Gava wines and also the Pio Cesare range. Not suitable for children after 8pm. **Seats 90** (private room 18/20; outdoor 30). Reservations required. Air conditioning. Open Mon-Sat, L12.30-4, D 6-11.15. A la carte. House wine about €20. SC discretionary. Closed Sun, 25 Dec-2 Jan. Amex, Diners, MasterCard, Visa, Laser, Switch. **Directions:** Near Shelbourne Hotel.

Dublin 2

Wagamama

RESTAURANT

Unit 4B South King Street Dublin 2 **Tel: 01 478 2152** Fax: 01 478 2154 Email: chris@wagamama-dublin.com Web: www.wagamama-dublin.com

The Dublin branch of this popular London-based noodle bar is full of groovy young things, who find it cool - both for the food and the interior, which is a huge basement canteen, simple and functional, but strikingly designed with high ceilings. The generous portions of noodles consist of ramen (thread noodles), udon (fat noodles) or soba (a round buckwheat noodle) served in soups or pan-fried, well seasoned and colourfully decorated with South Asian ingredients. The large menu gives plenty of information about ingredients and dishes - and also explains how orders are taken (kids love the electronic notepads used by servers); it includes a few Japanese dishes such as teriyaki (little kebabs) and edamame (freshly steamed green soya beans, served sprinkled with salt), also a selection of fruit and vegetable juices, some rice dishes and plenty of vegetarian options. All food served in Wagamama noodle bars is GMO free, and Sake and interesting soft drinks such as kombucha take their place on the drinks menu alongside wines and coffees. Service is friendly and efficient. It's noisy, and not a place for those who value comfort, but kids love it. Multi-storey carpark nearby. Children welcome. **Seats 136.** Air conditioning. Open daily, 12-11 (Sun to 10). A la carte. SC discretionary. Closed 25-26 Dec. Amex, Diners, MasterCard, Visa, Laser.

Dublin 2

Westbury Hotel

HOTEL / RESTAURANT

Grafton Street Dublin 2
Tel: 01 679 1122 Fax: 01 679 7078
Email: westbury@jurysdoyle.com Web: www.jurysdoyle.com

Possibly the most conveniently situated of all the central Dublin hotels, the Westbury is a very small stone's throw from the city's premier shopping street and has all the benefits of luxury hotels - notably free valet parking - to offset any practical disadvantages of the location. Unashamedly sumptuous, the hotel's public areas drip with chandeliers and have accessories to match - like the grand piano on The Terrace, a popular first floor meeting place for afternoon tea and frequently used for fashion shows. Accommodation is similarly luxurious, with bedrooms that include penthouse suites and a high proportion of suites, junior suites and executive rooms. With conference facilities to match its quality of accommodation and service, the hotel is understandably popular with business guests, but it also makes a luxurious base for a leisure break in the city. Laundry/dry cleaning. Mini-gym. Conference/banqueting (220/200). Business centre. Secretarial services. ISDN lines. Children welcome (Under 12s free in parents' room; cots available). No pets. **Rooms 204** (3 suites, 4 junior suites, 24 executive rooms, 160 no-smoking, 2 for disabled). Lifts. B&B about €200. SC15%. Open all year.

Russell Room: After a drink in one of the hotel's bars - the first floor Terrace bar and the Sandbank Bistro, an informal seafood restaurant and bar accessible from the back of the building - the Russell Room offers classic French dining, with some global cuisine and modern Irish influences. **Seats 100** (private room, 14). Air conditioning. SC 15%. L daily, 12 30-2.30; D daily 6.30-10.30 (Sun to 9). Set L from about €30, D à la carte. House wine about €20. Amex, Diners, MasterCard, Visa, Laser, Switch. **Directions:** City centre, off Grafton Street; near Trinty College & Stephens Green.

Dublin 2

The Westin Dublin

HOTEL

College Green Dublin 2 **Tel: 01 6451000** Fax: 01 6451401
Email: sales.dublin@westin.com Web: www.westin.com

Two Victorian landmark buildings were more or less rebuilt to create this impressive hotel although part of the former Allied Irish Bank bank was glassed over to create a dramatic lounging area, The Atrium, which has a huge palm tree feature and bedroom windows giving onto it like a courtyard (effective, if strangely airless). The magnificent Banking Hall provides the main conference and banqueting room and the adjacent Teller Room now makes an unusual circular boardroom, while the vaults have found a new lease of life as The Mint, a bar with its own access from College Street. It's an intriguing building, especially for those who remember its former commercial life, and it has many special features including a split-level penthouse suite, with views over Trinity College, which has a living room, board room and private exercise area; the business traveller's Westin Guest Office, designed to combine the efficiency and technology of a modern office with the comfort of a luxurious bedroom; and the so-called 'Heavenly Bed' designed by Westin and 'worlds apart from any other bed'. Very limited parking (some valet parking if it is arranged at the time of booking accommodation). Fitness room. **Rooms 164** (13 suites, 5 junior suites, 19 for disabled). Lift. Room rate from about €215 (max 2 guests). Open all year.

The Exchange: An elegant, spacious room in 1930s style, The Exchange has a welcome emphasis on comfort and simply oozes luxury. Everything about it, from the classily understated decor in tones of cream and brown to the generous-sized, well-spaced tables and large carver chairs says expensive but worth it. And, in the Guide's experience, that promise follows through onto the plate in well-executed menus - fairly contemporary, and distinguished by clear flavours and accurate cooking: top quality fresh ingredients, generous portions and confident, unfussy cooking endear this restaurant to visitors and discerning Dublin diners alike. Westin Smart Dining options (moderate in calories and fat) and vegetarian options are highlighted on menus. Friendly service from knowledgeable young waiting staff. More extensive, luxurious evening menus are à la carte, except for a 3-course pre-theatre menu which (like Chapter One - see entry) allows you to return to your table for dessert after the performance. **Seats 75.** Breakfast daily 6.30-10, L Sun-Fri 12-2.30, D daily 6.30-10 (Fri, Sat, Sun to 10.30). Restaurant closed L Sat. Amex, Diners, MasterCard, Visa, Laser. **Directions:** On Westmoreland Street, oppositeTCD. ◇

Dublin 2

The Winter Garden

CAFÉ The National Gallery Merrion Square West Dublin 2 **Tel: 01 661 5133**

A soaring glass-ceilinged space in the stunning new Millennium Wing of the National Gallery, provides an appropriately dramatic (if rather noisy) space or a break before or after a visit to the exhibition. It's minimalist and self-service, there's no menu except a blackboard (which may not have everything listed and can be confusing) but staff are very pleasant and helpful. International food is the order of the day and most of it is microwaved, but it still manages to be better than average gallery fare - just be careful to choose something robust which should stand reheating. Prices are reasonable. Open 12-5 daily; annual closures as for the gallery. **Directions:** In the new Millennium Wing of the National Gallery. ◇

Dublin 2

Yamamori Noodles

RESTAURANT 71 South Great George's Street Dublin 2
Tel: 01 475 5001 Fax: 01 475 5001

Good value speedy cooking with lots of flavour is the secret of Yamamori's success - and atmosphere too. It's just the kind of buzzy place that young people of all ages like to hang about in - a cool place for family outings. Specialities include Yamamori ramen, sushi and sashimi served in generous portions that give great value. Separate lunch and dinner menus are offered, with a more extensive choice in the evening. House wine (quarter bottles), about €5. **Seats 130.** Open daily, 12.30-11.30: L 12-5.30, D 5.30-11 (Sun-Wed 4-11). Closed Christmas, 1 Jan, Good Fri. Amex, MasterCard, Visa, Laser. **Directions:** City centre - 5 mins walk from Grafton Street. ◇

DUBLIN 3

Dublin 3

Clontarf Castle Hotel

HOTEL Castle Avenue Clontarf Dublin 3 **Tel: 01 833 2321** Fax: 01 833 0418
Email: info@clontarfcastle.ie Web: www.clontarfcastle.ie

This historic 17th century castle is convenient to both the airport and city centre. Located near the coast, Clontarf Castle has extensive conference and banqueting facilities along with luxurious bedrooms furnished to a high standard and well equipped for business guests with ISDN lines, voicemail and US electrical sockets in addition to the usual amenities found in an hotel of this standard. Bathrooms are well designed, and all south-facing rooms have air conditioning. The hotel has been imaginatively incorporated into the old castle structure, retaining the historic atmosphere; some rooms, including the restaurant and bar, have original features and the atrium linking the old castle to the hotel is an impressive architectural feature. Welcoming, friendly staff contribute to the atmosphere - but it is a pity that so little of the original grounds now remain. Conference/banqueting (550/450). Business centre. Secretarial services. Children welcome (Under 12 free in parents' room; cots available, baby sitting arranged). No pets. **Rooms 111** (3 suites, 2 junior suites, 4 executive rooms, 41 no-smoking, 6 for disabled). Lift. B&B €105 pps, ss €40. Templars Bistro: D Mon-Sat, 6.30-10.30 (Sun 6-9); L 12.30 -3 (Sun to 2.30). Closed 25 Dec.* A second hotel, the Crown Plaza at Dublin Airport, is under construction at the time of going to press. Amex, Diners, MasterCard, Visa, Laser. **Directions:** Take M1 from Dublin Airport, take a left on to Collins Avenue, continue to T junction, take left on to Howth Road. At second set of lights, take a right on to Castle Avenue, continue to roundabout, take right into hotel.

Dublin 3

Kinara Restaurant

Ⓝ RESTAURANT

318 Clontarf Road Dublin 3 **Tel: 01 833 6759** Fax: 01 833 6651
Email: info@kinara.ie Web: www.kinara.ie

ETHNIC RESTAURANT OF THE YEAR

This smart two-storey restaurant specialising in authentic Pakistani and Northern Indian cuisine opened in the autumn of 2001 in a scenic location overlooking Bull Island. Fine views - especially from the first dining room - are a feature at lunch time or on fine summer evenings, and there's a cosy upstairs bar with Indian cookbooks to inspire guests waiting for a table or relaxing after dinner. A warm welcome from the Sudanese doorman Muhammad ensures a good start as, with a mighty grin and a swirl of the traditional costume that has become the restaurant's trademark, he sweeps arriving guests into the little foyer. The restaurant has a very pleasant ambience, with soft lighting, some good antiques, interesting paintings, the gentlest of background music and streamlined table settings. The menu is unusual, beginning with a useful introduction to the cuisine that explains the four fundamental flavours known collectively as 'pisawa masala' - tomato, garlic, ginger and onions - and their uses, then offering a series of styles to choose from, opening with a range of traditional starters like kakeragh (local crab claws with garlic, yogurt, spices and a tandoori masala sauce) and main courses (such as Sumandari Badsha - lobster tails with cashew nuts, pineapple, chilli and spices). Each dish is described fully and there is a declared commitment to local produce - notably organic beef, lamb and chicken - and a section of the menu devoted to organic and 'lighter fare' main courses (typically Loki Mushroom, a vegetarian dish of courgettes and mushrooms in a light spicy yogurt sauce). Head chef Ashok Kumar and his team have over 80 years experience between them and the quality of both food and cooking is exemplary: dishes have distinct character and depth of flavour, and everything is appetisingly presented with regard for colour, texture and temperature - and fine food is backed up by attentive, professional service and fair prices. The care and attention that marks every aspect of this comfortable and attractive restaurant ensures that guests will return, time and again. **Seats 75** (private room 30). Air conditioning. Children welcome. L Thu, Fri & Sun, 12.30-3; D daily, 6-11.30. Set L €14.95; early D €19.95 (Mon-Thu, 6-7.30pm); also à la carte L&D. House wine €17.25. Closed 25-26 Dec, 1 Jan. MasterCard, Visa, Laser. **Directions:** 1.5 miles north of city centre on coast road to Howth (opposite wooden bridge).

Dublin 3

Ristorante Da Enzo

Ⓝ RESTAURANT

42a Fairview Strand Dublin 3 **Tel: 01 855 5274**

A Fairview cousin of the popular Blackrock restaurant, da Roberto, this basic little restaurant is wowing it to northsiders with its warm and friendly staff, great food and atmosphere - and terrific value. You'll be whisked to your table on arrival and presented with a complimentary mini-starter with the menu - a tomato and mozzarella bruschetta, perhaps - a lovely touch that really whets the appetite and sees you through what could be a longer time than anticipated deciding what to order, from a (very) long menu offering plenty to tempt, including many less usual dishes. Starters alone run to two pages - the second a range of pasta dishes, which you can have as a starter or main course - with each dish named in Italian and explained clearly in English. Fish, fowl, meat and so on each get their say - there really is a lot to choose from. Luckily the cooking follows through: authentic food - full of flavour and including a lot of fish, perfectly cooked, also a dozen or so dishes for vegetarians. And the best bit is the bill: the perfect neighbourhood restaurant. **Seats 45.** D Tue-Sun, 5-11, L&D Sun (1-10.30pm). Closed Mon. Diners, MasterCard, Visa, Laser.

DUBLIN 4

Dublin 4

Anglesea Townhouse

féile bia GUESTHOUSE

63 Angelsea Road Ballsbridge Dublin 4
Tel: 01 668 3877 Fax: 01 668 3461

Helen Kirrane's guesthouse brings all the best 'country' house qualities to urban Dublin - a delightful building and pleasant location near Herbert Park, Ballsbridge; comfortable, attractive bedrooms; good housekeeping; a warm, welcoming drawing room with a real period flavour and wonderful breakfasts that prepare guests for the rigours of the most arduous of days. Thoroughly recommended for its creativity and perfectionism in re-defining what a guesthouse can be, Anglesea Townhouse was the winner of our 1999 Irish Breakfast Award. Garden. Children welcome (Under 3s free in parents' room; cots available without charge). No pets. **Rooms 7** (5 shower only, all no-smoking). B&B about €65pps, no ss. Closed Christmas and New Year. Amex, MasterCard, Visa, Laser. **Directions:** Located near the Merrion Road South of the city centre.

Dublin 4

GUESTHOUSE

Aberdeen Lodge

53 Park Avenue Ballsbridge Dublin 4
Tel: 01 283 8155 Fax: 01 283 7877
Email: aberdeen@iol.ie Web: www.halpinsprivatehotels.com

IRISH BREAKFAST AWARD - DUBLIN

Centrally located (close to the Sydney Parade DART station) yet away from the heavy traffic of nearby Merrion Road, this handsome period house in a pleasant leafy street offers all the advantages of an hotel at guesthouse prices. Elegantly furnished executive bedrooms and four-poster suites offer air conditioning and all the little comforts expected by the discerning traveller, there's a drawing room with comfortable chairs and plenty to read - and a room service menu (with wine list). Staff are extremely pleasant and helpful (tea and biscuits offered on arrival), housekeeping is immaculate - and you can also look forward to a particularly good breakfast. An appealing buffet is set up with Nicholas Mosse spongeware to display an array of fresh and stewed fruits, cereals, home-made preserves, freshly-baked breads and muffins and big jugs of juice. Hot dishes cooked to order include scrambled eggs and smoked salmon, kippers and buttermilk pancakes with maple syrup, plus numerous variations on the traditional Irish breakfast. Everything is of the best quality, very nicely cooked and presented - appetising and not too fussy with small details that make a difference - real leaf tea, the sprig of fresh parsley on perfectly cooked eggs. While breakfast is usually included in the overnight rate, guests can join residents for breakfast and there's an option of having the buffet (€10) or buffet plus a cooked breakfast (€15) - a useful service for early morning meetings. Boardroom, business and fitness facilities for business guests - and mature secluded gardens. Small conferences (50). Children welcome. No pets. **Rooms 17** (2 suites, 6 executive rooms, 5 no-smoking).24 hour room service. B&B €70 pps, ss €35. Residents' meals available: D €30 + all-day menu. House wines from €25. SC 10%. Open all year. Amex, Diners, MasterCard, Visa, Laser. **Directions:** Minutes from the city centre by DART or by car, take the Merrion Road towards Sydney Parade DART station and then first left into Park Avenue.

Dublin 4

RESTAURANT

Bahay Kubo

14 Bath Avenue Sandymount Dublin 4
Tel: 01 660 5572 Fax: 01 668 2006

Don't be put off by trains rumbling overhead as you approach this unusual Filipino restaurant - once you get upstairs past the rather worn carpeted entrance and stairway, you will find yourself in a clean-lined modern room with pale beech flooring and matching panels on a vaulted roof space which, together with fresh flowers at the entrance (and on each table), uncluttered decor in warm colours and crisp white linen on the tables, creates a spacious, airy and welcoming atmosphere. Friendly staff seat new guests immediately and bring iced water with menus that are well organised with explanations about dishes - which are probably very necessary as most guests will not be familiar with the cuisine, which is related to Chinese food, with Malaysian, Indonesian and Thai influences. Several set menus are offered (a good choice on a first visit, perhaps), and an à la carte which is, by oriental standards, quite restrained; anyone who likes Chinese food should enjoy the Filipino versions, which are similar but with generally fresher flavours of lemongrass, ginger, chilli and coconut; no MSG is used and soups are refreshingly free of cornstarch. As in some other oriental cuisines, the weakness is in the dessert menu, so make the most of the excellent savoury dishes instead. Service is attentive, making up in willingness anything it may occasionally lack in training. Meals: D Tue-Sat, 6-11 (Sun 5-10), L Thu& Fri, 12-2.30. MasterCard, Visa. **Directions:** Above Lansdowne Bar, at railway bridge.

Dublin 4

Bella Cuba Restaurant

féile bia RESTAURANT

11 Ballsbridge Terrace Dublin 4 **Tel: 01 660 5539** Fax: 01 660 5539
Email: info@bella-cuba.com Web: www.bella-cuba.com

Authentic Cuban cuisine is presented in this small, intimate restaurant, which demonstrates the Spanish, Caribbean and South American influences on this unique country's cooking, with pork dishes prepared particularly well. Well worth a visit to experience something genuinely different: begin with a famous Cuban cocktail like a Daiquiri or Mojito and then try a speciality of roast pork in Cuban dressing, perhaps, or chicken with chorizo stuffing. Seafood is well represented too and the wine list, which offers a choice fairly balanced between the old world and the new, includes a pair of Cuban bottles. Unusually, the early evening 'Value Menu' allows you to choose from a limited selection on the à la carte. Not suitable for children after 7pm. **Seats 26.** D daily, 5.30-10.30pm (weekends to 11). Early D €20 (5.30-7). A la carte. House wine about €18. SC discretionary. Closed 25-26 Dec. Amex, MasterCard, Visa, Laser. **Directions:** Near the RDS.

Dublin 4

Berkeley Court Hotel

féile bia HOTEL / RESTAURANT

Lansdowne Road Ballsbridge Dublin 4
Tel: 01 665 3200 Fax: 01 661 7238
Email: berkeley_court@jurysdoyle.com Web: www.jurysdoyle.com

Set in its own grounds yet convenient to the city centre, this luxurious hotel has long been a haunt of the rich and famous when in Dublin. The tone is set by an impressively spacious chandeliered foyer, which has groups of seating areas arranged around it, with bars, restaurants and private conference rooms leading off. The hotel is famous for its high standards of service and accommodation; bedrooms have a safe, computer modem, mini-bars and extras such as robes and slippers as well as the more usual amenities, and refurbished rooms also have air conditioning. On-site facilities include health & beauty treatments, a barber shop and gift shop/newsagent. Conference/banqueting (400/380) Video-conferencing, business centre, secretarial services, ISDN lines. **Rooms 187** (1 penthouse suite, 6 luxury suites, 24 executive rooms, 35 no-smoking, 4 for disabled). Lift. B&B €182.50 pps, ss €142.50. SC15%. Open all year.

Berkeley Room: A fine hotel restaurant with very professional staff and some reliable specialities - seafood dishes are especially good and they are renowned for their roast beef. **Seats 60.** Air conditioning. L Sun-Fri,12.30-2.15; D Mon-Sat, 6.30-9.15. A la carte. SC 15%.Toilets wheelchair accessible. Restaurant closed L Sat, D Sun.Amex, Diners, MasterCard, Visa, Laser, Switch. **Directions:** Near Lansdowne Road rugby stadium; approx 13 Km from Airport.

Dublin 4

Berman & Wallace

RESTAURANT

Belfield Office Park Beaver Row Clonskeagh Dublin 4
Tel: 01 219 6252 Fax: 01 219 6219
Email: bermanandwallace@eircom.net Web: www.bermanandwallace.com

This pavilion-style restaurant, in a courtyard surrounded by office buildings, supplies the local business community with wide-ranging high quality brasserie style' daytime food. Choose from such all-time favourites as fish and chips, bangers and mash (made with Hicks sausages) and baguettes filled with chargrilled steak and garlic mayonnaise, to pasta dishes, lamb passanda, chicken piri-piri with herb risotto and a great deal more. There are also several revitalising or detoxing juices and smoothies for the diet conscious and there is a daily health lunch special on offer. Wines by the glass or by bottle. Full breakfast; takeaway/corporate platters. Delivery and party menus available. Restaurant available for evening functions. **Seats 80.** Open Mon-Fri, 7.30-3.30; Sun 11.30-3. Closed Sat; Christmas, bank hols. Amex, MasterCard, Visa, Laser. **Directions:** From Donnybrook, turn at Bus Station up Beaver Road towards Clonskeagh. Turn left at second set of lights into business park and follow signs.

Dublin 4

Bewley's Hotel, Ballsbridge

HOTEL / RESTAURANT

Merrion Road Ballsbridge Dublin 4
Tel: 01 668 1111 Fax: 01 668 1999
Email: bb@bewleyshotels.com Web: www.bewleyshotels.com

This new hotel has been cleverly built to incorporate a landmark period building next to the RDS (entrance by car is on Simmonscourt Road, via Merrion Road or Anglesea Road; underground carpark).

Like its sister hotel at Newlands Cross (see entry), you get a lot of comfort here at a very reasonable cost. *Restaurant: See O'Connells in Ballsbridge. Small conferences (30). ISDN lines. Children welcome (cots available without charge). No pets.Garden. Parking. **Rooms 304** (10 disabled). Lift. No room service. Room rate €99 (max. 2 adult guests, or 2 adults & 2 children). Closed 24 Dec - 26 Dec. Amex, Diners, MasterCard, Visa, Laser. **Directions:** At junction of Simmonscourt and Merrion Roads.

Dublin 4

Blakes Townhouse

GUESTHOUSE

50 Merrion Road Ballsbridge Dublin 4
Tel: 01 668 8324 Fax: 01 668 4280
Email: blakestownhouse@iol.ie Web: www.halpinsprivatehotels.com

One of Pat Halpin's small chain of quality guesthouses, Blakes is very handily situated for anyone attending exhibitions in Dublin, as it's directly opposite the RDS, and offers an attractive alternative to hotel accommodation. Comfortable bedrooms are well-equipped for business and professional travellers and executive rooms and four-poster suites also have whirlpool spas. Drawing room menu available all day (selection of quality wines, from €25); 24 hour room service. Children over 3 welcome. No pets. Complimentary use of nearby leisure centre. **Rooms 12** (2 suites,10 executive, 4 no smoking). B&B €60 pps, ss €35; SC 10%. Open all year. Amex, Diners, MasterCard, Visa, Laser. **Directions:** Opposite the RDS in Ballsbridge.

Dublin 4

Burlington Hotel

féile bia HOTEL

Upper Leeson Street Dublin 4
Tel: 01 660 5222 Fax: 01 660 8496
Email: burlington@jurysdoyle.com Web: www.jurysdoyle.com

Ireland's largest hotel, the Burlington has more experience of dealing with very big numbers efficiently and enjoyably than any other in the country. All bedrooms have been recently refurbished and banquets for huge numbers are not only catered for but can have a minimum choice of three main courses on all menus. Good facilities for business guests: a high proportion of bedrooms are designated executive, with ISDN lines, fax machines and air conditioning. Conference/banqueting (1200/1000). Business centre. Secretarial services. Video conferencing. No pets. Special offers often available. **Rooms 504.** B&B from about €90pps. Open all year. Amex, Diners, MasterCard, Visa, Laser.

Dublin 4

Butlers Town House

GUESTHOUSE

44 Lansdowne Road Ballsbridge Dublin 4
Tel: 01 667 4022 Fax: 01 667 3960
Email: info@butlers-hotel.com Web: butlers-hotel.com

On a corner site in Dublin's 'embassy belt' and close to the Lansdowne Road stadium, this large townhouse/guesthouse has been extensively refurbished and luxuriously decorated in a Victorian country house style and is a small hotel in all but name. Public rooms include a comfortable drawing room and an attractive conservatory-style dining room where breakfast is served; an attractive all-day menu is also offered. Rooms are individually decorated and furnished to a high standard, some with four-poster beds. Parking. **Rooms 19.** B&B about €95, ss about €45. Closed 23 Dec-3 Jan. Amex, Diners, MasterCard, Visa, Laser, Switch. **Directions:** Corner of Lansdowne Road and Shelbourne Road.

Dublin 4

Cedar Lodge

GUESTHOUSE

98 Merrion Road Ballsbridge Dublin 4
Tel: 01 668 4410 Fax: 01 668 4533
Email: info@cedarlodge.ie Web: www.cedarlodge.ie

Conveniently located near the RDS show grounds and conference centre, this owner-run guesthouse has been recently refurbished and is moderately priced. Spacious double-glazed rooms have a full range of amenities and some are on the ground floor. Public rooms are comfortably furnished, with an emphasis on relaxation and creating a 'home from home'. Children over 3 welcome. No pets. **Rooms 15** (all no-smoking, 1 for disabled). B&B from about €45pps. Closed 23-28 Dec. Amex, MasterCard, Visa, Laser. **Directions:** Directly opposite British Embassy on Merrion Road.

Dublin 4

Dish Restaurant

RESTAURANT

146 Upper Leeson Street Dublin 4 **Tel: 01 664 2135** Fax: 01 664 2719
Email: dish@indigo.ie Web: www.dishrestaurant.net

Gerard Foote moved his well-known under-stated Temple Bar restaurant up to this almost canalside location a while back and Dublin diners are now well used to its rather sleek modern reincarnation. He still uses only the best ingredients - organic beef and lamb, free-range chicken and a wide variety of fresh fish daily - providing a wholesome basis for concise, well-balanced menus that change regularly to make the most of seasonal produce. Six or eight choices on each course is plenty, if they are good ones - in this case they are, and also widened by a couple of intermediate sections offering salads suitable as starters or light main courses - and several pasta and noodle dishes, available as small or large portions. An imaginative vegetarian dish is a feature - crisp herbed parmesan polenta cake, perhaps, served with a ragoût of aubergine, red pepper, courgette, green beans and organic vinegar - and cheeses are supplied by Sheridan's cheesemongers, of South Anne Street. A compact wine list demonstrates same policy of careful selection and includes some interesting bottles - including the choice of house wines. Children welcome. **Seats 70.** Air conditioning. L daily 12-4, D 6-11. A la carte. House wine from about €17.95. SC 10% on parties of 6+. Closed 24-28 Dec & Good Fri. Amex, Diners, MasterCard, Visa, Laser. **Directions:** Near Burlington Hotel.

Dublin 4

Ernie's Restaurant

féile bia RESTAURANT

Mulberry Gardens Donnybrook Dublin 4
Tel: 01 269 3300 Fax: 01 269 3260

Named after the late Ernie Evans and still owned by the family, the dining-room of this famous restaurant overlooks a pretty courtyard garden, floodlit at night, though its main feature is the fantastic art collection, mostly of Ernie's beloved Kerry, that cover the walls entirely. Recent refurbishment has introduced a lighter, more contemporary tone and, although there is a generous nod to traditional values - in, for example, a house speciality of black sole on the bone with lemon butter, or rack of Wicklow lamb with ratatouille & rosemary jus - a young kitchen team has also transformed the cooking. While based on local Irish ingredients where possible, the style is modern international - so you could begin with colourful crostini, or Caesar salad (served in a wonton basket), then move on to pan-fried Atlantic prawns with angel hair pasta, wilted Chines leaves and dill & garlic butter. Desserts are deliciously classic - chocolate indulgence, perhaps, or a refreshing summer fruit compôte with vanilla ice cream and orange muscadet sabayon. Excellent service remains a strength, also the wine list, strong on clarets. The 3-course early dinner menu offers outstanding value. Not suitable for children under 12. Air conditioning. **Seats 60.** Open Mon-Sat, L12.30-2, D 6.30-10. Set L from €14.50, Early D €20 (6.30pm); Set D €32 (midweek), €40 (weekends). A la carte L&D also available. House wine from €19. SC discretionary. Closed Sun, Mon; 24 Dec-4 Jan. Amex, Diners, MasterCard, Visa. **Directions:** From city, first left after Victoria Avenue; to city, right turn opposite Ulster Bank in Donnybrook.

Dublin 4

Expresso Bar Café

CAFÉ

1 St Mary's Road Ballsbridge Dublin 4 **Tel: 01 660 0685** Fax: 01 660 0585
Email: expressosbmenus@hotmail.com

Colourful Cal-Ital food and classic brunches attract many a fan to Ann-Marie Nohl's clean-lined informal restaurant, which is renowned for diligently sourced ingredients that are well-prepared and carefully presented. The lively breakfasts for which they have become famous are served all morning and feature many of the best classic dishes, with a twist: thus a simple poached egg on toast comes with crispy bacon (from Dorans of Dalkey) and relish, or cooked-to-order pancakes are served with crispy bacon and maple syrup and French toast comes with bacon or winter berries and syrup. Lunch and dinner menus tend to favour an international style, but the same high standards apply: whether it's Caesar salad with bacon lardons, parmesan cheese and croûtons (with smoked chicken as an option), char-grilled fillet of beef with red onion marmalade or pan-seared scallops with chilli dressing, the concept is simple enough but it's the quality of the ingredients and cooking that make the difference. Weekend brunch is a must. Not suitable for children under 2 after 6pm. Air conditioning. * Also at IFSC and The Gables, Foxrock Village (see entries). **Seats 50.** Open Mon-Fri, 7.30am-9.30pm (B'fst 7.30-11.30, L12-5, D 6-9.30), Sun brunch 10-5. Closed 25 Dec. Amex, MasterCard, Visa, Laser. **Directions:** Opposite Hibernan Hotel, off Baggot Street.

Dublin 4

Four Seasons Hotel

féile bia HOTEL

Simmonscourt Road Ballsbridge Dublin 4
Tel: 01 6654000 Fax: 01 6654880 Web: www.fourseasons.com

Set in its own gardens on a three and a half acre site of the Royal Dublin Society's 42-acre show grounds, this luxurious hotel enjoys a magnificent site, allowing a sense of spaciousness while also being convenient to the city centre - the scale is generous throughout and there are views of the Wicklow Mountains or Dublin Bay from many bedrooms. Public areas are designed to impress, notably the foyer which is in the grand tradition; the rather small, traditional cherrywood-panelled Lobby Bar was recently joined by a second, larger bar called Ice: deliciously contemporary it has been well received. Accommodation is very luxurious and, with two-line speaker phones, data port, hi-speed Internet access, satellite TV, CD players, bar and safe, the air-conditioned rooms are designed to appeal equally to leisure and business guests. A choice of pillows (down and non-allergenic foam) is provided as standard, the large marble bathrooms have separate bath and shower, and also robes, among many desirable features - and there's great emphasis on service, with twice daily housekeeping service, overnight laundry and dry cleaning, one hour pressing and complimentary overnight shoe shine: everything, in short , that the immaculate traveller requires. Meeting planners will appreciate the hotel's state of the art conference and meeting spaces, which can accommodate corporate events, business meetings and parties in groups from 5-500. But the Spa in the lower level of the hotel is perhaps its most outstanding feature, offering: separate men's and women's saunas and steam rooms, a wide range of body and facial treatments, aromatherapy and massage services, plus a gym (with instructors) - and a naturally lit 14m lap pool and adjacent jacuzzi pool, overlooking an outdoor sunken garden. **Rooms 259** (67 suites, 192 executive rooms, 4 floors no-smoking rooms, 12 rooms for disabled). Room rate €395 (max. 2 guests). SC included. Off-season special breaks available. Open all year.

Seasons Restaurant: Guests dining in Seasons Restaurant may have an aperitif in the Lobby Bar or the new contemporary Ice Bar - or, as there is no dedicated reception area/cocktail bar for the restaurant, you may go straight to your table - a procedure which can make guests a little uncertain about procedures, although well-trained staff are generally very welcoming and attentive. No expense has been spared on the decor, and table settings are excellent, although the room does not perhaps have the elegance expected in a top hotel. Executive Head Chef Terry White states a commendable commitment to sourcing the best Irish ingredients for his contemporary international menus - citing, for example, organic produce from a west Cork farm, as well as Irish farmhouse cheeses and other speciality foods - so the quality of ingredients is not in question, and the standard of cooking is generally high, although the experience may not quite scale the heights that could be achieved. However, it is a good hotel restaurant with excellent service and a good pricing policy ensuring value for money in luxurious surroundings. Good wine list, compiled by sommelier Simon Keegan. Air conditioning. **Seats 90** (private room, 12). Breakfast 7-11 daily, L 12-2.30 daily, D 6.30-10 daily. Set L from €27; Set D €55; à la carte also available L&D). House wine from €24. No SC.*Less formal dining is available in The Café, open daily 11 am-midnight. Amex, Diners, MasterCard, Visa, Laser. **Directions:** Located on the RDS Grounds on corner of Merrion and Simmonscourt Roads.

Dublin 4

The French Paradox

WINE BAR / RESTAURANT

53 Shelbourne Road Ballsbridge Dublin 4
Tel: 01 660 4068 Fax: 01 663 1026
Email: tastingroom@thefrenchparadox.net Web: www.thefrenchparadox.com

On a busy road near the RDS, this inspired and stylish operation has brought a new dimension (and a whiff of the south of France) to the concept of wine and food in Dublin. A warm welcome sets the tone for an experience characterised by caring service, knowledge of the (short) menu and - the big story here - the wide range of wines available by the glass. At the time of going to press, a ground floor wine bar is due to open behind the wine shop - and will offer 50 wines by the glass, using a wine sommelier, with inert gas, to keep wines in perfect condition once open. Upstairs, over a continental style open fronted wine shop with a couple of pavement tables sectioned off with green canvas, there's a smart little bar - pale wood, glass, vases of lilies - with a display area for charcuterie and cheese and five tables set up with quality modern cutlery, a single flower and white linen napkins (even at lunch time). Food is simple - and superb: plates of charcuterie (cured meats from the Basque country and Spain); cured fish; pâtés (French style, with cornichons) and artisan cheeses, individual plates or shred ones for two, served with crusty bread baked twice daily on the premises and a green salad. If there is a signature dish it is probably the smoked duck breast salad, with quail's eggs, griottine and walnuts, with mixed leaves (€12.50) but salade Bill Hogan (Desmond and Gabriel cheese, mixed leaves & extra virgin oil dressing €9.90) is a worthy contender. Given the simplicity of the food, bills can mount alarmingly fast - probably because the seductive atmosphere of the place makes it too tempting to linger over another glass (or two) of wine - but this is quality and worth paying for. Wines offered change regularly, food can be purchased from the deli-counter to take home - and there's a more extensive menu in the evening, including tapas and, a wonderfully luxurious speciality: foie gras. Not very suitable for children. **Seats 25.** Air conditioning. Toilets wheelchair accessible. L&D Mon-Thu, 12-3 & 5-9.30; open all day Fri & Sat, 12-9.30. Set L €19.50; Set D €29. A la carte. House wines (4) change monthly. Closed Sun. Amex, Diners, MasterCard, Visa, Laser. **Directions:** Opposite Ballsbridge Post Office.

Dublin 4

Furama Restaurant

RESTAURANT

G/F Eirepage House Donnybrook Dublin 4
Tel: 01 283 0522 Fax: 01 668 7623
Email: info@furama.ie Web: www.furama.ie

In the sleek black interior of Rodney Mak's long-established restaurant, Freddie Lee, who has been head chef since the restaurant opened in 1989, produces terrific food with an authenticity which is unusual in Ireland. Even the menu does not read like other Chinese restaurants - dishes aren't numbered, for a start, and they are also presented and described individually. They do offer Set Dinners, which are more predictable - and many traditional Chinese dishes on the à la carte menu - but the option is there to try something different. Specialities include steamed seafood, roasted duck and Chinese vegetables. Service, under the supervision of Rodney Mak and manager Stephen Lee, is friendly and efficient. A Special Chinese Menu can be arranged for banqueting with one week's notice (up to 30 people) and outside catering is also available. Parking. **Seats 100.** L Mon-Fri 12.30-2, Sun 1.30-4; D daily: Mon-Fri 6-11, Sun 4-11. Various set menus from €35 pp. A la carte available. House wine from €17. Air conditioning. SC 10%. Closed 24-26 Dec & Good Fri. Amex, Diners, MasterCard, Visa, Laser. **Directions:** Opposite Bective Rugby Ground in Donnybrook, near RTE.

Dublin 4

Glenogra House

GUESTHOUSE

64 Merrion Road Ballsbride Dublin 4
Tel: 01 668 3661 Fax: 01 668 3698
Email: glenogra@indigo.ie Web: www.glengora.com

Seamus and Cherry McNamee make a point of providing personal service and good breakfasts at their comfortable Ballsbridge guesthouse. Old and new are carefully combined to create a homelike atmosphere and three new rooms were recently added. Conveniently located for the RDS and within 3 minutes walk of the Sandymount DART station. Children welcome (Under 12s free in parents' room; cots available free of charge). No pets. **Rooms 12** (2 shower only, all no-smoking). B&B €50pps, ss €25. Closed Christmas & New Year. MasterCard, Visa, Laser. **Directions:** Opposite Four Seasons Hotel, RDS.

Dublin 4

Herbert Park Hotel

HOTEL / RESTAURANT

Ballsbridge Dublin 4 **Tel: 01 667 2200** Fax: 01 667 2595
Email: reservations@herbertparkhotel.ie Web: www.herbertparkhotel.ie

This large, Irish-owned contemporary hotel is set in an 'urban plaza' near the RDS and the public park after which it is named. It is approached over a little bridge, which leads to an underground carpark and, ultimately, to a chic lower ground foyer and the lift up to the main lobby. Public areas on the ground floor are impressively light and spacious, with excellent light meals and drinks provided by efficient waiting staff. The bright and modern style is also repeated in the bedrooms, which have views over Ballsbridge and Herbert Park and are stylishly designed and well-finished with a high standard of amenities, including air conditioning, individual temperature control, 2 line ISDN phones with voice mail, mini bar, safe, interactive TV with email, Internet, PlayStation, in-house movies and bill view facility. Suites also have extras like robes, CD player, jacuzzi bath, complimentary mineral water, fruit and chocolates and a daily newspaper. Breakfast, lunch and dinner are all served in the hotel's attractive Pavilion Restaurant; snacks and light lunches are available all day in The Terrace lounge (8am-10pm). Team building, jazz events, golf packages and special breaks are all offered. A good choice for the business guest or corporate events as well as private guests, this hotel is also reasonably priced for the standard of accommodation and facilities offered. Conference/banqueting (120/150). Business centre. Secretarial services. Video conferencing. Gym. Garden. Children welcome (under 2 free in parents' room, cots available free of charge, playground). Pets by arrangement. **Rooms 153** (2 suites, 1 junior suite, 27 executive rooms, 65 no-smoking, 7 disabled). Lift. B&B €90pps. SS €90. No SC. Open all year.

Restaurant: This bright, elegant, contemporary room is pleasingly devoid of hard-edged minimalism and overlooks a garden terrace (where tables can be set up in fine weather). Prices are reasonable, especially when seen in comparison with nearby competition, and the lunch menu offers particularly good value. **Seats 150.** Air conditioning. L daily, 12.30-2.30 (to 3 on Sunday); D Mon-Sat, 5.30-9.30. Set L & early D (5.30-7.30) from €19.68; D à la carte. House wine €19. Closed D Sun & D bank hols. *Informal dining is offered at The Terrace, 8am-10pm daily. Amex, Diners, MasterCard, Visa. **Directions:** In Ballsbridge, shortly before RDS heading out of city.

Dublin 4

The Hibernian Hotel

HOTEL / RESTAURANT

Eastmoreland Place Ballsbridge Dublin 4
Tel: 01 668 7666 Fax: 01 660 2655
Email: info@hibernianhotel.com Web: www.hibernianhotel.com

It feels as if it's in a peaceful backwater, yet this splendid Victorian building is only yards from one of Dublin's busiest city centre roads. It's very friendly, with a country house feeling in the size and proportions of its rooms and an elegant decorative style with warm country colours. The names of the rooms evoke a homely atmosphere too - the drawing room, the library and so on. Bedrooms are all individually decorated to a high standard with excellent bathrooms featuring a wide range of amenities. Warm and friendly staff ensure that service is exemplary. Small conference/private parties (30/45). Business centre. Secretarial services. Garden. Children under 2 free in parents' room; cots available free of charge. No pets. **Rooms 40** (3 shower only, 10 junior suites, 28 no-smoking, 2 for disabled). Lift. B&B €111 pps. Closed Dec 24-26.

The Patrick Kavanagh Room: In keeping with the rest of the hotel, the restaurant is well-appointed, with elegance and charm - and there's a nice little patio area where tables can be set up on fine summer days. Head chef Jimmy Darcy presents lunch and dinner menus that change weekly: a speciality is roast rack of lamb with ratatouille of Mediterranean vegetables, confit of garlic, thyme jus, while fish lovers might try a nage of turbot with peppered rocket, spaghetti of vegetables with pink grapefruit - and there's always an unusual vegetarian choice. Desserts tend to be quite classic - sharp lemon tart with white peach sorbet, perhaps - and Irish and European cheeses are an option. Service is friendly and efficient. **Seats 45** (private room 20). L Mon-Fri 12.30-2 D Mon-Sat 6.30-10. Set L from €15, Set D €39; D also à la carte. House wine €21.95. SC 12.5%. Closed L Sat, all Sun, 24-27 Dec, bank hols. Amex, Diners, MasterCard, Visa, Laser, Switch. **Directions:** Turn off Upper Baggot Street just below Searsons pub (right turn heading into town).

Dublin 4

Jurys Ballsbridge Hotel

féile bia HOTEL

Pembroke Road Ballsbridge Dublin 4
Tel: 01 660 5000 Fax: 01 660 5540
Email: ballsbridge@jurysdoyle.com Web: wwwjurysdoyle.com

Centrally located in the Ballsbridge area, always busy, Jurys has the distinction of being both an international hotel providing high levels of service to business and leisure guests, while remaining a popular local hotel for Dubliners. Rooms and service are of a high standard (24 hour room service and laundry and dry cleaning services) and executive rooms also have a modem line, voice mail, mini-bar and 24 hour sports and news channels as well as multi-channel TV. The facilities offered by the hotel generally are excellent - Jurys was for a long time the only Dublin hotel with a swimming pool; the leisure centre currently also has a whirlpool, sauna and gym and there's a health & beauty salon, hairdresser and newsagent on site. There are two restaurants, Raglans and the informal Coffee Dock, and two bars - the larger Dubliner Bar is a great meeting place. Conference/banqueting (850/600). Business centre, secretarial services. Cabaret (May-Oct). No pets. Special offers often available. **Rooms 303** (3 suites, 300 executive rooms, 150 no-smoking, 2 for disabled). Lifts. B&B from €140. SC12.5%. Open all year.

Raglans Restaurant: Seats 120. Air conditioning. Open for L&D daily. Toilets wheelchair accessible. Open all year. Amex, Diners, MasterCard, Visa, Laser, Switch. **Directions:** About 11 km from the airport & 1 km from city centre.

Dublin 4

Jurys Ballsbridge The Towers

féile bia HOTEL

Lansdowne Road Dublin 4
Tel: 01 667 0033 Fax: 01 660 5540
Email: towers@jurysdoyle.com Web: www.jurysdoyle.com

The Towers is a quieter, more exclusive section of the main Jurys Hotel in Ballsbridge, a hotel within a hotel located to the rear of the main block with its own entrance on Lansdowne Road and a high level of security - entry to the inner foyer and thus to accommodation is by card key. Business and corporate guests are well looked after and constant maintenance and upgrading, plus a high level of service from a committed and well-trained staff, keep this hotel up with the leaders in an increasingly competitive market. The many little extras that make

The Towers especially desirable for business guests include complimentary tea, coffee and biscuits, served all day in a seating area known as the Hospitality Lounge, where guests can avail of a complimentary light breakfast (included in the room rate) and complimentary drinks are served, 6-7pm Monday-Thursday. Guests at The Towers also have the benefit of spacious rooms, queen/king size beds, dedicated work desk and lamp, luxurious bathrooms and towelling robes in addition to or of a higher grade than the usual 'executive' extras. There is direct access to the main hotel from The Towers and all its amenities. Business centre. **Rooms 107** (4 suites, 103 executive, 50 no-smoking, 2 for disabled). Lift. B&B from €160 pps, ss €130, SC12.5%. Open all year. Amex, Diners, MasterCard, Visa, Laser. **Directions:** Approx 11 km from the airport, 1 km from city centre.

Dublin 4

Jurys Montrose Hotel

féile bia HOTEL

Stillorgan Road Dublin 4 **Tel: 01 269 3311** Fax: 01 2691164
Email: montrose@jurysdoyle.com Web: www.jurysdoyle.com

This south-city hotel near the University College campus has undergone extensive refurbishment. Removing balconies and rebuilding the whole front has updated the exterior, while interior improvements include the addition of more rooms to executive standard and some wheelchair friendly accommodation. All rooms have quite good facilities (direct dial phone, multi-channel TV, tea/coffee-making facilities and trouser press/iron) and there's 12 hour room service and laundry/dry cleaning services. Executive rooms also have a modem line and complimentary newspaper and business magazines. Although conference facilities are not extensive (max. 70 delegates), there's a business centre, seven meeting rooms and free parking, making this an attractive venue for small events. Children welcome (cots available) **Rooms 180** (35 executive). B&B from about about €97pps, ss about €97; weekend specials available. Open all year. Amex, Diners, MasterCard, Visa. **Directions:** On Stillorgan dual carriageway near RTE studios.

Dublin 4

Kites Restaurant

RESTAURANT

15-17 Ballsbridge Terrace Ballsbridge Dublin 4
Tel: 01 660 7415 Fax: 01 660 5978 Web: www.kitesrestaurant.com

Lots of natural light with white painted walls, dark wooden fittings and a rich, dark carpet create a good first impression at this split-level Ballsbridge restaurant, and a mix of diners (Chinese and non-Chinese, business and pleasure) gives the place a nice buzz. The cuisine is a combination of Cantonese, Szechuan, Peking and Thai - predominantly Cantonese - and menus range from the standard set meals to a decent list of specials. Salt & chilli king prawns made a well-flavoured starter on a recent visit and, for the indecisive, a house platter of appetisers (€17.80 for two) makes a good beginning, offering a selection of spring rolls, wontons, sesame prawn toasts, spare ribs along with some more unusual additions. Duckling and seafood are specialities: half a crispy aromatic duck comes with fresh steaming pancakes, while a combination dish of salt & pepper jumbo king prawns and a stir-fry is interesting. Stir-fried lamb with ginger & spring onion (one of the few Peking dishes) is to be recommended. Desserts are not a strong point, but courteous, good humoured and charming service adds considerably to the experience. Air conditioning. **Seats 100** (private room 40). L Mon-Sat 12.30-2, D daily 6.30-11.30 (Sun to 11). Set L €18.50, Set D €35. House wine €18.50. SC10%. Closed 25-26 Dec, Good Fri. Amex, Diners, MasterCard, Visa, Laser. **Directions:** In the heart of Ballsbridge.

Dublin 4

The Lobster Pot

RESTAURANT

9 Ballsbridge Terrace Ballsbridge Dublin 4
Tel: 01 660 9170 Fax: 01 668 0025 Web: www.thelobster.ie

On the first floor of a redbrick Ballsbridge terrace, conspicuously located near the Herbert Park Hotel - and just a few minutes walk from all the major Ballsbridge hotels - this long-established restaurant has lost none of its charm or quality over the years. The whole team - owner Thomas Crean, restaurant manager (and sommelier) John Rigby and head chef Don McGuinness - have been working here together since 1980 and the system is running very sweetly. How good it is to see old favourites like dressed Kilmore crab, home-made chicken liver paté and fresh prawn bisque on the menu, along with fresh prawns Mornay and many other old friends, including kidneys turbigo and game in season. The menu is a treat to read but there's also a daily fish tray display for specials - dishes are explained and diners are encouraged to choose their own combinations. All this and wonderfully old-fashioned service too, including advice from John Rigby on the best wine to match your meal. If only there were more places like this - long may it last. L 12.30-2.30pm, D 6.45-9.45pm Mon-Sat. House wine €22.50. SC 12.5%. Closed Sun, 24 Dec-4 Jan. Amex, Diners, MasterCard, Visa, Laser.

ublin 4
UESTHOUSE

Merrion Hall

54 Merrion Road Ballsbridge Dublin 4
Tel: 01 668 1426 Fax: 01 668 4280
Email: merrionhall@iol.ie Web: halpinsprivatehotels.com

his Edwardian style townhouse opposite the RDS is handy to the DART (suburban rail) and makes a ood base for business or leisure, offering great value in comparison with hotels in the area. Major enovation has taken place over the last year and an additional 12 rooms were added; some rooms have our-posters and the suites have air conditioning and whirlpool spa baths. There's a well-stocked library nd a comfortable big drawing room where an all day menu is available (also 24 hour room service), ith a wine selection to complement it. Off-street parking at the back. Small conference/private arties (50/50). Garden. Children welcome (cots available free of charge). No pets. **Rooms 34** (6 suites, 4 executive, 20 no smoking, 2 disabled). Lift. B&B €60 pps, ss €35. Food available 7am-9pm daily; ouse wine €25. Open all year. Amex, Diners, MasterCard, Visa, Laser. **Directions:** Opposite the RDS in allsbridge.

ublin 4
AR

Merrion Inn

188 Merrion Road Dublin 4 **Tel: 01 269 6877**
Fax: 01 269 7669 Email: themerrioninn@o2.ie

ne McCormacks are a great pub family (see separate entry for their Mounttown establishment) and is attractive contemporary pub on the main road between Dublin and Dun Laoghaire has always had name for food. At lunchtime there's a good buffet, with a selection of hot main courses as well as a ide range of salads; it's a well-organised operation and details (such as having chilled drinks to hand) e well-planned. In the evening the style moves up a notch or two, with a menu including the likes of arm crispy bacon & croûton salad, pastas and serious main courses such as chargrilled sirloin steak erved with a choice of sauces and salads) as well as some good fish dishes, vegetarian options and e day's specials. Homely desserts always include home-made apple pie. Bar food served daily 12-10 12-3, D 3.30-10). Buffet/à la carte. House wine from about €16. Closed 25 Dec & Good Fri. Amex, ners, MasterCard, Visa, Laser. **Directions:** Opposite St. Vincent's Hospital.

ublin 4
HOTEL

Mespil Hotel

Mespil Road Dublin 4 **Tel: 01 667 1222** Fax: 01 667 1244
Email: mespil@leehotels.ie Web: www.leehotels.ie

is fine modern hotel enjoys an excellent location in the Georgian district of the city, overlooking the and Canal and within easy walking distance of St Stephen's Green and all the city centre attractions. blic areas are spacious and elegant in an easy contemporary style and bright, generously-sized drooms are comfortably furnished with good amenities including fax/modem connection and icemail. Dining options include the 200-seater restaurant 'Glaze Restaurant, which is open for lunch d dinner daily and offers a well-balanced choice of traditional and contemporary fare based on refully sourced ingredients at fair prices (main courses from €11.95), and the Terrace Bar, where lunch d light snacks are served. The hotel takes pride in the friendliness and efficiency of the staff and special eaks offer good value. Small meeting and seminars (20). Children welcome (Under 12 free in parents' om; cots available free of charge). No pets. **Rooms 256.** Lift. Room rate €145 (max. 3 guests). Closed -26 Dec. Amex, Diners, MasterCard, Visa. **Directions:** On the Grand Canal at Baggot St. Bridge.

ublin 4
RESTAURANT

O'Connells Restaurant

Bewleys Hotel Merrion Road Dublin 4
Tel: 01 647 3304 Fax: 01 647 3398
Email: info@oconnellsballbridge.com Web: www.oconnellsballbridge.com

cated in a large semi-basement under Bewley's Hotel, this remarkable restaurant continues to rive for the highest standards. It's run by Tom O'Connell, previously the general manager of the rkeley Court Hotel and a brother of Darina Allen (of Ballymaloe Cookery School in County Cork), and hat you will get here is quality ingredient-driven modern Irish cooking - simple food, with natural vours, often emphasised by cooking in a special wood-fired oven. It has dark wood-panelled walls d floor to ceiling windows overlooking a courtyard used for al fresco dining in summer - arriving by e courtyard steps rather than through the hotel helps the ambience considerably. A Swiss-trained ecutive chef, Felix Zund, joined the team in July 2002 and works closely with Rory O'Connell of llymaloe House, who visits regularly. Menus, which are arranged by course and price, are very asonable for the quality: the menu states that pork, beef, eggs and catering supplies are sourced ing Bord Bia's Quality Assurance Schemes, and also credits a number of individual producers and suppliers, often in dishes that have become house specialities - typically, a starter salad is made wit Fingal Ferguson's Gubbeen smoked bacon, from Schull in Co.Cork, an East Cork smoked fish plat comprises a selection from Frank Hederman's smokery in Cobh and smoked salmon from Bill Casey a Shanagarry (both Co.Cork) and beef comes from the Irish Hereford Prime Beef Society, Co. Offaly an Slaney Foods, Co.Wexford. Irish farmhouse cheese, matured on the premises, is served with home made biscuits and excellent classic desserts range from deliciously homely sugar crust apple ta served with lightly whipped cream to a light summery strawberry délice or (genuinely) home-mad ice creams. A highly informative wine list, which includes an extensive selection of house wine reflects the same philosophy and gives details of vintage, region, grape, grower/shipper, merchan taster's notes, suggested food partnership, bottle size (including some magnums) and price invariably moderate for the quality offered - for every wine on the list. **Seats 172** (summer courtya 60). Air conditioning. Buffet L daily 12.30-2.30 (Sun to 3). D daily 6-10.30 (Sun to 9.30). Early D fro €19,95 (6-7pm). Set D from €25. Also à la carte D available. SC discretionary (10% on parties of 6+ Closed D 24 -L 27 Dec. Amex, Diners, MasterCard, Visa, Laser. **Directions:** Off Merrion Road Simmonscourt Road, opposite the Four Seasons Hotel.

Dublin 4

Ocean Ba

BAR

Charlotte Quay Dock Ringsend Road Dublin 4 **Tel: 01 668 88**

Dramatically situated on the water's edge with lots of glass and outdoor seating to take full advanta of views over the Grand Canal Basin, Ocean has great atmosphere and makes an excellent meeting pla for people of all ages. The location, style and friendliness of the staff all make it a great place to rela and a particularly good choice for visitors to the city. There are three bars and dining areas to choo from and, while menus offering a wide range of contemporary favourites may not contain any surpris (and can seem a little expensive for what you get), food is freshly prepared and competently cooke and the ambience is exceptional. Tables are laid as you order - simple cutlery, paper napkins - and fo is served modern bistro style on big white plates. Food is pleasant rather than outstanding, but wh makes for a special feeling is the location - and the Sunday jazz brunches are a particular succe Children welcome. **Seats 80** (private room, 80). Air conditioning. Food served daily, 12 -10. House wi €21. Closed 25 Dec, Good Fri. Amex, MasterCard, Visa, Laser. **Directions:** On Grand Canal Basin.

Dublin 4

Pembroke Townhous

féile bia **GUESTHOUSE**

90 Pembroke Road Ballsbridge Dublin
Tel: 01 660 0277 Fax: 01 660 02
Email: info@pembroketownhouse.ie Web: www.pembroketownhouse

Conveniently located close to the RDS and Lansdowne Road, this luxurious guesthouse has all t amenities usually expected of an hotel. There's a drawing room and study for residents' use a individually designed rooms have a safe and fax facilities (on request) for business guests, as well direct dial phone, cable television, tea/coffee facilities and trouser press. Breakfast is the only me served but it is a point of pride (a Gourmet Menu offers dishes like sautéed lambs liver served on a b of sautéed onions and topped with bacon as well as the traditional cooked breakfast). Sm conferences (12). Children welcome (under 12 free in parents' room, cots available free of charge, ba sitting arranged). No pets. Lift. **Rooms 48** (7 suites, 2 shower only, 20 no-smoking, 4 for disabled). B€ €98 pps, ss €33. Closed 22 Dec-2 Jan. Amex, Diners, MasterCard, Visa, Laser. **Directions:** Pembroke leads onto Baggot St. On the right hand side going towards town.

Dublin 4

Radisson SAS St Helen's Hote

féile bia **HOTEL / RESTAURANT**

Stillorgan Road Dublin
Tel: 01 218 6000 Fax: 01 218 60
Email: info.dublin@radissonsas.com Web: www.radissonsas.cc

Set in formal gardens just south of Dublin's city centre, with views across Dublin Bay to Howth He the fine 18th century house at the heart of this impressive new hotel was once a private residen Careful restoration and imaginative modernisation have created interesting public areas, including t Orangerie bar and a pillared ballroom with minstrels' gallery and grand piano. Bedrooms, in a new fo storey block adjoining the main building, all have garden views (some of the best rooms also ha balconies) and air conditioning and are well-equipped for business guests (with desks and f machines). Rooms are comfortably furnished to a high standard in contemporary style, although le spacious than might be expected in a new development; small bathrooms, especially, fail to live up the opulence that the old house promises The hotel has two restaurants and lighter menus are a offered all day in the Orangerie bar and Ballroom lounge. Conference/banqueting (350/220). Fitne centre; beauty salon. Garden; snooker. Ample parking. Children welcome (Under 17s free in paren room; cots available). **Rooms 151** (25 suites, 70 no-smoking, 8 for disabled). Room rate €165 (max. 3 guests). Open all year.

Le Panto: The hotel's fine dining restaurant, offers international fine dining, including a 7-course "Chefs Surprise Menu" (€65). In common with other rooms at St Helen's, the name of the restaurant has military connections - a copper representation of the battle of Le Panto (as described in the G.K. Chesterton poem) hangs over the fire - but it's easy to forget all that when enjoying the view over the gardens. An à la carte menu tends towards the luxurious. Although mainly an evening restaurant, Le Panto is also open for lunch on Sundays and can be used for private lunch parties. **Seats 60.** Air conditioning, toilets wheelchair accessible. D Wed-Sat, 7-10.30; L Sun only, 12.30-3. A la carte. Closed D Sun-Tue, all Aug.

Talavera: In four interconnecting rooms in the lower ground floor, this informal Italian restaurant is decorated in warm Mediterranean colours and is atmospheric when candle-lit at night. It specialises in authentic dishes from Tuscany and Basilicata and features a fine antipasti buffet; the wine list offers a strong selection of regional Italian bottles to match the food. **Seats 110.** Air conditioning. Toilets accessible by wheelchair. L Mon-Sat 12.30-2.30; D daily, 6.30-10.30. Set L €29, D à la carte. House wine from €25. Closed L Sun. Amex, Diners, MasterCard, Visa, Laser. **Directions:** Just 3 miles south from the City Centre,on N11

Dublin 4

Raglan Lodge

GUESTHOUSE

10 Raglan Road Ballsbridge Dublin 4
Tel: 01 660 6697 Fax: 01 660 6781

Helen Moran's elegant mid 19th-century residence is peacefully situated near the US embassy, yet convenient to the city centre - and reasonably priced too. Well-proportioned, high-ceilinged reception rooms are reminiscent of more leisurely times and the en-suite bedrooms are exceptionally comfortable. Raglan Lodge is renowned for the high level of comfort and service provided, and particularly for outstanding breakfasts: a white-clothed sideboard displays freshly squeezed orange juice, fresh fruits and compôtes, home-made muesli and cereals, creamy porridge, yoghurt and cheeses, then a choice of kippers, scrambled eggs with smoked salmon or a fine traditional breakfast delivered piping hot under silver dome covers - a great start to the day. (Raglan Lodge was the Dublin winner of our Denny Irish Breakfast awards in 2001). Theatre reservations can be arranged. Children welcome. **Rooms 7** (3 shower only, 3 no-smoking). B&B €69.85pps, ss €65. Closed Christmas. Amex, Diners, MasterCard, Visa. **Directions:** Follow signs for South city to Baggot Street, turn right on to Raglan Road, Raglan Lodge is on the left.

Dublin 4

Roly's Bistro

féile bia **RESTAURANT**

7 Ballsbridge Terrace Ballsbridge Dublin 4
Tel: 01 668 2611 Fax: 01 660 8535
Email: ireland@rolysbistro.ie Web: www.rolysbistro.ie

This bustling Ballsbridge bistro has been a smash hit since the day it opened. Chef-patron Colin O'Daly (one of Ireland's most highly regarded chefs) and head chef Paul Cartwright present imaginative, reasonably priced seasonal menus at lunch and an evening à la carte menu. A lively style is based on Colin's classical French training but it also gives more than a passing nod to Irish traditions, world cuisines and contemporary styles. Carefully sourced ingredients are the sound foundation for cooking that never disappoints - Dublin Bay prawns are always in demand and may be served Newberg (a speciality that comes with a tian of mixed long grain and wild rice), or in prawn cocktail, when using fresh Dublin Bay prawns moves that old favourite up into a different class. Chicken stuffed with Clonakilty black pudding - which uses one of Ireland's best-loved contemporary products, made by Edward Twomey in West Cork - is another favourite, but the cooking is always innovative, colourful and appealing. Wholesomely delicious puddings are worth saving a little space for. Service is generally efficient but discreet. Offering quality with good value has been the philosophy of the restaurant from the outset and it continues to fulfil this promise well. **Seats 140.** Air conditioning. L daily 12-3, D daily 6-10 Set L about €18; carte. Early D menu (6-6.45); L&D also à la carte. SC10%. Amex, Diners, MasterCard, Visa.

Dublin 4

Rumm's D4

PUB

Shelbourne Road Ballsbridge Dublin 4
Tel: 01 667 6422 Fax: 01 667 6423
Email: cj@rummsd4.com Web: www.rummsd4.com

Good bar food and comfortable surroundings are a combination that's surprisingly hard to find in Dublin, so this large, well-maintained pub (which is quite handy to the RDS and only a drop kick away from Lansdowne Road Rugby Ground), is a useful spot to bear in mind. The pub is open-plan, with slightly tired decor - a bit worn, with shelves of books and bric-a-brac - but food is served in a pleasant conservatory. Examples from a well-balanced bar menu enjoyed on a recent visit include deep-fried St Killian cheese (from Wexford), served with a tossed salad & sweet chilli sauce, and grilled fillet of salmon with baby boiled potatoes & roast peppers: carefully cooked and well-presented - and well-trained staff are friendly, efficient and helpful. Wine is a weak point, but there is a selection of quarter bottles. L daily 12.30-3; D daily 6-9.30. Early D Sun-Wed €16-20. A la carte, with daily chef's specials. Live traditional music, Sat & Sun, from 9pm. Closed 25 Dec & Good Fri. Amex, MasterCard, Visa, Laser. **Directions:** Prominent corner position on Shelbourne Road.

Dublin 4

Schoolhouse Hotel

féile bia HOTEL

2-8 Northumberland Road Ballsbridge Dublin 4
Tel: 01 667 5014 Fax: 01 667 5015
Email: reservations@schoolhousehotel.com Web: www.schoolhousehotel.com

Dating back to its opening in 1896 as a school, this building beside Mount Street Bridge has seen many changes, culminating in its opening in 1998 as one of Dublin's trendiest small hotels. The Inkwell Bar is always a-buzz with young business people of the area, and the classrom theme continues to the restaurant, Satchels. Rooms are finished to a high standard, with air conditioning, power showers and the usual amenities expected of a quality hotel. Small conference (20). Wheelchair access. Parking. Children welcome (Under 5s free in parents room; cots available). No pets. Lift. **Rooms 31** (15 no-smoking, 2 for disabled). B&B about €125pps. SC discretionary. Closed 24-27 Dec. Amex, Diners, MasterCard, Visa. **Directions:** Southbound from Trinity College, at the end of Mount St. across the Grand Canal.

Dublin 4

Waterloo House

GUESTHOUSE

8-10 Waterloo Road Ballsbridge Dublin 4
Tel: 01 660 1888 Fax: 01 667 1955
Email: waterloohouse@eircom.ie Web: waterloohouse.ie

Evelyn Corcoran has combined two Georgian townhouses to make a luxurious and reasonably priced base in a quiet location very convenient to the city centre and also Lansdowne Road (rugby), RDS (equestrian & exhibitions) and some of the city's most famous restaurants. Equally attractive to the business or leisure traveller. ISDN lines. Conservatory & Garden. Wheelchair access. Own parking. Children welcome (under 4 free in parents' room, cot available). No pets. Garden. **Rooms 17** (1 disabled). Lift. B&B €59 pps, ss €20. Closed Christmas. MasterCard, Visa, Laser. **Directions:** South on Stephens Green on Merrion Row for 1 mile. First turn right after Baggot Street Bridge.

DUBLIN 6

Dublin 6

Antica Venezia

RESTAURANT

97 Ashfield Road Ranelagh Dublin 6
Tel: 01 497 4112 / 087 2505559

A real throw-back in time and refreshingly so: this entirely Italian-run restaurant has a classic Italian 70's interior with stained wooden floors and ceiling beams, Venetian trompe-l'oeil scenes on the walls and candlewax-dripped Chianti bottles on every table. The food is traditional Italian too, with a menu that could easily date back to the Seventies too: old-fashioned favourites like stuffed mushrooms and antipasto misto of Italian meats are followed by classics like chicken breast with mushroom and white wine sauce, salmon with lemon butter sauce, pork with marsala sauce and a choice of pasta dishes and pizzas, with predictable but good desserts such as banoffi, tiramisu and cassata as well as a selection of ice creams. Consistently good food, with service that is laid back but attentive - a perfect recipe for a popular neighbourhood restaurant. **Seats 45.** Air conditioning. D daily, 5-11.30, L Fri only 12-2.30. Set D from €30. House wine €18.50. SC 10%. Diners, MasterCard, Visa, Laser.

Dublin 6

Bijou Bistro

RESTAURANT

47 Highfiield Road Rathgar Dublin 6 **Tel: 01 496 1518**
Fax: 01 491 1410 Email: bijourestaurant@eircom.net

An intimate restaurant with four smallish rooms on two floors and a distinctly French atmosphere with curtained doorways, colourful turn-of-the-century style paintings, frilled lampshades and vases of lilies - and charming, efficient staff. Well made breads accompany an innovative menu with a dozen or so choices on each course and several fish specialities each evening (typically chargrilled loin of swordfish with chive mash and spiced chickpea salsa); other specialities include risotto of spiced cajun chicken with parmesan herb salad, while more traditional tastes will welcome dishes like pork fillet with sage & bacon potato cake, apple & raisin chutney and Vermouth cream, cooked with accuracy and style - and served on plates decorated with a colourful art deco flourish. Finish with classic desserts or an Irish cheese selection with muscat grapes. A good wine list, plus a couple of weekly specials. Booking at this popular neighbourhood restaurant is essential. Children welcome. **Seats 70** (private room, 14). Air conditioning. D daily, 5-11, L Sun only 12-3. Set Sun L about €20, early D about €17 (Mon-Fri, 5-6.45); wines from about €16. SC discretionary. Closed Christmas/New Year. Amex, Diners, MasterCard, Visa, Laser. **Directions:** Rathgar crossroads.

Dublin 6

Diep Noodle Bar

RESTAURANT

19 Ranelagh Dublin 6 **Tel: 01 497 6550** Fax: 01 497 6549
Email: info@diep.net Web: www.diep.net

Younger sister to Diep le Shaker off Fitzwilliam Square, this colourful little place opened late in 2002 and very quickly gained a reputation as the in place for discerning young things to meet. It has a great atmosphere, chic, clean-lined decor and - as if a mixture of Thai and Vietnamese food wasn't fashionable enough - a cocktail bar too. Closely packed tables reach a long way back down the long narrow room, and you can be fairly sure it will be packed, any night of the week, which adds to the ambience. Service is a strong point from the moment you arrive and the menu - which offers plenty of noodle dishes, and much else besides - points out that no monosodium glutamate is used and that food arrives, Asian style, just as soon as it's ready, rather than in courses. Eschewing MSG is a big bonus, allowing lots of different natural flavours and textures to come through in very fresh food that seems to be made for sharing. Whether the freefall attitude to meal structure works is, perhaps, more a matter of luck - if you order well, it's fine and adds to the fun, but you could end up with too much or too little of one thing, or a feeling that dishes are arriving in the wrong order. Individual dishes are not expensive - a classic Phad Thai, for example, is around €13.50, Tom Yaam Goong (hot & sour soup with prawns) €6.50, Vietnamese noodle soups all around €9-10, and curries and stir-fries in the €15-16 region; but by the time you've had a couple of cocktails, ordered a bit of everything and had an Asian beer or a bottle of wine with your food it can add up alarmingly. There's a sense of excitement to this little restaurant - it's a place to have fun; so first time out, order carefully - old hands know how to work the menu. Open 7 days: L 12.30-5.30, D 5.30-11 (Sun to 10.30). Set L from €15, Set D from €20; also à la carte. Wine from €17.50. Closed 25 Dec. Amex, MasterCard, Visa, Laser, Switch.

Dublin 6

Elysium

RESTAURANT

25 Dunville Avenue Ranelagh Dublin 6 **Tel: 01 496 8181**
Fax: 01 491 4583 Email: ledadeforge@hotmail.com

This popular neighbourhood restaurant is in a long narrow room with a conservatory at the end and decor in fashionable browns and beiges, softened by scatter cushions. An imaginative menu and sound, creative cooking - together with fair pricing - have earned Elysium a loyal local following: well-flavoured aubergine, feta and mint samosas, for example, come with a subtle cardamom yoghurt dip and an earthy oxtail & black pudding terrine is accompanied by a potato salad. Delicious Peking Duck may be served with a scrumptious bok choi roll filled with all sorts of vegetarian goodies, while excellent scallops come with raw, dressed baby spinach and, perhaps, an unusual accompaniment of crushed butternut squash. Desserts are classical and very good – mocha crème caramel with cinnamon espresso reduction, for example, or sticky toffee pudding with vanilla ice-cream. **Seats 45.** Air conditioning. L Tue-Sat, 12-2.45 (Sun 11.30-3); Set L €21. D Tue-Sat, 6-11; à la carte; wine from €18. Closed D Sun, all Mon. Amex, MasterCard, Visa, Laser. **Directions:** Just off Ranelagh Triangle.

Dublin 6

Ivy Court Restaurant

RESTAURANT

88 Rathgar Road Dublin 6 **Tel: 01 492 0633**

Swiss chef Josef Frei has been doing a good job at this reliable, quite traditional neighbourhood restaurant for many a year now, and it's greatly to his credit that he has maintained the standard of food - and kept prices to a reasonable level - at a time when the reverse is true in many more fashionable establishments. **Seats 80.** D only, Mon-Sat. Closed Sun, Christmas week. MasterCard, Visa.

Dublin 6

Poppadom Indian Restaurant

RESTAURANT

91a Rathgar Road Dublin 6 **Tel: 01 490 2383** Fax: 01 492 3900

Behind a neat but unremarkable frontage in a row of modern shops lies a treat: colourful and airy, with deep yellow walls, linen-clad tables, comfortable chairs and a bar, this new wave Indian restaurant demonstrates the delicious diversity of Indian cooking and offers some appealingly unusual dishes.

Complimentary poppadoms with fresh chutney dips are brought before menus which offer regional specialities including a starter of Karwari Prawns - deep-fried jumbo prawns marinated in ginger, garlic, yoghurt, garam masala and barbecued in the tandoor, then served with a fresh mint chutney - and main courses ranging in heat from Chicken Avadh, a mild and creamy dish with nuts that was a speciality of the erstwhile Avadh empire of central India, to Lamb Chettinad, a fiery festive dish of the Chettiyar clan in Tamil Nadu. Vegetarians are spoilt for choice, with plenty of dishes available as main courses or side orders. Variations like garlic, onion & coriander naan and lime rice offer a subtle change from the standard accompaniments, food presentation is contemporary and service solicitous. Make a point of trying the masala tea, made with leaf tea and cardamom pods. The wine list helpfully begins with some advice on the styles that partner spicy food well, wisely suggesting Alsace wines, notably Gewurtztraminer as the best all-rounder. Children welcome. **Seats 44.** Air conditioning. D daily, 6-12. A la carte. Wines from about €17. SC discretionary. Toilets wheelchair accessible. Closed 25-26 Dec. Amex MasterCard, Visa, Laser, Switch. **Directions:** A minute away on the same side as Comans Pub, Rathgar.

Dublin 6

Quality Charleville Hotel & Suites

HOTEL

121 Lr Rathmines Road Dublin 6
Tel: 01 406 6100 Fax: 01 406 620
Email: charleville@charleville.pressgroup.ie Web: pressgroup.ie

Well-equipped modern hotel, mostly with suites (including sitting room kitchenette), and the huge advantage of free parking for guests. Good business choice: fax machines, CD players, ISDN lines, modem sockets, cable TV, hairdryer, trouser press with ironing board and tea/coffee-making facilities all included as standard. Children welcome (under 4s free in parents' room; cots available). No pets. **Rooms 53** (43 suites, 4 shower only, 25 no-smoking rooms). B&B from about €85.50 pps. Lift. Open all year. Perhaps reflecting demands of the student population in the neighbourhood, pizzas and pasta are the backbone of menus in the restaurant which actually offer quite a wide choice. Closed 24-26 Dec Amex, Diners, MasterCard, Visa. **Directions:** 15 minutes stroll from the city centre on the South Side.

Dublin 6

Taipo Restaurant

RESTAURANT

2 Terenure Road East Rathgar Dublin 6
Tel: 01 490 0206 Fax: 01 490 0207 Email: taipo@eircom.net

Situated above a well-known Rathgar pub, this attractive Chinese restaurant is on two levels, with well spaced tables laid with crisp white linen and fresh flowers. The menu is shorter than most oriental restaurants, and all the better for that, offering Chinese cuisine with some diversions into neighbouring cultures with dishes such as Malaysian satay and some Thai dishes - and, while most of the dishes offered look quite familiar - dishes like sweet & sour king prawn and sizzling dishes like fillet steak with peppers and blackbean sauce, but are there - there are also simpler dishes like steamed sea bass with ginger & spring onion (€27) and a number of duck specialities including Cantonese roast duck (€16.80). Taipo is earning a place as a reliable neighbourhood restaurant - and it is greatly enhanced by charming Chinese staff who are eager to please. **Seats 100** (private room 40). Children welcome. Sun only, 1-3, D 6-11 daily. Set Sun L €19, D from €16.50; also à la carte. House wine €18. Closed 25-26 Dec, Good Fri. Amex, Diners, MasterCard, Visa, Laser. **Directions:** Above Coman's pub.

Dublin 6

Tribeca

RESTAURANT 65 Ranelagh Village Dublin 6 **Tel: 01 497 4174** Fax: 01 491 158

An outpost of the well-known Dublin restaurant Dish (see entry), this New York style restaurant was hit from the start for its good fast food and relaxed, casual feel, with bright and airy decor and wooden floors and tables. It's just right for food like carefully sourced burgers (made from 100% organic beef) salads, omelettes and chicken wings, which take their place beside the fusion inspired dishes that keep the more adventurous diners happy. It's not cheap, but portions are generous so it works out as quite good value for money. Air conditioning. **Seats 70** (outside seating 20). Open daily, 12-11. A la carte plus daily blackboard specials. Toilets wheelchair accessible. No reservations. Closed Dec 24-26, Good Fri. MasterCard, Visa, Laser. **Directions:** Heading southbound from city centre, halfway along Ranelagh main street, on right.

Dublin 6

Zucchini

Ⓝ **RESTAURANT**

47 Ranelagh Village Dublin
Tel: 01 497 8655 Fax: 01 497 903

The arrival of this striking, glass-fronted restaurant right in the middle of Ranelagh village in 2003 has introduced yet another smart neighbourhood restaurant to an area exceptionally well served with good eating places. It's stylish and minimalist, with a view of the busy street and décor in a mixture of dark wood, pale walls, glass and polished steel that works well with suede banquettes, small square tables and contemporary metal/leather - a small area used well, giving a feeling of spaciousness - and has the interest of an open kitchen behind a large lightbox and polished steel counter. Friendly, attentive staff are efficient, immediately bringing you to a very smart table with pretty glassware, cutlery and beautiful crockery (beautiful square and round plates and sculpted bowls do a lot for the food throughout). The menu comes with a variety of breads and dips, and majors in modern classics: start, perhaps with seared squid rings, served with a sweetish salsa and avocado dressing on tossed leaves, or moules marinières (overcooked on the Guide's visit, but a really tasty sauce compensated), and follow with a perfectly cooked steak and deliciously caramelised lyonnaise potatoes, or queen scallops, served on black squid-ink pasta and a subtle saffron cream sauce. Classic desserts - chocolate mousse (served with an orange sorbet), strawberry crème brulée - are prettily presented. This isn't adventurous food, but it is reliably good and enhanced by chic surroundings and service - although prices are on the high side for a neighbourhood restaurant. Interesting wine list. Meals: D Daily, from 6pm; L Mon-Fri 12-4; Brunch Sat-Sun, 11-4. A la carte. Wines from €17.50. MasterCard, Visa.

Dublin 6W

Vermilion

RESTAURANT

94-96 Terenure Road North Terenure Dublin 6W
Tel: 01 499 1400 Fax: 01 499 1300
Email: mail@vermilion.ie Web: www.vermilion.ie

This purpose-built restaurant on the first floor above the Terenure Inn pub opened to some acclaim a couple of years ago and the decor - a contemporary, smart interior in soft primary colours - reflects a forward-looking food philosophy, which offers colourful, beautifully presented and updated versions of many Indian favourites. Nibbles include little bowls of various condiments such as a rich tomato sauce, a vibrantly yellow, fragrant custard dip and grated carrots with ginger and black mustard seeds. The menu includes specialities from Kerala, Tamil-Nadu and Goa and pride is clearly taken in the quality of ingredients and cooking, reflecting attention to detail in every aspect of the operation including a good wine list and friendly service. A small selection of desserts is much more tempting than is usual in oriental restaurants (although only the kulfi is an Indian speciality). It has proved a very welcome addition to the city's ethnic dining scene and, during the summer of 2003, Vermilion ran an 11-week Indian Summer Festival, following a culinary trail around India - from the fiery southern dishes and curries with cooling coconut, to the Punjabi and Kashmiri styles of the north, and from western hot and spicy dishes to the rich and creamy dishes from the central Mogul region - and the ethnic experience was enhanced by performances by a popular belly dancer. This was a fascinating first for Dublin and will hopefully be repeated (midweek, Jun-Aug). It should perhaps be pointed out that, although the wide-ranging menu gives detailed explanations of each dish, some of which are well known, this is not a traditional Indian restaurant and it is necessary to come with an open mind rather than in the expectation of the usual, familiar experience of 'popular' Indian food. **Seats 90** (private area 35). Air conditioning. L Sun only, 1.30-5.30, D daily 5.30-11 Set Sun L, about €20; early D, 6-7, from €20; Set D €30. Tasting Menu €55. D à la carte. House wine €18. Closed 25-26 Dec, Good Fri. Amex, Diners, MasterCard, Visa, Laser, Switch. **Directions:** 200 yards from Terenure crossroads.

DUBLIN 7

Dublin 7

Chief O'Neill's Hotel

HOTEL

Smithfield Village Dublin 7 **Tel: 01 817 3822** Fax: 01 817 3811
Email: orlaomahony@chiefoneills.com Web: www.chiefoneills.com

This unusual hotel is central to the developing complex around Smithfield Village - and the ongoing upgrading of the areas along Dublin's north quays. Accommodation is a strikingly modern style which guests will either love or loathe - the bathroom arrangements, for example, are more sculptural than practical - but bedrooms have good facilities, including CD hi-fi systems, multi-channel TV, while penthouse suites have jacuzzis and rooftop balconies. Lines are simple, colours strong and there's a distinctly youthful air about the place. State of the art conference facilities and meeting rooms attract corporate guests and, for relaxation, Chief O'Neill's Café Bar features live traditional music at weekends and offers a combination of traditional and contemporary Irish food. Unusual attractions incorporated into the hotel complex include The Chimney Viewing Tower, which was once part of the distillery next door and now has two galleries reached by a glass-walled lift. It's open every day and panoramic views over the city can be spectacular on a good day (also available for private parties of up to 50 guests). Video-conferencing. Conference/banqueting (120/150). Children welcome (under 12 free in parents' room; cots available free of charge, baby sitting arranged). **Rooms 73** (3 suites, 63 shower only, 18 no-smoking, 5 disabled). Lift. Room service (limited hours). Room rates from €180. Closed 24-25 Dec. Amex, MasterCard, Visa, Laser, Switch.

Dublin 7

The Hole in the Wall

PUB

Blackhorse Avenue Phoenix Park Dublin 7
Tel: 01 838 9491 Fax: 01 868 5160

PJ McCaffrey's remarkable pub beside the Phoenix Park is named in honour of a tradition which existed here for around a hundred years - the practice of serving drinks through a hole in the wall of the Phoenix Park to members of the army garrison stationed nearby. Today the Hole in the Wall also claims to be the longest pub in Ireland - and it is certainly one of the most interesting. They do good food too - there's a carvery lunch (12.30-3pm) and a bar menu available throughout the day offers a wide choice including traditional Irish dishes like Beef & Guinness Pie, Dublin Coddle and Irish Stew. Children welcome. Pets allowed in certain areas. Music nightly and all day Sun. Wheelchair access. Parking. Bar menu served daily (12-9). Closed 25 Dec & Good Fri. Amex, MasterCard, Visa, Laser. **Directions:** Beside Phoenix Park.

Dublin 7

Kelly & Ping, Bar & Restaurant

RESTAURANT

Smithfield Village Dublin 7
Tel: 01 817 3840 Fax: 01 817 3841
Email: info@kellyandping.com Web: www.kellyandping.com

In common ownership with Chief O'Neill's Hotel, but with its own entrance from Duck Lane, this colourful, glass-fronted restaurant has established its own separate identity and is now serving a growing local population - both business and residential - well. The style is broadly Asian, mainly Thai, and many of the popular dishes are offered - chicken satay, vegetable spring rolls, Thai style sweet & sour pork, Nasi Goreng - along with many less well-known dishes, and a range of Kelly & Ping Thai curries which can be ordered red (hot), green (medium) or yellow (mild). There's also a sprinkling of international bistro dishes like goats cheese & home-dried tomato salad, baked salmon with caramelised onion mash and smoked chicken & mango quesadilla, all offered in generous portions and well-priced. As well as an inexpensive wine list, (house wine € 16.50), there's a good choice of Asian beers. **Seats 100** (outdoor, 50) Set D € 20. Open Mon-Sat 12-11 (L12-3, D 4-11). Closed Sun, bank hols. Amex, MasterCard, Visa, Laser, Switch. **Directions:** Behind the Four Courts, beside Old Jameson Distillery.

Dublin 7

The Old Jameson Distillery

PUB / CAFÉ

Bow Street Smithfield Dublin 7 **Tel: 01 807 2355** Fax: 01 807 2369
Email: reservations@ojd.ie Web: www.whiskeytours.com

While most visitors to Dublin will visit the restored Old Jameson Distillery to do the tour (which is fascinating), it's also a good spot for a bite to eat. There are special menus for groups (including evening functions, when the Distillery is not otherwise open) but The Still Room Restaurant is also open to individuals - light food served all day and lunch, featuring Irish specialities like John Jameson beef casserole, roast loin of pork with apple & Jameson sauce, and Jameson farmhouse whiskey cake - and the standard of cooking is generally high. Downstairs, the 1780 Bar is open from 12 noon daily, with bar food (mainly modern international - chicken Caesar, paninis etc) available at lunchtime (12.30-3). Conference centre recently opened. Wheelchair access. Children welcome. **Seats 100.** Food served daily, 9-5; L 12.30-2.30. Main course from €8. House wine €17.50. Air conditioning. Closed Christmas & Good Fri. Amex, Diners, MasterCard, Visa, Laser. **Directions:** 14km from Airport, 4km east of ferry port. On northside of Quays, off Arran Quay, near Four Courts.

DUBLIN 8

Dublin 8

Bar Italia

CAFÉ / RESTAURANT

Lr Exchange Street Essex Quay Dublin 8
Tel: 01 679 5128 Email: acrobat_ltd@yahoo.it

In a modern office block on the edge of Temple Bar and close to the Civic Offices known disparagingly to Dubliners as 'The Bunkers', this little Italian café has floor-to-ceiling glass to make the most of a splendid view across the Liffey towards the magnificent Four Courts - and there's plenty of space outside to enjoy lunch 'al fresco' when the weather's right. Attentive Italian waiters quickly seat new arrivals, service throughout is quick and professional and the banter lends a relaxed atmosphere - matched by colourful, flavoursome food, simply presented. The minestrone soup alone can be memorable, paninis and pasta dishes are the business and it's a place worth seeking out for their espressos alone. And it's great value too: magic. **Seats 25.** Outdoor seating. Open every day: Mon-Fri, 8-6, Sat 9-6, Sun 12-6. A la carte. Closed Christmas/New Year. Also at: La Corte 5a Custom Dublin 1 (Tel 01 672 1929). MasterCard, Visa. **Directions:** South quays, west end of Temple Bar (near Dublin Corporation head office).

Dublin 8

Brazen Head

ATMOSPHERIC PUB

20 Lower Bridge Street Dublin 8 **Tel: 01 679 5186**
Fax: 01 677 9549 Email: info@brazenhead.com

Dublin's (possibly Ireland's) oldest pub was built on the site of a tavern dating back to the 12th century and it's still going strong. Full of genuine character, this friendly, well-run pub has lots of different levels and dark corners. Food is wholesome and middle-of-the-road at reasonable prices. Live music nightly in the Music Lounge. L & D daily. Closed 25 Dec & Good Fri.

Dublin 8

Chorus Café

CAFÉ

Fishamble Street Dublin 8 **Tel: 01 616 7088** Fax: 01 616 7088

A small restaurant with a big heart, this bright and friendly little place is near the site of the first performance of Handel's Messiah, hence the name - and some features of the decor. Interesting breakfasts (Danish pastries, home-made scones and bagels with imaginative fillings, for example, as well as the 'full Irish'), are followed by an all-day procession of good things. Gourmet ciabatta and panini, and old favourites like tuna melts, jostle for space alongside wonderful salads: a great daytime place to know about if you're visiting anywhere in the Christchurch area. **Seats 24.** Open Mon-Fri, 7am-5pm, Sat 10-6. Closed Sun, Christmas, New Year. **No Credit Cards. Directions:** Opposite Dublin Corporation Offices, at Christchurch end of Fishamble Street.

Dublin 8

Gallic Kitchen

CAFÉ

49 Francis Street Dublin 8 **Tel: 01 454 4912**
Fax: 01 4733972 Email: galkit@iol.ie

This little spot in Dublin's "antique" district has been delighting locals and visitors alike for over five years. Patissière Sarah Webb is renowned for quality baking (quiches, roulades, plaits, tartlets, wraps) and also salads and delicious little numbers to have with coffee. A judicious selection from an extensive range is offered to eat in the shop: sourcing is immaculate, cooking skilful and prices reasonable, so you may have to queue. Outside catering offered (with stafff required). Open Mon-Sat, 9-5. * Sarah also has a stall at several markets: Temple Bar (Sat, 9-5); Dun Laoghaire (Thu, 10.30-5); Leopardstown (Fri, 11-5); Laragh, Co Wicklow (one Sun each month). MasterCard, Visa, Laser.

Dublin 8

Guinness Storehouse

PUB

St James's Gate Dublin 8
Tel: 01 408 4800 Web: www.guinness.com

The most spectacular pint of Guinness in Dublin - indeed, in all Ireland - awaits you in Gravity, the modern glass-walled bar providing panoramic views of the city from its unique position atop the impressive Guinness Storehouse, a handsome 1904 building. The Storehouse is commodious - with 170,000 square feet of floor space, it is one of the choicest pieces of real estate in Dublin. The space is imaginatively used to house the Guinness Museum, the story - told with fascinating high tech exhibits - of the famous company's 250-plus years in business. It also includes (on Level 5) the traditional Brewery Bar, serving nourishing Irish fare (seafood chowder, beef & Guinness stew, Guinness white & dark chocolate mousse) and the contemporary-style Source Bar. Slightly more formal evening menus, including a short children's menu, are available in Jul-Aug. Opened in the Autumn of 2000, the Guinness Storehouse has long since welcomed its millionth visitor: it has so much to offer that some folk spend an entire day there. The Storehouse is open daily, 9.30-5. Entrance fees apply. Bureau de Change. Free parking. **Seats 150.** Food served 11-4 daily. Closed 25-26 Dec, 31 Dec, 1 Jan, Good Fri.

Dublin 8

Havana Tapas Bar

CAFÉ

3 Camden Market Grantham Street Dublin 8 **Tel: 01 476 0046**
Email: info@havana.ie Web: www.havana.ie

This smashing little tapas bar is tucked away on a little street off Camden Street and, although understandably extremely popular with locals and people working in the area, it's otherwise one of Dublin's best kept secrets. Prices are very reasonable and lunch is a real bargain. Home-cooked food freshly made on the premises is the philosophy: Spanish tortilla, paella, Serrano ham and delicious breads from the famous Bretzel Bakery is the kind of food you'll get, along with tapas like marinated jumbo prawns. For music, be there on Friday and Saturday nights at 10 o'clock (until "late") for salsa music. **Seats 60** (private room 20). Open Mon-Sat 12-11.30 (Fri-Sat to 2 am, last orders 1.30). Tapas from €6.50. House wine €15. SC 12%. Closed Sun, bank hols. Amex, MasterCard, Visa, Laser. **Directions:** Adjacent to Cassidy's Pub, Camden St.

Dublin 8

Jurys Inn Christchurch

féile bia HOTEL

Christchurch Place Dublin 8 **Tel: 01 454 0000** Fax: 01 454 0012
Email: info@jurysdoyle.com Web: www.jurysdoyle.com

Jurys Inn Christchurch is well placed for both tourist and business travellers, offering reasonably priced accommodation within walking distance of the main city centre areas on both sides of the Liffey and close to attractions in Temple Bar, Dublin Castle and Dublinia (the museum of medieval Dublin). Rooms are comfortable and spacious, with large, well positioned work desks and practical bathrooms with economy baths and overbath showers. A large multi-storey car park at the rear has convenient access to the hotel. **Rooms 182.** Room rate from €103 (up to 3 adults or 2 adults and 2 children); breakfast from €9. Closed 24-26 Dec. Amex, Diners, MasterCard, Visa, Laser. **Directions:** Follow signs to city centre; opposite Christchurch Cathedral.

Dublin 8

Locks Restaurant

RESTAURANT

1 Windsor Terrace Portobello Dublin 8
Tel: 01 454 3391 Fax: 01 453 8352

In an old building with a lovely canal-side setting, this long-established two-storey restaurant is furnished and decorated in a warm country house style with soft lighting, open fires and a soothing atmosphere. There's a timelessness about the place which is extremely refreshing in contrast to the overdose of chic minimalism and international menus that has hit Dublin recently: short set menus for lunch and dinner offer the kind of food that might be served in a good country house; the seasonal à la carte menu is more ambitious in scale, but offers a similar combination of classic and country French and modern Irish cooking, with an occasional nod towards world cuisine. A new chef, Alan Kinsella, took over the kitchen shortly before the Guide went to press and had not, perhaps, completely settled in at the time of our visit, when cooking was a little uneven and made the à la carte, in particular, seem expensive. However, well-priced lunch and special dinner menus offer better value. The wine list favours France, notably Bordeaux, and offers several house choices (all French) by the glass. A la carte prices are high, but the set lunch and dinner menus offer good value. Children welcome. **Seats 60** (private room, 30). L Mon-Fri,12.30-2; D Mon-Sat, 7.15-10.30. Set L €28.95, Set D €30-48.95; L&D à la carte available. House wine from €23.15. SC 12.5%. Closed L Sat, all Sun, bank hols, Christmas week. Amex, Diners, MasterCard, Visa, Laser. **Directions:** Half way between Portobello and Harold's Cross Bridges.

Dublin 8

The Lord Edward

RESTAURANT / ATMOSPHERIC PUB

23 Christchurch Place Dublin 8
Tel: 01 4542 420 Fax: 01 4542 420
Email: ledward@indigo.ie

Dublin's oldest seafood restaurant/bar spans three floors of a tall, narrow building overlooking Christchurch Cathedral. Traditional in a decidedly old-fashioned way, The Lord Edward provides a complete contrast to the current wave of trendy restaurants that has taken over Dublin recently, which is just the way a lot of people seem to like it. There are a few non-seafood options - traditional dishes like Irish stew, perhaps, or corned beef and cabbage - and the seafood can be excellent: simplest choices are usually best. Bar food is also available Mon-Fri, 12-2.30. Children welcome. **Seats 40.** L Mon-Fri, 12-3. D 6-10.30 Mon-Sat. Set menu about €33. Reservations required. Closed Sun, Dec 24-2 Jan, bank hols. Amex, Diners, MasterCard, Visa, Laser. **Directions:** Opposite Christchurch Cathedral.

Dublin 8

Nancy Hands

PUB

30-32 Parkgate Street Dublin 8 **Tel: 01 677 0149** Fax: 01 677 0187
Email: nancyh@indigo.ie Web: www.nancyhands.com

A sister establishment to The Hole in the Wall (see entry), Nancy Hands is a newish pub, based on tradition but far from being a theme pub. It's a characterful place for a drink and the selection stocked is unusually extensive: it includes a wide choice of wines, also an extensive cocktail menu and a range of vodkas and whiskeys. Food was an important aspect of Nancy Hands from the outset and, on the whole, it is well done: Roland McLaughlin (who has been head chef since 2000) clearly takes it seriously. In both the bar and first floor restaurant his menus successfully straddle the divide between traditional bar food (seafood chowder, steaks; lunchtime carvery) and the lighter international fare that is becoming increasingly popular in pubs: spicy lamb wrap, crispy Japanese chicken, even Tahitian tuna - examples are from the restaurant menu, but bar food shares the same philosophy. Children welcome. Live music on occasion. Air conditioning. Toilets wheelchair accessible. Restaurant: **Seats 120**, L 12-3 (Sun to 4.30), D 6-10; Set L €16, Set D €30; à la carte L&D available. House wine €18. Meals available 10am-10pm. L 12-3 (Sun to 4.30), D 3.30-10 (Sun, 5-10). Closed 25-26 Dec & Good Fri. Amex, Diners, MasterCard, Visa. **Directions:** 100 metres from gates of Phoenix Park going towards Heuston Station.

Dublin 8

Ryan's of Parkgate Street

PUB

28 Parkgate Street Dublin 8 **Tel: 01 671 9352** Fax: 01 671 3590

Ryan's is one of Ireland's finest and best-loved original Victorian pubs, with magnificent stained glass, original mahogany bar fixtures and an outstanding collection of antique mirrors all contributing to its unique atmosphere. Good bar food is available at lunch time and in the evening, and there's a separate restaurant upstairs. Closed 25 Dec, Good Fri, first 2 wks Jan & bank hols.

Dublin 8

The Grass Roots Café

CAFÉ

Irish Museum of Modern Art Royal Hospital Kilmainham Dublin 8
Tel: 01 612 9900

This self-service café is a pleasant place for an informal meal, whether or not you are visiting the museum - it has good parking facilities and the spacious room, which is attractively located overlooking a garden area, has a pleasingly cool modern ambience. An appetising small menu offers home-made soup, salads and quiches, tarts and cakes plus several hot dishes - tortellini with pesto cream, perhaps, or tasty pork tacos, generously served - and about half the daily selection is vegetarian. Food quality and presentation is good (large white plates), cafeteria style service is efficient - and it's a handier choice for a quick lunch than city centre venues, perhaps. Wine choices are restricted to a few quarter bottles. Open: Museum opening hours. MasterCard, Visa. **Directions:** At Royal Hospital Kilmainham museum.

Dublin 8

The Old Dublin Restaurant

RESTAURANT

90/91 Francis Street Dublin 8
Tel: 01 454 2028 Fax: 01 454 1406 Email: olddub@indigo.ie

This is one of Dublin's longest-established fine restaurants and the dining area is in several domestic-sized rooms with special features - a marble fireplace, some very good pictures - creating a cosy old-world atmosphere. While most famous for its Russian and Scandinavian specialities like blini (buckwheat pancake with cured salmon, prawns and herrings), and planked sirloin Hussar, which still feature on the à la carte, recent menus have been noticeably modern. Set lunch and early evening menus are best value. Hospitable, thoughtful service. Children welcome. **Seats 65** (private room, 32). L Mon-Fri,D Mon-Sat. Closed L Sat, all Sun, bank hols. Amex, Diners, MasterCard, Visa, Laser.

DUBLIN 9

Dublin 9

Addison Lodge

PUB

Botanic Road Glasnevin Dublin 9 **Tel: 01 837 3534**
Fax: 01 837 5942 Email: addison@eircom.net

A very useful place to know about if you're visiting the Botanic Gardens, just across the road: this friendly family-run pub with accommodation is just the spot for wholesome, freshly-prepared food. Snacks like soup and sandwiches are available from opening time onwards and lunch-time brings hot food with a home-made flavour that is rare in carveries; traditional favourites like Irish stew and bacon & cabbage are especially welcome. Not suitable for children after 7pm. Food served daily, 12.30-8 (Sun to 6). Closed 25 Dec, Good Fri. Amex, MasterCard, Visa. **Directions:** Opposite entrance to the Botanic Gardens.

Dublin 9

Andersons Food Hall & Café

Ⓝ **CAFÉ / WINE BAR**

3 The Rise Glasnevin Dublin 9
Tel: 01 837 8394 Fax: 01 797 9004
Email: info@andersons.ie Web: www.andersons.ie

It is always sad to hear of a butchers shop closing, but the one that formerly operated on this premises has lived on, in a sense, through the delicious food now served to the lucky people of Glasnevin. It's quietly situated on a side road so the unexpected sight of jaunty aluminium chairs and tables outside - and a glimpse of many wine bottles lining the walls behind the elegant shopfront - should gladden the hearts of first-time visitors sweeping around the corner from Griffith Avenue. Noel Delaney and Patricia van der Velde opened this little gem in 2003, after refurbishing and extending the shop, which still has its original 1930s' tiled floor, high ceiling and façade - and oak fittings have been used throughout, including the wine displays. Chic little marble-topped tables for lighter bites suit the old shop well and, in the extension behind it, there are larger tables and space for groups to eat in comfort. Now, where cuts of meat were once displayed, there's a wonderful selection of charcuterie and cheese from Ireland and the continent: an Irish Plate offers a selection of Elliotts award-winning ham, corned beef and Irish farmhouse cheeses, for example, while The Iberian Selection comprises Serrano ham, salamis and Manchego sheep's milk cheese - and a Children's Selection educates the younger palate with the likes of ciabatta bread with Milano salami & Cheddar. A short blackboard menu of hot dishes and specials (penne pasta with tomato, spicy meat & aubergine for example), plus a daily soup, gourmet sandwiches, wraps, hot paninis, pastries and classic café desserts complement the charcuterie and cheese which have the gravitas to balance the extensive wine collection lining the walls - and, in addition to the wine list which charges regularly, you can choose any bottle to have with your food at a €5 corkage charge. **Seats 60.** Open Mon-Wed, 8am-7.30pm; Thu-Sat 8am-9pm; Sun 10am-7.30pm (last food orders half an hour before closing). MasterCard, Visa, Laser. **Directions:** Off Griffith Avenue, near junction with Mobhi Road.

Dublin 9

Egans House

GUESTHOUSE

7-9 Iona Park Glasnevin Dublin 9
Tel: 01 830 3611 Fax: 01 830 3312
Email: info@eganshouse.com Web: www.eganshouse.com

Within walking distance of the Botanic Gardens and convenient to the airport, north Dublin golf clubs, the Helix, Dublin port and the city centre, this family-run guesthouse offers comfortable, well-maintained accommodation at a reasonable price. All rooms are en-suite, with full bath, phone, tea/coffee trays. Wine licence. Wheelchair access. Parking. Children welcome (Under 3s free in parents' room; cots available, baby sitting aranged). No pets. **Rooms 32** (10 no-smoking). B&B €50, ss€10. Closed 20-28 Dec. MasterCard, Visa, Laser. **Directions:** North of city centre - Dorset Street - St. Alphonsus Road- Iona Park.

Dublin 9

Independent Pizza Company

RESTAURANT

28 Lr Drumcondra Road Dublin 9
Tel: 01 830 2044 Fax: 01 830 3952

A sister restaurant of the popular Gotham Café just off Grafton Street (see entry), the Independent Pizza Company is in smart new premises and the menu includes many of the Gotham favourites, so you can expect to find designer salads and contemporary pasta dishes, for example, alongside the excellent range of gourmet pizzas for which they are well known. Family-friendly (crayons, colouring books provided) and a handy place for a meal on the way to the airport. Air conditioning. Wheelchair friendly. **Seats 50** (Max table size 7). Open daily, 12 noon-midnight (Sun to 10.30). House wine €15; beer licence. A la carte; sc discretionary (except 10% on groups of 6+ adults). Closed Christmas, Good Fri. Amex, MasterCard, Visa, Laser. **Directions:** On the airport road - under the bridge at Drumcondra railway station.

Dublin 9

John Kavanagh (GraveDiggers)

ATMOSPHERIC PUB

1 Prospect Square Glasnevin Dublin 9
Tel 01 830 7978 Email: antokav@gofree.indigo.ie

John Kavanagh's lays claim to being the oldest family pub in Dublin - it was established in 1833 and the current family are the 6th generation in the business. Also known as "The Gravediggers' because of its location next to the Glasnevin cemetery and its attached folk history, this is a genuine Victorian bar, totally unspoilt - and it has a reputation for serving one of the best pints in Dublin. No music, "piped or otherwise". No food. Theme pub owners eat your hearts out. No children after 7pm. Closed Good Fri & Christmas. **Directions:** Old Glasnevin Cemetery Gate, off Botanic Road.

Dublin 9

The Washerwomans Hill Restaurant

RESTAURANT

60 Glasnevin Hill Glasnevin Dublin 9 **Tel: 01 837 9199**
Fax: 01 837 9492 Email: washerwomanrestaurant@eircom.net

Situated on a busy road, just across from the Met Office and convenient to the Botanic Gardens and the airport area, first impressions of this popular neighbourhood restaurant may be a little dusty but a prompt welcome and (if you are lucky) the offer of a choice of tables should help new arrivals warm to it. Traditional, even slightly old-world in style, the restaurant is quite dimly-lit, with simply-laid darkwood tables - place mats, pre-pack butter, a peppermill - and the work of a local artist displayed on the walls. Well-balanced traditional table d'hôte and à la carte menus offer the popular dishes that people of all ages feel comfortable with, sometimes with a contemporary twist - 'Fishysoisse' (leek & potato soup with smoked salmon & croûtons), deep-fried mushrooms (tossed in tandoori spices & serving with raita), crisp roast duck (on a bed of sweet & sour beetroot & red onion, with a citrus glaze) and char-grilled steak are all typical, and the cooking style is quite homely. Some suppliers are listed on the menu and special diets can be accommodated, but very ordinary bought-in desserts are a weak point. The ambience on the ground floor is warmer and more relaxed than a first floor room, which has rather gimmicky decor. Not suitable for children after 8pm. **Seats 70.** Reservations required. L Wed-Sun 12,30-3.30 (Sun 1.30-4.30); D daily 6-10.30. Set L €20, early D €26 (Sun-Thu, 6-8). Set D €35; also à la carte. House wine €16.50. Closed 25-26 Dec, Good Fri. Children - not after 8pm. Amex, MasterCard, Visa, Laser. **Directions:** Past Bon Secours hospital, opposite the Met Office.

DUBLIN 14

Dublin 14

Indian Brasserie

RESTAURANT

Main Street Rathfarnham Dublin 14 **Tel: 01 492 0261**

Samir Sapru's Indian Brasserie is just a minute's walk from Rathfarnham Castle, at the Butterfield Avenue end of the village. The restaurant, which is run as a buffet, offers freshly prepared wholesome food, aiming to make it the nearest to home cooking that can be achieved in a restaurant. The selection usually includes around eight starters, five or six salads and seven or eight main courses, with each dish individually prepared from scratch and the selection worked out so that all the dishes complement each other. Breads - which are baked quickly at a very high temperature - are cooked to order. The hospitality is intended to make each guest feel as if they are visiting a private house - customers are encouraged to try a little of everything that has been prepared on the night. Own parking. No children after 7pm. **Seats 50.** No-smoking area. Air conditioning D 5.15-11.30 daily. L Sun only 12.30-3. Set D about €20; early D, 5.30-7.30pm. House wine about €14. SC discretionary. Toilets wheelchair accessible. Closed 25-26 Dec. Amex, Diners, MasterCard, Visa. **Directions:** At the Butterfield Ave. end of Rathfarnham village, under TSB Bank.

Dublin 14

The Yellow House

RESTAURANT / BAR

1 Willbrook Road Rathfarnham Dublin 14
Tel: 01 493 2994 Fax: 01 494 2441

Named after the unusual shade of the bricks with which it is built, the landmark pub of Rathfarnham makes a perfect rendezvous, with no chance of confusion. The tall and rather forbidding exterior gives little hint of the warmth inside, where pictures and old decorative items relevant to local history repay closer examination. Traditional bar food is served in the lounge and there's a restaurant upstairs serving evening meals and Sunday lunch. Set L €21; D à la carte. House wine €19. Closed 25-6 Dec & Good Fri. Amex, Diners, MasterCard, Visa, Laser. **Directions:** Prominent corner building in Rathfarnham Village.

DUBLIN 15

Dublin 15

Ashbrook House

COUNTRY HOUSE

River Road Ashtown Castleknock Dublin 15 **Tel: 01 838 5660**
Fax: 01 838 5660 Email: evemitchell@hotmail.com

Eve Mitchell's lovely Georgian country house is set in 10 acres of grounds and gardens beside the Phoenix park just 15 minutes from the city and the airport. Large beautifully furnished bedrooms have power showers and two family rooms have a single bed as well as doubles. There are two magnificent drawing rooms, tennis court and walled gardens. Direct dial phones in rooms. B&B from about €45 pps. Single supplement about €10. Closed 19 Dec-2 Jan. MasterCard, Visa, Laser. **Directions:** Off M50, 15 minutes from airport; similar distance from city centre.

DUBLIN 16

Dublin 16 — Killakee House Restaurant

RESTAURANT

Killakee Road Rathfarnham Dublin 16 **Tel: 01 493 8849**

This famous old house - once the premises of the notorious Hellfire Club - was taken over in 2001 by George Smith, well known for his years as head chef at Kilkea Castle, Co. Kildare. The restaurant has settled well and a confident tone prevails: cheerful and willing staff provide a welcoming atmosphere, skilful cooking ensures that the promise of interesting menus (based on quality ingredients as ever) is carried through onto the plate - and happy punters create a pleasing ambience. **Seats 75.** D Tue-Sat 7-10, L Sun 12.30-5. Closed 25 Dec. Amex, MasterCard, Visa, Laser. **Directions:** Directions: From Rathfarnham, on right heading towards Dublin Mountains.

DUBLIN 17

Dublin 17 — Belcamp Hutchinson

COUNTRY HOUSE

Carrs Lane Malahide Road Balgriffin Dublin 17
Tel: 01 846 0843 Fax: 01 848 5703
Email: belcamhutchinson@eircom.net Web: www.belcamphutchinson.com

Dating back to 1786, this impressive house just outside Malahide (with good restaurants and shopping) takes its name from its original owner, Francis Hely-Hutchinson, 3rd Earl of Donoughmore. It is set in large grounds, with interesting gardens, giving it a very away-from-it-all country atmosphere - yet Belcamp Hutchinson is only about half an hour from Dublin city centre (off peak) and 15 minutes to the airport. The present owners, Doreen Gleeson and Karl Waldburg, have renovated the house sensitively: high ceilinged, graciously proportioned rooms have retained many of their original features and are furnished and decorated in keeping with their age. Bedrooms are very comfortable, with thoughtfully appointed bathrooms and views over the gardens and countryside. Although its convenient location makes this an ideal place to stay on arrival or when leaving Ireland, a one-night stay won't do justice to this lovely and hospitable place. Walled garden; maze. Golf, equestrian, walking, tennis, sailing nearby. Not suitable for children under. Pets welcome. **Rooms 8** (all with full bath & overbath shower). B&B €65 pps, no ss. Closed 20 Dec-31 Jan. MasterCard, Visa. **Directions:** From city centre, take malahide Road; past Campions pub, 1st lane on left (sign on right pointing up lane).

DUBLIN 18

Dublin 18 — Bistro One

féile bia **RESTAURANT**

3 Brighton Road Foxrock Village Dublin 18
Tel: 01 289 7711 Fax: 01 289 9858 Email: bistroone@eircom.ie

This popular first floor neighbourhood restaurant can get very busy but there is a little bar on the way in, where guests are greeted and set up in comfort, and the attitude throughout is laid back but not without care. Ingredients are carefully sourced - organic bacon and beef is from O'Toole's of Glasthule, cheeses from Sheridan's cheesemongers, fish from Caviston's of Sandycove - and seasonal menus offer about ten tempting choices per course. Starters might include West Cork smoked haddock fish cake with rocket and sauce béarnaise - or the ever-popular Bistro One's salad with pancetta, rocket & pine nuts - while the pasta and risotto selection can be starter or main course as preferred: typically, spaghetti with organic meatballs & fresh basil, perhaps, or risotto with fresh asparagus and a light lemon reduction. Main courses include classics - in seafood dishes, maybe, or roast duck - and organic meats like roast pork fillet, wrapped in Tuscan prosciutto, stuffed with apple & black pudding with organic cabbage is a typical autumn example. There are generous side vegetables and a choice of farmhouse cheese; home-made ice creams or classic puddings to finish. Children welcome. **Seats 45.** D Tue-Sat 6.45-10.30. A la carte. House wine €22. SC 10%. Closed Sun, Mon & Christmas/New Year. MasterCard, Visa, Laser, Switch. **Directions:** Southbound on N11, first right after Foxrock church.

Dublin 18

RESTAURANT

The Gables Expresso Bar & Café

The Gables Foxrock Village Dublin 18
Tel: 01 2892174 Fax: 01 289 2167
Email: info@thegables.ie Web: www.thegables.ie

A younger sister to Expresso Bar cafés in Ballsbridge and the IFSC, this is an imaginative joint venture with McCabes Wines, whose shop is part of the restaurant. So, in addition to the brunches and stylish contemporary food for which they are well known, the wine experience is now a major part of the attraction: the wine list (which begins at about €14, rising to about €47) offers quality wines at an unusually low mark-up- and you can have any wine from about 800 available in the shop at a corkage charge of just EUR8 : an exciting development all round. **Seats 65.** L daily, 12-6 (Sun 10-5); D Mon-Sat 6-9. A la carte; House wine €14. SC discretionary. Closed D Sun; 25-26 Dec, 1 Jan. Amex, Diners, MasterCard, Visa, Laser, Switch. **Directions:** At the crossroads in Foxrock Village.

Dublin 18

RESTAURANT

Rodney's Bistro

Horse & Hound Cabinteely Village Dublin 18
Tel: 01 285 3527

Rodney and Deirdre Doyle's popular restaurant has moved next door into the Horse & Hound pub, where friendly service, good cooking and fairly reasonable prices continue to attract a loyal following. Rodney's cooking style is updated classic/modern bistro style and, while the menu is short, limited choice is more than offset by the excellence of both food and cooking. Rodney has, of course, brought some favourite dishes with him so you can expect favourites like lamb kidneys with Meaux mustard & brandy cream with gorgeous treacly brown bread, warm salad of Indian spiced chicken with lime & tomato chutney, the goujons of sole - now as a main course with home-made tartare sauce and superb garlic fries - and the delicious boned roast crispy duck with fresh herb stuffing and port & orange jus: all combinations that work well. And of course there's a good steak, cooked perfectly as ordered, and served with juicy sautéed onions and those garlicky quick-roast 'fries'. (Only downside: no vegetables on the menu, and no vegetarian dishes offered.) Finish with a luscious crème brulée, perhaps - and leaving feeling you've had a great meal at a very reasonable price. Short, inexpensive wine list, with South African house wines and some half bottles. No reservations. **Seats 100.** L Mon-Fri, 12.30-2.30, also Sun, 12.30-4; D Wed-Sat, 5-9. Menu à la carte. House wine from €16. No smoking area; air conditioning. SC10%. Closed Sun, Mon, 2 weeks Jan, 2 weeks Jul. Amex, MasterCard, Visa, Laser. **Directions:** In Cabinteely village.

DUBLIN 22

Dublin 22

HOTEL

Bewley's Hotel at Newlands Cross

Newlands Cross Naas Road Dublin 22 **Tel: 01 464 0140** Fax: 01 464 0900
Email: res@bewleyshotels.com Web: www.bewleyshotels.com

The lobby gives a good first impression at this stylish budget hotel just off the N7. Bedrooms will confirm this feeling, especially at the price - a very reasonable room rate offers a large room with double, single and sofa-bed, a decent bathroom and excellent amenities including a trouser press, iron and ironing board and fax/modem lines. Many more expensive hotels might take note of these standards. Good business facilities too. The adjacent Bewley's Restaurant provides very acceptable food and there is free parking for 200 cars. Small conference (20). Wheelchair access. Parking. Children welcome. (under 16 free in parents' room; cots available). No pets. Lift. **Rooms 260** (5 shower only, 183 no-smoking, 7 for disabled). Room rate about €79 (max 3 adults). Closed Dec 24-26. Amex, Diners, MasterCard, Visa, Laser. **Directions:** Off N7 - take junction 9 from M50.

Dublin 22

RESTAURANT / PUB

Browns Barn

Citywest Bridge Naas Road Dublin 22
Tel: 01 464 0930 Fax: 01 464 0929
Email: info@brownsbarn.ie Web: www.brownsbarn.ie

This landmark listed building dates back to the late 17th century and once housed the Royal Garter Stables - today the old stone walls make a welcome contrast to new industrial developments along this stretch of road and it is especially impressive when floodlit at night. Now imaginatively restored as a contemporary bar and restaurant, it has proved a great asset to the area and retains many of the original features, including a courtyard that has been transformed into a light-filled bar - and a west-facing walled garden providing summer seating. Bar food is available all day (steak sandwiches, BLT etc.) and the first floor restaurant offers "casual fine dining". Menus are in the popular contemporary style - Caesar salad, goats cheese in filo and chargrilled steaks are typical, also more elaborate dishes such as trio of salmon (smoked salmon, poached fresh salmon and gravadlax with a lemon & dill dressing). Interesting vegetarian options are also given. Cooking, presentation and service are all generally good - and this, together with a friendly atmosphere and smart, efficient service, make it good value. Midweek visits might be more enjoyable as it gets very busy at weekends. Air conditioning **Seats 200** (private room, 10-100). Bar L&D daily; restaurant D daily, L Sun-Fri. Set L about €25; D à la carte. House wine about €20. SC discretionary, except 12.5% on parties of 6+. Restaurant closed L Sat. Bar closed 25 Dec, Good Fri. Amex, Diners, MasterCard, Visa, Laser. **Directions:** Opposite Citywest Business Park.

Dublin 22

Kingswood Country House

RESTAURANT / GUESTHOUSE

Naas Road Clondalkin Dublin 22 **Tel: 01 459 2428**
Fax: 01 459 2207 Email: kingswoodcountryhse@eircom.net
Web: www.kingswoodcountryhouse.com

Just off the Naas Road and very close to the industrial estates around Newlands Cross, the country house ambience of this guesthouse and restaurant comes as a very pleasant surprise. The restaurant has a lovely cosy atmosphere (with open fires, which is always a treat) and a loyal following, for service and friendliness as well as the food. This is an interesting combination of classic French and traditional and new Irish styles, using top quality ingredients - the policy is to use as much local and free range produce as possible, and both the cooking - which has a pleasing 'good home cooking with style' feel to it - and the ambience are invariably enjoyable. Private rooms are available for groups and small business meetings. Small conference/private parties (20/30). Garden. Children welcome (under 3 free in parents' room, cots available). **Seats 80** (private room, 30). L daily, 12.30 -2.30 (Sun to 3). Set L €23.95. D daily 6.30-10.30 (Sun to 10). House wine €18.40. SC 12.5%. Closed 25-26 Dec & Good Fri. Open on bank hols.

Accommodation: Guest rooms, like the rest of the house, have an old-fashioned charm. **Rooms 7** (all en suite). 24 hour room service. B&B €65 pps, ss €25. Amex, Diners, MasterCard, Visa, Laser. **Directions:** 1.5 miles past Newlands Cross heading south on N7.

Dublin 22

Lynch Green Isle Hotel

féile bia **HOTEL**

Newlands Cross Clondalkin Dublin 22 **Tel: 01 459 3406** Fax: 01 459 2178
Email: cro@lynchotels.com Web: www.lynchotels.com

Situated on the Naas Road, close to the major industrial estates, this is a popular hotel for conference and business. Half of the bedrooms are executive rooms and there are conference facilities for up to 500 delegates, four meeting rooms (up to 50 delegates each) and some business back-up service if required. Laundry/dry cleaning services available. Children welcome. No pets. **Rooms 90** (45 executive). Lift. 24 hour room service. B&B from €79pps, ss €26. Room-only rate: €135. Open all year. Amex, Diners, Visa, MasterCard, Laser.

Dublin 22

Red Cow Moran's Hotel

féile bia **HOTEL**

Red Cow Complex Naas Road Dublin 22
Tel: 01 459 3650 Fax: 01 459 1588
Email: info@morangroup.ie Web: www.moranhotels.com

Strategically located close to the motorway and known as a pub for many years, the Red Cow Hotel has a grand staircase sweeping up from the marble lobby to give an indication of the style to follow and although it may also be of interest to private guests, this is definitely a location to check out if you are considering visiting the area on business or wish to organise conferences or meetings. Bedrooms are all of executive standard, with excellent amenities for business guests including voice mail and fax/modem lines. The purpose-built conference centre offers a wide range of facilities and ample car parking. Conference/banqueting (700/550). Video conferencing. Wheelchair access. Parking. Children welcome (under 2 free in parents' room; cots available). No pets. **Rooms 123** (3 suites, 6 junior suites, 44 no-smoking, 5 for disabled). Lift. 24 hour room service. B&B about €95pps, ss about €50. Closed 24-27 Dec. Amex, Diners, MasterCard, Visa, Laser. **Directions:** Exit No.9 from M50 motorway, on the N7.

COUNTY DUBLIN

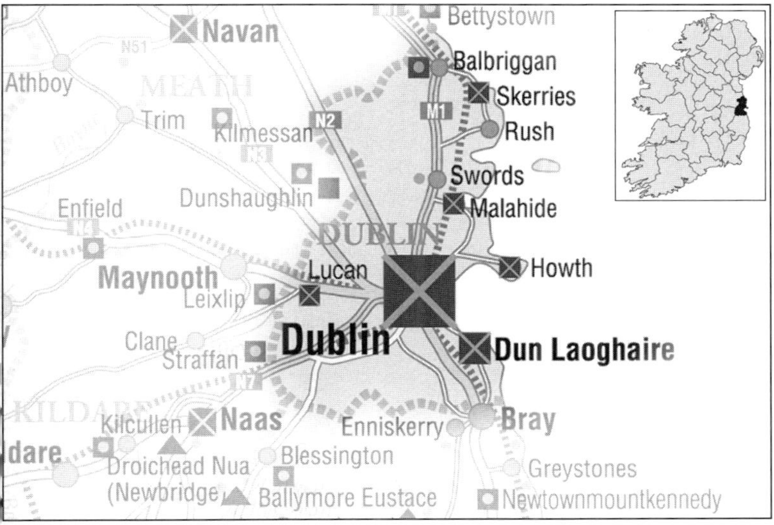

Blackrock — **Dali's Restaurant**

RESTAURANT 63-65 Main Street Blackrock Co. Dublin **Tel: 01 278 0660** Fax: 01 278 0661

Just across the road from the Library, these premises have been home to several of Dublin's most successful restaurateurs and Dali is no exception, having established a loyal local clientèle and a reputation beyond the immediate area. There's a chic little bar just inside the door and a dining area, at a slightly higher level, beyond - all very attractively set up in a style that is contemporary but without hard-edged minimalism. Menus are appealingly light and colourful, including zesty first courses salmon fishcakes with a chive beurre blanc, which are a speciality, followed by main courses that could include some unusual variations on old favourites - Dali's Irish Stew, for example, is excellent although it includes not just the hotly-disputed carrots, but celery and pearl barley too! Good, honest cooking based on quality ingredients and offering excellent value for money has them beating a path to the door, so booking is essential, especially at weekends. Set lunch menus offer a choice of four or five dishes on each course and are particularly good value. Professional, efficient service and a good (if slightly disorganised) wine list complete an appealing package. Children welcome. Air conditioning. **Seats 65.** L Tue-Sun, 12-3 D Tue-Sat 6-10.30. Set L from about €15. A la carte L&D available; house wine about €20, sc discretionary except 10% on parties of 6+. Closed D Sun, all Mon, 25-27 Dec. Amex, Diners, MasterCard, Visa, Laser. **Directions:** Opposite Blackrock Library.

Blackrock — **Ristorante da Roberto**

RESTAURANT 5 George's Avenue Blackrock Co. Dublin **Tel: 01 278 0759**

At Blackrock's most popular restarant, proprietor-chef Roberto Morsiani offers quite a few house specialities featuring dishes like - Prawns Roberto's Way, Greedy Man's Ravioli, Chef's Rustic Veal - plus a wide choice of fish (mostly local), a page of pastas and a vegetarian section. People like the food, of course, but it's the atmosphere that really singles it out and the overall experience provides a down-to-earth contrast to the chic contemporary restaurants nearby. The best tables are in the front section; the back room is very noisy. **Seats 70.** Air conditioning. D Sun-Sat. Closed Mon. Amex, MasterCard, Visa. **Directions:** Opposite the Post Office off the Main Street in Blackrock.

Dalkey — **Daniel Finnegan**

PUB 2 Sorrento Road Dalkey Co. Dublin **Tel: 01 285 8505**

An immaculately maintained pub of great character, much-loved by locals and visitors alike. It's bright, comfortable and cosy, with wood panelling and traditional Irish seating in 'snugs', has now 'blended in' the large extension built a couple of years ago. Food is served at lunchtime only - a full hot bar lunch, including starters such as baked Dalkey crab, brie fritters with apple coulis and main courses like roast stuffed pork steak, honey roast half duck and grilled cod steak, followed by traditional desserts like apple pie and lemon cheesecake. The fresh fish (from the harbour nearby) is excellent, the vegetables predictable but tasty and value good. No reservations - get there early to avoid a long wait. Carpark nearby. Bar food 12.30-3pm Mon-Sat. Closed 25 Dec, Good Fri & & New Year. Amex, Diners,MasterCard, Visa, Laser. **Directions:** Near Dalkey DART station.

Dalkey

IN

BAR / CAFÉ 115-116 Coliemore Road Dalkey Co Dublin **Tel: 01 275 0007** Fax: 02 275 0009 Email: info@indalkey.ie Web: www.indalkey.ie

This stylish contemporary café-bar in the centre of Dalkey opened to some acclaim in 2002 and seems to have found a niche, offering something rather different from pubs and restaurants in the area. The atmosphere is relaxed and what you get here is informal dining in chic surroundings: menus offer a choice ranging from the ubiquitous steak (accurately cooked) to more interesting seafood dishes - a speciality of Kimchee prawns (served in filo baskets) has attracted a particular following. Wheelchair accessible. Meals daily: L Mon-Fri 12-4.30, Sat & Sun 12-4. MasterCard, Visa. **Directions:** At the end of Dalkey's main street.

Dalkey

Kish Restaurant

RESTAURANT Coliemore Road Dalkey Co. Dublin **Tel: 01 285 0377** Fax: 01 285 0141 Email: book@kishrestaurant.ie Web: www.kishrestaurant.ie

The Delaney family's beautifully located restaurant is one of the area's finest - and takes full advantage of views over Dublin Bay and Dalkey Island. It's a great place for special treats like birthdays and anniversaries - the location is a huge asset and there is always something to watch, whether it be wildlife or watersports. The present head chef, Roisin Gavin, previously worked in Belfast with one of Ireland's finest chefs, Michael Deane. Her short seasonal à la carte menus offer about half a dozen choices on each course and favour seafood, notably local lobster - typically included in first course house specialities like lobster bisque with roasted langoustines & coconut (€13.90); main courses, which are in a similar style and also weighted heavily in favour of seafood - including a popular speciality of seared scallops with parsnip purée, puy lentils & bacon jus (€30) - but if you're not in the mood for fish there are a couple of options including a luxurious dish of duck breast with seared foie gras, with pomme boulangère, savoy cabbage, confit cabbage & a light Madeira jus (€29.50). Vegetarian dishes are available on request, so it would be wise to mention when booking if you would like a vegetarian choice. This is special occasion fare, and none the worse for that, although Sunday lunch is more accessible. Air conditioning. **Seats 50.** D Wed-Sun, 7-10, L Sun only 12.30-2.30. D à la carte; Set Sun L €40; house wine €22-24; SC10%. Closed Mon,Tue, 1 week Nov, last 3 weeks Jan, bank hols. Amex, Diners, MasterCard, Visa, Laser. **Directions:** 8 miles south of Dublin City just outside Dalkey Village.

Dalkey

Munkberrys Restaurant

RESTAURANT 22 Castle Street Dalkey Co. Dublin **Tel: 01 284 7185** Email: info@munkberrys.com Web: www.munkberrys.com

This chic, minimalist restaurant in the heart of Dalkey village has earned the favour of a local clientèle, who appreciate the stylish cooking and consistently high standard of cooking. An early dinner menu is particularly good value and Sunday brunch is a speciality, bringing fans from far and wide for good food and live jazz. Interesting, informative wine list. **Seats 50.** D daily: Mon-Sat from 5.30 (early D 5.30-6.45), Sun 6-10; Sun brunch 12-6. Closed public holidays. Amex, Diners, MasterCard, Visa, Laser. **Directions:** Main Street Dalkey (5 miles south of Dublin on the DART Rail Link).

Dalkey

Nosh

RESTAURANT 111 Coliemore Road Dalkey Co Dublin **Tel: 01 2840666** Email: comments@nosh.ie Web: www.nosh.ie

Samantha and Sacha Farrell's bright, contemporary restaurant is next to the famous Club Bar and, with its clean lines and lightwood furniture, no-nonsense menus, quality ingredients and fair prices, its niche in the Dalkey dining scene seems assured. Julie Sheils (previously at Dalis in Blackrock) took over as head chef in the autumn of 2002 and has kept up the practice of offering seasonal menus that also change throughout the day. There's brunch (hot dishes, anything from buttermilk pancakes with grilled bananas and maple syrup, to fish pie with Nosh mash and a wide range of coffees and other hot and cold drinks, including home-made lemonade) then lunch, where things move up a gear, with some overlap from the Brunch menu and a dozen or so choices, ranging up to the "Posh Nosh" special of the day. In the evening, you might begin with prawn pil-pils in sizzling garlic & chilli oil (an enduring favourite) and proceed to fish & chips with home-made chips & tartare sauce (another speciality) or an appealing vegetarian dish such as pea & asparagus risotto. Top prices range from around €16.50 for a vegetarian main course, to about €22.95 for rack of lamb. Desserts are home-made and there's a limited but well-chosen wine list, with a few half bottles, offered throughout the day. Not suitable for children after 8pm. Wheelchair accessible. Air conditioning. **Seats 45.** L Tue-Sun, 12-4; D Tue-Sun 6-10. A la carte. House wine €17.50. Closed Mon, bank hols. MasterCard, Visa, Laser. **Directions:** End of Dalkey town, take left.

Dalkey

The Queen's Bar & Restaurant

PUB / RESTAURANT

12 Castle Street Dalkey Co Dublin
Tel: 01 285 4569 Fax: 01 285 8345 Email: queens@clubi.ie

The oldest pub in Dalkey, and also one of the oldest in Ireland, The Queen's was originally licensed to 'dispense liquor' as far back as 1745. Recent renovations and improvements have been done with due respect for the age and character of the premises. As well as a busy, characterful bar, there are two restaurants on the premises - La Romana, which has offered good value Italian/Mediterranean food for some years and the first floor restaurant and piano bar, The Vico, which offers contemporary international food in a more formal atmosphere. Good bar food (member of BIM Seafood Circle): chowders, salads, pies, steak sandwiches etc also available every afternoon and and evening, and can be served to patio areas at the back and front in fine weather. Wheelchair accessible. Restaurants both **seat 70.** Vico D only Tue-Sat; Romana D daily. Bar menu daily, 12-5, light evening bar menu Mon-Fri. Closed 25 Dec & Good Fri. Amex, Diners, MasterCard, Visa, Laser. **Directions:** Centre of town,beside Heritage Centre.

Dalkey

Ragazzi

RESTAURANT

109 Coliemore Road Dalkey Co Dublin **Tel: 01 284 7280**

Possibly Dublin's buzziest little bistro, this is the pizza place where everyone goes to have their spirits lifted by theatrical Italian waiters and great value. Lovely pastas, luscious bruschettas - but best of all the pizzas, renowned for their thin, crisp bases and scrumptious toppings. But it's the atmosphere that counts - every town should have a place like this.

Dalkey

Thai House Restaurant

RESTAURANT

21 Railway Road Dalkey Co Dublin **Tel: 01 284 7304**
Email: info@thaihouseireland.com Web: www.thaihouseireland.com

Established in 1997, well before the current vogue for Thai food became established, Tony Ecock's restaurant has earned a loyal following and head chef Wilai Khruekhcai has maintained a reputation for including dishes that do not pander too much to bland western tastes. In typical oriental style, a number of set menus are offered for groups of various sizes and there is also an extensive à la carte which offers a wider choice. After an aperitif in the new wine bar/reception area, begin, perhaps, with the Thai House Special Starter Pack, a sampling plate of six starters, well-balanced in flavour and texture and including some vegetarian options: Thai prawn toast, chicken satay with peanut sauce, deep-fried corn cakes with herbs & curry paste, crispy vegetarian spring rolls, deep-fried prawn cakes with sweet chilli sauce. From a choice of soups that includes the famous Tom Yam Gung (spicy prawn soup with lemon grass and chilli) Tom Yam Rumit - a spicy soup with prawns, squid, crab and mussels is perhaps the most interesting. Main courses include a range of curries - a speciality is fresh monkfish dumplings in green curry sauce with wild ginger - and vegetarian dishes are listed separately. Groups of four can share a dessert platter (mostly with coconut and/or banana). The wine list includes a page of house favourites (all under €25) and a Thai beer. Not suitable for children after 8pm. Air conditioning. **Seats 34.** D Tue-Sun, 5.30-11.30. Set D €34, Early D €20 (5.30-7.15), house wine from €14.50; SC discretionary. Closed Mon. Amex, Diners, MasterCard, Visa, Laser. **Directions:** 100 metres from Dalkey DART Station.

Dublin Airport

Great Southern Hotel

féile bia HOTEL

Dublin Airport Co Dublin **Tel: 01 844 6000** Fax: 01 844 6001
Email: res@dubairport-gsh.ie Web: www.gshotels.com

This large, spacious modern hotel opened in the airport complex in 1998, and has already had an 82-bedroom wing added. It's s just two minutes drive from the main terminal building (with a coach service available), rooms are all double-glazed and there's a high proportion of executive rooms (12 of which are designated lady executive). It's a good choice for business guests and, should your flight be delayed, the large bar and Potters Bistro on the ground floor could be a welcome place to pass the time. Conference/banqueting (450/300); video conferencing; business centre. Children welcome (Under 2s free in parents' room; cots available free of charge). **Rooms 229** (2 suites, 4 junior suites, 82 executive rooms, 5 no-smoking floors, 4 rooms for disabled) Lifts. Room service (limited hours). Room rate €250 (1 or 2 guests). Closed 24-26 Dec. Amex, Diners, MasterCard, Visa, Laser. **Directions:** Situated in airport complex.

Dublin Airport

Holiday Inn Dublin Airport

féile bia HOTEL

Dublin Airport Dublin Airport Co Dublin **Tel: 01 808 0500** Fax: 01 844 6002
Email: reservations-dublinairport@6c.com Web: dublinairport.holiday-inn.com

This large, comfortable hotel makes an ideal meeting place and guests may use the ALSAA Leisure Complex swimming pool, gymnasium and sauna free of charge. Bedrooms all have TV and pay movies, mini-bar. Well-equipped meeting rooms/conference suites available for groups of up to 130, with secretarial and business services. Courtesy bus to and from the airport terminal (24 hr). Two restaurants (Bistro and Sampan) offer contrasting styles of cuisine. Live music in the bar at weekends. Parking. Children welcome (Under 12s free in parents' room; cots available without charge). Wheelchair accessible. **Rooms 249** (110 executive rooms, 102 no-smoking, 3 for disabled). Lift. 24 hour room service. Room rate from about €127. Closed 24-25 Dec. Amex, Diners, MasterCard, Visa, Laser. **Directions:** In airport complex, on the right when entering airport.

Dun Laoghaire

Brasserie Na Mara

féile bia RESTAURANT

1 Harbour Road Dun Laoghaire Co Dublin **Tel: 01 280 6767**
Fax: 01 284 4649 Email: brasserienamara@irishrail.ie

The old Kingstown terminal building beside the Dun Laoghaire DART station makes a fine location for this harbourside restaurant. Part of Irish Rail's art collection graces the walls - a Nora McGuinness, a Lambe, a Leech - and the current contemporary decor is stylish, with high ceilings and tall windows complemented by linen-covered tables and glistening glasses - and the bar faces in towards the reception area, so you look out over the harbour while enjoying your aperitif. Interesting menus are in a bright, modern style to suit the decor, and there is a special emphasis on seafood as one would expect: fried tuna risotto cake, pesto mayonnaise & sweetcorn relish for starters, for example, char-grilled, potato rösti, ratatouille, red pepper & saffron dressing for main course. Popular meat and poultry dishes include braised lamb shank and confit of duck, but they take pride in fish specials like monkfish, scallops, sole or seabass, and fresh Dublin Bay prawns, while vegetarians might be offered a wild mushroom risotto. Updated classic desserts: iced lemon & lime parfait, perhaps, with mango sorbet. Prices are not excessive and staff, who are charming and efficient, make a great team. **Seats 64** (private room, 50). Reservations required. L Mon-Fri 12.30-2.30; D Mon-Sat, 6.30-10. [Mon-Fri: Set L €20; Set 'Value' D €30.] A la carte L&D available; house wine €20.65. SC 12.5%. Closed L Sat & Sun, 25-26 Dec & 1 Jan, bank hols. Amex, Diners, MasterCard, Visa, Laser, Switch. **Directions:** Coast road, beside DART, opposite the Pavilion.

Dun Laoghaire

Caviston's Seafood Restaurant

RESTAURANT

59 Glasthule Road Dun Laoghaire Co Dublin
Tel: 01 280 9120 Fax: 01 284 4054
Email: caviston@indigo.ie Web: cavistons.com

Caviston's of Sandycove has long been a mecca for lovers of good food and was the Guide's Happy Heart Eat Out award-winner for 2001. Here you will find everything that is wonderful, from organic vegetables to farmhouse cheeses, cooked meats to specialist oils and other exotic items. But it was always for fish and shellfish that Caviston's were especially renowned - even providing a collection of well-thumbed recipe books for on-the-spot reference. At their little restaurant next door, they serve an imaginative range of healthy seafood dishes influenced by various traditions and all washed down by a glass or two from a very tempting little wine list. Caviston's food is simple, colourful, perfectly cooked - it speaks volumes for how good seafood can be. Children welcome. **Seats 26.** Air conditioning. L only Tue-Sat, 3 sittings: 12-1.30, 1.30-3, 3-5; all à la carte; sc discretionary. Toilets wheelchair accessible. Closed Sun, Mon & Christmas-New Year. Amex, Diners, MasterCard, Visa. **Directions:** Between Dun Laoghaire and Dalkey, 5 mins. walk from Glasthule DART station.

Dun Laoghaire

Eagle House

PUB

18 Glasthule Road Dun Laoghaire Co Dublin
Tel: 01 280 4740

This fine traditional establishment is full of interest and a great local. The interior is dark, but has a fascinating collection of model boats, ships and other nautical bric-à-brac and is arranged in comfortably sized alcoves and 'snugs' on different levels. Bar meals, available at lunchtime and in the evening, can be very good. Bar food daily, from 12.30. Closed 25 Dec & Good Fri. Amex, MasterCard, Visa, Laser. **Directions:** 5 mins walk from Glasthule DART station, opposite Caviston's.

Dun Laoghaire

The Forty Foot

PUB / RESTAURANT Pavilion Centre Dun Laoghaire Co Dublin **Tel: 01 284 2982**

Named after a well-known local swimming place, this ultra-modern two-storey bar and restaurant in the redeveloped Pavilion Centre is designed to make the most of views over the harbour and Dublin Bay - particularly from the first floor restaurant - and to impress. Bright, spacious and airy, with acres of wood and huge windows the restaurant, especially, is a lovely space and (except at very busy times when you may be directed down to the bar), you can settle into a comfortable sofa to read the menu before being shown to a table simply laid with good linen and cutlery and handsome,plain glasses. The choice is wide and the menu reads well: colourful, fresh-sounding starters are offered - typically mozzarella with roasted peppers & rocket salad, or tian of salmon & crab with crème fraîche; main courses in a similar vein : expect pleasant, attractively presented food and you will not be disappointed; well-informed, attentive staff will, together with the pleasing ambience, ensure you wish to return. If you hit it on a sunny day the large terraces outside both the bar and restaurant might also be a draw. Closed 25 Dec, Good Fri. MasterCard, Visa. **Directions:** At Pavilion Centre.

Dun Laoghaire

Glandore House

Ⓝ **GUESTHOUSE** Glandore Park Lr Mounttown Rd Dun Laoghaire Co Dublin
Tel: 01 280 3143 Fax: 01 280 2675
Email: info@glandorehouse.com Web: www.glandorehouse.com

Conveniently near the ferry terminal in Dun Laoghaire, this unusual guesthouse offers all the conveniences required by the discerning traveller in an old building of character. All the bedrooms are en-suite, with phone television, tea and coffee making facilities - and there's even a lift. Parking. **Rooms 12** (all en-suite). Lift. B&B from about €45. Closed mid Dec - late Jan. MasterCard, Visa. **Directions:** 5 minutes drive from Dun Laoghaire ferry teminal.

Dun Laoghaire

Gresham Royal Marine Hotel

féile bia **HOTEL** Marine Road Dun Laoghaire Co Dublin **Tel: 01 280 1911** Fax: 01 280 1069
Email: info@greshamroyalmarinehotel.com Web: www.gresham-hotels.com

Overlooking Dublin Bay and the ferry port, this grand old Victorian hotel has ample parking and extensive landscaped gardens, yet it's only a twenty minute DART ride to the centre of Dublin. On entering the marble floored foyer a few steps take you up and through arched columns into the Bay Lounge (popular for afternoon teas) and the Powerscourt Restaurant. Eight bay-windowed suites have four-poster beds and free-standing antique furniture - a reminder of the age and character of the original building - but most rooms have fitted furniture and standard facilities, including neat bathrooms. Reflecting its popularity as a venue for functions, conferences and meetings, rooms on the executive floor provide extras for business travellers. Conference/banqueting (450/250). Garden. No pets. **Rooms 103** (8 junior suites, 55 executive, 20 no smoking, 2 for disabled). Lift. B&B from €70 pps, SC15%. Open all year. Amex Diners, MasterCard, Visa, Laser. **Directions:** Town centre, 200 yards from ferry terminal.

Dun Laoghaire

Mao Café Bar

CAFÉ The Pavilion Dun Laoghaire Co Dublin **Tel: 01 2148090** Fax: 01 214 7064

This large, informal contemporary café-restaurant near the harbour is a younger sister establishment to the popular Café Mao in the city centre, which was one of Dublin's first - and enduringly successful - fusion cafés. It is run on the same lines, with the philosophy of providing simple, quick and healthy food with youthful appeal at a reasonable price. Dishes with nuts are highlighted on the menu, also chilli strength, low fat and vegetarian dishes. Daily specials are particularly good value, and there's a daily cake selection - e.g. cappuccino with walnut gateau, toffee & apple gateau, pecan pie & Mississippi mud pie. It's a good place for brunch, with tables outside for fine weather. Open every day for coffee, lunch & dinner. Bookings accepted. Closed Christmas, Good Fri. MasterCard, Visa, Laser. **Directions:** Dun Laoghaire seafront, near station.

Dun Laoghaire

PUB

McCormack & Sons

67 Lr Mounttown Rd Dun Laoghaire Co Dublin
Tel: 01 280 5519 Fax: 01 280 0145 Email: cormak@iol.ie

This fine pub (and 'emporium') has been run by the McCormack family since 1960. It's one of the neatest pubs around, with a landscaped carpark creating a pleasant outlook for an imaginative conservatory extension at the back of the pub. The main part of the pub is full of traditional character and the whole place has a well-run hum about it. Good bar food cooked to order includes fresh fish available on the day as well as classics like home-made hamburger (with mixed leaf salad, fries & a choice of toppings), sandwiches and salads. Evening menus offer tasty light dishes: zucchini fritters, warm crispy bacon and croûton salad, and steak sandwiches alongside more substantial dishes including a fish special, a 10 oz sirloin steak (with mushroom and Irish whiskey sauce perhaps) or pasta dishes with fresh parmesan. No children after 7pm. Wheelchair accessible. Bar food daily, 12-10 (Sun from 12.30). Closed 25 Dec, Good Fri. Amex, MasterCard, Visa, Diners, Laser, Switch. **Directions:** Near Dun Laoghaire at Monkstown end.

Dun Laoghaire

RESTAURANT

Roly @ The Pavilion

8 The Pavilion Dun Laoghaire Co Dublin
Tel: 01 2360 286 Fax: 01 2360 288

Roly Saul's purpose-built restaurant just across the railway line from the Royal St George Yacht Club is full of light, with gleaming contemporary decor balanced by some traditional gilded mirrors and leather upholstery in white and a shade that now looks black but (appropriately enough) will age to a deep burgundy; different levels and a mixture of banquettes and high-back chairs are used to break the area up and give it interest and semi-private areas. It's a favourite haunt of many from the area (and beyond) who appreciate both the hospitality and the work of a youthful kitchen team, who relish the international cuisine, produce starters like rare tuna with ginger risotto spring roll & shitake broth, tian of crabmeat with guacamole & chilled gazpacho and mains of organic salmon, mussels, leek and diced potato stew or roast rump of lamb with chilli polenta chips, ratatouille & thyme jus. True to his philosophy of offering an accessible wine list and real value, Roly has managed to keep the (French) house wines to about €12.70 and the list has many other good bottles at fair prices. Outside eating area. Air conditioning. Not Suitable for children under 7 after 7 pm. **Seats 100.** L&D daily. Closed 25-27 Dec, Good Fri. Amex, MasterCard, Visa, Laser. **Directions:** Opposite Railway Station.

Glencullen

féile bia **ATMOSPHERIC PUB**

Johnnie Fox's Pub

Glencullen Co Dublin
Tel: 01 295 5647 Fax: 01 295 8911
Email: 7nights@johnniefoxs.com Web: www.johnniefoxs.com

Nestling in an attractive wooded hamlet in the Dublin Mountains, south of Dublin city, this popular pub dates back to the eighteenth century and has numerous claims to fame, including the fact that Daniel O'Connell was once a regular, apparently (he lived in Glencullen at one time), and it's "undoubtedly" the highest pub in the land. Whatever about that, it's a warm, friendly and generally well run place just about equally famous for its food - the "Famous Seafood Kitchen" - and its music - "Famous Hooley Nights" (booking advisable). Unlike so many superficially similar pubs that have popped up all over the world recently, it's also real. Kitsch, perhaps, but real nonetheless - the rickety old furniture is real, the dust is real and you certainly won't find a gas fire here - there's a lovely turf or log fire at every turn. It's a pleasant place to drop into at quieter times too, if you're walking in the hills or just loafing around and Dubliners find it an amusing place to take visitors from abroad. Reservations recommended for food. Own parking. Children welcome (under supervision). Traditional Irish music and dancing. Seats 350 (private room, 150). Open all day (food 12.30-9.30); all food à la carte, house wine about €19. No SC. Closed 25 Dec & Good Fri. Amex, Diners, MasterCard, Visa, Laser. **Directions:** In Dublin Mountains, 30 minutes drive from Dublin city centre.

Howth

ATMOSPHERIC PUB / RESTAURANT

Abbey Tavern

Abbey Street Howth Co Dublin
Tel: 01 839 0307 Fax: 01 839 0284
Email: info@abbeytavern.ie Web: www.abbeytavern.ie

Just 50 yards up from the harbour, part of this famous pub dates back to the 15th century, when it was built as a seminary for the local monks (as an addition to the 12th century Chapter House next door). Currently owned by James and Eithne Scott-Lennon - James' grandfather bought it in 1945 - the entire establishment was refurbished in 1998 but this well-run and immaculately maintained pub retains features that have always made the Abbey special - open turf fires, original stone walls, flagged floors and gas lights. In 1960 the Abbey started to lay on entertainment and this, more than anything else, has brought the tavern its fame: it can cater for groups of anything between two and 200 and the format, which now runs like clockwork, is a traditional 5-course dinner followed by traditional Irish music. It's on every night but booking is essential, especially in high season. Bar food such as Howth seafood chowder, smoked salmon with home-made brown bread, a hot traditional dish such as corned beef and cabbage, and ploughman's salad is available at lunchtime. The first floor restaurant, The Abbot, is entered through the bar or separate entrance from the street, a wide carpeted staircase leads to a series of semi open-plan rooms on slightly different levels, with open turf fires and decor which has been gently updated (muslin drapes, wall lights, soft cream and dark green paint) and white-clothed tables set up in classic style - a welcoming sight. Fresh fish from the harbour. Restaurant **Seats 75.** D only, Mon-Sat, 7.-10.30. A la carte. House wine €18. Restaurant closed Sun. Banqueting for 200.

Abbot Restaurant: In 1956 a restaurant was opened, quite a novel move in a pub at the time; it is now called The Abbot and has its own separate entrance. Attractively and comfortably refurbished in keeping with the building, with open turf fires at both ends of the main room, it makes a fine setting for food which is generally well-cooked and not over-complicated - despite the fact that the house speciality "Sole Abbey", is an old-fashioned dish of sole fillets stuffed with prawns, mushrooms & herbs, served with a cream hollandaise sauce. Simpler dishes are usually the wisest choice. **Seats 70.** (private room, 40) Air conditioning. D only 7-10.30 Mon-Sat, all à la carte, house wine €16. SC discretionary Children welcome; carpark on harbour. Restaurant closed Sun; establishment closed 25-26 Dec & Good Fri. Amex, Diners, MasterCard, Visa, Laser. **Directions:** 9 miles from Dublin, in the centre of Howth.

Howth

Aqua Restaurant

RESTAURANT

1 West Pier Howth Co Dublin **Tel: 01 8320 690** Fax: 01 8320 687
Email: dine@aqua.ie Web: www.aqua.ie

In a stunning sea and harbourside location at the end of the west pier, overlooking the island of Ireland's Eye and with views west towards Malahide, this building was previously a yacht club and has been sensitively converted by the current owners to make a fine contemporary restaurant with plenty of window tables. Behind a glass screen, head chef Brian Daly and his team provide entertainment as well as zesty cooking of colourful food that is thoughtfully but quite simply presented - a refreshing change from the overworked presentation in many restaurants at the moment. What was once a snooker room is now a characterful bar - with an open fire and comfortable seating, it has retained a cosy, clubby atmosphere. Brian Daly's style of cooking is strong, simple and modern; he favours seafood strongly, notably lobster, but dry aged steak - with grilled peppers, roasted baby potatoes, balsamic vinegar and extra virgin olive oil, perhaps - is also a speciality. Menus offer a pleasing repertoire of broadly Cal-Ital origin - crostini of Serrano ham with rocket, asparagus & extra virgin oil, char-grilled breast of chicken with roasted corn salsa, red pepper coulis, herb oil - although changes could be introduced more often with benefit, to give new choices to a loyal local clientèle. The waterside location, well-sourced ingredients, skilful cooking and solicitous service all make dining at Aqua a pleasure; à la carte menus are pricey but well-balanced set menus (early dinner, lunch and the popular Sunday jazz brunch), offer good value. **Seats 100.** D Tue-Sat 5.30-10.30, Sun 6-9.30; L Sun 12.30-4 (Bar L Tue-Sat, 1-3). Early D from €19.95, Set Sun L €26.95. Also à la carte. House wine €21. SC discretionary. Closed Mon, 25 Dec, Good Fri. Amex, MasterCard, Visa, Laser. **Directions:** Left along pier after Howth DART Station.

Howth

Casa Pasta

RESTAURANT

12 Harbour Road Howth Co Dublin
Tel: 01 839 3823 Fax: 01 839 3104

Unbeatable atmosphere is what sets this first floor restaurant overlooking Howth harbour apart, and although this was partly due to its tiny size, doubling it in 1998 didn't diminish its appeal - it's still notoriously hard to get into, especially at weekends. The secret of Casa Pasta's success is its universal appeal for all age groups - it's the ideal place for family outings, with swift, good humoured young servers and blackboard menus featuring youthful international food (lots of pastas and salads) that is neither over-ambitious nor over-priced - although cooking standards might improve if the choice were reduced. Regulars that locals happily order without even consulting the menu include runny deep-fried brie with spicy chutney, big Caesar salads (possibly with slivers of chicken breast), home-made tagliatelle with mixed seafood in a creamy wine sauce - and desserts like gooey, boozy tiramisu and sticky banoffi pie. Wines are not quite as cheap and cheerful (house wine about €15.95) as might be hoped, given the style of food and surroundings. Children welcome: on Thursdays "kids eat free" (1 child under 10 per adult; 6-8pm) Open daily D 6-11, (Sun 12-10). A la carte, 10% SC on parties of 6+. Closed 25 Dec, Good Fri. Also at: 55 Clontarf Road, Dublin 3. Tel/Fax: 01 833 1402; Eirpage House,

Donnybrook, Dublin 4. Tel: 01 2608108. Amex, MasterCard, Visa, Laser, Switch. **Directions:** Harbour front, overlooking Howth Yacht Club.

Howth

Deer Park Hotel & Golf Courses

féile bia HOTEL

Howth Co Dublin **Tel: 01 832 2624**
Fax: 01 839 2405 Email: sales@deerpark.iol.ie

Set high up on the Hill of Howth, in the midst of Ireland's largest golf complex, the Deer Park Hotel enjoys wonderful views across Howth demesne (of which it is part) to the islands of Ireland's Eye and Lambay - and, on a clear day, right up the coast to the distant Mournes. Golf breaks are a particular attraction, especially in summer, and that guarantees that the hotel is always busy - also, perhaps, why it is so well-worn. However, although far from sumptuous, this makes a scenic base for anyone visiting the area. (Howth has lost several hotels to apartment developments recently, and an establishment aspiring to cater for discerning travellers is badly needed.) Golf (5 courses). Indoor swimming pool, sauna and steam room; all-weather tennis courts (2). Parking. Children welcome. Wheelchair accessible. No pets. **Rooms 80** (all en-suite) B&B from about €80. Closed Christmas. Amex, Diners, MasterCard, Visa. **Directions:** Follow coast road from the city centre to Howth, on right before reaching Howth Harbour.

Howth

King Sitric Fish Restaurant & Accommodation

féile bia RESTAURANT WITH ROOMS

East Pier Howth Co Dublin
Tel: 01 832 5235 Fax: 01 839 2442
Email: info@kingsitric.ie Web: www.kingsitric.com

Aidan and Joan MacManus' striking harbourside restaurant is named after an 11th century Norse King of Dublin who had close links with Howth and was a cousin of the legendary Brian Boru. It is one of Dublin's longest established fine dining restaurants - and, from its East Pier site, chef-patron Aidan MacManus can keep an eye on his lobster pots in Balscadden Bay on one side and the fishing boats coming into harbour on the other. Completely re-built in the recent past, this traditional restaurant has blossomed into a fine contemporary space, with first floor dining to take full advantage of the views (notably at lunch, which is especially good value too). Aidan's reputation for cooking seafood (and the excellent sauces that accompany) is of course what brings most people to The King Sitric, and lovers of game also wend their way here in winter, when it is likely to feature on both lunch and dinner menus. Always interested in using the best of local produce, informative notes on menu covers state the restaurant's commitment to local producers, some of whom are named, and gives a listing of Irish fish in six languages. Some specialities worth making a bee-line for include a luscious red velvet crab bisque, crab mayonnaise and calmar frites with tartare or tomato sauce; less well known seafood, such as locally fished razor shell clams in garlic butter, often shares the menu with classics like sole meunière and Dublin lawyer (lobster with sauce Dublin lawyer) - and make sure you leave room for the house dessert, meringue Sitric. But wine interests Aidan MacManus every bit as much as food; he has long had one of the country's finest wine lists, with an especially fine selection of Chablis, magnificent burgundies and a special love of the wine of Alsace. Hence a very special feature of the King Sitric: a temperature controlled wine cellar on the ground floor, where tastings are held. It is cleverly incorporated into the reception area, with only a glass door between them so diners, can enjoy the ambience while having aperitifs, or spill over to use stools around the table in the cellar area if the restaurant is very busy. The house wine, Pinot Blanc Cuvée Les Amours Hugel (a special reserve for the King Sitric) is outstanding for both quality and value. The King Sitric received the Guide's Wine List of the Year Award in 2001 and the restaurant operates a Food & Wine Club off-season. Banqueting (75). **Seats 70** (private room, 30). Air conditioning. L Mon-Fri,12.30-2.15; D Mon-Sat, 6.30-10. Set L from €22. 'Value' D €30 (Mon-Thu all year, no time restrictions); Set D from €49; also à la carte; house wine from €21; SC discretionary. Closed L Sat, all Sun, bank hols, last 2 weeks Jan.

Accommodation: There are eight lovely rooms, all with sea views and individually designed bathrooms. Rooms 8 (all no-smoking). B&B from €66 pps (penthouse, €92.25), ss €26. Amex, MasterCard, Visa, Laser, Switch. **Directions:** Far end of the harbour front, facing the east pier.

Howth

The Waterside & The Wheelhouse Restaurant

RESTAURANT / PUB

Harbour Road Howth Co Dublin
Tel: 01 839 0555 Fax: 01 839 3632

The ground floor of this attractive premises overlooking the harbour front is one of the pleasantest bars in the area - well-run, comfortable and full of character (although it can be very busy, especially at weekends). Upstairs, on the first floor, the Wheelhouse Restaurant is friendly and welcoming, with a cosy ambience and moderately priced middle-of-the-road food. They offer a wide choice on menus that naturally include a large selection of local fish dishes - but they're also known for good steaks and meat dishes; specialities include rack of Kildare lamb with honey & mustard crust, so non-fish eaters will be well looked after too. Main course dishes are consistently reliable and this is a popular neighbourhood restaurant. Children welcome. Car parking nearby. **Seats 60.** Air conditioning. D only (in restaurant) 6.30-10 daily. Bar Food also available. Closed 25 Dec, Good Fri. Amex, Diners, MasterCard, Visa. **Directions:** On Howth harbour front.

Howth/Sutton Area

Marine Hotel

HOTEL

Sutton Cross Dublin 13 Co Dublin **Tel: 01 839 0000** Fax: 01 839 0442
Email: info@marinehotel.ie Web: www.marinehotel.ie

Well-located on the sea side of a busy junction, this attractive hotel has ample car parking in front and a lawn reaching down to the foreshore at the rear. Recently renovated public areas give a good impression: a smart foyer and adjacent bar, an informal conservatory style seating area overlooking the garden and a well-appointed restaurant. Bedrooms, some of which have sea views, have recently been refurbished. A popular venue for conferences and social gatherings, especially weddings, the Marine is also the only hotel in this area providing for the business guest. Business centre; secretarial services. Conference/banqueting (80/190). Indoor swimming pool. Garden. Children welcome (under 5 free in parents' room; cots available, baby sitting arranged). No pets. **Rooms 48** (4 shower only, 27 executive rooms, 8 no-smoking, 2 disabled). Lift. 24 hour room service. B&B €90 pps, ss €30. Closed 25 Dec. Amex, MasterCard, Visa, Laser. **Directions:** Take coast road towards Howth from city centre, on right at Sutton Cross.

Killiney

Fitzpatrick Castle Dublin

HOTEL

Killiney Co Dublin **Tel: 01 230 5400** Fax: 01 230 5430
Email: dublin@fitzpatricks.com Web: www.fitzpatrickshotels.com

Located in the fashionable suburb of Killiney, this imposing castellated mansion overlooking Dublin Bay dates back to 1741. It is surrounded by landscaped gardens and, despite its size and grand style, has a relaxed atmosphere. Spacious bedrooms combine old-world charm with modern facilities, and a fitness centre has a 22 metre pool, jacuzzi, spa and relaxation deck. Although perhaps best known as a leading conference and function venue, Fitzpatrick's also caters especially well for business guests and 'The Crown Club', on the 5th floor functions as a 'hotel within a hotel', offering pre-arranged private transfer from the airport and a wide range of facilities for business guests. Five championship golf courses, including Druid's Glen, are nearby. Garden. Lift. **Rooms 113.** B&B about €130 pps. Closed 24-26 Dec. Amex, Diners, MasterCard, Visa, Laser. **Directions:** Take M50 from the airport, follow signs for Dun Laoghaire ferry port; south to Dalkey - top of Killiney hill.

Leixlip

Becketts Country House Hotel

HOTEL / RESTAURANT

Cooldrinagh House Leixlip Co Dublin
Tel: 01 624 7040 Fax: 01 624 7072

A handsome house on the County Dublin side of the river that divides Leixlip, this house was once the home of Samuel Beckett's mother and it is now an unusual hotel, offering a personalised service for business guests: from the moment you arrive a butler looks after all your needs, whether it be dining, laundry, limousine facilities or tailored requirements for meetings or conferences. Imaginatively converted to its present use, luxurious accommodation includes four boardroom suites and six executive suites, all furnished to a high standard in a lively contemporary style. All have a workstation equipped for computers, including modem/Internet connection and audio visual equipment, private fax machines etc. are also available on request. Public areas, including a bar and a stylish modern restaurant, have a far less business-like atmosphere. Cooldrinagh House overlooks the Eddie Hackett-designed Leixlip golf course, for which golf tee off times may be booked in advance. Conference/banqueting (350/250) Business centre/secretarial services. Wheelchair accessible. No pets. **Rooms 10** (4 suites, 6 executive rooms) B&B about €70. Open all year. Amex, Diners, MasterCard, Visa. **Directions:** Take N4, turn off at Spa Hotel, next left after Springfield Hotel.

Lucan

Finnstown Country House Hotel

HOTEL

Newcastle Road Lucan Co Dublin **Tel: 01 601 0700** Fax: 01 628 1088
Email: manager@finnstown-hotel.ie Web: www.finnstown-hotel.ie

Very much the hub of local activities, this fine old manor house set in 45 acres of woodland is impressive, but also full of charm. An open fire in the foyer sets a welcoming tone and all of the large, well-proportioned reception rooms - drawing room, restaurant, bar - are elegantly furnished in a traditional style well-suited to the house. Although quite grand, there is a comfortable lived-in feeling throughout. Bedrooms include some studio suites, with a small fridge and toaster in addition to the standard tea/coffee making facilities, and all rooms have good facilities including full bathrooms (with bath and shower). Residential golf breaks are a speciality. Conference/banqueting (300/200). Business centre; secretarial services. Leisure centre. Swimming pool. Tennis. Snooker; pool. Newsagent. Children welcome (Under 3 free in parents' room; cots available, baby sitting arranged). Pets permitted by arrangement. Own parking. Wheelchair accessible. **Rooms 53** (28 executive, 8 no-smoking, 1 for disabled). B&B €89, ss €32. Open all year. Amex, Diners, MasterCard, Visa, Laser. **Directions:** Off main Dublin-Galway Road (N4): take exit for Newcastle off dual carriageway.

Malahide

Beanos

RESTAURANT

1-3 The Green Malahide Co Dublin
Tel: 01 806 1880 Fax: 01 806 1881 Web: www.beanos.net

This contemporary bar and restaurant may look like an office block from the road, but the interior is pleasing and some tables have views over the marina. Welcoming staff give a good impression, and a deep red used selectively in lights, carpet and a feature create a warm atmosphere. Menus are simple and appealingly informal, split into five sections for appetisers, pizza & pasta, main courses - and a whole section on burgers - but this may not do the food justice: Beano's pizza, for example, is on a thin, crisp base topped with prawn tails, capers, red onion & tomato, while the mains are modern classics - tuna, salmon, fillet steak, chicken breast - simply cooked and attractively presented with roasted vegetables and interesting salads. Desserts tend towards the updated traditional - like pistachio flavoured bread & butter pudding, or there's an Irish cheese board to finish. Average main course about €18-22, but pizzas and burgers much less. Air conditioning. Not suitable for children after 8 pm. **Seats 100.** Open all day (12-10.30); short bar lunch menu 12-5; 'Value' D €30; otherwise D à la carte, 5-10.30. House wine from €18.50. SC discretionary. Closed 25 Dec. Amex, Diners, MasterCard, Visa, Laser. **Directions:** Facing the marina in Malahide Village.

Malahide

Bon Appetit

RESTAURANT

9 St James Terrace Malahide Co Dublin **Tel: 01 8450 314**
Fax: 01 8450 314 Email: info@bonappetit.ie Web: www.bonappetit.ie

In a Georgian terrace near the marina, Patsy McGuirk's highly-regarded basement restaurant is warmly decorated in shades of red and gold, enhanced by a collection of local watercolours - and there's a welcome emphasis on comfort. Patsy McGuirk is a very fine chef in the classic French style, sometimes tempered by Mediterranean and modern Irish influences; many years in the kitchen have resulted in a long list of specialities, each as tempting as the next, although if a choice had to be made it is probably his fish cookery that would top the bill - seafood, mostly from nearby Howth, predominates on menus although steaks, Wicklow lamb, farmyard duckling and ostrich, which is farmed nearby, also feature. Fresh prawn bisque with cognac is a regular and a long-established house speciality is Sole Creation McGuirk (whole boned black sole, filled with turbot and prawns, in a beurre blanc sauce), a dish so gloriously old-fashioned that it's now come full circle, while simple sole on the bone is presented whole at the table, then re-presented bone-free and neatly reassembled. Delicious roast crispy duckling Grand Marnier on a potato & herb stuffing is another speciality, also ostrich - medallions, perhaps, served on champ with onion marmalade and port wine jus. It's worth leaving room for pretty desserts: fresh strawberries in a crisp filo basket, sliced and sprinkled with Grand Marnier is typical, or there's an Irish cheese platter - and petits fours with your coffee. A fine wine list has its heart in France; there are helpful tasting notes and a special selection, as well as six fairly priced house wines. While not inexpensive, prices have held steady at the Bon Appetit; the set lunch menu is particularly good value. Not suitable for children under 12. Booking essential, especially for dinner. Small weddings catered for. **Seats 60** (private room, 20) Air conditioning. L Mon-Fri.12.30-2, D Mon-Sat 7-10; Set L €25, Set D €45, also à la carte; house wine from €20; SC discretionary. Closed Sun, bank hols & several days at Christmas. Amex, Diners, MasterCard, Visa, Laser. **Directions:** Coming from Dublin go through the lights and turn left into St James's Terrace at Malahide Garda Station.

Malahide

Cruzzo Bar & Restaurant

RESTAURANT

The Marina Malahide Co Dublin **Tel: 01 845 0599** Fax: 01 845 0602
Email: info@cruzzo.ie Web: www.cruzzo.ie

Built on a platform over the water, this attractive bar and restaurant is large and stylish in Florida style, with views over the marina. The interior is dashing, with a bar on the lower floor and a rather grand staircase rising to the main dining areas above, which are comfortable and well-appointed, with well-spaced tables in interesting groupings. Chef Tom Meenaghan, previously executive chef at Conran's Mezzo in London, presents contemporary menus of which Parma ham with niçoise salad and grilled black pudding with confit potato & shallot dressing are typical starters while main courses might include a couple of imaginative vegetarian choices, contemporary fish dishes like seared seabass with stir fried vegetables & black bean ginger jus and some dishes leaning towards comfort food - slow roast leg of lamb, for example, with creamed butter beans and beef tomato. Although prices on the à la carte are quite high (and vegetables are charged extra), the early dinner menu is exceptionally good value. **Seats 280.** L Tue-Sat 12.30-2.30, Sun 12.30-3; D Tue-Sun 6-10.15 (Sun to 10). Early D Mon-Fri, €14-19 (6-7pm); D also à la carte. Live music Tue, Fri & Sat. House wine from €21.50. SC discretionary. Closed Mon (except L on bank hols), 25-26 Dec, Good Fri. Amex, Diners, MasterCard, Visa, Laser. **Directions:** From Malahide Village through arch into Marina.

Malahide

Grand Hotel

HOTEL

Malahide Co Dublin **Tel: 01 845 0000** Fax: 01 845 0987
Email: info@thegrand.ie Web: www.thegrand.ie

Just 8 miles from Dublin airport in one of Ireland's most attractive coastal towns, The Grand Hotel is well-situated for business and pleasure; set in six acres of gardens, the original building at the heart of this large hotel dates back to 1835, which gives it a certain gravitas. Recent additions have included an excellent leisure centre and extensive conference and banqueting facilities. Many of the bedrooms have sea views, the beach (a tidal estuary) is just across the road, there are numerous golf courses nearby - also numerous other activities, including equestrian, fishing, tennis and watersports - and there is much of interest within walking distance in the town. Special breaks offered. Conference/banqueting (450/380). Business centre. Leisure centre (21 metre swimming pool, jacuzzi, gym). Own parking. Wheelchair accessible. Children welcome (under 12 free in parents' room; cots available, baby sitting arranged). No pets. **Rooms 150** (2 suites, 7 junior suites, 39 executive, 15 shower only, 60 no-smoking, 1 for disabled). Lift. B&B €175 pps. ss €85. Closed 24-27 Dec. Amex, Diners, MasterCard, Visa, Laser. **Directions:** Centre of Malahide; near Dublin Airport and about 30 mins from Dublin city centre.

Malahide

Jaipur

Ⓝ **RESTAURANT**

St. James's Terrace Malahide Co Dublin **Tel: 01 845 5455**

This chic new-wave Indian restaurant is the third Jaipur - the others are in Dublin 2 and Dalkey; it's in the basement of a fine Georgian terrace and, although Malahide is particularly well-served with interesting eating places, it has caused quite a stir. Cooking is crisp and modern - a contemporary take on traditional Indian food; head chef Sunil Ghai trained in the five-star Oberoi hotel in New Dehli and it shows in colourful, well-flavoured dishes that have a lot of eye appeal. Vegetarian choices are particularly appealing, old favourites like tandoori prawns take well to the contemporary treatment and even desserts - usually a total no-no in ethnic restaurants - are worth leaving room for. Meals: D daily, 5.30-11.30. (Early D 5-7pm). Amex, MasterCard, Visa, Laser. **Directions:** In Georgian terrace facing the tennis club in Malahide.

Malahide

Le Restaurant 12A

RESTAURANT

12 A New Street Malahide Co Dublin **Tel: 01 806 1928**
Email: jasonmccabe@ireland.com

Although not French-owned, this chic little restaurant is in the contemporary French style - clean-lined, with crisp linen and fine modern crystal - with a menu in the window to entice you in. The menu is sensibly limited to about half a dozen dishes on each course, which might typically include starters like rillette of pork & caramelised apple or marinated brochette of Dublin Bay prawns with a lime & rocket salad and main courses such as fresh loin of yellow fin tuna with niçoise salad and chargrilled fillet of beef bourguignonne style; vegetables are charged extra. Tempting desserts might include a simple crumble like apple & blueberry, with vanilla ice cream or summer pudding with fromage frais, or there's a European cheeseboard. Accurate cooking, attractive presentation and friendly, willing service make for an enjoyable occasion, although the pricing structure can make it quite an expensive outing - a competitively priced early dinner menu would be an attraction. **Seats 46.** D only, Tue-Sun 6-10. A la carte. House wine about €16. SC discretionary. Closed Mon, 3 weeks Jan. Amex, MasterCard, Visa, Laser. **Directions:** Opposite Gibneys pub, Malahide town centre.

Malahide — Siam Thai Restaurant

RESTAURANT Gas Lane Malahide Co Dublin **Tel: 01 845 4698** Fax: 01 8169460 Email: siam@eircom.net Web: www.siamthai.ie

Handily located in a laneway close to the marina, this large restaurant was one of Dublin's earlier Thai restaurants and still regularly fills its tightly-packed tables. Suracheto Yoodsang, head chef since 1996, presents menus that offer many of the Thai classics on an extensive à la carte as well as the set menus and, although perhaps blanded down a bit for local tastes, there's a willingness to vary the spiciness according to personal preference. Siam Combination Appetizers (including chicken satay, spring rolls, special coated prawns, marinated pork ribs, prawns wrapped in ham and bags of golden wonton with plum sauce) usually make a good beginning, followed by main courses like Ghung Phad Phong Garee (Tiger prawns with scallions, mushrooms and basil leaves and a spicy sauce) and Ped Makham (boneless crisp-skinned duck with crispy noodles and plum sauce). Staff are friendly, knowledgeable and efficient. No monosodium glutamate is used. Children welcome. Air conditioning. Piano at weekends. **Seats 105.** D daily 5-11.30. Early D €18; Set D €28-32; à la carte available. House wine €19.50. SC 10%. Closed 25-26 Dec & Good Fri. Amex, Diners, MasterCard, Visa, Laser. **Directions:** In Malahide village, near marina; turn left at Church to end of road.

Malahide — Silks

RESTAURANT 5 The Mall Malahide Co Dublin **Tel: 01 845 3331**

This smart Chinese restaurant is spacious, modern and airy, with cheerful decor and staff who are friendly and helpful, to match. Although the long menu offers no major surprises, the food is well above average and can show imagination and flair. Sizzlers and sweet & sours are there, but they are expertly done using quality ingredients, especially the seafood. Excellent crispy Peking duck with pancakes or a light, delicately spiced chicken and mushroom broth make good starters followed, perhaps, by fresh-flavoured main courses of crunchy salt & chilli squid and prawns with ginger and spring onions. Cantonese-style chicken is a speciality - tender slices of chicken in a light, fruit-based sauce with just a hint of spiciness - and desserts are unsurprising: banana fritters with an above average vanilla ice cream, perhaps, or a simple bowl of lychees. Reservations are essential as this restaurant has a loyal following and is busy every night of the week. **Seats 90** (private room 20). Air conditioning. D daily: Mon-Sat 6-12.30. Sun 5-11. A la carte. **Directions:** Opposite Garda Station.

Monkstown — Empress Restaurant

RESTAURANT Clifton Avenue Monkstown Co Dublin **Tel: 01 284 3200** Fax: 01 284 3188

Over more than a decade, owner-chef Burt Tsang has earned a strong local following for this pleasant first-floor restaurant just off Monkstown Crescent. A warm welcome and charming, efficient service complement regional Chinese dishes - Sichuan, Shandong and Beijing - plus Thai and Vietnamese cuisine, offered in set dinners for varying numbers in addition to an à la carte. Specialities include Beijing duck, carved at the table and served with fresh vegetables and hoi sin sauce on pancakes, which requires 24 hours notice. Thai dishes may may seem to have been blanded down for local tastes but cooking overall is consistently good, presentation attractive and prices reasonable; a good choice of vegetarian options is always available, typically Thai vegetable curries. D 6-12 Mon-Sat; Sun open from 3pm. MasterCard, Visa. **Directions:** Just off the Crescent.

Monkstown — The Purty Kitchen

ATMOSPHERIC PUB Old Dunleary Road Monkstown Co Dublin **Tel: 01 284 3576** Fax: 01 284 3576 Email: c-cm@iol.ie Web: purtykitchen.com

Established in 1728 - making it the second oldest pub in Dublin (after The Brazen Head) and the oldest in Dun Laoghaire - this attractive old place has seen some changes recently, but its essential character remains and it's well set up for enjoyment of the bar food for which it has earned a good reputation. Old favourites like the famous Purty Kitchen seafood chowder and Purty Seafood Platter are still there, but there's also creative cooking to be found here: smart little menus offer contemporary dishes like cous cous salad with black olives, peppers, sundried tomatoes and melted mozzarella alongside the more traditional bar food; more substantial dishes include 'all day breakfast', home-made beef burgers with salad and baked black sole, on or off the bone, all at reasonable prices. Bar food 12 noon-10pm daily. Amex, Diners, MasterCard, Visa, Laser.

Portmarnock

Portmarnock Hotel & Golf Links

HOTEL / RESTAURANT

Strand Road Portmarnock Co Dublin
Tel: 01 846 0611 Fax: 01 846 2442
Email: sales@portmarnock.com Web: www.portmarnock.com

Originally owned by the Jameson family, Portmarnock Hotel and Golf Links enjoys a wonderful beachside position overlooking the islands of Lambay and Ireland's Eye. Very close to the airport, and only eleven miles from Dublin city centre, the hotel seems to offer the best of every world - the peace and convenience of the location and a magnificent 18 hole Bernhard Langer-designed links course. Public areas, including an impressive foyer, are bright and spacious, with elegant modern decor and a relaxed atmosphere. The Jameson Bar, in the old house, has character and there's also an informal Links Bar and Restaurant next to the golf shop (open 12-9.30 daily). Accommodation is imaginatively designed so that all rooms have sea or golf course views, and all - including some in the original house which are furnished with antiques, two with four-posters and executive rooms with balconies or bay windows - are furnished to a high standard of comfort, with excellent bathrooms. Conference/banqueting (350/220) Business centre; secretarial services. Golf (18). Oceana, health & beauty, offers: gym, sauna, steam rooms & a wide range of treatments. Children welcome (under 3 free in parents' room, cots available without charge, baby sitting arranged). No pets. Garden. **Rooms 100** (17 executive, 16 no-smoking, 4 for disabled). Lift. 24 hour room service. B&B €155 pps, ss €75. Open all year.

☆ **The Osborne Restaurant:** Named after the artist Walter Osborne, who painted many of his most famous pictures in the area including the view from the Jameson house, the restaurant has been a major addition to the north Dublin dining scene since the hotel opened in 1996. Mark Doe, previously at Kilkea Castle, joined the hotel as executive chef in 2003 and the high standard set by his predecessors has been maintained. The room is very formal, with beautifully appointed tables and fresh flowers, and menus are constructed with the discerning international traveller in mind, making full use of the best quality ingredients available - especially seafood from the nearby fishing port of Howth. Food quality and cooking are reliably excellent, with great attention to detail - a duo of hot and cold foie gras comes with a brioche, plum & mango compôte & a little apple salad, for example, while beautifully tender loin of mountain lamb is wrapped in rösti and served with a delicious goat cheese crostini; presentation is notable for its formality - and, like the room itself, might benefit from relaxing a little. Attentive, helpful service by knowledgeable, well-trained staff. Luscious desserts include a signature dish of grilled white peaches with mascarpone cheese & pistachio biscotti. Air conditioning. **Seats 80** (private room, 22). D only Tue-Sat, 7-10. Set D from €45, Tasting Menu from €70. A la carte available; house wine from €18.95; SC discretionary. Closed Sun, Mon. Amex, Diners, MasterCard, Visa, Laser. **Directions:** On the coast in Portmarnock.

Saggart

Citywest Hotel Conference Leisure & Golf Resort

féile bia HOTEL

Saggart Co Dublin **Tel: 01 4010 500** Fax: 01 4588 756
Email: info@citywesthotel.com Web: www.citywesthotel.com

Only about 25 minutes from the city centre and Dublin airport (traffic permitting), this large hotel was planned with the needs of the rapidly expanding western edge of the capital in mind. It is set in its own estate, which includes two 18-hole golf courses and a comprehensive leisure centre with a large deck level swimming pool and a wide range of health and beauty facilities. The other big attraction is the hotel's banqueting, conference and meeting facilities, which include a convention centre catering for 6,500 delegates, making Citywest one of the largest venues in the country. All round, a much-needed amenity for West Dublin. Conference/banqueting (6,500/2,200); secretarial services, video-conferencing. Leisure centre, swimming pool. Hairdressing/beauty salon. Children welcome (under 6 free in parents' room, cots available free of charge). **Rooms 333.** Lift. B&B about €75 pps. Open all year.

Terrace Room: Well-appointed large restaurant serving above-average food at fair prices. **Seats 110.** Air conditioning. Children welcome. L Mon-Fri, D daily. Set D €40, house wine €18.40. Amex, MasterCard, Visa, Laser. **Directions:** Off Naas Road - N7 (from Dublin, take left after Independent printers & follow road for about a mile.

Sandycove — Provence

RESTAURANT 1 Martello Terrace Sandycove Co Dublin **Tel: 01 280 8788** Fax: 0404 45702

This appealing restaurant on the Dun Laoghaire seafront changed ownership shortly before the Guide went to press last year, taking on a new name and a colourful new livery. There was a good foundation in the kitchen, however, as the head chef (who had been with the restaurant, previously Southbank, since 1981) stayed on and has been very much involved in the gradual shift towards a more definitely French style - something which suited this classical kitchen well. Fresh produce, used with respect, has remained the ethos - and proficient, gimmick-free cooking, personal, friendly service and good value. Expect sound renditions of classics like moules marinières, chicken chasseur, plaice with lemon butter, and crème caramel and you should not be disappointed. A keenly priced midweek menu, offered without time restriction, offers particularly good value. Not suitable for children under 8. **Seats 45.** D Tue-Sat (and Sun in summer) 6.30-9.30. A la carte. House wine €18. Closed Mon, also Sun in winter, bank hols. Amex, MasterCard, Visa, Laser. **Directions:** From Dun Laoghaire, take coast road to Sandycove; restaurant is on the right.

Skerries — Red Bank House & Restaurant

RESTAURANT / GUESTHOUSE 5-7 Church Street Skerries Co Dublin
Tel: 01 849 1005 Fax: 01 849 1598
Email: redbank@eircom.net Web: www.redbank.ie

There's a double-entendre to the name of Terry and Margaret McCoy's restaurant - not only is there a sandbank of the same name nearby, but it's also in a converted banking premises, which makes a restaurant of character and practicality - even the old vault has its uses: as a wine cellar. A warm welcome, with aperitifs and crudités served in a comfortable bar/reception area, gets arriving guests off to a good start, and it's a pleasant place to consider Terry's high individual menus before heading through to the traditional restaurant. One of the great characters of contemporary Irish cooking, Terry is an avid supporter of local produce and suppliers and fresh seafood from Skerries harbour (including local razor fish) provides the backbone of his menus, but without limiting the vision - this is a man who goes out at dawn with a bucket to gather young nettles for soup. Dishes conceived and cooked with generosity have names of local relevance - thus, for example, grilled goats cheese St. Patrick is a reminder that the saint once lived on Church Island off Skerries. The dessert trolley is legendary (perhaps the traditional adjective 'groaning' should apply to the diners - a large space should be left if pudding is to be part of your meal). Should the sauces and accompaniments prove too much, plainly cooked food is provided on request and dishes suitable for vegetarians are marked on the menu. No smoking area. **Seats 55** (private room,10). D Mon-Sat, 6.30-10; L Sun only, 12.30-4.30. Early D €30 (6.30-8); Set D €39, Set Sun L €26. A la carte also available. Interesting selection of about two dozen house wines €20-28; sc discretionary. Children welcome. Closed D Sun, 24-27 Dec.

Accommodation: As well as comfortably furnished bedrooms with all the amenities normally expected of an hotel - twelve new ones were opened in 2003 - there are facilities for private parties (50). Gourmet golf breaks are a speciality. Children under 5 free in parents' room (cots available free of charge). Pets permitted by arrangement. **Rooms 18** (all no-smoking). B&B €55 pps, ss €10. Open all year. Amex, Diners, MasterCard, Visa, Laser, Switch. **Directions:** Opposite AIB Bank in Skerries.

Stillorgan — Beaufield Mews Restaurant & Gardens

RESTAURANT Woodlands Avenue Stillorgan Co Dublin
Tel: 01 288 0375 Fax: 01 288 6949
Email: beaumews@iol.ie Web: www.beaufieldmews.com

Dublin's oldest restaurant is located in a characterful 18th century coachhouse and stables - and, as the name implies, it is surrounded by beautiful mature gardens where guests can have an aperitif on the lawn before dinner, or take coffee afterwards, as they are lit up by night. The effect in a built-up area is quite startling, as you are just a few hundred yards off one of Dublin's busiest roads and yet, with its mature trees, spacious surroundings and old-fashioned feeling in both the buildings and gardens, you could be forgiven for thinking you have been mysteriously transported to the country - there's even an antique shop where guests are encouraged to have a browse before dining (Open 3-9pm). This impression has been reinforced by recent changes - including the installation of a new 'Hayloft' bar and a new 'garden' look for the restaurant: atmosphere really is the trump card at this legendary restaurant and the cooking style and courteous service are in tune with the old-fashioned surroundings. Good wine list. Not suitable for children after 8pm. **Seats 200** (private room, 60). D Tue-Sat, 6.30-10; L Sun only, 12.30-2.30. Closed Mon, bank hols, Good Fri. Amex, Diners, MasterCard, Visa, Laser. **Directions:** 4 miles from city centre, off Stillorgan dual carriageway.

Stillorgan

China-Sichuan Restaurant

RESTAURANT

4 Lower Kilmacud Road Stillorgan Co Dublin
Tel: 01 288 4817 Fax: 01 288 0882

David Hui's unique restaurant runs in co-operation with the cultural exchange programme of the State-run China Sichuan Catering Service Company, which supplies chefs and special spices direct from Sichuan province. Since 1986 their refusal to 'bland-down' the style to suit local tastes has earned the restaurant widespread recognition for authenticity. Strong flavours are a characteristic of Sichuan cuisine, and spicy and chilli-hot dishes are identified here on menus - 'Bon Bon Chicken' for example, is a dish of cold chicken shreds in a hot and spicy sauce - but spicing can be varied to suit individual tastes. A speciality worth seeking out is smoked duckling in Sichuan style (€19.05): seasoned duck is smoked over bay leaves, camphor wood and black Chinese tea leaves, then served hot with plum sauce as a dip; count your blessings when enjoying this dish at it is not widely available, even in London - which may seem the most cosmopolitan of cities yet it has no Sichuan restaurant. While set menus are relatively limited (especially at lunch time), the à la carte offers plenty to tempt the most jaded palate including a wide range of seafood dishes and a particularly strong vegetarian section. Children welcome. **Seats 60.** Air conditioning. L Mon-Fri 12.30-2.30, L Sun (& bank hols) 1-2.30. D daily 6-11. Set L about €15, Set D about €32; à la carte available; house wine about €15; SC10%. Toilets wheelchair accessible. Closed L Sat, 25-27 Dec & Good Fri. Amex, MasterCard, Visa, Laser. **Directions:** 5 miles south from city, through Stillorgan main road, turn right from Lower Kilmacud Road.

Stillorgan

Stillorgan Park Hotel

féile bia -HOTEL

Stillorgan Road Stillorgan Co Dublin **Tel: 01 288 1621** Fax: 01 283 1610
Email: sales@stillorganpark.com Web: www.stillorganpark.com

This hotel on the Stillorgan dual carriageway is notable for great improvements made in recent years and is furnished in a dashing modern style throughout. Public areas include the stylish reception and lounge areas and bedrooms - some with views of Dublin Bay - are spacious, attractively decorated in a bright contemporary style, with well-finished bathrooms. Ample free parking is an attraction and good facilities for business guests include work space and fax/modem lines in rooms. Conference/banqueting (500/400); business centre, secretarial services. Children welcome (under 4 free in parents' room, cots available without charge, baby sitting arranged). Pets permitted by arrangement. **Rooms 125** (4 suites, 125 executive rooms, 50 no-smoking, 4 for disabled) Lift. B&B €80 pps, ss €70. No SC.

The Purple Sage Restaurant: An attractive, informal restaurant with seating in several areas, and welcoming staff. Menus are appealing in a fairly contemporary style - potato, blue cheese, pear & rocket salad with pesto dressing, for example, or a speciality of stir-fried prawns & monkfish with peppers and pak choi, and Thai jasmine rice. Imaginative vegetarian cooking has always been a feature and the hotel regularly runs special themed dining weeks, including one when 'healthy options' are highlighted on the menu. Children welcome. **Seats 50.** Air conditioning. Toilets wheelchair accessible. L & D daily, 12-2.30 & 5.45-9.30. Set L €23, Set Sun L €23; à la carte D available; house wine €21; no SC. Closed 25 Dec. Amex, Diners, MasterCard, Visa, Laser. **Directions:** Situated on main N11 dual carriageway.

Stillorgan

TriBeCa

Ⓝ RESTAURANT

1 Kilmacud Road Lr. Stillorgan Co Dublin **Tel: 01 278 6024**

This Stillorgan outpost of the popular Ranelagh restaurant is on the first floor, above the Mill House pub. With all-white walls and lots of windows it's big, bright, open and buzzy - and the first thing you see as you enter is a round reception desk with square copper panels: very attractive and design - conscious, but also simple, with wooden floors and bare tables. A good setting for modern, international food with youth-appeal. As in Ranelagh, the menu offers a variety of options suitable for different times, ranging from sandwiches (only until 6pm) through omelettes, a range of burgers, pizzas, and a section offering a various international chicken, meat & fish dishes and a vegetarian option. Daily specials are given on a board too, and should be a good option. While the Guide's experience of this new restaurant was not wholly positive (very long delays, uneven cooking), its potential is obvious; it's a casual, buzzy spot in an area where it's badly needed and, given the experience behind the operation in Ranelagh, these teething problems should be sorted out. Light choices - starters, salads, chicken wings - are probably wiser choices than main dishes. Short wine list, also Budvar and Erdinger beer, which suits the food. Open 12 noon - 11pm, daily. MasterCard, Visa. **Directions:** Over the Mill House pub.

Swords

Old Schoolhouse Restaurant

féile bia RESTAURANT

Church Road Swords Co Dublin **Tel: 01 840 2846** Fax: 01 840 5060
Email: sincater@gofree.indigo.ie Web: www.oldschoolhouse.ie

In a quiet riverside site close to the Northern Cross motorway, and only a short drive from the airport, the Sinclair family's restored 18th century stone school building makes an attractive country-style restaurant, and major renovations quite recently saw the dining room restored to its original 20' height, and the garden and conservatory upgraded for al fresco dining. Personal service and good home cooking are the aims; all ingredients are locally sourced and fresh every day, which allows for a seasonal à la carte and table d'hôte menus (plus daily blackboard specials which include a lot of seafood). A la carte menus offer starters such as baked crab and an unusual Old Schoolhouse-style chowder, with big chunks of fish, whole crab claws and generous juices rather than soup. Main courses include plenty of seafood and maybe some less usual options like ostrich medallions (farmed locally) and wild boar (panfried with Madeira and figs), plus several vegetarian dishes. Children welcome. **Seats 70** (private room, 12) Air conditioning. L Tue-Fri, 12.30-2.30, D Tue-Sat 6.30-10.30. Set L €19.50. Early D €25 (Mon-Fri, 6.30-7.30); Set D €25; à la carte also available; house wine €18; SC discretionary. Closed Sun, Mon, Christmas/New Year,bank hols. Amex, Diners, MasterCard, Visa, Laser. **Directions:** Coming from Dublin, turn left after Lord Mayor's Pub.

COUNTY CARLOW

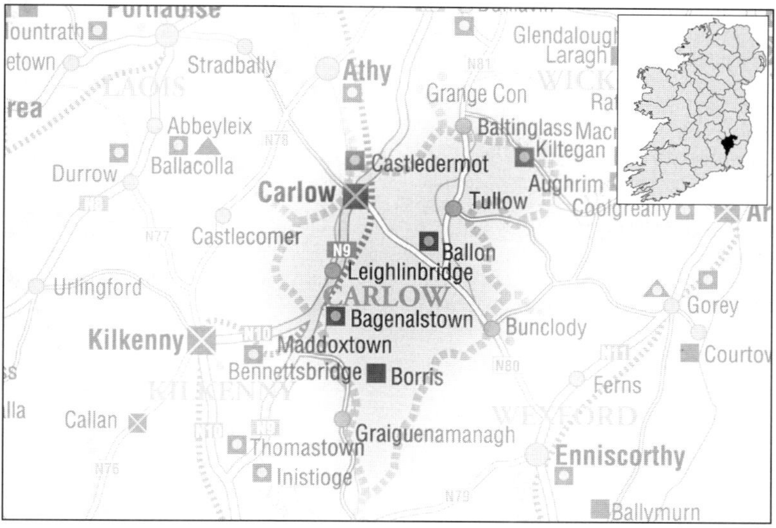

Carlow has character and charm, all within easy reach of Dublin. Although it is Ireland's second smallest county, it confidently incorporates such wonderful varieties of scenery that it has been memorably commented that the Creator was in fine form when He made Carlow. Whether you're lingering along the gentle meanderings of the waterway of the River Barrow, or enjoying the upper valley of the River Slaney while savouring the soaring outlines of the Blackstairs Mountains as they sweep upwards to the 793 m peak of Mount Leinster, this gallant little area will soon have you in thrall.

There's history a-plenty if you wish to seek it out. But for those who prefer to live in the present, the county town of Carlow itself fairly buzzes with student life and the energetic trade of a market centre, while a more leisurely pace can be enjoyed at riverside villages such as Leighlinbridge and Bagenalstown. Leighlinbridge - pronounced "Lochlinbridge" – has for many years been Barrowside's most community-conscious village, but as we go into 2004 there are also welcome improvements taking place to fulfill Bagenalstown's potential as a proper miniature river port.

The fine farmland of Carlow will be in national focus at the end of September 2004, when "Ploughtown" is established near the village of Grangeford between Tullow and Carlow town. For three days, Ireland's farming community - and those who wish to do business with them - will descend on Grangeford for the National Ploughing Championships. Appropriately, the defending champion in the senior section is a Carlow farmer, Eamonn Tracey, who was winner at the September 2003 Nationals at Ballybrackey in County Meath. If you wish to understand the festive heartbeat of rural Ireland, Ploughtown is the place to be.

Local Attractions and Information

Carlow town, Tourist Information 059 9131554

Carlow county, Carlow Rural Tourism 059 9130411/9130446

Carlow Craft Brewery, Micro-brewery 059 9134356

Grangeford, Nat. Ploughing Champs. (Autumn 04) 059 8625125

Tullow, Altamont Gardens 059 9159444

Bagenalstown

COUNTRY HOUSE

Kilgraney House

Borris Road Bagenalstown Co Carlow

Tel: 059 977 5283 Fax: 059 977 5595 Email: info@kilgraneyhouse.com

Web: www.kilgraneyhouse.com

In a lovely site overlooking the Barrow Valley, Bryan Leech and Martin Marley's charming late Georgian house - which (encouragingly) takes its name from the Irish 'cill greíne', meaning 'sunny hill or wood'

- is set in extensive wooded grounds that feature, amongst many other delights, a croquet lawn, a medicinal herb garden and fine cut-stone outbuildings. The kitchen garden provides much that Bryan will transform into delicious dinners, in contemporary cooking that makes creative use of local and artisan produce including their own home-smoked duck (with noodle salad & mirin/soy dressing, perhaps) and Lavistown cheese from Kilkenny - and your breakfast next morning will feature Rudd's dry-cured bacon from nearby Co Offaly. But it is for the sheer sense of style pervading the house that it is most famous - the enjoyment that Bryan and Martin have derived from their dedication to its restoration and furnishing is abundantly clear: elegant, yes, but with a great sense of fun too. Dinner is normally served at a communal table; private dining on request. Self-catering accommodation is also available, in two courtyard suites and the gate lodge. Herbal treatment room (massage & aromatherapy). Small conferences. Not suitable for children under 12. **Rooms 8** (2 suites, 3 shower only, all no smoking). No dogs. B&B €70, ss €15. D (non-residents welcome by reservation), 8 pm. Set 6-course D, €45. (Vegetarian meals or other special dietary requirements on request.) Wines from €18. Closed Sun-Thu off-season (Feb-Jun & Sep-Oct), closed 1 Nov-1 Mar. Amex, MasterCard, Visa, Laser. Helipad. **Directions:** Just off the R705, halfway between Bagenalstown and Borris.

Bagenalstown

Lorum Old Rectory

COUNTRY HOUSE

Kilgraney Bagenalstown Co Carlow
Tel: 059 977 5282 Fax: 059 977 5455
Email: reservations@lorum.com Web: www.lorum.com

This historic country house is close to many places of interest, including medieval Kilkenny, Altamont Gardens, New Ross (where river cruises are available), Kildare's National Stud and Japanese Gardens. Also close by is Gowran Park racecourse and activities such as golf and a riding school (offering both outdoor and indoor tuition). Elegant and spacious, there's a lovely drawing room for guests and accommodation includes a bedroom with a four-poster- all are very comfortable, with big beds, phones and tea/coffee trays. But it is Bobbie Smith's hospitality that keeps bringing guests back: Bobbie, who is a member of the international chefs' association, Euro-Toques, committed to defending local produce and suppliers, prepares good home cooking (rack of lamb, perhaps, with honey, mustard & rosemary dressing) based mainly on organic ingredients - dinner for residents is served at a long mahogany table (book by 3 pm). This relaxed place was the guide's Pet Friendly Establishment for 2000 and there are many interesting resident animals - so it is hardly surprising that this is a place where guests are welcome to bring their own dogs too, by arrangement. Not suitable for children. Private parties/small conferences (10). Cycling. Own parking. No smoking establishment. **Rooms 5** (all en-suite). B&B €55 pps, ss €15. Dinner available for residents (except Sunday). Closed 1 Dec-1 Feb. MasterCard, Visa, Laser. **Directions:** Midway between Borris & Bagenalstown on the R705.

Ballon

Ballykealey Manor Hotel

Ⓝ HOTEL

Ballon Co Carlow **Tel: 059 915 9288**
Fax: 059 915 9297 Email: ballykealeymanor@eircom.net
Web: www.ballykealeymanorhotel.com

Seat of the Lecky family for three centuries, the present house was designed by Thomas A Cobden (designer of Carlow cathedral) and built in the 1830s as a wedding present. Gothic arches and Tudor chimney stacks take you back to the architectural oddities of the time, but the house is set in well-maintained grounds and promising first impressions are well founded. The property moved into the energetic new hands in 2003 and the owners, Edward and Karen Egan, have completely refurbished the hotel - with considerable style. Significant touches in the entrance hall set a confident tone that is carried through into spacious reception rooms which are furnished in a pleasingly elegant mixture of contemporary style and period features, combining comfort with a friendly atmosphere. Individually designed bedrooms are in keeping with the character of the house and have all the necessary amenities, including direct-dial phones and multi-channel TV. Conferences/banqueting (20-250),. Wheelchair access; children welcome (under 6 free in parents' room, cot available without charge). Pets by arrangement. **Rooms 12** (1 junior suite, 4 shower only, 2 non-smoking). B&B about €70pps, ss €20; no SC. Closed 24 Dec.

Oak Room: Although perhaps a little lacking in colour - fresh flowers would help - promisingly well-appointed white-clothed tables and linen napkins look well against dark wood panelling, and interesting menus confirm impressions that the priorities here lie in the kitchen. Head chef Cian Irvine is doing a fine job and, while it is a little early for specialities to have been developed, dishes that impressed on our visit included an excellent oven-baked salmon fillet with cauliflower and saffron purée, beet and baby carrot. While not over-extensive, choices on well-balanced menus range from the classic (tournedos 'Rossini') to some dishes including exotic ingredients for the more adventurous diner, perhaps reflecting Cian Irvine's previous experience in Florida. Service, while friendly, may not match the professionalism in the kitchen, and the wine list could be improved but confident cooking and good value for money should offset minor weaknesses. **Seats 32** (private room 32). D daily, 7-9.30; L Sun only 12.30-3.30. D A la carte, Set Sun L €25.50. House wines €18. A la carte bar menu available 12.30-9.30. Closed 24 Dec. MasterCard, Visa, Laser. **Directions:** 10 miles from Carlow on the N80.

Ballon

Sherwood Park House

féile bia COUNTRY HOUSE

Kilbride Ballon Co Carlow **Tel: 059 915 9117** Fax: 059 915 9355
Email: info@sherwoodpark.ie Web: www.sherwoodparkh.ie

Patrick and Maureen Owens, who have run this delightful Georgian farmhouse next to the famous Altamont Gardens since 1970, accurately describe it as "an accessible country retreat for anyone who enjoys candlelit dinners, brass and canopy beds and the relaxing experience of eating out while staying in". Spacious accommodation is furnished in period style and thoughtful in the details that count - and Maureen takes pride in offering guests real home cooking based on the best of local produce. Dinner for residents is served at 8 pm - "best Carlow lamb from the excellent village butcher" is a speciality - and guests are welcome to bring their own wine and any other drinks. There's a lovely garden, Altamont Gardens are nearby and it's a good area for walking - and fishing the Slaney. Golf nearby. Private parties (max 14). **Rooms 4**, all en-suite & no-smoking. B&B €45, ss €10. Residents D €35 (must be booked ahead; no smoking in the dining room). Open all year except Christmas Day. Amex, MasterCard, Visa. **Directions:** Signed from the junction of the N80 and N81.

Ballon

The Forge Craft & Coffee Shop

N féile bia RESTAURANT

Kilbride Cross Ballon Co Carlow **Tel: 059 915 9939**

'The Forge for home baking and local produce' is their motto and it sums up nicely the appeal of Peadar and Mary Jordan's unpretentious daytime restaurant. Off the road but handy to it and with ample parking at the back, the granite building dates back to the 1700s and it makes a great place to break a journey, or for a wholesome bite before or after walking or visiting local attractions such as nearby Altamont Gardens. Mary takes pride in sourcing ingredients from local suppliers and her menus offer just the kind of food everybody loves on a day out - home-made vegetable soup with soda bread scones, ploughman's sandwiches and comforting hot lunch time favourites like baked ham, roast beef or lamb, and freshly made lasagne. Outside lunch service times you can always get simple treats like fresh scones with home-made jam for morning coffee or after noon teas - and they have a tourist information point as well as local art and craft work for sale. Walkers welcome and packed meals supplied on request. All round, a great little place for a break. Wheelchair friendly. Children welcome. Parking. **Seats 40.** Open 9.30-5 daily, L 12.45-2.30 (Sun to 3). Late opening by arrangement. A la carte. House wine €15.95. Closed 10 days at Christmas. MasterCard, Visa, Laser. **Directions:** Off the N80, between Ballon and Bunclody.

Borris

The Step House

GUESTHOUSE

66 Main Street Borris Co Carlow **Tel: 059 97 73209** Fax: 059 97 73395
Email: info@thestephouse.com Web: www.thestephouse.com

James and Cait Coady's attractive old house has undergone extensive renovation and has been stylishly decorated and furnished in period style, with antiques throughout. Well-proportioned reception rooms include a fine dining room (used for breakfast); a matching drawing room that overlooks the back garden and a putting green. Comfortable, elegant bedrooms include one with a four-poster and all are furnished to a high standard with smart shower rooms, TV and tea/coffee facilities. A great deal of commitment has been demonstrated in the renovation and upgrading of this fine old house, including the conversion of the whole of the lower ground floor to make a magnificently characterful kitchen and living room area with direct access to the garden - and decking beside the dining room where guests can enjoy breakfast outdoors on fine mornings. However, although apparently complete, this challenging project is far from finished, as there are plans for an extension which will take The Step House to hotel status in 2004/5. The Coadys also own the bar next door - and one of Ireland's finest classic pubs, Tynans Bridge Bar, in Kilkenny city. NB: there are several flights of stairs, including steps up to the front door. Not suitable for children under 10. Pets permitted in some areas by arrangement. Fishing, walking, garden. Own secure parking. **Rooms 5** (all no-smoking, 4 shower only). B&B €40pps, ss10. Closed 20 Dec-16 Mar. MasterCard, Visa. **Directions:** From main Carlow-Kilkenny road, take turning to Bagenalstown. 8 miles to Borris.

Carlow

Barrowville Townhouse

GUESTHOUSE

Kilkenny Road Carlow Co Carlow **Tel: 059 914 3324** Fax: 059 914 1953
Email: barrowvilletownhouse@eircom.net Web: www.barrowvillehouse.com

Ex-hoteliers Marie and Randal Dempsey have run this exceptionally comfortable and well-managed guesthouse just a few minutes walk from the town centre since 1989. Although immaculately maintained the house is old, so bedrooms inevitably vary in size and character, but all are comfortable and attractively furnished with a mixture of antiques and fitted furniture, plus direct dial phones, tea/coffee trays (for which there is a small charge, if used) and TV. Good housekeeping and thoughtfully designed, well-finished bathrooms contribute greatly to a generally high standard of comfort. Marie Dempsey is renowned for excellent breakfasts (buffet or traditional Irish, cooked to order) served in a handsome conservatory (complete with a large vine) overlooking the lovely back garden. There is also a particularly pleasant and comfortable residents' drawing room, with an open fire, grand piano and plenty to read. Barrowville was the guide's Guesthouse of the Year for 2000. Garden. Private parking. Not suitable for children under 15. No pets. **Rooms 7** (2 shower only, all no-smoking). B&B €40pps, ss €10. Open all year. Amex, MasterCard, Visa. **Directions:** South side of Carlow town on the N9.

Carlow

The Beams Restaurant

féile bia RESTAURANT

59 Dublin Street Carlow Co Carlow
Tel: 059 913 1824 Email: the.beams@ireland.com

Originally a coaching inn, this characterful building was restored by Betty and Peter O'Gorman, who opened it as a restaurant in 1986. Massive wooden beams create a warm atmosphere and are a reminder of the building's long history (it has held a full licence since 1760) and, while there are some eccentricities about the restaurant and the way it is run, the essentials are right and many of the country's trendy young restaurateurs would do well to come and learn some basics here. Classic French cuisine is the speciality of French chef Romain Chall, who has been at The Beams since it opened and was deservedly described by the late Peter O'Gorman as a "master craftsman". He has established a reputation for fine fare, including game in season and fish cooked with admirable simplicity; house specialities include filled pancakes (a favourite starter), quiches and home-made ice creams. Vegetarian dishes regularly feature on the menu (seasonal vegetables, many of them home grown, are a delight) and any special dietary requirements can be met at a day's notice. Extensive wine list. **Seats 40.** D Tue-Sat 7.30-9.30 pm (Sat to 10 pm); D€37.50; service discretionary. Closed Sun & Mon, bank hols, Christmas fortnight (from 24 Dec) & 1 wk July. Amex, MasterCard, Visa, Laser. **Directions:** Town centre, on main street.

Carlow

Lennon's Café Bar

féile bia PUB/CAFÉ

121 Tullow Street Carlow Co Carlow **Tel: 059 913 1575**

Sinéad Byrne runs this attractive modern café-bar with her husband, Liam, and their stylish contemporary design and deliciously healthy, reasonably priced food has clearly been a hit with both local business professionals and visitors to the town. In a manner reminiscent of that great Kerry speciality, the pub that gradually develops into a restaurant at the back without actually having a dedicated restaurant area, the design of the bar- which has a striking metal spiral staircase at the back - helps the atmosphere to shift into café gear as you move through it. Simple, uncluttered tables and speedy service of jugs of iced water bode well for menus that include a host of wholesome dishes: delicious home-made soups; open sandwiches (on freshly-baked home-made bread); ciabattas, wraps, some very tempting salads and a range of hot specials like steak & kidney pie topped with pastry & served with champ, or cod & mussel bake. Dishes suitable for vegetarians are highlighted, gluten free bread is available for coeliacs and everything is really wholesome and freshly made to order from top quality ingredients (some local sources are named on the menu). All this and good value too: with most main courses under €10, prices are very accessible, so it's a winning formula. Leave room for delicious home-made desserts - hazelnut meringue roulade with raspberry sauce, perhaps, or hot apple crumble. This is well-balanced good home cooking and was a worthy winner of our **Happy Heart Eat Out Award for 2003**. Breakfast 8.30-11; L Mon-Fri,12-3, Sat 12-4, Sun 12-5. Toilets wheelchair accessible. Closed 25 Dec, Good Fri. **Directions:** At Junction of Tullow Street & Potato Market. ◇

Leighlinbridge

Mulberry's Restaurant

Ⓝ féile bia CAFÉ

Arboretum Garden Centre Kilkenny Road Leighlinbridge Co Carlow
Tel: 059 97 21558 Fax: 059 97 21642 Email: arboretum@eircom.net

This pleasant self-service restaurant is in the main hall of the garden centre at the Arboretum and offers an attractive selection of wholesome, freshly-prepared food. A good place to break a journey. Children welcome. Wine licence. Open 9-5 Mon-Sat, Sun 11-5. Closed 2 or 3 days at Christmas. MasterCard, Visa, Laser.

COUNTY CAVAN

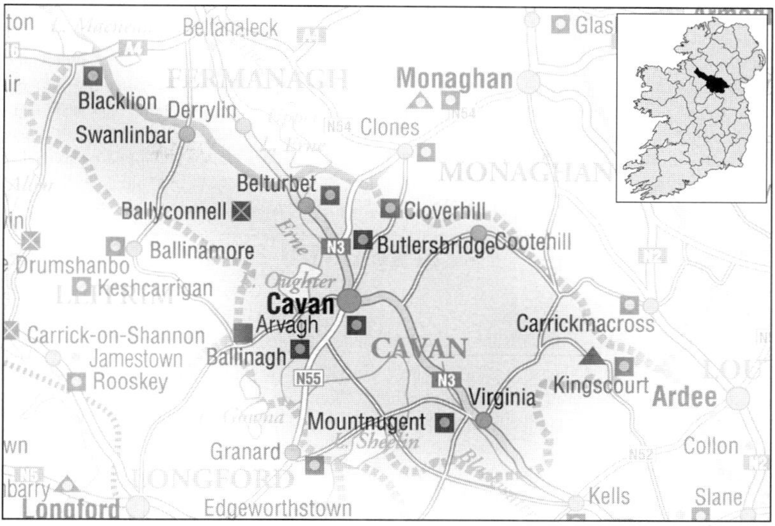

In its quiet way, lake-studded Cavan is one of Ireland's most watery counties. This is classic drumlin country, almost with more water than they know what to do with. But the very fact that the meandering waterways dictate the way of the roads means that much of Cavan is hidden. In 2004, this is a virtue. It is a place best discovered by the discerning visitor. Much of it has quiet and utterly rural charm, seemingly remote - yet it isn't so very far from Dublin or Belfast.

So if you take your time wandering through this green and silver land - particularly if travelling at the leisurely pace of the deservedly renowned Shannon-Erne Waterway which has joined Ireland's two greatest lake and river systems - then you'll become aware that this is a place of rewardingly gentle pleasures. And you'll have time to discover that it does have its own mountain, or at least it shares the 667 m peak of Cuilcagh with neighbouring Fermanagh. No ordinary mountain, this - it has underground streams which eventually become the headwaters of the lordly River Shannon.

In fact, Cavan is much more extensive than is popularly imagined, for in the northeast it has Shercock with its own miniature lake district, while in its southeast it takes in all of Lough Ramor at the charming lakeside village of Virginia. It also shares Lough Sheelin, that place of legend for the angler, with Westmeath and Meath, and always throughout its drumlin heartlands you can find many little Cavan lakes which, should the fancy take you, can be called your own at least for the day that's in it.

Local Attractions and Information

Bailieboro, Tourism Information	042 9666666
Ballyjamesduff, Cavan County Museum	049 8544070
Ballyjamesduff, International Pork Festival (June)	049 8544242
Belturbet, Tourist Office	049 9522044
Cavan town, Cavan Crystal	049 4331800
Cavan town, Tourist Information	049 4331942
Cootehill, Maudabawn Cultural Centre	049 5559504
Mullagh, Lakeview Gardens	046 42480
Shannon-Erne Waterway (Ballinamore-Ballyconnell)	078 45124

Arvagh

Bijou Cottage

Ⓝ B&B

Cornea Arvagh Co Cavan **Tel: 049 433 5466**
Fax: 049 433 5466 Email: bijoucottage@eircom.net

Monica and Robert Timmermans have offered hospitality in establishments as varied as the Wine Cellar in Dublin's Powerscourt Townhouse Centre to their famous lighthouse on Clare Island, so it should come as no surprise to find them in this pretty cottagey setting in deepest Cavan. A tidy gravelled courtyard, rock gardens and ample parking give a good impression from the outset, the welcome is warm and friendly, decor has an interesting continental flavour enhanced by unusual artwork, and rooms are thoughtfully furnished. This is a place for escape from city life, so don't expect things like TV or trouser presses here, but the essentials are in place - including good showers and even a seating area with a usable fireplace in your bedroom. Little caring touches at breakfast include toast that comes stamped 'Good Morning', hot dishes decorated with nasturtium flowers - and you might be offered a selection of delicious Dutch cheeses brought back from the continent. Dinner is available by arrangment. Activities in the area include angling and watersports, golf, horseriding, walks and cycling. Children welcome; dogs allowed by arrangement. **Rooms 2** (both en-suite). B&B €30, ss €10. Open all year. **No Credit Cards. Directions:** From Cavan (N55), take R198 through Crossdoney, R198 to Cornea and then to Arva.

Ballinagh

Lacken Mill House & Gardens

GUESTHOUSE

Lacken Lower Ballinagh Co Cavan
Tel: 049 433 7592 Fax: 049 433 7592
Email: info@lackenmillhouse.com Web: www.lackenmillhouse.com

This restored Victorian millhouse is set in gloriously unspoilt rolling countryside in a little known area about seven miles from Cavan town. Dubliners Eamon O'Donoghue and Naomi Brennan purchased the property several years ago and the restoration of the house - and, even more so perhaps, the gardens and woodland areas alongside the River Erne - has been a labour of love ever since. Their achievement is remarkable, especially as they remain relaxed and hospitable hosts to those lucky enough to find their home. Welcoming log fires are a feature of this warm and comfortable house (fuel is not in short supply) and the dining room, where both breakfast and evening meals are served, opens onto a patio and the gardens in fine weather. Spacious individually decorated bedrooms have well-finished shower rooms (there is also a luxurious bathroom, which any guest may use) tea/coffee trays, direct dial phones and TV (fax facility and iron available on request). Behind the house, the ruins of a corn and flax mill are still standing and awaiting restoration, but extensive areas of woodland have been cleared to make long walks (there are even hammocks dotted around, should you feel the need of a rest) and the river and its wildlife provide endless interest. Many guests never feel the need to wander, but restless souls will find plenty of other activities nearby, including fishing, golf and horseriding. Children under 2 free in parents' room, cot available without charge. Dogs allowed by arrangement. **Rooms 5** (all shower only); room service available (limited hours). B&B €38.50pps, ss €11.50. Closed Dec & Jan. MasterCard, Visa, Laser. **Directions:** N3 to Cavan, N55 to Ballinagh & follow signs.

Ballyconnell

Angler's Rest

PUB / ACCOMMODATION

Main Street Ballyconnell Co Cavan
Tel: 049 952 6391 Fax: 049 952 6777 Email: bycl@iol.ie

Golf, fishing, walking and cycling are among the pursuits that attract visitors to this lovely lakeland area and Francis McGoldrick's characterful pub makes a welcoming and moderately priced base for a relaxing stay. The premises have been greatly extended recently (and more rooms are planned) but the philosophy remains the same: accommodation is comfortable, staff hospitable and the bar has spirit - a real inn, in fact. There's a pleasantly informal restaurant and, as the proprietors are also the chefs, you can be sure of consistency in the kitchen. Live music some evenings (inquire for further details.) Children welcome; cot available free of charge. Garden; pool table. **Rooms 10** (all with en-suite shower, 4 non smoking) B&B €35pps, ss €15. Bar Food served 6-9 daily, L 12.30-2.30 pm, D 6-9. Closed 25 Dec & Good Fri. MasterCard, Visa. **Directions:** On N3, main street in Ballyconnell village.

Ballyconnell

Pólo'd Restaurant

RESTAURANT

Main Street Ballyconnell Co Cavan **Tel: 049 952 6228**

Owner-chef Paul O'Dowd's cottagey little restaurant consists of two small rooms on two floors with the country character of stripped pine, old brick and stonework - all of which suit its daytime persona. But Paul's talents really come into play at dinner time, when he presents imaginative contemporary menus - typically a trio of seafood with prawn & vermouth sauce, crispy duck with mango & peach sauce and an accomplished dessert selection - all cooked with a flair and confidence. A new dining room upstairs, with simple white table linen and candlelight, has added a pleasing space and comfort. Reasonable prices together with consistently good cooking and friendly, helpful service under the direction of Geraldine O'Dowd make this a great asset to the area. Children welcome. Wheelchair accessible. **Seats 80.** L12.30-2.30, Tue-Sat; D 6.30-9.30 Wed-Sat. Set D €35, early menu about €20 (5-7pm); house wine about €16. Bookings strongly recommended. Closed Sun & Mon. Amex, MasterCard, Visa, Laser. **Directions:** On main street of Ballyconnell village.

Ballyconnell

Slieve Russell Hotel & Country Club

HOTEL

Ballyconnell Co Cavan **Tel: 049 952 6444** Fax: 049 952 6046
Email: slieve-russell@quinn-hotels.com Web: www.quinn-hotels.com

Close to the attractive town of Ballyconnell, this striking flagship of the Sean Quinn Group is named after a nearby mountain and set amongst 300 acres of landscaped gardens and grounds, including 50 acres of lakes. Everything is on a generous scale - and it's very much the social and business centre of the area. In the foyer, generous seating areas are arranged around the marble colonnades and a grand central staircase, flanked by a large bar on one side and two restaurants at the other. All bedrooms have pleasant country views, extra large beds and spacious marble bathrooms as well as the usual amenities (direct dial, phone tea/coffee tray,TV, trouser press). Excellent conference and business facilities are matched by leisure facilities in the Golf and Country Club - the championship golf course has become one of the top golfing venues in Ireland and there's a putting green, practice area and nine hole, par 3 course. Off-season value breaks. Children under 3 free in parents' room, cot available free of charge; crèche. Conference/banqueting (800/550); video-conferencing available. Leisure centre; swimming pool. Golf, tennis, snooker, garden. Beauty salon; hairdresser. Shop. Garden. No pets. **Rooms 159** (14 suites, 96 executive rooms, 2 for disabled). Lift. B&B from €120 pps, ss about €15. Open all year. Amex, Diners, MasterCard, Visa, Laser. Helipad. **Directions:** Take N3 from Dublin to Cavan, proceed to Belturbet then Ballyconnell.

Belturbet

Erne Bistro

RESTAURANT / BAR

The Lawn Belturbet Co Cavan **Tel: 049 952 2443**

This well established restaurant and lounge bar is near the bridge over the River Erne and handy to the Emerald Star marina. Past a welcoming reception area with fresh flowers, there's a door to the comfortable bar and another takes you through to the restaurant, which is in two connecting rooms. Busy decor and friendly staff give it a warm ambience and it's an idea to order an aperitif quickly to allow the time required to consider an exceptionally long à la carte menu reminiscent of the '70s and early '80s, which may send out warning signals as short menus tend to be a good sign. But this is the exception that proves the rule, as everything is well done in classic style - good soups, for example, show that the basics are in place, and is matched by the home-made bread served with it. Quantities are generous, accompaniments correct and ingredients well-sourced; specialities include old favourites - tournedos chasseur, darne of salmon on a bed of fresh spinach, roast duckling and black sole and are all typical. Christmas Day Luncheon (2 sittings) and New Year Gala Dinner are much in demand. Special menus are available for private parties. Taxi service available. Live music (occasional). Not suitable for children after 8pm. **Seats 80** (private room, 40). D daily in summer, 7-11 (Sun to 10), L Sun only 1-3. All à la carte. Closed Mon off-season (Oct-Mar). MasterCard, Visa, Laser. **Directions:** At the bottom of Bridge Street in Belturbet.

Belturbet

International Fishing Centre

RESTAURANT / GUESTHOUSE

Loughdooley Belturbet Co Cavan
Tel: 049 952 2616 Fax: 049 952 2616
Email: michelneuville@eircom.net Web: www.angling-holidays.com

At this lovely waterside location, Michel Neuville offers residential fishing holidays, which are mainly for continental guests; however the restaurant is open to non-residents by reservation when there is room. The centre is like a little corner of France, with all signage in French, and neatly manicured lawns sweeping down to the river where, with in typical French style, the menu is clearly displayed. When the weather allows, tables are set out on the terrace and the restaurant provides an excellent facility for holidaymakers on river cruises, as there are pontoons at the bottom of the garden. A short French-style set menu is accompanied by compact French wine selection (all under €20) - and a refreshingly reasonable bill. **Seats 35.** Max preferred table size 10, (Private Room, 30). Set D 7-9pm daily, €18 & €28. Closed 1 Dec-1 Mar. MasterCard, Visa.

Belturbet

Seven Horseshoes

Ⓝ PUB

Belturbet Co Cavan **Tel: 049 952 2166**

This old pub in the centre of town is full of character, with an unusual wattle hurdle ceiling, plenty of local history, an open fire for cold days and the pleasingly dim atmosphere that makes Irish pubs so relaxing. This makes it very popular with boating folk, who also head up from the river for hearty home cooking at reasonable prices: steaks, mixed grills, lamb cutlets and panfried plaice are the order of the day. Just right for appetites fired up by plenty of fresh air. Food available daily: L 12.30-3 (Sun 1-4), evenings 5-9. MasterCard, Visa, Laser. **Directions:** Town centre.

Blacklion

MacNean House & Bistro

★ féile bia RESTAURANT WITH ROOMS

Main Street Blacklion Co Cavan
Tel: 072 53022 Fax: 072 53404

CHEF OF THE YEAR

Over the last decade Neven Maguire's cooking has put this little border town firmly on the culinary map and now that the small family restaurant has been refurbished, with elegant high-backed chairs, immaculate linen and restrained creamy white crockery, it makes a more appropriate setting for some of the best cooking in Ireland. Neven, who is a popular TV chef, shows no sign of being distracted from the restaurant and his cooking is better than ever: exact, perfectly judged food, that makes the most of meticulously sourced ingredients from the local and artisan producers he so strongly advocates, is an experience to treasure. Menus, which are admirably simply worded, include an 8-course 'surprise' tasting menu and a vegetarian menu, as well as a Sunday lunch which draws admirers from all over the country. Your meal begins with an absolutely gorgeous assortment of warm yeast breads and dipping oil, then a luscious little pre-starter soup before you launch into starters such as seared scallops on a coriander risotto, served with crab rolls & a light curry sauce: perfectly judged cooking, a little froth of sauce and just enough risotto to balance texture and taste; then perhaps a refreshing salad of Eden plants (supplied by the Eden Organic Centre at Rossinver), before an unusual main course of confit leg of rabbit with apple galette, with cabbage & onion purée, perhaps, or a beautiful fresh-looking dish of turbot fillets on a bed of cos lettuce, roast salsify and beetroot, and a light velouté - how good to find vegetables so wisely employed, and a dish so well-balanced that the delicate fish is not upstaged by the other components. Desserts have always been a particular passion for Neven and it's a must to leave a little room for one of his skilfully crafted confections - the grand finale is just that in this case: what could be more divine than a little pyramid of heart-shaped baked shortcake with raspberry pannacotta and lemon curd ice cream? This is outstanding cooking, served with charm and generosity of spirit - and it is exceptionally good value too, especially Sunday lunch, which somehow combines elements of the traditional meal with more adventurous choices - and is a snip at €25. **Seats 40.** D Wed/Thu-Sun 6-10pm (Sun to 9.30); L Sun only, 12.30-3.30, €25. Set D €30-€60, (Early D €30, 6-8pm); vegetarian menu €35 menus available, also à la carte. Service discretionary.

Accommodation: Rooms 6 (all en-suite, 2 shower only), about €35 pps. Direct-dial phone, tea/coffee tray & TV in rooms. Children welcome; cot available free of charge. Pets allowed by arrangement. Establishment closed Mon & Tue, 2 weeks Sep/Oct, 5 days Christmas. MasterCard, Visa, Laser.

Cavan

Cavan Crystal Hotel

Ⓝ HOTEL

Dublin Road Cavan Co Cavan **Tel: 049 436 0600** Fax: 049 436 0699
Email: info@cavancrystalhotel.com Web: www.cavancrystalhotel.com

This impressive new hotel on the Dublin side of Cavan town is a great asset to the area, bringing a state-of-the art health and fitness club, conference and banqueting facilities and a focal centre for local activities. In common ownership with the adjacent Cavan Crystal Showroom and Visitor Centre, it can offer guests the opportunity to tour the crystal factory - and even to cut your own crystal. Conference/banqueting (7 suites). 18m swimming pool, sauna, jacuzzi, steam room, gym. Children welcome (discounts available; children's meals; baby sitting). **Rooms 85** (3 suites incl. 1 'presidential', 66 executive; smoking rooms on request; 4 disabled); Lift. B&B €90, ss €25. SC incl. Amex, MasterCard, Visa, Laser. **Directions:** On N3, a few minutes from town centre in Dublin direction.

Cavan

Oak Room Restaurant

☆ féile bia RESTAURANT

Cavan Crystal Centre Dublin Road Cavan Co Cavan
Tel: 049 436 0099/436 2748 Fax: 049 433 2927

Proprietor-chef Norbert Neylon - one of the country's most talented younger chefs - has earned a well-deserved reputation for this fine restaurant, already making it a destination restaurant just a couple of years after opening. Large, well-proportioned and stylish, with a vibrant colour scheme in deep oranges and reds, big mirrors, a dramatic floral centrepiece, plenty of natural materials, this is an impressive restaurant - and classy, simple table settings with just a strip of white linen, plain glasses, restrained cutlery and white china hint at a commitment to quality which is to be followed through on the plate. A well-planned bar area has plenty of comfortable seating and arriving guests are welcomed well, with menus and aperitifs speedily offered. Ambitious menus offer a wide choice and the pricing structure is user-friendly: à la carte but you can choose anything to make up a 5-course dinner menu (€39.50), with only a couple of supplements (on shellfish, such as speciality warm salad of pan-fried scallops with a tomato and herb risotto, fresh pea and mint sauce, or perhaps a main course of Dover sole with a champagne & dill sauce). Creative variations lift familiar dishes out of the ordinary and the quality of both food and cooking is consistently outstanding. Home-baked bread, well-made salads, carefully cooked vegetables and gorgeous puddings are all impressive details - also the classic petits fours that arrive with coffee. Service can be a little patchy, but staff are invariably friendly and helpful. Overall, this is a fine restaurant, offering excellent cooking and good value. A carefully selected wine list may seem a little pricey for the area but it includes a fair number of bottles under €20. **Seats 75.** No smoking area; air conditioning. Toilets wheelchair accessible. D Tue-Sun, 6.30-10 (Sun to 9); L Sun only 12.30-3. Set D €39.50; Set L €19.50. D also à la carte. House wine €17.50. SC discretionary. Closed Mon, 25-26 Dec, 1 week Nov. MasterCard, Visa, Laser. **Directions:** At Cavan Crystal Centre.

Cavan

The Side Door

Ⓝ féile bia RESTAURANT

Drumalee Cross Cavan Co Cavan
Tel: 049 433 1819 Email: thesidedoor@tjgavigan.com

A younger sister restaurant to two successful and admirably consistent restaurants in Navan (The Loft) and Kells (The Ground Floor), The Side Door is based on the same principles of accessibility (good quality international food at a fair price), funky surroundings that make for an informal atmosphere that appeals equally to different age groups - and well-trained staff, who greet guests promptly on arrival and provide watchful service throughout. Popular starters like spicy chicken wings and Louisiana crab cakes are followed by a good selection of salads, speciality dishes (including a vegetarian Green Thai curry, perhaps) and old favourites like char-grilled steaks and home-made burgers. Ingredients are well-sourced, it's all cooked to order and there's something for everyone here within a wide price range, with starters about €3.50 - €8 and mains ranging from €11.50 (home-made burger) to about €23 ("Surf" - fillet steak with jumbo prawns). It's a great formula and pleases all the family. **Seats 90.** D 5.30-10.30 (Sun 5-10), early D €14.50 (Tue-Sat, 5.30-7.30), otherwise à la carte; L Sun only, from 12.30. House wine €15. 10% SC on parties of 4+. Closed Christmas, 1 Jan. MasterCard, Visa, Laser. **Directions:** On the Cootehill Road, quarter of a mile from Cavan town, above the Orchard Bar.

Cloverhill

The Olde Post Inn

☆ féile bia RESTAURANT WITH ROOMS

Cloverhill Co Cavan
Tel: 047 55555 Fax: 047 55111
Email: oldepostinn@eircom.ie
Web: www.theoldepostinn.com

NEWCOMER OF THE YEAR

This old stone building in a neatly landscaped garden served as a post office until 1974 and, since then, has made an attractive and popular inn. In the autumn of 2002 it was taken over by the talented young chef, Gearoid Lynch, and his fiancée, Tara McCann, who have worked hard to put their stamp on it both inside and out - and they are already earning a well-deserved reputation for fine food and genuine hospitality. There's a pleasant country atmosphere about the place, which has a proper bar to enjoy your pre/post-prandial drinks and an old-world style throughout, with bare walls, dark beams and simple wooden furniture - but, comfortably rustic as it may seem, that is far from the case in the kitchen. Gearoid's route to Cloverhill has included time in some fine establishments - at least one of which lives on in Cavan, in a house speciality: 'Le Coq Hardi' chicken breast (stuffed with potato, apple, bacon & herbs, wrapped in bacon and served with an Irish whiskey sauce). A committed Euro-Toques chef, Gearoid sources ingredients with great care and his respect for regional and seasonal foods shows in many ways, notably in adaptations of tradtional themes such as a speciality starter of warm bacon and cabbage terrinewith a baby leek cream sauce. This is a happy ship and the talent and dedication of a good kitchen team produces excellent cooking and there's a tangible sense of pride in the friendly, helpful service provided by local staff. Ample parking. **Seats 80** (private room 30); no smoking restaurant; toilets wheelchair accessible. D Tue-Sun, 6.30-9, L Sun only, 12.30-3. Set D from €30, also à la carte. Set Sun L €21. Closed Mon, bank hols. **Accommodation:** Some refurbishment of the rooms has taken place at the time of going to press and is expected to be completed, in appropriate country house style, for the 2004 season. Children welcome, under 3s free in parents' room. No pets. **Rooms 7** (all en-suite, 2 shower only), B&B €38 pps. MasterCard, Visa, Laser. **Directions:** N3 from Dublin, N54 from Butlersbridge - 3 miles.

Kingscourt

Cabra Castle Hotel & Golf Club

HOTEL

Kingscourt Co Cavan **Tel: 042 966 7030** Fax: 042 966 7039
Email: sales@cabracastle.com Web: www.cabracastle.com

Formerly known as Cormey Castle and renamed Cabra Castle in the early 19th century, this impressive hotel is set amidst 100 acres of garden and parkland, with lovely views over the Cavan countryside, famous for its lakes and fine fishing. (The nearby Dun A Ri Forest has many walks and nature trails on land once part of the Cabra estate.) Although initially imposing, with its large public rooms and antique furnishings, the atmosphere at Cabra Castle is relaxing. Due to the age of the building, the bedrooms vary in size and outlook, but all are comfortable and individually decorated. Accommodation includes some ground floor rooms suitable for less able guests and, in addition to rooms in the main building, the newer rooms in an extension are particularly suitable for families. There are also some romantic beamed rooms, in a courtyard that has been converted to provide modern comforts without sacrificing character. The combination of formal background and easy ambience make this a good venue for private and business functions; it is popular for both weddings and conferences (250/350 respectively). Garden, walking, golf (9), fishing. Off-season value breaks. Children welcome (under 3s free in parents' room, cots available without charge, baby sitting arranged); pets permitted by arrangement. **Rooms 80** (1 suite, 2 junior suites, 8 executive rooms). B&B €107pps, ss €32. Closed 24-26 Dec. Amex, MasterCard, Visa, Laser. **Directions:** Dublin - N2 - Navan - R162 - Kingscourt.

Kingscourt

Gartlans Pub

ATMOSPHERIC PUB

Main Street Kingscourt Co Cavan **Tel: 042 966 7003**

This pretty thatched pub is a delightfully unspoilt example of the kind of grocery/pub that used to be so typical of Ireland, especially in country areas. Few enough of them remain, now that the theme pub has moved in, but this one is real, with plenty of local news items around the walls, a serving hatch where simple groceries can be bought, all served with genuine warmth and hospitality. The Gartlans have been here since 1911 and they have achieved the remarkable feat of appearing to make time stand still. Closed 25 Dec & Good Fri. **Directions:** On the main street in Kingscourt village.

Mountnugent

Ross House & Castle

FARMHOUSE / B&B

Mountnugent Co Cavan **Tel: 049 854 0218** Fax: 049 854 0218
Email: rosshouse@eircom.net Web: www.ross-house.com

In mature grounds on the shores of Lough Sheelin, Peter and Ulla Harkort's old manor house enjoys a very lovely location and offers a good standard of accommodation at a modest price. Bedrooms, which are distinctly continental in style, have telephone, TV and tea/coffee trays and some unusual features: three have their own conservatories, four have fireplaces (help yourself to logs from the shed) and most have unusual continental style showers. Peace and relaxation are the great attraction, and there's a fine choice of activities at hand: a pier offers boats (and engines) for fishermen to explore the lake, there's safe bathing from a sandy beach, and also tennis. An equestrian centre at Ross House has 35 horses stabled, and offers hacking and trekking as well as instruction and schooling on the cross-country course. At the castle nearby, Peter and Ulla's daughter Benita Walker provides most unusual accommodation (it is a very real castle). Ulla cooks for everyone, making packed lunches, sandwiches, high tea and a 4-course dinner (about €20; wine list from €15). Equestrian, fishing, tennis. Children and pets welcome. **Rooms 6** (all en-suite, 5 shower only). B&B from about €35 pps, ss about €15. Closed 1 Nov-28Feb. MasterCard, Visa. **Directions:** 5 Km from Mountnugent, signposted.

VIRGINIA

This attractive town is on the the northern side of beautiful Lough Ramor, which has wooded shores and a great reputation for coarse fishing. It makes a good base for a fishing holiday, or simply exploring an attractive and unspoilt part of the country. For travellers between Northern Ireland and Dublin it's the ideal spot to take a break - up at **The Park Hotel (049 854 6100)**, perhaps, which isn't quite what it used to be but it's set in well-maintained parkland and its own golf course and you can get a bite in the bar then take a stroll along the shore; or - the preferred choice for discerning diners - at **The Cinnamon Stick (049 854 8692)** a clean-lined coffee shop in the village, where they do an excellent Illy coffee and serve wholesome home-made food.

COUNTY CLARE

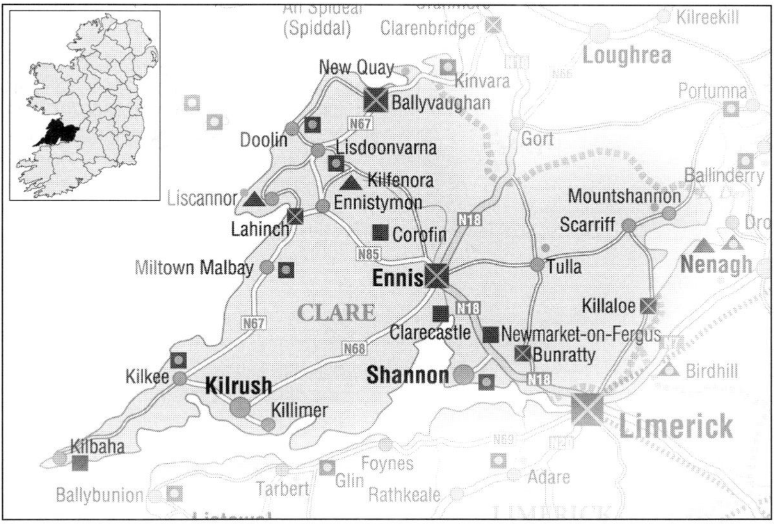

Clare is a larger-than-life county which is bounded by the Atlantic to the west, Galway Bay to the north, the Shannon and Lough Derg to the east, and the Shannon Estuary to the south. And it's typical of Clare that, even with its boundaries marked on such a grand scale, there is always something extra added. Thus the Atlantic coasts include not only the astonishing and majestic Cliffs of Moher, but also one of Ireland's greatest surfing beaches at Lahinch on Liscannor Bay. As for that Galway Bay coastline, it is where The Burren, the fantastical North Clare moonscape of limestone which is home to so much unexpectedly exotic flora, comes plunging spectacularly towards the sea around the attractive village of Ballyvaughan.

To the eastward, Lough Derg is one of Ireland's most handsome lakes, but even amidst its generous beauty, we find that Clare has claimed one of the most scenic lake coastlines of all. As for the Shannon Estuary, well, Ireland may have many estuaries, but needless to say the lordly Shannon has far and away the biggest estuary of all. Along its northern shore on the Fergus Estuary, Clare's county town of Ennis is a busy and energetic place.

"The Banner County" of sporting legend, Clare is somewhere special to call home - in the recent European survey, its population increased by 9.9%, above the Irish national average of 8%. It has many attractions, in recent years becoming the leading county for the study of dolphin life - the hundred-plus colony of bottle-nose dolphins which make the Shannon Estuary their summer home are monitored from the increasingly busy recreational port of Kilrush, while Doolin in the north of the county has its own exceptionally friendly dolphin.

Other places like Ennistimon, Milltown Malbay, Corofin and Mountshannon - they all have a very human and friendly dimension. For this is a county where the human spirit defines itself as being very human indeed, in the midst of scenic effects which at times seem to border on the supernatural.

Local Attractions and Information

Ballyvaughan, Aillwee Cave 065 707 7036
Bunratty, Bunratty Castle & Folk Park 061 360788
Cliffs of Moher, Tourist Information 065 708 1171
Corofin, Clare Heritage Centre 065 683 7955
Ennis, Tourist Centre 065 682 8366
Killimer, Killimer-Tarbert Ferry 065 53124
Kilrush, Kilrush Heritage Centre 065 905 1577
Kilrush, Scattery Island Interpretive Centre 065 905 2139
Kilrush, Vandeleur Walled Garden 065 905 1760
Quin, Craggaunowen (Celts & Living Past) 061 360788
Quin, Knappogue Castle 061 360788
Shannon Airport, Tourist Information 061 471664

BALLYVAUGHAN

This attractive little port is best known for its major attraction, the Aillwee Cave, but its seafood comes a close second - and, as it is in a leafy valley with a wide range of amenities close at hand, it makes a comfortable base for exploring the Burren. Hotel accommodation is available in the village at **Hylands Burren Hotel (065 707 7037; www.hylandsburren.com),** who offer all day food (speciality: seafood) and off-season breaks. Daytime food is also available at **The Whitethorn Restaurant (065 707 7044; www.thewhitethorn.com)**, also home to a good craft shop and The Burren Exposure interpretative centre. Of the pubs, the traditional **Monks Bar (065 707 7059),** on the pier, has open fires and, at its best, a name for good seafood, while those with a yen for a real old pub of character should drop in for a jar at nearby O'Loughlins, family-run for generations. For good Italian food it is worth checking out if **Holywell Italian Café (065 707 7322)** is open (near the Burren College of Art).

Ballyvaughan

Aillwee Cave

CAFÉ

Ballyvaughan Co Clare **Tel: 065 707 7036** Fax: 065 707 7107
Email: info@aillweecave.ie Web: www.aillweecave.ie

Visitors to this 2-million-year-old cave will see more than the amazing illuminated tunnels and waterfalls, for there is much of interest to foodlovers as well. Driving up to the entrance, look out for the sign to the cheese-making demonstrations - for it is here that the local Burren Gold cheese is made. Even if the process is in a quiet phase at the time of a visit, there is still plenty to see - and buy - as the cheesemaking takes place alongside a well-stocked food shop. Just inside the entrance to the cave there is a souvenir shop with a good book section (including travel and cookery books of Irish interest) and a themed potato bar café serving inexpensive, wholesome fare - typically baked potatoes with Burren Gold cheese. Fast food (coffee, paninis etc) also available outside - and a new mountain trail "guaranteed to work up an appetite". The Liscannor Rock Shop is a sister enterprise (see entry) - and it also provides wholesome, inexpensive food in its little café (and goodies, such as home-made preserves, to take home too). Children welcome. Café **Seats 80.** No-smoking area. Meals all day Mon-Sun (9.30-6.30). Closed 22-27 Dec. MasterCard, Visa. **Directions:** 2 miles south of Ballyvaughan.

Ballyvaughan

An Fear Gorta (Tea & Garden Rooms)

CAFÉ

Ballyvaughan Co Clare **Tel: 065 707 7157** Fax: 065 707 7127

Approached from the harbour side through a lovely front garden, Katherine O'Donoghue's delightful old stone restaurant dates back to 1790, when it was built as a residence for 'coast security officers'. Having been rebuilt by the present owners in 1981, it is now just the spot for a light bite to eat. In fine weather the beautiful back garden or the conservatory can be idyllic; otherwise the homely dining room offers comfort and shelter, with its informal arrangement of old furniture and a tempting display of home-baked fare. This is the speciality of the house - all laid out on an old cast-iron range and very reasonably priced - beginning at only €1.50 for scone, butter & home-made jam. Speciality teas are available as well as savoury choices including farmhouse cheeses, home-baked ham and Tea Room Specials including Open Smoked Salmon Sandwich on Brown Bread. 2-3 course lunch specials are available at around €10 and there's home-made jam and marmalade to take away. Open Jun-Sep, Mon-Sat:11-5.30 (L 12-4.30). Closed Oct-May. **No Credit Cards. Directions:** On the harbour front in Ballyvaughan.

Ballyvaughan

Drumcreehy House

GUESTHOUSE

Ballyvaughan Co Clare **Tel: 065 707 7377** Fax: 065 707 7379
Email: info@drumcreehyhouse.com Web: www.drumcreehyhouse.com

Just along the road beyond the Whitethorn restaurant and craftshop, Armin and Bernadette Grefkes' attractive purpose-built guesthouse makes a comfortable and moderately-priced base for a break in this lovely area and is a delightful place to stay. The furnishing style is a mixture of old and new with antiques and newer country furnishings blending well; front bedrooms have sea views across Galway Bay while those at the back have a pleasant outlook over the Burren - and all have phones and television. There's also a comfortable sitting room with an open fire available for guests' use and everything is spotless and full of character. Breakfasts are exceptional - a first class buffet includes local cheese, from Annaliese Bartelink in Kilnaboy, gravadlax and smoked salmon while hot dishes include unusual dishes such as herrings with horseradish sauce as well as the more usual dishes; 3-course evening meals are available by reservation, and there's an informal menu (chowders, open sandwiches, mixed meat/seafood platters, home baking etc), served in the lounge. Banqueting (40). Beach nearby (10 minute walk). Garden. **Rooms 10** (all en-suite & no smoking). Children welcome (cot available without charge. B&B €40pps, ss16. Residents D at 7pm (book by noon), €22; menus change daily. A la carte Lounge Menu served 12-1pm and 7-8pm. Wines from about €16. Closed Nov - Feb. (Open only on request.) MasterCard, Visa, Laser. **Directions:** N67 to Ballyvaughan, at Hylands Hotel turn right. Continue for 1 mile, Drumcreehy House on the right.

Ballyvaughan

COUNTRY HOUSE / RESTAURANT

Gregans Castle Hotel

Ballyvaughan Co Clare
Tel: 065 707 7005 Fax: 065 707 7111
Email: res@gregans.ie Web: www.gregans.ie

Gregans Castle has a long and interesting history, going back to a tower house, or small castle, which was built by the O'Loughlen clan (the region's principal tribe) between the 10th and 17th centuries and is still intact, while the present house dates from the late 18th century. It has been added to many times and was opened as a country house hotel with the name Gregans Castle in 1976 by Peter and Moira Haden who (true to the traditions of the house) have continued to develop and improve it, with the active involvement of their son Simon, who is Manager. The exterior is grey and stark, in keeping with the lunar landscape of the surrounding Burren, wonderfully heightening the contrast between first impressions and the warmth, comfort and hospitality to be found within. Peace and quiet are the dominant themes: spacious rooms are furnished to a very high standard, with excellent bathrooms and lovely countryside views - and deliberately left without the worldly interference of television. Yet this luxurious hotel is not too formal or at all intimidating; non-residents are welcome to drop in for lunch or afternoon tea in the Corkscrew Bar - named after a nearby hill which, incidentally, provides the most scenic approach to Ballyvaughan. In fine weather guests can sit out beside the Celtic Cross rose garden and watch patches of sun and shade chasing across the hills. In the morning, allow time to enjoy an excellent breakfast. Children welcome (no concessions, but cot available,€15). No pets. All day room service. **Rooms 21** (3 suites, 3 junior suites) B&B €99 pps; ss€79. No service charge.

The Dining Room: The restaurant is decorated in a rich country house style and elegantly furnished in keeping with the rest of the house. Most tables have lovely views over the Burren (which on fine summer evenings enjoys very special light effects as the sun sets over Galway Bay) and dinner is usually gently accompanied by a pianist. Head chef Norman Mueller joined Gregans Castle in 2003 and cooks contemporary meals with an international flavour tempered by experience on cruise liners and top hotels in France and Australia - Asian and Pacific Rim influences are noticeable, but also modern Irish themes with some French influence, offering a wide choice of dishes based on a combination of local produce (Kinvara organic smoked salmon, Carrigaholt crabmeat, Burren lamb, County Clare beef) and foods from further afield. There is always a fine selection of local cheeses, with homemade biscuits - and organic produce features on all menus, including breakfast (organic eggs from Hans & Ute Krewer in the East Burren, for example) and the wine list: 20% of the current wine list consists of organic and biodynamic wines, leading off with the house wines. Dinner is a treat at Gregans Castle, but they also offer an attractive short à la carte lunch menu (served in The Corkscrew Bar) and delicious Afternoon Teas too. **Seats 50** (Private Room, 30). No smoking restaurant. Well-behaved children welcome (not in the bar after 7.30). D daily, 7-8.30; 5-course D €49, any 2 courses €35.50. House wines from €23.50. No service charge. Short à la carte lunch is available in the Corkscrew Bar, 12-3 daily. Afternoon Tea, 3-5 daily. Hotel closed 1 Nov-31 Mar. Amex, MasterCard, Visa, Laser. **Directions:** On N67, 3 miles south of Ballyvaughan.

Ballyvaughan

ACCOMMODATION / GUESTHOUSE

Rusheen Lodge

Knocknagrough Ballyvaughan Co Clare
Tel: 065 707 7092 Fax: 065 707 7092
Email: rusheen@iol.ie Web: www.rusheenlodge.com

John and Rita McGann swapped houses with their daughter Karen, who now runs Rusheen Lodge to the high standards for which it is well known, and they live next door so there's no shortage of experienced hands nearby for very busy times - and, as it was John McGann's father, Jacko McGann, who discovered the Aillwee Cave, an immense network of caverns and waterfalls under the Burren which is now a major attraction in the area, the McGanns understand better than most the popularity of Ballyvaughan as a visitor destination. Fresh flowers in both the house and garden create a riot of colour in contrast to the overall green-greyness of the surrounding Burren, suggesting an oasis in a wilderness - which is just what Rusheen Lodge aims to provide. A 3-room executive suite introduced in 2002 has proved popular and all of the generously proportioned, well-appointed bedrooms have phones, tea/coffee trays, TV, trouser press and good bathrooms; all this, plus spacious public rooms, good food and warm hospitality make Rusheen Lodge a particularly pleasant place to stay. While evening meals are not provided, the pubs and restaurants of Ballyvaughan are only a few minutes' walk and breakfast - whether traditional Irish or continental - is a major feature of a stay. Children welcome (under 3s free in parents' room, cot available without charge, baby sitting arranged). No pets. **Rooms 9** (2 suites, 1 executive room, all no-smoking). B&B €45pps, ss€20. Closed mid Nov-mid Feb. MasterCard, Visa, Laser. **Directions:** 3/4 km from village on the N67.

Ballyvaughan

Trí na Chéile Restaurant

Ⓝ RESTAURANT

Main Street Ballyvaughan Co Clare
Tel: 065 707 7103 Fax: 065 707 7431

A convenient location, pleasant surroundings, friendly staff and menus offering a good choice - including vegetarian dishes and a children's menu - are among the attractions of this pleasing restaurant in the centre of Ballyvaughan. It has a warm and welcoming ambience - rustic ochre walls, candlelight, fresh flowers, soft music - and local foods (organic where possible) are offered in menus that have something for everyone, in terms of both choice and price. Galway Bay mussels, for example, may feature in dishes as varied as seafood vol-au-vent, the ubiquitous seafood chowder or a bourride of mussels (mussels cooked with white wine, herbs and spices), while lobster is available with 24 hours notice and Burren lamb is offered in season; other popular choices include straightforward steaks and a pasta selection - and you can finish off with classic desserts like a deeply-flavoured chocolate terrine or a refreshing fruit salad. Well-chosen wine list, efficent service and good value. Children welcome. No smoking restaurant. **Seats 45.** D daily, 6-10. Children's Menu 6-7.30, €5.50. Set D from €17.50, also à la carte. SC discretionary. Closed Oct-Mar. MasterCard, Visa, Laser. **Directions:** In centre of village.

BUNRATTY

With its famous medieval Castle and Folk Park, Bunratty attracts vast numbers of visitors and there is plenty of competition when it comes to accommodation, restaurants and, of course, entertainment. Of the hotels, the best known is **Fitzpatrick Bunratty Hotel (061 361177; www.fitzpatrickhotels.com)** which was built in the 1960s at the time when the castle was retored; it has good conference and leisure facilities and offers special breaks. **Avoca Handweavers (061 364029)** also have an outlet at Bunratty and, with wholesome daytime café food available, this can be a good place to break a journey

---

Bunratty

Bunratty Castle Hotel

HOTEL

Bunratty Co Clare **Tel: 061 478700** Fax: 061 364891
Email: info@bunrattycastlehotel.com Web: www.bunrattycastle.com

This modern hotel on a rise overlooking Bunratty Castle and Folk Park is attractively designed to reflect its Georgian origins. Public seating areas are spacious and comfortable, while traditionally furnished rooms have all the modern comforts, including air conditioning and satellite TV - and bathrooms with both (small) bath and good overbath shower; executive rooms are more luxurious, with extras including ISDN facilities and two-line phones. In addition to food and entertainment offered by the hotel (including the unique 'new Medieval bar'), the pubs and restaurants of Bunratty village are all close by. Some excellent quality shops are situated within the hotel grounds. Good business facilities for small to medium meetings (max 150; banqueting 200). Business centre. Ample parking. Children welcome (under 2 free in parents' room, cots available, babysitting arranged); pets allowed by arrangement. Lift. 24 hour room service. Shop. Garden. **Rooms 80** (8 junior suites, 11 executive, 50 no smoking, 2 for disabled). B&B €88pps, ss €20. Closed 25 Dec. Amex, Diners, MasterCard, Visa, Laser. Helipad. **Directions:** 5 miles from Shannon Airport.

Bunratty

Durty Nelly's

ATMOSPHERIC PUB / RESTAURANT

Bunratty Co Clare
Tel: 061 364861 Web: www.durtynellys.ie

Although often seriously over-crowded with tourists in summer, this famous and genuinely characterful old pub in the shadow of Bunratty Castle somehow manages to provide cheerful service and above-average food to the great numbers who pass through its doors. All-day fare is served downstairs in the bar (all day) and Oyster Restaurant (lunch and dinner), upstairs there is a more exclusive restaurant, The Loft, open in the evening only (Mon-Sat, 6-10). Both areas offer à la carte menus. Closed 25 Dec, Good Fri. Amex, Diners, MasterCard, Visa, Laser, Switch. **Directions:** Beside Bunratty Castle.

Bunratty

Muses Restaurant

RESTAURANT

Bunratty House Mews Bunratty Co Clare
Tel: 061 364 082 Fax: 061 364 350
Email: muses@oceanfree.net Web: www.musesrestaurant.com

Aidan McGrath's basement restaurant at the back of the Bunratty estate is all warmth and welcome: a small hall leads to a lovely bar area overlooking Bunratty Park and castle, with an open fire, a proper counter and deep sofa to relax in while enjoying a promptly served aperitif and consulting the menu, a well-balanced offering that promises well, with seafood and local organic produce much in evidence and imaginative vegetarian options - a starter of tempura of field mushrooms with various organic leaves and basil aioli, for example, or main course of grilled & roasted vegetables with herbs & olive oil, red pepper & basil pasta, tomato fondue & black olives - which might tempt the most dedicated carnivore. The restaurant consists of three small rooms in rustic cellar style, with well-appointed tables and lovely flowers, prints and bric-à-brac creating a soothing, restful atmosphere. High quality ingredients are the star, providing a sound foundation for creative cooking: excellent fresh local fish and shellfish, for example, meticulously sourced dry-aged beef and chicken - although not billed as organic or free-range - with real depth of flavour. Each dish has its own complementary vegetable garnish: a starter of naturally smoked haddock penne, for example, comes with fresh garden peas, broad beans & a grain mustard cream, or there's a black pudding terrine with sautéed potatoes, caramelised onions & mizuna - while a main course of roast rump of Burren lamb is served with roasted plum tomatoes, provençal vegetables and couscous. At an average of around €22 for a main course, prices are reasonable for the quality offered. Save a little space for luscious desserts such as strawberry and rhubarb tart or a classic vanilla crème brulée, which are beautifully presented. Service is very correct and the wine list is interesting and well-chosen, although there is little choice under €30. Private parties and small weddings can be catered for. Group lunch bookings accepted any day, also group dinner bookings Sun/Mon. Not suitable for children under 10 after 7.30 pm. No smoking restaurant. **Seats 45** (private room 14). D Tue-Sat, last orders 9.30; 2-course D €30 (6-7.30) otherwise à la carte. House wines from about €21.50; sc discretionary. Closed Sun, Mon, Christmas, all Jan. Amex, MasterCard, Visa, Laser. **Directions:** Bearing left at the village green, turn sharp left up the hill road for100 metres; restaurant parking spaces are on the right hand side.

Carron

Burren Perfumery Tea Rooms

Ⓝ CAFÉ

Carron Co Clare **Tel: 065 708 9102** Fax: 065 708 9200
Email: burrenperfumery@eircom.net Web: www.burrenperfumery.com

When touring Clare you will be pleased to find this charming spot - the perfumery is beautifully laid out, with a herb garden, pleasing old buildings and lovely biodynamic scents.The little tea rooms open onto a courtyard, opposite the perfumery shop - and beside the distillation room where essential oils are extracted in a traditional still. Although small and simple, the tea rooms are pretty, with floral waxed tablecloths, fresh flowers and cups and saucers all creating a happy mismatch of pastels - and what they do is of high quality and uses local organic produce. At lunchtime there might be spice lentil soup with brown bread (€5), or you could have a homemade scone with butter and jam (€2.10). All kinds of teas and tisanes, and coffee served in individual cafetières. Open daily in summer. **No Credit Cards. Directions:** In the Burren, east of Gort.

Clarecastle

Carnelly House

COUNTRY HOUSE

Clarecastle Co Clare **Tel: 065 682 8442** Fax: 065 682 9222
Email: info@carnelly-house.com Web: www.carnelly-house.com

Conveniently located for Shannon airport and touring the west of Ireland, Dermott and Rosemarie Gleeson's fine redbrick Georgian house is set on 100 acres of farm and woodland and offers discerning guests very special accommodation. Reception rooms include an impressive drawing room with Corinthian pillars, Francini ceiling, grand piano and a striking panelled dining room, while bedrooms are large and furnished to a high standard, with antiques, canopied king size or twin beds and luxurious private bathrooms. Yet the grandeur is not at all daunting and Carnelly - which is well-placed for a wide range of country pursuits, including many of the country's most famous hunts - has been described as "one of the warmest, friendliest and most entertaining houses in Ireland". Children welcome (cot available free of charge). There is also a gate lodge, which is available by the night, week or month. Conferences/banqueting (25/25). Pets permitted by arrangement. Garden, walks. **Rooms 5** (all deluxe, all no-smoking); limited room service; turndown service €115 pps (single occupancy €150 off-season, but single rate not available May-Oct). Licensed. SC discretionary. Open all year except Christmas/New

Corofin

Restaurant Lecatelinais

Ⓝ RESTAURANT

Market Street Corofin Co Clare **Tel: 065 683 7425**
Fax: 065 683 7425 Email: lecatelinais@eircom.net

This attractive restaurant in the village of Corofin gives a good impression on arrival - clearly signed, smart paintwork in warm tones, own carpark - all confirmed by a warm welcome that gets a meal in the calm, pleasant dining room off to a good start. Green and white linen clad tables with flowers and candles are equally welcoming and well-balanced, fairly classical, menus offer plenty of tempting dishes at very fair prices. The early dinner, in particular, is a snip and does not seem at all like a 'budget' menu, offering a choice of four really good dishes on each course including starters like steamed mussels in white wine with shallots & garlic or chicken & pistachio nut terrine with homemade pear chutney, main courses of honey roast half duck with tangy orange sauce (€2.95 extra), or grilled fillet of salmon with toasted almonds & citrus beurre blanc and delicious desserts such hazelnut parfait or Baileys bread & butter pudding with sauce anglaise - most of which are also included on the more expensive (and extensive) later menus. The wine list, which predictably favours France, is well-chosen, fairly priced and unusually informative, with a good selection of half bottles. All this and attentive, friendly service too. Children welcome. Reservations accepted. **Seats 45** (private room 16). D Tue-Sun from 5.30. L (Open daily in summer). Early D €21.50; Candlelight Menu €31.50; also à la carte. House wine €17.50. Closed Mon off-season; last 2 weeks Oct. MasterCard, Visa, Laser. **Directions:** North of Ennis town en route to the Burren.

Year. Amex, MasterCard, Visa, Laser. **Directions:** One mile south of Clarecastle on Limerick Road N18.

Corofin

Clifden House

COUNTRY HOUSE

Corofin Co Clare **Tel: 065 683 7692** Fax: 065 683 7692
Email: clifdenhousecountyclare@eircom.net
Web: www.clifdenhouse-countyclare.com

This unusual early Georgian manor on the shore of Lough Inchiquin was found "slipping gracefully into ruin" 25 years ago by Jim and Bernadette Robson who, while conceding that "the work is not yet finished nor will it be twenty years hence", have gone a considerable way towards restoration "following the criteria of respecting its tradition of hospitality and the comfort of our friends and guests". Bedrooms are highly individualistic (one bathroom in particular even more so), stylish and comfortable, with fresh flowers and views of the lake and countryside - do not be concerned that certain areas may be only partially restored. The Robsons enjoy their food, in every sense of the word - organic meats come from a nearby farm, fish and game are also local, while organic vegetables and fruit from their own lovely walled garden. Bernadette is the cook and a homely three-course meal is served by Jim, the genial host - who also dispenses wine from a short list and chats to guests around a large communal table, where everyone can get to know each other. Accommodation is also offered in two 3- and 4-bedroom holiday houses in a stable wing, with cobbled yard and riverside lawn; they can be either self-catering or serviced. Gardens, walking, fishing (boats available). Children welcome (cot available without charge; babysitting arranged). No pets. **Rooms 4** (1 shower only).€65 pps, ss€25. Communal dinner at 8 pm, €35 (book by noon). Closed Nov-mid Mar. Amex, MasterCard, Visa, Laser. **Directions:** Going north out of Corofin turn left at Grotto; take 2nd right then 1st right.

Corofin

Fergus View

FARMHOUSE

Kilnaboy Corofin Co Clare **Tel: 065 683 7606** Fax: 065 683 7192
Email: deckell@indigo.ie Web: www.fergusview.com

Mary Kelleher runs a very hospitable house and the care taken to ensure guests enjoy their visit to the full is shown in details like the the information packs on the area compiled by her and left in each bedroom - and interesting breakfasts that include home-made yogurt, freshly squeezed juice, home-made muesli, Anneliese Bartelink's excellent local Poulcoin cheeses and a wide range of teas as well as cooked breakfasts with free range eggs. Rooms are comfortable although a little on the small side, as often happens when family homes are converted to include en-suite facilities. Refurbishment is an ongoing business - traditional wooden windows were recently installed throughout the house, and the Kellehers also added a new entrance conservatory which opens onto the garden and has extensive views; soft furnishings in all the bedrooms have also been replaced recently - and there's always something else in progress on every re-visit. There's also a lovely stone cottage next door,Tigh Eamon, which has been charmingly converted for self-catering accommodation. Children welcome (cot available). Garden. No pets. **Rooms 6** (5 en-suite with shower only,1 with private bathroom, all no-smoking). B&B €34pps; ss €15. Closed mid Oct-Easter. **No Credit Cards. Directions:** 2 miles north of Corofin on Kilfenora Road.

Doolin

Aran View Hotel

HOTEL

Coast Road Doolin Co Clare **Tel: 065 707 4061** Fax: 065 707 4540
Email: bookings@aranview.com Web: www.aranview.com

Just outside Doolin, and commanding dramatic sea views across to the islands, the heart of the Linnane's family-run hotel is an eighteenth century house. It makes a good base for a family holiday - it is only a mile to a good beach, there is sea-angling and golf nearby and, of course, there is the traditional music for which Doolin is world famous. Public rooms include a comfortable bar for all weathers - it has a sea view and an open fire. Bedrooms vary considerably in size and outlook due to the age and nature of the building: rooms at the front are most desirable - several at the back have no view, but are otherwise pleasant. There are two extra large ones and two singles; all have phones, tea/coffee trays and TV (local stations). Children are welcome - outdoor play area and children's menu provided. The restaurant, which is open to non-residents daily, offers reasonably priced menus and a well-balanced selection of old favourites along with some more modern dishes. **Rooms 19** (2 superior, 6 shower only, 6 no smoking, 2 for disabled); B&B €60 pps, ss €15. Closed en Oct-mid Apr. Amex, Diners MasterCard, Visa. **Directions:** N67 exit off near Lisdoonvarna to Doolin.

Doolin

Ballinalacken Castle Country House & Restaurant

HOTEL

Doolin Co Clare **Tel: 065 707 4025** Fax: 065 707 4025
Email: ballinalackencastle@eircom.net Web: ballinalackencastle.com

Well away from the bustle of Lisdoonvarna, and with wonderful views of the Atlantic, Aran Islands, Cliffs of Moher and the distant hills of Connemara, Ballinalacken is easily identified by the 15th century castle still standing beside the hotel. In the O'Callaghan family ownership since opening in 1940, and currently managed by Marian O'Callaghan, Ballinalacken has retained a Victorian country house atmosphere with its welcoming fire in the hall and well-proportioned public rooms comfortably furnished with antiques. Public rooms and some bedrooms enjoy magnificent views and recent renovations have resulted in a major upgrade of accommodation, which now includes two suites - one with panoramic views, the other an historic room with a fireplace and luxurious bathroom. The grounds which are substantial - are being improved on an ongoing basis. Children welcome (under 4s free in parents' room, cot available without charge). Pets permitted by arrangement. **Rooms 12** (2 suites,1 room shower only; all no-smoking). B&B about €65pps, ss about €50. Closed end Oct-mid Apr.

Restaurant: The restaurant offers lovely views from window tables and provides a fitting setting for Frank Sheedy's modern cooking, which is based firmly on the best local produce although the style is international. Good home-made breads - traditional brown, walnut, tomato perhaps - set the tone and a choice of half a dozen starters might include local seafood (a tian of fresh crabmeat on pickled vegetables, with peanut pesto & sweet chilli dressing perhaps), two soups and a vegetarian option such as a Mediterranean salad, or goat cheese fritters. Well-balanced flavours and accurate cooking are evident throughout, making the most of prime ingredients like local lobster and Burren lamb. Good coffee, served at the table or in the drawing room, rounds off the evening nicely and refills are automatically offered. Open to non-residents. D daily, 6.45-9. A la carte. Service discretionary. Amex, MasterCard, Visa. **Directions:** Coast road, R477 North of Doolin Village. ◇

Doolin

Cullinans Seafood Restaurant & Guesthouse

RESTAURANT / GUESTHOUSE

Doolin Co Clare
Tel: 065 707 4183 Fax: 065 707 4239
Email: cullinans@eircom.net Web: www.cullinansdoolin.com

Proprietor-chef James Cullinan and his wife Carol, who looks after front of house, have earned a loyal following at their comfortable dining room overlooking the Aille river at the back of the house. Menus include an attractive early dinner, with three or four choices on each course (including vegetarian dishes) and an à la carte which is available at any time from opening. Local produce - including Burren smoked salmon, Inagh goats cheese, Doolin crabmeat and Aran scallops - is credited on the menu, providing a sound base for fairly modern Irish cooking with some French influence, as in specialities like starters of tian of prawn, avocado & smoked salmon (with horseradish cream and plum tomato compôte) and main courses such as pan-seared Aran scallops with root vegetable purée & balsamic reduction. Carnivores are well looked after too, of course - prime fillet steak on a shallot & fennel purée with burgundy jus is a speciality - and vegetarians will enjoy thoughtfully prepared dishes like an aubergine terrine with roast pepper coulis. Tempting desserts - a trio of chocolate, perhaps - or farmhouse cheeses to finish. A quite extensive wine list includes about ten half bottles. Children welcome. No smoking restaurant. **Seats 25** D Thu-Tue, 6-9. A la carte; early D €25 (6-7pm). House wines €18. SC discretionary. Closed Wed & Oct-Easter.

Accommodation: Warm hospitality, comfortable beds and a tasty breakfast make this a good place to stay. Cheerful modern rooms have all the necessities, including phones and tea/coffee trays - at a reasonable price. Children welcome (under 3s free in parents' room, cot available without charge). Garden. No pets. **Rooms 8** (3 shower only, all no-smoking). B&B €40 ss €30. Visa, MasterCard, Laser. **Directions:** Centre of Doolin between McGanns & O'Connors Pub.

Ennis

Hal Pino's Restaurant

RESTAURANT

7 High Street Ennis Co Clare **Tel: 065 684 0011** Fax: 065 684 0022
Email: halpinsrestaurant@eircom.net Web: www.halpins.com

Derek Halpin's first floor restaurant is up a staircase over a bar in the town centre and has become one of the area's most popular eating places since opening in 2001. You can have an aperitif and place orders from a sensibly compact menu in the comfortable reception/bar before going to your table (simply appointed but generous and well-spaced); the decor may not make very much impact, depending on the style of paintings exhibited all around the walls at the time - anyway the most noticeable feature is likely to be the buzz of lots of people enjoying themselves. Prawns in filo pastry, duck breast with blackberry jus (pink, tender with a welcome bit of bite in the sauce), Burren lamb with a herb crust are all typical of the food - also lovely Clare potatoes, imaginative seasonal vegetables and well-dressed side salads. Accurate cooking, excellent flavour and appetising presentation go a long way towards making a meal enjoyable, and a good atmosphere can make it memorable; service has tended to be inconsistent, in the Guide's experience. An early dinner menu offers good value. **Seats 70.** Not suitable for children under 8 after 7pm. D daily, 5-10.30 (Sun to 10). L Fri only, by arrangement. Closed Christmas. Amex, MasterCard, Visa, Laser. **Directions:** Just off main Town Square. ◇

Ennis

Jasmine Palace

RESTAURANT

Barrack Street Ennis Co Clare **Tel: 065 686 8188**
Fax: 061 410201 www.claretohere.com/jasminepalace

This delightful Chinese restaurant is a younger sister of the Jasmine Palace in Limerick and offers a full range of popular Chinese dishes, specialising in Cantonese cuisine, and is a good deal less expensive than comparable establishments in Dublin. Dishes singled out for praise on a recent visit include an appetizer of Crab Claws in Black Bean Sauce (€7.55) – six small pieces of crab claws cooked in a rich delicious sauce and beautifully presented - and Deep-fried Whole Fish (sea bream) with Garlic and Chilli Sauce, again beautifully prepared and cooked, though at €24, it is not cheap. Friendly and efficient service under the co-owner/manager Terry Yeung. Vegetarian Option. Family Friendly. Open Mon-Sat Lunch 12.30- 2.30, Dinner 4.30-11.30 Sun all day (12.30-10.30 pm) Early Bird 5.30-7.00 pm. House wine €13.90. Amex, Diners, MasterCard, Visa.

Ennis

Newpark House

FARMHOUSE

Ennis Co Clare **Tel: 065 682 1233** Fax: 065 682 123
Email: newparkhouse.ennis@eircom.net Web: www.newparkhouse.com

Strange as it may seem to find a genuine farmhouse in a country setting within easy walking distance of the pubs and restaurants of Ennis, the Barron family home is the exception that defies easy description. This 300 year old house is of great historic interest and has large homely rooms, furnished with old family furniture and a quiet atmosphere - and bedrooms which vary in size and character, as old houses do, but they are comfortable and full of interest. The en-suite bathrooms also vary considerably (remember this is a farmhouse), and first-time guests may need a fairly independent spirit in order to get into the ways of the house as information is not always forthcoming. However, regular guests adore the place and its exceptionally convenient location makes it a useful base for touring the area, following country pursuits (golf, horse riding, fishing, walking) or genealogy - there's a lot of useful material in the house and the Barrons can give advice on researching your roots. Local record centres - the library and courthouse - are just a few minutes' walk. Children welcome (under 2s free in parents' room, cot available); pets permitted in some areas. Communal dinner is available on request €25 at 6.30, please book by 3 pm. Bring your own wine. **Rooms 6** (all en-suite, 1 shower only; 4 triple rooms, 1 family room). B&B €50pps, ss €20. Closed Nov-Easter. **No Credit Cards. Directions:** R352, turn right at Roselevan Arms.

Ennis

Old Ground Hotel

HOTEL / RESTAURANT

O'Connell Street Ennis Co Clare
Tel: 065 682 8127 Fax: 065 682 8112
Email: oghotel@iol.ie Web: www.flynnhotels.com

This ivy-clad former manor house dates back to the 18th century and, set in its own gardens, creates an oasis of calm in the bustling centre of Ennis. One of the country's best-loved hotels, the Old Ground was bought by the Flynn family in 1995 and has been imaginatively extended and renovated by them in a way that is commendably sensitive to the age and importance of the building. Despite the difficulties of dealing with very thick walls in an old building, major improvements were made to existing banqueting/conference facilities in the mid '90s, then an extra storey was added to provide new rooms. Again, this was a sensitive development and, as the famous ivy-clad frontage continues to thrive, the external changes are barely noticeable to the casual observer. Major refurbishment has also taken place throughout the interior of the hotel, including all bedrooms - which have good amenities and well-designed bathrooms - and an additional 36 new executive rooms are due to open in April 2004. A traditional style bar, Poet's Corner (bar menu 12-9) features traditional music on some nights.* Town Hall Café (see entry), is an informal contemporary restaurant in an historic building adjacent to the hotel. Children welcome (under 2 free in parents' room, cot available without charge, baby sitting arranged). Conference/banqueting (130/200). No pets. Garden. **Rooms 83** (4 suites, 4 junior suites, 20 executive rooms, 3 shower only, 4 no-smoking, 1 disabled.) Lift. All day room service; turndown service. B&B €95pps; ss €32. Closed 24-26 Dec.

O'Brien Room Restaurant: The hotel's formal dining room is at the front of the hotel and has great character. Freddy Rynn took over as head chef from his old boss Gerry Walsh in 2002, maintaining a welcome continuity in a kitchen team which has been part of the hotel since 1980. Freddy takes pride in using local produce in enduring specialities dishes such as Burren lamb with rosemary & honey glaze or fillets of turbot with lemon & chive beurre blanc. **Seats 65** (private room, 70) Toilets wheelchair accessible. No smoking area; air conditioning. L&D daily: L12-2.30, D 6.30-9.30. Set L €12.50/17.50, Sun L €19.50; Set D €32.50, D also à la carte. House wine €16.50. SC discretionary. Closed 25-26 Dec. Amex, Diners, MasterCard, Visa, Laser. **Directions:** Town centre.

Ennis

Temple Gate Hotel

HOTEL

The Square Ennis Co Clare **Tel: 065 682 3300** Fax: 065 682 3322
Email: info@templegatehotel.com Web: www.templegatehotel.com

This family-owned hotel was built in the mid '90s on the site of a 19th century convent, to a clever design that retains the older features including a church, which is now the Great Hall Banqueting/Conference room. Existing Gothic themes have been successfully blended into the new throughout the hotel, creating a striking modern building of character which has relevance to its surroundings in the heart of a medieval town and succeeds in providing the comfort and convenience demanded by contemporary travellers, at a reasonable price. While guests' needs are well catered for on site - JM's Bistro offers lively contemporary menus and Preachers pub offers a bar menu and traditional music every weekend - the shops and many famous music pubs of the town centre are just a short walk across a cobble-stoned courtyard. Conference/banqueting (220/150). Children under 5 free in parents' room; cot available without charge, babysitting arranged. 24 hour room service. No pets. Garden. **Rooms 70** (2 junior suites, 2 executive rooms, 10 non-smoking). B&B€80 pps, ss €35. Closed 24-25 Dec. Amex, Diners, MasterCard, Visa, Laser, Switch. **Directions:** In Ennis, follow signs to tourist office: hotel is beside it.

Ennis

Town Hall Café

CAFÉ / RESTAURANT

O'Connell Street Ennis Co Clare
Tel: 065 682 8127 Fax: 065 682 8112
Email: oghotel@iol.ie Web: www.flynnhotels.com

Adjacent to (and part of) The Old Ground Hotel, the Town Hall Café has a separate street entrance and this contemporary space in no way feels like a 'hotel restaurant'. The old town hall has been well restored and the restaurant is in an impressive high-ceilinged room with sensitively spare decor - large art works which will be loved or loathed, big pots and simple table settings allow the room to speak for itself. Daytime menus are concise but varied, a mixture of modern bistro-style dishes (eg braised shank of Clare lamb, pommes parmentier, rosemary & port jus), daily specials, and tea-room fare - just what people need to re-charge during a day's shopping it seems, as the cooking is good, service swift and value excellent. In the evening it all moves up a notch or two, when a shortish à la carte menu comes on stream, offering about half a dozen choice per course. Starters might include baked Inagh goats cheese with sundried tomatoes & basil, pine nut salad & raspberry vinaigrette followed by main courses like beer battered monkfish with organic leaves & sweet chilli sauce, or prime 10oz sirloin steak with a grain mustard & Irish whiskey sauce. Desserts from a daily selection. Not fine dining, but stylish and great value. Reservations recommended except for snacks. **Seats 80.** Open 10-5 (coffee10-12, L 12-5, teas 4-5) & D 6-10. Set L €25, early D €25 (6-7.30); à la carte L&D also available. House wines from €16. SC discretionary. Closed 24-25 Dec, Good Fri. Amex, Diners, MasterCard, Visam Laser. **Directions:** On main street of Ennis town.

Ennis

West County Conference & Leisure Hotel

féile bia HOTEL

Clare Road Ennis Co Clare **Tel: 065 682 8421**
Fax: 065 682 8801 Email: cro@lynchotels.com Web: www.lynchhotels.com

This modern hotel just 5 minutes walk from the centre of Ennis town is not only a well-located and comfortable base for holidaymakers but also renowned for its exceptional business and conference facilities. The hotel's Island Convention Centre can seat 1,650 delegates in a range of four conference rooms and five meeting rooms that are almost infinitely variable. There is also video-conferencing, full business/office support services and an impressive Health and Leisure Club in which to wind down or shape up. Bedrooms include interconnecting rooms, mini-suites, family rooms and 43 newer Premier standard rooms with ISDN lines. This very busy hotel offers a range of dining options for different times and occasions, including Café West, a contemporary café offering gourmet sandwiches, cakes & speciality coffees. Off-season value breaks. Children welcome (under 3 free in parents' room; cots available free of charge; playroom, crèche.) Leisure centre, swimming pool; beauty salon. No pets. **Rooms 152** (1 suite, 3 executive, 17 non-smoking, 2 for disabled). Lift. 24 hour room service. B&B about €82.53 pps, ss about €25.40. Open all year. Amex, Diners, MasterCard, Visa. **Directions:** N18 main Limerick-Galway road.Ten minutes walk from Ennis Town. ◇

Ennis

Woodstock Hotel & Golf Club

féile bia HOTEL /RESTAURANT

Shanaway Road Ennis Co Clare
Tel: 065 684 6600 Fax: 065 684 6611
Email: info@woodstockhotel.com Web: www.woodstockhotel.com

This sister hotel to the Hibernian Hotel, Dublin, and McCausland Hotel, Belfast, is built around a 19th century manor house just outside Ennis on around 200 acres, now mostly utilised by the golf course. First impressions may be mixed: although it has settled down considerably since opening in 2000, it is not especially attractive from the road and a large car park dominates the approach to a rather grandiose foyer - where, however, a welcoming fire burning in the grate and helpful staff at the reception desk create a more positive mood. Spacious public areas are furnished with some style and the large, luxurious bedrooms have equally luxurious bathrooms and also ISDN lines in addition to the more usual amenities. Golf is the major attraction (championship course on site, residents' rates available) and there's a health and fitness club on the premises, also an equestrian centre half a mile away. Children are welcome (free in parents' room up to 2; cots available free of charge, baby sitting arranged). Conferences/banqueting (250/200). Golf (18); leisure centre (gym, swimming pool, sauna, jacuzzi). Walking. Garden. No pets. **Rooms 67.** (25 deluxe, 45 no-smoking, 1 shower only , 3 disabled) Lift. 24 hour room service.Turndown service. B&B €115 pp. Closed 23-27 Dec.

Restaurant: High-ceilinged, with very large abstract paintings and stylish classic table settings (white linen, fresh flowers), the restaurant offers an old-style dining experience in formal surroundings. Head chef Anthony Duggan's moderately priced Table d'Hôte and A la Carte menus are, perhaps, designed with golfers in mind and offer quite substantial fare alongside contemporary dishes. Seafood features, as in a speciality of roasted pavé of seabass, and red meats are always popular with golfers - roast rack of Burren lamb, perhaps, with minted potato rösti & niçoise vegetables; vegetarian options are also available. Cooking can be a little uneven (soups and starters outshone the main course on a recent visit), but service is attentive and pricing very fair. **Seats 100.** D 7-9.30 daily, L Sun only, 12.30-2.30. Set D from €32.95, Set Sun L €19.95. House wine from €21.95. (* Bar menu also offered daily, in Spikes Bar). Restaurant closed 23-27 Dec. Amex, Diners, MasterCard, Visa, Laser. **Directions:** From Ennis, take main road, N18; at the first roundabout take N85 to Lahinch for : km, then turn left and continue 1km to hotel.

Ennistymon

Byrne's Restaurant & Townhouse

RESTAURANT

Main Street Ennistymon Co Clare **Tel: 065 707 1080**
Fax: 065 707 2103 Email: byrnesennistymon@eircom.net

Located in a fine period house, Byrne's has views of Ennistymon's famous cascading river from the restaurant and terrace at the back of the dining room. Contemporary style, immaculate cleanliness genuine hospitality with wit and good humour are wedded to ambitious standards of food and cooking which do not disappoint. Menus are in the modern mode, but servings are generous. The early bird (exceptional value) and dinner menus are weighted towards dishes using carefully sourced local fresh fish : cod, turbot, scallops, mussels and wild salmon are usually bolstered by specials of the day; but meat lovers and vegetarians are also well catered for. Look out for the house Gravadlax, the pancetta-wrapped baked cod, the superbly cooked seared scallops and the lamb shank. Air conditioning. Not suitable for children after 8 pm. ◇

KILFENORA

One of the most famous music centres in the west of Ireland, traditional Irish music and set dancing at **Vaughan's pub (Tel: 065 708 8004; www.vaughanspub.com)** and (previously thatched) barn attract visitors from all over the world; it's been in the family since about 1800 and serves traditional Irish food (seafood chowder, bacon & cabbage, beef & Guinness stew) based on local ingredients. Discerning travellers looking for a snack head for the nearby Visitor Centre, which does a very nice line in good home baking.

Kilkee

Halpins Townhouse Hotel

HOTEL

Erin Street Kilkee Co Clare **Tel: 065 905 6032** Fax: 065 905 6317
Email: halpins@iol.ie Web: www.halpinsprivatehotels.com

Adapting the original Victorian building of the Halpin family's small townhouse hotel to provide en-suite bathrooms has meant that bedrooms are neat rather than spacious, but they are comfortable and well-appointed with direct-dial phone, TV, hospitality tray with mineral water as well as tea/coffee-making facilities and a laundry service. There's a characterful basement bar with an open fire where visitors, including the many who come to play the adjacent Kilkee Golf Course get together after dinner at the hotel's restaurant, Vittles. In common ownership with Aberdeen Lodge, Merrion Hall (see Dublin entries.) Conference/banqueting (50). Own parking. Off-season value breaks. Children welcome (under 3 free in parents' room, cots available without charge, baby sitting arranged). **Rooms 12** (2 suites) B&B €50 pps, ss €25. Bar food available 11-4 daily, D 6.30-9; Set D €35, à la carte also available L&D; house wine €25. Closed 15 Nov-15 Mar. Amex, Diners, MasterCard, Visa. **Directions:** Centre of Kilkee.

Killaloe

Cherry Tree Restaurant

☆ féile bia RESTAURANT

Lakeside Ballina Killaloe Co Clare
Tel: 061 375 688 Fax: 061 375 689

A lovely waterside location is a great bonus for chef proprietor Harry McKeogh's purpose-built restaurant and this impressive modern building - particularly its striking interior - makes a fine setting for consistently excellent contemporary cooking. Carefully sourced ingredients are the star here, providing a sound basis for a wide range of dishes - many of them admirably simple - produced by a strong kitchen team led by Harry and his head chef, Mark Anderson. Great salads are based on locally grown organic produce and creative signature dishes include luxurious starters like grilled asparagus with soft poached quail eggs, light truffle hollandaise and fresh truffle shavings - and superb dry aged beef, which is cut to order and cooked as requested; this outstanding ingredient has inspired more than one striking speciality dish at the Cherry Tree and received the guide's Irish Beef Award in 2001. Menus, while not over-complicated, offer a great deal of choice and there's tremendous verve and originality in their creation - including a dedicated vegetarian menu which is exciting enough to lure the most hardened carnivore into a dilemma of choice. Gorgeous desserts are mainly creative variations of classical themes, including such delights as apple tart tatin served warm with clotted cream from Glenilen Farm in West Cork and soup of organic Killaloe berries with cardamom scented panna cotta - and, of course, there's an Irish farmhouse cheese plate too. Although the exact origins of ingredients may not be mentioned on menus, there is a clear commitment to quality ingredients, especially organic produce, throughout. This is outstanding food, with service to match. A carefully chosen wine list offers lots of treats and is augmented by a good choice of aperitifs and digestifs. **Seats 60** (private room, 10). Toilets wheelchair accessible. No smoking area. Children over 7 welcome. D 6-10 Tue-Sat. A la carte except Set Vegetarian Menu €40. House wines €17.65. Closed Sun (except bank hol weekends), Mon; 24-26 Dec; last week Jan, 1st week Feb. Amex, MasterCard, Visa, Laser. **Directions:** At Molly's Pub in Ballina turn down towards the Lakeside Hotel, the Cherry Tree Restaurant is just before the hotel, on the left.

Killaloe

HOTEL

Waterman's Lodge Hotel

Ballina Killaloe Co Clare **Tel: 061 376 333** Fax: 061 375445
Email: info@watermanslodge.ie Web: www.watermanslodge.com

Views down to Killaloe and across the Shannon are among the many pleasing features of this former sporting lodge, which now makes an appealing country house hotel. Small weddings and private parties are a speciality and it is well suited to such occasions as both the bar and restaurant are well-placed on the front of the building, where groups can get together and enjoy the relaxing ambience created by a combination of country house style, lovely gardens and river views. Accommodation, in spacious, elegantly furnished rooms with generous beds and good bathrooms, is very comfortable. Golf, fishing, horse riding and pony trekking are all available nearby. Wheelchair accessible (including toilets). No pets. Rooms 10 (5 superior, 1 shower only); B&B about €90pps. Wheelchair accessible. Bar menu, 12.30-7.30 daily. Restaurant: **Seats 50.** D daily, 7-9.30; L Sun only, 12.30. Set D about €38; à la carte available; house wine about €19.90; sc discretionary. Bar L 12.30-2.30. Amex, MasterCard, Visa, Laser. **Directions:** N7 to Birdhill turn left 500yds after the bridge. ◇

Lahinch

RESTAURANT

Barrtra Seafood Restaurant

Lahinch Co Clare **Tel: 065 708 1280**
Email: barrtra@hotmail.com

Paul and Theresa O'Brien have been providing fine food and hospitality at their traditional, whitewashed restaurant on the cliffs just outside Lahinch for over a decade - and if there were an award for sheer value, Barrtra would have to be a contender. It's a cottagey building, made lighter and brighter by the addition of a conservatory - although the reception room (where the wait could sometimes seem rather long if you are waiting for a group to leave their table) is rather small. It's well worth a wait however and, once inside the restaurant, the sound of lots of people enjoying their meals and having a good time is infectious, the decor is appealingly simple and the views of Liscannor Bay - which can be magic from window tables on a fine evening - are a visual highlight. But local seafood is the star attraction and Theresa's excellent, unfussy cooking makes the most of a wide range of fish, while also offering a choice for those with other preferences, including vegetarian options - Paul, meanwhile, provides warm and easy hospitality and somehow manages to maintain a high level of service. Several menus are offered in high season, starting with their famous 5 O'clock Menu which is a real snip, then the regular dinner and à la carte menus, then (in summer) there's a late night Sushi Wave to round off the evening. Giving value has always been a priority here and local seafood, including lobster when available, - is all offered at the kind of prices that many restaurants claim to be "impossible" these days. Richly flavoured chowders, glorious crab salads with home-made mayonnaise and breads, perfectly cooked fish with excellent sauces; exact timing and perfect judgment of flavourings enhances while always allowing the fish to be "itself". Vegetables are also a strong point served on a platter will include beautiful Clare potatoes, and other respectfully presented vegetables such as wilted spinach, flavoursome flaked carrot - and some warm ratatouille as well. An interesting and keenly priced wine list, good cheeseboard, home-baked breads (the recipe for the walnut bread is cleverly given on the back of their business card) and aromatic cafetière coffee show an attention to detail in tune with an overall high standard which we have found consistently enjoyable over the years. Children welcome before 7pm. **Seats 32.** D Tue-Sun 5-10, Early D (3-course) 5-6.30, €20; Set 6-course D €35; also à la carte. The Sushi Wave 10-11.30 (Jun-Sep). House wines from €13. s.c. discretionary. Closed Mon (except Jul-Aug) & Jan-Feb. Phone to check opening hours off season. Amex, MasterCard, Visa, Laser. **Directions:** 3.5 miles south of Lahinch N67.

Lahinch

COUNTRY HOUSE

Moy House

Lahinch Co Clare **Tel: 065 708 2800**
Fax: 065 708 2500 Email: moyhouse@eircom.net
Web: www.moyhouse.com

This stunning house just outside Lahinch was our Country House of the Year in 2003. It's on a wooded 15 acre site on the river Moy and enjoys a commanding position overlooking Lahinch Bay, with clear coastal views.The house combines the best of materials with an inspired sense of design, making it one of Ireland's most appealing (and luxurious) country houses - greatly enhanced by manager Bernie Merry's genuine hospitality and great attention to detail. Although it appears to be quite small, low building as you approach, the scale is larger than at first appears and its hillside position allows for a lower floor on the sea side - a side entrance below has direct access to the dining room and lower bedrooms (useful for anyone who might have difficulty with the narrow spiral staircase which joins the two floors internally). On the main entrance level there are four bedrooms and also a large, elegant drawing room with an open fire and honesty bar, where guests are free to enjoy aperitifs before going down to dine, or to relax with coffee (or tea or herbal/fruit tea) and petits fours after dinner. The decor throughout is in rich country house tones, with rugs and beautiful heavy fabrics used to great advantage - antique furniture is lovely but it is the inspired use of fabrics which is memorable. Bedrooms, which all have sea views, are wonderfully spacious and luxuriously appointed, as are the bathrooms (with underfloor heating so tiles are always warm on bare feet). Dinner - which is mainly for residents - and breakfast are served at separate tables in a dining room which is elegant yet also cosy, which would be reassuring in wild weather. Dining here is a treat. The 4-course dinner menu offers three or four well-balanced choices on each course so you might start with deep-fried crab and vegetable spring roll, follow with one of a choice of soups or a refresher such as cherry & Malibu granita, then maybe a house speciality of honey roast duckling with courgette stuffing and an orange sauce and Tunisian orange cake with a citrus syrup; farmhouse cheeses are also offered and there's a short but interesting wine list (house wines are currently from California, but Europe is also well-represented). All round, this lovely house offers a unique experience and is worth a special trip. Children welcome (under 12 free in parents' room, baby sitting arranged). **Rooms 9** (3 shower only) B&B €114.50 pps. D 7-8.45 (reservations required), €45. House wine €21. Closed Christmas &1-14 Jan. Amex, MasterCard, Visa, Laser. **Directions:** On the sea side of the Miltown Malbay road outside Lahinch.

Liscannor

Liscannor Rock Shop Café

CAFÉ

Derreen Liscannor Co Clare **Tel: 065 7081930** Fax: 065 7081944

A useful place for anyone touring Clare to know about, the café is on the premises of the Liscannor Stone Story and The Rock Shop which are both extremely interesting and worth allowing some time to visit (especially if the weather is poor). It's a sister operation to the Aillwee Cave at Ballyvaughan (see entry) and makes a good place to factor in a bite to eat - not a major meal, perhaps, but a light lunch or a tea or coffee break. The café, which overlooks the stones and the hills, has a terrace outside for fine weather; it's quite simply set up with a servery display area, but everything is freshly home-made on the premises, giving dishes like cottage pie, Irish stew and (vegetarian) lasagne much more appeal - home-made ravioli is a speciality and there's a blackboard menu offering the day's home-made soup, various salads (served with French bread), a range of hot dishes (poached salmon, honey coated bacon with cabbage & jacket potatoes). Home-made scones, cakes (well-displayed and tempting by the slice) and desserts are lovely for morning or afternoon breaks - and you can also buy their home-made preserves to take home. **Seats 75.** Self service. Open daily 10.30-5.30 (Sun from 11.30). Closed Nov-Mar.(Hours not confirmed at time of going to press.) MasterCard, Visa, Laser. **Directions:** On road from Liscannor to Cliffs of Moher. ◇

Liscannor

Vaughans Anchor Inn

PUB / B&B

Main Street Liscannor Co Clare **Tel: 065 7081548**
Fax: 065 7068977 Web: www.vaughansanchorinn.com

A naturally characterful traditional bar, with lots of memorabilia and a newer restaurant area beyond the main bar, this is the place for some seriously good seafood at fair prices. Although famed locally for their seafood platters there's much more to it than that: Denis Vaughan cooks everything to order and patience is quite reasonably requested on this score, as it gets very busy and everything really is fresh - they offer about twenty varieties of fish and the menu may even be changed in mid-stream because there's something new coming up off the boats. However, you don't have to eat seafood to eat well here - vegetarian options are offered and they do excellent steaks too. Cooking combines old-fashioned generosity with some contemporary twists: succulent fresh salmon, for example, may be a good thick darne, grilled and served on a bed of just-cooked fennel, with a delicious creamy samphire sauce, while perfectly seared scallops may come on a brilliant bed of crisp-fried smoked haddock & scallion mash with a frothy white wine sauce. Understandably very popular and they don't take bookings so, if you want to have a reasonably quiet dinner without a long wait, get there before seven o'clock. Children welcome. **Seats 100.** Food served 12-9.30 daily. Toilets wheelchair accessible. Accommodation also available (not viewed by the Guide). Closed 25 Dec. (Open Good Fri for food, but bar closed.) MasterCard, Visa, Laser. **Directions:** 2.5 miles from Lahinch on Clifs of Moher route.

Lisdoonvarna

HOTEL / RESTAURANT

Sheedy's Country House Hotel

Lisdoonvarna Co Clare **Tel: 065 707 4026**
Fax: 065 707 4555 Email: info@sheedys.com
Web: www.sheedys.com

BREAKFAST AWARD WINNER - MUNSTER

John and Martina Sheedy's fine hotel has undergone major improvements over the last couple of years and now offers some of the best accommodation as well as the finest food in the area - yet it still has the warm ambience (in every sense - the sunny foyer has a comfortable seating area and an open fire for chillier days) and friendly hands-on management, which make Sheedy's one of the west of Ireland's best loved small hotels. All the bedrooms are spacious and individually designed to a high standard with generous beds, quality materials and elegant, quietly soothing colours; comfort is the priority, so bathrooms have power showers as well as full baths and there are CD music systems in addition to TV and the usual room facilities. Fine food and warm hospitality remain constant qualities however - and an original feature has already enhanced the exterior in a way that is as practical as it is pleasing to the eye: the gardens in front of the hotel are gradually being developed to include a potager (formal vegetable and herb garden) plus other similarly specialised areas, including an orchard and a rose garden: magic! Not suitable for children under 10. No pets. **Rooms 11** (3 junior suites, 1 for disabled, all no smoking). B&B €65pps, ss €25.

Sheedys Restaurant: That Sheedy's is a must-visit destination for so many discerning guests is due in no small part to the restaurant - and, specifically, John Sheedy's cooking. Prompt reception and a warm welcome immediately puts arriving guests at their ease, and amuse-bouches sent out from the kitchen while you are choosing your dinner (yummy bites likes beetroot and parsnip crisps, cherry tomatoes and black olives in spiced oil) sharpen the sense of anticipation of the delights to come. And there's plenty to choose from on well-balanced menus that are full of temptations: a wonderful fresh prawn soup, for example, or a starter like warm salad of roasted monkfish with Gubbeen smoked bacon, mushrooms & champagne dressing and main courses like baked hake on a risotto of garden herbs with Irish grain mustard sauce. But, while seafood choices are very strong, local meats are equally tempting - or poultry such as slow-roasted crispy duck with traditional accompaniments - potato stuffing, apple sauce and herb gravy. John's cooking is consistently excellent and the stylishly subdued olive-grey, curtainless dining room with plain candle-lit tables makes a suitably subtle setting for his carefully presented dishes to be consumed with relish. Hospitality and service are always exemplary too and prices are reasonable for the quality provided - and the same high standards apply at breakfast, where scrambled eggs with smoked salmon from the nearby Burren Smokehouse is a particular hit. Carefully selected, well-priced wine list. No smoking restaurant. Not suitable for children under10 after 7.30. **Seats 28.** D daily, 6.45-8.30. A la carte. House wine €18. SC discretionary. MasterCard, Visa, Laser. **Directions:** 200 metres from square of town on road to Sulphur Wells.

Loop Head

FARM / GUESTHOUSE

Anvil Farm Guesthouse

Kilbaha Loop Head Kilkee Co Clare
Tel: 065 905 8018 Fax: 065 905 8331
Email: info@anvilfarm Web: www.anvilfarm.com

Maura Keating is a member of Irrus, a group promoting marine ecotourism in West Clare, and she offers comfortable accommodation in a house beside the family's clifftop farm at the end of the Loop Head peninsula, one of the country's most remote and unspoilt areas. Rugged cliff scenery, angling, diving, bird watching and walking are some of the attractions that bring visitors to this wild and windblown beauty spot - the perfect antidote to city life. Simple en-suite bedrooms have tea/coffee making facilities with television, and guests may visit the farm, which has a variety of animals and a special interest in Irish sport horse breeding. Maura has all the details on things to do and visit in the area - and good local food for dinner, including Aberdeen Angus beef from their own farm, locally caught Atlantic salmon and local Inagh and Cratloe cheeses. Children welcome (under 6 free in parents room, cot available without charge, babysitting arranged). Dogs allowed in some areas. Walking, fishing. Short breaks. **Rooms 5** (all en-suite, 4 shower-only) B&B €30, ss €7. D by arrangement. Closed 1 Nov-1 Mar. **No Credit Cards. Directions:** Take Loop Head road from Kilkee; Anvil Farm is 2 miles after Cross village.

Miltown Malbay

Berry Lodge

RESTAURANT / B&B

Annagh Miltown Malbay Co Clare
Tel: 065 708 7022 Fax: 065 708 7011
Email: info@berrylodge.com Web: www.berrylodge.com

Near the coast of west Clare, between Kilkee and Lahinch, this Victorian country house is the family home of Rita Meade, who has run it as a restaurant with accommodation since 1994. The restaurant is set up welcomingly in an informal country style with pine furniture and is quite extensive, with a conservatory area at the back of the house, overlooking the garden. Wide-ranging menus offer local seafood of course but meats, from a local butcher, are exceptional and a simple dish like roast best end of lamb can be memorable; poultry is another strength - an updated classic of slow roast spiced duckling with Guinness honey & orange sauce & red onion marmalade is a speciality. Menus are interesting, food quality is very high and the cooking is sound - a combination which makes for an enjoyable dining experience. Local seafood features - in a starter of twice-baked crab soufflé with tomato chilli coulis, perhaps. Cookery classes - given by Rita in her own kitchen - are a special feature of Berry Lodge. **Seats 45.** D 7-9.30. Set D €36; also à la carte. House wines €18. SC discretionary. Closed 1 Jan-14 Feb.

Accommodation: Neat bedrooms, each with its own little shower room, are furnished with an attractive country mixture of old and new, including Irish craft items. Children welcome. No pets. Rooms 5 (all shower only). B&B about €38 pps, ss about €10. MasterCard, Visa, Laser. **Directions:** R460 to Milltown Malbay, N67 to Berry Lodge over Annagh Bridge, second left, first right to Berry Lodge. ◇

Miltown Malbay

Black Oak

RESTAURANT

Rineen Miltown Malbay Co Clare **Tel: 065 708 4408**

Set on a hillside with views over Liscannor Bay, this large modern house may not look like a restaurant, but it is well-established and very comfortable. The dining room is decorated in warm tones, with well-spaced, well-appointed tables - fresh flowers, good linen and glasses, comfortable chairs - setting a positive tone ahead of the meal. While not especially innovative, moderately priced menus offer a very fair choice, with starters like St Tola goat cheese, crab in filo pastry and mussels in wine then main courses such as rack of lamb and Seafood Pot (a house speciality - a generous and perfectly cooked selection of fish cooked in a tomato, leek, saffron & garlic sauce and served in its own pot), well-presented with a selection of side vegetables. Desserts tend towards the classics - lemon tarte, variations on crème brûlée. This restaurant delivers good fresh food, comfort and good service at reasonable prices - and is predictably popular, so booking is essential. Air conditioning. **Seats 65** (Max table size, 10). D Wed-Mon,5.30-9.30 pm.; early D 5.30-6pm about €20; Set D about €30 from 6.30pm. Closed Tue & Christmas-April. MasterCard, Visa. **Directions:** 7 km outside Lahinch village on the Miltown road.

Newmarket-on-Fergus

Carrygerry House

Ⓝ COUNTRY HOUSE / RESTAURANT

Newmarket-on-Fergus Co Clare
Tel: 061 360500 Fax: 061 360700
Email: info@carrygerryhouse.com Web: www.carrygerryhouse.com

Only 10 minutes from Shannon airport and in a beautiful rural setting, Carrygerry is a lovely residence dating back to 1793. It overlooks the Shannon and Fergus estuaries and, peacefully surrounded by woodlands, gardens and pastures, seems very distant from an international airport. A young couple, Niall and Gillian Ennis, took over as proprietors in the summer of 2003 and, while they hadn't yet put their stamp on the house at the time of the Guide's visit, it was very pleasant, with spacious, comfortable reception rooms, open fires and an hospitable atmosphere. Bedrooms are all non-smoking and those in the main house are quite traditional. While those in the coach yard are more modern. Children under 12s free in parents' room, cot available without charge. Pets permitted. Snooker; garden; walking. **Rooms 12** (3 shower-only, all no-smoking.) B&B €70 pps, ss €10. Closed Christmas week.

Restaurant: The restaurant, which is open to non-residents, is shared between the dining room and a conservatory, overlooking gardens. Set up classically, it's a pleasant spot to enjoy food cooked to order by head chef Ross Williams, who changes menus weekly and takes pride in using local ingredients. Good breads, some appealing dishes not found on other menus - a twice-baked goat's cheese soufflé for example - and excellent meats, as in a house speciality of grilled medallions of beef fillet with rösti potatoes & wild mushrooms. Vegetarian dishes are only available on request, so mention any special requirements when booking. Attractive surroundings, real food and pleasant, friendly service make for an enjoyable outing. Although open only a few weeks at the time of our visit, the restaurant should be a great asset to the area. Banqueting (80). **Seats 35** (private room 8). No smoking restaurant. Reservations required. D Tue-Sat 6.30-9.30. A la carte. House wine €17. Closed Sun & Mon. Amex, Diners, MasterCard, Visa, Laser. **Directions:** Very close to Shannon airport, on old Newmarket-on-Fergus road.

Newmarket-on-Fergus

HOTEL / RESTAURANT

Dromoland Castle Hotel

Newmarket-on-Fergus Co Clare
Tel: 061 368144 Fax: 061 363355
Email: sales@dromoland.ie Web: www.dromoland.ie

INTERNATIONAL HOSPITALITY AWARD

Dromoland is one of Ireland's grandest hotels, and also one of the best-loved. The ancestral home of the O'Briens, barons of Inchiquin and direct descendants of Brian Boru, High King of Ireland, it is one of the few Irish estates tracing its history back to Gaelic royal families. Today, the visitor is keenly aware of this sense of history, but will not find it daunting. Under the warm and thoughtful management of Mark Nolan, who has been General Manager since 1989, Dromoland is a very relaxing hotel, where the grandeur of the surroundings - the castle itself, its lakes and parkland and magnificent furnishings - does not overpower but rather enhances the pleasure for guests. It is an enchanting place, where wide corridors lined with oak panelling are hung with ancient portraits and scented with the haunting aroma of wood smoke. Public areas are very grand, with all the crystal chandeliers and massive antiques to be expected in a real Irish Castle, but the atmosphere suggests that a lot of fun is to be had here too. Bedrooms are all furnished to a very high standard, with luxurious bathrooms and nightly turndown service. The Brian Boru International Centre brought a new dimension to the Castle's activities a few years ago and can accommodate almost any type of business gathering, including exhibitions, conferences and banquets. A new wing, also built to blend in with the castle, was recently completed. Child under 12 free in parents' room (cot available free of charge, baby sitting arranged). Leisure centre (indoor pool, spa, beauty salon, hairdressing); golf (18); fishing, tennis, cycling, walking. Snooker, pool table. Boutique. No pets. **Rooms 100** (6 suites, 50 executive, all no smoking, 2 disabled). Lift. Room rate €397 (max 2 guests), SC15%. Open all year.

★**Earl of Thomond Restaurant:** The most beautiful room in the castle, the Earl of Thomond Dining Room is magnificent, with crystal, gilding and rich fabrics - and has a lovely view over the lake and golf course. Guests ease into the experience of dinner with an aperitif in the Library Bar, overlooking the eighth green, before moving through to beautifully presented tables and gentle background music provided by a traditional Irish harpist. In the evening a wide choice includes a table d'hôte menu, vegetarian menu and an à la carte offering a wonderful selection of luxurious dishes. The table d'hôte is more down-to-earth - a little less glamorous than the carte but with the same quality of ingredients and cooking. Although the style is basically classic French (with some of the current international influences) some dishes highlight local ingredients and are more Irish in tone: baked Inagh goats cheese with toasted sesame seeds, tomato salsa, garden leaves & lemon remoulade, for example, and poached native lobster with steamed greens or roast loin & cutlet of Clare lamb, salsa vert. Executive head chef David McCann's cooking is invariably superb, all the little niceties of a very special meal are observed and service, under restaurant manager Tony Frisby, is excellent. An good Sunday lunch menu offers a wide choice of interesting dishes - including a special Dromoland version of Irish Stew. The wine list - about 250 wines, predominantly French - is under the constant review of sommelier Pascal Playon, winner of our Sommelier of the Year Award in 2000, who is not only knowledgeable, but an exceptionally thoughtful and helpful wine host.(House wines from €24). A 15% service charge is added to all prices. **Seats 75** (private room 24). D daily, 7-9.30, L Sun only 12.30-1.30; Set Sun L €35; Set D €60 & €70, à la carte D also available.* The Gallery Menu offers a lighter choice of less formal dishes throughout the day (12-7), including Afternoon Tea. *Beside the castle, the Dromoland Golf and Country Club incorporates an 18-hole parkland course, a gym, a Health Clinic offering specialist treatments, also the Green Room Bar and Fig Tree Restaurant, which provide informal alternatives to facilities in the castle, including excellent food (10am-9.30pm). Open all year. Amex, Diners, MasterCard, Visa, Laser. **Directions:** 17 miles from Limerick, 8 miles from Shannon. Take N18 to Dromoland interchange; exit & follow signage.

Shannon

féile bia HOTEL

Great Southern Hotel

Shannon Airport Shannon Co Clare **Tel: 061 471122** Fax: 061 471982
Email: res@shannon.shannon-gsh.com Web: www.gshotels.com

Just two minutes walk from the main terminal building at Shannon Airport, the Shannon Great Southern is in an unexpectedly lovely location overlooking the estuary and, with its views and rather gracious atmosphere, it retains a little of the old romance of flight. On the practical side it also offers unbeatable convenience for travellers recovering from or preparing for international flights. The hotel is fully sound-proofed and bedrooms are spacious and comfortable, with all the amenities expected of a good modern hotel, including ISDN lines. Activities available include snooker and a mini-gym for residents, and there is golf and horseriding nearby. Day trips can be arranged to local sites, such as the Cliffs of Moher or the Aillwee Caves, including admission and full day transport. The hotel also has good conference facilities for groups of up to 250 (banqueting 200), backed up by a private business centre. Children welcome (under 2s free in parents' room, cot available without charge). **Rooms 115.** (1 suite, 56 executive rooms, 29 no-smoking rooms). Lift, limited room service. Room Rate €155 (fixed rate for up to 3 guests) Closed 24-26 Dec. Amex, Diners, MasterCard, Visa, Laser. **Directions:** Situated within airport complex.

Shannon

Oakwood Arms Hotel

HOTEL

Shannon Co Clare **Tel: 061 361500** Fax: 061 361414
Email: manager@oakwoodarms.com Web: www.oakwoodarms.com

John and Josephine O'Sullivan opened this mock-Tudor red brick hotel in 1991 and it created a good impression from the start, with its high standard of maintenance and neatly laid-out flower beds. The lounge bar and function room both have aviation themes: the bar honours the memory of the pioneer female pilot Sophie Pearse, who came from the area, and the restaurant is named after The Spruce Goose, Howard Hughes' famous flying boat. Public areas are quite spacious and comfortably furnished and although not individually decorated, rooms have all the necessary comforts and are double-glazed, with air conditioning, ISDN lines, hospitality trays, ironing facilities and TV. Conference/banqueting (300/250) facilities are good, with video-conferencing and back-up secretarial services available. Children welcome. No pets. **Rooms 100** (4 suites, 4 junior suites, 23 executive rooms, 37 no-smoking). B&B about €80 pps, ss about €35. No SC/Closed 24-26 Dec. Amex, Diners, MasterCard, Visa, Laser. **Directions:** Located on the N19, 2 kms from Shannon Airport. ◇

Shannon

Quality Hotel Shannon

HOTEL

Ballycasey Shannon Co Clare **Tel: 061 364 588** Fax: 061 364 045
Email: sales@qualityshannon.com Web: www.choicehotelsireland.ie

A recent addition to the choice of accommodation at Shannon airport, the Quality Hotel offers modern comforts at a reasonable price. Bright. comfortably furnished rooms all have multi-channel TV and modem points and the hotel is geared for the convenience of guests who are meeting or seeing off relatives, or want somewhere for a quick business meeting before heading off to another destination. Wholesome fare is served all day in the informal hotel restaurant, Lannigans. Conferences/banqueting (20/60). Ample parking. Children under 12 free in parents' room. No pets. **Rooms 54** (10 no-smoking, 3 for disabled). Lift. B&B from about €50 pps, ss about €20. Closed Christmas. Amex, Diners, MasterCard, Visa. **Directions:** On N19 coming to Shannon Town.

Tulla

Flappers Restaurant

RESTAURANT

Main Street Tulla Co Clare **Tel: 065 683 5711**

Jim and Patricia McInerney's simple little split-level restaurant (the lower part is non-smoking) is refreshingly free of decoration, except for a pair of striking pictures and fresh flowers on the tables. Lunchtime sees the emphasis on fairly hearty food and good value but, although the menu is limited, you can easily work up to a rather smart 3-course meal if you wish: organic mixed greens with honey mustard dressing to start, perhaps, lemon peppered chicken (breast of chicken grilled with a light lemon pepper sauce) and a home-made dessert such as fresh fruit meringues with banana cream. In the evening the mood changes and there's a pleasing, fairly priced à la carte menu offering a well-balanced choice of dishes which are a little out of the ordinary and make a change from the repetitive menus n the vast majority of restaurants. Specialities like a starter salad of fresh crabmeat with lemon tomato salsa & curried crème fraîche and a main course of roast rack of lamb with creamy flageolet beans or carrot & parsnip purée are deservedly popular, also tempting vegetarian choices like a red onion and goats cheese tartlet (using local Bluebell Falls soft goats cheese). But don't forget to leave room for delicious desserts - who could resist a tangy lemon mousse with sautéed raspberries and hazelnut shortbread cookies, for instance? A well-chosen wine list is well priced - and there's even a take-away service, which must be a boon for anyone in self-catering accommodation. **Seats 40.** No-smoking area; air conditioning. Wheelchair access to toilets. L12-3 Mon-Sat, D 7-10 Tue-Sat. (Shorter hours in winter - please phone for details) A la carte. House wine €16.95. SC discretionary (except 10% on groups of 8+). Closed all Sun, D Mon, bank hols; 2 weeks Nov & Jan. MasterCard, Visa, Laser. **Directions:** Main streetTulla village, 10 miles from Ennis.

CORK CITY

Cork's designation to be the European Capital of Culture for 2005 has reinforced the city's sense of itself. But in any case the sympathetic re-shaping of this ancient port - which is located on many islands among the several channels of the River Lee - has been steadily gathering momentum in recent years.

It is Cork, of all Ireland's cities, which most warmly gives the impression of being a place at comfort with itself through being set in the midst of a land flowing in milk and honey. Cork is all about the good things in life. While it may be stretching things a little to assert that the southern capital has a Mediterranean atmosphere, there's no doubting its Continental and cosmopolitan flavour, and the Cork people's relaxed enjoyment of it all.

The city's impressive literary tradition was given special recognition on September 22nd 2003 when the Minister for Arts & Culture officially opened a new centre for the Munster Literature Council at the refurbished birthplace of renowned short story creator Frank O'Connor (Michael O'Donovan) at 84 Douglas Street. The house had been restored to celebrate the Centenary of the writer's birth on September 17th 2003, and it now provides facilities to encourage and foster Cork's writing talent.

Cork's special qualities, and its people's appreciation of the pleasant commodities of life, make it a special destination for connoisseurs. Trading in life's more agreeable commodities has always been what Cork and its famous "merchant princes" are all about. At one time, the city was known as "the butter capital of Europe", and it continues to be unrivalled for the ready availability of the very best in fresh produce, with the Cork Free Choice Consumer Group (021 7330178) meeting each month to promote the cause of quality food.

The way in which sea and land intertwine throughout the wonderfully sheltered natural harbour, and through the lively old city itself, has encouraged waterborne trade and a sea-minded outlook. Thus today Cork is at the heart of Ireland's most dynamically nautical area, a place world-renowned for its energetic interaction with the sea, whether for business or pleasure.

In the city itself, we find two Irish stouts being brewed - Murphy's and Beamish. Each has its own distinctive flavour, each in turn is different from Dublin's Guinness, and it is one of life's pleasures - in a characterful Cork pub - to discuss and compare their merits while savouring the Cork people's delightful line in deflationary and quirky humour.

Local Attractions and Information

Cork Airport 021 431 3031
Cork Arts Society 021 427 7749
Cork City Gaol 021 430 5022
Cork Farmers Market Cornmarket St Sats 9am-1pm 021 733 0178
Cork Tourist Information 021 427 3251
Guinness Cork Jazz Festival (late October) 021 427 8979
Cork International Choral Festival (April/May) 021 430 8308
Cork International Film Festival (October) 021 427 1711
Cork Public Museum 021 427 0679
Crawford Gallery, Emmett Place 021 427 3377
English Market (covered, speciality food stalls),
corner between Grand Parade & Patrick Street .... 021 427 4920 / 086 240 0153
Firkin Crane Dance Centre, Shandon 021 450 7487
Frank O'Connor House (Writers Cntr) 84 Douglas St 021 431 2955
Good Food In Cork (Consumer Group) 021 733 0178
Opera House 021 427 0022
Railway Station 021 450 4888
Tig Fili, Arts Centre & Publishers, MacCreddin St 021 450 9274
Triskel Arts Centre, Tobin St off Sth Main St 021 427 2022

Cork

A Taste of Thailand

RESTAURANT

8 Bridge Street Cork **Tel: 021 450 5404**
Fax: 021 450 5404 Email: maryan@iol.ie

This authentic Thai restaurant has a loyal following, giving it a lively atmosphere, even early in the week. Refurbishment in 2003 has brought a more contemporary style, and the creation of a comfortable reception area is a big improvement. Menu changes were also made, but they continue to offer a wide choice, including vegetarian options (Thai food caters well for vegetarians) and the familiar set menus ('banquets') for groups of various sizes, as well as an à la carte which has a more interesting selection of dishes. All the well known Thai styles are represented - Pad Thai and red curry are among the house specialities and there are always a few appealing specials offered: Thai style ducking, for example, is half a farmyard duckling - crispy style and boneless - served on a bed of Thai spicy soft noodles. Fresh ingredients are all Irish, except for exotics, and mainly come from the English Market. Making everything to order, sound cooking and attractive presentation add up to an appealing package: good food, service and value explain this restaurant's popularity. A small European menu is also offered. **Seats 60.** D daily, 6-11; Early D €18 (6-7 pm); Set menus ('banquets') from €23.50, otherwise à la carte. House wine from €14.95 (beers, including Thai beers, available and BYO also allowed). Closed 24-26 Dec. Amex, MasterCard, Visa, Laser. **Directions:** 1 minute walk from city centre.

Cork

Amicus

RESTAURANT 14 A French Church Street Cork **Tel: 021 427 6455** Fax: 021 422 3547

Tucked into a small space in Cork's Huguenot district, Ursula and Robert Hales' restaurant looks interesting from the (pedestrianised) street and has a few tables outside in fine weather. It has youth appeal - bright, modern, with large prints and paintings on the walls - and, although small and tightly packed with tables (which adds to the sense of buzz), well placed mirrors give an impression of space. Arriving guests are promptly seated and offered quite extensive laminated menus featuring popular international dishes: salads (Cajun chicken), bruschetta (roasted vegetable with goat's cheese, olives & pesto), gourmet sandwiches and wraps, pastas on the daytime menu with some overlap onto the evening menu which offers more substantial dishes, notably seafood (grilled lemon sole, herb butter & pesto). Real food, fair pricing and a youthful atmosphere add up to an attractive package. Service, under Ursula's direction is efficient, with children made welcome. **Seats 38.** Open 10am-10pm daily; L 12-6, D 6-10.30; house wine about €14. MasterCard, Visa, Laser. **Directions:** Just off Patrick Street, between the Modern & the Ulster Bank.

Cork

Bodega/Café-Bar-Deli

BAR / RESTAURANT

Cornmarket Street Cork **Tel: 021 427 2878**
Fax: 021 427 2897 Email: bodega@indigo.ie

Alongside the youthful Bodega bar, which can get very noisy with its stone walls and wooden floors accentuating loud music and conversation, Café-Bar-Deli has a more relaxing atmosphere for eating. Housed in an old limestone warehouse building, this informal contemporary restaurant is run to the format now familiar in sister restaurants in Dublin and Sligo. The clever place-mat menu goes well beyond the pizzas which are its mainstay and the cooking has some style. Staff are friendly, prices moderate (average pizza €12, family-sized bowls of pasta from €20); a good choice for a family outing. Parking in the area is not difficult after 6.30pm. **Seats 80** (private room, 50). D Wed-Sun 5 -10.30. A la carte. House wine €14.50. *Daytime food available at Bodega, Mon-Sat 12-5 (L12-3); also Sat & Sun brunch. Restaurant (Café-Bar-Deli) closed Mon, Tue. Establishment closed 25 Dec, Good Fri. Amex, Diners, MasterCard, Visa, Laser. **Directions:** 2 minutes from Grand Parade in the historic Irish Market.

Cork

Bully's Restaurant

RESTAURANT 40 Paul Street Cork **Tel: 021 427 3555** Fax: 021 427 3555

A small, buzzy and inexpensive restaurant in one of the busiest little shopping streets in the city centre, Bully's has earned a reputation for good food at reasonable prices. A speciality is pizzas, which had ultra light, crisp bases long before they began to show up in fashionable restaurants; the dough is made on the premises every day using Italian flour. But their No. 10 pizza (€10.90) is a Cork Special, with ham, sausage, black and white pudding as well as tomatoes and mozzarella. They serve lots of other things too - freshly made burgers, steaks, omelettes, chicken dishes, seafood and freshly made pastas - and there's a short, reasonably priced wine list. Pavement seating outside the restaurant has eased the crush a bit of late and there are plans to open up extra seating upstairs in 2004, to cater for larger groups. A good place for a family meal out. **Seats 35.** Open daily: Mon-Thu 9.30 am-11.15, Fri & Sat 8am-11.15pm, Sun 9am-11pm. (Open for breakfast in Paul Street only.) L 12-2.30. A la carte. House wine €17.

Closed 25-26 Dec & 1 Jan. Also at: 7 Douglas Village East, Douglas, Cork (021-489 2415) Mon-Sat, 12-11, Sun 1-10; Open 1 Jan in Douglas only. Amex, MasterCard, Visa, Laser. **Directions:** In Cork city centre, next to Paul Street Shopping centre.

Cork

Café Gusto

CAFÉ

3 Washington Street Cork **Tel: 021 425 4446** Fax: 021 425 4446
Email: info@cafegusto.com Web: www.cafegusto.com

Big ideas are evident in this little designer coffee bar near Singer's Corner, which specialises in gourmet rolls, wraps and salads, either to go or eat on the premises. The brainchild of Marianne Delaney, previous manager of The Exchange on George's Quay, and her Ballymaloe-trained partner Denis O'Mullane, who take pride in sourcing the very best quality ingredients - small is indeed beautiful here, where coffee is made by baristas trained to master standard, using 100% arabica beans from the Java Roasting Company. The same philosophy applies to the food in this tiny café, in a short menu ranging from Simply Cheddar (freshly baked Italian bread filled with with beef tomato, white onion & relish) to The Flying Bacon (filled with chicken, bacon, Emmenthal, honey Dijon, lettuce & tomato). Food prices are not much more than supermarket sandwiches and the extensive selection of coffees, teas, herbal teas etc are good value too. No smoking area; air conditioning. **Seats 20.** Open Mon-Sat, 7.45 am-6pm. Closed Sun, bank hols. **No Credit Cards. Directions:** Across from Capitol Cinema.

Cork

Café Paradiso

☆ **RESTAURANT**

16 Lancaster Quay Western Road Cork **Tel: 021 4277 939**
Fax: 021 4274973 Email: info@cafeparadiso.ie Web: www.cafeparadiso.ie

Even the most committed carnivores love every mouthful at Denis Cotter and Bridget Healy's ground-breaking vegetarian restaurant, which has earned a national reputation for exciting mainstream cooking and great service. House specialities that people cross the country for include a delicious goats' cheese, pinenut and oven-roasted tomato charlotte, served with wilted greens and puy lentils in basil oil - which was selected as the guide's Vegetarian Dish of the Year in 2000 and remains a good example of the cooking style at this colourful little restaurant. It's a lively place with a busy atmosphere and the staff, under the direction of Bridget Healy, are not only friendly and helpful but obviously enthusiastic about their work. Seasonal menus based on the best organic produce available are topped up by daily specials, which might include a modish starter like vegetable sushi with tempura of cauliflower & aubergine, pickled ginger, wasabi and a dipping sauce and a broad beans salad with grilled haloumi, crispbreads & little gem lettuce with cherry tomatoes, radishes, Knockalara sheeps cheese and a mint & pinenut dressing. Irresistible desserts too - gooseberry and almond tartlet with amaretto custard, perhaps, or strawberry baked alaska with summer berry sauce - and a well-priced global wine list features a number of organic wines. The cooking is never less than stunning - and significantly, in this era of "cheffy" food and big egos, the creator of this wonderful food describes himself simply as "owner cook". Many of his creations are featured in the acclaimed Café Paradiso Cookbook and a second book, Café Paradiso Seasons, which was published in 2003. Café Paradiso may be small, but it packs a mighty punch. **Seats 45.** No Smoking area. Toilets wheelchair accessible. L Tue-Sat, 12.30-3, D Tue-Sat 6.30-10.30. A la carte. House wines from €12. Service discretionary. Closed Sun, Mon, Christmas week. Amex, MasterCard, Visa, Laser. **Directions:** On Western Road, opposite Jurys Hotel.

Cork

Citrus Restaurant

RESTAURANT

Barrycourt House East Douglas Village Cork
Tel: 021 436 1613 Fax: 021 489 1269

Harold Lynch and Beth Haughton's restaurant is a lovely bright space, with windows on two sides and simple uncluttered tables - not a lot to absorb the sound of lots of happy people enjoying Harold's cooking, but there's a good buzz. The style is international but as much as possible is based on local produce: meats and fish come from the famous butchers, O'Flynns, and fishmongers, O'Connells, for example, both at the English Market. Laminated menus are usually a big turn-off, but Harold's read simply and are full of things you'd love to try - so why not order a bottle of wine and a plate of anti pasta - a selection of salamis, prosciutto, olives, cheese & crostini - to nibble at while making the main choices. Starters are particularly attractive and many people choose two starters, or move on to a practical middle section offering dishes which can go either way - sautéed calamari with coriander, chilli, garlic

& lemon, for example, can be a starter (€7.50) or main course (€14) according to your mood. There's a fair sprinkling of highly tempting vegetarian dishes (papardelle with baby spinach, pinenuts, cherry tomatoes, cream and pesto for example) and updated classics such as a roast rack of lamb with aubergine & cherry tomato compôte, mint butter sauce; excellent raw materials are generally allowed to speak for themselves. Tempting desserts tend to be variations on favourite themes - meringue roulade with strawberry daiquiri sauce is typical- and the wine list is short but sweet. Service, under Beth's supervision, is charming and efficient. **Seats 55.** No smoking area. Toilets wheelchair accessible. Children welcome before 8pm. Open Mon-Sat 10am-10pm (L 12-3, D 5-10), Sun 5-9. House wine about €20. SC discretionary. Closed L Sun, Christmas Day. Amex, Diners, MasterCard, Visa, Laser, Switch.

Cork

Crawford Gallery Café

RESTAURANT / CAFÉ

Emmet Place Cork **Tel: 021 427 4415**
Fax: 021 465 2021 Web: www.ballymaloe.ie

This fine 1724 building houses an excellent collection of 18th- and 19th-century landscapes and has recently has a large modern extension added. It is also home to the Crawford Gallery Café, one of Cork city's favourite informal eating places, which is managed by Isaac Allen, grandson of Myrtle and Ivan Allen, founders of Ballymaloe House - and, by a remarkable coincidence, also a descendant of Arthur Hill, architect of a previous extension to the gallery, completed in 1884. Menus in this striking blue and white room reflect the Ballymaloe philosophy that food is precious and should be handled carefully, so the Gallery Café serves freshly prepared dishes made from natural local ingredients and offers Ballymaloe breads and many of the other dishes familiar to Ballymaloe fans. Except for a few specialities too popular to take off (such as savoury pancakes), the menu changes weekly but the style - a judicious mixture of timeless country house fare and contemporary international dishes featuring carefully sourced meats, fish from Ballycotton and the freshest of seasonal vegetables - remains reassuringly constant. Substantial dishes, such as an updated version of bacon & cabbage (glazed loin of bacon with spring cabbage mash & Irish Mist sauce) are great for a real meal and the home-made pickles, relishes, chutneys and preserves are delicious details. And, for a lighter bite, the home baking is outstanding. A short well-balanced wine list offers a good choice of half and quarter bottles. **Seats 70.** Toilets wheelchair accessible. Open Mon-Sat, 10am-5pm, B'fst 10-12, L 12.30-2.30 (Sat to 3). Set L about €18; also à la carte. House wine about €17.50. No SC. Closed Sun, 24 Dec (after lunch) to early Jan, bank hols. MasterCard, Visa, Laser. **Directions:** City centre, next to Opera House. ◇

Cork

Crow's Nest Bar & Restaurant

PUB / RESTAURANT

Victoria Cross Cork **Tel: 021 454 3330**
Email: thecrowsnestbarandrestaurant@eircom.net

This large, friendly pub is enormously popular in the locality. Both the bar and upstairs restaurant are bright and colourful in a contemporary (but emphatically not minimalist) style and the selection of past awards collected by the proprietor-chef indicates an encouraging commitment to good food. Bar food is always appealing and the restaurant menu is imaginative, with the provenance of some ingredients given, which is confidence-inspiring: steaks are a speciality, for example, and the local butcher who supplies them is credited on the menu. The standard of food and cooking is above average, although longish menus and a busy pub downstairs may make service a little slow noticeably as the pub fills up with the evening rush. An informative, well-priced wine list includes some lesser-known choices and a fair number of half bottles Not suitable for children after 7 pm. Bar meals 12.30-9 daily (carvery lunch & short à la carte afternoon menu). A large free carpark, on the Carrigrohane Road, is directly opposite. Restaurant **Seats 60.** Air conditioning. Toilets wheelchair accessible. Not suitable for children under 16 after 6pm. Food all day (12-10, Sun from 12.30). D 6-10pm daily (Sun to 9). Set Sun L about €20; also à la carte; SC discretionary. House wine about €20. Closed Christmas & Good Fri. Amex, Diners, MasterCard, Visa, Laser, Switch. **Directions:** One mile from City Centre via Western road. ◇

Cork

Dan Lowrey's Tavern

PUB

13 Mc Curtain Street Cork **Tel: 021 450 5071**

This characterful pub beside the Everyman Palace Theatre was established in 1875 and is named after its founder. Long before the arrival of the "theme pub", Lowrey's was famous for having windows which originated from Kilkenny Cathedral, but it also has many of its own original features, including a fine mahogany bar. It has been run by Catherine O'Riordan since 1995 and Catherine oversees the kitchen herself, so it's a good place for an inexpensive home-cooked meal - popular dishes like home-made quiche or lasagne served with salad or fries, for example, or seafood bake, filled with salmon, monkfish & cod, topped with creamed potatoes and toasted breadcrumbs. It's popular with local business people at lunch time, and heart-healthy dishes are considerately highlighted by a 'Happy Heart' symbol on the menu. There's also a nice little quarter-bottle wine list representing Chile, California, Italy and Portugal, sall €3.90. L Mon-Fri, 12-3; D daily 7.30-9.30 (Sandwiches available all day). Closed 25 Dec & Good Fri. **No Credit Cards. Directions:** Next to Metropole Gresham Hotel, across from Isaacs Restaurant.

Cork

Douglas Hide

féile bia PUB / RESTAURANT

63 Douglas Street Cork **Tel: 020 431 5695**
Email: douglashide@eircom.net

Tadhg and Aoife O'Donovan's narrow little bar is bright and cheerful, with contemporary paintings and a friendly, informal ambience. It has recently been extended and redecorated, which makes for greater comfort in the dining area beyond the bar and a young clientele creates a lively atmosphere. But it's the food that makes this a destination bar: careful sourcing of ingredients provide the building blocks for Aoife's good modern Irish cooking: local meat and fish come from O'Flynns butchers and O'Connells seafood at the English Market, for example, also olives from the Real Olive Co. Sensibly short menus change as the day progresses - imaginative soups, sandwiches, pastas and lightish bites for lunch include some tempting vegetarian options (O'Flynn's kassler pork on home-made tomato bread with a sweet apple chutney & side salad, for example) while more substantial dinner menus offer tasty starters like crab timbale with celeriac crisps & lime crème fraîche and mains like free range farmyard duck with red onion confit & spiced peach or fish specials (based on market availability). The standard of food and cooking is high, the service friendly and attentive - and it's very good value. Short, but interesting wine list. Outside meal times, it operates as a normal pub, with pub opening times. **Seats 52.** Toilets wheelchair accessible. Not suitable for children after 8pm. L daily 12-3 (Sun from 12.30), D Tue-Sun 6-10 (Sun to 9); all à la carte; house wines from €17.50. SC discretionary. Closed 25 Dec & Good Fri. MasterCard, Visa, Laser. **Directions:** Opposite South Presentation Convent.

Cork

Farmgate Café

féile bia RESTAURANT

English Market Cork **Tel: 021 427 8134** Fax: 021 427 8134
Email: knh@eircom.net

HAPPY HEART EAT-OUT AWARD

A sister restaurant to the Farmgate Country Store and Restaurant in Midleton, Kay Harte's Farmgate Café shares the same commitment to serving fresh food - and, as it is located in the gallery above the English Market, where ingredients are purchased daily, it doesn't come much fresher than this. The atmosphere is lively and busy, with constant movement (especially in the self-service area) as people come and go from the market below giving a great sense of being at the heart of things. With its classic black and white tiles, simple wooden furniture and interesting art work there's a combination of style and a comfortably down to earth atmosphere which suits the wholesome food they serve, including modern dishes as well as some famous old Cork ones with a special market connection like tripe & drisheen and corned beef & champ with green cabbage. Farmgate food is as healthy as it is delicious, meeting the Irish Heart Foundation's definition of a healthy choice, i.e. dishes with lots of fruit and vegetables that are high in fibre, low in fat, especially saturated fat. Menus depends on what is available in the English Market each day, including "the freshest of fish" - used, for example, in a chowder that market regulars love. And, however simple, everything is perfectly cooked, with careful matching of vegetables and judicious use of fresh herbs and seasonings: a delicious mushroom & Crozier Blue tart with thyme, for example, is perfectly balanced to allow the mushroom flavour to come through; chargrilled chicken comes with a delicate lemon thyme sauce and a delicious mixture of leeks, courgettes and rosemary flavoured roast potatoes, while traditionalists will love the classic Irish lamb stew, with its succulent chunks of lean lamb and perfectly cooked root vegetables. All this and delicious home-baked cakes and breads too, whether as a bite to accompany a coffee, or to finish off a meal, a wonderfully home-made seasonal sweet such as a classic raspberry sponge is always a treat. This is an interesting and lively place to enjoy good food - and it's great value for money. Meals Mon-Sat, from 8.30am: B'fast 8.30-10.30, L 12-4. Closed Sun, bank hols, Dec 25-2 Jan. Diners, MasterCard, Visa, Laser. **Directions:** English Market - off Oliver Plunkett Street and Grand Parade.

Cork

Fenns Quay Restaurant

RESTAURANT

5 Sheares Street Cork **Tel: 021 427 9527**
Fax: 021 4279526 Web: www.fennsquay.ie

Situated in a 250-year old listed building, this is a bright, busy restaurant with a welcoming atmosphere and simple decor enlivened by striking modern paintings. Both lunch and dinner menus offer plenty of interesting choices, including a number of vegetarian options (highlighted) and daily specials, including seafood sourced daily from the nearby English Market. Carefully sourced ingredients are local where possible (including meat from the owners' own business, which is a point of pride) presented in a pleasing bistro style. Starters of feta & olive salad with courgette fritters & yoghurt dip or the house salad are typical while aubergine mozzarella lasagne with fresh tomato sauce can be a starter or main course; more substantial dishes include char-grilled fillet steak "Wellie Style", an enduring speciality which comes with house cut potato chips. Lunch menus cross over the lighter, more informal dishes on the evening menu (minted lamb burger with red pepper hummus, tzatziki & house cut chips, for example). An interesting wine list offers variety at reasonable prices, with several by the glass - good value is a feature of both food and drink. Recent refurbishment has enabled wheelchair access to the restaurant but not, unfortunately, to toilets. Air conditioning. Children welcome. On street parking can be difficult during the day, but is easy to find after 6.30. **Seats 60.** Open all day Mon-Sat 10am-10pm; L 12.30-3, D 6-10. L à la carte; early D 6-7.30 Mon-Fri, €20; Set D €40, à la carte also available. House wine €16.95. Service discretionary. Closed Sun, 25 Dec, bank hols. Amex, MasterCard, Visa, Laser. **Directions:** Central city - 1/2 minute from the Courthouse.

Cork

Flemings

☆ RESTAURANT WITH ROOMS

Silver Grange House Tivoli Cork
Tel: 021 4821621 Fax: 021 4821800 Email: flemingsrestaurant@iolfree.ie

Clearly signed off the main Cork-Dublin road, this large Georgian family house is home to Michael Fleming's excellent restaurant - and it is high time this unsung culinary hero should be accorded the recognition which has been well-earned. On a hillside overlooking the river, the house is set in large grounds, including a kitchen garden which provides fruit, vegetables and herbs for the restaurant during the summer. It is a big property to maintain and the entrance is a little run down, but this is quickly forgotten when you enter the light, airy double dining room, which is decorated in an elegant low-key style that highlights its fine proportions, while well-appointed linen-clad tables provide a fine setting for Michael Fleming's classical and modern French cooking. Seasonal table d'hôte and à la carte menus offer a wonderful choice of classics, slightly influenced by current international trends but, even where local ingredients feature strongly, the main thrust of the cooking style is classical French - as in a superb speciality starter of pan fried foie gras de canard with Timoleague black pudding & glazed apple, or an early summer asparagus dish served hot (in puff pastry) or cold (with niçoise vinaigrette). Less usual choices might include roast saddle of rabbit, with herb stuffing and a morel mushroom sauce - and there are also confirmed favourites like roast loin of lamb (with an updated accompaniment of peppered couscous as well as a rosemary jus, perhaps) and grilled monkfish, served with a confit of vegetables, basil oil dressing and red wine sauce. Vegetables are imaginative in selection and presentation, while desserts may include a beautiful tasting plate. Michael's cooking is invariably excellent, presentation elegant and service attentive and knowledgeable. In the current rush of multi-cultural restaurants, places like this are becoming all too rare: a visit here is a treat to treasure. Good wine list - and good value all round. Banqueting (90). **Seats 85** (private room 40). Children welcome before 8pm. L12.30-3, D 6.30-9.30 every day; reservations advised. **Accommodation:** There are four spacious en-suite rooms, comfortably furnished in a style appropriate to the age of the house (B&B €55 pps, ss€25). Closed 24-27 Dec. Amex, Diners, MasterCard, Visa, Laser. **Directions:** Main Cork-Dublin route, 3 km from city centre.

Cork

G's Restaurant

CAFÉ

Grafton Mall Grand Parade Cork **Tel: 021 427 6430**

Gina Casey's informal café-style restaurant is open through the day and its situation in the Grafton shopping Mall (beside the multi-storey carpark) makes it an ideal meeting place. Gina sources ingredients with care and offers a concise menu that varies through the day, beginning with breakfast (from 9 am) and finishing with teas in the afternoon. A sensibly limited range of hot dishes includes a fish of the day, regular main courses might include a tasty vegetarian dish like warm char-grilled salad served on a basil potato cake and topped with vegetable crisps & balamic dressing - and there's a warning that hot food takes 15-20 minutes to prepare, which is reassuring if you value freshly cooked food. 'Special sambos' like bacon, cheese & tomato melt with relish in a pitta pocket are quicker and old favourites like meringue roulade and chocolate biscuit cake with caramel sauce are equally good as a snack with tea or coffee. A short wine list includes a couple of quarter bottles, but no halves. Children welcome. **Seats 107.** No smoking area; air conditioning. Open Mon-Sat, 9-4.30; L 12-3.30, (average main course about €10). House wine about €18. Closed Sun, bank hols, Christmas. MasterCard, Visa. ◇

Cork

Great Southern Hotel Cork Airport

HOTEL

Cork Airport Cork **Tel: 021 494 7500** Fax: 021 494 7501
Email: res@corkairport-gsh.com Web: www.gshotels.com

This stylish modern hotel is very handily located, within walking distance of the terminal. Ideal for a first or last night's stay, it's also a useful meeting place and is well equipped for business guests. Rooms have voice mail, fax/modem lines, desk space and TV with in-house movie channel as well as more usual facilities like radio, hair dryer, tea/coffee trays and trouser press. Gym, jacuzzi, sauna. Ample free parking. Business centre. Conference/banqueting (200/100). Children welcome (under 2 free in parents' room; cot available without charge). Rooms 81 (3 suites, 27 no smoking , 4 disabled). Room rate €155. Open all year except Christmas. Amex, Diners, MasterCard, Visa, Laser. **Directions:** Situated within Airport complex.

Cork

Gresham Metropole Hotel & Leisure Centre

féile bia HOTEL

MacCurtain Street Cork **Tel: 021 450 8122** Fax: 021 450 6450
Email: info@gresham-metropolehotel.com Web: www.gresham-hotels.com

This imposing city-centre hotel next door to the Everyman Palace Theatre and backing on to the River Lee, celebrated its centenary in 1998. Always popular with those connected with the arts and entertainment industry, there are many displays (photos and press cuttings) of stars past and present in the public areas and the atmospheric, traditionally-styled Met Tavern. Many of the hotel's original features remain, including the marble facade, exterior carved stonework and plaster ceilings. Recent refurbishment has greatly improved the bedrooms, most of which now combine a period feel with modern facilities, and care has been taken to bring previously neglected areas back to their former elegance by, for example, correcting ceiling heights which had been changed in previous 'improvements'. Unusually for an old city-centre hotel, there's a splendid leisure club with a large (and unconventionally shaped) indoor swimming pool, overlooked by the Waterside Café (where breakfast is served) and also a gym. State of the art conference and meeting facilities have air conditioning and natural daylight. (450). Children welcome (under 2 free in parents' room, cot available without charge, baby sitting arranged). No pets. Arrangement with nearby car park. **Rooms 113** (2 junior suites, 44 executive rooms,10 shower only, 55 no-smoking, 1 for disabled). B&B €127.50pps. Open all year. Amex, Diners, MasterCard, Visa, Laser. **Directions:** City centre hotel.

Cork City

Hayfield Manor Hotel

féile bia HOTEL

Perrott Avenue College Road Cork
Tel: 021 484 5900 Fax: 021 431 6839
Email: enquiries@hayfieldmanor.ie Web: www.hayfieldmanor.ie

Set in two acres of gardens next door to University College Cork, Hayfield Manor provides every comfort and a remarkable level of privacy and seclusion just a mile from the city centre. Although quite new - it only opened in 1996 - it has the genuine feel of a large period house. Conference rooms of varying sizes include a library/boardroom beside the drawing room that doubles as a private dining room. Spacious bedrooms vary in decor, are beautifully furnished to a very high standard with antiques and have generous marbled bathrooms with individual tiling, heated towel rails and quality toiletries. Conference/banqueting (140/90); business centre. Leisure centre, indoor pool, beauty salon; beauty and massage therapies by arrangement. Children welcome (under 12 free in parents' room, cot available without charge, baby sitting arranged). No pets. garden. **Rooms 88** (15 suites, 33 no-smoking, 4 for disabled). Lift. 24 hour room service. B&B €202 pps, ss about €65. Open all year. **The Manor Room:** As there is no dedicated reception area or cocktail bar attached to the restaurant, aperitifs must be taken in the bar (which can be noisy), at the table - or, perhaps, in the lobby - which is not an ideal way to begin a fine dining experience. However, once inside this well-appointed, traditional dining room, the view over the walled garden at the back of the hotel is soothing, giving it the quiet, serene atmosphere that head chef Philippe Farineau's fine cooking deserves. He joined the hotel in 2002, and makes good use of local produce, in impressive classical cuisine that may have an occasional contemporary twist; signature dishes include an unusual trio of

Irish lamb: ravioli set on aubergine salsa, roasted loin topped with basil compôte & cutlet served with gratin dauphinois, broad beans & lamb jus. But, complex as this may sound, he is not afraid of simplicity and, given the quality of ingredients and skilful cooking, this is a great strength. The combination of accomplished cooking and caring service should ensure an enjoyable dining experience. Seats 90. L daily, 12.30-2, D daily, 7-10. Set L €35. Set D €60; à la carte L & D also available. House wine from about €31. Service discretionary (10% on parties of 8+). *Informal meals are also available in the bar, 12.30-9.30pm daily: L 12.30-2.30; Aft Tea 2.30-5.30; D 5.30-9.30. Ames, Diners, MasterCard, Visa. **Directions:** Signed off College Road.

Cork

Hotel Isaacs

HOTEL

48 MacCurtain Street Cork **Tel: 021 450 0011**
Fax: 021 450 6355 Email: cork@isaacs.ie Web: www.isaacs.ie

Opposite the theatre and approached through a cobbled courtyard, this attractive hotel offers comfort in spacious rooms at a reasonable price. Major renovations during 2002/3 included the replacement of all front windows, which has considerably reduced traffic noise, and the addition of 14 superior bedrooms; the existing bedrooms are due to be refurbished as we go to press (Autumn 2003). The furnishing style is attractive and different from most hotels: bedrooms have attractive polished stripped wood floors, free-standing pine furniture and an unusually homely feeling. Conference/banqueting (60/40). Business centre; secretarial services, video conferencing by arrangement. Children welcome (under 3 free in parents room, cot available free of charge). All day room service. Car park nearby. No pets. Garden (courtyard). Self-catering apartments avilable (open all year). **Rooms 47** (2 suites, 14 executive, 6 shower-only, 21 no-smoking, 2 for disabled). Lift. B&B about from €58pps, ss25. Closed 24-27 Dec. **Greene's Restaurant:** The approach from the street is very attractive, under a limestone arch to a narrow courtyard with a waterfall - which is floodlit at night, making an unusual feature when seen from the restaurant. The reception and two restaurant areas have character and the atmosphere is more like an independent restaurant than an hotel dining room. Quite ambitious à la carte menus offer modern renditions of classic dishes, often based on local ingredients - starters like Cashel Blue twice-baked soufflé with dressed rocket salad & shallot vinaigrette, for example, or Greenes Irish crab bouillabaisse with grilled salmon & seaweed sour cream; main courses tend to be contemporary international in style and desserts more classical. Accurate cooking, attractive presentation and friendly, helpful service - plus a lively atmosphere and quite reasonable prices - should ensure an enjoyable meal. The early dinner menu is especially good value. **Seats 100** (private room, 40). Food served from 7.30 am. D daily 6-10 (Sun to 9.30), L Sun 12.30-2.30 (Bar L available daily). Early D €25 (6-7pm); also à la carte. Set Sun L €20. House wine €20. SC 10%. Bar Food: 12-6 daily. Closed 24 Dec (after lunch) - 27 Dec. Amex, MasterCard, Visa, Laser, Switch. **Directions:** Opposite Dan Lowrey's Pub.

Cork

Idaho.Café

CAFÉ

19 Caroline Street Cork **Tel: 021 427 6376**

This friendly and exceptionally well-located little café is hitting the spot for discerning shoppers, who appreciate Mairead Jacob's hearty food - this is good home cooking based on the best of ingredients and all the better for that. The day begins with breakfast (everything from porridge to Belgian waffles with organic maple syrup and the option of bacon) easing gently in to lunch, when tasty little numbers like crispy duck, spring onion and brie quesadillas and sheperdess's pie (using organic beef) are typical of the treats in store. But best of all perhaps, as baking is a speciality, are the 'Sweet Fix' temptations which are just ideal for that quick morning coffee or afternoon tea break - the coeliac friendly 'orange almond' cake has developed quite a following, and there's a wide range hot and cold drinks, including 'Hippy' specialist teas. **Seats 30.** No smoking area. Toilets wheelchair accessible. Children welcome. Open Mon-Sat, 8.30-6 (to 5 in summer); B'fst 8.30-12, L 12-4.30. House wine €3.90 (glass), specialist beers from €3.75. Closed Sun, 24-26 Dec. **No Credit Cards. Directions:** Directly behind Brown Thomas, Cork.

Cork

Imperial Hotel

HOTEL

South Mall Cork **Tel: 021 427 4040** Fax: 021 427 4040
Email: info@imperialhotelcork.ie Web: www.imperialhotelcork.ie

This thriving hotel in Cork's main commercial and banking centre was taken over by the Flynn family in 1998. It dates back to 1813 and has a colourful history - Michael Collins spent his last night here, no less, and that suite now bears his name. However, it's the convenient location - near the river and just a couple of minutes walk from the Patrick Street shopping area - that makes this hotel so popular for business and pleasure, also the free car parking available for residents. Rooms are all en-suite, with a mixture of furnishings, and there are attractive weekend and off-season rates. Conference/banqueting (300). Private car park. Children welcome; cots available. No pets. **Rooms 88** (some shower-only). B&B about €92pps. Closed 24-27 Dec. Amex, Diners, MasterCard, Visa, Laser. **Directions:** City centre Location.

Cork

Isaacs Restaurant

féile bia RESTAURANT

48 MacCurtain Street Cork **Tel: 021 450 3805**
Fax: 021 455 1348 Email: isaacs@iol.ie

This large, atmospheric modern restaurant in an 18th-century warehouse was a trend-setter in the modern Irish food movement. The co-owners, Michael and Catherine Ryan together with partner/head chef Canice Sharkey, present a combination of international influences and reassuring Irish traditions which was ahead of its time when they opened here in 1992: thus a comforting potato and leek soup might sit easily on the menu alongside modern tempura dish, and a traditional seafood chowder may come with garlic croûtons. Although it has been done in a quiet, low-key way, this restaurant played a leading role in the culinary revolution that has overtaken Ireland. Isaacs' exciting blend of Irish and international themes, together with a policy of providing great food and good value in an informal, relaxed ambience has attracted endless imitations. Over a decade later, it is no longer cutting edge but ingredients are still carefully sourced, the cooking is accomplished and menus are freshened by occasional inspired introductions (their plate of lunch tapas is a a good example) and specials that change twice daily; it remains one of the of Cork's best restaurants. **Seats 120.** L Mon-Sat 12.30-2.30, D daily 6.30-10.30 (Sun to 9). Short à la carte and daily blackboard specials; vegetarian dishes highlighted. Prices are reasonable, representing very good value for the high quality of food. House wine from €16. Service discretionary (10% on parties of 8+). Closed L Sun & L bank hols, Christmas week. Amex, Diners, MasterCard, Visa, Laser, Switch. **Directions:** Opposite Dan Lowrey's Pub.

Cork

Ivory Tower

féile bia RESTAURANT The Exchange Builldings Princes Street Cork **Tel: 021 427 4665**

Seamus O'Connell, one of Ireland's most original culinary talents, runs this unusual restaurant upstairs in an early Victorian commercial building - now familiar through his television series, Soul Food. Very best quality ingredients (all local and organic or wild, including game in season), creative menus and excellent details like delicious home-baked breads, and imaginative presentation are the hallmarks of The Ivory Tower. Menus start off with a "surprise taster" to set the mood and examples from a high summer menu that show the style include a signature starter of Roquefort soufflé baked in a globe artichoke & served with truffle beurre blanc, which might be followed by a little granita or sorbet (watermelon & blood orange, perhaps) then, from a choice of about nine dishes, perhaps wild wild sea trout hot smoked to order over oak, with whiskey & scallion sauce. Desserts are equally unconventional, so why not finish with another speciality - aphrodisiac of tropical fruits? A shortish wine list includes a number of rare treats, including some organic and biodynamic wines. Not suitable for children under 5. **Seats 35.** D Thu-Sun, 6.30-9.30. 5-course D €50; Surprise Menu €70. House wine from €18. SC discretionary. Closed Mon-Wed. Amex, MasterCard, Visa, Laser. **Directions:** Corner of Princes/Oliver Plunkett street.

Cork

Jacobs On The Mall

☆ féile bia RESTAURANT

30A South Mall Cork **Tel: 021 425 1530** Fax: 021 425 1531

Its location in the former Turkish baths has created a highly unusual and atmospheric contemporary dining space for one of Cork's leading restaurants (possibly the leader; the restaurant hierarchy in Cork city has never been the same since Declan Ryan sold Arbutus Lodge and took up baking). Mercy Fenton returned from abroad to take up the position of head chef here when the restaurant opened in 1998 and she has done a consistently superb job. Modern European cooking is the promise and, with close attention to sourcing the best ingredients allied to outstanding cooking skills, the results are commendably simple and never less than exceptional in terms of balance and flavour. Details like home-made breads are excellent - try the unusual black pepper soda bread - and fresh local and organic produce makes its mark in the simplest of dishes, like delicious mixed leaf salads. Reflecting the availability of local produce, lunch and dinner menus change daily and are sensibly brief - offering a choice of around five to seven dishes on each course, notably seafood and vegetables in season: a simple meal of Kinsale asparagus with lemon butter and seared scallops with potato and chive dressing could be memorable, for example. Creativity with deliciously wholesome and colourful ingredients, accurate cooking, stylish presentation and efficient yet relaxed service all add up to an outstanding dining experience. Finish on a high note - with a Jacobs Dessert plate, perhaps, or farmhouse cheeses, which are always so good in Cork, served here with homemade digestive biscuits and oatcakes. Pianist on some evenings. Children welcome. Special diets willingly accommodated with advance notice. **Seats 130** (Private room, 25, with own bar). No smoking area; air conditioning. Toilets wheelchair accessible. L Mon-Sat 12.30-2.30, D Mon-Sat 6.30-10pm. A la carte. House wines from €19; s.c.10%. Closed Sun, 25-26 D; L on bank hols. Amex, Diners, MasterCard, Visa, Laser, Switch. **Directions:** Beside Bank of Ireland, at the Grand Parade end of the South Mall.

Cork

☆ RESTAURANT

Jacques Restaurant

Phoenix Street Cork **Tel: 021 427 7387**
Fax: 021 427 0634 Email: jacquesrestaurant@eircom.net

An integral part of Cork life since 1982, sisters Eithne and Jacqueline Barry's delightful restaurant has changed with the years, evolving from quite a traditional place to the dashing Mediterranean-toned bistro it is today. There is always a personal welcome and, together with Eileen Carey, who has been in the kitchen with Jacque Barry since 1986, they are known for putting a high value on the provenance and quality of the food that provides the basic building blocks for their delicious meals. Menus have always been based on carefully sourced ingredients from a network of suppliers built up over many years and this care, together with skill and judgement in the kitchen, shows particularly in having the confidence to keep things simple and allow the food to speak for itself. Menus are refreshingly short, allowing this skilled team to concentrate on the delicious cooking that is their forte - in sun-filled starters such as roast marinated quail on tapenade crostini & hoummous (also available as a main course) and main courses including an updated classic of traditional roast duck with potato & apricot mash & apricot & tamarind sauce with roast vegetables, which is a speciality. Desserts could be lemon tart or orange & almond cake with cardamom & orange flower yoghurt. Consistently good cooking in stylish, relaxed surroundings and service which is unfailingly helpful and attentive have led to Jacques' present position as one of Cork's leading restaurants - and it's excellent value too, especially the early dinner. Sadly they are, at least temporarily, discontinuing their excellent lunches - we watch and hope. **Seats 50.** No-smoking area; air conditioning. An interesting, fairly priced wine list includes some organic wines and about ten half bottles. D Tue-Sat 6-10. Early D 6-7, €19.90. Also à la carte. House wine €16.90. Service discretionary. Closed Sun & Mon, bank hols & 24 Dec - 2 Jan. Amex, MasterCard, Visa, Laser. **Directions:** Near G.P.O.

Cork

féile bia HOTEL

Jurys Inn Cork

Anderson's Quay Cork **Tel: 021 494 3000** Fax: 021 427 6144
Email: julieann_brennan@jurysdoyle.com Web: www.jurysdoyle.com

In a fine central riverside site, this budget hotel has all the features that Jurys Inns have now become well known for: room prices include accommodation for up to two adults & two children (including a sofa bed) and there is space for a cot (by arrangement). No room service. Limited parking (22 spaces), plus arrangement with nearby car park (fee payable). **Rooms 133** (7 suitable for disabled guests). Room rate from €80. Closed 25-26 Dec. Amex, Diners, MasterCard, Visa. **Directions:** City centre, on quays.

Cork

féile bia HOTEL / RESTAURANT

Kingsley Hotel

Victoria Cross Cork **Tel: 021 480 0500**
Fax: 021 480 0526 Web: www.kingsleyhotel.com

BUSINESS HOTEL OF THE YEAR

Conveniently situated in an increasingly attractive location alongside the River Lee, just minutes from both Cork airport and the city centre, this modern hotel has been built and furnished to a high standard and is especially attractive for business visitors, for whom it quickly becomes a home from home. A large, comfortably furnished foyer has a homely yet luxurious feel to it - both it and an informal restaurant area a few steps up from it (and overlooking the weir), both make good meeting places. This hospitable feeling is noticeable throughout the hotel, from the moment guests are greeted on arrival, and accommodation is personally decorated and well-planned to make a good base away from home. Spacious rooms offer traditional comfort and are designed with care: air conditioning, work station with ISDN and modem, interactive TV with message facilities, safes, trouser press with ironing board and same day laundry service all increase the hotel's appeal for business guests - and these details are matched by excellent conference, business and leisure facilities. In addition to the attractive restaurant, private dining facilities are also available, in rooms catering for 16-80 guests. Conference/banqueting (9/80); secretarial services; video conferencing, on request; 24 hour room service. Leisure centre, swimming pool; treatment rooms, beauty salon. Children welcome (cot available without charge, baby sitting arranged). Garden. Riverside walks. Pets permitted by arrangement. Parking. **Rooms 69** (4 suites, 15 junior suites, 50 executive rooms, 40 no-smoking, 2 for disabled). Lift. B&B about €155pps, ss about €50. Open all year. **Otters at the Kingsley:** Set up in contemporary bistro style, with darkwood furniture, comfortable upholstered chairs and uncluttered table settings, this split level restaurant appeals to non-residents as well as hotel guests. A warm welcome, promptly presented menus and wine list, simple classy table settings and friendly, helpful staff all help both to impress and relax guests. International menus offer plenty of choice without being overlong, typically including starters of pan-seared diver sea scallops, with citrus & tomato purée and barbecue duck with dried fruit & minted green peppercorn jus and main courses such as a vegetarian dish of parmesan potato cake with sautéed spinach, button mushrooms, chive crème fraîche & truffle oil or medallions of monkfish with Caldine curry sauce & basmati rice - all excellent, in the recent experience of the Guide. Desserts - typically tiramisu or a classic lemon tart - are prettily presented and service is professional and, as elsewhere in the hotel, outstandingly friendly and helpful. Good wine list (although more wines by the glass would be an improvement). **Seats 100** (private room 80). L daily 12.30-2.30, (Sun L 12-3), D 6-10. Set L from €21; early D €23 (6-7pm); D also à la carte. House wine from €17. SC discretionary. *Lounge and bar food also available through the day. MasterCard, Visa. **Directions:** On Main N22 Killarney Road by Victoria Cross.

Cork

Lancaster Lodge

GUESTHOUSE

Lancaster Quay Western Road Cork **Tel: 021 425 1125** Fax: 021 425 1126
Email: info@lancasterlodge.com Web: www.lancasterlodge.com

This guesthouse opened in 1999 and it was built with vision, to offer hotel quality accommodation,with personal supervision, at a moderate price. Spacious rooms are furnished to quite a high standard (with ISDN lines, safes, 12 channel TV, trouser press, tea/coffee facilities and room service as well as the more usual facilities) and well-designed bathrooms (two with jacuzzi baths). Good breakfasts - attractive buffet and cooked to order hot dishes - are served in a contemporary dining room, or in your room. Maintenance seems to have slipped a little on recent visits by the Guide, but this remains a useful address and offers better value for money than many hotels. Children welcome (under 5s free in parents' room, cot available). Parking. 24 hour reception. **Rooms 39** (2 junior suites, 3 shower only, 2 for disabled). Lift. B&B from about €50 pps. Closed 23-25 Dec. Amex, Diners, MasterCard, Visa. **Directions:** On Western Road, opposite Café Paradiso. ◇

Cork

Les Gourmandises Restaurant

Ⓝ RESTAURANT

17 Cook Street Cork **Tel: 021 425 1959**

Just off South Mall, this simple little restaurant feels like an outpost of France - the menu in the window will draw you in and you'll be glad you noticed it. It's run by Patrick and Soizic Kiely - both previously at Restaurant Patrick Guilbaud but, although that says a lot about the key standards, this is an utterly down to earth place far more reminiscent of family-run restaurants in France. The long, narrow room is bright and functional, emphatically not smart - and with fairly bare walls relieved by a number of pictures on Venetian themes. Not, one suspects, a particular choice of the current proprietors. Staff - who are mainly French - are pleasant and helpful, swiftly bringing simple menus in the French style, and a lovely wine list. Lunch menus are very straightforward - warm salads are especially appealing: duck, or bacon, perhaps, with mixed leaves cherry tomatoes, olives, asparagus - whatever is in season, with a good dressing. Evening menus are more structured: ballotine of salmon or tian of crab to start, perhaps, confit of duck leg with sage pomme puree or pan-fried fillet of cod with roasted aubergine & tapenade followed by classic desserts (lemon tart with raspberries, creme brulée) and a French & Irish cheese selection. Good bread, lovely coffee; well-chosen, informative little wine list - smashing house wines. A good call. **Seats 30.** L Mon-Sat 12-3.30, D Fri/Sat 7.15-9.30. A la carte. House wine from €20. Closed Sun. MasterCard, Visa, Laser, Switch. **Directions:** City centre - access to Cook Street from South Mall.

Cork

Lotamore House

GUESTHOUSE

Tivoli Cork **Tel: 021 482 2344**
Fax: 021 482 2219 Email: lotamore@iol.ie

This large period house is set in mature gardens and, although not grand, it was built on a generous scale. Big, airy rooms have air conditioning, phones, TV and trouser press (tea/coffee trays on request), and they're comfortably furnished to sleep three, with room for an extra bed or cot and full bathrooms.

A large drawing room has plenty of armchairs and an open fire and, although only breakfast and light meals are offered, Fleming's Restaurant (see entry) is next door. Children welcome (Under 5 free in parents' room, cots available, baby-sitting by arrangement). Wheelchair access. Own parking. **Rooms 20** (5 no-smoking, 1 for disabled). Garden. Pets permitted. B&B about €45, ss about €10. Closed Christmas/New Year. Amex, MasterCard, Visa. **Directions:** On N8, 5 minutes drive from Cork City. ◇

Cork

Lovetts Restaurant & Brasserie

☆ RESTAURANT

Churchyard Lane off Well Road Douglas Cork
Tel: 021 429 4909 Email: lovetts@utvinternet.com

Home to both the restaurant and the Lovett family since 1977, this fine restaurant is in a late Georgian house situated in mature grounds. Management is now in the capable hands of Niamh Lovett and head chef is Marie Harding, a talented and creative cook committed to serious cooking, using the best of fresh, free range and local products. Just reading through Marie's list of suppliers is enough to whet the appetite: smoked salmon and eel from Cresswells of Ummera, Co Cork; mussels and oysters (in season) from Kellys of Clarenbridge; crab from Shellfish de la Mer, and most other fish from Denis Good, both in Castletownbere; Mrs Lombard of Minane Bridge supplies free range chickens, while ducks are from Barry's of Fort Farm, Fermoy and mushrooms from Fran & Jim Fraser. Better still, while the menus - which are based on daily availability, not over-extensive and admirably simple in style - are a mouth-watering read, the cooking matches the quality of ingredients, making for an outstanding dining experience. You might begin with an Ardrahan cheese & chilli chutney tart perhaps - Ardrahan is made nearby, in north Cork - followed by something as apparently ordinary as a sirloin steak; but this is Bresnan's Irish beef, selected for its exceptional quality - and it will come with a more-ish caramelised onion & rosemary mash and a wild mushroom bordelaise sauce: which all goes to show how delicious Ireland's most popular dish can be. A separate vegetarian menu is very appealing, desserts delicious (loganberry bakewell tart, with cream, perhaps) and, of course, there's a fine Irish farmhouse cheese plate. There's a fully licensed bar (the extensive wine list is Niamh's father Dermod Lovett's particular passion) and private dining is available in the 'Wine Geese' Room. **Seats 60.** (Private room 6-24). D à la carte; Vegetarian Menu €20. House wine about €18. Service discretionary. D Tue-Sat, 5.30-9.30. Closed Sun, Mon, bank hols, Christmas week, 1 week Aug. Amex, Diners, MasterCard, Visa, Laser. **Directions:** Close to south Cork city: from Douglas Road take turning to Mahon and Blackrock and go through a roundabout. Take the fourth turn on the left, Wells Road; Lovetts is off it in Churchyard Lane.

Cork

Maryborough House Hotel

féile bia HOTEL

Maryborough Hill Douglas Cork **Tel: 021 436 5555** Fax: 021 436 5662
Email: maryboro@indigo.ie Web: www.maryborough.com

The Maryborough House Hotel has at its heart a fine country house set in its own grounds and gardens and has been developed with sensitivity. The original house, which is beautifully proportioned, has many fine features, restored with care and furnished in period style with antiques. The main entrance is via the original flight of steps up to the old front door and, although there is no conventional reception area, guests receive a warm welcome at the desk just inside the front door. The new section of the hotel - which is modern and blends comfortably with the trees and gardens surrounding it - includes excellent leisure facilities and spacious public areas, which extend from the period rooms of the original house right across to the new accommodation wing through the Garden Room, a spacious contemporary lounge area recently refurbished in aubergine with smart leather sofas. Accommodation is exceptionally good in terms of design - simple, modern, bright, utilising Irish crafts: rooms are generously-sized, with a pleasant outlook, good amenities and extras including complimentary mineral water. Bathrooms are well-finished and well-lit, with plenty of marbled shelf space, generous towels and a robe; they have environmentally friendly toiletries, small baths and towels, and suggestions on saving water by avoiding unnecessary laundry. Conference/banqueting (500/400). Leisure centre (swimming pool); beauty salon. Children welcome (under 2 free in parents room, cots available, baby sitting arranged). No pets. **Rooms 79** (2 suites, 3 junior suites, 74 executive rooms, 18 no-smoking, 8 for disabled). Lift. 24 hour room service. B&B €85, ss €30. Closed 24-26 Dec. **Zings:** The hotel's design-led dining area is now more logically located next to the bar, which was recently moved up from its original position on the lower ground floor; it is cleverly designed to create separate areas without physical divisions, partly through careful use of lighting - and the tables of lone diners who wish to read are considerately spot lit. Gerry Allen, who has been head chef since the hotel opened in 1997, offers European cuisine with traditional and Mediterranean flavours - a speciality that sums up the style neatly is Thai baked sea bass with fragrant rice. International influences dominate, but local produce is used. Pretty desserts include some good ices - real vanilla, for example, and passion fruit parfait. Not suitable for children after 7pm. **Seats 140.** Air conditioning. L daily 12.30-2.30, D 6.30-9.30. Set L €24, Set D €50, also à la carte. House wine €22. SC discretionary.* Bar meals also available every day, 9.30am-9.30pm. Amex, Diners, MasterCard, Visa, Laser. **Directions:** Near Douglas village; signed from roundabout where Rochestown Road meets Carrigaline Road.

Cork

Nakon Thai Restaurant

RESTAURANT

Tramway House Douglas Village Cork **Tel: 021 436 9900**
Fax: 021 488 8002 Web: www.nakonthai.com

Efficient reception gets guests off to a good start at this smart restaurant in Douglas village. The aim is to provide traditional Thai cuisine in a relaxed and friendly atmosphere, although the flavours typical of Thai cuisine - coriander, lime, chilli, saltiness - seem to have been tamed somewhat, presumably to meet local demand. Several set menus are offered and an à la carte that may seem overlong, but everything is freshly cooked, without any artificial flavourings or MSG. If in doubt try some of the house specialities such as hot & sour prawn soup, or a sizzling dish of fried beef with chilli, onion, pepper, garlic & spring onions. A simple dessert selection includes exotic Thai fruit salad for a refreshing finish. Informative fairly priced wine list, also imported Thai beers. Not suitable for children after 7pm. **Seats 46.** No smoking area. Air conditioning. D Mon-Sat 5.30-11, Sun 5-10. Set menus from €22.95; à la carte also available. House wine from about €19.95. SC discretionary. Closed 24-26 Dec, Good Fri. Amex, Diners, MasterCard, Visa, Laser. **Directions:** Douglas Village opposite Rugby Club.

Cork

Proby's Bistro

féile bia **RESTAURANT**

Proby's Quay Crosses Green Cork **Tel: 021 431 6531** Fax: 021 4975882
Email: info@probysbistro.com Web: www.probysbistro.com

Handier to the city centre than it first appears, this is a pleasant spot for a bite to eat during the day (tables outside for fine weather) as well as in the evening, when menus are more likely to include less usual dishes, such as a Gascon duck & bacon soup, or roast pigeon. The style - established before the current wave and competently executed - is global cuisine, with an emphasis on things Mediterranean. Menus - which include a fast lunch and early dinner as well as à la carte choices - offer lively fare with an international tone yet plenty of local produce; West Cork black pudding is a favourite starter(served with grainy mustard sauce & garlic mash), and duck confit (honey glazed duck with rosemary jus, sautéed courgette & pepper and fondant potatoes) is a speciality main course. Specials change daily and there's a special seafood night on Wednesdays (2-course Set D about €25). Children welcome. **Seats 120** (private room 40; outdoor seating, 20). Air conditioning. Open Mon-Sat, 10 am-10pm (Fri & Sat to 11): L 12-5, D 6-10 (Fri & Sat to 11). Early D €20 (6-7.30), otherwise à la carte; SC discretionary (except 10% on parties of 8+). House wine €16.75. Closed Sun, Mon bank hols, 24-27 Dec. Amex, MasterCard, Visa, Laser. **Directions:** Adjacent to St. Finbarre's Cathedral and Beamish & Crawford brewery.

Cork

Rochestown Park Hotel

féile bia **HOTEL**

Rochestown Road Douglas Cork **Tel: 021 489 0800** Fax: 021 489 2178
Email: info@rochestownpark.com Web: www.rochestownpark.com

Formerly a home of the Lord Mayors of Cork, this attractive hotel stands in lovely grounds and the original parts of the building feature gracious, well-proportioned public rooms. Since opening in 1989 the hotel has seen many changes under the watchful eye of General Manager Liam Lally. Rooms are furnished to a high standard with all the comforts - including air conditioning, ISDN lines, fax and safe in executive rooms, as well as the more usual conveniences like tea/coffee trays, multi-channel TV and trouser press, all of which make this a popular base for business guests, who are well looked after in an executive wing. Facilities include a fine leisure centre with a Roman style 20-metre swimming pool, sauna, steam room and computerised gymnasium, as well as a Thalasso Therapy centre which predates the current fashion for spas by a good few years: seaweed baths, seaweed wraps, hydrojets, therapeutic pools and massage aim to provide relaxation and renewal for both body and mind. They also offer reflexology and beauty treatments including Yonka facials. Conference and meeting facilities are amongst the best in the country. Conference/banqueting (900/550); video conferencing on request. Children welcome (under 6 free in parents' room; cots available). Leisure centre, indoor swimming pool, beauty salon. Garden. Parking. No pets. **Rooms 165** (1 suite, 6 junior suites, 70 executive rooms, 20 no smoking, 4 for disabled). Lift. 24 hour room service. B&B €70pps, ss €25. SC 12.5%. Short breaks offered. Open all year.

Gallery Restaurant: The restaurant is in a pleasant position overlooking the hotel gardens; the ambience and service are both good and head chef Gerry Kirwin ensures that the food goes beyond the expectations of a hotel dining room, making dining-in a positive option for residents, especially business guests. Menus, which change monthly, are well-balanced and always include some strong vegetarian options; prime Irish beef is a speciality, also a choice of local seafood. L&D daily. SC 12.5%. Amex, Diners, MasterCard, Visa, Laser. **Directions:** Adjacent to South Ring Road which links all main routes into Cork city.

Cork

Silver Springs Moran Hotel

féile bia HOTEL

Tivoli Cork **Tel: 021 450 7533** Fax: 021 450 7641
Email: silversprings@morangroup.ie Web: www.silverspringshotel.ie

This well-known hotel situated in 25 acres of landscaped gardens about five minutes drive from the city centre is a modern tower block overlooking the River Lee and has an eye-catching external glass lift; spacious bedrooms are furnished to a high standard, with good bathrooms and some of them share the view. Self-contained conference/banqueting suites can each accommodate up to 700 guests & there's a business centre. A well-equipped leisure centre has indoor tennis and squash, as well as a 25-metre pool, and there's a 9-hole golf course on site. **Rooms 109** (3 suites, 2 mini-suites, 29 executive rooms, 16 no-smoking rooms and 5 for disabled). B&B about €100 pps. Amex, Diners, MasterCard, Visa, Laser. **Directions:** At the Tivoli flyover above the main Cork Dublin road and clearly signed off it. (From Cork, take first left then right at the flyover.) ◇

Cork

Table 8

RESTAURANT

8/9 Careys Lane Cork **Tel: 021 427 0725** Fax: 021 427 0694

Husband and wife team Chris and Eleanor O'Brien took over this bright, modern restaurant in a characterful area of the city in 2002 and it seems to have found a niche. It's on an interesting narrow street of specialist shops and wine bars and, being upstairs in a tall narrow building, they've sensibly gone to some trouble to highlight its appeal from the street, with bright fresh paintwork and encouraging menus on display. Eleanor is the restaurant manager while Chris, who trained at Ballymaloe House, offers moderately priced menus with strong Mediterranean and some modern Irish influences - typically in starters like bruschetta of char-grilled peppers, anchovy and capers, and main courses such as a speciality dish of roast cod with prawn colcannon & chive velouté or grilled chicken breast parmesan & fresh herb risotto cake, with wild mushroom cream. Chris bakes all the breads on the premises and desserts - vanilla ice cream with rhubarb & strawberry compôte - are also home-made. Ground floor wheelchair accessible. Reservations advised. **Seats 100.** L Mon-Sat, 12-3; D Mon-Sat, 5.30-"late". Early D €20 (5.30-7.30), Set D Menus from €30, also à la carte. Closed L Sun, 25-26 Dec. MasterCard, Visa, Laser. **Directions:** On Carey's Lane, pedestrian street between Patrick St & Paul Street in the centre of Cork.

COUNTY CORK

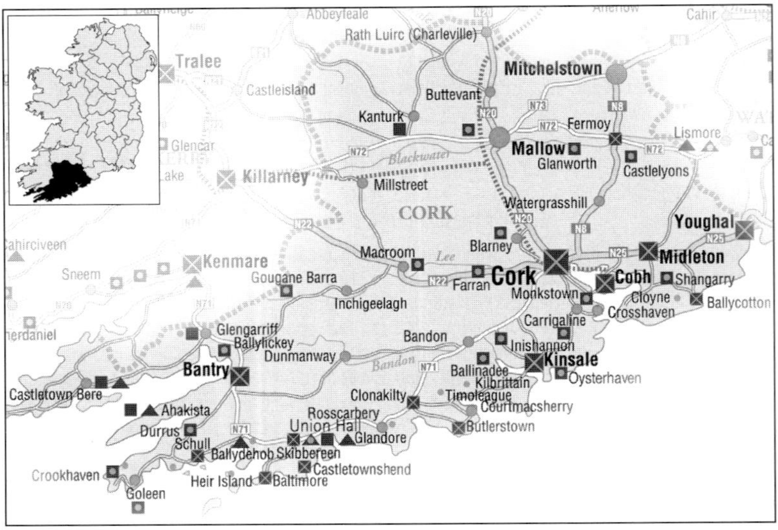

Cork is Ireland's largest county, and its individualistic people take pride in this distinction as they savour the variety of their territory, which ranges from the rich farmlands of East Cork, away westward to the handsome coastline of West Cork where the mighty light of the famous Fastnet Rock swings across tumbling ocean and spray-tossed headland.

The counties many towns and villages have their own distinctive character. In the far west of the county, way down towards the end of the rugged Beara Peninsula, the colourful little village of Eyeries has been making the most of itself. At the National Tidy Town awards ceremony in Dublin Castle on September 8th 2003, it was announced that Eyeries was the closest possible runner-up to the overall winner, with a score of 269, which is 89.7%. And the Beara village was of course the winner of a Gold Medal.

Eyeries is set in big country, on the edge of the Atlantic. By contrast, East Cork is lush farming country. In the midst of it, Midleton is home to the Jameson Heritage Centre, where the fascinating story of whiskey is entertainingly told in a town which is also the locality for Irish Distillers' manufacturing headquarters, producing Jameson, Power's and Paddy whiskey together with many variants, as well as Huzzar Vodka and Cork Dry Gin.

At the far end of East Cork, the new by-pass around the ancient port of Youghal has removed excessive through-traffic from an intriguing place which is re-discovering itself. The spectacularly located township of Cobh - facing south over Cork Harbour - is also asserting its own identity, with a renewed sense of its remarkable maritime heritage being expressed in events such as a Sea Shanty Festival, while the town's direct link with the Titanic is celebrated in many ways.

The county is a repository of the good things of life, a treasure chest of the finest farm produce, and the very best of seafood, brought to market by skilled specialists. Not surprisingly, it is County Cork which is at the forefront in developing the very commendable international Slow Food Movement in Ireland (028-31179) But it isn't all work by any means. As Ireland's most southerly county, Cork enjoys the mildest climate of all, and it's a place where they work to live, rather than live to work. The arts of living, in fact, are probably seen at their most skilled in County Cork, and they are practised in a huge territory of such variety that it is difficult to grasp it all, even if you devote your entire vacation to this one county.

Local Attractions and Information

Ballydehob, Nature Art Centre 028 37323
Bantry, Bantry House 027 50047
Bantry, Murphy's International Mussel Fair (May) 027 50360
Bantry, Tourism Information 027 50229
Blarney, Blarney Castle 021 438 5252
Cape Clear Island, International Storytelling Festival (early September) 028 39157

Carrigtwohill Fota Estate (Wildlife Park, Arboretum) 021 481 2728
Castletownroche, Annes Grove (gardens) 022 26145
Clonakilty, Lisselan Estate Gardens 023 33249
Cobh, The Queenstown Story 021 481 3591
Cobh, Sirius Arts Centre 021 481 3790
Cork Airport, ... 021 431 3131
Glanmire, Dunkathel House 021 482 1014
Glanmire, Riverstown House 021 482 1205
Glengarriff, Garinish Island 027 63040
Kinsale, Gourmet Festival (early October) .... c/o 021 477 2234
Kinsale, Charles Fort 021 477 2263
Kinsale, Desmond Castle 021 477 4855
Kinsale, Tourism Information 021 477 2234
Macroom, Brierly Gap Cultural Centre 026 42421
Mallow, Cork Racecourse 022 50207
Midleton, Farm Market Sats 9am-1.30pm .... 021 464 6785 / 463 1096
Midleton, Jameson Heritage Centre 021 461 3594
Millstreet, Country Park 029 71810
Mizen Head, Mizen Vision, Signal Station 028 35591
Shanagarry, Ballymaloe, Cookery School Gardens 021 464 6785
Schull, Ferries to Sherkin, Cape Clear and Fastnet 028 28278
Schull, Schull Planetarium 028 28552
Skibbereen, Creagh Gardens 028 22121
Skibbereen, Tourism Information 028 21766
Skibbereen, West Cork Arts Centre 028 22090
Slow Food Ireland, (c/o Glenilen Farm, Drimoleague) 028 31179
Youghal, Myrtle Grove 024 92274

Ahakista

Ahakista Bar

ATMOSPHERIC PUB

Ahakista Durrus Bantry Co Cork **Tel: 027 67203**

Anthony and Margaret Whooley run one of the most relaxed bars in the country: known affectionately as "the tin pub" because of its corrugated iron roof, it has a lovely rambling country garden going down to the water at the back, where children are very welcome to burn off excess energy. It's been in the family for two generations now and, other than succumbing to the telephone after years of resistance, it's a place that just doesn't change. Normal pub hours don't apply in this part of the world, but they're open from 12 noon and evenings all year, except 25 Dec & Good Fri. **Directions:** Sheeps Head from Durrus.

Ahakista

Hillcrest House

FARMHOUSE

Ahakista Durrus Bantry Co Cork **Tel: 027 67045**
Email: hillcrestfarm@ahakista.com Web: www.ahakista.com

Agnes Hegarty's traditional farmhouse attracts many types of visitor, including walkers, who revel in the 55 mile "Sheep's Head Way" - and hospitality comes first at this working farm overlooking Dunmanus Bay, where guests are welcomed with a cup of tea and home-baked scones on arrival. The bedrooms have all been recently refurbished and have power showers, very comfortable beds, tea/coffee making facilities and clock radios. Families are well catered for as there's a swing and a donkey on the farm - and rooms are big enough for an extra child's bed. There is also a ground-floor room suitable for less able guests, with parking at the door and direct access to the dining room, which is furnished with antiques; moderately priced evening meals and fine cooked-to-order breakfasts are both served here. Hillcrest House was our Farmhouse of the Year for 2001. Rooms 4 (3 en-suite & no-smoking, 2 shower only) B&B €30-34 pps (Under 12s 25% discount in parents' room, cot available without charge.) Evening meals by arrangement (7 pm; about €22); light meals also available. *Self-catering cottage and farmhouse also available, all year - details on the website. Closed 1 Nov-15 Mar. Visa. **No Credit Cards. Directions:** 3 km from Bantry, take turn for Durrus.

Ballycotton

Bayview Hotel

RESTAURANT / HOTEL

Ballycotton Co Cork **Tel: 021 464 6746** Fax: 021 464 6075
Email: info@bayviewhotel.net Web: www.bayviewhotel.net

Overlooking Ballycotton Harbour, John and Carmel O'Brien's hotel enjoys a magnificent location on the sea side of the road, with a path down to the beach through its own gardens - and there are miles of sandy beaches nearby. The O'Briens completely rebuilt the hotel in the early 1990s, keeping the building fairly low and in sympathy with the traditional style and scale of the surrounding buildings and harbour, and it creates an excellent first impression with its immaculate grounds, classy cream paintwork and smart black railings. The style is quite traditional throughout and comfortable, homely public areas include a very pleasant bar with clubby leather furniture and a cosy atmosphere - and friendly, helpful staff do their best to make guests feel at home. Well-furnished bedrooms all have sea views although they vary according to their position in the building - first floor rooms include two corner suites (with jacuzzi) and they all open onto small balconies, while those on the top have smaller dormer windows (and may seem cosy or a little claustrophobic depending on your taste). All rooms have decent bathrooms although, like the rest of the interior of the hotel, small signs of wear and tear may spoil an otherwise good impression. Small conferences/banqueting (40/80). Garden, tennis, fishing, walking. Children welcome (under12 free in parents' room, cot available without charge, baby sitting arranged). No pets. * The nearby Garryvoe Hotel is in the same family ownership and currently undergoing impressive redevelopment; some new rooms are already operational and the entire scheme, including a leisure centre, is due to open in 2005. Its beachside location makes it a popular base for family holidays (see website above for details.) **Rooms 35** (2 suites, 5 no-smoking rooms). B&B €97pps, ss €32. Closed end Oct-mid Apr.

Capricho at the Bayview: Head chef Ciaran Scully has been at the Bayview since 1995 and his creative cooking has attracted a loyal following. The restaurant is smartly furnished, with good carpeting, generous use of wood, glass screens and classical table settings with fresh flowers all adding up to give a nice old-fashioned feel; the best tables have lovely harbour and sea views, although you may not be guaranteed a window table when booking. However, whether for dinner or Sunday lunch, you can safely anticipate an interesting and satisfying dining experience, complemented by pleasant service. Menus, changed daily, are refreshingly straightforward in tone, reflecting the confidence of a talented chef whose cooking style is modern Irish (developed from a classic French base, with contemporary international overtones). Ciaran Scully's wide-ranging menus are never less than creative and sometimes offer unusual dishes (a speciality is honey & mustard pig's cheek with swede purée & caramelised crispy cabbage) or game in season, in addition to a predictably wide selection of local seafood (seared fillet of cod with sautéed bok choi, Chinese leaves & teriyaki sauce, perhaps, although more traditional combinations are also offered) and well-sourced meats. Vegetable lovers will be pleased to find that imaginative individual garnishes enhance each main dish, although a plainer side dish may be less impressive - and vegetarian dishes are sometimes overlooked on the menu, so you may have to ask for a special dish to be made to order. Finish with a classic dessert like tangy lemon tart, served with vanilla bean custard, perhaps, or a farmhouse cheese selection. In fine weather, light meals may be served in the garden. Nice wine list - unusually good choice of half bottles. Not suitable for children under 12. No smoking area. **Seats 65** (private room 36) D 7-9 daily, L Sun only, 12.30-6. Set D e47, Set Sun L e26. A la carte also offered. Wines from about e25. (Bar meals available 12.30-5.30 daily). Amex, Diners, Visa, Laser. **Directions:** At Castlemartyr on the N25, turn onto the R632 in the direction of Garryvoe.

Ballycotton

Grapefruit Moon

☆ RESTAURANT

Main street Ballycotton Co Cork **Tel: 021 464 6646**

Clear signage and a tempting menu displayed in the window will tempt many an indecisive visitor into Ivan Whelan and Jean Manning's smartly painted restaurant - and, for anyone lucky enough to get in, it will be a smart move. It's a smashing little place, done up in an uncluttered low key style in neutral tones that allow people to provide colour, with some carefully-chosen modern paintings, comfortable leather chairs and simple table settings - fine glasses, fresh flowers - on classic white cloths. A warm welcome from Jean, an aperitif over the (rather too) simply presented menu in the neat little reception area - and it's decision time. While not over-extensive, menus are adventurous and wide-ranging, offering a choice of half a dozen or so dishes on each course in an unusually satisfying blend of the great classic dishes and original creations. They are changed daily, depending on the availability of fresh produce, especially fish landed on the pier just a couple of hundred yards away - which could inspire a starter of panfried brill with mango, watermelon & chilli salsa, for example, or a main course like poached monkfish with red pepper sauce & buttered asparagus. And there's plenty else to tempt the tastebuds - roast loin of wild boar might take your fancy, for instance, served with caramelized apples, cider & calvados jus, or a seriously appealing vegetarian dish like couscous crusted aubergine filled with goats parmesan, cream cheese, spring onions and toasted nuts & raisins. Classic desserts include old favourites like strawberry meringue roulade and bread & butter pudding, with butterscotch sauce & vanilla ice cream - or Irish farmhouse cheese, of course. Creative, consistently excellent cooking teamed with superb presentation and attention to detail - lovely bread, interesting side vegetables - makes for a very special dining experience here, enhanced by friendly and attentive staff and a good atmosphere. In its first year this great little restaurant has confirmed its special niche in an area already well-served by good eating places - so book early and enjoy the anticipation. The wine list has been improved considerably in the last year. **Seats 44.** No smoking area. Children welcome. D Tue-Sat, 7-10. A la carte (average main course about €23). House wine €18. SC discretionary. Reservations advised. Closed Sun, Mon, Christmas, 1 week Feb, 1 week Oct. Amex, Diners, MasterCard, Visa , Laser. **Directions:** From Castlemartyr on the N25, take R632 signed Garryvoe. On right hand side driving into the village.

Ballycotton

Spanish Point Seafood Restaurant

RESTAURANT WITH ROOMS

Ballycotton Co Cork **Tel: 021 464 6177**
Fax: 021 464 6179 Email: spanish@indigo.ie

Halfway through the village of Ballycotton you suddenly come upon the entrance to Spanish Point, an attractive old building on the seaward side of the road with a clear view across the bay. The Tattan family's two trawlers are the key to the reputation of this relaxed seafood restaurant, which has had a loyal following for over a decade. Menus are interesting without being over complicated: dishes like goujons of lemon sole with a basil & lime mayonnaise, or panfried monkfish on a hot smoked Gubbeen cheese risotto with crispy Parma ham & sundried tomato pesto are typical of a style which respects the strength of classical dishes and applies the best of contemporary influences to make for a livelier repertoire. Menus change weekly and offer a good choice - majoring on local seafood, of course, but also offering dishes based on other local produce, usually including vegetarian options - ask if this is not mentioned on the menu. The welcome is prompt and aperitifs are served in a little lounge/bar at the back, or the sun lounge, where you can mull over the menu and place your order. The restaurant is in two rooms (one a conservatory) overlooking the harbour - a fitting setting for good food, cooked and presented with care, and with service to match. The wine list includes an interesting house selection. Small conferences/banqueting (60) by arrangement. Sun deck for outside dining. **Seats 60.** No smoking area. Open daily, 8am-9.30pm, L 12.30-3 (if there are bookings), D 6.30-9.30; Set L about €20, Set D about €36. House wine about €18. A la carte also offered. Service discretionary. Low season open weekends only - phone for details.

Accommodation: Comfortable, well-furnished bedrooms all have sea views and good amenities including phone, TV and tea/coffee trays. Children welcome (under 3s free in parents' room, cot available without charge). Pets permitted. Rooms 5 (all shower only & no smoking) B&B about €38 pps, ss about €7. Closed Sun before Christmas-mid Feb. MasterCard, Visa, Laser. **Directions:** From N25, turn onto the R632 at Castlemartyr (signed Garryvoe). ◇

Ballydehob

Annie's Restaurant

RESTAURANT

Main Street Ballydehob Co Cork **Tel: 028 37292**

Anne and Dano Barry have been running their famous restaurant since 1983 - and, for many, a visit to West Cork is unthinkable without a meal here. A couple of years ago they extended into the building next door, almost doubling the number of covers and upgrading the whole restaurant so all facilities, including disabled, are on the ground floor. But you needn't worry that it's all been changed, as the fundamentals are thankfully intact and it's not at all designerish or minimalist - pretty much the same Annie's, just a bit bigger. Annie makes a great host, welcoming everybody personally, handing out menus - and then sending guests over to Levis' pub across the road for an aperitif. Then she comes over, takes orders and returns to collect people when their meals are ready - Annie's does have a wine licence but there has never been room for waiting around until tables are ready, so this famous arrangement works extremely well. As to the food at Annie's, everything is freshly made on the day, using local ingredients - fish is delivered every night, meat comes from the local butcher (who kills his own meat), farmhouse cheeses are local (including one of Ireland's most renowned cheeses, Gubbeen, which is made by Annie's sister-in-law Giana Ferguson) and all the breads, ice creams and desserts for the restaurant are made on the premises. As for Dano's cooking, it is simple and wholesome, the nearest to really good home cooking you could ever hope to find in a restaurant. Dano cooks fish like a dream and this place is still magic. Wine list features interesting half dozen house selection. Not suitable for children after 9 pm. Toilets wheelchair accessible. **Seats 40.** D Tue-Sat 7-9.30, Set D from about €38 (priced by choice of main course), à la carte also offered. House wines €17. Service discretionary. Closed Sun & Mon, 12 Oct-1 Dec & 24-27 Dec. MasterCard, Visa, Laser **Directions:** Street side midway through village.

Ballydehob

Levis' Bar

ATMOSPHERIC PUB Corner House Main Street Ballydehob Co Cork **Tel: 028 37118**

Julia and Nell Levis have run this 150-year-old bar and grocery for as long as anyone can remember. It is a characterful and delightfully friendly place, whether you are just in for a casual drink or using the pub as the unofficial 'reception' area for Annie's restaurant across the road (see entry for Annie's above). Closed 25 Dec & Good Fri. **Directions:** Main street, opposite Annie's.

Ballylickey

Ballylickey Manor House

COUNTRY HOUSE

Ballylickey Bantry Bay Co Cork
Tel: 027 50071 Fax: 027 50124
Email: ballymh@eircom.net Web: www.ballylickeymanorhouse.com

Built some 300 years ago by Lord Kenmare as a shooting lodge and home to the Franco-Irish Graves family for four generations, Ballylickey Manor enjoys a stunning, romantic setting overlooking Bantry Bay, with moors and hills behind. There are ten acres of gardens, through which the Ouvane river (trout and salmon fishing) flows. Choose between the elegant and grand bedrooms in the Manor, all lavishly furnished, or more rustic accommodation in the garden - cottages and chalets, some grouped around the outside swimming pool. Dinner is served in a lovely period dining room (the chef, Céline Poux, previously worked in a 2 star restaurant in France) and non-residents are welcome by reservation. Garden, outdoor heated swimming pool, walking, fishing. Family accommodation details "on application" (cot available, baby sitting arranged). Small conferences (15) Pets allowed in some areas. Private parking. **Rooms 12** (7 suites, 1 shower only) B&B €110 pps, ss €110. Closed Nov-Mar. Amex, Diners, MasterCard, Visa. **Directions:** On N71 between Bantry & Glengariff.

Ballylickey

Seaview House Hotel

HOTEL / RESTAURANT

Ballylickey Bantry Co Cork
Tel: 027 50462 Fax: 027 51555
Email: info@seaviewhousehotel.com Web: www.seaviewhousehotel.com

Personal supervision and warmth of welcome are the hallmarks of Kathleen O'Sullivan's restorative country house hotel close to Ballylickey Bridge. Spacious, well-proportioned public rooms include a graciously decorated drawing room, a library, cocktail bar and television room, while generously-sized bedrooms - some especially luxurious ones in a new wing, and many with sea views - are all individually decorated, with good bathrooms. Family furniture and antiques enhance the hotel and standards of maintenance and housekeeping are consistently outstanding. Children welcome (free in parents' room under 4, cot available without charge, baby sitting arranged). Pets permitted by arrangement. **Rooms 25** (2 junior suites, 2 for disabled). B&B about €65pps, ss about €26.

Restaurant: Overlooking the garden, with views over Bantry Bay, the restaurant is elegant and well-appointed with antiques, fresh flowers and plenty of privacy. Set five-course dinner menus change daily and offer a wide choice on all courses, with the emphasis firmly on local produce, especially seafood, in dishes like simple Irish oak smoked salmon, blackberry sorbet, Dover sole on the bone with lemon butter or roast rack of lamb with rosemary. Choose from classic desserts - dark chocolate mousse with white chocolate sauce, strawberry shortcake - or local cheeses to finish. Tea or coffee and petits fours may be served out of doors on fine summer evenings. Seats 50. No-smoking restaurant. Toilets wheelchair accessible. D 7-9 daily, L Sun only 12.30-2; Set D about €40, Set Sun L €25. House wines from €16. 10% sc. Hotel closed mid Nov-mid Mar. Amex, MasterCard, Visa, Laser. **Directions:** 10 mins drive from Bantry, on N71 to Glengarriff.

Baltimore

Baltimore Bay Guest House & La Jolie Brise

GUESTHOUSE / RESTAURANT

The Waterfront Baltimore Co Cork
Tel: 028 20600 Fax: 028 20495
Email: joliebrise@youenjacob.com Web: www.youenjacob.com

Just along from Bushe's Bar, La Jolie Brise has brought a breath of fresh air to eating out in Baltimore. Run by Youen Jacob the younger (see below), this cheerful continental-style café spills out on to the pavement and provides holiday-makers with good, inexpensive meals to be washed down with moderately priced wines. Breakfast menus include regular continental and full Irish breakfast and several fish choices, including hot smoked salmon, plus a range of drinks including hot chocolate and expresso. Generous, well-made pizzas (also available to take away) and pastas are available and for lunch and dinner there's a good choice of well-priced local seafood including a half dozen Sherkin Island oysters (with brown bread & butter) for just €6 - and various "European & Irish" specialities like traditional mussels & chips and char-grilled sirloin steaks with salad & chips: all youthful, contemporary use of local ingredients. The only downside to this great little place is that it can get very crowded in summer and it's hard to keep pristine. **Seats 50.** Smoking unrestricted. Open 8am-11pm daily; à la carte & special menus. Wine from €13.50. Service discretionary. Open all year. [***Chez Youen (Tel: 028 20136),** the Youen family's original Breton restaurant, is just a few doors away. Classic seafood (eg Shellfish Platter €50); D 6-10.30 Tue-Sun. Fine wine list.]

Accommodation: The Jacobs have eight very attractive, well-equipped bedrooms in their guesthouse overlooking the harbour. Everything in it is big - the rooms, the beds, the bathrooms. Amenities are good - direct-dial phones, tea/coffee-making facilities, TV with video. Furniture is modern, with a light sprinkling of Georgian and Victorian pieces and, in addition to a good sitting area in each room, there's a comfortable residents' lounge. Children up to 4 free in parents' room (cot available). Pets permitted. No private parking. Rooms 8 (7 en-suite,1 shower only for wheelchairs). B&B €50 pps, ss €20. Open all year. Amex, MasterCard, Visa, Diners, Laser. **Directions:** The Square, Baltimore. ◇

Baltimore

Baltimore Harbour Resort Hotel & Leisure Centre

féile bia **HOTEL**

Baltimore Co Cork **Tel: 028 20361** Fax: 028 20466 Email: info@bhrhotel.ie

Since the Cullinane family took over this old hotel, they have done a prodigious amount of work, beginning with the complete refurbishment of the original building prior to re-opening in 1995. The hotel enjoys a lovely position overlooking Roaring Water Bay and is well located for deep sea fishing and visits to nearby islands, including Sherkin and Cape Clear. Modern furnishings, with plenty of light wood and pastel colours, create a sense of space in public areas and the accommodation includes family rooms, junior suites and luxury suites. All rooms are comfortably furnished, with neat bathrooms and sea views, and the larger ones have double and single beds. Public areas include a bar that can be reversed to serve the Sherkin Room (banqueting/conferences for 140) and a bright semi-conservatory Garden Room for informal meals and drinks. Children are well looked after - there's a playroom, a children's club in school holidays and under 3s are free in parents' room (cots available). Off-season breaks are good value. No pets. Leisure centre; swimming pool; gym. Lift. **Rooms 64** (12 suites, 1 mini-suite). B&B about €70pps. Closed early Jan. Amex, Diners, MasterCard, Visa. **Directions:** Signposted on the right as you enter Baltimore on the R595 from Skibbereen.

Baltimore

Bushe's Bar

BAR / B&B

The Square Baltimore Co Cork **Tel: 028 20125** Fax: 028 20596
Email: tombushe@eircom.net Web: www.bushesbar.com

Everyone, especially visiting and local sailors, feels at home in this famous old bar. It's choc-a-bloc with genuine maritime artefacts such as charts, tide tables, ships' clocks, compasses, lanterns, pennants et al - but it's the Bushe family's hospitality that makes it really special. Since Richard and Eileen took on the bar in 1973 it's been "home from home" for regular visitors to Baltimore, for whom a late morning call is de rigeur (in order to collect the ordered newspapers that are rolled up and stacked in the bar window each day). Now there's a new generation of Bushes involved with the business, so all is humming nicely. Simple, homely bar food starts early in the day with tea and coffee from 9.30, moving on to home-made soups and a range of sandwiches including home-cooked meats (ham, roast beef, corned beef), salmon, smoked mackerel or - the most popular by far - open crab sandwiches, served with home-baked brown bread. And all under €8. This is a terrific pub, at any time of year, and was a very worthy recipient of our Jameson Pub of the Year Award in 2000. Not suitable for children after 9pm. Bar food served 9.30am-8pm daily. Bar closed 25 Dec & Good Fri.

Accommodation: Over the bar, there are three big, comfortable bedrooms, all with a double and single bed, bath & shower, TV and a kitchenette with all that is needed to make your own continental breakfast. There are also showers provided for the use of sailors and fishermen. No pets. **Rooms 3.** B&B €22.50-27.50 (depending on the room) pps, single rate €35. Amex, MasterCard, Visa, Laser. **Directions:** In the middle of Baltimore, on the square overlooking the harbour.

Baltimore

Casey's of Baltimore

HOTEL / RESTAURANT

Baltimore Co Cork **Tel: 028 20197** Fax: 028 20509
Email: caseys@eircom.net Web: www.caseysofbaltimore.com

The Casey family's striking dark green hotel is just outside Baltimore as you approach and enjoys dramatic views over Roaring Water Bay to the islands beyond. It has grown, organically it seems, from the immaculately maintained bar/restaurant that the Caseys had run for twenty years to the characterful hotel they operate today. The old back bar and restaurant have been ingeniously developed to extend the ground floor public areas and make best use of the view, and bedrooms are spacious and well-furnished, with good facilities (phone, TV, tea/coffee tray, trouser press) neat bathrooms with full bath and shower - and those wonderful views. Friendly, helpful staff create a relaxed atmosphere and there are well-organised outdoor eating areas for bar food in fine weather. On less favoured days, the open fires are very welcome - and there's traditional music at weekends. Children are welcome (cots available without charge), although not in public areas after 7 pm. No pets. Rooms 14 (1 shower only) B&B €77.50 pps, ss €25. Bar meals daily 12.30-2.30 & 6.30-9. Restaurant **seats 100.** D daily, 6.30-9, L Sun only 12.30-2.30. Set D €35, Set Sun L €19; à la carte also available). Closed 20-27 Dec.

Casey's of Baltimore Restaurant: A comfortable informal dining room overlooking the bay provides just the setting for good, unpretentious food. Baltimore seafood naturally takes pride of place - crab and lobster are specialities and there will always be other fish of the day on the blackboard. Dinner menus may well begin with the local version of smokies (creamed smoked mackerel, topped with cheese and served hot) and soups will certainly include the Casey's chowder - and Roaring Water Bay mussels are served as a main course, steamed in the shell with white wine, garlic and onion. Steaks (served with pepper sauce or garlic butter) are almost as popular and there's always a vegetarian option, such as a vegetable stir-fry. Friendly, relaxed service adds to the enjoyment. Seats 65: L 12.30-2.30, D 6.30-9.30 daily. Set L (Sun) €17, Set D €32. House wine from €15.24; à la carte also available; service discretionary. Amex, Diners, MasterCard, Visa, Laser. **Directions:** From Cork take the N71 to Skibereen & then R595 to Baltimore.

Baltimore

Customs House Restaurant

☆ **RESTAURANT**

Baltimore Co Cork **Tel: 028 20200**

SEAFOOD RESTAURANT OF THE YEAR

Susan Holland and Ian Parr's uncluttered contemporary restaurant is rightfully recognised as one of the finest in the land and draws dedicated followers from every corner of Ireland - and beyond. The secret of their achievement is an unswerving philosophy of using only the best and freshest of local produce in season, keeping it simple - and giving real value for money. They do great daily menus - menus that highlight local seafood, especially, which is cooked by Susan with flair and served by Ian with unflappability - and are incredibly keenly priced. The couple, who are Australian, have been running the Customs House as a seasonal restaurant since 1995, then use the winter months to travel. They have worked in some very distinguished kitchens indeed and, between them, have over 60 years experience in hospitality, in half a dozen countries - and, each summer, visitors to the little town of Baltimore are the fortunate beneficiaries of all this talent and commitment. Superb ingredients are presented with deceptive simplicity, mostly in classic French and Italian dishes served with organic salads, or simple, perfectly cooked organic side vegetables like new potatoes and spinach. You may well begin the €35 menu with a wonderful seafood tapas plate, typically of of langoustine (Dublin Bay prawns), ceviche of john dory, peppers stuffed with brandade of salt cod and crab claws, each with its own dressing or garnish; alternatively there might be a rocket salad zinging with vitality, with parmesan, pine nuts & balsamic vinaigrette - and perhaps one or two unlisted ingredients added, like semi-dried tomatoes and puy lentils; thoroughly satisfying. Main courses depend on the catch but at least three of five or six main courses will probably be fish - including a classic sole meunière perhaps, and grilled monkfish with rösti potatoes and saffron & langoustine sauce. Then there are those unbeatable timeless desserts - rich chocolate fondant with house triple sec ice cream, tarte tatin with house vanilla ice cream, or farmhouse cheese - Cooleeney, Ardagh, Carraig goat - in perfect condition. All this is complemented by an interesting, highly informative and keenly-priced wine list, and Ian Parr's efficient, refreshingly low-key service. **Seats 30.** No smoking area. D Thu-Sun (also Wed in Jul-Aug), 7-9.30; Set D €25 (3-course, 1 choice on main course only) & €35 (3-course, more choices);

house wines €15. Vegetarian dishes on request; not suitable for children under 12. Closed Mon, Tue (also Wed except Jul-Aug); 1 week June & end Sept - Apr. (Cheques, incl sterling cheques, accepted). **No Credit Cards. Directions:** Beside the Garda Station 50 metres from Pier.

Baltimore

Rolf's Restaurant "Café Art" & Wine Bar

WINE BAR / RESTAURANT Baltimore Co Cork **Tel: 028 20289** Fax: 028 20289
Email: rolfsholidayhostel@eircom.net Web: www.rolfsholidays.com

It's a bit of a trek up from the village if you are on foot, but a visit to Rolf's is well worth the effort. The Haffner family have been here for 20 years and, although part of the business is still a holiday hostel, it's a hostel with a difference; the complex has been extensively renovated and sensitively developed over the last few years, to include self-catering accommodation of some character - and the restaurant and wine bar, which is attracting a loyal following. Discerning locals appreciate both the food and the fact that it remains open after the summer visitors have left and, for the casual visitor, the café is open all day and serves an à la carte lunch as well as excellent light food with morning coffee or afternoon tea. In the evening, a more extensive dinner menu is served in the Restaurant 'Café Art' which has views over Baltimore harbour - and is named after the contemporary art exhibitions held in the restaurant. Euro-Toques chef Johannes Haffner uses as much home-grown, organic and local produce as possible and all pastries, desserts and breads are home-made; his wide-ranging menus include quite a few classics and retro dishes - starters like house paté with cranberry sauce & toast and smoked salmon with crusty brown bread for example, or main courses such as beef stroganoff (authentically cooked with vodka), which sit easily beside updated dishes such as steamed mussels with lemongrass and fresh ginger (starter or main course) and stunningly fresh fish simply cooked in the contemporary style; vegetarians are well looked after (dishes highlighted on the menu) and there's also a better choice than in most other restaurants in the area for carnivores. Desserts include some continental treats - Flemish apple tart, "Linzer" almond tart - and coffees are delicious. The wine bar - with an open fire - is just the place for a drink before (or after) dinner; many wines not given on the wine list are available here by the glass. Garden terrace and seaview terrace available for fine weather. Self-catering accommodation also available. **Seats 50.** Toilets wheelchair accessible. Open daily in summer, 8.30am-9.30pm (B'fst 8-9.30, L 12.30-3, D 6-9.30). A la carte. Closed Mon & Tue off season. Open all year. MasterCard, Visa, Laser **Directions:** Baltimore Hill

---

Baltimore

Slipway

B&B The Cove Baltimore Co Cork **Tel: 028 20134** Fax: 028 20134
Email: theslipway@hotmail.com Web: www.theslipway.com

Quietly located just beyond the bustle around the square, Wilmie Owen's delightful and hospitable house has uninterrupted views of the harbour and distant seascape from all the bedrooms and the lovely first floor breakfast room, which has a balcony. This unusual and imaginatively designed house has a charming oyster bar in a converted outbuilding; very much intended for residents, it is only open when Wilmie's husband Dave Owen is not away on his travels. Not suitable for children; no pets. Garden. **Rooms 4** (all shower only & no-smoking). B&B €34 pps, ss €26. Closed Nov-Mar officially, but phone to check. **No Credit Cards. Directions:** Through Baltimore village, to the Cove, 500 metres.

Baltimore

The Mews

RESTAURANT Baltimore Co Cork **Tel: 028 20390** Fax: 028 20390

Owner-chef Lucia Carey's hospitable and atmospheric restaurant is a romantic spot, with white- linen-clad candlelit tables and strategically placed plants, well-chosen art on the stone walls and an adjacent conservatory that is bright and fresh for early dining, turning into an equally romantic setting by candle light as darkness falls. Menus are contemporary and the cooking is excellent, based on carefully sourced fresh ingredients in dishes that are are bursting with flavour, generous and light. Freshly-baked breads and tapenade get the evening off to a good start and starters like a wonderfully fresh salad of mixed leaves with fresh feta cheese and ripe peaches or a long time favourite speciality of prawn, crab and coriander filo parcels (with a delicious citrussy crème fraîche) will not disappoint. Main courses could include a variation on traditional themes such as a superb fillet steak with a crunchy blue cheese & walnut butter, served with imaginative and well-cooked vegetables. Delicious desserts (a perfect pannacotta, perhaps, brimming with tiny vanilla seeds and accompanied by luscious rosemary-flavoured poached pears), or you could finish with a local cheese plate and freshly brewed coffee. **Seats 30.** No smoking area. D only; à la carte. Closed Oct-May. **No Credit Cards. Directions:** In village of Baltimore (signed in laneway just before the harbour). ◇

Baltimore Area

Island Cottage

RESTAURANT

Heir Island Skibbereen Co Cork **Tel: 028 38102** Fax: 028 38102
Email: ef@islandcottage.com Web: www.islandcottage.com

Just a short ferry ride from the mainland yet light years away from the "real" world, this place is unique. Hardly a likely location for a restaurant run by two people who have trained and worked in some of Europe's most prestigious establishments - but, since 1990, that is exactly what John Desmond and Ellmary Fenton have been doing at Island Cottage. Everything about it is different from other restaurants, including the booking policy: a basic advance booking for at least six people must be in place before other smaller groups of 2 to 4 can be accepted - not later than 3pm on the day; changes to group numbers require 24 hours notice and a booking deposit of about €6.50 per head is required to reserve a table. The no-choice 5-course menu (about €25) depends on the availability of the fresh local, organic (where possible) and wild island ingredients of that day. A vegetarian dish can be accommodated with advance notice. An early autumn menu will give an idea of John's attachment to the island and the kind of meal to expect: roast duck legs on a bed of turnip with duck jus (using hand-reared ducks "of exceptional quality" from Ballydehob), local turbot with shrimp sauce on a bed of sea beet or spinach (the shrimp is caught by local fishermen; sea beet is a wild foreshore vegetable, rather like spinach) and a classic terrine of vanilla ice cream with meringue served with a blackberry sauce, using berries picked by children holidaying on the island. Cookery courses and demonstrations can be arranged, also private dinner parties (October-May). Details of cottages for rent also available from the restaurant. **Seats 24** (max table size 10; be prepared to share a table). D €25 approx. Wed-Sun, 8.15-11.45 pm; one sitting served at group pace. L by arrangement only, off-season: groups of 8-24. Closed Mon & Tue, and mid Sep-mid May (please phone to check opening days/times - not confirmed at time of going to press). **No credit cards. Directions:** From Skibbereen, on Ballydehob road, turn left at Church Cross, signposted Hare Island and Cunnamore. Narrow winding road, past school, church, Minihan's Bar. Continue to end of road, Cunnamore car park. Ferry departs Cunnamore pier at 7.55 returns at 11.55 (journey: 4 minutes). ◇

Baltimore Area

The Islander's Rest

HOTEL

Sherkin Island Skibbereen Co Cork **Tel: 028 20116** Fax: 028 20360
Email: info@islandersrest.ie Web: wwww.islandersrest.ie

Just a 10 minute ferry trip from Baltimore harbour, Sherkin is a small island about 3.5 miles long by 1.5 miles wide with a population of only a hundred or so and three lovely safe beaches. This recently-built hotel would make a comfortable base for a break and is understandably becoming a popular place for weddings - it may not have a great deal of character as yet, but the island location is highly romantic. The bar offers a good choice of dishes like: poached monkfish with brandy and peppercorn sauce, warm goats' cheese salad with honey and pear dressing and great steaks with garlic butter and chips, all around €15. Pleasant service by staff and owner. Conference/banqueting (30/110). **Rooms 21** (all en-suite). Large bedrooms include some family rooms with four beds, and most have stunning views; all have good quality pine beds and soft furnishings, television, phone and ensuite bathroom, although the price may seem high for the standard offered. There's a large breakfast room for guests as well as a sitting room with open fire place - still a little unfinished, in the summer of 2003. Children welcome (under 3s free in parents' bedroom, cot available). Fishing, walking, garden. No pets. B&B €55 pps, ss €20. SC discretionary. Open all year but a phone call is essential to check in winter. MasterCard, Visa, Laser. **Directions:** Cork-Skibbereen- Baltimore. 10 minute ferry.

Baltimore Area

Windhoek

GUESTHOUSE

Sherkin Island Baltimore Co Cork **Tel: 028 20275** Fax: 028 20275
Email: windhoek@esatclear.ie Web: windhoeksherkin.com

Dutch-born Ingrid van Maarle and Peter van de Ruenen's beautifully located renovated farmhouse reaches down to the waterfront and, across a narrow strip of land, it is flanked to the rear by two deserted beaches. Accommodation is in three studio apartments, situated around a central paved herb garden; roof windows bring in extra light and a pretty, Scandinavian-style greyish-blue and white colour scheme is used to great effect throughout – a veritable showcase for the couple's talents in interior design and building restoration. Rooms are comfortably and stylishly furnished, with TV and tea/coffee-making facilities provided. Meals are available by arrangement and, although primarily self-catering, breakfast can also be provided for guests taking the apartments. Windhoek is available for corporate hospitality (10-16 guests). **Rooms 3** (all with en-suite shower). Children welcome. Pets permitted by arrangement. Garden. B&B €35 pps, ss €5. Studio apartment €70 (35pps), also available for short or long lets. Closed Jan-Feb. **Directions:** Cork - Skibbereen - Baltimore- 10 min ferry to Sherkin.

Bantry

O'Connor's Seafood Restaurant

féile bia **RESTAURANT**

The Square Bantry Co Cork **Tel: 027 50221**
Email: oconnorseafood@eircom.net Web: www.oconnorseafood.com

O'Connor's long-established seafood restaurant is right on the main square (site of Friday markets and the annual early-May mussel festival) and, after over thirty years in the family, the business was taken over by Peter and Anne O'Brien in 2003. But the entire staff has stayed on and the O'Briens' plan to keep everything as it was seems to be working out just fine. What's more, there's an even longer family connection here, as Anne's great-grandmother was the original owner of the bar license back in 1914 - how's that for continuity! The lobster and oyster fish tank by the entrance still sends all the right messages and, beyond the front room, the are booths and a seated bar (full bar facilities include beers on draft) in the back are just the same, all decorated in a nautical theme. Bantry Bay mussels, cooked all ways, are a speciality - a starter of them grilled with herbs and lemon butter fits the bill perfectly, followed perhaps by fresh scallops and salmon mornay in shells, served with an abundance of vegetables, or else mussels marinière with a fish pie as a main course. There are some non-fish dishes available, all using local produce - roast rack of mountain lamb is another speciality. At lunchtime you can have soup and a sandwich in the bar or daily-changing dishes off the blackboard. No children after 8 pm. **Seats 50.** Air conditioning. Open 12.15-9.30 daily, L 12.30-3, D6-9.30. A la carte. House wine €18.50. 10% SC. Open all year, but telephone to confirm opening times off-season. MasterCard, Visa, Laser. **Directions:** Town Centre. Prominent location on square.

Bantry

The Snug Bar

féile bia **PUB**

The Quay Bantry Co Cork **Tel: 027 50057**

Maurice and Colette O'Donovans' well-named bar is a cosy and welcoming place, bustling with life and ideal for a wholesome bite at moderate prices. Maurice is the chef and takes pride in using local produce and giving value for money; his menus feature a wide range of popular dishes, many of which are in the house style. At lunch time, home-made soups - chicken & leek, perhaps, or carrot & coriander - top the bill and are followed by other equally good things like pan-fried fresh wild salmon, traditional Irish stew, home-made beefsteak & onion pie and lasagne "house style" (which is available with meat or for vegetarians). More extensive evening menus offer dressier dishes as well, including starters like Bantry Bay prawn cocktail or oak smoked salmon salad, and a good choice of main courses like steaks, home-made beefburgers and farmyard duckling with orange sauce as well as a number fish dishes - including Bantry Bay mussels, of course. This wholesome fare is good value (lunch main courses about €8.50, evening all except steaks €16 or less). Children welcome (but not after 9pm). Food served daily, 10.30am-9pm. Closed 25 Dec & Good Fri. MasterCard, Visa, Laser. **Directions:** Beside Garda Station, near the harbour.

Bantry Area

Larchwood House Restaurant

RESTAURANT / ACCOMMODATION

Pearsons Bridge Bantry Co Cork **Tel: 027 66181**

The gardens are a special point of interest here, complementing the restaurant, which is in a relatively modern house with both the traditionally-furnished lounge and dining room enjoying lovely views. Sheila Vaughan, a Euro-Toques chef, presents seasonal dinner menus: smoked salmon with citrus salad, an unusual soup such as carrot, peach & paprika, quite traditional main courses such as loin of lamb with lemon and mint, and classical desserts with a modern twist, such as crème caramel with apple & brandy coulis - good cooking and, although a meal can take longer than might be expected, the view of the garden is ample compensation. This is a haven for garden lovers, who often make it a base when visiting the many gardens in the locality; here there are acres to explore, river boulders to cross and nothing prettier than the wild bluebell wood in spring. (B&B accommodation is also offered, €40pps, no ss). **Seats 25.** D Mon-Sat, 7-9.30. Set D €40. House wine €22. SC discretionary. Closed Sun & Christmas week. (Limited opening in winter). Amex, Diners, MasterCard, Visa. **Directions:** Take the Kealkil Road off N71 at Ballylickey; after 2 miles signed just before the bridge.

Blarney

Blairs Inn

féile bia **PUB / RESTAURANT**

Cloghroe Blarney Co Cork
Tel: 021 4381470 Email: blair@eircom.net

John and Anne Blair's delightful riverside pub is in a quiet, wooded setting just outside Blarney yet, sitting in the garden in summer, you might see trout rising in the Owennageara river (or perhaps a heron out fishing), while winter offers welcoming open fires in this comfortingly traditional country pub. It's a lovely place to drop into for a drink or a session - and the Blairs have built up a special reputation for their food. Anne supervises the kitchen personally, and care and commitment are evident in menus offering a wide (but not over-extensive) range of interesting but fairly traditional dishes including seafood (from Kenmare and Dingle); old favourites like corned beef with champ & cabbage & parsley sauce, casserole of beef & stout and Irish stew sit easily alongside some fancier fare and make a pleasing change from many other menus; there's always a vegetarian dish on, and game in season too. Lunch is served in the restaurant and bar area; later, there's a separate evening bar menu and à la carte dinner, which can be booked in the candlelit Snug or Pantry dining areas. Interesting wine list. Children welcome, but not after 7.30 pm. **Seats 40/50** (restaurant/bar) & 60 in garden. Bar menu 12.30-9.30 daily. Restaurant L 12.30-3.30, D 6.30-9.30. A la carte. House wine €18.75. Service discretionary. Closed 25 Dec & Good Fri. Amex, Diners, MasterCard, Visa, Laser **Directions:** 5 minutes from Blarney village, on the R579.

Blarney

Blarney Castle Hotel

Ⓝ HOTEL

Blarney Co Cork **Tel: 021 4385116** Fax: 021 4385542
Email: info@blarneycastlehotel.com Web: www.blarneycastlehotel.com

This attractive family-run hotel overlooks the village green in the centre of Blarney, just beside the castle. It has been in the Forrest family since 1837 but, with the exception of the restaurant, reception area and a very characterful old bar with original Victorian tiling and an open fire, they completely rebuilt the hotel a couple of years ago. The resulting new accommodation is very pleasing: spacious, bright bedrooms have a view over the green or a pleasant outlook at the back and all have both a double and single bed, wide screen TV, tea/coffee-making; well-finished bathrooms have classic black and white tiles and full bath. Helpful, friendly staff create a welcoming atmosphere and prices are reasonable for the high standard offered. Numerous golf courses nearby. Children welcome (under 5 free in parents' room, cot available without charge, baby sitting arranged.) Pool table. Private parking. **Rooms 13** (1 shower only, all no smoking). B&B €60 pps, ss €20. [Meals: The Lemon Tree Restaurant: D 7-9.30. Bar food 12-4 & 6-9.30 daily.] Closed 25 Dec. Amex, MasterCard, Visa, Laser. **Directions:** Centre of Blarney, on village green (next to Blarney Castle entrance).

Blarney

Blarney Park Hotel

HOTEL

Blarney Co Cork **Tel: 021 438 5281** Fax: 021 438 1506
Email: info@blarneypark.com Web: blarneypark.com

There is always something going on at the Blarney Park; close proximity to Cork city (just half an hour on the Limerick road) makes this a very convenient location for business, while a leisure centre with 40-metre water slide and 20-metre pool is an attraction for families. 2 all-weather tennis courts. Conference/banqueting (270/250); business centre, secretarial services, video-conferencing. **Rooms 91** (11 shower only; 1 junior suite, 14 executive rooms, 2 no-smoking, 2 disabled). Lift. B&B about €100 pps, ss about €25. Closed Christmas. Amex, MasterCard, Visa, Diners **Directions:** In centre of Blarney, on left on entering town from Cork. ◇

Butlerstown

Atlantic Sunset

B&B

Dunworley Butlerstown Bandon Co Cork **Tel: 023 40115**

Mary Holland provides comfortable accommodation and a genuinely warm welcome in her neat modern house with views down to the sea at Dunworley. The house is wheelchair accessible and the ground floor rooms are suitable for less able guests. The breakfast room and some bedroom windows have sea views and, weather permitting, the sight of the sun setting over the Atlantic can indeed be magnificent. Sandy beaches and coastal walk nearby. **Rooms 4** (2 en-suite, shower only). B&B about €25pps. Closed 20 Dec-1 Jan. **Directions:** From Bandon Road R602 to Timoleague, then Butlerstown Village, Atlantic Sunset 1 km. ◇

Butlerstown

O'Neill's

ATMOSPHERIC PUB

Butlerstown Bandon Co Cork **Tel: 023 40228**

Butlerstown is a pretty pastel-painted village, with lovely views across farmland to Dunworley and the sea beyond. Dermot and Mary O'Neill's unspoilt pub is as pleasant and hospitable a place as could be found to enjoy the view - or to admire the traditional mahogany bar and pictures that make old pubs like this such a pleasure to be in. O'Neill's is now a popular stopping off point for the "Seven Heads Millennium Coastal Walk" so it may be useful to know that children (and well-behaved pets) are welcome.*A point of historical interest: the anchor from the S.S. Cardiff Hall, which sank off the nearby coast in 1925, has found a permanent home on a platform beside the pub. Closed 25 Dec & Good Fri. **No Credit Cards. Directions:** On the Courtmacsherry - Clonakilty coast road.

Butlerstown

Otto's Creative Catering

RESTAURANT WITH ROOMS

Dunworley Butlerstown Bandon Co Cork
Tel: 023 40461 Email: ottokunze@eircom.net
Web: www.ottoscreativecatering.com

With the help of their talented son who lives nearby and is a creative and practical woodworker, Hilde and Otto Kunze have created a dream of a place here, very close to the spot where they originally started the famous Dunworley Cottage restaurant many years ago. The house is unusual and only reveals its true personality once you are inside; words cannot do it justice, so you must go and see it for yourself. Deeply committed to the organic philosophy, Otto and Hilde are members of both Eiro-Toques and the Slow Food movement - and their vegetable gardens provide a beautiful and satisfying view from the vine-clad dining room, where meals of wonderful simplicity cooked by Otto are presented by Hilde. Take time to marvel at the sheer originality and ingenuity of their home over a drink (brought with you, if you like - no corkage is charged - or chosen from a short list of biodynamically produced wines) in the sitting room, while also pondering a unique dinner menu that offers several choices on each course. Typically you will start with a vegetarian salad platter, with organic leaves and several dips or, perhaps, a fish plate of Anthony Cresswell's smoked wild salmon and Frank Hederman's eel and mussels, again with organic leaves. Freshly baked breads and butter will be left temptingly close by on the table - try to resist trying everything as there are still marvellous soups (most likely based on whatever vegetable is most prolific at the time, and perhaps Otto's wonderful beef consommé), before you even reach the main courses. Here Otto moves up another gear and, as well as classics - wild salmon caught off the Seven Heads, panfried and served with, perhaps, browned butter & capers, or organic T-bone steak well hung in local butcher Dan Moloney's cold room, pan-fried and served with its own gravy, mushrooms, onions and garlic butter - there are unusual choices like braised ox tongue with a rich red wine gravy and a vegetarian dish such as nettle & St Tola organic goats cheese pie. A magnificent selection of vegetables, with potatoes and rice, accompanies the main course and everything is presented with originality and palpable pleasure. Then there are desserts - apfelstrudel with vanilla ice cream, perhaps, or home-grown strawberries with cream. Or, if you are very lucky, there might be freshly picked top fruit, warm from the trees in the growing tunnels - cherries, plums, apricots, white peaches... This wonderful food needs no embellishment, it is extraordinarily good value for the quality given - and it clearly gives Otto and Hilde great satisfaction to see their guests' appreciation. This place is a must for any food lover travelling in west Cork. Organic farm. Seats 30 (max table size 12). D €45, by reservation (24 hours notice if possible); L Sun only, 1.30-3 pm; Set Sun L €30. Organic house wine from €20, or BYO (no corkage). Closed Feb.

Accommodation: The two bedrooms share the fresh originality of the rest of the house and are furnished in a simple Scandinavian style which, like the cleverly designed shower rooms, is intensely practical. And, of course, you will wake up in a most beautiful place - and have more of that superb food to look forward to, at a breakfast that counts home-made sausages and home-produced rashers among its gems. Children welcome (under 4 free in parents' room, cot available without charge.) Walking. Garden. **Rooms 2.** B&B €50 pps, ss €20. MasterCard, Visa, Laser. **Directions:** Bandon to Timoleague to Dunworley.

Butlerstown

Sea Court

COUNTRY HOUSE

Butlerstown Bandon Co Cork **Tel: 023 40151** / 40218
Email: seacourt-inn@yahoo.com
Web: www.tourismresources.ie/cht/seacort.htm

Set in 10 acres of beautiful parkland (source of the fallen trees used in the construction of Otto's Creative Catering, nearby) Sea Court is at the heart of an unspoilt wonderland for bird-watchers and walkers - and a restful retreat for any discerning traveller. Since 1985, David Elder - an American academic who spends his summers in Ireland - has devoted his energies to restoring this gracious Georgian mansion and, while the task is nowhere near completion, the achievement is remarkable - and ongoing. Recent improvements - upgrading bathrooms, restoring sash windows and "eliminating the rattles in windy weather" - have made the house more comfortable, a lot of painting has been done and the Drawing Room was redecorated. David was particularly pleased to have restored a Victorian couch ('the one with with a collapsible arm"), although the search for Victorian roll-top baths continues. The grounds and exterior generally are always a credit to him and, although it is wise not to expect too much luxury, what Sea Court has to offer guests is comfortable and very reasonably priced accommodation in a real and much-loved country house; bedrooms are, for the most part, elegantly proportioned with bathrooms that are already adequate and gradually being upgraded. Breakfast, cooked by David himself, is served at a long dining table, where dinner is also available if there are reservations for at least four people - and, after dinner, guests can chat around the fire in the drawing room, or browse through David's books. The house is also available for small conferences or celebrations (usually 12-16 people, but they did a small wedding last year and managed to seat 28!) and for rental off-season (sleep 8-12). **Rooms 6** (5 en-suite, 1 with private bathroom). B&B €40, no s.s. D 8pm, €32.50 (by arrangement, except Sun - min 4 persons). No SC. Closed 21 Aug-7 June. **No Credit Cards. Directions:** Butlerstown is signposted from Timoleague.

Carrigaline

Carrigaline Court Hotel

féile bia **HOTEL / RESTAURANT**

Main Street Carrigaline Co Cork
Tel: 021 485 2100 Fax: 021 437 1103
Email: carrigcourt@eircom.net Web: www.carrigcourt.com

This modern hotel has only been open since 1998 but has already undergone major changes, with an new extension creating 39 new bedrooms, extra meeting rooms and The Bistro (see below) - and giving the whole hotel a completely different atmosphere. Fresh primrose yellow paintwork creates a good first impression which is carried through into bright, spacious public areas - a little bland perhaps, at the time of our visit, but perhaps not quite finished. Interesting contemporary furniture is an attractive feature throughout, in both public areas and bedrooms, which are quite stylishly decorated and well-equipped for business guests with work desks, ISDN lines and safes as well as the more usual amenities (TV, tea/coffee making, trouser press); smart marbled bathrooms are quite luxurious, with good quality toiletries. Friendly staff are invariably pleasant and helpful. Conference/banqueting facilities (350/250), also smaller meeting rooms; secretarial services. Leisure centre; swimming pool, spa, crèche, beauty salon. Children welcome (under 5s free in parents' room, cot available without charge, baby sitting arranged). Weekend breaks available all year. No pets. **Rooms 88** (2 suites, 1 executive). Lift. B&B €80 pps, ss €20. Closed 25 Dec.

The Bistro: Although it can be reached from the hotel, The Bistro also has its own entrance from the car park giving it the feeling of an independent restaurant rather than a hotel dining room. A large semi open plan area, is divided up into three separate dining spaces, each with a distinctly different atmosphere and decor ranging from quite traditional to contemporary - a clever idea which allows for personal preference and ensures a more intimate atmosphere for quieter times. The menu is interesting, clearly described and very affordable, with local produce providing a sound base for popular dishes. Seafood is a strength, all supplied by O'Connells of Cork: an impressive seafood cassoulet is served in a soup plate (with a spoon provided for a tasty lobster & chive sauce). Finish off with prettily presented classic desserts such as orange crème brulée and bavarois. Good food, efficient service and a pleasing ambience make for an enjoyable meal - and value for money will keep people coming back. Good wine list too. Air conditioning. Toilets wheelchair accessible. Children welcome. **Seats 150** (private room, 70). L 12.30-2.15, D 6-10 daily. A la carte. Amex, MasterCard, Visa, Diners, Laser. **Directions:** Town centre.

Carrigaline

Glenwood House

GUESTHOUSE

Ballinrea Road Carrigaline Co Cork **Tel: 021 4373 878** Fax: 021 4373 878
Email: info@glenwoodguesthouse.com Web: www.glenwoodguesthouse.com

This well-respected guesthouse is in purpose-built premises, very conveniently located for Cork Airport and the ferry and set in gardens, where guests can relax in fine weather. Comfortable, well-furnished rooms (including one designed for disabled guests) have all the amenities normally expected of hotels. Breakfast has always been a strong point - available from 7am for business guests, until 10 am for those taking a leisurely break. A guest sitting room with an open fire makes a cosy retreat on dark winter evenings. Secretarial service available. Children welcome (Under 12 free in parents' room, cot available without charge, baby sitting arranged). Golf nearby. Garden. **Rooms 10** (2 shower only, 1 for disabled, 9 no smoking). No pets. B&B €45pps, ss €10. Closed mid Dec-early Jan. MasterCard, Visa. **Directions:** Entering Carrigaline from Cork, turn right at Ballinrea roundabout.

Carrigialine

Gregory's Restaurant

féile bia **RESTAURANT**

Main Street Carrigaline Co Cork **Tel: 021 437 1512**

Owner-chef Gregory Dawson and his partner and restaurant manager Rachelle Harley celebrate a decade in business at this bright, comfortable and friendly restaurant this year - and it's still going strong, with plenty of buzz. Shortish à la carte menus, changed monthly, provide plenty of variety and are based on local produce. Although there's an occasional modern twist, the cooking style is pleasingly classical. Enduring favourites like lambs kidney & mushroom fricassée and baked stuffed mushrooms with Cashel Blue cheese are as welcome as the flowers in spring to frequent diners out, who will be equally pleased by a main course fricassée of prawns with dill or roast rack of lamb with a herb & mustard crust and fresh herb jus. Desserts are in a similar vein - rum & raisin parfait with caramel cream sauce perhaps, or a luscious chocolate roulade with raspberry coulis - and there's always an an Irish cheese plate as well.

Service is friendly and helpful - and it's good value for money. **Seats 40.** No-smoking area. Air conditioning. Toilets wheelchair accessible. D Wed-Sat 6.30-10, L Sun only 12.30-3; D à la carte, Sun L €21.95. House wine €18.95. Closed D Sun, all Mon & Tue; bank hols, 3 weeks annual holiday (TBC). Amex, Diners, MasterCard, Visa, Laser. **Directions:** On main street, opposite Bank of Ireland.

Castletownbere

MacCarthy's

ATMOSPHERIC PUB

The Square Castletownbere Co Cork
Tel: 027 70014 Email: adrimac22@yahoo.com

Dating back to the 1870s, and currently run by Adrienne MacCarthy, this famous old pub and grocery store really is the genuine article. Fortunately, it shows no signs of changing. Atmosphere and live traditional music are the most obvious attractions, but the grocery is real and provisions the local fishing boats. Simple bar food - seafood chowder, open seafood sandwiches - is available Mon-Sat, 10.30am-6pm. Closed 25 Dec & Good Fri. **No Credit Cards. Directions:** In town square.

Castletownbere

The Old Presbytery

B&B

Brandy Hall House Castletownbere Co Cork
Tel: 027 70424 Fax: 027 70420
Email: marywrigley@eircom.net Web: midnet.ie/oldpresbytery/index.htm

On the edge of Castletownbere and well-signposted from the road, this very pleasant old house on 4 acres is in a magnificent position - on a little point with the sea on two sides and clear views of Berehaven Harbour. The house dates back to the late 1700s and has been sensitively restored by the current owners, David and Mary Wrigley. The five bedrooms vary in size and outlook but all have phone, tea/coffee tray and TV and are furnished to a high standard, in keeping with the character of the house. Breakfast - which includes a vegetarian menu - is served in a pleasant conservatory overlooking the sea. Children welcome (under 5s free in parents' room, cot available); pets permitted by arrangement. **Rooms 5** (all en-suite, 4 shower only). B&B about €32, ss about €13. Closed Oct-Mar. MasterCard, Visa. **Directions:** Turn left as the road narrows by Brandy Hall bridge and follow the sign.

Castletownshend

Bow Hall

B&B

Main Street Castletownshend Co Cork **Tel: 028 36114**

Castletownshend is one of west Cork's prettiest villages and this very comfortable 17th century house on the hill is a wonderful place to stay. With a pleasant outlook over beautiful well-tended gardens to the sea, excellent home-cooking and a warm welcome by enthusiastic hosts, Dick and Barbara Vickery, a visit to this lovely home is a memorable experience. The house is full of interest but its most outstanding feature is perhaps the food, which is not only imaginative but much of it is home-grown too. Residents' dinner is available by reservation and this treat will be a truly seasonal menu, based on their own produce fresh from the garden - potatoes, courgettes, swiss chard, salads, fresh herbs and fruit - picked just before serving with other local specialities such as fresh crab or salmon. Menus change daily and breakfasts are also a highlight, with home-baked breads and muffins, home-made sausages, home-made preserves, pancakes and rhubarb from the garden among the delights. Non-smoking house. Children welcome (under 2 free in parents' bedroom, cot available without charge, babysitting arranged). Garden, tennis. No pets. **Rooms 3** (1 en-suite, 2 with private bathrooms), B&B €45, ss €5; min 2 night stay preferred. Advance bookings essential, especially in winter. Residents D 8 pm, by reservation; €32 (no wine licence). Closed Christmas week. **No Credit Cards. Directions:** 5 miles from Skibbereen.

Castletownshend

Mary Ann's Bar & Restaurant

PUB / RESTAURANT

Castletownshend Skibbereen Co Cork
Tel: 028 36146 Fax: 028 36377 Email: maryanns@eircom.net

Mention Castletownshend and the chances are that the next words will be 'Mary Ann's', as this welcoming landmark has been the source of happy memories for many a visitor to this picturesque west Cork village over the years. (For those who have come up the hill with a real sailor's appetite from the little quay, the sight of its gleaming bar seen through the open door is one to treasure.) The pub is as old as it looks, going back to 1846, and has been in the energetic and hospitable ownership of Fergus and Patricia O'Mahony since 1988. Any refurbishments at Mary Ann's have left its original character intact. The O'Mahonys have built up a great reputation for food at the bar and in the restaurant, which is split between an upstairs dining room and The Vine Room at the back, which can be used for private parties. Seafood is the star, of course, and comes in many guises, usually along with some of the lovely home-baked brown bread which is one of the house specialities. Another is the Platter of Castlehaven Bay Shellfish and Seafood - a sight to behold, and usually including langoustine, crab meat, crab claws, and both fresh and smoked salmon. Much of the menu depends on the catch of the day, although there are also good steaks and roasts, served with delicious local potatoes and seasonal vegetables. Desserts are good too, but local West Cork cheeses are an excellent option.* A Wine Club was started at Mary Ann's in September 2001 and is proving a great success. Restaurant **Seats 30** (private room 20). Toilets wheelchair accessible. Children welcome. D daily in summer, 6-9; L Sun only in winter, 12-2.30. A la carte House wine from about €15.25. SC discretionary. *Bar food 12-2.30 & 6-9 daily. Closed Mon, from Nov-Mar; 25 Dec,Good Fri & 3 weeks Jan/Feb. MasterCard, Visa, Laser. **Directions:** Five miles from Skibbereen. ◇

Clonakilty

An Sugan

féile bia **BAR / B&B**

41 Wolfe Tone Street Clonakilty Co Cork **Tel: 023 33498** / 33719
Email: sineadcrowley@hotmail.com

The O'Crowley family has owned An Sugan since 1980 and they have done a great job: it's always been a friendly, well-run place and their reputation for good food is generally well-deserved. Recent changes have extended the informal dining area and introduced a contemporary café restaurant "Hasta Pasta Pizza" (with outside seating in a sheltered courtyard at the back), in contrast to the traditional atmosphere of the original bar and restaurant, which remain equally popular and have kept their character. Menus changes daily and are very strong on seafood - specialities include smoked salmon parfait, baked crab and An Sugan seafood basket while daily fish specials could include a choice of ten, ranging from cod on a bed of champ to lobster salad. If you're not in the mood for seafood you might try a terrine of the famous Clonakilty puddings or a prime Hereford sirloin steak - or head next door for the pizzas and pastas. [*B&B accommodation is also available - call 023 33719 for details.] No private parking. Restaurant **seats 48.** Food served 12.30-9 daily. A la carte. House wine from €16. Service discretionary. Closed 25 Dec & Good Fri. MasterCard, Visa, Laser. **Directions:** From Cork on the left hand side as you enter Clonakilty.

Clonakilty

Dunmore House Hotel

féile bia **HOTEL**

Muckross Clonakilty Co Cork **Tel: 023 33352** Fax: 023 34686
Email: dunmorehousehotel@eircom.net Web: www.dunmorehotel.com

The magnificent coastal location of Jeremiah and Mary O'Donovan's family-owned and managed hotel has been used to advantage to provide sea views for all bedrooms and to allow guests access to their own stretch of foreshore. Comfortable public areas include a traditional bar and lounges so the dining room - which is light, bright, much more contemporary and home to a fine collection of paintings - is quite a contrast. Bedrooms, which all have sea views, are furnished to a high standard and make a comfortable base for the numerous leisure activities in the area including angling and golf - green fees are free to residents on the hotel's own (highly scenic) nine hole golf course - cycling, horse-riding and watersports; packed lunches are provided on request. Hands-on owner-management, a high standard of maintenance and housekeeping (down to the fresh flowers ordered for the hotel on a weekly basis) and a professional and exceptionally friendly and helpful staff make this a hotel that guests return to again and again. Conference/banqueting 200/250. Wheelchair accessible. Children welcome (under 3 free in parents' room, cot available without charge; junior evening meal 5.30-6.30). Golf, fishing, walking. Dogs allowed in some areas. **Rooms 23** (2 junior suites, 4 shower only, 1 for disabled). B&B €705pps, ss€10. Bar food available all day (12-8.30). Restaurant Seats 80. Toilets wheelchair accessible. Air conditioning D daily, 7-8.30 (€40), L Sun only, 1-2.30 (€25). Closed Christmas; 19 Jan-11 Mar. Amex, Diners, MasterCard, Visa, Laser. **Directions:** 4 km from Clonakilty town,well signed.

Clonakilty

Emmet Hotel

féile bia **HOTEL / RESTAURANT**

Emmet Square Clonakilty Co Cork
Tel: 023 33394 Fax: 023 35058
Email: emmethotel@eircom.net Web: www.emmethotel.com

This friendly hotel is hidden away in the centre of Clonakilty on a lovely serene Georgian square that contrasts unexpectedly with the hustle and bustle of the nearby streets; it's a most attractive location, although parking is likely to be difficult. Rooms vary a little due to the age of the building, but all are comfortable and have phone, air conditioning, TV and tea/coffee making facilities. The standard of furnishing and comfort is high for the prices charged, with management in the capable hands of Tony and Marie O'Keeffe (who run a separate restaurant next door, see below). Conference/banqueting

(40/55). Children welcome (under 3s free; cots available without charge). Pets permitted by arrangement. **Rooms 20** (2 executive). B&B about €60pps. Open all year.

O'Keeffe's of Clonakilty: Although located in separate premises next door, O'Keeffe's also has direct access from the hotel and bookings are made through the hotel. Overlooking Emmet Square, the restaurant is creatively decorated in a colourful style that is most unexpected in an old house and allows a complete change of atmosphere. Marie O'Keeffe's cooking is based on the best of seasonal local produce, much of it organic, and her reputation for creative modern cooking is well established. Although there are some very strong alternative choices, seafood takes the starring role on her concise, moderately priced menus and there are always some daily specials. Examples that give a flavour of O'Keeffe's might include garlic breaded mussels or lobster cocktail, followed by main courses like Ballycotton brill simply panfried in butter with sea asparagus - and loin of lamb with a rosemary & red wine jus is a likely alternative. Vegetarian dishes are offered (ask if necessary) and there is an awareness of special dietary requirements in, for example, a dessert of non-dairy citrus mousse with organic Irish strawberries & a peach coulis. Friendly, helpful staff enhance a visit to either hotel or restaurant. D 6.30-10 daily; L 12.30-2.30 (in the hotel); Set D about €36. House wine from about €16. SC discretionary. Restaurant closed 25 Dec. Amex, Diners, MasterCard, Visa, Laser, Switch. **Directions:** In the centre of Clonakilty - turn left into Emmet Square at the Catholic Church. ◇

Clonakilty

Gleesons

Ⓝ RESTAURANT

3/4 Connolly Street Clonakilty Co Cork **Tel: 023 21834**
Fax: 023 21944 Email: gleesonrestaurant@eircom.net

Robert and Alex Gleeson opened their new restaurant in April 2003 and, since then, word has gradually been filtering through to an admiring following who see it as the hottest new place to dine out in the area. The couple put a great deal of commitment into refurbishing the premises, which has a discreet frontage and rather mysterious interior, with dark woods and deep, rich tones in furnishings which exude quality and include many original touches (such as beautifully simple slate place mats). Robert's cooking style is modern French and his experience in famous kitchens - The Dorchester, for example and, closer to home, The Lodge & Spa at Inchydoney Island - should give an idea of what to expect. His menus, which offer about seven choices on each course on the à la carte and three on the early dinner menu, are not over-elaborate but with dishes like tian of Clonakilty Bay lobster & Ummera organic smoked salmon with mango, red onion & coriander salsa among the starters, this is emphatically fine dining. Not everything is so high falutin' however, as down to earth ingredients like the famous Clonakilty black pudding make their appearance too, in a tempting starter salad of poached egg with black pudding, bacon, sauté potatoes and herb vinaigrette. Skeaghanore duck, from Ballydehob, is another speciality - the breasts is pan-fried and served with braised red cabbage, garlic potatoes & red wine sauce; side orders are offered but it is pleasing to find that each dish is individually garnished. Vegetarian dishes are imaginative (woodland mushroom & red onion tart, perhaps, served with a mushroom ragoût & chive beurre blanc) and desserts classical. Cooking and service both measure up to the high level of expectation: this is a fine restaurant and deserves to succeed. A wide-ranging wine list offers an interesting house selection (all New World, although Europe is well represented in the main list). Children welcome (until 7.30). **Seats 44.** No smoking area. D Mon-Sat, 6-10. Early D €29.50 6-7.30; also à la carte. House wine from €17.65. SC discretionary. Closed Sun in summer, Sun & Mon in winter; 24-26 Dec, 3 weeks Feb. MasterCard, Visa, Laser **Directions:** Town centre; next door to Scanner's Pub.

Clonakilty

Harts Coffee Shop

Ⓝ féile bia CAFÉ

8 Ashe Street Clonakilty Co Cork **Tel: 023 35583**

Good home cooking is the attraction at Aileen Hart's friendly coffee shop in the town centre. A nifty little menu offers all kinds of healthy little meals - ranging from a breakfast ciabatta with bacon, eggs & cheese, through warm baguettes (peppered steak strips, perhaps, with lettuce and mayo), sandwiches toasted and cool - all served with side salad & home-made vinaigrette dressing - to specials such as a West Cork salmon plate with home-made brown bread or an Irish cheese plate with a choice of crackers or bread. But best of all, perhaps, is the choice of home-baked scones just like your granny used to make, served with home-made jam, and tarts - everything from savoury quiches to old-fashioned apple tart served with cream - and cakes ranging from healthy carrot cake to gooey orange chocolate drizzle cake. Simple, wholesome, home-made: just lovely! Great selection of drinks too, including freshly squeezed juices teas and Green bean coffees. Wine licence. **Seats 30.** No smoking area. Children welcome. Open 10-5.30 Mon-Sat. Closed Sun. **No Credit Cards. Directions:** Clonakilty town centre.

Clonakilty — The Lodge & Spa at Inchydoney Island

HOTEL / RESTAURANT

Inchydoney Island Clonakilty Co Cork
Tel: 023 33143 Fax: 023 21164
Email: dod@inchydoneyisland.com Web: www.inchydoneyisland.com

This hotel enjoys great views over the two 'Blue Flag' beaches at Inchydoney and, although architecturally uninspired, it has mellowed as landscaping of the large carpark on the seaward side fills in - and it has proved a great success. Once inside the hotel (as opposed to the Dunes Pub, which has a more down to earth atmosphere), that pampered feeling soon takes over. Public areas are spacious and impressive, notably a large, comfortably furnished first-floor residents' lounge and library, with a piano and extensive sea views. The spacious bedrooms are all furnished and decorated in an uncluttered contemporary style, with air conditioning, safe and all the more usual amenities (including tea/coffee making), and most have wonderful views; those on the third and fourth floors were refurbished in 2003 and the lower floors are due for completion in time for the 2004 season. Outstanding health and leisure facilities include a superb Thalassotherapy Spa, which offers a range of special treatments and makes Inchydoney a particularly attractive venue off-season. However, even without taking up any of the these amenities, there is something in the air that makes this a very relaxing place. Special breaks are a major attraction - fishing, equestrian, golf, therapies or simply an off-season weekend away. Conferences/banqueting (300); video-conferencing (by arrangement). Thalassotherapy spa (24 treatment rooms); beauty salon, hairdressing; leisure centre, swimming pool; fishing, equestrian, walking; snooker. Children welcome (under 4s free in parents' room; cots available without charge, baby sitting arranged). Pets allowed in some areas. **Rooms 67** (3 suites, 1 junior suite,16 no smoking; 2 for disabled). Lift. 24 hour room service. B&B €155, ss €27. SC10%. Closed 25-26 Dec.

Gulfstream Restaurant: Located on the first floor, with panoramic sea views from the (rather few) window tables, this elegant restaurant offers fine dining in a broadly Mediterranean style. Head chef Mark Kirby, who has been with the hotel since 1999, uses organic produce where possible and his menus change monthly. Imaginative vegetarian options are always included on the main menu and any special dietary requirements are willingly catered for. **Seats 80** (private room 80). Not suitable for children under 5, or after 8.30pm. Toilets wheelchair accessible. No smoking area; air conditioning. D 6.30-9.45, early D €30, Set D €48. House wine from €20. SC10%. [*Informal/ bar meals also available 12-9 daily.] Amex, Diners, MasterCard, Visa, Laser. **Directions:** N71 from Cork to Clonakilty, then causeway to Inchydoney.

Clonakilty — Malt House Granary Restaurant

Ⓝ **RESTAURANT / WINE BAR**

30 Ashe Street Clonakilty Co Cork **Tel: 023 34355**
Email: malthousegranary@eircom.net

Elaine McCarthy took over the premises of the well-known restaurant Fionnula's Little Italian Restaurant in 2003 and, inspired by the history of the building, re-named it and completely re-vamped the interior to create a very pleasing restaurant and wine bar. The style is modern classic, with warm colours and quality materials giving it a quality feeling - and her interesting, accessible menus confirm that impression. Clonakilty black pudding features, of course - in a starter dish with mango, green onion & yellow pepper salsa & garlic croûtons - and so does other local produce: warm Ummera organic smoked salmon comes with a spiced prawn dressing, for example and there's also a salad of their smoked chicken, while Bantry Bay mussels are cooked in the classic style, with white wine, and served with a delicious Guinness bread. This restaurant has its heart in the right place, the service is friendly and attentive and it gives good value for money. The wine list, which is interesting, well-priced and informative, includes a number of organic wines - and half a dozen house wines from old and new world countries. **Seats 50** (private room 10). Reservations accepted but not required. Air conditioning. Toilets wheelchair accessible. Children welcome. D daily, 5-10.30. A la carte. House wines €15.90. Closed 24-25 Dec. **Directions:** Town centre, on main street.

Clonakilty — Randles Clonakilty Hotel

HOTEL

Wolfe Tone Street Clonakilty Co Cork **Tel: 023 34749** Fax: 023 35035
Email: clonakilty@randleshotels.com Web: www.randlehotels.com

This sister hotel to the Randles hotels in Killarney opened in 2002, after renovations. Staff are friendly and helpful, the public face is impressive - deep carpets, elegant furnishings in public areas - and, while not luxurious, accommodation offers a comfortable base in West Cork, with the convenience of a town centre location. Conferences (50); secretarial services. **Rooms 31** (5 no smoking, 2 disabled). Lift. Children welcome (under 5s free in parents' room, cot available, babysitting arranged). B&B €80 pps, ss €30. No SC. Closed 21-27 Dec. Amex, Diners, MasterCard, Visa, Laser. **Directions:** Town centre, beside An Sugan.

Cloyne — The Cross of Cloyne

PUB / RESTAURANT

Cloyne Co Cork **Tel: 021 465 2401**

The long narrow bar of this traditional pub has been sensitively renovated, with an open fire for colder times. You can reach the restaurant through the pub, or directly from the street; the welcome is warm and you may be shown to a small reception area to consider the menu, or go straight to attractively set up tables, discreetly well-lit by spotlights that also pick up modern oil paintings on the walls. Anyone who remembers Colm Falvey's previous restaurants - The Clean Slate in Midleton, The Earl of Orrery in Youghal - will have high expectations of a meal here and should not be disappointed. The hallmarks are here: a menu based on local ingredients and not over-extensive, a tempting selection of imaginative dishes, with the emphasis on fish but not to the exclusion of well-balanced choices. Ballycotton seafood chowder is predictable, perhaps, but very good nonetheless; panfried fishcake comes with a fresh tarragon mayonnaise dressing and main courses of fillet of hake with a fresh crab and herb crust and roast rack of lamb with chargrilled Mediterranean vegetables and a red wine jus are all excellent choices. Accomplished cooking, generous portions and attractive presentation are all good points but, best of all, are the flavours - and service, which is friendly and efficient, the better to enjoy this fine fare. Imaginative desserts too - walnut & armagnac tart, for example, with crème anglaise - and a short but well-chosen wine list. **Seats 60.** D Mon-Sat high season (Jun-Aug), otherwise Wed-Sat, 6-9.30; Sun 4-9.30, all year. A la carte (average main course about €20). Closed Mon & Tue except Jun-Aug, 25 Dec & Good Fri. Diners, MasterCard, Visa, Laser. **Directions:** Approaching from Midleton, straight through cross in centre of town (Ballycotton is indicated to the left); pub/restaurant 50 yards on left. ◇

Cobh — Mansworth's Bar (Est 1895)

ATMOSPHERIC PUB

Midleton Street Cobh Co Cork **Tel: 021 481 1965**

Cobh's oldest established family-owned bar dates back to at least 1895 and is currently in the capable hands of John Mansworth, who is a great promoter of the town and a knowledgeable provider of local information. Bar snacks are available but it's really as a character pub that Mansworth's is most appealing. It's a bit of a climb up the hill to reach it but well worth the effort, especially for anyone with an interest in the history of Cobh as a naval port - the photographs and memorabilia on display here will provide hours of pleasure. Not suitable for children after 7 pm. Pets permitted. Open from 10.30 am. Closed 25 Dec & Good Fri. **Directions:** Above St. Colman's Cathedral.

Cobh — Robin Hill House & Restaurant

GUESTHOUSE / RESTAURANT

Lake Road Rushbrooke Cobh Co Cork
Tel: 021 481 1395 Fax: 021 481 4680
Email: robinhillhouse@eircom.net Web: www.robinhillhouse.com

A neat driveway leads steeply up to Colin and Teresa Pielow's smartly-painted Victorian rectory and its hillside position gives it an open feeling, with views across the harbour. Good first impressions are confirmed as guests are welcomed into a comfortable reception area (with a real fire) and, alongside it, a stylishly bright restaurant with high-back chairs and handsomely-laid tables with very fine glasses - all overlooking a terrace and gardens to the sea beyond. Well-made freshly-baked breads, bowls of butter and jugs of iced water arrive immediately, along with a wine list deserving of some serious consideration. (Colin, a real wine buff, has even set up a tasting room in his wine cellar). Seasonal menus offer about four choices on each course, plus daily specials, and always include some especially tempting and unusual dishes, with a strong selection of fresh seafood all year and game in season. Starters like carpaccio of tuna with citrus fruit & mint, basil oil or smoked loin of venison salad with hazelnut oil and juniper berry dressing are light and interesting and might be followed by an unusual speciality like pan-fried saddle of rabbit with a creamy whole-grain mustard sauce or a chargrilled selection of seafood. Updated classic desserts like a cappuccino of tiramisu or homely rhubarb crumble with custard round a meal off satisfyingly, and there's always an Irish & continental cheese selection. Some dishes - daily specials and the cheeseboard, for example - attract a supplement. **Seats 50.** Not suitable for children under 12. D Wed-Sat, 7.30-9.30; L Sun only 12.30-2.30. Set D €40, Set Sun L €22. House wines from €19; SC discretionary. Restaurant closed D Sun, all Mon.

Accommodation: En-suite accommodation is offered in rooms imaginatively furnished in an uncluttered contemporary style, with specially made furniture in different woods - hence the Beech Room, the Sycamore Room, the Cherry Room and so forth.(The same craftsman also made a magnificent cigar humidor for the restaurant, which is an exceptional piece of work.) Rooms all have phones, TV and tea/coffee-making facilities. Garden. **Rooms 6** (2 shower only, all no smoking) B&B €50, ss €15. Establishment closed 25-27 Dec & 7 Jan -7 Feb. MasterCard, Visa, Laser **Directions:** Over the bridge past Fota, take right turn right for Cobh 4 miles past the Statoil garage, next turn left, 300 yards on the left.

Cobh

WatersEdge Hotel

HOTEL

Cobh Co Cork **Tel: 021 481 5566** Fax: 021 481 2011
Email: watersedge@eircom.net Web: www.watersedgehotel.ie

The name says it all at Michael and Margaret Whelan's enterprising hotel, which is neatly slotted between the road and the harbour, taking full advantage of its unique waterside setting. There's a carpark underneath the hotel and public areas include an impressive foyer and attractively located dining areas, while the spacious bedrooms - some of which have French windows opening onto a verandah, most have a sea view - include a suite which is designed to be used for small conferences as well as accommodation. Children welcome (under 2s free in parents' room, cot available without charge). Pets permitted by arrangement. **Rooms 19** (1 suite, 1 for disabled, 5 no-smoking). B&B from about €50 pps, ss about €26. Closed 23-28 Dec.

Jacob's Ladder: Michael Whelan has been in the tugboat business for many years (there may well be a tug berthed alongside the hotel when you visit) and the restaurant name has particular maritime relevance. Well-located within the hotel, with large windows affording views across the harbour - and a new waterside deck where guests can make the most of fine weather - this stylish restaurant is well-appointed, with colourful high back chairs and tables arranged brasserie style, creating a light, bright atmosphere. Local seafood is, of course, the star here - including Ballycotton bay mussels (cooked in a tomato & garlic broth then finished with fresh herbs, perhaps) Rossmore oysters and Shanagarry smoked salmon as well as sea fish landed nearby, but vegetarians are not overlooked and red meats (typically in rack of lamb on roasted baby aubergines, with a red wine & mint jus), duck and pigeon feature regularly too. Good value, high quality fresh ingredients, accurate cooking and attentive service should ensure a dining experience to match the attractive location. As the hotel is beside the station, a pleasant way to go for a meal from Cork city is by train. L&D daily. House wine about €18; sc discretionary. Amex, Diners, MasterCard, Visa, Laser. **Directions:** R624 off the N25. Follow signs for Cobh Heritage Centre. ◇

Courtmacsherry

Travara Lodge

Ⓝ **RESTAURANT WITH ROOMS**

Courtmacsherry Co Cork
Tel: 023 46493 Email: travaralodge@eircom. net

Richard May and Brendan Murphy have built up an enviable reputation at their restaurant in an early Victorian seafront terrace overlooking Courtmacsherry Bay. Arriving guests are welcomed to a comfortable sofa in their colourful sitting room for an aperitif and time to consider the menu, before heading across the hall to the dining room which is small, but attractively furnished in an uncluttered style with high back chairs and bare table tops enhanced by linen napkins, individual pepper mills and fresh flowers from the garden. Brendan uses lots of local produce and his carefully sourced menus offer generous choices - about seven on each course - but are refreshingly simple in style: grilled mussels, garlic crumbs; crab cakes Travara, Thai dipping sauce; warm black pudding salad, mustard dressing & apple chutney are all typical appetisers and main courses follow in the same vein - blue cheese pork fillet, apple & mustard sauce; roast wild salmon on buttered spinach, balsamic dressing; vegetable ragoût, cheese & polenta stuffing. If this all sounds highly appetising, you're very right. Brendan, who describes his cooking style as "Irish with a French twist" is a talented and experienced chef (White's on the Green, Arbutus Lodge) and you can look forward to fine creative cooking - and, with most starter well under €10 and main courses from €19, excellent value too. Short, well-chosen wine list. Service, under Richard's direction, is hospitable and helpful, making sure everyone has a good time. Jazz at weekends. Reservations advised. Not suitable for children under 7 after 9pm. **Seats 30.** D Fri-Tue, 6.30-9.30. Set D €40, also à la carte. House wine from €15. Closed Wed & Thu; closed 2 weeks end Sep/Oct, 2 weeks mid Jan.

Accommodation is offered in six moderately priced rooms; they vary somewhat depending on their position in the house (some are in an extension at the back) but all are en-suite (5 shower only, 1 with bath) and have tea/coffee-making. Children under 12 free in parents' rooms. Pets permitted. B&B €40 pps, ss €10. MasterCard, Visa, Laser. **Directions:** N71 to Bandon, on to Timoleague & follow signs to Courtmacsherry: beside Anchor Bar.

Crookhaven

O'Sullivans Bar

ATMOSPHERIC PUB

Crookhaven Skibbereen Co Cork **Tel: 028 35319**
Fax: 028 35319 Email: o'sullivans@crookhaven.ie

This long-established family-run bar is in an attractive location right on the harbour at Crookhaven, with tables beside the water - when it's not too busy, it can be heaven on a sunny day. Angela O'Sullivan personally supervises all the food served in the bar - home-made soups and chowders, baskets of shrimps (in summer) with homemade brown bread and butter, open sandwiches, home-baked scones and desserts - all good homely fare. Bar food daily 12.30-8. Closed 25 Dec & Good Fri. MasterCard, Visa **Directions:** From Cork, take the N71 and turn left on to the R591 just before Bantry.

Durrus

☆ RESTAURANT WITH ROOMS

Blairs Cove House

Durrus Bantry Co Cork **Tel: 027 61127**
Fax: 027 61487 Email: blairscove@eircom.net

Philippe and Sabine de Mey's beautiful property enjoys a stunning waterside location at the head of Dunmanus Bay. Although additions over the years have enlarged the restaurant considerably - including an elegant conservatory overlooking a courtyard garden - the original room at this remarkable restaurant is lofty, stone-walled and black-beamed. However, while characterful, any tendency to rusticity is immediately offset by the choice of a magnificent chandelier as a central feature, gilt-framed family portraits on the walls, generous use of candles - and the superb insouciance of using their famous grand piano to display an irresistible array of desserts. They have things down to a fine art at Blairs Cove - and what a formula: an enormous central buffet displays the legendary hors d'oeuvre selection, a speciality that is unrivalled in Ireland. Main course specialities of local seafood or the best of meat and poultry are char-grilled at a special wood-fired grill right in the restaurant and, in addition to those desserts on the piano, full justice is done to the ever-growing choice of local farmhouse cheese for which West Cork is rightly renowned. The food is terrific, service friendly and efficient and, as a tribute to its memorable ambience, Blairs Cove was selected as our Atmospheric Restaurant of the Year in 2003. **Seats 80.** D 7.30-9.30 Tue-Sat. Set D €46 (2-course - starter buffet & desserts - €35); house wine about €20, SC discretionary. Closed Sun & Mon & Nov-Mar. **Accommodation:** Three small apartments, offered for self-catering or B&B, are furnished in very different but equally dashing styles and there is also a cottage in the grounds. Children welcome, cot available. B&B €100 pps, ss €30; SC incl. Diners, MasterCard, Visa, Laser. **Directions:** 1.5 miles outside Durrus on Mizen Head Road, blue gate on right hand side.

Durrus

☆ Ⓝ CAFÉ

Good Things Café

Ahakista Road Durrus Co Cork **Tel: 027 61426** Fax: 027 61426

Superb ingredients-led contemporary cooking is drawing a growing band of happy diners to Carmel Somers' excellent restaurant just outside Durrus village. Well-placed to make the most of fine west Cork produce, she also sells some specialist foods from Ireland and abroad and a few books including the great little guide to Local Producers of Good Food in Cork, produced by Myrtle Allen and Cullen Allen for the Cork Free Choice Consumer Group, which details many of the artisan producers who supply Good Things Café. The daytime café menu offers a short enough choice of about eight dishes - but what dishes: superb salads (mixed leaves with fresh beetroot, fresh broad beans, cherry tomatoes, smoked salmon, quails eggs among the goodies), West Cork fish soup (available, like most dishes on the daytime menu, as a starter or main course), West Cork Ploughmans (a trio of local cheeses served with an onion cassis compôte), Durrus cheese, spinach & nutmeg pizza (perfect thin, crisp pizza with a topping which would tempt the most pizza-resistant) Fingal's baked ham with eggs and potato cake (a generous portion of Fingal Ferguson's superb local ham, with a wedge of swiss-style potato cake), then there are irresistible desserts to choose from a display (raspberries and cream, St Emilion chocolate cups...) Dinner brings a more formal menu, with a choice of four on each of two/three courses, and will feature some of the daytime treats, along with main courses like ragoût of monkfish with Ahakista prawns and braised shank of lamb with mash. Service is prompt and attentive from the moment a choice of breads and iced water is brought to your table to the arrival of home-made chocolate truffles with your coffee - and it's terrific value. This place is a one-off - whatever you do, plan your travels in West Cork around a visit here. Interesting, well-priced wine list. Ample parking. Children welcome. **Seats about 30** (plus 14 outdoor in fine weather). In summer, open all day (10-5) Wed-Mon, also D Wed-Sat (7-8.30); off-season, open daytime only, Wed-Mon. Daytime café menu à la carte; restaurant D from €32.50. House wine €14.80. Closed Tue in summer, also Wed off-season; all Jan & Feb. MasterCard, Visa, Laser **Directions:** From Durrus village, take Ahakista/Kilcrohane Rd.

Farran

COUNTRY HOUSE

Farran House

Farran Co Cork **Tel: 021 7331215** Fax: 021 7331450
Email: info@farranhouse.com Web: www.farranhouse.com

Set in 12 acres of mature beech woodland and rhododendron gardens in the rolling hills of the Lee valley, this impressive house was built in the mid 18th century, although its present elegant Italianate style only dates back to 1863. It is beautifully situated with views over the medieval castle and abbey of Kilcrea and its location west of Cork city makes it a good base for exploring Cork and Kerry. In the present energetic and caring ownership of Patricia Wiese and John Kehely, the house has been carefully restored and, although there are some contemporary touches as well as antiques, none of its original charm has been lost. Despite its considerable size, there are just four bedrooms - both they and their adjoining bathrooms are exceptionally spacious and decorated with style and comfort, adding greatly to the sense of luxury that the house imparts. There's a fine drawing room for guests' use (complete with grand piano) and a billiard room with full size table. Golf nearby (six 18 hole courses within 20 km). Children welcome (under 12s free in parents' room, cot available without charge). No pets. Garden. B&B €80 pps, ss €30 (advance bookings only - 10% discount on 3 night stays; off-season rates reduced); residents D €40 (24 hours notice; not available Sun or Mon, but nearby pub does good meals). Self-catering coach house (4-6 people, from €500 pw); house also available for self-catering (groups of 8-9, from €3,500 pw). Closed 1 Nov-31 Mar. MasterCard, Visa, Laser. **Directions:** Take N22 between heading west: 5 miles after Ballincollig, turn right to Farran village, up hill, 1st gate on left.

Fermoy

Castlehyde Hotel

HOTEL / RESTAURANT

Castlehyde Fermoy Co Cork **Tel: 025 31865** Fax: 025 31485
Email: cashyde@iol.ie Web: www.castlehydehotel.com

In a lovely unspoilt area only a short drive from Cork, this delightful hotel is retained within the original buildings of a beautifully restored 18th century courtyard building and would make a soothing base for exploring a wide area. Warm hospitality, gracious surroundings, open fires and a high level of comfort combined with the character of the old buildings and courtyard make this an unusually appealing hotel. Bedrooms, which are individually furnished to a high standard, have a great style and the feeling of a private home; ground floor rooms are along a courtyard verandah. Small conferences/banqueting (60/70). Tennis. (Spa & other leisure facilities due 2005). Children welcome. No pets. **Rooms 14** (plus 5 cottage suites; all no-smoking). B&B €75 pps, ss €20. Closed 24-26 Dec. **Sir Henry's Restaurant:** The restaurant is pleasantly situation, overlooking a lawn and mature woodland. Lunch and dinner menus in a creative Irish international style offer some unusual choices; reliable cooking and attentive service make a meal here an enjoyable experience. Children welcome (but not after 8pm.) Reservations advised. **Seats 70.** (Private room, 20). Restaurant open 7.30am-9pm (Sun to 8). L12.30- 3, D 5.30-9 (Sun 6-8); Set Sun L about €25; Early D €25 (5.30-7, Mon-Fri), Set D €36; also à la carte. House wine from €18. Service discretionary (10% on groups of 6+); air conditioning. Toilets wheelchair accessible. Amex, MasterCard, Visa, Laser. **Directions:** At Fermoy, turn off the N8 and take the N72 (Mallow direction) for about 2 miles.

Fermoy

La Bigoudenne

RESTAURANT

28 MacCurtain Street Fermoy Co Cork **Tel: 025 32832**

At this little piece of France in the main street of a County Cork town, Noelle and Rodolphe Semeria's hospitality is matched only by their food, which specialises in Breton dishes, especially crèpes - both savoury (made with buckwheat flour) and sweet (with wheat flour). They run a special pancake evening once a month or so, on a Saturday night. But they do all sorts of other things too, like salads that you only seem to get in France, soup of the day served with 1/4 baguette & butter, a plat du jour and lovely French pastries. Opening times are a little complicated, but it's worth taking the trouble to work them out as it's a lovely spot - and even the bill is a pleasant surprise. **Seats 18.** D Tue-Sun, 5.45-10: Early D Tue-Thu 5.45-7 (€20.95), later à la carte; L Thu & Sat only, 12.30-4. Fri & Sat D 7-10: Gourmet Menu €34.50; Sun: D 6.30-10, Set D (Gourmet Menu) €34.50, also à la carte. House Wine €15.17. Closed Mon. Amex, MasterCard, Visa. **Directions:** On the main street, opposite ESB.

Fermoy Area

Ballyvolane House

COUNTRY HOUSE

Castlelyons Fermoy Co Cork
Tel: 025 36349 Fax: 025 36781
Email: ballyvol@iol.ie Web: www.ballyvolanehouse.ie

Jeremy and Merrie Greene's gracious mansion is surrounded by its own farmland, magnificent wooded grounds, a recently restored trout lake and formal terraced gardens, all carefully managed and well maintained - a major replanting of 400 rhododendrons, azaleas and specimen trees is the current project and garden lovers will find a stay here especially rewarding. The Italianate style of the present house - including a remarkable pillared hall with a baby grand piano and open fire - dates from the mid 19th century when modifications were made to the original house of 1728. This is a very lovely house, elegantly furnished and extremely comfortable, with central heating and big log fires; bedrooms vary according to their position in the house - all are roomy and, like the rest of the house, are furnished with family antiques and look out over attractive gardens and grounds. Ballyvolane has private salmon fishing on 8km of the renowned River Blackwater, with a wide variety of spring and summer beats. Fishing is Merrie's special enthusiasm and a brochure is available outlining the fishing services she provides. Delicious food is another high point at Ballyvolane, where memorable modern Irish dinners cooked by Maeve Crofts are served in style around a long mahogany table (no smoking in the dining room). There is much of interest in the area - the beautiful Blackwater Valley is well worth exploring, with its many gardens and historic sites, and Lismore, the Rock of Cashel and Waterford Crystal are among the many interesting places which can easily be visited nearby. The standard of hospitality, comfort and food at Ballyvolane are all exceptional, making this an excellent base for a peaceful and very relaxing break. French is spoken. Banqueting (25). Children welcome (cot available, €5). No pets. Garden; fishing; walking. **Rooms 6** (1 shower only, 1 for disabled). B&B €85pps ss €20. Residents D €40 at 8pm, book by 10am (no-smoking dining room); menu changes daily. House wine from €18.50. Closed 23-31 Dec. Amex, MasterCard, Visa, Laser, Switch. **Directions:** Turn off main Dublin-Cork road N8 just south of Rathcormac (signed Midleton), following house signs on to R628.

GLANDORE

The attractive village of Glandore is beautifully situated in a sheltered location overlooking Glandore Harbour and its guardian rocks, Adam and Eve. The all year population is small and it will never be a place for mass tourism but there is comfortable accommodation to be found at guesthouses in the area and at the family-run **Marine Hotel (Tel: 028 33366)**, right beside the little harbour in the village and, next door, a relaxed restaurant, **Café Sativa (Tel: 028 34746)**, where proprietor-chef Bevan Fleming sources food carefully and serves it with flair. Glandore is also fortunate in its pubs, which have different characters and are all special in their own way: The Glandore Inn, for example, acts as unofficial clubhouse for the local sailing community (and serves sound food), while the old-fashioned Casey's (at the 'top of the town') only opens in the evenings and is a place for impromptu sessions and late-night craic.

Glandore

Hayes' Bar

PUB The Square Glandore Co Cork **Tel: 028 33214** Email: dchayes@tinet.ie

Hayes Bar overlooks the harbour, has outdoor tables - and Ada Hayes' famous bar food. The soup reminds you of the kind your granny used to make and the sandwiches are stupendous. Everything that goes to make Hayes' special - including the wines and crockery collected on Declan and Ada's frequent trips to France (which also affect the menu, inspiring the likes of Croque Monsieur) - has to be seen to be believed. Just order a simple cup of coffee and see what you get for about €2. Wine is Declan's particular passion and Hayes' offers some unexpected treats, by the glass as well as the bottle, at refreshingly reasonable prices. Great reading too, including a lot of background on the wines in stock - and you can now see some of Declan's paintings exhibited, from June to August. By any standards, Hayes' is an outstanding bar. Meals 12-6, Jun-Aug; weekends only off-season. Closed weekdays Sep-May except Christmas & Easter. **No Credit Cards. Directions:** The Square Glandore. ◇

Glanmire

The Barn Restaurant

féile bia **RESTAURANT** Glanmire Co Cork **Tel: 021 486 6211** Fax: 021 486 6525

This long-established neighbourhood restaurant has earned a devoted local clientèle for its good French/Irish cooking and professional service. An attractive entrance conservatory leads to a comfortable lounge/reception area, where the welcome is warm and you can choose from menus which offer a good choice of quite traditional dishes - starters like home-smoked salmon with a dill mayonnaise, duet of chef's duck & chicken liver patés with Cumberland sauce and main courses of roast farmyard duckling with port and orange sauce, steaks various ways, fillet of sole & prawns topped with puff pastry lattice are all typical. Comfort is a high priority throughout this large restaurant, which is divided up into several dining areas. with well-spaced tables attractively set up with fresh flowers. While not aiming to be in any way cutting edge, everything is cooked to order, with the emphasis on flavour and wholesomeness - and professional, attentive service; all round a reassuringly old-style approach which makes a welcome contrast to the sameness of many contemporary restaurants. Vegetarians are well looked after, saucing and presentation are good and accompaniments are carefully selected. Sunday lunch is very popular and menus are similar in style. Car park. Reservations advised (essential at weekends). **Seats about 160.** D daily, 6.30-9.30, L Sun only 12-2.30. Set D about €36, Set Sun L about €22. House wine about €22. Closed Ash Wed & Good Fri. Amex, Diners, Visa, Laser, Switch. **Directions:** On the edge of Cork city, on the old Youghal road at Glanmire. ◇

Glanworth

Glanworth Mill Country Inn

GUESTHOUSE

Glanworth Co Cork **Tel: 025 38555** Fax: 025 38560
Email: glanworth@iol.ie Web: www.glanworthmill.com

Set in landscaped riverside gardens beside a Norman castle on the banks of the River Funcheon, this imaginatively converted stone mill - complete with the old mill wheel which has been restored, encased in glass and worked into the interior design - makes an unusual place to stay. There's a restful sitting room and the Mill Tea Rooms, where informal meals are served (12 noon-9.30 pm). Bedrooms - styled on the era and taste of the writer each is named after, including Anthony Trollope, Elizabeth Bowen and William Trevor - all have good en-suite bathrooms, phones, complimentary water and fruit. A leisure garden, with giant chess, maze, boules and deck was added recently. Small conferences/private parties (46). Fishing. No pets. **Rooms 10** (1 junior suite, all no-smoking). B&B from about €60pps, ss about €20. Children welcome; cot available without charge. More formal meals are served in the Fleece'n'Loom Restaurant, which includes a conservatory area (D Mon-Sat 7-9.30 & L Sun, à la carte.) Restricted hours in winter - phone for details. Amex, Diners, MasterCard, Visa, Laser. **Directions:** 5 miles off N8 between Mitchelstown and Fermoy. ◇

GLENGARRIFF

Famous for its mild Gulf Stream climate and lush growth - especially on nearby Garinish Island, with its beautiful gardens - Glengarriff has been a popular tourist destination since Victorian times and a little of that atmosphere still exists today. The rather grand looking **Eccles Hotel (Tel: 027 63319 www.eccleshotel.com)** overlooks the harbour and actually dates as far back as 1745, while the smaller, moderately priced and very hospitable family-run **Casey's Hotel (027 63010)** nearby, was established in 1884 and has been run by the same family ever since. Interesting places to eat in the village include **The Martello Restaurant** (Tel: 027 63860, L&D Tue-Sun in summer), which made a promising start in 2003, and a good ethnic restaurant **The Night Kitchen (Tel: 027 63555; D Thu-Sun)**. For daytime food you might check out **The Church Café** (previously the Glengarriff Protestant Church), which has some unusual features (including an open log fire in the candlelit church - and outdoor tables for fine weather) and offers a casual menu from lunchtime onwards.

Goleen

The Heron's Cove

RESTAURANT WITH ROOMS

The Habour Goleen Co Cork **Tel: 028 35225** Fax: 028 35422
Email: suehill@eircom.net Web: www.heronscove.com

When the tide is in and the sun is out there can be few prettier locations than Sue Hill's restaurant overlooking Goleen harbour. The Heron's Cove philosophy is to use only the best of fresh, local ingredients and there's a natural leaning towards seafood - typically in wholesome starters like plump, perfectly cooked Bantry Bay moules marinières or a delicious Fisherman's Broth and main courses such as fillet of John Dory in a a caper butter sauce or perfectly cooked Roaring Water Bay scallops, pan-fried and served with a smoked bacon cream sauce. If you're not in a fishy mood, Goleen lamb cutlets with a redcurrant sauce are a speciality and there's always at least one vegetarian dish. More-ish desserts might include a luscious mocha panna cotta (coffee and chocolate flavoured mascarpone, with a dollop of home-made ice cream too, perhaps, from a wide selection - passion fruit, blackcurrant, blackberry, rum & Michigan cherry to name a few of the less usual ones). Good food, accurately cooked and pleasingly presented, plus friendly attentive service - and, with main courses at €17-24, all at very fair prices: what more could anyone ask? An unusual Wine on the Rack system offers a great selection of interesting, well-priced wines that change through the season - they are listed but the idea is that you can browse through the bottles and make your own selection. Children welcome at discretion of the management. **Seats 30.** D daily in summer, from 7pm (bookings Oct-Mar); à la carte. SC discretionary Closed Christmas & New Year. **Accommodation:** Comfortable en-suite rooms, some with private balconies, have satellite TV, phones, tea/coffee-making facilities and hair dryers. Garden. **Rooms 5** (4 shower only, all no smoking). B&B €35 pps, ss about €8. Open for dinner, bed & breakfast all year except Christmas week, but it is always advisable to book, especially off-season. Amex, Diners, MasterCard, Visa, Laser **Directions:** Turn left in middle of Goleen to the harbour, 300m from village.

Goleen Area

Fortview House

Farmhouse

Gurtyowen Toormore Goleen Co Cork **Tel: 028 35324** Fax: 028 35324
Email: fortviewhousegoleen@eircom.net
Web: http://homepage.eircom.net/~fortviewhousegoleen/

Violet & Richard Connell's remarkable roadside farmhouse in the hills behind Goleen is immaculate. It is beautifully furnished, with country pine and antiques, brass and iron beds in en-suite bedrooms (that are all individually decorated) and with all sorts of thoughtful little details to surprise and delight. Richard is a magic man when it comes to building - his recent work around the house includes a lovely conservatory dining room that he has completed with great attention to detail. For her part, Violet loves cooking, and provides guests with a great choice at breakfast - including Tom & Giana Ferguson's Gubbeen cheese, made down the road - and she provides residents' dinners, by arrangement, to the great delight of her guests. Children under 2 free in parents' room. No pets. Garden. **Rooms 5** (4 shower only). B&B €40 pps. Closed 1 Nov-1 Mar. **No Credit Cards. Directions:** 2 km from Toormore on main Durrus-Bantry road (R591).

Gougane Barra

Gougane Barra Hotel

HOTEL

Gougane Barra Co Cork **Tel: 026 47069** Fax: 026 47226
Email: gouganebarrahotel@eircom.net Web: www.gouganebarra.com

In one of the most peaceful and beautiful locations in Ireland, this delightfully old-fashioned family-run hotel is set in a Forest Park overlooking Gougane Barra Lake (famous for its monastic settlements). The Lucey family has run the hotel since 1937, offering simple, comfortable accommodation as a restful base for walking holidays. Rooms are comfortable but not over-modernised, all looking out on to the lake or mountain. There are quiet public rooms where guests often like to read; breakfast is served in the lakeside dining room. No weddings or other functions are accepted. Shop. Garden, walking. No pets. **Rooms 27** (all en-suite & no smoking, 9 shower only). B&B €60 pps, ss €10. Closed mid-Oct-mid Apr. Amex, Diners, MasterCard, Visa, Laser. **Directions:** In Gougane Barra National Forest; well signposted.

Innishannon

Innishannon House Hotel

HOTEL

Innishannon Co Cork **Tel: 021 477 5121** Fax: 021 477 5609
Email: innishannon@tinet.ie

This lovely house was built in 1720 in the 'petit chateau' style and both it and the riverside location and gardens have great charm. There's a residents' sitting room, a bar that is open to non-residents and bedrooms that vary in shape and character - the best rooms have river views, while others overlook the lovely gardens and all have their original wooden shutters. After many years as a family-run business, the hotel is now operated by a consortium, who have plans for major upgrading and a new bedroom block. So far everything seems much the same, but changes are probably inevitable in the near future. While the hands-on care of family ownership is sadly missed, this remains a good place to break a journey for a bite in the bar - or outside at a table overlooking the garden and river if the weather is fine. Garden, fishing, boating. **Rooms 13** (1 suite). B&B about €100pps. Closed 23-27 Dec. **Directions:** Off the Cork-Bandon road, north of Kinsale. ◇

Kanturk

Assolas Country House

COUNTRY HOUSE

Kanturk Co Cork **Tel: 029 50015** Fax: 029 50795
Email: assolas@eircom.net Web: www.assolas.com

Home to the Bourke family for generations and currently managed by Joe and Hazel Bourke, this gracious 17th century manor house is famous for generous, thoughtful hospitality, impeccable housekeeping and wonderful food. Hazel was the winner of the guide's Euro-Toques Natural Food Award in 2000 and very deservedly so - she is renowned for imaginative and skilled use of organic produce from their own garden and the surrounding area, offered in a daily residents' dinner menu which documents in detail the produce used in their kitchen and the people who supply it. Memorable dinners are served in a lovely dining room - high-ceilinged and elegantly proportioned with deep red walls, antique furniture and crisp white linen - which is not over-decorated, providing an appropriate setting for food that is refreshingly natural in style as well as substance. Bedrooms vary according to their position in this lovely old house - some are very spacious and overlook the garden and river, and there are some courtyard rooms which are especially suitable for families. A lovingly maintained walled kitchen garden, a little river with tame swans and a couple of boats for guests to potter about in all add to the charm - even boots kept beside the front door for the use of anyone who may feel like looking up the local otters at dusk. The wine list concentrates on European wine, notably Maison Guigal, which has supplied the house wines since 1983. Children welcome (under 4 free in parents' room,cot available without charge, baby sitting arranged). Pets allowed by arrangement. garden, walking, tennis, fishing. Small conferences/banqueting (18/30). **Rooms 9** (all en-suite). B&B €99 pps, ss €16.

Dining Room: Seats 18. Residents' D €49, 7-8 pm; house wine €22. Service is included in prices and tipping is discouraged. Closed 1 Nov-1 Apr. MasterCard, Visa, Laser **Directions:** Signposted off N72, 8 miles west of Mallow.

Kanturk

The Vintage

PUB

O'Brien Street Kanturk Co Cork **Tel: 029 50549** Fax: 029 51209

Stephen Bowles has been running this attractive pub since 1985, and its well-maintained exterior draws people in. Once through the door, the comfortable, pleasingly traditional interior encourages visitors to linger, if only for a pint or a quick bowl of home-made soup. Meals 12.30-10 Mon-Sat, 6-10 Sun. Closed 25 Dec & Good Fri. MasterCard, Visa **Directions:** In a terrace of houses, alongside river. ◇

Kilbrittain

Casino House

☆ féile bia **RESTAURANT**

Coolmain Bay Kilbrittain Co Cork
Tel: 023 49944 Fax: 023 49945 Email: chouse@eircom.net

While Kerrin and Michael Relja's delightful restaurant is just a few miles west of Kinsale, it has been one of the country's best kept secrets for a long time and is only now achieving well-deserved recognition. The couple's cool continental style makes a pleasing contrast to their lovely old house and the warmth of Kerrin's hospitality is consistently matched by the excellence of Michael's food. He cooks with verve and confidence, offering imaginative, wide-ranging menus based on the finest seasonal ingredients - and with clear respect for local produce. Ummera smoked organic salmon, for example, is produced nearby and appears regularly - typically in a carpaccio, with a parmesan & crème fraîche dressing - and fresh seafood from nearby fishing ports features in many dishes including a wonderful speciality lobster risotto which is offered as a starter but a variation with mixed seafood is also available as a main course. Local duck is another speciality and appears in many forms - roast breast of Ballydehob duck may be served on a lentil potato cake with a honey & port sauce (house style is rare - ask if you prefer it cooked longer). Vegetarian dishes are not only tempting but, unusually, listed ahead of the other main courses - spaghetti with basil oil, lamb's lettuce & feta cheese is typical - which often include less usual dishes like saddle of rabbit; saddle of lamb is another speciality (with a stuffed courgette rosemary jus, for example) and nightly specials will include extra seafood dishes, all with individual vegetable garnishes and deliciously simple seasonal side vegetables. Variations on classic desserts are delicious but local cheeses are always tempting in this area - and here they are handled with particular respect (earning our Farmhouse Cheese Award in 1999). This is a lovely restaurant and, while the style is constant, cooking consistently excellent and hospitality genuine, it never stands still - somehow, there is always noticeable improvement on each visit. *Casino Cottage: sleeps two €65 per night everything provided except breakfast - which can be supplied if needed. Weekly & winter rates available. **Seats 35** (private room 22). D Thu-Tue, 7-9, L Sun only,1-3; all à la carte; house wine from €18.50; sc discretionary. Closed Wed and 1 Jan-17 Mar. MasterCard, Visa, Laser, Switch. **Directions:** On R600 between Kinsale and Timoleague.

KINSALE

One of Ireland's prettiest towns, Kinsale has the old-world charm of narrow winding streets and medieval ruins tucked in around Georgian terraces - all contrasting with the busy fishing harbour and marina of today. It was known several decades ago as the 'gourmet capital of Ireland' and, while that claim would now be hotly disputed by several other contenders, it still has a remarkable variety of good restaurants and and an exceptionally active programme of culinary activities- and, less widely recognised but of equal interest to the visitor, some of the best accommodation in the country. For outstanding self-catering accommodation in the centre of town, for example, you might consider **Boland Townhouse (Tel: 021 477 2161; www.bolandkinsale.com)** and, just around the corner, one of the town's most famous small hotels is **The Blue Haven (Tel 021 477 2209; www.bluehavenkinsale.com)** has small but well-designed bedrooms and characterful public areas. The town's many pubs offer a judicious mixture of music and food - especially seafood - while **The Bulman (021 477 2131)** at Summercove is near Charles Fort and has the best view of the town (and sunny aspect); across the bridge, in the opposite direction, Castle Park has a sandy south-facing beach and **The Dock Bar (Tel: 021 477 2522)** is a friendly pub.

Kinsale

Actons Hotel

féile bia HOTEL

Pier Road Kinsale Co Cork **Tel: 021 477 2135** Fax: 021 477 2231
Email: info@actonshotelkinsale.com Web: www.actonshotelkinsale.com

Overlooking the harbour and standing in its own grounds, this attractive quayside establishment is Kinsale's most famous hotel, dating back to 1946 when it was created from several substantial period houses. Extensive renovations recently included the refurbishment of bedrooms and public areas, which now include a new look modern bar (Waterfront Bar & Bistro) - and the restaurant was given a contemporary makeover. A new Health & Fitness Club offers a brand new swimming pool with separate children's pool, hot tub, sauna, steam room and whirlpool spa; there's also a gym (with Technogym equipment), aerobics room, solarium and treatment facilities. Good conference/banqueting facilities too (300/250). Children welcome (under 2 free in parents' room, cots available without charge.) No pets. Wheelchair access. Lift. Garden. **Rooms 76** (3 junior suites, 14 executive, 1 shower only, 2 for disabled). B&B €100 pps, ss €40 (wide range of special breaks available). Captain's Table Restaurant, L&D daily (speciality: the 'Derek Davis' steamed local seafood platter). Bar food available daily, 12-9. Closed 24-26 Dec, all Jan. Amex, MasterCard, Visa, Laser. **Directions:** On the waterfront, short walk from town centre.

Kinsale

Blindgate House

GUESTHOUSE

Blindgate Kinsale Co Cork **Tel: 021 477 7858** Fax: 021 477 7868
Email: info@blindgatehouse.com Web: www.blindgatehouse.com

Maeve Coakley's purpose-built guesthouse is set in its own gardens high up over the town and, with spacious rooms, uncluttered lines and a generally modern, bright and airy atmosphere, Blindgate makes a refreshing contrast to the more traditional styles that prevail locally. All bedrooms are carefully furnished with elegant modern simplicity, have full en-suite bathrooms and good facilities including fax/modem sockets as well as phones, satellite TV, tea/coffee trays and trouser press. Maeve is an hospitable host - and well-known in Kinsale for her skills in the kitchen, so breakfast here is a high priority: there's a buffet displaying all sorts of good things including organic muesli, fresh fruits and juices, farmhouse cheese and yogurts, as well as a menu of hot dishes featuring, of course, the full Irish Breakfast alongside catch of the day and other specialities - so make sure you allow time to enjoy this treat to the full. **Rooms 11.** B&B €67.50 pps, no ss. Closed 23 Dec-1 Mar. Amex, MasterCard, Visa, Laser, Switch. **Directions:** From Fishy Fishy Café: Take left up the hill, keeping left after St Multose Church. Blindgate House is after St Joseph's Primary School, on the left.

Kinsale

Chart House

B&B

6 Denis Quay Kinsale Co Cork **Tel: 021 477 4568** Fax: 021 477 7907
Email: charthouse@eircom.net Web: www.charthouse-kinsale.com

Billy and Mary O'Connor's delightful 200 year old house has been completely renovated, with commendable attention to period details, and now offers luxurious accommodation. Beautifully furnished bedrooms have orthopaedic mattresses, phone, TV, hair dryer and a trouser press with iron; tea and coffee are served by the fire in a cosy reception/sitting room. An imaginative breakfast menu is served communally on a fine William IV dining room suite. Not suitable for children. No pets. **Rooms 4.** (2 suites with jacuzzi baths, 2 shower only, all no-smoking). B&B €55-85 pps (depending on room), single occupancy 75%; single room €50. Closed Christmas week. Amex, MasterCard, Visa, Laser. **Directions:** On Pier Road between Actons and Trident Hotels, turn rght after Actons, last house on right.

Kinsale

Crackpots

féile bia RESTAURANT / WINE BAR

3 Cork Street Kinsale Co Cork
Tel: 021 477 2847 Fax: 021 477 3517
Email: crackpots@iol.ie Web: www.crackpots.ie

Carole Norman's attractive and unusual restaurant has a lot going for it - not only can you drop in for a glass of wine at the bar, as well as the usual meals, but all the pottery used in the restaurant is made on the premises so, if you take a fancy to the tableware, you can buy that too. Menus are imaginative and considerate, with plenty for vegetarians and many of the specialities are seafood, notably shellfish: a seafood platter is available hot or cold, mussels are offered gratinated (with pesto & garlic breadcrumb topping) or marinière, oysters are served on the shell - and old favourites like chowder and smoked salmon are sure to make an appearance. If you feel like a change from fish there will be a vegetarian dish of the day - and maybe organic roast duck, with a Calvados & prune sauce, or a classic fillet steak on the dinner menu. Children welcome. **Seats 50.** No smoking area; air conditioning. L Fri-Sun, 12.30-2.30; D daily 6-10. Early D €20 (6.30-7.30pm); otherwise à la carte, house wines €17. Amex, MasterCard, Visa, Laser, Switch. **Directions:** Between Garda Station and Wine Museum.

Kinsale

Fishy Fishy Café @ The Gourmet Store

CAFÉ

Guardwell Kinsale Co Cork **Tel: 021 477 4453**

This delightful fish shop, delicatessen and restaurant is a mecca for gourmets in and around Kinsale and was our Seafood Restaurant of the Year in 2001. The café, which has tables both indoors, alongside the shop, and outside under an awning, sports trendy little aluminium chairs and an agreeably continental air. Although all sorts of other delicacies are on offer, seafood is the serious business here - and, as well as the range of dishes offered on the menu & specials board, you can ask to have any of the fresh fish on display cooked to your liking. Not that you'd feel the need to stray beyond the menu, in fact, as it makes up in interest and quality anything it might lack in length - and you can have anything you like from seafood chowder or smoked salmon sandwich to grilled whole prawns with lemon garlic & sweet chilli sauce or fresh lobster, crayfish or crab. Vegetarian dishes available on request. Not suitable for children under 7. Wheelchair accessible. No reservations. **Seats 36.** L daily 12-3.45 (Mon-Sat only, Oct-Mar); à la carte; house wines from €18. Closed Sun from Oct to Mar; 24-28 Dec. **Directions:** Opposite St Multose church, next to Garda station.

Kinsale

Harbour Lodge

GUESTHOUSE

Scilly Kinsale Co Cork **Tel: 021 477 2376**
Email: relax@harbourlodge.com Web: www.harbourlodge.com

Everything has recently been refurbished at Raoul and Seiko de Gendre's quietly located guesthouse, with new carpets, top of the range beds and bedding and upgraded bathrooms, which are now luxurious, with the largest, thickest possible towels and bathrobes - and in-house laundry to take care of them. The position, away from the bustle of the town centre is lovely and peaceful; some bedrooms have balconies and there's a large conservatory "orangerie" (where breakfast is served). for the leisurely observation of comings and goings in the harbour and a sitting room with an open fire for chilly days. A high level of personal attention and service is the aim, including the arrangement of transport to and from their restaurant, The Vintage, for guests wishing to dine there. Simple meals are available on request - salads, sandwiches, soup, steaks, moules marinière - and there's a limited laundry and pressing service. Walking, cycling. Golf and many other activities nearby. Special breaks offered. **Rooms 8** (1 suite, 1 wheelchair accessible, all no smoking). B&B from about €80 pps. Open all year. Amex, Diners, MasterCard, Visa, Laser. **Directions:** Half a mile from town centre,beside the Spinnaker.

Kinsale

Jean Marc's Chow House

RESTAURANT

7 Pearse Street Kinsale Co Cork **Tel: 021 477 7117**
Fax: 021 477 8929 Email: thechowhouse@msr.com

Jean-Marc Tsai is no stranger to Kinsale - many will remember his exquisite combination of classica French and Chinese cooking in his previous restaurant, Chez Jean Marc. But this little place is something different; very Asian and very accessible with average prices for a meal only around €27 Jean Marc's stylish combination of Chinese, Thai and Vietnamese cuisines goes down a treat with the area's discerning diners, who cite the Chow House as a favourite evening destination. It's bright and modern, with comfortable seating and a lively atmosphere - a patio at the back has been ingeniously turned into a covered 'Monsoon Garden', which increases the seating significantly, and recent redecoration makes the most of Lao and Kemlan handicrafts from Jean-Marc's annual travels. Although specialist ingredients must obviously be imported, Jean-Marc uses a lot of fresh local produce and everything is very authentic, colourful, attractively presented and fresh-flavoured - all this with friendly helpful service and terrific value for money makes for a thoroughly enjoyable experience: truly a winning combination. Unusually for an Asian restaurant, desserts are made on the premises - and here we catch a glimpse of Jean-Marc in his classic French mode: crêpes suzettes and a 'crème brulée du jour' are typical! An 'Asian Libations' wine list, has been researched to compliment the food and complimetary partnerships are suggested - full marks for this initiative. Chinese & Thai beers available also an extensive range of herbal and Asian speciality teas. Not suitable for children after 8.30. **Seats 70** (private room 20). Toilets wheelchair accessible. D Wed-Mon (daily in Jul-Aug), 6.30-10.30. A la carte (av. price for meal with wine €28). House wine €17.50. Closed Tue (except Jul-Aug); 1 Jan -17 Mar MasterCard, Visa, Laser. **Directions:** Next door to AIB bank.

KINSALE

Man Friday

RESTAURANT

Scilly Kinsale Co Cork **Tel: 021 477 2260** Fax: 021 477 226.

High up over the harbour, Philip Horgan's popular, characterful restaurant is housed in a series o rooms. It has a garden terrace which makes a nice spot for drinks and coffee in fine weather. Marti Fox, who has been head chef since 1996, presents seasonal à la carte menus that major on seafood bu offer plenty else besides, including several vegetarian choices and duck, steak and lamb. While geared to fairly traditional tastes, the cooking is generally sound and can include imaginative ideas. Simple, well-made desserts include good ice creams. Service is, for the most part, cheerful and efficient and, unlike many other restaurants in the area, which are seasonal, Man Friday is open in the winter. **Seats 130** (private room, 35) Air conditioning. Toilets wheelchair accessible. D Mon-Sat; à la carte, house wine from about €19; sc discretionary. Closed Sun, Dec 24-26. Amex, MasterCard, Visa, Laser **Directions:** Overlooking the harbour, at Scilly.

Kinsale

Max's Wine Bar

RESTAURANT 48 Main Street Kinsale Co Cork **Tel: 021 477 2443** Fax: 021 477 2443

Max's is run by a young couple, Anne Marie Galvin, who supervises front of house, and chef-owner Olivier Queva and they have earned a loyal following in the locality. It's a characterful little place with stone walls at the bar end, varnished wooden tables and an attractive conservatory area at the back. They offer a light snack lunch and a short menu that's available at lunch or in the early evening, as well as the main dinner menu. Olivier's seasonal menus change regularly (some seasonal, others daily) and offer a balance of meats and poultry, as well as the seafood from the pier - langoustines and oysters (in season), mussels, black sole, salmon, ray and so on - which is always so much in demand. Roast rack of Irish lamb is a consistent favourite - served with a basil and tomato dice jus, perhaps - and imaginative vegetarian dishes are always offered too. An informative wine list offers a range of house wines (available by the glass) and a fair sprinkling of half bottles. Not suitable for children under 5 after 8pm. **Seats 30.** No smoking area. L Wed-Mon,12.30-2.45 (Sun 1-3), D Wed-Mon, 6.30-10.30 (Sun to 10). Set L/Early D (6.30-7.30) €17.90; à la carte available; house wine €15.90, SC discretionary. Closed Tue; 1 Nov-1 Mar. Amex, MasterCard, Visa, Laser, Switch. **Directions:** Street behind the petrol station on pier.

Kinsale

Perryville House

ACCOMMODATION Long Quay Kinsale Co Cork **Tel: 021 477 2731** Fax: 021 477 2298
Email: sales@perryville.iol.ie Web: www.perryvillehouse.com

One of the prettiest houses in Kinsale, Laura Corcoran's characterful house on the harbour front has been renovated to an exceptionally high standard and provides excellent accommodation only 15 minutes from the Old Head of Kinsale golf links. Gracious public rooms are beautifully furnished, as if for a private home. Spacious, individually decorated bedrooms vary in size and outlook (ones at the front are most appealing, but the back is quieter) and all have extra large beds and thoughtful extras such as fresh flowers, complimentary mineral water, quality toiletries, robes and slippers. The suites have exceptionally luxurious bathrooms although all are well-appointed. Breakfasts include home-baked breads and local cheeses; morning coffee and afternoon tea are available to residents in the drawing room and there is a wine licence. No smoking establishment. Own parking. Not suitable for children under 12. No pets. **Rooms 26** (6 junior suites,8 superior, all no-smoking). B&B about €100 pps, SC discretionary. Closed Nov-1 Apr. Amex, Diners, MasterCard, Visa. **Directions:** Central location, on right as you enter Kinsale from Cork, overlooking marina. ◇

Kinsale

Pier House

Ⓝ **GUESTHOUSE** Kinsale Co Cork **Tel: 021 477 4475** / 477 4169 Fax: 021 477 4475
Email: pierhouseaccom@eircom.net Web: www.pierhousekinsale.com

Ann and Pat Hegarty's newly refurbished guesthouse is one of the latest additions to the choice of quality accommodation in Kinsale, and can be entered from the pier or, at the other side of the block, from Main Street. First impressions are very favourable - an enclosed garden is professionally landscaped and includes a barbecue area with a wood burning stove overlooking the harbour, that catches the evening sun - and everything about this stylishly decorated house reinforces initial good impressions. There are 'extras' everywhere: an 'outdoor' balcony area on the first floor, for example, has large hot tub and sauna room, while a communal room has laundering and ironing facilities, and also an ice machine, glasses and openers for guests' use. A gallery seating area for guests' use features highlighted paintings done by Pat's brother Michael, an accomplished artist - creating a bright, airy atmosphere. Bedrooms vary somewhat in size and outlook, but all have television (many in cabinets), direct dial phones and ISDN connections for laptops. Some bathrooms are quite small (with power showers rather than baths) but luxurious features include under floor heating, good shaving mires, heated towel rails and mirrors. An attractive breakfast room on the ground floor has proved too small and is to be relocated to a new dining room with a conservatory extension for the 2004 season. Children welcome (under 4 free in parents' room, cot available without charge, baby sitting arranged). Garden. **Rooms 10** (9 shower only, 1 with full bath. all no smoking). B&B €120 per room (2 sharing). Open all year. MasterCard, Visa. **Directions:** At the top of Pier Road, opposite Tourist Office. ◇

Kinsale

The Spaniard Inn

PUB

Scilly Kinsale Co Cork **Tel: 021 477 2436** Fax: 021 477 3303
Email: thespaniard@eircom.net Web: www.spaniardinn.com

Who could fail to be charmed by The Spaniard, that characterful and friendly old pub perched high up above Scilly? Although probably best known for music (nightly), it offers bar food all year round and there's a restaurant in season. Popular traditional fare (Spaniard seafood chowder, smoked salmon platter, moules marinières) for which The Spaniard is well known is served informally in the bar alongside more contemporary dishes such as warm blue cheese tartlet, chicken stir-fry with noodles and gourmet sandwiches such as char-grilled sirloin steak in ciabatta bread. Evening restaurant meals (Dublin Bay prawns, fillet of lamb, roast monkfish) are more extensive. Bar meals: 12.30-5.30 (average main dish about €10); evening meals: 6.30-10 (main courses around €22). House wine €18. Closed 25 Dec & Good Fri. Amex, MasterCard, Visa, Laser.

Kinsale

The Old Bank House

GUESTHOUSE

11 Pearse Street Kinsale Co Cork **Tel: 021 477 4075** Fax: 021 477 4296
Email: oldbank@indigo.ie Web: www.oldbankhousekinsale.com

Marie and Michael Riese's townhouse in the middle of Kinsale has earned a high reputation for quality of accommodation and service - it has an elegant residents' sitting room, a well-appointed breakfast room and comfortable countryhouse-style bedrooms with good amenities, antiques and quality materials. All rooms are furnished and decorated to the same high standard, with lovely bathrooms, phone, TV. Breakfast is a treat - an extensive menu is served in the Dining Room (8.30-9am) and continental breakfast is available in bedrooms by request. All-day (8am-10pm) room service for coffee, tea, wine, mineral water etc (which may also be served in the sitting room). ISDN line and safe available at reception. No smoking in public areas. Babies up to 1 year free in parents' room; cot €15. Golf friendly: tee-off times, hire of clubs, transport to course, golf tuition can all be arranged; golf storage room. **Rooms 17** (1 suite, 3 junior suites). Lift. B&B €170 per room (max 2 guests). Closed 23-26 Dec. Amex, MasterCard, Visa, Laser, Switch. **Directions:** Next to the Post Office.

Kinsale

The Old Presbytery

ACCOMMODATION

43 Cork Street Kinsale Co Cork **Tel: 021 477 2027** Fax: 021 477 2166
Email: info@oldpres.com Web: www.oldpres.com

This old house in the centre of the town has provided excellent accommodation for many years and the current owners, Philip and Noreen McEvoy, recently added three new self-catering suites, each with two en-suite bedrooms, sitting room, kitchenette and an extra bathroom. The new rooms are well proportioned and furnished in the same style and to the same high standard as the original refurbished bedrooms (with stripped pine country furniture and antique beds); they can be taken on a nightly basis (min 2 nights), sleeping up to six adults. The top suite has an additional lounge area leading from a spiral staircase, with magnificent views over the town and harbour. **Rooms 6** (3 suites, 2 shower only, all no-smoking). B&B €115pps, ss €25. Closed Dec-mid Feb. Amex, MasterCard, Visa, Laser, Switch. **Directions:** Follow signs for Desmond Castle - in same street.

Kinsale

Toddies Restaurant

☆ **RESTAURANT**

Eastern Road Kinsale Co Cork **Tel: 021 477769**
Email: toddies@eircom.net Web: toddieskinsale.com

Facing south-westwards over Kinsale harbour, Pearse and Mary O'Sullivan's fine restaurant enjoys one of the best locations in the area - easy to find, yet secluded in well-maintained gardens, with views across the water from the restaurant. Commitment, hard work - and that magic ingredient of great delight - have clearly gone into converting the house and furnishing it in a pleasingly personal contemporary style enhanced by an impressive collection of modern art. After a warm welcome from Mary in the attractive little entrance lobby (too small for a bar, unfortunately, although aperitifs can be taken outside in fine weather), guests are usually taken straight to a table in one of two rooms - the larger one, at the front, has harbour views and a lively atmosphere while a smaller one towards the back of the house overlooks the patio and gardens and has a more intimate ambience. Well-balanced compact menus are changed monthly, and offer a choice of about five on each course (the addition of one or two daily specials would give more variety for regulars). Starters range from soup (cream of potato and watercress, perhaps) to sophisticated speciality dishes like terrine of foie gras with creamed black truffle vinaigrette and home-made ravioli of crab and spinach with cherry tomato butter sauce & shaved Parmesan, while main courses start range from an imaginative vegetarian dish (a strudel of spinach, wild mushrooms and ricotta with asparagus spears, pine nuts & a roasted pepper coulis another house speciality) to prime fish like Dover sole (meunière, perhaps) and roasted rump of Munster lamb with a confit of Mediterranean vegetables and a thyme & garlic jus. An Irish farmhouse cheeseboard is offered, or you can finish with classic desserts - which might include a baked Granny Smith apple tart (well worth a 15 minute wait)- and home-made petits fours with your coffee. Accurate, creative cooking makes the most of carefully sourced ingredients here and each dish is carefully presented, complete with its own garnish, to look its best against simple white plates; well-judged textures and excellent flavour make for a very satisfying dining experience, complemented by flawless service. A wide-ranging and informative wine list includes an interesting Sommelier's Choice selection. **Seats 40** (private room 10-12). Children over 10 welcome. D Tue-Sun, 6.30-10, L Sun only 12-2.30. D A la carte. (Starters about €6-16; main courses about €20-30), Sun L €25. House wine €18.50. SC discretionary. Closed Mon & Jan-Mar. Amex, MasterCard, Visa, Laser. **Directions:** 4th house on left hand side past Texaco Station as you enter Kinsale.

Kinsale

Trident Hotel

féile bia HOTEL / RESTAURANT

World's End Kinsale Co Cork
Tel: 021 477 2301 Fax: 021 477 4173
Email: info@tridenthotel.com Web: www.tridenthotel.com

While this blocky, concrete-and-glass 1960s waterfront hotel cannot match the luxurious accommodation offered by some of the town's best guesthouses at similar rates, it enjoys an exceptional location and, under the watchful management of Hal McElroy, is a well-run, hospitable and comfortable place to stay for those who prefer the ambience and services of an hotel. The genuinely pubby Wharf Tavern is a good meeting place and Gerry O'Connor, head chef for the main restaurant, also has responsibility for the bar food (12-9 daily). Bedrooms include two suites, with private balconies directly overlooking the harbour and, while slightly dated, all bedrooms are quite spacious and comfortable, with phone, TV and tea/coffee trays (iron and board available on request) and small but adequate bathrooms. Conference/banqueting (220); secretarial services, video-conferencing on request. Children welcome (under 12 free in parents room, cot available without charge, baby sitting arranged). No pets. Lift. **Rooms 58** (2 suites, 2 wheelchair accessible). B&B from €75 pps, ss €33. **Savannah Waterfront Restaurant:** While it is difficult for a hotel restaurant to compete with the exceptional number and variety of restaurants in Kinsale, the Savannah - which is named after the first steam-powered vessel to cross the Atlantic from west to east - does a good job. The restaurant has plenty of atmosphere and is well-located on the first floor with views over the harbour - which also makes it an exceptionally pleasant room for breakfast. The food is good and especially welcome in winter, when many of the smaller restaurants are closed. **Seats 80.** D daily, 7- 9.30, L Sun only 1 & 2.30. Set Sun L €21.50; Set D €35, D also à la carte. House wine from €18.40. SC discretionary. Toilets wheelchair accessible. Amex, MasterCard, Visa, Laser. **Directions:** Take the R600 from Cork to Kinsale - the hotel is at the end of the Pier Road.

Kinsale

Vintage Restaurant

féile bia RESTAURANT

50, Main Street Kinsale Co Cork **Tel: 021 477 2502** Fax: 021 477 4828
Email: info@vintagerestaurant.ie Web: www.vintagerestaurant.ie

Raoul and Seiko de Gendre have been running the cottagey Vintage restaurant successfully since 1994, specialising in 'continental cuisine with an Irish accent'. Wide-ranging à la carte menus are especially strong on seafood in summer and game in the winter: specialities include an hors d'oeuvre of home-smoked wild fish and seafood from Irish waters, terrine of white and black pudding, foie gras and pork. Many of the main course choices are luxurious: Dublin lawyer (a speciality lobster dish), scallops, sole, turbot and game (venison, wild duck) all feature in season. Details are good - tasty little amuse-bouches are served with aperitifs, tables are beautifully appointed, service professional. Wine appreciation evenings and other special events are held regularly off-season. Not suitable for children under 8. No-smoking area; air conditioning. **Seats 56** (private room 25). D Tue-Sun 6.30-10; Tasting Menu €75, otherwise à la carte, house wine €27.50, SC discretionary. Open 7 days Easter-15 Oct; closed 2 Jan-13 Feb, also Mon. *Accommodation also offered: see under Harbour Lodge. Amex, Diners, MasterCard, Visa, Laser. **Directions:** From the Post Office, turn left at the Bank of Ireland - restaurant is on the right.

Kinsale Area

Glebe House

COUNTRY HOUSE

Ballinadee nr Kinsale Bandon Co Cork
Tel: 021 477 8294 Fax: 021 477 8456
Email: glebehse@indigo.ie Web: http://indigo.ie/~glebehse/

Everybody loves this charming old rectory near Kinsale which dates back to 1690 (Church records provide interesting details: it was built for £250; repairs and alterations followed at various dates, and the present house was completed in 1857 at a cost of £1,160). More recently, under the hospitable ownership of Gill Good, this classically proportioned house has been providing a restful retreat for guests since 1989. Set in beautiful, well-tended gardens (including a productive kitchen garden), it has a beautiful wisteria at the front door, spacious reception rooms and large and generous, stylishly decorated bedrooms with good bathrooms and phone and tea/coffee making facilities. The Rose Room is on the ground floor, with French doors to the garden. A 4-course candle-lit dinner for residents, much of it supplied by the garden, is served at a communal table (please book by noon). Although unlicensed, guests are encouraged to bring their own wine. The whole house may be rented by parties by arrangement and several self-catering apartments are also available. Children welcome (under 5s free in parents' room, cots available) without charge. Pets allowed by arrangement. **Rooms 4** (2 shower only, all no-smoking), B&B €45 pps, ss €12. Residents' D Mon-Sat, €30, at 8pm (please book by noon). No D on Sun. Closed Christmas. Diners, MasterCard, Visa. **Directions:** Take N71 west from Cork to Innishannon Bridge, follow signs for Ballinadee (6 miles). After village sign, 1st on right.

Leap

All Things Nice

Ⓝ CAFÉ

Main Street Leap Co Cork **Tel: 028 34772**

A handsome dark green building set back from the road in the centre of the village attracts the eye - and the sight of contented people sipping coffee (organic fair trade of course) at outdoor tables should be enough to arouse the curiosity. Do make a point of stopping here at Kathleen Woumans' smashing little delicatessen and café whether for a quick break (an organic milk shake, perhaps, with home-made ice cream and local strawberries) or maybe something a little more substantial, such as a plate of Irish and continental cheeses and salamis with olives and a freshly-baked roll. Baking is a strong point and organic loaves with pumpkin & sunflower seeds or currants, or organic wholegrain seeds crackers go perfectly with local cheeses Gubbeen and Durrus, which are offered alongside a careful selection of other Irish and continental speciality cheeses and treats like kulmata olives and semi-sundried tomatoes, olive oils and vinegars. An interesting range of meats includes salamis and other Gubbeen specialities - smoked dry-cured bacon and free range pork sausages. All this and much more, either to eat in the café or load up to stock your larder. Parking. **Seats 16.** Open daily,10-6 (Sun 12-4). MasterCard, Visa. **Directions:** On main road between Clonakilty and Skibbereen; shop is in village next to post office.

Macroom

The Mills Inn

PUB / B&B

Ballyvourney Macroom Co Cork **Tel: 026 45237**
Fax: 026 45454 Email: millinn@eircom.net Web: www.millinn.ie

One of Ireland's oldest inns, The Mills Inn is in a Gaeltacht (Irish-speaking) area and dates back to 1755. It was traditionally used to break the journey from Cork to Killarney - and still makes a great stopping place as the food is good and freshly cooked all day - but is now clearly popular with locals as well as travellers. New owners took over in 2003 and they are renovating the premises while retaining its old-world charm and a genuine sense of hospitality. Toilets wheelchair accessible. L&D daily. Closed 25 Dec.

Accommodation: Rooms vary considerably due to the age of the building, but all are comfortably furnished with neat bathrooms and good amenities - and, like the rest of the premises, are undergoing refurbishment at the time of going to press. A large ground-floor room is suitable for less able guests, who can use the residents' car park right at the door - in a courtyard shared with a vintage car and an agricultural museum. Full room service is available for drinks and meals. **Rooms 13** (1 for disabled). Amex, Diners, MasterCard, Visa, Laser. **Directions:** On N22, 20 minutes from Killarney. ◇

Macroom

The Castle Hotel & Leisure Centre

Ⓝ féile bia HOTEL

Macroom Co Cork **Tel: 026 41074** Fax: 026 41505
Email: castlehotel@eircom.net Web: www.castlehotel.ie

In the ownership of the Buckley family since 1952, this well-managed hotel is ideally located for touring the scenic south-west. Major recent developments include the addition of superior executive bedrooms and suites, an extensive new foyer and reception area, an impressive new bar and the stylish 'B's' Restaurant. Extensive leisure facilities include a fine swimming pool (with children's pool, spa and massage pool), steam room, solarium and gym. Conferences/banqueting (60). Special breaks are offered, including golf specials (tee times reserved at Macroom's 18-hole course). 'The Next Door Café' has a separate entrance from the street and offers informal continental style fare; it is a popular meeting place for locals and visitors alike. Friendly staff take pride in making guests feel at home. Children welcome (under 4s free in parents' room, cots available without charge; playroom). Conference/banqueting (150). No pets. **Rooms 60.** B&B €77.50 pps, ss €25. Food available 9.30am-9pm. Closed 24-28 Dec. Amex, Diners, MasterCard, Visa, Laser. **Directions:** On N22, midway between Cork & Killarney.

Mallow — Longueville House

COUNTRY HOUSE

Mallow Co Cork **Tel: 022 47156** Fax: 022 47459
Email: info@longuevillehouse.ie Web: www.longuevillehouse.ie

When Longueville House opened its doors to guests in 1967, it was one of the first Irish country houses to do so. Its history is wonderfully romantic, "the history of Ireland in miniature", and it is a story with a happy ending. Having lost their lands in the Cromwellian Confiscation (1652-57), the O'Callaghans took up ownership again some 300 years later. The present house, a particularly elegant Georgian mansion of pleasingly human proportions, dates from 1720, (with wings added in 1800 and the lovely Turner conservatory - which has been completely renovated - in 1862), overlooks the ruins of their original home, Dromineen Castle. Many things make Longueville special, most importantly the warm, informal hospitality and charm of the O'Callaghans themselves - Michael and Jane, their son (and talented chef) William and his wife Aisling. The location, overlooking the famous River Blackwater, is lovely. The river, farm and garden supply fresh salmon in season, the famous Longueville lamb and all the fruit and vegetables. In years when the weather is kind, the estate's crowning glory (and Michael O'Callaghan's great enthusiasm) is their own house wine, a light refreshing white, "Coisreal Longueville". Graciously proportioned reception rooms include a bar and drawing room both elegantly furnished with beautiful fabrics and family antiques. Accommodation is equally sumptuous and bedrooms are spacious, superbly comfortable and stylishly decorated to the highest standards (under the personal supervision of Jane O'Callaghan) - and, after a good night's sleep, a Longueville breakfast is a treat to be cherished: a wonderful array of local and home-cooked foods assured Longueville's place as winner of our Denny Irish Breakfast Awards, for Munster and all Ireland in 2003. Worth dropping in for even if you can't stay overnight - what a way to break a journey! As well as being one of the finest leisure destinations in the country, the large cellar/basement area of the house has been developed as a conference centre with back-up services available. The house is also available for small residential weddings throughout the year. Conference/banqueting (50/110). Children welcome (under 2s free in parents' room, cot available without charge, baby sitting arranged). No pets. **Rooms 20.** (3 suites, 4 junior suites, 13 superior rooms, all no-smoking). B&B €100pps. Closed Christmas and second fortnight in Feb (but may open for groups of 20+ excl. Christmas/New Year. Shooting weekends available Nov, Dec, Jan; telephone for details).

★**Presidents' Restaurant:** Named after the family collection of specially commissioned portraits of all Ireland's past presidents (which made for a seriously masculine collection until Ireland's first woman president, Mary Robinson, broke the pattern) this is the main dining room and opens into the beautifully renovated conservatory, which makes a wonderfully romantic setting in candlelight; there is a smaller room alongside the main restaurant and also the Chinese Room, which is suitable for private parties. William O'Callaghan is a highly accomplished chef and home- and locally-produced food is at the heart of all his cooking. His well-balanced dinner menus are not over-extensive, offering a choice of four or five dishes on each course, plus some extra daily dishes - and a no-choice 8-course Menu Gourmand for complete parties. Local ingredients star, in a starter of house smoked salmon with a garden salad, for example, followed by rack of Longueville lamb - with rosemary sauce and roasted garden vegetables, perhaps - or home reared pork loin or duck, all worked into creative dishes which sound simple enough on the menu but can be complex. Home produce influences the dessert menu too, as in garden raspberry vacherin, and it is hard to resist the local farmhouse cheeses. Delicious home-made chocolates and petits fours come with the coffee and service, under Jane or Aisling O'Callaghan's direction, is invariably excellent. A fine wine list includes many wines imported directly by Michael O'Callaghan. Children welcome. **Seats 110** (private room 18). D daily, 6.30-9; Set D €50, Menu Gourmand €65; light meals 1-5 daily (set L for groups of 20+). House wine €25, sc discretionary. Annual closures as above. Amex, MasterCard, Visa, Laser. **Directions:** 3 miles west of Mallow via N72 to Killarney.

Midleton — Farmgate

féile bia RESTAURANT

Coolbawn Midleton Co Cork **Tel: 021 4632771** Fax: 021 4632771

This unique shop and restaurant has been drawing people to Midleton in growing numbers since 1985 and it's a great credit to sisters Maróg O'Brien and Kay Harte. Kay now runs the younger version at the English Market in Cork while Maróg looks after Midleton. The shop at the front is full of wonderful local produce - organic fruit and vegetables, cheeses, honey - and their own super home baking, while the evocatively decorated, comfortable restaurant at the back, with its old pine furniture and modern sculpture, is regularly transformed from bustling daytime café to sophisticated evening restaurant (on Friday and Saturday) complete with string quartet. Maróg O'Brien is a founder and stall holder of the hugely successful Midleton Farmers Market, which is held on Saturday mornings. Meals all day Mon-Sat, D Fri & Sat. Closed Sun, Bank Hols. MasterCard, Visa. **Directions:** Town centre. ◇

Midleton

Finíns

PUB

75 Main Street Midleton Co Cork **Tel: 021 463 1878** Fax: 021 463 3847

Finín O'Sullivan's thriving bar and restaurant in the centre of the town has long been a popular place for locals to meet for a drink and to eat some good wholesome food. This attractive, no-nonsense place offers a wide range of popular home-made dishes, mostly based on local produce notably fresh seafood from Ballycotton harbour. Meals available 10.30am-10pm. Bar menu à la carte; D from €25. House wine €18. Closed Sun, bank hols, 24 Dec-1 Jan. **Directions:** Town centre.

Midleton

Glenview House

COUNTRY HOUSE

Midleton Co Cork **Tel: 021 4631680** Fax: 021 4634680
Email: info@glenviewmidleton.com Web: www.glenviewmidleton.com

When Ken & Beth Sherrard acquired their lovely Georgian house near Midleton in 1963 it was virtually derelict. Two years later, Ken bought the entire contents of the Dublin Georgian buildings infamously demolished to make way for the new ESB offices - and today this well-tended, comfortable and elegantly furnished house is the richer for that act of courage. Now, with a welcoming fire in the hall and classically-proportioned reception rooms on either side, it's hard to imagine it any other way. Except for one adapted for wheelchair users, bedrooms in the main house are on the first floor, all comfortably furnished with en-suite bathrooms (one has an old bath with a highly original - and practical - shower arrangement built in), hair dryers and tea/coffee-making facilities. There is also some delightful self-catering accommodation in converted outbuildings - with the agreeable arrangement of dinner in the main house as an option. Dinner is cooked by Beth and served at a communal table (8pm, usually residents only; book by noon). There is much to do in the area: the heritage sites at Cobh and Midleton are nearby, also Fota Wildlife Park, Arboretum & Golf, wonderful walks and much else besides. Midleton Market (every Saturday) is a must for food lovers. Garden, terrace, croquet, lawn tennis, forest walks, cycling. Children welcome, baby sitting arranged. Pets allowed by arrangement. **Rooms 7** (4 in main house, 3 in converted coach house, 2 suites (coach house), 4 shower-only, 2 fully wheelchair accessible, all no smoking). B&B €70pps, ss €18. Residents D €40, by arrangement. Open all year. Amex, MasterCard, Visa, Laser **Directions:** Drive into Midleton (do not take the by-pass). When you come to the AIB bank, take the L35 (R626) Fermoy road. Continue towards Fermoy for 2.5 miles until reaching a forestry area; look for a sign for Leamara, Watergrasshill and Glenview House. Turn left and immediately right, following signage for Glenview House. Exactly 3 miles from Midleton.

Midleton

Loughcarrig House

COUNTRY HOUSE

Midleton Co Cork **Tel: 021 463 1952** Fax: 021 461 3707
Email: info@loughcarrig.com Web: www.loughcarrig.com

Bird-watching and sea angling are major interests at this relaxed and quietly situated country house, which is in a beautiful shore side location. Comfortable rooms have tea/coffee making facilities and there's a pleasantly hospitable atmosphere. Children welcome (free in parents' room under 2, cot available without charge). Pets permitted by arrangement. Fishing, walking, Garden. **Rooms 4** (all en-suite & no smoking). Closed Christmas/New Year. B&B €35 pps, ss €5. SC discretionary. **No Credit Cards. Directions:** From roundabout at Midleton on N25, take Whitegate Road for 2 miles.

Midleton

Midleton Park Hotel & Spa

HOTEL

Old Cork Road Midleton Co Cork **Tel: 021 463 5100** Fax: 021 463 5101
Email: reso@midletonpark.com Web: www.midletonpark.com

This pleasant hotel situated in the town of Midleton, close to the Old Midleton Distillery, has recently been completely refurbished and upgraded. Renovations include a new bar and restaurant, and an impressive leisure centre with 18-metre deck level swimming pool, gymnasium, outdoor Canadian hot tub and much else besides - including a Wellness Centre and Spa, with a wide range of treatments such as seaweed wraps, Indian head massage and reflexology as well as Yonka revitalising beauty treatments. Comfortable en-suite bedrooms - which are all furnished to a high standard with interactive TV with video and movie channel, phone/ISDN line, trouser press & ironing facilities, hairdryer and tea/coffee facilities - include some suitable for disabled guests and some non-smoking rooms as well as a 'presidential suite' for visiting VIPs. Although it is used a lot by the business community, the hotel also makes a good base for touring east Cork - Fota Island wildlife park, Cobh harbour (last port of call for the Titanic) are nearby and golf packages are arranged. Banqueting/conferences (300). Children welcome (under 3 free in parents' room, cot available without charge, baby sitting arranged). Wheelchair access. Ample parking. Leisure centre; beauty salon, hairdressing. Garden, walking. No pets. **Rooms 80** (1 suite, 1 junior suite, 41 executive, 23 no smoking, 3 disabled). Lift. B&B €100pps, ss €25. Closed 25 Dec. Amex, Diners, MasterCard, Visa, Laser. **Directions:** 12 miles east of Cork city, off N25.

Midleton

Old Midleton Distillery

CAFÉ

Distillery Walk Midleton Co Cork **Tel: 021 461 3594** Fax: 021 461 3642
Email: bookings@omd.ie Web: www.whiskeytours.ie

The Old Midleton Distillery is a fascinating place to visit - that such visiting can be thirsty work is acknowledged at the door (a whiskey tasting is part of the tour) but it can also be hungry work. Sensibly, the Centre has a pleasant restaurant, which was greatly extended in 2003, to include a new bar. Menus change daily and a wide range of dishes is offered, including simple fare like Irish stew, shepherd's pie and lasagne - and there are always vegetarian options and a good selection of home-made cakes. Children welcome. Toilets wheelchair accessible. **Seats 120** (private room 30). Air conditioning. Food available 10-5 daily. Closed Christmas period & Good Fri. Amex, Diners, MasterCard, Visa, Laser. **Directions:** 12 miles east of Cork on main Waterford (N25) road.

Midleton Area

Ballymaloe House

RESTAURANT / HOTEL

Shanagarry Midleton Co Cork
Tel: 021 465 2531 Fax: 021 465 2021
Email: res@ballymaloe.ie Web: www.ballymaloe.ie

Ireland's most famous country house hotel, Ballymaloe was one of the first country houses to open its doors to guests when Myrtle and her husband, the late Ivan Allen, opened The Yeats Room restaurant in 1964. Accommodation followed in 1967 and since then a unique network of family enterprises has developed around Ballymaloe House - including not only the farmlands and gardens that supply so much of the kitchen produce, but also a craft and kitchenware shop, a company producing chutneys and sauce, the Crawford Gallery Café in Cork city and, of course, Darina Allen's internationally acclaimed cookery school. Yet, despite the fame, Ballymaloe is still most remarkable for its unspoilt charm: Myrtle - now rightly receiving international recognition for a lifetime's work "recapturing forgotten flavours, and preserving those that may soon die"- is ably assisted by her children, and now their families too. The house, modestly described in its Blue Book (Irish Country House & Restaurants Association) entry as "a large family farmhouse" is in the middle of the amily's 400 acre farm, but the description fails to do justice to the gracious nature of the original ouse, or the sensitively designed later additions. The intensely restorative atmosphere of Ballymaloe s still as strong as ever; there are few greater pleasures than a fine Ballymaloe dinner followed by the elaxed comforts provided by a delightful, thoughtfully furnished (but not over decorated) country edroom. Ground floor courtyard rooms are suitable for wheelchairs. Children welcome (cot available, €45; baby sitting arranged). Special winter breaks offered. Pets allowed by arrangement. Outdoor wimming pool, tennis, walking, golf (9 hole). Gardens. Shop. **Rooms 33** (2 shower only). B&B €107.50pps, ss€60. Service discretionary.

★ **Restaurant:** The restaurant is in a series of domestic-sized dining rooms (some for non-smokers) and uests are called to their tables from the conservatory or drawing room, where aperitifs are served. A ood philosophy centred on using only the highest quality ingredients is central to everything done at allymaloe, where much of the produce comes from their own farm and gardens. The rest, including eafood from Ballycotton and Kenmare, comes from leading local producers. Rory O'Connell (who is arina Allen's brother) has been head chef at Ballymaloe since 1995 and presents a daily 7-course inner menu, with vegetarian dishes given a leaf symbol. He is doing an inspired job in the kitchen, reating generous, beautiful, daringly simple meals: Ballymaloe brown bread, crudités with garlic nayonnaise, paté de campagne with pickles, superb roast loin of free-range pork with herbs, garlic, ramley apple sauce & piquante beetroot, Irish farmhouse cheeses with home-made biscuits and a essert trolley that include rhubarb compôte and vanilla ice cream are typical of the truly impressive et homely dishes that invariably leave us lost in admiration - and, as if a 7-course dinner isn't enough, hey even offer second helpings of the main course! The teamwork at Ballymaloe is a sight to behold: his is, quite simply, as good as it gets. Finish with coffee or tea and home-made petits fours, served in the drawing room - and perhaps a drink from the small bar before retiring contentedly to bed. Children welcome at lunchtime, but the restaurant is not suitable for children under 7 after 7pm. (Children's high tea is served at 5.30.) Buffet meals only on Sundays. **Seats 100.** L daily 1-1.30, D daily 7-9.30 (Sun 7.50-8.30); Set D €55, Set L €35. House wine from €22. Service discretionary. Reservations essential. House closed 23-26 Dec. Helipad. Amex, Diners, MasterCard, Visa, Laser. **Directions:** Take signs to Ballycotton from N 25. Situated between Cloyne & Shanagarry.

Midleton Area

Ballymaloe Shop Café

CAFÉ

Ballymaloe House Shanagarry Co Cork **Tel: 021 465 2032**
Fax: 021 465 2021 Email: ballymaloeshop@eircom.net

At the back of Wendy Whelan's magnificent crafts and gift shop at Ballymaloe, there is a very nice little family-run café selling wholesome home-bakes and just the kind of light, nourishing fare that is needed to sustain you through a shopping expedition that may well be taking longer than you had planned. So take the weight off your feet, settle down with an aromatic cup of coffee and a slice of quiche and organic salad leaves - or why not an almond slice or some hazelnut meringue cake? *Wendy has a charming self-catering cottage, Rockcliffe House, in Ballycotton; details from the shop. Café open shop hours. Closed 25-26 Dec. Amex, MasterCard, Visa, Laser. **Directions:** 2 miles beyond Cloyne on Ballycotton road.

Midleton Area

Barnabrow Country House

féile bia **COUNTRY HOUSE / RESTAURANT**

Barnabrow Cloyne Midleton Co Cork
Tel: 021 465 2534 Fax: 021 465 2534
Email: barnabrow@eircom.net Web: www.barnabrowhouse.ie

John and Geraldine O'Brien's sensitive conversion of an imposing seventeenth century house optimises on stunning views of Ballycotton, and the decor is commendably restrained. Innovative African wooden furniture (among items for sale in an on-site shop) is a point of interest and spacious bedrooms are stylishly decorated and comfortable (although only two have a bath). Some bedrooms are in converted buildings at the back of the house, but (good) breakfasts are served in the main dining room, at a communal table. Recent developments have increased the dining capacity at Barnabrow, so they can now cater for weddings and other functions (up to 150) as well as normal private dining; word has clearly got out to discerning would-be-weds that weddings at Barnabrow are conducted with style and personal interest, as this is now an important side of the business. Head chef Eamonn Harty is Ballymaloe trained and brings to Barnabrow's Trinity Rooms Restaurant and catering operations the philosophy and cooking style that has earned such acclaim (Shanagarry smoked salmon and gratin of cod with Imokilly cheese & mustard topping are typical specialities.) Children welcome (cots available, €6.50). Pets permitted by arrangement. Conference/banqueting. **Rooms 19** (17 shower only, 2 with private bathrooms, 3 disabled, all no smoking). B&B €55pps, ss €20. D 7-9 Thu-Sun, L Sun Only 12.30-3; D à la carte; Set Sun L €25. House wine from €22; service discretionary (10% on parties of 10+). Restaurant closed Mon-Wed; house closed 23-27 Dec. Diners, MasterCard, Visa, Laser. **Directions:** From Cork N25 to Midleton rounddabout, right for Ballinacurra, left for Cloyne, then on to Ballycotton road for 1.5 miles.

Midleton Area

Rathcoursey House

COUNTRY HOUSE / RESTAURANT

Ballinacurra Midleton Co Cork
Tel: 021 461 3418 Fax: 021 461 3393
Email: beth@rathcoursey.com Web: rathcoursey.com

Set in 35 acres of woodland above an inlet of Cork Harbour, this peaceful small Georgian manor was opened to guests in 1999 by the food writer and former restaurateur Beth Hallinan. Book well ahead as this has become a favourite destination for discerning travellers in the know. Children welcome; pets permitted by arrangement. **Rooms 6** (1 junior suite, 1 shower only, 1 suitable for disabled guests). B&B about €85 pps, ss about €15. Residents' dinner about €40, house wine about €18. Open all year. MasterCard, Visa. **Directions:** At Midleton roundabout take Whitegate road. After 4km turn right for East Ferry, then small village of Rathcoursey and follow green arrows to the left. ◇

Mitchelstown

O'Callaghan's Delicatessen, Bakery & Café

féile bia **CAFÉ**

19/20 Lower Cork Street Mitchelstown Co Cork
Tel: 025 24657 Fax: 025 24657 Email: ocalhansdeli@eircom.net

The ideal place to break a journey, O'Callaghans have an impressive deli and bakery as well as tasty fare for a snack or full meal in the café, where lovely things to look forward to include steak sandwiches, goats cheese on a croûton, salmon & potato cakes and Mediterranean sandwich. If you're going home to an empty house, this is the place to stock up with delicious home-baked breads and cakes, home-made jams and chutneys - and, best of all perhaps, there's a range of home-made frozen meals. And if you have a wedding coming up in the family, ask about their wedding confectionery, made to order... The only downside to this life-saving stopping place is that it's closed on Sundays. They've always had a no-smoking section, of course, but at the time of going to press the O'Callaghans are refurbishing part of the garden to allow smoking after the ban is expected to come into force (January 2004). To avoid the busy main street, park around the corner on the road to the creamery - or, coming from Dublin, parking is also available on the new square (on right after second set of lights); but remember the square is not available for parking on Thursday - market day. Restaurant **Seats 110.** Food served Mon-Sat, 8.30 am-5.30 pm; L 12.3-2.30. Closed Sun, bank hols. MasterCard, Visa, Laser. **Directions:** On main street, right side heading towards Dublin.

Monkstown

The Bosun

PUB / RESTAURANT / GUESTHOUSE

The Pier Monkstown Co Cork
Tel: 021 484 2172 Fax: 021 484 2008
Email: info@thebosun.ie Web: www.thebosun.ie

Nicky and Patricia Moynihan's waterside establishment close to the Cobh car ferry, has grown a lot over the years, with the restaurant and accommodation growing fast and becoming an increasingly important part of the enterprise. Bar food is still taken seriously, however; seafood takes pride of place and afternoon/evening bar menus include everything from chowder or garlic mussels through to real scampi and chips, although serious main courses for carnivores such as lamb cutlets,pork escalopes and beef stroganoff are also available. Next to the bar, a well-appointed restaurant provides a more formal setting for wide-ranging table d'hôte and à la carte menus - and also Sunday lunch, which is especially popular. Again seafood is the speciality, ranging from popular starters such as crab claws or oysters worked into imaginative dishes, and main courses that include steaks and local duckling as well as seafood every which way, from grilled sole on the bone to medallions of marinated monkfish or a cold seafood platter. There's always a choice for vegetarians and vegetables are generous and carefully cooked. Finish with home-made ices, perhaps, or a selection of Irish farmhouse cheeses. Not suitable for children after 7pm. Restaurant **Seats 80** (max table size 12). No-smoking area; air conditioning. D daily 6.30-9, L Sun 12-2.30, Set D €37.50, Set Sun L €23.50; à la carte also available; house wine €19.50, sc discretionary. Bar food available daily 12-9.30 (L12-2.30, D 6.30-9.30). Closed 24-26 Dec, Good Fri.

Accommodation: Bedrooms are quite simple but have everything required (phone, TV, tea/coffee trays); those at the front have harbour views but are shower only, while those at the back have the advantage of a full bathroom and are quieter. Guests tend to be working in the area and resident all week, with weekends bringing more leisure visitors. Fota Island Golf Course is only 12 minutes away, also Fota House and Wildlife Centre. **Rooms 15** (9 shower only). Lift. B&B €49 pps, ss €7. Children welcome (under 5s free in parents' room, cot available without charge). No pets. Closed 24-26 Dec. Amex, Diners, MasterCard, Visa, Laser. **Directions:** On sea front, beside the Cobh ferry.

Oysterhaven

Finders Inn

RESTAURANT

Nohoval Oysterhaven Co Cork
Tel: 021 477 0737 Web: www.findersinn.com

Very popular with local people (but perhaps harder for visitors to find) the McDonnell family's well-named restaurant is in a row of traditional cottages eastn of Oysterhaven, en route from Crosshaven to Kinsale. It is a very charming place, packed with antiques and, because of the nature of the building, broken up naturally into a number of dining areas (which gives it an air of mystery). Seafood stars, of course - smoked salmon, Oysterhaven oysters, bisques, chowders, scallops and lobster are all here, but there are a few other specialities too, including steaks, lamb and lovely tender crisp-skinned duckling with an orange-sage sauce. Good desserts, caring service and a great atmosphere. Well worth taking the trouble to find. Not suitable for children under 8 after 8 pm. **Seats 90** (private room, 70). D Tue-Sat (also bank hol Sundays), 7-9.30. A la carte; sc discretionary. Toilets wheelchair accessible. Closed Sun (except bank hol weekends) & Mon; Christmas week. MasterCard, Visa, Laser. **Directions:** From Cork, take Kinsale road, turn left at The Huntsman roadhouse, follow Oysterhaven road and, at crossroads, go straight ahead to Nohaval.

Oysterhaven

Oz-Haven

RESTAURANT

Oysterhaven Co Cork **Tel: 021 477 0974**
Fax: 021 477 0974 Web: www.ozhaven.com

In a delightful waterside location at the head of Oysterhaven creek, Australian Paul Greer has transformed what was once a cosy cottage restaurant into something very different. The stone walls and open fires are still there, but the whole place has been done over in a highly idiosyncratic, colourful modern style; there's a great sense of fun about the whole approach (the latest addition is a giant fish tank with two huge Amazon fish) and, despite its modernism, the wacky decor works surprisingly well with the old building. The restaurant is divided between three separate areas, with open fires in two; well-spaced tables have comfortable high-back carver chairs and are simply laid in quality contemporary style, with generous wine glasses and white plates decorated only with the restaurant logo. Frederic Pastorino - previously at The Vintage in Kinsale - took over as head chef in 2002, bringing an element of classicism to new menus (it is unlikely that the OTT jokey descriptions of dishes are his doing). Underlying the wordy descriptions, the best of local ingredients - Bandon lamb, Ballydehob duck, lots of seafood - feature in variations of time-tested combinations such as steak with a potato & black pudding fritter, streaky bacon etc; lamb with rosemary, cod with bayonne ham... and so on. However, if that sounds like a U-turn on earlier menus, there are still plenty of world flavours in there and diners looking for an unusual experience should not be disappointed. Service is under the personal direction of Paul and Lydia Greer, who take pride in getting to know everyone - and continuing to present food with a difference, in entertaining surroundings. **Seats 50** (private room 30, outside dining 25). Toilets wheelchair accessible. Children welcome. D Wed-Sat, 7-10; L Sun & bank hols, 1-5. D à la carte, Set Sun L €27. House wine €17.95. Open all year except Christmas. Amex, MasterCard, Visa, Laser. **Directions:** 30 min from Cork city, turn left for Oysterhaven just before Kinsale.

Oysterhaven

Walton Court

COUNTRY HOUSE

Oysterhaven Co Cork **Tel: 021 477 0878** Fax: 021 477 0932
Email: info@waltoncourt.com Web: www.waltoncourt.com

Walton Court dates back to 1645, and when Paul and Janis Rafferty took it over on their return from Kenya in 1996, it was derelict. Five years of restoration work brought this listed building back to its former glory and the courtyard has been converted to stylish bedrooms and self-contained cottages, each with its own personality. There is also a small conference room (ISDN, video & lecture facilities), a bar with an open fireplace where guests can have a drink before dining in a plant-filled courtyard conservatory at the back of the main house, or the restored Georgian dining room. Walton Court is a member of the Slow Food movement and Paul & Janis prepare everything using fresh organic and home-grown ingredients. This unusual place will please those who value character above the hotel conveniences (television, room service) and it helps to like animals as you will certainly be greeted by the dogs as well as their owners, and quite probably cats and other household animals too. Small conferences/banqueting (30). Indoor exercise pool, sauna, treatment rooms. Private berthing facilities for visiting sailors planned for spring 2004. Pets permitted by arrangement. **Rooms 6** (all en-suite & no smoking). B&B €54, ss €21. D Tue-Sat; Set Menu from €42, at 8pm - non-residents welcome by reservation. House wine €16. Not suitable for children under 15, except in self-catering cottages. Closed 25 Dec. MasterCard, Visa, Laser. **Directions:** 6 miles from Kinsale (Cork side); R600 to Belgooly, signs to Oysterhaven.

Rosscarbery

Celtic Ross Hotel, Conference & Leisure Centre

féile bia **HOTEL**

Rosscarbery Co Cork **Tel: 023 48722**
Fax: 023 48723 Web: www.celticrosshotel.com

This modern hotel is close to the sea, overlooking Rosscarbery Bay (although not on the sea side of the road), and well placed as a base for touring west Cork; the facilities in the leisure centre of this modern hotel offer alternative activities for family holidays if the weather should disappoint. It's an attractive building with an unusual tower feature containing a bog oak, which is quite dramatic; public areas are spacious, and the bedrooms - many of which have sea views - have all the usual facilities. However, shortage of accommodation in the area means that this hotel is always busy, and a fair degree of wear and tear has been noted on recent visits. Children welcome (cots available, baby sitting arranged). Conference/banqueting (250/200). No pets. **Rooms 66** (3 suites, 3 for disabled, 10 no smoking). Wheelchair access. Lift. B&B €90 pps, ss €25. Closed mid Jan-mid Feb. Amex, Diners, MasterCard, Visa, Laser. **Directions:** Take N71 from Cork City, 10 miles west of Clonakilty.

Rosscarbery

RESTAURANT

O'Callaghan-Walshe

The Square Rosscarbery Co Cork **Tel: 023 48125**
Fax: 023 48125 Email: funfish@indigo.ie

ATMOSPHERIC RESTAURANT OF THE YEAR

This unique restaurant on the square of the old village (well off the busy main West Cork road) has a previous commercial history that's almost tangible - exposed stone walls, old fishing nets and glass floats, mismatched furniture, shelves of wine bottles and candlelight all contribute to and its unique atmosphere - which is well-matched by proprietor-host Sean Kearney's larger-than-life personality. Then there's the exceptional freshness and quality of the seafood, (steaks theoretically share the billing, but seafood steals the scene): Martina O'Donovan's menus change weekly but specialities to look out for include a superb Fruits de Mer platter (available as small or large but, in the Guide's experience, the small one is very large indeed) which has an exceptional range and quality of fish and shellfish included. The famous Rosscarbery Pacific oysters feature, of course, also char-grilled prime fish such as turbot, steamed lobster with lemon butter. Ultra-freshness, attention to detail in breads and accompaniments - and a huge dose of personality - all add up to make this place a delight. Not suitable for children after 8 pm. **Seats 40.** D 6.30-9 Tue-Sun, all à la carte, house wine about €24, sc discretionary. Closed Sun; phone ahead to check opening times in winter. MasterCard, Visa, Laser. **Directions:** Main square in Rosscarbery village.

Schull

CAFÉ

Adèle's

Main Street Schull Co Cork **Tel: 028 28459** Fax: 028 28865
Email: adeles@oceanfree.net Web: adelesrestaurant.com

If you happen to be in Schull early in the morning, you'll find it hard to squeeze in to Adèle Connor's little bakery and coffee shop, never mind trying to find a table for a cup of coffee and a home-baked scone - although there might be room upstairs if the ground floor tables are full. Hand-made bread, cakes and biscuits made on the premises are the main draw, but there are tempting savoury things too, such as ciabatta with Gubbeen cheese served with a small tossed salad and home-made chutney - or an omelette with roasted red pepper and garlic. Hand-made bread, cakes and biscuits are the main speciality, made on the premises. Times of opening vary according to the season. Children welcome. No wheelchair access. **Seats 40.** Open Wed-Sat, 9.30- 5 or 6, Sun 11-6 (last orders 5). A la carte. House wine €16 (quarter bottles also available), sc discretionary. Closed Nov-Easter. Amex, MasterCard, Visa. **Directions:** Turn off N71 at Ballydehob for Schull - in town centre.

Schull

Ⓝ GUESTHOUSE

Corthna Lodge Country House

Air Hill Schull Co Cork **Tel: 028 28517** Fax: 028 28032
Email: info@corthna-lodge.net Web: www.corthna-lodge.net

Situated up the hill from Schull, commanding countryside and sea views, Martin and Andrea Mueller's roomy modern house just outside Schull is one of the best located places to stay in the area. The house has been refurbished since the Muellers took over a year or two ago and, although fairly compact (most have standard double, rather than queen size, beds) bedrooms are comfortable with good amenities, and there's plenty of space for guests to sit around and relax - both indoors, in a pleasant and comfortably furnished sitting room and outdoors, on a terrace overlooking the lovely garden towards the islands of Roaring Water Bay. House computer available for guests' internet access; unusually, there's also a gym - and a putting green. Children over 5 welcome. Pets by arrangement. **Rooms 9** (all shower only & no smoking). B&B €45 pps, ss €20. Closed 15 Oct-28 Dec & early Jan- early April. MasterCard, Visa, Laser. **Directions:** Through village, up hill, first left, first right - house is signposted.

Schull

GUESTHOUSE

Grove House

Colla Road Schull Co Cork **Tel: 028 28067** Fax: 028 28069
Email: billyoshea@yahoo.com Web: www.grovehouseschull.com

Overlooking Schull Harbour, this beautifully restored period house offers quality accommodation just a few minutes walk from the main street. The approach is less than immaculate, but landscaping is beginning to mature and slight untidiness around the house is not typical of the interior, where housekeeping is exemplary. It is a pleasing house, and any period features have been retained in well-proportioned reception rooms and bedrooms, which are large, with individual character and well-finished shower rooms. A lovely dining room is used for breakfast - featuring local foods such as Gubbeen smoked bacon or Sally Barnes' smoked fish - and there's a panelled reading room as well as a guest sitting room. Not suitable for children. No pets. **Rooms 4** (all shower only, & no smoking); B&B €60, ss €15. Closed Nov-mid Mar. Amex, MasterCard, Visa, Laser. **Directions:** On right beyond C of I, Colla Road, 4 mins walk from village.

Schull

La Coquille - Restaurant Francais

RESTAURANT

Main Street Schull Co Cork **Tel: 028 28642**

Jean-Michel Cahier's little restaurant is situated in the main street, convenient to the harbour. Like the restaurant itself, the à la carte menu appears to have remained more or less the same since it opened, which is perhaps unsurprising as competently handled classics are the main feature. M. Cahier offers more red meats and poultry than most restaurants in the area as well as a wide range of seafood, but the menu in the window doesn't do it justice as there is also a blackboard brought promptly to the table with the day's specials - which extend the choices very considerably. Specials usually include a lot of seafood - possibly including lobster (from about €17 as a starter), prawns, scallops, oysters and a seafood platter (about €50, including half a lobster) as well as black sole, plaice and angler- but also local lamb, and less usual meats such as rabbit. Desserts, also classic, usually include tarte tatin, meringue suisse and, perhaps, a featherlight chocolate gateau. Simple presentation, accurate cooking and, for the most part, fair pricing make this an attractive dining option when in Schull - and a mixture of French and local staff provide quietly efficient, friendly service that contributes to a relaxing atmosphere. **Seats 35.** D 7-9.30. Opening hours can be erratic, a phone call to check would be wise, especially off-season. Amex, Diners, MasterCard, Visa. **Directions:** In the village, across from the church. ◇

Schull

Lasair Choille

B&B

Ardmanagh Schull Co Cork **Tel: 028 27982**
Email: venita@gofree.indigo.ie Web: www.lasair-choille.com

A mile or so outside Schull, at the foot of Mount Gabriel, Venita and David Galvin's guesthouse offers modern, clean-lined accommodation in an area of natural beauty. Moderately priced, with spruce en-suite bedrooms and hard floors throughout, it would make a good base for the many activity holidays in the area - walking (several short or long routes of 2-10 miles, also maps for serious hill walkers), horse riding, angling, diving, canoeing and so on. A large lounge has communal tea/coffee making facilities and television and packed lunches are available; also residents' dinner on request, based on local foods and organic produce from the garden. (€15). Children welcome (under 2s free in parents' room but no cot available). Small conferences (10). No pets. Garden. **Rooms 4** (all shower only) B&B €30 pps. Closed Sep-May. **No Credit Cards. Directions:** Turn right at bank on main street, then right at T. Junction.

Schull

Stanley House

B&B

Schull Co Cork **Tel: 028 28425** Fax: 028 27887
Email: stanleyhouse@eircom.net Web: www.stanley-house.net

Nancy Brosnan's modern guesthouse provides a west Cork home from home for her many returning guests. Compact bedrooms are comfortably furnished with tea/coffee making facilities and there's a pleasant conservatory running along the back of the house, with wonderful sea views over a field where guests can watch Nancy's growing herd of deer and sometimes see foxes come out to play at dusk. Good breakfasts too. Children welcome (under 3s free in parents' room, cots available without charge). No pets. **Rooms 4** (all shower only, all no-smoking). B&B €30 pps, ss €12.50. Closed 31 Oct-28 Feb. MasterCard, Visa. **Directions:** At top of main street, follow signs for Stanley House.

Schull

T J Newman's

ATMOSPHERIC PUB

Main Street Schull Co Cork **Tel: 028 27776**

Just up the hill from the harbour, this characterful and delightfully old-fashioned little pub has been a special home-from-home for regular visitors, especially sailors up from the harbour, as long as anyone can remember. The premises was sold in 2000 but, although Kitty Newman is missed, there is little obvious change - except that bar food is now offered, 12-6pm daily. Closed 25 Dec & Good Fri. MasterCard, Visa. **Directions:** Main West Cork route to Mizen Head.

Schull Area

Rock Cottage

Ⓝ COUNTRY HOUSE

Barnatonicane Schull Co Cork **Tel: 028 35538** Fax: 028 35538
Email: rockcottage@eircom.net Web: mizen.net/rockcottage

Barbara Klotzer's beautiful slate-clad Georgian hunting lodge near Schull is an absolute delight. Garden-lovers, especially, will thrill to the immediate surroundings which are on a south-facing slope away from the sea (at nearby Dunmanus Bay) and offer a fascinating combination of well-tended lawns and riotous flower beds, the rocky outcrop which inspired its name - and even great estate trees in the 17 acres of parkland (complete with peacefully grazing sheep) that have survived from an earlier period of its history. The main house has style and comfort, with welcoming open fires and bright bedrooms which - although not especially large - have been thoughtfully furnished to allow little seating areas as well as the usual amenities. Behind the house a walled courtyard creates a wonderfully sheltered feeling and very appealing self-catering accommodation is offered in converted stables. And, as if all this were not enough, Barbara is an accomplished chef - so dinner at Rock Cottage is an experience to savour; a set menu based on the best of local produce might include starters like fresh crab salad or warm Ardsallagh goats cheese, main courses of Rock Cottage's own rack of lamb, monkfish kebab, or even lobster or seafood platters (prices for these options on request) and classic desserts like home-baked vanilla cheesecake or bread and butter pudding. Breakfast options include a Healthy Breakfast and a Fish Breakfast as well as traditional Irish and continental combinations - just make your choice before 8pm the night before. Not suitable for children under 10. No pets. **Rooms 3** (2 with en-suite showers, 1 with private bathroom, all no smoking). B&B €45 pps, ss €15. Breakfast, 8.30-9.30 (order by 8pm the night before). Residents D Mon-Sat, €35, at 7.30; house wine €16. No D on Sun. Open all year. MasterCard, Visa. **Directions:** From Schull, 6 miles, at Toormore, turn into R591 after 1.5 miles. Sign on left.

Skibbereen

Kalbo's Bistro

RESTAURANT

48 North Street Skibbereen Co Cork **Tel: 028 21515**
Fax: 028 21515 Email: kalbo's@eircom.ie

Siobhan O'Callaghan and Anthony Boyle are doing a great job at this bright, buzzy town-centre restaurant. It's informal but there has always been an air of quality about it - staff are quick and helpful and Siobhan's simple food is wholesome and flavoursome in a light contemporary style - good soups, pastas, tarts, ciabattas, and salads at lunchtime and more serious dishes of local seafood, rack of lamb, steaks and so on in the evening. Home-made burgers come with a choice of toppings and vegetarian options are imaginative. The dishes are popular, but this is real food; consistently delicious, it is well-sourced, accurately cooked, appetisingly presented - and has real flavour. **Seats 42.** Open daily, L 12.30-3.30 (Sun 12.30-2.30), D daily, 6.30-9.30. A la carte; house wine €15.95, sc discretionary. Closed Christmas & Good Fri. Amex, MasterCard, Visa, Laser. **Directions:** In town centre.

Skibbereen

Ty Ar Mor Seafood Restaurant

RESTAURANT

46 Bridge Street Skibbereen Co Cork **Tel: 028 22100** Fax: 028 22834
Email: tyarmor@iol.ie Web: www.tyarmor.com

Chef-patron Michel Philippot and front-of-house manager Rosaleen O'Shea's delightful little Breton restaurant in the centre of Skibbereen has a lively atmosphere and gives an exceptionally high quality of ingredients, cooking and service - and all at very moderate prices. A limited choice Menu Touristique offers great value on weekdays (two excellent choices per course), while the Menu Gastronomique is a class act at €45, offering choices of eight starters and main courses within the menu price - and solitary supplements of just €6/€16.50 respectively for lobster starters and main courses. Begin, perhaps, with a traditional Breton fish soup or a crab bisque with rouille and croûtons, half a dozen Sherkin Island oysters with shallot sauce and lemon or Roaring Water Bay prawns mayonnaise. Outstanding main courses might include classics like black sole on the bone with lemon or garlic butter and grilled fillet of turbot beurre blanc alongside more contemporary renditions such as fillet of John Dory with lime & ginger and carnivorous dishes like chargrilled rack of spring lamb with grain mustard sauce or fillet steak sauce poivrade. And desserts will not disappoint: for those who crave it, gateau maison is made with chocolate and Grand Mariner, while other classics such as île flottante, pears poached in red wine & cinnamon or even a wonderful caramelised tarte tatin provide a memorable - and lighter - end to a magnificent meal. For those with the appetite to appreciate them, local cheeses are beautifully presented, French style, with a walnut salad. The value for money is exceptional and very professional service, from mostly French staff, matches the food: this place is a gem - and was our Seafood Restaurant of the Year in 2003. Not suitable for children under 12. **Seats 30** (Max table size, 10). D Wed-Sun 6.30-9.30 (Wed-Mon in Jul-Aug); closed Mon & Tue in winter, Tue only in summer (Jun-Sep) Set D from €33, Menu Gastronomique €45; s.c 10%. House wine from €18.50. *In 2003 **Thai@Ty Ar Mor** noodle and wine bar opened upstairs, serving absolutely delicious authentic Thai food for lunch (Mon-

Sat); it also operates as a wine bar for aperitifs from 6pm (same openings as the main restaurant downstairs), allowing seafood restaurant customers to relax in a Thai atmosphere. (Thai opening hours may be extended for 2004, to serve Thai food in the evening). Restaurant closed mid Oct-end Nov & 2 weeks Feb/Mar. MasterCard, Visa, Laser. **Directions:** Skibbereen town centre, towards road to Schull.

Skibbereen

West Cork Hotel

féile bia **HOTEL**

Ilen Street Skibbereen Co Cork **Tel: 028 21277** Fax: 028 22333
Email: info@westcorkhotel.com Web: www.westcorkhotel.com

John Murphy's welcoming family-run hotel enjoys a pleasant riverside site beside the bridge, on the western side of the town, and recent refurbishment has been completed with style. The entrance is quite small, but the hotel opens up behind the foyer, to reveal a bright and airy bar along the river side of the hotel, and a pleasant modern restaurant, where breakfast is served to residents, as well as main meals. Bedrooms are not especially large, but they are comfortably furnished in a gently contemporary style and have all the necessary amenities (phone, tea/coffee tray, TV) and neat, well-designed en-suite bathrooms - this would make a good base from which to explore this beautiful area. Rooms at the back are quieter and have a pleasant outlook over trees and river. Conference/banqueting (250). Children welcome (under 4 free in parents' room, cot available without charge, baby sitting arranged). Pets permitted by arrangement. Garden. Private parking. **Rooms 30** (3 suites, 4 junior suites, 23 superior rooms, 6 shower only). B&B €85, ss €5. Food available in restaurant and bar: 12.30-2.30 & 6-9.315. Closed 22-28 Dec. Amex, Diners, MasterCard, Visa, Laser, Switch. **Directions:** Follow signs N71 to Bantry through Skibbereen.

Timoleague

Dillon's

RESTAURANT

Mill Street Timoleague Co Cork **Tel: 023 46390**

On the main road to West Cork, Dillons was one of the first café-bars and has always laid the emphasis on good food. Although still very much involved, times have changed since Isabelle Dillon did all of the cooking herself - she now has a chef to help her, so you may be less likely to find dishes inspired by her native Brittany than creative international food, on menus that change daily. A la carte. Open daily in summer, 6.30-9.30; closed Mon in Oct; closed Mon & Tue, Nov-17 Mar. No bookings. **No Credit Cards. Directions:** On main street of village. On M71. ◇

Union Hall

Casey's

PUB / B&B

Union Hall Co Cork **Tel: 028 33590**
Email: caseysbar@tinet.ie Web: htt://web.ukonline.co.ukcaseybar

This friendly traditional family-run pub has the best location in Union Hall, by far, with a walled outside seating area on the sea side of the building for the better enjoyment of Martha Casey's homely food on fine days. Seafood is the speciality here, available seven days a week for six months a year. No food in winter. B&B also available; fishing holidays are a speciality. Closed 25 Dec-6 Jan. ◇

Union Hall

Shearwater

B&B

Keelbeg Pier Union Hall Co Cork **Tel: 028 33178**
Fax: 028 34020 Email: shearwater@esatclear.ie

Adela Nugent's B&B is located close to Keelbeg pier, on an elevated site overlooking Glandore harbour and the surrounding countryside. All bedrooms are good-sized and comfortably furnished with en-suite facilities (only one with bath); most rooms overlook the harbour. The breakfast room and TV room also have views, and there's a patio for guests' use in fine weather. Children welcome. No pets. **Rooms 4** (3 shower only; all no smoking). B&B about €35pps, ss about €15. Closed 31 Oct-1 Apr. Amex, Diners, MasterCard, Visa. **Directions:** Off N71 between Clonakilty and Skibbereen. ◇

Youghal

Aherne's Seafood Restaurant & Accommodation

RESTAURANT WITH ROOMS

163 North Main Street Youghal Co Cork
Tel: 024 92424 Fax: 024 93633
Email: ahernes@eircom.net Web: www.ahernes.com

Now in its third generation of family ownership, one of the most remarkable features of Aherne's is the warmth of the FitzGibbon family's hospitality and their enormous enthusiasm for the business which, since 1993, has included seriously luxurious accommodation. It is for its food - and, especially, the ultra-fresh seafood that comes straight from the fishing boats in Youghal harbour - that Aherne's is best known, however. While John FitzGibbon supervises the front of house, his brother David reigns over a busy kitchen. Bar food tends pleasingly towards simplicity - oysters, chowder, smoked salmon (all served with the renowned moist dark brown yeast bread) - its sheer freshness tells the story. Restaurant meals are naturally more ambitious and include some token meat dishes - rack of lamb with a rosemary jus or mint sauce, char-grilled fillet steak with mushrooms and shallot jus or pepper sauce - although seafood is still the undisputed star of the show and David is not afraid of simplicity when it is merited. Specialities like prawns cooked in garlic butter or fresh crab salad can make memorable starters, for example, and hot buttered Youghal Bay lobster are all, in a sense, simple dishes yet they have plenty of glamour too. A wine list strong on classic French regions offers a fair selection of half bottles and half a dozen champagnes. **Seats 60** (private room, 20). Toilets wheelchair accessible. D 6.30-9.30 daily; set D €30-42; also à la carte; house wine €18.50, sc discretionary. *Bar food daily, 12-10. **Rooms:** The stylish rooms at Aherne's are generously sized and individually decorated to a very high standard; all are furnished with antiques and have luxurious, beautifully finished bathrooms. Housekeeping is exemplary and excellent breakfasts are served in a warm and elegantly furnished residents' dining room. Rooms more recently added are equipped to give the option of self-catering if required. Conference room (25); banqueting (75). Safe & fax available at reception. Children under 5 free in parents' room (cot available without charge, baby sitting arranged). No pets. **Rooms 13** (5 junior suites, 3 for disabled). B&B €90 pps, ss €20. Wheelchair access. Closed 23-29 Dec. Amex, Diners, MasterCard, Visa, Laser. **Directions:** on N25, main route from Cork-Waterford.

Youghal

Ballymakeigh House

FARMHOUSE / COUNTRY HOUSE

Killeagh Youghal Co Cork
Tel: 024 95184 Fax: 024 95370
Email: ballymakeigh@eircom.net Web: www.ballymakeighhouse.ie

Winner of our Farmhouse of the Year Award in 1999, Ballymakeigh House provides a high standard of comfort, food and hospitality in one of the most outstanding establishments of its type in Ireland. Set at the heart of an east Cork dairy farm, this attractive old house is immaculately maintained and run by Margaret Browne, who is a Euro-Toques chef and author of a successful cookery book. The house is warm and homely with plenty of space for guests, who are welcome to use the garden and visit the farmyard. The individually decorated bedrooms are full of character and equally comfortable and Margaret's hospitality is matched only by her energetic pursuit of excellence - ongoing improvements and developments are a constant characteristic of Ballymakeigh. Margaret Browne has a national reputation for her cooking; an impressive dinner menu is offered every night, and non-residents are very welcome in the restaurant. Garden, tennis, walking. Off-season value breaks, special interest breaks. Children welcome (under 3 free in parents' room, cot available, baby sitting arranged). Pets allowed in some areas. **Rooms 5** (all en-suite & no smoking, 3 shower only). B&B €50 pps, ss €10. D daily, 7-9, non-residents welcome by reservation; Set D €35 & €40; house wine from €20; SC discretionary. House closed 1 Nov-1 Feb. MasterCard, Visa. **Directions:** Off N25 between Youghal & Killeagh (signed at Old Thatch pub).

Youghal

Glenally House

Ⓝ COUNTRY HOUSE

Copperalley Youghal Co Cork **Tel: 024 91623** Fax: 024 91623
Email: enquiries@glenally.com Web: www.glenally.com

Situated on seven acres in a tranquil rural setting with its own productive walled kitchen garden, Glenally House dates back to 1828 and has been stylishly restored by the current owners, Fred and

Herta Rigney. A classical layout allows for a large drawing room and dining room on either side of the hall, and many period features have been retained as a backdrop for individualistic contemporary decor - all done by the owners themselves. It's a labour of love for the Rigneys, who have created for guests the kind of place they would like to stay in themselves, and emphasise that guests are free to use the house and gardens at any time of day. Large, airy bedrooms painted in soft pastels have very comfortable beds, tea/coffee-making facilities, TV and views of the gardens and surrounding countryside; three of the well-appointed bathrooms are en-suite, and the fourth bedroom has a private bathroom on the landing. The gardens, paddocks and wild areas around the house provide a constant supply of flowers and foliage for the house and, as members of the Slow Food movement, the Rigneys believe in sourcing local produce where possible for both breakfast and dinner, which is available by prior arrangement - preferences are discussed at the time of booking. [The house is not signed as the Rigneys wish to create a relaxed country house atmosphere, but this does make it quite difficult to find - approaching Youghal from the Waterford side, turn left at the first roundabout; follow signs for St Martins B&B, which is located nearby, then ask for directions. However, although it feels delightfully remote, it is actually within walking distance of the town centre.] Not suitable for children under 12. Pets allowed by arrangement. No smoking establishment. **Rooms 4** (3 en-suite, 1 private bathroom; 3 shower only). B&B €60, ss €15. Residents D, by arrangement, €40, at 8pm. Closed mid Dec-1 Mar. MasterCard, Visa. **Directions:** Just off N25, east of the town (Waterford side).

Youghal

Old Imperial Hotel with Coachhouse, Bar & Restaurant

HOTEL / PUB

27 North Main Street Youghal Co Cork
Tel: 024 92435 Fax: 024 90268
Email: theoldimperialhotel@eircom.net Web: www.theoldimperialhotel.com

James and Mary Browne's new hotel presents an attractive, sprucely-painted face to the world. There's a separate entrance to the hotel off the street, but it would be a pity to miss the downstairs bar, which incorporates the wonderful old-world bar previously known as D. McCarthy ("A lovely little low-ceilinged bar of great character with an open fire and a long history to tell...") as well as the newer and much larger Coachman's Bar, where bar meals are served: lack of a staff uniform may create a bad impression here, but waiting staff are friendly and helpful - and, in the Guide's experience, the quality of the food is excellent. The limitations of the site have resulted in a shortage of space in the hotel, which is on three rather steep floors, with no space for a lift or a residents' sitting room/separate reception area for the first-floor restaurant (where breakfast is also served). Bedrooms also tend to be on the small side, although there are two quite impressive junior suites and all rooms are furnished and fitted to a high standard with all the usual amenities including a trouser press with steam iron. **Rooms 18.** B&B €65pps, ss €10.

Restaurant: Menus show individuality and an impressive freshness of approach; a choice of eight or nine courses will include several dishes featuring local seafood well-balanced by a fair selection of meats and poultry - and at least one imaginative vegetarian dish. Carefully sourced ingredients, accurate cooking and simple, attractive presentation make for a pleasant dining experience. Service is friendly. Private parking. **Seats 40.** Air conditioning. D daily, 6.15-9.15. * Bar meals served daily, 12.30-9; L12.30-3.30 (Sat 1-2.30); D 6.30-9 [Times not confirmed at time of going to press.]. Diners, MasterCard, Visa, Laser. **Directions:** On the N25 - 30 miles from Cork Airport. ◇

COUNTY DONEGAL

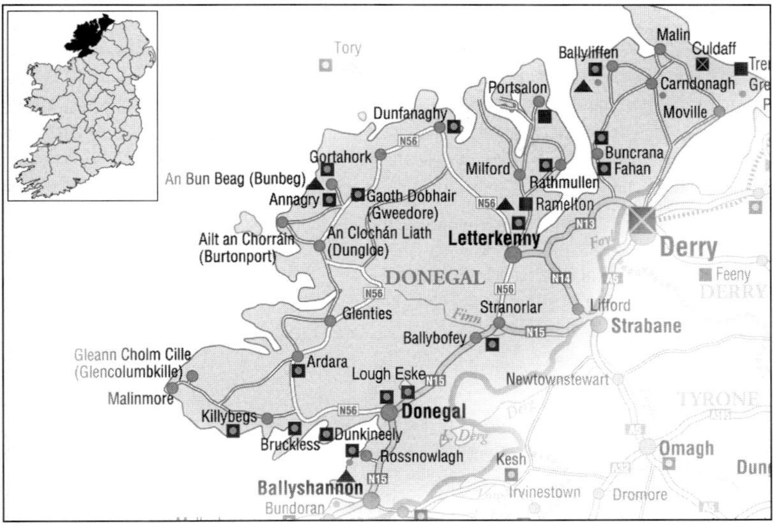

Golden eagles are no flight of fancy in Donegal. The spectacular Glenveagh National Park in the northern part of the county has been selected for the re-introduction of the golden eagle to Ireland. Last seen here in 1912, the first six Scottish-born chicks of the new wave were released at Glenveagh in June 2001. Over a five year period, 50 birds are being released, and there are high expectations of success for the programme. The initial arrivals are now almost mature, soaring over the valley, and it is just possible that the first native born offspring will appear in 2004, though 2005 is more likely.

Travel at sea level is also an increasingly significant element in visits to Donegal, one of Ireland's most spectacularly beautiful countries. It is much-indented by the sea, but the introduction of car ferry services is shortening journeys and adding interest. The new ferry between Greencastle and Magilligan across the narrow entrance to Lough Foyle has been very popular since starting in June 2002, and eventually another car ferry - between Buncrana and Rathmullan across Lough Swilly – will add to the travel options.

For many folk, particularly those from Northern Ireland, Donegal is the holiday county par excellence. But in recent years, despite the international fluctuations of trading conditions, there has been growth of modern industries and the re-structuring of the fishing, particularly at the developing harbour of Killybegs, home port of the world's largest fishing vessel, the Atlantic Dawn. This entrepreneurial spirit has led to a more balanced economy, with the pace being set by the county town of Letterkenny, where the population has increased by 50% since 1991.

But much and all as Donegal county is increasingly a place where people live and make a living, nevertheless it is still a place of nature on the grand scale, a place assaulted by the winds and weather of the Atlantic Ocean if given the slighest chance. Yet at communities like Bundoran and Rossnowlagh, where splendid beaches face straight into the Atlantic, enthusiastic surfers have demonstrated that even the most demanding weather can have its sporting uses.

For most folk, however, it is the contrast between raw nature and homely comfort which is central to Donegal's enduring attraction. For here, in some of Ireland's most rugged territory, you will find many sheltered and hospitable places whose amenities are emphasised by the challenging nature of their broader environment. And needless to say, that environment is simply startlingly utterly beautiful as well.

Local Attractions and Information

Arranmore Ferry, Burtonport-Arranmore 074 952 0532
Ballintra, Ballymagroarty Heritage Centre 074 973 4966
Buncrana, National Knitting Centre 074 936 2355
Bundoran, Tourism Information 071 984 1350
Burt, Grianan of Aileach Centre 074 936 8512

Churchill, Glebe House & Gallery (Derek Hill) 074 913 7071
Donegal Airport, Carrickfin 074 954 8232
Donegal Highlands, Hillwalking/Irish lang.(adults).. 074 973 0248
Donegal town, Donegal Castle 074 972 2405
Donegal town, Tourism information 074 972 1148
Donegal town, Waterbus Cruises 074 972 1148
Dunfanaghy, Workhouse Visitor Centre 074 913 6504
Dungloe, Mary from Dungloe Int. Festival (July/August)
Dungloe, Tourism Information 074 952 1297
Glencolumbcille, Folk Museum 074 973 0017
Glencolumbcille, Tourism Information 074 973 0017
Glenties, Patrick Mac Gill Summer School (August)
Glenveagh National Park (Castle, gardens, parkland) 074 913 7088
Greencastle, Lough Foyle Ferry 074 938 1901
Greencastle, Maritime Museum 074 938 1363
Inishowen, Inishowen Tourism (Carndonagh) 074 937 4933
Letterkenny, An Grianan Theatre 074 912 0777
Letterkenny, Arts Centre 074 912 9186
Letterkenny, County Museum 074 912 4613
Letterkenny, Newmills watermill 074 912 5115
Letterkenny, North West Tourism 074 912 1160
Lifford, Cavanacor Historic House 074 914 1143
Tory Island Ferry 074 953 1320

Annagry

Danny Minnie's Restaurant

RESTAURANT WITH ROOMS Annagry Co Donegal **Tel: 074 954 8201** Fax: 074 954 8880

The O'Donnell family has run Danny Minnie's since 1962, and a visit is always a special treat. There's nothing about the exterior as seen from the road to prepare first-time visitors for the atmosphere of this remarkable restaurant: hidden behind a frontage of overgrown creepers a surprise awaits when, after a warm welcome from Terri O'Donnell, guests are suddenly surrounded by antiques and elegantly appointed candle-lit tables. The menu is presented in both Irish and English and Brian O'Donnell's cooking is a good match for the surroundings - fine, with imaginative saucing, but not at all pompous. On a wide-ranging à la carte menu, seafood stars in the main courses - lobster and other shellfish, availability permitting - and there is also a strong selection of meats including Donegal mountain lamb, typically served with honey, garlic and rosemary gravy and Donegal beef, served various ways including classic Beef Wellington. Vegetables are a strength and gorgeous desserts such as crêpes suzette with orange and Grand Marnier can be relied on to create an appropriately dramatic finale. Under Terri's direction, helpful service from attentive waitresses is another bonus. There's nowhere quite like Danny Minnie', our winner of the Guide's Atmospheric Restaurant of the Year in 2000. Not suitable for children after 8pm. Reservations required. **Seats 80.** Air conditioning. D daily in summer, 6.30-9.30. A la carte, house wine €17; sc10%. (Phone ahead to check opening hours, especially off peak season) Closed Christmas & Sun/Mon off season. [Accommodation is also offered in eight non-smoking rooms, five of them en-suite and one suitable for disabled guests]. MasterCard, Visa, Laser. **Directions:** R259 off N56 follow Airport signs.

Ardara

The Green Gate

B&B Ardvally Ardara Co Donegal **Tel: 074 954 1546**

Paul Chatenoud's amazing little B&B is a one-off. Above Adara, up a steep and twisting boreen (follow his unique signing system) that will reward you with a stunning view on arrival, Paul offers simple but comfortable accommodation in his unspoilt traditional cottage and converted outbuildings. It's a far cry from the Parisian bookshop he once ran, but this little place is magic. In the morning (or whenever you wake up - he will be working around his lovely garden and is happy to stop at any time it suits his guests), he cooks up breakfast while you take in the laid-back homeliness of his cosy cottage sitting room. If the morning is fine he may serve breakfast in the garden (just where is that beautiful music coming from?) while he regales you with stories of famous people who have fallen in love with The Green Gate. Just be glad you found it, because he's probably right - it may well be "the most beautifu place anywhere in Ireland". Just leave the Merc at home - and come with an open mind. Children welcome (Under 10s free in parents' room, cot available). Pets permitted. **Rooms 4** (all with en-suite bathrooms). B&B €30pps, ss €15. Open all year. **Directions:** One mile on the hill from Ardara.

Ardara

Nancy's

PUB

Front Street Ardara Co Donegal **Tel: 074 954 1187**

This famous pub, in the village renowned for its tweeds and handknits, is a cosy, welcoming place in its seventh generation of family ownership, with five or six small rooms packed with bric à brac and plenty of tables and chairs for the comfortable consumption of wholesome home-made food, especially seafood. Famous for their chowder - maybe try it with a "Louis Armstrong" (smoked salmon on brown bread topped with grilled cheese) and finish with an Irish coffee. Or there's "Charlie's Supper", a speciality of prawns and smoked salmon warmed in a chilli & garlic sauce. Live music too. Bar food served daily 12-9, from Easter to September. Wheelchair access. Closed 25 Dec & Good Fri. **No Credit Cards. Directions:** In Ardara village; half an hour's drive from Donegal Town.

Ardara

Woodhill House

GUESTHOUSE / BAR

Woodhill Ardara Co Donegal
Tel: 074 954 1112 Fax: 074 954 1516
Email: yates@iol.ie Web: www.woodhillhouse.com

Formerly the home of Ireland's last commercial whaling family, John and Nancy Yates' large country house is set in its own grounds overlooking the Donegal Highlands and the hard restoration work they have put in over more than fifteen years is now bearing fruit. This hospitable house has a full bar where light lunches are served and unusual accommodation in the main house and nearby converted outbuildings - rooms are all en-suite but vary greatly in position, size and character so it is worth spending a few minutes discussing your preferences when booking. There's also a restaurant (booking recommended as it's very popular locally) offering quite traditional food based on local ingredients at reasonable prices: specialities include oysters, Donegal mountain lamb, duck off the bone and carrageen pudding. Gradually restoring the garden is perhaps Nancy's greatest challenge and it's turning out beautifully, not only on the kitchen garden side but as a pleasure garden too. Renovations, on both the main house and some fine outbuildings, continue on an ongoing basis. Small conferences (20). Children welcome (free in parents' room up to 6, cot available without charge). Pets permitted by arrangement. **Rooms 9** (6 shower-only). B&B €55 pps, ss €30. Restaurant: **Seats 40** (private room, 15). No smoking area. Children welcome. Reservations required. D 6.30-10 daily, Set D €38, house wine €16.50; sc discretionary. * Bar lunch available 1-3 pm daily (a phone call ahead is advised). House closed 24-27 Dec. Amex, Diners, MasterCard, Visa, Laser. **Directions:** 1/4 mile from Ardara town.

Ballybofey

Jackson's Hotel

HOTEL

Ballybofey Co Donegal **Tel: 074 913 1021** Fax: 074 913 1096
Email: bjackson@iol.ie Web: www.jacksons-hotel.ie

Although it has a town centre location, this attractive family-run hotel is set in its own gardens and enjoys a tranquil position alongside the River Finn. The spacious, elegantly furnished foyer (with open fire) creates a good first impression and this is followed through in other public areas including the restaurant, which overlooks the garden. Bedrooms, all recently refurbished to a high standard, are very comfortable with direct-dial phones, tea/coffee trays and TV with video channel, and the best have river views. Conference/banqueting (400/800); business centre, ISDN lines, secretarial services. Leisure centre (22m pool). Children welcome (under 2 free in parents' room, cots available, baby sitting arranged, playroom). Bank Holiday and other special breaks throughout the year offer particularly good value. Horse-riding, golf, fishing and bike hire all nearby. Pets permitted in some areas. Garden. *Food available all day at the Ballybuffet self-service bistro/restaurant (9am-11pm); Garden Restaurant open for dinner. **Rooms 89** (2 suites, 5 executive rooms, 2 disabled).Wheelchair access. Lift. B&B €70 pps, ss €19. Open all year. MasterCard, Visa. **Directions:** Beside the river, in the centre of town.

Ballybofey

Kee's Hotel

HOTEL / RESTAURANT

Stranorlar Ballybofey Co Donegal
Tel: 074 913 1018 Fax: 074 913 1917
Email: info@keeshotel.ie Web: www.keeshotel.ie

This centrally located, all-year hotel has an unusually long line of continuous family ownership, having been in the Kee family since 1892. Public areas have recently undergone radical renovations, including a new foyer, meeting rooms and a lift. Bedrooms are regularly refurbished and have good bathrooms;

those at the back of the hotel, with views of the Blue Stack Mountains, are most desirable and avoid the problems caused by through traffic which may be disturbing at the front. Residents have direct access from the hotel to the excellent leisure facilities. Golf and fishing nearby. Conference/banqueting (150/250). Children welcome, under 3 free in their parents' room; cots and high chairs available, baby sitting arranged. Special breaks offered by the hotel include golfing holidays and a novel "Post Christmas Recovery Break". **Rooms 53** (1 junior suite, 30 executive rooms,1 for disabled). Lift. Limited room service. B&B €80 pps, ss €15. Closed 24-26 Dec.

The Looking Glass: Good food has been a particular attraction at Kee's for some years and Frank Pasquier, who has been head chef since 2001, is continuing the tradition in both the informal Old Gallery bistro, and the fine dining Looking Glass Restaurant, which is decorated with hand-worked tapestries made by Arthur Kee's mother. It's a pleasant warm-toned restaurant in two areas, with plenty of alcoves for privacy - a comfortable setting for Frank Pasquier's balanced menus, which change daily. The best of local produce is presented with a French accent in starters like fresh grilled langoustine (Dublin Bay prawns), with armagnac and garlic butter and main courses like best end of Donegal lamb with truffle mash potato, provençal garnish & rosemary jus. Vegetarian dishes are available on request (mention any special requirements when booking). Classic desserts might include warm dark chocolate fondant with crème anglaise and cheese is served with a tossed salad. Children welcome. Toilets wheelchair accessible. **Seats 75** (private room, 60). D 6.30-9.30 daily, L Sun only, 12.30-2.30, Set Sun L €20; Set D €38; house wine €17. SC discretionary. [Informal meals served in the Old Gallery, 12.30-3 and 5.30-9.30 daily.] Amex, Diners, MasterCard, Visa, Laser. **Directions:** On the Main Street in the village of Stranorlar.

Ballyliffin

Rossaor House

B&B

Ballyliffin Inishowen Co Donegal **Tel: 074 937 6498** Fax: 074 937 6498
Email: rossaor@gofree.indigo.ie Web: www.ballyliffin.com/rossaor.htm

Brian and Anne Harkin's very pleasant and hospitable house is in a beautiful area that deserves to be better known and it has amazing views down over two golf courses to Pollen Strand and Malin Head. Bedrooms are furnished to a high standard (generous beds, direct dial phone, tea/coffee facilities and TV) and personally decorated by Anne herself. Spacious, comfortably furnished public rooms include a large sitting room, which takes full advantage of the view, and a conservatory (considerately situated overlooking the lovely front garden and away from the full blast of morning sunshine) where excellent breakfasts are served with commendable efficiency. There is also self-catering accommodation on the property - details from the Harkins. Children welcome (cot available). No pets. **Rooms 4** (all en-suite). B&B €40pps, ss €10. Closed 1 Dec-14 Jan. MasterCard, Visa. **Directions:** Take signs to Buncrana, to Clonmany to Ballyliffin (R238).

Bruckless

Bruckless House

FARMHOUSE

Bruckless Co Donegal **Tel: 074 913 7071** Fax: 074 913 7070
Email: bruc@bruckless.com Web: www.iol.ie/~bruc/bruckless.html

Clive and Joan Evans' lovely 18th-century house and Connemara pony stud farm is set in 18 acres of woodland and gardens overlooking Bruckless Bay - an ideal place for people who enjoy quiet countryside and pursuits like walking, horse-riding and fishing. The gardens are not too formal but beautifully designed, extensive and well-maintained - they really enhance a visit here, as does the sea: guests have direct access to the foreshore at the bottom of the garden. Family furniture collected through a Hong Kong connection add an unexpected dimension to the elegant reception rooms and generous, comfortably furnished bedrooms. Bedrooms include two single rooms and there is a shared bathroom. No pets. **Rooms 4** (2 en-suite, all no-smoking) B&B €50pps, no ss. Weekly rates also offered. * A two-bedroom Gate Lodge, sleeping four, is available for self-catering. Closed 1 Oct-31 Mar. Amex, MasterCard, Visa. **Directions:** On N56, 12 miles west of Donegal.

Bunbeg

Ostan Gweedore

HOTEL

Bunbeg Co Donegal **Tel: 074 953 1177** Fax: 074 953 1726
Email: reservations@ostangweedore.com Web: www.ostangweedore.com

Although its blocky 1970's architectural style may not be to today's taste, Ostan Gweedore was built to make the most of the location - and this it does very well. Spacious public areas, including the recently refurbished restaurant and the Library Bar ("the most westerly reading room on the Atlantic seaboard") have superb views over the shoreline and Mount Errigal - as do most of the bedrooms (and three suites), all of which are comfortable if a little dated. It's ideal for families, with its wonderful beach and outdoor activities, including tennis, pitch & putt and day visits to nearby Tory Island. Wet days are looked after too, with indoor leisure facilities, including a 19-metre swimming pool, jacuzzi and gym, all supervised by qualified staff. A new Beauty & Body clinic was due to open as the Guide went to press.

This romantic setting is predictably popular for weddings (conferences/banqueting 200/300). Fishing and golf (9 hole) available locally. Under 4s free in parents' room (cot available without charge, baby sitting arranged). No pets. * Donegal Airport, Carrickfin is nearby. **Rooms 36** (3 suites). B&B €85 pps, ss €10. Closed 4 Nov-14 Feb. Amex, MasterCard, Visa, Laser. **Directions:** From Letterkenny, take coast road past hospital.

Bundoran

Brennans

ATMOSPHERIC PUB

Criterion Bar Main Street Bundoran Co Donegal
Tel: 071 984 1810

The discerning drinker visiting this part of the country should make a point of calling in at this delightful pub in the centre of Bundoran town - it's as fine an unspoilt Irish pub as you'll find anywhere in the country: "no television, just conversation". Friendly, welcoming, just 'itself': magic. Closed 25 Dec & Good Fri. **Directions:** Town centre.

Bundoran

Le Chateaubrianne

RESTAURANT

Sligo Road Bundoran Co Donegal **Tel: 071 984 2160** Fax: 071 984 2160

Brian and Anne Loughlin celebrated a decade at this welcoming and very professionally run establishment in 2003 and it remains the leading restaurant in the area. The approach is pristine, creating positive first impressions which are confirmed by a warm welcome from Anne and the offer of aperitifs in a comfortable reception room/bar where you can take time to consider the menu. Brian is a Euro-Toques chef and a strong supporter of local produce; the cooking style is classic French with modern Irish and international overtones and his imaginative dinner menus are considerately offered as a two- or three-course meal. The half dozen or so choices on each course are well-balanced with some long-term specialities included and local seafood well represented (crab and prawn profiteroles are a speciality starter), also game in season, and interesting vegetarian options such as a wild mushroom risotto. In the restaurant, which is quite traditional, lovely freshly-baked breads set the tone for sound, quite classical, cooking with some contemporary twists; a successful dish of baked collops of monkfish with a herb crumb coating, for example, is served on a bacon mash, with a grain mustard sauce, while rack of lamb has a mint crust and comes with rösti, with a port & orange sauce. Side vegetables, while perhaps a little dated, are served pleasingly crunchy. Sunday lunch provides something for everyone by offering a well-judged combination of traditional roasts and more adventurous fare; the same high standard of cooking applies and the meal will be nicely finished off with coffee and petits fours. **Seats 56** (private room, 20). D Tue-Sat 6.30-9.30, L Sun only 12.30-3, Set Sun L €25, Set D €33/39; house wine about €18; sc discretionary. Closed Mon, Christmas, 3 wks Jan & bank hols. Amex, MasterCard, Visa. **Directions:** On left entering Bundoran from Sligo. ◇

BURTONPORT

BURTONPORT (Ailt an Chorrain) is a small fishing port and sea angling centre in The Rosses, renowned for its catches of salmon, lobster and crab in the summer months - fresh seafood which (along with many other varieties) finds its way onto menus in family-run pubs such as **Skippers Tavern (074 954 2234)** and **The Lobster Pot (074 954 2012)** both of which have a national reputation for fresh home-cooked food and warm hospitality.

Carndonagh

Corncrake Restaurant

RESTAURANT

Millbrae Carndonagh Co Donegal **Tel: 074 937 4534**

Brid McCartney and Noreen Lynch made a decision to live and work in this lovely (and, so far, unspoilt) part of the country some years ago, when they established the original Corncrake in its old 'downtown' premises. It became one of the hottest addresses in Donegal for food lovers, not least because of the off-season residential cookery courses they have run for some years at the restaurant, together with Rossaor House (see entry) who provide the accommodation element. A recent move to larger premises on the edge of the town has allowed for a dedicated reception area as well as more spacious dining - and will enable them to run the cookery courses with greater comfort and, perhaps, slightly larger numbers. Meanwhile, they continue to relish the area and take pleasure in its produce - typically in a speciality starter of twice-baked fresh crab soufflé, main courses (about €17-23) like roast rack of Donegal lamb with rosemary & redcurrant gravy or one of several seafood dishes - roast loin of monkfish in a light Thai curry sauce with pilau rice, perhaps. Vegetarian dishes are available on request (mention when booking your table). This is an hospitable house and Brid's cooking is a delight, having that elusive home-made quality that is so rarely encountered in restaurants - and Noreen supervises the service with quiet efficiency. Not suitable for children after 7.30 pm. **Seats 28.** D Tue-Sat from June-October (Fri & Sat off season), 6-9 (approx); à la carte; house wine €15; sc discretionary. Closed Mon

& Tue, in summer (Sun-Thu, off season); establishment closed Christmas-17 Mar. **No Credit Cards.** **Directions:** On the Derry road as you enter the town.

Clonmany

Glen House

B&B

Straid Clonmany Co Donegal **Tel: 074 937 6745**

Doris Russo's charming period house is beautifully located with an ocean view and would make a most comfortable and hospitable base for any of the many activities this lovely area offers - including visiting the nearby waterfall, which has recently been opened to the public. Rooms are appealing decorated in a genuinely country style which will take many guests back to their childhood. Several hill walks start at Glen House and there are plans to establish a major centre nearby as a base for walkers in the region as a whole. There is also a beach and two golf courses nearby, while festivals in June, July and August highlight music and culture of the area. No dinner, but Ballyliffin is not far away and guests also like The Rusty Nail pub, nearby at Clonmany. (Children welcome (under 5s free in parents' room, cot available without charge). **Rooms 3** (2 en-suite & shower only, all no smoking). B&B about €30, ss 10. Open all year. Visa, MasterCard. **Directions:** From Derry NI, A2 to Buncrana, right sign to Clonmany. Through village, left over bridge, signed to house; half mile. ◇

Culdaff

McGrory's of Culdaff

féile bia **PUB / GUESTHOUSE**

Culdaff Inishowen Co Donegal
Tel: 074 937 9104 Fax: 074 937 9235
Email: mcgr@eircom.net Web: www.mcgrorys.ie

In an area that has so much to offer, in terms of natural beauty and activities like golf, angling and walking, McGrory's would make an ideal base. An inn in the true sense of the word, offering rest and refreshment to travellers, this north-western institution was established in 1924 and remains in the active care of the McGrory family, who set great store by the traditions of hospitality and personal care while also keeping an eye on changing tastes and the requirements of a fast-moving society. Having recently undergone a major makeover, it is now a pleasing combination of old and new which is easy on the eye and includes a new restaurant as well as an overhaul of the whole premises. Comfortable bedrooms vary in size and outlook but are attractively furnished in a classic contemporary style that is both practical and appropriate; all have well-planned bathrooms and all the necessary amenities (phone, tea/coffee tray, TV), although their popularity has been seen in minor signs of wear and tear on recent visits. For anyone touring the Inishowen peninsula this is a logical place to take a break, as popular bar food is available throughout the day. But it is probably for music that McGrory's is most famous - as well as traditional sessions in The Front Bar on Tuesday and Friday nights, Mac's Backroom Bar (constructed on the site of the old outhouses of McGrory's shop) is a major venue for live shows featuring international names. (Live music Wednesday and Saturday; events listings on the web.) Conference/banqueting (40/100). Special interest/off season breaks offered. **Rooms 10** (all en-suite, 4 shower only). Children welcome (under 12 free in parents' room; cot available free of charge, baby sitting arranged). No pets. B&B €50, ss €10. Restaurant: D Tue-Sun, L Sun. Bar meals daily, 12.30-8. Restaurant closed Mon (also Tue in winter); establishment closed 23-27 Dec. Amex, MasterCard, Visa, Laser. **Directions:** On R238 around Inishowen Peninsula.

DONEGAL TOWN

Donegal Town was originally a plantation town and is now best known as the main centre for the tweed industry and crafts. A visit to the area would be unthinkable without calling into **Magee's on The Diamond** where there are hand loom weaving demonstrations; wholesome fare is avilable at the in-store restaurant, and also **The Blueberry Tea Room,** just off The Diamond, on Castle Street. **The Craft Village,** on the edge of the town, is well worth a visit and there's a very nice little coffee shop, **Aroma,** serving good home cooking, notably baking.

Donegal

St. Ernan's House Hotel

HOTEL

Donegal Co Donegal **Tel: 074 972 1065** Fax: 074 972 2098
Email: info@sainternans.com Web: www.sainternans.com

Set on its own wooded island connected to the mainland by a causeway, tranquillity is the main characteristic of Brian and Carmel O'Dowd's unique country house hotel. Spacious public rooms have log fires and antique furniture and, while they vary in size and outlook, the individually decorated bedrooms are furnished to a high standard and have good amenities including (surprisingly perhaps) television, while most also have lovely views. Room service (limited hours). Children under 6 not catered for. No pets. Garden. **Rooms 10** (2 suites; 1 shower only) B&B €135pps.

Restaurant: The dining room is mainly for resident guests, but non-residents are welcome by reservation if there is room. Daily 5-course country house-style dinner menus based on local produce; vegetarian dishes on request. **Seats 2.** D 6-8 daily, D from about €25 (semi-à la carte, priced by course); house wine €23. Closed end Oct-Easter. MasterCard, Visa, **Directions:** 1.5 mile south of Donegal Town.

Dunfanaghy

The Mill Restaurant

RESTAURANT / B&B

Figart Dunfanaghy Co Donegal
Tel: 074 913 6985 Fax: 074 913 6985
Email: themillrestaurant@oceanfree.net Web: www.themillrestaurant.com

Beautifully located on the shore of the New Lake, which is a special area of conservation, the mill was the home of Susan Alcorn's grandfather and, as they are a family of accomplished painters, the walls are hung with wonderful water colours. Susan and her husband Derek, who is the chef, have earned a dedicated following here, as the location is superb, the welcome warm and the cooking both imaginative and assured. The dining room is on two levels, with plenty of windows framing the views, fresh flowers on the tables, soft lighting and some well-placed antiques - a room of character and atmosphere. Menus are based firmly on the best ingredients, local where possible, and change every 4-6 weeks. While based on the classics, the house style is quite contemporary: purée of aubergine & coconut soup is unusual, while roast rack of new season lamb with dauphinoise potatoes & rosemary makes the most of a classic combination. Delicious desserts might include a seasonal rhubarb crumble tart with custard & ginger ice cream, or there's a good Irish cheese plate. (Lovely breakfasts too.) No-smoking restaurant; air conditioning. Children welcome. **Seats 46.** D Tue-Sat 7-9pm, Set D €35; house wine €14; sc discretionary. Closed Mon; mid-week Nov-Dec; all Jan-Feb).

Accommodation is offered in six individually decorated rooms, which have opened gradually as they have been finished. The decor is simple but stylish, with good new beds and some antique pieces, and there's also a lovely little sitting room off the dining room, with comfy big chairs and sofas to relax in. Children welcome (under 5s free in parents' room, cot available without charge, baby sitting arranged). Walking; garden. **Rooms 6** (all en-suite & no-smoking, 2 shower only). B&B €40 pps, ss €10. Closed midweek Nov-Dec; all Jan-Feb. Amex, MasterCard, Visa, Laser. **Directions:** N56 from Letterkenny to Dunfanaghy. 1/2 mile outside Dunfanaghy on Falcarragh Rd on right hand side at the lake.

Dunkineely

Castle Murray House Hotel

HOTEL / RESTAURANT

St. John's Point Dunkineely Co Donegal
Tel: 074 973 7022 Fax: 074 973 7330
Email: castlemurray@eircom.net Web: www.castlemurray.com

This beautifully located clifftop hotel has wonderful sea and coastal views over the ruined castle after which it is named. It is a comfortable and relaxing place to stay, with a little bar, a residents' sitting room and a large verandah that can be covered with an awning in a good summer, so meals can be served outside. Since 2002 the hotel has been owned by Martin and Marguerite Howley, previously of The Fleet Inn in nearby Killybegs, and it is to their credit that no major changes have been made: many people who have been coming here for some time like it just the way it is. Bedrooms have a mixture of modern and antique pieces that give each room its own character, and are gradually being refurbished; most have sea views and all are quite large with a double and single bed, good bathrooms (most with full bath) and facilities including digital TV as well as phone and tea/coffee trays. A sun area on the sheltered flat roof at the back of the building has direct access from some bedrooms. Good breakfasts are served in in the restaurant, or in bedrooms on request. Banqueting (50). Pets permitted by arrangement. Children welcome; cots available without charge. Off-season value breaks. **Rooms 10** (all en-suite). B&B €70pps, ss €25. Closed mid Jan-mid Feb.

Restaurant: The restaurant is on the seaward corner of the hotel and maximises the impact of the dramatic view, including the castle (which is floodlit at night) and an open fire makes for real warmth in this dramatic location, even in winter. Remy Dupuis, who has been head chef since 1994 now works alongside Marguerite Howley and there is a consistent house style, with a strong emphasis on local produce. Multi-choice menus (basically 3-course, plus options of soup and sorbet), are sensibly priced according to the choice of main course and offer a wide choice, including vegetarian dishes. Seafood is the speciality of the house in the summer months; in winter there are more red meats, poultry and game. The location, helpful staff and consistently good cooking ensure an enjoyable visit. **Seats 65.** No smoking restaurant. Not suitable for children after 8pm. D daily 7-9.30, L Sun only 1.30-3.30; D from €40 (depending on choice of main course); Set Sun L €22.50; house wine €19; SC discretionary. Closed as above, but phone to check restaurant opening in low season, which may vary according to demand. MasterCard, Visa. **Directions:** Situated on the N56.8km from Killybegs,20 km Donegal Town on the coast road to St Johns Point; first left outside Dunkineely village.

Fahan

St. John's Country House & Restaurant

féile bia: COUNTRY HOUSE / RESTAURANT

Fahan Inishowen Co Donegal
Tel: 074 936 0289 Fax: 074 936 0612
Email: stjohnsrestaurant@eircom.net Web: homepage.eircom.net/~stjohnscountryhouse

In this substantial period house overlooking Lough Swilly, Reggie Ryan and Phil McAfee have run Restaurant St John's to growing acclaim since 1980. It's one of the most hospitable houses in Ireland - Reggie has a way with guests (and there's many an international figure among them) which must be pretty well unrivalled, making each one feel especially welcome so the whole occasion is relaxed and fun. A conservatory extension allows lough views in addition to the original cosy inside rooms, all a fit setting for Phil's cooking, which combines a respect for tradition and understanding of the value of simplicity with a willingness to experiment, ensuring that the many guests who regularly return always have a meal that is both stimulating and relaxing. Given the location, seafood is very popular (a seafood platter as a starter, perhaps) but Phil's menus are based on a wide range of local ingredients, including game in winter. Donegal mountain lamb, which she cooks in many different ways is an established favourite (an excellent speciality is "Rack of Donegal Mountain Lamb with Rosemary and Mascarpone Risotto"), and her crispy roast duckling is also a real treat. Vegetarian dishes are on the regular menu. A carefully selected wine list includes nine house wines, a special seasonal selection and a good choice of half bottles. **Seats 70** (private room, 25) Air conditioning. D Tue-Sun 7.30-9.30, Set D from €30; L Sun only, 12.30-3.30pm, Set Sun L about €18. house wines from about €16.50; SC discretionary. Restaurant closed Mon & Nov-Feb.

Accommodation: The five stylish, comfortable rooms are beautifully furnished with antiques and have many thoughtful details to make a stay more enjoyable, including well-finished bathrooms; rooms at the front also have lovely lough views. Breakfasts are a real treat. Golf, fishing, walking nearby. Children welcome (cot available, baby sitting arranged). No pets. garden. **Rooms 5** (2 junior suite, 2 shower only, all no-smoking) B&B about €56 pps, ss about €6. Closed Nov-Feb. Amex, MasterCard, Visa, Switch. **Directions:** In Fahan village on R238 Derry-Buncrana road.

GLENVEAGH NATIONAL PARK

Glenveagh National Park (Tel: 074 9137090; www.heritageireland.ie) is open to visitors all year, although visitor facilities are seasonal (mid March-early November). The Victorian castle, which is the focal point for visitors to the Park, was donated to the State by the last private owner, Henry Plummer McIlhenny, together with most of its contents - and the gardens are among the most interesting in Ireland, with many unusual and rare plants displayed in a series of garden rooms - the Pleasure Grounds, the Walled Garden the Italian Garden and so on; garden tours are given regularly by experienced gardeners, but guests are also free to wander freely. The Interpretative Centre includes a restaurant, but there's a treat in store if you go to the **Tea Rooms** at the castle itself; they are in an attractive stone courtyard attached to the castle and specialise in excellent home baking.

Greencastle

Harbourside Café

Ⓝ CAFÉ

Greencastle Co Donegal **Tel: 086 382 6670**

This nice little café beside the Maritime Museum is open all day in summer and offers lots of tasty little bites - sandwiches, plain, toasted and gourmet sandwiches, plus homely bakes (scones, muffins and tray bakes, which change daily). Freshly squeezed orange juice is a tempting option on the drinks list - and there's delicous Illy coffee too. Overlooks the ferry, so you can be sure not to miss it. Open Mon-Sun, 10am-5.30pm. **No Credit Cards. Directions:** Beside the Maritime Museum.

Greencastle

Kealys Seafood Bar

RESTAURANT

The Harbour Greencastle Co Donegal **Tel: 074 938 1010**
Fax: 074 938 1010 Email: kealys@iol.ie

Under-stated quality remains a fair description of the tone of James and Tricia Kealy's excellent seafood restaurant, which has always valued simplicity. Since 1989 the restaurant has been a key establishment in a major fishing port and still retains the original bar at its heart. Until the arrival of the new ferry between Greencastle and Magilligan Point in Northern Ireland in 2002, Greencastle seemed quite remote but the ferry has brought many new visitors to the area - and to Kealys, who have responded to this sudden increase in demand by extending their opening hours. Even if it's just to pop in for a bowl of Greencastle chowder and some home-baked bread, don't miss the opportunity of a visit to Kealys - although simple, this place is really special. (If we did an award for seafood chowder, theirs would take the prize!) James takes a creative and balanced approach to seafood, presenting this precious resource as a component in complete dishes which are modern in tone but also echo traditional Irish themes.

House specialities demonstrating this healthy and (ecologically sound) philosophy include baked fillet of hake on braised fennel with a tomato & saffron butter sauce and baked Atlantic salmon with a wholegrain mustard crust served on Irish spring cabbage and bacon. James also bakes a variety of breads and uses local organic vegetables (from Greencastle organic farm) and farmhouse cheeses - typically Gubbeen, St Killian, Boilie and Cashel Blue. Not suitable for children after 8 pm. **Seats 70.** L 12.30-3pm (Sun 1-3), D 7-9.30 (Sun to 8.30); Set D €35, also à la carte L&D, house wine about €13.30. Closed Mon, 2 weeks Nov. Amex, MasterCard, Visa, Laser. **Directions:** On the harbour at Greencastle, 20 miles north of Derry City.

Gweedore

An Chuirt - Gweedore Court Hotel

HOTEL

Gweedore PO Co Donegal **Tel: 074 953 2900** Fax: 074 953 2929
Email: anchuirt@eircom.net Web: www.anchuirt-hotel.ie

This immaculate family-run hotel is beautifully situated in the heart of the Donegal Gaeltacht and provides a very comfortable base for exploring the area. There has been a hotel here for many years - quotations from the Visitors' Book go back as a far as 1845 - but it has been re-built under the present ownership, re-opening in 1999. Past and present are brought together neatly - not only in the hotel, which is furnished in a traditional style throughout - but in an impressive heritage centre and art gallery alongside, which is run by the hotel and also used for conferences and banqueting. Conference/banqueting 100/120. Children welcome (under 4s free in parents' room, cot available without charge, baby sitting arranged). Garden, walking. **Rooms 19** (2 junior suites, 1 disabled, 10 no smoking). about B&B €90, ss about €20. Closed Christmas. MasterCard, Visa, Laser. **Directions:** N56 main road from Letterkenny to Gweedore.

Kincasslagh

Iggy's Bar

ATMOSPHERIC PUB

Kincasslagh Co Donegal **Tel: 074 954 3112**

Just a short walk up from the harbour - it's also called the Atlantic Bar - Ann and Iggy Murray have run this delightfully unspoilt pub since 1986 and it's an all year home-from-home for many a visitor. The television isn't usually on unless there's a match and Ann makes lovely simple food for the bar, mainly seafood - home-made soups, delicious crab sandwiches and Rombouts coffee. Children welcome. Bar open 10-12.30 daily, light food available 12-7, Mon-Sat. No food on Sundays. Closed 25 Dec & Good Friday. **No Credit Cards. Directions:** On the corner of the Main Street, where the road turns off to the harbour.

Laghey

Coxtown Manor

RESTAURANT / COUNTRY HOUSE

Laghey Co Donegal
Tel: 074 973 4575 Fax: 073 973 4576
Email: coxtownmanor@oceanfree.net Web: www.coxtownmanor.com

Just a short drive from the county town, this welcoming late Georgian house set in its own parkland is in a lovely, peaceful area close to Donegal Bay. Belgian proprietor, Edward Dewael - who fell for the property a few years ago and is still in the process of upgrading it - personally ensures that everything possible is done to make guests feel at home. A pleasant wood-panelled bar - well-stocked, notably with Belgian beers and a great selection of digestifs to accompany your after dinner coffee - caters for all weathers, with an open fire and a new conservatory planned alongside it (due for completion in 2004). The elegant period dining room is the heart of the house and is well-appointed - and, like the food served here, attractive but not too formal. Friendly staff settle guests in with the prompt offer of aperitifs and presentation of à la carte menus which offer a wide choice of mostly classic dishes with an emphasis on seafood from Donegal Bay (wild salmon, lobster, prawns), Mulroy Bay (crab, scallops), Mullaghmore (crab) and Lissadell (clams). Thornhill duck, Moyallon Farm boar Charolais beef from a named butcher (McGettigan's) also feature, as (unusually) does organic red label chicken - all interesting and highly reassuring information and a sound foundation for head chef Michel Aerts' proficient cooking: starters will certainly include several shellfish dishes (lobster mayonnaise, perhaps), while a good home-made soup of the day might be chicken & vegetable (excellent clear stock with fine vegetables); main course choices include less usual dishes like squab pigeon (with deep-fried celeriac) and house specialities like John Dory à l'Ostendaise. The aim is to serve (mostly) local produce in a Belgian way and offer a different experience from other dining options in the area, with a high standard of cooking and good value. Belgian chocolate features every which way on the dessert menu (Dame blanche, a speciality of home-made vanilla ice cream with hot chocolate sauce and cream is worth leaving room for) but fresh fruit salad is a refreshing option, on request. Not suitable for children after 8pm. **Seats 45.** D 7-9 Tue-Sun, L Sun only 1-4; D à la carte; Set Sun L €21.50. House wine €19.50. Closed Mon; 3 weeks Feb.

Accommodation: The atmosphere is more restaurant with rooms than country house, although there is a growing emphasis on accommodation since the coachouse at the back has been converted to create five new bedrooms, offering higher standard than those in the main house (due for completion Christmas 2003). But the older rooms, while not luxurious, are large, well-proportioned and comfortable (some with countryside views and open fireplaces). Breakfast buffet 8-10am; cooked options include delicious Fermanagh dry-cured black bacon. Children welcome (under 10 free in parents'room, cot available without charge, baby-sitting arranged). Walking; garden. No pets. **Rooms 10** (3 superior, 9 en-suite, 1 shower only, 1 with private bathroom). B&B about €55 pps, ss €19 (price depends on the room). Closed 3 weeks Feb. MasterCard, Visa, Laser, Switch. **Directions:** Main sign on N15 between Ballyshannon & Donegal Town.

Letterkenny

Castle Grove Country House Hotel

HOTEL / RESTAURANT Letterkenny Co Donegal **Tel: 074 915 1118** Fax: 074 915 1118
Email: reservation@castlegrove.com Web: www.castlegrove.com

Parkland designed by "Capability" Brown in the mid 18th-century creates a wonderful setting for Raymond and Mary Sweeney's lovely period house overlooking the lough. Castlegrove is undoubtedly the first choice for discerning visitors to the area, especially executives with business in Letterkenny: it is, as Mary Sweeney says, an oasis of tranquillity. Constant improvement is the policy and the last few years have seen major changes, including a new conservatory, a larger new restaurant and, most recently, the adjoining coach house has been developed to make seven lovely bedrooms - all carefully designed and furnished with antiques to feel like part of the main house - and a small conference room. The original walled garden is also under restoration as part of an ongoing development of the gardens which will continue for several years. Bedrooms are spacious and elegantly furnished to a high standard with antiques, and bathrooms are gradually being upgraded where practical, to provide walk-in showers as well as full bath. Good breakfasts include a choice of fish as well as traditional Irish breakfast, home-made breads and preserves. Mary Sweeney's personal supervision ensures an exceptionally high standard of maintenance and housekeeping and staff are friendly and helpful. Two boats belonging to the house are available for fishing on Lough Swilly and there is a special arrangement with three nearby golf clubs. Conference/banqueting (25/50). House available for private use (family occasions, board meetings etc) Not suitable for children under 12. No pets. **Rooms 14** (1 suite, 2 junior suites, 2 shower only, 2 disabled, all no-smoking) B&B €80 pps, no ss. Closed 20-29 Dec.

Green Room: Although the style of the room is similar to the rest of the house, the restaurant is actually in a recent extension and, while not quite as warmly furnished as the other receptions (carpet rather than the present wooden floor might make all the difference), it is big enough to allow generous well-spaced tables. Pascal Desnet, who has been doing an excellent job as head chef since 1998, neatly combines classic French and modern Irish cooking. Carefully sourced specialist and local ingredients are the sound base for his cuisine and it would be interesting to see more about this on menus, as many of the herbs, vegetables and soft fruit are home grown, the seafood - such as wild salmon and Swilly oysters - is local, and local meats are regularly used in, for example, a speciality dish of pan fried fillet of beef with grilled horseradish polenta and caramelised chicory which is an enduring favourite. Desserts might include a juicy rhubarb tart with home-made ice cream, or crème caramel with orange segments and fresh cream - well-balanced treats that make a refreshing ending to a fine meal. Not suitable for children under 10 after 7pm. **Seats 50** (private room, 15). B'fst 8-9.30 daily, L 12.30-2 Mon-Sat, D 6.30-9 daily. Set L from €22, light L €15; Set D €30-48, D also à la carte; house wines from €15; sc discretionary. Reservations required. Closed L Sun; 20-29 Dec. Amex, Diners, MasterCard, Visa, Laser. **Directions:** N 245 off main road to Letterkenny.

LETTERKENNY

Originally a fishing village, which developed on the banks of Lough Swilly, Letterkenny is now one of the largest and most densely-populated towns in Donegal - and one of the fastest-growing towns in Ireland. The Donegal County Museum is in the town and, for those who need accommodation in an hotel with leisure facilities, the new **Holiday Inn Letterkenny (Tel: 074 912 4369; www.holidayinnletterkenny.net)** is a good choice, conveniently situated on the edge of town. For moderately-priced town centre hotel accommodation, try the **Quality Hotel Letterkenny (Tel: 074 912 2977; www.qualitydonegal.com)**, which offers apartment-style suites as well as en-suite bedrooms.

Lough Eske

Ardnamona House

COUNTRY HOUSE Lough Eske Donegal Co Donegal **Tel: 074 972 2650**
Email: info@ardnamona.com Web: www.ardnamona.com

The glorious gardens, which were first planted by Sir Arthur Wallace in the 1880s, are central to the special atmosphere of Kieran and Annabel Clarke's secluded Victorian house overlooking Lough Eske and it's hard to credit that it's only a few miles from Donegal town. It's a gentle, hospitable house and draws people who value its peace and beauty. Front rooms have lovely views over the Lough to the mountains beyond, but all are individualistic with private bathrooms (and a peaceful outlook through rhododendrons and azaleas which have received international acclaim). Gardeners will enjoy doing the garden trail (guide leaflet provided and all plants labelled) and special interest groups are welcome to visit the gardens by arrangement. There are also miles of walks through ancient oak forests full of mosses and ferns and private boating and fishing on the Lough. No evening meals, but restaurants, including Harvey's Point, nearby. Children welcome (under 12 months free in parents' room, cot available without charge, baby sitting arranged; playroom). Dogs allowed in some areas. Cycling, walking, fishing. **Rooms 6** (all with en-suite or private bathrooms). All day room service provided. B&B €70, ss €20. Closed 'occasionally'; reservations essential. MasterCard, Visa. **Directions:** From Donegal, follow signs to Harvey's Point.

Lough Eske

Harvey's Point Country Hotel

HOTEL / RESTAURANT

Lough Eske Donegal Co Donegal
Tel: 074 972 2208 Fax: 074 972 2352
Email: info@harveyspoint.com Web: www.harveyspoint.com

In a stunning location on the shores of Lough Eske, this unusual hotel has a distinctly alpine atmosphere, with chalet-style buildings, pergolas and covered walkways joining the residential area to the main bars and restaurant. Maintenance is immaculate and the atmosphere can be deeply peaceful. Rooms, which are based on a Swiss design with show-wood furniture and four-posters, have all been refurbished recently; generally they have good amenities and direct access to verandah and gardens, although some are shower-only (and of continental design, ie without shower cubicle, which can be messy). A further 30 new rooms (all suites) are due to come on stream for 2004. Conferences/banqueting (200/350). Dinner dances and special breaks are often offered; telephone for details. Not suitable for children under 10 years. Pets permitted. **Rooms 20** (6 executive, all no smoking, some shower only). B&B €99 pps, ss €25. Open all year, but closed D Sun, all Mon & Tue in winter (Nov-Mar).

Restaurant: The restaurant extends right down to the shores of Lough Eske, taking advantage of the beautiful view. Service has always been attentive and professional; the wine list includes a range of 'everyday easy drinking' wines (all under €25) and a good selection of half bottles. Head chef, Martin Lynch, who took over the kitchens in August 2002, is continuing in the classical style of previous chefs and doing a good job - a meal here is always an enjoyable experience. **Seats 100** (private room, 20). Air conditioning. Toilets wheelchair accessible. L 12.30-2.30 (Sun 12-6) & D 6-9.30 daily in summer (Sun to 8). [Nov-Mar: open only Wed D-Sun L]. Set D €50, Set L €25; house wine from €19.50; no sc. Closed D Sun, all Mon & Tue off season. (Nov-Mar). Amex, Diners, MasterCard, Visa, Laser. **Directions:** 6km from Donegal town.

Lough Eske

Rhu-Gorse

B&B

Lough Eske Co Donegal **Tel: 074 972 1685**
Fax: 074 972 1685 Email: rhugorse@iol.ie

Beautifully located, with stunning views over Lough Eske (and windows built to take full advantage of them), Grainne McGettigan's modern house is not architecturally outstanding but it has some very special attributes, notably the warmth and hospitality of Grainne herself. Bedrooms and bathrooms are all ship-shape and residents can have afternoon tea as well as breakfast, although not evening meals (however Harvey's Point is very close, see entry, and Donegal town is only a short drive). Animals are central to Rhu-Gorse, which is named after a much-loved pedigree dog bred by Grainne's father-in-law (a descendant now follows her around everywhere), and one of her special interests is breeding horses: not your average B&B, but a comfortable, hospitable and very interesting base for a walking holiday or touring the area. **Rooms 3** (2 en-suite, 1 shower only); B&B about €40, ss €10. Closed 1 Nov-Easter. Visa, MasterCard, Laser. **Directions:** Take N15 /N56 from Donegal Town. Take signs for Lough Eske & Harvey's Point Hotel. Pick up signs for Rhu-Gorse. ◇

Malin

Malin Hotel

N féile bia HOTEL

Malin Co Donegal **Tel: 074 937 0606**
Fax: 074 937 0770 Email: malinhotel@eircom. net

This attractive hotel came into new ownership in 2003 and has been quite extensively refurbished within the limitations of the building. The friendly bar is a popular meeting place for visitors and locals alike and neat bedrooms - which have been been redesigned in three different styles, in rich natural colours - have phones, tea/coffee making facilities and TV (local stations) and full bathrooms, with over bath shower. While not very large, rooms are inviting and comfortable, - offering a moderately priced base for exploring this beautiful area. Conference/banqueting 100/350. Pool table; playroom. Walking.

Rooms 15 (all en-suite & no smoking). Children welcome (under 5 free in parents' room, cot available free of charge, baby sitting arranged.) Limited room service. B&B €55 pps, ss €5. Diners, MasterCard, Visa, Laser. **Directions:** Overlooking the village green in Malin town.

Portsalon

Croaghross

COUNTRY HOUSE Portsalon Letterkenny Co Donegal **Tel: 074 915 9548** Fax: 074 915 9548
Email: jkdeane@croaghross.com Web: www.croaghross.com

John and Kay Deane's latter-day country house enjoys a lovely location on the Fanad peninsula, overlooking Lough Swilly. It's within 5 minutes walk of a great beach - and the renowned 100-year old Portsalon Golf Course - and very convenient to Glenveagh National Park. Three bedrooms open onto a sun terrace, while the two side rooms overlook a landscaped rock garden - one is especially suitable for wheelchair users, who can park beside it. Residents' dinner is, like breakfast, based on local ingredients and 'good Irish cuisine', with home-made breads and farmhouse cheeses always available (please book ahead; very reasonably priced short wine list offered). Barbecues are sometimes arranged when the weather is favourable and, although officially closed in winter, bookings can be made by arrangement. This is an attractive option for a group, as the house is centrally heated throughout and the living room has a big open fire. The Deanes also have a 3-bedroom self-catering cottage available nearby. Children welcome (cot available without charge). Pets permitted. Garden. **Rooms 5** (all en-suite & no smoking, 1 for disabled). B&B from €35 pps, ss €6.50. Residents D 7.30 pm Mon-Sat, from €27.50; wines from €13.50. No D on Sun. Closed mid Oct-14 Mar. MasterCard, Visa, Laser. **Directions:** Letterkenny - Ramelton - R246 (Milford direction) through Kerrykeel to Portsalon; opposite golf course, turn up hill.

Ramelton

Ardeen

COUNTRY HOUSE Ramelton Co Donegal **Tel: 074 915 1243** Fax: 074 915 1243
Email: ardeenbandb2@eircom.net Web: www.ardeenhouse.com

Overlooking Lough Swilly, set in its own grounds on the edge of the heritage town of Ramelton and well-located for touring Donegal and Glenveagh National Park, Anne Campbell's mid-nineteenth century house is not too grand and has the comfortable atmosphere of a family home. Individually decorated bedrooms with views over the Lough or nearby hills all have their own character and are charmingly furnished (Anne is very handy with a sewing machine and time available in the winter is well used for guests' comfort). The drawing room and dining room are both furnished with antiques and have open fires, making this a very warm and comfortable place to return to after a day out. No dinners, but Anne can recommend pubs and restaurants nearby. Children welcome (under 3 free in parents' room, cots available free of charge). Garden, tennis. Pets allowed by arrangement. * Self-catering also available in the 'Old Stables'; details on request. **Rooms 5** (4 en-suite with shower, 1 twin has private bathroom, all no smoking). B&B from €30, ss €10. Open all year (Oct-Easter by prior arrangement only). MasterCard, Visa. **Directions:** Follow river to Town Hall, turn right; 1st house on right.

Ramelton

Frewin

COUNTRY HOUSE Ramelton Co Donegal **Tel: 074 915 1246** Fax: 074 915 1246
Email: flaxmill@indigo.ie Web: www.accommodationdonegal.net

Thomas and Regina Coyle have restored this unspoilt Victorian house with the greatest attention to period detail and guests have the opportunity to drink in the atmosphere on arrival while having a cup of tea in the little book-lined library, where the old parish safe is still set in the wall. Beautifully furnished bedrooms have snowy white bedlinen and a robe provided in case of night-time forays along the corridor and a delicious breakfast, including freshly baked breads warm from the oven, is taken communally at a long polished table - at night lit only by candlelight. This beautiful house is most unusual, notably because Thomas Coyle specialises in restoring old buildings and is a collector by nature - much of his collection finds a place in the house, some is for sale in an outbuilding at the back. Not suitable for children under 8. No dogs. No smoking except in sitting room & library. Garden. **Rooms 4** (1 suite, 3 en-suite, 1 shower only, 1 with private bath, all no smoking). B&B from €50, ss €20. D about €35 (by arrangement). Closed 23 Dec-1 Jan. MasterCard, Visa. **Directions:** Take R245 from Letterkenny. Travel 7 miles approx and take right turn on approach to Ramelton. Located 400 yards on right.

Rathmullan

Fort Royal Hotel

HOTEL / RESTAURANT Rathmullan Co Donegal **Tel: 074 915 8100** Fax: 074 915 8103
Email: fortroyal@eircom.net Web: www.fortroyalhotel.com

Overlooking the sea, and with direct access to a sandy beach, the Fletcher family's attractive Victorian hotel is set in 19 acres of lawn and woodland above Lough Swilly. It's a good base for family holidays or visiting places of local interest, including Glenveagh National Park and Glebe House, the late artist

Derek Hill's former home, which has a museum and gallery next door. Public rooms, which include a recently refurbished bar, are spacious, well-proportioned and comfortably furnished in country house style, with big armchairs and open fires. Well-appointed bedrooms (all en-suite, most with bath and shower, a few bath only) are designed for relaxation and enjoy a pleasant outlook over wooded grounds. Croquet, tennis, golf, pitch & putt are available on the premises and activities such as riding and fishing nearby. Special interest breaks offered. Children welcome (under 4 free in parents' room, cot available without charge, baby sitting arranged). Pets permitted.* Self-catering cottages available in the hotels grounds; details on application. **Rooms 15.** B&B €90pps, ss €30. Closed Nov-Mar.

Restaurant: This attractive traditional dining room overlooking lawns and woodland is well-appointed with crisp white linen and fresh flowers - just the right setting for good country house cooking. Much of the food at Fort Royal comes from the hotel's own walled gardens (although this is not mentioned on menus, which is a pity) and is cooked by Tim Fletcher, who has been head chef since 1995 and proprietor since 2000. He offers nightly dinner menus with about five classic choices on each course, considerately priced to allow two- or three-course options. Typical examples from a summer menu include a starter of cornets of smoked salmon filled with smoked trout mousse; sole meunière (and vegetable selection) and crème brulée with mixed berry compôte. Tea or coffee is served in the lounge afterwards - or, on fine evenings, you could take it outside and enjoy the view down over the lough. Staff are very pleasant and helpful. **Seats 50.** Not suitable for children under 10. D daily, 7.30-8.45 (last orders). Set D €32/38. *Light lunches are also served in the bar or at tables in the garden, 12-2 daily. Phone ahead to check availability. Amex, Diners, MasterCard, Visa, Laser. **Directions:** Ramelton road from Letterkenny, straight on to Rathmullan.

Rathmullan

Rathmullan House

HOTEL / RESTAURANT

Rathmullan Co Donegal **Tel: 074 915 8188** Fax: 074 915 8200
Email: info@rathmullanhouse.com Web: www.rathmullanhouse.com

Built as a summer house by the Batt banking family of Belfast in the 1800s, Rathmullan has been run as a country house hotel since 1961 by Bob and Robin Wheeler who have now semi-retired and it's currently managed by their sons William and Mark and daughter-in-law Mary. Set in lovely gardens on the shores of Lough Swilly, this gracious early nineteenth century house is fairly grand with public areas which include three elegant drawing rooms, but it's not too formal - and there's a cellar bar which can be very relaxed. Bedrooms vary in decor, facilities and cost to suit different requirements and budgets - there are luxurious garden suites (close to the swimming pool and leisure facilities) as well as the unpretentious old-fashioned comforts of family rooms at the top of the house, which many guests like best. Donegal has an other-worldliness that is increasingly hard to capture in the traditional family holiday areas, and the laid-back charm of Rathmullan House - albeit given invisible backbone by the professionalism of the Wheeler family and their staff - somehow symbolises that special sense of place. Small conferences (15-20); banqueting (100) Swimming pool, steam room, tennis. Children welcome; cot €10, baby sitting arranged. Pets permitted by arrangement.*At the time of going to press the hotel plans to close from November 2003 to April 2004 to build 10 new bedrooms, new conference./private dining area and an extension to the present dining room. **Rooms 24** (2 room for disabled). B&B €95 pps, ss €20.

Pavilion Dinning Room: The dining room with its unusual tented ceiling (designed by the late Liam McCormick, well known for his striking Donegal churches) makes the most of the garden outlook and provides a fine setting for Peter Cheesman's country house cooking as well as the tremendous breakfasts for which Rathmullan is justly famous. Cooking here is upbeat traditional and carefully-sourced menus offer a wide choice - a speciality of Rathmullan loin of lamb on boulangère potato, with roast carrots & courgettes & rosemary jus and desserts like compôte of garden fruit with carrageen moss pudding convey the style. The carrageen is equally at home at breakfast too - each morning a tremendous buffet is laid out, offering a huge variety of juices, fresh and poached fruits with yogurt and carrageen pudding to go with them, cooked ham, smoked salmon and farmhouse cheeses, plus home-baked breads, scones and preserves from the garden - and all this before anything from the menu of hot dishes is even contemplated. (Rathmullan was the 2002 winner of our Denny Irish Breakfast Awards for the Ulster region). **Seats 80.** No smoking restaurant. D daily 7.30-8.45, Set D €35/45 house wine from €18; sc 10%. *Informal meals are available in the Cellar Bar: L, 1-2.30pm daily; Early D, 5-8pm daily; children's menu available. Closed for renovations, Nov-Apr. Amex, MasterCard, Visa, Laser. **Directions:** Letterkenny to Ramelton - turn right to Rathmullan at the bridge, through village and turn right to hotel.

Rossnowlagh

Sand House Hotel

féile bia **HOTEL**

Rossnowlagh Co Donegal **Tel: 071 985 1777** Fax: 071 985 2100
Email: info@sandhouse-hotel.ie Web: www.sandhouse-hotel.ie

Perched on the edge of a stunning sandy beach two miles long, Mary and Brian Britton's famous hotel lost its trademark crenellated roof-line in major renovations over the winter of 2001/2 and has emerged with an extra storey and an elegant new look, reminiscent of a French chateau. The wonderful sea views and easy access to the beach have always been the great attractions of the Sand House, which started life as a fishing lodge in the 1830s and has now completed its latest metamorphosis with a new floor of bedrooms, a panoramic lift (who will bother with the stairs when the lift has the best view in the house?), a new boardroom and a marine spa, where seaweed products are used for a range of exclusive body and skincare treatments. Existing bedrooms were also refurbished and upgraded and many have a superb outlook; all are very comfortable, with excellent bathrooms - and everyone can enjoy the view from the new sun deck which has replaced the Atlantic Conservatory, and allows a sheltered retreat from which to soak in the sea view. Things that haven't changed at the Sand House include the ever-burning welcoming fire in the foyer- and the hospitality of the Britton family and staff (not to mention Mary Britton's reputation for exceptional housekeeping), which is the real appeal of this remarkable hotel. Jacuzzi, steam room, balneo bath, beauty salon. Fishing, cycling, tennis, walking, tennis on site; golf, horse riding, boating and many other activities available nearby. Conference/banqueting (90). Children welcome (cots available, baby sitting arranged). Pets permitted in some areas by arrangement. **Rooms 60** (4 junior suites, 10 shower only, 15 no-smoking, 1 disabled). 24 hour room service. B&B €85pps, ss €30. Closed Dec.

Seashell Restaurant: The restaurant is rather unexpectedly at the front of the hotel (and therefore faces inland) but is well-appointed, in keeping with the rest of the hotel. Sid Davis, Head Chef since 1994, presents seasonal 5-course dinner menus, changed daily, that are based on local/carefully sourced ingredients - although that may not be obvious from the menus. Fresh seafood and locally sourced lamb and beef (also game, in season) provide the foundation for a traditional repertoire which is quite conservative but offers plenty of choice on all courses. Finish with a choice of Irish cheeses or hotel-style desserts. Staff are helpful and attentive. Good choice of wines by the glass. **Seats 70** (private room, 18). Children welcome. D daily 7-9, L Sun only, 1-2.30. Set D €45, Set Sun L €25; house wines from €13.50. SC 10%. Amex, Diners, MasterCard, Visa, Laser. **Directions:** Coast road from Ballyshannon to Donegal Town.

Tory Island

HOTEL

Ostan Thoraig (Hotel Tory)

West End Tory Island Co Donegal **Tel: 074 913 5920**
Fax: 074 913 5613 Email: hoteltory@tinet.ie

The Gaeltacht (Irish-speaking) island of Tory lies eight miles off the north-west corner of Donegal and, in spite of its exposed position, has been inhabited for four thousand years. Perhaps not surprisingly, this other-worldly island managed quite well without an hotel until recently, but once Patrick and Berney Doohan's Ostan Thoraig was built in 1994 it quickly became the centre of the island's social activities - or, to be more precise, The People's Bar in the hotel quickly became the centre. The hotel is beside the little harbour where the ferries bring in visitors from mainland ports. Although simple, it provides comfortable en-suite accommodation with telephone and television. A special feature of the island is its 'school' of primitive art (founded with the support of well-known artist the late Derek Hill of nearby Glebe House and Gallery, Church Hill). It even has a king as a founder member: the present King of the Tory is Patsy Dan Rogers, who has exhibited his colourful primitive paintings of the island throughout the British Isles and in America. A tiny gallery on Tory provides exhibition space for the current group of island artists. Small conferences. Children welcome (cot available, small charge). Pets permitted by arrangement. **Rooms 14** (1 for disabled) B&B about€40pps, ss about €13. Wheelchair access. Closed Oct-Easter. [NB: Current data not confirmed at time of going to press; a phone call ahead is strongly advised.] MasterCard, Visa. **Directions:** Tory is accessible by ferry (subject to weather conditions) from several mainland ports: telephone 074-913 1320 for details, or ask at the hotel. ◇

Tremone

FARMHOUSE

Trean House

Tremone Lecamy Inishowen Co Donegal
Tel: 074 936 7121 Fax: 074 936 7227
Email: treanhouse@oceanfree.net Web: www.treanhouse.com

Way out on the Inishowen peninsula, Joyce and Mervyn Norris's farmhouse is tucked into a sheltered corner in stonewalled countryside beside the sea. Surrounded by a large garden with mature trees and welcoming flowers, it is a substantial house and offers a comfortable base for a a relaxing holiday in a homely atmosphere. Guests have the use of a cosy sitting room with an open fire and simple country bedrooms have everything that is needed - the only room without an en-suite shower room has a private bathroom nearby - and, if any other guest prefers a bath, it can be used by arrangement. Joyce's home cooking is another attraction - breakfasts to set you up for the day, evening meals by arrangement. **Rooms 3** (all en-suite, shower only & no smoking). B&B €30. No SC. Open all year except Christmas. MasterCard, Visa. **Directions:** From Moville follow R238 5kms, turn right & follow house signs.

COUNTY GALWAY

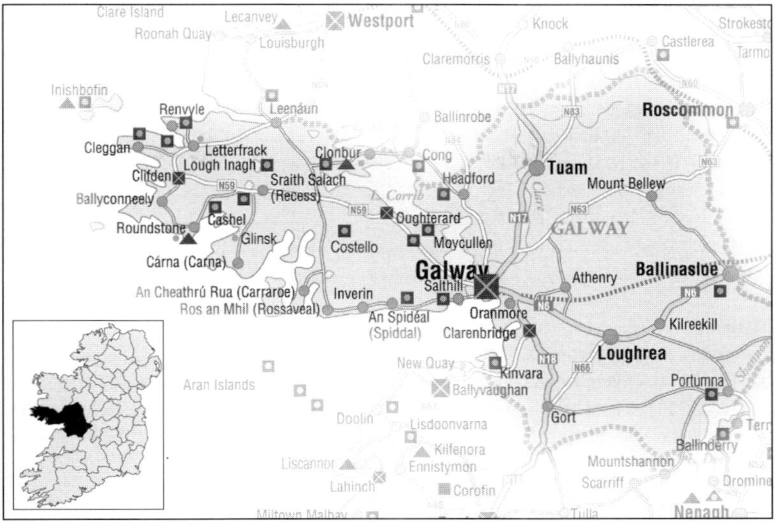

Galway can more than match any other Irish county for the variety and charm of its many scenic routes. But it also has more to offer than any other Irish county in the way of slightly offbeat expeditions and experiences, in addition to all the usual visual attractions of Ireland's Atlantic seaboard.

Visiting the Aran Islands, for instance, can be done by air as well as by sea, and in 2004-2005 there's the prospect of this facility being extended to Inishbofin off Galway's west coast, with an airstrip planned for the island. matched by one on the nearby mainland just north of Clifden. Clifden is a very long way from Ireland's largest centres of population on the east coast, so although it can be an entertaining journey, the prospect of a quick flight across country to Clifden will appeal to those whose time is limited.

However, as the much-visited Aran Islands have shown, the presence of an air service doesn't seem to lessen the popularity of ther ferries – many people seem to think that you haven't properly visited an island unless you go there by boat. Then, too, there are many coastal boat trips, including an informative seaborne tour from Killary Harbour, Ireland's only genuine fjord, while Lough Corrib is also served by miniature cruise liners.

As for sport ashore, the Galway Races at the end of July have developed into a six day meeting which is firmly established as Ireland's premier summer horse racing event, while the Ballinasloe International Horse Fair in the Autumn is simply unique. It dates back more than 280 years.

This has to be Ireland's most generous county, for in effect you get two counties for the price of one. They're neatly divided by the handsome sweep of island-studded Lough Corrib, with the big country of many mountains to the west, and rolling farmland to the east. As a bonus, where the Corrib tumbles into Galway Bay, we find one of Ireland's - indeed, one of Europe's - most vibrant cities. Galway is a bustling place which cheerfully sees itself as being linked to Spain and the great world beyond the Atlantic.

The theme of double value asserts itself in other ways. As Autumn ripeness makes its presence felt, the county and city provide not one, but two, Oyster Festivals. Once September has ushered in the traditional oyster season, Galway's long and distinguished connection with the splendid bivalve mollusc is celebrated first with the Clarenbridge Oyster Festival on the southeast shore of Galway Bay, and then a week or so later, right in the heart of the city with the International Galway Oyster Festival itself. This now has a truly international flavour. 2003's Festival – the 49th - was from September 25th to 28th, and it saw the coveted World Oyster-Opening Championship going to Dieter Berner from Sweden.

Lough Corrib is both a geographical and psychological divide. East of it, there's flatter country, home to hunting packs of mythic lore. West of the Corrib - which used itself to be a major throughfare, and is now as ever place of angling renown - you're very quickly into the high ground and moorland which sweep up to the Twelve Bens and other splendid peaks, wonderful mountains which enthusiasts would claim as the most beautiful in all Ireland.

Their heavily indented coastline means this region is Connemara, the Land of the Sea, where earth, rock and ocean intermix in one of Ireland's most extraordindary landscapes. Beyond, to the south, the Aran Islands are a place apart, yet they too are part of the Galway mix in this fantastical county which has its own magical light coming in over the sea. And yet all its extraordinary variety happens within very manageable distances.

Local Attractions and Information

GALWAY CITY:

Arts Centre, 47 Dominick St	091 565886
Galway Airport	091 752874
Galway Arts Festival (July)	091 565886
Galway Crystal Heritage Centre	091 757311
Galway Races (late July/early August, Sept & Oct)	091 753870
50th Galway International Oyster Festival (late September)	091 527282 / 522066
Kenny's Bookshops & Art Galleries, High Street	091 562739
O'Brien Shipping (Aran Island Ferries)	091 563081
Tourist Information	091 563081
Town Hall Theatre	091 569755

CO GALWAY:

Aran Islands, Heritage Centre	099 61355
Aran Islands, Ferries from Rossaveal	091 568903 / 561767
Aran Islands, Flights from Inverin Airport	091 593034
Aughrim, Battle of Aughrim Centre	090 967 3939
Ballinasloe, International Horse Fair (Sept/Oct)	090 964 3453
Clarenbridge, Oyster Festival (September)	091 79 6342
Clifden, Connemara Pony Show (mid August)	095 21863
Clifden, Connemara Safari - Walking & Islands	095 21071
Gort, Thoor Ballylee (Yeats' Tower)	091 63 1436
Inishbofin, Arts Festival (Biennial, September)	095 45909
Inishbofin Ferries (Cleggan)	095 44642
Inisheer, Duchas Inis Oirr (Arts Centre)	099 735576
Killary, Cruises on Connemara Lady	091 566736
Kinvara, Dungaire Castle	061 360788
Letterfrack, Connemara Bog Week (May)	095 43443
Letterfrack, Connemara Sea Week (October)	095 43443
Letterfrack, Kylemore Abbey & Gardens	095 41146
Loughrea, Dartfield Horse Museum	091 843968
Roundstone, Roundstone Arts Week (July)	095 35834
Roundstone, Traditional bodhran makers	095 35808
Tuam, Little Mill (last intact cornmill in area)	093 25486

GALWAY CITY

Galway City — Antons

Ⓝ CAFÉ

12 Father Griffin Road Galway Co Galway **Tel: 091 582067**

Antons is a popular, family-run Galway café, a five minute walk from Jurys Inn over the bridge. It's a simple, place a long room with local artists' paintings and a lot of wood - floors, tables, chairs and benches - mugs and unmatching ware. It offers excellent value and has been feeding a loyal lunch time trade for many years, so it's just the kind of place visitors need to know about. Particularly recommended for home baking, consistently good salads and desserts (Raspberry and almond tart, Italian chocolate cake) in an unfussy atmosphere. Great coffees, teas, infusions and freshly squeezed juice too. **Seats 30.** Open all day Mon-Sat. Closed Sun. **Directions:** Over the bridge from Jurys Inn, towards Salthill.

Galway City — Ardawn House

GUESTHOUSE

College Road Galway Co Galway **Tel: 091 568833** Fax: 091 563454
Email: ardawn@iol.ie Web: wwwgalway.net/pages/aedawn-house/

Mike and Breda Guilfoyle's hospitable guesthouse is easily found, just a few minutes walk from Eyre Square. Accommodation is all en-suite and rooms are comfortably furnished, with good amenities. But it's Mike and Breda who make Ardawn House special - they take great pride in every aspect of the business, (including an extensive breakfasts) and also help guests to get the very best out of their visit to Galway. Children welcome. Pets permitted by arrangement. **Rooms 8** (all shower only & no-smoking). B&B €60pps, no ss. Closed 21-27 Dec. Amex, MasterCard, Visa, Laser. **Directions:** Off N6, take city east exit; follow signs to city centre. First house on right after greyhound track.

Galway City

Ardilaun House Hotel

féile bia HOTEL / RESTAURANT

Taylors Hill Galway Co Galway
Tel: 091 521433 Fax: 091 521546
Email: ardilaun@iol.ie Web: www.ardilaunhousehotel.ie

Ardilaun House Hotel has an interesting history - it dates back to about 1840, when it was built as a townhouse for prominent members of Galway society, the Persse family (Augusta Persse became Lady Gregory, co-founder of the Abbey Theatre) - and recently celebrated 40 years in the ownership of the Ryan family, who opened it as an hotel in 1962. While convenient to the city, its wooded grounds give it a country feeling. Friendly, helpful staff make a good impression on arrival and everything about the hotel - which has recently been extensively renovated, extended and refurbished - confirms the feeling of a well-run establishment. Public areas are spacious, elegantly furnished and some - notably the dining room - overlook gardens at the back. Bedrooms are traditionally furnished to a high standard (and have modem lines as well as the usual amenities) and excellent in-house leisure facilities include snooker and a new leisure centre with indoor swimming pool, gym, solarium, beauty salon and treatment rooms. Purpose-built conference facilities offer a wide range of options for large and small groups (max 400), with back-up business services, including video conferencing on request. An attractive banqueting room is especially suitable for weddings. Conference/banqueting (400/270). Children welcome (under 3s free in parents' room, cots available without charge, baby sitting arranged). Pets permitted in some areas. **Rooms 89** (1 suite, 2 junior suites, 9 executive rooms, 6 shower only, 24 no-smoking, 3 for disabled). Lift. B&B €115 pps, ss €25. Closed 24-28 Dec.

Camilaun Room: The restaurant is in a fine old-fashioned hotel dining room with crystal chandeliers and bay windows overlooking a colourful garden, traditional white-clothed tables, warm decor and a welcome emphasis on comfort - and friendly staff make guests feel welcome. Head chef John Kelly has been with the hotel since 1985 and knows his market well, using the best of ingredients in a traditional style with a light sprinkling of words like balsamic, red onion marmalade and lemongrass on the menu, giving the tiniest nod to fashion here and there. Menus offer a predictably wide choice of prime meats and fish - a house speciality is chateaubriand, also braised shank of lamb and a medley of scallops and prawns - competently cooked and attractively served with an exceptional variety of side vegetables - perhaps as many as seven or eight - all perfectly cooked. The grande finale is an excellent traditional dessert trolley - sherry trifle, tiramisu, charlotte royale, apple tart - and an invitation to double up on the sweets reinforces the overall feeling of being generously treated in pleasant, formal surroundings that is the essential pleasure of dining here. Good coffee to finish. Extensive wine list. **Seats 140** (private room 30). No smoking restaurant. L&D daily: L1-2.15, D 7-9.15. Set L €20. Set D from €21 (5-course Set D €39), D also à la carte. House wine €16.50. SC 10%. Amex, Diners, MasterCard, Visa, Laser. **Directions:** 1 mile west of city centre (towards Salthill).

Galway City

Da Roberta

N RESTAURANT

169 Upper Salthill Galway Co Galway
Tel: 091 585808 Fax: 091 583455

Roberta and Sandro Pieri see their tightly-packed little restaurant is Salthill as 'a piece of Italy' - and they convey this so successfully that queues regularly form at the door. Sunny, yellow walls are hung with still life prints and posters of "Touring Club Italiano", tables sport linen cloths with peach paper covers, it's child-friendly and buzzes with the chatter of happy diners. Roberta smiles as she takes orders, Sandro moves from table to table with bottles of wine exchanging wry banter with customers as he pours wine, stuffing corks in his pocket. The menu offers many familiar Italian dishes (also available to take away) starting with a daily soup (€4, home-made) rising to a maximum of about €16 for a speciality main course Involtini alla Roberta (veal stuffed with Parma ham , baked with cheese & cream sauce). Between lie many authentic dishes : prosciutto and salad leaves with soft cheese and a salad of rocket with olives, capers and parmesan can both be excellent, for example, also pizzas with thin, crisp bases and a good choice of toppings (Luisa, with sun-dried tomatoes, rosemary, feta and mozzarella, for example) although fritto misto di Mare may disappoint, if consisting of canned squid rings, mussels and tiny prawns sautéed with tomatoes. Desserts - not a strong point and augmented by the familiar plastic card of ice creams - come with good coffee and an appropriate all-Italian wine list also offers Italian beer. So what you get here is charming hospitality, an authentic Italian atmosphere and good value - a great recipe for success. **Seats 46.** Open daily 12 noon-10.45 (Sun to 11). A la carte. House wine €16. Reservations required. Amex, Diners, MasterCard, Visa, Laser. **Directions:** Central Salthill, opposite the Church.

Galway City

Devondell

B&B

47 Devon Park Lr. Salthill Galway Co Galway **Tel: 091 528306**
Email: devondel@iol.ie Web: www.devondell.com

Although quite unremarkable from the road, Berna Kelly's immaculate house has won many admirers and it's easy to see why: a warm welcome, pretty bedrooms with crisp white linen and many homely touches and Berna's special breakfasts served in a fine dining room overlooking the back garden, are just a few of the reasons guests keep coming back. It's a little difficult to find on the first visit, but well worth the effort. **Rooms 4** (all en-suite & no smoking, 3 shower only). B&B €40 pps, no ss. Closed Dec-Mar. **No Credit Cards. Directions:** Fr Griffin Road to T Junction-take left after 400 - 500 yds, take right at Devon Park House, go to fork 100 yds up, take left and sharp left.

Galway City

Galway Bay Hotel

féile bia **HOTEL**

The Promenade Salthill Galway Co. Galway **Tel: 091 520520** Fax: 091 520530
Email: info@galwaybayhotel.net Web: www.galwaybayhotel.net

This well-named hotel has clear views over Galway Bay to the distant hills of County Clare from public rooms on the ground floor as well as many of the spacious, well-equipped bedrooms. The large marbled foyer and adjacent public areas are very spacious and facilities for both business and leisure are particularly impressive. A good choice for business guests as well as the usual facilities, all rooms have modem points and interactive TV for messages, internet and preview of the bill. Conference/banqueting (1000/600), video-conferencing. Leisure centre, swimming pool, gym; beauty salon. Children welcome (free in parents' room under 2, cot available, baby sitting arranged; playroom) Rooftop garden. Parking (inc underground). No pets. **Rooms 153** (4 suites, 7 executive, 24 no smoking, 5 for disabled). Lifts. B&B €115 pps, ss €25. Open all year. Amex, Diners, MasterCard, Visa, Laser. **Directions:** Located on Salthill Road beside Leisureland, overlooking Galway Bay.

Galway City

Glenlo Abbey Hotel

HOTEL / RESTAURANT

Bushypark Galway Co Galway
Tel: 091 526666 Fax: 091 527800
Email: info@glenloabbey.ie Web: www.glenlo.com

Originally an eighteenth century residence, Glenlo Abbey is just two and a half miles from Galway city yet offers all the advantages of the country - the hotel is on a 138-acre estate, with its own golf course and Pavilion. It enjoys views over Lough Corrib and the surrounding countryside. The scale of the hotel is generous throughout, public rooms are impressive and bedrooms are well-furnished in a traditional country house style, with good amenities and marbled bathrooms. The old Abbey has been restored to provide privacy for meetings and private dining, and there is a fully equipped business service bureau to back up seminars, conferences and presentations; (conference/banqueting 200/160). For indoor relaxation there's the Oak Cellar bar (where light food is served) and, in addition to the classical River Room restaurant, the hotel operates an historic Pullman train carriage as a restaurant in the hotel grounds (see below). Golf (9 & 18 hole), fishing, equestrian, walking. Garden. Children welcome (cot available without charge). No pets. Own parking. **Rooms 46** (4 suites, 1 junior suite, 16 no-smoking,1 shower only, 1 for disabled). Wheelchair access. Lift. Room rate about €270. Open all year.

Pullman Restaurant: This must be one of the most novel dinner venues in the country – four carriages, two from the original Orient Express that featured in scenes from "Murder on the Orient Express", filmed in 1974 with a catalogue of famous stars including Albert Finney, Ingrid Bergman and Peter Ustinov. Adapting it to restaurant use has been achieved brilliantly, with no expense spared in maintaining the special features of a luxurious train. There is a lounge/bar area leading to an open dining carriage and two private 'coupes'. Compartments, each seating a maximum of six. Background clackity-clack and hooting noises lend an authenticity to the experience and the romance is sustained by discreetly piped music of the 1940s and 50s – Sinatra, Nat King Cole, Bing Crosby and the Andrews Sisters. The view from the windows is of a coiffeured golf course, Lough Corrib and Connemara hills in the distance. Welcome by smart staff is pleasant, service throughout exemplary. Tables are set up as on a train, with silver cutlery, simple glassware and white linen - and the food is suitably inclined to Asian influences; while not cutting edge, it is very enjoyable. In line with the fun of the theme, you could begin your meal with a Pullman Paté - and even end it with Poirot Pie (apple tart); more typically, try an excellent 'Assiette of Oriental Appetisers' includes sushi, smoked salmon, nori, prawn and hot green mustard paste - and follow with a main course of (deliciously crisp-skinned) roast half duck in plum sauce. Short, well-chosen wine list. Recommended as much for its unique, special occasion experience as for the fare. **Seats 66.** D daily 6.30-9.30 Amex, Diners, MasterCard, Visa, Laser. **Directions:** 4 km from Galway on N59 in the Clifden direction.

Galway City

Goya's

CAFÉ

2/3 Kirwans Lane Galway Co Galway **Tel: 091 567010**
Email: goyas@eircom.net Web: www.goyas.ie

If only for a cup of cappuccino or hot chocolate and a wedge of chocolate cake or a slice of quiche, a restorative visit to this delightful contemporary bakery and café is a must on any visit to Galway. There's something very promising about the cardboard cake boxes stacked up in preparation near the door, the staff are super, there's a great buzz and the food is simply terrific. What's more, you don't even have to be in Galway to enjoy Emer Murray's terrific baking - contact Goya's for her seasonal mail-order catalogues "Fabulous Festive Fancies" (Christmas cakes, plum pudding, mince pies etc) and "Easter Delights" (simnel cake and others); wedding cakes also available. If you're wondering where to start, why not try a speciality: Goya's 3-layer chocolate gateau cake. Open all day Mon-Sat. MasterCard, Visa, Laser. **Directions:** Behind McDonaghs Fish Shop, off Quay Street.

Galway City

Great Southern Hotel

féile bia HOTEL

Eyre Square Galway Co Galway **Tel: 091 564041** Fax: 091 566704
Email: res@galway.gsh.ie Web: www.gshotels.com

Overlooking Eyre Square right in the heart of Galway, this historic railway hotel was built in 1845 and has recently undergone a major refurbishment programme which - like the renovation of their Killarney hotel - was intended mainly to reinstate the grandeur and elegance of its 19th century heyday; this has been achieved most notably in the public areas, where marble flooring, high ceilings, chandeliers and rich fabrics have all contributed to re-creating the grandeur of old. Accommodation has been treated similarly - the wide corridors (designed so that ladies in hooped dresses could pass without inconvenience) are especially impressive in these days of compact modern buildings and all the rooms are spacious and opulently decorated, with bathrooms to match. On the top storey, the old swimming pool has given way to a new health spa with panoramic views over Galway city and harbour (interesting rather than scenic); new facilities include a Canadian hot tub, hydrotherapy baths, jacuzzi and steam room , a state of the art gym and fitness area - and treatment rooms offering a wide range of therapies. The Oyster Room Restaurant (overlooking Eye Square) has not changed significantly but O'Flaherty's Pub, which is in the basement of the hotel and also has direct access from the street, had undergone a complete revamp and is much more modern, with a big screen and a high-tech sound system. Conference/banqueting (350/300); business centre, secretarial services. Leisure centre, indoor swimming pool. Children under 2 free in parents' room, cots available without charge, baby sitting arranged. No pets. Arrangement with nearby car park. 24 hour room service.* A sister hotel, the Corrib Great Southern (Tel 091 7555281; www.gshotel.com) is nearby on the main Dublin road entering the city. Larger & newer with extensive conference & leisure facilities, it is especially suitable for conference/banqueting and family breaks. **Rooms 99** (12 suites, 8 junior suites, 34 executive, 21 no-smoking, 2 for disabled). Lift. B&B €140 pps, ss €35 (Room only rate: €250, max 3 guests). Closed 25-26 Dec. Amex, Diners, MasterCard, Visa, Laser. **Directions:** In heart of the city overlooking Eyre Square.

Galway City

Harbour Hotel

HOTEL / RESTAURANT

New Docks Road Galway Co Galway
Tel: 091 569466 Fax: 091 569455
Email: stay@harbour.com Web: www.harbour.ie

This contemporary style hotel is conveniently situated at the heart of the city and offers comfortable, moderately priced accommodation with secure parking adjacent. Functional bedrooms with all the usual facilities (TV, trouser press) and well-fitted bathrooms have already been refurbished less than two years after the hotel opened - a clear indication of Galway's current popularity as a holiday destination. Furthermore, at the time of going to press, work is in progress on an extension, to provide extra dining space, a separate breakfast room and a residents lounge - all due for completion by January 2004. Krusoes Restaurant (Tel: 091 539115) is entered directly from the hotel lobby and bar but run as a separate operation by well-known local restaurateur Michael O'Grady (who also provides breakfast and bar lunches). Chic and trendy, with colourful big paintings and a large mirror at one end giving a sense of depth, it has minimalist shiny black table tops and paper napkins. Background jazz is pleasant and the food style is, predictably, contemporary international; it's above-average as an hotel restaurant and particularly popular at lunch time. L daily 12-2.30 (Sun to 3.30), D daily 6.30-9.30 (Sun to 8.30). Closed 24-25 Dec. Amex. Diners, MasterCard, Visa, Laser, Switch. **Directions:** Beside the docks in Galway, 5 mins from Eyre Square.

Galway City

Jurys Inn Galway

féile bia HOTEL

Quay Street Galway Co Galway **Tel: 091 566444** Fax: 091 568415
Email: jurysinngalway@jurysdoyle.com Web: bookajurysinn.com

Jurys Galway Inn is magnificently sited to make the most of both the river - which rushes past almost all the bedroom windows - and the great buzz of the Spanish Arch area of the city (just outside the door). Like the other Jurys room-only 'inns', the hotel offers a fair standard of basic accommodation without frills. Rooms are large (sleeping up to three adults or two adults and two children) and well finished, with everything required for comfort and convenience - ample well-lit work/shelf space, neat en-suite bathroom, TV, phone - the only downside is that the high occupancy rate can sometimes show in wear and tear. Beds are generous, with good-quality bedding, and open wardrobes are more than adequate. Neat tea/coffee-making facilities are built into the design, but there is no room service. Public areas include an impressive, well-designed foyer with seating areas, and a modern café/bar with good atmosphere. Arrangement with next door car park. Garden. **Rooms 128.** Room Rate from €72 (max 3 adults/2 adults & 2 children; 2 rooms for disabled). Closed 24-26 Dec. Amex, Diners, MasterCard, Visa. **Directions:** City centre, beside Spanish Arch, overlooking the bridge.

Galway City

K C Blakes

RESTAURANT

10 Quay Street Galway Co Galway **Tel: 091 561826** Fax: 091 561829

K C Blakes is named after a stone Tower House, of a type built sometime between 1440 and 1640, which stands as a typical example of the medieval stone architecture of the ancient city of Galway. The Caseys' restaurant, with all its sleek black designer style and contemporary chic could not present a stronger contrast to such a building. Proprietor-chef John Casey sources ingredients for K C Blakes with care and cooks with skill in wide-ranging menus that offer something for every taste: traditional Irish (beef and Guinness stew), modern Irish (pan-fried scallops and black pudding with potato purée and basil cream, perhaps, or breast of chicken with morel and tarragon stuffing with creamy mash and port jus), classical French (sole meunière) to global cuisine (a huge choice here - oriental duck with warm pancakes stuffed with cucumber and spring onion, perhaps, tiger prawns in filo or pasta dishes such as tagliatelle carbonara). Very professional service, creative cooking and smart surroundings make for quite a sense of occasion - yet this remarkable operation is aimed at a wide market and fairly priced. Closed 25 Dec. Amex, MasterCard, Visa. **Directions:** City centre, near Spanish Arch. ◇

Galway City

Kilkenny Café

CAFÉ

6-7 High Street Galway Co Galway **Tel: 091 566110**

On the top floor of the new 3-storey Kilkenny store in Galway city, this bright modern café is run on similar lines to the successful Dublin operation. It's an attractive space with comfortable corners to tuck into for a chat - and foot-weary shoppers will be particularly glad of the fact that, unlike Dublin, it is not self-service but provides waitress service. Wholesome, flavourful, good-home-cooking style food is available throughout the day; breakfast and lunch menus are offered, otherwise a tempting selection of panini, wraps and sandwiches plus the home-bakes for which Kilkenny is well-known (scones with butter, preserves and cream, pear & almond tart) are available all day. The drinks menu includes a range of Java Republic coffees and a short wine list (a house wine available by the bottle and a couple of quarter bottles) as well as juices, smoothies and other soft drinks. Vegetarian and gluten-free options are highlighted on the menu. The only disadvantage is its location within the building (no lift). **Seats 48.** Open Mon-Thu & Sat, 10-5; Fri 10-6.30. B'fast, 9-11.30; L, 11.30-3.30 (Sat to 4.30). Closed Sun, bank hols, 25-26 Dec. Amex, Diners, MasterCard, Visa, Laser. **Directions:** City centre.

Galway City

Killeen House

COUNTRY HOUSE

Bushy Park Galway Co Galway
Tel: 091 524179 Fax: 091 528065
Email: killeenhouse@ireland.com Web: www.killeenhousegalway.com

Catherine Doyle's delightful house really has the best of both worlds. It's on the Clifden road just on the edge of Galway city yet, with 25 acres of private grounds and gardens reaching right down to the shores of Lough Corrib, offers all the advantages of the country, too. Catherine has been welcoming guests to Killeen House for over a decade and her quiet, thoughtful hospitality and high standards make a stay here very special, beginning with tea on arrival, properly served on a beautifully arranged tray with fine linen and polished silver - a house speciality extending to the tray provided in your bedroom, which manages to bring real class to that most practical of facilities. The house was built in 1840 and has the features of a more leisurely era, when space was plentiful - not only in the reception rooms, which include a guest drawing room and an elegant dining room overlooking the gardens (where delicious breakfasts are served in style), but also the bedrooms. These are luxuriously and individually furnished, each in a different period, e.g. Regency, Edwardian and (most fun this one) Art Nouveau; the bedding is exquisite and they have lovely bathrooms too - again, highly individual in style and with every possible comfort provided. As in all the very best guesthouses, your hostess seems to have thought of all the little things that make people feel at home (and some of the bigger ones too, like comfortable armchairs and flat screen TV); her attention to detail is an object lesson in how to do things right: there are fresh flowers everywhere (including the bathroom), there's a turn-down service (and fresh towels in the bathroom while you're out for dinner) and, although the menu is not especially extensive, breakfast is a delight - lots of fresh juice and aromatic coffee, free range eggs - and little details like a separate toast rack and butter dish for each guest - delicious home-made preserves too. Just lovely. Not suitable for children under 12. Garden; walking. No pets.* Killeen House was our Guesthouse of the Year in 2003. **Rooms 6** (1 shower only). Lift. B&B €80pps, ss €45. Closed 23-27 Dec. Amex, Diners, MasterCard, Visa. **Directions:** On N59 between Galway city and Moycullen village.

Galway City

Kirwan's Lane Restaurant

RESTAURANT Kirwans Lane Galway Co Galway **Tel: 091 568266** Fax: 091 561645

This well-known contemporary restaurant is in a laneway just beside the Hotel Spanish Arch. When it opened in 1996, it was Galway's first cutting-edge restaurant - and such a success that it was extended to double the capacity less than three years later. The formula has since been changed from contemporary fine dining to a more informal bistro style, offering extensive international menus (Asian influences, quite a lot of grills, popular desserts like tiramisu) at relatively moderate prices. But good fish cookery - which has always been a feature - remains a strong point and and piano playing can add to the atmosphere at weekends. No parking (multi-storey carpark nearby). **Seats 100** (private room 50). No smoking area; air conditioning. L& D daily: L12.30-2.30, D 6-10.30. Closed Christmas. Amex, MasterCard, Visa, Laser, Switch. **Directions:** Just off Cross Street and Quay Street. ◇

Galway City

Martine's Quay Street Wine Bar

Ⓝ **RESTAURANT / WINE BAR** 21 Quay Street Galway Co Galway
Tel: 091 565662 Fax: 091 563232
Email: info@winebar.ie Web: www.winebar.ie

In the buzz of Quay Street, across from the famous McDonagh seafood restaurant (in the same family ownership), this quaint old terraced house is painted a trademark maroon and has a few tables outside for fine weather. Don't be put off by the higgledy piggledy little reception area - which leads to the wine bar and restaurant on the ground floor and stairs to a smaller first floor dining room - as you'll soon get into the swing of things. Lots come to sit around the tiny bar, everyone seems to know everyone and it's a bit chaotic, but that's all part of the charm. It was originally a small house and the atmosphere is cosy, with candles in bottles, old mirrors and mismatched furniture - the ideal retreat from hard-edged minimalism. The menu offers a good choice - lots of starters including favourites like chicken liver paté and warm salad of smoked bacon & blue cheese, a pasta section, poultry and classic red meats like herb-crusted rack of lamb and the perennial steaks - but, of course seafood is the main speciality, in dishes like Claddagh fish stew (prawns, salmon, mussels, silver hake with vegetables in a rich tomato based stew, starter or main course), 'Salmon of the Night' and many more, including popular international dishes. Cooking is good (portions are large, but the food is really tasty), service casual but interested and an extensive wine list is designed to be fun, with new additions every week. This is a restaurant with a following, so booking is advised. **Seats 39.** Open daily, 12.30-10.30. A la carte. Wines from €15. Clsed 25 Dec. Amex, MasterCard, Visa, Laser. **Directions:** City centre, near Spanish Arch.

Galway City

Nimmo's Restaurant & Wine Bar

RESTAURANT / WINE BAR Spanish Arch Galway Co Galway **Tel: 091 561114**

Good food and a friendly, bustling atmosphere have made Harriet Leander's restaurant in a characterful old stone building on the water's edge one of Galway's most popular dining places. Pleasant staff meet and seat guests efficiently, presenting short but balanced à la carte menus. The style is fairly modern but there is no question of presentation taking precedence over flavour and texture: a fresh-tasting salmon & chive terrine comes wrapped in smoked salmon and served with horseradish cream while a perfectly cooked canon of lamb may come with red roast peppers, spring onion mash and asparagus; plentiful side vegetables are full of flavour and the overall impression is of excellent ingredients in safe hands. Desserts are bought-in but their provenance is impeccable (from Goya's, see entry); good coffee is refilled without charge - and there's a good wine list too. Prices may seem a little steep for the surroundings (quite basic furnishings and table settings), but this is offset by good cooking - and the ambience has the happy informality of a busy French bistro. Open Tue-Sun, 7-10pm. Closed Sun. No bookings. *Nimmo's Wine Bar, downstairs, is a sister to the first floor restaurant and, although much more informal, offers similarly delicious food at reasonable prices. It has a bit of style - flowers in wine buckets, lots of prints and memorabilia on the walls - and the French chef adds that special something to classics like pork and prune terrine, or a traditional fish soup. L Tue-Sat, 12.30-3, D Tue-Sun 7-10 (live music Sun, 6.30-9.30). Closed Mon. MasterCard, Visa. **Directions:** Harbour front, beside Spanish Arch. ◇

Galway City

Norman Villa

GUESTHOUSE

86 Lower Salthill Salthill Galway Co Galway
Tel: 091 521131 Fax: 091 521131
Email: normanvilla@oceanfree.net Web: www.normanvilla.com

Dee and Mark Keogh's guesthouse is exquisite. It's a lovely old house, immaculately maintained and imaginatively converted to make the most of every inch, ensuring guest comfort without spoiling the interior proportions. Dee and Mark are dedicated hosts and their home is dashingly decorated, with lovely rich colours and a great collection of modern paintings looks especially magnificent juxtaposed with antique furniture. Bedrooms have neat shower rooms ingeniously fitted into tiny spaces and also phones and tea/coffee-making facilities, while a converted coach house at the end of the lovely little back garden makes an unusual self-contained suite. Children welcome. No pets. **Rooms 6** (all shower only & no-smoking). B&B €55 pps, ss €15. Closed Nov-Feb. MasterCard, Visa. **Directions:** Follow signs from Galway city centre toSalthill, then Lower Salthill - house is beside P.J. Flaherty's Pub.

Galway City

Oscars Restaurant

Ⓝ RESTAURANT

Dominick Street Galway Co Galway **Tel: 091 582180**

Oscars is an extraordinary restaurant: a startlingly black and red room, the ceiling covered in a billowing tent-like material, low lights; tables, well apart, are draped in imitation leather, seating is zebra-patterned, framed film posters decorate the walls - the effect is nightclubby, with overloud jazz adding to the slightly decadent atmosphere. The menu, in an old-fashioned wine list cover, lists about 60 separate items: cooking influences are eclectic, leaning particularly towards Thailand and the East. Lovely waitresses are helpful, interested and attentive - and, while it's difficult to know what to make of the place at first, delicious amuse-bouches (demi-tasses of gazpacho perhaps) indicate something serious going on in the kitchen. A starter platter for two consists of onion badjis, spiced chicken wings, mushrooms in garlic butter, fish cake, spare ribs and dip (€17) or there are various combinations in filo baskets - Tiger Prawns tossed in garlic and lemon butter, perhaps, or Florida style chilli pepper poppers – hot chillis stuffed with prawns, deepfried and served with a sweet/sour salad (both about €9). Main courses are served in large portions on big, heavy plates: a properly cooked sirloin steak with smoked garlic sauce on potato purée (€23), an amazing, well-made Thai Green Fish Curry served spectacularly on a banana leaf and including a wide variety of fish and along with coconut milk, lemon grass, sliced aubergine and rice (€26). Most remarkable, perhaps, is chargrilled supreme of chicken with sweet and sour sauce and rice served on a lotus leaf big as an elephant's ear. Desserts (€8.50) are less dramatic - good Baileys crème brulée in a gratin dish, a deeply flavoured lemon sorbet perhaps.The wine list features bottles from France, Italy, Australia and Chile, with two half bottles offered. In spite of presentation that is sometimes bizarre, chef/patron, Michael O'Meara's expressive, confident cooking stands out in Galway. **Seats 50.** D Tue-Sun. A la carte. House wines from €19.50. Closed Mon. ◇

Galway City

Park House Hotel

féile bia HOTEL

Forster St. Eyre Square Galway Co Galway **Tel: 091 564924** Fax: 091 569219
Email: parkhousehotel@eircom.net Web: www.parkhousehotel.ie

It would be hard to beat the location of this attractive and welcoming owner-run hotel just off Eyre Square - and it is furnished to a high standard and warmly decorated throughout. Rooms are spacious and cosily furnished, with all the comforts that make you feel at home when travelling, including good bathrooms. Providing a high level of personal service is a particular point of pride, making this an especially comfortable base for visitors on business or leisure. There are facilities for small conferences and banqueting (40/50) and one of the hotel's greatest assets in this busy city is a private residents' car park. Park Room Restaurant (D daily & L Sun); bar food L&D daily. Children welcome (under 12s free in parents' room, cots available). No pets.* At the time of going to press major building work was in progress at the hotel;. completion expected before the 2004 season. **Rooms 57** (2 junior suites, 1 for disabled). Lift. 24 hour room service. B&B from about 60 € pps. Closed 24-26 Dec. Amex, Diners, MasterCard, Visa, Laser. **Directions:** Located adjacent to Eyre Square. ◇

Galway City

Radisson SAS Hotel

HOTEL

Lough Atalia Road Galway Co Galway **Tel: 091 5383000** Fax: 091 538380
Email: sales@radissonsas.com Web: www.radissonsas.com

Ideally situated on the waterfront, overlooking Lough Atalia, this dashing new hotel is much more central than its scenic location might suggest, as the railway and bus stations are very close and the shops and restaurants of Eyre Square are only a few minutes walk. A high, airy foyer with satellite reception desk, unusual sculptures, audacious greenery and a glass-walled lift is designed to impress and lift the spirits, a feeling confirmed by the atmosphere in adjacent public areas, including a very pleasant big lounge area a few steps up, in a sunny position looking over the roman-style leisure centre to Lough Atalia, and the cosier Backstage Bar. Bedrooms are designed in three distinct styles - Scandinavian, Maritime or Classic - all furnished to a high standard, with excellent bathrooms and facilities (air conditioning, phone/voice mail & modem, safe, TV with video channel as well as the more mundane but necessary tea/coffee making and trouser press); all of this plus 3-hour express laundry and 24 hour room service make this the ideal business accommodation; an extra floor was added in 2003, providing luxurious new suites with superb views. Facilities for conferences and meetings are excellent: the main conference room (appropriately named Inis Mór) can seat 1,000 delegates, and there are also five boardrooms and six meeting rooms (all named after the Tribes of Galway), with cutting edge equipment and business support services available. The hotel restaurant, Marinas, is a large split-level room with decor in blues and browns inspired by Lough Atalia, and works equally well for formal dining (where Galway seafood features strongly) and as a place to make the most of the famous Scandinavian buffet breakfast. Conference/banqueting (750/570). Video-conferencing, business centre, secretarial services. Leisure centre (17m pool, children's pool, gym, sauna, steam bath, jacuzzi, outdoor hot tub). Pitch & putt. No pets. **Rooms 204** (3 suites, 10 junior suites, 138 no smoking, 10 for disabled.) Lift. Children welcome (under 10s free in parents' room, cot available without charge) B&B about €185, ss about €90, no SC. Amex, Diners, MasterCard, Visa, Laser. **Directions:** 200 m from Bus & Train Station. ◇

Galway City

Revive Coffee & Sandwich Bar

CAFÉ

35 Eyre Street Galway Co Galway **Tel: 091 533779**

This popular day-time rendezvous offers a wide choice of quality sandwiches, wraps, salads, panini, made-up to order at the counter, where you pay and will be served at tables, or at a 'bar' counter - or in a small, covered courtyard with hanging baskets of flowers under a perspex roof at the back - a welcome relief from the heat of the main café in summer. Good soups, wraps - chicken, cheddar salad and pesto with tortilla chips and sweet and sour dip on the side makes a generous lunch portion, packed with chicken. Or, there are: gourmet sandwiches, panini or house salads, such as Caesar or smoked salmon. There are scones, croissants, muffins and other treats, good coffees and smoothies available all day. Although busy at lunchtime Revive is a pleasant drop-in for breakfast (toasted ciabatta filled with smoked bacon, Cumberland sausage, tomatoes and fried eggs), morning coffee, or afternoon tea. Staff are pleasant and efficient - and complimentary newspapers are provided. Open Mon-Sat, 8am to 6pm. ◇

Galway City

The Malt House

RESTAURANT

High Street Galway Co Galway **Tel: 091 567866** Fax: 091 563993
Email: info@malthouse.com Web: www.malt-house.com

The Cunninghams' welcoming old restaurant and bar in a quiet, flower-filled courtyard off High Street has great character and a friendly attitude. There's a lunchtime bar menu with soups and salads, served with good home-made bread, classic starters and light dishes like duck liver paté with Cumberland sauce or deep-fried camembert with pear sauce & salad, popular hot seafood dishes - baked garlic mussels, panfried crab claws - steaks and vegetarian dishes. Dinner menus are more formal but the emphasis is still on fairly traditional dishes - and none the worse for that. This is one of Galway's most consistent restaurants and its cosy atmosphere and comfortingly familiar food make a welcome alternative to contemporary fare served in hard-edged minimalist surroundings. Multi-storey carpark nearby. **Seats 50** (private room, 20). No smoking restaurant; air conditioning. L & D Mon-Sat: L12.30-2.30, D 6-10. Bar Food also available. Set L about €20, Early D about €20 (6-7pm), Set D about €35, à la carte L&D available, house wine about €18; no SC. Closed Sun & Christmas/New Year. Amex, Diners, MasterCard, Visa, Laser. **Directions:** Located in a courtyard just off High Street. ◇

Galway City

Tigh Neachtain

ATMOSPHERIC PUB

Cross Street Galway Co Galway
Tel: 091 568820 Fax: 091 563940

Tigh Neachtain is one of Galway's oldest pubs - the origins of the building are medieval and it has been in the same family for a century - the interior has remained unchanged since 1894. Quite unspoilt, it has great charm, an open fire and a friendly atmosphere - and the pint is good too. Simple bar food (sandwiches and a variety of coffees) are available but perhaps the nicest thing of all is the way an impromptu traditional music session can get going at the drop of a hat. Closed 25 Dec & Good Fri. **No credit cards. Directions:** Situated on crossroads Quay Street/Cross Street/High Street. ◇

Galway City

Viña Mara Restaurant & Wine Bar

Ⓝ **RESTAURANT / WINE BAR**

19 Middle Street Galway Co Galway
Tel: 091 561610 Fax: 091 562607
Email: vinamara@hotmail.com

Jarlath and Eileen Feeney's total refurbishment of an old building in the Spanish Arch area has brought a little bit of the Mediterranean to deepest Galway - and, with its authentic decor and full cocktail bar, it succeeds remarkably well in creating a relaxed holiday atmosphere. Better still, the food is excellent too. Head chef Padraic Kielty has been building up a well-deserved reputation for Vina Mara since they opened in November 2002 and his pride in freshness and quality shows in vibrant dishes that are full of flavour - there is an emphasis on presentation, but this food tastes even better than it looks. A seasonal à la carte considerately includes a section of vegetarian and vegan dishes (good enough to make tempting mainstream choices) and is augmented by daily specials: a speciality of crisp crusted stuffed loin of veal, perhaps, with Cambozola & figs and a saffron mash. The range offered is wide, with some seafood but also more red meats and poultry than many other restaurants in the area - and smaller dishes that are equally appealing - a warm Mediterranean salad, for example, comes with olives, garlic, crispy pancetta, sundried tomatoes hot feta and raspberry black pepper oil: colourful, refreshing, ideal for a summer evening. A well-balanced wine list includes one or two organic wines and might be more interesting if it specialised more - there are only two sherries, for example, although there's also a full page of cocktails. Live music at weekends. **Seats 70** (private room 30). No smoking restaurant; air conditioning. Children welcome. Reservations required. D daily, 6-10. A la carte, House wine €18.50. Amex, MasterCard, Visa, Laser. **Directions:** Behind Shop St. turn down alley at Anthony Ryan's shop - at end, next to church.

Galway City

Westwood House Hotel

HOTEL

Dangan Upper Newcastle Galway Co Galway **Tel: 091 521442** Fax: 091 521400
Email: info@westwoodhousehotel.com Web: www.westwoodhousehotel.com

A sister hotel to The Schoolhouse Hotel in Dublin and the Station House Hotel, Clifden, Westwood House is well located, on the edge of Galway and convenient to both the city and Connemara, it's set well back from the road and offers a high standard of accommodation for business and leisure at fairly reasonable prices. Air-conditioned throughout, the hotel has good conference/banqueting facilities (350/275) with back-up services and fax/ISDN lines in bedrooms. A leisure centre and dedicated business centre are among improvements planned for 2004. A range of 2-3 night leisure breaks offers particularly good value. No pets. **Rooms 58** (6 junior suites, 8 executive, 26 no smoking, 3 for disabled). Lift. B&B about €100pps, ss €25. Closed 24-25 Dec. Amex, Diners, MasterCard, Visa, Laser. **Directions:** 1.5 km from Eyre Square (N59 for Clifden).

COUNTY GALWAY

Aran Islands

An Dún

Ⓝ **B&B / RESTAURANT**

Inis Meain Aran Islands Co Galway
Tel: 099 73047 Fax: 099 73047
Email: anduninismeain@eircom.net Web: www.inismeainaccommodation.com

A short jump from Inis Mor, this interesting island is the most traditional of the group - very few cars, wonderful walks, and some people still wearing traditional clothes; by contrast the Inis Meain Knitting Co. factory and showroom offers great bargains on unique products only to be found in specialist outlets in Milan and Japan. At the foot of Dun Conchubhar (Connor's Fort) is Teresa and Padraic

Faherty's restaurant and B&B, An Dún, which was the home of Padraig's grandfather and was the first restaurant on the island when it opened in 1989. In 2000 it was refurbished and extended to include en-suite bedrooms (modern, well fitted out, comfortable, great views), a new dining room and a mini-spa; Teresa is qualified in aromatherapy and can arrange packages for the new spa, especially off-season. Once you get here you may not be in a hurry to leave - one Swiss lady came for a week and stayed 31 days... The island's pretty traditional pub is just five minutes' walk. Children welcome (under 5 free in parents' room, cot available without charge, baby sitting arranged). Walking, cycling. Garden. Mini-spa; aromatherapy. Shop. **Rooms 4** (all en-suite & no smoking). B&B €32, ss €6 (off season €25, no ss; advance booking only in winter).

Restaurant: There are two dining rooms - the inner one is original and cottagey, while a modern extension has wooden floors and windows on two sides, with wonderful sea and mountain views. The style and atmosphere is homely and some of the best traditional food on the islands is to be found here. Local foods star: fish straight from currachs, (sometimes in time for breakfast); their own floury Inis Meain potatoes, fertilized in the traditional manner, with seaweed; freshly squeezed orange juice for breakfast...scones, crumbles and tarts using local fruits. Specialities include fish dishes like home-made chowder or a trio of ultra fresh mackerel, pollock and wild salmon on a lemony apricot sauce, then there's local lamb shank served with fresh herbs and interesting desserts like Baileys or brandy carrageen or blackberry tart. A short wine list includes a Concannon, from the Livermore vineyard in California, which has local connections. **Seats 30.** Reservations required (non residents welcome). No smoking restaurant. Wheelchair accessible. D daily in summer, 6.30-10. Set D available fore residents (€20), otherwise à la carte. House wine €15. Open all year except 1-2 weeks taken off-season. MasterCard, Visa. **Directions:** Centre of island.

Aran Islands

Ard Mhuire

Ⓝ **B&B** Inis Oirr Aran Islands Co Galway **Tel: 099 75005** Email: unamcdonagh@hotmail.com

On this the smallest and most beautiful of the islands, this fine pebble-dashed house is the first you pass when you get off the ferry and the Conneely family have taken guests here since the house was built in 1934 - Sean Keating stayed with the Conneely family on and off from 1915 till the '50s, as did Brendan Behan; on arrival, all guests get tea and scones by order of Una's mother, Maura, and she'll always find accommodation for anyone she can't fit in. Bedrooms are all newly refurbished, there's a comfortable sitting room, large gardens - and great views, of course. Good home cooking too: set dinner could be curried parsnip and apple soup, local pollock, mackerel or salmon, McGeogh's lamb (from the famous Oughterard butcher, who kills his own lambs), and a dessert of white chocolate, strawberries and mascarpone cheese with cream. Children welcome (under 8 free in parents' room, cot available without charge; baby sitting arranged). Pets permitted by arrangement. Walking, cycling, fishing. Garden; children's playground. Five minutes walk to all amenities. **Rooms 3** (3 en-suite & shower only, 1 with separate bath; all no smoking). B&B €30. No ss. Residents D by arrangement. Closed 10 Dec-10 Jan. **No Credit Cards. Directions:** Turn left at top of pier on Inish Oirr; first house on right.

Aran Islands

Gairdín an Maighdean Mhara/Mermaid's Garden

Ⓝ **RESTAURANT / B&B**

Castle Village Inis Oirr Aran Islands Co Galway
Tel: 099 75062
Web: http://homepage.eircom.net/~mermaidgarden

A walk along the beach, up the hill past the old graveyard and just on the other side nestled a little below is a lovely 2-storey house with a spacious deck in front, overlooking the sea and the majestic Clare coast to the east. On the way in, a happy child-like mermaid on the garage wall greets you - in mosaic tiles collected from everybody on the island. The café is an expression of Padraic and Anita Poil's love of working with the earth and seasons and a means of sharing that bounty, serving delicious organically grown food in a peaceful holiday atmosphere. Padraic has been growing his own meat and produce on Inis Oirr his entire life, using seaweed as a fertiliser. Anita offers an extensive range of food; her à la carte lunch menus can be as light or as serious as the fancy takes you: a good chowder, perhaps, and a super grilled sandwich platter, with mozzarella, rocket pesto, sundried tomato, tapenade and an herbed yogurt mayo - or pasta dishes, Inis Oirr beef (in a wholesome stew perhaps) and a range of seafood dishes. Gorgeous desserts range from seasonal fruit tarts - rhubarb, blackberry & apple - to deeply delicious chocolate almond torte served with vanilla ice cream... Dinner menus are more structured, offering a three-course meal priced by choice of main course. Many who have been here say they'd go to the island for the food alone. Bring your own wine. Children welcome. *Accommodation also available - details on request. **Seats 30** (outdoor, 18). L 12-4, D 6-9 daily. L à la carte; D €30-35. D reservations required. Closed Nov-Easter. **No Credit Cards. Directions:** On top of hill, above the airstrip.

Aran Islands

Kilmurvey House

GUESTHOUSE

Kilronan Inis Mor Aran Islands Co. Galway
Tel: 099 61218 Fax: 099 61397
Email: kilmurveyhouse@eircom.net Web: wwww.kilmurveyhouse.com

This 150 year old stone house stands out as a beacon at the foot of the island's most famous attraction, Dun Aonghasa. On the west side of the island away from the bustle of Kilronan, it is just 3 minutes' walk from the island's only blue flag beach (ideal for a swim before breakfast) and a brisk 15-minute walk to the nearest pub. It's a fine house, with a large high-ceilinged hall and wide stairs giving a feeling of space and grandeur; it has been extended to provide extra en-suite accommodation - all with unrestricted views - and four extra bedrooms and a small function room are planned for 2005.The house is steeped in history - with portraits of the ferocious O'Flahertys, who owned it and the lands around, and one of the godfather of Oscar Wilde (Oscar O'Flaherty Fingall Wilde) hanging in the sitting room. Well kept, with neat manicured front garden and a feeling of space all around it, it has a walled garden at the back where vegetables, salads and herbs are grown - residents' dinners, served about five evenings each week, are based on home-grown and local produce: wonderful Inis Mor floury potatoes, wild salmon, homemade soups, fruit tarts... Comfortable accommodation, good food, and Treasa Joyce's warm and chatty personality that make this an ideal place to stay for a cycling or walking holiday, or just to relax. Children welcome (under 5s free in parents' room, cots available free of charge). Walking; garden. **Rooms 12** (all en-suite, 7 shower only, all no smoking), B&B €40, ss €10. Residents' D by arrangement - please check when booking. Closed 31 Oct-1 Apr.* Café An Sunda Caoch (The Blind Sound) is a café at the Dun Aonghusa visitor centre, run independently by Treasa Joyce. An impressive long stone building in keeping with its surrounding craft shops, it serves delicious home-made food - notably good home baking - every day in summer, 11am-5pm. MasterCard, Visa, Laser. **Directions:** 4.5 miles from Kilronan.

Aran Islands

Mainistir House Hostel

Ⓝ RESTAURANT

Inis Mor Aran Islands Co Galway **Tel: 099 61169**
Fax: 099 61351 Web: www.mainistirhousearan.com

Eleven years since Joel d'Anjou opened this long single storey whitewashed building on a hill overlooking Galway Bay as a hostel and restaurant, it is still the most talked about place on the islands. Despite the name - and the hostel-type outer hall with lots of notices on the walls - twin and double rooms are available as well as small dormitories; guesthouse comfort at a hostel rate is the offer and that's what it delivers, although you'd probably need to be a good mixer to get the most from this type of accommodation. But you don't even have to be staying here to experience Joel's famous 'Vaguely Vegetarian Buffet' which is served nightly and written on a blackboard. It's a quirky system, which everybody loves; on arrival you wait at a table outside, or on the wall, and mix with visitors from around the world until you're called through at 8 o'clock sharp. Six large tables are set up with checked cloths and everyone is served a starter - say a delicious lentil soup - then there are half a dozen dishes displayed on a big round table: a great white dish of wild salmon, paella, one of steaming puy lentils, fresh mixed salad leaves, green beans and great hunks of olive and onion foccacia with a wonderful home-made pesto sauce - and all this for just €12. If you want to push out the boat and spend another €3 you can finish off with home-made ice creams - a delicious expresso cream, perhaps, or classic brown bread - or a baked cheesecake. The actual dishes change daily, but this inventive and enthusiastic cook should not disappoint. Service is prompt (and colourful), this is great food - and amazing value. Bring your own wine. Christmas and New Year packages available. Restaurant **Seats about 48.** D daily, 8pm. €12. BYO.

Accommodation: (8 private rooms plus hostel accommodation for up to 70). B&B €12pps (includes a simple breakfast of porridge/cereals & freshly baked bread each morning). MasterCard, Visa. **Directions:** A short walk from the harbour.

Aran Islands

Man Of Aran Cottages

RESTAURANT / B&B

Kilmurvey Inis Mor Aran Islands Co Galway
Tel: 099 61301 Fax: 099 6132[illegible]
Email: manofaran@eircom.net Web: www.manofarancottage.com

Despite its fame - this is where the film Man of Aran was made - Joe and Maura Wolfe make visiting their home a genuine and personal experience. The cottage is right beside the sea and Kilmurvey beach, surrounded by wild flowers, and Joe has somehow managed to make a productive garden in this exposed location, so their meals usually include his organically grown vegetables (even artichokes and asparagus), salads, nasturtium flowers and young nettle leaves as well as Maura's home-made soups, stews and freshly-baked bread and cakes. In summer they're open for lunch (soups, sandwiches, desserts) and you can eat in the little restaurant or, on fine days, take your food out to benches in the garden with stunning views across the sea towards the mountains. Packed lunches are available too. **Seats 22.** No smoking restaurant. L 12-3; D at 7.30, reservations required. Set D from about €28; house wine from €15-18. SC discretionary (10% at D). No regular weekly closures, but check availability of meals when booking.

Accommodation: The three little bedrooms are basic but full of quaint, cottagey charm and they're very comfortable, although only one is en-suite. Breakfast will probably be a well cooked full-Irish - made special by Joe's beautifully sweet home-grown cherry tomatoes if you are lucky - although they'll do something different if you like. Garden, walking. No pets. Rooms 3 (1 en-suite, all no smoking). B&B €35, ss €7. Closed Nov-1 Mar. **Directions:** Mini-bus or cycle from Kilronan, 4 miles.

Aran Islands

Pier House Guest House

GUESTHOUSE

Kilronan Inishmore Aran Islands Co. Galway
Tel: 099 61417 Fax: 099 61122 Email: pierhouse@iol.ie

In a new building, right on the pier where the boats arrive, Maura & Padraig Joyce run this large well-kept guesthouse. As you walk from the ferry you will be offered tours of the island (mini-bus or pony and trap) or invited to hire one of the thousand or so bikes available on the island. Kilronan is the action centre of the island and Pier House is around the corner from pubs, cafés, a supermarket and the local hall; the attractive beach is round the next corner. While perhaps less characterful than some of the older houses, rooms are comfortable, with more facilities than most island accommodation (TV and phones as well as communal tea/coffee making facilities downstairs to use at any time) and views over sea and hills, and flagstoned fields at the back. There's also a large residents' lounge and the house generally is comfortable and well-run. The **46-seater** restaurant is currently franchised to an Australian chef, Dave Goggin.

*Four attractive new self-catering apartments are also offered and there are plans for major additions to Pier House, to include a conference centre, leisure centre, a new dining room and extra sitting areas; no doubt existing accommodation will also be upgraded to match the new facilities, which are due for completion early in 2005. **Rooms 12** (all en-suite & no smoking). B&B about €35, ss about €16.50. MasterCard, Visa, Laser. **Directions:** Galway to Rosamhil then Ferry, 30 minutes to Island. ◇

Aran Islands

Radharc An Chlair

Ⓝ **GUESTHOUSE**

Castle Village Inis Oirr Aran Islands Co Galway
Tel: 099 75019 Fax: 099 75019 Email: bridopoil@iolfree.ie

Brid Poil's welcoming dormer house looks over the Cliffs of Moher, with views of Galway Bay on the left, and has a great reputation for many years - she came over from Clare twenty years ago when she married Peadar and thought this would be a nice thing to do. Her many regular guests clearly agree - when the ferry from Doolin started, all Clare came over and are still coming so you need to book a month ahead. A keen cook, Brid makes all sorts of treats for different times of day (prune and apricot compôtes, tea and scones, home-made grapefruit marmalade, strawberry pavlova, bread and butter pudding...) and makes dinner for guests. Children over 5 welcome (under 6 free in parents' room). Walking; garden. No pets. **Rooms 6** (5 shower, 1 bath, all no smoking). B&B €30, ss €5. Residents' D €20. MasterCard, Visa, **Directions:** At Castle village, overlooking Clifs of Moher.

Aran Islands

Tig Congaile

Ⓝ **B&B / RESTAURANT**

Moore Village Inis Meain Aran Islands Co Galway
Tel: 099 73085 Fax: 099 73085 Email: tigcongaile@eircom.net

Arriving on Inis Meain, Tigh Congaile is a lovely pale primrose painted, green silled house on the hill above the harbour, with neatly manicured gardens within stone walls, just a 5-minute walk from the pier and from the beach. Vilma Conneely, who came here eleven years ago when she married her husband Padric, is from Guatemala - so you may look forward to freshly brewed Guatemalan coffee while taking in the pictures by local artists, which are for sale. All rooms, including the dining room, have views to die for and Vilma uses organic food where possible including home-grown vegetables - and also an unusual speciality (available on request), a wonderful Sea Vegetable Soup. The all day /evening menu on the wall is ideal for the non-stop visitors coming onto the island off the different ferries and it's best to go for dishes which are definitely home-made like a beautiful green pea soup, vegetable & herb quiche, deep-fried black pudding (in the lightest of batters) and freshly-baked scones or luscious desserts like a more-ish chocolate gateau... *En-suite accommodation is also available in clean-lined modern rooms with wooden floors and comfortable beds. **Seats 45.** Toilets wheelchair accessible. Children welcome. All day menu from 10.30am-9pm (D6-9, reservations required). A la carte. Closed Christmas. MasterCard, Visa. **Directions:** Five minutes from the pier. ◇

Aran Islands

Tigh Fitz

BAR / GUESTHOUSE / RESTAURANT

Killeaney Inis Mor Aran Islands Co Galway
Tel: 099 61213 Fax: 099 61386
Email: penny@tighfitz.com Web: www.tighfitz.com

Over 100 years ago Penny Fitzpatrick's grandfather opened his bar in the village of Killeaney, little knowing then that the island's airport would be a few fields away. This long 2 storey bar and lounge and adjacent guesthouse looks on to Teampall Beanann, dated 846 A.D. and reputedly the smallest church in Europe. Penny extended and refurbished the house a few years ago, creating the luxurious rooms she now offers, all with great views, tea/coffee making facilities; TV and direct line phones. There's a comfortable sitting room in the house - and the bar with great music sessions next door. The food, cooked by Declan Branigan, an enthusiastic and talented Dubliner, is very good quality and probably the best value on the island. Menus have a broad appeal - minute steak, Cajun chicken or chicken curry - but are most notable for fish, bought from a local fisherman, and a speciality Aran-style bouillabaisse using mussels picked by Declan himself. Simple food, great cooking. Children welcome (under 3 free in parents room, cot available by arrangement, baby sitting arranged). No pets. Walking, cycling, fishing. Garden; children's playground. **Rooms 11** (all shower only). B&B €45, ss €20. Restaurant open Mon-Sat, 12-6.(Will also cook dinner for groups, on reservation) Restaurant closed Mon. Guesthouse closed Nov-late Dec. MasterCard, Visa, Laser. **Directions:** 1 mile from Kilronan village.

Ballinasloe

Tohers Bar & Restaurant

RESTAURANT / PUB

18 Dunlo Street Ballinasloe Co Galway
Tel: 090 96 44848 Fax: 090 96 44844

This family-run pub on the main street is very attractive, with a traditional style bar on the ground floor and the restaurant in three separate dining rooms upstairs. A tempting bar lunch menu offers simple but tasty fare: if you can hit Ballinasloe at the right time, this is the spot to be and it's only a short walk up from the new marina too. Restaurant evening meals offer a wide choice of interesting international dishes. Bar meals L & D Mon-Sat, Restaurant D Tue-Sat. Closed Christmas, Good Fri, 2 weeks Oct. MasterCard, Visa, Laser. **Directions:** Town centre, just off market square.

Ballyconneely

Emlaghmore

B&B

Ballyconneely Co. Galway **Tel: 095 23529** Fax: 095 23860
Email: info@emlaghmore.com Web: www.emlaghmore.com

Built in 1862 as a small fishing lodge, Nicholas Tinne's magically located house is situated halfway between Roundstone and the 18-hole links golf course at Ballyconneely, in an Special Area of Conservation. It has been in the Tinne family for 75 years and is quite a modest house in some ways, but it is comfortably (and interestingly) furnished in keeping with its age and feels gloriously remote and has its own river running through the garden with fly fishing for sea trout, brown trout and even the occasional salmon, yet it is only a few hundred yards from sandy beaches and there are good pubs and restaurants nearby. Not that you will necessarily feel the need to wander in search of sustenance as Nick (who may be remembered from his famous restaurant, Snaffles, in Dublin) cooks dinner for residents: seafood treats like lobsters and mussels, rack of Connemara lamb and fillet of beef béarnaise... Not suitable for children. Pets allowed by arrangement. Golf, pony trekking, windsurfing nearby. Walking, fishing, garden. *Self-catering cottage also available nearby. **Rooms 4** (2 en-suite, 1 shower only; 2 private bathrooms; all no smoking). B&B €50-65 (depending on room), ss 50%. Residents D, €40 at 8.30 (please book by 10am.). House wine €15. Closed Nov-Easter. MasterCard, Visa. **Directions:** Turn inland off coast road 100 yards on Roundstone side of Callon Bridge. 6 miles from Roundstone, 2.5 from Ballyconneely.

Barna

O'Grady's on the Pier

RESTAURANT

Sea Point Barna Co Galway **Tel: 091 592223** Fax: 091 590677

In a stunning position, with views over the harbour and beach to distant mountains, Michael O'Grady's charming seafood restaurant has earned a loyal clientèle. There are some contemporary elements (especially on the first floor) but tradition has also been allowed its place - the old fireplace has been kept, for example, which bodes well for cosy sessions in wild weather - and Michael's aim is for his seafood to be "simply prepared and very fresh as my father did it years ago". This he and head chef John Moran are doing very well, although world cuisine is allowed a little space too, notably among the daily blackboard specials which might include dishes like cajun crusted hake with fruit chutney and - a house speciality - baked seabass with sweet chilli glaze alongside the ultimate classic, grilled whole black sole with lemon butter. Shellfish is perennially popular - crab cocktail, prawn and crab salad and grilled lobster are all typical and O'Grady's Seafood Platter combines crab, smoked salmon, prawns, smoked mackerel, oyster and salad. There's always some choice for non seafood eaters too: starters of deep-fried farmhouse cheese or chicken liver paté and main courses like braised lamb shank. (Vegetarian dishes on request.) Always innovative, Michael was joint winner of our Creative Seafood Dish Award in 2001 (together with Cathal Reynolds of Cré-na-Cille, Tuam). Children welcome. **Seats 85** (private room 22). Air-conditioning. D daily 5-10 (Sun 6-10), L Sun only 12-2.45. Set Sun L €21.95, also à la carte L&D; house wine €17.50. Closed 23-27 Dec. Amex, MasterCard, Visa, Laser, Switch. **Directions:** 4 miles west of Galway city on the Spiddal Road.

Cashel

Cashel House Hotel

HOTEL / RESTAURANT

Cashel Co Galway **Tel: 095 31001** Fax: 095 31077
Email: info@cashel-house-hotel.com Web: www.cashel-house-hotel.com

Dermot and Kay McEvilly were among the pioneers of the Irish country house movement when, as founder members of the Irish Country Houses and Restaurants Association (now known as The Blue Book) they opened Cashel House as an hotel in 1968. The following year General and Madame de Gaulle chose to stay for two weeks, an historic visit of which the McEvillys are justly proud - look out for the photographs and other memorabilia in the hall. The de Gaulle visit meant immediate recognition for the hotel, but it did even more for Ireland by putting the Gallic seal of approval on Irish hospitality and food. Comfort abounds here, even luxury, yet it's tempered by common sense, a love of gardening and the genuine sense of hospitality that ensures each guest will benefit as much as possible from their stay. The gardens, which run down to their own private beach, contribute greatly to the atmosphere, and the accommodation includes especially comfortable ground floor garden suites, which are also suitable for less able guests (wheelchair accessible but no special grab rails etc in bathrooms). Relaxed hospitality combined with professionalism have earned an international reputation for this outstanding hotel and its qualities are perhaps best seen in details - log fires that burn throughout the year, day rooms furnished with antiques and filled with fresh flowers from the garden, rooms that are individually decorated with many thoughtful touches. Service (with all day room service, including all meals) is impeccable and superb breakfasts include a wonderful buffet display of home-made and local produce. (Cashel House was the Connaught winner of the Guide's Denny Breakfast Award in 2001.) Not suitable for children under 5, although cots are available for young babies (€15). Pets permitted. Walking, tennis, garden. * Special breaks offered - details on application. **Rooms 32** (13 suites, 9 superior rooms, 1 shower only, 16 no-smoking, 4 suitable for less-able guests). B&B €120pps, ss €60; SC 12.5%.

Dining Room: A large conservatory extension enhances this well-appointed split-level restaurant, which is open to non-residents. Although ably assisted by head chef Florent Foulard since 2000, Dermot McEvilly has overseen the kitchen personally since the hotel opened, providing a rare consistency of style in five-course dinners that make imaginative use of local produce and seafood - lobster, oysters, fresh and home-smoked wild salmon, mussels, turbot, monkfish - is a great strength. Connemara lamb regularly stars and garden produce is also a welcome presence throughout, in soups, salads, side dishes, fine vegetarian dishes and desserts, such as rhubarb tart or strawberries and cream. Farmhouse cheeses come with home-baked biscuits and a choice of coffees and infusions is offered to finish. Service, under the personal supervision of Kay McEvilly and restaurant manager Ray Doorly, is excellent. An interesting wine list includes four house wines (€24). An attractive little à la carte bar lunch menu offers interesting snacks and sandwiches, but also hot meals, including lobster if you want it; afternoon teas are also served daily in the bar (Bar L12.30-2.30, Afternoon Tea 2-5). Restaurant **Seats ?0.** D daily 7-8.30. Set D €45; also à la carte. 12.5% s.c. Closed 5 Jan-5 Feb. Amex, MasterCard, Visa, Laser, Switch. **Directions:** South off N59 (Galway-Clifden road), 1 mile west of Recess.

Cashel

Zetland Country House

HOTEL / RESTAURANT

Cashel Bay Cashel Co Galway **Tel: 095 31111** Fax: 095 31117
Email: zetland@iol.ie Web: www.zetland.com

Originally built as a sporting lodge in the early 19th century, Zetland House is on an elevated site, with views over Cashel Bay and still makes a good base for fishing holidays. This is a charming and hospitable house, with a light and airy atmosphere and an elegance bordering on luxury, in both its spacious antique-furnished public areas and bedrooms. The latter are individually decorated in a relaxed country house style. The gardens surrounding the house are very lovely too, greatly enhancing the peaceful atmosphere of the house. Its unusual name dates from the time when the Shetland Islands were under Norwegian rule and known as the Zetlands - the Earl of Zetland (Lord Viceroy 1888-1890) was a frequent visitor here, hence the name. Small conferences/banqueting (20/65). Special breaks offered (details on request). Garden, tennis tennis, walking, snooker. Children welcome (under 2 free in parents' room, cot available €10). Pets permitted by arrangement in some areas. **Rooms 19** (10 executive rooms, 5 no smoking). B&B €95pps, ss €35; SC 12.5%. Wheelchair access.

Restaurant: Like the rest of this lovely hotel, the dining room is bright, spacious and elegant. Decorated in soft, pretty shades of pale yellow and peach that contrast well with antique furniture - including a fine sideboard where plates and silver are displayed - the restaurant is in a prime position for taking full advantage of the view and makes a wonderful place to watch the light fading over the mountains and the sea. A warm welcome and quietly efficient service from staff who are clearly happy in their work greatly enhances the pleasure of dining here. The kitchen makes good use of the vegetables and herbs grown by Mona Prendergast in the hotel garden, along with the best of local produce, notably lobster - and also game in season, which head chef Jason Le Gear transforms into dishes like a starter of char-grilled wild mallard with oyster sauce & shiitake mushrooms and main course of whole roast wild partridge, stuffed with mushroom duxelle, with a saffron & raisin pilaf cooking. Excellent breakfasts are also served in the restaurant - home-made preserves are an especially delicious feature. Children welcome. **Seats 40** (private room 20). D 7.30-9 daily. Set D €47.50; house wine €24; s.c. 12.5%. Closed 1 Dec-1 Feb. Amex, Diners, MasterCard, Visa, Laser. **Directions:** N59 from Galway. Turn left after Recess

---

Cashel Area

Le Bistrot Cottage Restauran

RESTAURANT

Gowla Cashel Co Galway **Tel: 095 3121**

About an hour and a half's drive from Galway, Le Bistrot is a delightful traditional cottage overlookin a rocky inlet near Cashel. It's in a sheltered corner planted with privet and roses growing among th wild fuchsia and sycamore (a pretty view from the window) and the location itself is part of its charm along with its cottagey ambience and the genuine hospitality of Anne Marie (the chef) and Jean Paul Perrotton (host). The three-table restaurant takes up what was the front room and kitchen of the cottage, now simply restored with wooden flooring and wall panels in soft, autumnal tones, with a tur and wood-burning stove replacing the old open fire. A short menu offers about five starters - classi French onion soup is a speciality and a good choice - and three main courses, possibly including chicke fondue with three sauces, which has to be ordered 24 hours in advance. Beef braised in Guinness i another likely choice - well-cooked in a rich, beery sauce - and also fried pollock (crisp on the outside moist within) which comes with a chive butter sauce. Lovely local potatoes may share the plat possibly also a green vegetable which (surprisingly) has been known to be frozen. This homely fa seems splendidly appropriate in the surroundings - former owners of this old cottage would have dine on much the same: beef or pollock, with peas and spuds. Le Bistrot offers a very different experienc from sophisticated city restaurants - an experience greatly enhanced by Jean Paul's solicitous servic Short all-French wine list. **Seats 14.** D Wed-Sun in summer (Fri-Sun off-season), 7-9pm; à la carte. Hous wine €14. Closed Mon, Tue (off season Mon-Thu). **No Credit Cards. Directions:** Carna road, R340, 8.5 k from the main Galway-Clifden road.

Clarinbridge

The Old School House Restauran

RESTAURANT

Clarinbridge Co Galway **Tel: 091 79689**
Fax: 091 796117 Email: kenc@iol.

Kenneth Connolly's old schoolhouse restaurant is full of character: a bright, tall-windowed room wi simple varnished tables is lifted by quality china and linen napkins - and welcoming staff who offer men promptly, in the bar/reception area or at your table. The choice offered is wide and well-organised perhaps a dozen starters (with local oysters getting a little section to themselves) and at least as ma main courses. It's the kind of menu that can be difficult to choose from as everything seems equal appealing, with some really tempting first courses (black & white pudding with griddle potato, perhap or steamed Galway Bay mussels with a classic white wine cream sauce) and, although fish main cours are predictably strong, there will also be some attractive meat and poultry dishes (braised lamb sha with fondant potato & shallot jus for example, or chicken breast with smoked bacon stuffing & mushroo cream sauce) and a couple of creative vegetarian options. While not especially adventurous, head ch Daire Hanrahan's skilful cooking makes the most of carefully sourced quality Irish produce (although mo information on the menu would be welcome) and classic dishes like black sole - beautifully fresh a served off the bone with butter, lemon & capers - are perfectly executed and presentation is, like t cooking, really good. Service, from knowledgeable and attentive staff, greatly enhances a meal here. finish, the Irish cheeseboard (served with pear & raisin chutney) is a good bet. **Seats 60** (private room 2 Toilets wheelchair accessible. Not suitable for children after 8pm. D Tue-Sun, 6.30-10; L Sun only 12.3

2.30. Set D from €25, also à la carte. Set Sun L, €21. House wine €17.50. Closed Mon. Amex, MasterCard, Visa, Laser, Switch. **Directions:** 6 miles from Galway city, on N18 Galway-Limerick road.

Clifden

Abbeyglen Castle

HOTEL

Sky Road Clifden Co Galway **Tel: 095 21201** Fax: 095 21797
Email: info@abbeyglen.ie Web: abbeyglen.ie

Set romantically in its own parkland valley overlooking Clifden and the sea, Abbeyglen is family-owned and run in a very hands-on fashion by Paul and Brian Hughes. It's a place that has won a lot of friends over the years and it's easy to see why: from the minute arriving guests meet the parrot at reception it's clear that this place is different; it's big and comfortable and laid-back - and there's a generosity of spirit about the place which is very charming. Complimentary afternoon tea for residents is a particularly hospitable speciality, served in a spacious drawing room or in front of an open peat fire in the relaxing, pubby bar, where many a late night is spent. Bedrooms (all with good bathrooms) are quite big and have been recently refurbished, as part of an ongoing improvement programme. Helipad. Garden. Pitch & putt. Snooker. Outdoor swimming pool. Live music. No pets. Not suitable for children. Wheelchair accessible. **Rooms 38** (18 superior, 20 standard, all en-suite) Lift. B&B €80pps, ss €30. 12.5% s.c. Closed 6 Jan-1 Feb. Amex, Diners, MasterCard, Visa, Laser. **Directions:** About 300 yards out of Clifden on the Sky road, on the left.

Clifden

Ardagh Hotel & Restaurant

HOTEL / RESTAURANT

Ballyconneely Road Clifden Co Galway
Tel: 095 21384 Fax: 095 21314
Email: ardaghhotel@eircom.net Web: www.ardaghhotel.com

Beautifully located, overlooking Ardbear Bay, Stephane and Monique Bauvet's family-run hotel is well known for quiet hospitality, comfort and good food. Public areas have style, too, in a gentle sort of way - not "decorated" but furnished in a relaxed homely style with good fabrics and classic country colours. Turf fires, comfortable armchairs and a plant-filled conservatory area upstairs all indicate that peaceful relaxation is the aim here. Bedrooms vary according to their position but are well-furnished with all the amenities required for a comfortable stay, and have been recently renovated. (Not all have sea views - single rooms are at the back with a pleasant countryside outlook, and have shower only). Bedrooms include some extra large rooms, especially suitable for families. Children welcome (under 5s free in parents' room, cot available without charge, baby sitting arranged); pets permitted by arrangement. Pool table. **Rooms 17** (2 junior suites, 2 shower only, all no smoking). B&B €85 pps, ss €25.

Restaurant: The restaurant is on the first floor and set up to take full advantage of the view, providing an appropriate setting for fine cooking, which specialises in local seafood. Imaginative use is made of local ingredients, including home-grown organic vegetables, in à la carte or nightly 5-course dinner menu offering plenty of choice - typically in a starter such as house marinated fresh wild salmon gravlax with a mustard & dill sauce, followed by a soup - Ardagh's fresh mussel chowder perhaps - and main course of Connemara lamb (with roasted celeriac wedges, perhaps, and red wine jus with rosemary & thyme) or lobster, various ways (€2.50 supplement per 100g). The dinner menu includes home-made petits fours with your coffee (or tea/tisane) and is good value. A fairly priced wine list strong on old world wines, especially Bordeaux and Burgundy, offers a good choice of half bottles and several magnums. **Seats 50.** (Bar meals, including oysters, fresh crab, smoked salmon, seafood chowder etc, 11-5 daily.) D 7.15-9.30 daily, Set D €46, à la carte also available; house wine €19; sc discretionary. Closed Nov-Easter. Amex, Diners, MasterCard, Visa, Laser, Switch. **Directions:** 2 km outside Clifden on Ballyconneely Road.

Clifden

Clifden Station House Hotel

HOTEL

Clifden Co Galway **Tel: 095 21699** Fax: 095 21667
Email: info@stationhousehotel.com Web: www.stationhousehotel.com

Built on the site of the late lamented railway station this large new hotel suits those who require a leisure centre and conference/banqueting facilities (250/150). Public areas are impressively spacious and modern, while bedrooms are a good size, contemporary in style and comfortably furnished with ISDN lines as well as more usual amenities such as direct-dial phones, tea/coffee making and TV. The old Station House has become a themed bar and restaurant, operated independently (see separate entry, The Signal Restaurant) and the complex includes an upmarket range of shops and boutiques. Leisure centre, indoor swimming pool, beauty salon. Children welcome (under 2s free in parents' room; cots available without charge; playroom). No pets. Short breaks. **Rooms 78** (2 junior suites, 8 executive, 18 no-smoking, 4 for disabled). Lift. B&B €70pps, ss €20. No SC. Closed 24-25 Dec. Amex, Diners, MasterCard, Visa, Laser, Switch. **Directions:** Follow N59 from Galway city. 80 km.

Clifden

Dolphin Beach Country House

COUNTRY HOUSE

Lower Sky Road Clifden Co Galway
Tel: 095 21204 Fax: 095 22935
Email: dolphinbeach@iolfree.ie Web: www.connemara.net/dolphinbeachhouse

Billy and Barbara Foyle's stunning beachside house is set in 14 acres of wilderness, which only serves to emphasise the style and comfort within. It started as an early 19th century farmhouse, now totally renovated and extended to include new bedrooms. Those familiar with the old Foyle magic (Rosleague Manor, Quay House) will find it much in evidence here. Something family members have in common is a talent for creating original interiors - an example here is Billy's unusual woodwork - bedheads, mirror frames, anything that takes his fancy - which is a key to the fresh style at Dolphin Beach. They have also spared no cost to ensure that the best materials are used throughout which creates a wonderful feeling of quality: bedrooms are finished to a very high standard, with antique furniture, pristine bedlinen, lovely bathrooms and underfloor heating; television and tea/coffee making facilities are available on request. They grow their own organic vegetables too, and these, together with other local produce, notably seafood and Connemara lamb, are used for evening meals which are served in a dining room overlooking the beach (ask about dinner when booking your room). Breakfast follows the same philosophy - you can even collect your own free-range eggs for breakfast. (Dolphin Beach was winner of our Irish Breakfast Award for Connacht in 2003). Not suitable for children. No pets. Walking, garden, safe swimming off rocky beach. **Rooms 8** (4 shower only, all no smoking). B&B €70 pps, ss €30. Residents dinner 7pm, €40 (booking essential); house wine €20. Visa, MasterCard, Laser. **Directions:** Left off Sky Road, about 3 miles from Clifden.

Clifden

Mitchell's Restaurant

RESTAURANT

Market Street Clifden Co Galway **Tel: 095 21867** Fax: 095 2177C

This attractive and well-managed family-run restaurant offers efficient, welcoming service and very agreeable "good home cooking" all day, every day throughout a long season - and they have been doing so, with admirable consistency, since 1991. An all-day menu offers a wide range of lightish fare everything from sandwiches and wraps to seafood chowder and seafood tagliatelle; the internationa flavours are there but how refreshing it is to find old friends like deep-fried Gubbeen cheese and bacor & cabbage there amongst the home-made spicy fishcakes and fresh crab salad with home-made browr bread. There's some overlap onto an à la carte evening menu, which offers a judicious selection from the snack menu but a wider choice of main dishes, including traditional Irish stew and a range o seafood. This is a very fair place, offering honest food at honest prices: half dozen local oysters a €9.50, for example, and a seafood platter €18.25. **Seats 70.** Air conditioning. Not suitable for childre after 6 pm. Open daily, 12-10; early D 5-6.30, €22.50. otherwise à la carte. House wine from €17.50 Closed 10 Nov-10 Feb. Amex, MasterCard, Laser, Switch. **Directions:** Next to SuperValu Supermarket.

Clifden

Quay House

GUESTHOUSE

Beach Rd Clifden Co Galway **Tel: 095 21369** Fax: 095 2160
Email: thequay@iol.ie Web: www.thequayhouse.com

In a lovely location - the house is right on the harbour, with pretty water views when the tide is in - The Quay House was built around 1820. It has the distinction of being the oldest building in Clifden and has also had a surprisingly varied usage: it was originally the harbourmaster's house, then a convent, then a monastery, was converted into a hotel at the turn of the century and finally, since 1993, has been enjoying its most recent incarnation as specialist accommodation in the incomparable hands of long time hoteliers, Paddy and Julia Foyle. Airy, wittily decorated and sumptuously comfortable rooms include not only two wheelchair-friendly rooms but a whole new development alongside the origina house - seven stunning studio rooms with small fitted kitchens and balconies overlooking the harbour As in the older rooms, excellent bathrooms all have full bath and shower. Breakfast, including deliciou freshly-baked breads and scones straight from the Aga, is served in the conservatory. Although officiall closed in winter it is always worth inquiring. Children under 12 free in parents' room (cots availabl without charge, baby sitting arranged). No pets. **Rooms 14** (all with full bathrooms, 2 for disabled) B&B €75pps, ss €15. Closed Nov-mid Mar. MasterCard, Visa, Laser. **Directions:** 2 minutes from town centre, overlooking Clifden harbour - follow signs to the Beach Road.

Clifden

Rock Glen Country House Hotel

HOTEL

Clifden Co Galway **Tel: 095 21035** Fax: 095 2173
Email: rockglen@iol.ie Web: www.connemara-net/rockglen-hote

Beautifully situated in quiet grounds well away from the road, Rock Glen was built in 1815 as a shootin lodge for Clifden Castle and enjoys views over a sheltered anchorage. Since 1973 it has been run by th

Roche family as a delightful hotel in which the public rooms and some of the bedrooms have the full advantage of the view- indeed the whole hotel is very restful and comfortable, with a pleasing outlook from all windows. Rooms are furnished in country house style, with good bathrooms (all have a full bath and over-bath shower) and amenities - some, such as tea/coffee trays, are not in the rooms but available on request. In addition to local activities - fishing, pony trekking, golf - there's a putting green on site, also all-weather tennis and croquet; indoors there are plenty of places to read quietly and a full size snooker table. Special interest short breaks available, notably tutored painting holidays. Children welcome (under 3s free in parents' room, cots available without charge). Pets permitted by arrangement. Walking, tennis, garden, snooker. **Rooms 26** (2 for disabled). Wheelchair access. B&B €95 pps, ss €40; sc 12.5%. Closed end Oct-Easter.

Restaurant: Traditionally furnished in country house style, the emphasis in this pleasant restaurant is on comfort and relaxation. Head chef Gee Nazri cooks in a style that blends Irish traditions with French and Asian influences and the five-course dinner menus, which change daily, are considerately also available as individually priced courses, making it semi à la carte - any starter chosen separately is €11.50, for example, any main course €25); local ingredients, especially seafood, play a major role in dishes ranging from sauté shrimp & angel hair pasta with Thai coconut broth, to roast leg of Connemara lamb with petit ratatouille & mint jus, or roast lime & chilli monkfish tail with sweet & sour cabbage, dill beurre blanc. Finish with tempting desserts, or Irish farmhouse cheese & biscuits. Service is friendly and efficient and an excellent breakfast is served in the restaurant. Seats 60 (private room, 12). No-smoking restaurant. D 7-9 daily; Set D €45, also à la carte; house wine €18; sc 12.5%. Toilets wheelchair accessible. Closed end Oct-Easter. Amex, MasterCard, Visa, Laser. **Directions:** 1.5 miles from Clifden, on Ballyconneely road.

Clifden

Sea Mist House

B&B

Clifden Co Galway **Tel: 095 21441**
Email: sgriffin@eircom.net Web: www.accommodation-connemara-ireland.com

Sheila Griffin's attractive house was built in 1825, using local quarried stone. Major renovations undertaken over the last few years have retained its character while adding modern comforts, allowing her to offer stylish and comfortable accommodation. The most recent improvement has been the addition of a conservatory, which provides a spacious room overlooking the garden, where guests can relax - and fruit from the garden is used in spiced fruit compôtes and preserves which appear at breakfast along with home-made breads, American-style pancakes with fresh fruit salsa and scrambled eggs with smoked salmon. This year there is also a special of the day which could be anything from scrambled eggs with smoked salmon to American pancakes with maple syrup - a surprise to start each day. Private parking (3). **Rooms 6** (all shower only & no-smoking). B&B €50pps, ss €15. Closed Christmas week. MasterCard, Visa. **Directions:** Left at square, a little down on right.

Clifden

Sunnybank House

GUESTHOUSE

Clifden Co Galway **Tel: 095 21437** Fax: 095 21976
Email: info@sunnybankhouse.com Web: www.sunnybankhouse.com

Set in its own mature gardens, with panoramic views, Sunnybank is owned and run by the O'Grady family, of O'Grady's restaurant fame and has recently been refurbished throughout. At a reasonable price they offer very comfortably appointed en-suite bedrooms with good facilities (phone, tea/coffee-making, iron/trouser press and TV) and day rooms for guests' use. This comfortable and peaceful base also has lovely gardens, a heated outdoor swimming pool, sauna and tennis court. Not suitable for children under 7; no pets. **Rooms 8** (1 suite, 4 shower only, all no-smoking). B&B about €55 pps, ss about €15. Closed Nov-Mar. MasterCard, Visa, Laser. **Directions:** from Galway - right at Esso station & first left, house 200 m on right.

Clifden

The Signal Restaurant

N RESTAURANT

Clifden Station House Clifden Co Galway
Tel: 095 22946 Email: smatz@esatclear.ie

Visitors to Clifden are in for a treat at the courtyard across from the Station House Hotel - where the first floor restaurant is now known as The Signal. Indeed it may become something of a place of pilgrimage, as it here that the brothers Matz - Christian and Stefan, famed for their time at Erriseask House at nearby Ballyconneely - have returned to spin a little of their magic in Connemara again, this time together with head chef Michael Gleeson.The restaurant itself will certainly bring on a sense of déja-vu for anyone who was there under previous management, as the high-ceilinged room has changed little - with warm wood tones and colourful high-back chairs and banquettes creating a stylish backdrop, and big windows which overlook a courtyard below. A comfortable little reception/bar and classy, simple table settings create a good impression. Menus (a no-choice four course Table d'Hôte and a short à la carte)offer first course specialities like potato-wrapped prawn tails and roulade of foie gras & apples and main courses including tempting vegetarian dishes (strudel of goat's cheese & sun-dried tomatoes,perhaps) unusual fish main courses such as turbot fillets in a sauce of smoked oysters. Red meats are equally appealing - Connemara mountain lamb, served perfectly pink and beautifully juicy, on a bed of oven-roasted vegetables, perhaps, or a delicious fillet of beef with a fresh horseradish crust, parsley champ and wild mushrooms (crusty without and tender within), cheese (Irish farmhouse, with Stefan's trademark fruit bread - magic with cheese) or, perhaps,...a hot soufflé of dark chocolate and oranges, with vanilla ice cream. Mmm... Not suitable for children under 12. **Seats 45.** Reservations accepted. D Wed-Sun, 6.30-9.30. Set D €39; also à la carte. House wine €19. SC discretionary. Closed Mon,Tue & Oct-Mar. Amex, MasterCard, Visa, Laser. **Directions:** Opposite Station House Hotel.

Clifden

Two Dog Café

Ⓝ CAFÉ

2 Church Hill Clifden Co Galway **Tel: 095 22186** Fax: 095 2219
Email: janehackett@eircom.net Web: www.twodogcafe.i

This smashing little café just off the square in Clifden is a gem, combining home-made cakes, gourme sandwiches and aromatic Illy coffee with a laid-back newspaper-reading atmosphere and an Interne cafe upstairs. Drop in for a light lunch, maybe - home-made soup with freshly-baked brown bread & butter, and a panini of marinated mushrooms and smoked Gubbeen cheese - or maybe a tortilla wra of spicy pork fillet & coriander. But, luscious as all the wholesome savoury choices may be, it's reall the display of home bakes that proves irresistible to any with the slightest hint of a sweet tooth. Jus like granny used to make - magic! Children welcome. **Seats 30.** Open daytime. No reservations MasterCard, Visa. **Directions:** Behind the Alcock & Brown Hotel in Market Square.

Clonbur

Ballykine House

FARMHOUSE

Clonbur Co Galway **Tel: 094 954 6150** Fax: 094 954 615
Email: ballykine@eircom.net Web: www.dirl.co

Comfortable accommodation and Ann Lambe's warm hospitality make this an appealing base for peaceful holiday. There are guided forest walks from the house, angling on Lough Corrib, an equestria centre (at nearby Ashford Castle) and bikes for hire locally. It's also well-placed for touring Connemara Moderately priced rooms have TV, tea/coffee making facilities and hairdryers. No evening meals bu the pubs and restaurants of Clonbur - including **J.J. Burke's pub (Tel: 094 954 6175)**, which is renowne for its food (and music) - are all within walking distance. There's plenty of comfortable seating in th sitting room and conservatory for lounging and chatting, also a pool table - and a drying room fo anglers. Garden. **Rooms 5** (4 with en-suite shower; 1 with private bath, restricted use), B&B €30, s €10. Closed 1 Nov-31 Mar. **No Credit Cards. Directions:** 3 km from Cong, on Cong/Clonbur Rd - R345.

Costello

Fermoyle Lodge

COUNTRY HOUSE

Costello Co Galway **Tel: 091 786111** Fax: 091 78615
Email: fermoylelodge@eircom.net Web: www.fermoylelodge.co

COUNTRY HOUSE OF THE YEAR

One of Ireland's best-kept secrets, Nicola Stronach delightful sporting lodge seems to enjoy the best of a possible worlds. Although only 29 miles from Galwa (and six miles from the ferry to the Aran Islands), it hidden from the road in one of the wildest and mo remote parts of Connemara. Protected by matu woodland and shrubs, it has stunning lake an mountain views, with both salmon and sea tro fishing on the doorstep. All this and creature comfor too. The spacious, well-proportioned house has bee sensitively renovated and beautifully furnished an decorated. Nicola has used the best of materials wisely, in a warm, low-key style that allows for eve comfort without detracting from the wonderful setting that is its greatest attribute. Bedrooms are all ve comfortable, with private bathrooms - and Nicola has yet another ace up her sleeve in the form of h French husband, Jean-Pierre Maire, who's a wizard in the kitchen as well as on the lough. A set dinn changes nightly - lobster tail & viagrette au Pernod, braised shoulder of lamb with cream of aubergine ar poached 'pêche de vigne' au Montbasillac is a typical menu (yes, really) - and is served for residents 7.30pm; 24 hour notice is required and any particular dislikes or allergies should be mentioned on bookin Not suitable for children. Pets permitted in certain areas. Fishing, garden, walking. **Rooms 6** (all en-sui

& no smoking). B&B €85pps, ss €25. D €40. No sc. Closed Nov-Mar. MasterCard, Visa, Laser. **Directions:** From Galway, take Clifden road (N59). At Oughterard turn left by Bridge Restaurant; Lodge is 10 miles along this road on right.

Clonbur

John J. Burke & Sons

New **PUB**

Mount Gable House Clonbur Co Galway
Tel: 094 954 6175 Fax: 094 954 6290
Email: tibhurca@eircom.net Web: www.burkes-clonbur.com

Clonbur is a most attractive village - and this characterful old family-run pub is one of its greatest assets. It's a friendly, welcoming place no matter when you might drop in and the business of feeding people with good traditional meals is taken seriously both in the bar, during the day, and the more formal dining area overlooking the garden at the back of the pub in the evening. Bar meals are quite traditional - egg mayonnaise, spicy wedges, roasts, home-made lasagne, apple tart. There's a much wider range offered in the evening: starters like baked mussels or venison sausage, for example, followed by the likes of steaks, rack of lamb and fish from sea and river. Irish stew is a speciality - a unique version, using prime cuts of locally farmed lamb with herb dumplings. Open from 10 am. Bar meals available Mon-Sat, 1-5pm (except 23-28 Dec & 31 Dec); D daily 6-9 in summer, weekends only off season (Oct-Mar). Closed 25 Dec, Good Fri. MasterCard, Visa, Laser. **Directions:** 30 miles north of Galway city, between Lough Corrib & Lough Mask.

Furbo

Connemara Coast Hotel

féile bia **HOTEL**

Furbo Co Galway **Tel: 091 592108** Fax: 091 555047
Email: sinnott@iol.ie Web: www.sinnotthotels.com

Like the other Sinnott hotels - Connemera Gateway and Brooks Hotel in Dublin - this beautifully located hotel is an attractive building which makes the best possible use of the site without intruding on the surroundings. Set on the sea side of the road, in its own extensive grounds, it is hard to credit that Galway city is only a 10 minute drive away. An impressive foyer decorated with fresh flowers sets the tone on entering, public areas are spacious and facilities are particularly good - a fine bar, two restaurants, a children's playroom and a leisure centre (which has a Canadian hot tub) among them. A policy of constant refurbishment and upgrading of facilities ensures that the hotel has a warm, well-cared for atmosphere. This most likeable of hotels is understandably popular for conferences - the facilities and service are both excellent and the location is magic. Conference/banqueting facilities (500/280) with secretarial back-up. A range of special breaks is offered (details on application). Children welcome (under 3 free in parents' room; cots available without charge, baby sitting arranged; playroom). Leisure centre, indoor swimming pool; pool table. No pets. Walking, tennis, garden. **Rooms 112** (1 suite, 9 executive rooms). B&B €80pps, ss €30. Gallery Restaurant, D 7-9.30pm daily; bar food also available. Open all year. Amex, MasterCard, Visa, Laser. **Directions:** 6 miles from Galway city on Spiddal road.

Headford

Lisdonagh House

COUNTRY HOUSE

Caherlistrane Headford Co Galway **Tel: 093 31163** Fax: 093 31528
Email: cooke@lisdonagh.com Web: www.lisdonagh.com

Situated about 15 minutes drive north of Galway city in the heart of hunting and fishing country, Lisdonagh House is on an elevated site with beautiful views overlooking Lake Hackett. It is a lovely property, with large well-proportioned reception rooms, a fine staircase and luxurious bedrooms, furnished with antiques and decorated in period style, with marbled bathrooms to match. A 4-course residents' dinner (choice limited to one of two main courses), about €40, is served between 7 and 9pm. House wine €25. Children welcome. Pets permitted in some areas. Equestrian, fishing, walking, cycling. *Two luxurious villas in the courtyard are also available, either for self-catering or fully serviced. The main house can also be rented exclusively for family celebrations and get-togethers, either weekly or for two-night lets. **Rooms 10.** B&B €140 pps, ss €30. Wheelchair access. Closed 1 Nov-1 May. Amex, MasterCard, Visa, Laser, Switch. **Directions:** N17 to within 4 miles of Tuam, R333 to Caherlistrane.

Inishbofin

Day's Inishbofin House Hotel

HOTEL

Inishbofin Co Galway **Tel: 091 798031**

This hospitable family-run hotel beside the harbour has been first (and last) port of call for many visitors to the island over the years. Very extensive renovations were required and, at the time of going to press it is being re-built; the Days expect to re-open with 34 new bedrooms, leisure centre and conference facilities in April 2004. Visa, Laser. **Directions:** Ferries to the island run regularly from Cleggan, with ticket offices in Clifden (regular buses between Clifden and Cleggan) and also at Kings of Cleggan. For bookings and enquiries, phone: 091 44642 or 091 21520. Credit card bookings are accepted.

Kilcolgan

Moran's Oyster Cottage

ATMOSPHERIC PUB

The Weir Kilcolgan Co Galway
Tel: 091 796113 Fax: 091 796503
Email: moranstheweir@eircom.net Web: www.moransoystercottage.com

This is just the kind of Irish pub that people everywhere dream about. It's as pretty as a picture, with a well-kept thatched roof and a lovely waterside location (with plenty of seats outside where you can while away the time and watch the swans floating by). It's also brilliantly well-run by the Moran family - and so it should be, after all they've had six generations to practise. They're famed throughout the country for their wonderful local seafood, including lobster, but especially the native oysters (from their own oyster beds) which are in season from September to April. Willie Moran is an ace oyster opener, a regular champion in the famous annual competitions held in the locality. Farmed Gigas oysters are on the menu all year. Then there's chowder and smoked salmon and seafood cocktail and mussels, delicious crab salads - and lobster, with boiled potatoes & garlic butter. Private conference room. Morans was our Seafood Pub of the Year in 1999. **Seats 120** (privates rooms, 6 and 8) Meals 12 noon -10pm daily. House wine €17. Closed 24-26 Dec & Good Fri. Amex, MasterCard, Visa, Laser. **Directions:** Just off the Galway-Limerick road, signed between Clarenbridge and Kilcolgan. ◇

Kinvara

Keogh's Bar & Restaurant

RESTAURANT / BAR

Main Street Kinvara Co Galway **Tel: 091 637145**
Fax: 091 637028 Email: keoghsbar@eircom.net

Michael and Mary Keogh took over this old pub in 1996 and refurbished it to create a cosy bar with an open fire and a more modern restaurant behind it, with wooden floors and benches and oilcloth-covered tables - with character added by a large fireplace with a traditional black stove. The food is modern Irish bar meals, served by charming Filipino and French staff, and there are tables outside in summer. Local seafood is the main speciality -a fine, creamy, fishy chowder and steamed mussels, for example, both come with home-made brown bread - although there are other choices too, such as a good goats cheese salad, or Irish stew. Homely desserts might include a freshly-baked apple and rhubarb crumble. Weekly music sessions in summer. **Seats 60.** Food available 10am-10pm daily. Closed 25 Dec, Good Fri. MasterCard, Visa, Laser. **Directions:** Kinvara village.

Kinvara

The Pier Head Bar & Restaurant

PUB / RESTAURANT

The Quay Kinvara Co Galway **Tel: 091 638188**

Mike Burke took over this well-known harbourside establishment in the picturesque village of Kinvara in 2000 and, with the help of an excellent Belgian chef Philippe de la Roux, has earned and retained a reputation for serving the best food in the area. Seafood is, of course, the star - especially lobster - served in the shell with garlic butter and a side salad, it makes a meal for about €33 - and the other thing they take pride in doing well is top of the range steak, using local beef (totally traceable) which is salughtered and butchered specially. Excellent service, under the direction of Mike's Filipino right hand man, Louis, who combines a warm personality with a lot of knowledge and skill. A well-balanced wine list includes some interesting faiveley bottles and house wines are good value; no half bottles. As well as good food, there's also music, all year: bands on on Friday & Saturday nights, usually also traditional on Sunday afternoon. Children welcome. **Seats 100** (private room 50). No smoking area Food served daily in summer, 5-10 (Sun 12-8); off-season 5-8 (end Oct-May). A la carte. House wine €15 Closed 25 Dec & Good Fri. Diners, MasterCard, Visa, Laser. **Directions:** Kinvara harbour front. ◇

Kinvara

Tully's

ATMOSPHERIC PUB

Kinvara Co Galway **Tel: 091 637146**

Definitely a spot for traditional music, this is a real local pub in the old tradition, with a little grocery shop at the front and stone-floored bar at the back. Tully's has a fine old stove in the bar for cosy winter sessions, which is always a good sign (They also have a small enclosed garden with a few parasoled tables for fine weather). Not a food place, although sandwiches, teas and coffees are always available Normal pub hours. Closed 25 Dec & Good Fri. **No credit cards.**

Leenane

Blackberry Café & Coffee Shop

CAFÉ

Leenane Co Galway **Tel: 095 42240**

Sean and Mary Hamilton's lovely little restaurant is just what the weary traveller hopes to happen on when touring or walking in this beautiful area. They're open through the afternoon and evening every day during the summer, serving home-made soups and chowders with home-baked bread, substantial snacks such as fish cakes and mussels, and delicious desserts like rhubarb tart and lemon meringue pie with cream. Extra dishes such as hot smoked trout and a chicken main course might be added to the menu in the evening, but the secret of the Blackberry Café's appeal is that they don't try to do too much at once and everything is freshly made each day. **Seats 40.** Open 12-9 daily in high season. A la carte. House wine about €14 (1/4 bottles also available). Closed Tue in shoulder seasons. Closed end Sep-Easter. Visa, Laser, Switch. **Directions:** On main street,opposite car park. ◇

Leenane

Delphi Lodge

COUNTRY HOUSE

Leenane Co Galway **Tel: 095 42222** Fax: 095 42296
Email: delfion@iol.ie Web: www.delphilodge.ie

One of Ireland's most famous sporting lodges, Delphi Lodge was built in the early 19th-century by the Marquis of Sligo. It is beautifully located in an unspoilt valley, surrounded by the region's highest mountains (with the high rainfall dear to fisherfolk). Owned since 1986 by Peter Mantle - who has restored and extended the original building in period style - the lodge is large and impressive in an informal, understated way, with antiques, fishing gear and a catholic selection of reading matter creating a stylish yet relaxed atmosphere. The dozen guest rooms are all quite different, but they are en-suite (four bathrooms were dramatically upgraded in 2003) and very comfortably furnished (with lovely lake and mountain views). Dinner, for residents only, is taken at a long oak table. It is cooked by Cliodhna Prendergast, who has "a range of dishes that is vast and eclectic" - some traditional, some 'nouveau', some oriental. (To illustrate the point; home made ravioli of wood pigeon is a speciality, also nephrops from Killary Bay, with warmed rocket butter; reading the menu is a mouth-watering exercise.) The famous Delphi Fishery is the main attraction, but people come for other country pursuits, painting, or just peace and quiet. A billiard table, the library and a serious wine list (great bottles at a very modest mark-up) can get visitors through a lot of wet days. Just across the road, four restored cottages offer self-catering accommodation. Small conferences/banqueting (20/26). Not suitable for children under 12. No pets. Garden, fishing, walking, snooker.* Short breaks (3D B&B from €250); also fly fishing weekends (€595); off season wine weekends from €395. **Rooms 12** (all executive standard). B&B €95 pps, ss €47.50. Meals 1pm and 8pm. Residents L €15, D €45; House wine €19; SC discretionary. Closed 20 Dec-10 Jan. MasterCard, Visa. **Directions:** 8 miles northwest of Leenane on the Louisburgh road.

Leenane

Delphi Mountain Resort & Spa

HOTEL

Delphi Leenane Co Galway **Tel: 095 42987** Fax: 095 42303
Email: delphigy@iol.ie Web: www.delphiescape.com

Stunningly located on a 300-acre estate in one of the most beautiful and unspoilt areas of the west of Ireland, this luxurious retreat offers a wide range of health and fitness programmes designed as an antidote to the stresses of contemporary life. The building (which is to have a grass roof by 2004) is inspired by and designed to reflect the natural beauty and materials of the area: a big turf fire is lit in the reception area every morning, ensuring a warm welcome for newcomers and setting the tone for the whole enterprise. Storm-felled timber and local stone is used throughout, incorporating traditional craftsmanship and modern detailing - curving corridors echo ring forts, luxurious contemporary bedrooms are wood-themed (beech room, oak room etc), with complementary natural fabrics and furnishings. Considered simply as an hotel offering understated luxury in uniquely beautiful surroundings, it has a great deal to offer. The bedrooms (especially those at the back) have beautiful views and all have either a window balcony or patio; furnished to a high standard in a simple, clean-lined style and neutral colours - and the suites have a loft bedroom over a downstairs living room. Normal hotel facilities include a full bar and fine dining restaurant on the first floor (open to non-residents), with big windows to take full advantage of the mountain view; enjoyment and relaxation are the aim. A brochure detailing the very wide range of facilities and therapies offered (both residential and day programmes) is available from the hotel; children can be accommodated at the adventure centre next door, providing an unusual choice for a family holiday, with much to offer different age groups. It is also an interesting and well-equipped centre for conferences and team building. Conference/banqueting (200/70). Equestrian, fishing, cycling, walking; beauty salon. **Rooms 22** (8 suites, 2 for disabled, all no smoking.) B&B €120 pps, ss €45. Light L daily (phone ahead to check), 1-2 (Sun to 4). D daily 6.30-9, reservations required. Closed mid Dec-mid Jan. Amex, MasterCard, Visa, Laser. **Directions:** From Galway take the N59 to Leenane - then 7 miles to Delphi.

Leenane

Killary Lodge

GUESTHOUSE

Leenane Co Galway **Tel: 095 42276** Fax: 095 42314
Email: lodge@killary.com Web: www.killary.com

Situated on the shores of Killary harbour, Jamie and Mary Young's former hunting lodge has been renovated in a relaxed modern style and now offers a very comfortable place to stay in a beautiful location. Those with an interest in outdooor pursuits will get particular enjoyment from the many activities operating from here, but it also makes a good base for touring Connemara. Friendly staff, an informal atmosphere and home cooked evening meals are all part of the attraction and there is plenty of walking - and other activities such as water-skiing and kayaking, available on site - for the energetic. Conferences and corporate training are among the many programmes offered at this unusual establishment - contact the manager, Kathy Evans, for further details. Garden, tennis, walking, cycling. **Rooms 21** (11 shower only, 2 for disabled). B&B €53 pps, ss €19. Residents D €30; house wine €16. Closed mid Dec-end Jan. MasterCard, Visa, Laser. **Directions:** Off the N59, 3 miles outside the village of Leenane on the Clifden Road.

Leenane

Portfinn Lodge

RESTAURANT WITH ROOMS

Leenane Co Galway **Tel: 095 42265** Fax: 095 42315
Email: rorydaly@anu.ie Web: www.portfinn.com

There are few views in Ireland to beat the sight of the sun sinking behind the mountains over Killary Harbour. On a good evening that's something you can look forward to at Rory and Brid Daly's seafood restaurant, Portfinn Lodge. The dining area is in a room of the main house and an adjoining conservatory. The reception area is small but the welcome is warm and a lobster tank at the entrance bodes well for a good meal - a high proportion of the menu is likely to be seafood: prawns, salmon, brill, turbot and many of their cousins make a nightly appearance. Rory's cooking style is classic: examples from a selection of specialities that are changed weekly include turbot fillets in caper & dill sauce and traditional roast half duckling à l'orange (half a Cavan duckling, roasted & served with a port & orange sauce); there is also at least one vegetarian dish daily. Rory's classical cooking is consistently good and portions generous, including a selection of side vegetables. Good brown bread comes with country butter, which is quite a feature in these parts, and there's always an Irish cheeseboard. Not suitable for children under 12. **Seats 35.** D 6.30-9 daily. A la carte; house wine from €17.50; sc discretionary. Closed 1 Nov-1 Apr.

Rooms: Modest but comfortable accommodation is offered in eight neat purpose-built en-suite rooms, all sleeping three and one with four beds; one room has wheelchair access. Pets permitted by arrangement. Fishing, walking. Rooms 8 (all en-suite). B&B €40pps, ss €30, no sc. MasterCard, Visa. **Directions:** Midway between Westport and Clifden (N59).

Letterfrack

Kylemore Abbey Restaurant & Tea House

RESTAURANT

Kylemore Letterfrack Co Galway **Tel: 095 41146** Fax: 095 41368
Email: info@kylemoreabbey.ie Web: www.kylemoreabbey.ie

Kylemore Abbey, with its stunning mountain and waterside setting, would make a dramatic location for any enterprise. But what the Benedictine nuns are doing here is truly astonishing. The abbey is not only home for the nuns but is also run as an international girls' boarding school. In addition, the nuns run a farm and a restored walled garden, which is open to the public. A short walk further along the wooded shore leads to the Gothic church, a miniature replica of Norwich Cathedral. In a neat modern building beside the carpark is one of the country's best craft shops - and an excellent restaurant. Everything at this daytime self-service restaurant is made on the premises, and the range of wholesome offerings includes a good selection of hot and cold savoury dishes, including traditional beef & Guinness casserole, Irish stew and several vegetarian options - typically black eye bean casserole or vegetarian lasagne. Home baking is a special strength and big bowls of the nuns' renowned home-made jams are set up at the till, for visitors to help themselves. Beside them are neatly labelled jars to buy and take home. **Seats 240.** Meals daily 9.30-5.30. Closed Christmas week & Good Fri. (The Garden Tea House, in the restored walled garden, is open Easter-Hallowe'en, 10.30-5, using produce from the garden.) Amex, MasterCard, Visa, Laser. **Directions:** 2 miles from Letterfrack, on the N59 from Galway. ◇

Letterfrack

Oceans Restaurant

RESTAURANT

Derryinver Letterfrack Co Galway **Tel: 095 43842**

The Curran family's pretty little restaurant close to Derryinver harbour is a useful place to know about if you're staying in the area or, if you are touring or walking nearby during the day, it's a pleasant place to break a journey. A short lunch menu offers a choice of soups - chowder perhaps, with home-baked brown bread - and a range of open sandwiches, including wild smoked salmon and fresh crabmeat (both about €8. Ordinary sandwiches too, plain or toasted, a few hot dishes, including Irish Stew, plus several desserts (chocolate fudge cake, about €3.50). A much wider range is offered in the evening, when the emphasis is understandably on seafood (Connemara crab with avocado & mango, fillet of cod with bacon & scallion mash) but there's also a choice of meats and poultry (including roast rack of lamb with rosemary & garlic, perhaps), served by hospitable and obliging staff. The early dinner menu is particularly good value

[Opening times not confirmed at time of going to press, please phone for details.] MasterCard, Visa. **Directions:** Overlooking Derryinver Bay, beside Oceans Alive sea life centre. ◇

Letterfrack

Pangur Bán Restaurant

RESTAURANT

Letterfrack Co Galway **Tel: 095 41243**
Email: pban@indigo.ie Web: www.pangurban.com

John Walsh and Mairead Tucker's pretty, whitewashed roadside cottage has a tiny front garden and a large carpark at the back; you enter into a reception / bar area which is unexpectedly bright and airy, with a raised wooden ceiling and plenty of light from the cottage door as well as windows although, with whitewashed walls and an old fireplace, it retains its natural cottagey character, and table settings in the adjoining dining rooms are appropriately simple. A relaxing meal with John's good home cooking and Mairead's caring service is the aim, and this they achieve well. Local produce is used whenever possible (mountain lamb is sourced from John's brother) in dishes that vary widely in style from quite traditional specialities like venison and Guinness stew to those with international influences, such as Thai chicken & peanut curry or Taiwanese stir-fry pork with cashew nuts & cabbage. But leave some room for a little indulgence from a wide choice of desserts, ranging from homemade ice creams and rhubarb fool through fresh fruit and ricotta sponge and, perhaps, a tangy lime & lemon cheesecake. *Cookery classes at weekends: Nov/Dec & Mar/Apr. **Seats 50.** D 6-9.30/10; daily in high season (Jul-Aug); 6 nights in shoulder seasons(Mar-May & Sep-Oct) closed Mon; 5 nights low season (Nov-Dec) closed Sun & Mon. (A phone call to check opening times any time except high season is advised.) A la carte. House wine €14.95. Closed Jan-1Feb. MasterCard, Visa, Laser. **Directions:** In Letterfrack village.

Letterfrack

Rosleague Manor Hotel

COUNTRY HOUSE / RESTAURANT

Letterfrack Co Galway
Tel: 095 41101 Fax: 095 41168
Email: rosleaguemanor@eircom.net Web: www.rosleague.com

A lovely pink-washed Regency house of gracious proportions and sensitively handled modernisation, Rosleague looks out over a tidal inlet through gardens planted with rare shrubs and plants. Although the area offers plenty of activity for the energetic, there is a deep sense of peace and it's hard to imagine anywhere better to recharge the soul. The hotel changed hands within the Foyle family a couple of years ago and is now run by Anne Foyle's nephew, Mark Foyle, who has undertaken considerable refurbishment and renovations are continuing on an ongoing basis. Children welcome (cot available, €15, baby sitting arranged) Garden, tennis, fishing, walking. Pets permitted. **Rooms 20** (4 junior suites,10 no smoking). B&B €95pps, ss €25. D 7-9 daily, non-residents welcome by reservation; Set D €45. House wine €19. Wheelchair access. Closed 16 Nov-15 Mar. Amex, MasterCard, Visa, Laser, Switch. **Directions:** On N59 main road, 7 miles north of Clifden.

Moyard

Rose Cottage

FARMHOUSE / RESTAURANT

Rockfield Moyard Co Galway **Tel: 095 41082**
Email: info@connemaratourism.org

This long-established farmhouse is situated on a working farm in a scenic location surrounded by the Twelve Bens mountains. John O'Toole, who is a qualified chef, took over management in 2002 (with his mother Mary, who ran the business for many years, still lending a hand when necessary). There's a sitting room with an open turf fire and the moderately priced, comfortable bedrooms have tea/coffee making trays and hair dryers. John uses local produce, including lamb from the farm (rack, served with its own jus perhaps, or braised shank with herbs and garlic, served with a redcurrant & mint sauce perhaps) and herbs and vegetables from their own garden. Children welcome. **Rooms 6** (all en-suite, 5 shower only). Free cots available, baby sitting arranged; pets by arrangement. Garden; walking. B&B €26 pps, no ss. D daily 6-9.30; L Sun 12.3-2.30 & by request. Set D from €30, Sun L €25; L&D also à la carte. House wine €17. Open all year. MasterCard, Visa, Laser. **Directions:** Main Westport Rd,6 miles from Clifden.

Moycullen

Moycullen House & Restaurant

RESTAURANT WITH ROOMS

Moycullen Co Galway
Tel: 091 555621 Fax: 091 555566
Email: info@moycullen.com Web: www.moycullen.com

Overlooking Lough Corrib, and set peacefully in 30 acres of rhododendrons and azaleas, Moycullen House was built as a sporting lodge in the arts and crafts style at the beginning of the century and has been run as a country house for some years by the Casburn family. When Richard and Louise Casburn opened this very professionally run restaurant in the house in 1998, it quickly earned a loyal following. A great deal of thought and work went into getting the changes right, and the effort has paid off handsomely: Louise looks after front-of-house beautifully and Richard is the chef - his well-balanced and fairly priced menus are ambitious but he offers a sensibly short à la carte with daily extras, including seafood. Having worked with Gerry Galvin at nearby Drimcong House in its heyday and been influenced by its philosophy, Richard seeks out quality ingredients, which he treats with due respect and with very pleasing results. The 'progressive Irish' style is fairly modern but based on classics: menus could include starters of sautéd scallops & Parma ham salad and grilled goats cheese on a garlic & tomato brioche, for example, while typical main courses could include turbot as one of the daily specials and, from the à la carte, roast loin of Connemara lamb with roasted shallots, spinach and potato - simply delicious. (Moycullen was selected for the Guide's Bord Bia Irish Lamb Award in 2001). Presentation is not overworked and cooking is consistently excellent. Banqueting (45). **Seats 40.** D Thu-Tue 6.30-9.30; L Sun only, 3.30-4.30 pm. Set D €50; also à la carte; Set Sun L from €22.50. House wine €17.95. SC discretionary. Restaurant not suitable for children after 7pm. Closed Wed & 5 Jan-15 Mar.

Accommodation: Large bedrooms furnished with antiques all have private baths and there's a spacious residents' sitting room with an open log fire. Children welcome; under 5s free in parents' room, cot/extra bed available without charge; baby-sitting by arrangement. No pets. Garden, walking. Rooms 3 (1 superior room, all no-smoking). B&B €45.50 pps, ss€15. House closed Christmas & 8 Jan-10 Mar. Amex, MasterCard, Visa, Laser. **Directions:** N59 Galway to Moycullen; at the cross roads, take left turn onto Spiddal Road, signed on left after about 1.5km.

Moycullen

White Gables Restaurant

RESTAURANT

Moycullen Village Moycullen Co Galway
Tel: 091 555744 Fax: 091 556004
Email: info@whitegables.com Web: www.whitegables.com

Kevin and Ann Dunne have been running this attractive cottagey restaurant on the main street of Moycullen since 1991 and it's now on many a regular diner's list of favourites. Entry is directly into the dining room, where open stonework, low lighting and candlelight (even at lunch time) create a soothing away-from-it-all atmosphere (a bar/reception area is to be completed for the 2004 season). Kevin sources ingredients with care and offers weekly-changing dinner and à la carte menus and a set Sunday lunch (which is enormously popular and has two sittings). Cooking is consistently good in a refreshingly traditional style and, while there is much else to choose from - roast half duckling with orange sauce is one of their most popular dishes - fresh fish is the main speciality, including lobster (served thermidor, perhaps) from their own tank and other classics like sole on the bone, scallop mornay, monkfish panfried in garlic butter and poached turbot in martini sauce. Well-cooked seasonal vegetables are always particularly enjoyable at this fine restaurant and their roast beef, as served for Sunday lunch, is like no other. Good desserts, including home-made ices, and friendly, efficient service all help make this one of the area's finest restaurants. **Seats 45.** Children welcome. Air conditioning. D Tue-Sat, 7-10; L Sun only, 12.30-3. Set D €37.50 (with some supplements); Set Sun L €23. House wine €18; sc discretionary. Closed Mon; 23 Dec-14 Feb. Amex, MasterCard, Visa, Laser. **Directions:** On N59 in Moycullen village, 8 miles from Galway city.

Oranmore

Lynch Galway Bay Hotel

HOTEL

Oranmore Co Galway **Tel: 091 790500** Fax: 091 790510
Email: cro@lynchotels.com Web: www.lynchotels.com

Well located, just eight miles from Galway city, this rather handsome modern hotel looks out over an 18-hole championship golf course (designed by Christy O'Connor Jnr.) towards Galway Bay; it has a wide range of facilities for both business and leisure and is potentially one of the pleasantest hotels in the area. Generous-sized bedrooms are comfortably furnished with all the necessary facilities and many have lovely views across the bay, although maintenance and routine refurbishment is sometimes less than perfect. However, prices are quite moderate and special packages, especially, give good value on both golf and non-golfing breaks. Conference/banqueting (275/250); business centre. Children welcome (under 2 free in parents room, cot available, baby sitting arranged). No pets. **Rooms 92** (5 suites; 6 rooms for disabled). B&B €79 pps, ss €26. Golf (18), garden, walking. Open all year. Amex, Diners, MasterCard, Visa, Laser. **Directions:** Signposted from Oranmore.

Oughterard

Corrib Wave Guesthouse

GUESTHOUSE

Portcarron Oughterard Co Galway **Tel: 091 552147** Fax: 091 55273
Email: cwh@gofree.indigo.ie Web: www.corribwave.com

A fisherman's dream, Michael and Maria Healy's unpretentious waterside guesthouse offers warm family hospitality, comfortable accommodation, an open turf fire to relax by and real home cooking

All rooms have phone, tea/coffee-making, TV, radio and a double and single bed; some are suitable for families. Best of all at Corrib Wave is the location - utter peace and tranquillity. Golf and horseriding nearby and everything to do with fishing organised for you. **Rooms 10** (all en-suite). B&B €35. Closed 20 Dec-2 Jan. MasterCard, Visa, **Directions:** From Galway, signed from N59, 1 km before Oughterard.

Oughterard

Currarevagh House

COUNTRY HOUSE

Glann Road Oughterard Co Galway **Tel: 091 552312** Fax: 091 552731
Email: currarevagh@ireland.com Web: www.currarevagh.com

Tranquillity, trout and tea in the drawing room - these are the things that draw guests back to the Hodgson family's gracious, but not luxurious early Victorian manor overlooking Lough Corrib. Currarevagh, which was built in 1846 as a wedding present for Harry Hodgson's great, great, great grandfather, is set in 150 acres of woodlands and gardens with sporting rights over 5,000 acres. Guests have been welcomed here for over half a century and the present owners, Harry and June Hodgson, are founder members of the Irish Country Houses and Restaurants Association (known as Ireland's Blue Book). Yet, while the emphasis is on old-fashioned service and hospitality, they are adamant that the atmosphere should be more like a private house party than an hotel, and their restful rituals underline the differences: the day begins with a breakfast worthy of its Edwardian origins, laid out on the sideboard in the dining room; lunch may be one of the renowned picnic hampers required by sporting folk. Then there's afternoon tea, followed by a leisurely dinner. Fishing is the ruling passion, of course - notably brown trout, pike, perch and salmon - but there are plenty of other country pursuits to assist in building up an appetite for June's good home cooking, all based on fresh local produce. Not suitable for children. Garden, walking, tennis. **Rooms 15** (all en-suite). B&B €90, ss €32. SC10%. D €37, at 8pm (non residents welcome by reservation). Wines from €15. Closed mid Oct-1 Apr. MasterCard, Visa, Laser. **Directions:** Take N59 to Oughterard. Turn right in village square and follow Glann Road for 4 miles.

Oughterard

River Run Lodge

RESTAURANT WITH ROOMS

Glann Road Oughterard Co Galway
Tel: 091 552697 Fax: 091 552669
Email: riverrun@indigo.ie Web: www.connermara-bedandbreakfast.com

Tom and Anne Little's modern guesthouse and restaurant is quietly located in landscaped gardens just outside the village of Oughterard, on the banks of the Owenriff River. A welcoming fire in the reception area sets a caring note that is evident throughout the house, especially in the thoughtful planning of spacious bedrooms which all have exceptional facilities including minibar, hospitality tray, satellite television, radio, trouser press with iron and writing desk - there's even a suite, The Corrib: overlooking the back garden, it has a double and single bed, comfortable chairs, a separate dressing room and separate bath and shower. A ground floor room beside the front door has less privacy than others. **Rooms 8** (1 suite, 3 shower only, all no smoking). B&B about €50pps. ss €12. Closed Nov-Jan.

Restaurant: The well-appointed restaurant is in the prime spot, towards the back of the house and overlooking maturing gardens and the little river - and dinner is likely to be the highlight of your visit. Ingredients are carefully sourced and everything is freshly prepared and cooked to order. There's a shortish à la carte menu, with half a dozen choices on each course and the style is modern international. Delicious starters typically include crispy duck wontons with spring onions, cucumber & hoi sin sauce and potato cakes with smoked salmon & horseradish with salad, followed perhaps by a well-cooked roast half duck with plum compôte, burnt orange & port sauce, darne of salmon en papillotte or a vegetarian special. Finish with an unusual dessert such as rhubarb jelly with home-made vanilla ice cream, perhaps, or an Irish coffee. Not surprisingly this little gem is popular with locals as well as resident guests, so booking is required. Not suitable for children under 4. **Seats 32.** D Mon-Sat, 6.30-9.30. D from €27.50. A la carte. House wine from €17. Closed Sun. Amex, MasterCard, Visa, Laser, Switch. **Directions:** In Oughterard village take turning for Glann Road - it's a few hundred yards down on the right.

Oughterard

Ross Lake House Hotel

Ⓝ HOTEL

Rosscahill Oughterard Co Galway
Tel: 091 550109 Fax: 091 550184
Email: rosslake@iol.ie Web: www. rosslakehotel.com

Quietly located in six acres of beautiful gardens, this charming country house was built in 1850 and is now a protected building. The current owners, Henry and Elaine Reid, bought the property in 1981 and have gradually refurbished it, so the hotel now offers luxurious accommodation in spacious rooms and suites individually furnished with antiques - including some with four-poster beds. Small conferences and weddings are a speciality, especially off season. Walking, cycling, fishing. Short breaks offered. Pets allowed in some areas. **Rooms 13** (3 suites, 4 superior) B&B from €75. Closed 1 Nov-15 Mar. Amex, MasterCard, Visa, Laser. **Directions:** Signed off Galway-Oughterard road.

Oughterard

Sweeney's Oughterard House

HOTEL Oughterard Co Galway **Tel: 091 552207** Fax: 091 552161 Email: phiggins@iol.ie

The Sweeney-Higgins family have owned and run this attractive creeper-clad old hotel for several generations. Prettily situated opposite the river and surrounded by mature trees (on the Clifden side of the town), it is genuinely old-fashioned with comfortable, cottagey public rooms furnished with antiques - a very pleasant place to break a journey. (Very acceptable light food is served in the bar during the day.) Bedrooms vary considerably - some have four-posters. Fishing is the main attraction, but there are plenty of other outdoor pursuits including the gentle pleasure of taking tea on the lawn. Closed about 22 Dec-mid-Jan. **Directions:** From Galway: through Oughterard, across river, on right. ◇

Portumna

Shannon Oaks Hotel & Country Club

féile bia **HOTEL** St. Josephs Rd Portumna Co Galway **Tel: 0509 41777** Fax: 0509 41357 Email: sales@shannonoaks.ie Web: www.shannonoaks.ie

Situated near the shores of Lough Derg and adjacent to the 17th century Portumna Castle and estate (with recently restored gardens), this privately-owned hotel opened in 1997. The interior is spacious - a large lobby is quite impressive, with polished wooden floor, faux-marble pillaring and ample (if clearly well-used) seating in contemporary style, while other public rooms include a warm-toned restaurant, which can be opened out in summer, and a cosy, pub-like bar with an informal mezzanine restaurant. It's a good choice for business and corporate events - bedrooms have air conditioning and fax/modem lines as standard, conference and meeting facilities are designed for groups of all sizes, with full back-up services. Off-duty delegates will find plenty to do too, a fine leisure centre on-site has an air-conditioned gymnasium as well as a swimming pool and ancillary services and nearby activities include river cruising, fishing, golf, horseriding, cycling and clay pigeon shooting. Conference/banqueting (600/350). Children welcome (under 5s free in parents' room). No pets. **Rooms 63** (3 suites, 4 no smoking, 2 for disabled). B&B from about €75 pps ss about €25. Amex, Diners, MasterCard, Visa, Laser. **Directions:** Situated on St Joseph Road,Portuma. ◇

Recess

Ballynahinch Castle Hotel

HOTEL Recess Co Galway **Tel: 095 31006** Fax: 095 31085 Email: bhinch@iol.ie Web: www.ballynahinch-castle.com

Renowned as a fishing hotel, this crenellated Victorian mansion enjoys a most romantic position in ancient woodland on the banks of the Ballynahinch River. It is impressive in scale and relaxed in atmosphere - a magic combination which, with a high level of comfort and friendliness (and an invigorating mixture of residents and locals in the bar at night) all combine to bring people back. Renovations and extensions have been undertaken with great attention to period detail, a policy also carried through successfully in furnishing both public areas and bedrooms. Most bedrooms and some reception rooms - notably the dining room - have lovely views over the river. It's a lovely setting for head chef Robert Webster's fine meals based on the produce of the area - specialities with enduring popularity include poached wild Atlantic salmon and oven-roasted rack of Connemara lamb. It's also a wonderful place to start the day with an excellent breakfast to give you a good start ahead of a day's fishing or touring the area: a host of fresh juices, fruits, freshly-baked breads and other good things are displayed on the buffet - and a wide range of hot dishes cooked to order including, of course, that delicious black pudding and rashers, from McGeough's famous butchers shop in Oughterard. (Ballynahinch was the Connaught winner of Guide's Denny Irish Breakfast Awards in 2002.) The bar food is consistently good too - a great place to drop into for a bite when touring Connemara. Facilities for small conferences (15); Fishing, cycling, walking; garden, tennis. Children welcome (under 3s free in parents' room; cots available without charge, baby sitting arranged). No pets. **Rooms 40** (3 suites). B&B €95 pps, ss €27. Owenmore Restaurant open daily, D only 6.30-9 (Set D €45), house wine €22.50. Bar meals 12.30-3 & 6.30-9 daily. SC 10%. Closed Christmas & Feb. Amex, Visa. **Directions:** N59 from Galway left after Recess (Roundstone Rd), 2km.

Recess

Lough Inagh Lodge

HOTEL Country House Recess Co Galway **Tel: 095 34706** Fax: 095 34708 Email: inagh@iol.ie Web: www.loughinaghhotel.ie

Maire O'Connor's former sporting lodge on the shores of Lough Inagh makes a delightful small hotel with a country house atmosphere. It has large, well-proportioned rooms, interesting period detail and lovely fireplaces with welcoming log fires, plus all the modern comforts. Public areas include two drawing rooms, each with an open fire, a lovely dining room - with deep green walls and graceful spoonback Victorian mahogany chairs (non-residents welcome by reservation) - and a very appealing bar with a big turf fire and its own back door and tiled floor for wet fishing gear. Bedrooms, some with four-posters, are all well-appointed and unusually spacious, with views of lake and countryside. Walk-in dressing rooms lead to well-planned bathrooms and tea/coffee-making facilities are available in rooms on request. While it has special appeal to sportsmen, Lough Inagh is only 42 miles from Galway and makes a good base for touring Connemara. Walking, cycling, golf and pony trekking all nearby; garden. Off-season breaks offer especially good value. Small conferences/banqueting (55). Children welcome (under 4s free in parents' room, cots available without charge). Pets permitted. **Rooms 12** (7 junior suites, 5 executive); room service (limited hours) B&B €97 pps, ss €20. Restaurant open daily 7-8.30 (reservations required), Set D from €20 - €42; house wine €20; Bar meals 12.30-5 & 7-8.30 daily. SC10%. Closed mid Dec-mid Mar. Amex, Diners, MasterCard, Visa, Laser. **Directions:** From Galway city travel on N59 for 40 miles. Take right N344 after Recess; 3 miles on right.

Renvyle

Renvyle House Hotel

féile bia HOTEL

Renvyle Co Galway **Tel: 095 43511** Fax: 095 43511
Email: info@renvyle.com Web: www.renvyle.com

In one of the country's most appealingly remote and beautiful areas, this famous Lutyens-esque house has a romantic and fascinating history, having been home to people as diverse as a Gaelic chieftan and Oliver St John Gogarty - and becoming one of Ireland's earliest country house hotels, in 1883. Although it was in a state of decline for some time, recent (and continuing) investment is gradually bringing this magic place back to its old self. It is approached via a stunning scenic drive along a mountain road with views down into a blue-green sea of unparalleled clarity. However, once reached, the hotel seems to be snuggling down for shelter and has only limited views. This sheltered feeling is reinforced by the cosy atmosphere of the original building, with its dark beams, rug strewn floors and open fires - and a snug conservatory where guests can survey the garden and landscape beyond from a comfortable vantage point. Photographs and mementoes recording visits from the many famous people who have stayed here - Augustus John, Lady Gregory, Yeats and Churchill among them - keep guests happily occupied for hours, but there is plenty to distract you from this enjoyable activity. There's a heated outdoor swimming pool and other on-site activities include tennis, trout fishing, golf (9 hole) and croquet - while the surrounding area offers more challenging activities including archaeological expeditions, horse riding, hill walking, scuba diving and sea fishing. Just loafing around is perhaps what guests are best at here, however, and there's little need to do much else. Head chef Tim O'Sullivan looks after the inner man admirably in lovely dinners featuring local seafood and Connemara produce, including Renvyle rack of lamb, local lobster and game in season - and the hotel's bar food is also excellent. All this, plus the scent of a turf fire and a comfortable armchair, can be magic. Continuing refurbishment and improvements have now brought most bedrooms up to a high standard. Special breaks (midweek, weekend and bank holiday) are very good value and Renvyle makes an excellent conference venue. (conference/banqueting 200); business centre, secretarial services. Children welcome (cots available without charge; crèche, playroom, children's playground, children's tea, baby sitting arranged). Archery, all-weather tennis court, clay pigeon shooting, croquet, lawn bowls, snooker. **Rooms 69** (6 suites, 40 no smoking, 1 for disabled). B&B €115, ss about €15, SC incl. Restaurant open 7-9 daily (Set D €45). Bar meals 11-7 daily (exc 25 Dec, Good Fri). Closed Jan. Amex, Diners, MasterCard, Visa, Laser. **Directions:** 12 miles north of Clifden.

Roundstone

O'Dowd's

féile bia PUB / RESTAURANT

Roundstone Co Galway **Tel: 095 35809**
Fax: 095 35907 Email: odowds@indigo.ie

The O'Dowd family have been welcoming visitors to this much-loved pub overlooking the harbour for longer than most people care to remember - and, although there are some new developments from time to time, the old bar is always the same. It's one of those simple places, with the comfort of an open fire and good pint, where people congregate in total relaxation - if they can get in (it can be very busy in the summer months). A reasonably priced bar menu majoring in seafood offers sustenance or, for more formal meals, the restaurant next door does the honours: seafood chowder, mussels, crabmeat etc; Connemara a lamb; blackberry & apple pie. All day food also available at the adjacent family-run coffee shop. Own parking. Meals 12-10 daily (to 9.30 in pub). Reservations required in restaurant. Tourist menu €20. House wine from €16. SC 10% on parties of 6+. Closed 25 Dec. Amex, MasterCard, Visa, Laser. **Directions:** On harbour front in Roundstone village.

Roundstone Area

The Anglers Return

Ⓝ COUNTRY HOUSE / B&B

Toombeola Roundstone Co Galway
Tel: 095 31091 Fax: 095 31091

This charming and unusual house near Roundstone was built as a sporting lodge in the eighteenth century and, as the name implies, fishing remains a major attraction to this day. But you don't have to be a fisherperson to warm to the special charms of The Anglers Return: peace and tranquillity, the opportunity to slow down in a quiet, caring atmosphere in this most beautiful area - this is its particular appeal. The house is set in three acres of natural gardens (open every day in spring and summer; best in late spring) and makes a good base for the Connemara Garden Trail - and, of course, for painting holidays. Bedrooms are bright and comfortably furnished in a fresh country house style, although only one is en-suite (the other four share two bathrooms between them); bathroom arrangements are gradually being improved, although it is not a major problem and the overall level of comfort is high. As well as fishing, riding and boat trips can be arranged for guests - and there are maps and information for walkers too. Tea and snacks are available at any time during the day or evening, (out in the secluded back garden in fine weather, or beside the fire in the soothing drawing room, perhaps); dinner is available for groups staying several days, otherwise bookings can be made in nearby restaurants. Breakfast will include treats from the garden - and you are even invited to collect your own egg. Children over 4 welcome, baby sitting arranged. No pets. Walking, fishing, garden. **Rooms 5** (1 en-suite, 4 with shared bathrooms; all no smoking). B&B €40, ss 35. Closed Dec-Feb. **No Credit Cards. Directions:** From Galway, N59 Clifden road; turn left onto R341 Roundstone road for 4 miles; house is on the left.

Tuam

Cré-na-Cille

féile bia **RESTAURANT**

High Street Tuam Co Galway **Tel: 093 28232** Fax: 093 28232
Email: crenacille@eircom.net

Cathal and Sally Reynolds' consistently excellent restaurant in Tuam makes a fine stopping place en-route to Galway city or Connemara but, as it is deservedly popular with the locals both at lunchtime and in the evening, booking is strongly advised. Evenings are a little more formal and the setting softer, but the common link is Euro-Toques chef Cathal Reynolds' confident use of local ingredients in generous food at remarkably keen prices. A number of menus - set lunch, early evening special, set dinner and à la carte - offer a wide range of seafood, meats, poultry and game in season: delicious specialities regularly on the menu include a starter of John Begley's black pudding with apple and onion in a balsamic sauce, and main course of herb-crusted rack of Connemara mountain lamb with red wine & rosemary jus, while vegetarian dishes might include a roast vegetable & pasta bake with mozzarella in a spicy tomato & nut sauce. Lunchtime menus, which are particularly good value, include a 2-course light lunch such as chowder & brown bread followed by courgette & mushroom quiche with side salad - just right for a busy weekday. Always an inventive chef, Cathal was the joint winner of the Guide's 2001 Creative Seafood Dish Award (together with Mike O'Grady of O'Grady's on the Pier, Barna). Another nice feature of the restaurant is a customer-friendly wine/drinks list, which offers an exceptional range of whiskeys and after-dinner drinks, including nearly thirty Irish whiskeys. Arrangement with nearby carpark. Children welcome to 7.30 pm. **Seats 50** (private room 30). Air conditioning. L&D Mon-Sat, 12.30-2.30 & 5.45-10. Set L €16; Early D €18 (5.45-6.30pm); Set D €20-45. À la carte available at L&D. House wine from €15.75. No SC. Closed Sun, 24-28 Dec & all bank hols. Amex, Diners, MasterCard, Visa, Laser, Switch. **Directions:** 200 mtrs from square, opposite old churchyard.

Tuam

Finns Restaurant

féile bia **RESTAURANT / BAR**

Milltown Tuam Co Galway **Tel: 093 51327** Fax: 093 51426
Email: johnfinn.indigo.ie

John and Lucy Finn's attractive restaurant is on the river, in a charming little award-winning tidy town a few miles north of Tuam - a welcome sight for hungry travellers between Galway and Sligo. John cooks an eclectic mix of international (cajun chicken, stir-fried beef with pepper sauce) and traditional (smoked salmon chowder, steaks, honey roasted duck) dishes - reasonably priced and served in a relaxed atmosphere. The cooking is sound, it's good value for money and the small village setting - where everyone seems to know someone at another table - makes a welcome change from busy towns. Children welcome. **Seats 80** (Private rooms, 2 x 10); air conditioning. D Tue-Sun, 5-9pm. A la carte, house wines from €16. Service discretionary. Closed 25 Dec & Good Fri. Children welcome. Visa, Laser. **Directions:** 8 miles from Tuam, main N17 to Sligo.

Tuam

Waterslade House

Ⓝ **RESTAURANT WITH ROOMS**

Waterslade Place Tuam Co Galway
Tel: 093 60888 Fax: 093 60838
Email: info@waterslade house.ie Web: www.watersladehouse.ie

It would be hard to miss this late eighteenth century house in the centre of Tuam as it has a large turreted entrance beside the river Nanny, creating an air of expectation for locals and visitors alike. Although no longer surrounded by gardens (an attractive apartment development has been built to the side of the original house) the house remains impressive, and the welcome from owners Adrian and

Vicky Brennan is genuinely warm. The Brennans took on the derelict property five years ago and opened in February 2003 after total refurbishment - no mean task, especially considering the high standards achieved. There are now two dining rooms on each side of an entrance enhanced by white lilies - formal, high-ceilinged, classically proportioned rooms with marble fireplaces and cool schemes of blue and grey which, with wooden floors and lacquered tables, may seem cold, although warmed by candles and firelight at night. A bar downstairs (the Medici room), in what was the old kitchen, is more lived-in and adds an extra dimension to a visit. Head chef Richard Harte (perviously with Paul Rankin in Belfast and Gleneagles, Perth) provides a fine dining experience in line with the surroundings, through an updated/classical French repertoire on a short à la carte menu - terrine of ham & foie gras with shallot dressing (€8.95), spatchcock of poussin with crushed new potatoes & fricassé of baby veg €19.95) are typical, with seasonal specialities such as game often included - and this is very sensibly augmented by a simpler early evening grills menu, which is ideal for golfers. The quality of food and standard of cooking are exemplary - and service, by black-uniformed staff under the direction of restaurant manager Gerry Sinnott, is outstandingly attentive and professional. Adrian Brennan is personally responsible for a shortish but carefully selected wine list. Not suitable for children after 6 pm. **Seats 60** (private room 35). Reservations required. Toilets wheelchair accessible. Grills Wed-Sun, 5-6.30; D Wed-Sun 6-9.30 (Sun 5-7.30); L Sun only 12-3. Grills & D à la carte; Sun L €14-25. House wine €16.95. Restaurant closed Mon, Tue.

Accommodation: There are four luxurious, highly individual rooms available - and visitors to the restaurant are invited to ask for "the tour". All day room service; turndown service. Conference/banqueting (35/70); secretarial services. Children under 14 free in parents' room (cot available, free of charge, baby sitting arranged. No pets. Walking; garden. **Rooms 4** (1 with bath & shower; 3 shower only - 1 wet room; all no smoking). B&B €160. Establishment closed last 2 wks Jan, first 2 wks Nov. Amex, MasterCard, Visa, Laser. **Directions:** 2 minutes walk from town square, down Shop Street.

COUNTY KERRY

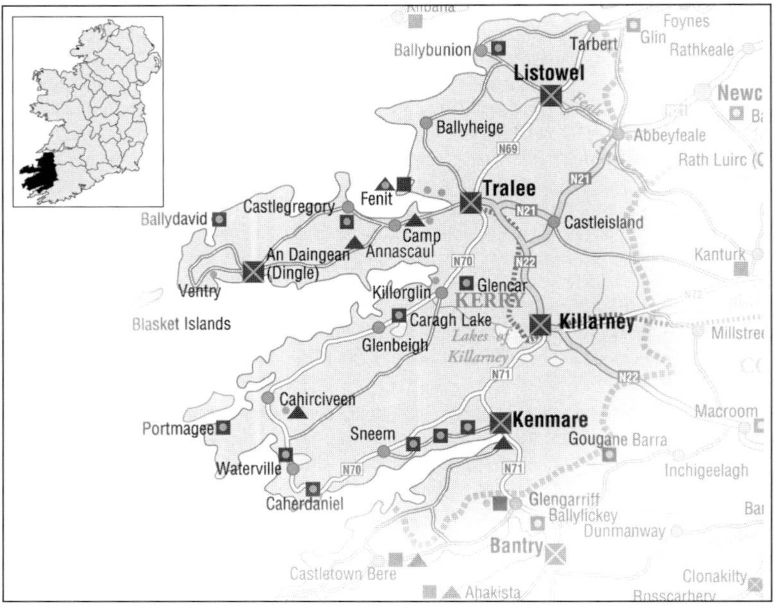

It's something special, being Kerry. This magnificent county in the far southwest has Ireland's highest and most varied mountains, and certain favoured areas also have our longest-lived citizens. Then, too, it's a region which has long been a global pioneer in the hospitality business - in 2004, the scenically-blessed town of Killarney will be celebrating 250 years in the forefront of Irish tourism, while its most senior hotel, the Great Southern, is celebrating its 150th anniversary.

So visitors inevitably arrive with high expectations. Kerry, however, can face the challenge. This magnificent county really is the Kingdom of Kerry. Everything is king size. For not only has Kerry mountains galore - more than anywhere else in Ireland - but there's a rare quality to Carrantuohill, the highest of all.

By international standards, this loftiest peak of MacGillicuddy's Reeks (try pronouncing it "mackil-cuddy") may not seem particularly notable at just 1038 m. But when you sense its mysterious heights in the clouds above a countryside of astonishing beauty, its relative elevation is definitely world league. And all Kerry's mountains sweep oceanwards towards a handsome coastline which rings the changes between sheltered inlets and storm tossed offshore islands. Visually, Kerry has everything.

But these days, spectacular scenery isn't enough on its own. Like other leading visitor destinations, Kerry is well aware of the need to provide accessible entertainment and an increasing choice of places with cultural and historical interest. Here too, the Kingdom can oblige

The oldest fossil footprints in the Northern Hemisphere are in Kerry, and they're about 350 million years old. You'll find tham way down west, on Valentia Island, and they're reckoned one of the seven wonders of Ireland. In much more modern times, the Antarctic explorer Tom Crean was from Kerry. He came from the little village of Annascaul on the majestic Dingle Peninsula, and when he had finished with adventuring, he returned to Annascaul and opened the South Pole Inn.

The town of Killarney among the lakes and mountains has long been a magnet for visitors, but Killarney is determined not simply to rest on its laurels after a Quarter Millennium as Ireland's oldest tourist destination, for it was in 1754 that its attractions were first internationally promoted. However, the people of Killarney continue to look forward, and in 2003 the publication of Re-imagining Killarney: The Killarney Urban Masterplan, envisaged boulevards, a civic theatre, and a museum with a new town movement towards underground carparks, for at times Killarney seems a victim of its own popularity. Meanwhile, on the more immediate question of keeping the place clean, Killarney scored well in the latest national Tidy Town contest, announced on September 8th 2003 – it came in with an excellent score of 87.7%.

Across the mountains, the lovely little town on Kenmare in South Kerry is both a gourmet focus, and another good touring centre. As one of the prettiest places in Ireland, Kenmare puts the emphasis on civic pride, and the latest Tidy Town results made it the tidiest small town in all Ireland, with a rating of 89.3%.

In the far northeast of this large county, Listowel – famed for its writers – has the restored Lartigue Monorail, part of which was re-opened in the summer of 2003. It's unique. And if you want to know how unique, well, you'll just have to go and see for yourself.

Local Attractions and Information

Beaufort, Hotel Dunloe Castle Gardens	064 44583
Castleisland, Crag Cave	066 714 1244
Dingle, Ocean World	066 915 2111
Dunquin, Great Blasket Centre	066 915 6444 / 915 6371
Farranfore, Kerry International Airport	066 976 4644
Glencar, Into the Wilderness Walking Tours (May-Sep)	066 60104
Kenmare, Walking Festivals	064 41034
Kenmare, Heritage Centre	064 41233
Killarney Muckross House, Gardens & Traditional Farm	064 31440
Killarney, Tourism Information	064 31633
Killorglin, Kerry Woollen Mills	064 44122
Killorglin, Puck Fair (ancient festival), mid-August	066 976 2366
Lauragh, Dereen Gardens	064 83103
Listowel, St John's Art Centre	068 22566
Listowel, Writers' Week (June)	068 21074
Tralee, Kerry County Museum	066 712 7777
Tralee, Rose of Tralee Festival (late August)	066 712 3227
Tralee, Siamsa Tire Arts Centre	066 712 3055
Valentia Island, The Skellig Experience	066 947 6306
Valentia Island, Valentia Heritage (Knightstown)	066 947 6411
Waterville Craft Market	066 947 4212

Annascaul

South Pole Inn

ATMOSPHERIC PUB

Annascaul Co Kerry **Tel: 066 915 7388**
Email: info@southpoleinn.com Web: www.southpoleinn.ie

Annascaul, on the Dingle peninsula, is one of the most-photographed villages in Ireland – mainly because of the brilliantly colourful and humorous frontage painted onto his pub by the late Dan Foley (which is still a fine pub). Nearby, The South Pole, which is down at the lower end of the street is equally interesting - the name becomes clear when you realise there is a connection with the great Irish explorer Sir Ernest Shackleton and, more particularly, his second officer, Tom Crean, who was a native of Annascaul and has only recently achieved the recognition he deserved for his own part in antarctic exploration. On retiring in 1920, he returned to Annascaul, married and ran the South Pole Inn. As well as being a delightful, well-run pub, The South Pole Inn is full of fascinating Shackleton and Crean memorabilia. Bar food available 12-8 daily. Closed 25 Dec & Good Fri. MasterCard, Visa, **Directions:** On the main road between Tralee & Dingle.

Ballybunion

Harty-Costello Townhouse Bar & Restaurant

GUESTHOUSE

Main St. Ballybunion Co Kerry **Tel: 068 27129** Fax: 068 27489
Email: hartycostello@eircom.net Web: www.hartycostello.com

Although styled a townhouse, Davnet and Jackie Hourigan's welcoming town centre establishment is really an inn, encompassing all the elements of hospitality within its neatly painted and flower bedecked yellow walls, albeit at different times of day. The spacious bedrooms have television, direct dial phones, tea & coffee-making facilities and hair dryer, and also comfortable chairs and curtains thoughtfully fitted with blackout linings to keep out intrusively early summer light. Although always comfortable, rooms had become a little dated and, along with the residents' lounge, are to be completely refurbished in time for the 2004 season. There's a choice of no less than three bars in which to unwind and an evening restaurant where seafood is the speciality in the restaurant, complemented by an extensive wine list. It all adds up to a relaxing and hospitable base for a golfing holiday, or for touring the south-west. Children welcome (under 12s free in parents' room). No pets. **Rooms 8** (all en-suite). B&B €70 pps, ss €20. Food available Mon-Sat, 12-7 (bar); 6.30-9.30 (restaurant). No food on Sun; establishment closed Nov-Mar. Amex, MasterCard, Visa, Laser. **Directions:** 50 miles from Limerick N69 40 miles from Killarney.

Ballybunion

Iragh Ti Connor

COUNTRY HOUSE

Main Street Ballybunion Co Kerry **Tel: 068 27112** Fax: 068 27787
Email: iraghticonnor@eircom.net Web: www.golfballybunion.com

The name, which translates as "the inheritance of O'Connor", says it all: what John and Joan O'Connor inherited was a 19th century pub with potential and, thanks to their scrupulous attention to detail when planning and sourcing materials like real slates and wooden windows for its transformation, their inheritance has now been transformed into a fine establishment with exceptionally large, comfortable bedrooms. All rooms have been carefully refurbished and furnished with antiques to complement the convenience of satellite television, direct dial phones and generous bathrooms with cast-iron tubs and power showers - and many rooms even have working fireplaces, where fires can be lit on request. Public areas, which include the original public bar, a lounge bar and a fine dining restaurant with a baby grand to add to the atmosphere, are also generous in scale, and furnished with style and individuality. Golfing holidays are a serious attraction here and Iragh Tí Connor is fast establishing a reputation as one of the best places to stay on the discerning golfers' circuits. Children welcome (cot available without charge.) Small conferences (60). Garden. No pets. Meals daily: bar food 5-8; restaurant Mon-Sat 6-9.30; Sun 1-9.30. **Rooms 17** (3 junior suites, 14 superior rooms, all no smoking). B&B €95 pps, ss €55. Closed 20-31 Dec. Amex, MasterCard, Visa, Laser. **Directions:** Opposite statue of Bill Clinton.

Ballybunion

Teach de Broc

GUESTHOUSE

Links Road Ballybunion Co Kerry **Tel: 068 27581** Fax: 068 27919
Email: teachdebroc@eircom.net Web: www.ballybuniongolf.com

You don't have to play golf to appreciate this highly popular guesthouse, but it certainly must help as it is almost within the boundaries of the famous Ballybunion links. Aoife and Seamus Brock offer an extremely high standard of comfort, with direct dial phones and satellite television in all rooms and there is a commitment to constant upgrading and improvement: additions completed in 2003 include a new sitting room, dining room and another four fine new bedrooms and also a lift. But, however comfortable and well-located this exceptional guesthouse may be, it's the laid-back and genuinely hospitable atmosphere that really gets them coming back for more. Always keen to provide the best possible service for the discerning golfer, breakfast is served from 6am, with freshly baked scones and croissants among the good things offered. Internet for guests' use. Laundry service. Horse riding available nearby. Own parking. Garden. Not suitable for children. No pets. Wine licence. **Rooms 10** (all en-suite & no-smoking, 1 for disabled). B&B €65pps, ss €25. Closed Dec-Feb. MasterCard, Visa, Laser. **Directions:** Directly opposite entrance to Ballybunion Golf Club.

Caherdaniel

Derrynane Hotel

féile bia HOTEL

Caherdaniel Co Kerry **Tel: 066 947 5136** Fax: 066 947 5136
Email: info@derrynane.com Web: www.derrynane.com

If only for its superb location – on the seaward side of the Ring of Kerry road – this unassuming 1960s-style hotel would be well worth a visit, but there is much more to it than the view, or even its waterside position. The accommodation is quite modest but very comfortable, the food is good and, under the excellent management of Mary O'Connor and her well-trained staff, this hospitable, family-friendly place provides a welcome home from home for many a contented guest. Activity holidays are a big draw - there are beautiful beaches, excellent fishing with local fisherman Michael Fenton (who supplies all necessary equipment and has a fully licensed boat), Waterville Golf Course offers special rates at certain times - and the hotel has published its own walking brochure. Don't leave the area without visiting Daniel O'Connell's beautiful house at Derrynane – or the amazing Ballinskelligs chocolate factory. Children welcome (under 4s free in parents' room, cots available without charge; playroom) Heated outdoor swimming pool, tennis, pool table. Walking. Well-behaved small dogs with their own beds may stay with their owners. Garden. **Rooms 70** (all en-suite, 10 no smoking). B&B €79.50 pps, ss €19. Closed Oct-Apr.

Restaurant: Beautifully located, overlooking the heated outdoor swimming pool and the hotel's gardens (which reach down to the shore), the restaurant enjoys stunning sea views on a good day and the best of local ingredients are used in imaginative, very fairly priced four-course dinner menus. **Seats 80.** D 7-9 daily, Set D € 29/38, sc disc retionary. House wine €19. Air conditioning. * All day salad bar avalable for light meals. Hotel closed Oct-mid Apr. Amex, Diners, Visa, Laser. **Directions:** Midway on Ring of Kerry.

Caherdaniel

Iskeroon

COUNTRY HOUSE

Iskeroon Caherdaniel Co Kerry **Tel: 066 947 5119** Fax: 066 947 5488
Email: info@iskeroon.com Web: www.iskeroon.com

Geraldine and David Hare's beautiful old house is in a secluded position overlooking Derrynane Harbour. The effort taken to get there makes it all the more restful once settled in. All three of the comfortable and interestingly decorated bedrooms overlook the harbour - and the islands of Deenish and Scarriff - and each has its own private bathroom just across a corridor. The private pier at the bottom of the garden joins an old Mass Path which, by a happy chance, leads not only to the beach but also to Keating's pub (known as Bridie's) where a bit of banter and some good seafood is also to be had in the evenings, although it's wise to check on this beforehand. Unsuitable for children. Pets allowed by arrangement. Fishing, walking, garden. *Self-catering studio apartment for two also available. **Rooms 3** (all with private bathrooms, all no smoking). B&B €60 pps, ss ss €20. Closed 31 Oct-30 Apr. MasterCard, Visa, Laser. **Directions:** Between Caherdaniel and Waterville (N70), turn off at the Scariff Inn, signed to Bunavalla Pier. Go to the pier and left through "private" gate; cross beach and enter through white gate posts.

Cahirciveen

O'Neills "The Point Bar"

ATMOSPHERIC PUB

Renard Point Cahirciveen Co Kerry
Tel: 066 947 2165 Fax: 066 947 2165

In the same family for 150 years, Michael and Bridie O'Neill's pub, The Point Bar, is beside the Valentia Island car ferry. Renovated in true character by the present owners, it's always neat and makes an appealing place to drop into for a quick one while you're waiting for the ferry - but even better to stay awhile and make the most of their super fresh seafood, served during the summer. The menu covers everything from a whole range of salads and open sandwiches on brown bread - fresh and smoked wild salmon, smoked mackerel, crabmeat, crab claws - to hot dishes like deep-fried squid and a couple of hake and monkfish dishes with garlic and olive oil. Not very suitable for children. The Valentia Island ferry runs continuously - i.e. not to a time table - from April-September inclusive. L Mon-Sat, D daily. Closed L Sun. Food available only from April to October (Phone ahead to check food service, especially off season). **No Credit Cards. Directions:** Beside the Valentia Island ferry slip. ◇

Cahirciveen

QC's Seafood Bar & Restaurant

RESTAURANT

3 Main Street Cahirciveen Co.Kerry **Tel: 066 947 2244** Fax: 066 947 2244
Email: kate@qcbar.com Web: www.qcbar.com

Kate and Andrew Cooke renovated this old building with style and sensitivity - introducing a pleasingly continental tone (Spanish to be exact) while retaining interesting and characterful features such as the original stone wall and a big fireplace that must be a great draw on cold winter days. The bar counter is also over a century old and there are numerous nautical antiques and pictures of local interest. Although there are plenty of other things on the menu, local fish is the main feature - supplied by the family company, Quinlan's Kerry Fish at Renard's Point - cooked Basque-style on a charcoal grill specially imported from Spain, so expect delicious chargrills, with lots of olive oil and garlic. Wild Kerry salmon, smoked in the family factory, is another speciality, served simply with leaves and home-made brown bread, and also chargrilled fillet steak to balance up all that ultra-fresh seafood. There are some tempting vegetarian starters - main courses on request. The wine list leans strongly towards Spain, especially the reds (but house wines are from France & Chile, €16.95). Children welcome. **Seats 48.** Meals: Easter-end Oct, L Mon-Sat 12-2.30 & D daily, 6-9.30; Nov-mid Dec & Feb 12-Easter, D only Thu-Sun; Christmas period open all day. Closed Sun until 6 pm; Nov-mid Dec & 12 Feb-Easter no L & closed D Mon-Wed; also closed 25 Dec, Good Fri; annual closure 7 Jan-12 Feb. The minimum transaction for credit cards is €25. MasterCard, Visa, Laser. **Directions:** In the centre of Caherciveen.

Cahirciveen

The Quarry Restaurant

RESTAURANT

Kells Post Office Cahirciveen Co Kerry
Tel: 066 947 7601 Fax: 066 947 7660
Email: patscraftshop@eircom.net Web: www.patscraftshop.com

Pat Golden's family-run "one stop shop" on the Ring of Kerry is extremely useful to know about - not only will you get good home cooking here, but there's a post office and foodstore, filling station, tourist information point and bureau de change. Aside from these practical points, there are more interesting aspects to this many-sided venture as it also includes a fine craft shop, with quality Irish clothing and gift items and a unique attraction in the shape of 'The Golden Mile Nature Walk' up behind the quarry, which is just the place to walk off your lunch. The restaurant is on the first floor with large windows to take in panoramic views over Kells Bay to the Dingle Peninsula and - another surprise - the cooking style includes genuine Mediterranean influences as well as Irish dishes as head chef Elena Stavri is a Greek Cypriot and "cooks with the heart". So you'll find real home-made Greek food like moussaka, hummous, tzatziki and baklava sitting happily alongside Irish stew and wild Dingle Bay salmon. The pricing is reasonable (most main courses around €9; top price, for sirloin steak, about €16.95) and, best of all perhaps, this is somewhere you can get a decent bite to eat during the day on a Sunday, when most of our recommendations in the area are closed. * On alternate Friday nights in July & August Greek mezza style banquets are held - ring the restaurant for information and booking. **Seats 86.** No smoking area; air conditioning. Children welcome. Open daily 9am-6pm, Easter-Oct. A la carte; house wine €13.95. Closed Nov-Easter. Amex, Diners, MasterCard, Visa, Laser. **Directions:** Midway between Glenbeigh & Cahirciveen.

Camp

Barnagh Bridge Country House

GUESTHOUSE

Cappaclough Camp Co Kerry **Tel: 066 713 0145** Fax: 066 713 0299
Email: bbguest@eircom.net Web: www.barnaghbridge.com

Snuggled into the hillside overlooking Tralee Bay, Heather Williams' unusual architect-designed guesthouse is in extensive grounds between the mountains and the sea. Attractive and comfortable, it was purpose-built, with five individually furnished guest bedrooms (decor themed on local wild flowers), all with en-suite shower rooms. In the dining room guests can drink in the view of Tralee Bay while doing justice to Heather's breakfasts – fresh juices, newly baked breads and scones, locally made preserves, and Dingle smoked salmon and scrambled eggs or a traditional fry (plus daily specials such as kippers or French toast). The stylishly decorated guest drawing room opens onto a patio overlooking the Maharees islands and their spectacular sunsets, and there's a conservatory, which extends the reception area and dining room - and maximises still further on the wonderful view. Garden, fishing, walking. Not suitable for children under 10. No pets. **Rooms 5** (all shower only & non-smoking). B&B about €40 pps, ss about €10. Closed 31 Oct-17 March. Amex, MasterCard, Visa, Laser. **Directions:** Take N86 from Tralee for 10 miles, then R560 for 1 mile.

Camp

The Cottage Restaurant

RESTAURANT

Camp Co Kerry **Tel: 066 713 0022** / 7130176 Web: www.ireland.view.com

Although quite newly built, both the design and materials of Frank & Gretta Wyles' bright, airy restaurant are in the local idiom so it fits in well and is maturing gracefully. Local ingredients feature in wholesome, quite traditional fare (west coast chowder, boxty, roast stuffed loin of Kerry lamb, with colcannon mash and garlic & rosemary sauce). Seafood is a speciality (pan-fried sole on the bone with butter & parsley, daily specials) and also steaks, various ways; vegetarian dishes - typically an aubergine stack of grilled aubergine filled with goats cheese and semidried tomato, baked & finished with chunky tomato sauce - are always on the main menu. Pleasant service and reasonable prices too. Ample parking; children welcome. Reservations advised. **Seats 60.** (private room, 14). D daily in summer, 6-10; L12-3.30; à la carte; house wine from about €13.50; SC discretionary. Closed Mon & Tue off season. Establishment closed Jan-Mar. Amex, MasterCard, Visa, Laser. **Directions:** On the Tralee-Castlegregory-Conor Pass-Dingle road (10 miles from Tralee). ◇

Camp

James Ashe

ATMOSPHERIC PUB

Camp Co Kerry **Tel: 066 413 0133**

This fine old pub just off the Tralee-Dingle road has been in the family for 200 years and the present owners Rory and Gertie Duffin, intend to keep things pretty much the way they've been, at least in the recent past. It's a delightful place, full of genuine character and hospitality - ideal for a drink and a chat. Even when very busy staff do their best to deliver prompt service, even accommodating special requests without fuss. Bar lunch dishes include a good home-made chowder (good value too at €4.95) and main dishes like sirloin steak with pepper sauce (€15.95), while evening menus offer popular dishes with more sense of occasion like crispy duck with orange & plum sauce. Closed 25 Dec & Good Fri. Phone ahead to check opening times off season. Amex, Diners, MasterCard, Visa. **Directions:** On the main Tralee-Dingle road, 10 miles from Tralee. ◇

Camp

Suan Na Mara

B&B

Lisnagree Castlegregory Rd Camp Co Kerry **Tel: 066 7139258**
Fax: 066 7139258 Email: suanmara@eircom.net

Fionnuala Fitzgerald's welcoming modern B&B near the sea is set well back from the road in spacious grounds and even has its own pitch & putt course in an adjoining field, whilst a path leads to a long deserted sandy beach, where the friendly golden retrievers eagerly join guests (when invited) for a walk along the shore. It's a relaxed and very pleasant place to stay, with comfortable sitting rooms for guests and bedrooms that are a little on the small side but pretty, with bright fabrics and well-equipped, with hair dryer, TV, radio and tea/coffee making facilities and neat shower rooms. Maintenance is immaculate, hospitality genuine - and breakfast will be a treat, with unusual offers as well as the traditional Irish breakfast: warm home-made compôtes and yoghurt, scrambled eggs with chives and thick slices of smoked salmon, or freshly-made apple fritters with minted strawberries. No dinners, but Fionnuala sends guests along to one of the local pubs, such as Tomasín's olde-worlde thatched bar and restaurant just down the road at Stradbally (Tel: 066 71 39179). Garden, pitch & putt, walking. **Rooms 6** (all en-suite & no smoking). B&B €35 pps, ss €30 (high season). Children welcome (cot available, €7, baby sitting arranged). Closed 31 Oct-28 Feb. Visa, Laser. **Directions:** Take N86 to Camp Junction and then R560 for approx 5 Km.

Caragh Lake

Caragh Lodge

COUNTRY HOUSE / RESTAURANT

Caragh Lake Killorglin Co Kerry
Tel: 066 976 9115 Fax: 066 976 9316
Email: caraghl@iol.ie Web: www.caraghlodge.com

Less than a mile from the Ring of Kerry, Mary Gaunt's lovely Victorian house and gardens nestling on the shores of the startlingly beautiful Caragh Lake is an idyllic place, with views of Ireland's highest mountains, the McGillicuddy Reeks. The house – which is elegantly furnished with antiques but not too formal – makes a cool, restful retreat. Bedrooms include some newer garden rooms with wonderful views, their own entrance and sitting room (complete with open log fire), and are all sumptuously furnished with lovely bathrooms. Salmon and trout fishing, boating and swimming are all available at the bottom of the garden. Not suitable for children under 12. No pets. Banqueting (50). **Rooms 15** (1 suite, 8 junior suites, 6 superior). B&B €90, ss €40. Closed mid Oct-end Apr.

Restaurant: In the elegant dining room overlooking the lake, Mary's real love of cooking shines through. Local produce (such as freshly caught seafood, often including wild salmon from Caragh Lake, Kerry lamb and home-grown vegetables) takes pride of place. Wide-ranging menus tempt with starters like twice-baked goats cheese soufflé with a herb cream sauce, followed by soup or sorbet of the day then main courses such as pan-fried turbot with olive oil scented potato purée & coriander cream sauce, Caragh Lodge crispy half duck with plum sauce or noisette of Kerry lamb niçoise. Baking is a particular strength, not only in delicious home-baked breads, but also baked desserts and treats for afternoon tea - including recipes handed down by Mary's family through the generations. **Seats 34** (private room, 12). D daily, 7-8.30; about €40 (average, à la carte). Good wine list, unusually strong on South African wines. House wine €22. SC discretionary. Open to non-residents by reservation. Not suitable for children under 12. Establishment closed mid Oct-end Apr. Amex, Diners, MasterCard, Visa. **Directions:** From Killorglin on N70, Glenbeigh direction, take second road signed Caragh Lake; at end of road go left again. The house is on the right.

Caragh Lake

Carrig House Country House & Restaurant

RESTAURANT / COUNTRY HOUSE

Caragh Lake Killorglin Co Kerry
Tel: 066 976 9100 Fax: 066 976 9166
Email: info@carrighouse.com Web: www.carrighouse.com

At the heart of Frank and Mary Slattery's sensitively extended Victorian house lies a hunting lodge once owned by Lord Brocket - and he chose well, as it is very attractive and handsomely set in fine gardens with the lake and mountains providing a dramatic backdrop. The house is welcoming and well-maintained, with friendly staff (Frank himself carries the luggage to your room) and a very relaxed atmosphere, notably in a series of sitting rooms where you can chat beside the fire or have a drink before dinner. This is a place where you can lose yourself for hours with a book, or playing chess, cards or board games in the games room, or boating out on the lake. Individually decorated bedrooms furnished with antiques (some with their own patio) are large, high-ceilinged and airy, with generous, well-designed bathrooms with bath and shower - a Presidential Suite has a sitting room with panoramic views across the lake to the Magillicuddy Reeks, two separate dressing rooms and jacuzzi bath. The extensive gardens are of great interest and a laminated map is available, naming the various areas - Waterfall Garden, Pond Garden, Rock Walk etc - and the main plantings in each; a more detailed list is available on request and personalised tours can be arranged with head gardener Mark Skidmore. Not suitable for children under

8 except small babies (under 1 free of charge, cot available, baby sitting arranged). Dogs allowed in some areas. Swimming (lake), fishing (ghilly & boat available), walking, garden, croquet. **Rooms 16** (1 suite, 1 junior suite, 3 no smoking) B&B €75 pps, ss about €45. Closed Dec-Feb.

Lakeside Restaurant: Beautifully situated overlooking the lake, the restaurant moved up a gear in 2003 with the arrival of head chef Helen Vickers, who brought experience from highly regarded kitchens including the K Club, and pastry chef Patricia Teahan who ensures there are many daily temptations on the dessert menu. The style is confident and refined but the atmosphere is warm and relaxed - and there is a wholesome regard for local produce: trout and salmon from the lake, Kerry lamb and home grown vegetables from their own walled kitchen garden all feature in dishes that taste as good as they look. Vegetarian dishes are always available. **Seats 50** (private room, 15). D daily, 6.30-9. Extensive à la carte. House wine €25. SC discretionary. Non-residents welcome (booking essential). Establishment closed Dec-Feb. Diners, MasterCard, Visa, Laser. **Directions:** Left after 2.5 miles on Killorglin/Glenbeigh Road N70 (Ring of Kerry).

Caragh Lake

Hotel Ard-na-Sidhe

HOTEL

Caragh Lake Co Kerry **Tel: 066 976 9105** Fax: 066 976 9282
Email: sales@kih.liebherr.com Web: www.iol.ie/khl

Set in woodland and among award-winning gardens, this peaceful Victorian retreat is in a beautiful mountain location overlooking Caragh Lake. Decorated throughout in a soothing country house style, very comfortable antique-filled day rooms provide plenty of lounging space for quiet indoor relaxation and a terrace for fine weather – all with wonderful views. Bedrooms – shared between the main house and some with private patios in the garden house – are spacious and elegantly furnished in traditional style, with excellent en-suite bathrooms. This is a sister hotel to the Hotel Europe and Dunloe Castle (see entries), whose leisure facilities are also available to guests. Dooks, Waterville, Killeen and Mahony's Point golf courses are all within easy reach. Not very suitable for children, although concessions are given (under 12s free in parents' room; cots available). No pets. **Rooms 20** (5 no smoking). B&B Room Rate from about €215 (max 2 guests), SC included. 24 hr room service. Closed 1 Oct-30 Apr. Amex, Diners, MasterCard, Visa, Laser. **Directions:** Off N70 Ring of Kerry road, signed 5 km west of Killorglin. ◇

Castlegregory

Spillanes

PUB

Fahamore Maharees Castlegregory Co Kerry **Tel: 066 713 9125** Fax: 066 713 9538

It's a long way down from the main road to reach the Maharees, but well worth it for many reasons, not least a visit to Marilyn and Michael Spillane's great traditional pub - they work hard at both the food and hospitality and have earned loyal following as a result. There's a tempting display of salads and desserts to choose from and seafood stars on the menu - mussels grilled with garlic breadcrumbs, crab claws served in shell with brown bread and a cocktail dipping sauce, fresh and wild salmon in salads and open sandwiches, scampi made from Dingle prawns. And there's plenty for meat-lovers too, such as chargrilled steaks and several chicken dishes (in the evening), some vegetarian dishes and some with child-appeal too. Meals daily in high season (Jun-Aug), 1-9.30 (Sun 2-9), evenings only early in early and late season. No food in winter (Nov-mid March). MasterCard, Visa, Laser. **Directions:** Dingle Peninsula, 3.5 miles north of Castlegregory, between Bandon and Tralee bays.

Dingle

Bambury's Guesthouse

GUESTHOUSE

Mail Road Dingle Co Kerry **Tel: 066 915 1244** Fax: 066 915 1786
Email: info@bamburysguesthouse.com Web: www.bamburysguesthouse.com

Just a couple of minutes walk from the centre of Dingle, Jimmy and Bernie Bambury's well-run, purpose-built guesthouse has spacious modern rooms with tea/coffee trays, phone, satellite TV, hair dryer and complimentary mineral water. Bernie Bambury's breakfasts include griddle cakes with fresh fruit and honey – a house speciality – and vegetarian breakfasts are offered by arrangement. Not suitable for children under 4; no pets. Own parking. **Rooms 12** (all shower only & no smoking, 3 for disabled) B&B €60, ss €20. Open all year. MasterCard, Visa, Laser. **Directions:** On N86, on the left after the Shell garage, on entering Dingle.

Dingle

Beginish Restaurant

RESTAURANT

Green Street Dingle Co Kerry **Tel: 066 915 1588**
Fax: 066 915 1591 Email: patmoore@eircom.net

Pat Moore has returned to run her renowned restaurant after a break of several years and, while the high ceilinged room (unusual in cottagey Dingle) remains elegant, it's now lighter and brighter with mainly contemporary paintings, white lilies on the bar and freesias on bare tables. On the ball as ever,

Pat's other big change is in the menu: compact, unfussy and very accessible, it's a simple printed affair offering eight or nine concisely named dishes on each course, including the night's catch from the harbour. Starters like a classic soupe de poissons, served en cocotte with croûtons and rouille (not to be missed), Smokies (smoked haddock in béchamel with scallions and melted cheddar), steamed mussels, and grilled organic goats cheese with shallot jam all come in at under €10, main courses begin at little more for the vegetarian dish of the day - peaking with poached lobster, which is a snip at €25 per lb, served plain or with garlic butter. Prime fish include a wonderful turbot dish with a leek fondue and there are local meats - organic beef and Kerry lamb - a simple rack, for example, with rosemary jus and an excellent selection of roasted vegetables. Classic desserts - citrus scented crème brulée (light and crisp-topped with a couple of pretty tuile leaves), perhaps, or a meltingly delicious chocolate fondue with pistachio ice cream & raspberry sauce - or there's an Irish farmhouse cheese plate. Good coffee to finish and a genuine sense of having been restored; this is superb classic cooking, refreshingly simple and with wonderful flavours - and caring service to match. The wine list has (with a little sadness perhaps) abandoned all the great wines of yore and now offers an interesting, manageable selection of affordable bottles kicking off with a house selection of ten well-chosen wines. **Seats 52.** Air conditioning. D Tue-Sun, 6-9.30, L Sun only 12.30-2.30. A la carte. House wine €18.50; no SC. Closed Mon & Tue; also all Nov-mid Mar. Amex, Diners, MasterCard, Visa, Laser. **Directions:** Below the Catholic Church, on the opposite side of the street.

Dingle

Captains House

GUESTHOUSE

The Mall Dingle Co Kerry **Tel: 066 915 1531** Fax: 066 915 1079
Email: captigh@eircom.net Web: homepage.eircom.net/ncaptigh/

When Jim, a retired sea captain, and Mary Milhench bought this guesthouse in the late 80s they were renewing a seafaring tradition going back to the original captain, Tom Williams, who first took lodgers here in 1886. Today this charming house is as relaxed and hospitable a place as could be wished for: approached via a little bridge over the Mall River then through a lovely garden, it has been renovated and furnished with the antiques and curios collected by Jim on his voyages. The age and nature of the building - which extends into the next door premises - has created a higgledy-piggledy arrangement of rooms that adds to the charm; rooms vary considerably, as would be expected, but all have comfort (orthopaedic beds, phones, satellite TV, hospitality trays, plenty of hot water) as well as character. A welcoming turf fire in the reception area encourages guests to linger over tea, or with a book, and breakfast - which is a very special feature of a stay here - is served in the conservatory. Not suitable for children. No pets. **Rooms 9** (1 suite, 7 shower only, all no smoking). B&B about €45pps, ss about €5. Closed 1 Dec-mid Mar. Amex, MasterCard, Visa. **Directions:** Turn right at town entrance roundabout; Captains House is 100 metres up on left. ◇

Dingle

The Chart House

féile bia **RESTAURANT**

The Mall Dingle Co Kerry **Tel: 066 9152255**
Email: charthse@iol.ie Web: www.charthousedingle.com

In an area exceptionally well-endowed with good eating places, Jim McCarthy's informal purpose-built restaurant is one of the natural leaders. It's attractively built in local stone to a low-key design that matches the proportions of the town well and there's a smart little bar just inside the door - where Jim McCarthy, the perfect host, always seems to be meeting, seating and seamlessly ensuring that everyone is well looked after and generally having a good time. And he has a good kitchen team to match his warm professionalism: while based mainly on local ingredients, notably seafood, head chef Gary Fitzgerald's well-judged menus are international in tone - a superb speciality starter of Annascaul black pudding, for example, is wrapped in filo pastry and served with apple chutney and a lemongrass jus, while roast rack of Kerry lamb - supplied by Ashe's butchers in Annascaul - is served with red onion and feta tart tatin & vanilla gravy; high quality ingredients and accurate, confident cooking give these traditional foods a new character and a large selection - perhaps half a dozen or more - of simple, perfectly cooked side vegetables are the ideal complement. Seafood is well represented, of course (pan roast monktail, perhaps, with stuffed vine tomato & sweetcorn pancakes) and vegetarian dishes - probably two or more on each course - offer mainstream contemporary cooking of the same high standard and have wide appeal. Desserts include classics like a basket of home-made ice creams or intriguing variations on familiar themes such as apple & clove tartlet topped with ginger nut crumble, served with a Calvados – but the smart money is on the Irish cheeses, which are cannily offered with a glass of vintage port and served with delicious home-made oat biscuits and two varieties of grapes. Prices are fairly moderate (starters around €8.75, main courses average €20). An interesting wine list has helpful tasting notes as well as a clear layout of country of origin as well as vintages - and, of course, there's always a Chateau MacCarthy in stock. *Jim McCarthy was the Guide's Host of the Year for 2003. **Seats 45.** Children welcome. Air conditioning. D Wed-Mon, 6.30-10; à la carte. House wine €18.50. Closed Tue & 7 Jan-13 Feb. MasterCard, Visa, Laser. **Directions:** Left at the roundabout as you enter the town.

Dingle

Cleevaun

GUESTHOUSE

Lady's Cross Milltown Dingle Co Kerry **Tel: 066 915 1108** Fax: 066 915 2228 Email: cleevaun@iol.ie Web: www.cleevaun.com

A cup of tea or coffee and a slice of home-made porter cake welcomes guests to Charlotte and Sean Cluskey's well-run, recently renovated guesthouse just outside the town. Set in an acre of landscaped gardens overlooking Dingle Bay, it's near enough to Dingle to be handy and far enough away to enjoy the peace that the peninsula promises. Furnishing throughout is in a pleasant country pine style: bedrooms are all non-smoking, have good facilities and are well organised, with quality beds, quilted bedspreads and well-finished en-suite bathrooms; one bedroom has a separate dressing room. Charlotte's breakfasts – served in a large south-facing dining room overlooking Dingle Bay – are quite a speciality and she is a most hospitable hostess. No pets. **Rooms 8** (all with full bath). B&B €48, ss €30. Closed Nov-17 Mar. MasterCard, Visa, Laser. **Directions:** Just outside the town, on the Slea Head/Ventry scenic route R559.

Dingle

Dingle Benners Hotel

HOTEL

Main Street Dingle Co Kerry **Tel: 066 915 1638** Fax: 066 915 1412 Email: reservations@dinglebenners.com Web: www.dinglebenners.com

Major refurbishment and the addition of spacious new rooms at the back have greatly improved this 300 year old centrally-located hotel. Public areas include a streetside bar which has more character than expected of an hotel (food available 11-9.30 daily) and a large, bright, dining room towards the back of the building. Bedrooms in the older part of the hotel have more character (some have four-posters), but the new back bedrooms are quieter and make a very comfortable base within comfortable walking distance of all parts of the town. Private parking. Banqueting (100). Children welcome (under 3 free in parents' room, cot available without charge, baby sitting arranged). No pets. **Rooms 52** (6 superior, 9 no smoking, 2 disabled). Lift. B&B €97 pps, ss €32. Closed 25-26 Dec. Amex, Diners, MasterCard, Visa, Laser. **Directions:** Town centre, half way up Main Street on left beside Bank of Ireland.

Dingle

Dingle Skellig Hotel

HOTEL

Dingle Co Kerry **Tel: 066 915 0200** Fax: 066 915 1501 Email: dsk@iol.ie Web: www.dingleskellig.com

It may be modest-looking from the road, but this 1960s hotel enjoys a shoreside location on the edge of the town and has won many friends over the years. It is a particularly well-run, family-friendly hotel, with organised entertainment for children, an excellent leisure centre and a luxurious health and beauty centre (opened in 2003). Roomy public areas are comfortably furnished with a fair degree of style and good use is made of sea views throughout, especially in the conservatory restaurant, which has special anti-glare glass. Good-sized bedrooms are regularly refurbished and have small but neat bathrooms; an especially attractive feature of the hotel is their policy of dedicating floors for family use to avoid disturbing those without children. Although best known as a holiday destination, the Dingle Skellig also has excellent conference and business meeting facilities, with back-up services including French and German translation on request. Conference/banqueting 250/230); business centre, secretarial services. Children under 3 free in parents' bedrooms; cots available free of charge; all year crèche, playroom, children's playground. Garden, fishing, leisure centre, swimming pool, health & beauty centre. [* Dingle Benner's Hotel (see entry) is in the same ownership, also the Dingle Marina Cottages.] **Rooms 112** (3 suites, 36 executive, 10 no-smoking). B&B about €120, ss about €19. Restaurant: D daily 7-9.30 (cl Sun & Mon; Nov & Jan-Feb); bar meals 12.30-9 all year. Hotel closed Christmas week. Amex, Diners, MasterCard, Visa, Laser. **Directions:** On the sea side of the road as you approach Dingle from Tralee & Killarney. ◇

Dingle

Doyle's Seafood Restaurant & Townhouse

RESTAURANT WITH ROOMS

John Street Dingle Co Kerry **Tel: 066 915 1174** Fax: 066 915 1618 Email: cdoyles@iol.ie Web: www.doylesofdingle.com

In the hospitable hands of Sean Cluskey, his wife Charlotte (who runs Cleevaun guesthouse) and their son John, this restaurant has lots of character with flagstone floors and old furniture - and local seafood is the main attraction. Nightly specials depend on the day's landings and lobster - selected from a tank in the bar - is a speciality (€35 per lb). Aside from lobster, speciality seafood dishes include hot oysters glazed with a horseradish sabayon, a West Coast platter and baked fish pie 'Doyle's style' (a tasty mixture of fish in a creamy wine sauce with crumb & cheese crust, moderately priced at €19.50). There are also some concessions to non-seafood eaters, such as Kerry lamb pie (braised lamb with roasted parsnips, topped with pastry), and vegetarian dishes. Puddings are nice and traditional or there's a plated selection of farmhouse cheeses to finish. **Seats 45.** Air conditioning. D only, Mon-Sat 6-10. Early D €30 (6-7pm); also à la carte; house wine from €19.95; sc 10%. Closed Sun.

Accommodation: Quality accommodation includes a residents' sitting room as well as spacious bedrooms with well-designed en-suite bathrooms. B&B about €88 pps, ss about €68. Establishment closed mid Nov-mid Feb. Amex, Diners, MasterCard, Visa, Laser. **Directions:** On entering Dingle, take third exit from roundabout into The Mall; turn right into John Street.

Dingle

Emlagh House

COUNTRY HOUSE

Dingle Co Kerry **Tel: 066 915 2345** Fax: 066 915 2369
Email: info@emlaghhouse.com Web: www.emlaghhouse.com

The Kavanagh family's luxurious country house style guesthouse is tucked into a site close to the Dingle Skellig Hotel, on the sea side of the road; it has been built with exceptional attention to detail and is maturing gracefully as the landscaping fills in. The style throughout the house is gracious, in large, well-proportioned rooms furnished in traditional country house style but with a contemporary streak that gives it a great lightness of touch. Bedrooms (most of which have harbour views) are elegant and extremely comfortable, with fresh flowers, fruit and chocolates to greet guests on arrival and many features, including individually controlled heating/air conditioning, trouser press with iron, direct dial phone with modem, satellite TV, video, radio & CD - the latter wired to lovely marbled bathrooms with underfloor heating, separate shower and bath, double basins, heated mirror and towel rails and thick bathrobes. Some interconnecting rooms are available to provide private accommodation for groups. Hosts Marion and Grainne Kavanagh do everything possible to make guests comfortable, and their attention to detail includes an evening turndown service. Delicious breakfasts are served in a stylish dining room with contemporary influences in the decor alongside the antiques. Many activities (golf, fishing, sailing, equestrian) available nearby. Not suitable for children under 8. No pets. Own parking. **Rooms 10** (all no smoking, 1 for disabled). Lift. B&B about €120pps, ss about €40. Closed early Jan-end Feb. MasterCard, Visa, Laser. **Directions:** Enter Dingle, take first left after Shell Service Station. ◇

Dingle

The Half Door

RESTAURANT

John Street Dingle Co Kerry **Tel: 066 915 1600**
Fax: 066 915 1883 Web: halfdoor@iol.ie

Denis and Teresa O'Connor's cottagey restaurant is one of the prettiest in town and well-known for great seafood. Menus go with the seasons but whatever is available is perfectly cooked and generously served without over-presentation. An outstanding speciality of the house is the seafood platter, available hot or cold as either a starter or main course with (depending on availability of individual items) lobster, oysters, Dublin Bay prawns, scallops, crab claws and mussels (attractively presented with garlic or lemon butter). Good traditional puddings or Irish farmhouse cheeses to follow. **Seats 50.** Air conditioning. D Mon-Sat, 6-10. Early D 6-6.30 only; later, à la carte. Closed Sun; several days at Christmas. [Times not confirmed at time of going to press.] MasterCard, Visa. **Directions:** On entering Dingle, turn right onto The Mall at roundabout, then right onto John Street. ◇

Dingle

Heatons House

GUESTHOUSE

The Wood Dingle Co Kerry **Tel: 066 915 2288** Fax: 066 915 2324
Email: heatons@iol.ie Web: www.heatonsdingle.com

Cameron and Nuala Heaton's fine purpose-built guesthouse is set in well-maintained gardens just across the road from the water and, although convenient to the town, it's beyond the hustle and bustle of the busy streets. An impressive foyer-lounge area sets the tone on arrival and spacious bedrooms confirm first impressions: all have bathrooms finished to a very high standard and phones, TV and hospitality trays - and the two new junior suites and three superior rooms added this year are not only luxurious but very stylish in a refreshingly contemporary idiom. Getting guests off to a good start each day is a point of honour and breakfast includes an extensive buffet (everything from fresh juices to cold meats and Irish cheeses) as well as a full hot breakfast menu. All day room service. Fishing, walking, garden. No pets. **Rooms 16** (2 junior suites, 3 superior, all no smoking). B&B €59 pps, ss €34. Closed 5 Jan-1 Feb. MasterCard, Visa, Laser. **Directions:** 600 yards beyond marina, at front of town.

Dingle

James Flahive

ATMOSPHERIC PUB

The Quay Dingle Co Kerry **Tel: 066 915 1634**

They don't make them like this any more - James Flahive's welcoming, friendly old pub has been a home from home for many a regular visitor for over 30 years. It's hard to imagine any call for a tailor's shop in Dingle these days, but that's how it started off in the 1890s; more recently it's long been a special favourite of sailing people and has had some very distinguished visitors and photos of many of them adorn the walls - along with several of Dingle's best-loved resident, Fungie the dolphin. No food, but a good pint and good company. Opening hours are irregular. **Directions:** On the harbour front.

Dingle

Lord Baker's Restaurant & Bar

féile bia RESTAURANT / BAR

Dingle Co Kerry **Tel: 066 915 1277**
Fax: 066 915 1274 Email: lordbaker@tinet.ie

Believed to be the oldest pub in Dingle, this business was established in 1890 by a Tom Baker. A popular businessman in the area, a colourful orator, member of Kerry County Council and a director of the Tralee-Dingle Railway, he was known locally as "Lord Baker" and as such is now immortalised in John Moriarty's excellent bar and restaurant in the centre of Dingle. A welcoming turf fire burns in the front bar, where bar food such as chowder and home-baked bread or crab claws in garlic butter is served. At the back, there's a much more sophisticated dining set-up in the restaurant proper (and, beyond it, a walled garden). Seafood (notably lobster from their own tank) stars, of course, and speciality dishes include monkfish wrapped in bacon, with garlic cream sauce and classic seafood mornay; but there's also a good choice of other dishes – local lamb (roast rack or braised shank, perhaps), also Kerry beef, chicken and local duckling – all well-cooked and served in an atmosphere of great hospitality. In addition to the main menu there are chef's specials each evening - and an unusual house speciality features on the dessert menu: traditional plum pudding with brandy sauce! Sunday lunch in the restaurant is a particularly popular event and very well done (booking strongly advised); on other days the lunchtime bar menu, plus one or two daily specials such as a roast, can be taken in the restaurant. An informative wine list includes a Connoisseur's Selection of ten wines. John is an excellent host, caring and watchful - no detail escapes his notice, ensuring that every guest in Dingle's largest restaurant will leave contented. **Seats 120.** L Fri-Wed, 12.30-2; D Fri-Wed, 6-9.45. Set D menus & à la carte; light lunch, €9.90. Closed Thurs, 24-25 Dec & Good Fri. Amex, MasterCard, Visa, Laser. **Directions:** Town centre.

Dingle

Milltown House

GUESTHOUSE

Dingle Co Kerry **Tel: 066 915 1372** Fax: 066 915 1095
Email: milltown@indigo.ie Web: www.indigo.ie/~milltown/

The Kerry family's attractive guesthouse, on the western side of Dingle, is set in immaculate gardens running down to the water's edge and enjoys beautiful views of the harbour and distant mountains. Day rooms include an informal reception room, a comfortably furnished sitting room and a conservatory breakfast room overlooking the garden - breakfast is quite an event, offering everything from fresh juices and fruit, through cold meats and cheeses, freshly baked breads and an extensive cooked breakfast menu. The bedrooms – all very comfortable and thoughtfully furnished with phone, TV with video channel, tea/coffee making facilities and iron/trouser press - include two with private patios. Constant upgrading is the policy here: a number of rooms have recently been increased in size and a new lounge, with sea and mountain views, has been added to the front of the house. Room service (limited hours). Not suitable for children. No pets. Garden. **Rooms 10** (3 junior suites, all with full bath en suite and no smoking). B&B €75 pps, ss €45. Closed early Oct-mid Mar. Amex, MasterCard, Visa, **Directions:** West through Dingle town, 0.75 miles from town centre.

Dingle

Number Fifty Five

Ⓝ B&B

55 John Street Dingle Co Kerry **Tel: 066 915 2378**
Email: stelladoyle@eircom.net Web: stella.thewob.com

Stella Doyle's charming B&B in the centre of Dingle offers accommodation with character - and a high level of comfort at a very affordable price. The house is furnished with antiques and original art and bedrooms are delightfully furnished in a fresh country house style, with television and full bathrooms (bath and power shower). Guests are welcomed with a cup of tea on arrival - and breakfast is sure to be a treat. Not suitable for children. No pets. Rooms 2 (both en-suite with full bath & no smoking). B&B €35, ss €15. **No Credit Cards. Directions:** At main road roundabout, turn right up the Mall; turn right up John Street - the house is at the top on the left side.

Dingle

Out of the Blue

Ⓝ RESTAURANT

Waterside Dingle Co Kerry
Tel: 066 915 0811 Email: timmason@eircom.net

Tim Mason's deli, fish shop and seafood restaurant is an absolute delight. Discerning locals are clearly thrilled to have such an exciting little place on their doorstep and it's just the kind of thing that visitors dream of finding. Although its brightly-painted exterior has a kind of temporary look from the road, once you get inside, it is immediately obvious that this is a highly focussed operation, where only the best will do: fresh fish - a huge variety of whatever is available from the boats on the day - is sold in the shop at the front, along with a carefully selected range of specialist foods and deli items and, in the casual little restaurant at the back, seriously delicious seafood cookery is the order of the day for those lucky enough to get a table. Everything depends on the fresh fish supply and menus - changed twice daily, at lunch and dinner - are given on blackboards: if there's no fresh fish, they don't open. Breton chef Eric Maillard cooks wonderful classics, sometimes with a modern twist: langoustines (Dublin Bay prawns) may come with garlic butter or sweet chilli sauce, for example, John Dory may come with a pepper sauce & garlic aubergines - or on a bed of stir-fry vegetables. Lobster is very reasonably priced at €27.50 per 500g and crayfish (a rarity on Irish menus) at €32.50. A short but skilfully assembled wine list complements the food perfectly: this place is a little gem. **Seats 30** (+ 16 outdoors). L Thu-Tue, 12.30-3.30 (Sun 12.30-7), D Thu-Tue, 6.30-9.30. Reservations required for D. A la carte. House wines from €17.50. Closed Wed ('usually'), also days when fresh fish is unavailable & Dec-Feb. MasterCard, Visa, Laser. **Directions:** Opposite the pier on Dingle harbour.

Dingle

Pax Guest House

GUESTHOUSE Upper John Street Dingle Co Kerry **Tel: 066 915 1518** Fax: 066 915 2461
Email: paxhouse@iol.ie Web: www.pax-house.com

Just half a mile out of Dingle, this modern house enjoys what may well be the finest view in the area – and, thanks to the exceptional hospitality and high standards of the owners, Joan Brosnan and Ron Wright, is also one of the most comfortable and relaxing places to stay. The furnishing style is daringly bright and fresh and thoughtfully furnished bedrooms have every amenity (including little fridges as well as phone, TV, tea/coffee making facilities and iron/trouser press) and well-finished bathrooms, most with full bath. Two suites have their own terraces where guests can lounge around and enjoy that stupendous view. Breakfast is a major event with lots of home-made goodies - yogurt, preserves, breads - and some unusual dishes like sardines on toast and home-made white drisheen (also known as white pudding) served on a waffle, with raspberry sauce. Freshly smoked Dingle Bay mackerel (when available), as well as the more usual kippers. Children welcome (cots available, €10). Pets permitted by arrangement. **Rooms 13** (3 suites, 1 junior suite, all no-smoking). B&B €60 pps, no ss (suite prices vary). Wine licence. Closed 1 Dec-31 Jan. MasterCard, Visa, Laser. **Directions:** Turn off at sign on N86.

Dingle

Wild Banks Restaurant

N féile bia **RESTAURANT** Main Street Dingle Co Kerry **Tel: 066 915 2888**
Email: thewildbanks@eircom.net Web: www.thewildbanks.com

Paul and Laura Walker opened this little restaurant in 2002 and it has found a niche. After a warm welcome in the little bar/reception (too tiny to sit in) you'll be taken through to a well-appointed table in the light and airy restaurant, where menus are promptly presented with the offer of a drink. Laura is the chef and offers about half a dozen dishes on each course, in an updated classical style: dishes like local black pudding filled with smoked Gubbeen cheese, served with plum chutney and home-made seafood chowder make a wholesome start, and there's a 'middle course' - soup, sorbet or salad - which extends the choice. Main courses offer seafood, of course - pan-fried black (Dover) sole on the bone with prawn butter & tomato butter sauce is good value at €21 - but the balance is perhaps better than most other nearby restaurants, as at least half of the main courses are meat, poultry or vegetarian; roast rack of Kerry lamb with a parmesan & herb crust with roast vegetables & balsamic cream sauce is a speciality. Pineapple upside down cake, perhaps, for dessert or more usual dishes like crème brulée and ice creams. This is a pleasant restaurant, well liked by local diners and offering good value, especially on the early dinner menu. **Seats 34.** Air conditioning. Toilets wheelchair accessible, Children welcome. D Tue-Sun, 6-10. Set early D €21.50 (6-8pm), also à la carte. House wine €18.70. SC discretionary. Closed Mon, except bank hols; 7 Jan-14 Feb. MasterCard, Visa, Laser. **Directions:** Town centre; on the right going up Main Street.

Dingle Area

Gorman's Clifftop House & Restaurant

GUESTHOUSE / RESTAURANT Glaise Bheag Ballydavid Dingle Peninsula Co Kerry
Tel: 066 915 5162 Fax: 066 915 5003
Email: gormans@eircom.net Web: www.gormans-clifftophouse.com

Beautifully situated near Smerwick Harbour on the Slea Head scenic drive and Dingle Way walking route, Sile and Vincent Gorman's guesthouse is, as they say themselves "just a great place to relax and unwind". It's also a very comfortable place to do this, as the whole premises has recently been virtually rebuilt and upgraded to a high standard. Natural materials and warm colours are a feature throughout the house and open fires, newspapers and books in two generous lounging areas (and a lot of pottery from the nearby Louis Mulcahy workshops) create a welcoming laid-back atmosphere. Bedrooms, which include some on the ground floor with easy access from the parking area, are not luxurious but very comfortable and attractively furnished in country style with thoughtfully finished bathrooms (some with jacuzzi bath) as well as phones and TV; superior rooms have king size beds. The Gormans are knowledgeable and helpful hosts too, giving personal advice where it's needed in addition to the interesting information about the area provided at reception. Breakfast - an excellent buffet with home-baked breads, freshly squeezed juices, fruits, cheeses and cold meats as well as hot dishes cooked to order - is a treat and will set you up well for the day. Gorman's was the Guide's Guesthouse of the Year in 2002. Children welcome (under 3s free in parents' room, cot available free of charge). No pets. Garden, cycling, walking. **Rooms 9** (all en-suite & no smoking, 2 junior suites, 2 superior, 1 for less able, 1 shower only). B&B €60 pps, ss€30.

Restaurant: The restaurant - which is open to non-residents by reservation - is on the sea side of the house, with large windows commanding superb sea views and, on fine evenings, spectacular sunsets. Vincent Gorman is the chef and Sile, who is a warm and solicitous host, supervises front of house; it's a good team, ensuring service that is both friendly and efficient. Vincent offers a couple of soups - fresh salmon chowder or petit pois & mint, perhaps - and four or five other starters, such as potato cake & black pudding sandwich with mushroom & bacon sauce (attractively presented and lighter than it sounds) and a pretty smoked Irish salmon with cream cheese & chives. Well-balanced main courses include several seafood dishes and the ever-popular sirloin steak (with mushroom & brandy sauce perhaps); vegetarian choices are always given - a main course of grilled aubergine and spinach mille feuille is typical - and copious dishes of delicious vegetables are left on the table. But don't forget to leave a little room, as desserts are a strong point: home-made ice creams, chocolate fondants and baby meringues with whipped cream and loganberry sauce are just a few of the temptations on offer, or you can finish with a cheese plate. Tea or coffee can be served in the lounge, which smokers will prefer as the dining room is no smoking. **Seats 35.** D daily, 7-9. Set D € 30/37.50. House wine from €17.50. Closed Nov-Mar except by reservation. MasterCard, Visa, Laser. **Directions:** 8 miles from roundabout west of Dingle Town - sign posted An Fheothanach. Keep left at V.

Dingle

Greenmount House

GUESTHOUSE

Upper John Street Dingle Co Kerry **Tel: 066 915 1414** Fax: 066 915 1974
Email: greenmounthouse@eircom.net Web: www.greenmounthouse.com

Just five minutes walk from the centre of Dingle, John and Mary Curran have run one of Ireland's finest guesthouses since the mid-70s. It's an exceptionally comfortable place to stay, quietly located on the hillside, with private parking and uninterrupted views across the town and harbour to the mountains across the bay. The spacious, well-appointed bedrooms are mainly junior suites with generous seating areas and particularly good amenities, including fridges as well as tea/coffee-making trays, phone and TV (and, in most cases, also their own entrance and balcony). There's a comfortable residents' sitting room with an open fire and a conservatory overlooking the harbour, where breakfast - which has always been a special feature of Greenmount and won our Breakfast Award (Munster Region) in 2001 - is served. The buffet - laden down with all kinds of fresh and poached fruits, juices, yogurts, cheeses, freshly baked breads - is augmented by an extensive choice of hot dishes, including the traditional full Irish breakfast. Home baking is a speciality and all the preserves are home-made too - the wonder is that anyone ever leaves this place of a morning at all. Not suitable for children under 8. No pets. Garden. Parking. **Rooms 9** (7 junior suites, 1 shower only, all no smoking). Room rate €140 (2 guests), SC discretionary. Closed 15-27 Dec. MasterCard, Visa, Laser. **Directions:** Turn right and right again on entering Dingle.

Fenit

The Tankard

BAR / RESTAURANT

Kilfenora Fenit Tralee Co Kerry **Tel: 066 713 6164** Fax: 066 713 6516
Email: emailtankard@eircom.net Web: adlib.ie.eaterie/tankard

Easily spotted on the seaward side of the road from Tralee, this bright yellow pub and restaurant has built up a great reputation, especially for seafood. An imaginative bar menu, which overlaps to some extent with the restaurant à la carte, is available from lunchtime to late evening (12.30-10) serving a good range of food. Seafood chowder with home-made brown bread, hot snacks such as steamed mussels Tankard style or warm salads/cold seafood dishes like fresh crab and apple salad (€9.50) and - a house speciality - The Tankard seafood platter (€19.95), for example, and plenty of other dishes too, including warm chicken salad, home-made burgers, pastas sandwiches and wraps. Children's menu.

Restaurant: Except on Sunday this is an evening restaurant, although lunch is available by arrangement. A phone call is worthwhile to get the best of seafood cooking, which can be exceptional: although bar menus give a passing nod to current trends, the restaurant style is quite traditional and beyond fashion, mainly classic French with Irish overtones. Simple well-cooked food, based on the finest local ingredients with excellent saucing and unfussy presentation makes a refreshing change from the ubiquitous 'world cuisine'. An extensive à la carte offers some irresistible seafood dishes and quite a wide choice of others, especially steaks in various guises, duckling, Kerry lamb and some strong vegetarian options and pasta dishes. There are sea and mountain views from the restaurant, which has recently been extended and opened out to make the most of its location, with a patio area and a path down to the sea. Good wine list, well matched to the menu. **Seats 100.** D daily 6-10, L Sun only; à la carte. House wines from about €14; sc discretionary Closed 25 Dec & Good Fri. Amex, Diners, MasterCard, Visa, Laser. **Directions:** 5 miles from Tralee on Spa/Fenit road.

Fenit

West End Bar & Restaurant

PUB / RESTAURANT / B&B

Fenit Co Kerry **Tel: 066 713 6246** Fax: 066 713 6599

The O'Keeffes' family-run pub is exactly seven minutes walk from the marina. Good food is available in both the bar and the restaurant, which has earned a sound reputation in the area and includes an attractive conservatory dining area. Head chef Bryan O'Keeffe is a member of the Panel of Chefs of Ireland and his style is "classic French with Irish popular cuisine", with seafood and meats billed equally as specialities. Expect starters ranging from Tralee Bay seafood chowder with brown bread, through warm salad of avocado and crab (the West End's signature dish), to deep-fried 'Roulet Brie' pieces. Main courses include old favourites - steaks, half roast duckling, home-made beefburger - and a range of seafood dishes including sole on the bone (with lemon butter) and strips of monkfish deep fried in beer batter, at quite reasonable prices. Simple, moderately priced accommodation is offered in ten en-suite rooms (B&B €30, no ss). Bar/restaurant Meals 5.30-10 daily in season. A la carte; house wine from about €13. Phone ahead to check food service off-season. Not suitable for children after 7.30pm. Closed Jan & Feb. MasterCard, Visa, Laser. **Directions:** 7 miles from Tralee, well signposted.

Kenmare

An Leath Phingin

RESTAURANT

35 Main Street Kenmare Co Kerry **Tel: 064 41559**

As the ground floor is cosy in a traditional Irish way, visitors may be surprised to find that Cornelius Guerin's long-established restaurant specialises in northern Italian food. All is revealed as soon as the menu appears, however, or when going up to the first floor which is more stylish and arty, with Italian posters. Cornelius takes pride in sourcing the best of local ingredients - organic green salads from Billy Clifford, Kenmare smoked salmon for risotto, meats from the local "A Taste of Kerry" butcher - and interpreting Italian dishes with a certain amount of individualistic flair. First course choices range from old favourites like salad Caprese with mozzarella, tomato & basil, through home-made pork sausages to bruschetta with freshly cut Parma ham, tomato, fresh basil & Durrus cheese, on home-made foccacia. Cooking on an oak fire makes for a special house style when grilling fish and marinated skewered Kerry lamb and there's a range of interesting home-made pastas (tortelloni, perhaps, with spinach, ricotta and parmesan), risotto (typically with smoked salmon) and half a dozen crispy-based pizzas. Reasonable prices (main courses in the €15-18 region) and friendly, helpful service add to the enduring appeal of this attractive restaurant. Concise, carefully selected wine list. D only Thu-Mon. A la carte. House wine about €18. Closed Tue & Wed; all Dec & Jan. Amex, MasterCard, Visa, Laser. **Directions:** Town centre.

Kenmare

d'Arcys Restaurant

RESTAURANT

Main Street Kenmare Co Kerry **Tel: 064 41589** Fax: 064 41589
Email: patgath@iol.ie Web: www.neidin.net/darcys

Formerly a bank – you can still make out where the vault used to be – Pat Gath's well-known restaurant has earned a reputation for consistent quality and the head chef, Brendan Byrne, offers well-balanced contemporary menus, based on seasonal local ingredients - often used in dishes with a global flavour. Start, perhaps, with specialities like local crab & smoked salmon cakes or home made beef sausages with Asian spices, stir-fried greens and lime & sesame dressing and move on to a vegetarian dish with mainstream appeal, like fresh vegetable risotto - topped with chilli tapenade & a light herb oil and - or pan-seared wild salmon with braised baby leeks. Confit of Skeaghanore Duck is another speciality, this time with rösti potato, salsify and spinach & a sultana & hazelnut dressing - the imaginative use of vegetables, in particular, makes interesting and well-balanced dishes that are different from other restaurants. Finish with farmhouse cheeses or delicious desserts such as rhubarb fool with hazelnut shortbread or hot chocolate fondant with vanilla ice cream. A good wine list, home-made breads, and pleasant, efficient service all add to the appeal of this pleasantly cosmopolitan and fairly priced restaurant. Not suitable for children under 2 after 7 pm. **Seats 50.** D daily in summer, 6-10 (phone to check opening off season); Set D from €22, also à la carte. House wine €17.50; sc discretionary. Closed Christmas & mid Jan- mid Feb. Amex, MasterCard, Visa, Laser, Switch. **Directions:** Top of Main Street on left.

Kenmare

The Horseshoe

RESTAURANT / ATMOSPHERIC PUB

3 Main St Kenmare Co Kerry **Tel: 064 41553**
Email: thehorseshoe@eircom.net

Chef-proprietor Irma Weeland's pleasingly old-fashioned bar and restaurant is cosy and well-run – and the good home cooking she offers in the informal oil-cloth-tabled restaurant at the back, with its open fire and original cattle stall divisions, is unpretentious and wholesome. Laminated menus give the wrong impression, as what you get here is fresh home-style cooking at fairly moderate prices. Soups, chowders, steamed mussels and crab claws rub shoulders with the house speciality, Horseshoe barbecued spare ribs - a half or whole rack, served with salad, home-made chips (rare enough for comment these days), steaks and much else, including some tempting vegetarian options. Desserts include some classic puddings - bread & butter pudding with hot custard – and an unusual ice cream bombe. Shortish wine list, also laminated. No children after 8.30. **Seats 45.** Food daily 3-10 (Sun from 5); à la carte. House wine about €17; sc discretionary. Closed 25 Dec, Good Fri; end Jan, all Feb. MasterCard, Visa, Laser. **Directions:** Centre of Kenmare.

Kenmare

Jam

CAFÉ 6 Henry St Kenmare Co Kerry **Tel: 064 41591** Fax: 064 40790 Email: info@jam.ie

James Mulchrone's delightful bakery and café has been a great success since the day it opened, in March 2001 and, unlikely as this may seem in the town that has the highest concentration of good eating places in Ireland, it brought something new and very welcome. Affordable prices, friendly service and an in-house bakery have proved a winning combination; everything is made on the premises using the best of local produce and you can pop into the self-service café for a bite at any time all day. To give a flavour of the wide range offered, lovely main course choices include salmon baked in pastry with spinach; a selection of quiches (roast vegetable with goats cheese, basil & pinenuts, for example, or bacon, onion & cheddar). This is the place to visit if you are planning a fine day out as they have all you could want for a delicious picnic, including a wide range of sandwiches and salads, terrines and all sorts of irresistible cakes and biscuits. The café menu changes daily and party platters and celebration cakes are made to order (48 hours notice required for special orders). The stated aim is "to provide fresh, quality, imaginative food at affordable prices in nice surroundings"; this they seem to be doing very well. * A second restaurant has now opened in Killarney (High Street); Tel: 064 31441. **Seats 60.** Air conditioning. Open Mon-Sat, 8am-6pm. Closed Sun, 3 days Christmas. **No Credit Cards. Directions:** Lower Henry Street on the left.

Kenmare

Lime Tree Restaurant

☆ **RESTAURANT**

Shelburne Street Kenmare Co Kerry
Tel: 064 41225 Fax: 064 41839
Email: benchmark@iol.ie Web: www.limetreerestaurant.com

Tony and Alex Daly's restaurant is an attractive cut stone building built in 1832 and set well back from the road. An open log fire, exposed stone walls, original wall panelling and a minstrels' gallery (which provides an upper eating area) all give character to the interior and, once it fills up, there's always a real buzz. The team here have worked together since the restaurant opened in 1994, which makes for a great sense of continuity and a relaxed, well organised atmosphere. Menus change with the seasons, and there are always daily specials, including several imaginative vegetarian options - a starter of deep-fried aubergine with slow roasted tomatoes, perhaps, and an equally unusual main course such as a cous cous cake, oven-baked with fresh vegetables and mild organic goats' cheese and served with red onion relish. Cooking is consistently excellent and local produce – Sneem black pudding, local free-range duck and Kerry lamb (oven-roasted, with honey mint jus perhaps) – is highly valued; local seafood such as Killmakillogue mussels appear in delicious specialities like seafood potpourri "en papillotte". Finish, perhaps, with a traditional dessert like warm apple & date pudding, or rhubarb with shortbread and crème anglaise. A user-friendly wine list is organised by style ('light, crisp and appealing', 'soft bodied and fruity'...) and includes some interesting bottles. Warm hospitality and excellent service add greatly to the enjoyment of the dining experience - and you can have more than a good meal here too, as part of the first floor is given over to an impressive contemporary art gallery (open daily from 4pm until the restaurant closes). It might be wise to budget a little extra for dinner here - you could be taking home a modern masterpiece. Toilet wheelchair accessible. No-smoking area; air conditioning. Not suitable for children after 7 pm. **Seats 60.** D daily 6.30-10; à la carte (average main course about €22). House wine about €20; sc discretionary. Closed-Nov-Mar. MasterCard, Visa, Laser. **Directions:** top of town, next to Park Hotel.

Kenmare

The Lodge

GUESTHOUSE

Killowen Road Kenmare Co Kerry **Tel: 064 41512** Fax: 064 42724
Email: thelodgekenmare@eircom.net Web: www.thelodgekenmare.com

This large, purpose-built guesthouse just 3 minutes walk from the centre of town offers hotel-style accommodation in spacious rooms which have everything you could possibly need - including phone, TV, safe, iron/trouser press and tea/coffee facilities, as well as well-finished bathrooms - at guesthouse prices. There is also plenty of comfortable seating and a bar was installed in 2003. Children welcome (under 3 free in parents' room, cot available without charge). 24 hour room service. No pets. Garden. **Rooms 11** (all en-suite & no smoking; 1 disabled with shower). B&B €50-54 pps, ss from €29. Open all year (weekends only Nov-Mar). MasterCard, Visa. **Directions:** Cork road, 150m from town opposite golf course.

Kenmare

Mickey Neds

BAR / RESTAURANT

The Square Kenmare Co Kerry **Tel: 064 40200** Fax: 064 40222
Email: info@mickeyneds.com Web: www.mickeyneds.com

Owned by former Kerry All-Ireland winning football captain Mickey Ned O'Sullivan and his wife Marian - who are friendly and efficient hosts - this recently renovated pub and restaurant is in a quiet corner of Kenmare, overlooking the square. The building dates back to 1795 and Mickey Ned was born here; today, while the exterior has clearly undergone some renovation, there is little about it to prepare the first-time visitor for the ambitiously re-designed interior, which is refreshingly modern in a town known for its quaint, old world style – a spacious and airy mixture of concrete, dark wood, plain white walls and mirrors, cubed seats, leather sofas and low dark oak tables. Fresh flowers, warm lighting effects and old photographs alongside some pieces of modern art emphasise the aim to create a stimulating contemporary environment which is also cosy and reflects traditional local values - this it clearly does very successfully and it has gone down a treat with the locals, particularly at lunch time. Menus read well and the food on the plate follows through - really fresh ingredients (some of which come straight from the farmers' market outside) are used in generous contemporary dishes, attractively served. The bar menu is quite extensive, offering a wide range of gourmet sandwiches, salads and hot dishes ranging from traditional Irish stew, through tempura battered prawns with wasabi cocktail sauce and chips to a vegetarian choice of ricotta and spinach tortelloni with sundried tomato sauce. There's some overlap between dishes on the bar menu and those served in the more serious evening restaurant upstairs (their very popular seafood chowder, for example, and a speciality dessert of baked cheesecake, which changes daily) although the restaurant menus are changed regularly with nightly specials. The wine list includes half a dozen sold by the glass or by quarter bottles. Music at weekends (traditional; jazz; rock). Restaurant **Seats 100** (private room, 60). Toilets wheelchair accessible. Children welcome. D Tue-Sat, 6-9; L Sun,12-4. D, à la carte; Set L from €14; house wine €15. SC discretionary. Bar Meals daily, 11-3 & 6-9 (Sun 12-6). Closed D Sun, 25 Dec, Good Fri. Diners, MasterCard, Visa, Laser. **Directions:** Next to Tourist Office and Heritage Centre in Square.

Kenmare

Mulcahys Restaurant

RESTAURANT

16 Henry Street Kenmare Co Kerry **Tel: 064 42383** Fax: 064 42383

The decor at Bruce Mulcahy's wacky restaurant is definitely different, with all sorts of influences jumbled up; it's funky but warm, fairly comfortable and sympathetically lit - and it certainly gives people something to talk about while waiting to eat. Eclectic menus offer a wide choice of fashionable fare, of which some dishes have become house specialities - such as sushi & sashimi (Japanese nori sheets filled with local seafood and served with wasabi, pickled ginger & mirin dip) which is available as a starter or main course. Another, more classical speciality is pan-fried loin of Kerry lamb with cep powder & pistachio nut crust (along with many other things) which sits happily alongside fish dishes like paupiettes of sole with seafood colcannon, baby spinach & tomato brown butter. Vegetarians are offered a daily special and, while the menu is a bit wordy, there's genuine enthusiasm here both in the cooking and front of house, and a mainly youthful clientèle makes for an enjoyably lively atmosphere. Not suitable for children after 7pm. **Seats 35.** D Wed-Mon, 6-10. A la carte. Set D from €38; also à la carte. House wines from €18. SC discretionary. Closed Tue, 10 Nov-10 Dec & 10 Jan -10 Feb. MasterCard, Visa, Laser. **Directions:** Halfway down Henry Street, on the left hand side.

Kenmare

Muxnaw Lodge

COUNTRY HOUSE

Castletownbere Haven Road Kenmare Co Kerry
Tel: 064 41252 Email: muxnawlodge@eircom.net

Within walking distance from town (first right past the double-arched bridge towards Bantry), Mrs Hannah Boland's wonderfully cosy and homely house was built in 1801 and enjoys spectacular views across Kenmare Bay. Disregard any imperfections in the rather steep driveway or cobwebs around the door - this is very much a home where you can relax in the TV lounge or outside in the sloping gardens (you can even play tennis on the all-weather court). Bedrooms are tranquil and comfortable, individually furnished with free-standing period pieces and pleasant fabrics - and have cleverly hidden tea/coffee-making facilities. Notice is required by noon if you would like dinner – a typical meal cooked in and on the Aga might be carrot soup, oven-baked salmon and apple pie, but guests are always asked beforehand what they like. Not suitable for children. Garden. **Rooms 5** (all en-suite & no-smoking). B&B about €30-35. Residents D about €20. Closed 24-25 Dec. Visa, **Directions:** 2 minutes drive from Kenmare Town.

Kenmare

P F McCarthy

PUB / RESTAURANT

14 Main Street Kenmare Co Kerry **Tel: 064 41516**
Fax: 064 42766 Email: failtebar@eircom.net

This fine establishment has been in the McCarthy family since 1913 and was previously known as the Failte Bar. It is now run by mother and daughter Maureen and Margaret McCarthy, who recently renovated the premises and re-opened it under its new name: stylishly designed to bring natural light into bright rooms, it has a spacious feeling and a dining area separated from the bar by low partitions, topped by wine bottles for privacy. Everyone loves it, whether for a snack lunch or more leisurely dinner - or just for the craic. Modern food shows an underlying classical French influence - at lunchtime there are home-made soups, salads and light international snacks - bruschetta, melts, ciabatta pizza, enchiladas - and a wide range of regular and hot sandwiches. Evening menus are more extensive. There's a great buzz (without overcrowding), a friendly atmosphere and efficient service. **Seats 36.** Toilets wheelchair accessible. Children welcome. L Mon-Sat 12-3. D Mon-Sat 6-10. No food on Sun. A la carte; house wine from about €15; SC discretionary. Closed 25 Dec, Good Fri. MasterCard, Visa, Laser. **Directions:** First Pub/Restaurant on the right hand side as you travel up Main Street. ◇

Kenmare

Packie's

☆ féile bia RESTAURANT

Henry Street Kenmare Co Kerry **Tel: 064 41508** Fax: 064 42135

Many regular visitors to Kenmare would quote Tom and Maura Foley's buzzy little restaurant as their favourite in a town blessed with an unrivalled choice of wonderful eating places: it is stylish but unpretentious, with small tables and a big heart - a combination that finds great favour with discerning Irish diners. Maura Foley, who has been in the kitchen herself since 1992 and built up a great following, has now moved aside to a new role as executive chef, so Martin Hallissey - who has worked with her since 2000 - has become head chef. The preparation for this change has paid off well, and there is no obvious change. Menus - which are augmented by perhaps nine or ten extra dishes each evening - continue to be based mainly on great local ingredients, especially organic produce and seafood, and the cooking style retains its essential characteristics of simplicity and intense flavouring. While there's a clear awareness of international trends, the underlying influence is classic and the judgement of complementary food combinations is sure. Many of these combinations are traditional and that is why they have lasted - crab cake with tartare sauce, for example, or rack of lamb with rosemary & garlic gravy for example - while others are a well-judged interpretation of contemporary international trends. Close examination of menus will probably reveal more dishes that have stood the test of time than new ones, but what remains impressive is the quality of both food – especially local seafood – and the cooking. Puddings include good ices (vanilla or praline, for example) and old favourites like sticky toffee pudding – or there are Irish farmhouse cheeses to finish. Interesting and well-priced wine list. **Seats 38.** D Mon-Sat, 6-10; à la carte. House wine from €16.50; sc discretionary. Closed Sun & Christmas to end Feb. Amex, MasterCard, Visa, Laser. **Directions:** Town centre.

Kenmare

Park Hotel Kenmare

HOTEL / RESTAURANT

Kenmare Co Kerry **Tel: 064 41200** Fax: 064 41402
Email: info@parkkenmare.com Web: www.parkkenmare.com

This renowned hotel enjoys a magnificent waterside location in the midst of Ireland's most scenic landscape, with views over gardens to the ever-changing mountains across the bay - yet only a short stroll to the Heritage Town of Kenmare and its quality shops, characterful pubs and a choice of fine restaurants unrivalled in Ireland. Many travellers from all over the world have found a home from home here since the hotel was built in 1897 by the Great Southern and Western Railway Company as an overnight stop for passengers travelling to Parknasilla, 17 miles away. More recently, its star has been in the ascendant ever since Francis Brennan became proprietor in 1985, and subsequently earned international acclaim for exceptional standards of service, comfort and cuisine which have made it the benchmark against which all other Irish hotels are judged. It is a most hospitable and relaxing place, where a warm welcome and the ever-burning fire in the hall set the tone for a stay in which guests are happy to do very little except relax in great comfort, looked after by exceptionally friendly and professional staff. Now that relaxation can be taken to an art form with the opening (just as we go to press) of the hotel's deluxe destination spa, Sámas, which translates from the Gaelic as 'indulgence of the senses'. A true world class spa, unlike anything else offered in Ireland, Sámas adjoins the hotel on a wooded knoll and is designed to rejuvenate the body, mind and spirit; there are separate male and female areas (also two day suites for couples) and guests can choose from over forty holistic treatments, designed by a team of professionals to meet individual needs. Lifestyle programmes incorporating spa treatments with other activities - walking on the Kerry Way, golf, fishing, horse trekking etc - are available, offering a unique way to enjoy the deeply peaceful atmosphere of this luxurious hotel. And, as for the guest accommodation, spacious suites and bedrooms are individually furnished to the highest standards, with personally selected antiques and many special details. Golf club adjacent (18 hole). Horseriding, sea and game angling, mountain walks and stunning coastal drives are all nearby. Garden, tennis, croquet, cycling, walking, snooker. **Rooms 46** (9 suites, 24 superior, 12 no smoking, 3 for disabled). Lift. 24 hour room service. Children welcome (under 4 free in parents' room, cots available without charge), baby sitting arranged. No pets (but kennels available on grounds). B&B €205 pps, (single occupancy €230); Lifestyle programmes from €855 (3 days, low season). Hotel closed 1-23 Dec & 4 Jan-6 Feb.

★**Restaurant:** The views from window tables in this elegant dining room are simply lovely – a fitting setting for very fine food. A stylishly restrained classicism has characterised this distinguished kitchen under several famous head chefs and Joe Ryan - who has been head chef since 1999 - demonstrates a traditional leaning towards local seafood, including lobster (try the house selection of Kenmare Bay seafood with leeks, lemon beurre blanc). Kerry lamb and local Skeaghanore duck are also specialities: a treat of a dish for two people is roast Skeaghanore duck with sautéed mouli & pomme paille with Kenmare honey & sherry vinegar sauce. Admirably disciplined dinner menus offer just three dishes on each course, making up in quality and flavour anything they lack in length. Superb attention to detail - from the first trio of nibbles offered with aperitifs in the bar, through an intriguing amuse-bouche served at the table, well-made breads, punctilious wine service and finally the theatrical little Irish coffee ritual and petits fours at the end of the meal - all this contributes to a dining experience that is exceptional. The wine list, although favouring the deep-pocketed guest, offers a fair selection in the €30-40 bracket and includes a wine suitable for diabetics. Service, under the direction of restaurant manager John O'Sullivan since 1995, is immaculate. A short à la carte lounge menu is available, 11am-6pm. Not suitable for children under 4 after 8 pm. **Seats 80** (private room, 40). D, 7-9 daily; Set D menus €49-64. House wine from €31.50; sc discretionary. Amex, Diners, MasterCard, Visa. **Directions:** Top of town.

Kenmare

The Purple Heather

BAR / RESTAURANT

Henry Street Kenmare Co Kerry **Tel: 064 41016**
Fax: 064 42135 Email: oconnellgrainne@eircom.net

Daytime sister restaurant to Packie's, Grainne O'Connell's traditional darkwood and burgundy bar gradually develops into an informal restaurant at the rear as is the way in many of the best Kerry bars. Run by the O'Connell family since the mid-1970s, The Purple Heather was among the first to establish a reputation for good food in Kenmare. What they aim for – and achieve, with commendable consistency – is good, simple, home-cooked food. Start with refreshing freshly squeezed orange juice, well-made soups that come with home-baked breads or salad made of organic greens with balsamic dressing. Main courses include a number of seafood salads, vegetarian salads (cold and warm), pâtés – including a delicious smoked salmon pâté – plus a range of omelettes, sandwiches and open sandwiches (Cashel Blue cheese and walnut, perhaps, or crabmeat with salad) or Irish farmhouse cheeses (with a glass of L.B.V Offley port if you like). This is a great place, serving wonderfully wholesome food in a relaxed atmosphere - and it's open almost all year. *Grainne O'Connell also has accommodation available nearby at 'Rockcrest', a beautifully furnished 3-bedroom detached house in mature gardens, 2 minutes walk from town. Email or telephone, as above, for details. **Seats 40.** Bar open 10.45-7; food served Mon-Sat, 11.45-5. Closed Sun, 25-30 Dec, Good Fri. MasterCard, Visa, Laser. **Directions:** Town centre.

Kenmare

Sallyport House

COUNTRY HOUSE

Kenmare Co Kerry **Tel: 064 42066** Fax: 064 42067
Email: port@iol.ie Web: www.sallyporthouse.com

The Arthur family's renovated country house on the edge of Kenmare is in a quiet and convenient location overlooking the harbour, with fine garden and mountain views at the rear. It is spacious throughout, from the large entrance hall (with welcoming fire) to bedrooms that are thoughtfully furnished with a mixture of antique and good quality old-style furniture, plus orthopaedic beds, TV, phone, tea/coffee facilities and (still unusual enough to merit mention) lights and mirrors correctly placed for their function. All rooms have practical, fully-tiled bathrooms with powerful over-bath showers and built-in hair dryers. Under Janie Arthur's eagle eye, housekeeping is outstanding - and delicious breakfasts are served in a sunny dining room overlooking the garden. Not suitable for children. No pets. Rooms 5 (all with full bath & shower, all no-smoking). B&B €75, ss €25. Closed 1 Nov- 1 Apr. **No Credit Cards. Directions:** South of town on N71, between town and bridge.

Kenmare

Sea Shore Farm Guest House

GUESTHOUSE

Tubrid Kenmare Co Kerry **Tel: 064 41270** Fax: 064 41270
Email: seashore@eircom.net Web: http://homepage.eircom.net/~saeshore

The O'Sullivans' well-named farm guesthouse is beautifully situated overlooking the Beara peninsula. with field walks through farmland down to the shore - and, despite its peace and privacy, it's also exceptionally conveniently located, just a mile from Kenmare town. Mary Patricia O'Sullivan provides old-fashioned Irish hospitality at its best, with friendly, welcoming and efficient reception and spotlessly clean accommodation. A pleasant guest lounge has stunning views and plenty of tourist information and Irish heritage books - and Mary Patricia is herself a veritable mine of local information who obviously delights in her job of telling guests about it. Spacious, comfortably furnished bedrooms have the considerate small touches that make all the difference to the comfort of a stay: a hairdryer that is placed conveniently in front of a mirror, shelves beside the washbasin for toiletries and a chaise-longue in front of a huge window so you can make the most of those unforgettable views. No dinner, but breakfast is a feast of fruit salads, yoghurt, cereals etc as well as a choice of scrambled eggs draped with locally smoked salmon, pancakes or traditional Irish. Garden, walking. *Glen Inchaquin Park is nearby and should not be missed. **Rooms 6** (all en-suite & no smoking, 3 shower only, 2 for disabled). B&B €65 pps, ss about €15. Closed 15 Nov-1 Mar. MasterCard, Visa, **Directions:** Off Ring of Kerry N70 Kenmare/Sneem road.

Kenmare

Sheen Falls Lodge

HOTEL / RESTAURANT

Kenmare Co Kerry **Tel: 064 41600** Fax: 064 41386
Email: info@sheenfallslodge.ie
Web: www.sheenfallslodge.ie

HOST OF THE YEAR

Set in a 300-acre estate just across the river from Kenmare town, this stunning hotel made an immediate impact from the day it opened in April 1991; it has continued to develop and mature most impressively since. The waterside location is beautiful and welcoming fires always burn in the elegant foyer and in several of the spacious, elegantly furnished reception rooms, including a lounge bar area overlooking the tumbling waterfall. Decor throughout is contemporary classic, offering traditional luxury with a modern lightness of touch and a tendency to understatement that adds up to great style; accommodation in spacious suites and bedrooms - which now include a presidential suite, in a five bedroom extension added in 2003 - is luxurious: all have superb amenities, including video/DVD and CD players, beautiful marbled bathrooms and views of the cascading river or Kenmare Bay. Outstanding facilities for both business and private guests include state-of-the-art conference facilities, a fine library (with computer/internet), an equestrian centre (treks around the 300 acre estate) and The Queen's Walk (named after Queen Victoria), which takes you through lush woodland. A Health & Fitness Spa includes a pretty 15 metre pool (and an extensive range of treatments including seaweed wraps and aromatherapy massages) and, alongside it, there's an informal evening bar and bistro, "Oscars", which has its own separate entrance as well as direct access from the hotel. But it is the staff, under the guidance of the exceptionally warm and hospitable General Manager, Adriaan Bartels, who make this luxurious and stylish international hotel the home from home that it quickly becomes for each new guest: Adriaan has a particular talent with people, and nothing is ever too much trouble to ensure that guests get the best possible enjoyment and relaxation from a stay at Sheen Falls - an absolute natural for our Host of the Year Award for 2004. *Two luxuriously appointed self-contained two-bedroomed thatched cottages, Little Hay Cottage and Garden Cottage, are also available to rent, singly or together. Conference/banqueting (120/140); business centre, secretarial services, video-conferencing. Health & Fitness Spa (swimming pool, jacuzzi, sauna, steam room, treatments, beauty salon), snooker, equestrian, walking, fishing, gardens, tennis, cycling. Children welcome (cots available, €45, baby sitting arranged; playground). No pets. **Rooms 66** (11 suites, 9 junior suites,10 no-smoking bedrooms, 1 disabled). Lift. 24 hour room service; turndown service. B&B €229.50 pps, ss €50 [Room rate €395 (1 or 2 guests)].

★ **La Cascade:** This beautifully appointed restaurant is arranged in tiers to take full advantage of the waterfalls – floodlit at night and providing a dramatic backdrop for Chris Farrell's modern Irish cooking, with the backing of faultless service under restaurant manager Johnny Le Poël. An admirably concise table d'hôte offers about seven choices on each course - perhaps three seafood, one vegetarian and a balanced selection of meats and poultry. Cooking is consistently impressive and the range of dishes offered often includes variations on a number of specialities: seared Valentia Island scallops are a great favourite, for example, served with foie gras, apple salad, hazelnut cream and liquorice jus - and pigeon, rabbit and crab from Castletownbere are all also likely to feature amongst the starters. Main courses are in a similar vein – Kerry lamb is almost de rigeur, of course, and predictably delicious (typically it might be a saddle with fig purée, ravioli of lamb shank, lambs liver and fresh peas) and there may be wild salmon from the estate, perhaps served with lobster risotto, mussels and clams alongside a summer vegetable nage. Speciality desserts include updated classics like hot soufflés (caramel, with Baileys sabayon & malt milk ice cream perhaps, perhaps) and farmhouse cheeses, served with scrumptious parmesan biscuits. The hotel's atmospheric wine cellar is a particular point of pride and guests can choose their own bottle from nearly 950 wines - and port can also be served in the cellar after dinner. *Light lunches (smoked salmon, club sandwiches etc) and afternoon tea are available in the sun lounge, 12-6 daily, and the informal Oscar's Bistro offers an extensive à la carte dinner menu every night, 6-10pm. Restaurant **Seats 120** (private room, 24). D daily 7-9.30. Set D €65. House wines from about €33. SC discretionary. Hotel closed 2 wks Dec, all Jan. Amex, Diners, MasterCard, Visa, Laser. **Directions:** Take N71 from Kenmare to Glengariff, take 1st left at Riversdale Hotel.

Kenmare

Shelburne Lodge

COUNTRY HOUSE

Cork Road Kenmare Co Kerry **Tel: 064 41013**
Fax: 064 42135 Web: www.shelburne@kenmare.com

Shelburne Lodge is the oldest house in Kenmare and has all the style and attention to detail that would be expected from Tom and Maura Foley, proprietors of the dashing Kenmare restaurant, Packies. A fine stone house on the edge of the town, the lodge is set back from the road in its own grounds and lovely gardens. Spacious day rooms include an elegant, comfortable drawing room and a large, well-appointed dining room where excellent breakfasts are served. Accommodation, in seven rooms individually decorated to a high standard, is extremely comfortable and everything (especially beds and bedding) is of the highest quality; individual decoration extends to the excellent bathrooms – all with full bath except the more informal conversion at the back of the house, which is especially suitable for families and has neat shower rooms. No evening meals are served, but residents are directed to the family's restaurant, Packies. Garden, tennis. Own parking. No pets. **Rooms 9** (2 shower-only). B&B €65, ss €15. Closed mid Dec-28 Feb. MasterCard, Visa, Laser. **Directions:** 500 yards from town centre, on the Cork road R569.

Kenmare Area

Avoca Handweavers

CAFÉ

Moll's Gap Kenmare Co Kerry **Tel: 064 34720** Fax: 064 35742
Email: info@avoca.ie Web: www.avoca.ie

High up at a famous viewing point on the Ring of Kerry, this outpost of the County Wicklow weaving company sells its fine range of clothing and crafts - and offers wholesome, home-made fare to sustain the weary sightseer. Restaurant **seats 80.** Food service all day 10-5. Closed 20 Nov -10 Mar. Amex, Diners, MasterCard, Visa, **Directions:** on Ring of Kerry, 14 miles from Killarney, 6 from Kenmare at famous panoramic crossroads.

Killarney

Aghadoe Heights Hotel

HOTEL / RESTAURANT

Killarney Co Kerry **Tel: 064 31766** Fax: 064 31345
Email: aghadoeheights@eircom.net Web: aghadoeheights.com

A few miles out of town, this famous low-rise hotel, built in the '60s, enjoys stunning views of the lakes and the mountains beyond and also overlooks Killarney's two 18-hole championship golf courses. Major refurbishments have recently been undertaken and, while the controversial exterior was still undergoing modifications in 2003, the renovation of the interior is complete. The new rooms - junior suites and a Presidential Suite - have superb views and balconies and are equipped and furnished to a high standard in a contemporary style. The whole hotel is luxuriously furnished and decorated, with lots of marble, antiques and good paintings, and the famous first-floor restaurant, Fredrick's, has been extended and incorporated into an open-plan lounge area, where traditional Afternoon Tea is served (2-5.30pm). Conference/banqueting facilities have also been increased and upgraded (150/80); business centre. Leisure centre, swimming pool, beauty salon, garden, tennis. Children welcome (Under 2s free in parents' room; cot available, about €20). No pets. Garden. **Rooms 69** (2 suites, 7 junior suites, 36 superior rooms, 2 for disabled). Lift. B&B about €199 pps, ss about €45. Weeekend breaks from bout €245. Open all year.

Fredrick's: The restaurant itself may have changed somewhat - while still on the first floor it is now integrated into an open plan area - but the same team is still in place and the classic style of food and service for which the hotel is famous remains the same. A la carte menus offer updated variations on well-loved dishes - fresh seafood cakes may come with a tomato chilli salsa, for example, and roast loin of lamb with girolles & rösti potatoes - but there will also be the great classics, like grilled chateaubriand sauce béarnaise and sole meunière. Piano 7-11pm. Not suitable for children under 10 after 7 pm. **Seats 120** (private room 40). D daily, L Sun only 12.30-2. Set D about €60 (also semi-à la carte); house wine from about €25, sc discretionary. Amex, Diners, MasterCard, Visa. **Directions:** Two miles west of Killarney; signposted off N22. ◇

Killarney

Bricín

RESTAURANT

26 High Street Killarney Co Kerry **Tel: 064 34902** Fax: 064 39030

Upstairs, over a craft shop (which you will find especially interesting if you like Irish pottery, of which there is a very wide range), Paddy & Johnny McGuire's country-style first-floor restaurant has been famous for restoring weary shoppers since 1990 and, although they are no longer open during the day, an early dinner can still round off an afternoon in the town. It's a large area, but broken up into "rooms", which creates a surprisingly intimate atmosphere - and the country mood suits wholesome cooking, in menus offering popular starters like bruschetta and spring rolls with peanut sauce (not perhaps an ideal combination although the spring rolls should be very good). Some main courses (such as chicken stuffed with blue cheese and wrapped in both smoked bacon and filo) may seem over-complicated but simpler dishes, including well-cooked fish, are a good choice. Vegetarian dishes are always available and an interesting range of desserts includes excellent home-made ice cream - an unusual 'creamy berry crumble' ice came in for special praise on a recent visit. **Seats 80.** Air conditioning. Children welcome. D Mon-Sat, 5.30-9.30. Set D €40, early D (6-7 only), about €20; also à la carte. House wine about €16. Closed Sun and Dec-Mar. Amex, Diners, MasterCard, Visa, Laser. **Directions:** On the High Street, Killarney. ◇

Killarney

Coolclogher House

COUNTRY HOUSE

Mill Road Killarney Co Kerry **Tel: 064 35996** Fax: 064 30933
Email: info@coolclougher house.com Web: www.coolclougher house.com

Mary and Maurice Harnett's beautiful early Victorian house is just on the edge of Killarney town and yet, tucked away on its 68 acre walled estate, it is an oasis of peace and tranquillity. The house has been extensively restored in recent years and has many interesting features, including an original conservatory built around a 170 year-old specimen camellia (when camellias were first introduced to Europe, they were mistakenly thought to be tender plants). Spacious reception rooms are stylishly furnished and comfortable for guests, with newspapers, books, fresh flowers - and open fires in inclement weather - while the four large bedrooms have scenic views over gardens, parkland and mountains. Mary and Maurice enjoy sharing their local knowledge with guests to help them get the most of their stay at what they quite reasonably call 'perhaps the most exclusive accommodation available in Killarney'. Children over 5 welcome. Garden, walking. **Rooms 4** (1 shower only, all no smoking). B&B €95, ss €50.*Coolclogher House is also offered as a weekly rental (from €4,000) for special occasions; staff can be arranged if required. MasterCard, Visa, **Directions:** Leaving Killarney town, take 3rd turning left off the N71 (Muckross Road); gates 1 mile along Mill Road, on right.

Killarney

RESTAURANT

The Cooperage Restaurant

Old Market Lane Killarney Co Kerry **Tel: 064 37716**
Fax: 064 37716 Email: chezmart@iol.ie

In an excellent location, in a pedestrianised laneway just off the Glebe public carpark, Martin McCormack and Mo Stafford's striking contemporary restaurant has been pleasing discerning diners consistently since it opened in 1998. A lot of thought went into the decor, which is more than just eye-catching and (unlike many contemporary restaurants) the dining space is comfortable as well as visually impressive - especially since the addition of a lounge area where you can have a relaxing aperitif or after dinner drink. Moody background jazz, played just loud enough for appreciation without interfering with conversation, helps make this a restaurant with lots of atmosphere - and, better still, the food and service live up to the surroundings: a friendly welcome sets the tone from the outset, followed through by contemporary menus, a pleasing element of simplicity and recognition of seasonality and provenance of ingredients as well as eye appeal. Apart from a lively atmosphere and great professionalism, what you get here is imaginative good food, stylishly prepared and at reasonable prices (average evening main course about €18). Shortish fairly priced wine list. The Cooperage was the Guide's Atmospheric Restaurant of the Year in 2001.* At the time of the Guide's visit (July 2003), Martin and Mo were in the midst of ambitious developments in Kenmare, where they are opening **The Club Restaurant,** in a listed building opposite the Heritage Centre. Menus, created by Martin, are to be similar to The Cooperage. Also in Kenmare, they are re-building a bar in Main Street (opposite Super-Valu); bar food will be served. **Seats 80.** No-smoking area; air conditioning. Children welcome (under parental control). L Mon-Sat 12.30-2.30, D 6-10 daily. A la Carte. House wine €16.45. Closed L Sun; 24-25 Dec. MasterCard, Visa, Laser. **Directions:** Located in the heart of Killarney, just off Main St.

Killarney

HOTEL

Dromhall Hotel

Muckross Road Killarney Co Kerry **Tel: 064 39300** Fax: 064 39301
Email: info@dromhall.com Web: www.dromhall.com

A sister hotel to the traditional Randles Court Hotel next door, this more contemporary hotel provides complementary services and has been completed to a high standard, to include a leisure centre situated between the two hotels, for their common use. A fine marbled reception area give a good first impression which is confirmed by other well-appointed public areas - including Kayne's bar and restaurant (accessible from the hotel or its own separate entrance), where good contemporary food is served, and the hotel's main dining area, the Abbey Restaurant, which was upgraded in 2003. Accommodation is very comfortable, in unusually spacious bedrooms which are stylishly furnished, with well-designed bathrooms. Conference/banqueting (350/300); business centre, secretarial services; video-conferencing available by arrangement. Children welcome (under 5 free in parents' room, cot available without charge, baby sitting arranged.) Leisure centre (17 m indoor pool, gym, sauna, steam room, therapy suites, beauty salon.) Ample parking. Pets allowed by arrangement. **Rooms 72** (49 no smoking, 1 for disabled). Lift. 24 hour room servoce. B&B about €70 pps, ss €30. Abbey Restaurant: D daily, 7-10; L by reservation only. Set D €35; Set L €21. Kaynes Bistro: Seats 76. D daily, 6-10. Bar meals 12.30-8 daily. Closed Christmas. Amex, MasterCard, Visa, Laser. **Directions:** On right going out of Killarney on the Muckross road, beside Randles Court Hotel.

Killarney

GUESTHOUSE

Earls Court House

Woodlawn Junction Muckross Road Killarney Co Kerry
Tel: 064 34009 Fax: 064 34366
Email: info@killarney-earlscourt.ie Web: www.killarney-earlscourt.ie

GUESTHOUSE OF THE YEAR

This purpose-built guesthouse quite near the town centre offers exceptionally comfortable accommodation at moderate prices and is run with warmth and professionalism by Roy and Emer Moynihan. A neat, functional exterior does little to prepare first-time visitors for the comfort and character within: a large beautifully furnished foyer (with an open fire) and an adjoining guest sitting room have plenty of comfortable seating for guests - an ideal rendez-vous, or simply a place to relax - and, as elsewhere in the house, antiques, books, paintings and family photographs are a point of interest and emphasise the personality of this spacious home from home. Emer's personal attention to the details that make for real comfort - and the ever-growing collection of antiques that guarantees individuality for each room - are the hallmarks of the outstanding accommodation offered, which includes four suites with canopy beds. All the bedrooms are well-planned and generously-sized, with double and single beds, well finished bathrooms, phone and satellite TV; tea/coffee-making facilities are available on request. Breakfast is served in a large, antique-furnished dining room, where guests are served - charmingly and efficiently - a superb breakfast that includes home-made compôtes and breads, a choice of different teas (served in antique silver teapots), fruits, yoghurts and cereals as well as a full Irish breakfast, and other treats including beautifully garnished scrambled eggs with smoked salmon, kippers, pancakes and cheeses. Earls Court offers friendly professionalism and hotel standard accommodation at a moderate price and is a fine example of Irish hospitality at its best; in recognition, this quiet, generously and efficiently owner-run guesthouse has been selected as our Guesthouse of the Year for 2004. Children welcome (under 2s free, cot available without charge). Garden. **Rooms 19** (4 suites, 18 no smoking). Lift. Room service (limited hours). B&B €60 pps, ss €40. Closed 30 Nov-1 Feb. Amex, MasterCard, Visa. **Directions:** Take the first left at the traffic lights on Muckross road, then 3rd premises.

Killarney

Gaby's Seafood Restaurant

RESTAURANT

27 High St Killarney Co Kerry **Tel: 064 32519** Fax: 064 32747

One of Ireland's longest established seafood restaurants, Gaby's has a cosy little bar beside an open fire just inside the door, then several steps lead up to the main dining area, which is cleverly broken up into several sections and has a pleasantly informal atmosphere. Chef-proprietor Gert Maes offers well structured seasonal à la carte menus in classic French style – and in three languages. Absolute freshness is clearly the priority – a note on the menu reminds that availability depends on daily landings – but there's always plenty else to choose from, with steaks and local lamb as back-up. Specialities include wild Atlantic salmon, with chive & lemon cream and red onion marmalade, Atlantic prawns on a bed of tagliatelle in a light garlic sauce and lobster "Gaby": fresh lobster, cognac, wine, cream and spices - cooked to a secret recipe! Lovely desserts include "my mother's recipe" - an old-fashioned apple & raspberry crumble with warm wild honey scented berries, sauce anglaise and caramel ice cream - or you can finish with an Irish cheese selection and freshly brewed coffee. Toilets wheelchair accessible. **Seats 75.** D only, Mon-Sat 6-10pm; à la carte; house wine about €22; sc discretionary. Closed Sun, Christmas/New Year & mid Feb-mid Mar. Amex, Diners, MasterCard, Visa, **Directions:** On the Main Street.

Killarney

Great Southern Hotel Killarney

HOTEL

East Avenue Road Killarney Co Kerry **Tel: 064 31262** Fax: 064 35300
Email: mking@killarney-gsh.com Web: www.gshotels.com

This classic railway hotel was established in 1854 and its pillared entrance and ivy-clad facade still convey a sense of occasion - and, since a major refurbishment programme, which was completed with due respect for its age and history, the sparkle has also been restored to the interior of this fine building. A welcoming open fire just inside the door draws guests through to a spacious pillared foyer (where afternoon tea is served) and the adjacent areas - including a homely residents' drawing room and a fine bar, which has also been redeveloped- are also elegant, high-ceilinged rooms with some sense of grandeur, and also a soothing atmosphere which makes a refreshing contrast to the bustle of Killarney town. New suites and executive rooms are designed to regain the original sense of grandeur in generously-proportioned rooms (floor space of up to 500 square feet), elegantly furnished to individual designs with all the necessary modern facilities (modem, email, fax, mini-bar etc). But the pièce de résistance in restoration terms is the great gilt-domed restaurant which has been meticulously refurbished and is now once again a prime example of Victorian opulence. Conference and recreational facilities have also been upgraded - the leisure centre (now known as the Innisfallen Spa) has an extensive range of facilities including an 18 metre pool, jacuzzi, steam room, plunge pool and gym - but perhaps the greatest leisure asset is outside as, belying its central position, the hotel is set in 20 acres of landscaped gardens, providing peace and relaxation on the premises. Conference/banqueting (1,000/650); business centre; secretarial services. Leisure centre, swimming pool, spa, beauty salon. Tennis. Children welcome (under 2 free in parents room, cots available, baby sitting arranged; crèche, playground; children's tea 5.30-6). Pets allowed in some areas. Gardens. **Rooms 172** (2 suites, 34 junior suites, 70 superior rooms, 119 no smoking, 4 disabled). Lift. 24 hour room service. B&B €140 pps, ss about €30; no SC. Open all year (off-season breaks available). *The moderately priced Torc Great Southern Hotel, is a sister hotel; it makes a good base for a family holiday and for Killarney's championship golf courses - special breaks available. Tel: 064 31611 Fax: 064 31824 email: res@torc.gsh.ie.

Peppers: While the newly restored Garden Room Restaurant is very grand, Peppers is the hotel's newer bistro-style restaurant - and very much in demand. Situated quietly in a corner position behind the bar and overlooking the gardens, it is dashingly decorated in contemporary style, with high-back chairs, an elegant black, brown and beige/gold colour scheme and (in common with other areas of the hotel) fine paintings. The ambience, professional service and head chef José Claro's imaginative Mediterranean menus and sound cooking made it an immediate success and - unusually for an hotel restaurant - it is well established as one of Killarney's leading eating places. **Seats 70.** D daily, 6.30-9.30; advance reservations required. Amex, Diners, MasterCard, Visa, Laser. **Directions:** In the heart of Killarney town beside Railway Station.

Killarney

Jam

Ⓝ CAFÉ

High Street Killarney Co Kerry **Tel: 064 31441**

James Mulchrone's delightful bakery and café in Kenmare has been such a success that he opened a second one in Killarney last year, bringing the same principles of affordable prices, friendly service and real home-made food using the best of local produce (see entry under Kenmare for details). Open Mon-Sat, 8am-6pm. Closed Sun, 3 days Christmas. **Directions:** Town centre.

Killarney

Kathleen's Country House

GUESTHOUSE

Tralee Road Killarney Co Kerry **Tel: 064 32810** Fax: 064 32340
Email: info@kathleens.net Web: www.kathleens.net

Long before the new wave of purpose-built guesthouses, Kathleen O'Regan Sheppard was offering hotel standard accommodation at guesthouse prices, and this family-run business - which is off the main Tralee road, just a mile from the town centre - continues to offer good value, hospitality and comfort. Individually decorated, non-smoking rooms are furnished to a high standard, with orthopaedic beds, phone, TV and tea/coffee-making facilities, and the fully tiled bathrooms all have bath and shower. An ongoing programme of maintenance and refurbishment ensures that everything is immaculate, including spacious public areas that provide plenty of room for relaxing - there are several sitting areas and even a library. Excellent breakfasts are served in a spacious dining room overlooking the garden, setting you up for a day that's as energetic or as relaxing as you choose to make it. Special rates are offered off-season. Not suitable for very young children (over 5s welcome). No pets. garden, walking. **Rooms 17** (all no smoking, 1 for disabled). B&B €65 pps, ss €25. Closed early Nov-mid Mar. MasterCard, Visa, Laser. **Directions:** 1 mile north of Killarney Town off N22 (Tralee road). ◇

Killarney

Killarney Lodge

GUESTHOUSE

Countess Road Killarney Co Kerry **Tel: 064 36499** Fax: 064 31070
Email: klylodge@iol.ie Web: www.killarneylodge.net

Catherine Treacy's fine purpose-built guesthouse is set in private walled gardens just a couple of minutes walk from the town centre and offers a high standard of accommodation at a fairly moderate rate. Large en-suite air-conditioned bedrooms have all the amenities expected of an hotel room, including direct dial phone and TV, and large public rooms to relax in. Children welcome (under 10 free in parents room; cot available without charge, baby sitting arranged). Wheelchair accessible. No pets. Garden. Own parking. **Rooms 16** (2 junior suites, 14 superior, 1 shower only, 1 for disabled, all no smoking). Room service (limited hours).B&B €60 pps, ss €40; no sc. Closed 15 Nov-15 Feb. Amex, Diners, MasterCard, Visa, Laser. **Directions:** 2 minutes walk from town centre off Muckross Road.

Killarney

Killarney Park Hotel

HOTEL / RESTAURANT

Kenmare Place Killarney Co Kerry
Tel: 064 35555 Fax: 064 35266
Email: info@killarneyparkhotel.ie Web: killarneyparkhotel.ie

Situated in its own grounds, a short stroll from the town centre, the Treacy family's luxurious, well run hotel is deceptively modern - despite its classical good looks, it only celebrated its first decade in March 2002. However it has already undergone more than one transformation, indeed, constant improvement is so much a theme here that it is hard to keep up with developments as they occur. The exceptionally welcoming atmosphere strikes you from the first greeting from the doorman as you pass through the new outer lobby to Reception and then into a series of stylish seating areas, with fires and invitingly grouped sofas and armchairs; the same sense of comfort characterises the Garden Bar (which has a sheltered terrace for fine days) and also the quiet Library, which provides a relaxing haven. Elegant public areas are enhanced by a sweeping staircase that leads to bedrooms that are luxuriously furnished in warm tones, with great attention to detail. Spacious suites have a private entrance hall and a sitting area with fireplace creating a real home from home feeling - and all rooms have been thoughtfully and individually designed, with air conditioning, well-planned bathrooms, judiciously selected antiques and the many small details that make a hotel room really comfortable - a decent hair dryer, iron as well as trouser press, bathrobes & slippers, multi music system as well as satellite TV, and the security of an in-room safe. House keeping is never less than immaculate and, most importantly, of course, the staff at this wonderful hotel are committed to looking after guests with warmth and discretion, making it an ideal choice for both business and pleasure. This year's big news at the hotel is the opening of a wonderfully away-from-it all health spa within the hotel, with eight treatment rooms, outdoor hot tub, plunge pool and jacuzzi; the menu of treatments offers is seriously seductive and it may well happen that some guests never feel the need to leave the hotel at all during their stay. Park Hotel Killarney was a most deserving winner of our Hotel of the Year Award in 2002 - and it's nothing short of amazing to see how much they have done since then. (The much older Ross Hotel, nearby, is a smaller sister hotel and equally delightful in its characterful way - so it is with a little sadness that the Guide has learned that the Ross Hotel is to re-built. However, given the Treacy family track record at Killarney Park Hotel, it will be a resounding success). Conference/banqueting (150); business centre; secretarial services, video conferencing (on request). Spa, hot tub, jacuzzi. Leisure centre, swimming pool (20m), sauna, plunge pool, jacuzzi pool. Library; billiard room. Garden, walking, cycling. Children welcome (under 2 free in parents room; cots available without charge, playroom). No Pets. **Rooms 70** (3 suites, 18 junior suites, 30 no-smoking, 1 for disabled). Lift. 24 hour room service. Turndown service. B&B €185 pps, ss €185; no sc. Closed 24-27 Dec.

The Park Restaurant: This large and opulent room has just undergone major refurbishment, emerging with the essential elements of grandeur still in place (the ornate ceiling, glittering chandeliers) but with a much lighter, more contemporary tone in the furnishings. The restaurant underlines this hotel's respect for the best of traditional hospitality and it is appropriate that head chef Odran Lucey (who joined the hotel in 1999) should have come here from The Merrion Hotel, Dublin, where the same values are upheld. His menus, while offering plenty of choice, are not overlong or unnecessarily wordy; an enduring house speciality that illustrates the style is pan-seared foie gras served with Clonakilty black pudding, apple compôte and toasted brioche, which is a nicely judged combination of classical and modern influences - and there are many other examples. Pan-fried beef fillet, that most conservative of dishes, is offered with tomato ragoût, potato rösti, garlic confit and tarragon jus - not so very different, but much more in tune with the times; similarly a main course of roast fillet of cod may come with creamed salsify, pink grapefruit and lemon cream with samphire. But when it comes to a real classic - Dover sole (on or off the bone) - it comes as nature intended, with lemon and caper butter. Courteous service and the presence of a pianist, who plays throughout dinner, add to the sense of occasion. A wide-ranging wine list includes many of the classics and, not only a fair choice of half bottles, but also a sommelier's choice of the week, offering half a dozen good wines by the glass. An interesting feature of the restaurant is an open wine cellar which guests are free to browse. Restaurant **seats 150** (private room,40). Air conditioning. D daily 7-9.30; Set D €52; also à la carte. House wines from €23. SC discretionary. * Food is also served in the bar, 12 noon-9pm daily. Amex, MasterCard, Visa, Laser. **Directions:** Located in Killarney town - all access routes lead to town centre.

Killarney

Killarney Royal

HOTEL

College Street Killarney Co Kerry **Tel: 064 31853** Fax: 064 34001
Email: royalhot@iol.ie Web: www.killarneyroyal.ie

Another of Killarney's unrivalled collection of fine hotels, this family-owned establishment is a charming older sister to the luxurious Hayfield Manor Hotel in Cork city (see entry). Joe and Margaret Scally have recently lavished care and investment on it and the impressive result is a beautifully furnished hotel in an elegant period style that is totally appropriate to the age and design of the building. No expense has been spared on the highest quality of materials and workmanship, air conditioning has been installed throughout the hotel and rooms have been individually designed, all with marble bathrooms and sitting areas. But what is most remarkable, perhaps, is the warm and friendly atmosphere that prevails throughout the hotel, conveyed partly through the soft warm tones chosen for furnishing schemes, but also through the attentive attitude of friendly, caring staff. Interesting modern food is served every day in the bar, which is popular meeting place for an informal meal, while the main dining room - where refurbishment was completed in the late summer of 2003 - is more traditional and reservations are required; however lobster is a speciality in both areas. Conference/banqueting (50/120); business centre. Wheelchair accessible. Children welcome (under 7 free in parents' room; cots available, baby sitting arranged). Pets permitted by arrangement. No on-site parking (arrangement with nearby car park). **Rooms 29** (5 junior suites, 10 no-smoking, 1 disabled). Lift. 24 hour room service. B&B €115 pps, ss €60. Restaurant **Seats 110** (reservations required): L daily, 12.30-2.30; D daily, 7-9.30; bar meals 12.30-9.30 daily. Closed 23-27 Dec. Amex, Diners, MasterCard, Visa. **Directions:** In Killarney town centre on College Street, off the N22.

Killarney

Killeen House Hotel

HOTEL

Aghadoe Killarney Co Kerry **Tel: 064 31711** Fax: 064 31811
Email: charming@indigo.ie Web: killeenhousehotel.com

Just 10 minutes drive from Killarney town centre and 5 minutes from Killeen and Mahoney's Point golf courses, this early nineteenth century rectory has become Michael and Geraldine Rosney's "charming little hotel". You don't have to be a golfer to stay here but it must help, especially in the pubby little bar, which is run as an "honour" bar with guests' golf balls accepted as tender; most visitors clearly relish the bonhomie, which includes addressing guests by first names. Rooms vary in size but all have full bathrooms (one with jacuzzi) and are freshly-decorated, with phone and satellite TV. There's a comfortable traditional drawing room with an open fire for guests, furnished with a mixture of antiques and newer furniture. The hotel is popular with business guests as well as golfers; secretarial services are available, also all day room service. The dining room is open to non-residents. Children welcome (under 12 free in parents' room; cots available without charge). Pets permitted by arrangement. Garden. **Rooms 23** (all en-suite). B&B from about €60 pps, ss about €42.50; sc10%. D daily, 7-10; Set D €40, house wine about €20, restaurant sc discretionary. Closed 1 Nov-mid April. Amex, Diners, MasterCard, Visa. **Directions:** 4 miles from Killarney - just off Dingle Road.

Killarney

The Old Presbytery Restaurant

féile bia RESTAURANT

Cathedral Place Killarney Co Kerry **Tel: 064 30555** Fax: 064 30557
Email: oldpresbytery@eircom.net Web: www.oldpresbytery.com

Gerry Browne and Mary Rose Hickey's restaurant is in an impressive, beautifully restored 3-storey building and now well-established as one of the area's leading fine dining establishments. Friendly, efficient reception and a comfortable, spacious bar area for aperitifs get things off to a good start and Simon Regan's well-balanced modern menus should provide plenty to ponder on. The style is classical/contemporary international, sophisticated and based on high quality ingredients (many of them local); he usually offers a balanced choice of nine or ten dishes on each course, including several attractive vegetarian dishes, such as a spinach & herb wrap with chilli ratatouille, parmesan & cheddar cheese. Braised Kerry lamb shank is perennially popular, served with rosemary mash, honey glazed vegetables and a tarragon & wholegrain mustard sauce - good wholesome fare, attractively presented and fairly typical of the meat dishes, while poultry and fish tend to be lighter and more adventurously flavoured. The restaurant is divided into elegant, well-appointed dining areas on two floors - the ground floor space is broken up into several small areas, while the first floor provides a large dining room which can be used for private parties. Desserts are particularly good - pannacotta served with brandy snap with orange creme chantilly and a sweet white wine & Cointreau sauce is definitely worth leaving room for - and also a speciality warm melting chocolate cake, with white chocolate sauce and vanilla ice cream... or sautéed strawberries in port, with hazelnut ice cream... or farmhouse cheese. They definitely save the best until last here. Good home-baked breads are another plus and a generally high standard of food and able cooking are enhanced by pleasing surroundings and staff who are professional, cheerful and tolerant of groups of friends having a good time. The early dinner menu is great value. Good wine list, above-average selection of house wines. Children welcome. Private car park. **Seats 60** (private room, 45). Air conditioning. Toilets wheelchair accessible. D Wed-Mon, 6.30-10. Early D €23 (6.30-7); otherwise à la carte; house wines, €21. SC discretionary. Closed 24-25 Dec, Good Fri and 7 Jan-5 Feb; otherwise off-season (between 1 Nov & 11 Mar) closed Mon-Wed. Amex, Diners, MasterCard, Visa, Laser. **Directions:** Opposite St Mary's Cathedral.

Killarney

Panis Angelicus

CAFÉ

15 New Street Killarney Co Kerry **Tel: 064 39648**

New Street is just the place for this stylish contemporary café and breadshop - the tempting display of freshly baked breads, scones and gateaux will draw you in and then you'll be hooked by the aroma of freshly brewed Italian coffee - which is served with homemade biscuits or Belgian chocolates. No matter what time you drop in there will be plenty to tempt, even if it's just homemade soup with a gourmet sandwich (home baked Limerick ham with wholegrain Irish mustard, perhaps) or a hot Irish potato cake with garlic butter, green salad and crusty bread. Outside of meal times you can just have that cup of tea or coffee - and maybe take some goodies home for later. Dinner menus are more ambitious and offer a wide choice while retaining a fresh, youthful approach. Unusually, Panis Angelicus not only offers interesting vegetarian food but also specialises in gluten free breads, soups, sauces and desserts. **Seats 54.** Children welcome. Open daily from 10am-5.30; also, in summer, D to 9 pm Thu-Mon; (L 12-4.30, D Thu-Mon 6-9). House wine from €15. Closed D Tue & Wed in summer; closed at night from Oct. MasterCard, Visa, Laser. **Directions:** Opposite Credit Union.

Killarney

Randles Court Hotel

HOTEL

Muckross Road Killarney Co Kerry **Tel: 064 35333** Fax: 064 35206 / 39301
Email: info@randlescourt.com Web: www.randlescourt.com

Within easy walking distance of the town centre, but also convenient to attractions such as Muckross House and Killarney National Park, this family-owned and managed hotel has been developed around an attractive house originally built in 1906 as a family residence, and extensively refurbished before opening as an hotel in 1992. Although it has grown a little since then, it still has some of the domesticity and warmth of the family home - period features, including fireplaces and stained glass windows, have been retained and comfortably furnished public rooms include a small bar, a large drawing room with log fire, tapestries and antiques and an elegant restaurant, Checkers, which opens onto a sheltered patio. Spacious bedrooms are furnished to a high standard, with direct dial telephones, satellite television, radio, hair dryers and well-appointed bathrooms - less "country house" than the public areas. perhaps, but very comfortable. Leisure facilities shared with the neighbouring sister hotel, Dromhall (and accessible from both hotels), include a 17 metre pool, sauna, steam room, gym and treatment rooms. Conferences(80), business centre. Children welcome (under 5 free in parents' room, cot available without charge, baby sitting arranged). Own parking. Pets permitted by arrangement.* There is a sister hotel in Clonakilty, Co Cork (see entry). **Rooms 52** (3 junior suites, 12 executive, 2 shower only, some no smoking). Lift. 24 hour room service. B&B about €85 pps, ss about €35, SC inc. Checkers Restaurant: D daily, 7-9.30; Light L 12.30-2. Closed 23-27 Dec. Amex, Diners, MasterCard, Visa, Laser. **Directions:** On way out of Killarney by Muckross Road, on left just before Dromhall Hotel.

Killarney Area

The Beaufort Bar & Restaurant

féile bia BAR / RESTAURANT

Beaufort Killarney Co Kerry **Tel: 064 44032** Fax: 064 44390
Email: beaurrest@eircom.net Web: www.beaufortbar.com

In the fourth generation of family ownership, Padraig O'Sullivan's immaculate establishment near the Gap of Dunloe is a pleasure to visit. The old tree at the front was left safely in place during renovations which, together with features like the stonework and an open fire in the bar for winter, all contribute to the genuine character that can easily be lost in refurbishments. The pride taken by the family in running this fine pub is palpable and the upstairs restaurant (which can be reached through the bar or by a separate entrance from the carpark) is a logical extension of the existing business. Head chef Tim Brosnan, who joined the team in 1999, presents quite extensive, well-balanced à la carte dinner menus with a generous, traditional tone (seafood cocktail, chilled galia melon with a seasonal fruits & strawberry sorbet, chicken liver paté; roast rack of Kerry lamb or duckling, sole meunière) plus a few more international dishes. There's a pleasingly local feel to some dishes - Aghadoe black pudding is singled out for mention, for example; finish with classic desserts or farmhouse cheeses. Pricing is fairly moderate (main courses about €12.50-30) and Sunday lunch, which is very popular, is especially good value. Children welcome. Restaurant **Seats 76** (private room 20). D Tue-Sat, 6.30-9.30, à la carte; L Sun only, 1-3; Set Sun L €19. House wine about €17. SC discretionary. Restaurant closed D Sun, Mon. Establishment closed Nov. MasterCard, Visa, Laser. **Directions:** Follow the N72 to Killorglin. Turn left at Beaufort bridge, first stone building on left in village.

Killarney Area

Hotel Dunloe Castle

HOTEL

Beaufort Killarney Co Kerry **Tel: 064 44111** Fax: 064 44583
Email: sales@kih.liebherr.com Web: www.iol.ie/khl

Sister hotel to the Hotel Europe (Fossa) and Ard-na-Sidhe (Caragh Lake), Dunloe Castle is a wonderfully relaxing place to stay and has many features in common with the larger Europe: the style of the building is similar and the same priorities apply – generous space is allowed for all areas throughout, the quality of furnishing is exceptionally high and both maintenance and housekeeping are superb. The original castle is still part of the development, but the hotel is mainly modern and, like the Europe, the atmosphere is distinctly continental. Everything is on a large scale, with wide corridors leading to spacious bedrooms, some with dining areas and all with magnificent views, satellite TV & in-house video, air conditioning and ironing facilities. Major improvements have been made recently, including a re-styling of the exterior to include a new entrance and foyer, a lobby bar, terrace and a new café. The park around the hotel is internationally renowned for its unique botanical collection, which includes many rare plants and, as well as an equestrian centre, the hotel also has its own fishing rights on the River Laune (fishing free of charge to residents; ghillie available on request). Conference/banqueting (150/180). Leisure centre, swimming pool. Snooker, pool table. Garden, fishing, walking, tennis, equestrian. Children welcome (under 2s free in parents' room, cot available without charge; playroom, playground). No pets. **Rooms 110** (1 suite, 40 no smoking). Lift. B&B from about €80 (weekend specials from about €210). Closed 1 Oct-mid April. Amex, Diners, MasterCard, Visa. **Directions:** Off main Ring of Kerry road. ◇

Killarney Area

Hotel Europe

HOTEL

Fossa Killarney Co Kerry **Tel: 064 31900** Fax: 064 32118
Email: sales@kih.liebherr.com Web: www.iol.ie/khl

Although now around thirty five years old, the Europe was exceptionally well built and has been so well maintained through the years that it still outshines many a new top level hotel. A facelift to the front façade and improvements to the approach, with landscaping that included the planting of a large number of trees, are the most obvious recent changes but maintenance has always been excellent, notably in public areas which are very large and impressive, furnished to the highest standards and make full use of the hotel's wonderful location. Bedrooms follow a similar pattern, with lots of space, quality furnishings, beautiful views and balconies all along the lake side of the hotel. Leisure facilities include a 25-metre swimming pool, fitness suite and sauna; the hotel adjoins the three Killarney golf clubs - Killeen, Mahony's Point and Lackabane - and the two nine hole courses, Dunloe and Ross, are nearby. The hotel's continental connections show clearly in the style throughout but especially, perhaps, when it comes to food - breakfast, for example, is an impressive hot and cold buffet. Excellent conference and meeting facilities include a 450-seat auditorium with built-in microphones and translation system. Given the high standards and facilities offered, rates are reasonable, and it is also worth inquiring about special breaks. Leisure centre, swimming pool, beauty and hair salons. Equestrian, fishing, (indoor) tennis, snooker. Children welcome (under 12s free in parents room, cot available without charge; playroom, playground). No pets. Lift. **Rooms 204** (8 suites, 60 no smoking, 154 twin rooms). Room Rate from about €80, SC incl. Closed mid Nov-mid Mar.

Panorama Restaurant: Aptly-named, this beautifully situated and elegantly appointed restaurant has views over the Lakes of Killarney with the mountains beyond providing a haunting backdrop - a fine setting for classic European cooking which makes full use of local produce like Kerry lamb and salmon through wide-ranging international menus. Table d'hôte and à la carte menus are accurately descriptive (which is unusual at the moment) and offer something to please everyone, including vegetarians. Lovely breads are made in-house - and there's a very extensive range offered at breakfast. Starters might include a well-flavoured seasonal soup and Westphalian ham (presumably from the excellent German butchers shop across the road, which is well worth a visit) appropriately served with a freshly-made coleslaw. This might be followed by a sorbet, or maybe marinated local salmon with rösti & horseradish cream then main courses such as suckling pig in caraway jus, or duck breast in Madeira sauce, served with well-matched vegetables. Delicious desserts - chocolate marquise with redcurrants, maybe, or cherry clafoutis with Black Forest ice cream - then a slow coffee as you watch the light fading behind the mountains... Service is pleasant and very efficient. [*A separate informal restaurant, The Brasserie, offers popular all day food, 11am-11pm daily.] **Seats 450.** D daily, 7-9.30. Set 4-course D about €54. House wine about €25. Hotel closed mid Nov-mid Mar. Amex, Diners, MasterCard, Visa. **Directions:** On main Ring of Kerry road. ◇

Killorglin

Nick's Seafood Restaurant & Piano Bar

RESTAURANT

Lr Bridge Street Killorglin Co Kerry **Tel: 066 976 1219** Fax: 066 976 1233

This is one of the famous old restaurants of Ireland and Nick Foley's is clearly thriving. Nick's cooking – classic French with an Irish accent– has earned a particular reputation for his way with local seafood, although there are always other choices, notably prime Kerry beef and lamb. Moules marinière or provençale, lobster thermidor, shellfish mornay and peppered steak in brandy cream sauce are all typical of his classic style. Vegetarians aren't forgotten either – there's a choice of three dishes on the regular menu. Dessert choices are changed daily and there's a good cheeseboard. Aside from providing excellent food, Nick's is also renowned for its music and great atmosphere. Children welcome. **Seats 80** (private room,30). Air conditioning. D Wed-Sun 6.30-10 in winter, daily in summer. Set D about €40. Extensive wine list; house wine about €20; sc discretionary. Closed all Nov, Mon-Tue in Dec-Mar & Christmas. Amex, Diners, MasterCard, Visa. **Directions:** On the Ring Road of Kerry, 20 km from Killarney. ◇

Listowel

Allo's Restaurant, Bar & Bistro

féile bia BAR / RESTAURANT WITH ROOMS

41/43 Church St Listowel Co Kerry
Tel: 068 22880 Email: allo's@eircom.net

Named after the previous owner ("Alphonsus, aka Allo"), Helen Mullane's café-bar seems much older than it is as the whole interior was reconstructed with salvaged materials (the flooring was once in the London Stock Exchange). It is convincingly done with the long, narrow bar divided up in the traditional way, although the restaurant has since been extended into the house next door. Expect lively combinations of traditional and new Irish cooking with some international influences, based on carefully sourced ingredients. Theme nights, eg Australian, are held on Thursdays. **Seats 50** (private room, 20). Open Tue-Sat, L12-7, D 7-9 L & D à la carte; House wine €22. Closed Sun & Mon, 25 Dec & Good Fri. D reservations required.

Accommodation: There are three beautiful guest bedrooms. Spacious and stylishly furnished with antiques, they have four-poster beds and luxurious Connemara marbled bathrooms. **Rooms 3** (1 shower only), B&B about €60, ss about €20. Amex, MasterCard, Visa, Laser. **Directions:** Coming into Listowel on the N69, located half way down Church Street on the right hand side (almost opposite Garda Station).

Listowel

Listowel Arms Hotel

féile bia HOTEL

Listowel Co Kerry **Tel: 068 21500** Fax: 068 22524
Email: listowelarms@ireland.com

This much-loved old hotel is rich in history and especially famous as the main venue for the annual Listowel Writers Week. Since 1996 the hotel has been blessed with the energetic and discerning ownership of Kevin O'Callaghan, who has overseen a major extension and overhaul of the whole premises during the last few years. The extension has provided a new restaurant, kitchen, banqueting area and new bedrooms, all overlooking the River Feale; improvements have all been done with great sensitivity, so greater comfort has been gained throughout the hotel without loss of character. Non-residents find this a handy place to drop into for a bite in the bar where they serve lovely traditional dishes like braised beef & stout casserole (L12-3, D 5.30-9.30) and you can have tea or coffee in the lounge at other times. Conference/banqueting (500/400); video-conferencing, ISDN lines. Wheelchair accessible. Lift. Children welcome (under 5s free in parents' room, cots available without charge). Pets permitted by arrangement. **Rooms 37** (all en-suite). B&B from about €55 pps, ss about €20. (Higher rates apply to Festival weeks, incl Irish Open & Listowel Race Week.) Closed 24-26 Dec. **Directions:** In the corner of the historic old square in Listowel town centre.

Portmagee

The Moorings

GUESTHOUSE / BAR

Portmagee Co Kerry **Tel: 066 947 7108** Fax: 066 947 7220
Email: moorings@iol.ie Web: www.moorings.ie

Gerard & Patricia Kennedy's guesthouse overlooks the harbour and many bedrooms - which are comfortably furnished with phone, TV, tea/coffee making facilities and full bathrooms - have a sea view. Children welcome (under 3 free in parents' room, cot available without charge, baby sitting arranged). No pets. **Rooms 14** (all en-suite, 5 shower only) B&B €40 pps, ss €12.50. Reliably good food is available in the Bridge Bar (12-8 daily) and the restaurant (D Tue-Sun 6-9.30, L Sun only 12-8) all à la carte. Seafood stars and the style is fairly traditional - chowder, seafood selection, deep-fried brie for starters; main courses of seafood platter, poached salmon, steaks - and lobster, which is quite moderately priced. House wine €17.95. Restaurant closed Mon (except bank hols). Establishment closed 1 Nov-1 Mar. Amex, MasterCard, Visa, Laser. **Directions:** 3 miles outside Caherciveen on the Waterville Road.

Sneem

Great Southern Hotel, Parknasilla

féile bia HOTEL

Sneem Co Kerry **Tel: 064 45122** Fax: 064 45323
Email: res@parknasilla-gsh.com Web: www.gshotels.com

Set in 300 acres of sub-tropical parkland, overlooking Kenmare Bay, this classic Victorian hotel is blessed with one of the most beautiful locations in Ireland. The spacious foyer with its antiques and fresh flowers sets a tone of quiet luxury, enhanced by the hotel's impressive collection of original art (currently being catalogued). Whether activity or relaxation is required there are excellent amenities at hand – including an outdoor swimming pool and Canadian hot tub - and an abundance of comfortable places (including a no-smoking drawing room) for a quiet read or afternoon tea. Public rooms include an impressive restaurant and a library (added in 1995 for the hotel's centenary and available for the use of all guests, although also ideal for meetings and small conferences). Bedrooms vary in size and outlook but most have been upgraded recently and all have en-suite bathrooms with bath and shower, tea/coffee making facilities, direct-dial telephone, radio, TV with in-house movie channel, trouser press and hair dryer. Afternoon tea at Parknasilla is a relaxing affair, served in the spacious interconnecting lounges along the front of the hotel. An impressive range of outdoor activities available on-site includes walking (routes marked, map available), golf (9 hole), horseriding, inshore and deep sea fishing and cruises on the hotel's own boat, Parknasilla Princess - this is a place to slow down and take time for yourself. Conference/banqueting (50/150); secretarial services. Children welcome (under 2 free in parents room; cots available without charge; children's tea 5.30-6, baby sitting arranged) Leisure centre, swimming pool. Golf (9 hole), tennis, fishing, equestrian, walking. Snooker, pool table, games room. Pets by arrangement. **Rooms 84** (1 suite, 8 junior suites, 13 superior rooms, 1 for disabled). Lift. 24 hour room service. B&B €140, ss €30. No SC. Short breaks/special interest breaks offered. Open all year. Amex, MasterCard, Visa, Laser. **Directions:** 25 km west of Kenmare, on Ring of Kerry.

Sneem

Tahilla Cove Country House

GUESTHOUSE

Tahilla Cove Sneem Co Kerry **Tel: 064 45204** Fax: 064 45104
Email: tahillacove@eircom.net Web: www.tahillacove.com

This family-run guesthouse feels more like a small hotel – it has a proper bar, for example, with its own entrance (which is used by locals as well as residents). This is a low-key place, with an old country house in there somewhere (which has been much added to) and there is a blocky annexe in the garden. It has two very special features, however: the location, which is genuinely waterside, is really lovely and away-from-it-all; and the owners, James and Deirdre Waterhouse. Tahilla Cove has been in the family since 1948, and run since 1987 by James and Deirdre – who have the wisdom to understand why their many regulars love it just the way it is and, apart from regular maintenance (and some recent major refurbishment) little is allowed to change. Comfort and relaxation are the priorities. All the public rooms have sea views, including the dining room and a large sitting room, with plenty of armchairs and sofas, which opens onto a terrace (where there are patio tables and chairs overlooking the garden and the cove with its little stone jetty). Accommodation is divided between the main house and another close by; rooms vary considerably but all except two have sea views, many have private balconies and all are en-suite, with bathrooms of varying sizes and appointments (only one single is shower-only). All rooms have phone, TV, hair-dryer and individually controlled heating. Food is prepared personally by the proprietors and, although the dining room (20) is mainly intended for residents, others are welcome when there is room – James and Deirdre cook for guests and their simple 4-course country house style menus change daily. (It's a lovely place to drop into for a cup of tea overlooking the little harbour). Garden; walking; fishing. Wheelchair accessible. Children welcome. Pets allowed in some areas. **Rooms 9** (1 shower only, 6 no smoking). B&B €65 pps, ss €25. Dining room closed Tue & Wed evenings. Closed Oct-Easter. Amex, MasterCard, Visa, Laser. **Directions:** 11 miles west of Kenmare and 5 miles east of Sneem (N70).

Tralee

Ballygarry House Hotel

féile bia HOTEL

Killarney Road Tralee Co Kerry **Tel: 066 712 3322** Fax: 066 712 7630
Email: ballygarry@eircom.net Web: ballygarry.com

Recently renovated and upgraded to a high standard, this pleasant roadside hotel presents a neat face to arriving guests and also has extensive landscaped gardens. The furnishing style is traditional with occasional contemporary twists; warm colours, notably in oriental rugs used on wooden floors, create a welcoming atmosphere in public areas and darkwood furniture in bedrooms is used to effect against contrasting furnishings and pale walls. Accommodation is very pleasing, with many thoughtful details adding to the comfort of a stay. This is an appealing hotel and moderately priced - rooms at the back should be quieter. It is understandably popular for weddings. Conference/banqueting 300/390. Hairdressing. Children welcome (cot available without charge, baby sitting arranged). Walking, cycling, garden. No pets. **Rooms 46** (5 junior suites, 23 no smoking, 1 for disabled) Lift. 24 hour room service. Turndown service. B&B €75pps, ss about €45, no sc. Special breaks available. Closed 20-27 Dec & 5-20 Jan.

Riverside Restaurant: This well appointed restaurant pleasingly set up towards the back of the hotel and head chef Padraig Kerrins' modern classical food has great appeal. He offers quite an extensive a la carte menu, based largely on local produce, and its strength is in the presentation of traditional dishes with a successful modern twist. Cooking is very sound, presentation attractive - and, best of all, staff are attentive and hospitable. Music Sun & Tue, 9pm. Children welcome. **Seats 90** (+ outdoor seating for 16). D daily 6.30-9.30; L Sun only 12.30-2.30,House wine from €18. No SC. Bar meals also available 12.309 daily (except Fri & Sat 3.30-6). Amex, MasterCard, Visa, Laser. **Directions:** 1 mile outside Tralee town on the Killarney road.

Tralee

The Brandon Hotel

féile bia HOTEL

Princes Street Tralee Co Kerry **Tel: 066 712 3333** Fax: 066 712 5019

Overlooking a park and the famous Siamsa Tire folk theatre, and close to the Aquadome, Tralee's largest hotel is at the heart of activities throughout the area. Spacious public areas are impressive since recent refurbishment, and while some bedrooms are on the small side, all have been refurbished or are due for refurbishment and have direct-dial phone, radio and TV (no tea/coffee-making facilities) and tiled bathrooms. There's a well-equipped leisure centre and good banqueting/conference facilities. B&B from about €45 pps. Closed 22-29 Dec. Amex, Diners, MasterCard, Visa, **Directions:** Town centre. ◇

Tralee

Brook Manor Lodge

GUESTHOUSE

Fenit Road Tralee Co Kerry **Tel: 066 712 0406** Fax: 066 712 7550
Email: brookmanor@eircom.net

Set back from the road, in 3.5 acres of grounds, Vincent and Margaret O'Sullivan's large purpose-built guesthouse offers immaculate accommodation and warm hospitality. Public rooms and bedrooms are spacious and very comfortably furnished - bedrooms have generous beds and all the usual modern facilities - TV, phone, trouser press, tea/coffee making, hair dryer and radio/alarm - everything, in short, that the traveller (and, specifically, the golfing traveller) could need. Breakfast is a special point of pride, cooked to order from an extensive menu. Not very suitable for children, but concessions are given (under 5 free in parents' room, cot available free of charge). No pets. **Rooms 8** (1 suite, 1 junior suite, 2 superior rooms, 2 shower only, 1 for disabled, all no smoking.) B&B €55, no ss. Open all year. MasterCard, Visa, Laser. **Directions:** 2 km from town centre on Fenit road.

Tralee

Castlemorris House

ACCOMMODATION

Ballymullen Tralee Co Kerry **Tel: 066 718 0060**
Fax: 066 712 8007 Email: castlemorris@eircom.net

Mary and Paddy Barry's attractive creeper-clad Victorian house makes a lovely place to stay, with good home baking (complimentary afternoon tea in front of the drawing room fire on arrival) and the friendly atmosphere of a family home. Bedrooms are spacious and well-furnished for comfort with style. Breakfast is a speciality and dinner is available by arrangement. Garden. Children welcome (cot available). Pets allowed in some areas. Rooms 6 (4 shower only). B&B €52 pps, no ss. Closed 24-29 Dec (TBC). Amex, MasterCard, Visa. **Directions:** on Killorglin road (Ring of Kerry) leaving Tralee.

Tralee

Meadowlands Hotel

HOTEL

Oakpark Tralee Co Kerry **Tel: 066 718 0444** Fax: 066 718 0964
Email: info@meadowlands-hotel.com Web: www.meadowlands-hotel.com

This hotel in a peaceful part of the town is set in 3 acres of grounds and landscaped gardens, within walking distance of the town centre. Open since 1998, the high quality of materials and workmanship is now paying off as the building mellows and takes on its own personality - and this, together with caring service from well-trained staff, is ensuring its position as one of Tralee's leading hotels. A new conference centre and bedrooms were added in 2003 and conference facilities are to be extended further by May 2004. The interior layout and design of the hotel are impressive; notably the whole hotel is wheelchair friendly and furniture, commissioned from Irish craft manufacturers, is interesting, well-made and practical. Stylish, well-designed bedrooms are spacious and comfortable, with striking decor and the suites have jacuzzis. The main restaurant, An Pota Stoír, is open in the evening only (except Sunday lunch) and booking is advised as it is popular with locals as well as residents. Informal meals (notably seafood, from the proprietor's fishing boats) are available in the bar, Johnny Franks, every day (12.30-9, Sat to 8). Conference/banqueting (200/180). Leisure centre: 17m swimming pool, gym, steam room, sauna, jacuzzi, therapies. Garden. Children welcome (cots available, free of charge, baby sitting arranged). Wheelchair accessible. No pets. **Rooms 58** (3 suites, 9 superior rooms, 17 no smoking, 1 for disabled). Lift. 24 hour room service. B&B €100 pps, ss €20. Off-season value breaks available. Closed 24-26 Dec. Amex, Diners, MasterCard, Visa, Laser. **Directions:** 1km from Tralee town centre on the N69.

Tralee

Oyster Tavern

PUB / RESTAURANT

The Spa Tralee Co Kerry **Tel: 066 7136102** Fax: 066 7136047

This well-maintained roadside bar and restaurant has achieved high standards of food and service over a long period of time, earning a loyal local following. Wide-ranging menus specialising in seafood are moderately priced and, although the style is largely traditional, there are some unusual dishes - a starter terrine of cray fish & crab with seaweed, for example - and some unfamiliar varieties, such as Black Scabbard and Red Emperor. A shorter choice of non-seafood dishes offers prime meat and poultry and a couple of vegetarian dishes. Sunday lunch is especially good value and very popular. Bar open usual hours (no food served in the bar). Restaurant **Seats 140.** D daily, 5-10.15 (Sun from 6), L Sun only 12.30-2.30. Set Sun L about €16, D à la carte, House wine from about €15. Closed 25 Dec, Good Fri. Diners, MasterCard, Visa, Laser. **Directions:** 4 miles outside Tralee, on the Fenit road.

Tralee

Restaurant David Norris

☆ **RESTAURANT**

Ivy House Ivy Terrace Tralee Co Kerry **Tel: 066 718 5654**
Fax: 066 712 6600 Email: restaurantdavidnorris@eircom.net

Restaurant David Norris opened to some acclaim in December 2000 and is now established as Tralee's leading fine dining restaurant. Although located on the first floor of an unprepossessing modern building, it has a nice little reception area with a sofa and stools at a small bar and simple, tasteful decor with lots of plates on the walls and lightwood furniture in the Charles Rennie Macintosh style. Well-spaced tables are dressed with quality linen, plain glasses and white china, relieved by fresh flowers. A Euro-Toques chef, David Norris's sourcing is immaculate: ingredients are organic wherever possible and everything served is handmade on the premises (breads, pasta, ice creams). The emphasis is on taste, and presentation that is beautiful but not over-elaborate - and the aim is to offer the best of food at reasonable prices. This he seems to be achieving quite successfully: there's a sense of excitement and energy in seasonal menus which are simply written and, while very promising, are not over-ambitious in extent. About seven choices are offered on each course of an à la carte menu: seafood is well-represented, as would be expected in this area, but the range of foods offered is wide - Kerry beef may top the bill, for example (with with crisp potato rösti, potato confit and tarragon cream, perhaps), also lamb (roast loin, with sautéed new potatoes and onions, red wine & rosemary juices is typical of a summer menu) - and vegetarian dishes like warm puff pastry box of seasonal vegetables with poached egg, asparagus tips and parmesan cream. Classic desserts, which include speciality handmade ice creams, round off the meal in style, or there are Irish farmhouse cheeses, served with fresh fruit, home-made preserves and biscuits. Thoughtful detail is evident throughout, from the complimentary amuse-bouche that arrives with your aperitif to the home-made fudge served with your tea or coffee. Good cooking, professional service, an informative but sensibly limited wine list and good value for money are all winning this fine restaurant many friends. **Seats 40.** D Tue-Sat, 6.30-1.; à la carte. House wine €18.95; sc discretionary, except 10% (charged on food only) on parties of 10+. Closed Sun, Mon, 1 week Nov, 2 weeks Jan/Feb. Amex, MasterCard, Visa, Laser. **Directions:** Facing Siamsa Tire.

Tralee

RESTAURANT

Restaurant Uno

14 Princes Street Tralee Co Kerry **Tel: 066 718 1950**
Fax: 066 718 1951 Email: uno1@eircom.net

Patrick Fitzgibbon and Maeve Duff's restaurant just across the road from the town park is very popular with both locals and visitors. The restaurant is in several areas: a cosy front room doubles as reception and opens into a second high-ceilinged room which is brightly lit and more modern in style, with extra seating also in a balcony area above it. Menus favour the contemporary style with a leaning toward Cal-Ital and global influences with a seasoning of more traditional dishes - thus starters like crispy duck spring roll with sweet chilli dip and main courses range from Thai red chicken to honey roast duckling and steaks, most under €20, and there will always be about five daily specials on. Desserts are quite traditional - home-made tiramisu, crème brûlée, hot apple pie with cream - and the wine list is short (on choice and information) but well-balanced and includes half a dozen house wines. All round this buzzy place is offering a fair deal. Not suitable for children after 8 pm. **Seats 65** (private room 25). No smoking area. L Tue-Fri, 12.30-2.15; D Tue-Sun 5.30-9.30 (Sun from 4); à la carte. House wine from about €16. Closed L Sat & Sun, all Mon, 25-27 Dec, 1 Jan, 2 weeks in Jan. Amex, Diners, MasterCard, Visa, Laser. **Directions:** Beside Brendan Hotel. ◇

Tralee

BAR / RESTAURANT

Val O'Shea's Bar & Bistro

Bridge Street Tralee Co Kerry **Tel: 066 712 1559**
Fax: 066 712 5495 Email: vals@ohallorangroup.com

This is the happening place for informal dining and music. Very stylish, designer-driven, it's all of a piece with tinted windows, very dark woods and very dark leather on seats and bar stools - and traditional music most week nights (phone for details). Differing floor heights are cleverly exploited, and there's a mammoth feature area at the bottom of the stairs up to the bistro, which looks like an enormous three-sided sofa seating about 10 people. Although gloomy if you come in out of bright sunlight, the lighting is subtle and effective once your eyes adjust. Consistent standards, of both bar and the upstairs bistro food, have been maintained even when there have been changes of personnel, so the policy of providing quality and good value is likely to continue. Bistro **Seats 60.** Air conditioning. L Mon-Sat,12.30-2.30; D daily 6-10. Closed Sun L, 25 Dec, Good Fri. MasterCard, Visa, Laser. **Directions:** Town centre, beside Abbey carpark.

Tralee Area

COUNTRY HOUSE

Barrow Country House

West Barrow Ardfert Tralee Co Kerry
Tel: 066 713 6437 Fax: 066 713 6402
Email: info@barrowhouse.com Web: www.barrowhouse.com

In a stunning shoreside position on Barrow Harbour, this recently renovated guesthouse dates back to 1723 and was once home to the Knight of Kerry. Despite occasional reminders of the modern world from a nearby road, the house has largely retained its unique tranquil setting - and the front bedrooms and public rooms, which include a period drawing room and a breakfast room, where both buffet and hot breakfasts are served, all have wonderful views across water to the Slieve Mish Mountains and Dingle peninsula. Bedrooms are spacious and extremely comfortable, with orthopaedic beds, phone/ISDN lines, satellite TV, bathrobes, tea/coffee facilities and lovely bathrooms, some with jacuzzi baths; everything has has been completed to a very high standard, albeit with a hint of the hotel about some of the furnishings. Angling and golf are major attractions - the Arnold Palmer designed Tralee Golf Club is next door and Killarney, Ballybunion and Waterville are within range - and a helicopter service makes travelling to neighbouring golf courses easier. Children welcome (under 3 free in parents' room; cot available). No dinner, but good restaurants nearby (see entries under Fenit and Tralee). Some rooms are in an adjacent courtyard. Garden, fishing walking. **Rooms 16** (1 suite, 3 superior rooms, 1 for disabled, all no-smoking). B&B from about €50 pps, ss about €20. Amex, MasterCard, Visa, Laser. **Directions:** Follow the R558 after Oyster Tavern, follow signs to Churchill and straight on for 4kms.

Waterville

Butler Arms Hotel

HOTEL

Waterville Co Kerry **Tel: 066 947 4144** Fax: 066 947 452C
Email: reservations@butlerarms.com Web: www.butlerarms.com

One of Ireland's best-known hotels – it is one of several to have strong links with Charlie Chaplin – Pete and Mary Huggards' Butler Arms Hotel dominates the seafront at Waterville. Like many hotels which have been owner-run for several generations, it has established a special reputation for its homely atmosphere and good service. Improvements are constantly being made and public areas, including two sitting rooms, a sun lounge and a cocktail bar, are spacious and comfortably furnished, while the beamed Fisherman's Bar (which also has a separate entrance from the street) has a livelier atmosphere and can be a useful place for a break on the Ring of Kerry route. Bedrooms vary from distinctly non standard rooms in the old part of the hotel (which many regular guests request) to smartly decorated spacious rooms with neat en-suite bathrooms and uninterrupted sea views in a wing constructed in the early '90s and 12 new junior suites which opened in 2002. Off season value breaks; shooting (woodcock snipe) Nov-Jan. Garden; fishing; tennis. Snooker. Wheelchair accessible. Own parking. Children welcome (free cot, baby sitting arranged). No pets. **Rooms 44** (12 junior suites, 38 no-smoking rooms 8 disabled). Lift. B&B €107 pps, ss €45. No SC. Fisherman's Restaurant: D daily, 7-9.30. Fisherman's Bar bar food available daily 12-3 & 6.30-9. Closed Oct-Mar. Amex, MasterCard, Visa, Laser. **Directions:** O Ring of Kerry road.

Waterville

The Smuggler's Inn

BAR / RESTAURANT / B&B

Cliff Road Waterville Co Kerr
Tel: 066 947 4330 Fax: 066 947 442
Email: thesmugglersinn@eircom.net Web: www.welcome.to/the smugglersinn.co

Harry and Lucille Hunt's famous clifftop inn enjoys a remarkable location right beside the world famou championship Waterville Golf Course - and it's a real inn, providing food, drink and shelter. It can loc a little windswept (exterior maintenance is not easy in this exposed site) but it's a good place to tak a break from the Ring of Kerry – garden tables for fine sunny weather overlook a mile of sandy beac to the sea and mountains beyond, or you can eat in the comfortable bar or restaurant on chillier day Local ingredients provide the base for both modern and traditional cooking by Harry and son Henr who is also a chef - with seafood (including lobster from their own tank) being the speciality. Nc seafood-lovers have plenty of other choices, including Kerry lamb and beef, of course, and there's separate vegetarian menu available. Restaurant/Bar **Seats 100.** Air conditioning. L12.30-3, D 6-9.3 (snack menu only 3-6 pm). Set Sun L €21.50. Early D €30 (4.30-7.15). Set D €39.50, also à la cart House wine €17.50

Accommodation is also offered, in modest but pleasantly decorated rooms which vary in size, outloc and facilities (one has a balcony) and price, but all are comfortably furnished, if a little dated. There a first-floor residents' sitting room with sofas and armchairs, books, television – and magnificent se views. Children welcome (under 6 free in parents' room, cots available without charge). Pets b arrangement. Garden, walking, fishing. **Rooms 17** (11 shower only). B&B €38, ss €25. Closed 1 Nov Mar. Amex, Diners, MasterCard, Visa, Laser. **Directions:** Before village of Waterville, on coast road ne to Golf Club.

COUNTY KILDARE

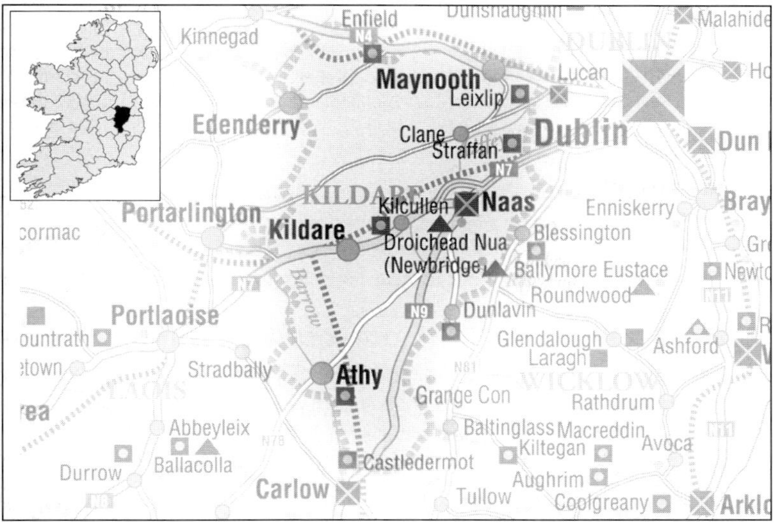

As you'd expect from a place which includes the famed racecourses of The Curragh, Punchestown and Naas among its many amenities, Kildare is the horse county par excellence. The horse is so central and natural a part of Irish life that you'll find significant stud farms in a surprisingly large number of counties. But it is in Kildare that they reach their greatest concentration in the ultimate equine county. Thus it's ironic that, a mere 400 million years ago, Kildare was just a salty ocean where the only creatures remotely equine were the extremely primitive ancestors of sea horses.

However, things have been looking up for the horse in County Kildare ever since, and today the lush pastures of the gently sloping Liffey and Barrow valleys provide ideal country for nurturing and training champions. Apart from many famous private farms, the Irish National Stud in Kildare town just beyond the legendary gallops of The Curragh is open for visitors, and it also includes a remarkable Japanese garden, reckoned the best Japanese rock garden in Europe, as well as the Museum of the Horse.

2004 sees Kildare town finally by-passed by motorway, and though there'll be bottlenecks further west on what is the main road from Dublin to Cork and Limerick, the people of the county town and their visitors can look forward to a pleasanter pace of life. Once you get away from the busy main roads, the County of Kildare is full of surprises. In fact, getting off the main roads is what enjoyment of life in Kildare is all about. The county's proximity to Dublin means that in the most recent population survey of 1996-2002, Kildare was second only to neighbouring Meath in its increase, the numbers growing by 21.5% to 164,000. Yet it is surprisingly easy to get away from the traffic, and you'll quickly find areas of rural enchantment and unexpected swathes of nature in the raw.

In the northwest of the county is the awe-inspiring Bog of Allen, the largest in Ireland, across whose wide open spaces the early engineers struggled to progress the Grand Canal on its route from the east coast towards the Shannon. Such needs of national transport are intertwined through the county's history. But between the arterial routes, railroads and canals, there is an easier pace of life, and gentle country with it. A southern leg of the Grand Canal curves away to become the Barrow Navigation, winding it way to Waterford. Beyond Athy, it goes near Kilkea, birthplace of Antarctic explorer Ernest Shackleton, whose growing fame is increasingly celebrated in his native county where his ancestors were involved in building the meeting -house which is now the Quaker Museum in Ballitore.

Local Attractions and Information

Athy, Heritage Centre 059 863 3075
Ballitore, Quaker Museum & Library 059 862 3344
Carbury, Ballindoolin House & Garden 046 953 1430
Celbridge, Castletown House 01 628 8252
Curragh, The Curragh Racecourse 045 441205
Edenderry, Grange Castle & Gardens 046 973 3316

Kilcock, Larchill Arcadian Gardens (follies) 01 628 7354
Kildare (Tully), Irish National Stud 045 521617
Kildare (Tully), Japanese Gardens 045 521251
Kildare, Tourism Information 045 522696
Kill, Goff's Bloodstock Sales (frequent) 045 886600
Naas, Kildare Failte 045 898888
Naas, Naas Racecourse 045 897391
Newbridge, Riverbank Arts Centre 045 433480
Punchestown, Punchestown Racecourse 045 897704
Straffan, Lodge Park Walled Garden 01 628 8412
Straffan, Steam Museum 01 627 3155
Timolin-Moone, Irish Pewtermill 059 862 4164

Athy

Coursetown Country House

COUNTRY HOUSE Stradbally Road Athy Co Kildare **Tel: 059 863 1101** Fax: 059 863 1101

Jim and Iris Fox's fine 200 year old house just off the Stradbally road is attached to a large arable farm. The house is large, welcoming, immaculately maintained and very comfortable, with some unusual attributes, including Jim's natural history library (where guests are welcome to browse) and extensive, well-tended gardens stocked with many interesting plants, including a number of rare fruit trees. Bedrooms vary according to their position in the house, but all are thoughtfully furnished in a pleasantly homely country house style and have direct dial phones, tea/coffee facilities and hair dryers. Iris takes pride in ensuring that her guests have the comfort of the very best beds and bedding - and the attention to detail in the pristine shower rooms is equally high, with lots of lovely towels and quality toiletries. (A bathroom is also available for anyone who prefers to have a good soak in a tub.) Another special feature is a ground floor room near the front door which has been specially designed for wheelchair users, with everything completed to the same high standard as the rest of the house. Then there is breakfast - again, nothing is too much trouble and the emphasis is on delicious healthy eating. The wide selection offered includes fresh juices and fruit salad, poached seasonal fruit (eg plums from the garden) pancakes, French toast with banana & maple syrup, Irish farmhouse cheeses, home-made bread and preserves - and the traditional cooked breakfast includes lovely rashers specially vacuum-packed for Iris by Shiel's butchers, in Abbeyleix. Small weddings catered for (20). Not suitable for children under 12 and older children must have their own room. Pets allowed in some areas by arrangement. Garden. **Rooms 5** (all with en-suite shower, all no smoking, 1 for disabled). B&B €50, ss €10. Closed 20 Dec- 6 Jan. MasterCard, Visa. **Directions:** Just outside Athy, on R428. Well signposted.

Athy

Tonlegee House & Restaurant

GUESTHOUSE / RESTAURANT Athy Co Kildare **Tel: 0507 31473**
Email: marjorie@tonlegeehouse.com
Web: www.tonlegeehouse.com

Marjorie Molloy's elegant country house just outside Athy was built in 1790 and now combines modern comfort with a pleasing element of old-fashioned style. The individually decorated en-suite bedrooms include one single room and all are comfortably furnished to a high standard with phones, TV and complimentary mineral water and well-finished bathrooms. Children welcome (under 10 free in parents' room, cot available without charge, baby sitting arranged). Pets permitted in some areas by arrangement. **Rooms 12** (5 superior, 2 shower only). Room service (limited hours). B&B €65 pps, ss €25.

Restaurant: Hugh Johnston has been head chef since 1998 and his seasonal menus are in a modern European style, based on home-grown and local produce. Over an aperitif in the drawing room, imaginative, fairly priced menus make good reading and offer a balanced choice, including house specialities such as a starter of quail in pastry with wild mushroom sauce. Local Kildare lamb is an especially strong option, also beef (typically, fillet with celeriac purée, shallot & red wine sauce) also vegetarian dishes like baked aubergine stuffed with roasted vegetables topped with mozzarella, coriander sauce. Tempting desserts might include a thin apple tart with cinnamon cream (cooked to order) or home made ice creams - or make the most of a good Irish farmhouse cheeseboard. An informative wine list offers a wide choice, including half bottles. The early dinner is particularly good value. **Seats 40.** D Tue-Sat 6-9.30pm (closed Sun & Mon). Non-residents welcome by reservation. Early D €25 (6-7.30), otherwise à la carte. House wines from €17.95. SC discretionary. Restaurant closed Sun, Mon; establishment closed 24 Dec-10 Jan. Amex, MasterCard, Visa, Laser. **Directions:** From Dublin, take M7, then onto M9 to N78, through Athy, across 2 bridges, passing by the canal take 1st left after Tegral factory.

Ballymore Eustace

RESTAURANT / PUB

Ballymore Inn

Ballymore Eustace Co Kildare **Tel: 045 864585**
Fax: 045 864747 Email: theballymoreinn@hotmail.com

It's the food that draws people to the O'Sullivan family's pub and it's wise to book well ahead to get a taste of the wonderful things this country kitchen has to offer, especially at weekends. The outside of the Ballymore Inn gives little away, although the blackboard menu at the door is a hint of what's to come. Inside, the clues begin to add up: unusual craft furniture, imaginative use of colour and striking fresh flowers and plants all add up to the kind of place where details count so the menu, when it arrives, fits into the pattern. Top quality ingredients have always been at the heart of the food operation here: fresh produce is sourced from a local organic grower, while beef, bacon and eggs come from recognised Quality Assurance Schemes and chicken and lamb from approved Irish farms. Careful sourcing, careful cooking and a relaxed ambience have proved a winning formula - so much so, in fact, that the bar has been refitted to allow more eating space and food service has been extended to Sundays to meet demand. Menus have plenty to choose from: delicious soups, Caesar salad with crispy bacon, excellent meats - Kildare sandwich with baked ham, farmhouse cheese & apricot chutney, for example, or minute sirloin steak with herb butter or grilled Ardrahan cheese, served with sauté potatoes or champ - and delicious, homely desserts. Creative crisp-based modern pizzas that marry artisan Irish food products with traditional methods are a house speciality, baked in a special pizza oven; their Grilled Fennel, Roasted Peppers, Basil and Ardrahan Cheese Pizza one was a previous winner of our Vegetarian Dish of the Year. You can also construct your own pizza, starting with a choice of five bases (tomato plus a range of cheeses) and select from ten toppings. Evening menus are more structured and offer a much wider choice of dishes: vegetables and salads have always been especially interesting here and it's no surprise to find that starters major on flavourful garden combinations - chargrilled aubergine & tomato salad with mature Ardrahan, for example, and roast red pepper mousse with black olive dressing - and home-cured salmon is a speciality too, with pickled cucumber & dill dressing. Main courses offer a wider range of more substantial dishes - including roast rack of lamb (with creamed spinach and garlic jus) and fillet of beef with Doneraile mushrooms) - and will always include an imaginative vegetarian option (grilled vegetable couscous with halloumi cheese, perhaps) and fish of the day. Side dishes are a far cry from the usual tired offering - organic vegetable sauté, for example, and broad bean salad with Irish bacon. Children welcome. **Seats 50.** No smoking area; air conditioning. Food served daily, 12.30-8 (Sun 12.30-?); L12.30-3, D 6-8 (restaurant menu to 9). House wine about €13; sc discretionary. No food 3-6pm Mon-Thu. Closed bank hols, 25 Dec & Good Fri. Amex, MasterCard, Visa, Laser. **Directions:** Turn right at 2.5 miles after Blessington on Baltinglass Road.

Carbury

RESTAURANT

Tyrrells Restaurant

Ballindoolin House & Gardens Carbury Edenderry Co Kildare
Tel: 046 973 2400 Fax: 046 973 2377
Email: tyrrells@ballindoolin.com Web: www.ballindoolin.com

Fairly well signed, off the Edenderry-Kinnegad road (R401), David and Nikki Molony's unusual country restaurant is in converted outbuildings at the back of a large house of historical interest (currently undergoing renovations) and adjacent to a lovely recently restored kitchen garden (which supplies produce to the restaurant) and charming woodland walks. The restaurant has more character than first impressions suggest, with a welcoming open fire, flagstone flooring, attractive simply laid wooden tables and large windows overlooking a yard inhabited by rare breed farm stock and the occasional strutting peacock, all of which is both interesting and entertaining. A prompt warm welcome, with menu and wine list delivered to your table, is swiftly followed by a plate of bread - a dark, close-textured loaf with a hint of spice - and your choice from a wine list weighted heavily in favour of the New World. Well-constructed menus offer starters like a soup of the day (smoked haddock chowder, perhaps) or a pesto potato cake with garlic, slow roasted tomato, feta cheese & chilli oil, and main courses such as prime Irish char-grilled rib eye steak with mustard & peppercorn butter or fish of the day. Finish off with a classic dessert - strawberry & crème fraîche bavarois, perhaps or maybe a liqueur coffee. Quality ingredients, a sure hand in the kitchen, characterful surroundings, caring service by well-trained staff and good value add up to a great outing for all age groups - no wonder they have built up a loyal following. **Seats 50.** No smoking restaurant, wheelchair accessible. L Wed-Sun, 12-2.30 (Sun to 4), D Wed-Sat, 6.30-10. Set D from €30; Set L €25. House wines (Tyrrells Old Winery - what else - from €20.50. Closed D Sun, all Mon & Tue; 25-26 Dec, 1st 2 wks Jan, Good Fri. Visa, MasterCard, Laser. **Directions:** signed to Ballindoolin House & Gardens.

Castledermot

Kilkea Castle Hotel

féile bia HOTEL / RESTAURANT

Castledermot Co Kildare **Tel: 0503 45156** Fax: 0503 45187
Email: kilkea@iol.ie Web: www.kilkeacastle.ie

The oldest inhabited castle in Ireland, Kilkea dates back to the twelfth century and has been sensitively renovated and converted into a hotel without loss of elegance and grandeur. Rooms, many with lovely views over the formal gardens and surrounding countryside, are splendidly furnished to incorporate modern comforts. Public areas include a hall complete with knights in armour and two pleasant ground floor bars - a cosy back one and a larger one that opens onto a terrace overlooking gardens and a golf course. Some of the bedrooms in the main castle are very romantic - as indeed is the whole setting making it understandably popular for weddings. The adjoining (architecturally discreet) leisure centre has an indoor swimming pool, saunas, jacuzzi, steam room, well-equipped exercise room and sun bed. Outdoor sports include clay pigeon shooting, archery, tennis and fishing. An 18-hole championship golf course, which has views of the castle from every fairway, uses the River Greese flowing through the grounds as a natural hazard and a couple of extra lakes were added to increase the challenge still further; informal meals are served in the golf club. Special weekend breaks at the castle are good value. Conferences/banqueting (300/200). Leisure Centre, swimming pool. Garden. Tennis, Golf (18). Children welcome. No pets. **Rooms 35** (1 suite, 3 junior suites, 8 executive, 2 shower only). 24 hour room service B&B from about €110 pps, ss about €40. SC 12.5%. Closed Christmas week.

Named after Hugh de Lacy, who built Kilkea Castle in 1180, this beautiful first-floor restaurant has a real 'castle' atmosphere and magnificent views over the countryside. It also overlooks the delightful formal kitchen garden (source of much that appears on the table in summer) and has a bright, airy atmosphere. Guests may take coffee on the terrace in summer and wander around to see the old fruit trees, vegetables and herbs. Cooking, service and surroundings make this a very special venue. Restaurant **Seats 60** (private room 40). L (daily by reservation) 12.30-2.00, D 7-9.30. Set L about €26. Set D about €45. House wine about €21; sc 12.5%. Toilets wheelchair accessible. Closed 3 days at Christmas. Amex, Diners, MasterCard, Visa, Laser. **Directions:** 3 miles from Castledermot (off M9) signed from village. ◇

Curragh

Martinstown House

COUNTRY HOUSE

Curragh Co Kildare **Tel: 045 441 269** Fax: 045 441 20
Email: info@martinstown.com Web: www.martinstown.com

Just on the edge of the Curragh, near Punchestown, Naas and The Curragh race courses, this delightful 200 year old 'Strawberry Hill' gothic style house is on a farm, set in 170 acres of beautifully wooded land, with free range hens, sheep, cattle and horses and a well-maintained walled kitchen garden that provides vegetables, fruit and flowers for the house in season. Meryl Long welcomes guests to this idyllic setting, aiming to offer them 'a way of life which I knew as a child (but with better bathrooms!), a warm welcome, real fires and good food.' It is a lovely family house, with very nicely proportioned rooms - gracious but not too grand - open fires downstairs, and bedrooms that are all different, very comfortably furnished with fresh flowers and each with its own special character. A stay here is sure to be enjoyable, with the help of a truly hospitable hostess who offers a delicious afternoon tea on arrival - and believes that holidays should be fun, full of interest and with an easy-going atmosphere. Golf and equestrian activities nearby. Not suitable for children under 12. No pets. **Rooms 4** (2 en-suite, 2 with private bathrooms, all no smoking) B&B from about €80 pps, ss €20. Residents D €45 (by arrangement - book the previous day). House wine about €22.50. Closed mid Dec-early Jan. Amex, MasterCard, Visa. **Directions:** Kilcullen exit off M9 then N78 towards Athy. Sign at 1st crossroads. ◇

Leixlip

Leixlip House Hotel

HOTEL / RESTAURANT

Captains Hill Leixlip Co Kildare
Tel: 01 624 2268 Fax: 01 624 417
Email: info@leixliphouse.com Web: www.leixliphouse.com

Up on a hill overlooking Leixlip village, this lovely Georgian house is just eight miles from Dublin city centre. It opened as an hotel in 1996 after extensive renovations and is furnished and decorated to a high standard in period style. Gleaming antique furniture and gilt-framed mirrors enhance thick carpeted public rooms in soft country colours, all creating an atmosphere of discreet opulence. Bedrooms include two suites furnished with traditional mahogany furniture; the strong, simple decor particularly pleases the many business guests who stay here and there is a welcome emphasis on service - there is all day room service (tea/coffee complimentary), and a nightly turndown service which includes complimentary mineral water and chocolates - and a shoe valet service. Hotel guests also have complimentary use of a nearby gym. Conference/banqueting (100/140). Secretarial services. Children welcome (under 12s in parents' room charged only for breakfast, cots available without charge, babysitting arranged). No pets. **Rooms 19** (5 executive, 14 shower only). All day room service. B&B from €82.50 pps, ss €52.50.

The Bradaun Restaurant: The commitment to quality evident in the hotel as a whole is continued in the restaurant, a bright, high-ceilinged, formally appointed dining room. Sean Hicks, who has been head chef since the hotel opened, offers consistently good modern Irish cooking; his imaginative, wide-ranging menus change weekly (with extra Chef's Recommendations daily), are based on fresh seasonal produce and well executed with admirable attention to detail. Specialities that show the style include a deep-fried parcel of crabmeat and nori, served with a citrus salsa and loin of lamb with a provençal stuffed tomato, courgette ribbons & rosemary jus. Set menus offer particularly good value for money and there's an attractive lounge menu for those who prefer an informal meal. An extensive, informative and carefully chosen wine list would make good bedtime reading; it includes an interesting and well-balanced Recommended Wines of the Month selection within an accessible price range, and a fair selection of half bottles. Not suitable for children after 7.30pm. **Seats 45.** D Tue-Sun, 6.30-10 (Sun to 8.30); L (Sun only, except group bookings on other days) 12.30-4; Early D €27 (6.30-7.30); Set D €30 & €43; also à la carte. Set Sun L €25. House wine from €18.50; sc discretionary. Restaurant closed Mon (except for group bookings). Hotel closed 25-26 Dec. Amex, Diners, MasterCard, Visa, Laser. **Directions:** Leixlip exit off M4 motorway. Take right in Leixlip village at traffic lights.

Maynooth

Glenroyal Hotel & Leisure Club

HOTEL

Straffan Road Maynooth Co Kildare **Tel: 01 629 0909** Fax: 01 629 0919
Email: info@glenroyal.ie Web: www.glenroyal.ie

Situated on the outskirts of the university town of Maynooth, and only 20 minutes from Dublin city centre, this large hotel meets local demand for essential facilities covering a wide range of events - conferences, corporate events and weddings - and provides extensive leisure facilities, including a dramatically designed 20 metre pool (with underwater loungers, whirlpool and children's splashpool), a gymnasium and much else besides. Bedrooms are all comfortably furnished - mostly in contemporary style - with all the amenities of a good modern hotel and neat en-suite bathrooms. Conference and business facilities are the best in a wide area; a new conference centre with five syndicate suites was added in 2002. * A branch of Lemongrass, a small chain of authentic Asian restaurants based in Naas, is located in the hotel and very popular with locals as well as residents. Conferences/Banqueting (550/350); business centre; secretarial services; video conferencing. Leisure centre (now with 2 pools; a new one with hydro-spa is for adult use only); beauty salon. Children welcome (under 4 free in parents room, cots available without charge, baby sitting arranged). No Pets. **Rooms 112** (66 executive, 7 shower only, 12 no smoking, 5 for disabled). Lift. All day room service. B&B €81 pps, ss €15, no SC. **Lemongrass Restaurant:** Seats 80 (private room 20). Reservations required. Air conditioning. L daily 12-5, D daily 5-10. Special L €14.20, otherwise à la carte. House wine from €15. Restaurant closed 25 Dec & Good Fri. Hotel closed 25 Dec. Amex, Diners, MasterCard, Visa, Switch. **Directions:** From Dublin, M4 to Maynooth; turn right off sliproad for Maynooth.

Maynooth

Moyglare Manor

HOTEL /RESTAURANT

Maynooth Co Kildare
Tel: 01 628 6351 Fax: 01 628 5405
Email: info@moyglaremanor.ie Web: www.moyglaremanor.ie

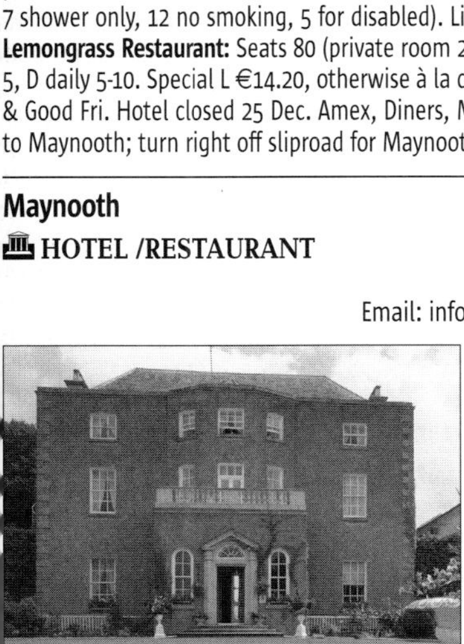

Country hedges and workaday farmland give way to neatly manicured hedging, rolling parkland then beautifully tended gardens as one approaches this imposing classical Georgian manor - and it comes as no surprise to find that the owner, Norah Devlin, lavishes her love of beautiful things on the place, with a passion for antiques that has become legendary. Gilt-framed mirrors and portraits are everywhere, shown to advantage against deep-shaded damask walls. The remarkable abundance of chairs and sofas of every pedigree ensures comfortable seating, even when the restaurant is fully booked with large parties milling around before and after dining. First-time visitors sometimes describe it as 'like being in an antique shop' but, after recovering from the stunning effect of its contents, guests invariably reflect on the immaculate maintenance and comfort of the place under the careful stewardship of long-time manager Shay Curran. Spacious bedrooms are also lavishly furnished in period style, some with four-posters or half testers, and include a ground-floor suite; all have well-appointed bathrooms with quality appointments and careful attention to detail. All rooms have recently been upgraded to a very high standard and, despite a long-standing aim for peacefulness, the modern world seem to have caught up with Moyglare and televisions have been installed in bedrooms. Golf nearby (four courses within 10 miles), also tennis and horse riding nearby. Small conferences/banqueting (30); secretarial services. Not suitable for children under 12. No Pets. Garden; walking. **Rooms 16** (1 suite, 4 executive, 2 rooms for disabled). B&B from about €115 pps, ss about €25.

Restaurant: Hotel manager Shay Curran personally supervises the formally-appointed restaurant, which is in several interconnecting rooms; the middle ones nice and cosy for winter, those overlooking the garden and countryside pleasant in fine weather. Grand and romantic, it's just the place for a special occasion and there's a pianist playing background music in the evening. Lunch and dinner menus offer a nicely balanced combination of traditional favourites and sophisticated fare, attractively presented, with a vegetarian option always available. There is an emphasis on seafood and game in season - roast pheasant, perhaps, hung long enough to give it a gamey flavour, perfectly cooked and served off the bone accompanied by a nice little serving of green-flecked champ as well as game chips and Cumberland sauce. Lunch menus offer less choice than dinner, but are nevertheless quite formal and convey a sense of occasion. Fine meals are complemented by an exceptional wine list of special interest to the connoisseur (Moyglare Manor was the winner of our 1999 Wine List of the Year Award). Not suitable for children under 12. Restaurant **seats 40** (private room, 25). L Sun-Fri 12.30-2; D daily 7-9. Set L about €32. Set D about €45, also à la carte. House wine from about €22; sc 12.5%. Restaurant closed L Sat. House closed 24-26 Dec. Amex, Diners, MasterCard, Visa, Laser. **Directions:** From Dublin, N4 west; exit for Maynooth, keep right at church; after 2 .5 miles, turn left at Moyglare crossroads, then next right. ◇

Naas

Killashee House Hotel

féile bia HOTEL

Old Killcullen Road Naas Co Kildare **Tel: 045 879277** Fax: 045 879266
Email: sales@killasheehouse.com Web: www.killasheehouse.com

Set in 80 acres of gardens and woodland just outside Naas town, this fairly recently opened hotel is approached along an attractive driveway through gardens and the setting is impressive, although spoilt a little by the car parking arrangements in front of the building. The entrance and lobby areas are striking and a fine inner courtyard is planted with Virginia creeper, which will be attractive when mature. A rather grand staircase leads to a large traditionally furnished lounge area on the first floor, with views of the grounds and courtyard and well-grouped seating areas; this could be a pleasant place for afternoon tea and informal socialising - there is a pianist at certain times. Conference and business events are well catered for, with conference and meeting rooms of various sizes available, and it is a popular venue for weddings. Bedrooms, which have been designed with practical requirements of business guests as well as comfort in mind, include a number of suites and some with four-poster beds; all rooms have multi-line phones, data ports, voicemail, fax (on request), and safe as well as the more usual amenities. Formal dining is offered at the main restaurant, Turners (where a harpist plays at weekends), and informal food is available in other areas. The hotel is well located for many of the county's sporting activities including horse racing (four courses nearby), golf (five clubs nearby), car racing (Mondello Park) and attractions such as the Wicklow Mountains, The Japanese Gardens and The National Irish Stud. On site facilities include archery, cycling, woodland walks; leisure centre with 25m pool. Conference/banqueting 1600/800. Business centre; secretarial services; video conferencing. Children welcome (under 4 free in parents' room, cot available without charge), but not in restaurant after 8pm. Garden, walking, cycling. **Rooms 84** (6 suites, 8 junior suites, 4 superior, 5 shower only, 24 no smoking, 3 for disabled). Lift. B&B €129 pps, ss €45. Amex, MasterCard, Visa, Laser. **Directions:** 30 minutes from Dublin on N7 to Naas, then 1 mile on R448, Kilcullen road.

Naas

Lemongrass

Ⓝ RESTAURANT

Abbey Street Naas Co Kildare **Tel: 045 871544**

The parent restaurant of a small chain that now has franchises in half a dozen other places, this is an attractive contemporary restaurant which combines comfort with style. There's a friendly welcome on your arrival at the reception desk - and a small bar with some seating if you should have to wait for a table. The split-level restaurant is divided into several appealing areas and well-spaced tables, good lighting and simple stylish table settings - plain modern crockery, glass and cutlery, a single fresh flower - provide just the right setting for food that is well-executed and good value. You can take your pick of dishes from a very large menu offering a wide range of broadly Asian dishes, many of them familiar - and the hot ones obligingly indicated with a red chilli pepper. A combo platter of starters is great value at €9.85, with generous quantities of chicken saté, Thai beef salad, prawn & salmon cake & vegetable spring roll for two - and a main course dish of crispy roast duck with plum sauce also attracted particular praise on a recent visit. Vegetarians are well looked after, with a section of the menu dedicated to suitable dishes in addition to other choices in the main menu. Desserts are not an Asian strong point, but you can have a tropical fresh fruit platter or banana fritters with ice cream along with a few other popular dishes. Smart, attentive staff work well together and add an extra dimension to a dining experience. Short wine list, Asian beers, Bento box lunch special available until 5pm. Open Mon-Fri 12.30-10pm, Sat & Sun 1-10pm. **Directions:** Behind the main street, in Naas.

Naas

Les Olives

RESTAURANT

10 South Main Street Naas Co Kildare
Tel: 045 894788 Email: lesolive@indigo.ie

Olivier and Maeve Pauloin-Valory's successful little restaurant is on the first floor over Kavanagh's pub, in the centre of Naas and regulars are drawn from a wide area around the town. It's an attractive room with sunny yellow walls, comfortable ladder back chairs, formal white-clothed tables and a lobster tank all setting a positive tone. Seafood is a particular attraction, especially oysters and lobsters which you can choose from the tank yourself, and in addition to dishes on the main menu - which may include some unusual items, such as fresh water crayfish cassolette - daily fish specials (prawn kebab, lobster salad) are shown on a blackboard, where you may also find some less likely soul mates, such as ostrich (which is farmed nearby) and, of course, local meats like Kildare beef and lamb. Olivier's good cooking, friendly efficient service under Maeve's direction and a wine list which offers an extensive range of wines, including champagnes, rare vintages and a full page of magnums all promise a good night out. Not suitable for children under 10. **Seats 45.** D Tue-Sun, 7-10; Set D about €45, also à la carte. House wine about €17; sc discretionary. Closed Sun, Mon; Christmas, Good Fri. MasterCard, Visa, Laser. **Directions:** Town Centre. ◇

Naas

The Storehouse

Ⓝ **RESTAURANT**

Friary Lane Naas Co Kildare **Tel: 045 889333**

Pat Brophy's converted railway storehouse gives out all the right messages with stone walls, exposed beams and old wooden floor contrasting with shiny bare wooden tables set up simply in contemporary style and fashionable high-backed chairs. It makes a warm and comfortable (if rather noisy) setting for meals that echo the same philosophy of updating classics - onion marmalade replaces the classic Cumberland sauce with chicken liver paté, for example, and steaks might come with Guinness battered onions instead of the familiar onion rings of yore although a few dishes, such as Storehouse Caesar salad, need no improvement and remain a pretty faithful rendition of the original with only minor variations. Offering more contemporary side orders is used to liven up the old favourites too - spiced stir-fried greens will perk up a piece of plain grilled or pan-fried meat or fish in a flash, for instance, and the choice is yours: ideal in a fairly conservative area, where a restaurant has to appeal to all age groups and a wide range of tastes. A user-friendly wine list is organised by style. Open Tue-Sat, 6-10.30, L Sun 12-4. MasterCard, Visa.

Naas

Thomas Fletcher

ATMOSPHERIC PUB

Commercial House Main Street Naas Co Kildare
Tel: 045 897328 Fax: 045 897328

This great old pub goes back well into the 1800s and has been in the Fletcher family since Tom Fletcher's father ran it in the 1930s. It's the kind of place that puts Irish theme pubs to shame, with its simple wooden floor and long, plain mahogany bar broken up in the traditional way with mahogany dividers and stained glass panels. They did up the back lounge recently, but there's no need to worry - it shouldn't need more work for another couple of hundred years. Open 2-11.30. Closed 25 Dec, Good Fri & Bank Hols. **Directions:** Main street Naas, at the Dublin end of town, beside Superquinn.

Narraghmore

The Pond House

B&B

Narraghmore Co Kildare **Tel: 045 485456** Fax: 045 485456

No need to explain the name of Nuala Clarke's unusual house, which will become obvious as soon as you reach it. Although it's in a different county, The Pond House is handy enough to Rathsallagh (see entry, Dunlavin, Co Wicklow) to be a regular recipient of overflow custom, a system which pleases all concerned - word has got around and some very interesting people stay here. The house is quietly located and spacious with a large patio area at the back, the atmosphere is distinctly laid back and, unusually for a guesthouse, it even has a proper bar where race-goers and wedding guests can enjoy a small one or two before heading upstairs. Bedrooms are pleasant in a country pine way, but by no means luxurious (no phone or TV and they're all shower only). Nuala is a natural hostess and clearly enjoys making people feel at home. Children welcome (under 4s free in parents' room, cots available without charge). Garden, fishing, walking. Pets allowed by arrangement. **Rooms 5** (all shower only). B&B about €40pps, ss about €15. Open all year. MasterCard, Visa. **Directions:** 1 mile off main Dublin Carlow road to Narraghmore, next right- sign posted. ◇

Newbridge

Keadeen Hotel

HOTEL

Newbridge Co Kildare **Tel: 045 431666** Fax: 045 434402
Email: keadeen@iol.ie Web: keadeenhotel.kildare.ie

Centrally located and easily accessible off the M7 motorway, this family-owned hotel is set in ten acres of fine landscaped gardens just south of the town (and quite near the Curragh racecourse). The hotel has recently been refurbished and generously spacious accommodation is furnished to a high standard. A fine romanesque Health & Fitness Club has an 18-metre swimming pool and aromatherapy room among its attractions, plus a staffed gymnasium. Extensive conference and banqueting facilities (1,000); secretarial services. Video conferencing can be arranged. Leisure centre, swimming pool. Garden. Parking. No Pets. Children welcome (under 3s free in parents rooms; cots available). Weekend specials available. **Rooms 77** (1 suite, 3 junior suites, 20 executive, 1 for disabled) B&B from about €87. Weekend specials from about €140. Closed 24-27 Dec. Amex, Diners, MasterCard, Visa. **Directions:** From Dublin take N7 off M50, take sliproad sign posted Curragh race course & follow signs for Newbridge. ◇

Newbridge

The Red House

HOTEL / RESTAURANT

Newbridge Co Kildare **Tel: 045 431657** Fax: 045 431934
Email: info@redhouse.ie

Proprietor-manager Brian Fallon runs a tidy ship at this cosy inn just off the motorway. It has a very relaxed atmosphere, especially in the characterful bar and the restful conservatory and garden at the back, and bedrooms all have good amenities. Conference/Banqueting (400/300); secretarial services. Garden. Children under 5 free in parents' room; cots available. **Rooms 12** (1 suite, 1 junior suite, 2 no-smoking rooms, 1 for disabled). B&B about €85 pps, ss €15. No sc.

Restaurant: Nigel Teague cooks for the Red House café-brasserie, Café Tomat. In a lovely comfortably furnished room with warm contemporary decor at the back of the inn, overlooking well-maintained gardens, it specialises in deliciously flavourful modern food at reasonable prices (with some rather more traditional dishes on the more extensive evening menu); service is friendly, professional and very efficient. Children welcome. **Seats 45.** L&D daily 12.30-3, D 6.30-10; à la carte. Toilets wheelchair accessible. Closed 25-26 Dec, 1 week early Jan & Good Fri. Amex, Diners, MasterCard, Visa, Laser. **Directions:** On the N7 between Naas and Newbridge.

Straffan

Barberstown Castle

HOTEL / RESTAURANT

Straffan Co Kildare **Tel: 01 628 8157** Fax: 01 627 7027
Email: castleir@iol.ie Web: www.barberstowncastle.com

Barberstown Castle is fascinating; steeped in history through three very different historical periods, it's one of the few houses in the area to have been occupied continuously for over 400 years. The oldest part is very much a real castle - the original keep in the middle section of the building, which includes the atmospheric cellar restaurant, was built by Nicholas Barby in the early 13th century. A more domestic Elizabethan house was added in the second half of the 16th century and Hugh Barton (also associated with nearby Straffan House, now the Kildare Hotel & Country Club, with whom it shares golf and leisure facilities) then built the 'new' Victorian wing in the 1830s. Most recently, in the current ownership of Kenneth Healy, the property has been thoroughly renovated and appropriately refurbished, in keeping with its age and style, to offer a high standard of modern comfort. Very comfortable accommodation is provided in well-appointed, individually decorated en-suite rooms - some are in the oldest section, the Castle Keep, others are more recent, but most are stylish and spacious. Public areas, including two drawing rooms and an elegant bar, have been renovated with the same care, and there are big log fires everywhere. Conferences/Banqueting (30/150); Children welcome (under 6s free in parents' room; cot available without charge). Garden. No pets. **Rooms 22** (1 suite, 1 shower only, 1 for disabled). All day room service. B&B €110 pps, ss EU27.50; sc inc.

The Castle Restaurant: The restaurant is in a series of whitewashed rooms in the semi-basement of the old Castle Keep, which gives it great atmosphere, heightened by fires and candles in alcoves. Head chef Bertrand Malabat, who joined the castle in 1998, presents a number of menus including a six-course Tasting Menu (served to complete parties only) and a seasonal à la carte with about seven choices on each course. The style is classic French with the occasional nod to international fashions; local beef or lamb usually feature, also game in season, and there will be several prime fish dishes. Imaginative vegetarian dishes are offered on the main menu - a wild mushroom, spinach & ricotta feuillette, for example, with truffle oil & herb butter sauce. Finish with a classic sweet like Barberstown bread & butter pudding with vanilla ice - or a selection of Irish farmhouse cheeses and home-baked breads. Not suitable for children under 12. **Seats 75** (private room 30). Reservations advised. L daily 12.30-2.30 (Sun to 3.30) D 7-9.30 (Sun,6-8); Daily L menu à la carte; Set Sun L €29.50; Set D €45, Tasting Menu €55; à la carte L&D also available. House wine €22.50; sc discretionary. Closed 24-27 Dec & 2nd week Jan. Amex, Diners, MasterCard, Visa, Laser. **Directions:** West N4 - turn for Straffan exit/ South N7 - Kill Exit.

Straffan

Kildare Hotel & Golf Club

HOTEL / RESTAURANT

Straffan Co Kildare
Tel: 01 601 7200 Fax: 01 601 7299
Email: hotel@kclub.ie Web: www.kclub.ie

The origins of Straffan House go back a long way - the history is known as far back as 550 AD - but it was the arrival of the Barton wine family in 1831 that established the tone of today's magnificent building, by giving it a distinctively French elegance. It was bought by the Smurfit Group in 1988 and, after extensive renovations, opened as an hotel in 1991. Set in lush countryside, and overlooking its own golf course, the hotel boasts unrivalled opulence. The interior is magnificent, with superb furnishings and a wonderful collection of original paintings by famous artists, including Jack B.Yeats, who has a room devoted to his work. All bedrooms and bathrooms are individually designed in the grand style, with superb amenities and great attention to detail. Under the guidance of Ray Carroll, who has been with the hotel from the outset and is Chief Executive of the Resort, it is run with apparently effortless perfection. The hotel and golf course are in the midst of major developments in preparation for the Ryder Cup, which the K Club will host in 2006; these include a new bedroom extension, an extension to the Byerley Turk Restaurant and a second 18-hole golf course, which are all complete, and a spa which is due to open early in 2004. Although most famous for its golf, the hotel also offers river fishing for salmon and trout and coarse fishing with a choice of five stocked lakes (equipment bait and tackle provided; tuition available). For guests interested in horticulture there is a mapped garden walk, with planting details. Conferences/ Banqueting (500/300); secretarial services; video conferencing. Leisure centre, swimming pool; specialist therapies; beauty salon. Golf (18), tennis, garden, walking, fishing, cycling, equestrian. Snooker, pool table. Children welcome (cots available without charge, baby sitting arranged). Lift. 24 hour concierge. 24 hour room service, twice daily housekeeping. No pets. **Rooms 69** (4 suites, 5 junior suites, 60 executive rooms). Room rate from €270 (max 2 guests). No SC.

★**The Byerley Turk:** Dramatically draped tall windows, marble columns, paintings of racehorses, tables laden with crested china, monogrammed white linen, gleaming modern crystal and silver - these all create an impressive background for the hotel's fine food. While the style has not changed noticeably since the restaurant was extended in 2001, the room is now a more interesting shape (enabling one end to be closed off for private parties without affecting normal dining arrangements) and as the old trompe l'oeil cocktail bar has been seamlessly absorbed into the entrance to the new accommodation. A larger bar has been created, with dark green walls creating a pleasingly clubby atmosphere and - the stroke of genius that is the making of this extension - it opens onto an elegant terrace with a distinctly French tone, thus reflecting the changes made in the Barton years. Here, on fine summer evenings, guests consider menus over an aperitif and admire the new golf course across the river (completed in 2003). Executive chef Michel Flamme, who has been with the hotel since it opened, bases his cooking on classical French cuisine, using the best of local and estate-grown produce; his Menu du Jour (about €70) is concise, with just three choices on each course but all the little touches - a complimentary amuse-bouche, home-made petits fours with the coffee - that make a special dining experience memorable will be in place. A seasonal à la carte is also offered, and a surprise "Tasting Menu" (on request), for complete parties. All menus are luxurious and notable for a growing number of specialities, which include crispy wontons of Dublin Bay prawns, with basil, pine kernels and olive oil, and some dishes with a definite Irish flavour such as braised loin of organic bacon with Savoy cabbage & onion sauce, also a range of wonderful hot soufflés. Service, under the direction of restaurant manager Martin Meade is friendly and professional - and the best wine choices for your meal are in the sure hand of sommelier Didier Fiat; given the intertwined history of Straffan House and the Barton family, it is appropriate that the Bordeaux Reserve from Barton and Guestier should be the label chosen for the hotel's house wine. Children welcome. **Seats 115** (private room 14). No smoking area; air conditioning. Piano at certain times. D 7.30-10 daily. Set D about €70; also à la carte. House Wine from €30; sc discretionary. *A less formal dining option is available at The Legends Restaurant at the golf club (12.30-11 daily). Amex, Diners, MasterCard, Visa, Laser. **Directions:** 30 mins south west of Dublin airport and city (M50 - N4).

COUNTY KILKENNY

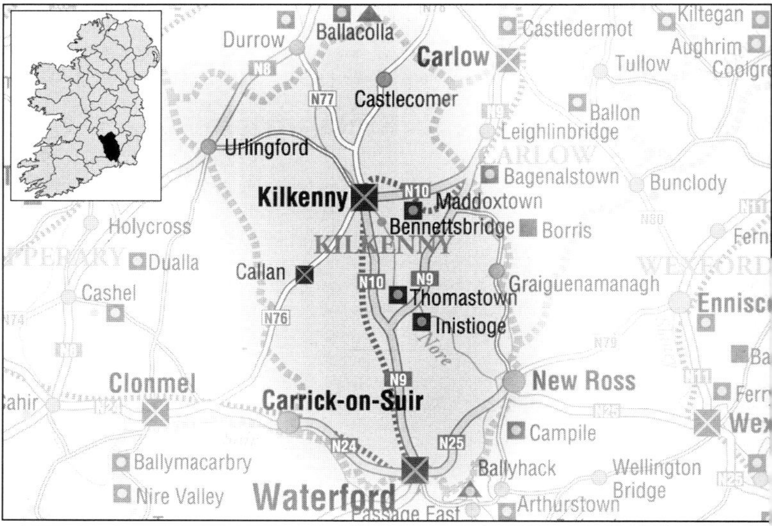

Kilkenny is a land of achingly beautiful valleys where elegant rivers weave their way through a rich countryside spiced by handsome hills. So naturally it's a place whose people care passionately about their county, and the miniature city at its heart. For Kilkenny - the Marble City - is one of Ireland's oldest cities, and proud of it. Its array of ancient buildings is unrivalled. But, by today's standards of population, this gem of a place is scarcely a city at all. Yet it's a city in every other way, with great and justified pride in its corporate status.

Civic pride is at the heart of it, and in 2004 the city is already benefitting from the refurbishment of its ancient quay walls along the River Nore, and the increase in pedestrian zones. Enjoying its reputation as a major centre for civilisation and culture for well over 1500 years, Kilkenny city thrives on a diverse mixture of public debates about conservation, arts festivals, and a comedy festival of international standing.

Rivers define the county. Almost the entire eastern border is marked by the Barrow, which becomes eve more spectacularly lovely as it rolls gently through the beautiful Graiguenamanagh, then thrust towards the sea at the tiny river port of St Mullins. The southern border is marked by the broad tida sweep of the Suir, and this fine county is divided diagonally by the meandering of the most beautifu river of all, the Nore.

Invaders inevitably progressed up its tree-lined course past what is now the lovely river village of Inistioge towards the ancient site of Kilkenny city itself. They quickly became Kilkenny folk in the process, for thi is a land to call home. And a county that is passionate about its sport, too. Kilkenny retained the Al Ireland Hurling Champions in a courageously fought display against Cork in the fabulous Croke Par Stadium in Dublin on September 14th 2003. For good measure, the Kilkenny Minor Team (under 21s achieved victory over Galway on the same day The celebrations will be continuing well into 2004.

Local Attractions and Information

Callan, Edmund Rice House 056 772 5993
Gowran, Gowran Park Racecourse 056 772 6225
Inistioge, Woodstock Gardens 056 52699
Graiguenamanagh, Cushendale Woollen Mills 059 972 4118
Kilkenny, Kilkenny Castle 056 772 1450
Kilkenny, Cat Laughs Comedy Festival (May) 056 776 3416
Kilkenny, Rothe House (16c house, exhibitions) 056 772 2893
Kilkenny, City Tourist Information 056 779 4130
Thomastown, Jerpoint Abbey 056 772 4623
Thomastown, Kilfane Glen & Waterfall 056 772 4558
Thomastown, Mount Juliet Gardens 056 777 3000
Tullaroan, Kilkenny GAA Museum 056 69202

Bennettsbridge

Nicholas Mosse Pottery

CAFÉ

The Mill Bennettsbridge Co Kilkenny **Tel: 056 772 7105** Fax: 056 772 7491
Email: reception @nicholas mosse.com Web: www. nicholasmosse.com

One of the best reasons to venture out from Kilkenny city to nearby Bennettsbridge is to visit the Nicholas Mosse Pottery in their old riverside mill. Major renovations have been ongoing for some years and several storeys have now been converted to make spacious premises that allow visitors to watch potters at work and see the full range of products - including hand blown glass and table linens, blankets, quilts and knitwear, Clive Nunn furniture and even jewellery from leading craftspeople - as well as acres of the famous spongeware. Their informal little tea shop is on the first floor, overlooking the river, and offers reasonably priced wholesome snacks - including, of course, delicious freshly-baked scones made with the local Mosse's flour. Home baking is their thing, sold with good coffee or tea, not savoury food. **Seats 30.** Children welcome. Open Mon-Sat 9-6, Sun 1.30-5. Closed 25-26 Dec & 1 Jan. Amex, Diners, MasterCard, Visa, Laser. **Directions:** 4 miles south of Kilkenny, just before bridge turn off.

Callan

Ballaghtobin

Ⓝ COUNTRY HOUSE

Ballaghtobin Callan Co Kilkenny
Tel: 056 772 5227 Fax: 056 772 5712
Email: catherine@ballaghtobin.com Web: www.ballaghtobin.com

Set in parkland in the middle of a five hundred acre working farm, this immaculately maintained house has been in the Gabbett family for three hundred and fifty years. Graciously proportioned rooms are beautifully furnished and the spacious bedrooms - which Catherine Gabbett has decorated stylishly - all have antique furniture and every comfort, including lovely bathrooms with bath and overbath shower. The house is surrounded by large gardens, with a hard tennis court, croquet lawn - and even a ruined Norman church - for guests' use. No dinners, but there are good restaurants within a short drive, including The Motte at Inistioge (see entry). Children welcome (under 3 free in parents' room; cot available, €10). Pets allowed by arrangement. Garden, walking, tennis, croquet. **Rooms 3** (all en suite & no smoking). B&B €50, ss 10. Closed at Christmas. MasterCard, Visa. **Directions:** Past Golf Club on left, 2.3 miles, bear left; bear left at junction, entrance on left opposite Lodge.

Callan

The Old Charter House

Ⓝ PUB / B&B

Green Street Callan Co Kilkenny **Tel: 056 775 5902**

This attractive pub in the centre of Callan village serves appetising meals that are a cut above the usual bar food and offers accommodation too. There's a nice little breakfast menu in the morning and the choices for main meals cover everything from home-made soup of the day with freshly baked bread, through bruschetta and Greek salad, to serious main courses like chargrilled ribeye of beef with grain mustard dressing, sautéed onions & mushrooms, grilled tomatoes and fries. Desserts are home-made too (rare enough these days) and include old favourites like lemon meringue pie and cheesecake. Food served 10-3 & 6-8 daily: Breakfast menu 10-12 daily; L 12-3; D6-8.

Accommodation: Brand new rooms were opened in summer 2003; pleasantly furnished in pine, they are light and bright, with en-suite showers. B&B €35 pps. Closed 25 Dec, Good Fri. MasterCard, Visa, Laser, Switch. **Directions:** Centre of Callan villege.

Graiguenamanagh

Waterside

RESTAURANT / GUESTHOUSE

The Quay Graiguenamanagh Co Kilkenny
Tel: 059 972 4246 Fax: 059 972 4733
Email: info@waterside.iol.ie Web: www.watersideguesthouse.com

Brian and Brigid Roberts run a characterful restaurant with accommodation at this attractive old stone warehouse on the quayside, which was converted some years ago. A comfortable reception area leads into the restaurant, which is well-appointed and offers modern European food on varied and enticing menus - in very pleasant waterside surroundings. Brigid's à la carte dinner menus offer about half a dozen dishes on each course, using fresh local produce wherever possible,possibly including a speciality starter of Graiguenamanagh smoked eel with side salad & horseradish sauce - the eel fishery at Graiguenamanagh dates back to the Cistercian monks who built the town and weirs on the river, and is now active again. Aside from a range of mainstream choices (salmon, pork steak, striploin beef steaks) game might be offered in season (venison fillet in redcurrant & wild berry sauce, perhaps) and interesting vegetarian choices, such as puff pastry with roasted vegetables and orange scented hollandaise sauce, are always included. Finish with a nice homely dessert such as rhubarb fool with ginger cream, or an Irish cheese plate (choice of half a dozen ports to accompany, if you wish). Sunday lunch menus are more restricted, but similar in style. Service is friendly and willing under Brian's supervision - and the wine list is interesting and fairly priced. **Seats 35.** D 6.45-9.30 daily; L Sun only 12.30-2.30. Set L about €18, Set D about €30, also à la carte. Wines from about €19.

Guesthouse: The accommodation is quite simple but comfortable, with direct dial phones, tea/coffee making facilities and TV in all rooms. Some rooms at the top of the building are especially spacious and all overlook the river. Hillwalking holidays for small groups are offered (guide, maps, packed lunch, transport etc all arranged). Children welcome (under 3 free in parents' room, cot available without charge, baby sitting arranged). No pets. **Rooms 10** (all shower only) B&B €50pps, ss €15. * Weekend packages/ short breaks from €79 pps. No lift. Closed Christmas week. Amex, MasterCard, Visa, Laser. **Directions:** 17 miles south east of Kilkenny on banks of the River Barrow.

Inistioge

The Motte Restaurant

RESTAURANT

Plas Newydd Lodge Inistioge Co Kilkenny **Tel: 056 775 8655**
Email: atmotte@gofree.indigo.ie

On the edge of the picturesque village of Inistioge, with views of extensive parklands and the River Nore, The Motte is situated in the classically proportioned Plas Newydd Lodge, named in honour of the ladies of Llangollen, who eloped from Inistioge in the late 18th century. Although small in size, this unique country restaurant is big on personality - of the host, the irrepressible Tom Reade-Duncan, who makes every guest feel as welcome as the flowers in spring and greatly adds to the enjoyment of the occasion with his offbeat humour and helpful way with local knowledge, and of the chef, Alan Walton, as conveyed through his imaginative menus and distinctive style of cooking. The pair of them combine a special blend of classical style and (sometimes wacky) artistic inspiration. Menus are sensibly limited to five or six choices on each course - starters might include Mediterranean mezze with hummus, aubergine & pitta bread and quail terrine with dressed leaves, while main courses range from variations with local meats - classic sirloin steak with grain mustard sauce, perhaps, or pork tenderloin with black pudding and Hoi Sin sauce, to a sound fish dish such as lemon & garlic cod with tomato & basil. Vegetarians are always catered for (penne with spinach and blue cheese sauce is typical), side vegetables invariably imaginative and perfectly cooked and desserts - a delicious baked white chocolate cheesecake is a speciality. A private dining room has recently been added and small weddings or parties can be catered for. Toilets wheelchair accessible. **Seats 40** (Private room, 16). D only, Wed-Sat 7-9.30. Set D €33. House wine €16.; sc discretionary (except 10% on groups of 6+). Closed Mon & Tue, a1so Sun except on bank hol weekends; week Christmas, 1 week autumn. Amex, MasterCard, Visa, Laser, Switch. **Directions:** Opposite Village "name sign" on Kilkenny side of village.

Kilkenny

Butler House

GUESTHOUSE

16 Patrick Street Kilkenny Co Kilkenny
Tel: 056 772 2828 Fax: 056 776 5626
Email: res@butler.ie Web: www.butler.ie

Located close to Kilkenny Castle, this elegant Georgian townhouse was restored by the Irish State Design Agency in the 1970s - and the resulting combination of what was at the time contemporary design and period architecture leads to some interesting discussions. However bedrooms are unusually spacious - some have bow windows overlooking the gardens and Kilkenny Castle - and the accommodation is very adequate, with all the amenities now expected of good 3-star guesthouse accommodation (although bathrooms are curiously utilitarian and only have showers, even though there is plenty of space for more comfort). Three magnificent bow-windowed reception rooms are available for receptions and dinners. An excellent breakfast is served at the Kilkenny Design Centre, which is just across the gardens in the refurbished castle stables. Conferences/banqueting (120/70). Children welcome (under 4 free in parents' room; cot available without charge). Parking. Walking, garden. No pets. **Rooms 13** (1 suite, 4 superior,12 shower only, baby sitting arranged) B&B €85, ss €30, sc discretionary. Closed 23-29 Dec. Amex, Diners, MasterCard, Visa, Laser. **Directions:** City centre, close to Kilkenny Castle.

Kilkenny

Café Sol

Ⓝ **RESTAURANT / CAFÉ**

William Street Kilkenny Co Kilkenny **Tel: 056 776 4987**
Fax: 056 775 6720 Email: cafesolkk@eircom.net

Hugh Bergin and Noel McCarron took over this brightly painted terrace house just off the High Street in 2002, and it is a very popular daytime café and evening restaurant. A small interior porch leads in to a large room warmly decorated in yellow and terracotta with large paintings by local artist Catherine Barron, giving it a sunny, Mediterranean feeling; daytime is very casual with oilcloths or plain wooden table tops, and in the evening - when the building is floodlit and heavy white paper cloths and candles are used - there's a distinct change of atmosphere. Head chef Bill Tremewan's style is colourful and punchy - modern Irish dishes show some international influences based on local produce like delicious Lavistown sausages, beef and lamb from Mullins butchers, Ballyraggett free range eggs and fish from Duncannon, Co Wexford. An unusual speciality is slow-roasted Kilkea lamb with date & forest mushroom stuffing, with port & honey jus and roasted vegetables but some dishes are quite spicy - a beef or chicken salad with Thai chilli dressing, for instance, which is served as a starter or light lunch dish. Vegetarians always do well here, too - provençal bean stew with fresh herbs and sour cream is typical - - and lovely desserts might include almost-forgotten classics like lemon possett with home-made shortbread - delicious. Presentation - on stylish plain white plates - does a lot for the food, and is not over-worked. This is an interesting restaurant, offering something different from the 'sameness' of so many menus, and at reasonable prices. **Seats 60.** Air conditioning. Open all day Mon-Sat, 10-5, & Tue-Sat D from 6.30. A la carte. Wines from €13.80. Amex, MasterCard, Visa. **Directions:** Coming from castle - up High St. - 2nd turn left opposite Town Hall.

Kilkenny

Kilkenny Design Centre

féile bia **RESTAURANT**

Castle Yard Kilkenny Co Kilkenny **Tel: 056 772 2118** Fax: 056 776 5905
Email: info@kilkennydesign.com Web: Kilkennydesign.com

CREATIVE USE OF VEGETABLES AWARD

Situated in what was once the stables and dairy of Kilkenny Castle - and overlooking the craft courtyard - this first floor self-service restaurant (above the temptations of a different sort on display in the famous craft shop below) is deservedly popular. Wholesome, healthy and absolutely delicious fare is consistently provided at very reasonable prices here, and the room is well-designed to allow attractive and accessible display of their wonderful food. Everything is freshly prepared every day, home baking is a strong point and salads, especially, are always colourful and full of life - fresh beetroot, asparagus, spinach, red onion, coriander & crumbly Lavistown local cheese makes a salad worth travelling for, for example, and the selection changes all the time. Vegetarian dishes like penne with tomato & parmesan, or red onion & brie tart, for example, are invariably tempting, and contemporary cooking generally is well-represented - in, for example, a soup plate option that changes daily and offers an unusual sandwich such as foccacia with caramelised red onion & Lavistown cheese, with the daily soup choice - an unusual carrot & mint, perhaps, served piping hot. There are also delicious old-fashioned bakes like chicken & broccoli crumble, and vegetables are taken seriously: carrots, for example, are served seasoned with cracked pepper, cream and a little olive oil, and baby potatoes are seasoned with honey, cumin, ginger, balsamic vinegar and olive oil, while broccoli and cauliflower have a tangy dressing to give them a lift: details that make all the difference to simple foods. It is good to see local ingredients used so well in such a fresh and appetising way - if only every town could have a place like this. Toilets wheelchair accessible. Lift. **Seats 180** (private room 50). Meals Mon-Sat 10-7 (Sun & bank hols from 11). Self service. Closed Sundays Jan-Mar. Amex, Diners, MasterCard, Visa, Laser. **Directions:** Opposite Kilkenny Castle.

Kilkenny

Kilkenny Ormonde Hotel

féile bia **HOTEL / RESTAURANT**

Ormonde Street Kilkenny Co Kilkenny
Tel: 056 772 3900 Fax: 056 772 3977
Email: info@kilkennyormonde.com Web: www.kilkennyormonde.com

Sister establishment to the famous Aghadoe Heights Hotel, Killarney (see entry), this modern hotel enjoys an outstandingly convenient central location for both business and leisure guests, beside (but not adjacent to) a multi-storey carpark and within walking distance of the whole city. Spacious public areas include an impressive foyer, the informal Earls Bistro - where sassy international cooking is available at lunch and dinner daily - and an elegant restaurant, Fredricks (see below). Generously large bedrooms are furnished to a high standard in a pleasing contemporary style, with ISDN lines and safes in addition to the more usual amenities, and both business/conference and on-site leisure facilities are excellent. Friendly, professional staff provide outstanding service, ensuring a pleasant stay or well-run business event - the hotel's excellent conference centre and 10 fully equipped meeting rooms offer the region's premier conference and business venue and well-trained staff to match. Conference/banqueting (500/400). Business centre, video conferencing. Leisure centre, 21m swimming pool, crèche. **Rooms 118** (6 suites, 6 executive rooms, 59 no smoking, 4 disabled). Lift. 24 hour room service. B&B €127.50pps, ss €32.50. Children welcome (under12s free in parents' room, cots available without charge, bay sitting arranged). Earls Bistro: L Mon-Fri 12.30-2, D Thu-Sat 6.30-9.30; bar meals also available: Sun 1-2.30. Wed-Sat 3-9pm. Closed 25 Dec.

Fredricks: The restaurant bears the same name as the Killarney restaurant that has earned such a high reputation for Aghadoe Heights over the years. It is a very comfortable, rather clubby, room with well-spaced, elegantly appointed tables and a pleasing ambience. Head chef Mark Gafney, who is also responsible for the food at Earls Bistro (see above), presents international menus based mainly on carefully sourced produce - some, such as Lavistown cheese, is clearly local; cooking is quite ambitious and service, as in other areas of the hotel, is a strong point. The restaurant is also used for breakfast. **Seats 68.** Air conditioning. Toilets wheelchair accessible. Open D daily 7-9.30, L Sun only12.30-2.30. Set D from €30. House wine €24.95. sc discretionary. Closed L except Sun. Amex, MasterCard, Visa, Laser. **Directions:** Kilkenny city centre off the parade opposite castle.

Kilkenny

Kilkenny River Court Hotel

féile bia HOTEL

The Bridge John Street Kilkenny Co Kilkenny
Tel: 056 772 3388 Fax: 056 772 3389
Email: reservations@kilrivercourt.com Web: www.kilrivercourt.com

Beautifully situated in a courtyard just off the narrow, bustling streets of the city centre, with only the River Nore separating it from Kilkenny Castle, this fine hotel enjoys the city's premier location. While equally attractive for business or leisure - bedrooms and public areas are all finished to a high standard and the Health & Leisure Club provides excellent facilities for health, fitness and beauty treatments - the hotel has established a special reputation for conferences and incentive programmes, with state-of-the-art facilities for groups of varying numbers and plenty to do when off duty in the city, as well as outdoor pursuits - golf, fishing, equestrian - nearby. Conference/Banqueting (210/160). Leisure centre, indoor swimming pool. Children welcome (under 3 free in parents' room, cot available without charge, baby sitting arranged). Limited private parking (access can be a little difficult). Short breaks/ special interest breaks offered. **Rooms 90** (2 suites, 41 executive, 19 no smoking, 2 for disabled). Lift. 24 hour room service. B&B from about €80pps, ss about €40. Closed 25-26 Dec.

The Riverside Restaurant: The restaurant, which is well-located within the hotel to take full advantage of the riverside setting, is an elegant room, with beautifully appointed tables, silver candle sticks and a grand piano conveying a sense of occasion. The atmosphere is that of a restaurant rather than a hotel dining room and head chef Mark Phelan's menus and cooking style reinforce that impression. The à la carte offers 8-10 choices on each course and, while it would be interesting to see evidence of local ingredients on the menu, cooking is generally good - and an unusual house speciality worth trying is baked saddle of rabbit with pink roasted wood pigeon, with quails egg & chervil vinegar. The early dinner and Sunday lunch menus are particularly good value, and charming service adds to the occasion. **Seats 80** (private room 40). D daily 6-9.15, L Sun only 12.30-3. Early D €24 (6-7.30); Set D €40, also à la carte. Set Sun L €24. [Food is also served in the Riverview Bar, 12-6 daily.] Amex, Diners, MasterCard, Visa. **Directions:** Follow city centre signs,directly opposite Kilkenny Castle. Two archways on the Dublin side of Bridge - use the castle as a landmark.

Kilkenny

Lacken House

féile bia RESTAURANT WITH ROOMS

Dublin Road Kilkenny Co Kilkenny
Tel: 056 776 1085 Fax: 056 776 2435
Email: info@lackenhouse.ie Web: www.lackenhouse.ie

This period house on the edge of Kilkenny city has been home to the leading restaurant in the area for over 15 years. It was taken over by Jackie and Trevor Toner in 2001 and they have achieved their intention to run it in the same way and to maintain the high standards of food and hospitality for which it was well- known. The existing staff were retained, and head chef Barry Foley continues the practice of using the best local produce and mainly organic vegetables and fruit. The style is a combination of traditional and modern cooking - and there is a willingness to meet any special requests wherever possible, whether for dietary reasons or simply preference. Menus are well-balanced, with more seafood than might be expected in a midlands restaurant, but local meats are exceptional: a speciality fillet beef dish, with Clonakilty mash, toasted black pudding and crispy bacon and wholegrain mustard sauce is not to be missed - and the rack of Kilkenny lamb, cooked with a crunchy herb crust and served with rosemary jus - is just as good. In addition to vegetarian options on the main menu, a short separate menu is also offered. An irresistible dessert selection offers treats fir different moods ('The Refreshing', 'The Indulgent') some unusual home-made ice creams - and a farmhouse cheese selection comes with scrumptious home-baked biscuits. Private parties and functions are also catered for (conference/banqueting 25/40). Children welcome. **Seats 40.** (Private room, 20). D Tue-Sun, 6.30-10; 'Value' menu €30 (Sun-Thu), Set D €39; house wine €19. Closed Mon (also Sun during winter except bank hol weekends) 24-27 Dec.

Accommodation: Guest bedrooms vary in size and outlook but all have phone, TV, tea/coffee-making trays. Excellent breakfasts are served in the restaurant. Room service (limited hours). Children welcome (under 4 free in parents' room, cot available free of charge, baby sitting arranged). Garden. Gourmet Weekend/short breaks offered. **Rooms 10** (2 junior suites, 5 shower only, all no smoking). B&B €60 pps, ss €15. Amex, MasterCard, Visa, Laser. **Directions:** On N10 Carlow/Dublin Road into Kilkenny City.

Kilkenny

Marble City Bar

ATMOSPHERIC PUB

66 High Street Kilkenny Co Kilkenny **Tel: 056 776 1143**
Email: langtons @oceanfree.net

This historic bar has quite recently been redesigned by the cutting edge international designer David Collins, who was brought in to cast his highly original eye over the premises. Although initially controversial (especially the ultra-modern stained glass window which now graces the otherwise traditional frontage and looks strange from the street but much better from the inside looking out), it is a wonderful space to be in and attracts a varied clientèle, ranging from the merely curious to fans of all ages and many walks of life who are there to enjoy the vibrant atmosphere - and make the most of their excellent contemporary European bar food. The food side of the operation is taken commendably seriously and standards have, on the whole, been maintained; although it is not be immediately obvious from the menu, ingredients are well-sourced and many local ingredients are used - so that, for example, a dish like confit of pork sausages with creamy potatoes and caramelised onion gravy is most likely to be based on the superb lean sausages hand-made nearby by Olivia Goodwillie (who also makes the wonderful Lavistown cheese), and the fresh cod'n'chips in a crispy beer batter will be just in from Dunmore East. Good service, even at busy times; well chosen small wine list; wines available by the glass. Food service begins with breakfast, from 10am daily; main menus from 12 noon-8.30 pm. Closed 25 Dec & Good Fri. Diners, MasterCard, Visa. **Directions:** Main Street, city centre.

Kilkenny

Rinuccini Restaurant

RESTAURANT / ACCOMMODATION

1 The Parade Kilkenny Co Kilkenny
Tel: 056 776 1575 Fax: 056 775 1288
Email: info@rinuccini.com Web: www.rinuccini.com

Antonio and Marion Cavaliere's well-established Italian restaurant is in a semi-basement in the impressive terrace opposite Kilkenny Castle and the closely packed tables are an indication of its popularity. When empty it looks a little bleak, but the room quickly fills up with a healthy mixture of locals (who clearly have their preferred tables) and tourists. The cooking style is mainly classic Italian, with quite an extensive à la carte evening menu plus a shorter one available as an option at lunchtime. Service is prompt, from the time fresh bread and butter is delivered speedily with the menu. Food is characterised by freshness of ingredients and a high standard of cooking: excellent minestrone (a classic test), a superb plate of house antipasti (Parma ham, smoked pork, two different salame, barbecue-seared aubergine slices, pungent roast peppers, black olives & garlic toasted foccacia) delicious seafood and memorable pasta. The simple things are right, which is always a good sign - but that doesn't necessarily preclude luxury: spaghetti with fresh lobster is one of the house specialities. Great service and outstanding value for money too - no wonder this place is always so full of happy people. **Seats 56.** L daily 12-2.30, D daily 6-10.30 (Sun D 6-9.30); à la carte. House wine from €19.95

Accommodation: Seven large, en-suite rooms are offered with air conditioning, TV, tea/coffee facilities and trouser press with iron. A breakfast tray is supplied, for you to make up your own continental breakfast in the room. **Rooms 7** (1 junior suite, all shower-only & no-smoking) Room rate: €50 (max 2 guests). Amex, Diners, MasterCard, Visa, Laser. **Directions:** Opposite Kilkenny Castle.

Kilkenny

Zuni

HOTEL / RESTAURANT

26 Patrick Street Kilkenny Co Kilkenny **Tel: 056 772 3999**
Fax: 056 775 6400 Email: info@zuni.ie Web: www.zuni.ie

Although Zuni is an hotel, it is for the restaurant that most people come here: an oasis of contemporary chic in this bustling city, it is well established as an important address for discerning diners. There's a separate entrance on the side of the building so you don't have to go through the hotel and the room is large and airy, overlooking a courtyard which is set up with tables in fine weather. A warm reception is promptly followed by the offer of delcious breads - and the tone is set for an enjoyable, highly proficient meal. Head chef Maria Raftery, who joined the hotel in spring 2001, has a great kitchen team who cook calmy and efficiently in full view of diners; Maria offers eclectic menus at lunch and dinner, her colourful, attractively presented food clearly pleases locals as much as visitors. Smart salads make sassy starters and an example of simple excellence, taken from a lunch menu, might be beer battered cod with French fries: perfectly cooked, succulent fish in a light batter that stays crisp to the last bite, served with excellent crisp, floury chips and well-judged chilli mayonnaise: perfectly seasoned, perfectly cooked. Restaurant **Seats 60.** (Breakfast); L Tue-Sun 12.30-2.30 (Sun from 1), D 6.30-19.30 (Sun 6-9). 'Value' D €30 (Sun-Thu only). A la carte. House wine from €19.50. Restaurant closed Mon.

Accommodation: This contemporary hotel offers a more youthful style of accommodation than other comparable establishments; although comfortable, the minimalist decor is difficult to keep immaculate and there is evidence of wear and tear (major refurbishment is planned). Rooms have phones (& ISDN lines) and TV, although no tea/coffee-making facilities. Breakfast is served in the restaurant. Children welcome (under 3s free in parents' room; cot available, €25.) No pets. **Rooms 13** (8 shower only, 1 for disabled). Lift. B&B €80ps, no ss. Hotel closed 24-28 Dec. Amex, MasterCard, Visa, Laser, Switch. **Directions:** 200 yards from Kilkenny Castle.

Maddoxtown

Blanchville House

COUNTRY HOUSE Dunbell Maddoxtown Co Kilkenny **Tel: 056 772 7197** Fax: 056 772 7636
Email: info@blanchville.ie Web: www.blanchville.ie

Tim and Monica Phelan's elegant Georgian house is just 5 miles out of Kilkenny city, surrounded by its own farmland and gardens. It's easy to spot - there's a folly in its grounds. It's a very friendly, welcoming place and the house has an airy atmosphere, with matching well-proportioned dining and drawing rooms on either side of the hall and the pleasant, comfortably furnished bedrooms in period style all overlook attractive countryside. Dinner is available to residents (bookings required before noon) and, like the next morning's excellent breakfast, is taken at the communal mahogany dining table. Not suitable for children under 10, although a cot is available for young babies (baby sitting arranged). Well-behaved dogs are permitted by arrangement. The Coach House has been renovated to make four self-catering coach houses. Walking, garden, cycling. **Rooms 6** (5 en-suite, 1 with private bathroom, 3 shower only, all non-smoking). B&B €50-60 pps, ss €10. Closed 1 Nov-1 Mar. MasterCard, Visa, Laser, Switch. **Directions:** From Kilkenny take N10, 1st right 1/2 mile after 'The Pike'. Continue 2 miles to crossroads (Connolly's pub). Take left, large stone entrance 1 mile on left.

Thomastown

Ballyduff House

COUNTRY HOUSE Thomastown Co Kilkenny **Tel: 056 775 8488**
Email: ballyd@gofree.indigo.ie

Set in fine rolling countryside in its own farmland and grounds, Breda Thomas's lovely 18th century house overlooking the River Nore is blessed with an utterly restful location. Breda is a relaxed and welcoming host and offers exceptionally spacious and comfortable accommodation in large period bedrooms with generous bathrooms and beautiful views over the river or gardens. Guests also have the use of spacious well-proportioned day rooms furnished with family antiques - and many return often, finding this rural retreat a warm and welcoming home from home. Beautiful walks on the estate. Fishing (salmon, trout). Riding, hunting and other country pursuits can be arranged. Children welcome. *Self-catering accommodation also offered at Ballyduff Castle, adjoining Ballyduff House (2-4 bedrooms). **Rooms 3.** B&B about €40, ss about €10. **No Credit Cards. Directions:** 3 miles south of Thomastown.

Thomastown

Hudsons

Ⓝ RESTAURANT Station Road Thomastown Co Kilkenny
Tel: 056 779 3900 Fax: 056 779 3901

Richard and Kyra Hudson opened their stylish, confident new restaurant in the summer of 2003 and it has been an immediate hit. The interior is lovely, with comfortable dark brown leather high-back chairs, wooden floors and rich, warm colours; a dramatic flower arrangement sets the tone on entering and a small bar, with heavy cream curtains, leather sofas and stools, offers a comfortable spot to look at menus and take in the atmosphere, before proceeding to the restaurant - which overlooks a charming old stone-walled garden at the back, with a romantic arch and trailing climbers: a delightful contrast to the modern interior. Head chef Steve Smith's menus are contemporary, as would be expected, with plenty of modern classics to choose from (Caesar salad, beef carpaccio, seared salmon) and a range of char-grills (which should please golfers down from nearby Mount Juliet, especially), but there are also some less usual dishes - Cornish crab potato boxty with wholegrain mustard & tarragon aioli, for example, and pot roast duck, on a bed of mixed greens, with puy lentils & hoi sin jus. Side orders are charged separately on the à la carte, which can mount up quickly, but set menus offer very good value. This is a very pleasing restaurant, offering stylishly presented lively, accurate cooking, and friendly, attentive service under the management of the proprietors. It is a very welcome addition to dining choices in the area and deserves to succeed. Children welcome (separate menu available on application). **Seats 70.** D Tue-Sun 6-10, L Sun only 12.30-3. Set D (Wed & Fri) €24.95; otherwise D à la carte. Set Sun L €26. House wine €24. MasterCard, Visa, Laser. **Directions:** On road to Mount Juliet from Dublin to Waterford.

Thomastown

Mount Juliet Conrad

HOTEL / RESTAURANT

Thomastown Co Kilkenny
Tel: 056 777 3000 Fax: 056 777 3019
Email: mountjulietinfo@conradhotels.com Web: www.mountjulietconrad.com

Built over 200 years ago by the Earl of Carrick, and named in honour of his wife, Mount Juliet House is one of Ireland's finest Georgian houses and retains an aura of eighteenth century grandeur. Lying amidst 1500 acres of unspoilt woodland, pasture and formal gardens beside the River Nore, it is one of Europe's greatest country estates, with world class sporting amenities and conference facilities. The elegance of the old house has been painstakingly preserved, so that the hand-carved Adam fireplaces, walls and ceilings decorated with intricate stucco work and many other original features can still be enjoyed today - and, since forming an alliance with the Conrad group of hotels in 2002, refurbishment and maintenance programmes have been scaled up. Bedrooms have period decor with all the comfort of modern facilities and, as well as the main house, additional rooms on the estate are in The Club, and the Rose Garden two-bedroom lodges. The top-ranking Jack Nicklaus-designed golf course hosted the Irish Open for three years consecutively (from 1993 to 1995) and, more recently, the WGC American Express World Golf Championships in September 2002. Conference/banqueting (75/70). Children welcome (under 12 free sharing with two adults; cot available, €25). Equestrian; angling. Clay pigeon shooting, archery, tennis, croquet, cycling, walking trails. Spa & Health Club (15m swimming pool). No pets. **Rooms 59** (2 suites, 2 for disabled). No lift. Room rate about €290. Open all year.

Lady Helen Dining Room: Although grand, this graceful high-ceilinged room, softly decorated in pastel shades and with sweeping views over the grounds, is not forbidding and has a pleasant atmosphere. To match these beautiful surroundings, classic daily dinner menus based on local ingredients are served, including wild salmon from the River Nore, vegetables and herbs from the Mount Juliet garden and regional Irish farmhouse cheese. Service is efficient and friendly. Extensive international wine list. **Seats 55** (private room, 25). Toilets wheelchair accessible. D daily 6-10, L Sun only 12-3. A la carte. House wine about €23. * It can be difficult to get a reservation at the Lady Helen Dining Room, especially for non-residents, so booking well ahead is advised. A very attractive alternative dining option is offered at the newer contemporary restaurant, Kendals, which is open for breakfast & dinner daily, 7.30am-10pm. *Informal dining is available in The Club, Presidents Bar (8am-9pm). Amex, Diners, MasterCard, Visa. **Directions:** M7 from Dublin, then M9 towards Waterford, arriving at Thomastown on the N9 via Carlow and Gowran.

COUNTY LAOIS

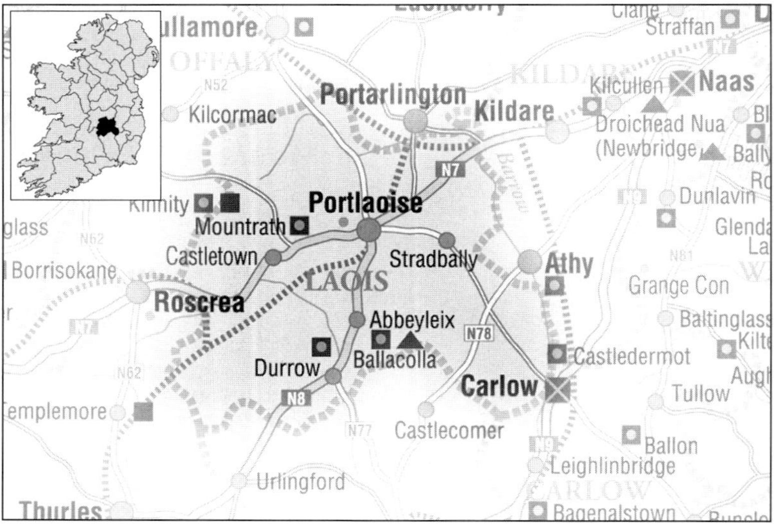

With its territory traversed by the rail and road links from Dublin to Cork and Limerick, Laois is often glimpsed only fleetingly by inter-city travellers. But as with any Irish county, it is a wonderfully rewarding place to visit as soon as you move off the main roads. And a salutary place to visit as well. For, in the eastern part, between Stradbally and Portlaois, there's the Rock of Dunamase, that fabulous natural fortress which many occupiers inevitably assumed to be impregnable. Dunamase's remarkably long history of fortifications and defences and sieges and eventual captures has a relevance and a resonance for all times and all peoples and all places.

But there's much more to Laois than mournful musings on the ultimate vanity of human ambitions. With its border shared with Carlow along the River Barrow, eastern Laois comfortably reflects Carlow's quiet beauty. To the northwest, we find that Offaly bids strongly to have the Slieve Bloom Mountains thought of as an Offaly hill range, but in fact there's more of the Slieve Blooms in Laois than Offaly, and lovely hills they are too. And though the River Nore may be thought of as quintessential Kilkenny, long before it gets anywhere near Kilkenny it is quietly building as it meanders across much of Laois, gathering strength from the weirdly-named Delour, Tonet, Gully, Erskina and Goul rivers on the way.

Along the upper reaches of the Nore in west Laois, the neat little village of Castletown has long been a tidy place. Castletown has for the past seventeen years climbed steadily up the rankings in the annual Tidy Towns contest. Having been the tidiest village in all Ireland in 2001, Castletown repeated the performance and then some in 2002, and at the annual awards ceremony in Dublin Castle, it was announced that Castletown was both the tidiest village, and the national overall winner in all categories. This high standard has been maintained, and the most recent National Awards ceremony on September 8th 2003 saw Castletown receiving a Gold Medal.

Local Attractions and Information

Abbeyleix, Abbeyleix Heritage House 0502 31653
Abbeyleix, Sensory Gardens 0502 31325
Ballinakill, Heywood (Lutyens gardens) 0502 33563
Donaghmore, Castletown House Open Farm 0505 46415
Donaghmore, Donaghmore Workhouse Museum 0505 46212
Emo, Emo Court (Gandon house & gardens) 0502 26573
Portlaois, Dunamaise Theatre & Arts Centre 0502 63356
Portlaois, Tourist Information 0502 21178
Slieve Bloom, Slieve Bloom Rural Development Assoc. 0509 37299
Stradbally, National Steam Traction Rally (August) 0502 25444

Abbeyleix

Morrissey's

ATMOSPHERIC PUB

Main Street Abbeyleix Co Laois **Tel: 0502 31281**

One of Ireland's finest and best-loved pubs, Morrissey's is a handsome building on the wide main street of this attractive little town. It's a great place to lift the spirits while taking a break between Dublin and Cork – food is not its strength but a quick cup of coffee and enjoyment of the atmosphere is sometimes all that's needed. It first opened as a grocery in 1775, when it started life as a thatched one-storey house and has been in the ownership of the current proprietor, P.J. Mulhall, since 1934. In 1880 it was rebuilt as the lofty two-storey premises we see today, with high shelf-lined walls and a pot belly stove to gather round on cold days. They have a list of people who have served their time at Morrissey's since 1850 – and, true to the old tradition, television, cards and singing are not allowed. No children after 7 pm. Closed 25 Dec & Good Fri. **Directions:** In the village, on the right heading south.

Abbeyleix

Preston House

féile bia **RESTAURANT WITH ROOMS**

Main Street Abbeyleix Co Laois
Tel: 0502 31432 Fax: 0502 31432

A sign on the pavement outside Michael and Allison Dowling's attractive creeper-clad house welcomes people to their friendly and informal country-style restaurant. Allison's good home cooking starts off with delicious scones, served with tea or coffee and home-made preserves before lunch, at which time the choice widens to a short but tempting à la carte – typically including starters like smoked haddock chowder with freshly-baked brown bread or chicken liver paté with toast and salad followed, perhaps, by fish of the day or a speciality such as stirfry beef with roast vegetables. Vegetarians do very well here too, so if you're in a meat-free mood you can look forward to dishes like grilled goats cheese with salad and relish or penne pasta with tomato & basil sauce. Delicious desserts include sophisticated classics like crème brûlée but there are always simple, wholesome options too, like apple crumble or fresh fruits with low fat yogurt. Dinner menus are also à la carte and, although more formal and offering a wider choice, the same philosophy applies: this is deliciously healthy, well-balanced food with the emphasis on freshness and making best use of local produce - and thanks to the long opening hours and reasonable prices, it is exceptionally accessible. A first-floor ballroom runs across the whole width of the building and, with a library area up a few stairs at one end providing comfortable seating for non-participants and a minstrels' gallery at the other, it makes a superb venue for local events. Not suitable for children under 4 after 6 pm. **Seats 45.** No smoking restaurant. L Tue-Sun,12.30-2.45 (Sun 1-3); D Thu-Sat 6.30-9. Early D €22 (6-8pm); Set D €35; also à la carte. House wine €18.50; sc discretionary (10% on parties of 6+). Closed Mon, Christmas period.

Accommodation: The four large, high-ceilinged bedrooms are interestingly furnished with antiques and unusual en-suite facilities have been cleverly incorporated without spoiling the proportions of these fine rooms – by hiding them in what appears to be a long wardrobe but which opens up to reveal a row of individual facilities - shower, WC etc. Children welcome (under 5 free in parents' room). Pets permitted by arrangement. No smoking establishment. **Rooms 4** (all shower only). Room service (limited hours). B&B from €42.50 pps, ss €5. MasterCard, Visa, Laser. **Directions:** In the village, a few doors down from Morrisey's.

Ballacolla

Foxrock Inn

PUB / B&B

Clough Ballacolla Co Laois **Tel: 0502 38637** Fax: 0502 38637
Email: foxrockinn@eircom.net Web: www.foxrockinn.com

Sean and Marian Hyland run a very friendly, relaxed little place here for lovers of the country life. Hill walking, fishing (coarse and game), golf and pitch & putt are all in the neighbourhood (golf and fishing packages are a speciality) and they'll make packed lunches to see you through the day. Evening meals, an open fire and traditional music (Tuesdays, May-September) make the pub a welcoming place to come back to and there is accommodation just up the stairs, in five simple but comfortable rooms (all en-suite). Children welcome (under 2 free in parents' room, cot available without charge) B&B €35 pps, ss €5. Closed 25 Dec & Good Fri. Visa. **Directions:** On the R434, which links Durrow (N4) and Borris-in-Ossory (N7). Sign-posted off N7 and N8.

Durrow

Castle Durrow

HOTEL

Durrow Co Laois **Tel: 0502 36555** Fax: 0502 36559
Email: info@castledurrow.com Web: www.castledurrow.com

The restoration of this substantial 18th century country house and grounds has clearly been a labour of love for proprietors Peter and Shelly Stokes - and its position roughly halfway between Dublin and Cork makes it easily accessible for short breaks from either city, or a good place to break the journey. It is an impressive building with some magnificent features and very spacious, luxurious accommodation in high-ceilinged, individually decorated rooms and suites with views over the surrounding parkland and countryside; some equally luxurious ground floor rooms were opened in 2003 in a wing - particularly suitable for guests attending the weddings which have become a speciality, as they are convenient to the banqueting suite and avoid disturbing guests in the main house. Public rooms include a large drawing room/bar, which is furnished in a rather wacky style (the bar is strangely out of character with the rest of the house, especially when a commercial radio station is playing loudly); but it is quite comfortable nonetheless, and there is a lovely dining room with a gently pastoral outlook at the back of the house, where dinner is available to guests and also non-residents by reservation (Peter Stokes previously owned Coopers restaurants in Dublin). Major restoration work has been done in the grounds, including the old walled garden at the back which showed signs of beginning a new lease of life at the time of the Guide's visit. Much work clearly remains to be done (including staff training) but this brave venture has made noticeable progress since opening and is an interesting place to visit. **Rooms 24.** B&B about €120 pps. Open all year. Amex, Diners, MasterCard, Visa. **Directions:** On main Dublin-Cork road, N8.

Mountrath

Roundwood House

COUNTRY HOUSE

Mountrath Co Laois **Tel: 0502 32120** Fax: 0502 32711
Email: roundwood@eircom.net Web: hidden-ireland.com/roundwood

Ah, Roundwood - it is not, perhaps, for everyone but it is difficult to see how anybody could fail to love this unspoilt early Georgian house, which lies secluded in mature woods of lime, beech and chestnut, at the foot of the Slieve Bloom mountains. A sense of history and an appreciation of genuine hospitality are all that is needed to make the most of a stay here – forget about co-ordinated decor and immaculate maintenance, just relax and share the immense pleasure and satisfaction that Frank and Rosemarie Kennan derive from the years of renovation work they have put into this wonderful property. Although unconventional in some ways, the house is extremely comfortable and well-heated (with central heating as well as log fires) and all the bathrooms have been recently renovated (all have full bath). The Kennans also have several beautifully converted rooms at the back and further outbuildings, The Coach House, The Forge and The Cottage, available for self-catering. Restoration is an ongoing process and an extraordinary (and historically unique) barn is possibly the next stage; this enterprise defies description, but don't leave Roundwood without seeing it. Children, who always love the unusual animals and their young in the back yard, are very welcome and Rosemarie does a separate tea for them. Residents dinner (8 pm) is based on the best local and seasonal ingredients (notably locally reared beef and lamb); Rosemarie's food suits the house perfectly – good home cooking without unnecessary frills – and Frank is an excellent host. A relatively extensive wine list includes a generous choice of half bottles. Children welcome (under 3 free in parents' room, cot available without charge; playroom; baby sitting arranged). Garden, croquet, boule, walking - there is a mile long walk in the grounds and garden renovation is scheduled for 2004. Stabling available at the house; horse riding nearby. Golf nearby. Pets allowed in some areas. **Rooms 10** (all en-suite & 4 no-smoking). B&€75 pps, ss €25. No sc. D €45 (non-residents welcome by reservation if there is room); please book by noon. Closed Sun & Mon except for guests, 25 Dec & all Jan. Amex, Diners, MasterCard, Visa, Laser. **Directions:** On the left, 3 miles from Mountrath, on R440.

Portlaoise

Ivyleigh House

GUESTHOUSE

Bank Place Church Street Portlaoise Co Laois
Tel: 0502 22081 Fax: 0502 63343
Email: info@ivyleigh.com Web: www.ivyleigh.com

This lovely early Georgian house is set back from the road only by a tiny neatly box-hedged formal garden, but has a coachyard (with parking), outhouses and a substantial lawned garden at the back. It is a listed building and has clearly fallen into good hands as the present owners, Dinah and Jerry Campion, have restored it immaculately and furnished it beautifully in a style that successfully blends period elements with bold contemporary strokes, which gives it great life. Two sitting rooms (one with television) are always available to guests and there's a fine dining room with a large communal table and a smaller one at the window. Bedrooms are the essence of comfort, spacious, elegant, with working sash windows and everything absolutely top of the range including pocket-sprung mattresses and even real linen sheets and pillowcases. Large shower rooms have many excellent details and terrific power showers (and, unusually, the space to make the most of them) although those who would give anything for a bath to soak in will be disappointed. But it is perhaps at breakfast that this superb guesthouse is at its best. An extensive menu shows a commitment to using quality local produce that turns out to be even better than anticipated: imaginative, perfectly cooked and beautifully presented. Fruits and yogurts include natural yogurt with geranium jelly and poached fruit in season; 'perfect porridge' comes with cream - cereals include home-made muesli - and hot dishes include wonderfully creamy baked free range eggs with cream & cheese, and Cashel Blue cheesecakes - light and delicious, like fritters - come with mushrooms and tomatoes. There is also, of course, the option of a Full Irish Breakfast and - very unusually - there's a vegetarian variation on the great traditional fry. The details that count - freshly-baked brown bread, leaf tea or freshly brewed coffee, smooth, friendly service and meticulous timing of hot dishes - all add up to an exceptional experience. And through it all Dinah Campion (who must rise at dawn to bake the bread) is charming, efficient and hospitable. This is one of the best guest houses in Ireland and is well placed for touring the midlands, to break a journey, or for a short break from Dublin. No evening meals, but the Campions direct guests to good restaurants nearby. **Rooms 6** (all shower only & no smoking); phone, tea/coffee facilities. B&B€55, ss €20. Closed Christmas period. MasterCard, Visa. **Directions:** Centre of town follow signs for multi-storey car park, 30 metres from carpark.

Portaoise

The Kitchen & Foodhall

féile bia **RESTAURANT** Hynds Square Portlaoise Co Laois **Tel: 0502 62061** Fax: 0502 62075

Jim Tynan's smashing restaurant and food shop is definitely worth a detour into town. Delicious home-made food, an open fire, relaxed atmosphere - a perfect place to break a journey or for a special visit. The foodhall stocks a wide range of Irish speciality food products (and many excellent imported ones as well) and also sells products made on the premises: home-made terrines and breads for example (including gluten-free breads - which are also available in the restaurant) lovely home-bakes like Victoria sponges, crumbles and bread & butter pudding. You can buy home-made ready meals too and any of the wines from the shop can be bought for the restaurant without a corkage charge. The restaurant offers a great choice of wholesome fare, including at least three vegetarian dishes each day - old favourites like nut roast, perhaps and others like roasted vegetable & cream cheese flan and spinach roulade with cream cheese & pepper. Hereford premium beef is typical of the Irish produce in which such pride is taken - and lunches are served with a wholesome selection of vegetables or salads. **Seats 200** (daytime). Open all day Mon-Sat, 9-5.30; L12.30-2.30. Set L from about €9. D à la carte. House wine €9.99. Wheelchair access. Closed 25 Dec-3 Jan. Amex, Diners, MasterCard, Visa, Laser. **Directions:** In the centre of Portlaoise, beside the Courthouse.

Portlaoise

Kingfisher Restaurant

féile bia **RESTAURANT** Old AIB Bank Main Street Portlaoise Co Laois
Tel: 0502 62500 Fax: 0502 62700
Email: kingfisherrestaurant.com Web: www.kingfisherrestaurant.com

Situated in the centre of Portlaoise in the old AIB bank, this atmospheric and highly regarded Indian restaurant specialises in Punjabi cuisine. You enter into a very large, high-ceilinged room (the former banking hall), with a reception area off it where you are greeted by immaculately attired and genuinely friendly staff. The decor is unusual, using pale washes to portray the crumbling sandstone walls of an ancient Indian temple, including disintegrating murals with some entertainingly mischievous details. The relaxed ambience and people of all ages enjoying themselves makes for a very atmospheric room. Simple table presentation and enormously long menus may send out warning signals, but there are poppadums with dipping sauces to see you through the decision-making phases and, once food appears, it is clearly accomplished cooking, without recourse to elaborate presentation but well-flavoured with the fresh flavours of individual ingredients and authentic spicing creating satisfying combinations - in dishes that vary from creamy styles with almonds, to very spicy dishes with 'angry' green peppers. Tandoori, balti, biryani, 'exquisite' dishes and 'old favourite' dishes like korma, rogan josh, do piaza are all there, but they are well executed, served with professionalism and charm, and very reasonably priced (main courses about €11.50-17.95). **Seats 65.** L Wed-Fri 12.30-2, à la carte; D daily, 5.30-11; early D €15 (5.30-7); otherwise set D menus from €23.50 per person, also à la carte. House wine about €14.75. Closed 25 Dec, Good Fri. Amex, Diners, MasterCard, Visa, Switch. **Directions:** Town Centre.

COUNTY LEITRIM

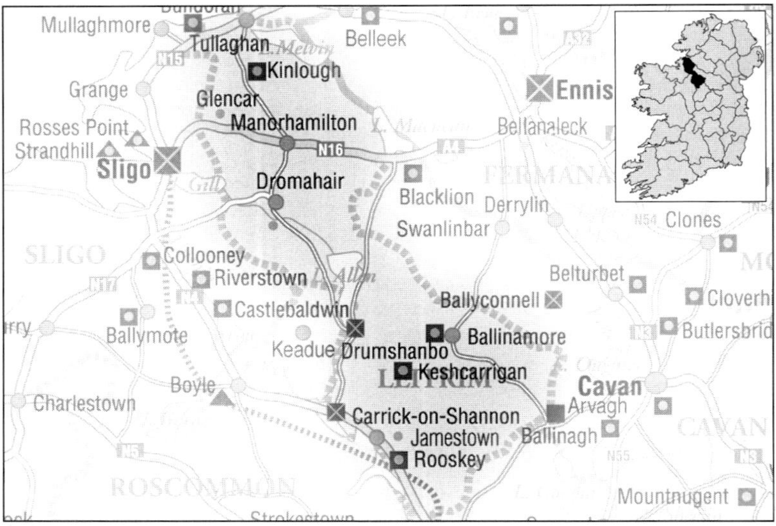

If you seek a county which best symbolises the resurgence of Ireland, you need look no further than Leitrim. In times past, it was known as the Cinderella county. Official statistics admitted that Leitrim did indeed have the poorest soil in all Ireland, in places barely a covering of low fertility. Back in the sad old days of the 1950s, the little county's population had fallen to 30,000. It was doubted that it was still a viable administrative entity.

You'd be hard put to visualise those gloomy times now, fifty years on. Today, Leitrim prospers. The county town, Carrick-on-Shannon, is one of Ireland's brightest and best, a bustling river town. Admittedly, there are drawbacks. Going into 2004, Carrick-on-Shannon has its first-ever set of traffic lights. Until this year, there were no traffic lights in Leitrim. Or at least, not on the roads. The modern automatic locks on the restored Shannon-Erne Waterway – whose vitality has contributed significantly to Leitrim's new prosperity – may have their own boat traffic lights. But until 2004, the roads had managed without any.

Yet despite the new energy, Leitrim is rightly seen as a pleasantly away-from-it-all sort of place which has many attractions for the determined connoisseur. So with some of Ireland's better known holiday areas suffering if anything from an excess of popularity, the true trail-blazers may find the relaxation they seek in Leitrim. But is it so remote? Popular perceptions may be at variance with reality. For instance, Leitrim shares the shores of Lough Gill with Sligo, so much so that Yeat's legendary Lake Isle of Innisfree is within an ace of being in Leitrim rather than Sligo of Yeatsian fame. To the northward, we find that more than half of lovely Glencar, popularly perceived as being one of Sligo's finest jewels, is in fact in Leitrim. As for the notion of Leitrim being the ultimate inland and rural county - not so. Leitrim has an Atlantic coastline, albeit of only four kilometres, around Tullaghan.

It's said this administrative quirk is a throwback to the time when the all-powerful bishops of the early church aspired to have ways of travelling to Rome without having to cross the territory of neighbouring clerics. Whatever the reason, it's one of Leitrim's many surprises, which are such that it often happens that when you're touring in the area and find yourself in a beautiful bit of country, a reference to the map produces the information that, yes indeed, you're in Leitrim, a county which also provides most of the land area for Ireland's first Ecotourism 'Green Box'. Leitrim's significance within this scheme achieved additional recognition in Dublin on 18th September 2003 when the first An Taisce National Awards were announced. The prize for the most appropriate building in the countryside – a concept which is surely central to An Taisce's very existence – went to Rossinver Organic Centre, whose buildings in North Leitrim near Lough Melvin were designed by Colin Bell.

Local Attractions and Information

Ballinamore, Shannon-Erne Waterway 071 9644855
Ballinamore, Slieve an Arain Riverbus Cruises 071 9644079
Carrick-on-Shannon, Moonriver Cruises 071-9621777
Carrick-on-Shannon, Tourism Information 071 9620170

Carrick-on-Shannon, Waterways Ireland 071 9650898
Dromahair, Parke's Cas. (restored 17c fortified hse) 071 9164149
Drumshanbo, Sliabh an Iarainn Visitor Centre 071 9641522
Manorhamilton, Glens Arts Centre 071 9855833
Mohill, Lough Rynn House and Gardens 071 9631427
Rossinver, The Organic Centre (Ecotourism) 071 9854338

Ballinamore

Glenview House

RESTAURANT / FARM GUESTHOUSE Aghoo Ballinamore Co Leitrim **Tel: 071 964 4157**
Fax: 071 964 4814 Email: glenvhse@iol.ie

Teresa Kennedy's farm guesthouse beside the Shannon-Erne Waterway is a great place for a family holiday as there's lots to do in the area, and there's a tennis court and outdoor play area as well as an indoor games room with a pool table and table tennis - and they also have an impressive little agricultural museum in outbuildings. But what many more people come here for is Teresa's restaurant, which attracts a balanced mixture of locals and holidaymakers, including people on leisure cruisers. Guests for dinner gather in the bar - a long room with a fire and many chairs indicating the numbers she sometimes expects; menus and drinks are dispatched in rapid succession before diners are brought to formally-laid polished tables in the large dining room. A piano in the corner suggests that parties can get going in here (and there's even a little dance floor); meanwhile, your 5-course dinner might start with crab claws in garlic butter or a tastily dressed mixed leaf salad with avocado, then a soup or sorbet before a hearty main course - escalope of pork with a creamy Baileys and red apple sauce, perhaps, or a deliciously moist brace of quail, with a little stuffing and an orange and brandy sauce (cooked to order) served with well-cooked side vegetables. Finish with fairly traditional 'Sunday lunch' style desserts and coffee before heading back to the bar or upstairs to bed. (Rooms are simple but moderately priced, with compact shower rooms.) Children welcome (under 2s free in parents' room, cot available without charge; baby sitting available). No pets. **Rooms 6** (all en-suite & no smoking) B&B about €38 pps. Restaurant: **Seats 50** (private room 25). D daily, 6-8.30 pm. Set D €35. House wine about €18. Reservations advised. Open all year. MasterCard, Visa. **Directions:** 2 miles south of Ballinamore. ◇

Ballinamore

Riversdale Farm Guesthouse

Ⓝ **FARM GUESTHOUSE** Ballinamore Co Leitrim **Tel: 071 964 4122** Fax: 071 964 4813
Email: riversdaleguesthouse@eircom.net Web: www.riversdaleguesthouse.com

Attractively situated on rising ground, overlooking the Shannon-Erne Waterway, the Thomas family's farm guesthouse is an unusual establishment surrounded by their 80 acre farm. The house was built on quite a grand scale and looks impressive against a background of mature trees as you approach past a paddock which is home to newborn lambs in spring: a truly rural escape if ever there was one. Inside, the tone is that of a homely B&B rather than country house, which is totally appropriate for a farm guesthouse - so it is very surprising to find the exceptional amenities offered, which include a small but well-maintained leisure complex comprising an indoor heated swimming pool, fitness suite, squash court, and a loft with table tennis (ideal for teenagers), as well as the colourful barges moored below the house, which Riversdale offer for holidays afloat. Simply furnished bedrooms are all en-suite and spacious, with lovely views, and there are three family suites in the courtyard, which can be let by the week. Meals are taken in a lovely conservatory overlooking green countryside and the river, and there are two large sitting rooms with open fires and plenty of space for guests to relax in. What Riversdale offers is a easy going rural holiday at moderate price, with unusually good facilities for a farm guesthouse and easy access to the town of Ballinamore and the many interesting activities and excursions in this unspoilt area. **Rooms 13.** B&B from about €38. Closed mid Dec-early Jan. MasterCard, Visa. **Directions:** Just outside Ballinamore, beside Aghoo Lock, on Shannon-Erne Waterway.

CARRICK-ON-SHANNON

This thriving town is cosmopolitan in its outlook, with a growing range of restaurants and some fascinating shops: the Market House Centre is a good browsing spot and, beside the bridge, an excellent delicatessen **Cheese Etc (Tel: 071-962 2121),** offers wonderful selection of specialist foods, notably farmhouse cheeses. Beside the bridge, **Cryan's Bar & Restaurant (Tel: 071-962 0409)** is well known for steaks and music and the two hotels - **The Bush Hotel (071- 962 0014; www.bushhotel.com)** and **The Landmark Hotel (Ferraris/CJs Restaurant: 071 962 2222; www.thelandmarkhotel.com)** - provide for traditional and international tastes, respectively. For exotic flavours, the new **Lemongrass (087 257 5513),** is due to open near the Rowing Club at the time of going to press. For accommodation, don't overlook **Glencarne Country House (see entry)** which is across the bridge on the Boyle road, with a Co Roscommon postal address.

Carrick-on-Shannon — Hollywell Country House

COUNTRY HOUSE

Liberty Hill Cortober Carrick-on-Shannon Co Leitrim
Tel: 071 962 1124 Fax: 071 962 1124 Email: hollywell@esatbiz.com

After many years as hoteliers in the town (and a family tradition of inn-keeping that goes back 200 years), Tom and Rosaleen Maher moved some years ago to this delightful period house on a rise over the bridge, with beautiful views over the Shannon and its own river frontage. It's a lovely, graciously proportioned house, with a relaxed family atmosphere. Tom and Rosaleen have an easy hospitality (not surprisingly, perhaps, as their name derives from the Gaelic "Meachar" meaning hospitable), making guests feel at home very quickly and this, as much as the comfort of the house and its tranquil surroundings, is what makes Hollywell special. Bedrooms are all individually furnished in period style and have tea & coffee making facilities. Delicious breakfasts are worth getting up in good time for: fresh juice, fruits and choice of teas, coffees and herbal teas, freshly-baked bread, home-made preserves, lovely choice of hot dishes - anything from the "full Irish" to Irish pancakes with maple syrup or grilled cheese & tomato with black olive pesto on toast. No evening meals, but Tom and Rosaleen advise guests on the best local choices and there's a comfortable guests' sitting room with an open fire to gather around on your return. A pathway through lovely gardens leads down to the river; fishing (coarse) on site. Lots to do in the area - and advice a-plenty from Tom and Rosaleen on the best places to visit. Not suitable for children under 12. Pets allowed by arrangement. **Rooms 4** (2 junior suites, 2 shower only). B&B €55 pps, ss about €10. Closed Christmas-New Year. Amex, MasterCard, Visa, Laser. **Directions:** From Dublin, cross bridge on N4, keep left at Gings pub. Hollywell entrance is on left up the hill.

Carrick-on-Shannon — The Oarsman Bar & Café

BAR / RESTAURANT

Bridge Street Carrick-on-Shannon Co Leitrim
Tel: 071 962 1733 Fax: 071 962 1734
Email: info@theoarsman.com Web: www.theoarsman.com

This attractive and characterful pub moved into a new era when Conor and Ronan Maher took it over in 2002. The brothers are sons of Tom and Rosaleen Maher (see entry for Hollywell) and clearly have what's known as "the hotelier's gene": numerous visits by the guide at different times of day and days of the week have found everything spick-and-span, very welcoming and efficiently run, even at busy times. The bar - which is very pleasantly set up in a solidly traditional style with a fire, comfortable seating arrangements for eating the excellent bar meals, and an occasional gesture towards contemporary tastes in the decor - leads off towards a sheltered patio at the back, which makes a spot for a sunny day and gives the bar an open atmosphere; just the place for one of their delicious Illy coffees with a complimentary Illy chocolate. A strong kitchen team led by head chef Shaun Hanna and sous-chef Sheila Sharpe produce consistently excellent food, offered on sassy lunchtime bar menus (warm wraps, healthy options (with Weight Watchers points) and enticing organic pastas and main course salads) and exciting à la carte evening menus offered upstairs three evenings a week. As Sheila Sharpe is one of the country's foremost pastry chefs, you should definitely save a space for a wonderful ending - such as orange and Malibu pannacotta, served with an orange confit & light caramel sauce. Definitely worth a detour! Bar meals: L Mon-Wed 12-3.30, Thu-Sat 12-2.30. Restaurant **Seats 36.** (private room 6-8): D Thu-Sat 7-9.30. Not suitable for children after 7pm. Closed 25 Dec. Amex, MasterCard, Visa, Laser. **Directions:** Near the bridge in Carrick-on-Shannon, towards the centre of the town.

Carrick-on-Shannon — Shamrat

RESTAURANT

Bridge Street Carrick-on-Shannon Co Leitrim
Tel: 071 965 0934 Fax: 071 965 0935

This appealing Indian restaurant has earned a loyal following since it opened in 2001. Although the entrance is small from the street, first-time visitors will be surprised to find a spacious L-shaped first floor dining area and enough room for a comfortable reception area at the top of the stairs. Uncluttered contemporary decor and well-spaced tables with comfortable high-back chairs add to the sense of thoughtful design that prevails - all of which, together with attentive service from friendly and helpful staff, add to the enjoyment of interesting, authentic and well-cooked food. L&D daily; Mon-Sat: L 12.30-2.30, D 6-11.30; Sun, special family lunch 1-4, à la carte 4-10. Set L from €8.85 (Sun €11.35); Set D €15.95; also à la carte. House wine €16.50. Closed 25 Dec, Good Fri. MasterCard, Visa, Laser. **Directions:** Near the bridge, on right-hand side walking into town.

Carrick-on-Shannon Area

Lynch's Bar/The Sheermore

Atmospheric Pub

Kilclare Carrick-on-Shannon Co Leitrim **Tel: 071 964 1029**

Well away from the bustle of nearby Carrick-on-Shannon, Padraig and Christina Lynch's friendly traditional bar, grocery and hardware shop on the Shannon-Erne Waterway is known from the road as "The Sheermore" - but presents its much more attractive side to the water. You can sit outside at the back in fine weather and watch the boats going by, or choose between a conservatory overlooking the bridge or a move right into the bar if the weather dictates. This isn't really a food place, but Christina Lynch makes home-made soup every day and cuts sandwiches freshly to order - which can be just the right thing, in the right place. Children welcome. Pets allowed in certain areas. Bar food available 12.30-9.30 daily. Wheelchair accessible. Closed 25 Dec, Good Fri. MasterCard, Visa, Laser. **Directions:** 6 miles from Carrick-on-Shannon towards Ballinamore, on the Shannon-Erne Waterway.

Cootehall

Cootehall Bridge Restaurant & Coffee House

RESTAURANT / CAFÉ

Cootehall Co Leitrim **Tel: 071 96 67173**

Cootehall is one of those places which can't decide which county it is in but, whether it is in Roscommon or Leitrim, Manfred Kan's seasonal waterside restaurant provides a very complete service once it gets going. A substantial à la carte dinner menu is offered, (typically including French onion soup, steaks, Wiener Schnitzel and a separate vegetarian menu) and Manfred's good cooking and great value for money send many a customer happy into the night. There's also a children's menu, varied desserts and waffles and a range of novelty ice cream dishes. Open from St Patrick's Day. Early season Wed-Sun from 6pm; in summer (after May): Tue-Sun,12.30-10 pm. (L23.30-3, then teas, ices etc; Dinner 6-10pm). Closed Oct-mid Mar & Mon-Tue early season. Dinner reservations recommended. A phone call to check opening times is recommended, especially off season. MasterCard, Visa. **Directions:** Right of the bridge as you approach the village. ◇

Drumshanbo

LOUGH ALLEN

On the shores of Lough Allen, Drumshanbo is an interesting little town with a number of characterful pubs - we like the unspoilt **Conway's Corner House (Tel 071 96 41020),** where you can buy the papers and read them in front of the fire. And, at the time of going to press, big changes are afoot with the imminent opening of the area's first destination hotel, **Lough Allen Hotel & Spa (Tel 071 96 40044; www.loughallenhotel.com).**

Jamestown

Al Mezza

RESTAURANT

Jamestown Co Leitrim **Tel: 071 962 5050**

This colourful little Lebanese/Mediterranean restaurant on the edge of the pretty village of Jamestown is run by proprietor-chef Milad Serhan (previously at The Pyramids in Carrick-on-Shannon) and offers quite extensive authentic middle eastern menus - mixed dishes are probably the best choice on a first visit. It's an unusual little place for a country area, with friendly service as well as good food. For those arriving in Jamestown by boat, it's about half a mile from the quay, but it's a pleasant walk through the village - pavement all the way and past two particularly enticing pubs for a visit in each direction, perhaps. Open Wed & Thu 6-11, Fri & Sat 6-11.30/12; Sun & Mon 6-10. Closed Tue. Open all year. MasterCard, Visa, Laser. **Directions:** On right just before entering Jamestown village. ◇

Keshcarrigan

Canal View House & Restaurant

RESTAURANT / GUESTHOUSE

Keshcarrigen Co Leitrim

Restaurant **Tel: 071 964 2404** Accommodation **Tel: 071 964 2056**

A fireside cup of tea and home-baked scones or biscuits in the comfortable residents' lounge (with views of the cruisers passing) welcomes guests on arrival at Jeanette Conefry's immaculate guesthouse overlooking the Shannon-Erne Waterway. Bedrooms – some with water views, all with a pleasant outlook – are comfortably furnished, with direct-dial telephones and neat en-suite shower rooms. Peace and quiet are an attraction here, but television is available in bedrooms on request. Families are welcome and well looked after. Pets permitted by arrangement. **Rooms 6.** B&B about €35 pps, ss about €7. Closed Christmas week. **Restaurant:** Michael and Cathy Flahertys have run the restaurant here for some years and it has both a local following and particular appeal for boating guests who may use the private mooring facilities overnight when dining here. Michael offers traditional cooking in a mainly classical style with some international influences - and many house specialities feature on menus that could include home-made pâté with Cumberland sauce, steaks various ways, poached salmon with mushroom & dill sauce and a good choice of vegetarian dishes cheese & spinach vol-au-vent, perhaps, or a spicy vegetable stir-fry. There might be game in season - venison & mushroom pie is a speciality. Children welcome. A simple early dinner, offering Irish stew and home-made brown bread for a tenner sounds like a winning number. **Seats 40.** D daily, 6-10 (Sun to 9); L Sun only 12-4; Set Sun L €19.95; early D €10 (5-7pm); D à la carte. House wine €15.50; sc discretionary. Wheelchair accessible. Open all year except Christmas. Amex, Visa. **Directions:** 100 metres from jetty.

Kinlough

Courthouse Restaurant

RESTAURANT / B&B

Main Street Kinlough Co Leitrim **Tel: 071 984 2391**
Fax: 071 984 2824 Email: thecourthouserest@eircom.net

In the old courthouse of the attractive village of Kinlough, Piero and Sandra Melis's stylish little restaurant is a particularly welcoming place and offers good contemporary cooking in the Mediterranean style with some more down to earth local influences - especially at lunchtime - which attracts a following from a wide area. A wide ranging menu includes specialities like local free range Thornhill duck, with spinach and wild mushrooms and there are always daily specials; ostrich has become popular and the house specialities include ostrich fillet (tender, tasty, beautifully sauced) with chargrilled vegetables in a reduced balsamic vinegar sauce. More traditional dishes include starters like seafood risotto (with smoked salmon, smoked tuna & prawns) and pasta dishes such as the perennially popular vegetarian penne four cheeses (pasta cooked in a creamy gorgonzola, cheddar, parmesan and smoked cheese sauce), served with a side salad. Consistently accurate cooking ensures that vegetables are served à point - and traditional desserts (which can be tasted as a selection) include an irresistible panna cotta with just the right degree of delicate wobble! Not suitable for children after 8 pm. **Seats 35** (private room 15). D Wed-Mon, 6.30-9.30, L Sun only 12.30-2.30. D à la carte; Set Sun L about €18. House wines about €18; sc discretionary except 10% on parties of 6+. Closed Tue, 3 days Christmas, 2 weeks Nov & 2 weeks Feb. [A phone call to check opening times and prices is advised.] **Accommodation:** Neat, freshly decorated bedrooms offer comfortable accommodation at a very reasonable price. **Rooms 4** (all shower only). B&B about €35 pps, ss about €10. MasterCard, Visa, Laser. **Directions:** Off main Donegal-Sligo road (N15), 5 km towards Sligo from Bundoran. ◇

Leitrim

The Barge Steakhouse

RESTAURANT / BAR

Leitrim Village Carrick-on-Shannon Co Leitrim
Tel: 071 962 0807 Fax: 071 962 2957

This inviting stone building on the main street has been extensively renovated and gradually developed under the current ownership of John and Rose Pierce. It began with the characterful bar, which they opened in 2001, and has since developed to include a spacious restaurant and conservatory - and, most recently, a beer garden at the back, which is very popular for barbecues when weather permits and, like everything else in this immaculate maintained establishment, kept scrupulously clean and tidy. Head chef Margaret Melia provides a daytime bar menu as well as an à la carte for the restaurant; while there's the occasional nod to fashion (hot paninis on the barfood sandwich menu, for example), the style is quite traditional - as the name implies, steaks various ways are the speciality of the house. Other regulars include crispy duck and there's always at least one vegetarian dish; there may sometimes be really traditional dishes like beef & Guinness casserole or bacon & cabbage too. Fresh, attractive food, responsive service, pleasing surroundings and good value add up to an unusually appealing package. There's a little children's menu too, and a short list of popular wines. Open 12.30-9.30 daily, L 12-6, D 6-9.30. A la carte. House wines from €15.50. **Seats 90** (32 in conservatory; private room 21). Not suitable for children after 7pm. Toilets wheelchair accessible. Closed 25 Dec & Good Fri. Amex, Diners, MasterCard, Visa, Laser, Switch. **Directions:** In Leitrim village.

Rooskey

Shannon Key West Hotel

HOTEL

The River Edge Rooskey Co Leitrim **Tel: 071 963 8800** Fax: 071 963 8811
Email: shnkywst@iol.ie Web: www.keywest.firebird.net

This well-run riverside hotel on the Leitrim/Roscommon border has brought valuable facilities to the area and is open all year (except Christmas), making it a particularly good venue for off-season short breaks, meetings and conferences. Comfortably furnished bedrooms have all the usual amenities - direct dial phones, TV with video channel, tea & coffee-making facilities and trouser press; two rooms also have fax machines and there is a safe available on request. On-site amenities include a gym, jacuzzi, solarium and steam room (but no swimming pool) and there is plenty to do and see in the area. Reliable bar food also makes this a useful place to bear in mind for breaking a journey. Conference/banqueting (220); video conferencing and back-up secretarial services available. Leisure centre. Children welcome (under 3 free in parents' room, cots available without charge, baby sitting arranged). **Rooms 38** (7 no smoking, 1 for disabled). B&B €70 pps, ss €19. Closed 24-28 Dec. Amex, MasterCard, Visa, Laser, Switch. **Directions:** On N4, main Dublin-Sligo route, midway between Longford and Carrick-on-Shannon.

COUNTY LIMERICK

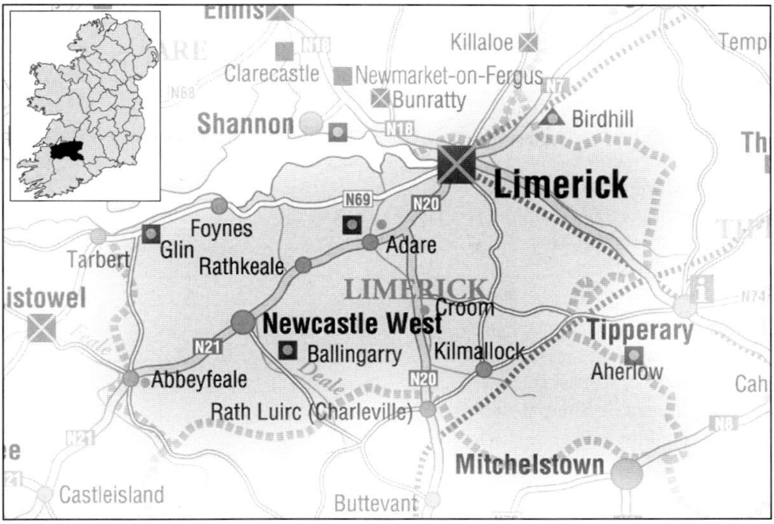

2004 sees Limerick city's renewed focus on its waterfront and waterways being further emphasised with plans to restore the Park Canal, which will provide the possibility of a waterbus link between the city centre and the University. Added to the "Riverside City" European Investment Initiative which was launched in March 2003, this becomes an impressive vote of confidence in the city's potential for people-friendly development based around the Shannon.

The story of Limerick city and county is in many ways the story of the Shannon Estuary, for in times past it was the convenient access provided by Ireland's largest estuary - it is 60 miles long - which encouraged the development of life along the estuary's southern shore and into the River Shannon itself. Today, the area's focal point for national and global transport is of course Shannon International Airport, which is actually located in south County Clare, but is very much a part of the shores of the Shannon Estuary, the region's dominant geographical feature.

In recent years, the opening of improved waterway links through the heart of town has seen the welcome regeneration of the old city continuing in tandem with the attractive new developments. But significant and all as this is, there's much more to Limerick county than the city and its waterways.

Inland from the river, the very richness of the countryside soon begins to develop its own dynamic. Eastern Limerick verges into Tipperary's Golden Vale, and the eastern county's Slieve Felim hills, rising to Cullaun at 462 m, reflect the nearby style of Tipperary's Silvermine Mountains.

Southwest of Limerick city, the splendid hunting country and utterly rural atmosphere of the area around the beautiful village of Adare makes it a real effort of imagination to visualise the muddy salt waters of the Shannon Estuary just a few miles away down the meandering River Maigue, yet the Estuary is there nevertheless. Equally, although the former flying boat port of Foynes and the nearby jetty at Aughinish may be expanding to accommodate the most modern large ships, just a few miles inland we find ourselves in areas totally remote from the sea in countryside which lent itself so well to mixed farming that the price of pigs in Dromcolliher (a.k.a. Drumcolligher) on the edge of the Mullaghareirk Mountains reputedly used to set the price of pigs throughout Ireland.

The growth of the computer industry in concert with the rapid expansion of the remarkably vibrant University has given Limerick a completely new place in Irish life, and the city's energy and urban renewal makes it an entertaining place to visit, while the eclectic collection on stunning display in the unique Hunt Museum in its handsome waterside setting has a style which other areas of Limerick life are keen to match.

With newfound confidence, Limerick has been paying greater attention to its remarkable heritage of Georgian architecture, with Limerick Civic Trust restoring the Georgian house and garden at 2 Pery Square. It acts as the focal point for an area of classic urban architecture which deserves to be better known.

That said, Limerick still keeps its feet firmly on the ground, and connoisseurs are firmly of the opinion that the best pint of Guinness in all Ireland is to be had in this no-nonsense city, where they insist on being able to choose the temperature of their drink, and refuse to have any truck with modern fads which would attempt to chill the rich multi-flavoured black pint into a state of near-freezing tastelessness aimed at immature palates.

Local Attractions and Information

Adare, Heritage Centre	061 396666
Adare, May Fair	061 396894
Ballysteen, Ballynacourty Gardens	061 396409
Bruree, Heritage Centre and de Valera Museum	063 91300
Croom, Waterwheel and Heritage Centre	061 397130
Foynes, Flying Boat Museum	069 65416
Glin, Glin Castle Pleasure Grounds & Walled Garden	068 34364
Limerick, Belltable Arts Centre, 69 O'Connell St	061 319866
Limerick, Georgian House & Garden, 2 Pery Square	061 314130
Limerick, Hunt Museum, Customs House, Rutland St	061 312833
Limerick, King John's Castle	061 360788
Limerick, Limerick City Art Gallery, Pery Square	061 310633
Limerick, Limerick Museum, John's Square	061 417826
Limerick, Tourism Information	061 317522
Limerick, University of Limerick	061 333644
Lough Gur, Interpretive centre, 3000BC to present	061 360788
Patrickswell Limerick Racecourse (Greenmount Park)	061 355055

Limerick

BAR / RESTAURANT

Aubars Bar & Restaurant

49-50 Thomas Street Limerick Co Limerick
Tel: 061 317799 Fax: 061 317572
Email: padraic@aubars.com Web: www.aubars.com

Padraic Frawley's modern city centre bar and restaurant typifies the renewal of Limerick itself - a university city with a youthful population and city, it is said, with more cafés, pubs and restaurants than any other in Ireland. Padraic, a hotel management graduate who trained at the highly respected catering college nearby in Shannon, returned to his home city at the grand old age of 27 bursting with ideas collected during experience abroad and proceeded to transform an old pub into this dashing contemporary bar and restaurant. The layout is on several levels with no hard divisions and a mixture of seating in various areas, which can lead to confusion between customers coming in to eat rather than have a drink, although watchful staff soon have new arrivals sorted. While the style is uncompromisingly modern, down to the designer crockery, chef Michael Ryan's values are quite traditional and sound cooking is inspired by the admirable Gary Rhodes' style: 'dishes that are simple to make, tasty and look great'. Appealing, well-balanced menus change frequently and offer a number of different options for bar food (AuBars) and more structured meals in the restaurant/wine bar (Hush); there's a very likeable house style that integrates vegetables into each dish and often includes lesser known ones - a dish that found particular favour on a recent visit, for example, was grilled fillet of plaice with saffron potatoes, Swiss chard and a piquant caper jus: perfectly cooked, delicious and a lovely surprise to find a vegetable like Swiss chard on a popular menu. There may be a few small niggles - a bare window onto the street does not make for a comfortable dining ambience at some tables, for example, and the wine list needs a little more work if this is a serious wine bar - but the overall experience is very enjoyable and the contrast between the casual, lively bar area and Hush, with its crisply starched napkins, is pleasing. Vegetarians are well looked after, with appealing dishes marked clearly on menus, and the early dinner offers very good value. **Seats 42.** L 12.30-3 daily (Sun to 4.30; Mon-Sat gourmet sandwiches & salads to 4.30pm); D 5.30-9.30; early D €22 (5.30-7.30) A la carte L & D offered. SC discretionary. Amex, MasterCard, Visa, Laser. **Directions:** Left after Brown Thomas, O'Connell St, second block on the right.

Limerick

féile bia **RESTAURANT**

Brûlées Restaurant

Corner of Henry St & Mallow St Limerick Co Limerick
Tel: 061 319931 Email: brulees@eircom.net

Just a stroll across from Jurys Limerick Inn, Donal and Teresa Cooper's restaurant is on a busy corner and can sometimes look a little unappealing from the road, but the interior is well-appointed and it is a first choice destination for many discerning diners visiting the city. Dining areas on several levels break groups up nicely and are elegantly furnished in a simple classic style that makes the most of limited space. A soothing ambience and welcoming details - olives and freshly baked breads to nibble - get guests off to a good start while reading Teresa's appealing menus. She takes pride in using the finest of ingredients, both local and imported, in imaginative, colourful modern Irish cooking, which is as good as it sounds - a speciality starter of pan-fried goats cheese & pancetta parcels with mixed leaves and pecan oil makes a good beginning, or a vegetarian dish like a tartlet of cherry tomato, buffalo mozzarella, pine nut & basil drizzled with truffle oil might be a tempting option. Main courses offer a balanced combination of ingredients in sound modern Irish cooking, such as a speciality dish of pan-fried escalope of pork in a herb crumb, with caramelised apples, baby spinach and a mustard & caper fruit sauce. Menus are consistently appealing - vegetarian dishes are invariably imaginative, also fish and seafood, which will always include daily specials. Cooking is accurate, presentation attractive without being fussy and, with main courses averaging around €23, this is good value for the quality. Simple, attractively prepared and carefully cooked side vegetables are another plus point, also a good cheese selection - and gorgeous puddings include (what else) a classic crème brûlée, served with crunchy shortbread and warm berry compôte. Lunch menus offer especially good value. Interesting, fairly priced wine list. Seats 30. No smoking area. L 12.30-2.30; D 6.30-9.30. Set L €12.50-21.50; D à la carte. House wine €17; SC discretionary (12.5% on groups of 6+). Closed Sun, Mon; 24-25 Dec, New Year. Amex, Diners, MasterCard, Visa, Laser. **Directions:** On the corner of Henry St. and Lower Mallow Street, near Jury's Inn roundabout.

Limerick

Castletroy Park Hotel

féile bia HOTEL

Dublin Road Limerick Co Limerick **Tel: 061 335 566** Fax: 061 331 117
Email: sales@castletroy-park.ie Web: www.castletroy-park.ie

This blocky redbrick hotel is not especially architecturally pleasing, but it has mellowed a little with time - and the surroundings gardens are maturing well and (like the rest of the hotel) always immaculately well-maintained. Generous car parking is kept at a discreet distance from the building and the walkway, through trellises clothed in honeysuckle and vines (and past a window that affords a glimpse into an impressive leisure suite and deck level pool), creates a good impression, immediately reinforced by a warm and welcoming atmosphere in the large foyer. Outstandingly friendly staff are welcoming and helpful in all areas of the hotel and, while not individually decorated, spacious bedrooms are regularly refurbished and thoughtfully furnished with special attention to the needs of the business traveller (good desk space, second phone, fax and computer points). The hotel is much sought after as a conference venue and, after work, excellent leisure facilities (which include a 1 km jogging track) and The Merry Pedlar pub offer a change of scene. Conferences / Banqueting (450-260). Video conferencing. Leisure/fitness centre, swimming pool. Children welcome (under 12s free in parents room, cot available without charge, baby sitting arranged). Garden. **Rooms 107** (7 suites, 5 junior suites, 22 executive, 69 no-smoking, 1 for disabled). Lift. 24 hour room service. B&B €115 pps, ss €90. SC incl. Hotel closed 24-25 Dec.

Mc Laughlin's: The hotel's fine dining restaurant is an airy room with an attractive outlook (making it more appealing at breakfast time); it has recently been refurbished in a lighter, more contemporary style and provides an impressive and comfortable setting for head chef Tom Flavin's international cuisine. In addition to the table d'hôte menus, a wide-ranging à la carte ensures that guests staying in the hotel for several days have plenty of choice. Starters include several soups and specialities like Carrigaholt crab spring roll with mango salsa, sweet chilli oil & soy dressing, while main courses are almost equally balanced between meat/poultry, seafood and vegetarian dishes. Some are quite unusual, but there are plenty of enduring favourites too including a speciality of prime Hereford beef fillet with celeriac and shallot purée & morel cream sauce. And to end on a high note, you could try the soufflé of the day. An informative wine list includes a fair selection of half bottles. Seats 75. No smoking area; air conditioning. B'fst 7-11 daily; L 12.30-2 (Sun to 2.30), D 5-9.30 (Sun 5.30-9.30) Set L €26, Set D €40; D also à la carte. House wine, €17.65. SC discretionary except 12.5% on groups of 8+. Amex, MasterCard, Visa, Laser. **Directions:** Dublin road, directly opposity the University of Limerick.

Limerick

Clarion Hotel

HOTEL

Steamboat Quay Limerick Co Limerick **Tel: 061 444100** Fax: 061 444101
Email: info@clarionhotellimerick.com Web: www.clarionhotellimerick.com

This exciting cigar-shaped 17-storey hotel right on the River Shannon waterfront in the centre of Limerick city opened in the autumn of 2002 and enjoys panoramic views over the city and the Shannon region - although, strangely, bedroom windows are quite high in the walls so the full benefit of the location is missed while sitting. Like the Clarion IFSC in Dublin (see entry), clean-lined contemporary elegance is the theme throughout and there are many similarities between the two hotels, including the semi-open plan arrangement of foyer, bars and dining spaces (which take full advantage of the location). As at IFSC, business facilities are excellent and bedrooms - which vary more than usual in hotels due to the unusual shape of the building - are offered in several pleasingly simple, modern colour schemes. All, however, have striking maple furniture, the best of beds and bedding, air conditioning,

ISDN lines, cable TV - everything, in short, that makes an hotel room the perfect retreat. Leisure facilities are also good - a health and fitness club up on the nth floor (it's easy to lose count) has a gym, sauna, jacuzzi and even a 12 metre swimming pool, with personal fitness consultant and nutritionist on hand to advise. Several decked balconies and terraces at different levels allow guests to take full advantage of fine weather - and the top two floors have suites and penthouses available for long lets. On the down side, after the first year of operation the hotel (which is not easily accessible for those unfamiliar with the city) would benefit from better signage in the one-way system and, once inside, signs of wear and tear in the foyer and rather off-hand reception are unwelcoming - and recent experience of Sinergie Restaurant (which is excellent at its best) is also mixed, undermining the achievements at this otherwise exciting hotel. Conference/banqueting 93/70. Business centre. Video-conferencing. Leisure centre; swimming pool. **Rooms 123.** (4 suites, 3 junior suites, 21 executive, 97 no smoking, 4 disabled). Lift. 24 hour room service. Children welcome (under 4 free in parents' room; cot available without charge). B&B 60pps, ss €25. (Room-only rate €120). Sinergie Restaurant: B'fst from 7am; L Sun-Fri,12.30-2.30; D daily, 7-9.45; (closed L Sat). Kudos Bar serves Asian food, 12-8.30 daily. Closed 24-25 Dec. Amex, Diners, MasterCard, Visa, Laser. **Directions:** Take Dock Road exit off the Shannon Bridge Roundabout, then first right.

Limerick

Copper & Spice

N RESTAURANT

2 Cornmarket Row Limerick Co Limerick
Tel: 061 313 620 Fax: 061 313 922
Email: copperandspice@eircom.net Web: www.copperandspice.com

Well situated near the recently restored Milk Market buildings, this attractively named restaurant is bright orange and would be hard to miss. You have to ring a bell to get in, so you are assured of immediate attention from agreeable (orange-uniformed) staff, who show arriving guests directly to tables. Indian background music contributes to the atmosphere and the orange theme is continued in stylish modern (distinctly Indian) decor and on promptly presented, clearly laid out menus, which offer an unusual combination of Indian and Thai cuisine. Each dish on the menu is explained and dishes suitable for vegetarians - and also wheat-free dishes - indicated. The feeling is there is a stronger leaning towards authentic Indian food, than the Thai dishes offered; mango chutney, lime pickle and minted yoghurt are provided on tables and food is presented on steel plates – as you would find if ordering a thali in India. Some less usual dishes are offered - an Indian starter of paneer rolls, for example, is made of home-made Indian cheese mixed with potatoes, bread-crumbed and fried - and podina chicken, "a 'must try dish of chicken', with strong yet refreshing flavours of mint and coriander". Saag meat - which one might expect to be beef, but here it is lamb - comes with a tasty, sharply flavoured spinach sauce and an unusual type of naan bread, rather thin to mop up juices. This is quite a stylish restaurant, offering a different experience from other ethnic restaurants in the city and giving fair value for money. It would be a particularly good choice for anyone with a preference for a meat-free meal as the range of vegetarian dishes offered is wide - and, a nice touch at the end of your meal, you can finish off with some locally hand-crafted chocolate truffles in most unusual flavours - Chilli, for example, is topped with a fresh chilli, and Spice is a combination of cardamom, chilli and ginger. D Mon-Sat, 5pm-10.30. Closed Sun. MasterCard, Visa. **Directions:** Near Milk Market buildings.

Limerick

DuCartes at the Hunt Museum

RESTAURANT

Hunt Museum Old Custom House Rutland Street Limerick Co Limerick
Tel: 061 312662 Fax: 061 417929

At the back of the museum, overlooking the river, with tables outside on the terrace, this bright modern café/restaurant is the perfect place for lunch in fine weather. As well as providing an appropriately elegant space to restore visitors to the museum, it is a popular lunchtime venue for locals who enjoy a light meal in pleasing surroundings - a generous smoked chicken salad, perhaps, with well-dressed fresh leaves All ingredients are sourced locally and prepared daily: attractively presented and healthy home-cooked food in the modern idiom should not disappoint, although it may be a little short on personality. [D, for groups only by arrangement] Seats 70. Air conditioning. Meals daily 5-5 (Sun 2-5), L 12-3. Wine licence. Closed Sun morning, 25 Dec. MasterCard, Visa. **Directions:** On the ground floor of the Hunt Museum. ◇

Limerick

Finn's Bar & The Milestone

BAR

62 William Street Limerick Co Limerick **Tel: 061 313495** Fax: 061 313496
Email: info@finnsbar.ie Web: www.finnsbar.ie

The Flannerys, father and sons, have reason to be proud of this fine city centre pub - Michael Flannery, who has been in charge since 1960, handed over the reins to Seamus and Liam in 1999 and, while it still has a traditional pub front, the new generation decided that the building, which is over 200 years old, needed a complete makeover - and it's now uncompromisingly 21st century. Changes were made with great care, however, and the new design is both striking and warm: 'modern but comfortable' was the brief. A dramatic sculptural chandelier makes an unusual focal point in the high-ceilinged front bar, which also has a gallery around it, creating interesting spatial relationships which can be studied from above as well as below. Clean lines are emphasised by another feature which is unusual, possibly unique, in Irish pubs: a total absence of advertising; the only branding allowed is their own and their swirling black and gold logo appears on everything. Providing a comfortable place where quality food and drink is served by friendly staff is the aim, and it is achieved with commendable consistency at The Milestone. After breakfast (mini-Irish, muffins, scones), then a lunch menu offering a tasty selection of soups, sandwiches and salads; hot dishes are cooked to order and attractively presented; seafood is quite prominent (try the Kerry crab open sandwich, with home-made brown bread, side salad & citrus mayonnaise, perhaps) and everything is home-made, including a speciality chowder, scones and desserts of the day. (Average main course about €8, seafood a little more). Service is pleasant and informal - and speciality coffees come with complimentary chocolates. DJ music on weekend evenings; the more traditional Milestone bar downstairs is quieter. **Seats 60.** Food available Mon-Sat, 9.30am-3.30pm (Sat to 4pm): B 9.30-11.30, L 11.30-3.30. (No food on Sun). House wine about €17. Closed 25 Dec & Good Fri. Amex, MasterCard, Visa, Laser. **Directions:** 100 metres off Wiliam Street/O'Connell Street junction.

Limerick

Green Onion Caffé

RESTAURANT

Rutland Street Limerick Co Limerick **Tel: 061 400 710**

Just across the road from the Hunt Museum in the old town hall, visiting this popular café-restaurant on two levels is a bit like going to the theatre, especially given the funky style and dimly lit tables up in the "gods". Interesting decor, light jazz music (not too loud), pleasant and efficient staff and good modern café style table settings give out all the right messages and the comfortable atmosphere makes this a place you can drop into, without being rushed. All day menus offer interesting sandwiches made to order on homemade brown bread or bap and served with a seasonal salad garnish and salads – Greek, chicken caesar - and pasta dishes. Good value - and useful to know about if you need to eat outside the usual lunch hour. Open all day Mon-Sat. Closed Sun & bank holidays. Amex, Diners, MasterCard, Visa. **Directions:** Opposite Hunt Museum. ◇

Limerick

Jurys Inn Limerick

féile bia **HOTEL**

Lower Mallow St Limerick Co Limerick **Tel: 061 207000** Fax: 061 400966
Email: aileen_phelan@jurysdoyle.com

Like other Jurys Inns, this budget hotel enjoys a prime city centre location and has car parking available in an adjacent multi-storey carpark. Rooms are large, comfortable and furnished to a high standard, especially considering the moderate cost, although maintenance may not always be up to the high standard required of relatively spartan budget accommodation. Bathrooms are fairly basic but have everything required including a small bath as well as overbath shower. Don't expect high levels of service - that's what keeps the costs down - but there is a restaurant and pub-like bar as part of the development. Traffic noise can be disturbing in front rooms, as the trucks head to and from the west all night. Children welcome. (under 12s free in parents' room, cot available without charge, baby sitting arranged,) B&B €45.50 pps, ss €37.50; Room rate from €75 (max 3 guests). Closed 24-26 Dec. Amex, Diners, MasterCard, Visa, Laser. **Directions:** City centre.

Limerick

Lynch South Court Hotel

féile bia **HOTEL**

Raheen Roundabout Adare Road Limerick Co Limerick
Tel: 061 487487 Fax: 061 487499
Email: cro@lynchotels.com Web: www.lynchotels.com

Ideally located for Shannon Airport and the Raheen Industrial Estate, the South Court Hotel presents a somewhat daunting exterior, but once inside visitors soon discover that it caters especially well for business guests, both on and off-duty - hence the Guide's Business Hotel Award to Lynch Hotels in 2000; since then, a 1,250 seater International Convention Centre has been added. In addition to excellent conference and meeting facilities, comfortable bedrooms are impressively spacious and well equipped, with generous desk areas and the latest technology, including fax/modem/ISDN points, in every room. Executive bedrooms have a separate work area providing a 'mini-office' with a leather desk chair and private fax machine - and there are 67 'lifestyle suites' with in-room gym, designed by the internationally recognised Irish designer Paul Costelloe. Leisure facilities were improved dramatically in 2002 with the opening of a 'Polo Lifestyle Club', designed with international rugby player (and local hero) Keith Wood and, continuing the hotel's policy of working with internationally recognised specialists in their field, Paul Costelloe was again involved in a new design, this time of a stylish new café bar, The CreamRoom, which has become a popular meeting place for coffee or speciality sandwiches. Conference/banqueting (1250/1000); business centre; video conferencing. Gym, sauna, solarium (swimming pool due late 2003). Hairdressing. Children welcome (under 2 free in parents' room, cot available without charge, baby sitting arranged). No Pets. **Rooms 127** (1 suite, 15 junior suites, 55 executive, 14 no-smoking). Lift. 24 hour room service. B&B €79 pps, ss €26; room-only rate also available, €135 (max 3 guests). Amex, Diners, MasterCard, Visa, Laser. **Directions:** Located on the main N20 Cork/Killarney road, 20 minutes from Shannon Airport.

Limerick

River Bar & Restaurant

Ⓝ CAFÉ / BAR

4 Georges Quay Limerick Co Limerick **Tel: 061 401883**

This French-run riverside restaurant and bar is a recent addition to the Limerick dining scene and has proved a hit with discerning diners of the area. A compact menu offers classics like French onion soup, darne of salmon with white wine sauce and French farmhouse cheeses among less obviously French dishes - it's the delivery that makes it special. Dinner daily, 6.30-12. Lunch "sometimes" (phone for details). MasterCard, Visa, Laser. **Directions:** City centre.

Limerick

Rogue Traders Restaurant at The Bank

Ⓝ RESTAURANT / BAR

63 O'Connell Street Limerick Co Limerick
Tel: 061 481546 Fax: 061 483819
Email: info@thebank.ie Web: www.thebank.ie

Entrance to the first floor restaurant at this former bank is through the Bank Bar downstairs, which is large, with the air of a gentleman's club, with leather armchairs, shelves of real books, various alcoves and split level areas for private chats. It bills itself as Limerick's only late night bar, and also Ireland's biggest sporting venue, with four big screens – mostly for watching sport – rugby in particular. Yet, at other times, it has a mixed clientele and a quiet buzz; the banking references, while quite gimmicky, don't detract from the fact that it is a very comfortable place to sit and talk and drink. Upstairs, in a large reception area that sets the tone for the spacious split-level restaurant - high-ceilinged, airy, beautifully lit with wall lights and candles - a piano has a large vase of lilies on it. The restaurant is comfortable, with low background music and a relaxed atmosphere; reception is prompt, menus are brought immediately to the table (beautifully set up, except for paper napkins), then a jug of water and interesting breads are brought, with tapenade and unsalted butter, while you wait for the first course. The banking theme continues on to the menu, where starters are billed as Quick Returns, fish dishes are Off Shore Investments etc. A wide choice includes several vegetarian dishes - such as a tomato and parmesan gratinée tart, served with rocket leaf, balsamic reduction - which might double as main courses, and some unusual dishes, such as wild mushroom and lamb's liver filo parcel, taking their place alongside excellent renditions of ever-popular dishes like crisply roast duck with kumquats – an entire half duck and an unctuous passion fruit & orange sauce: excellent. Desserts (Sweet Deals) include an interesting coconut crème brulée. Good service - pleasant and relaxed but on the ball; good food, well-presented; an interesting, informative wine list and very pleasant surroundings make this a great addition to the city's dining choices - and it's good value too, especially the early dinner menu. D daily, 5-10.30. Early D €24.95 (5-7pm). Otherwise à la carte. Closed 25 Dec, Good Fri. MasterCard, Visa **Directions:** City centre. On a corner at the Clarion Hotel end of O'Connell Street. ◇

Limerick

The Radisson SAS Hotel

féile bia HOTEL

Ennis Road Limerick Co Limerick **Tel: 061 326666** Fax: 061 327418
Email: elaineryan@radissonsas.com Web: www.radissonsas.com

This low rise hotel is set well back from the road in its own grounds and, although just a short drive from the city centre, enjoys an almost rural setting and views of the Clare Mountains. The original building dates back to the 1970s but, having been taken over by Radisson SAS, it opened in a completely new and elegant guise in July 2002. The size and layout of the building suits the Radisson style well - public areas, notably the large open-plan foyer/lounge, have a great a great sense of space and style, with seating groups arranged around glass-topped tables on marbled floors softened by beautiful specially commissioned rugs and a few dramatic pieces of art. A sense of generosity characterises the whole hotel - and accommodation is also notable for its spaciousness: all rooms are styled deluxe, with the comfort and amenities that implies (air conditioning, TV with video, ISDN line, personal safe, bathroom with full bath and shower) but, for people who like a bit of room around them, the sense of space is the main attraction of this hotel over its city centre rivals. Fine conference and business facilities have ample parking. Conference/banqueting (500/375); secretarial services. Leisure centre (indoor swimming pool, steam room, sauna, fitness room, treatment rooms). Tennis courts. Children welcome (under 17 free sharing parents' room; cots available without charge; baby sitting arranged). Children's adventure playground; playroom. Gardens. Parking. Helipad. **Rooms 154** (2 executive). Lift. 24 hour room service. B&B €60pps, ss€30. Room-only rate available: €110 (max 2 guests). Porters Restaurant: L 12-3 daily; D 6-9 daily. Set D €20 & €35. Bar food also available daily. Amex, MasterCard, Visa, Laser. **Directions:** On N18, 5 minutes from city centre.

Limerick

Tiger Lilies Bistro

RESTAURANT 9B Ellen Street Limerick Co Limerick **Tel: 061 317484** Fax: 061 317868

The black beams, exposed stone walls and wooden floors and beams of an old bonded warehouse in a redevelopment area provide a characterful setting for this terrific informal restaurant. Pleasant lighting, fresh flowers, light background jazz and changing art displays by local artists all add up to a very pleasing ambience. It's attractive from the outside too, with plants and tables for al fresco dining in fine weather although, unfortunately, it faces a carpark (although this does have its compensations). The upbeat tone of the interior is reflected in stylish table settings - even if ordinary paper napkins do seem a bit out of place - and modern menus (colourfully presented) with fashionable global influences offer some more down to earth dishes too, like venison sausage with champ potato (albeit with chilli jam). Seafood is the main player on this menu however and the many strong fish options include less usual choices like chargrilled swordfish (with mango salsa, guacamole & crème fraîche) alongside more familiar dishes - and vegetarian dishes are imaginative too. Prices may seem high for the casual ambience (evening main courses rise to as much as €26.95) but this is above average bistro food, based on fresh local produce, accurately cooked and complemented by well-trained service. Well selected, interesting wine list. **Seats 95.** Toilets wheelchair accessible. L Mon-Sat 12-2.30, D Tue-Sat 6-10 (Fri/Sat to 11). A la carte. House wine about €18. Closed all Sun, D Mon, 24-28 Dec, bank hols *Also at 18 Abbey Street, Ennis, Co Clare. Tel: 065 6829264 (Ennis branch open Sun, Closed Mon.) Amex, MasterCard, Visa, Laser. **Directions:** Between Cruises Street and the Gateway. ◇

Abbeyfeale

Whytes Restaurant & Bar

RESTAURANT / BAR The Square Abbeyfeale Co Limerick
Tel: 068 32917 Fax: 068 32916

Style and panache - that pretty well sums up Armel Whyte's sassy restaurant. Creamy floor tiles, colourful contemporary furniture and (a lot of) good modern paintings make a strong design statement and, better still, you'll get a genuinely warm welcome and efficient service from caring staff - and food to match. It has changed a little since opening in 2002 - the booths which previously divided the ground floor area have been removed, creating a more stylish, comfortable space, and the cooking style has settled down to become less international, more modern Irish. And it's well executed: top quality local ingredients are used in generous, accurately cooked dishes - sometimes a variation on a traditional theme, like chicken breast wrapped in Tralee smoked bacon on a bed of colcannon and seafood dishes - usually from a separate listing of half a dozen - such as fresh Fenit Bay crab claws, tossed in a garlic, lemon & chive butter. Good details include vegetables that are presented simply yet with panache, great home-made breads and desserts worth leaving room for. A shortish international wine list includes some Wine Specials, which are changed and updated regularly. Stylish surroundings, excellent food, efficient service and value for money are proving a winning combination for Abbeyfeale. **Seats 70** (private room 35). Air conditioning. Toilets wheelchair accessible. D Wed-Sun, 4-9; Set menus from €25, also à la carte. House wine from €19. SC discretionary. Reservations advised (the best tables are allocated to advance bookings). Closed Mon & Tue, 25 Dec & Good Fri. MasterCard, Visa, Laser. **Directions:** In the square across from Bank of Ireland.

ADARE

The chocolate-box village of Adare is not only an interesting and well-located destination in it's own right, but also an excellent place to break a long journey. Useful places to know about in the pretty row of cottages along the main street include **The Inn Between (061 396633),** an informal restaurant belonging to The Dunraven Arms across the road, is a good choice but only open in summer, while **The Blue Door (061 396481)** is open for most of the year. **Fitzgeralds Woodlands House Hotel (Tel 061 605100; www.woodland-hotel.ie)** is a little way out of the village on the Limerick side; especially popular for weddings and large gatherings, they offer special breaks and have excellent leisure/health facilities including a wide range of therapies and treatments.

Adare

Adare Manor Hotel & Golf Club

HOTEL

Adare Co Limerick **Tel: 061 396566** Fax: 061 396124
Email: sales@adaremanor.com Web: www.adaremanor.com

The former home of the Earls of Dunraven, this magnificent neo-Gothic mansion is set in 900 acres on the banks of the River Maigue. Its splendid chandeliered drawing room and the glazed cloister of the dining room look over formal box-hedged gardens towards the Robert Trent Jones golf course. Other grand public areas include the Gallery, named after the Palace of Versailles, with its unique 15th century choir stalls and fine stained glass windows. Luxurious bedrooms have individual hand carved fireplaces, fine locally-made mahogany furniture, cut-glass table lamps and impressive marble bathrooms with powerful showers over huge bathtubs. Quite recent additions include a new clubhouse in the grounds (complete with full conference facilities) and a state of the art Spa, which offers a wide variety of massage and beauty treatments. A new "golf village" of two and four bedroom townhouses provides a comfortable accommodation option for longer stays, large groups and families. Conference/banqueting (220/150). Leisure centre, swimming pool, spa treatments; beauty salon; hairdressing. Shop. Golf (18), equestrian; fishing; walking; cycling. Garden. Children welcome (cots available without charge, baby sitting arranged). No pets. **Rooms 135** (1 state room, 5 suites). Wheelchair access. Lift. Room service (all day). Room rate from €360. SC discretionary. Open all year.

Oakroom Restaurant: The beautifully appointed Oak Room Restaurant provides a fine setting for cooking based on local produce, including vegetables from the estate's own gardens. Head chef Thomas Andrews' seasonal menus change every two days and, while based on classical French cuisine, the style includes some modern Irish food - as in honey glazed rack of lamb with potato rösti, leek & onion compôte and rosemary jus, for example. A separate vegetarian menu is offered. Not suitable for children after 7pm. Seats 76 L (12-2), D (7-9.30) daily; Set D €58; house wine €25; SC discretionary. * More informal bistro style dining is offered all day at the Clubhouse Bar & Restaurant, breakfast-9.30 pm daily. Open all year. Amex, MasterCard, Visa, Laser. **Directions:** On N21 in Limerick.

Adare

Carrabawn Guesthouse

GUESTHOUSE

Killarney Road Adare Co Limerick **Tel: 061 396 067**
Email: carrabaw@indigo.ie Web: www.carrabawnhouseadare.com

In an area known for high standards, with prices to match, this immaculate owner-run establishment set in large mature gardens provides a good alternative to the luxury accommodation nearby. Bernard and Bridget Lohan have been welcoming guests here since 1984 - and many of them return on an annual basis because of the high level of comfort and friendly service provided. Bedrooms are very well maintained with all the amenities required (and a good Irish breakfast is served in a conservatory dining room overlooking lovely gardens. Children welcome (cot available without charge). No pets. **Rooms 8** (all shower only & no smoking). Room service (limited hours). B&B €45 pps, ss€20. Open all year except Christmas. MasterCard, Visa, Laser. **Directions:** On N21, 8 miles south of Limerick.

Adare

Dunraven Arms Hotel

HOTEL / RESTAURANT

Adare Co Limerick
Tel: 061 396 633 Fax: 061 396 541
Email: lmurphy@dunravenhotel.com Web: www.dunravenhotel.com

HOTEL OF THE YEAR

Established in 1792, and set in one of Ireland's most picturesque villages, the Dunraven Arms has seen many changes over the last few years and is now a large hotel. Yet, under the personal management of Bryan and Louis Murphy, it somehow manages to retain the comfortable ambience of a country inn. A very luxurious inn nevertheless: the furnishing standard is superb throughout, with antiques, private dressing rooms and luxurious bathrooms, plus excellent amenities for private and business guests, all complemented by an outstanding standard of housekeeping. It's a great base for sporting activities - equestrian holidays are a speciality and both golf and fishing are available nearby - and also extremely popular for both conferences and private functions, including weddings, which are held beside the main hotel (with separate catering facilities). In recent times the hotel has earned an unrivalled reputation for the value and quality of short breaks offered, something which has endeared it to many new guests who will no doubt be loyal customers for many years to come - this, and an ongoing determination to provide personal service and quality in all aspects of its operation, makes Dunraven Arms an outstanding example of contemporary Irish hospitality at its best. Equestrian; hunting; fishing; shooting; archery. Bike hire; walking. Leisure centre, indoor swimming pool, beauty salon. Snooker. Walking. Garden. Pets permitted by arrangement. **Rooms 74** (6 suites, 12 junior suites, 56 executive, 2 disabled, 12 no smoking). Lift. 24 hour room service. B&B €128 pps, ss €72. Room-only rate €190. SC 12.5% . Hotel closed 25 Dec.

Maigue Restaurant: Named after the River Maigue, which flows through the village of Adare, the restaurant is delightfully old fashioned - more akin to eating in a large country house than in an hotel. Sandra Earl, who has been head chef since 1998, takes pride in using the best of local produce in meals that combine the traditions of the area with influences from around the world on menus that offered a balanced selection of about half a dozen dishes on each course. Although particularly renowned for their roast rib of beef (carved at your table from a magnificent trolley), other specialities like River Maigue salmon and local game in season, especially pheasant, are very popular. Menus are not overlong but always offer some dishes not found elsewhere - a main course of pan-fried calves liver on a bed of champ with confit of bacon and onions rings, for example, and an unusual fig and almond tart with Madeira syrup and home-made vanilla ice cream. Ingredients are of the highest quality and Sandra Earl has the confidence to treat them with commendable simplicity when necessary. Little home-made touches add an extra dimension - Cashel Blue and Milleens cheese are served with home-made biscuits as well as grapes and a truffle oil vinaigrette, for example. And, as elsewhere in the hotel, service is exemplary. **Seats 80** (private room 40). D daily 7-10, Set D €38, also à la carte; L Sun only 12.30-2.30, Set L €27. House wines €19.50, SC 12.5%. [*The Inn Between, across the road in one of the traditional thatched cottages, is an informal restaurant in common ownership with the Dunraven Arms; D Tue-Sat, 6-10. * Light bar food (soup and sandwiches) available daily, 12.30-6.] Amex, Diners, MasterCard, Visa, Laser. **Directions:** First building on RHS as you enter the village coming from Limerick (approx. 11 miles).

Adare

The Wild Geese Restaurant

féile bia RESTAURANT

Rose Cottage Adare Co Limerick **Tel: 061 396451** Fax: 061 396451
Email: wildgeese@indigo.ie Web: www.wilde-geese.com

David Foley and Julie Randles' restaurant is in one of the prettiest cottages in the prettiest village in Ireland - and a charming atmosphere, caring service and consistently good modern Irish cooking all add up to an irresistible package. David Foley is a fine chef who sources ingredients with care - and his dinner menus are considerately priced by course, so you're not tied into the full meal, and offer about half a dozen choices for starters and main courses. Typical starters might include a terrine of smoked bacon, guinea fowl and Clonakilty black pudding with a plum chutney and seasonal salad and steamed mussels with a lemon butter sauce, while well-balanced main courses might include a speciality fish dish of grilled Castletownbere lobster with snow peas & shallot, topped with a chive mayonnaise and a local poultry dish of roast duckbreast with an onion tartlet and mushroom flavoured rice with a beetroot sauce. Finish off with an interesting dessert - hot apple soufflé with Calvados ice cream for example - or a selection of Irish cheeses, served with treacle bread and water biscuits. There's a separate vegetarian menu, offering a choice of three tempting dishes on each course, and friendly, caring service from long-serving staff adds greatly to the dining experience. An interesting, informative wine list is fairly priced. Not suitable for children after 7 pm. **Seats 45** (private room 30). D Tue-Sun 6.30-10; L Sun only, 12.30-2.30. Set D from €30 (2-course), also à la carte; Set Sun L €24. House wine €22. Closed Mon May-Sep; also Sun, Oct-Apr. Annual; closure 20 Dec-18 Jan. Amex, Diners, MasterCard, Visa, Laser. **Directions:** From Limerick,at top of Adare village, opposite Dunraven Arms Hotel.

Ballingarry

The Mustard Seed at Echo Lodge

COUNTRY HOUSE / RESTAURANT

Ballingarry Co Limerick
Tel: 069 68508 Fax: 069 68511
Email: mustard@indigo.ie Web: www.mustardseed.ie

One of the country's prettiest and most characterful restaurants, Dan Mullane's famous Mustard Seed started life in Adare in 1985. Having celebrated its first decade it began the next one by moving just ten minutes drive away to Echo Lodge, a spacious Victorian country residence set on seven acres of lovely gardens, with mature trees, shrubberies, kitchen garden and orchard - and very luxurious accommodation. Elegance, comfort and generosity are the key features - seen through decor and furnishings which bear the mark of a seasoned traveller whose eye has found much to delight in while wandering the world. The main house and garden having been put in order, Dan's next project was the conversion of an old schoolhouse in the garden, to provide three new superior suites, a new residents' lounge and a small leisure centre with sauna and massage room. This stylish development offers something quite different from the older accommodation and is in great demand from regulars who make Echo Lodge their base for golf and fishing holidays. Small conferences (20); banqueting (65). Children welcome; under 2 free in parents' room, cots available without charge, baby sitting arranged). Pets allowed by arrangement. Garden, walking. **Rooms 16** (3 suites, 6 shower only, 10 no smoking, 1 for disabled). Room service (limited hors). B&B €86 pps, ss €20. Special winter breaks offered, depending on availability. Closed Christmas week, 2 wks Feb.

The Mustard Seed: Food and hospitality are at the heart of Echo Lodge and it is in ensuring an enjoyable dining experience, most of all, that Dan Mullane's great qualities as a host emerge (he was the Guide's Host of the Year in 2001). The evening gets off to an auspicious start when aperitifs, served in the Library, come with a tasty amuse-bouche, and it is evident that attention to detail is the hallmark here - an impression confirmed when you go in to the beautiful dining room to find fresh flowers on each table, carefully selected to suit the decor. Head chef Tony Schwartz cooks in modern classical Irish" style. The kitchen gardens supply much of the produce for the restaurant, other ingredients are carefully sourced from organic farms and artisan food producers. Menus are wide-ranging and very seasonal - the components of a delicious tossed salad (with chorizo sausage, garlic croûtons & parmesan shavings, with soya & balsamic dressing, perhaps) will be dictated by the leaves and herbs in season and the soup course - typically of roast vegetable - may also be influenced by garden produce. Main courses are based on the best local meats (typically, Irish beef (sirloin or fillet) with basil-flavoured potato cakes, buttered melange of vegetables and Palmer mustard cream, seafood just up from the south-western fishing ports and game, in season - and, with so such an abundance of garden produce, vegetarians need no fear of being overlooked. Using the best Irish farmhouse cheeses at their peak of perfection is another point of honour - or you can finish with gorgeous puddings, which are also likely to be inspired by garden produce. Finally, irresistible home-made petits fours are served with tea or coffee, at the table or in the Library. All absolutely delicious - and the hospitality element is truly exceptional. **Seats 65.** D 7-9.30 (Sun to 9. Non residents welcome by reservation. Early D €25 (7-8pm); Set D €50. House wines from €25. Closed Christmas week, 2 weeks Feb. Amex, MasterCard, Visa, Laser. **Directions:** From top of Adare village take first turn to left, follow signs to Ballingarry - 8 miles.

Glin

COUNTRY HOUSE

Glin Castle

Glin Castle Glin Co Limerick **Tel: 068 34173** Fax: 068 34364
Email: knight@iol.ie Web: www.glincastle.com

The Fitzgeralds, hereditary Knights of Glin, have lived in Glin Castle for 700 years and it is now the home of the 29th Knight and his wife Madame Fitzgerald. The interior is stunning, with beautiful interiors enhanced by decorative plasterwork and collections of Irish furniture and paintings. Guests are magnificently looked after by manager Bob Duff. Accommodation was originally all in suites - huge and luxurious, but not at all intimidating because of the lived-in atmosphere that characterises the whole castle - but additional rooms ("smaller, friendly, with a family atmosphere") have more recently been opened. Furnished and decorated in traditional country house style (there was no need for this family to haunt the auctions in order to furnish the new rooms), everything has been done just right and every room feels as if it has always been that way; attention to detail is seen in all sorts of small thoughtfulnesses - the guests' information pack, for example, is exceptionally well-presented, with possible outings and itineraries listed under different interests (gardens, historical or whatever) and the amount of time required. When the Knight is at home he will take visitors on a tour of the house and show them all his pictures and old furniture. Not to be missed while in Glin is O'Shaughnessy's pub, just outside the castle walls; one of the finest pubs in Ireland, it is now in its sixth generation of family ownership and precious little has changed in the last hundred years. The garden and house are open to the public at certain times. Small conferences/private parties (20). Not suitable for children under 10 except babies (cot available without charge, baby sitting arranged). Pets permitted by arrangement. Garden , walking, tennis. **Rooms 15** (3 suites, all no-smoking). B&B €140pps. Dinner is available for residents by reservation; an attractive menu with about four choices on each course is offered. Dining Room Seats 30. D 7-9.30, Set D €48. House wine from about €21; sc discretionary. Closed 2 Nov-1Apr. Amex, Diners, MasterCard, Visa, Laser. **Directions:** 32 miles west of Limerick on N69,4 miles east Tarbert Car Ferry.

COUNTY LONGFORD

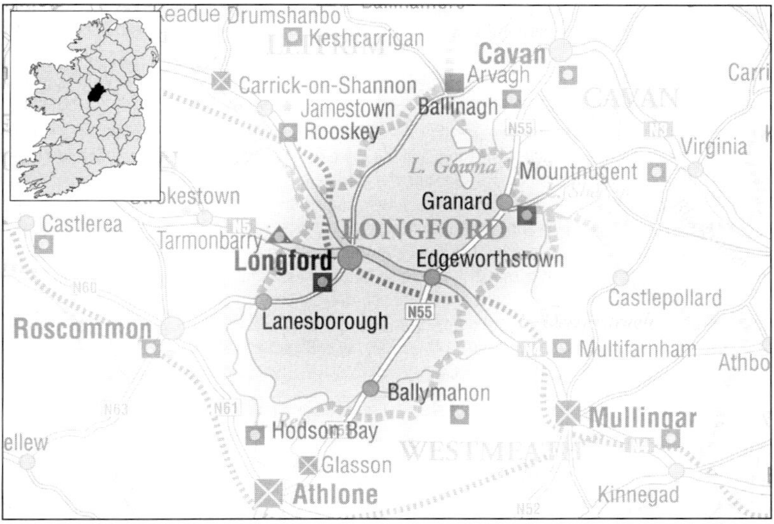

Longford is mostly either gently undulating farming country, or bogland. The higher ground in the north of the county up towards the intricate Lough Gowna rises to no more than 276m in an eminence which romantics might call Carn Clonhugh, but usually it's prosaically known as Corn Hill. The more entertainingly named Molly Hill to the east provides the best views of the lake in an area which arouses passionate patriotism. A few miles to the north is Ballinamuck, scene of the last battle in the Rising of 1798 in a part of Longford renowned for its rebellions against foreign rule.

To the southeast, there is even less pulling of the punches in the name of the little market town in its midst, for Granard - which sounds rather elegant - may be translated as "Ugly Height". Yet this suggests a pleasure in words for their own sake, which is appropriate, for Longford produced the novelist Maria Edgeworth from Edgeworthstown, a.k.a Mostrim, while along towards that fine place Ballymahon and the south of its territory on the Westmeath border, Longford takes in part of the Goldsmith country.

Goldsmith himself would be charmed to know that, six kilometres south of the road between Longford and Edgeworthstown, there's the tiny village of Ardagh, a place of just 75 citizens which is so immaculately maintained that it has been the winner of the Tidiest Village in the Tidy Towns awards three times during the past ten years.

Another award-winner is Newtowncashel in the southwest of the county, atop a hill immediately eastward of Elfeet Bay on northern Lough Ree, where the scenery becomes more varied as County Longford has a lengthy shoreline along the Shannon's middle lake. On September 8th 2003, Newtowncashel was yet again mentioned in dispatches as the winner of a Gold Medal in the latest Tidy Town contest, with an impressive score of 89.3%.

West of Longford town at Clondra, the attractive Richmond Harbour is where the Royal Canal - gradually being restored along its meandering track from Dublin - finally gets to the Shannon. And as for Longford town itself, they're working on it, and some day the rest of Ireland will wake up to find that there's life a-plenty going on there, if you just know where to look for it.

Local Attractions and Information

Ardagh, Heritage Centre 043 75277
Ballinamuck, 1798 Memorial & Visitor Centre 043 24848
Ballymahon, Bog Lane Theatre 0902 32252
Kenagh, Corlea Trackway (Bog Road) Visitor Centre 043 22386
Longford, Backstage Theatre & Arts Centre 043 47885
Longford, Carrigglas Manor (Gandon stableyard, lace museum) 043 41026
Longford, Tourism Information 043 46566
Newtowncashel, Heritage Centre 043 25021

Granard

Toberphelim House

FARMHOUSE

Granard Co Longford **Tel: 043 86568**
Email: tober3@eircom.net Web: www.toberphelinhouse.com

Dan and Mary Smyth's Georgian farmhouse is about half a mile off the road, on a rise that provides a lovely view of the surrounding countryside. Very much a working farm – cows, beef cattle and sheep plus an assortment of domestic animals, (but no more hens "they're gone with the fox") – it is an hospitable, easy-going place. Guests are welcome to wander around and walk the fields. ("Rubber boots are a must"). There's a guests' sitting room with television, and the three bedrooms are all comfortably furnished and well-maintained - the front bedroom, overlooking the garden, has a lovely old wooden floor and TV - but don't expect too much in the way of amenities. Always improving, the Smyths have given the house a facelift for their 25th wedding anniversary - solid mahogany interior doors, re-tiling the bath- shower-rooms, re-painting the hall, stairs and landing - and the programme continues next year. Families are welcome – and light meals and snacks can usually be arranged. Children welcome (under 6s free in parents' room); children's playground & playroom; pool table. Garden, fishing, walking. Pets allowed in some areas. **Rooms 3** (2 en-suite shower only, 1 private bathroom). B&B €40pps, ss €10. Minimum stay 2 nights; prior booking advisable. Closed 23 Sep-1 May. Visa. **Directions:** Granard, N55 (Cavan end), turn at the Statoil station, taking right at the next junction. About 0.5 miles towards Abbeylara, to the left.

Longford

Ilia A Coffee Experience

Ⓝ CAFÉ

38 Ballymahon Street Longford Co Longford **Tel: 043 42958**
Fax: 044 40050 Email: iliacoffeeshop@eircom.net

Discerning travellers who know Julie Kenny's coffee shop Ilia, in Mullingar, will be pleased to find this newer branch in the centre of Longford town. The café may be quite different in style - it is a ground floor premises, approached via an entrance shared with the butcher's shop next door - but devotees of her wholesome fare will be able to get their morning fix of freshly squeezed orange juice here, and the bagel combo (toasted bagel with crispy bacon, poached egg, melted cheese & tomato relish)... and, come lunchtime, tuck into a mountain of mixed leaves with diced crispy bacon, red onion, peppers, black olives, tomatoes, grated carrots & croûtons, with home-made vinaigrette and an avocado fan. Of course, there's a great little coffee menu (Java Republic speciality hand-roasted coffees), a speciality tea menu (and irresistible home-bakes to go with them), smoothies and soft drinks - plus a carefully selected choice of wines. **Seats 58.** Open Mon-Sat, 9-5.30 (B'fst 9-12). Closed Sun; Christmas week. MasterCard, Visa, Laser.

LONGFORD

Country pursuits, notably fishing, are an attraction for visitors to this pleasant area, and Longford town can also be a useful place to break a journey. **The Longford Arms Hotel (Tel 043 46296; www.longfordarms.ie)** always presents a smart face to the world (and offers wholesome all-day food), and there are several appealing cafés and restaurants, including **Café Torc** (a must-visit for chocolaholics). And the big news as we go to press is that brother and sister team Stephen and Linda Devlin - who did so much to put Longford town on the diners map with their delightful Aubergine Gallery Café (Tel: 043 48633), are re-opening with a new restaurant of the same name a hundred yards down Ballymahon Street at The White House pub (entrance on right of ground floor shop).

Longford

Viewmount House

Ⓝ COUNTRY HOUSE

Dublin Road Longford Co Longford
Tel: 043 41919 Fax: 043 42906
Email: info@viewmounthouse.com Web: www.viewmounthouse.com

James and Beryl Kearney's lovely 1750s Georgian house just on the edge of Longford town was once owned by Lord Longford and is set in four acres of beautiful wooded gardens. It has been sensitively restored with style, combining elements of grandeur with a human scale that makes guests feel very comfortable. Its warmth strikes the first-time visitor immediately on arrival in the hall, which has a welcoming open fire and warm red walls contrasting strongly with a graceful white-painted staircase. Each room has its own character - there is an elegant period drawing room, and the six guest bedrooms all have their particular charm (one is especially large, but all are delightful); but perhaps the handsomest room of all is the unusual vaulted dining room, where an extensive breakfast menu is served. The original intention was to operate a restaurant here and that may well still happen, although it is now more likely to be out in the classic stone outbuildings that are currently under restoration. This is a most appealing house, with old wooden floors, rugs, antique furniture - and, most importantly, a great sense of hospitality. Golf nearby. Children welcome (under 4 free in parents' room, cot available without charge). Garden. No pets. **Rooms 6** (1 suite, 3 bath & shower, 3 shower only, all no smoking). B&B €50, ss €10. *Self-catering also available - details on application. Amex, MasterCard, Visa. **Directions:** Signed off Ardagh/Longford Road (R393).

COUNTY LOUTH

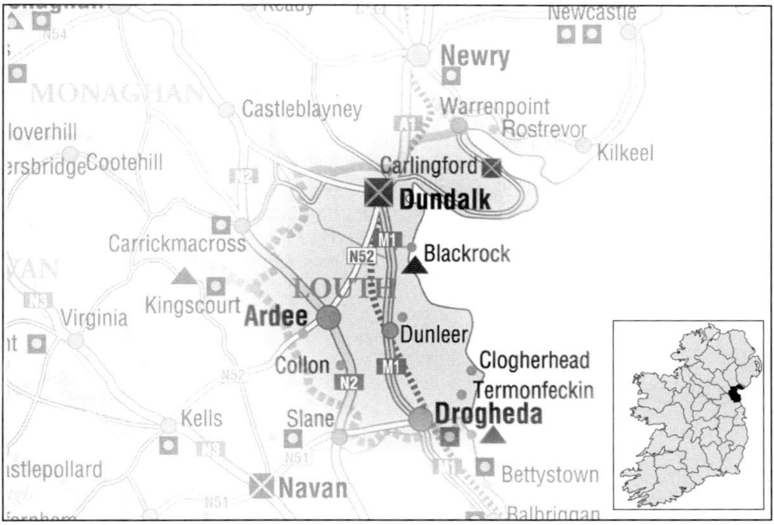

Plumb in the middle of the main East Coast corridor between Dublin and Belfast, Louth is leaping at the opportunities provided by the extension of the M1, which crosses the River Boyne near Drogheda on a handsome modern structure which is the largest cable-stayed bridge of its type in Ireland. With traffic pressure removed from its other roads, Louth begins to find itself. And though it may be Ireland's smallest county at only 317 square miles (it's just an eighth the size of Cork, the largest) Louth still manages to be two or even three counties in one.

Much of it is fine farmland, at its best in the area west of the extensive wildfowl paradise of Dundalk Bay, on whose shores we find the attractive village of Blackrock, one of Ireland's better kept secrets. But as well there are the distinctive uplands in the southwest, whose name of Oriel recalls an ancient princedom. And in the north of the county, the Cooley Mountains sweep upwards in a style which well matches their better-known neighbours, the Mountains of Mourne, on the other side of the handsome inlet of Carlingford Lough.

Its name might suggest that this is a genuine fjord, but it isn't. However, its beauty is such that there's more than enough to be going along with, and on its Louth shore the ancient little port of Carlingford town used to be a best-kept secret. It was a quiet little place imbued with history, but today it is happily prospering both as a recreational harbour for the Dundalk and Newry area, and as a bustling visitor attraction in its own right.

The county's three main townships of Ardee, Dundalk and Drogheda each have their own distinctive style, and all three have been coming vibrantly to life in recent years. The historic borough of Drogheda is the main commercial port, its river valley crossed by the Boyne Viaduct of 1855 vintage, such a remarkable piece of engineering work that it is reckoned one of the seven wonders of Ireland. Dundalk is the county town, and home to the Louth Museum, where a recent acquisition is the riding jacket worn by William of Orange at the Battle of the Boyne in 1690.

Local Attractions and Information

Ardee (Tallanstown), Knockabbey Castle & Gardens 042 937 4690
Carlingford, Heritage Trust, Tourism Information 042 937 3888
Carlingford, Carlingford Adventure Centre 042 937 3100
Carlingford, Carlingford Sea School 042 937 3879
Castlebellingham, Farm Market 0404 43885
Drogheda, Beaulieu House and Garden 041 983 8557
Drogheda, Droichead Arts Centre 041 983 3946
Drogheda, Millmount Museum 041 983 3097
Drogheda (Tullyallen), Old Mellifont Abbey 041 982 6459
Drogheda, Tourism Information 041 983 7070

Dundalk, Louth County Museum 042 932 7056
Dundalk, Tourism Information 042 933 5484
Termonfeckin, Irish Countrywomens Assoc. College 041 982 2119

Ardee — ARDEE

Ardee is an attractive little town of historical interest - its thirteenth century castle is prominent in the main street and there's evidence of contemporary interest for the traveller too: look out for a smart new bar called **Indigo (Tel 041 686 0060)**, on the northern edge of the town. Just opening on the Guide's visit, and offering light modern bar food - paninis, wraps etc - it could be a promising place to break a journey. About 4 miles south of Ardee, the fourteenth century **Smarmore Castle (Tel 041 6857167; www.smarmorecastle.com)** is an extraordinary place offering accommodation, a restaurant (Italian, run separately) and, most unlikely of all, an impressive leisure centre with 22 metre swimming pool, sauna, steam room, jacuzzi and fully equipped gym.

Ardee — Rolf's Bistro

Ⓝ RESTAURANT

52 Market Street Ardee Co Louth
Tel: 041 685 7949 Fax: 041 685 7949
Email: rolfsbistro@eircom.net Web: www.rolfsbistro.com

Paul and Bernadette Svender opened their attractive restaurant in the centre of Ardee in 2002 and it now draws a loyal following from a wide area around the town. It's a pleasingly informal place with a relaxed atmosphere and a refreshing determination to provide quality food and attentive service at affordable prices. The menu, which changes daily, is well-balanced and well-judged - not over-long yet allowing plenty of choice for regulars, with about ten dishes on each course. Paul is the chef and his speciality dishes reflect his background - Scandinavian prawn toast with Swedish caviar and Swedish beef Lindstrom (a main course based on minced meat, capers and beetroot), for example - but he uses local produce a lot and there really is something for everyone here, including popular starters like steamed mussels (with a sparky tomato & chilli sauce and aoïli bread) and a first course vegetarian tartlette with mushrooms, onions and gratinated Bellingham Blue cheese. There will always be at least a couple of fish dishes, some kind of pasta (perhaps for vegetarians, with goats cheese and sweet peppers) and old favourites like fillet steak (with Stilton gratinated tomato & brandy & black pepper sauce). Deft cooking, professional service, a relaxed ambience and fair prices add up to a successful formula and, with a reception area with squashy sofas planned for 2004, there will be more emphasis on comfort too. An early dinner menu is particularly good value. **Seats 36.** Toilets wheelchair accessible. Children welcome - but not after 9pm. D Tue-Sun, 5.30-10 (Sun 5-9). Early D €15 (5.30-7). House wine from €14.50. SC discretionary. Closed Mon; 1 wk summer,1 wk winter. MasterCard, Visa, Laser, Switch. **Directions:** Centre of Ardee, opposite SuperValu & Wogan Interiors. Beside Hatch Castle.

Blackrock — The Brake

PUB / RESTAURANT

Main Street Blackrock Co Louth
Tel: 042 932 1393 Fax: 042 932 2568

There is little about the neat but plain exterior to prepare first-time visitors for the warmth and country charm of The Brake – all old pine and rural bric-à-brac, it has open fires and friendly staff. It's a great place to stop just for a late afternoon cup of tea, but even better if you're hungry – it has a well-deserved reputation for good bar meals, and not just the usual pub staples, but a very wide choice including home-made chicken kiev, for example and all kinds of seafood including prawn or crab cocktail, wild smoked salmon, smoked mussels and prawns or crab claws in garlic butter - and that's just for starters. Main course seafood includes a seafood platter (hot or cold), poached wild salmon in season, jumbo prawns and maybe even lobster. There are lots of meat dishes, too, especially steaks (beef and gammon) with a range of sauces and creamy dishes that come with rice, such as prawns provençal, beef stroganoff and pork in a cream & herb sauce. Salads and accompaniments are particularly good, all arranged buffet style. Prices are fairly moderate - hot main courses range from about €14.50 (chicken curry or pork in cream & herb sauce) to €19.95 for jumbo prawns and €22.95 for fillet steak, but many of the lighter dishes and salads are much less. Beware of the unusual opening hours though – this is a late afternoon into evening place. No children under 12. **Seats 130.** Air conditioning. Toilets wheelchair accessible. Bar open 5-11.30. D daily 6.30-10.30 (Sun 6-9.30). A la carte; house wine €15; sc discretionary. * The Clermont Arms, a few doors along the front, is in the same family ownership. Closed 25 Dec, Good Fri. MasterCard, Visa, Laser, Switch. **Directions:** Turn off the main Dublin-Belfast road 3 miles south of Dundalk.

Carlingford

Beaufort House

GUESTHOUSE

Ghan Road Carlingford Co Louth **Tel: 042 937 3879** Fax: 042 937 3878
Email: michaelcaine@beauforthouse.net Web: www.beauforthouse.net

Michael and Glynnis Caine's immaculate property is well-placed to maximise on the attractions of a quiet and beautiful waterside position with wonderful sea and mountain views, while also being just a few minutes walk from Carlingford village. All areas are spacious and furnished to high specifications: hotel standard bedrooms have phone, TV with video channel and tea/coffee making facilities. The Caines were previously restaurateurs and dinner is available by arrangement for parties of eight or more. (Set D about €35). Associated activities include a sailing school and yacht charter - corporate sailing events (team building and corporate hospitality), including match racing in Carlingford Lough, are a speciality. Golf nearby. Helipad; ample car parking. Small conference/banqueting (25). Children welcome (under 2s free in parents' room). Fishing, cycling, hill walking, bird watching walking, garden. No pets. **Rooms 5** (2 shower only, all no smoking). B&B €43 pps, ss €43. Open all year. MasterCard, Visa. **Directions:** Approaching from Dundalk, turn right just before the village and harbour; house on shore.

Carlingford

Georgina's Tearooms

CAFÉ

Castle Hill Carlingford Co Louth **Tel: 042 937 3346** Email: tedf@eircom.net

Georgina Finegan's little daytime restaurant high up in the web of small roads above King John's Castle is well worth seeking out. The bakery has been going for over twenty years now, specialising in meringues and desserts and, since opening the tea rooms in 1997, Georgina has built up a loyal customer base including "people who return on a daily, weekly or even annual basis for the good food and friendly tea room setting." They come from Belfast, Dublin and "places in between", they're local, and they're visitors from all over the world - the fact is that there is something for everyone at this friendly and unpretentious café. Although a relatively recently added conservatory has brought some extra space, the original café is really quite small, but it's cosy and seems just right for simple wholesome fare like soup of the day (Italian Peasant, perhaps, made with carrots, parsnips, fennel, basil & sun-dried tomatoes) with a traditional sandwich like egg, tomato & parsley, or open sandwiches like ham & apple salad or ploughman's cheese platter, made with home-made wholemeal or white soda bread. Then there are toasted sandwiches -pastrami and gouda, perhaps, with sweet beetroot - and contemporary snacks like tortilla wraps, like smoked salmon & cream cheese, for example. But many people just drop in for a wedge of lemon meringue pie or Austrian apple pie, or maybe a slice of carrot cake and a cup of tea - after all, that's where it all started. **Seats 35.** Children welcome. Open daily, 10.30-6. Closed 1 week Sep, Christmas, 1 week Jan. **No Credit Cards. Directions:** Opposite King Joh's Castle.

Carlingford

Ghan House

COUNTRY HOUSE / RESTAURANT

Carlingford Co Louth
Tel: 042 937 3682 Fax: 042 937 3772
Email: ghanhouse@eircom.net Web: www.ghanhouse.com

This 18th century house is attractively located in its own walled grounds on the edge of Carlingford village and - and there's more to it than comfortable accommodation and the delicious meals you will enjoy for dinner or breakfast, as the Carroll family also run a cookery school on the premises. Accommodation is in four very different country rooms of character in the main house, each with sea or mountain views, and eight new bedrooms, which have been finished to a high standard in a separate building. In addition to the cookery school (contact Paul Carroll for the 2004 programme), Ghan House is also an increasingly popular venue for small conferences and meetings, including team development and corporate hospitality; details of services and rates available on request. A great little bar was added in 2003, creating a relaxing space where guests can mingle - in a more convivial atmosphere, perhaps, than beside the drawing room fire, although that too has its moments; it's very pleasant for residents to return to, and especially welcoming for non-residents just coming in for dinner. Conference/banqueting (55/80). Garden; walking. Children welcome (under 5s free in parents' room; cots available without charge). No pets. **Rooms 12** (all en-suite, 1 shower only, all no-smoking) B&B €80 pps, ss €20. (Discounts applied on stays of 2 or more nights.) Closed 23 Dec-10 Jan.

Restaurant: Dinner is, of course, a high priority at Ghan House – the style is contemporary, based mainly on quality home-grown (vegetable, fruit and herbs), home-made (breads, ice creams, everything that can be made on the premises) and local produce, notably Cooley lamb, dry cured bacon, free range eggs - and seafood: oysters are synonymous with Carlingford, smoked salmon and crab come from nearby Annagassan. A user-friendly set dinner menu with about five choice on each course is also priced by course, allowing considerable flexibility without having a separate à la carte: typical dishes on a late summer menu might include crab cakes with spinach, fennel & butter sauce, lemon roast cornfed chicken with crispy sage, prosciutto and mash and red wine roast plum and pecan strudel turnovers, with home-made vanilla ice cream and orange jus. Interesting, fairly priced wine list. Non-residents are welcome by reservation. **Seats 54.** D only, Fri & Sat 7-9.30 (other times by arrangement); Set D €47; special 8-course Gourmet Night menu about €68 (available six times a year); house wine €18; sc discretionary. Children welcome. Restaurant closed Sun-Thu , except for groups by arrangement. House closed 23 Dec-10 Jan. Amex, MasterCard, Visa, Laser. **Directions:** On edge of Carlingford village, Dundalk side.

Carlingford

Kingfisher Bistro

RESTAURANT

Darcy Ma Gee Court Dundalk Road Carlingford Co Louth
Tel: 042 937 3716

Mark and Claire Woods' little restaurant at the heritage centre has a great following. Although tiny, it packs quite a punch; it's amazing how much variety Mark manages to create a kitchen with very limited space and how well Claire manages the service. Modern menus begin with a "something soup" and a selection of eight starters (risotto of ham and pea with basil oil & fresh parmesan and smoked fish cakes with olive tapenade & crème fraîche are typical), while a similar number of main courses offers dressed up old favourites like sirloin steak (with potato rösti, garlic & parsley butter and onion sauce) alongside ideas from further afield like Thai spiced pork with sticky rice, curry oil, sweet soy & Asian salad. There are quite a few vegetarian dishes (including a house special). Desserts are not a particular priority (choice of four, possibly including apple strudel) but the wine list is another surprise for such a tiny place - not long by some standards, but interesting and fairly priced. Pricing generally is very reasonable and the minimum charge given on the menu is fair. Not suitable for children. **Seats 26.** D Tue-Sun 6.30-9.30 (Sun 5.30-8.30). A la carte (minimum charge about €16 per person). House wine about €21. MasterCard, Visa. **Directions:** Dundalk Road, Carlingford. ◇

Carlingford

O'Hares

ATMOSPHERIC PUB

Carlingford Co Louth **Tel: 042 937 3106**

Thankfully, at least the heart of this renowned pub seems to be resistant to change. It's one of those lovely places with a grocery at the front and an unspoilt hard-floored pub with an open fire at the back, and the food is simple but good: the speciality is Carlingford oysters – with a pint of stout of course. On the Guide's most recent visit there was building work in progress in the yard which, we suspect, will be covered over in 2004 - but, locals say, it won't be spoilt... Live music: traditional on Thursday nights, jazz on Sunday afternoons. Closed 25 Dec & Good Fri. **Directions:** In centre of village.

Carlingford

The Oystercatcher Lodge & Bistro

féile bia **RESTAURANT WITH ROOMS**

Market Square Carlingford Co Louth
Tel: 042 937 3922
Email: bmckev@eircom.net Web: www.theoystercatcher.com

Brian and Denise McKevitt's popular little restaurant with rooms has been doing great business on the square in Carlingford village since 1997. The arrival of a new chef, Connor Woods, in 2003 has brought some change of style towards modern Irish cooking, but everything is still local and seafood stars: Carlingford oysters, of course (several ways, cooked and fresh), seafood chowder, tempura of cod with crushed peas and a light tartare sauce - all this is typical and the house policy is not to use warm water fish, which makes a refreshing change from the majority of Irish restaurants. And they have another ace up their sleeves too, in the shape of delicious Cooley mountain lamb - typically a braised shank on champ with a red wine sauce; other favourites like steak and duck are equally well handled, also some vegetarian choices, all of which come fully garnished. Children welcome, but not after 7 pm. **Seats 40** (private room, 24) No smoking area. D Mon-Sat, 6.30-9.30; Sun 2.30-7.30. A la carte, plus specials. House wine €18; sc discretionary. Phone to check opening times off season. Closed 22-27 Dec.

Accommodation: Guest rooms are bright, spacious and very clean, with polished floors; phone, TV, tea/coffee making facilities, iron/trouser press provided. **Rooms 8** (all shower only) B&B €65 pps. ss €20. Children welcome (under 4 free in parents' room, cot available, €5; baby sitting arranged). MasterCard, Visa. **Directions:** In the centre of Carlingford village.

Carlingford area

Lily Finegans

Ⓝ **ATMOSPHERIC PUB**

Whitestown Co Louth

What a delight this pretty, traditional pub is - although now predictably popular with a young set who bring life and plenty of noise at busy times, it is a friendly and welcoming place without a sense of cliquishness so even the first time visitor will feel very much at home sipping a pint or a glass of whiskey in the bar or a little room at the back that feels as if it hasn't changed in fifty years. Open evenings. Closed 25 Dec.

Clogherhead

Little Strand Restaurant

RESTAURANT Strand Street Clogherhead Co Louth **Tel: 041 988 1061** Fax: 041 988 1062

This neat modern building, on the righthand side as you go through the village of Clogherhead to the beach, is set back a little from the road, with steps up to the front door. The fairly large ground floor restaurant is surprisingly formally appointed for the location and, upstairs, there's an impressive lounge area, used for aperitifs and coffee at busy times. You don't have to be a fish-lover to enjoy a meal here - menus offer a range of meat and vegetarian dishes including, intriguingly, Skipper's Choice (a 12 oz sirloin steak topped with Clogherhead prawns) but local seafood, brought in to the nearby fishing harbour of Port Oriel, is of course the speciality and very good it is too. House specialities include crab claws in garlic/lemon butter, lobster thermidor and sole on the bone with lemon, lime and dill butter; an exceptional dish is Clogherhead scampi, cooked and served the traditional way with sauce tartare. The restaurant is still fairly new, but the proprietor, Catherine Whelahan, continues to work hard to get the details right. **Seats 60** (Private room 12-16). Air conditioning. D Wed-Sun, 7-"late" (Sun from 5); à la carte; also autumn & spring special menus, about €20; house wine about €17, sc discretionary. Closed Mon, Tue, bank hols. MasterCard, Visa. **Directions:** 7 miles from Drogheda, 3 miles from Termonfeckin village.

Collon

Forge Gallery Restaurant

RESTAURANT WITH ROOMS Church Street Collon Co Louth **Tel: 041 982 6272**
Fax: 041 982 6584 Email: forgegallery@eircom.net

For the best part of twenty years this charming two-storey restaurant has been providing good food, hospitality and service - and guarding its reputation as the best eating place for miles around. It's a most attractive place – the building itself is unusual and has been furnished and decorated with flair, providing a fine setting for food that combines country French and New Irish styles, with a few other influences along the way. Seasonal produce stars, much of it local – seafood, game in season, vegetables, fruit – and typical main course selections include a special vegetarian dish as well as local meat, such as rack of tender Cooley lamb, and seafood like the 'Forge Rendezvous' of prawns and scallops in chablis & cream. Quality ingredients, well-cooked and generously served make for good value - and a loyal following. **Seats 60.** Air conditioning. D Tue-Sat, 7-9. Set D €40; à la carte also available. House wine from €23; sc discretionary). Closed Sun & Mon; Christmas & 1 week Jan. Amex, Diners, MasterCard, Visa, Laser. **Directions:** On N2, 35 miles from Dublin due north, midway between Slane and Ardee, in centre of village.

Drogheda

Boyne Valley Hotel & Country Club

HOTEL Drogheda Co Louth **Tel: 041 983 7737** Fax: 041 983 9188
Email: reservations@boynevalleyhotel.ie Web: www.boynevalleyhotel.ie

Set in large gardens just on the Dublin side of Drogheda town - and handy to the motorway - this substantial hotel has an 18th century mansion at its heart. It is not as obvious as it used to be since developments created a completely new entrance, but it is still there and provides some unspoilt, graciously proportioned rooms that contrast well with the later additions, including 34 new rooms added in May 2003. Owner-run by Michael and Rosemary McNamara since 1992, it has the personal touch unique to hands-on personal management and is popular with locals, for business and pleasure, as well as a base for visitors touring the historic sites of the area. While rooms in the old building have more character, the new ones are finished to the high standard demanded by today's discerning travellers. Fine conference facilities and excellent leisure centre add greatly to the hotel's attraction. Conference/banqueting (450/450); secretarial services. Leisure centre, indoor swimming pool; beauty salon. All weather tennis; pitch & putt. Garden. Pets allowed by arrangement. **Rooms 72** (1 suite, 13 shower only, 35 no-smoking, 1 disabled). B&B from about €80 pps. Open all year. Amex, Diners, MasterCard, Visa, Laser. **Directions:** On southern edge of Drogheda town. From Dublin turn off M1 to N1 at Julianstown; from Belfast turn off M1 to N1 at Drogheda north.

Dundalk

Ballymascanlon House Hotel

HOTEL Dundalk Co Louth **Tel: 042 935 8200** Fax: 042 937 1598
Email: info@ballymascanlon.com Web: www.ballymascanlon.com

Set in 130 acres of parkland, this hotel just north of Dundalk has developed around a large Victorian house. It has been in the Quinn family ownership since 1948 and major improvements made over the last few of years have been done with panache, lifting the hotel into a different class; bright and spacious public areas are furnished and decorated in a warm, comfortably contemporary style with plenty of table lamps, good pictures and a variety of seating - comfy sofas and armchairs, Lloyd loom chairs - all of which combines to create a stylishly homely atmosphere. Spacious and very attractive new bedrooms share the same qualities, with specially commissioned furniture adding interest - and, in many cases, views over lovely gardens, the golf course or the attractive old stable yard, which is in the process of restoration. Corporate facilities include three versatile meeting rooms, with back-up business services available. Impressive new leisure facilities include a 20 metre deck level pool and tennis courts. With so much to do on the premises and easy access to areas of great natural beauty and historical interest, this hotel makes a good base for a break (special interest and off-season deals available). Conference/banqueting (250/250); secretarial services. Leisure centre, swimming pool; tennis, golf (18), garden, walking. Children welcome (under 2s free in parents' room; cots available without charge, baby sitting arranged). **Rooms 90** (4 suites, 2 junior suites, 90 executive rooms, 26 no smoking, 2 for disabled). Lift. 24 hour room service. B&B about €80 pps, ss €25. Open all year. Amex, Diners, MasterCard, Visa, Laser. **Directions:** N1 from Dublin; on the Carlingford road, 3 miles north of Dundalk.

Dundalk

Cube

Ⓝ CAFÉ / RESTAURANT

5 Roden Place Dundalk Co Louth
Tel: 042 932 9898 Fax: 042 935 6656
Email: dine@cuberestaurant.ie Web: www.cuberestaurant.ie

Probably one of the country's most style-conscious new restaurants, Cube is up a few steps just across from St Patrick's Cathedral and crammed with visual tricks and fancies - if not persuaded by the cool aubergine walls and leather armchairs in the bar or the imaginative lighting (including uplighters set into the floor), or the cream leather banquettes in the restaurant, the dramatic plates used for presenting sushi and desserts (actually far too big for the table and difficult to eat off) - or, indeed, the Cube logo itself - you might just pop down and check the loos. What it costs to kit out a restaurant like this heaven only knows - about the price of a small semi perhaps - but it does have impact. Given all that, it's a surprisingly friendly, almost laid-back place, the simple modern place settings have class and they work hard at the menus so, although understandably expensive, Cube does offer something different from other restaurants in the area and, for the most part, it's an interesting package. A a carte lunches ('Cube Café') are quite reasonable, offering a wide choice of popular café fare (fashionable salads, wild boar bangers and mash, deep-fried cod with mushy peas & chunky ships) with virtually nothing over €10 - except a listing headed 'Seafood Bar' which loses the run of itself completely, rising to €85 for the Cube Seafood Platter for two, and appears on the evening menu also. By contrast there's also a 'Value Menu' offered at €30 - just too much choice, perhaps, causing confusion and indecision. Grilled turbot fillet is a speciality and sounds simple enough - until you realise that it comes with crab and langoustine ravioli, poached oysters, a little bouillabaisse of baby vegetables with saffron and garlic... Of a range of dishes sampled by the Guide, the best was a rack of Cooley lamb, which was also the simplest dish by far; however, especially given that entertainment is high on the agenda here, high marks also go to an excellent and dramatically presented sushi starter plate. Service can be noticeably slow, but staff are friendly and helpful, albeit with varying degrees of professionalism. This is a young enterprise, there is obvious commitment to attaining high standards and the underlying feeling at the end of a meal here is that it might be achievable by offering less choice in all areas allowing the team to focus on getting things just right. An interesting wine list beginning at €20 includes an unusually wide range of over twenty wines offered by the glass, a proprietors' list of fine wines and a good choice of dessert wines and digestifs. Children welcome, but not after 8pm. **Seats 54** (private room, 16). L Mon-Fri, 12-3; D Tue-Sat, 7-11. Set D (2-course) €30; also à la carte L&D. No SC. Closed L Sat, D Sun & Mon; 25-26 Dec. MasterCard, Visa. **Directions:** Opposite St. Patrick's Cathedral.

Dundalk

McKeown's

ATMOSPHERIC PUB

16 Clanbrassil Street Dundalk Co Louth **Tel: 042 933 7931**

This well-run pub of character has a great atmosphere and friendly staff - just the place for a pint and welcome reassurance that the great Irish pub is alive and well in Dundalk. Closed 25 Dec, Good Fri. **Directions:** Town centre - across the road from Quaglino's Restaurant.

Dundalk

Number Thirty Two Restaurant

RESTAURANT

32 Chapel Street Dundalk Co Louth **Tel: 042 933 1113**
Email: no.32@ireland.com Web: www.no32.ie

Attractively situated in a leafy corner of town near the museum, Susan Heraghty's great little place is the neighbourhood restaurant par excellence and a great asset to Dundalk. It occupies a corner site, with windows all along one side giving it a sense of space, a feeling emphasised by the smart simplicity of the decor and table settings. Menus are written in an admirably down-to-earth style - and the same can be said of the prices, notably an exceptional early evening menu (the 'Express') which allows you two courses (from a generous selection of about half a dozen starters and main courses, plus several daily fish and vegetarian specials) and includes coffee with a mini-dessert - and the later set menu is not far behind. On whichever, you might get such delicious starter combinations as deep-fried tempura aubergine & courgette with red onion marmalade & curry oil, or a beautifully light crisp-pastried baked tartlette of smoked chicken, tarragon & semi-dried tomato cream - and main courses like Creole salmon with green beans, tossed salad & citrus sour cream, or a provençal style lamb shank with root vegetables & broccoli purée. There has always been a terrific generosity of spirit here - not in overladen plates, but in quality of food and service; the later menu is like the Express but with a little more choice and slightly more sophisticated dishes - but prices are still very reasonable. Everything is just as delicious as it sounds (or even more so), service is good-humoured and efficient. Would that every town in Ireland had a place like this. **Seats 35.** Reservations required. Children welcome. D Mon-Sat, 5.30-10.30. Early 'Express' D €15 (Mon-Thu 5.30-7), 'Gourmet Express' D €20 (Fri & Sat); Set D €26. House wine €18.95. No SC. Closed Sun, bank hols. Amex, MasterCard, Visa, Laser. **Directions:** First left turn after courthouse at "home bakery".

Dundalk

Quaglinos at the Century

N féile bia **BAR / RESTAURANT**

The Century Bar 19 Roden Place Dundalk Co Louth
Tel: 042 933 8567 Fax: 042 933 4147

Pat and Eileen Kerley relocated their long-established and highly regarded restaurant in Dundalk, to interesting new premises at The Century Bar, which is a listed building on a corner site opposite St Patrick's Cathedral. It's a romantic building dating back to 1902, with an ornamental turret on the corner, above the front door - and it has retained many features of historical interest, including the original bar counter and hand-carved bar backdrop. The restaurant is over the bar and here Pat Kerley - a committed Euro-Toques chef - continues to take great pride in the active promotion of Irish cuisine and uses as much local produce as possible: Carlingford oysters, Annagassan salmon, lobster and, of course, Cooley lamb all make their mark on menus that offer an appealing blend of traditional and modern Irish cooking. As in most Louth restaurants, generosity remains the keynote and providing good service with good value is a priority. Quaglino's has always had a strong following and loyal customers (plus many new ones) have taken to the new restaurant with great enthusiasm, so reservations are essential. Children welcome. **Seats 30.** D daily, 6-10. Set D from €35, also à la carte; no SC Bar meals Mon-Sat, 12-3. Closed 25 Dec, Good Fri. Amex, Diners, MasterCard, Visa, Laser, Switch. **Directions:** Just off town centre by St. Patrick's Cathedral.

Dundalk

Rosemount

N **B&B**

Dublin Road Dundalk Co Louth **Tel: 042 933 5878** Fax: 042 933 5878

Maisie Meehan's spick and span B&B is easily recognisable by the garden which is a colourful mass of flowers - all home raised in their own greenhouse, from seed, each year. The house is very homely and immaculately maintained, with a comfortable guests' sitting room and an attractive breakfast room overlooking the back garden. Neat, individually decorated bedrooms, have tea and coffee-making facilities, television and well-finished shower rooms. **Rooms 9** (all en-suite). B&B about €40 pps. **No Credit Cards. Directions:** 1.5 miles south of town centre, off N1.

Dundalk

The Spirit Store

N **ATMOSPHERIC PUB**

The Harbour Dundalk Co Louth

This pub of great character and friendliness is right on the quay, where coasters dock, so you never know what country visiting sailors may come from. But everyone mixed well in the wackily-furnished bars downstairs and - although a youthful place best known for its music (regular events are held in the upstairs bar, often famous names) people of all ages and backgrounds are welcomed here, even if only for a cup of tea to break a journey. Closed 25 Dec, Good Fri. **Directions:** On the quayside, beside the bridge.

Dundalk Area

Fitzpatrick's Bar & Restaurant

féile bia **PUB / RESTAURANT**

Jenkinstown Rockmarshal Dundalk Co Louth
Tel: 042 937 6193 Fax: 042 937 6274

Flowers and a neat frontage with fresh paintwork always draw attention to this attractive and well-run establishment. It has plenty of parking and is well organised for the informal but comfortable consumption of food in a series of bar/dining rooms, all with character and much of local interest in pictures and artefacts. Prompt reception, friendly service and traditional home-cooked food (sometimes with a modern twist) at reasonable prices all add up to an appealing package - and its obvious popularity with locals and visitors alike is well deserved. **Seats 60** (private room 40). Air conditioning. Open daily in summer, otherwise Tue-Sun 12.30 -10pm (Sun to 9pm), L from 12.30, D 6-10. A la carte menus. Closed Mon (except high season), Good Fri, 25 Dec. MasterCard, Visa, Laser. **Directions:** Just north of Dundalk town, take Carlingford road off main Dublin-Belfast road.

Dunleer

Carlito's

RESTAURANT

Main Street Dunleer Co Louth **Tel: 041 686 1366**

People come from miles around to eat at this unassuming Italian restaurant, so it is wise to book well ahead, especially at weekends. Although quite unremarkable from the street, the interior is welcoming, in warm shades of deep red and orange and a comfortable seating area just inside the door where groups can assemble over an aperitif before heading for their table. Tables are simply set (night light, cutlery and a paper napkin) but the welcome is very friendly and you'll quickly be settled into a menu that is well-constructed to please everyone, regardless of age or the occasion. Expect lovely home-baked bread, real minestrone soup with heaps of flavour, mixed leaf salads with creamy home-made dressing, deliciously crisp thin-based pizzas, a range of pastas and daily specials - such as herb-crusted cod, perfectly cooked and served with local vegetables (choice of boiled or chipped potatoes). Desserts are equally good: real tiramisu, crème brulée with fresh strawberries perhaps, and freshly brewed coffee to finish. Great value, great place. D Tue-Sat, 6pm -"late", Sun 5-9pm. MasterCard, Visa. **Directions:** On main street. ◇

Termonfeckin

Triple House Restaurant

RESTAURANT

Termonfeckin Co Louth **Tel: 041 982 2616** Fax: 041 982 2616

The pretty village of Termonfeckin provides a fine setting for Pat Fox's popular restaurant, which is in a 200-year-old converted farmhouse in landscaped gardens surrounded by mature trees. In winter you can settle in front of a log fire in the reception area on cold evenings while pondering the menu over a glass of wine (there's also a conservatory, used for aperitifs in summer). Committed to using the best of local produce, Pat offers wide-ranging menus and daily blackboard seafood extras from nearby Clogherhead – fresh Clogherhead prawns, Annagassan crab, and a dish he entitles, intriguingly, Port Oriel Pot-Pourri. But locally-reared meats feature too, in roast Drogheda smoked loin of pork with a nectarine & Calvados sauce, for example. Specialities include lovely spinach-filled crêpes(baked with cream sauce, tomato sauce and Parmesan) and, for dessert, a chewy meringue dacquoise that varies with the season's fruits. Plated farmhouse cheeses typically include Cashel Blue, Cooleeney and Wexford Cheddar. The wine list reflects Pat's particular interests and special evenings are sometimes held for enthusiasts off-season. Children welcome. **Seats 40.** D Tue-Sat 6.30-9.30, L Sun only 1-3; Set D about €30, à la carte available; early D about €22, 6.30-7.30 only; Set Sun L about €22. House wines about €17-20; sc discretionary. Toilets wheelchair accessible. Closed Mon, Christmas. MasterCard, Visa. **Directions:** 5 miles north east of Drogheda. ◇

COUNTY MAYO

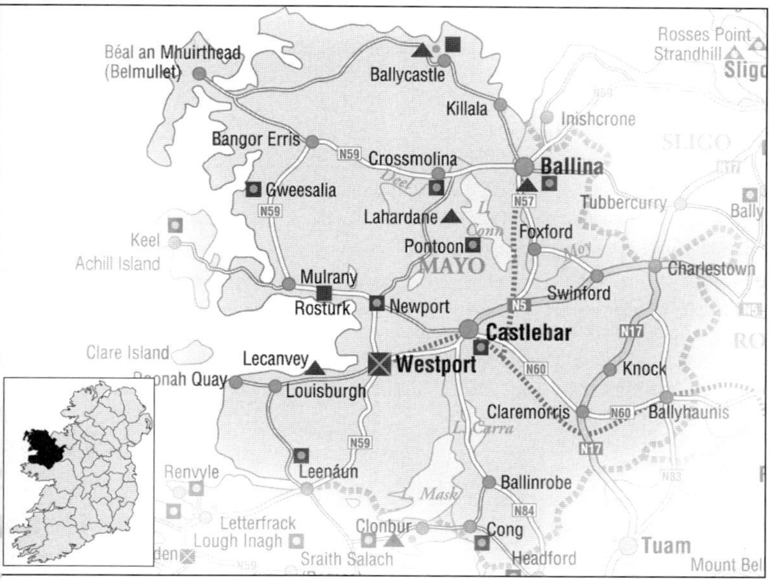

Mayo - far Mayo - might have been a byword for remoteness and declining population in times past, but now it is thriving. The recent six year Census showed a population increase of 5.3% (to 118,000), and they are people who enjoy the present as much as savouring the past. No more so than at Westport on Clew Bay, near the famed Holy Mountain of Croagh Patrick. Westport is a planned town which responds to TLC, and on September 8th 2003, it was declared the best kept large town in Ireland in the annual Tidy Towns awards.

Five kilometres east of the bustling county town of Castlebar, the Museum of Country Life at Turlough Park House, the first fully-fledged department of the National Museum to be located anywhere outside Dublin, celebrates Irish country life as it was lived between 1850 and 1960 with a remarkable display of artefacts which were in regular everyday use, yet now seem almost exotic.

As often, indeed, does Mayo itself - for Mayo is magnificent. All Ireland's counties have their devotees, but enthusiasts for Mayo have a devotion which is pure passion. In their heart of hearts, they feel that this austerely majestic Atlantic-battered territory is somehow more truly Irish than anywhere else. And who could argue with them after experiencing the glories of scenery, sea and sky which this western rampart of Ireland puts on ever-changing display?

Yet among Mayo's many splendid mountain ranges we find substantial pockets of fertile land, through which there tumble fish-filled streams and rivers. And in the west of the county, the rolling hills of the drumlin country, which run in a virtually continuous band right across Ireland from Strangford Lough, meet the sea again in the island studded wonder of Clew Bay.

Along Mayo's rugged north coast, turf cutting at Ceide Fields near Ballycastle has revealed the oldest intact field and farm system in existence, preserved through being covered in blanket bog 5,000 years ago. An award-winning interpretive centre has been created at the site, and even the most jaded visitor will find fascination and inspiration in the clear view which it provides into Ireland's distant past. A few miles eastward, the charming village of Ballycastle is home to the internationally-respected Ballinglen Arts Foundation, creative home-from-home for artists worldwide.

Nearby, the lively town of Ballina is where the salmon-rich River Moy meets the sea in the broad sweep of Killala Bay. It takes a leap of the imagination to appreciate that the sheltered Moy Valley is in the same county as the spectacularly rugged cliffs of Achill Island. But leaps of the imagination is what Mayo inspires.

Local Attractions and Information

Ballina, Street Festival/Arts Week (July) 096 70905
Ballina, Tourism Information 096 70848

Ballycastle, Ballinglen Arts Foundation .... 096 43184 / 43366
Castlebar, Linenhall Arts Centre 094 902 3733
Castlebar, Tourism Information 094 902 1207
Castlebar Turlough House (see entry under Turlough) 094 903 1589
Ceide Fields, Interpretive Centre 0996 43325
Clare Island Ferries 098 27685
Foxford, Woollen Mills Visitor Centre 094 925 6756
Inishkea Island Tours, Belmullet 097 85741
Inishturk Island Ferries .... 098 45520 / 45541
Killasser(Swinford)Traditional Farm Heritage Centre 094 925 2505
Kiltimagh, Glore Mill Follain Arts Centre 094 82184
Knock International Airport 094 936 7222
Moy Valley Holidays 096 70905
Turlough,Turlough Park House. Museum of Country Life.
Open Tuesday to Saturday 10am to 5pm, Sundays 2pm to 5pm, closed Mondays 094 903 1589
Westport, Clew Bay Archaeological Trail 087 293 5207
Westport, Westport House & Children's Zoo .... 098 25430 / 27766
Westport, Tourism Information 098 25711

Achill

Gray's Guest Hous

GUESTHOUSE

Dugort Achill Island Co Mayo **Tel: 098 43244** / 4331

Vi McDowell has been running this legendary guesthouse in the attractive village of Dugort since 197 and nobody understands better the qualities of peace, quiet and gentle hospitality that have bee bringing guests here for the last hundred years. It is an unusual establishment, occupying a series houses, and each area has a slightly different appeal. There's a large, traditionally furnished sittin room with an open fire and several conservatories for quiet reading. Bedrooms and bathrooms va considerably due to the age and nature of the premises, but the emphasis is on old-fashioned comfor they all have tea & coffee-making trays, phones for incoming calls have been introduced recently ar there are extra shared bathrooms in addition to en-suite facilities. Children are welcome and have a indoor playroom and safe outdoor play area, plus pool and table tennis for older children. It's a nic place to drop into for coffee, light lunch or afternoon tea (which is served in the garden in fine weathe and the dining room is open to non-residents for evening meals by arrangement.(Lovely old-fashione menus like hot spiced grapefruit, roast lamb or beef, poached Keem Bay salmon with hollandai sauce, apple tart with cream or fresh fruit meringue. Packed lunches supplied. Pets permitted in som areas by arrangement. Children welcome (under 3s free in parents' room). Garden, croquet, fishin walking. **Rooms 15** (all en-suite, 14 shower only). B&B €40 pps, ss €6, SC10%. D 7pm. Set D €26 (nc residents €32, by reservation), house wine €16. Closed 25 Dec. Personal cheques accepted. **No Cred Cards. Directions:** Castlebar,Westport, Newport, Achill Sound - Dugort!

Achill Island

Bervi

Ⓝ **B&B**

Keel Achill Island Co Mayo **Tel: 098 43114** Fax: 098 434
Email: bervie@esatclear.ie Web: www.bervieachill.co

John and Elizabeth Barrett's magical beachside house was once a coast guard station and, since 193 has been the ultimate escape for the many guests who have stayed here. It's a low, tucked-in kind of place with a little wicket gate giving direct access to the beach and an other-worldliness which is ve rare these days. Elizabeth was born here and, aside from the location and the charm of the house its - which has style without being at all 'decorated' - it is the sense of continuity that makes it speci and, of course, she has the 'hotelier's gene' which makes hospitality come naturally. Bedrooms, wh not especially large, are comfortably furnished with everything you need to feel at home, there is large dining room, where Elizabeth serves a home-cooked dinner with several choices on each cours and plenty of room for sitting around the turf fire; while meals are primarily for residents, there's natural hospitality here - beginning with the hot-buttered scones and home-made jam Elizabeth mak for afternoon tea - and a willingness to fit in extra guests if there is room. Children welcome (c available without charge). Pets allowed in some areas. Pool table, playroom, garden. **Rooms 14** (all e suite & no smoking, 11 shower only). Room service (all day). B&B €45 PPOs. ss €15. Weekend Dini Room seats 40. D from €25 (reservations required; non-residents welcome if there is room). Vi **Directions:** Follow signs to Keel from bridge onto island; turn left in village, towards beach.

Achill Island — The Beehive

CAFÉ

Keel Achill Island Co Mayo **Tel: 098 43018** / 43134 Fax: 098 43018

At their informal restaurant and attractive craft shop in Keel, husband and wife team Patricia and Michael Joyce take pride in the careful preparation and presentation of the best of Achill produce, especially local seafood such as fresh and smoked salmon, mussels, oysters and crab. Since opening, in 1991, they have extended both the menu and the premises more than once and now offer all-day self-service food, which you can have indoors or take out to a patio overlooking Keel beach in fine weather Everything is homemade, and they make great soups such as cheddar & onion, courgette & onion, leek & mussel, seafood chowder and traditional nettle soup (brotchán neantóg) all served with homemade brown scones. As baking is a speciality, there's always a tempting selection of cakes, bracks, teabreads, fruit tarts, baked desserts and scones with home-made preserves or you can simply have a toasted sandwich, or an Irish farmhouse cheese plate (with a glass of wine perhaps). * The family also has accommodation on the island; details from the restaurant. **Seats 150** (private rooms, 50). Toilet wheelchair accessible; baby changing facility. Meals 10-6 daily, Easter-early Nov. A la carte; wine licence: house wines about €15-19 (plus large selection of quarter bottles, around €3.75). Amex, Diners, MasterCard, Visa, Laser. **Directions:** Situated in the centre of Keel overlooking beach and Minuan cliffs.

Ballina — Crockets on the Quay

PUB

Ballina Co Mayo **Tel: 096 759340** Fax: 096 70069
Web: www.crocketsonthequay.ie

Gina and Padraig McLoughlin's well-known hostelry is attractively situated on the quay in Ballina, overlooking the River Moy (which may well provide some of the wild salmon on the menu), and it's a surprisingly large premises once you start exploring. At the front there's seating outside for fine weather and a very pleasant old-style bar with an open fire (gas, alas) and plenty of pictures and artefacts of local interest giving it a sense of history. Extending behind the traditional bar is a series of contemporary bar areas with trendy low seating and big tables, finishing up with a stylish big bar right at the back, which has access to a carpark behind the building. Coming in from the sunshine on a bright summer's day, all this seems quite surreal, but it leaps into life at night. It's a hospitable place, where bar food is available all day and interesting evening menus are offered in a restaurant - quite modern, stylish - overlooking the river; here the à la carte menus offer some unusual dishes based on local produce such as rabbit terrine with bacon (not as traditional as it sounds, when it comes with truffled papaya salad), Carramore eels (in a spring roll, with sweet & sour pear) and imaginative vegetarian dishes, like aubergine-wrapped courgettes with slow cooked tomatoes, smoked Bally Oak cheese and green herb salsa - and there's even a side dish of cabbage & bacon with chilli. This is a welcoming, laid-back place for local and visiting customers, and service is a priority. Not suitable for children after 7.30pm. **Seats 58** (outdoor seating, 30). Air conditioning. Toilets wheelchair accessible. D daily, 6-10.30; L Sun only, 12.30-2.30, A la carte. House wine €16. bar menu available daily, 12.30-8.30. Accommodation also offered (B&B €35pps). Closed 25-26 Dec. **Directions:** On the edge of Ballina ; from town, take main Sligo road, turn left at first traffic lights.

Ballina — Gaughans

ATMOSPHERIC PUB

O'Rahilly Street Ballina Co Mayo
Tel: 096 70096 Email: edmg@eircom.net

This is one of the great old pubs of Ireland and has a gentle way of drawing you in, with the menu up in the window and a display of local pottery to arouse the curiosity. It's a fine old-fashioned bar, with everything gleaming and a great sense of the pride taken in its care. Michael Gaughan opened the pub in November 1936 and his son, Edward, took over in 1972. Edward's wife Mary is a great cook and, once they started doing food in 1983 they never looked back; everybody loves the way they run the place and Mary still does all the cooking. Her specialities (all good home cooking) include home-made quiche Lorraine with salad, fresh crab salad and good old-fashioned roasts - roast stuffed chicken with vegetables and potatoes, perhaps, or baked gammon. There's always a daily special (€8) and old favourites like lemon meringue pie and pineapple upside down pudding for dessert. There are lighter options on the menu too, like open smoked salmon or crab sandwich, smoked salmon salad, ploughman's lunch. Seasonal ingredients like crab and wild salmon depend on availability and it's all great wholesome fare. And, charmingly listed along with the Bewley's tea and coffee, the wine and Irish coffee "Glass of spring water: Free." Now that's style. Children welcome. Opening hours: Mon-Sat from 11 am (Mon-Thu to 11.30; Fri & Sat to 12.30) Sun 8-11pm. Bar food served Mon-Sat, 11am-6pm. Closed 25 Dec & Good Fri. Amex, Diners, MasterCard, Visa, Laser. **Directions:** Up to post office on left.

Ballycastle

Mary's Bakery & Tea Rooms

RESTAURANT Main Street Ballycastle Co Mayo **Tel: 096 43361**

Mary Munnelly's homely little restaurant is the perfect place to stop for some good home cooking. Baking is the speciality but she does "real meals" as well - home-made soups like mushroom or smoked bacon & potato, wild salmon various ways and free range chicken dishes. And, if you strike a chilly day, it's very pleasant to get tucked in beside a real fire too. There's also a garden with sea views for fine weather - and home-made chutneys and jams on sale to take home. **Seats 30.** Toilets wheelchair accessible. Open 10am-7pm in summer (shorter hours off season); Closed Sun Oct-Easter & first 3 weeks Jan. **No Credit Cards. Directions:** From Ballina - Killala - main road to Ballycastle, on way to Ceide Fields. ◇

Ballycastle

Polke's

ATMOSPHERIC PUB Main Street Ballycastle Co Mayo **Tel: 096 43016**

This lovely old-established general merchants and traditional pub is just across the road from Mary's Bakery and well worth a visit. It was established in 1820 and has remained in the family since then - the present proprietor, Brian Polke, has had responsibility for this national treasure since 1962. Not much has changed it seems: the long, narrow bar behind the shop is completely unspoilt, friendly and a joy to find yourself in. The whole place is immaculate too (including the outside loo in a whitewashed yard at the back), giving the lie to the widely-held view that "character" pubs are, by definition, scruffy. A nice touch of modernity which reflects the close-knit nature of the local community is the collection of pictures donated by artists from the nearby Ballinglen Arts Centre, which are exhibited in the bar and make a fascinating talking point for new arrivals. Closed 25 Dec & Good Fri. **Directions:** On main street.

Ballycastle

Stella Maris Hotel

HOTEL / RESTAURANT Ballycastle Co Mayo **Tel: 096 43322** Fax: 096 43965
Email: info@stellamarisireland.com Web: www.stellamarisireland.com

IRISH BREAKFAST AWARD - CONNAUGHT

Built in 1853 as a coast guard regional headquarters, Frances Kelly and Terence McSweeney's fine property was later acquired by the Sisters of Mercy who named it Stella Maris and, most recently, opened as an hotel under the current management in 2002. Extensive renovations have restored the building to its original impressive condition and then some - Frances has acquired a remarkable collection of antiques and interesting pieces for the hotel and mixed them with contemporary furniture, creating a warm and interesting interior with a welcome emphasis on comfort. But the location is this hotel's major asset and a conservatory built all along the front takes full advantage of it, allowing guests to relax in comfort and warmth while drinking in the majestic views of the surrounding coastline and sea. Accommodation blends style with comfort in uncluttered rooms furnished with antiques that enjoy the best of both worlds, with modern bathrooms and power showers. Dinner- cooked by Frances - is a very enjoyable experience: menus are well balanced and imaginative without being over-influenced by fashion: sautéed lambs kidneys (in season), roasted pepper and red onion soup, rack of Mayo lamb with puy lentils and sage-flavoured jus are all typical and there is usually a choice of two fish dishes (vegetarian option on request). Classic desserts include refreshing seasonal fruits - poached peach with vanilla ice cream, glazed Italian meringue & mango coulis, perhaps - or there's an Irish farmhouse cheese plate - then it's back to the conservatory for a digestif... This is indeed a wonderful retreat. Concise, well-chosen wine list. And, next morning residents will have another treat in store as the Stella Maris breakfast is worth lingering over: lashings of freshly squeezed juice, a beautiful fruit plate, gorgeous freshly-baked brown bread, hand-made preserves and perfect hot food cooked to order, be it a traditional Irish or a special like creamy scrambled eggs with smoked salmon - not a grand display, but exceptionally delicious. **Rooms 12** (suite, 4 shower only, all no smoking, 1 disabled). B&B €90 pps, ss €45. Children welcome (under 4 free in parents' room, cot available without charge, baby sitting arranged). Restaurant **Seats 24.** D Tue Sun, 7-10, L Sun only, 1-3; D à la carte, Sun L €25; house wine €16.95. Restaurant closed Mon; hote closed 5 Oct-8 Apr. MasterCard, Visa, Laser. **Directions:** West of Ballina on R314.

Bangor Erris

Teach Iorrais Hotel

HOTEL

Geesala Bangor Erris Ballina Co Mayo **Tel: 097 86888** Fax: 097 86855
Email: teachior@iol.ie Web: www.teachiorrais.com

Facilities in this remote and fascinating Gaeltacht area were pretty thin on the ground before this new hotel opened in 1998 and it has proved a great success. It's a great place to drop into during the day for a bite to eat or just a cup of tea - there's always a welcoming fire in the bar (which has character, although the hotel is modern) and staff are very friendly. Bedrooms are comfortably furnished, with neat en-suite bathrooms, direct dial phone, tea/coffee facilities and television with video channel. Off-season breaks offer especially good value and there are many activities nearby, including golf, horse riding, walking, boating and fishing (there's a drying room for tackle and bait). Teach Iorrais is a popular place for weddings and would also be an interesting choice for conferences and corporate events - or for a very different Christmas or New Year break. Conference/banqueting (400/325); secretarial services. Pets permitted by arrangement. Children welcome (under 5s free in parents' room; cots available without charge). Garden, fishing, walking. **Rooms 31** (all en-suite,1 suite, 10 no-smoking, 1 for disabled). B&B about €55 pps, ss about €10. Light bar food 1-5pm daily. L & D offered daily, 12.30-3 (Sun to 4), 7-9.30. Open all year. Amex, MasterCard, Visa, Laser. **Directions:** 40 minutes drive from Ballina. ◇

Castlebar

An Carraig

Ⓝ féile bia RESTAURANT

Chapel Street Castlebar Co Mayo **Tel: 094 26159**

Limar Horan's family-run restaurant in a quiet street just off the town centre has earned a loyal local following. It's an attractive, quite traditional restaurant with cut stone walls and a nautical theme with lots of wood, portholes and an arch that links smaller dining areas and also provides visual interest, a cosier atmosphere and privacy - a feeling enhanced by gentle lighting and candles. Menus are updated traditional, with seafood taking the starring role in dishes like seafood chowder, steamed mussels, lobster - many of the old favourites are there; also home-made paté, honey roast duckling, char-grilled steaks various ways - but most will have some kind of twist in the presentation, bringing them up to date. Finish with the shared dessert platter for two. Healthy options are offered and there's willingness to provide for special diets and allergies (advance notice preferred). Good customer care and home cooking is the aim, achieved very successfully - and they give good value too. Guests are even urged to take home a loaf of the home-made bread. part catering. **Seats 55.** D Tue-Sun, 6-10pm. Closed Mon, 10 days Jan. **Directions:** Opposite Church of the Holy Rosary. ◇

Castlebar

Café Rua

Ⓝ RESTAURANT

New Antrim Street Castlebar Co Mayo **Tel: 094 23376**

Colleen McMahon's attractive little restaurant is well located near the Linenhall Arts & Exhibition Centre and you can't miss it, with its cheerful red frontage. The same lighthearted tone prevails inside too - it's not a very large room but pine tables (some covered in red oilcloths) are quite well-spaced and most have a good view of the large blackboard menu that lists all kinds of good things to raise the spirits of weary shoppers and culture vultures. Careful sourcing of ingredients is a point of pride (organic vegetables are supplied by a nearby organic scheme in summer) and wholesome, home-made fresh food is the order of the day here. Typically there might be a main course special of free range turkey with red cabbage, turnip puree and champ (€10.95) or a warm chicken salad with chilli mayonnaise and boiled potato (€9.50). There are lots of lighter dishes too, like Café Rua paté (served with toast, €6), paninis (eg Parma ham, with buffalo mozzarella & pesto, €7.50) and freshly-cut sandwiches made to order, from €2.30. Luscious desserts and good home bakes too: great little place. **Seats 30.** Open all day Tue-Sat, 9.30-6. **Directions:** Opposite Tourist Information Office. ◇

Castlebar

Lynch Breaffy House Hotel & Spa

féile bia HOTEL

Castlebar Co Mayo **Tel: 094 902 2033** Fax: 904 902 2276
Email: cro@lynchhotels.com Web: www.lynchhotels.com

This handsome hotel set in its own grounds just outside Castlebar town dates back to 1890 and retains some of its original country house atmosphere. It has undergone major renovation and refurbishments over the last few years and, since a change of ownership in 2000, the restaurant and some of the bedrooms have already been refurbished and sixty five new deluxe bedrooms (including two presidential suites and 20 interconnecting family rooms) opened in 2003. But the most exciting development - and one that is certain to make this a key all-year destination for short breaks - is the recent opening of a new five star leisure complex and health spa - 'Life Spa' and Ku'dos Aqua & Fitness Club, which features an array of treatment rooms and therapy suites, complete with gymnasium, 20 metre pool, Café West (for informal refreshments at the leisure complex) and an exhaustive range of treatments, some of which are unique in Ireland. Conference/banqueting (500); business centre. Preferential local golf rates. Garden. Off season value breaks. Children welcome (under 2 free in parents' room, cots available without charge, baby sitting arranged). No pets. Garden, walking. **Rooms 125** (9 suites, 10 no smoking, 2 disabled). Lift. B&B €79pps, ss €29. (Room only rate also available: €135, max 3 guests). SC incl. Open all year. Amex, Diners, MasterCard, Visa, Laser. **Directions:** 4km outside Castlebar on the Claremoris Road.

Cong

Ashford Castle

HOTEL
☆ RESTAURANT

Cong Co Mayo **Tel: 092 46003** Fax: 092 4626(
Email: ashford@ashford.ie Web: www.ashford.ie

Ireland's grandest castle hotel, with a history going back to the early 13th century, Ashford is set in 35(acres of beautiful parkland. Grandeur, formality and tranquillity are the essential characteristics, first seen in the approach through well manicured lawns, in the entrance and formal gardens and, once inside, in a succession of impressive public rooms that illustrate a long and proud history – panelled walls, oil paintings, balustrades, suits of armour and magnificent fireplaces. A new General Manager, Nial Rochford, and a talented young Executive Chef Stefan Matz (see below), have recently joined the Ashford team, bringing the energy and enthusiasm that will revitalise this wonderful place. Accommodation varies considerably due to the size and age of the building, and each room in some way reflects the special qualities of this unique hotel. The best bedrooms and the luxurious suites at the top of the castle - many with magnificent views of Lough Corrib, the River Cong and wooded parkland - are elegantly furnished with period furniture, some with enormous and beautifully appointed bathrooms, others with remarkable architectural features, such as a panelled wooden ceiling recently discovered behind plasterwork in one of the suites (and now fully restored). A bijou fitness centre has computerised exercise equipment; steam room; sauna and whirlpool, all strikingly designed in neo-classical style. A specialist team backs up impressive conference facilities and the hotel's exceptional amenities and sports facilities are detailed in a very handy little pocket book; in it you'll find everything you need to know about the equestrian centre, falconry hunting, clay target shooting, archery, cycling, pony & trap tours, golf (resident instructor & equipment hire), tennis, lake & river fishing, lake cruising, jogging, guided walking & cycling tours on the estate and a guide to scenic routes and attractions in Mayo and Galway - this little book is a gem. Conference/banqueting (120/80); business centre; secretarial services; video conferencing. Fitness centre, beauty salon, hairdressing. Snooker, pool table. Children welcome (under 12 free in parents' room, cot available without charge, baby sitting arranged). No pets. **Rooms 83** (6 suites, 5 junior suites, 32 executive, 60 no smoking). Lift. 24 hour room service. Turn down service. Room rate about €414 (max 2 guests); SC 15%.

The Connaught Room: This small room is the jewel in Ashford Castle's culinary crown and one of Ireland's most impressive restaurants. A talented new executive head chef, Stefan Matz, joined the team in 2003 and oversees the cooking for both this and the George V Dining Room. Changes to menus will be introduced gradually, meanwhile the style remains classical French using the best of local ingredients – Atlantic prawns, Galway Bay sole, Cleggan lobster, Connemara lamb – in sophisticated dishes that will please the most discerning diner. Irish farmhouse cheeses and warm soufflés are among the tempting endings for luxurious meals which are, as always, greatly enhanced by meticulous attention to detail. Service is discreet and extremely professional. **Seats 20.** D only, 7-9.30 (usually residents only).

George V Dining Room: Lunch and dinner are served in this much larger but almost equally opulent dining room, and an light daytime menu is also available. Changes envisaged by the Executive Chef Stefan Matz are gradually being introduced to all the menus at the castle. The new signature dishes are not in place at the time of going to press, but this is an exciting time at the castle and there is a sense of anticipation, together with a new lightness of tone in the dining experience generally - and service, under the direction of Maitre d'Hôtel Seamus Judge, is sensitively attentive and friendly. A five course dinner menu offers a choice of about five dishes on the first and main courses, while a separate vegetarian menu has less choice but is more modern and includes some tempting suggestions. If at least two people (preferably a whole party) are agreed, a 7-course Menu Surprise tasting menu is available - and after dinner you will be presented with a souvenir copy of the Menu Surprise: a wonderful way to commemorate a special occasion. Lunch offers a shortened and somewhat simplified version of the dinner menu, but the same high standards apply. **Seats 130.** L daily 1-2.30, D daily 7-9.3[illegible] Set L €35, Set D from €45 (2-course). Menu Surprise €100. A la carte D also available; house wine fro[illegible]

€26. SC.15%. *All meals in the castle are by reservation, but Afternoon Tea is served at The Cottage, for day visitors to the grounds. Amex, Diners, MasterCard, Visa, Laser. **Directions:** 30 miles north of Galway on Lough Corrib.

Crossmolina

Enniscoe House

COUNTRY HOUSE

Castlehiill Crossmolina Ballina Co Mayo
Tel: 096 31112 Fax: 096 31773
Email: mail@enniscoe.com Web: www.enniscoe.com

In parkland and mature woods on the shores of Lough Conn, Enniscoe is stern and gaunt, as Georgian mansions in the north-west of Ireland tend to be, but any intimidating impressions of "the last great house of North Mayo" are quickly dispelled once inside this fascinating old place. Built by ancestors of the present owner, Susan Kellett, (they settled here in the 1660s), Enniscoe attracts anglers and visitors with a natural empathy for the untamed wildness of this unspoilt - and still surprisingly little known - area; the house has great charm and makes a lovely place to come back to after a day in the rugged countryside. Family portraits, antique furniture and crackling log fires all complement Susan's warm hospitality and deliciously simple, wholesome dinners (Irish country house cooking), which non-residents are welcome to share by reservation. All this would be more than enough without any extra attraction, but Susan has been very busy at the back of the house in recent years and developments here have been attracting a growing amount of interest: In the old farm buildings, the local Historical Society operates a genealogy centre, The Mayo North Family History Research Centre (096 31809) that researches names and families of Mayo origin; alongside, a small but growing agricultural museum displays old farm machinery and a blacksmith works on the restoration of machinery that has been donated. There's also a small conference centre in the courtyard, along with three delightful self-catering units. Perhaps the most exciting developments are in the gardens and woodlands, however; a network of paths has made much of the beautiful woodland area around the house more accessible to guests and major renovations have recently taken place in the walled gardens, which are now open to the public and have tearooms - and, most recently, a shop stocking a good range of quality "non-tourist" items and some garden plants. Another garden produces organically grown vegetables, herbs and fruit for the house. There is brown trout fishing on Lough Conn and other trout and salmon fishing nearby; boats, ghillies, tuition and hire of equipment can be arranged. Children are welcome (under 2s free in parents' room, cot available without charge) and dogs are also allowed by arrangement. Small conferences (30). **Rooms 6** (all en-suite, 2 no smoking) B&B €86 pps, ss €20. Restaurant: **Seats 16.** D daily, 7.30-8pm; non residents welcome by reservation. Set D €40-45, house wines €15-18. Closed 1 Nov-1 Apr. Amex, MasterCard, Visa. **Directions:** 2 miles south of Crossmolina on R315.

Foxford

Healy's Hotel

féile bia HOTEL / RESTAURANT

Pontoon Foxford Co Mayo
Tel: 094 925 6443 Fax: 094 925 6572
Email: info@healyspontoon.com Web: www.healyspontoon.com

This famous old hotel, loved by fisherfolk, landscape artists and many others who seek peace and tranquillity, changed hands in 1998, and there has since been considerable renovation and refurbishment, without spoiling the old-fashioned qualities that have earned this hotel its special reputation: just a good bit of painting and decorating, some overdue refurbishment in the bar and a general tidy up around the front while, at the back, old gardens have been re-established (500 new roses have been planted), and a beer garden has been created. Accommodation is modest but comfortable - and also fairly moderately priced. There's a great feeling of people happy in what they're doing around here (notably the fisherfolk); it's all very relaxed and the hotel has lots of information on things to do in the area - including golf at around a dozen courses within an hour's drive. Aside from fishing, other country pursuits available nearby include shooting, horse racing, mountain climbing and golf (links and parkland courses nearby). Small banqueting facilities (60); garden, fishing. Packed lunches available. Children welcome (under 3s free in parents' room; cots available). Pets permitted by arrangement. The restaurant is open for dinner every evening and lunch on Sunday. **Rooms 14** (all shower only). B&B €59pps, ss €10.* Bar food available 12-9 daily. Closed 25 Dec. Amex, Diners, MasterCard, Visa, Laser. **Directions:** R310 from Castlebar - 10 min drive; R318 from Foxford to junction R310; R310 from Ballina - 10 min drive.

Lahardane

Leonard's

ATMOSPHERIC PUB

Lahardane Ballina Co Mayo **Tel: 096 51003**

This unspoilt roadside traditional pub & grocery shop was established in 1897 and the original owners would be proud of it today. If you get hungry, there's always the makings of a picnic on the shelves. Closed 25 Dec & Good Fri.

Lecanvey

T.Staunton

ATMOSPHERIC PUB

Lecanvey Westport Co Mayo **Tel: 098 64850** / 64891

Thérèse Staunton runs this great little pub near the beginning of the ascent to Croagh Patrick - genuinely traditional, with an open fire it has the feeling of a real 'local'. Not really a food place, but home-made soup and sandwiches or plated salads are available every day until 9pm. Occasional traditional music sessions - and frequent impromptu sing-songs. Closed 25 Dec & Good Fri. **No Credit Cards. Directions:** 8 miles from Westport on Louisburgh Road.

Mulrany

Rosturk Woods

B&B

Mulrany Westport Co Mayo **Tel: 098 36264** Fax: 098 36264
Email: stoney@iol.ie Web: www.rosturk-woods.com

Beautifully located in secluded mature woodland, with direct access to the sandy seashore of Clew Bay, Louisa and Alan Stoney's delightful family home is between Westport and Achill Island, with fishing, swimming, sailing, walking, riding and golf all nearby. It is a lovely, informal house; the three guest bedrooms are all en-suite and very comfortably furnished. Children welcome (under 4 free in parents' room, cot available without charge, baby sitting arranged). Garden. Pets allowed by arrangement. **Rooms 3** (all en-suite & no-smoking, 1 shower only). B&B about €45 pps, ss €30. Self-catering cottages also available. Closed Christmas. **No Credit Cards. Directions:** 7 miles from Newport on Achill Road.

Newport

Newport House

COUNTRY HOUSE / RESTAURANT

Newport Co Mayo **Tel: 098 41222** Fax: 098 41613
Email: info@newporthouse.ie Web: www.newporthouse.ie

WINE AWARD OF THE YEAR

Cathal Murray (Sommelier) & Catherine Flynn (Manager)

To its many visitors, a stay at Newport House symbolises all that is best about the Irish country house, which was the Guide's Country House of the Year in 1999. Currently in the caring hands of Kieran and Thelma Thompson, Newport has been especially close to the hearts of fishing people for many years, but the comfort and warm hospitality of this wonderful house is accessible to all its guests – not least in shared enjoyment of the club-fender cosiness of the little back bar. The house has a beautiful central hall, sweeping staircase and gracious drawing room, while bedrooms, like the rest of the house, are furnished in style with antiques and fine paintings. The day's catch is weighed and displayed in the hall and the fisherman's bar provides the perfect venue for a reconstruction of the day's sport. Fishing, garden, walking, snooker. **Rooms 18** (16 en-suite, 2 with private bathrooms, 2 with bath & separate shower) Children welcome. Limited wheelchair access. Pets allowed in some areas. Rooms 18 (2 shower only, 2 private, 16 en-suite) B&B about €112, ss about €25, no S.C. Closed 10 Oct-18 Mar.

Restaurant: The restaurant is all that a country house dining room should be - high-ceilinged and elegant with tall windows, and fresh flowers from the garden, the perfect backdrop for "cooking which reflects the hospitable nature of the house" and creates fine meals from home-produced and local foods. John Gavin has been head chef since 1983 and his five-course country house style menus are invariably rewarding. Fresh fish is, of course, a speciality – not only freshwater fish caught on local lakes and rivers, but also three or four varieties of fish delivered daily from nearby Achill island - and, of course, the freshest of produce from their own walled garden appears regularly in soups, salads, delicious desserts and preserves as well as main courses. Wild salmon from the house smoking room is a particular speciality, and also wild gravalax, with dill and mustard sauce. Local meats are not overlooked however - charcoal grilled Irish beef medallion makes a regular appearance with a croûton of paté, red wine & Madeira sauce, for example, and there will always be local lamb - and, equally, game - in season, while classic desserts may use fruit from the garden. And then there is Kieran's renowned wine list that, for many, adds an extra magic to a meal at Newport. It includes a great collection of classic French wines – about 150 clarets from 1961-1996 vintages, a great collection of white and red burgundies, excellent Rhônes – and a good New World collection too. The foundations of this cellar go back many decades to a time when Kieran was himself a guest at Newport; great wines are a great passion for him and, while acknowledging that they are irreplaceable, he offers them to guests at far less than their current retail value. Great lists of this scale and quality are almost a thing of the past, so it is a cause for great celebration that a collector such as Kieran should also be blessed with the generosity that allows others to share his passion. **Seats 38.** D daily 7-9.30; Set D €55; house wines €24. Toilets wheelchair accessible. Non-residents welcome by reservation. Amex, Diners, MasterCard, Visa, Laser. **Directions:** Newport village.

Westport

Ardmore House Hotel & Restaurant

HOTEL

The Quay Westport Co Mayo **Tel: 098 25994** Fax: 098 27795
Email: ardmorehotel@eircom.net Web: www.ardmorecountryhouse.com

Pat and Noreen Hoban's small family-run hotel is well-located near Westport harbour with lovely views over Clew Bay and, since recent major refurbishment, offers a tempting combination of warm hospitality, very comfortable accommodation and good food. Open fires in the foyer and bar set a welcoming tone and there is usually a family member at hand to greet arriving guests. Bedrooms are spacious, individually decorated and furnished to a high standard - the style is quite luxurious, they have the full range of facilities expected of better hotel rooms (including an iron and ironing board) and most have separate bath and shower. A more flexible price structure has been introduced for 2004, to give the choice of seaview or back of house rooms and allow for a less expensive option; this also applies to short breaks offered. Small conferences (12-15). Not suitable for children under 12. No pets. Garden. **Rooms 13** (all superior, all no smoking). Room service (limited hours); turndown service. B&B (high season, back of house) €85 pps, ss €25.

Restaurant: Owner-chef Pat Hoban presents pleasingly classic menus with a strong emphasis on seafood, which make good reading over an aperitif in the comfortable bar. An unusually wide selection of first and middle courses is offered - cold and warm starters, soups and sorbets - including an hors d'oeuvre plate - while main courses offer a good range of meat and poultry as well as the dominant seafood dishes, which includes shellfish such as scallops and lobster when available. The restaurant is well-appointed, bright and airy with tables well separated by plants, and staff work well to ensure that an enjoyable evening is had by all. Seats 50. D (daily in summer, Mon-Sat low season), 7-9. Set D €40, also à la carte. House wine €19.50. Closed Sun in low season, 24-26 Dec, mid Jan-end Feb. Amex, MasterCard, Visa, Laser. **Directions:** 1.5 kms from Westport town centre.

Westport

Atlantic Coast Hotel

HOTEL

The Quay Westport Co Mayo **Tel: 098 29000** Fax: 098 29111
Email: info@atlanticcoasthotel.com Web: www.atlanticcoasthotel.com

Behind the traditional stone façade of an old mill on Westport harbour, this bright and interesting modern hotel has spacious public areas designed and furnished in a pleasing combination of traditional and contemporary themes and materials. and the tone is continued through to good-sized bedrooms, which may occasionally lack attention to detail in maintenance but have good facilities and stylish Italian bathrooms. Although it may seem like an impersonal city hotel in some ways, staff (including those in the excellent leisure centre) are exceptionally friendly and efficient. The same is true of The Blue Wave Restaurant, which is situated right up at the top of the building (a good idea, although the view is somewhat restricted by sloping roof windows and the room can be very warm in summer). Here Frank Walsh, who took over as head chef in 2003, presents interesting and well-balanced menus offering plenty of local produce, especially seafood. Conferences/banqueting (150/140). Business centre; secretarial services; video-conferencing. Children welcome (under 4s free in parents' room, cots available without charge). Leisure centre, swimming pool; fishing; discount at local golf club. Prices are high, making it worthwhile to shop around, but better value off-season/special interest breaks are often available. **Rooms 85** (3 suites, 10 superior, 40 no smoking, 3 for disabled). Lift. All day room service. B&B €135, ss €20; SC incl. Closed 24-26 Dec. Amex, MasterCard, Visa, Laser. **Directions:** Located at Westport harbour, 1 mile from town centre on main Louisburgh and coast road.

Westport

Hotel Westport

HOTEL

Newport Rd Westport Co Mayo **Tel: 098 25122** Fax: 098 26739
Email: sales@hotelwestport.ie Web: www.hotelwestport.ie

Just a short stroll from Westport town centre this large modern hotel is set in its own grounds and offers excellent facilities for both leisure and business guests. It makes a good base for a holiday in this lovely area and numerous short breaks are offered, including family breaks at times when special children's entertainment is available (June-August). The conference and business centre provide a fine venue for corporate events of all kinds, including incentive breaks, and the hotel and surrounding area provide all the activities and amenities necessary for off-duty delegates. Bedrooms, which include some with four-poster beds, are well-appointed, with phone/ISDN lines, TV/video, tea/coffee facilities and trouser press; constant refurbishment and upgrading is an ongoing feature of this well-managed hotel:

bedrooms, corridors, public and banqueting areas have recently received special attention and this current improvement programme will continue into 2004. The whole hotel is unusually wheelchair-friendly, without steps or obstacles, and staff are invariably helpful and friendly. Conference/banqueting (500/350); video conferencing; business centre. Leisure centre, swimming pool (a spa and treatment rooms are planned for 2004, as part of a development that will link the hotel and leisure centre). Garden. Children welcome (under 3s free in parents' room; cots available without charge, baby sitting arranged). **Rooms 129** (6 suites, 7 for disabled). Lift. B&B €130 pps, ss €20. No SC. Open all year. Amex, Diners, MasterCard, Visa, Laser. **Directions:** On Castlebar road, turn right onto north mall, then turn onto Newport Road, 1st left and at the end of the road.

Westport

Knockranny House Hotel

féile bia HOTEL / RESTAURANT

Knockranny Westport Co Mayo **Tel: 098 28600**
Fax: 098 28611 Email: info@khh.ie Web: www.khh.ie

Set in landscaped grounds on an elevated site overlooking the town, this Victorian-style hotel opened in 1997. The spacious foyer, friendly staff and the sight of a welcoming fire create an agreeably warm atmosphere: the foyer sets the tone for a hotel which has been built on a generous scale and is full of contrasts, with spacious public areas balanced by smaller ones - notably the library and drawing room - where guests can relax in more homely surroundings. Bedrooms are also large - the suites have four poster beds and sunken seating areas with views and, while a visit in 2003 suggested that some rooms might be awaiting refurbishment, most are very comfortable; some have jacuzzi baths, and phones with ISDN. Guests currently have use of a nearby leisure centre, but on-site facilities are expected to be completed by mid-2004. **Rooms 54** (3 suites, 9 deluxe, 3 shower only, 4 no smoking, 2 for disabled.) Lift. 24 hour room service. B&B €120, ss €50. Closed 22-27 Dec.

La Fougère: Contemporary Irish cooking is offered in the hotel dining room, La Fougère ("the fern"), which is at the front of the hotel, with views across the town to Clew Bay and Croagh Patrick. A new head chef, Paul Moran, took over shortly after the Guide's most recent visit but menus remain similar - wide-ranging in a classic/modern style - and some specialities, such as home-smoked salmon and haddock, remain; you might try the smoked salmon in a terrine with spinach, dill & tzatziki for example. Restaurant manager John Masterson runs a happy ship, which adds greatly to the enjoyment of guests, and this is pleasant spot for an outing. A user-friendly wine list blends entertainment and information in various ways, including colour coding different weights of wine. **Seats 100.** D 6.30-9 (Sun 7-9). L 12.30-2.30. Set D €45; Set Sun L €24. House wine €20. SC discretionary. Amex, MasterCard, Visa. **Directions:** Take N5/N60 from Castlebar. Hotel is on the left just before entering Westport.

Westport

The Lemon Peel

RESTAURANT

The Octagon Westport Co Mayo **Tel: 098 26929** Fax: 098 26965
Email: robbie@lemonpeel.ie Web: www.lemonpeel.ie

Proprietor-chef Robbie McMenamin's simply-furnished little town centre restaurant just off The Octagon has been a favourite with locals and visitors alike ever since it opened in 1997 - and, despite the arrival of more restaurants in the area, it remains the most popular restaurant in town. The atmosphere is buzzy and friendly and the food interesting. Robbie sources ingredients with care - local seafood features but there's also a wide choice of other local produce, including organic vegetables - and his cooking is creative and accurate. Menus are considerately sprinkled with symbols to help your selection meet the mood: so you might start off gently with a luscious duck liver parfait with redcurrant and cranberry & port sauce, then progress to a medium-hot Cajun roast salmon with fruit salsa, lemon & basil cream, or maybe a more cautious (but equally interesting) house speciality of beef with blue cheese - these and lots more like them keep tempting people back for more. Specials change on a weekly basis and everything comes with a choice of mashed potatoes - plain, basil, champ, garlic, or olive olive - in addition to the vegetables of the day. Lovely homely puddings like rhubarb & apple crumble and gorgeous chocolate mousse and freshly brewed coffee to finish. The early dinner menu is outstanding for value and friendly, helpful staff create a relaxed atmosphere: good food, good service - good place. Not suitable for children under 12. **Seats 32.** No smoking area; air conditioning. D only 6-9.30 (Sun 6-9). Early menu €21.95 (6-7pm), Also à la carte. House wines €16.50-19.50; SC discretionary. Closed Mon (Sun & Mon Nov-Feb) & all Feb. (Telephone off season to check opening times.) Amex, MasterCard, Visa, Laser. **Directions:** Westport Town Centre.

Westport

Linenmill Restaurant

N féile bia RESTAURANT

The Linenmill The Demesne Westport Co Mayo
Tel: 098 29500 Fax: 098 29861

The Linenmill Restaurant - which is part of a museum and shop selling upmarket household furnishings and accessories - gives a good first impression, with classy signage and a large, open-plan reception area decorated with dramatic white floral arrangements and large plants. A pleasing blend of old and new materials throughout, and formally laid white-clothed tables, bode well for a special dining experience. Head chef Philip Brazil's quite extensive and well-balanced modern à la carte menus include some ambitious dishes alongside straightforward ones: for example a demanding and well-executed starter such as pan-seared scallops on grilled courgettes with creamed spinach and saffron & chive cream, appears alongside a simple (and much less expensive) Linenmill house salad of feta cheese, sundried tomatoes, baby gem lettuce, bacon lardons and black olives. Sophisticated main courses such as charred breast of Peking duck with Parmesan polenta & plum tomato ragout or a special of monkfish on parsnip & potato puree with rocket salad & crisp pancetta work well and there is always an equally impressive vegetarian option. The wine list is proprietor Vincent Coakley's special enthusiasm and he travels to France to buy for the restaurant. Service, under the direction of restaurant manage Luca Lualot, is a highlight. The Linenmill aims to please discerning diners at a fair price and, with main at about €13.95 to €19.95, they seem to be doing this very well. **Seats 80** (Outdoor, 15). Toilets wheelchair accessible. Not suitable for children after 7.30pm. L 12-3; D 7-10; Sun brunch 11-2. A la carte. Closed Nov-Jan. Reservations advised - also a phone call to check opening times. MasterCard, Visa, Laser. **Directions:** On the Newport road from Westport, just before entrance to Hotel Westport.

Westport

Matt Molloy's Bar

ATMOSPHERIC PUB

Bridge Street Westport Co Mayo **Tel: 098 26655**

If you had to pick one pub in this pretty town, this soothingly dark atmospheric one would do very nicely – not least because it is owned by Matt Molloy of The Chieftains, a man who clearly has respect for the real pub: no TV (and no children after 9 pm). Musical memorabilia add to the interest, but there's also the real thing as traditional music is a major feature in the back room or out at the back in fine weather. Matt is often away on tour, but he's a real local when he's back and takes great pride in this smashing town. It's worth noting that normal pub hours don't apply – this is an afternoon into evening place, not somewhere for morning coffee. Closed 25 Dec & Good Fri. **No Credit Cards. Directions:** Town centre.

Westport

McCormack's at the Andrew Stone Gallery

Ⓝ RESTAURANT / CAFÉ

Bridge Street Westport Co Mayo
Tel: 098 25619 Fax: 098 25619

Go under the archway beside Kate McCormack's sixth generation butcher's shop and up the stairs, where you will find an art gallery on your right and, on your left, this small, unpretentious restaurant with brightly coloured oilcloths on the tables and an open counter displaying an array of good things, including home-baked cakes, quiches and pates - the product of generations of family recipes and particularly of Annette McCormack's table, where family and friends have tasted great dishes. Here, her two daughters, Katrina and Mary Claire, carry on the tradition - and the welcome. Treats especially worth trying include a leek and bacon quiche; fresh crab on home-made baps; beef stir-fry - made with locally reared beef, obtained, of course, from their butchers shop next door. And don't leave without one of the gloriously home-made desserts like almond Madeira pie with seasonal fruits like rhubarb or blackcurrants. Many of the deli dishes from the shop are on the menu, as well as farmhouse cheeses including the local Carrowholly cheese. Works by local artists like John Brady, Michael McCarthy and Henry Blackmoor hang in the restaurant and adjacent rooms: well worth a visit. **Seats 40.** Children welcome. Open all day Thu-Sat and Mon. Closed Sun, Tue, Wed. MasterCard, Visa. **Directions:** Westport town centre - on the main street (the one with the clock tower at the top).

Westport

The Olde Railway Hotel

HOTEL

The Mall Westport Co Mayo **Tel: 098 25166** Fax: 098 25090
Email: railway@anu.ie Web: www.theolderailwayhotel.com

Once described by William Thackeray as 'one of the prettiest, comfortablist hotels in Ireland', The Olde Railway Hotel was built in 1780 as a coaching inn for guests of Lord Sligo. Attractively situated along the tree-lined Carrowbeg River, on the Mall in the centre of Westport, it remains a hotel of character, well known for its antique furniture and a slightly eccentric atmosphere. Warm, friendly reception and a complimentary cup of tea on arrival (and at any other time during your stay) immediately makes guests feel welcome - and certain concessions have been made to the demands of modern travellers, including en-suite bathrooms, satellite television and private car parking. There's a conservatory dining room quietly situated at the back of the hotel and several very spacious ground floor rooms with smart en-suite shower rooms were recently added. The large bar, which is the public face of an otherwise quite private hotel, serves very acceptable bar food - a private garden now supplies organic herbs and vegetables for the hotel. Own parking. Garden, fishing, cycling (bicycles provided without charge). Children welcome (cots available). No pets. **Rooms 26** (12 superior rooms, some shower only, all no-smoking). 24 hour room service. B&B €75 pps, ss €30. Food served 12.30-2.30 & 6-9.30 daily. Open all year. Amex, Diners, MasterCard, Visa, Laser. **Directions:** Entering Westport from N5 (Dublin-Westport) road, turn right just before bridge. Hotel is on the mall overlooking the river.

Westport

Quay Cottage

RESTAURANT

The Harbour Westport Co Mayo **Tel: 098 26412** Fax: 098 28120
Email: kirsten@oceanfree.net Web: www.quaycottage.com

Kirstin and Peter MacDonagh have been running this charming stone quayside restaurant just outside Westport since 1984, and it never fails to delight. It's cosy and informal, with scrubbed pine tables and an appropriate maritime decor, which is also reflected in the menu (although there is also much else of interest, including steaks and imaginative vegetarian options). But seafood really stars, typically in starters of chowder or garlic grilled oysters and main courses like fillet of monkfish Kiev, with glazed asparagus tips and a white wine & garlic sauce - or whole seabass, pan-fried and served on rice salad, drizzled with salsa verde. Daily specials are often especially interesting (duckling, turbot, scallops, lobster for example) and there are nice homely desserts – or a plated farmhouse cheese selection such as Cashel Blue, smoked Gubbeen and an Irish brie. Freshly-brewed coffee by the cup to finish. Service, supervised by Kirstin, is friendly and efficient. Children welcome. **Seats 85** (private room, 45). Air conditioning. Toilets wheelchair accessible. D 6-"late" daily. Set D from about €35; also à la carte; house wine €16.50; SC discretionary (except 10% on parties of 6+). Closed 24-26 Dec, all Jan. Amex, MasterCard, Visa, Laser. **Directions:** On the harbour front, at gates to Westport House.

Westport

The Creel Restaurant

RESTAURANT

The Quay Westport Co Mayo **Tel: 098 26174**
Email: bennettf@gofree.indigo

Frank and Julie Bennett run this attractive daytime restaurant on the harbour front - it's a pleasant, informal place with pine furniture and warm tones in the terracotta tiled floor, nautical bric-a-brac and traditional baskets used for display. There's some comfortable seating too, and magazines lying around - the idea is to make it a homely place where people can lounge about and relax awhile. An imaginative blackboard menu offers an eclectic range of hot dishes and snacks, mostly under €15 - typically hot meals like lamb hotpot, chicken korma and linguine with seafood sauce, lighter dishes such as seafood chowder or chicken liver paté and light bites like toasted paninis (with brie and crispy bacon for example). Home-made desserts are temptingly displayed at the counter (where you'll also find some well-priced wines alongside the juices and mineral waters). Tasty, lively food well-cooked, pleasant service and surroundings - and good value - make this the perfect place for a daytime bite. **Seats 70.** Open Wed-Sun, 11-6. Closed Tue and all Jan. MasterCard, Visa, Laser. **Directions:** Head for Westport follow signs for the Quay.

COUNTY MEATH

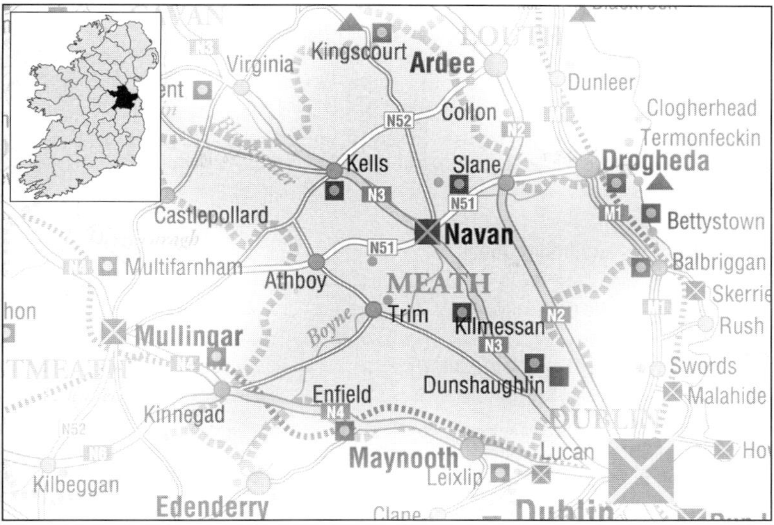

Royal Meath. Meath of the pastures. Meath of the people. Meath of many people.......The recent six year Census confirmed what had been expected. The population of Ireland may have increased by 8%, but Meath is the fastest-growing place of all, its increase clocking in at 22.1% to bring the county total to 134,000 and counting.

Not a huge number in today's overcrowded world, perhaps, but nevertheless Meath in 2004 is a county which finds itself living in interesting times. The proximity of Dublin - with the inevitable pressures of prosperity and population – can be challenging. But it also brings benefits. With an increasingly affluent and discerning population, Meath is able to support its own Good Food Circle with an impressive total of 23 member establishments, ranging from beachside restaurants of international quality to characterful pubs deep in the heart of the country – details on the Good Food Circle from 046-9073426.

And the inevitable changes – for instance, the need to find ways through the county for new major roads - are projects which you feel Meath can absorb. For this is a county which is comfortable and confident with itself, and rightly so. The evidence of a rich history is everywhere in Meath. But it's a history which sits gently on a county which is enjoying its own contemporary prosperity at a pace which belies the bustle of Dublin just down the road.

Yet the further you get into Meath, the more peaceful it becomes, and in late September 2003, Kells in the north of the county saw the very symbol of this, the 33rd National Hot Air Balloon Championship. Despite its title, this proved to be a truly international event, with entries from the USA, Chile, Singapore, Sri Lanka and Britain in addition to the home squad. A beautiful and peaceful activity, ideal for our times.

That said, anyone with an interest in the past will find paradise in Meath, for along the Boyne Valley the neolithic tumuli at Knowth, Newgrange and Dowth are awe-inspiring, Newgrange in particular having its remarkable central chamber which is reached by the rays of sun at dawn at the winter solstice.

Just 16 kilometres to the southwest is another place of fascination, the Hill of Tara. Royal Tara was for centuries the cultural and religious capital of pre-Christian Ireland. Its fortunes began to wane with the coming of Christianity, which gradually moved the religious focal point to Armagh, though Tara was a place of national significance until it was finally abandoned in 1022 AD.

Little now remains of the ancient structures, but it is a magical place, for the approach by the road on its eastern flank gives little indication of the wonderful view of the central plain which the hill suddenly provides to the westward. It is truly inspiring, and many Irish people reckon the year is incomplete without a visit to Tara, where the view is to eternity and infinity, and the imagination takes flight.

On a more down to earth note, late September 2003 saw that extraordinary Irish agricultural festival, the National Ploughing Championships, being staged in County Meath in fine Autumn weather over three days with an attendance of nearly 170,000 farming folk and their friends. As President McAleese commented when performing the opening ceremony, this is where the traditional Irish fair meets the modern business fair, and it buzzes.

In effect, an entire trading township – "Ploughtown" - is created on several hundred acres of farmland. Astonishingly, it was the first time the championship had ever been staged in Royal Meath in its 72 years. And it was barely in Meath at that, for the location was at Ballinabrackey immediately south of Kinnegad. Ballinabrackey is within an ace of being in Offaly, and of Westmeath and Kildare too. But it remains staunchly on a peninsula of Meath, and Ploughtown revelled in the fact. The winners in 2003 were from a goodly selection of Irish counties – Carlow, Wexford, Louth, East Cork, Kilkenny, Offaly, West Cortk, Tyrone, Derry, Meath and Kildare – well reflecting the event's national appeal.

In the Autumn of 2004, the festival will be at Grangeford, which is well within County Carlow. And the success stakes will be even higher, as it will be part of the buildup to the staging of the World Ploughing Championship in Ireland in 2006.

Local Attractions and Information

Donore, Bru na Boinne Visitor Centre	041 988 0300
Dunboyne, Hamwood House & Gardens	01 825 5210
Good Food Circle (Meath)	c/o 046 907 3426
Kells, Grove Gardens & Tropical Bird Sanctuary	046 923 4276
Laytown, Sonairte (National Ecology Centre)	041 982 7572
Navan, Tourism Information	046 907 3426
Navan, Navan Racecourse	046 902 1350
Newgrange (inc Dowth & Knowth)	041 988 0300 / 982 4488
Oldcastle, Loughcrew Historic Gardens	049 854 1922
Oldcastle, Loughcrew Passage Tombs (3000BC)	049 854 2009
Ratoath, Fairyhouse Racecourse	01 825 6167
Summerhill, Larchill Arcadian Gardens	01 628 7354
Tara, Interpretive Centre	046 25903
Trim, Butterstream Garden	046 943 6017
Trim, Tourism Information	046 943 7111
Trim, Trim Castle (restored Norman stronghold)	046 943 8619

Bettystown

Bacchus At The Coastguard

RESTAURANT

Bayview Bettystown Co Meath **Tel: 041 982 8251** Fax: 041 982 8236

Right beside the beach, with views over Bettystown Bay - where, even at night, it is interesting to see the lights of the ships waiting in the bay to go up the river to the port at Drogheda - Kieran Greenway and Anne Hardy have been running this fine restaurant since 1996; during that time they have earned recognition as the leading restaurant in the area and play a key role in the Meath Good Food Circle, which is an independently assessed group formed to highlight good food in County Meath, and to raise standards. The entrance to the restaurant is from the road side (actually the back of the building, as the sea is at the front) and opens into a pleasant bar overlooking the sea, where aperitifs are served. Menus offer a generous, well-balanced choice - including a growing number of house specialities which are eagerly anticipated by returning guests - and there is a strong leaning towards seafood, supplied by local fishermen and from the west coast: updated classic starters like tian of white Clogherhead crab meat with croquant of cucumber & gazpacho sauce, are typical, and main courses such as deliciously crispy goujons of monk fish with tartare sauce and chilli & coriander salsa. But the choice is far from being restricted to seafood; a good selection of poultry and red meats is likely to include succulent honey roast farmyard duckling with savoury potato stuffing and bitter orange sauce and Duleek lamb - a roast rack, perhaps, with rosemary & redcurrant sauce. Imaginative vegetarian dishes are usually offered too - just ask if there doesn't happen to be one on the day. Desserts are always a treat - a more-ish roast peach and hazelnut parfait, perhaps, with strawberry & basil salsa - and you can relax afterwards in the bar with a digestif. This is an excellent restaurant offering creative, accurately-cooked food, a cosy ambience and friendly, efficient service. Early dinner menus and Sunday lunch are particularly good value. Not suitable for children after 8pm. **Seats 90** (private room, 20). D Tue-Sat, 6-10 (Mon-Sat in summer); L Sun only, 12.30-2.30. Early D €30 (6-7.30pm), also à la carte; Set Sun L €30. House wines from €17; SC discretionary. Closed Mon, Christmas, 2 weeks Feb. Amex, MasterCard, Visa, Laser. **Directions:** N1 to Julianstown, then coast road to Bettystown.

Bettystown

Neptune Beach Hotel

HOTEL

Bettystown Co Meath **Tel: 041 982 7107** Fax: 041 982 7412
Email: info@neptunebeach.ie Web: www.neptunebeach.ie

In a great location overlooking the famous long sandy beach at Bettystown and adjacent to a golf links, this striking modern hotel also has excellent in-house leisure facilties, notably a leisure club with 20m swimming pool. There's a characterful traditional lounge bar on the road side of the building plus a large bar with sea views and a central lounge area designed around a well feature and a second bar overlooking the beach. Bedrooms are generous and have all the usual modern amenities (best ones at the front have the view). Restaurant meals are well above the standard expected of an hotel - both for Sunday lunch (a jazz buffet, served in a funtion room overlooking the beach) and dinner, in Le Pressage restaurant. **Rooms 38.** B&B from about €120 pps; midweek specials offered. Restaurant D daily, L Sun only. Open all year. Amex, MasterCard, Visa. **Directions:** N1 to Julianstown follow coast road through Laytown to Bettystown. ◇

Castletown

Mountainstown House

COUNTRY HOUSE

Castletown Kilpatrick Navan area Co Meath
Tel: 046 905 4154 / 905 4195 Fax: 046 905 4154
Email: pollock@oceanfree.net

If you want to experience something out of the ordinary in a really rural setting, this is the place for you: on a 750-acre farm amidst unspoilt rolling countryside, John and Diana Pollocks' home is a huge house of great character. It was bought by the Pollock family in 1796, from Samuel Gibbons who ran it as a sporting estate. The front door is approached up seriously impressive steps, which give some inkling of what is to come - not only does this magnificent place have the grandly proportioned reception rooms and large countryhouse bedrooms that might be expected, but there's a wonderful 18th century courtyard at the back, complete with a spring well and original carriagewash. Peacocks and all kinds of poultry stroll around this amazing place with measured insouciance... It's a marvellously romantic venue for a wedding reception (max 80). Snooker/billiards. Children welcome (under 3s free in parents' room, cots available, children's playground & playroom. Pets by arrangement. Garden. **Rooms 6** (1 suite, 3 en-suite, 2 with private bathrooms, all no smoking). B&B €72pps, ss €12. Residents' D at 8 pm, about €32 (24 hrs notice required). *Self-catering accommodation also available. Closed 22 Dec-2 Jan. **No Credit Cards. Directions:** From Dublin - N3 Navan.Turn right 3rd set of traffic lights for Kingscourt - Wilkinstown.

Dunboyme

Caldwell's Restaurant

féile bia RESTAURANT

Summerhill Road Dunboyne Co Meath **Tel: 01 801 3866**
Email: d_caldwell2002@yahoo.com

In a neat modern building in the centre of Dunboyne, this smart new two-storey restaurant is simple and modern in style - clean lines, unfussy table settings, comfortable high-back chairs; the high-ceilinged ground floor area overlooks a large patio, which gives it a light, bright atmosphere, while tables on the balcony area above have a cosier ambience. Guests are shown straight to their tables to look over the menu and order aperitifs; home-made breads are offered (probably more than once before food is served). Promising menus are refreshingly simply worded and sources highlighted - suppliers named, vegetables from the family garden - along with membership of Féile Bia, which is all interesting and confidence-inspiring. Set menus offer a choice of three on each course (celeriac & apple soup; pan-fried striploin of beef with peppered Jameson whiskey sauce (certified Irish Hereford beef); Caldwell's sorbet & fruit plate, perhaps) while the à la carte is wider ranging and dishes sound more luxurious. There will always be several seafood specialities but, unusually, the leaning is towards red meats - and, like the vegetables, very tasty they are too. Desserts tend to be enjoyable variations on classics, with a welcome emphasis on fruits in season. Caldwell's has its heart in the right place - it's great to see the provenance of ingredients given due recognition on a menu - and offers good cooking and a pleasant ambience at fair prices. **Seats 55** (private balcony area 20). Children welcome for Sun L. D Wed-Sat, 6-10; L Sun only 1.30-5.30. Set D(Wed-Fri) & Sun L €24, D also à la carte. House wine €18. Closed D Sun, all Mon & Tue, bank hols. Amex, MasterCard, Visa, Laser. **Directions:** Dunboyne village, through lights, 2nd building on left.

Dunshaughlin

The Olde Workhouse

COUNTRY HOUSE

Dunshaughlin Co Meath **Tel: 01 825 9251**
Fax: 01 82 5951 Email: comfort@a-vip.com

It's hard to imagine that this striking cut-stone listed building was once a workhouse – having been restored by Niamh and Dermod Colgan it makes a beautiful old house of great character and charm, with highly individual bedrooms, one of which has a kingsize four-poster bed. Each has been furnished and decorated with great attention to detail, using carefully sourced antiques and an ever-growing collection of old plates. Of the five rooms, three are officially shower-only but the Colgans have got around the problem of space with ingenuity by installing half-baths instead of shower trays. More power to them for their thoughtfulness (others please take note). Indeed, there are thoughtful touches everywhere and Niamh, who is an enthusiastic cook, lavishes attention on breakfast: freshly squeezed orange juice, fresh fruit salad, dried fruit compôte poached in tea, bananas in orange juice with lime zest, homegrown rhubarb with star anisé, fresh strawberries, fresh citrus segments, home-made granola and other cereals, smoked salmon ham cooked in cider, farmhouse cheeses (including Silke Cropp's Corleggy and Drumlin cheeses, from Cavan) and an array of home-baked breads, scones and croissants with home-made preserves. And, of course, there's a delicious traditional Irish hot breakfast cooked to order as well. Wheelchair accessible. Not suitable for children. Garden. Pets permitted. **Rooms 5** (1 junior suite, 1 with four-poster, all no-smoking). B&B €55pps, ss €25. Closed Oct-June (and possibly some other times). MasterCard, Visa. **Directions:** On N3 1 mile south of Dunshaughlin Village.

Enfield

Johnstown House Hotel

féile bia **HOTEL / RESTAURANT** Enfield Co Meath **Tel: 046 954 0000** Fax: 046 954 0001
Email: mmuller@johnstownhouse.com Web: www.johnstownhouse.com

This new hotel opened in August 2001 and has still some work to complete at the time of going to press, including the Spa and leisure centre which is to be a central theme. It's well-located in 80 acres of woods and parkland only about half an hour's drive from Dublin's western suburbs (traffic permitting), and has at its heart a mid-18th century house which has been carefully restored. Although the original house is only a small part of the hotel it is the focal point and the main entrance; the original wings have been replaced by a large, well-designed banqueting area on one side and the spa and leisure centre (now due to open in 2005) on the other. An unusually fine feature of the old house is a drawing room with a ceiling by the renowned Francini brothers, who were responsible for some of Ireland's finest plasterwork in great houses of the time; as the house was not of comparable importance with others they worked on, there is a theory that they did it in return for a favour, such as free use of a hunting lodge on the estate. Bedrooms are elegantly and very comfortably furnished. The hotel has become extremely popular as a wedding venue (sometimes two in one day), but this side of the business is very well run and, with separate entrances and car parks, does not intrude unduly on other activities in the hotel. Conference/banqueting 600; business centre; secretarial services; video conferencing. Children welcome (under 12 free in parents' room, cots available without charge). Walking, fishing, garden. No pets. **Rooms 82** (4 for disabled). Lift. 24 hr room service. Room rate €200 (1 or 2 guests).

Pavilion Restaurant: All accommodation is in new areas, but a fine dining restaurant, The Pavilion, and a private dining room are among the rooms in the old building. A new head chef, Sean McDonald took over in 2002 and is doing a good job. For The Pavilion - which is a lovely, elegantly appointed room, with a relaxing ambience - he presents quite classical à la carte menus with a contemporary tone, and he is also responsible for the Atrium Brasserie, where lively popular menus offer an informal dining experience and good value. Good food and exceptional staff make a visit here an enjoyable experience - and many discerning travellers now cite the hotel as a favourite place to break the journey between Dublin and the west. Food served all day (12.30-10); L 12.30-2.30 (Sun to 5), D 6-10 (Sun to 9.30). Set L from €20, Set D from €25. A la carte also available L&D. House wine €18. SC discretionary. Closed 24-25 Dec. Amex, Diners, MasterCard, Visa, Laser. **Directions:** Take N4 from Dublin - first village after motorway.

Kells

The Ground Floor Restaurant

féile bia **RESTAURANT** Bective Square Kells Co Meath **Tel: 046 924 9688** Fax: 046 922 8347

A bright and attractive contemporary restaurant in the centre of Kells, The Ground Floor is a younger sister of The Loft in Navan and has much in common with it: wacky paintings and a youthful buzzy atmosphere, plus interesting, colourful food at accessible prices - the most expensive dish on the regular menu is a fillet steak at about €20, but most main courses are much less. Popular dishes from around the world abound in starters like kofta kebabs, spicy buffalo wings and crostini and main courses ranging from Greek and caesar salads, through home-made burgers to steaks, pastas and pizzas. Interesting daily blackboard specials are often a good bet - and there are new weight-watching options on the menu. Exceptionally pleasant and helpful staff add greatly to the relaxed ambience. Children welcome up to 8pm (baby changing facility available). Wheelchair access. **Seats 60.** Air conditioning. D daily, 5.30-10.30 (Sat 5-11.30, Sun 5-10). A la carte. House wine €16.50. 10% SC on parties of 4+. MasterCard, Visa, Laser. **Directions:** Centre of Kells on the Athboy/Mullingar Road, in Bective Square.

Kells

Vanilla Pod Restaurant

féile bia RESTAURANT

Kells Co Meath **Tel: 046 924 0084** Fax: 046 924 0587
Email: headfortarms@eircom.net Web: www.headfortarms.ie

Although reached through an entrance just inside the foyer of the Headfort Arms Hotel and in common ownership, The Vanilla Pod is run as an independent entity. In contrast to the rest of the hotel, it is very modern, with lots of pale wood, recessed lighting and sleek informal table settings. Efficient staff show you straight to your table to choose from a well-structured contemporary menu, which offers a significant number of dishes (including some vegetarian) as starter or main course options - grilled goats cheese salad on crostini, with rocket leaves & plum chutney, char-grilled cajun spiced chicken marinated in natural yogurt and served on a bed of noodles are typical of the style. The wine list is a strong point and include a wine of the month; 'Pod Wine Club' gourmet wine evenings, hosted by wine producers, are held bi-monthly. **Seats 65.** Air conditioning. D Tue-Sun, 5.30-10 (Fri & Sat to 11, Sun to 9.30), L Sun only, 12-3. Set L from €20.25. Early D (5.30-7.30) €15.50, also à la carte. SC10% on parties of 4+. House wine €17.50. Closed Mon, 25 Dec, Good Fri. Amex, MasterCard, Visa, Laser. **Directions:** On main Dublin road, black &white building on right.

Kells

White Gables

B&B

Headfort Place Kells Co Meath **Tel: 046 924 0322**
Fax: 046 924 9672 Email: kelltic@eircom.net

Just across the road from the Heritage Centre, Joe and Penny Magowan's old house is on a slip road with trees and a little park between it and the main road, although light sleepers may find the traffic noise disturbing. It has a restful garden at the back - overlooked by the residents' sitting room and dining room - for guests' use and the comfortable, cottagey bedrooms have all been recently refurbished. Penny is a Cordon Bleu cook and previously ran a restaurant in the town: breakfasts are extensive and evening meals are available by arrangment for groups of eight or more. "Kelltic Walking Holidays" operates from White Gables, so a range of information on the locality is available for guests. **Rooms 4** (3 en-suite, 1 with private bathroom & all no smoking). B&B about €30 pps, ss about €10. Children welcome, cots available. Open all year. **No Credit Cards. Directions:** On the edge of Kells. ◇

Kilmessan

The Station House Hotel

féile bia HOTEL / RESTAURANT

Kilmessan Co Meath **Tel: 046 902 5239** Fax: 046 902 5588
Email: info@thestationhousehotel.com Web: www.thestationhousehotel.com

Chris and Thelma Slattery's unique establishment is an old railway junction, which has been closed since 1963, and all the various buildings have been converted to a new use. Major renovations have recently been completed - new rooms, an upgraded reception area and a larger bar, which overlooks a large patio (platform) and gardens, which are a particularly attractive aspect of the hotel and supply all the fresh flowers. The old engine and goods building is now a conference and banqueting suite which, with its original stone walls and natural light giving it character, is now understandably popular for both business and leisure gatherings, notably weddings (and the old signal box is now a 2-room honeymoon suite). Conference/banqueting (350/180); business centre; secretarial service; video conferencing. Children welcome (under 5 free in parents' room, cot available without charge, baby sitting arranged). No pets. **Rooms 20** (1 suite, 2 executive, 20 no-smoking, 5 disabled). B&B €76, ss €25.

The Signal Restaurant: The bar is a pleasant spot to have an aperitif and look at the menu before going into the restaurant, which is spread over two rooms and furnished with antiques in a comfortable. homely style. Daily set dinner menus and an à la carte that take both traditional tastes and current food trends into account are offered, and there is always an imaginative vegetarian choice. Speciality dishes include home-made duck liver paté with Cumberland sauce and melba toast, rack of Kilmessan lamb (with rosemary & redcurrant jus perhaps), but there are also some more contemporary offerings and, to finish, farmhouse cheeses or desserts such as chocolate and orange parfait or warm lemon tart. Live music (mandolin/piano) give a sense of occasion to dinner on Saturday night. Sunday lunch is extremely popular and justifies two sittings - staff somehow remain calm and cheerful throughout. **Seats 90.** Children welcome. L 12.30-3 (Sun to 5.30), D7-11 (Sun to 10) Set L& early D (Mon-Fri) €23.95. Set D Sat €43.95); L&D also à la carte; house wine from €17; SC discretionary. Food is also served in the bar, 11-5.30 daily. Amex, Diners, MasterCard, Visa, Laser. **Directions:** From Dublin N3 to Dunshaughlin and follow signposts.

Navan

Adam & Eve's

RESTAURANT

Ludlow Street Navan Co Meath **Tel: 046 907 1444** Fax: 044 906 4378
Email: adamandeves@eircom.net Web: meathtourism.ie

This small restaurant is just across the road from one of the area's finest old pubs, P Bermingham (unspoilt and friendly - well worth dropping into for an aperitif or digestif). Decor is light and airy in smart neutral tones, with stylish high-back chairs, white linen and primrose napkins - and service is confident and friendly. Colourful international menus of mainly Mediterranean in influence are offered and, in the Guide's experience, have always been well executed and attractively presented. A new chef, Gary Beattie, took over shortly after the Guide's most recent visit - and, with previous experience in several distinguished Northern Ireland kitchens, this attractive restaurant should be entering an exciting new phase. Sunday menus change weekly, early dinner menus monthly and seasonal à la carte menus are to change completely every four months. Children welcome. **Seats 50.** D Tue-Sat, 5-10 (to 9.30 on weekdays, later at weekends), L Sun, 1-5.30. Early D €18 (Tue-Fri, 5-7pm), otherwise à la carte. House wines from €16. Closed Mon (unless by arrangement), 24-25 Dec, 1 Jan. MasterCard, Visa, Laser. **Directions:** Town centre, opposite Bermingham's pub.

Navan

Ardboyne Hotel

féile bia HOTEL

Dublin Road Navan Co Meath **Tel: 046 902 3119** Fax: 046 902 2355
Email: ardboyne@quinn-hotels.com Web: quinn-hotels.com

Standing in its own grounds on the outskirts of town, this modern hotel has a thriving conference and function trade. The entrance and all public areas give a good first impression, although bedrooms are on the small side and could be more comfortable with a little more attention to detail. Restaurant: The restaurant is above average for a country hotel. The atmosphere may leave a lot to be desired but friendly, helpful staff and an interesting, well-balanced menu are plus points, and the cooking is sound and generous. Conference/banqueting (600/400). Parking. Children under 2 free in parents' room; cots available. Wheelchair accessible. **Rooms 29** (all en-suite). B&B from about €65ps, ss about €20. Children welcome. Restaurant **seats 80.** Air conditioning. L 12.30-3 & D 6-10 daily. Toilets wheelchair accessible. Closed 24-26 Dec. Amex, Diners, MasterCard, Visa. **Directions:** From Dublin, N3 to Navan, hotel on left approaching town. ◇

Navan

Fada Coffee Rooms

CAFÉ

31 Railway Street Navan Co Meath **Tel: 046 907 4285**
Fax: 046 902 1459 Email: callon@eircom.net

A light, airy atrium room at the back of an arty gift shop, this daytime coffee shop has flagstones and plants that give it a soothing greenhouse feeling - and make it the perfect place to drop into for a break when shopping. Simple menus offer a choice of soup, sandwiches, toasties and paninis - and a 'lite bites' menu with a Weightwatchers-pointed option and low fat cappuccino and café bainne. Imaginative sandwiches might include open smoked salmon with walnuts on Spicers country white bread and a typical panini could be spicy sausage in tomato fondue & caramelised onions. Savoury and sweet crêpes too - hot pear with chocolate sauce, perhaps. Immaculately clean too, with friendly, helpful staff. **Seats 50.** Open 10am-4.45pm. Closed Christmas. MasterCard, Visa, Laser. **Directions:** Town centre, near Tourist Office.

Navan

Hudson's Bistro

féile bia RESTAURANT

30 Railway St Navan Co Meath **Tel: 046 902 9231** Fax: 046 907 3382

Richard and Tricia Hudson's stylish, informal bistro has a strong following and is well-established as a leading restaurant in the area. Richard's menus include an exciting à la carte based on wide-ranging influences – Cal-Ital, Mexican, Thai, French and modern Italian. Appealing vegetarian and healthy options are a feature and there are fish specials nightly – and, traditionalists will be pleased to hear, the ever-popular sirloin steak (from Kilmessan) has not been overlooked - it comes with a rich Madeira jus and local vegetables; on the whole, menus taste as well as they read, although some of the spicier dishes may be toned down. There are Irish cheeses and/or some very tempting puddings to finish. The wine list echoes the global cooking and is informative and keenly priced. Service can be a weak point, with new arrivals sometimes left waiting for directions and the pace can be uneven throughout a meal. The early dinner menu is very good value. Children welcome. **Seats 54.** D Tue-Sat 6-10. Early D €20 (6-7 pm only); also à la carte. House wine €16.75; no SC. Closed Sun (except bank hol weekends), Mon, 24-26 Dec, Easter Sun. Amex, MasterCard, Visa, Laser. **Directions:** Follow directions to town centre,take right off roundabout, 5th house down on left.

Navan

Killyon House

B&B '

Dublin Road Navan Co Meath **Tel: 046 907 1224** Fax: 046 907 2766
Email: info@killyonguesthouse.com Web: www.killyonguesthouse.com

Just across the road from the Ardboyne Hotel, Michael and Sheila Fogarty's modern guesthouse immediately attracts attention, with its striking array of colourful flowers and hanging baskets. The house is furnished with interesting antiques, and made comfortable by modern double-glazing which reduces traffic noise. The back of the house, which leads down to the banks of the Boyne, is unexpectedly tranquil, however, and the dining room overlooks the river, giving guests the added interest of spotting wildlife, sometimes including otters and stoats, along the bank from the window. The Fogartys are extremely hospitable hosts and nothing (even preparing a very early breakfast) is too much trouble. The house is very well run and rooms are all en-suite and comfortable. There's also a separate guests' sitting room and, although they are too close to the restaurants of Navan to make evening meals a viable option, they do a particularly good breakfast. Own parking. Children welcome (under 5 free in parents' room; cots available without charge, baby sitting arranged). Garden; fishing. **Rooms 6** (all en-suite, 4 shower only, all no smoking). Room service (limited hours). B&B €40 pps, ss €10. Closed 3 days at Christmas. MasterCard, Visa, Laser. **Directions:** On N3, opposite Ardboyne Hotel on River Boyne.

Navan

Ryan's Bar

PUB 22 Trimgate Street Navan Co Meath **Tel: 046 902 1154** Fax: 046 907 8333

This pleasantly refurbished pub makes a good meeting place for a drink or lunch, when contemporary light meals are offered - soups, hot panini bread (stuffed with smoked salmon, cream cheese & tomato perhaps, or chicken with a satay sauce), wraps (including a vegetarian one filled with grated cheese, apple, carrot and a chive mayonnaise) and toasties (honey baked ham, perhaps, with a salad garnish). Apple pie and cream may be predictable but it's enjoyable nonetheless - and there's always a dessert among the daily specials. It's good value, the airy bar makes for a comfortable atmosphere and staff are friendly and efficient. Disc parking. Open from 11.30 am; L Mon-Fri. 12.30-2.30. Closed 25 Dec & Good Fri. MasterCard, Visa, Laser. **Directions:** Main Street Navan. ◇

Navan

Shahi Tandoori

RESTAURANT 19 Watergate Street Navan Co Meath **Tel: 046 902 8762**

Mahammad Kahlid's attractive, well-maintained and conveniently located restaurant is beside a carpark in the main street. Once inside, the traditional Indian decor is welcoming - and hospitable staff promptly offer the menu and wine list. An extensive menu includes a couple of set dinners and an à la carte that offers many dishes not usually encountered in Irish/Indian restaurant - and also some simple western dishes - steak and chips, roast chicken - providing an alternative if someone in a group wants the choice. It is clear that they know and love Indian food: after a complimentary starter of poppadoms and various dips, appetising main dishes are served Indian style, with silver dishes on table heaters, with dips and excellent breads to accompany. This well-run establishment offers good food and service at very fair prices). An otherwise fairly standard wine list includes several especially suited to spicy food. Open from 5.30pm daily. MasterCard, Visa. **Directions:** Main street, Navan town centre.

Navan

The Loft Restaurant

RESTAURANT 26 Trimgate Street Navan Co Meath **Tel: 046 907 1755**
Fax: 046 902 8347 Email: theloft@tgavigan.com

Older sister to The Ground Floor in Kells (and the newer Side Door in Cavan), this thriving two-storey restaurant has much in common with it, notably strong modern decor (including some interesting original paintings by the Northern Ireland artist Terry Bradley), exceptionally pleasant, helpful staff and a lively global menu at reasonable prices that lays the emphasis on accessibility: this is a place for all ages and every (or no particular) occasion. The menu is similar to The Ground Floor (see entry), also with daily blackboard specials - typically a main course of poached supreme of Boyne salmon with a light yogurt & prawn sauce and desserts like bread & butter pudding, served presented, surrounded by strawberry coulis. Children welcome. **Seats 70.** Air conditioning. D daily: Mon-Thu 5.30-10.30, Fri & Sat 6-11.30, Sun 5-10. Early D about €16 (Mon-Fri 5.30-7.30 only), otherwise à la carte. House wine €16.50. 10% sc added to tables of 4+. Closed 25 Dec, 1 Jan. MasterCard, Visa, Laser. **Directions:** Centre of Navan, corner of Trimgate Street and Railway Street.

Navan

The Willows Restaurant

RESTAURANT Old Bridge Inn Navan Co Meath **Tel: 046 902 2682**

A warm welcome, good cooking and a sprinkling of less usual dishes are all part of the appeal of this attractive Chinese restaurant on the edge of Navan town. A long menu offers a mixture of Cantonese and Szechuan dishes, with a few western ones as well. A starter platter of house specials immediately indicates a confident cook at work and service details, such as the hot towels provided with finger foods and a big pottery bowl with a lid to keep the rice warm, are authentic and pleasing. The standard set meals are available but the more unusual dishes may be a better bet. Carpark (entrance via a side road). D daily, Sun all day (12.30-9.30 pm). Set menus & à la carte. MasterCard, Visa. **Directions:** On Dublin-Navan road, on left after the bridge as you approach the town.

Slane

Boyles Licensed Tea Rooms

ATMOSPHERIC PUB

Main St Slane Co Meath **Tel: 041 982 4195**

Boyle's has been run for over a decade by Josephine Lenehan (née Boyle), the third generation of the family to do so. The tea rooms lie behind a superb traditional black shopfront with gold lettering, with an interior that has barely changed since the 1940s. Visitors from all over the world come here, often after visiting nearby Newgrange – hence the unlikely facility of menus in 12 languages! Traditional afternoon tea (Devon style, with scones, jam and cream) is perhaps the main event, although soup and sandwiches are available for those with more savoury tastes. But the food – which includes home-made soups, scones, desserts, cakes, pancakes and preserves – is not really the point here, as people come for the character. Theoretically, at least, there's food service all day 11-11 (Sun from 12.30), but this is a place where they decide for themselves when to close the door - if you're going specially, a phone call might be wise. Closed Tuesdays, 25 Dec & Good Fri. MasterCard, Visa. **Directions:** From Dublin direction, turn left at square in Slane village; 2nd business house.

Slane

Conyngham Arms Hotel

féile bia HOTEL

Slane Co Meath **Tel: 041 988 4444** Fax: 041 982 4205
Email: enquiry@conynghamarms.com Web: www.conynghamarms.com

This attractive stone hotel creates a good impression with its lovely signage and twin bay trees at the main entrance - and chintzy fabrics and wood panelling make for a cosy country feeling in the restaurant and bar areas. All the bedrooms have recently been refurbished and are comfortably furnished in appropriate traditional style; some have four poster beds, all have direct line phones and tea/coffee-making facilities and iron & ironing boards are available on request. The hotel is understandably popular for weddings, but it is also well placed as a base to visit the great historic sites of Newgrange, Knowth and Dowth, the site of the Battle of the Boyne, and the Hill of Tara. Golf nearby. Conference/banqueting (350/22). **Rooms 15** (1 suite, all en-suite). B&B about €50 pps. Children welcome (cots available without charge). Closed 23-27 Dec. Diners, MasterCard, Visa, Laser. **Directions:** Centre of Slane in Navan direction. ◇

Tara Area

O'Connell's

ATMOSPHERIC PUB

Skryne Nr. Tara Co Meath **Tel: 046 902 5122**

Three generations of O'Connells have been caretakers of this wonderfully unspoilt country pub. The present owner, Mary O'Connell, has been delighting customers old and new for over ten years now. It's all beautifully simple – two little bars with no fancy bits, lots of items of local interest, and a welcoming fire in the grate. What more could anyone want? As for directions: – just head for the tower beside the pub, which is visible for miles around. Closed 25 Dec & Good Fri. **No Credit Cards.**

Trim

Franzini O'Briens

féile bia RESTAURANT

French's Lane Trim Co Meath **Tel: 046 943 1002** Fax: 046 943 1118

Modern, spacious and with an exceptional location looking out onto Trim Castle, this smart restaurant has well-trained staff who greet and seat arriving guests with commendable professionalism, immediately presenting menus, taking drink orders and ensuring that everyone settles in comfortably from the start and setting a tone of relaxed efficiency that prevails throughout. Space is attractively broken up around a central carpeted square with leather sofas to provide a variety of seating areas (the more intimate ones, with banquette seating, are towards the back) and simple, uncluttered table settings are modern and elegantly functional - tall water carafes, finger bowls for nachos and paper napkins (replaced with each course). Light-hearted menus offer an excellent range of choices in the international style and, together with an informal, buzzy atmosphere, indicate that this is a place for a good night out. And attractively served food should not disappoint - typically, a tomato-based seafood chowder is served with delicious dark treacle bread, and skilfully prepared fajitas come with a generous amount of tasty nachos and well-made accompaniments - service is excellent, even at very busy times. Interesting wine list (supplied by Jim Nicholson), but no wine offered by the glass (quarter bottles only). [Benninis daytime restaurant next door is under the same ownership but run separately.] **Seats 110.** Children welcome. Toilets wheelchair accessible. Air conditioning. D Mon-Sat, 6.30-10 (Sun 5-9). A la carte. House wines from €15. Closed 25-26 Dec, Good Fri. Amex, Diners, MasterCard, Visa, Laser, Switch. **Directions:** Beside Trim Castle, adjacent to car park.

COUNTY MONAGHAN

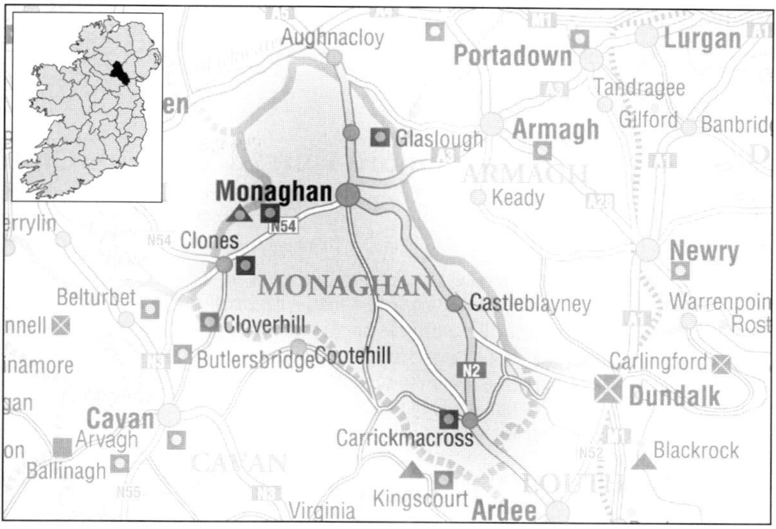

Of all Ireland's counties, it is Monaghan which is most centrally placed in the drumlin belt, that strip of rounded glacial hills which runs right across the country from Strangford Lough in County Down to Clew Bay in Mayo. Monaghan, in fact, is all hills. But as very few of them are over 300 metres above sea level, the county takes its name from Muineachain - "Little Hills". Inevitably, the actively farmed undulating country of the little hills encloses many lakes, and Monaghan in its quiet way is a coarse angler's paradise.

Much of the old Ulster Canal is in Monaghan, while the rest is in Armagh and Tyrone. Once upon a time, it connected Lough Erne to Lough Neagh. It has been derelict for a very long time, but with the success of the restored Shannon-Erne Waterway along the line of the old Ballinamore-Ballyconnell Canal bringing added vitality to Leitrim, Cavan and Fermanagh, the even more ambitious vision of restoring the Ulster Canal is being given serious consideration.

Vision of a different sort is the theme at Annaghmakerrig House near the Quaker-named village of Newbliss in west Monaghan. The former home of theatrical producer Tyrone Guthrie, it is now a busy centre for writers and artists who can stay there to complete 'work in progress'.

In the east of the county at Castleblayney, there's a particularly attractive lake district with forest park and adventure centre around Lough Mucko. Southwards of Castleblayney, we come to the bustling town of Carrickmacross, still famous for its lace, and a Tidy Towns trophy winner. Civic pride will continue to grow in Carrickmacross, for September 19th 2003 finally saw the signing of the contract to provide a proper bypass round an attractive town which has endured excessive through traffic for too long.

In the Tidy Town awards of September 2003, Monaghan's second highest scorer was the pretty village of Glaslough towards the north of the county. And at Clontibret in northeast Monaghan, there's gold in them thar little hills. Whether or not it's in sufficient quantities to merit mining is a continuing matter of commercial debate, but the fact that it's there at all is another of Monaghan's more intriguing secrets. Another is the county's uncrowded character. The recent six year Census revealed that Monaghan's population has risen by only 2.8%, the smallest increase of any county, bringing Monaghan's total population to a modest 52,772. In an overcrowded world, this is surely interesting news.

Local Attractions and Information

Carrickmacross, Carrickmacross Lace Gallery	042 966 2506
Carrickmacross (Kingscourt Rd) Dun a Ri Forest Park	042 966 7320
Castleblayney, Lough Muckno Leisure Park	042 974 6356
Clones, Clones Lace Exhibits	047 51051
Glaslough, Castle Leslie Gardens	047 88109
Inniskeen, Patrick Kavanagh Centre	042 937 8560

Carrickmacross

Nuremore Hotel & Country Club

féile bia HOTEL / RESTAURANT

Carrickmacross Co Monaghan
Tel: 042 966 1438 Fax: 042 966 1853
Email: nuremore@eircom.net Web: nuremore.com

This fine owner-managed country hotel just south of Carrickmacross is set in a parkland estate, with its own 18-hole golf course, and serves the sporting, leisure and business requirements of a wide area very well. As you go over the little bridge ("Beware - ducks crossing") and the immaculately maintained hotel and golf club open up before you, worldly cares seem to recede - this is a place you can get fond of. The hotel invariably gives a good impression on arrival and this sense of care and maintenance is continued throughout. Spacious, comfortably arranged public areas and generous bedrooms with lovely views over the gardens and lakes are regularly refurbished. It would make an excellent base to explore this little known area - and there is plenty to do on site. The superb country club has a full leisure centre and a wide range of related facilities - including a new gymnasium and spa, opened in 2003 - and there are conference and meeting rooms for every size of gathering, with state-of-the-art audio-visual equipment available. Conference/banqueting (500/350); business centre, secretarial services on request, video conferencing. Leisure centre, swimming pool, spa; beauty salon; golf (18), fishing, walking, tennis, garden; snooker. Children welcome (cots available, €13; baby sitting arranged). **Rooms 72** (7 junior suites, 11 executive, 1 for disabled, 23 no smoking). B&B €130 pps, ss €50.

☆ **The Restaurant at Nuremore:** The restaurant is well-appointed in a fairly formal country house style, with generous white-clothed tables and a couple of steps dividing the window area and inner tables, allowing everybody to enjoy the view over golf course and woodland. Good food has always been a high priority at the Nuremore, which is well established as the leading restaurant in the area, and this aspect of the hotel has been sharply pinpointed since Raymond McArdle, previously head chef at Deane's Brasserie in Belfast took over as head chef in 2000. His ambitious plans for the restaurant have had the full backing of proprietress Julie Gilhooly and their spacious, state-of-the art kitchen is now the envy of chefs throughout the country. Raymond sources ingredients meticulously, using local produce as much as possible in top rank daily set lunch and dinner menus, a separate vegetarian menu and an evening à la carte. Recent visits by the Guide have confirmed the excellence of the cooking, seen in perfectly executed and well-flavoured dishes like an exquisitely luxurious signature dish, roast tranche of foie-gras with spiced brioche and with smoked duck and artichoke salad. From a choice of six or seven equally appealing main courses on the dinner menu, dishes like fillet of turbot in lobster bisque with tortellini, organic spinach and thermidor sauce vie with other house specialities such as a glorious celebration of pork - roast fillet, braised stuffed trotter& crisp confit, with fried cabbage, apple chutney & Midleton jus. Everything, it seems, is similarly impressive - and, on the dessert menu also he continues his liking for taking a single ingredient and presenting it in three ways, in dishes like a deliciously light and refreshing apple & ginger crème caramel, with apple jus and apple crisps - and rhubarb and custard, cooked three ways. A selection of French and Irish cheeses comes with a walnut brioche - and wonderful petits fours are served with cappuccino or espresso. This is exceptional cooking and, since the arrival of restaurant manager Frank Trutet in 2003 brought a new element of professionalism to the front of house team, service is being brought into line with the standard of cuisine. The dining room, while well-appointed in a traditional style, is somewhat at odds with this cutting edge cuisine and there is no dress or behaviour code; it is a privilege to experience food of this quality and it would be a compliment to the exceptional dining experience offered by this fine kitchen if guests could contribute to the sense of occasion by dressing up a little - and, perhaps, the official policy that the restaurant is not suitable for children after 7.30, might be enforced. As well as exceptional quality, the Restaurant at Nuremore offers outstanding value for money, especially at lunch time. **Seats 100** (private room, 50). Air conditioning. L Sun-Fri, 12.30-2.30; D daily 6.30-9.30 (Sun to 9). Set L €28 (Set Sun L €30); Set D €45 (vegetarian €25); Tasting Menu €70. House wine €19.50; sc discretionary. Closed L Sat. Open all year. Amex, Diners. MasterCard, Visa, Laser. **Directions:** Just south of Carrickmacross, 55 miles from Dublin on N2.

Clones — Hilton Park

COUNTRY HOUSE

Clones Co Monaghan **Tel: 047 56007** Fax: 047 56033
Email: mail@hiltonpark.ie Web: www.hiltonpark.ie

Once described as a "capsule of social history" because of their collection of family portraits and memorabilia going back 250 years or more, Johnny and Lucy Madden's wonderful 18th century mansion is set in beautiful countryside, amidst 200 acres of woodland and farmland. With lakes, Pleasure Grounds and a Lovers' Walk to set the right tone, the house is magnificent in every sense, and the experience of visiting it a rare treat. Johnny and Lucy are natural hosts and, as the house and its contents go back for so many generations, there is a strong feeling of being a privileged family guest as you wander through grandly-proportioned, beautifully furnished rooms. Four-posters and all the unselfconscious comforts that make for a very special country house stay are part of the charm, but as visitors from all over the world have found, it's the warmth of Johnny and Lucy's welcome that lends that extra magic. The gardens are also of particular interest - formal gardens have recently been restored to their former glory and Lucy, an enthusiastic organic gardener and excellent cook, supplies freshly harvested produce for meals in the house, while other ingredients are carefully sourced from trusted suppliers of organic and free-range products. Residents' dinners are served in a beautiful dining room overlooking the gardens and lake - and memorable breakfasts are taken downstairs in the Green Room next morning. This is exceptional hospitality, with an Irish flavour – and, in recognition, Hilton Park was presented with the Guide's International Hospitality Award in 1999. Not suitable for children under 8 (except babies, free in parents' room, cot available, baby sitting arranged), playroom for older children. Pets allowed in some areas. Gardens, fishing (own lake), walking, cycling. *Special weekend breaks, and discounts offered for 2-night stays; they also have a picturesque, comfortably furnished gate lodge available for self-catering (sleeps 4); each weekly let gets a free round of golf (18 hole) for four! **Rooms 6** (all en-suite & no smoking). B&B €110 pps, ss €40. Residents D Tue-Sat, €50 at 8 pm (Fri, 8.30); please give 24 hours notice. House wine €20-22.50. SC discretionary. Closed 1 Nov-3 Jan. MasterCard, Visa. **Directions:** 3 miles south of Clones on Scotshouse Road.

Glaslough — Castle Leslie

féile bia RESTAURANT / HOTEL

Glaslough Co Monaghan **Tel: 047 88109** Fax: 047 88256
Email: info@castleleslie.com Web: www.castleleslie.com

During the three centuries that this extraordinary place has been in the Leslie family it has changed remarkably little - and its fascinating history intrigues guests as much as the eccentricity of Castle Leslie as they find it today. Once inside the massive front door (guarded by family dogs who snooze in beds flanking the stone steps) there is no reception desk, just a welcoming oak-panelled hall (and afternoon tea in the drawing room), and there are no phones, television sets or clocks in the rooms, although concessions to the 20th century have been made in the form of generous heating and plentiful hot water. The fourteen bedrooms are all different, furnished and decorated around a particular era, with en-suite bathrooms a feature in their own right with huge baths, wacky showers and outrageous toilets, all done in a tongue-in-cheek style, reflecting the family's eccentric history and the wonders of Victorian plumbing. In a charming reverse of circumstances, the family lives in the servants' wing, so guests can enjoy the magnificence of the castle to the full – it has all the original furniture and family portraits. The estate has wonderful walks, and pike fishing; boating and picnic lunches on the estate are available by arrangement. Due to the nature of the castle (and the fact that the Leslies see it as a wonderful refuge from the outside world for adults) this is not a suitable place to bring children. Despite the extreme eccentricity suggested by details such as the answering machine ("please leave your message after the (scream)", which makes callers think they are just nuts, this is actually a professionally run business and a little more 'hotel-like' than the publicity suggests. Conferences/banqueting (24/98). Garden, walking, fishing, tennis. No children. No pets. **Rooms 14** (3 suites; 13 en-suite, 1 with private bathroom - 9 with bath, 5 shower only; all no smoking). B&B €107, ss €25. Open all year.

Restaurant: Good food is an important element of a visit to Castle Leslie and non-residents are welcome to come for dinner, by reservation. It is all done in fine old style with pre-dinner drinks in the drawing room (or the Fountain Garden in summer) and dinner, which is served in rooms including the original dining room, unchanged for over a century, by waitresses wearing Victorian uniforms. However, despite the obvious oddities of faded grandeur - tables with a slight list, chairs and sofas which have long since lost their stuffing - Noel McMeel, head chef since 2000, is essentially offering a restaurant dining experience rather than a country house dinner. Many entertaining wine and food events are held during the year - contact the Castle for details - and the Castle Leslie range of preserves and speciality foods is available from the castle and Brown Thomas, in Dublin. **Seats 90.** D daily 6.30-9.30; Set D €48.50 (Gourmet Menu €54). House wine from €19. MasterCard, Visa, Laser. **Directions:** 10 mins from Monaghan Town: Monaghan -Armagh road-Glaslough.

Monaghan

Andy's Bar and Restaurant

féile bia **BAR / RESTAURANT**

12 Market Street Monaghan Co Monaghan
Tel: 047 82277 Fax: 047 84195 Web: www.andysmonaghan.com

Right in the centre of Monaghan, opposite the old market house, the Redmond family's bar is furnished and decorated in traditional Victorian style, with a lot of fine mahogany, stained glass and mirrors. It has a strong local following, and it is easy to see why: everything is gleaming clean and arranged well for comfort, with high-backed bar seats and plenty of alcoves set up with tables for the comfortable consumption of their good bar food. Substantial bar meals include a range of mid-day specials on a blackboard as well as a concise written menu. The evening restaurant upstairs, which has recently been refurbished but retains its old-fashioned ambience, offers a much more extensive range of popular and classic dishes, including a good choice of prime fish and steaks various ways - specialities include garlic Monaghan mushrooms and crispy half roast duckling (with orange & brandy sauce); while not adventurous, this is good cooking based on quality ingredients and the results are extremely tasty, satisfying - and good value. Traditional desserts like pavlova, lemon cheesecake, fresh fruit salad and home-made ices are served from a trolley, and there might be something comforting like a hot treacle sponge pudding in cold weather. Members of the Redmond family are everywhere, keeping an eye on things, and service is charming and efficient. Bar meals daily, 12-3 & 6-10 (Sat, all day). Restaurant D Tue-Sun, 6-10.15 (Sun 4-9.30). Set D €32.95; house wine €14.60. Closed L Sun, D Mon, 25 Dec, Good Fri, bank hols & 1-14 July. MasterCard, Visa, Laser. **Directions:** Town centre, opposite the Market House.

Monaghan

Hillgrove Hotel

HOTEL

Old Armagh Rd Monaghan Co Monaghan **Tel: 047 81288** Fax: 047 84951
Email: hillgrove@quinnhotels.com Web: quinnhotels.com

Overlooking the town from a fine hillside location,the appropriately named Hillgrove is the leading hotel in the town. Like its sister properties in the Quinn Group, an impressive foyer sets the tone and it is generally well-run, although maintenance and refurbishment can sometimes be a little disappointing. Conference/banqueting (1000/600). Garden. Children welcome. No pets. **Rooms 44.** B&B about €70 pp. Closed 25-26 Dec. Amex, Diners, MasterCard, Visa. **Directions:** Take N2 from Dublin to Monaghan town. ◇

COUNTY OFFALY

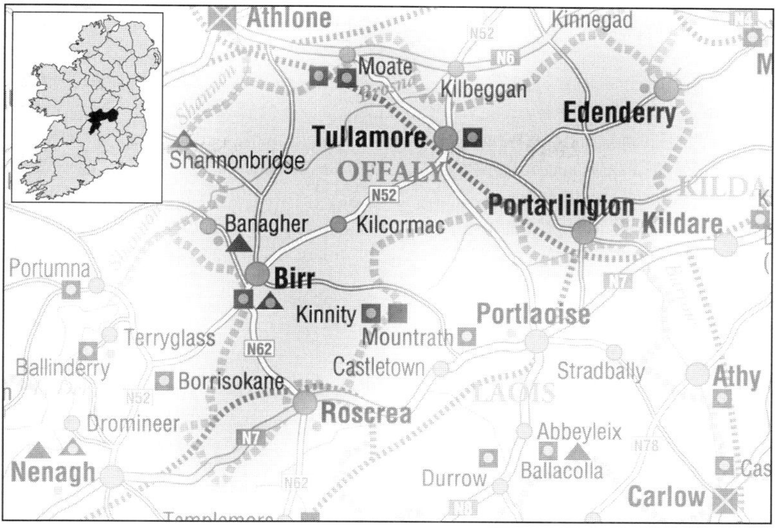

At the heart of the old Ely O'Carroll territory, Offaly is Ireland's most sky-minded county. In the grounds of Birr Castle, there's the Parsons family's famous restored 1845-vintage 1.83m astronomical telescope – rated one of the Seven Wonders of Ireland - through which the 3rd Earl of Rosse observed his discovery of the spiral nebulae. And in Tullamore, there's a thriving amateur Astronomical Society whose members point out that the wide clear skies of Offaly have encouraged the regular observation of heavenly bodies since at least 1057 AD, when astronomy was the province of moon-minded monks.

On a more modern note, the Tullamore Dew Heritage Centre is housed in the restored 1897 canal-side bonded warehouse, which formerly stored the famous local whiskey. The Centre explores Tullamore's distilling, canal and urban history with entertaining style. Style is also the theme of the new County Hall in Tullamore, which on September 18th 2003 was given the An Taisce sustainable building award.

Back in Birr meanwhile, the restored gardens of Birr Castle are an added attraction, but still the sky calls, and the annual Irish Hot Air Balloon Meeting has been run with increasing success since 1970. It attracts serious international balloonists who welcome the opportunity for participation in a relaxed fun event where everyone wins a prize, and is equally suitable for beginners, as Offaly's bogs provide a soft landing - "there's a bit of give in a bog".

Offaly is also historic hunting country. It is home to the Ormonde, which may not be Ireland's largest or richest hunt, "but it's the oldest and undoubtedly the best." Once upon a time, they invited the neighbouring County Galway Hunt for a shared meet, and afterwards the carousing in Dooley's Hotel in Birr reached such a hectic pitch that the hotel was joyously torched by the visitors. Dooley's was rebuilt to fulfill its central role in Birr, and the hunt from across the Shannon has been known as the Galway Blazers ever since.

The Grand Canal finally reaches the great river at Shannon Harbour in Offaly, after crossing Ireland from Dublin through Tullamore, and on the river itself, waterborne travellers find that Offaly affords the opportunity of visiting Clonmacnoise, where the remains of an ancient monastic university city give pause for thought. In the south of the county, the Slieve Bloom Mountains rise attractively above Offaly's farmland and bogs. These are modest heights, as they attain just 526 m on the peak of Arderin. However, it is their understated charms which particularly appeal, and in the Slieve Blooms we find Ireland's first organised system of gites, the French concept whereby unused farmhouses have been restored to a comfortable standard for self-catering visitor accommodation.

Nestling in a valley of the Slieve Blooms is the unspoilt village of Kinnitty, where Offaly's quality of life is most in evidence. And in the far east of the county, where Offaly marches with Kildare, we find Clonbulloge, top title holder in Offaly in the current Tidy Towns awards, a pretty place on the banks of the stream known as the Figile River.

Local Attractions and Information

Banagher Cloghan Castle (15C Tower House) 0509 51650
Birr, Castle Demesne & Historic Science Centre .... 0509 20336 / 22154
Birr, Tourism Information 0509 20110
Clonmacnoise Visitor & Interpretive Centre 090 967 4195
Edenderry, Canal Festival (June) 046 973 2071
Shannonbridge, Clonmacnoise & West Offaly Railway 090 967 4114
Slieve Bloom, Rural Development Society 0509 37299
Tullamore, Offaly Historical Society 0506 21421
Tullamore, Tullamore Dew Heritage Centre 0506 25015
Tullamore, Tourism Information 0506 52617

Banagher

J.J. Hough

ATMOSPHERIC PUB

Main Street Banagher Co Offaly
Tel: 0509 51893 Email: houghsheila@eircom.net

Hidden behind a thriving vine, which threatens to take over in summer, this charming 250-year old pub is soothingly dark inside – making a fine contrast to the cheerful eccentricity of the current owner, Michael Hough. A world famous music pub, it's authentic and unique, family-run and with a wealth of Irish art on the walls. It's a great local and also popular with people from the river cruisers, who come up from the harbour for pints, music and craic - for the last thirty years there's been traditional Irish music here every night from March to November, and on Friday, Saturday & Sunday in winter. Children and pets welcome. Open 10.30 am - 1 am. No food. Closed 25 Dec & Good Fri. **Directions:** Lower Main Street.

Banagher

The Vine House

RESTAURANT

Banagher Co Offaly **Tel: 0509 51463** Fax: 0509 51463

This atmospheric bar and restaurant is the perfect haven for boating people - head chef Adam Ashton has been sending guests happy into the night for over 10 years now. Music nightly May-August (bands at weekends, weekdays ballads & traditional); Saturday nights only off-season. Food served: 12 noon - 3.30 pm and 7-9.30 pm daily in summer; off-season: evenings only, probably Wed-Sun. A phone call to check opening times is advised, especially off season. MasterCard, Visa. **Directions:** Near harbour.

BIRR

Birr is a lovely old town steeped in history and it makes a good holiday centre, with plenty to do locally – Birr Castle, with its observatory and magnificently restored gardens to visit, also golfing, fishing, riding and river excursions. The charmingly old-fashioned **Dooly's Hotel (Tel 0509 20032 www.dooleyshotel.com)** is one of Ireland's oldest coaching inns, dating back to 1747 and is right on Emmet Square, the centre of Georgian Birr (food served all day); for those who like a little more space, the late Georgian **County Arms Hotel (Tel 0509 20791; www.countyarmshotel.com)** is set in its own grounds nearby, with gardens and glasshouses to supply the hotel, and also a leisure centre. Food and moderately priced accommodation is also available at the riverside **Maltings Guesthouse (Tel 0509 21345),** which also has a bar.

Birr

The Chestnut

Ⓝ PUB

Green Street Birr Co Offaly **Tel: 0509 220011**

Clodagh Fay, sister of Caroline Boyd of The Stables, has re-vamped and re-opened the old Chestnut pub in Birr town, which poured its first pint back in 1823. She has refurbished the place beautifully with no expense spared on the stylish dark wood interior, slick bar and comfy layout. It is a great place to while away a Sunday afternoon reading the papers by the fire. They serve great cappucinos and mochacinos along with some of the best Guinness you are likely to find anywhere in the country. Look out for the mouthwatering BBQs they host in the summer. Open: Mon-Fri 5pm-closing; Sat & Sun 12 noon-closing. Closed 25 Dec, Good Fri.

Birr

Spinners Town House & Bistro

RESTAURANT / GUESTHOUSE

Castle Street Birr Co Offaly
Tel: 0509 21673 Fax: 0509 21672
Email: spinners@indigo.ie Web: www.spinners-townhouse.com

This unusual establishment in the centre of Birr runs through five Georgian townhouses and, after a change of ownership in 2000, was restored and refurbished throughout in a simple contemporary style. Four spacious new rooms (similar in style but "with a hint of the baronial gothic") were added, and then the bistro refurbished making the central courtyard garden and its surrounding arches a major feature. Stylish, thoughtfully designed bedrooms include family rooms, doubles and twins, all with en-suite or private bathrooms. In addition to their own sitting room and a breakfast room, where a traditional hot Irish breakfast based on organic bacon and sausages is served, guests have the use of the enclosed courtyard garden. Children welcome (cots available). No pets. **Rooms 13** (10 en-suite, 3 with private bathrooms, all shower only and no smoking). B&B from €32.50 pps, ss €12.50. Closed 5-31 Jan; phone to check opening in winter.

Spinners Bistro: Everything is based on fresh ingredients, local and organic wherever possible, with fish and seafood the main speciality, accounting for about four starters (try their house special of wild salmon, potato & herb cakes, served with chive mayonnaise) and a similar number of main courses. But there is plenty else to choose from too, including interesting vegetarian alternatives (a starter tomato & goat's cheese tart and main course yoghurt & lentil chicken curry are typical). Meats are organic - a 12 oz sirloin steak, perhaps, with a choice of sauces or Somerset pork, where the fillet is pan-fried and dressed with fresh apple & cider cream. Desserts tend to be old favourites, like warm pear and almond flan and home-made lemon meringue pie. Open to non-residents; full bar licence. **Seats 46.** D Tue-Sat, 5-10 (Sun 4-9); à la carte.House wine from €12.50. SC discretionary. Closed Mon, 5-31 Jan (Phone to check opening off season.) Amex, Diners, MasterCard, Visa, Laser. **Directions:** Beside Birr Castle.

Birr

The Stables Restaurant & Townhouse

RESTAURANT WITH ROOMS

6 Oxmantown Mall Birr Co Offaly
Tel: 0509 20263 Fax: 0509 21677
Email: cboyd@indigo.ie Web: www.thestablesrestaurant.com

The Boyd family's characterful establishment is in a lovely old Georgian house overlooking the tree-lined mall and it has a strong local following. The restaurant is in the converted stables and coach house and has lots of atmosphere, with attractive exposed bricks and stonework, arches and an open fire in the period drawing room (which is used as a bar and reception area). The cooking style is quite traditional – a blend of Cordon Bleu and traditional Irish, but with some unexpectedly adventurous options like pan-fried ostrich and more seafood than might be expected in the midlands – and hearty country portions are the norm. Children welcome. Banqueting (90). **Seats 65.** D Tue-Sat, 5.30-9.30 (also Sun 6-8 Jun-Sep) L Sun only, 12.30-3. Set D €36.50, à la carte also available; Set Sun L €22; house wine €17.50; SC discretionary. Air conditioning. Closed all Mon, also D Sun Oct-May, Ash Wednesday, Good Fri. * Open Christmas day, 12-3.

Accommodation: Old world en-suite bedrooms overlooking the mall or the courtyard include two large newer rooms added in 2000. Children welcome (under 10 free in parents' room, cot available without charge). Pets allowed by arrangement. **Rooms 6.** B&B €40 pps, ss €10. Amex, Diners, MasterCard, Visa, Laser. **Directions:** Town centre, opposite original gates of Birr castle.

Birr

The Thatch Bar & Restaurant

PUB / RESTAURANT

Crinkle Birr Co Offaly **Tel: 0509 20682**
Fax: 0509 21847 Email: thethatchcrinkle@eirom.net

This characterful little thatched pub and restaurant just outside Birr shows just how good a genuine, well-run country pub with imaginative, freshly cooked food can be. Since 1991 the energetic owner, Des Connole, has worked tirelessly to improve standards - recently with the help of head chef Duncan West, who is responsible for imaginative bar food as well as the restaurant, which offers both set menus and an à la carte. Expect a mixture of traditional dishes such as ever-popular sirloin steaks (with garlic mash, braised wild mushrooms & rosemary jus) and more unusual things – plenty of seafood for a midland restaurant, and exotics like ostrich (which is farmed in Ireland) and kangaroo; local produce is there as well, of course, in a house speciality of apricot & spinach stuffed pork fillet with a light creamy Irish whiskey sauce, for example, and there are some vegetarian options. Good food and warm hospitality make this one of the best eating places in the area. Children welcome. Parking. **Seats 50** (private room, 15-20). D 6.30-9.30 daily, Set D €37, also à la carte; L Sun-12.30 & 2.30; Set Sun L €20; early evening bar menu Mon-Sat 5-7.30 (except Jul-Aug), à la carte; house wine €18; SC discretionary. Bar meals Mon-Sat, 12.30-3.30 & 5-7.30. Toilets wheelchair accessible. Restaurant closed D Sun, establishment closed 25 Dec, Good Fri. Diners, MasterCard, Visa, Laser. **Directions:** 1 mile from Birr (Roscrea side).

Kinnitty

Ardmore House

COUNTRY HOUSE

The Walk Kinnitty Co Offaly **Tel: 0509 37009**
Email: info@kinnitty.net Web: www.kinnitty.net

Set back from the road in its own garden, Christina Byrne's stone-built Victorian house offers old-fashioned comforts: brass beds, turf fires and home-made bread and preserves for breakfast. Bedrooms are deliberately left without amenities, in order to make a visit to Ardmore a real country house experience and encourage guests to spend less time in their rooms and mix with each other - tea is available downstairs at any time. All bedrooms are decorated to a high standard - one with jacuzzi bath - and a ground floor room is wheelchair friendly. Christina can provide you with maps and guides to walking in the Slieve Blooms. There's a traditional Irish night on Friday nights, at nearby Kinnitty Castle. Children welcome (under 3s free in parents' room); pets allowed in certain areas. **Rooms 5** (4 en-suite, 3 shower only, 1 with private bathroom, all no smoking). B&B €32 pps, ss €11. Closed 25 Dec. **No Credit Cards. Directions:** In village of Kinnitty, 9 miles from Birr.

Kinnitty

The Glendine Bistro

RESTAURANT / B&B

Kinnitty Co Offaly **Tel: 0509 37973** Fax: 0509 37975

Situated in a charming village at the foot of the Slieve Bloom mountains, the clean-lined simplicity of Percy and Phil Clendennan's attractive contemporary restaurant provides a welcome contrast to other, more traditional, dining options nearby, giving visitors to this unspoilt area a choice of styles. Head chef Jamie Owens offers wide-ranging menus that suit the surroundings: this is steak country and prime Hereford beef features in steaks various ways, but there are also many more international dishes like barbecued tiger prawns & king scallops with chargrilled peppers or Irish ostrich on a bed of pesto courgettes, with balsamic dressing - and sound cooking is backed up by friendly service. Vegetarian options, typically stir-fries and fresh pasta dishes, are always available. Children welcome. **Seats 60** (private room 15). Air conditioning. D Thu- Sun, 6.30-9.30. L Sun only, 12.30-2.30. Set D €32.50, also à la carte. Set Sun L €20. House wine €17.50. Closed all Mon-Wed; all Jan.

Accommodation: Bright, comfortably furnished en-suite bedrooms are offered, all with direct dial phones, TV and tea/coffee-making facilities. Children under 6 free in parents' room. **Rooms 5** (all shower-only & no smoking). Accommodation open all year. B&B €32 pps, ss €7. MasterCard, Visa, Laser. **Directions:** 7 miles from Birr, in centre of Kinnitty Village.

Kinnitty

Kinnitty Castle

HOTEL

Kinnitty Co Offaly **Tel: 0509 37318** Fax: 0509 37284
Email: kinnittycastle@eircom.net Web: www.kinnittycastle.com

Furnished in keeping with its dramatic history and theatrical character, this luxurious Gothic Revival castle in the foothills of the Slieve Bloom Mountains is at the centre of a very large estate (accessible for horse-riding and walking) with 650 acres of parkland and formal gardens. Public areas – a library bar, Georgian style dining room, Louis XV drawing room and an atmospheric Dungeon Bar where there is traditional music on Friday nights all year – are mainly furnished in the style expected of a castle hotel. The accommodation, however, is slightly different: bedrooms are all interesting and comfortable but vary considerably according to their position in the castle: the best are big and romantic, with stunning views over the estate (and sumptuous, dramatically styled bathrooms). There are new, but atmospheric, medieval-style banqueting/conference facilities for up to 180/200 in a courtyard at the back of the castle, which are understandably popular for weddings, also a small leisure centre (no swimming pool as yet). Apart from its olde-worlde character, what makes this hotel special is the staff, for whom nothing is too much trouble and who contribute greatly to the overall sense of fun. Tennis, fishing, equestrian, garden. Children welcome (Under 12s free in parents' room; cots available without charge). No pets. **Rooms 37** (10 suites, 11 junior suites). No lift (long corridors and a lot of stairs). B&B about €120 pps, s.c.12.5%. Open all year. Amex, Diners, MasterCard, Visa, Laser, Switch. **Directions:** On the R422- Emo to Birr Road,off main N7 Limerick Road. ◇

Shannonbridge

The Old Fort

Ⓝ **RESTAURANT**

Shannonbridge Co Offaly **Tel: 0905 74973**

In a very pleasant site right beside the Shannon, this restaurant is in an attractively restored fort and has oodles of character. The proprietor, Fergal Moran, grew up here and started restoration of the fort about eight years ago, working with Dúchas to make sure it was done correctly. Initial impressions on arrival are confirmed in the large reception area, which has lovely old timbers, fresh flowers, good lighting and comfortable sofas beside an open fire - a great start by any standards, and a useful extra dining space for for elderly guests, or anyone in a wheelchair, who may not be comfortable with stairs. The main dining room is upstairs (also a second room used for busy times or for private functions) and the ambience is lovely, with old wooden floors, well-spaced polished wood tables smartly laid with starched linen napkins and candles, which are also everywhere in sconces. The head chef, Brian Maher, (well known in the area as he was previously at The Thatch in Crinkill) offers three attractive evening menus - an early dinner, a more extensive set dinner and an à la carte, which is wide ranging and includes several vegetarian dishes. The simplest dishes are often best - a good steak, cooked as ordered comes with a creamy mushroom sauce and perfectly cooked, very good quality vegetables; most people will go home happy after such a dish. Presentation can be a little fussy (drizzles of this and that) but, overall, this is very good food, enhanced by attentive service and lovely surroundings. It's a great asset to the area and should certainly do well. **Seats 75.** D Wed-Sat, from 5pm; L Sun only 12.30-2.30 (or later, when busy). MasterCard, Visa. **Directions:** Beside the bridge in Shannonbridge.

Shannonbridge

The Village Tavern

ATMOSPHERIC PUB

Main Street Shannonbridge Co Offaly **Tel: 0905 74112**

At J.J. Killeen's wonderful pub weary travellers can be restored, particularly by the house special of hot rum and chocolate - perfect after a damp day on the river. Meanwhile you can also top up on groceries, fishing bait and gas. Music nightly May-September; weekends only off-season. **Directions:** On the main street of Shannonbridge, between Ballinasloe and Cloghan.

Tullamore

Tullamore Court Hotel Conference & Leisure Centre

HOTEL

Tullamore Co Offaly **Tel: 0506 46666** Fax: 0506 46677
Email: info@tullamorecourt.hotel.ie Web: www.tullamorecourthotel.ie

An attractive building, set back from the road a little and softened by trees, this large modern hotel has an extensive foyer and public areas are bright and cheerful. It serves the local community well, with fine conference and banqueting facilities (750/550) and an excellent leisure centre and it's an ideal base for business or pleasure. Bedrooms are very pleasantly decorated in an easy modern style, using warm colours and unfussy fabrics and the staff are exceptionally friendly and helpful. Food is generally above the standard expected in hotels and this can be a refreshing place to break a journey. Leisure centre, swimming pool, garden. Children welcome. **Rooms 72.** Lift. B&B €120 pps. Closed 24-26 Dec. Amex, Diners, MasterCard, Visa, Laser. **Directions:** South end of town. ◇

Tullamore Area

Annaharvey Farm

FARM GUESTHOUSE

Tullamore Co Offaly **Tel: 0506 43544** Fax: 0506 43766
Email: info@annaharveyfarm.ie Web: www.annaharveyfarm.ie

Henry and Lynda Deverell's restored grain barn, with pitch pine floors and beams, open fires and comfortable accommodation, provides a good base for a holiday offering all the pleasures of the outdoor life. Equestrian activities are the main attraction (including tuition in indoor and outdoor arenas), but walking, cycling and golfing also lay their claims - and, for the rest days, major sights including Clonmacnoise and Birr Castle are nearby. Small conference/banqueting (40/20). Children welcome (under 2 free in parents' room; cot available without charge). No pets. **Rooms 7** (6 shower only, 1 with bath; all no-smoking). B&B €36 pps, ss €10. Meals available - details on application. Closed Dec & Jan. MasterCard, Visa, Laser. **Directions:** R420 Tullamore - Portarlington.

COUNTY ROSCOMMON

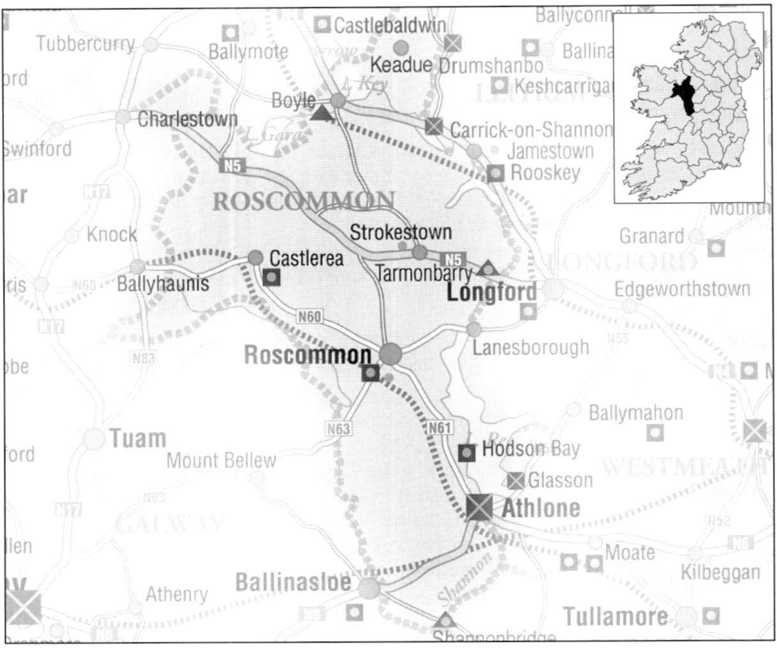

The National Tidy Town Awards ceremony in early September in Dublin Castle is one of those occasions when the Irish countryside comes to town, and metropolitan interests move into the background. The most recent awards were made on September 8th 2003, and it was vintage stuff. Irish villages are small places, but even by those standards Keadue in north Roscommon is small indeed. It has just two shops, two pubs, a church and a health centre. The population is barely 150 people. But a third of them seem to be on the local Tidy Towns Committee. They keep their very Irish little village a neat as a new pin. And in 2004, they can celebrate the fact that Keadue (try pronouncing it "Kay-doo") is the Tidy Towns overall winner with an impressive score of 270 (90.0%).

It could be said that in times past, Roscommon was a county much put upon by the counties about it. Or, put another way, to the casual visitor it seemed that just as Roscommon was on the verge of becoming significant, it became somewhere else. In one notable example - the hotel complex at Hodson's Bay on the western shores of Lough Ree - the location is actually in Roscommon, yet the exigencies of the postal service have given it to Athlone and thereby Westmeath.

But Roscommon is a giving sort of county, for it gave Ireland her first President, Gaelic scholar Douglas Hyde (1860-1949), it was also the birthplace of Oscar Wilde's father, and as well the inimitable songwriter Percy French was a Roscommon man. Like everywhere else in the western half of Ireland, Roscommon suffered grieviously from the Great Famine of the late 1840s, and at Strokestown, the handsome market town serving the eastern part of the county, Strokestown Park House has been sympathetically restored to include a Famine Museum. A visit to it will certainly add a thoughtful element to your meal in the restaurant.

Roscommon town itself has a population of barely 1,500, but the presence of extensive castle ruins and a former gaol tell of a more important past. The gaol was once noted for having a female hangman, today it has shops and a restaurant. Northwestward at Castlerea - headquarters for the County Council - we find Clonalis House, ancestral home of the O'Conor Don, and final resting place of O'Carolan's Harp.

In the north of the county, the town of Boyle near lovely Lough Key with its outstanding Forest Park is a substantial centre, with a population nearing the 2,000 mark. Boyle is thriving, and symbolic of this is the restored King House, a masterpiece from 1730. Reckoned to have been the most important provincial town house in Ireland, it is today filled with exhibits which eloquently evoke the past. Nearby, the impressive riverbank remains of Boyle Abbey, the largest Cistercian foundation in Ireland, date from 1148.

Lough Key is of course on one of the upper reaches of the inland waterways system, and a beautiful part it is too. In fact, all of Roscommon's eastern boundary is defined by the Shannon and its lakes, but as the towns along it tend to identify themselves with the counties across the river, Roscommon is left looking very thin on facilities. But it has much to intrigue the enquiring visitor. For instance, along the Roscommon shore of Lough Ree near the tiny village of Lecarrow, the remains of a miniature city going back to mediaeval times and beyond can be dimly discerned among the trees down towards Rindown Point.

These hints of of an active past serve to emphasise the fact that today, Roscommon moves at a gentler pace than the rest of Ireland - something which is reflected in its pubs to people ratio. It is second only to Leitrim on this scale, as Leitrim has just 153 people for every pub licence, while Roscommon has 170. Slainte!

Local Attractions and Information

Boyle, Boyle Abbey (12th C Monastery)	071 966 2604
Boyle, Frybrook House (18thC town hse)	071 966 2513
Boyle, King House (500 years of Irish life)	071 966 3242
Boyle, Lough Key Forest Park	071 966 2363
Boyle, Tourism Information	071 966 2145
Castlerea, Clonalis House	094 962 0014
Elphin, Restored windmill	071 963 5181
Frenchpark Dr Douglas Hyde Interpretive Centre	0907 70016
Roscommon town, Arts Centre	090 662 5824
Roscommon town, County Museum	090 662 5613
Roscommon Town, Race Course	090 662 6231
Roscommon town, Tourism Information	090 662 6342
Strokestown, Park House, Garden & Famine Museum	071 963 3013
Strokestown, Roscommon County Heritage Centre	071 963 3380

Carrick-on-Shannon

Glencarne House

COUNTRY HOUSE / FARMHOUSE

Ardcarne Carrick-on-Shannon Co Roscommon
Tel: 071 966 7013 Fax: 071 966 7013

On the border between Leitrim and Roscommon - Glencarne House is physically in Leitrim, but the postal address is Roscommon - the Harrington family's large Georgian house is set well back from the road, with a large garden in front and farmland behind, so it is easy to find, yet without interference from traffic. Spacious and elegantly furnished with antiques, this is very much a family home and Agnes Harrington has won many awards for hospitality and home-cooked food based on their own farm produce. Garden. Children welcome; pets permitted by arrangement. **Rooms 4** (all en-suite & no smoking). B&B about €35 pps, ss about €5. Set D €25.50, 7.30pm (book by 6pm); wine licence. Closed Oct-Mar. **No Credit Cards. Directions:** On the N4,halfway between Carrick-on-Shannon and Boyle.

Castlerea

Clonalis House

COUNTRY HOUSE

Castlerea Co Roscommon **Tel: 094 962 0014**
Fax: 094 962 0014 Email: clonalis@iol.ie

Standing on the land that has been the home of the O'Conors of Connacht for 1,500 years, this 45-roomed Victorian Italianate mansion may seem a little daunting on arrival, but it's magic - and the hospitable owners, Pyers and Marguerite O'Conor-Nash, enjoy sharing their rich and varied history with guests, who are welcome to browse through their fascinating archive. Amazing heirlooms include a copy of the last Brehon Law judgment (handed down about 1580) and also Carolan's Harp. Everything is on a huge scale: reception rooms are all very spacious, with lovely old furnishings and many interesting historic details, bedrooms have massive four poster and half tester beds and bathrooms to match and the dining room is particularly impressive, with a richly decorated table to enhance Marguerite's home cooking. A reduction is offered for stays of three or more nights. Horse riding, fishing, shooting and golf (9) are all nearby. Garden. Unsuitable for children. No pets. B&B €80 pps, ss €15. Residents D Tue-Sat, €36 (24 hrs notice required); wines €12-19. (D not available Sun or Mon.) Closed Oct-Apr. MasterCard, Visa, Laser. **Directions:** N60 west of Castlerea.

Cootehall

M. J. Henry

ATMOSPHERIC PUB

Cootehall Boyle Co Roscommon **Tel: 071 966 7030**

The more theme pubs and superpubs there are, the better everyone likes James Henry's bar, which hasn't changed in at least 30 years and, in true country Irish fashion, is also a food store 'that caters for all your grocery needs'. A visit to Cootehall (the village of well-known writer John McGahern) would be unthinkable without checking on this little gem They don't make them like this any more, alas, but this delightful old pub - complete with formica from the most recent renovation - is a gem. Get in beside the fire with a hot whiskey and the world will do you no harm. No bar food. Closed 25 Dec & Good Fri. **No Credit Cards. Directions:** 2 miles off Sligo - Dublin road.

Knockvicar

Italia

RESTAURANT

Knockvicar Boyle Co Roscommon
Tel: 071 966 7788 Email: brunoboe@eircom.net

Bruno Boe took over this beautifully located contemporary restaurant in the summer of 2003 and it was an immediate hit with discerning diners in the area. The interior is well-designed on two levels to take full advantage of views over the river and Knockvicar marina, and enhanced by dashing decor which is colourful, comfortable and stylishly appointed - fashionable high-back chairs, classy tableware, fine glasses - an unusually cosmopolitan approach for a rural restaurant. Expect a real Italian welcome, authentic Italian cooking - and very fair prices. Service can be slow, but the overall package is so attractive that everybody keeps coming back. **Seats 56.** D 6- "late", L Sun only 1-4. A la carte. House wine €17. No SC. (reservations required; ring off-season to check opening hours.) Closed Mon & a few weeks Oct-Nov & Feb. Amex, MasterCard, Visa, Laser. **Directions:** Near Carrick-on-Shannon, on the Knockvicar-Cootehall road.

Roscommon

Abbey Hotel & Leisure Centre

HOTEL

Abbeytown Galway Road Roscommon Co Roscommon
Tel: 090 662 6240 Fax: 090 662 6021
Email: sales@abbeyhotel.ie Web: www.abbeyhotel.ie

The heart of this pleasing hotel is an old manor house and, despite major developments that have recently been completed, the atmosphere of the original building prevails and there's a romantic honeymoon suite with a four-poster in the old house. Big changes that have been taking place recently include the addition of a contemporary wing with spacious new bedrooms, all designed and decorated to a high standard and with pleasant views. A new restaurant was almost complete at the time of the Guide's most recent visit, also a redesigned bar serving food all day. A high level of comfort, together with excellent leisure facilities and good value offered, adds greatly to the hotel's appeal for short breaks - and it would make an excellent base for exploring an area that deserves to be better known. Conference/banqueting (250/280); business centre. Leisure centre (20m swimming pool, sauna, steam room, gym, jacuzzi). Children welcome (under 12s free in parents' room; cots available, baby sitting arranged). Garden. No pets. **Rooms 50** (1 junior suite, 26 executive, 35 no smoking, 2 disabled, 1 shower only). Lift. Room service (limited hours) B&B €75 pps, ss €10. Short breaks offered. Restaurant L 12.45-2.45, D 7-9.30 (Sun to 9). Set L €25, Set Sun L €30; D à la carte. House wines from €16.50, no SC. Hotel closed 25-26 Dec.

Restaurant: A fairly recent addition, the restaurant is designed on two levels in a semi-brasserie style and makes a popular meeting place, where friendly, helpful staff serve unpretentious wholesome fare. Seats 70 (private room, 50). L 12.45-2.30 daily. D 7-9.30 daily. Set L about €19; Set Sun L about €21.50; à la carte available. House wine about €14.No smoking area. Toilets wheelchair accessible. Hotel closed 24-25 Dec. Amex, Diners, MasterCard, Visa, Laser. **Directions:** N4 to Roscommon, Galway Road.

Tarmonbarry

Keenans Bar & Restaurant

BAR / RESTAURANT

Tarmonbarry (via Clondra) Co Roscommon
Tel: 043 26052 Fax: 043 26198
Email: info@keenans.ie Web: www.keenans.ie

Just beside the bridge over the Shannon in Tarmonbarry, this well-run bar and restaurant is a favourite watering hole for river folk and makes a great place to break a journey between Dublin and the north-west. The bar is comfortably set up for food and informal meals - mostly quite traditional, but with more international influences in the more expensive evening dishes - are served all day; open sandwiches on home-made wholemeal or soda bread, toasted sandwiches, salads and scones with jam & cream are typical, plus half a dozen daily specials (including specialities such as fish casserole and bacon & cabbage at lunch, perhaps, and more elaborate dishes like roast half duckling on a peach stuffing with a red onion, ginger and orange marmalade in the evening). A la carte menus are similar in tone but more extensive - wholesome, hearty fare that pleases all age groups; the steak sandwich (served with onions, chips, garlic butter & home-made horseradish sauce) is not to be missed - while the set dinner menu is a little more formal. Good unpretentious food and cheerful, efficient service keep happy customers coming back. Restaurant **seats 30.** Food served daily 12.30-8.30; L 12.30-2.30, D 6.30-8.30. Set D €32, Set Sun L about €20. House wine about €12. Restaurant closed D Sun. Establishment closed 25 Dec, Good Fri. Amex, Diners, MasterCard, Visa, Laser, Switch. **Directions:** On N5, west of Longford town.

COUNTY SLIGO

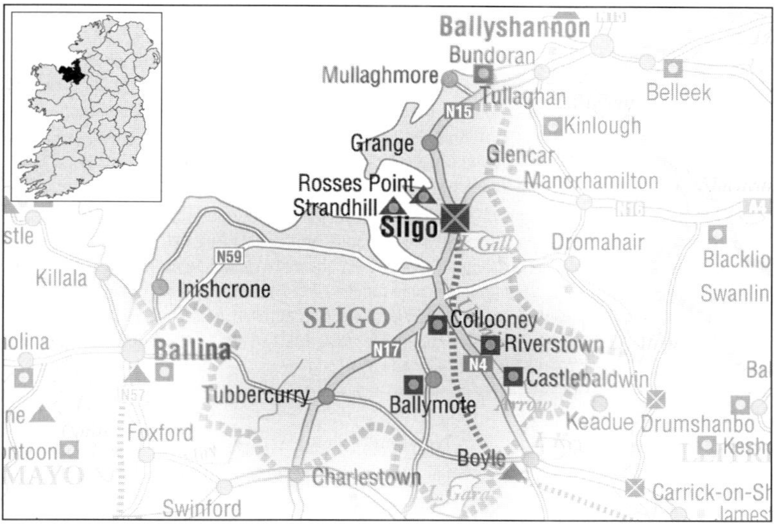

There's a stylish confidence to Sligo which belies its compact area as one of Ireland's smallest counties. Perhaps it's because they know that their place and their way of life have been immortalised through association with two of the outstanding creative talents of modern Ireland, W.B.Yeats and his painter brother Jack. The former's fame seems beyond question, while the latter's star was never higher than it is today.

But whatever the reason for Sligo's special quality, there's certainly something about it that encourages repeat visits. The town itself is big enough to be reassuring, yet small enough to be comfortable. And civic pride in Sligo received a double boost on September 18th 2003, when two "environmental excellence" national awards went its way, one for the refurbished Courthouse, the other for the restored Town Hall.

And the countryside about Sligo town also has lasting appeal. Mankind has been living here with enthusiasm for a very long time indeed, for in recent years it has been demonstrated that some of County Sligo's ancient monuments are amongst the oldest in northwest Europe. Lakes abound, the mountains are magnificent, and there are tumbling rivers a-plenty.

Yet if you wish to get away from the bustle of the regular tourist haunts, Sligo can look after your needs in this as well, for the western part of the county down through the Ox Mountains towards Mayo is an uncrowded region of wide vistas and clear roads.

Local Attractions and Information

Carrowmore, Largest Megalithic Cemetry in Ireland 071 916 1534
Drumcliff, Drumcliffe Church & Visitor Centre (Yeats) 071 914 4956
Drumcliff, Lissadell House 071 916 3150
Inniscrone, Seaweed Bath House 096 36238
Lough Gill, Waterbus Cruises 071 916 4266
Sligo, Discover Sligo Tours 071 914 7488
Sligo, Model Arts & Niland Gallery 071 914 1405
Sligo Abbey, (13thC Dominican Friary) 071 914 6406
Sligo, Sligo Airport, Strandhill 071 916 8280
Sligo, Sligo Art Gallery 071 914 5847
Sligo, Tourism Information 071 916 1201
Sligo Yeats Memorial Building, Hyde Bridge 071 914 2693
Strandhill Seaweed Baths, Maritime House 071 916 8686

Aughris Head
Beach Bar/Aughris House

B&B / ATMOSPHERIC PUB

Aughris Head Templeboy Co Sligo
Tel: 071 916 6703 / 917 6465

The McDermott family's picturesque and beautifully located thatched pub seems too good to be true when you first find it in this quiet and unspoilt place, but there it has been since the 18th century when, apparently, it was a shibín known as Maggie Maye's. Today, after sensitive restoration, it has retained some of the best characteristics of the past and makes a lovely stopping place, with food served in the flag-stoned bar - and access to a beach just a hop across the wall from the car park. Bar food available all day (10.30am-8pm); phone to check opening off season.

Accommodation: In a neat bungalow just behind the pub, the McDermotts also offer comfortable, inexpensive, B&B accommodation, with neat shower rooms and TV. Children welcome (under 2 free in parents' room, cot available, baby sitting arranged); pets allowed in some areas. **Rooms 9** (8 en-suite & shower only, all no smoking). Children welcome (under 2 free in parents' room, cot available, baby sitting arranged); pets allowed in some areas. Pool table. Garden; walking, fishing. B&B €30, ss €4. (Short breaks & family rates available). Open all year. MasterCard, Visa. **Directions:** Off N59 Sligo/Ballina Road, Coast Rd to Aughris Head/Pier.

Ballymote
Temple House

COUNTRY HOUSE

Ballymote Co Sligo **Tel: 071 918 3329** Fax: 071 918 3808
Email: guests@templehouse.ie Web: www.templehouse.ie

One of Ireland's most unspoilt old houses, this is a unique place – a Georgian Mansion situated in 1,000 acres of farm and woodland, overlooking the original lakeside castle which was built by the Knights Templar in 1200 A.D. The Percevals have lived here since 1665 and the house was redesigned and refurbished in 1864 – some of the furnishings date back to that major revamp. The whole of the house has retained its old atmosphere and, in addition to central heating, has log fires to cheer the enormous rooms. Spacious bedrooms are all furnished with old family furniture and guests have the use of an elegant sitting room with open fires. Deb Perceval's evening meals are served in the very beautiful dining room and are a treat to look forward to – she is a Euro-Toques chef and takes pride in preparing fine meals based on produce from the estate and other local suppliers. A typically delicious menu might include: mushroom tartlet on salad leaves, baked local salmon with seasonal vegetables, raspberry parfait and Irish cheeseboard. NB: Sandy Perceval is seriously allergic to scented products, so guests are asked to avoid all perfumes, aftershave and aerosols. Children welcome (under 2s free in parents' room; cots available, baby sitting arranged). No pets in house. **Rooms 6** (5 en-suite, 2 shower only, 1 with private bathroom). B&B €65pps, ss €20. Residents D €32, 7.30pm (book by 1pm); house wine €12. Children's tea 6.30pm; SC discretionary. Closed Feb & Mar. Amex, MasterCard, Visa, Laser. **Directions:** Signposted on N17 south of Ballinacarrow Village.

Castlebaldwin
Cromleach Lodge

HOTEL / RESTAURANT

Castlebaldwin via Boyle Co Sligo
Tel: 071 916 5155 Fax: 071 916 5455
Email: info@cromleach.com Web: cromleach.com

HIDEAWAY OF THE YEAR

Quietly situated in the hills just above Lough Arrow, Christy and Moira Tighe's small hotel enjoys one of the finest views in Ireland - and it makes a luxurious retreat for the most discerning of guests. Cromleach is rightly renowned for exceptionally high standards of both food and accommodation - and, most importantly, the Tighe family and their staff have the magic ingredient of genuine hospitality, doing everything possible to ensure comfort and relaxation for their guests. Spacious bedrooms have an emphasis on comfort rather than fashion, and are thoughtfully furnished, with king-size and single beds, seating areas overlooking the lough with easy chairs to relax in, and well-planned bathrooms with lots of luxurious little extras. Hospitality, housekeeping and attention to detail are all outstanding: immaculately maintained rooms have fresh flowers, a basket of fruit and a complimentary miniature of Baileys - and this is one of the very few hotels to provide not only a mini-bar but, more importantly, a jug of fresh milk in the fridge for your tea and coffee, a telling gesture typical of these thoughtful hosts. The area around Cromleach is beautiful and unspoilt, and the Tighes like nothing better than to introduce guests to the many places of interest and activities nearby but, for many, just being here is more than enough. Small conferences (12). Children welcome (under 7 free in parents' room, cot available without charge, baby sitting arranged). Pets permitted by arrangement. Garden; walking; fishing. **Rooms 11** (6 junior suites, 1 shower only, 6 no-smoking) B&B €158 pps, ss €45. Short breaks and off-season value breaks available. Closed Nov-Jan.

★**Restaurant:** The restaurant is the heart of Cromleach Lodge and dinner is the high point of every guest's visit to this special place. The restaurant is arranged as a series of rooms, creating a number of individual dining areas for varying numbers of people – a system which tends to work better for groups than couples dining alone. Lovely simple table settings – crisp linen, modern silver and crystal, fine, understated china and fresh seasonal flowers – provide a beautifully understated setting for memorable meals. Moira Tighe and her personally trained kitchen team work superbly well together and, as the growing number of specialities are in constant demand, menus include these as a base, with new dishes added as appropriate. The cooking style is modern Irish (without being slavishly fashionable), but it is Moira's scrupulously careful sourcing of ingredients, pride in local produce and outstanding cooking that makes this restaurant so special. Menus offered include an 8-course Gourmet Tasting Menu (for residents only, included in the dinner bed & breakfast rate) and a 5-course table d'hôte, with specialities ranging from simple starters like warm smoked salmon on creamed organic spinach to a sophisticated tasting selection of award-winning desserts - with many wonderful dishes in between. The wine list leads with 32 accessible house wines from around the world, in the €23-39 bracket, and the dessert menu comes with helpful suggestions of dessert wines and ports. Moira, who was the Guide's Chef of the Year in 2000, is an exceptional, totally dedicated chef - and well-trained, friendly, staff provide excellent service to complement the high standards of the kitchen. **Seats 50** (private rooms, 4-24).D only, 6.30-9 daily (Sun to 8) Set D about €55, also à la carte; house wines from about €23; sc discretionary. Toilets wheelchair accessible. Closed Nov-Jan. Amex, MasterCard, Visa. Helipad. **Directions:** Signposted from Castlebaldwin on the N4.

Cliffoney

La Vecchia Posta

RESTAURANT

Cliffoney Co Sligo **Tel: 071 917 6777** Fax: 071 917 7688

After thirty years in Italy the Dunlevy family returned to their native Sligo to open a modern Irish/continental restaurant in this attractively stone-faced former post office, which has views of Donegal Bay, Classiebawn Castle, and Mullaghmore headland in the distance. Have an aperitif in a spacious seating area, where old furniture lends atmosphere, or at your table in a large high-ceilinged room featuring uncurtained windows with sweeping coastal views. Promptly presented menus have a strong emphasis on shellfish (including a wide variety of fish from Killybegs, and lobster all year round from nearby Mullaghmore), also locally sourced lamb and beef, served with mainly organic vegetables, salads and herbs - some grown by the Donlevys themselves. Head chef Shane McAuley trained in Brittany and takes pride in using locally sourced ingredients on wide-ranging seasonal menus. Samples that give a flavour of the style might include filo parcels filled with herbed cream cheese & prawns, served with organic leaves and lime & chilli marmalade, a man course of roast rack of lamb encrusted with honey, mustard and tarragon - or maybe rabbit, cooked with garlic, shallots, tomatoes & herbs. Desserts may include a seasonal fruit dish such as pears poached in red wine & cinnamon, served with fresh almond cream. Italian coffees are predictably good, and children are warmly welcomed. An interesting and unusual Italian wine list includes a number of organic wines and is imported directly. **Seats 60.** Air conditioning. D Tue-Sun, 6-10, L Sun only, 12.30-3.30. D à la carte; Set Sun L €17.50. House wine €18.50; s.c. discretionary. Closed Mon (inc bank hols), all Feb. MasterCard, Visa, Laser. **Directions:** On side of main Sligo/Bundoran/Donegal road in the village of Cliffoney.

Collooney

Markree Castle

HOTEL / RESTAURANT

Collooney Co Sligo **Tel: 071 916 7800** Fax: 071 916 7840
Email: markree@iol.ie Web: markreecastle.ie

Sligo's oldest inhabited house has been home to the Cooper family for 350 years. Set in magnificent park and farmland, this is a proper castle, with a huge portico leading to a covered stone stairway that sweeps up to an impressive hall, where an enormous log fire always burns. Everything is on a very large scale, and it is greatly to the credit of the present owners, Charles and Mary Cooper, that they have achieved the present level of renovation and comfort since they took it on in a sad state of disrepair in 1989 - and they have always been generous with the heating. Ground floor reception areas include a comfortably furnished double drawing room with two fireplaces (where light food – including afternoon tea – is served). There is a lift and also disabled toilets, but the layout of the castle makes it difficult for elderly people or wheelchair users to get around; a phone call ahead to ensure the (very willing) staff are available to help would be wise. The dining room is a very beautiful room and open to non-residents for dinner, and lunch on Sunday. While by no means perfect - investment is clearly needed to bring it up to the standard that many people expect of a castle, and there are many idiosyncrasies, in bedrooms, for example - this slightly eccentric place has got real heart. Horse riding. Conferences/banqueting (50/150). Children welcome (under 4s free in parents' room; cots available). Pets permitted. **Rooms 30** (all en-suite, 5 executive rooms, 1 for disabled). Lift. B&B from about €92 pps, ss about €10. Restaurant seats 80 (private room, 40) D 7.30-9.30 daily; L 1-2.30 Sun only. Closed 24-27 Dec. There is a beautiful dining room, where head chef Tom Joyce has been serving very good food since 1993. Standards of food and service here have generally remained high - and the surroundings alone make dining here a memorable occasion. Non-residents are welcome. (Reservations recommended). **Seats 80** (private room, 40) D 7.30-9.30 daily; L 1-2.30 Sun only. Set D about €30, Set Sun L about €18; house wine about €14; no sc. No smoking restaurant. Hotel closed 24-27 Dec. Amex, Diners, MasterCard, Visa. **Directions:** Just off the N4, take the Dromohair exit at Collooney roundabout. ◇

Mullaghmore

Eithna's Seafood Restaurant

RESTAURANT

The Harbour Mullaghmore Co Sligo **Tel: 071 916 6407**
Email: eithnasrestaurant@eircom.net Web: www.eithnaseafood.com

Situated right on the harbour at Mullaghmore, Eithna O'Sullivan Huel's atmospheric seafood restaurant specialises in fish and shellfish caught by local fishermen in Donegal Bay. Since opening in 1990 she has gradually built up a reputation that extends far beyond the local population - those in the know now travel specially for Eithna's cooking, particularly lobster (served various ways) and the seafood platter which, at €29, is much better value than the various lobster dishes served separately. For this you get a cold half lobster, prawns, crab, crab claws, razor fish, mussels and clams; all served in the shell - the exact ingredients may vary a little according to availability but it will balance out. The platter is attractively served and comes with tossed organic salad greens, mayonnaise, fresh lemon, a bread basket and a dish of potatoes (quite probably from Normandy). There are fish specials too, offering two or three varieties daily, and some options other than seafood offered, including starters like smoked chicken salad, also vegetarian dishes - and tempting desserts might include a refreshing choice like rhubarb with strawberries. **Seats 55** (private room 30). Children welcome. D daily in high season, 6.30-9.30, also L Sat & Sun, 12.30-3 in Jul-Aug. (Opening variable Sep-Easter; phone for information). Set D from about €32, also Set L in high season. House wine €15. Diners, MasterCard, Visa, Laser. **Directions:** 16 miles from Sligo on N15 (Donegal) turn at Cliffoney.

Riverstown

Coopershill House

COUNTRY HOUSE

Riverstown Co Sligo **Tel: 071 916 5108** Fax: 071 916 5644
Email: ohara@coopershill.com Web: www.coopershill.com

Undoubtedly one of the most delightful and superbly comfortable Georgian houses in Ireland, this sturdy granite mansion was built to withstand the rigours of a Sligo winter – but its numerous chimneys suggest there is warmth to be found within its stern grey walls. Peacocks wander elegantly on the croquet lawns (and roost in the splendid trees around the house at night) making this lovely place, home of the O'Hara family since it was built in 1774, a particularly perfect country house. Nothing escapes Brian O'Hara's disciplined eye: in immaculate order from top to bottom, the house not only has the original 18th century furniture but also some fascinating features – notably an unusual Victorian free-standing rolltop bath complete with fully integrated cast-iron shower 'cubicle' and original brass rail and fittings, all in full working order. Luxurious rooms are wonderfully comfortable and have phones and tea/coffee making facilities. Lindy runs the house and kitchen with the seamless hospitality born of long experience, and creates deliciously wholesome, country house home cooking which is served in their lovely dining room (where the family silver is used with magnificent insouciance – even at breakfast). Tennis, cycling, boating, fishing, garden, croquet; snooker room. Children welcome (under 2 free in parents' room; cots available without charge, baby sitting arranged). No pets. **Rooms 8** (7 en-suite, 1 shower only, 1 private). B&B €96 pps, ss about €21 (10% discount on stays of 3 days or more). Dining Room **Seats 16-20.** D 8.30 daily (non-residents welcome by reservation); Set D €40-€45, house wines from €13; sc discretionary. Closed end Oct-31 Mar. (Off season house parties of 12-16 people welcome.) Amex, Diners, MasterCard, Visa, Laser, Switch. **Directions:** Signposted from N4 at Drumfin crossroads.

Rosses Point

Austie's

ATMOSPHERIC PUB

Rosses Point Co Sligo **Tel: 071 917 7111** / 087 2634216

This 200 year-old pub overlooking Sligo Bay has always been associated with a seafaring family and is full of fascinating nautical memorabilia. It has a very nice ship-shape feeling about it and friendly people behind the bar - and this, rather than food, is its main appeal. However, the sea stars on the simple bar menu too, with local seafood in dishes like garlic mussels, seafood chowder and in open sandwiches or salads made with crab, prawns and salmon - although there are other choices, including ever-popular steaks and home-made burgers: definitely not cutting edge, but wholesome nonetheless and with traditional appeal. Not a daytime pub (except in high summer the usual opening time is 4 pm). If you're going out to Rosses Point specially, it's wise to ring ahead and check opening times off-season. **Seats 70.** Children welcome. Food served daily 4-9.30 in summer (12.30-9.30 at weekends), evenings only off-season (Sept-Mar). A la carte menu; house wine from about €15; sc discretionary. Check times off season. Closed 25 Dec & Good Fri. MasterCard, Visa, Laser. **Directions:** On the seafront. ◇

Rosses Point

The Waterfront

Ⓝ féile bia RESTAURANT / BAR

Rosses Point Co Sligo **Tel: 071 917 7122**
Fax: 071 917 7040 Email: jgrogan@eircom.net

Joe Grogan and Miriam Harte's busy bar and restaurant on the front at at Rosses Point is hard to describe as there are big changes in the offing, which should see it substantially upgraded in the near future. Meanwhile, the exterior would not draw you in and it can look rather forbidding before opening, when the door is locked, but that doesn't put off those in the know around here, who pile in of an evening from Sligo town to make the most of chef Alan FitzMaurice's fine food. The bar menu includes the usual dreary children's fare (it's great to see families welcomed, but why do so few places offer children real food?) but plenty of good things for their parents including light bites like oysters, local mussels, garlic mushrooms, panini with smoked Appelwood cheddar (good to see a Fermanagh cheese) and a tempting à la carte. Here there's a choice of about ten starters (mussels with organic salad, linguine of crabmeat, glazed roasted quail) and equally interesting mains, like slow roast duck with goats cheese brulée & blackcurrrant sauce or absolutely magic seared king scallops fresh herb mash & basil cream froth. Finish with a delicious dessert (whole pear stuffed with cinnamon & pear cream, with port syrup & honeycomb ice cream...) or Irish cheeses. Pretty good by any standards, even better if you book a table in the the dining room next door. **Seats 60** (private room 25). Toilets wheelchair accessible. D daily 5-10. L Sun only 12.30-3. A la carte. Wines from €16.95. Closed 25 Dec, Good Fri, 1st 2 weeks Oct. Amex, MasterCard, Visa, Laser. **Directions:** In Rosses Point village, looking out on the bay.

SLIGO

A fascinating town, with a rich heritage, Sligo has several hotels: if business and leisure facilities are important, the **Sligo Park Hotel (Tel 071 91 60291; www.leehotels.com)** is on the edge of the town and has ample parking, while those who like to be within an easy walk of everything around the town might prefer the modern well-maintained **Tower Hotel (Tel 071 914 4000 www.hotelsligo.com).** There are plenty of popular little coffee shops and cafés to sustain a day around the town: informal food, people-watching and entertainment are to be found at **Garavogue & Café Bar Deli (Tel 071 914 0100)** - a brilliantly located contemporary riverside bar and café with outside seating for fine weather. Across the nearby pedestrian bridge, **The Riverbank Restaurant (Tel: 071 917 1097; www. sligoaccommodation.com/riverbank)** also offers informal fare, in a small, more intimate setting, as does **Fiddler's Creek (071 914 1866),** a cosy bar which could make a welcome retreat on a bad day. A new hotel, **Radisson SAS Sligo Hotel,** is under construction on the site of the old Ballincar Hotel out towards Rosses Point, as we go to press, and will bring excellent facilities to the area in 2004 (Tel: 071 914 0008, or email sligo@RadissonSAS.com for information). Rosses Point, a few minutes' drive from Sligo town has views across to Oyster Island and Coney Island (after which the island off New York was named), golf and a lovely beach; the restaurant and bar with the best view is **The Moorings (Tel: 071 917 7112)** which looks across to the islands and the famous Metal Man navigation mark.

Sligo

Atrium Restaurant

Ⓝ CAFÉ

The Niland Model Arts Centre The Mall Sligo Co Sligo
Tel: 071 914 1418 Fax: 071 914 3694
Email: info@modelart.ie Web: www.modelart.ie

A magic combination seems to have come together here as Brid Torrades, Euro-Toques chef formerly of the Glebe at Collooney, and Roy Kinsley, formerly of Ta Se Mahogani Gaspipes in Stoneybatter, Dublin, are now jointly running the delightful Atrium restaurant at Sligo's Model Arts Centre. The open-plan café is light and contemporary in style, spilling out into the bright atrium area of the gallery - stylish, yet accessible. Blackboard menus offer some seriously tempting simple, light food with an emphasis on good quality and flavour: superb soup (carrot & fennel, perhaps), for example, and delicious omelettes (prettily presented with herbs and leaves from Rod Alston's Organic Centre); a couple of blackboard specials indicate daily dishes and there are gourmet sandwiches too. Finish, perhaps, with gorgeous looking compôtes topped with cream - rhubarb, blackberry - simply delicious; and good coffee too. This is an important little place, now in first-class professional hands, and anyone visiting Sligo should make a beeline here. Parking (up the steep hill, behind the gallery). Meals: Tue-Sat 10-5, also Sun in summer, 1-5. Closed Sun morning, all Mon. **Directions:** Sligo town centre; prominent building on The Mall.

Sligo **Coach Lane Restaurant @ Donaghy's Bar**

féile bia **PUB / RESTAURANT**

1-2 Lord Edward Street Sligo Co Sligo
Tel: 071 916 2417 Fax: 071 917 1935

The restaurant over Orla and Andy Donaghy's pub is approached by an attractive side alley, with a menu board dislayed on the street. It's a long narrow room, furnished in a comfortable mixture of traditional and contemporary styles, with well-appointed white-clothed tables, soft lighting and neatly uniformed waitresses in black polo shirts and trousers with white aprons all creating a good impression. Andy's menus are lively and attractive - and the cooking is confident, although service can be slow. Specialities using local produce include a porterhouse steak (marinated in herbs and chargrilled), fresh whole lobster and Sligo Bay salmon. There's also a wide choice of salads, pasta dishes and chicken - and the cooking style ranges from traditional (steak with home-made fries, crispy onion rings & HP sauce) to spicy (cajun chicken with a fresh fruit salsa). **Seats 65** (plus 40 on an outside terrace, weather permitting). Air conditioning. Toilets wheelchair accessible. D daily 6.30-10, Set D about €32, also à la carte; L Sun 12-4. House wine about €15; service discretionary except 10% on parties of 8+.Closed 25 Dec & Good Fri. Amex, MasterCard, Visa, Laser. **Directions:** N4 to Sligo,Left at Adelaide St. make a right into Lord Edward St.

Sligo **Hargadon Bros.**

ATMOSPHERIC PUB

O'Connell Street Sligo Co Sligo **Tel: 071 917 0993**

Unquestionably one of Ireland's greatest old pubs, the best time to see Hargadon's properly is early in the day when it's quiet – they'll give you good coffee (and probably a newspaper to go with it) and you can relax and take in the detail of this remarkable old place. It still has the shelves which used to hold the groceries when it was a traditional grocer-bar, the snugs and the old pot belly stove – and it's still owner-run and unspoilt. Later in the day it gets very busy, especially at weekends – but by then it's time for a bit of craic anyway. **Seats 100.** Light food available in the morning; meals served Mon-Sat, 12-4. Air conditioning. Toilets wheelchair accessible. Closed 25 Dec & Good Fri. Amex. **Directions:** In town centre on the main street.

Sligo **Montmartre**

féile bia **RESTAURANT**

Market Yard Sligo Co Sligo **Tel: 071 916 9901** Fax: 071 914 0065
Email: montmartre@eircom.net

French run and staffed, this restaurant has been thriving since opening in December 1999 and, as it is now well-established as the area's leading restaurant, bookings are strongly advised, especially at weekends. Although not big, it has a light and airy feel and a restful atmosphere enhanced by strategically placed potted palms and a lack of clutter. A small bar area doubles as reception, staff are smartly uniformed and the restaurant is well-appointed in the French style, with comfortable chairs and white crockery. Proprietor-chef Stephane Magaud presents varied menus offering imaginative French cuisine in a light, colourful style, matched by sound cooking and attractive presentation. Local produce features in some dishes, especially seafood - Lissadell oysters and mussels, for instance, and there may also be game in season. Examples that give a flavour of the place, include a speciality of hot smoked wild salmon with wine & shallot glaze, or a vegetarian starter of peppered cheese parcel with smoked onion & tomato coulis and a main course dish of honey & mustard roast leg of rabbit, with tarragon & coriander seeds jus. This interesting, wide-ranging menu always includes some imaginative vegetarian dishes - and Lissadell lobster is excellent value at €25 per lb. Finish with classic desserts - white & dark chocolate bavarois, tarte à l'orange et aux amandes - or a cheese plate. The wine list is mostly French, with a token gesture to the New World, and includes ten wines available by the glass. **Seats 50.** Air conditioning. Toilets wheelchair accessible. D Tue-Sun, 5-11. A la carte. Early D €14 (5-7pm); Set D from €27. House wines from €11 Closed Mon, 24-27 Dec, 5-21 Jan. Amex, Diners, MasterCard, Visa, Laser, Switch. **Directions:** 150 yards from theatre & tourist office.

Strandhill **Strand House Bar**

PUB

Strandhill Co Sligo **Tel: 071 916 8140** Fax: 071 916 8593

Just ten minutes drive from Sligo, close to the airport and one of Europe's most magnificent surfing beaches, this well-known bar has a big welcoming turf fire, cosy snugs and friendly staff. No children after 9pm. Bar meals served all day (12-3pm). Toilets wheelchair accessible. Air conditioning. Closed 25 Dec & Good Fri. **No Credit Cards. Directions:** Follow signs to Sligo airport (Strandhill). Strand House is situated at the end near the beach. ◇

COUNTY TIPPERARY

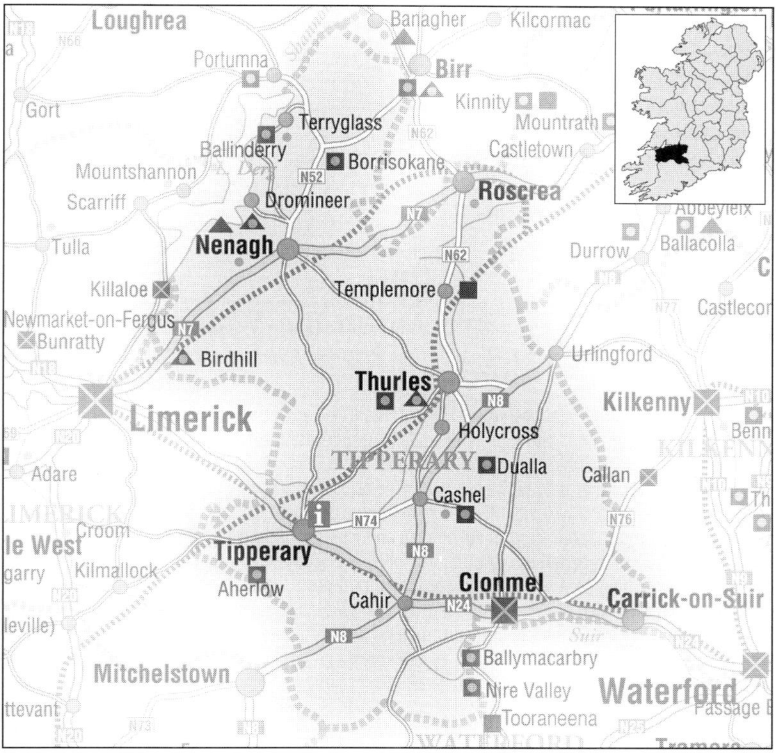

The cup of life is overflowing in Tipperary. In this wondrously fertile region, there's an air of fulfilment, a comfortable awareness of the world in harmony. And the placenames reinforce this sense of natural bounty.

Across the middle of the county, there's the evocatively-named Golden Vale, with prosperous lands along the wide valley of the River Suir and its many tributaries, and westwards towards County Limerick across a watershed around Donohill.

The county's largest town, down in the far south under the Comeragh Mountains, is the handsome borough of Clonmel - its name translates as "Honey Meadow". Yet although there are many meadows of all kinds in Tipperary, there's much more to this largest inland county in Ireland than farmland, for it is graced with some of the most elegant mountains in the country.

North of the Golden Vale, the Silvermine Mountains rise to 694 m on Keeper Hill, and beyond them the farming countryside rolls on in glorious profusion to Nenagh - a town much improved by by-passes on either side - and Tipperary's own "sea coast", the beautiful eastern shore of Lough Derg. Inevitably, history and historic monuments abound in such country, with the fabulous Rock of Cashel and its dramatic remains of ancient ecclesiastical buildings setting a very high standard for evoking the past.

But Tipperary lends itself every bit as well to enjoyment of the here and now. Tipperary is all about living life to the full, and they do it with style in a place of abundance.

Local Attractions and Information

Aherlow, Glen of Glenbrook Trout Farm 062 56214
Birdhill, Tipperary Crystal Visitor Centre 061 379066
Cahir, Cahir Castle 052 41011
Cahir Farmers Market Sats 9am-1pm 086 648 2044
Carrick-on-Suir, Ormond Castle 051 640787
Carrick-on-Suir, Tipperary Crystal Visitor Centre 051 641188
Cashel, Bru Boru Culture Centre 062 61122

Cashel, Rock of Cashel 062 61437
Cashel, Tourism Information 062 61333
Clonmel, Clonmel Racecourse 052 23422
Clonmel, Tourism Information 052 22960
Nenagh, Heritage Centre 067 32633
Nenagh, Tourism Information 067 31610
Roscrea, Roscrea Heritage - Castle & Damer House 0505 21850
Thurles, Holy Cross Abbey 0504 43241
Thurles, Race Course 0504 21040
Tipperary Race Course (Limerick Junction) 062 51357
Tipperary town, Tourism Information 062 51457

Ballinderry

Brocka-on-the-Water Restaurant

RESTAURANT

Kilgarvan Quay Ballinderry Nenagh Co Tipperary
Tel: 067 22038 Fax: 067 22995

Anthony and Anne Gernon's almost-waterside restaurant has attracted a following disproportionate to its size over the years and, although it has been extended at the back to include a high-ceilinged conservatory style room which opens on to a garden patio, it is still basically carved out of the lower half of a family home that is by no means huge. The atmosphere is very much a "proper restaurant" - yet with all the warmth of welcome that the family situation implies. There's a reception room with an open fire, comfy chairs, interesting things to read and look at (Anthony's a dab hand at wood carving) - and aperitifs served in generous wine glasses, while you read a menu that promises good things to come in the adjoining dining room and conservatory. Guests arriving in daylight will notice hens clucking around a garden well-stocked with fruit and vegetables - promising the best of all possible beginnings for your dinner. Seasonal menus depend on availability of course - if you are here in late spring, for example, you might be offered avocado pear with local goats cheese, yogurt capers & wild garlic - but there are always some specialities retained by popular demand, including Cooleeney cheese croquettes with home-made chutney (Cooleeney is one of Ireland's finest cheeses, made by Breda Maher on the family farm near Thurles). A late summer menu might include pork medallion in a herb crust with plum & cranberry - and there will always be home-grown vegetables in season. **Seats 50** (private room, 30). Air conditioning. Toilets wheelchair accessible. Booking essential. D 7-9.30 Mon-Sat in summer (call to check opening times off season). Set D about €40, also à la carte. SC discretionary. House wine about €22. Closed Sun. **No Credit Cards. Directions:** Lough Derg drive, half way between Nenagh and Portumna.

Borrisokane

Ballycormac House

COUNTRY HOUSE

Aglish Roscrea Co Tipperary **Tel: 067 21129** Fax: 067 21200
Email: ballyc@indigo.ie Web: www.ballyc.com

John and Cherylynn Lang's farmhouse is a charming, cottagey place, delightfully furnished and very comfortable in a laid-back way – and one of the five bedrooms is a romantic suite with a four-poster bed and its own fireplace. Country pursuits are the big attraction here, especially equestrian activities - the Langs have up to 30 horses and ponies on site so there's something to suit everyone, from the novice to the experienced rider. They are approved by A.I.R.E. (Irish Association of Riding Establishments) and offer trail riding and cross country riding in spring and summer, also fox hunting breaks in winter. Golf, fishing, watersports and rough shooting can also be arranged. Cherylynn cooks a country house style dinner for guests, based on fresh local ingredients (including produce from their own organic garden) and non-residents are welcome for dinner by reservation, if there is room, also for Sunday lunch. Mention any special dietary requests (including vegetarian meals) when booking. Children and well-behaved pets welcome (children under 2 free in parents' room; cot available). A hot tub is available for guests' use (€8 per hour). **Rooms 5** (1 suite, all no smoking). B&B €45, no ss). Dining Room **Seats 16.** D 7.30-8 (book by 12).; Sun L 12-2. Set D €35. House wine €16. SC discretionary. Open all year. MasterCard, Visa. **Directions:** N52 through Borrisokane towards Portumna. Right out of Borrisokane at sign.

Borrisokane

Dancer Cottage

COUNTRY HOUSE

Curraghmore Borrisokane Co Tipperary **Tel: 067 27414** Fax: 067 27414
Email: dcr@eircom.net Web: dancercottage.cjb.net

A neat well planned garden and plenty of parking make a good impression at Carmen and Wolfgang Roedder's modern tudor style house near Borrisokane. An extensive array of tourist literature in the big hall guarantees that no guest here will ever be short of things to do in the area and there's a comfortable L shaped sitting/dining room to relax in when you get back, with a wood-burning stove and lots of books. Bedrooms include two recently purpose-built ones with wheelchair access and a family room with an extra bed; all are comfortably furnished with some lovely pieces of antique furniture, immaculate bathrooms and tea/coffee facilities. Carmen and Wolfgang do everything possible to ensure that their guests enjoy a stay here and extensive breakfast menus include several home-baked breads, speciality porridge, stuffed pancakes and French toast as well as the traditional Irish fry - and, like the evening meals, breakfast is served at a communal table overlooking the lovely back garden, which has seating for guests' use. A small sauna is available by arrangement - ask for details. Children welcome (under 2s free in parents' room, cot available without charge, small children's playground). Pets allowed by arrangement. Garden, cycling. **Rooms 4** (all with shower & no smoking, 2 for less mobile guests). Residents D €24 (when booked in advance). B&B from €29-34, ss €7. Closed 12 Dec-10 Jan. Amex, MasterCard, Visa. **Directions:** N 52 from Nenagh or Birr to Borrisokane; road signs in town.

Cashel

Café Hans

Ⓝ CAFÉ Moor Lane Cashel Co Tipperary **Tel: 062 63660**

Hans and Stefan Matthia opened this smashing little contemporary café in 2003 and it is the perfect complement to the parent establishment, Chez Hans, next door. A neat renovation job has been done with clean-lined style, creating a bright and airy space out of very little; bare-topped tables are laid café-style and a canny little menu offers just the kind of food that's needed during the day: colourful, sassy dishes including lots of salads - several versions of Caesar salad include a vegetarian one, and there's an irresistible house salad with pear Cashel Blue cheese (what else?) and Parma ham; open sandwiches come with home-made French fries and there are half a dozen hot dishes - grilled lamb cutlets with mushroom sauce, poached salmon with new potatoes, green beans and salsa verde. Good desserts and afternoon tea (2-5.30), lovely coffee; wine list. Well worth planning a journey around a break here - everyone travelling the Dublin-Cork route should make a note of this place and its hours. There is some menu overlap with Chez Hans, where, together with Jason Matthia, Stefan is also responsible for the early dinner. Children welcome. Seats 30. Open Tue-Sat, 12-5.30. Closed Sun & Mon. No reservations. **No Credit Cards. Directions:** Off N8 in Cashel, 50m in Rock of Cashel direction.

Cashel

Cashel Palace Hotel

féile bia HOTEL Main Street Cashel Co Tipperary **Tel: 062 62707** Fax: 062 61521
Email: reception@cashel-palace.ie Web: www.cashel-palace.ie

One of Ireland's most famous hotels, and originally a bishop's residence, Cashel Palace is a large, graciously proportioned Queen Anne style house (dating from 1730) set well back from the road in the centre of Cashel town. The beautiful reception rooms and some of the spacious, elegantly furnished bedrooms overlook the gardens and the Rock of Cashel at the rear. The present owners, Patrick and Susan Murphy, took over the hotel in 1998 and, since then, have been gradually renovating and refurbishing both public areas and bedrooms; the whole hotel was redecorated in 2003 and a new function room opened. Conference/banqueting (85/94). Children welcome (Under 3 free in parents' room, cot available without charge, baby sitting arranged). No pets. Garden. **Rooms 23** (5 suites). Lift. Room service (limited hours). B&B €111, €35. Closed 24-26 Dec.

Meals: Lunch and dinner are served every day in the vaulted basement restaurant, The Bishops' Buttery, and there is also a formal ground floor Dining Room, overlooking the gardens. Head chef Declan Hayes, who has been here since 2001, successfully juggles the various demands of a mixed clientele ranging from passing trade to local business people, corporate guests, families out for a treat - and, of course, residents. His menus are well-balanced, offering the traditional choices like steak and chicken breast alongside more adventurous ones (ostrich, perhaps); cooking is sound and quite modern, with the generosity expected in country areas - although, in the Guide's recent experience, the food has been good although a little let down by off-hand service. **Seats 60.** L 12.30-2.30 (Sun to 3.30); D 6-9.30. Set D €35, Set L (1-3 courses) €11.50-22.50, D also à la carte. House wines €20.50 *Food is also available in the Guinness Bar, 10.30am-8pm (Fri & Sat to 6pm). Amex, Diners, MasterCard, Visa, Laser. **Directions:** On N8 which runs through main street - Cashel. Just off main road.

Cashel

Chez Hans

RESTAURANT Moor Lane Cashel Co Tipperary **Tel: 062 61177** Fax: 062 61177

Although many others have since followed suit, the idea of opening a restaurant in a church was highly original when Hans-Peter Matthia did so in 1968. The atmosphere and scale – indeed the whole style of the place – is superb and provides an excellent setting for the fine food which many diners travel great distances to sample. Hans-Peter's son, Jason, returned here in 1998 after gaining experience in some great kitchens (Le Gavroche, La Tante Claire, Restaurant Marco Pierre White...) bringing new energy to one of Ireland's best-loved restaurants and recent investment in new staff - and the opening of Café Hans, next door - confirm the status of Chez Hans as the leading restaurant in a very large area. Ably assisted by P.J.Hartnett and a strong kitchen brigade, menus offered by Jason include an Early Bird dinner which is definitely worth travelling for - with an outstanding choice of about ten excellent dishes on each course, it offers some of the best value to be found in Ireland. The à la carte offers an even wider range including many specialities - such as starter pâté of chicken liver and foie gras with chutney & hot toast - and main courses like their famous cassoulette of seafood (half a dozen varieties of fish and shellfish with a delicate chive velouté sauce), classics like sole on the bone, crispy roast duck - and, of course, the great lamb and beef for which the area is renowned. Finish perhaps with lemon tart and orange curd ice cream, and coffee with home-made chocolates. A wine list strong on classic old world wines offers some treats for the deep-pocketed as well as half a dozen special recommendations under €25. Booking ahead is essential. **Seats 80.** D Tue-Sat, 6-10. Set D €40-50, also à la carte; early D 2-3-course, €22-29 (6-7.30). House wine from €21.50. Closed Sun, Mon. MasterCard, Visa, Laser. **Directions:** First right from N8, 50m.

Cashel

Legends Townhouse & Restaurant

féile bia **GUESTHOUSE / RESTAURANT**

The Kiln Cashel Co Tipperary
Tel: 062 61292 Fax: 062 62876
Email: info@legendsguesthouse.com Web: wwww.legendsguesthouse.com

Tucked just under the Rock of Cashel (and with direct access from the Bru Boru carpark at the back), Rosemary and Michael O'Neill's neat purpose-built guesthouse makes a comfortable and hospitable base for visiting the area's many sites. Open fires and old furniture give the house a pleasingly old-world feeling and, as Michael is an experienced chef, food is an important part of the visit. He offers shortish but well-balanced menus based on carefully sourced ingredients and including familiar dishes: starters like warm black pudding and apple salad or Cashel Blue in filo pastry with a walnut salad, are typical and main courses are likely to include Tipperary lamb, typically a roast rack in a herb crust. Cheerful, efficient serving staff under Rosemary's supervision. D Tue-Sat and Sun L, open to non-residents. **Rooms 7** (3 shower only), B&B about €35 pps. ss about €15. Closed mid Feb-mid Mar. Amex, MasterCard, Visa. **Directions:** Adjacent to Rock of Cashel carpark. ◇

Cashel

Spearmans Bakery & Tea Room

CAFÉ

97 Main Street Cashel Co Tipperary **Tel: 062 61143**

At their home-bakery and tea rooms on a slip road in the centre of Cashel, David and Louise Spearman, use only the best ingredients - including butter in all their pastries - to make a wide range of breads, cakes and pastries: sponges of every kind, swiss rolls, flans and cheesecakes, real sherry trifle, apple slices, meringues and strawberry shortcake. Freshly-made sandwiches, home-made soup and brown bread are also available daily, and chutneys & relishes like home-made pesto and honey & mustard dressing. "Greenbean" coffee is freshly ground for every cup - and you can choose between sitting in or taking out. A good place to break a journey with a wholesome little bite - and pop a few goodies into the car too. [Wheelchair accessible toilets under construction at time of going to press.] **Seats 25.** Open Mon-Sat, 9-6. Closed Sun. Amex, Diners, MasterCard, Visa, Laser. **Directions:** Opposite turn for Clonmel on the main street.

Cashel Area

Carron House

FARM GUESTHOUSE

Carron Cashel Co Tipperary **Tel: 052 62142**
Fax: 052 62168 Email: hallyfamily@eircom.net

Mary Hally's country home is on an award-winning farm, in a peaceful location in the heart of the Golden Vale, yet only minutes from Cashel and just an hour from Kilkenny. Approached up a long, well-maintained drive, first impressions are very encouraging, as there's a lovely front garden in front of the large, modern house - and separate entrances for the house and farm. Good-sized individually decorated bedrooms include one on the ground floor and all are very comfortably furnished, with generous beds, television, tea/coffee facilities, hair dryers and neat en-suite shower rooms. Housekeeping throughout is immaculate and there's a guest sitting room with antique furniture and interesting books, which is always available to guests. Mary, who is a friendly, attentive and informative hostess, gives guests a good send-off in the morning, with a generous, well-cooked and nicely presented breakfast in a large sun room overlooking the garden. Not suitable for children. **Rooms 4** (all with en-suite shower & all no smoking). B&B €33pps, ss €20. Closed 1 Oct-1 Apr. MasterCard, Visa. **Directions:** Take N8 south bound from Cashel for 2.5 miles. Signposted at left of crossroads.

Cashel Area

Dualla House

COUNTRY HOUSE

Dualla Cashel Co Tipperary **Tel: 062 61487** Fax: 062 61487
Email: duallahse@eircom.net Web: www.tipp.ie/dualla-house.htm

Set in 300 acres of of rolling Tipperary farmland in the "Golden Vale" , Martin and Mairead Power's fine Georgian manor house faces south towards the Slievenamon, Comeragh, Knockmealdown and Galtee Mountains. Just 3 miles from the Rock of Cashel, this is a convenient base for exploring the area but its special appeal is peace and tranquillity which, together with comfortable accommodation in large airy bedrooms (with tea/coffee trays), great hospitality and Mairead's home cooking, keep guests coming back time and again. An extensive breakfast menu includes local apple juice as well as other fresh fruits and juices, farmhouse cheeses, porridge with local honey, also free-range eggs and sausages from the local butcher in the traditional cooked breakfast - and home-made bread and preserves. Children welcome (under 3s free in parents' room, cot available without charge). **Rooms 4** (3 en-suite, 1 with private bathroom, all no smoking). B&B about €40 pps, ss about €10. Closed Dec-Feb. MasterCard, Visa. **Directions:** 3 miles from Cashel on R691. Coming from Dublin signed from N8, 5 miles after Horse & Jockey. Sign on left. 2.5 miles to house. ◇

Clonmel

Angela's Restaurant

féile bia RESTAURANT

14 Abbey Street Clonmel Co Tipperary **Tel: 052 26899**

A great little daytime restaurant in the centre of town, Angela's is renowned for delicious, wholesome food - and wholefoods. Baking is a speciality and seasonal and organic produce goes into an imaginative range of dishes with both traditional and contemporary influences. There will always be savoury flans - chargrilled peppers, vegetables, Cashel Blue, perhaps and special sandwiches include bruschetta (typically with mozzarella cheese, semidried tomato & basil oil - vegetarians do well here) and warm croissants like grilled chicken with cheese, bacon and relish. Hot specials might include roasted lamb peperonata and desserts tend to towards the comforting - bread & butter pudding, plum & almond tart. They're open all day for tea, coffee and sandwiches - La Scala coffee is served ("skinny" and decaff available) - and cuppa with one of their special oaten Anzac biscuits is just ace. Takeaway and outside catering service also available. Children welcome. **Seats 50.** L 12.30-3 Mon-Sat. All à la carte. Wine licence. Closed Sun, Christmas, Good Fri, bank holidays. **Directions:** Near Friary Church on River Suir.

Clonmel

Clifford's Restaurant

Ⓝ féile bia RESTAURANT

29 Thomas Street Clonmel Co Tipperary **Tel: 086 8353217**

Michael and Deirdre Clifford's renowned restaurant - which has been in Cahir for several years - is moving to new premises in Clonmel as we go to press. Michael, who is a classical French chef with Irish influences, sources his ingredients with immense care: meats come from two butchers - Kennedy's of Cahir and O'Dwyers of Cashel - the weekly Cahir country market is a source of local vegetables and flowers and Deirdre's father also supplies home-grown garden produce. Followers of these renowned restaurateurs will quickly feel at home in the old stone building - formerly a CIE coal house - where their precious art collection and many well-earned accolades will line the walls. Starters will, of course, include Michael's famous gateau of Clonakilty Black Pudding and main courses are sure to offer another speciality, of roast rack of Tipperary lamb with roasted pear & thyme sauce (Michael's saucing is invariably excellent) - and it will be worth travelling to Clonmel for lunch as well as dinner. Children welcome. Toilets wheelchair accessible. **Seats 50** (Private room, 40) Air conditioning. D Tue-Sat 6.30-10, L Tue-Sun 12.30-2.30 (Sun to 3) . Set L €12; early D €27, D also à la carte. House wines from about €20. PSC discretionary. Closed D Sun, all Mon; Christmas, 1st week Jan. Amex, Diners, MasterCard, Visa, Laser. **Directions:** Beside C.I.E. Rail & Bus Station.

Clonmel

Hotel Minella

féile bia HOTEL

Coleville Road Clonmel Co Tipperary **Tel: 052 22388** Fax: 052 24381
Email: hotelminella@eircom.net Web: www.hotelminella.ie

Sparky, the Old English sheepdog, establishes a friendly tone from the outset as he welcomes arriving guests to this pleasant hotel, which is attractively located in its own grounds, overlooking the River Suir. The original house was built in 1863 as a private residence and was purchased in 1961 by the current owners, Jack and Babs Nallen - the Nallen family are great racing enthusiasts and have stables nearby, where their Minella horses are trained and the racing theme is carried throughout the hotel. They've expanded the hotel over the years, to provide extensive banqueting and conference facilities and, most recently, self-catering apartments beside their fine leisure centre. Public areas in the old house - including a cocktail bar, restaurant (where reliable traditional food is served) and lounge areas

- have a lovely view over well-kept lawns and the river. Accommodation includes suites with four-posters and steam rooms, and junior suites with jacuzzis; all are furnished to a high standard with well-finished bathrooms - and housekeeping is exemplary. Excellent facilities and the romantic situation make the hotel especially popular for weddings. Leisure centre with 20 metre swimming pool and outdoor Canadian hot tub, jacuzzi, steam room and gym. Children welcome (under 2 free in parents' room, cot available without charge, baby sitting arranged). Tennis, fishing. Garden. **Rooms 70** (3 suites, 5 junior suites, 10 no smoking, 1 disabled). B&B €90 pps, ss €30. Closed 23-29 Dec. Amex, MasterCard, Visa, Laser. **Directions:** Edge of Clonmel town.

Clonmel

Mr. Bumbles

RESTAURANT / B&B

Kickham St. Clonmel Co Tipperary
Tel: 052 29188 Fax: 052 29380

With a stylish seating area at reception, attractively laid tables and plenty of plants, the atmosphere of Declan Gavigan's large bistro-style restaurant in the centre of town is relaxed and informal. Catering for a changing clientèle throughout the day and evening, seven days a week the menus – a light morning and afternoon menu, a fairly short à la carte lunch menu and a choice of à la carte or set dinner in the evening – offer straightforward, popular dishes with an international tone as well as the hearty steaks (char-grilled with green peppercorn sauce or garlic & parsley butter) and Tipperary lamb (cutlets with a basil crust, garlic mash potatioes & its own jus) for which the area is renowned. Lunchtime main courses may include home-made burgers, pasta dishes and a roast of the day with hot vegetables, while evening menus are more extensive and offer more ambitious dishes. Consistently high standards, friendly service, fair pricing - and long opening hours - make this cheerful restaurant a great asset to the area. **Seats 65.** L 12.30-2.30 daily (Sun to 3); D 6-10 daily (Sun to 9.30). Set Sun L about €22, Set D about €35, also à la carte; house wine about €16; sc discretionary (10% on parties of 6+). Closed Christmas. MasterCard, Visa, Laser. **Directions:** Situated beside Superquinn car park, opposite the Omniplex Cinema. ◇

Clonmel

Sean Tierney

PUB

13 O'Connell Street Clonmel Co Tipperary **Tel: 052 24467**

This tall, narrow pub is packed with "artefacts of bygone days – in short a mini-museum". A giant screen is discreetly hidden around the corner, for watching matches. Upstairs (and there are a lot of them – this is a four storey building) there's a relaxed traditional family-style restaurant. Expect popular, good value food like potato wedges, mushrooms with garlic, steaks and grills rather than gourmet fare, although the evening restaurant menus are more ambitious. Toilets are at the very top, but grand when you get there. Children welcome before 8.30 pm. Food served daily: Mon-Sat,10.30-9 (Sun to 8.30). Air conditioning. Closed 25 Dec, Good Fri. Visa. **Directions:** Situated 1/2 way down O'Connell St. on the left opposite Dunnes Stores.

Clonmel Area

Kilmaneen Farmhouse

FARMHOUSE

Ardfinnan Newcastle Clonmel Co Tipperary
Tel: 052 36231 Fax: 052 36231
Email: kilmaneen@eircom.net Web: www.kilmaneen.com

As neat as a new pin, Kevin & Ber O'Donnell's delightfully situated farmhouse is on a working dairy farm, surrounded by three mountain ranges - the Comeraghs, the Knockmealdowns and the Galtees - and close to the river Suir and the Tar, making it an ideal base for walking and fishing holidays. Kevin is trained in mountain skills and leads walking groups and trout fishing in the Suir and Tar on the farm is free (hut provided for tying flies, storing equipment and drying waders). It's an old house, but well restored to combine old furniture with modern comforts. Bedrooms are not especially big, but they are very thoughtfully furnished (including tea/coffee facilities and iron/trouser press) and, like the rest of the house, immaculate. There's a large, well-maintained garden, where guests can relax and enjoy the peaceful setting, and Ber's dinners are based on fresh farm produce. Fishing, walking. **Rooms 3** (2 shower only, all en-suite & no smoking). B&B €37.50 pps, ss €10. Children welcome (under 2s free in parents' room, cots available without charge, baby sitting arranged). Dining room seats 12. Residents' D from 7pm except on Sun (book in advance); Set D €22.50. No SC. Closed Nov-Mar. MasterCard, Visa. **Directions:** In Ardfinnan, follow signs at the Hill Bar.

Dromineer

The Whiskey Still

féile bia **PUB**

Dromineer Nenagh Co Tipperary **Tel: 067 24129**

Dromineer is one of the Shannon's most-visited places, popular with cruisers, anglers, sailing folk (and even walkers) alike. Declan Collison and Fiona Neilan, who took over The Whiskey Still in 1999, have made great improvements to the building - and established a well-deserved reputation for good food.

It's a characterful old place just up from the harbour, with a stove in the bar for cold days and table service to wherever you're sitting. The cooking style is lovely - the kind of thing a good home cook would make when not too pressured for time but with a some professional flair in the presentation. Baked garlic mussels, poached chicken breast in a lovely spring onion cream and a generous smoked haddock bake are all typical, followed by a well-made lemon meringue pie, perhaps, or apple cobbler with fresh cream. For fine weather there's a big deck facing the water, with patio heaters to extend the long summer evenings. Food served all year: Mon-Sat 12.30-9.30 pm, Sun & bank hols to 9pm. Closed 25 Dec & Good Fri. MasterCard, Visa, Laser. **Directions:** In Dromineer village. ◇

Fethard

Mobarnane House

COUNTRY HOUSE

Fethard Co Tipperary **Tel: 052 31962** Fax: 052 31962
Email: info@mobarnanehouse.com Web: www.mobarnanehouse.com

Approached up a stylish gravel drive with well-maintained grass verges, Richard and Sandra Craik-White's lovely 18th century home has recently been restored to its former glory and makes a wonderfully spacious house for guests. A large, beautifully furnished drawing room is the only room where smoking is allowed and has plenty of comfortable seating for everyone when there's a full house - and the dining room, where Richard's good country cooking is served (usually at a communal table, although separate tables can be arranged on request), is equally well-appointed in every sense of the phrase. Accommodation is to a similar standard: all rooms have lovely views and comfortable seating (two have separate sitting rooms), quality bedding and everything needed for a relaxing stay, including tea/coffee making facilities, phones and television. Bathrooms vary somewhat (bedrooms without sitting rooms have bigger bathrooms), but all have quality towels and toiletries. An excellent breakfast gets the day off to a good start - and, as well as being well-placed to explore a large and interesting area blessed with beautiful scenery, an interesting history, local crafts and sports, there's plenty to do on-site (extensive walks in the grounds, tennis). Pets by arrangement. **Rooms 4** (2 junior suites, all no smoking). Not suitable for children under 5 except babies (cot available, €5). B&B €75 pps, ss 25. Residents D 8pm, €40. House wine €15. SC discretionary. Closed Nov-Feb. MasterCard, Visa. **Directions:** From Fethard, take Cashel road for 3.5 miles, turn right, signed Ballinure and Thurles; 1.5 miles on left.

GARRYKENNEDY

Garrykennedy is a charming little harbour about six miles from Nenagh, but it's really in a world of its own. Despite its tiny size, it has two harbours - one used to shelter Guinness barges en route from Dublin to Limerick - and two pubs. The older pub at this delightful little port is **Ciss Ryan's (067 23364),** where there's music on Saturdays, and other - a pretty thatched cottage with fresh bright red and white paintwork - is **Larkins (067 23232),** where you'll get traditional bar food daily in summer, and music several days a week.

Glen of Aherlow

Aherlow House Hotel

HOTEL

Glen of Aherlow Co Tipperary **Tel: 062 56153** Fax: 062 56212
Email: aherlow@iol.ie Web: www.aherlowhouse.ie

Romantically located in a forest on the slopes of a famous glen, this hotel - which was originally a hunting lodge - enjoys stunning views of the surrounding mountains and countryside. The old house is lovely, with well-proportioned rooms furnished in an appealing country house style; the drawing room, bar and dining room are all well-placed to take advantage of the view, and there is a large terrace for fine weather. The bedrooms in the original house also reflect the gracious style, while newer ones have less character, but are comfortably furnished and have all the modern conveniences. Recently added self-catering lodges unfortunately dominate the site although their "mountain lodge" style is not inappropriate. Outdoor pursuits like horse riding, fishing, walking and mountain climbing are all on site or nearby; special breaks available. Popular for weddings. Conference/banqueting (400/300); secretarial services. Children welcome (under 6s free in parents' room). No Pets. **Rooms 29** (all en-suite). B&B about €82pps, ss about €15.50. Open all year. Amex, Diners, MasterCard, Visa, Laser. **Directions:** From Tipperary town take the R664 road. Signposted to the right after 4 miles. ◇

NENAGH

This quietly prosperous town in the heart of Irelands best farmland can provide a convenient base within easy reach of many attractions in the mid-west, including Lough Derg, or makes a handy place to break a journey - the modern **Abbey Court Hotel (Tel: 067 41111; www.abbeycourt.ie)** is located on the edge of town, with ample parking and good facilities.

Nenagh — Country Choice Delicatessen & Coffee Bar

CAFÉ

25 Kenyon Street Nenagh Co Tipperary
Tel: 067 32596 Fax: 067 32736
Email: peter@countrychoices.com Web: www.countrychoice.ie

NATURAL FOOD AWARD

Food-lovers from all over the country make sure of building in a visit to Peter and Mary Ward's unique shop when planning a journey anywhere near Nenagh. Old hands head for the little café at the back first, fortifying themselves with simple home-cooked food that reflects a policy of seasonality – if the range is small at a particular time of year, so be it. Meats, milk, cream, eggs, butter and flour: "The economy of Tipperary is agricultural and we intend to demonstrate this with a finished product of tantalising smells and tastes." Specialities developed over the years include Cashel Blue and broccoli soup – served with their magnificent home-baked breads (made with local flours) – savoury and sweet pastry dishes (quiches, fruit tarts) and tender, gently-cooked meat dishes like lamb ragout and beef and Guinness casserole. The shop carries a very wide range of the finest Irish artisan produce, plus a smaller selection of specialist products from further afield, such as olive oil and an unusual range of quality glacé fruits that are in great demand for Christmas baking (they probably make Ireland's best Christmas puddings for sale in the shop too). Several specialities deserve special mention: there's a great terrine, made from the family's saddleback pigs; the preserves - jam (Mary Ward makes 12000 pots a year!) and home-made marmalade, based on oranges left to caramelise in the Aga overnight, producing a runny but richly flavoured preserve; then there is Peter's passion for cheese. He is one of the country's best suppliers of Irish farmhouse cheeses, which he minds like babies as they ripen and, unlike most shops, only puts on display when they are mature: do not leave without buying cheese. As well as all this, they run regular art exhibitions in the shop, wine courses and poetry readings. Definitely worth a detour. **Seats 40.** Picnic service available. Open all day (9-5.30); L 12-3.30 daily, à la carte; house wine from about €31. Children welcome. Closed Mon, bank hols & Good Fri. **No Credit Cards. Directions:** Centre of town,on left half way down Kenyon Street.

Nenagh Area — Coolbawn Quay

Ⓝ HOTEL

Coolbawn Nenagh Co Tipperary **Tel: 067 28158** Fax: 067 28162
Email: info@coolbawnquay.com Web: www.coolbawnquay.com

Spas and retreats are appearing all over Ireland at the moment, but few could rival the beauty of this magic place. This unique resort on the eastern shores of Lough Derg (with its own marina) is modelled on the lines of a 19th century Irish village with quietly understated luxurious accommodation in suites and rooms scattered throughout the village - with hotel style service throughout. Whether you want to pamper yourself at the spa, hold a small conference or board meeting - or simply to unwind with style - this unusual resort village could be the ideal destination. The inner man will be well looked after too, with excellent cooking by Rob Oosterban. (Small conference/banqueting (35). Spa; beauty treatments. Walking, fishing. Pool table. Children welcome (cot available, baby sitting arranged). Garden. No pets. **Rooms 40** (3 suites, 9 shower only, all no smoking). Room service (limited hours). Restaurant **Seats 38.** Non residents welcome by reservation if there is room (not suitable for children under 7). D daily, 7-9; Set D €35, also small à la carte menu. Bar food daily in high season, 12.30-2 (residents & members only); also barbecues. Amex, MasterCard, Visa, Laser. **Directions:** On eastern side of Lough Derg; access from N7.

Roscrea Area — Saratoga Lodge

COUNTRY HOUSE

Barnane Templemore Co Tipperary **Tel: 0504 31886** Fax: 0504 31491

In a particularly unspoilt and peaceful part of the country, just below the famous Devil's Bit in the Silvermine mountain range, Valerie Beamish's lovely classically proportioned house on a working stud farm is well-situated on an open, sunny site looking out over the hills. Good equestrian paintings enhance the large, traditionally furnished reception rooms opening off a spacious hall and there is also a little TV room for children (under 3s free in parents' room, cots available free of charge). Bedrooms are very comfortably furnished, although the bathroom arrangements are a little complicated: two share a well-appointed intercommunicating bathroom and the third shares with the hostess (who uses a downstairs bathroom if guests want it to themselves). However, guests seem to cope with this unusual arrangement quite happily - no doubt the breakfasts that Valerie takes great pride in are more important, also the fact that she's willing to cook 4-course dinners on request (using home-produced vegetables, herbs and honey), and make picnics - and be extremely hospitable all round. **Rooms 3** (2 en-suite but shared, 1 shower only, all no smoking). B&B €40 pps, no ss. Residents' D €30, on request. House wine, €15. Closed 23 Dec-3 Jan. MasterCard, Visa, Laser. **Directions:** N7 from Dublin/Limerick, N62 Templemore, R510 from Templemore/Borrisoleigh 2 miles. First turn right,first turn left.

Roscrea Area

Fiacrí Country House Restaurant

féile bia RESTAURANT

Boulerea Knock Roscrea Co Tipperary **Tel: 0505 43017**
Fax: 0505 43018 Email: fiacrihouse@eircom.net

FÉILE BIA AWARD

It was curiosity about their Feile Bia membership that first led us to this restaurant, to see how Enda & Ailish Hennessy had diversified from farming into the food side of hospitality rather than the more usual B&B or farmhouse holidays. It's not the easiest place to find (it is sensible to get directions when booking) but, once discovered, what a welcome sight their neat pink-painted farmhouse presents - and a lot of people obviously think it is worth seeking out, as they are regularly booked out at weekends and always busy, even midweek. If you have ever wondered how a handsome young farmer might take to front of house work in a restaurant, it is instructive to observe the easy hospitality at work here, as Enda shows guests through to a comfortable leather sofa in the bar, speedily offers menus and an aperitif, and then leaves you to enjoy the open fire and relax with Ailish's five-course menu. Excellent management, but not so surprising perhaps - after all, he's well used to running a demanding business with a particular emphasis on attention to detail. Ailish sources ingredients carefully, to make full use of local and Quality Assured products, and her menus offer a good choice of six or seven dishes on each course - a salad of baked Clonakilty black pudding & caramelised apple, perhaps, or warm smoked salmon potato cake with horseradish cream, to start, and fairly traditional main courses like rack of Tipperary lamb with a pinenut stuffing & rosemary jus, or pan-fried medallions of pork with caramelised apple, calvados & wholegrain mustard cream sauce. (It's surprising how rarely pork comes up on Irish menus, considering the place of the pig in our culinary heritage; here it makes a fine house speciality). Menus are balanced, to include fish, poultry and vegetarian choices, but local meats are especially good, and large portions of seasonal vegetables are served separately - in fact, as is to be expected in a farming area, generosity is a key feature here. The restaurant has a pleasing country house ambience, decorated in warm, traditional shades of deep green and red, with an open fire and tables elegantly set up with white linen and mahogany chairs - it all creates a relaxed atmosphere. To finish, try the excellent Assorted Dessert Plate - miniature servings of the day's desserts such as hazelnut meringue roulade, rhubarb ginger & strawberry crumble, strawberry shortcake - or farmhouse cheese. A compact, informative and fairly priced wine list spans the old and new worlds. The bill, which is reasonable for the standard offered, is presented in a Feile Bia cover, explaining their commitment to the Feile Bia Charter and products from recognised Quality Assurance Schemes: a neat way to reinforce the Feile Bia message. Flavoursome, generous country house cooking, enhanced by professional well-paced service and a real sense of hospitality make a great combination - and, at Fiacri, it's clearly a recipe for success. Barbecues in summer; cookery classes also available. **Seats 80.** Not suitable for children under 12. D Wed-Sat, 7-9.15. Set D €40. House wine €17. Full bar licence. Closed Sun, Mon & Tue. Amex, MasterCard, Visa, Laser. **Directions:** Roscrea 6.5 miles,Erril 4.5, Templemore 8.

Terryglass

Kylenoe

COUNTRY HOUSE

Balinderry Terryglass Nenagh Co Tipperary
Tel: 067 22015 Fax: 067 22275

Virginia Moeran's lovely old stone house on 150 acres of farm and woodland offers homely comfort and real country pleasures close to Lough Derg. The farm is home to an international stud and the woodlands provide a haven for an abundance of wildlife, including deer, red squirrel, badgers, rabbits and foxes. With beautiful walks, riding (with or without tuition), golf and water sports available on the premises or close by, this is a real rural retreat. Spacious, airy bedrooms are furnished in gentle country house style, with antiques and family belongings, and overlook beautiful rolling countryside. Downstairs there's a delightful guests' sitting room and plenty of interesting reading. Virginia enjoys cooking – her breakfasts are a speciality – and dinner is available to residents by arrangement. Importantly for people who like to travel with their dogs, this is a place where man's best friend is also made welcome – and Kylenoe was the recipient of the Guide's Pet Friendly Establishment Award in 1999. Children welcome (under 4 free in parents' room; cot available). Garden, walking. **Rooms 4** (2 en-suite, 2 with private bathrooms, all no-smoking) B&B €50 pps, ss €15. Residents D 8pm, €38 (book by noon). Wines €8-25. Closed Christmas. Visa. **Directions:** Nenagh - Borrisokane - through Terryglass, 1.5 miles out on left hand side.

Terryglass

The Derg Inn

féile bia RESTAURANT / PUB / BAR

Terryglass Co Tipperary **Tel: 067 22037**
Fax: 067 22297 Email: derginn@eircom.net

Tables set up outside the Derg Inn please the summer crowd and a crackling fire is a welcome sight on a cold day - like many country pubs, this is a place perhaps seen at its best off season. This is one of the area's best pubs for food and the sight of tables set up for the comfortable enjoyment of a good meal quickly gets hungry guests into a relaxed mood (especially boating visitors, after the walk up from the harbour). Everything is sourced with great care, using the best of local produce including organic food when possible; traditional Irish dishes like bacon & cabbage and beef & Guinness pie are always a treat here and evening menus are quite wide-ranging with a choice that usually includes delicious house specialities like home-made paté with Derg Inn mango chutney & garlic bread and salmon in filo pastry with lemon & caper sauce - and maybe fillet steak with wholegrain mustard sauce (Lakeshore mustard is made nearby, at Ballinderry) along with more-ish desserts like praline parfait with cinnamon syrup. Sea fish is more prominent on the menu than might be expect in a river and lakeland area a grilled mixed platter for two, for instance, is served with green salad new potatoes and proving very popular. Sunday lunch is also quite a speciality, but you don't have to eat at the Derg - there's an interesting little wine list to enjoy with or without food and a very pleasant bar. Music in summer - Friday, Saturday and Sunday, various styles; Sunday night is the one for traditional music enthusiasts. Seats 150 (private function room, 70+). Toilets wheelchair accessible. Open daily: food available 10-10. Breakfast from 10am, L 12-5, D 6-10. A la carte. House wine €15. SC discretionary. Closed Good Fri, 25 Dec. Amex, MasterCard, Visa, Laser. **Directions:** In the heart of Terrryglass Village.

Thurles Area

Inch House Country House & Restaurant

féile bia RESTAURANT / COUNTRY HOUSE

Bouladuff Thurles Co Tipperary
Tel: 0504 51348 Fax: 0504 51754
Email: inchhse@iol.ie Web: www.tipp.ie/inch-house.htm

Built in 1720 by John Ryan, one of the few landed Catholic gentlemen in Tipperary, this magnificent Georgian house managed to survive some of the most turbulent periods in Irish history and to remain in the Ryan family for almost 300 years. John and Norah Egan, who farm the surrounding 250 acres, took it over in a state of dereliction in 1985 and began the major restoration work which has resulted in the handsome, comfortably furnished period house which guests enjoy today. Reception rooms on either side of a welcoming hallway include an unusual William Morris-style drawing room with a tall stained glass window, a magnificent plasterwork ceiling (and adjoining library bar) and a fine dining room which is used for residents' breakfasts and is transformed into a restaurant at night. Both rooms have period fireplaces with big log fires. The five bedrooms are quite individual and are furnished with antiques. Children welcome (under 3 free in parents' room; cot available, baby sitting arranged). No Pets. **Rooms 5** (all en-suite, 1 shower only). B&B €52.50 pps, ss €7.50. Room service (limited hours.) Closed Christmas week.

Restaurant: The restaurant, which is open to non-residents by reservation, has polished wood floors, classic country house decor and tables laid with crisp white linen and fresh flowers, which provide a pleasing setting for dinner, especially when the atmosphere is softened by firelight and candles. Head chef Kieran O'Dwyer's menus offer a well-balanced choice in a fairly traditional style that combines French country cooking and Irish influences. Dishes like boned stuffed quail on mixed berries, with red wine sauce and entrecôte steak with mixed hole peppercorn brandy sauce illustrate the style. Anyone with special dietary needs, including vegetarians, should mention this on booking to allow for preparation of extra dishes. Not suitable for children under 10 after 7 pm. **Seats 45.** D Tue-Sat 7-9.30; Set D from €38; house wine about €17; sc discretionary. Closed Sun & Mon, Christmas week. Amex, MasterCard, Visa, Laser. **Directions:** Four miles from Thurles on Nenagh Road.

COUNTY WATERFORD

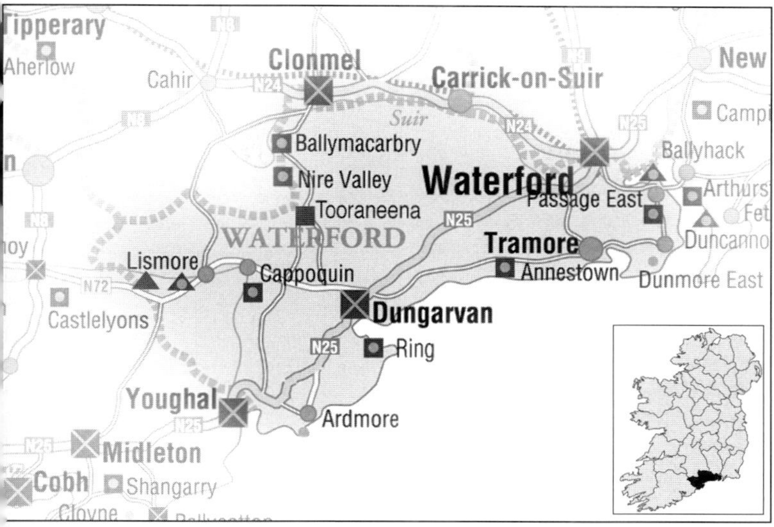

2004 should see a major construction project getting under way for the benefit of Waterford city in particular, and southeast Ireland in general. At present, the compact city has only one bridge across the tidal waters of the River Suir. But the plan for a new cable-stayed bridge of "distinct and impressive, light and elegant" design three miles upriver will greatly ease traffic pressures, and much improve the ambience of the quays.

On the quays of Waterford city, we are witness to a trading and seafaring tradition which goes back at least 1,150 years. But this sense of history also looks to the future, as Waterford - the city of crystal and quality glassware - has been selected as the assembly port for the Tall Ships of all nations at the beginning of their European sail training programme in July 2005. Today's larger commercial ships may be berthed downstream on the other side of the river at Belview, but the old cityside quays on the south bank retain a nautical flavour which is accentuated by very useful marina berthing facilities in the heart of town.

This fine port was founded in 853 AD when the Vikings - Danes for the most part - established the trading settlement of Vadrefjord. Its strategic location in a sheltered spot at the head of the estuary near the confluence of the Suir and Barrow rivers guaranteed its continuing success under different administrators, particularly the Normans, so much so that it tended to overshadow the county of Waterford, almost all of which is actually to the west of the port.

But for many years now, the county town has been Dungarvan, which is two-thirds of the way westward along Waterford's extensive south coast, which includes the attractive Copper Coast - between Fenor and Stradbally - in its midst. This spreading of the administrative centres of gravity has to some extent balanced the life of the Waterford region. But even so, the extreme west of the county is still one of Ireland's best kept secrets, a place of remarkable beauty between the Knockmealdown, Comeragh and Monavullagh mountains, where fish-filled rivers such as the Bride, the Blackwater, and the Nire make their way seawards at different speeds through valleys of remarkable variety and beauty, past pretty towns and villages such as lovely Lismore which, on September 8th 2003, was awarded the Gold Medal for small towns in the national Tidy Towns competition,

West Waterford is a place of surprises. For instance, around the delightful coastal village of Ardmore, ancient monuments suggest that the local holy man, St Declan, introduced Christianity to the area quite a few years before St Patrick went to work in the rest of Ireland. And across the bay from Ardmore, the Ring neighbourhood is a Gaeltacht (Irish-speaking) area with its own bustling fishing port at Helvick.

Dungarvan itself is in the midst of an attractive revival. It has relinquished its role as a commercial port, but is enthusiastically taking to recreational boating and harbourside regeneration instead. Along the bluff south coast, secret coves gave smugglers and others access to charming villages like Stradbally and Bunmahon. Further east, the increased tempo of the presence of Waterford city is felt both at the traditional resort of Tramore, and around the fishing/sailing harbour of Dunmore East. Meanwhile, inland along the River Suir, 13 miles northwest of Waterford city, Portlaw is of interest as one of

Ireland's "model" industrial townships. In September 2003, an ambitious conservation plan was unveiled, for the industry – mostly leather – has long since gone elsewhere, leaving much of its former premises derelict. An intriguing project.

Local Attractions and Information

Ballymacarbry, Nire Valley & Comeraghs on Horseback	052 36147
Cappoquin, Mount Melleray Activity Centre	058 54322
Cappoquin, Tourism Information	058 53333
Dungarvan, Tourism Information	058 41741
Kilmeaden, Old School House Craft Centre	051 853567
Lismore, Lismore Castle & Gardens	058 54424
Passage East, Car Ferry (to Ballyhack, Co Wexford)	051 382480
Tramore, Tramore House Gardens	051 386303
Waterford Airport	051 875589
Waterford, Christ Church Cathedral (18c Neoclassical)	051 858958
Waterford, Waterford Crystal Glass Centre	051 332500
Waterford, Heritage Museum	051 871227
Waterford, Int. Festival of Light Opera (Sept)	051 375437
Waterford, Reginald's Tower 13th C Circular Tower	051 304220
Waterford, Theatre Royal	051 874402
Waterford, Tourism Information	051 875823
Waterford, Waterford Treasures at the Granary	051 304500

Annestown

Annestown House

COUNTRY HOUSE

Annestown Co Waterfor
Tel: 051 396160 Fax: 051 39647
Email: relax@annestown.com Web: www.annestown.com

John and Pippa Galloway's relaxed and comfortable home is in a magic location on Waterford's 'Coppe Coast', overlooking a small bay, with a private path leading to the beach below. In front of the house ar manicured lawns – one for croquet, one for tennis – while inside there are several lounges with lo burning fires and a billiard room with full-size table. Everywhere you look there are books – a catholi collection ranging from classics to thrillers. An evening meal is available for residents (they call th cooking "new comfort"!) and there will be satisfying home-cooked dishes such as warm goats chees salad, rack of lamb and raspberry brulée and, next morning, a hearty Irish breakfast (with exceller breads) will set you up for the day ahead. All the centrally-heated bedrooms are attractively an comfortably furnished with twin or king size beds, direct-dial telephone and tea-making facilities (an hot water bottles are thoughtfully provided for those who still feel cold). **Rooms 5** (all en-suite, 1 showe only; all no-smoking), B&B €60 pps, ss €15. Residents' D Mon-Sat €35, at 7.45pm; wines €16 & 23 (€ by the glass). D must be booked by the previous evening; not available on Sun. Closed 31 Oct-15 Fe Amex, MasterCard, Visa. **Directions:** Midway between Tramore and Burmahon on coast road R675.

Ardmore

White Horses Restauran

RESTAURANT

Ardmore Co Waterford **Tel: 024 94040** Fax: 024 9404

Christine Power and Geraldine Flavin's delightfully bright and breezy café-restaurant on the main stree of this famous little seaside town is one of those places that changes its character through the day b always has style. They're open for all the little lifts that visitors need through the day - morning coffe afternoon tea - as well as imaginative lunches (plus their traditional Sunday lunch, which runs a afternoon) and a more ambitious à la carte evening menu. Vegetarian dishes feature on both menus a noodle stir-fry during the day perhaps, and Ardsallagh goat's cheese with sesame seed salad in th evening - and there's a good balance between traditional favourites like steaks and more adventurou fare: the daytime fish could be deep-fried plaice with tartare sauce, for example, while its evenir counterpart might be Helvick salmon with a crust of couscous, served with a sauce verte. Attracti and pleasant to be in - the use of local Ardmore pottery is a big plus on the presentation side - this is friendly, well-run place and equally good for a cuppa and a gateau or pastry from the luscious hom made selection on display, or a full meal. Even when very busy, service is well-organised and efficien **Seats 60.** Air conditioning. In summer (May-Sep) open: Tue-Sun 11am-"late" (around 11pm); L 11-4, D

11; (also open Mon in Aug). In winter (Oct-Apr) open weekends only: Fri from 6 pm, Sat 11 am-late & Sun 12-4. A la carte except Sun Set L, about €18. Licensed; sc discretionary. Closed Mon all year, except Aug. MasterCard, Visa. **Directions:** Centre of village. ◇

Ballymacarbry

Glasha Farmhouse Accommodation

FARMHOUSE

Glasha Ballymacarbry Co Waterford **Tel: 052 36108** Fax: 052 36108
Email: glasha@eircom.net Web: www.glashafarmhouse.com

Paddy and Olive O'Gorman's spacious farmhouse is set in its own gardens high up in the hills and provides a very comfortable and hospitable base for a relaxed rural break. Fishing is a major attraction (the Nire runs beside the farmhouse and permits are available locally), also walking (Glasha links the Comeragh and Knockmealdown sections of the famous Munster Way), pony trekking, golf (available locally) and painting this beautiful area. Glasha was the national winner of the Bord Failte Irish Welcome Awards in 2002 and it is easy to see why: Olive thinks of everything that will help guests feel at home and bedrooms have lots of little extras including TV/radio, hair dryers, electric blankets, tea/coffee-making, spring water and magazines; all rooms are en-suite and the newer ones have lovely bathrooms with jacuzzi baths. There's plenty of comfortable lounging room for guests' use, including a conservatory too - and the nearest pub is just 3 minutes' walk from the house. Children welcome, cots available. **Rooms 9** (4 with jacuzzi, 5 shower only, all no-smoking). B&B from €45 pps, ss €8. Closed 20-28 Dec. MasterCard, Visa. **Directions:** Off 671 road between Clonmel and Dungarvan; signed on 671.

Ballymacarbry

Hanora's Cottage

RESTAURANT / GUESTHOUSE

Nire Valley Ballymacarbry Co Waterford
Tel: 052 36134 Fax: 052 36540
Email: hanorascottage@eircom.net Web: www.hanorascottage.com

The Wall family's gloriously remote country guesthouse is now a very substantial building, yet Hanora's still nurtures the spirit of the ancestral home around which it is built. The Walls are caring and hospitable hosts and this, plus the luxurious accommodation and good food they provide, makes Hanora's a very special place - and especially wonderful for foot-weary walkers. Spacious, thoughtfully furnished rooms all have jacuzzi baths and there is an especially romantic one for honeymooners or special occasions - and there's also a spa tub in a conservatory overlooking the garden, with views of the mountains. Overnight guests have the privilege of starting the day with Hanora's legendary breakfast buffet, which was the Munster and National Winner of the Denny Irish Breakfast Awards in 2002; it takes some time to get the measure of this feast, so make sure you get up in time to make the most of it. Local produce and an amazing variety of exotics (some of which you may not previously have encountered) jostle for space on the beautifully arranged buffet: there's freshly squeezed juices and luscious Crinnaghtaun Apple Juice from Lismore, more fresh fruits, Seamus Wall's homemade muesli and Mary's Nire Valley Porridge, then the bread section... Seamus is the baker, beginning at 6am every day so that, when guests come down for breakfast, he'll have an incredible dozen or more types of bread, scones, muffins and buns ready, including organic and gluten free varieties. Then there are local farmhouse cheeses, smoked salmon and home made jams - and the cooked breakfast options are yet to come: for your hot dish you can have Syl Murray's home-made sausages, Clonakilty black & white puddings, Biddy Cooney's free-range eggs (various ways) and much else besides. This is truly a gargantuan feast, designed to see you many miles along the hills before you stop for a little packed lunch (prepared that morning) and ultimately return for dinner...Small weddings (40). **Rooms 10** (1 suite, 3 junior suites, all no smoking). Not suitable for children. No pets. B&B from about €75 pps. Closed 22-27 Dec.

Restaurant: Dinner visitors travel from far and wide to mingle with residents at the fireside to have an aperitif and ponder on Eoin and Judith Wall's imaginative, well-balanced menus. Then, difficult choices made, you move through to the restaurant, which overlooks a lovely garden and the riverside woodland. Enthusiastic supporters of small suppliers, Eoin and Judith use local produce whenever possible and credit them on the menu - fresh fish from Dunmore East, free range chickens from Stradbally and local cheeses, for example. There's a separate vegetarian dinner menu on request as well as an à la carte which offers a choice of six or seven dishes on each course, usually including some vegetarian options. A typical menu might include starters of sautéed lambs kidneys with wholegrain mustard mash and mushroom paté on crostini with mixed salad and, as lamb is abundant locally, roast rack of lamb makes an excellent main course choice (served, perhaps, with a delicious mint hollandaise), while fish doesn't have far to travel either and is beautifully fresh and accurately cooked. Classical desserts include home-made ice creams, and are often fruit based. Not suitable for children under 12. **Seats 30/40.** D Mon-Sat, 7-9, Set D about €40, also à la carte. House wine about €14.50. Closed Sun, bank hols. MasterCard, Visa, Laser. **Directions:** Take Clonmel/Dungarvan Road to Ballymacarbry.

Ballymacarbry — Melody's Nire View Bar

PUB

Ballymacarbry Co Waterford **Tel: 052 36147** / 36169

This hospitable, well-run pub in the upper reaches of the Nire Valley has been in the family for over a hundred years - and it's a great place to take a break if you're walking or simply touring the area. When something simple but good is needed, Melody's is just the spot for a bowl of Carmel's home-made soup served with freshly baked brown bread, or a freshly-cut sandwich and a bit of crisp-crusted apple tart. The soup might be mulligatawny, mixed vegetable, simple mushroom or carrot & tomato, but it will certainly be made from fresh ingredients that morning and the sandwiches - typically turkey, ham, cheese or salad - are freshly made up to order. Recent renovations and extensions have made the pub brighter and more comfortable without losing its atmosphere and its most important features - genuine hospitality, real open fires and simple good food - remain unchanged. Live music on Tuesdays & Fridays. Maps are available for a number of walks taking from 11/2-4 hours. Light meals. Closed 25 Dec & Good Fri. **Directions:** On Nire Valley scenic drive, R671, Dungarvan/Clonmel road.

Cappoquin — Richmond House

COUNTRY HOUSE / RESTAURANT

Cappoquin Co Waterford
Tel: 058 54278 Fax: 058 54988
Email: info@richmondhouse.net Web: www.richmondhouse.net

Genuine hospitality, high standards of comfort, thoughtful service and excellent food are all to be found in the Deevy family's fine 18th century country house and restaurant just outside Cappoquin - no wonder this is a place so many people like to keep as a closely guarded secret. There's a sense of pleasurable anticipation from the outset, as you approach through parkland along a well-maintained driveway, which is lit up at night - a feeling confirmed by the climbing plants beside the door, and the warm welcome from one of the family when you arrive. Inside, a fine high-ceilinged hall has a wood-burning stove and a well-proportioned, elegantly furnished drawing room and restaurant opening off it, and there are nine individually decorated en-suite bedrooms. They vary in size and appointments, as is the way with old houses - some love the smallest cottagey bedroom, while others may prefer the larger ones - but all are comfortably furnished in country house style with full bathrooms. As well as creating wonderful dinners in the restaurant (see below), the Deevys make sure that you also have a memorable breakfast to see you on your way. It is, of course, a wonderful area to explore and this would make an excellent base. Children welcome (under 3 free in parents' room, cot available without charge, baby sitting arranged). Garden; walking. **Rooms 9** (all en-suite with full bathrooms). B&B €80 pps, ss €15. Closed 23 Dec-20 Jan.

Restaurant: The restaurant is the most important single element at Richmond House, and non-residents regularly make up a high proportion of the guests. Warm and friendly service begins at the front door, then menus are presented over aperitifs - in front of the drawing room fire, or in a conservatory overlooking the garden. Herbs, fruit and vegetables are grown on the premises for use in the kitchen and Paul is an ardent supporter of local produce, buying seafood from Dunmore East and Dungarvan, beef, lamb, bacon and sausages from his trusted local butcher, and extra organic produce grown nearby. Paul constantly seeks ways to improve the range and style offered and there is a sureness of touch in his kitchen, seen in stimulating menus that always include imaginative vegetarian choices and offer a balance between traditional country house cooking and more adventurous dishes inspired by the current trend towards global cuisine. Dinner menus offering about five choices on each course are changed daily, and a slightly shorter separate vegetarian menu is also offered. Dishes particularly enjoyed on a recent visit included a starter of perfectly cooked pan-seared Dunmore East scallops, served with a parmesan risotto and a lovely fennel cream sauce - and a speciality dish, roast rack of delicious West Waterford lamb on braised puy lentils with a feta croquette, home-made mint jelly and rosemary jus; vegetables, served separately, as invariably imaginative and cooked 'au point'. Classic desserts are always a treat - raspberry & yogurt mousse, perhaps, with brandysnap biscuits... Service, under Claire's direction, is attentive and discreet. A carefully selected and fairly priced wine list includes interesting house wines and a dozen half bottles. Children welcome. **Seats 40** (private room, 16). D 7-9 daily Set D €48 (Vegetarian Menu €43); house wine €18; sc discretionary. Amex, Diners, MasterCard, Visa, Laser. **Directions:** Half a mile outside Cappoquin on N72.

Cheekpoint

The Cottage Bistro

Ⓝ RESTAURANT

Cheekpoint Village Co Waterford **Tel: 051 380854**
Email: mcalpinscottage@eircom.net

Aidan and Marian McAlpin's neat cottagey restaurant is actually brand new, but it fits in well with neighbouring houses. Inside, everything is spick and span and the style is pleasingly simple, with a small bar area and plain handsomely-laid tables softened by warm lighting and fresh flowers. Good home-made brown bread and iced water are served promptly, along with hand written menus that offer plenty of choice, although local seafood is a speciality and starters, in particular, offer a lot of popular dishes like prawn cocktail, mussels or crab claws in garlic butter, along with a few other classics, typically duck liver terrine with sauternes. Main courses offer a wider choice - including a vegetarian shepherd's pie, no less - cheese topping optional - as well as steaks, pork and chicken - but seafood is dominant in dishes like fresh salmon mayonnaise, fillets of sole baked in chive sauce with (perhaps a little too much) creamed potato topping and seafood gratin, which is a house speciality. A side salad is served after the main course, and desserts are home-made; (some food is apparently bought in, so it would be wise to ask when ordering). What you get here is Marian McAlpin's sound home cooking, simply presented - and, with nothing over €20 on the menu, prices are very reasonable, especially for seafood. An interesting, informative and well-priced wine list includes unusual house wines and a decent choice of half bottles. **Seats 40.** D Tue-Sat, 6-9.45 (Sun, summer only, 5.30-8.30).A la carte. House wine €16.95. Closed Mon (also Sun off season), 1st week Oct, 1st 2 weeks Jan. MasterCard, Visa, Laser. **Directions:** Above the harbour.

Cheekpoint

The Suir Inn

féile bia RESTAURANT

Cheekpoint Co Waterford **Tel: 051 382 220**
Email: frances@mcalpins.com Web: www.mcalpins.com

This immaculately maintained black-and-white painted inn is 300 years old and has been run by the McAlpin family since 1972. During that time they have earned an enviable reputation for hospitality and good food served at a moderate price, notably local seafood. It's a characterful, country style place with rustic furniture, cottagey plates and old prints decorating the walls. Seasonal menus offer a choice of about six starters (nearly all seafood and under €7) and ten main courses, including three cold dishes and two vegetarian ones, again all moderately priced - specialities include a generous seafood platter and home-made seafood pie. All meals come with brown soda bread, butter and a side salad – and there's a nice little wine list. Own parking. No children after 8 pm. **Seats 62.** D Mon-Sat, 5.45-9.45; à la carte; sc discretionary. House wine €15. Closed Sun. MasterCard, Visa, Laser. **Directions:** 7 miles east of Waterford.

Dungarvan

Powersfield House

féile bia GUESTHOUSE / RESTAURANT

Ballinamuck West Dungarvan Co Waterford
Tel: 058 45594 Fax: 058 45550
Email: powersfieldhouse@cablesurf.com Web: www.powersfield.com

You could be forgiven for thinking that Edmund and Eunice Power's fine guesthouse has been here for a long time - although new, the garden has matured well and this, together with traditional country house style furnishing, gives it an unexpected sense of age. Antiques and interesting fabrics creating a soothing and relaxing atmosphere throughout the house, including a comfortable, homely sitting room as well as bedrooms which have been individually decorated and finished to a high standard, with smart bathrooms and all the necessary comforts: phones (with ISDN & fax facilities)TV and tea/coffee trays). Eunice also runs a small restaurant at the house several nights a week, offering a set menu based on local produce such as Helvic seafood (typically, in a speciality of lemon sole en papillotte with Thai herbs & lemon butter), local organic vegetables and Ardsallagh goats cheese. Children are welcome (under 4 free in parents' room; cot available without charge; children's playground, baby sitting arranged). **Rooms 6** (all en-suite and no smoking, 4 shower only, 1 for disabled). B&B €50 pps, ss €10. Restaurant **seats 22.** D Thu-Sat, 7-9.30. Set D €39.50; House wine €19.50; sc discretionary. Closed Sun-Wed, 24-28 Dec. Amex, MasterCard, Visa, Laser. **Directions:** Take the main Killarney road R672 from Dungarvan, second turn left first house on right.

Dungarvan

★ RESTAURANT

The Tannery Restaurant

10 Quay Street Dungarvan Co Waterford **Tel: 058 45420**
Fax: 058 45518 Email: tannery@cablesurf.com

RESTAURANT OF THE YEAR

Paul and Maire Flynn's stylish contemporary restaurant has put Dungarvan firmly on the culinary map in recent years, making it a destination for discerning diners from all over Ireland (and beyond). It is in an old leather warehouse, imaginatively converted a few years ago so that Paul and his team can be seen at work in the open kitchen as guests arrive - and, perhaps, have an aperitif in the little bar/reception area before going upstairs to the first-floor dining area. The tannery theme is imaginatively echoed throughout the light, clean-lined interior, creating a sense of history that, along with dramatic paintings and fresh flowers, adds greatly to the atmosphere. Menus are wonderfully simple, written with a confidence that transfers to the hungry guest: you just know that every dish will be an experience. While inspired to some extent by global trends and regional cooking - particularly of the Mediterranean countries - cooking is based mainly on local ingredients, which Paul supports avidly and sources with care: local seafood stars in Mediterranean fish soup, for example - and in a speciality gratin of crayfish and asparagus, which comes with a tomato and avocado salsa. Pork and bacon supplied by local butcher JD Power are rightly a source of pride (in a delectable frisée and bacon salad with parmesan crisp and warm poached egg, perhaps) and meatless magic is also there for the tasting in, for example, a provençal vegetable tart, made with filo pastry and served with rocket and basil mash. Dashing desserts are invariably (very) tempting, and often appealingly simple - pannacotta is a speciality, for example, and anyone who despairs of the way trifle has been presented to the dining public in recent decades should not miss Paul's rendition of raspberry trifle. But the farmhouse cheese selection is equally unmissable: a carefully balanced selection is presented in perfect condition with oatcakes and chutney. The à la carte is fairly priced for food of this quality, but interesting and frequently changed lunch and early evening menus are outstandingly good value. The ambience, attentive and efficient service under Maire's direction, an interesting and kindly priced wine list - and, above all, Paul's exceptional cooking - make for memorable meals at The Tannery, a very fine winner of our Restaurant of the Year for 2004. Toilets wheelchair accessible. Children welcome before 8.30pm. **Seats 52** (private room up to 28, wheelchair accessible). L Tue-Sun, 12.30-2.15; D Tue-Sat (also Sun in Jul & Aug), 6.30-9.30. Early D €24 (Tue-Fri, 6.30-7.30); Set Sun L €24; house wine €18; sc discretionary (10% on parties of 6+). Closed late Jan-early Feb & 1st week Sep. Amex, Diners, MasterCard, Visa, Laser. **Directions:** End of lower main street beside old market house.

Dungarvan Area

FARMHOUSE / B&B

Gortnadiha House

Ring Dungarvan Co Waterford **Tel: 058 46142**
Email: ringcheese@tinet.ie

Eileen and Thomas Harty's home is on a working dairy farm in a lovely setting, with woodland gardens and sea views. Accommodation in the family home is comfortable, hospitality is warm and breakfasts offer a very wide selection of local and home produce, including fresh fish in season. Children welcome (under 5 free in parents' room, cot available without charge, baby sitting arranged). Pets permitted. [* 'Sometime soon', the Hartys are planning to exchange houses with their son, who lives nearby; no definite date has been decided but, while the accommodation will be more modern (the house was purpose-built, with all rooms en-suite), Eileen's hospitality will remain unchanged.] **Rooms 3** (2 shower only). B&B €40 pps, ss €5. Closed Nov-Mar. Visa. **Directions:** N25 Rosslare to Cork, 3 km from Dungarvan: follow the sea.

Lismore

HOTEL

Ballyrafter Country House Hotel

Lismore Co Waterford **Tel: 058 54002** Fax: 058 53050
Email: info@waterfordhotel.com Web: ballyrafter@waterfordhotel.com

Fishing is a big draw to Joe & Noreen Willoughby's welcoming country house hotel, but a relaxing atmosphere, log fires and good home cooking also appeal to a growing number of people who simply enjoy the area and have come to see the unpretentious comforts of Ballyrafter as a home from home. The bar, where informal meals are served, is lined with photographs of happy fisherfolk - if you are dining in the restaurant, you can have an aperitif here while looking at the menu, or beside the fire in the drawing room next door. Bedrooms in the main house are simple and comfortable and one side of the the courtyard area at the back of the hotel has been thoughtfully developed to provide five new executive bedrooms, all carefully designed to replicate the older ones. (New PVC windows were installed for practical reasons, but they were carefully sourced to match existing sash windows); there is also a large new first floor room which could be used as a boardroom or for small functions and, on the ground floor, the existing function area overlooking the yard has been completely rebuilt as a conservatory, which allows light through to the bar and transforms that section of the hotel. **Rooms 14** (5 shower only). B&B about €51 pps, ss about €20. Closed Dec-Feb.

Restaurant: An open fire, family antiques and flowers from the garden create a caring atmosphere in the restaurant and the Duke of Devonshire's fairytale castle looks magical from window tables when floodlit at night. Appetising home-cooked meals are based on local ingredients including, of course, fresh and smoked Blackwater salmon, along with home-produced honey and local cheeses like Knockanore, and service is friendly and helpful. **Seats 30.** D 7.30-9.30 daily (Mon residents only); Set D about €32; L Sun only 1-3 pm, Set L about €17. House Wine: about €14; 10% sc. Bar Meals 12-6.30 daily, L 1-2.30. Closed Dec-Mar. Amex, Diners, MasterCard, Visa. **Directions:** On the edge of Lismore town, from Cappoquin direction. ◇

Lismore Area

Buggys Glencairn Inn

féile bia ATMOSPHERIC PUB / B&B RESTAURANT

Glencairn Lismore Co Waterford
Tel: 058 56232 Fax: 058 56232
Email: Buggys@lismore.com Web: www.lismore.com

Ken and Cathleen Buggy's dream of a country pub just oozes character throughout - everything, from the little fire-lit bar to the beckoning old-world bedrooms, is full of charm. Ken is a talented artist - his delightfully quirky drawings have become symbolic of the West Waterford hospitality scene - but his artlessly rustic food (he describes it as "non-gourmet") is the main attraction here. Everything in this miniscule pub is based on top quality fresh ingredients and "made on the day" so be prepared for limited choice, especially towards the end of service. There's no particular statement about local produce but you'll usually notice sources mentioned in the descriptions of many of the dishes; up to six are offered on each course, and food is served in the bar as well as two little dining rooms charmingly set up with a stylish country informality. Paté de campagne is a favourite starter, full of texture and rich flavours, or there's something less usual like smoked eel, with horseradish sauce and salad (all served with home-made brown soda bread); this could be followed by fish (from Helvick) as available on the day - cooked simply in butter, olive oil and lemon juice - or pot-roasted guinea fowl with wild herbs and apples, all served with crisp little home-made chips, vegetable of the day and a side salad. Finish up with something like fresh lime and lemon pie (with home-made ice cream), or farmhouse cheeses (Durrus, Milleens, Carrigaline, Cashel Blue & Dubliner), then cafetière coffee or an Irish coffee in the bar. An unusual wine list is assembled on individual inserts in a business card index book, a flexible system that allows for weekly changes: brilliant. Cathleen supervises the restaurant and service is both charming and efficient. Upstairs there are five delightful en-suite rooms, all no smoking (€60 pps). Not suitable for children under 12. **Seats 30.** D daily in summer, 7.30-9, Wed-Sun in winter; à la carte; house wine €17.95; SC 10%. Closed Mon & Tue off season, Christmas period & occasionally throughout the year. (Times of opening are somewhat flexible - a phone call ahead is wise, especially off season; dinner reservations strongly advised).*Traditional 4-bedroom cottage also available, for self-catering. MasterCard, Visa, Laser, Switch. **Directions:** Between Tallow & Lismore.

Millstreet

The Castle Country House

FARMHOUSE

Millstreet Dungarvan Co Waterford **Tel: 058 68049** Fax: 058 68049
Email: castlefm@iol.ie Web: www.castlecountryhouse.com

Set in 1.5 acres of recently landscaped gardens overlooking the River Finisk, the Nugent family's unusual farmhouse is in the 18th century wing of a 16th century castle. Although most of the house seems quite normal inside, it blends into the original building in places - so, for example, the dining room has walls five feet deep and an original castle archway. Spacious, comfortably appointed rooms have king size beds, television, tea/coffee facilities and neat shower rooms; (there is also a full bathroom available for any guest who prefers a bath). Meticulous housekeeping, a very pleasant guests' sitting room and fresh flowers everywhere all add up to a very appealing farmhouse indeed, and Joan uses their own produce

- fruit, vegetables, meats and herbs - in her cooking. Excellent breakfasts. Children welcome (under 3 free in parents' room, cot available without charge, baby sitting arranged). Pets permitted.Garden, walking, fishing. **Rooms 5** (all en-suite). B&B €40-45 pps, ss €15. Dining Room Seats 20; Residents D €25. Closed 1 Nov-1 Mar. MasterCard, Visa. **Directions:** Off N72 on R671.

Tallowbridge

The Brideview Bar

PUB / RESTAURANT

Tallowbridge Co Waterford **Tel: 058 56522** Fax: 058 56729

This attractive bar and restaurant is beautifully located just outside Tallow, beside an old stone bridge over the River Bride and with parking space in a yard beside the pub. Recent extensions and renovations have kept some character in the older bar - which is along the road side of the building and has an open fire - while creating a fine informal dining space with large windows maximising on views over the river and a large garden and apple orchard which is well away from the road, with picnic tables set up for sunny days. Menus are not over-ambitious and change weekly (plus daily blackboard specials); the emphasis is on providing home-cooked food and good value. Home-cooked bar food is available all day, making this a useful place to know if you are touring or walking in the area. Children welcome. Food available daily, 12.30-9. (restaurant more limited hours) Closed 25-26 Dec & Good Fri. Amex, MasterCard, Visa, Laser. **Directions:** Near Tallow on N72 12 miles Fermoy - 3 Lismore.

Touraneena

Sliabh gCua Farmhouse

Ⓝ FARMHOUSE

Touraneena Ballinamult Dungarvan Co Waterford **Tel: 058 47120**
Email: breedacullinan@sliabhgcua.com Web: www.sliabhgcua.com

Breeda Cullinan's lovely creeper-clad farmhouse is in a beautiful area for lovers of the rural life; it is not as old or as large as it looks, but it was built with the classical proportions that create handsome, light-filled rooms, and has a happy atmosphere. Bedrooms, individually furnished and decorated with great care by Breeda, are very comfortable and have tea/coffee making facilities - and wholesome food, based on fresh farm produce, is served in a lovely dining room overlooking the garden: there are home-made cereals, fruit salads, freshly baked breads, local cheeses and hot cooked dishes to set guests up for the day. Children welcome (under 3 free in parents' room, cot available without charge, baby sitting arranged, playground). Walking; garden. **Rooms 4** (all en-suite, shower-only & no smoking). B&B €35, ss €10. Closed Nov-Mar. **Directions:** 16km off the N25, signposted on main Dungarvan- Clonmel Road (R672).

Tramore

Coast Restaurant

Ⓝ RESTAURANT

Upper Branch Road Tramore Co Waterford
Tel: 051 393646 Fax: 051 393647
Email: coastrestaurant@eircom.net Web: www.coast.ie

Renovation work on Turlough McNamara and Jenny McNally's fine restaurant was still on-going at the time of the Guide's visit and there are plans to have accommodation and an outside dining terrace in place for the 2004 season. Meanwhile, the existing restaurant is impressive, with a lovely bar area for pre-dinner drinks and an attractive dining room which overlooks Tramore - and uses mirrors well to maximise on this natural asset; polished tables are well-appointed, with linen napkins, lovely plates and fine glasses. Excellent breads are served with a choice of dips (pesto & sundried tomato), and Jenny McNally's well-balanced à la carte menus offer a choice of six to eight dishes on each course, with a strong emphasis on seafood (presumably local, although not stated on the menu). The cooking style is modern - seen in an outstanding starter of fresh chorizo with polenta cake & tomato cream, for example, and a main course of cod fillet with a garlic & parsley crust and warm olive oil mayonnaise, served with baby potatoes & wilted spinach. Angus beef, lamb and corn-fed chicken may be among other choices - and vegetarian dishes, such as home-made ravioli stuffed with mushroom duxelle, with mushroom cream, truffle oil and shaved parmesan, are very tempting. Finish with a gorgeous dessert like iced berries with a hot white chocolate sauce - and a delicious Illy coffee. Cooking is confident, flavours well-judged and presentation excellent: in short, this is a gem of a restaurant that will light up the south-east. An otherwise interesting wine list offers no house wine - and only one bottle under €20; (haphazard wine service was also the only negative on the Guide's visit). **Seats 45** (private room 20). D Tue-Sun 6.30-10 (D Sun Jul-Aug & bank hol weekends only), L Sun 1-3 & bank hols. Amex, MasterCard, Visa, Laser. **Directions:** First turn right after main roundabout.

Tramore

Rockett's of "The Metal Man"

ATMOSPHERIC PUB

Westown Tramore Co Waterford
Tel: 051 381496 Fax: 051 391125
Email: Rocketts@iolfree.ie Web: www.RockettsforRibs.com

Open fires and a friendly, welcoming atmosphere will always draw you into this unusual pub but it's the speciality of the house, Crubeens (pig's trotters) which has earned it fame throughout the land.

Crubeens (cruibíns) were once the staple bar food in pubs everywhere in Ireland but, as they've been supplanted by crisps, peanuts and lasagne & chips, Rockett's is one of the few places to keep up the old tradition. Two bars are set up with tables for the comfortable consumption of these porcine treats - and you can forget about finger bowls here: the back room even has a sink in the corner for rinsing sticky fingers! Other traditional foods like boiled bacon & cabbage, spare ribs, colcannon and apple pie are also very much on the menu at Rockett's - and all prepared freshly. Food served in summer (Jun-Oct): Tue-Sat 6-9.30 pm & Sun 1-7 (Oct-May: Wed-Sun). Closed Mon. A phone call is advised to check times off-season. Closed 25 Dec & Good Fri. MasterCard, Visa, Laser. **Directions:** From Waterford, straight through Tramore, one mile far side.

Waterford

Bodega!

Ⓝ **RESTAURANT / WINE BAR**

54 John St Waterford Co Waterford
Tel: 051 844177 Fax: 051 384868
Email: cormac_cronin@hotmail.com Web: www.bodegawaterford.com

With its warm Mediterranean colours, this place would bring the sun out on the darkest of days: pine tables, covered with the occasional oilcloth, a mix'n'match collection of seating - sofas, wooden chars, fashionable high-backs and some pretty basic high stools bask in a sea of golden light. And the food isn't half bad either: here's a talented French chef using fresh local ingredients with imagination in a relaxed setting, and the lucky locals are lapping it up. There's a written menu offering everything from soup of the day to steaks - or fresh foie gras, pan-fried with truffle and walnut oil, and paté de campagne (€12.50)... There are also blackboard specials, which are likely to be the best bet - and friendly staff are well-informed to advise. Duck and pork rillettes, for example, come well recommended and prove a winner, served with an excellent relish, and the same is true of chicken breast Provençal: well-cooked, well presented and well flavoured. At lunch time the place fills up with young people, some with children - who are made especially welcome - and there are lots of regulars. Dinner is a little more structured - and the prices heat up too, with main courses like pan-fried scallops with julienne vegetables, roast fennel & a mussel jus clocking in at well over €20. Wide choice of wines by the glass. What you get here is good food and good fun - Bodéga! is so cool that it's hot. **Seats 60** (private room 18). L Mon-Sat 12.30-2.30, D Mon-Sat 6.30-10 (Mon to 9.30). A la carte. House wine €16.50-18. SC discretionary. Closed Sun. Amex, MasterCard, Visa, Laser, Switch. **Directions:** A few doors down from the Applemarket, in city centre.

Waterford

Chez K's Steak & Seafood Restaurant

RESTAURANT

20-22 William Street Waterford Co Waterford
Tel: 051 844180 Fax: 051 844520
Email: info@chez-ks.com Web: www.chez-ks.com

This popular steak and seafood restaurant moved to a stylish new home in 2003 and has now acquired a lot of things lacking in the previous premises: it's an appealing restaurant, with an open kitchen and well-spaced polished tables attractively set up with linen napkins, good glasses and cutlery and fresh flowers - and there's a small bar area where you can look over head chef Conor Foran's interesting menus (plus nightly specials) before going to your table. The food is good - specialities worth looking out for include smoked haddock & mussel chowder and lemon sole on a bed of peperonata, with tartare cream & basil mash - and staff are charming and friendly. On the downside, service seems to be disorganised, causing confusion and delays - a pity as both ingredients and cooking have class, the surroundings are pleasing - and there's also a well thought out wine list; it is to be hoped that glitches on the service side can be smoothed out to enable this restaurant reach its considerable potential during 2004. **Seats 114.** D daily 6-11, L Sun only 12.30-3.30. D à la carte, Set Sun L €24. MasterCard, Visa, Laser. **Directions:** Left at traffic lights at Tower Hotel- on the left 400m.

Waterford

Henry Downes

PUB

8-10 Thomas St Waterford**Tel: 051 874 118**

Established in 1759, and in the same (eccentric) family for six generations, John de Bromhead's unusual pub is one of the few remaining houses to bottle its own whiskey. Although not the easiest of places to find, once visited it certainly will not be forgotten. Large, dark and cavernous – with a squash court on the premises as well as the more predictable billiards and snooker – it consists of a series of bars of differing character, each with its own particular following. It achieves with natural grace what so-called Irish theme pubs would dearly love to capture (and can't). Friendly, humorous bar staff enjoy filling customers in on the pub's proud history – and will gladly sell you a bottle of Henry Downes No.9 to take away. Wine about €9 (to drink in pub). Open from 4.30pm to normal closing time. Closed 25 Dec & Good Fri. **No credit cards. Directions:** Second right after Bridge Hotel, halfway up Thomas Street on right.

Waterford

Dwyers Restaurant

féile bia RESTAURANT

8 Mary Street Waterford Co Waterford
Tel: 051 877478 Fax: 051 877480
Email: info@dwyersrestaurant.com Web: www.dwyersrestaurant.com

Quietly located in an elegantly converted old barracks, chef-proprietor Martin Dwyer and his wife Sile have been running this highly regarded restaurant since 1989 - the Clive Nunn designed refurbishments have more recently introduced a classy contemporary tone to the decor. Without show or fuss, they consistently provide excellence: low-key presentation of some of the country's finest food is invariably accompanied by discreet, thoughtful service. Martin carefully sources the best seasonal local produce which he prepares in a style that is basically classic French, with some country French and modern Irish influences. He sums up his philosophy with admirable simplicity: "We feel that the basis of good food is taste rather than presentation or fashion". Menus change monthly and main courses lean towards seafood – seared fillet of salmon with Escoffier's walnut & horseradish relish, and scallops Torrades with crisped bacon, whiskey and cream would both be typical – but there are strong choices for carnivores and vegetarians too. Classic desserts are well worth leaving room for (rhubarb ice cream with ginger is a speciality), and there's always an Irish cheese plate. Espresso and herbal teas are offered as well as regular cafetière coffee and tea. Like the cooking, the wine list favours France, although Spain, Italy, Germany and the New World are also represented. The early evening menu is particularly good value. Children welcome before 8 pm. **Seats 32** (private room, 8). D Mon-Sat,6-10; early D €27.50 (6-7); à la carte also available; house wine €18.50; sc discretionary. No private parking. Toilets wheelchair accessible. Closed Sun, Christmas week & bank hols. Amex, Diners, MasterCard, Visa, Laser. **Directions:** 25 yards south of Bridge, turn right into Mary Street.

Waterford

Foxmount Farm & Country House

COUNTRY HOUSE / FARMHOUSE

Passage East Rd Waterford Co Waterford
Tel: 051 874 308 Fax: 051 854 906
Email: Info@foxmountcountryhouse.com Web: www.foxmountcountryhouse.com

Foxmount Farm, the Kent family's 17th century country house and working dairy farm, is just 15 minutes drive from the centre of Waterford city. The house is lovely, with classically proportioned reception rooms, and it is a haven of peace and tranquillity. Margaret Kent's home-cooked food is one of the main reasons guests keep returning to Foxmount - dinner, prepared by her personally and based on the farm's own produce, is available for residents by arrangement; vegetarian or other special dietary requirements can be built into menus if mentioned on booking. Margaret is a great baker, as guests quickly discover when she serves afternoon tea in the drawing room (or in the morning, when freshly-baked breads are presented at breakfast). Five very different rooms are all thoughtfully furnished, but bear in mind that peace and relaxation are the aim at Foxmount, so don't expect phones or TVs in bedrooms or a very early breakfast. There is a hard tennis court on the premises (plus table tennis). Children welcome, pets by arrangement. **Rooms 5** (all en-suite & no-smoking). B&B €50 pps, ss 15. Residents' D €30, at 7pm (book by noon). BYO wine. Closed 1 Nov-10 Mar. **No Credit Cards. Directions:** From Waterford city, take Dunmore Road - after 4 km, take Passage East road for 1 mile.

Waterford

Gatchell's Restaurant

féile bia RESTAURANT

Waterford Crystal Visitor Centre Kilbarry Waterford Co Waterford
Tel: 051 332575 Fax: 051 332561
Email: visitorreception@waterford.ie Web: www.waterfordvisitorcentre.com

If you intend visiting the Waterford Crystal Visitor Centre it could be useful to know that a tasty bite to eat can be part of the plan. Well-known Waterford restaurateur, Paula Prendiville, runs this stylish all-day restaurant at the centre - and don't be put off by the fact that it's self-service, as Paula cooks interesting, wholesome fare based on local produce, albeit with some international themes (and, due to the high turnover, a few dishes may sometimes be bought in). Irish potato & coriander soup, prawn pasta & pineapple salad and fresh salmon salad are all typical home-cooked fare - and visitors who despair of ever finding traditional Irish food in the current tidal wave of global cooking will be pleased to see dishes with a respect for tradition here, such as Murphys Irish beef. Seats 160. Children welcome. Open daily 8.30am-5.30 (in winter 9-5). A la carte (average main course about €9). House wine about €12. Closed 21 Dec-2 Jan. Amex, Diners, MasterCard, Visa, Laser. **Directions:** Waterford Crystal Visitor Centre.

Waterford

The Gingerman Bar

féile bia PUB 6/7 Arundel Lane Waterford Co Waterford **Tel: 051 879522** Fax: 051 879522

Michael Tierney's renovated pub is in the old Norman area of the city, in a pedestrianised lane just off Broad Street. It can be very busy but, at quieter times it's a very pleasant place, with welcoming open fires in several bars, and a commitment to serving good food. Open 10am-11.30pm. Food served Mon-Sat, 12-6. No food on Sun. Closed 25 Dec, Good Fri. Amex, Diners, MasterCard, Visa, Laser, Switch. **Directions:** Off John Roberts Square. ◇

Waterford

Goose's Barbecue Restaurant

RESTAURANT 19 Henrietta Street Waterford Co Waterford
Tel: 051 858426 Fax: 051 858426

Here, in an historic site (the details of which are given on the menu), the aim is to provide high quality at a reasonable price, so a self-service salad buffet keeps costs down - and all the main meals are freshly prepared when you order them and cooked in view of customers. There are little starters like cajun chicken wings and saucy sausages and main dishes like boozy beef steaks and medallions of lamb barbecued with rosemary & herbs, served with jacket potato. Vegetarians can have mixed veg & tofu skewers and there's a blackboard giving the fish of the night and desserts. Not suitable for children after 7pm. **Seats 40.** D Tue-Sat, 6-'late'. à la carte (average main course €16-18). House wine €18. Closed Sun, Mon, 1 week in winter, 1 week in summer. MasterCard, Visa, Laser. **Directions:** Across from Plaza on the quay.

Waterford

Granville Hotel

féile bia HOTEL The Quay Waterford Co Waterford **Tel: 051 305 555** Fax: 051 305 566
Email: stay@granville-hotel.ie Web: www.granville.hotel.ie

One of the country's oldest hotels, this much-loved quayside establishment in the centre of Waterford has many historical connections - with Bianconi, for example, who established Ireland's earliest transport system, and also Charles Stuart Parnell, who made many a rousing speech here. Since 1979, it's been owner-run by the Cusack family, who have overseen significant restoration and major refurbishment. It's a large hotel - bigger than it looks perhaps - with fine public areas and well-appointed bedrooms (all with well-designed bathrooms with both bath and shower). This is a good choice for business guests and would also make a comfortable base for touring the area or participating in the many activities available locally, including boating, fishing, golf, walking and horse riding. Off season value breaks available. Conference/banqueting (200/200), secretarial services. Parking nearby. Children welcome (under 3s free in parents' room; cots available without charge). No pets. **Rooms 98** (3 suites, 50 executive rooms, 20 no-smoking). Lift. B&B €70 pps, ss €20. Closed 25-26 Dec. Amex, Diners, MasterCard, Visa. **Directions:** In city centre, on the quays opposite Clock Tower.

Waterford

Tower Hotel Waterford

HOTEL The Mall Waterford Co Waterford **Tel: 051 875801** Fax: 051 870 129
Email: reservations@the.ie Web: www.towerhotelwaterford.com

A central location, within easy walking distance of everything in the city, ample private parking, large conference/banqueting capacity and excellent on-site leisure facilities are major attractions at this big hotel. Considerable investment over the last few years has seen an improvement in standards throughout the hotel: an impressive new bistro, a carvery restaurant and a new state of the art conference centre are all quite recent additions and the lobby and reception area have been renovated. However, refurbishment is still on-going at the time of going to press and some bedrooms may not yet have been completed - it is worth checking on this when making a reservation as there is a big difference between old and new rooms. Conference/banqueting facilities (450/350). Leisure Centre, indoor swimming pool. Children welcome (cots available free of charge). Own parking. No pets. **Rooms 140** (3 suites, 3 executive, 3 for disabled). Lift. B&B about €75 pps, ss about €40. Closed 24-27 Dec. Amex, Diners, MasterCard, Visa, Laser, Switch. **Directions:** Waterford city centre overlooking the marina. ◇

Waterford

Waterford Castle Hotel & Golf Club

HOTEL The Island Ballinakill Waterford Co Waterford **Tel: 051 878 203** Fax: 051 879 316
Email: info@waterfordcastle.com Web: www.waterfordcastle.com

This beautiful hotel dates back to the 15th century. It is uniquely situated on its own 310 acre wooded island (complete with 18-hole golf course) and is reached by a private ferry. The hotel combines the elegance of earlier times with modern comfort, service and convenience - and the location is uniquely serene. Its quietness (and the golf facility for off-duty relaxation) makes the castle a good venue for small conferences and business meetings, but it is also a highly romantic location and perfect for small weddings. All guest rooms have recently been refurbished and, although they inevitably vary in size and outlook, all are very comfortably furnished in a luxurious country house style. There are plans to extend the accommodation and add a health spa in 2004. Conference/banqueting (30/70). Golf, fishing, tennis, walking. Children welcome (under 4 free in parents' room; cots available). No Pets. **Rooms 19** (5 suites, 14 en-suite) Lift. Room rate €325 (2 guests). 24 hour room service. Closed Jan.

Munster Room: This beautiful dining room is appointed to the highest standard and head chef Michael Quinn and a fine kitchen brigade will provide the food to match: menus are peppered with luxurious ingredients like lobster, foie gras, scallops, prawns, black sole, aged Irish beef and game, such as wild Irish venison; local produce is used as much as possible, including organic vegetables, and the cooking, in a modern classical style, is excellent. A set dinner menu is offered, but considerately priced by course, allowing for a semi à la carte selection. **Seats 60.** D daily, from 7pm; Set D €58. L Sun only €30. House wines €25-30. MasterCard, Visa, Laser. **Directions:** Outskirts of Waterford City just off Dunmore East road.

Waterford

The Wine Vault

féile bia RESTAURANT

High Street Waterford Co Waterford **Tel: 051 853 444**
Fax: 051 853 784 Email: wineshop@waterfordwinevault.com
Web: www.waterfordwinevault.com

Situated in the medieval part of the city, in an 18th century bonded warehouse with the remains of a 15th century tower house, David Dennison's informal little wine bar and restaurant includes a vaulted wine merchant's premises, and has great atmosphere. A new (laminated) menu was introduced just after the Guide's most recent visit; in contrast to previous menus, which were brief, with a 'daily' feel and blackboard extras, the new menu is quite extensive and more 'popular', with pizzas and grills taking centre stage. However it remains quality ingredient led and is sprinkled encouragingly with the names of artisan products - Ardsallagh goats cheese, Gubbeen bacon, Fingal Ferguson salami - and other well sourced ingredients include local and Quality Assured beef, pork, eggs and poultry. And, of course, you can always rely on wine-man David to ensure a great choice of bottles for every conceivable occasion. Toilets wheelchair accessible. Children welcome **Seats 60** (private room 28). L& D Mon-Sat, 12.30-2.30 & 5-10.30 Set L €10; early D €14.50 (5-7.30 only), otherwise a la carte. House wines (20) €1-€23. sc discretionary. Closed Sun (except bank hol weekends), 25-26 Dec, Good Fri. Amex, MasterCard, Visa, Laser. **Directions:** Take right turn off quay - City Square car park. Take next left to High Street.

Waterford Area

Faithlegg House Hotel

HOTEL

Faithlegg Co Waterford **Tel: 051 382000** Fax: 051 382010
Email: reservations@fhh.ie Web: www.faithlegg.com

This lovely 18th century house is set in wooded landscape with magnificent views over its own golf course and the Suir estuary. The house has been sensitively developed as a luxury hotel - the tone is set in the reception area, with its original stone floor, classic fireplace and Waterford Crystal chandelier and a similar sensitivity to the essentials of conversion is evident throughout. Public areas are spacious and elegant and bedrooms, in both the old house and a discreetly positioned new wing, are furnished to a high standard with excellent facilities, including ISDN lines; large, graciously proportioned rooms and suites in the old house are really lovely, while those in the new wing are more practical. (Self-catering accommodation is also offered in the grounds.) Numerous health, fitness and beauty treatments are available in the more recently added leisure centre, which has a 17m swimming pool. Conference/banqueting (180/140); secretarial services. Ample parking. Golf (18), fishing, tennis, gardens, walking; leisure centre, swimming pool; snooker. Children welcome (under 3s free in parents' room; cots available without charge). No pets. **Rooms 82** (14 suites, 14 executive, 10 no-smoking, 6 for disabled). Lift. B&B from about €90 pps, ss about €25. Weekend specials offered. Closed Christmas.

Roseville Rooms: The bar is comfortably furnished in a clubby style - a good place to have an aperitif and look at the menu; orders may be taken here and you will be called through when your table is ready. Chef de Cuisine Eric Thèze's classic French menus change daily, which is ideal for residents staying for several nights, and offers a balanced choice of about four on each course. Rosette of local smoked salmon with lemon, caper, red onion and crème fraîche, cream of asparagus soup (or champagne sorbet); sautéed noisette of venison sauce vigneronne with red wine pear; and marinated strawberries in balsamic syrup flavoured with fresh mint and vanilla ice cream give a fair indication of the style. The restaurant is shared between two lovely classical, formally appointed dining rooms and cooking is reliable, although service can be a little uneven, notably on busy nights. **Seats 80** (private room 40). Not suitable for children after 7pm. D daily, 6.30-9.30; L 12.30-2.30. Set menu €42, House wines from €18. Amex, Diners, MasterCard, Visa, Laser. **Directions:** Off Dunmore East Road 6 miles from Waterford city. ◇

COUNTY WESTMEATH

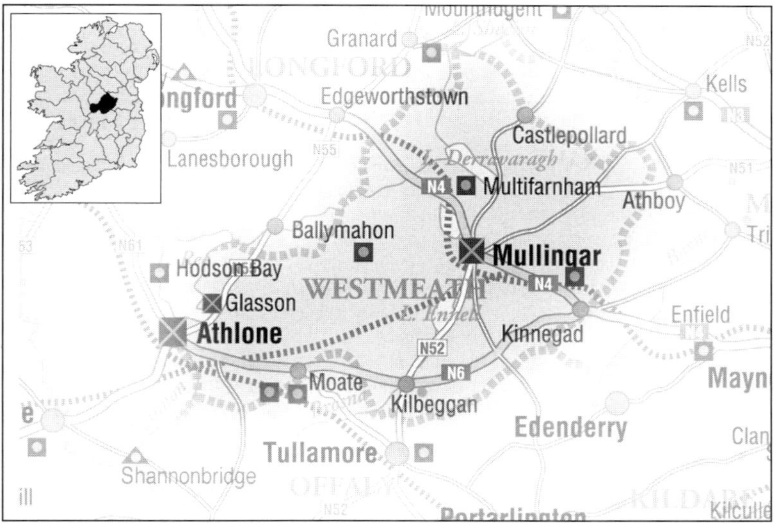

As its name suggests, in the distant past Westmeath tended to be ruled by whoever held Meath. But today, Westmeath is a county so cheerfully and successfully developing its own identity that perhaps they should find a completely new name for the place. For this is somewhere that makes the very best of what it has to hand.

Its highest "peak" is only the modest Mullaghmeen of 258 m, 10 kilometres north of Castlepollard. But this is in an area where hills of ordinary height have impressive shapes which make them appear like miniature mountains around the spectacularly beautiful Lough Derravaragh, famed for its association with the legend of the Children of Lir, who were turned into swans by their wicked step-mother Aoife, and remained as swans for 900 years until saved by the coming of Christianity.

Westmeath abounds in lakes to complement Derravaragh, such as the handsome expanses of Lough Owel and Lough Ennell on either side of the fine county town of Mullingar, where they've been making life even more watery in recent years with schemes to speed the restoration of the Royal Canal on its way through town from Dublin to the north Shannon.

Meanwhile, Athlone to the west is confidently developing as one of Ireland's main inland river towns, its Shannonside prosperity based on its riverside location and a useful mixture of electronics, pharmaceuticals and the healthcare industry.

Despite such modern trends, this remains a very rural place - immediately south of the town, you can hear the haunting call of the corncrake coming across the callows (water meadows). But Athlone itself has a real buzz, particularly in the compact area around the old castle by the west bank quayside. And north of it, there's Lough Ree in all its glory, wonderful for boating in an area where, near the delightful village of Glasson, the Goldsmith country verges towards County Longford, and they have a monument to mark what some enthusiasts reckon to be the true geographical centre of all Ireland. You really can't get more utterly rural than that.

Local Attractions and Information

Athlone, All Ireland Amateur Drama Festival (May)	090 647 3358
Athlone, Athlone Castle Visitor Centre	090 649 2912
Athlone, River Festivals	090 649 4981
Athlone, Tourism Information	090 649 4630
Ballykeeran, MV Goldsmith Lake & River Cruises	090 648 5163
Castlepollard, Tullynally Castle & Gardens	044 49060
Clonmellon, Ballinlough Castle Gardens	046 943 3135
Glasson, Glasson Rose Festival (August)	090 648 5677
Kilbegggan, Locke's Distillery Museum	0506 32134
Kilbeggan, Race Course	0506 32176

Athlone

ATHLONE

This bustling, youthful centre town of Ireland has much of historical interest - and, although other towns along the mighty Shannon will no doubt be keen to mount a challenge, Athlone is presently the culinary capital of the inland waterways, with a cluster of good eating places in the town itself and surrounding area. Too many, in fact, to mention here, but they include the leisurely **Manifesto (0902 73241),** a cool first floor restaurant (and night club) on the east side of the bridge and, nearby, the entertaining pub and informal restaurant mix of **Gertie Browne's (0902 74848)** pub and its restaurant **Hatter's Lane Bistro (0902 73077),** which is around the corner or down the stairs through the pub, depending on where you start off. Quality accommodation has been in shorter supply in the town than good restaurants in recent years, but The Prince of Wales Hotel is due to re-open in the centre of the town shortly after we go to press, after a complete re-build, and there are other hotel plans due to mature shortly. On the edge of town, **Creggan Court Hotel (Tel 0902 77777; www.creggancourt.com)** offers moderately priced accommodation and parking.

Athlone

Hodson Bay Hotel

féile bia HOTEL

Hodson Bay Athlone Co Westmeath **Tel: 090 644 2000** Fax: 090 644 2020
Email: info@hodsonbayhotel.com Web: www.hodsonbayhotel.com

This waterside hotel adjoins Athlone Golf Club on the western shores of Lough Ree, just four miles outside Athlone town. With lovely lake and island views and a wide range of leisure activities on site – including boating and fishing and a fine leisure centre – it's in great demand as a venue for both business and social occasions. It is the only establishment providing such facilities in the locality and, to meet the demand, it has grown considerably since opening in 1992. Bedrooms are bright and comfortable, with contemporary decor, well-finished en-suite bathrooms and double and single beds in most rooms; many also have lough views. If there is a downside, it is that the hotel is almost always so busy that it is difficult for maintenance and routine refurbishment to keep pace with ongoing wear and tear, especially in public areas - and, similarly, keeping food standards up to the high quality to which the hotel clearly aspires is a challenge which can be difficult to meet. Excellent banqueting/conference facilities (700/500); secretarial services, business centre; video conferencing. Helipad. Leisure centre, swimming pool; beauty salon. Golf (18), fishing, equestrian, tennis, walking, garden. Children welcome (under 2 free in parents' room; cots available without charge; baby sitting arranged; playroom, children's playground). No pets.* Weekend breaks and midweek activity breaks offered. **Rooms 133** (2 suites, 6 junior suites, 36 executive rooms, 1 for disabled). 2 Lifts. Room service (limited hours). B&B €110pps, ss €25. Informal food service all day; L'Escale Restaurant, L&D daily, by reservation. Open all year.

The restaurant is on the lake side of the hotel, well-appointed in traditional style. Head chef Tony Hanevy has been at the hotel since 1992 and food is generally above the usual expectation for hotels. In addition to the basic à la carte, daily set menus ensure variety for residents. While not adventurous, the quality of ingredients, cooking, presentation and service all ensure an acceptable meal. Expect popular dishes: steaks may be predictable but this is great beef country and they are well-cooked, with a choice of sauces. The seafood selection sometimes includes lobster, along with several fish. There is a short vegetarian menu and farmhouse cheese is always available in addition to traditional desserts. **Seats 150.** No smoking area; air conditioning. L 12.30-2.30 & D 7-9.30 daily. Set L €17, (Sun L €20), Set D €32, à la carte available, house wines from €17; sc discretionary. [Bar food available 10-9 daily). Open all year. Amex, Diners, MasterCard, Visa, Laser. **Directions:** Roscommon road (N61) - off N6 Athlone bypass.

Athlone

The Left Bank Bistro

RESTAURANT

Fry Place Athlone Co Westmeath **Tel: 090 649 4446** Fax: 090 649 4509
Email: info@leftbankbistro.com Web: www.leftbankbistro.com

Athlone has always been a great place to break the journey if you're travelling across the country, but it's much more than a handy stopover: now recognised as the culinary capital of the inland waterways, it has become a destination town for discerning travellers, whether by car or by boat. Annie McNamara and Mary McCullough's original, wacky little Left Bank Bistro was one of the cornerstones of that reputation - and their philosophy lives on in their elegant and spacious newer premises near the river. Here architectural salvage materials and interesting, subtle colours combine well with contemporary wooden furniture and a gently minimalist style to create a space which is both impressive and relaxing. Bare tables and paper napkins convey an informal atmosphere that suits their lively food: short, keenly-priced lunch menus - plus several extra lunch-time savoury dishes chalked up on a blackboard - offer a wide range of delicious-sounding dishes with the multi-cultural stamp which, together with carefully sourced ingredients and good cooking, make this the number one choice for an informal meal in Athlone. Wraps, bruschetta, focaccia feature a lot, especially on the lunch menu (try the tandoori chicken on focaccia), and accompanying salads and vegetables are always outstanding - colourful and full of zing. Fresh fish dishes have their own menu, and vegetarians can choose between blackboard specials and regular dishes from the menu, including Greek salad, Left Bank Salad (with a wedge of foccacia) and Vegetable Spring Rolls (or samosas). Dinner menus are more extensive and tend to be based on more expensive ingredients, but the style is similar and, here again, vegetarian dishes are especially attractive. After a choice of delicious desserts or farmhouse cheeses, dip into a nice little drinks menu that offers a range of coffees, teas and hot chocolate. **Seats 70.** Air conditioning. Wheelchair access. Open 10.30-9.30. L 12-5 & D 5.30-9.30 Tue-Sat; Midweek 2-3 course D, €21-25 (Tue-Thu, all evening), otherwise à la carte; main courses from about €8 (L), €19 (D); house wine €18. Closed Sun & Mon, bank hols & Christmas/New Year. Amex, MasterCard, Visa, Laser. **Directions:** Behind Athlone Castle, west side of the Shannon.

Athlone

Restaurant Le Chateau

féile bia **RESTAURANT**

St. Peter's Port The Docks Athlone Co Westmeath **Tel: 090 649 4517** Fax: 090 649 3040 Email: lechateau@eircom.net

Steven and Martina Linehan's quayside restaurant is in a converted Presbyterian Church, just west of the bridge, and it makes a two-storey restaurant of character which complements the couple's well-earned reputation for good food and hospitality. Designed around the joint themes of church and river, the upstairs section has raised floors at each end, like the deck of a galleon, while the church theme is reflected in the windows – notably an original "Star of David" at the back of the restaurant. Steven Linehan is a talented chef and, backed up by a well-trained staff, is providing a fine dining experience at formal meal times, notably their renowned Candlelight Dinners, when candles are used generously to create a relaxed, romantic atmosphere. Opening hours have been extensive during the last year or two, making it difficult to maintain the highest of standards all the time, but local produce is very much in evidence - notably Angus beef and rack of lamb - and, at its best, it is for real flavour, attention to detail and professional service that a meal at Le Chateau will be remembered. The cooking style is modern, with some international influences - but there is a welcome sense that the chef is in control rather than the fashion. The early dinner menu is popular locally, and very good value. Children welcome. **Seats 100** (private room, 20) Air conditioning. Open 12.30-10 daily: L 12.30-3 (Sun to 5.30), D 5.30-10; Set L €12, Set Sun L about €23, Early D about €23 (5.30-6.45 pm only); also à la carte; house wines from about €18.75; SC10%. Full bar. Closed Christmas. Amex, MasterCard, Visa, Laser. **Directions:** Heading west through Athlone, over Shannon and left at castle, left again and onto bank of Shannon. ◇

Athlone

Sean's Bar

ATMOSPHERIC PUB

13 Main Street Athlone Co Westmeath **Tel: 090 642 92358**

West of the river, in the interesting old town near the Norman castle (which has a particularly good visitors' centre for history and information on the area, including flora and fauna of the Shannon), Sean Fitzsimons' seriously historic bar lays claim to being the pub with the longest continuous use in Ireland – all owners since 900 AD are on record. (It has actually been certified by the National Museum as the oldest pub in Britain and Ireland - and the all-Europe title is currently under investigation.) Dimly-lit, with a fine mahogany bar, mirrored shelving, open fire and an enormous settle bed, the bar has become popular with the local student population and is very handy for visitors cruising the Shannon (who have direct access to the river through the back bar and beer garden). The sloping floor is a particularly interesting feature, cleverly constructed to ensure that flood water drained back down to the river as the waters subsided (it still works). A glass case containing a section of old wattle wall original to the building highlights the age of the bar, but it's far from being a museum piece. Food is restricted to sandwiches (Mon-Sat), but the proper priorities are observed and they serve a good pint. Closed 25 Dec & Good Fri. **Directions:** On the west quayside, just in front of the castle.

Athlone

The Olive Grove Restaurant

RESTAURANT

Bridge Street Custume Place Athlone Co Westmeath **Tel: 090 647 6946** Fax: 090 647 1248

Garry Hughes and Gael Bradbury opened their charming little restaurant in the autumn of 1997 and it is popular for its pleasant, informal atmosphere (seasoned with a good dash of style), excellent home-cooked food from noon until late (light food in the afternoon), good value and a great willingness to do anything which will ensure a good time being had by all. The cooking style is Mediterranean-influenced international and youthful – as seen in starters such as traditional Greek salad and lunchtime pastas like prosciutto & ricotta tortellini; vegetarians have particularly good choice here on both lunch and the more ambitious evening menus – although this is beef country and the speciality of the house has always been chargrilled steaks. The entire restaurant was refurbished in 2003, and more extensive new menus introduced - a kind of coming of age. Children welcome. Parking nearby. Seats 50. L &D Tue-Sun,12-4 & 5.30-10); à la carte (average main course about €10 (L); €18-20 (D); house wines €16.75, sc discretionary. Closed Mon, 24-28 Dec. Amex, MasterCard, Visa, Laser. **Directions:** Travelling from Dublin, take the left before the bridge in Athlone town centre.

Athlone Area

Glasson Golf Hotel & Country Club

HOTEL

Glasson Athlone Co Westmeath **Tel: 090 648 5120** Fax: 090 648 5444
Email: info@glassongolf.ie Web: www.glassongolf.ie

Beautifully situated in an elevated position overlooking Lough Ree, the Reid family's impressive new hotel has been developed around their fine old family home (now the clubhouse) and, despite the name, it will delight all discerning visitors to this lovely area equally. The golfing dimension pre-dated the hotel (Christy O'Connor Junior course) and has earned an international reputation as one of Ireland's premier inland courses, but the hotel is equally geared to business guests and those looking for peace and relaxation in beautiful surroundings. The hotel is bright and contemporary, with a welcoming atmosphere; guest rooms are spacious, thoughtfully furnished with the needs of business travellers in mind and decorated in an attractive modern style which is not over-designed and allows views over the lough and golf course to take centre stage. The bar and restaurant are in the clubhouse section of the hotel, and both have been refurbished in a more traditional style appropriate to the older building. There's also a private jetty between the 15th and 17th greens, where visiting cruisers coming to the hotel may berth, or residents can arrange a private cruise. The hotel has proved a welcome addition to the limited accommodation choice around Athlone and a great asset to the area. *A gym and beauty/therapy salon is due to open in April 2004. Conference/banqueting 150/120. Children welcome (under 5 free in parents' room, cots available without charge, baby sitting arranged). Walking, fishing. Garden. No pets. **Rooms 29** (1 junior suite, 12 executive, 1 disabled). Lift. B&B from €85pps, ss€50. Special breaks offered. Food available to non-residents all day (7.30am-10pm; hot food from 1pm). Closed 25-26 Dec. Amex, Diners, MasterCard, Visa, Laser. **Directions:** 6 miles north of Athlone on the N55 Cavan-Longford road.

Glasson

Glasson Village Restaurant

RESTAURANT

Glasson Co Westmeath **Tel: 090 648 5001**

In an attractive stone building which formerly served as an RIC barracks, chef-proprietor Michael Brooks opened the Village Restaurant in 1986, making his mark as a culinary pioneer in the area. On the edge of the village, there's a real country atmosphere about the place, enhanced by old pine furniture and a conservatory which is particularly pleasant for Sunday lunch. As has been the case since they opened, fresh fish features strongly on the menu – Michael takes pride in having introduced fresh seafood at a time when it wasn't popular locally, and aims to maintain the special reputation earned for fresh fish (including shellfish in season and freshwater fish like Lough Ree eel). His cooking has long set the standard for the area which, together with caring service under the supervision of Marie Brooks, who is restaurant manager, has earned the restaurant enduring popularity with a loyal following. The style is imaginative and fairly traditional – country French meets modern Irish perhaps; à la carte menus change with the seasons, set menus weekly and there are always a couple of vegetarian dishes. Consistent standards and good value are the hallmarks of this restaurant. Parking. Children welcome. **Seats 50.** D Tue -Sat 6-9.30; L Sun only 12.30-2.30. Set D €33.50, also à la carte; early D €23.50 (6-7pm only). Set Sun L €21. House wines €18-24; SC discretionary. Closed D Sun, all Mon, 3 weeks from mid Oct, 24-26 Dec. Amex, Diners, MasterCard, Visa, Laser. **Directions:** 5 miles from Athlone on Longford/Cavan road (N55).

Glasson

Grogan's Pub

ATMOSPHERIC PUB

Glasson Co Westmeath **Tel: 090 648 5158**

It's hard to cross the Midlands without being drawn into at least a short visit to this characterful pub in Goldsmith's "village of the roses". It's one of those proudly-run, traditional places with two little bars at the front (one with a welcome open fire in winter) and everything gleaming; it was established in 1750 and feels as if the fundamentals haven't changed too much since then. There's traditional music on Wednesday nights, when three generations of the same family play and visiting musicians are also welcome. Closed 25 Dec, Good Fri. Visa, MasterCard, Laser. **Directions:** Centre of village. ◇

Glasson

Wineport Lodge

féile bia RESTAURANT WITH ROOMS

Glasson Co Westmeath
Tel: 090 643 9010 Fax: 090 648 5471
Email: lodge@wineport.ie Web: www.wineport.ie

Ray Byrne and Jane English's lovely lakeside lodge styles itself 'Ireland's first wine hotel' - and their stunning new accommodation has certainly had great impact. A covered boardwalk in front of the restaurant brings you to the front door: you enter your guest key card and step into a different world. A lofty residents' lounge with a stove and its own bar simply oozes style and comfort, a hint of the high pamper quota waiting above in the ten spacious new bedrooms, all with private balconies overlooking the lake. Superbly comfortable beds with goose down duvets and extra large pillows face the view - a clear invitation to relax and take it all in. There's flat screen TV too, if the view is not enough, and you can even have a little drink courtesy of your hosts - Ray and Jane decided to build on the history of the townland of Wineport by naming each room after a wine or a region famous for its wine and including related artefacts in the decor - and a little taste of that particular wine to enjoy with your hosts' compliments! The careful planning, inspired design and attention to detail throughout is exceptional: seriously luxurious bathrooms have separate double-ended bath and walk-in shower, de-mist mirrors, underfloor heating and many little extras; complimentary drinks trays include individual cafetières - and fresh milk in the fridge; business guests will be delighted by the amount of state-of-the-art technology that is hidden discreetly away yet instantly accessible. Nothing has been overlooked - even the decor, which is designed around a palette of warm neutrals and natural materials, complements the view rather than distracting from it, and has universal appeal. Skilful use of a wide range of woods is perhaps the strongest design theme throughout and, not only is it a perfect complement to the natural backdrop, but Jane's brother, the cabinetmaker and designer Robert English, did all the woodwork for them. Wineport has a huge amount to offer discerning guests and has quickly become a hot choice for business and corporate events - every technological requirement has been thought of and one look at the first floor board room, which is also dramatically planned to take full advantage of the beautiful location, would sway anyone arranging a meeting. Luxurious, romantic, beautiful, businesslike, this boutique hotel is a place of many moods: Wineport has everything. * More accommodation and even more luxury is planned for 2005. **Rooms 10** (all no smoking; 1 for disabled, shower only). All day room service. Conference/banqueting (50/110). Video conferencing. Garden, fishing, walking. Massage. Children welcome (cots available). No pets. B&B €137.50pps, ss from €37.50; (single rate €175 available Sun-Thu); no SC.

Wineport Lodge: This lovely lakeside restaurant is almost a second home to many regulars guests. Its stunning location and exceptional hospitality draw guests back time and again – guests who return with additions to the now famous Wineport collections (nauticalia, cats) and find the combination of the view, the company and a good meal irresistible. Head chef Feargal O'Donnell is a member of Euro-Toques and presents strongly seasonal menus based on local ingredients including game in season, eels, home-grown herbs, free range eggs and wild mushrooms. However, the style is diverse - international, with an occasional nod to traditional Irish themes - so you could start a meal with crispy tiger prawn wontons, sweet chilli, lime & sesame jam and follow with dishes diverse as whole lobster & a selection of fresh fish with three sauces (for two to share) and seared Irish Angus beef, with sundried pepper & Auburn herb salsa (there's always at least one dish based on certified Irish Angus beef). Finish with an unusual seasonal dessert like smoked Abbey brie & walnut tart, with pear & pickled ginger compôte, perhaps as an alternative to an Irish Cheese Plate. Ray and Jane were the Guide's Hosts of the Year in 1999 - and Wineport was our Hideaway of the Year in 2003. **Seats 110** (private room, 60). Air conditioning. Children welcome. D daily 5.30-10 (Sun 5-9); L Mon-Fri, 12.30-2.30 (Sun 3-5). Set L €20. Set D from €30 (2-course), to €65; D also à la carte; house wine €19; sc discretionary. Closed 24-26 Dec. Amex, Diners, MasterCard, Visa, Laser. **Directions:** Midway between Dublin and Galway: take the Longford/Cavan exit off the Athlone relief road; fork left after 2.5 miles at the Dog & Duck; 1 mile, on the left.

Kilbeggan

The Loft Restaurant

Ⓝ RESTAURANT

Main Street Kilbeggan Co Westmeath
Tel: 0506 32243 Email: loftkilbeggan@eircom.ie

Beautifully located overlooking a waterfall and watermill on the River Brosna, this old building was used as a wool store in the nineteenth century - and now makes a lovely spot to break a journey and enjoy some of Breda Kelly's good home baking: freshly baked scones, breads, home-made tarts and crumbles - you name it, if it's cooked, it's done freshly on the premises by Breda. Lasagne, quiches, beef stroganoff and other savoury dishes too. And the motto of this family business? "To keep things simple, but serve the best of freshly prepared foods". Definitely the place to plan a break. **Seats 60.** Open Mon-Sat, 9am -4.45pm. L €8.50. Closed Sun, bank hols, 1 week Christmas. MasterCard, Visa, Laser. **Directions:** On main Dublin-Galway road (N6).

Moate

P. Egan

ATMOSPHERIC PUB

Main Street Moate Co Westmeath
Tel: 0902 82014 Email: peganspub@eircom.net

Easy to recognise with its bright red and black paintwork and the bikes outside, this cheerful traditional pub in the centre of Moate has a turf range in the back bar and it's a friendly place to drop in for a drink and some low-down on the area. Traditional Irish music is a speciality. Own parking. Children welcome up to 6pm. Visa. **Directions:** Beside the Bank of Ireland on the Main Street.

Moate

Temple Country House & Spa

COUNTRY HOUSE

Horseleap Moate Co Westmeath **Tel: 0506 35118**
Fax: 0506 35008 Web: spiders.ie/templespa

Relaxation is the essence of Declan and Bernadette Fagan's philosophy at Temple, their charming and immaculately maintained 200 year-old farmhouse in the unspoilt Westmeath countryside. On its own farmland – where guests are welcome to walk – close to peat bogs, lakes and historical sites, outdoor activities such as walking, cycling and riding are all at hand. There are three lovely country style en-suite rooms in the house and a further five newer ones in the courtyard. Relaxation programmes and healthy eating have always been available at Temple, but when they introduced Spa, this side of the operation moved into a new phase, offering yoga, hydrotherapy, massage, reflexology and specialist treatments such as Yon-Ka spa facial and seaweed body contour wraps. Temple is a member of the Health Farms of Ireland Association, which means that Bernadette gives special attention to healthy eating guidelines (and caters for vegetarian, vegan and other special diets). She uses the best of local produce – lamb from the farm, their own garden vegetables, best midland beef, cheese and yogurts – in good home cooking. And, although the Spa is a major attraction, you do not have to be a Spa guest to enjoy a stay at Temple. Garden, cycling, sauna, steam room, children's playground. **Rooms 8** (all en-suite, 5 no-smoking). B&B about €70 pps, ss about €25 (min 2-night stay at weekends). Spa weekends from about €300 pps (ss about €40). Residents' D Tue-Sat, about €30 (book by 10 am; no D Sun, Mon). Wine licence. Closed Christmas-New Year. Amex, MasterCard, Visa. **Directions:** Just off N6, 1 mile west of Horseleap. ◇

MULLINGAR

This thriving midland town is really booming at the moment - a new hotel on the Dublin side of the town was opening just as the Guide went to press **Mullingar Park Hotel (044 44446 www.mullingarparkhotel.com),** bringing extra facilities to the area, including a new leisure centre; meanwhile the attractive old town-centre hotel the **Greville Arms Hotel (Tel 044 48563)** continues to be the hub of local activities. In the town centre also, **Canton Casey's** pub is a place for those who appreciate traditional bars (at its best at quiet times - it can get very busy); upstairs, over the bar, **Fat Cats Brasserie (044 49969)** offers informal dining. New restaurants - including several ethnic ones - are opening all the time, so it's worth taking a browse around the town.

Mullingar

The Belfry Restaurant

féile bia RESTAURANT

Ballynegall Mullingar Co Westmeath **Tel: 044 42488**
Fax: 044 40094 Email: belfryrestaurant@eircom.net

The tall spire will lead you to the Murphy family's restaurant in a magnificently converted church near Mullingar. The design is brilliant, with (excellent) toilets near the entrance, perfect for a quick freshen up before heading up thickly carpeted stairs to a mezzanine lounge which is luxuriously furnished with big lounge-around leather sofas, striking lamps and fresh flowers. A second staircase descends to the dining area, which is very striking and extremely atmospheric, especially when seen in candlight with a room full of people enjoying themselves, with background music from the grand piano where the altar used to be. Everything has been done to the very highest specifications, colours schemes are subtle and elegant - and the whole set-up is highly atmospheric. Head chef Thérèse Gilsenan has a very down to earth approach to cooking, sourcing ingredients well (herbs and some fruit are home grown) and working in a style that is refreshingly unselfconscious - professionally presented but never over the top, with more elements of good home cooking than cheffy tricks. Menus are carefully constructed to offer a good balance of ingredients and styles, to suit big country appetites and also more urban tastes - a house speciality that pleases everyone is roast half rack of local lamb with redcurrant, mint & port sauce - and younger guests also get special choices, which is a good way to introduce children to quality dining. Well-made breads and soups, everything cooked freshly to order - all the signs of a good cook are here, right down to the choice of coffees. Charming, helpful and well-timed service adds greatly to the enjoyment of the visit - and there's a pianist on some nights. 'Wines from the Crypt' are listed - and you are invited to browse. Catering offered for private parties, small weddings (up to 75);

private room for meetings. Cookery classes given: evening and day courses, including children's courses in summer - call the restaurant for details. **Seats 65** (private room 22). Air conditioning. Children welcome. D Wed-Sun, 5.45-10; L Sun only, 1-4. Early D €28.50 (5.45-6.45), otherwise D à la carte, Set Sun L €26.50; house wine €21. Closed Mon,Tue, & last 3 weeks Jan. MasterCard, Visa, Laser. **Directions:** Castlepollard road off the Mullingar bypass.

Mullingar

Gallery 29 Café

CAFÉ

16 Oliver Plunkett St Mullingar Co Westmeath **Tel: 044 49449**
Fax: 044 49449 Email: corbetstown@eircom.net

Ann & Emily Gray's smart black-painted traditionally-fronted premises is really bright and welcoming - and the buzz of an open kitchen and beautiful freshly cooked food on display draws people in. They're great bakers and, although there's much more on offer than that (and the choice has grown during their first year in business here) their food reflects that interest - freshly baked breads, scones, muffins, baked puddings, tarts and gateaux are all on display. Good soups, salads (warm bacon salad with avocado, croutons & toasted pine nuts, perhaps), savoury tart of the day "tailor-made" sandwiches, fashionable focaccia with every imaginable filling and hot main courses, like oven-baked salmon with sweet chilli sauce, champ & salad and steak sandwich on ciabatta, with spicy salsa & mixed salad. It's a good place for any time of day, including breakfast (with freshly squeezed juice) and afternoon tea; it's vey popular and often busy, but well-trained staff seem well able to cope. Outside catering, picnics and freshly made dishes for home freezing are also offered. **Seats 50.** Open Mon-Sat, 9.30-5.30 (late opening with a bistro menu Thu-Fri evenings). All a la carte. Wine licence. Closed Sun, Christmas/New Year. **No Credit Cards. Directions:** From Dublin through traffic lights at Market Square in town centre. About 60 - 70 m on right hand side. ◇

Mullingar

Ilia A Coffee Experience

CAFÉ

28 Oliver Plunkett Street Mullingar Co Westmeath **Tel: 044 40300**
Fax: 044 40050 Email: juliekenny@eircom.net

Julie Kenny's delightful 2-storey coffee house and informal restaurant in the centre of Mullingar is attractively set up - the first floor area is particularly pleasing, with a seating area of sofas, low tables and plants at the top of the stairs setting a relaxed tone and making a good place to wait for a friend or to sip a cup of coffee while reading the paper at quiet times; the rest is more conventionally furnished in café style - and a more comfortable height for eating a real meal. Menus cater for all the changing moods though the day, beginning with an extensive breakfast (everything from porridge with brown sugar and cream to traditional breakfast, to toasted bagels (their Bagel Combo - toasted bagel with crispy bacon, poached egg, topped with melted cheddar & tomato relish 'just walks out of the door'!)), then there are the mid-day bites like home-made soup, paninis, steak baguettes, bruschetta, Ilia salad and much more (plenty for vegetarians) - and lots of pastries and desserts including a range of crêpes, both savoury and sweet. More predictably, there's a nice little drinks menu offering everything from big glasses of freshly squeezed orange juice through iced teas, smoothies, teas - and, of course, coffees (Java Republic), any way you like, including flavoured coffees. Everything is deliciously fresh and wholesome, staff are charming and efficient, prices reasonable - you'd be hard pushed to find anything over €8. Takeaway also available. Wine licence. **Seats 50.** Air conditioning. Open Mon-Sat 9 am-6pm. Closed Sun. MasterCard, Visa, Laser. **Directions:** Centre of Town.

Mullingar

Oscars Restaurant

RESTAURANT

21 Oliver Plunkett Street Mullingar Co Westmeath
Tel: 044 44909 Fax: 044 44909 Web: www.oscarsrestaurant.com

This smartly painted centrally located restaurant is extremely popular locally, pleasing people of all ages for its lively atmosphere and mix of traditional and contemporary favourites at reasonable prices. This is beef country, so a section of the menu given over to steaks should come as no surprise, but there's much else besides, ranging from 80s classics like deep-fried mushrooms with garlic & cucumber dip, through spicy chicken wings to simple smoked salmon with lemon, capers & home-made bread. Main courses cover a similar range, also specialities which, apart from steaks various ways, offer everything from chicken Italienne to crispy Silver Hill duckling with cranberry stuffing and port & orange jus. Pastas and pizzas too - this is popular food, well executed at fair prices - the dearest main course is about €23.50 (large fillet steak) but the average is about €16 - and with cheerfully efficient service to match. An affordable outing with something for everyone and wines starting at about €10. D daily, L Sun only. A la carte. Closed Christmas week, Good Fri. MasterCard, Visa, Laser. **Directions:** Centre of town opposite town mall.

Multyfarnham

An Tintáin Restaurant

N féile bia RESTAURANT WITH ROOMS

Main Street Multyfarnham Co Westmeath
Tel: 044 71411 Fax: 044 71434
Email: antintain@ireland.com Web: www.antintain.info

This is a characterful old building in an attractive village and has recently been renovated by Jack and Caroline Sleator to make a fine restaurant with rooms, and a bar - and it would make an excellent base for a break in an interesting and appealing part of the country that deserves to be better known. You may start your visit in the bar, looking over head chef Mervyn O'Connell's menus - which, naturally enough, feature the meats for which the area is renowned, especially beef, but also offer a good variety of dishes that would appeal to local diners looking for something that you wouldn't have at home - in generous quantities! There's a great sense of being in a community here, it's a very different experience from visiting a restaurant in a town or city. The restaurant is divided into large-ish domestic-sized areas - one has a large feature fireplace which would be welcoming in winter - and, with membership of Feile Bia and the Happy Heart Eat Out highlighted on menus, there is a clear commitment to sourcing ingredients carefully and offering customers healthy choices. Children welcome. **Seats 55.** D Wed-Sun, 6-9.30, L Sun only 12.30-3.30. Early D €20; Set Sun L €21.50; D also à la carte. House wine €16.50. Closed Mon,Tue, bank hols, 23-29 Dec.

Accommodation: Bedrooms are a good size, comfortably furnished and freshly decorated - and residents have the use of a sitting room alongside the restaurant, and the bar: a comfortable set-up at a reasonable price. Children welcome (under 5 free in parents' room, cot available without charge, baby sitting arranged). Walking, fishing. Garden. No pets. **Rooms 6** (all en-suite, 1 shower only, 2 no smoking). Room service (limited hours). B&B €38, ss €10. Closed Christmas week. Amex, MasterCard, Visa, Laser. **Directions:** At bottom of Main St in Multyfarnham village beside the bridge.

Multyfarnham

Mornington House

COUNTRY HOUSE

Mornington Multyfarnham Co Westmeath
Tel: 044 72191 Fax: 044 72338
Email: info@mornington.ie Web: www.mornington.ie

Warwick and Anne O'Hara's gracious Victorian house is surrounded by mature trees and is just a meadow's walk away from Lough Derravarragh where the mythical Children of Lir spent 300 years of their 900 year exile. The Lough is now occupied by a pleasing population of brown trout, pike, eels and other coarse fish. It has been the O'Hara family home since 1858 and is still furnished with much of the original furniture and family portraits and, although centrally heated, log fires remain an essential feature. Bedrooms are typical of this kind of country house – spacious and well-appointed, with old furniture (three have brass beds) – but with comfortable modern mattresses. Anne cooks proper country breakfasts and country house dinners for residents and Warwick does the honours front-of-house. Pets allowed by arrangement. Garden; fishing. Not suitable for children under 12 except babies (cot available without charge, baby sitting arranged). **Rooms 5** (3 en-suite, 2 with private bathrooms, all no smoking). B&B €60 pps, ss €20. Set residents D €40, at 8pm (book by 2pm). House wine €14. Closed Nov-Mar. Amex, MasterCard, Visa. **Directions:** Exit N4 for Castlepollard.

COUNTY WEXFORD

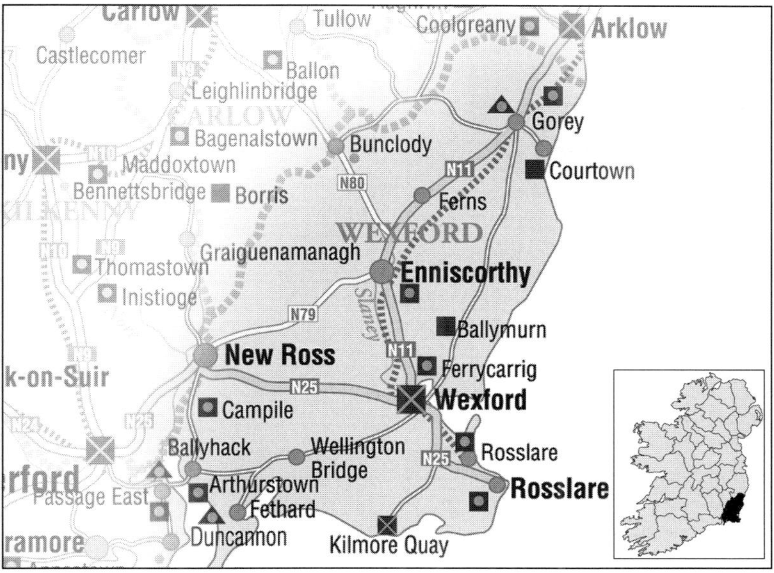

The popular view of Wexford is beaches, sunshine and opera. The longest continuous beach in all Ireland runs along the county's east coast, an astonishing 27 kilometres from Cahore Point south to Raven Point, which marks the northern side of the entrance to Wexford town's shallow harbour. As for sunshine, while areas further north along the east coast may record marginally less rainfall, in the very maritime climate of the "Sunny Southeast" around Wexford, the clouds seem to clear more quickly, so the chances of seeing the elusive orb are much improved.

And opera.....? Well, the annual Wexford Opera Festival every October is a byword for entertaining eccentricity - as international enthusiasts put it, "we go to Wexford town in the Autumn to enjoy operas written by people we've never heard of, and we have ourselves a thoroughly good time."

All of which is fine and dandy, but there's much more to this intriguing county than sun, sand and singing. Wexford itself is but one of three substantial towns in it, the other two being the market town of Enniscorthy, and the river port of New Ross. While much of the county is relatively low-lying, to the northwest it rises towards the handsome Blackstairs Mountains. There, the 793m peak of Mount Leinster may be just over the boundary in Carlow, but one of the most attractive little hill towns in all Ireland, Bunclody, is most definitely in Wexford.

In the north of the county, Gorey is a pleasant and prosperous place, while connoisseurs of coastlines will find the entire south coast of Wexford a fascinating area of living history, shellfish-filled shallow estuaries, and an excellent little harbour at the much-thatched village of Kilmore Quay inside the Saltee Islands.

Round the corner beyond the impressive Hook Head, home to Ireland's oldest lighthouse, Wexford County faces west across its own shoreline along the beauties of Waterford estuary. Here, there's another fine beach, at Duncannon, while nearby other sheltered little ports of west Wexford - Arthurstown and Ballyhack - move at their own sweet and gentle pace.

In New Ross, where the authentic re-creation of a 19th Century emigrant ship - the impressive Dunbrody - is proving to be a very effective focal point for the revival of the picturesque waterfront, a fitting place for the lovely River Barrow to meet ships in from sea in an area historically linked with President John F Kennedy.

Local Attractions and Information

Ballygarrett, Shrule Deer Farm 055 27277
Ballyhack, Ballyhack Castle 051 389468
Campile, Kilmokea Gardens 051 388109
Dunbrody, Abbey & Visitor Centre 051 388603

Duncannon, Duncannon Fort 051 388603
Enniscorthy, National 1798 Visitor Centre 054 37596
Enniscorthy, Tourism Information 054 34699
Enniscorthy, Wexford County Museum 054 46506
Ferrycarrig, National Heritage Park 053 20733
Gorey (Coolgreany), Ram House Gardens 0402 37238
Hook Head, Hook Head Lighthouse 051 397055
Johnstown, Castle Demesne & Agricultural Museum 053 42888
Kilmore Quay, Saltee Island Ferries 053 29684
New Ross, Dunbrody - re-creation of 19th C ship 051 425239
New Ross, Galley River Cruises 051 421723
New Ross, John F Kennedy Arboretum 051 388171
New Ross, John F Kennedy Homestead, Dunganstown 051 388264
New Ross, Tourism Information 051 421857
Rosslare Ferry Terminal 053 33622
Saltmills (nr Fethard-on-Sea), Tintern Abbey 051 562650
Wexford, North Slobs Wildfowl Reserve 053 23129
Wexford, Opera Festival (October) 053 22144
Wexford, Tourism Information 053 23111

Arthurstown

Dunbrody Country House Hotel & Cookery School

HOTEL / RESTAURANT

Arthurstown Co Wexford
Tel: 051 389600 Fax: 051 389601
Email: dunbrody@indigo.ie Web: www.dunbrodyhouse.com

IRISH BREAKFAST AWARD - MUNSTER

Set in twenty acres of parkland and gardens on the Hook Peninsula, just across the estuary from Waterford city, this elegant Georgian manor was the ancestral home of the Chichester family and the long tradition of hospitality at this tranquil and luxurious retreat is very much alive and well. Catherine and Kevin Dundon are thoughtful and caring hosts and there is a feeling of true welcome here - beginning, perhaps, with a gentle greeting from their affectionate dogs (who look out for newcomers from their vantage point on the granite steps at the front door). Well-proportioned public rooms, which include an impressive entrance hall and gracious drawing room, are all beautifully furnished and decorated with stunning flower arrangements and the occasional unexpectedly modern piece that brings life to a fine collection of antiques. Spacious bedrooms, including those in a newer wing which blends admirably with the original building, have superb bathrooms and offer all the comforts expected of such a house - and fine views over the gardens. Constant improvement is the on-going quest at Dunbrody and a recent development was converting outbuildings into Ireland's most stylish cookery school. An exceptional breakfast offers a magnificent buffet - fresh juices, fruit compôtes, cheeses - as well as hot dishes from a tempting menu - and is a worthy national winner of the Guide's Breakfast Award for 2004. While Dunbrody provides a wonderfully relaxing place for a leisure break, they also cater for business meetings, small conferences, product launches and incentive programmes (full details available on request). Conference/banqueting (60/110). Business centre, secretarial services. Cookery school. Garden, walking. Children welcome (cot available without charge). No pets. **Rooms 22** (all en-suite, 8 suites, 8 junior suites, 4 executive, 1 disabled). B&B €120 pps; ss €25. Closed 22-27 Dec.

☆ **The Harvest Room:** The restaurant looks out onto a pleasure garden and, beyond, to an organic vegetable and fruit garden. A well-proportioned, elegant room with an open fire in winter and stunning flower arrangements all the time, it presents a striking blend of classic and contemporary style - bold choices which bring life to the room include some beautiful modern rugs, specially commissioned from Ceadogan Rugs at Wellington Bridge. Likewise, chef/proprietor Kevin offers tempting à la carte and set menus that succeed unusually well in combining classical and international influences with local produce and Irish themes: specialities of the house include, for example, roast loin of bacon with a clove and Irish Mist, served on a bed of braised cabbage leaves & potato cake, a dish which brilliantly marries traditional and contemporary tastes. Rack of Wexford lamb with a whiskey marmalade crust, leek confit & caramelised kumquat jus perhaps, is another such dish and, while beautifully presented, this is not ostentatious cooking - Kevin's creations are outstanding for flavour before all else. Catherine leads a well-trained and efficient dining room staff with the charm and panache that typifies all aspects of the hospitality at this exceptional country house. An informative wine list which leans towards the classics includes a nice selection of half bottles and wines by the glass. Seats 100. Toilets wheelchair accessible. D Mon-Sat 6.30-9.15. Sun L 1.15-2.30. Set Sun L €32. Set D €50. House wines €18. SC discretionary. Not suitable for children after 8pm. Closed 22-27 Dec. Amex, Diners, MasterCard, Visa, Laser. **Directions:** N11 from Dublin, R733 from Wexford to Arthurstown.

Arthurstown

Glendine Country House

Ⓝ B&B

Arthurstown New Ross Co Wexford **Tel: 051 389258** Fax: 051 389677
Email: glendinehouse@eircom.net Web: www.glendinehouse.com

Ann and Tom Crosbie's spacious nineteenth century house is approached up a driveway off the main road to Arthurstown and it offers a very comfortable and hospitable place to stay at a reasonable price. There's a guest drawing room with comfortable seating and excellent views down to the harbour, and across the estuary, and the immaculately maintained bedrooms are very large, as are the en-suite bathrooms. The couple are committed to making major improvements - five new guest rooms will be ready for the 2004 season and a restaurant is due to open at about the time of going to press - a promising development with head chef Joe de Castro, who previously ran a respected restaurant nearby. Service at Glendine House is excellent - the Crosbies take pride in giving their guests personal attention and lots of advice on local amenities - and sending everyone off well-fed for the day after a particularly good breakfast. Children welcome (cot available, baby sitting arranged). Pets allowed by arrangement. **Rooms 5** (2 suites, 3 superior, 4 shower only) B&B €50pps, ss €15. Room service (limited hours) Restaurant **Seats 60.** D Tue-Sun 6-10, L Sun only 12-3. Sun L €20, D from €30, also à la carte. Children welcome until 8.30. Closed at Christmas. Diners, MasterCard, Visa, Laser. **Directions:** From Wexford, R733 to Arthurstown, entrance on right before village.

Bunclody

Chantry Restaurant

RESTAURANT

Bunclody Co Wexford **Tel: 054 77482** Fax: 054 76130

The Chantry is especially attractively situated within the lovely little town of Bunclody. Originally a Wesleyan chapel, it enjoys a position of unexpected serenity above its own lovely waterside gardens, where guests can relax and enjoy the fine trees and plants, including many rare species. The restaurant is in a high room with a little gallery (just the right size for a grand piano) but, with its deep red walls and chandeliers, it doesn't feel too churchy. Menus offered vary considerably depending on the time of day - all day food tends to be casual, with a carvery lunch from 12.30, but evening service is more formal. At dinner, the self-service buffet is removed and an à la carte menu with table service is offered instead. Typical main courses include a speciality of traditional honey-glazed baked Chantry ham, with fresh parsley sauce and vegetarian dishes like tofu & vegetable stirfry. Early bird specials are good value - and what all the various menus have in common is good home cooking. **Seats 50** (private room, 14). Children welcome. Toilets wheelchair accessible. Own parking. Pets in certain areas. Open 9am-9pm Mon-Sat, 10-4 Sun. Sun L 12.30-4. House wine about €16. All a la carte menus. SC discretionary. Open all year. MasterCard, Visa. **Directions:** In town centre. ◇

Campile

Kilmokea Country Manor & Gardens

COUNTRY HOUSE

Great Island Campile Co Wexford **Tel: 051 388 109** Fax: 051 388 776
Email: kilmokea@indigo.ie Web: www.kilmokea.com

Mark and Emma Hewlett's peaceful and relaxing late Georgian country house is set in 7 acres of Heritage Gardens, including formal walled gardens (open to the public, 9-5; cream teas, for guests and garden visitors, are served in a Georgian conservatory). The house is elegantly and comfortably furnished, with a drawing room overlooking the Italian Loggia, an honesty library bar, and a classic country house dining room. The individually-designed and immaculately maintained bedrooms command lovely views over the gardens and towards the estuary beyond. They have no television to disturb the tranquillity (though there is one in the drawing room). In an adjoining coach house there's a billiards room, newer rooms and self-catering suites; they have a separate entrance and lighter, more contemporary atmosphere than the main house - as they are so different it is wise to discuss your preferences when booking. Mark and Emma have also continued their on-going programme of improvements to the property - the latest additions are a tennis court and an indoor swimming pool, no less, plus a gym and aromatherapy treatment rooms (Emma is a trained aromatherapist). As if that isn't enough, they're also working on a large organic vegetable garden, planted in the old potager design - it's great to see a revival of this charming fashion. Conferences/banqueting (30/50). Garden, fishing, tennis, walking; games room (billiards, table tennis), swimming pool, gym, aromatherapy. Children welcome (cots available without charge; playground, playroom, baby sitting arranged). Pets allowed by arrangement. **Rooms 6** (5 en-suite, 1 with private bathroom, 2 shower only, 1 for disabled). B&B €75 pps; ss €25. Self-catering also available. Residents D €42; book by noon. Light meals in conservatory 10-5 daily when house and gardens are open. Closed 5 Nov-1 Mar. MasterCard, Visa, Laser, Switch. **Directions:** Off R733 from New Ross to Ballyhack, sign posted for Kilmokea Gardens.

Duncanon

Sqigl Restaurant & Roches Bar

féile bia RESTAURANT / ATMOSPHERIC PUB

Quay Road Duncannon New Ross Co Wexford
Tel: 051 389700 Fax: 051 389700
Email: sqigl2003@eircom.net

Bob and Eileen Roche's fine traditional bar in the centre of Duncannon village serves the local community (and discerning visitors) well. There's an old bar at the front, pleasingly free of improvements, and it gradually develops more towards the back which keeps the younger crowd and the oldies in their preferred spaces. The bar food menu offers a selection of hot dishes, salads and sandwiches, plus some daily specials - a well-balanced mixture of traditional (breaded cod with french fries tartare sauce & side salad) and contemporary (grilled goat's cheese with red onion salad & pesto dressing). While it is not an especially long menu, there is something for everyone - and, in a rather nice piece of role reversal, adult portions of the children's menu are also offered. Bar Food served 12.30-5 daily. Pub closed 25 Dec, Good Fri.

Sqigl Restaurant: Sqigl (pronounced Squiggle) is located in a converted barn behind the pub and is run by Bob and Eileen's daughter Cindy Roche, supported by chef Wayne Neville. Sqigl aims to make the most of local produce and does it well with a sensibly limited menu, particularly the white fish landed at the harbour round the corner, wild locally caught salmon and Wexford beef and lamb. Décor is light, bright and modern and the cooking style is modern too, except that portions are aimed at generous Wexford appetites: sweet potato cake, Clonakilty pudding with peppered quails eggs and paprika hollandaise, for example, makes a fine substantial starter. There's local seafood of course - a speciality to keep an eye open for is pan-fried scallops, which they do with pancetta & salsa verde. And there's always an interesting vegetarian option too - an asparagus & garden pea risotto parcels with a beetroot froth, perhaps... Finish off with a rich dessert like warm chocolate pudding with brown bread ice cream, or something lighter and refreshing such as a trio of citrus desserts. Seats 32. D Tue-Sat, 7-10; L Sun only, 1-3. House wine from €15. Closed D Sun & Mon, 24-27 Dec, 3 weeks Jan. MasterCard, Visa, Laser **Directions:** R733 from Wexford & New Ross. Centre of village.

Enniscorthy

Ballinkeele House

COUNTRY HOUSE

Ballinkeele House Enniscorthy Co Wexford
Tel: 053 38105 Fax: 053 38468
Email: info@ballinkeele.com Web: www.ballinkeele.com

Set in 350 acres of parkland, game-filled woods and farmland, this historic house is a listed building; designed by Daniel Robertson, it has been the Maher family home since it was built in 1840 and remains at the centre of their working farm. It is a grand house, with a lovely old cut stone stable yard at the back and some wonderful features, including a lofty columned hall with a big open fire in the colder months, beautifully proportioned reception rooms with fine ceilings and furnishings which have changed very little since the house was built. Nevertheless, it is essentially a family house and has a refreshingly hospitable and down-to-earth atmosphere. Large bedrooms are furnished with antiques and have wonderful countryside views. Margaret Maher is a keen cook and enjoys preparing 4-course dinners for guests (nice little wine list to accompany); she's also an enthusiastic amateur painter and runs small art workshops at Ballinkeele with Patricia Jorgensen, who is well-known for her botanical paintings. Croquet and bicycles are available for guests' use and horse riding, fishing and golf can be organised nearby. Garden. Not suitable for children under 5. No pets. **Rooms 5** (all en-suite, 2 executive, 4 shower only). B&B €70 pps; ss 20. Residents Set D €38 at 7.30 (book by noon; no D on Mon); house wine from €15. Private parties up to 14. Closed 12 Nov-28 Feb. MasterCard, Visa, Laser. **Directions:** From Wexford N11 north to Oilgate Village, turn right at signpost.

Enniscorthy

Monfin House

COUNTRY HOUSE

St Johns Enniscorthy Co Wexford **Tel: 054 38582** Fax: 054 38583
Email: info@monfinhouse.com Web: www.monfinhouse.com

This classic Georgian house just outside Enniscorthy was built in 1823 and has all the simplicity and elegance of that period. Having carried out major refurbishment, Chris and Avril Stewart opened their house to guests in 2001, with the aim of providing a quiet and relaxing haven, with the emphasis on comfort, personal service and, particularly, the joys of food and wine. This they do very well: guests are free to stroll around the grounds and see the walled garden (which is destined for restoration to its original design and purpose) and your bedroom will provide a tranquil sanctuary - spacious and very comfortably furnished with a whirlpool or antique bath, although kept without the worldly intrusion of amenities like television (phone and modem connection are available on request however). Avril sources food carefully, using local and organic produce wherever possible in her country house style cooking. A candlelit dining room with an open fire provides a soothing setting for a 5-course, no-choice dinner, and there is an interesting wine list with refreshingly low mark-up prices. (Chris has a "day job" in the wine business.) A typical dinner might start with a salad of fresh crab with red pepper chutney, then a seasonal soup such as pea & coriander; there might be roast rack of Wexford lamb for the main course, then a classic dessert like orange soufflé. This is not the end, however, as there is still a cheese plate to come - and chocolates with your coffee, which is served in front of another fire, in the drawing room. Breakfast is to the same high standards - and you may well need a walk afterwards. Not suitable for children under 12. Pets permitted.* Weekend/short breaks offered- call Avril for details. **Rooms 4** (all en-suite). B&B €65 pps, ss €20. Residents' D 8 pm; €35; wine from €15. MasterCard, Visa. **Directions:** From Enniscorthy take New Ross road - turn left after Grain Mill. 0.5 mile up on right hand side.

Enniscorthy

Riverside Park Hotel

HOTEL

The Promenade Enniscorthy Co Wexford **Tel: 054 37800** Fax: 054 37900
Email: info@riversideparkhotel.com Web: www.riversideparkhotel.com

While this riverside hotel may be visually at odds with the pleasing traditional style of the area, it brings welcome amenities to the town and is always immaculately maintained. Public areas are quite impressive and rooms are comfortably furnished in a moderate, contemporary style that people feel comfortable with - and there are good facilities for conferences and functions. Off-season and special interest breaks are offered and there is plenty to do in this beautiful area, including fishing, golf and horse riding. There is a pleasant riverside path in a linear park beside the hotel and this can be a useful place to break a journey to stretch the legs and have a bite to eat; head chef David Anderson has been with the hotel since it opened and, in the Guide's experience, does a good job. Conference/banqueting facilities (800/600), secretarial services. New leisure centre and pool opening in 2004. Own parking. Children welcome (under 3 free in parents' room, cots available without charge, baby sitting arranged). No pets. Garden. **Rooms 60** (1 junior suite, 2 for disabled, 10 no smoking). Lift. 24 hour room service. B&B €87 pps. ss €20. Bar food available 12.30-7.30 daily; Moorings Restaurant D daily (Set D €28) & L Sun (Set Sun L €23.50); also à la carte. House wine from €20; Alamo Bar & Grill (Tex-Mex) D daily from 6pm. Closed 25-26 Dec.

Moorings Restaurant: In the Guide's experience, food and ambience are both above the standard expected of a country hotel. David Anderson's seasonal à la carte and daily set menus successfully marry the demands for both traditional and contemporary dishes and the cooking is sound. There is also an informal Tex-Mex restaurant in the hotel and bar food is available 12.30-7.30 daily. L 12.30-2.30, D 7-9. Set Sun €18.50, Set D from €29; à la carte also available L&D. MasterCard, Visa, Laser. **Directions:** 0.5 km from the new bridge centre Enniscorthy Town. Just off N11 Dublin - Rosslare road.

Enniscorthy

Salville House

B&B

Enniscorthy Co Wexford **Tel: 054 35252** Fax: 054 35252
Email: info@salvillehouse.com Web: www.salvillehouse.com

Set high on a hillside outside Enniscorthy, Gordon and Jane Parker's large mid-19th century house has sweeping views over the Slaney River Valley but the main point of interest is indoors, in the dining room where Gordon Parker's confident modern cooking is offered to guests around a communal table in the evening - and splendid breakfasts are served next morning. Seasonal dinners have an emphasis on local seafood and organic produce from the garden - but there isn't a formal menu with choices, so it's wise to mention any allergies or dislikes when booking. After dinner, guests can relax in front of the drawing room fire, or play a game of backgammon before heading up to one of the three large rooms in the main house , which have views over the Slaney and are comfortably furnished with some style, or one of the two in a self-contained apartment at the back. (All have tea/coffee making facilities, but no TV.) A really good breakfast sends everyone on their way in good heart - freshly squeezed juice, lovely fruit compôte, freshly-baked bread warm from the oven and hot dishes cooked to order, like undyed smoked haddock with rösti and poached eggs, or local smoked salmon with scrambled egg. Laid back hospitality, great food and good value make this comfortable house a fine base for exploring the area, or somewhere to break a journey. Children welcome. Pets allowed by arrangement. Garden; Tennis. **Rooms 5** (2 en-suite, 3 with private bathrooms, 1 shower only). B&B €40, ss €10. Residents' 3-course D €30, at 8pm (book a day ahead; no D on Sun). BYO wine. Closed Christmas. **No Credit Cards.** **Directions:** 2 miles from Enniscorthy on Wexford side (not signed until off main road).

Ferrycarrig Bridge

Ferrycarrig Hotel

féile bia HOTEL / RESTAURANT

Ferrycarrig Bridge Co Wexford **Tel: 053 20999** Fax: 053 20982
Email: ferrycarrig@griffingroup.ie Web: www.griffingroup.ie

Although very close to the main Rosslare road - steeply sloping gardens have steps from the main entrance up to the car park which is almost adjacent to the road - this modern hotel is in a lovely location overlooking the Slaney estuary and has excellent amenities, including a superb health and fitness club with 20 metre swimming pool and state-of-the-art facilities for conferences and business meetings. Neatly uniformed staff are exceptionally welcoming and friendly; service generally is caring without being intrusive. All bedrooms have splendid views across the water and some have balconies with wooden loungers; in-room facilities are generally good, including a safe (which uses the room key card) and an iron/trouser press unit as well as the usual phone, television, tea/coffee tray. Housekeeping is of a high standard and generous bathrooms have a phone extension and large baths with good showers. Special interest and off-season value breaks are offered. Conference/banqueting (400/350). Leisure centre. Garden. Children welcome (cots available, €6.50; playroom). No pets. **Rooms 102** (4 suites, 5 junior suites, 2 for disabled). Lift. All day room service. B&B €120 pps; ss €35. Open all year.

Restaurant: The smaller of the hotel's two restaurants, Tides, offers discerning guests modern cooking in the atmosphere of an independent restaurant rather than an hotel dining room. It has its own reception/bar area and is formally appointed with linen cloths and napkins, quality tableware, fresh flowers and chilled water in stoppered bottles. Head chef Tony Carty presents imaginative and well-balanced à la carte menus offering a selection of about eight on each course, always including interesting vegetarian options; expect updated classics - like organic chicken Cordon Bleu: supreme of chicken filled with smoked Gubbeen cheese and honey roast ham with wholegrain mustard sauce - and a sprinkling of more international dishes. Tables are set up to maximise on the waterside position and most have a lovely view in which to enjoy specialities based on local produce, such as a well-judged Kilmore crabmeat spring roll with Asian greens & hoi sin sauce, and fillet or sirloin of prime Hereford beef, which is outstanding for its excellent flavour and served various ways; menus are quite informative about the provenance of their ingredients, and side vegetables are organic. Imaginative desserts may include an intriguing home-made banana pizza with rum ice cream & caramel sauce and home-made chocolates come with coffee (including cappuccino/espresso) or tea (herbal teas available). Food presentation is fashionable but not over the top and service is pleasant and professional. **Seats 45.** Air conditioning. D Tue-Sat 6.30-9.45 (limited opening in winter). A la carte. House wines from €18.95. sc discretionary. Not suitable for children after 7.30. *The popular 150-seater Boathouse Bistro, serves modern Irish/international cooking L & D daily; three seasonal evening menus are used in rotation, ensuring variety for guests staying several nights; the calorie content of dishes is given alongside the price... Children welcome up to 7.30 - no restrictions on Friday, which is family night. *Bar food is also available daily: Mon-Thu, 12.30-8.30; Fri-Sun 12.30-6. Amex, Diners, MasterCard, Visa, Laser. **Directions:** Located on N11, 2 miles north of Wexford Town.

Gorey

Ashdown Park Hotel

N HOTEL

Gorey Co Wexford **Tel: 055 30501** Fax: 055 80777
Email: info@ashdownparkhotel Web: www.ashdownparkhotel.com

This new hotel has brought badly needed amenities to the Gorey area, offering quality accommodation at fairly reasonable prices and providing facilities for conferences, weddings and other large functions. The 60 bedrooms are modern, classical in style, with all the latest conveniences, and the Ashdown Club provides an impressive health and leisure centre. An attractive restaurant, the Rowan Tree, is promising - well-located in a bright and airy first floor, it features fresh local produce on its menus. An above-average carvery and light menu is available in the Ivy Bar - a useful place to break a journey. **Rooms 60** (all en-suite, 6 suites, 1 for disabled) B&B €100pps. ss €25.* Short breaks offered. Restaurant open daily. D 6.30-9.30. Set D €45, also a la carte. Set Sun L €25. House wine from €18. Bar meals 12.30-9 daily. Closed 25 Dec. MasterCard, Visa, Laser. **Directions:** Dublin Road, turn left before entry to Gorey town.

Gorey

Marlfield House

COUNTRY HOUSE / RESTAURANT

Courtown Rd Gorey Co Wexford
Tel: 055 21124 Fax: 055 21572
Email: info@marlfieldhouse.ie Web: www.marlfieldhouse.com

Often quoted as 'the luxury country house hotel par excellence', Marlfield House was once the residence of the Earls of Courtown and, thanks to the dedication and professionalism of Ray and Mary Bowe, has now been a leading light in the quest for excellence in Irish hospitality for 25 years. During that time they have lavished care and attention on this lovely house, creating an elegant oasis of unashamed luxury, where guests are cosseted and pampered in sumptuous surroundings - and matching these exceptional standards with a reputation for outstanding hospitality and service. Imposing gates, a wooded drive, a fine kitchen garden all set the scene - and the interior features marble fireplaces, antiques, notable paintings, glittering chandeliers and fine fabrics: all the creation of Mary Bowe, who has also ensured that housekeeping is immaculate throughout, service from committed staff thoughtful and unobtrusive. Although Mary and Ray Bowe are still very much involved, the house is now under the direction of daughter Margaret Bowe, continuing the family tradition. Conference/banqueting (40/30). Secretarial services. Dogs and children are welcome by prior arrangement. (Cots available without charge, baby sitting arranged). Tennis, cycling, walking. Garden. **Rooms 20** (5 state rooms, 1 suite, 14 superior). B&B €130pps. All day room service. Closed mid Dec-1 Feb.

Restaurant: The graceful dining-room and Turner style conservatory merge into one, allowing views out across the gardens. The conservatory, with its hanging baskets, plants and fresh flowers (not to mention the odd stone statue), is one of the most romantic spots in the whole of Ireland, further enhanced at night by candlelight – a wonderful setting in which to enjoy chef Henry Stone's accomplished cooking. Henry sources ingredients with care and a lot of the fruit, vegetables and herbs are grown in their own gardens, ensuring a strongly seasonal dimension to menus which are always interesting and attractive without being slavishly fashionable. The main emphasis is on flavour and this fine chef has a down to earth quality which is most refreshing in a fine dining restaurant. Specialities that indicate the style include ravioli of veal shank with oven-roasted tomatoes, spinach & gorgonzola cream - and wild Irish sea trout with fennel, baby leek, spring onion & mussel sauce. Vegetarian choices are always offered and an Irish cheeseboard, which is temptingly displayed on a side table. Elegant desserts might include a dashing high-rise banana gratin with Malibu sabayon topped with a ball of superb dark chocolate sorbet, then it's off to the drawing room for coffee and petits fours to round off the feast. An extensive wine list, long on burgundies and clarets, is informative. Not suitable for children under 8 at D. **Seats 65** (private room, 20). Air conditioning. D daily, 7-9 (Sat to 9.30, Sun to 8); L Sun only 12.30-1.45. Set D about €55 & à la carte; Set Sun L about €37. House wine €24. SC discretionary. Light à la carte lunches are served daily in Library, 12.30-5. Amex, Diners, MasterCard, Visa, Laser. **Directions:** 1 mile outside Gorey on Courtown Road (R742).

Gorey

Pooles Porterhouse

PUB

78 Main Street Gorey Co Wexford **Tel: 055 21271**
Fax: 055 80856 Web: www.poles.ie

With its traditional darkwood decor and open fires, this substantial town-centre premises looks and feels as if it has always been a pub - and it has, in fact, been in the family for three generations and was run as a restaurant for some years by the parents of the three Poole brothers, Eric, Colin and Brian. Its renewed success is down to these energetic young men, who did up the building, obtained a licence and re-opened it as a pub and restaurant. Eric, a chef with wide-ranging experience beginning nearby at Marlfield House, started the food side of the Porterhouse himself while Colin and Brian looked after other aspects of the business. Daytime fare tends to be light and snacky, augmented by daily main course specials on the blackboard: everything is cooked to order. Evening menus are more formal, offering a choice of about eight starters and a dozen or so main courses ranging from updated versions of the traditional meat and poultry dishes popular in rural areas to some sophisticated seafood and game in season. **Seats 65.** Air conditioning. Children welcome (but not after 6 pm). Food available daily, 12.30-9: L 12-2.30; Bar menu 2.30-9 (Sat & Sun to 8); D 7-9. Set Sun L about €16, otherwise à la carte. House wines about €16. Closed 25 Dec, Good Fri. Amex, Diners, MasterCard, Visa, Laser. **Directions:** Centre of Main Street. ◇

Kilmore Quay

Kehoe's Pub & Maritime Heritage Centre

féile bia PUB

Kilmore Quay Co Wexford **Tel: 087 239 5363** Fax: 01 298 8648
Email: info@kehoe.iol.ie Web: kehoes.com

Recent harbour developments, and especially the marina, have brought an extra surge of activity to this thriving fishing village – and well-informed visitors all head straight for Kehoe's. It has been family-owned for generations - James and Eleanor Kehoe have been running it since 1987 - and, among the changes made over the years, the most challenging was in 1994 when they decided to do a really good refurbishment job, to enhance the pub's traditional ambience – everything was done correctly, from the roof slates to the old pitch pine flooring (and ceiling in the Parlour). At the same time, the interior was used to display a huge range of maritime artefacts, some of them recovered from local wrecks by James and his diving colleagues. They have created what amounts to a maritime museum; even the beer garden at the back of the pub is constructed from a mast and boom discarded by local trawlers -

it now also has patio heaters to encourage people to eat outdoors on summer evenings. The other major change has been to the food side of the business, which has crept up on Kehoe's gradually: a few years ago they did little more than soup and sandwiches but now the pub has an established reputation for the quality and range of its bar meals – seafood, such as Ocean Pie (a selection of locally caught fish, topped with sauce and baked) - as well as vegetarian dishes and other main courses such as lasagne and stuffed chicken breasts wrapped in bacon. There's a short but very adequate wine list in addition to normal bar drinks. Children welcome. Wheelchair access. Open daily for food 12.30-8pm. Closed 25 Dec, Good Fri. Visa. ◇

Kilmore Quay

GUESTHOUSE / RESTAURANT

Quay House Guesthouse

Kilmore Quay Kilmore Quay Co Wexford
Tel: 053 29988 Fax: 053 29808
Web: hhll://quayhouseguesthouse.com

Siobhan and Pat McDonnell's pristine guesthouse is centrally located in the village (not on the quay as might be expected) and is especially famous for its support of sea angling and diving – they have an annexe especially geared for anglers with drying/storage room, fridges and freezers, live bait and tackle sales. Packed lunches can be provided and non-residents are welcome for breakfast as well as evening meals. The whole place is ship shape, with attractive, slightly nautical bedrooms ("a place for everything and everything in its place"), practical pine floors and neat en-suite rooms (most shower only). The breakfast room and restaurant, Quay Plaice, offers a full à la carte menu is offered, in a contemporary style, majoring in seafood. Children welcome (infants free in parents' room, cots available without charge). Pets by arrangement. Garden. **Rooms 7** (all en-suite, most shower-only). B&B about €36 pps; ss about €20.

Restaurant: D daily in summer, 6-9.30 pm. Set D about €45, also à la carte; house wine about €15. Accommodation open all year; restaurant closed Mon & Tue in winter. MasterCard, Visa, Laser. **Directions:** Wexford 14 miles, Rosslare Ferry route.

NEW ROSS

This interesting old town has much of interest to the visitor - especially, of course, its key attraction, the recreation of the nineteenth century sailing ship The Dunbrody. **Kennedy's Pub (Tel 051 425188),** just opposite the Dunbrody, has recently been renovated with some style by a young couple who run the place in a friendly fashion and offer tasty modern food. Just outside the town, on a hillside site with river views, the **Brandon House Hotel (Tel 051 421703; www.brandonhousehotel.ie)** has been developed around a house of character and offers some surprises (including an interesting art collection) as well as much-needed facilities.

Rosslare Area

COUNTRY HOUSE

Churchtown House

Tagoat Rosslare Co Wexford **Tel: 053 32555** Fax: 053 32577
Email: info@churchtownhouse.com Web: wwwchurchtownhouse.com

Patricia and Austin Cody's Georgian house is extremely handy for the Rosslare ferryport, about four miles away, but it is a really lovely place and deserves a longer stay - it would make a beautifully relaxing base for a few days exploring the area. It's set in about eight and a half acres of wooded gardens and dates back to 1703 but it has been completely renovated by the Codys, and elegantly furnished to make a comfortable country house retreat for discerning guests. Public areas are spacious, with plenty of seating in rooms of different character allowing a choice of mood for guests. Bedrooms are equally pleasing - large, and furnished to the highest standards in ciountry house style, with generous beds, phones, TV and well-finished bathrooms. The Codys are renowned for their hospitality and, if you're lucky enough to arrive at this well-run house at around teatime, you'll be served delicious home-made cake and tea in the drawing room. Good food is an important feature here and a fine Irish breakfast is served in the bright dining room, where dinner is also available for residents by arrangement. Garden. Not suitable for children under 10. Pets by arrangement. **Rooms 12** (2 junior suites, 4 shower only, 1 for disabled). B&B about €80 pps; ss about €20. Residents' D, 8pm; Set D about €40, book by noon. House wines about €25. Closed 30 Nov-1 Mar. MasterCard, Visa, Laser. **Directions:** On R736 half mile from N25, at Tagoat.

Rosslare Strand

féile bia **HOTEL / RESTAURANT**

Kelly's Resort Hotel

Rosslare Co Wexford **Tel: 053 32114**
Fax: 053 32222 Web: www.kellys.ie

The history of this renowned family-run hotel spans three centuries - yet constant renovating, refurbishing and building work each winter keep raising standards ever higher. Quite simply, the hotel has everything, for both individuals and families, many of whom return year after year (the number of children is limited at any one time, so as not to create an imbalance). The many public rooms range from a quiet reading room and the snooker room to a supervised crèche and gallery lounge: pictures (mostly modern) throughout the hotel form an outstanding art collection. Many of the bedrooms have sea views, some with balconies; housekeeping throughout is immaculate. Leisure facilities include a therapeutic spa, two indoor swimming pools, indoor tennis, and, a bit of fun for Francophiles, boules. Outside the summer holiday season (end June-early Sept), ask about special breaks (including special interest breaks - everything from wine appreciation to golf clinics), when rates are reduced. Conferences (30). Leisure centre, swimming pools. Tennis. Fishing (sea). Snooker. Hair dressing. Health & beauty centre. Playroom & children's playground. Garden. Parking. No pets. **Rooms 99** (all en-suite, 1 for disabled). Lift. B&B about €85 pps, ss €10; sc10%. Hotel closed 7 Dec-20 Feb.

'Beaches' Restaurant: This L shaped room, which has been run under the eagle eye of Pat Doyle since 1966, was completely re-designed in 2003 to retain a sense of traditional opulence with the use of rich colours and textured finishes whilst treating them with a fresh, almost gallery-esque approach - the perfect home for selected examples from the hotel's famous art collection. Executive Chef Jim Aherne has been pleasing guests with his classic cuisine for over thirty years now - and the value of that tradition is also reflected in the new restaurant. Jim's menus reflect the value placed on fresh local produce: Rosslare mackerel, Slaney salmon and locally sourced vegetables, for example, are used in daily-changing menus that ensure variety for residents who may be staying for some time. The hotel's renowned wine list is meticulously sourced, always changing, and excellent value. **Seats 250** (private room 40); air conditioning. L 1-2.15 D 7.30-9; Set L €21; Set Sun L €25; Set D €39. House wine €20; s.c. discretionary.

La Marine: This contemporary restaurant adjacent to the hotel complements the style of the main restaurant and has its own separate entrance. A zinc bar imported from France is the focal point of an adjacent area where you can have an aperitif (although the turnover is brisk and you will be encouraged to go directly to your table if it is ready). Offering a popular informal dining option, La Marine is the place to see and be seen - and it can be hard to get a table, especially for dinner at weekends. The atmosphere can be electric, although comfort is not a top priority; fashionably sparse tables have fresh flowers, good quality cutlery and paper napkins, but space is at a premium so be prepared for a bit of a squeeze. Ingredients are carefully sourced, using local seasonal produce as much as possible and a finely judged balancing act between traditional and fusion fare is achieved. Desserts are deliciously classic - panna cotta with summer fruits, perhaps, or there's a selection of Irish cheese. Service is swift and friendly. The downside of the popularity of this bar and restaurant is that heavy usage can take its toll, especially towards the end of season, so that it loses the pristine appearance so necessary to the modern style. Sunday lunch is more traditional and may feature upbeat versions of traditional roasts. A light snack menu is also available every afternoon, 3-6pm. Wines reflecting the style of food, are fairly priced (selection off main list). **Seats 60.** L daily, 12.30-3; D 6.30-9.30. Amex, MasterCard, Visa, Laser. **Directions:** Take the signs for Wexford/Rosslare/Southeast. Outside Wexford Town alongside Rosslare Strand beach.

Rosslare Strand

Le Colleseo

Ⓝ RESTAURANT

Strand Road Rosslare Strand Co Wexford **Tel: 053 73975**

This friendly family restaurant offers an enjoyably informal dining experience - there's a good understanding of Italian cooking and excellent value for money, especially considering the quality of the seafood. Lunches are good, but the dinner menu is much more ambitious and gives a fairer impression of the scope of the kitchen. Food is well presented and service is friendly and efficient - staff are attentive and knowledgeable. Wine list a little limited but house wine good value at €13.95. Open all day from 11.0am Tue-Sun. Reservations advised. Closed Mon. Amex, MasterCard, Visa, Laser. **Directions:** Beside Kelly's Hotel.

WEXFORD TOWN

Wexford is a fascinating old town and offers much of interest, notably the annual Opera Festival which takes place every autumn. Visitors who prefer to be a little away from the bustle of the town might like the **Riverbank House Hotel (Tel: 053 23611;www.riverbankhousehotel.com)** just across the bridge; recent renovations have been completed with deference to the character of the building and, although rooms are a little small, it offers a pleasingly personal style of hospitality and food service. Those looking for an interesting daytime bite should look out for the big green, red & white canopy over Roberto Pons' new restaurant and specialist Italian food emporium off Main Street, **La Dolce Vita (Tel: 053 70806).**

Wexford

Forde's Restaurant

féile bia **RESTAURANT** Crescent Quay Wexford Co Wexford **Tel: 053 22816** Fax: 053 23832

In a renovated building near the Ballast Office, proprietor-chef Liam Forde's bistro-style first-floor restaurant overlooking the harbour has great atmosphere - created by happy customers and excellent use of lighting, with mirrors reflecting lots of candles. Tables are quite well-spaced and comfortable and the varied seasonal à la carte menus offer a wide choice, with vegetarian (and vegan) options prominently listed and a leaning towards seafood. From a dozen or so starters, try button mushrooms filled with brie & garlic then deep-fried in an almond coating (a nice little twist on the old favourite) or a delicious salad of marinated seared scallops, with mini crab spring rolls and a lemon dressing. Main courses might include a fish special trio of salmon, scallops & turbot in a light cream sauce and rack of local lamb with rosemary and raspberry jus and accompanying vegetables (small buttered steamed potatoes in their jackets, a mixture of julienne courgette, finely sliced onion & broccoli florets, stir fried briefly in butter and spring rolls filled with mashed potato). Everything is made on the premises - stocks, pastas, ice creams - the cooking is spot on and details excellent. Interesting, informative wine list. The early evening menus is particularly good value. **Seats 100.** Air conditioning. Children welcome. D Mon-Sat, 6-9.30. Early D, €22 (5-6pm only). Set Sun L €20 (12-6pm). Set D €34, also à la carte. House wine €18.50; s.c. discretionary. Closed Sun (except during Opera Festival), 24-26 Dec. MasterCard, Visa, Laser. **Directions:** The Quay Front.

Wexford

La Riva

féile bia **RESTAURANT** 2 Henrietta Street Crescent Quay Wexford Co Wexford
Tel: 053 24330 Fax: 053 24330
Email: warrengillen@dol.ie Web: www.larivawexford.com

Warren Gillen took over this first floor restaurant in May 2001 and, since then, has earned the respect of discerning diners from Wexford and beyond. The restaurant is bright and pleasant, with views out across the harbour - and through to the kitchen, where you can watch the team at work. Furnishings and table settings are simple, but staff are welcoming and efficient, and the opening details - really delicious breads and a complimentary amuse-bouche are very impressive. Warren takes pride in using as much local and organic produce as possible and hopes to be totally organic within two years. Judging by the Guide's most recent visit (summer of 2003) he is serving some of the finest food in the area: menus are quietly impressive; without resorting to long or flowery descriptions, dishes like sautéed John Dory with shitake mushrooms & spinach, crushed new potatoes & truffle oil, or cumin roasted new season lamb with shitake mushrooms & spinach, warm red wine & raspberry vinaigrette are extremely appealing - and they follow through on the plate, in memorable dishes which are beautifully balanced in presentation, flavour and texture. Creative vegetarian dishes are particularly tempting too and you can finish off with an updated classic dessert, like almond macaroons with mascarpone cream, Wexford strawberries & cream: simply delicious. Well-trained, attentive staff complement the creative cooking. An eight-course tasting Menu is now available (€55). **Seats 42.** Air conditioning. Children welcome. D daily, 6-10. L Sun only 1-4pm. 'Value' D, Mon-Fri, €30. Set D €30-35; also à la carte. House wine about €20; sc discretionary. MasterCard, Visa, Laser. **Directions:** Opposite Commodore Barry Statue.

Wexford

Mange 2

RESTAURANT 100 South Main St Wexford Co Wexford **Tel: 053 44033**
Email: thierryb@gofree.indigo.ie

Although the setting is simple - farmhouse-style pine tables, terracotta walls - and may not give away any clues about the standard of the food, it does have views through to the kitchen, where Richie Trappe and his team work hard to retain their reputation as one of Wexford's most exciting restaurants. The menu is also very understated - a single A4 page plainly laid out in a double column, but it is in fact ambitious: what you get here is genuinely creative cooking which is also good value for money. And it is a warm and welcoming place; tables are cleared very promptly and everything possible is done to ensure guests enjoy the food. Vegetarians are well looked after (there are blackboard specials daily in addition to à la carte menus) and vegetables are used creatively within each dish. Expect colourful starters and main dishes such as roast loin of pork with orange and black pepper crust, sweet potato dauphinoises and caramelised onion glaze. There is something here to please everyone, speedy service - and good value; this team lives up to their policy "that customers will never leave disappointed." Seats 40. Wheelchair access. Air conditioning. D 6-10.30 daily. A la carte. House wines from about €12.50 SC discretionary 10% on parties of 8+). Children welcome. Open all year. Amex, MasterCard, Visa, Laser. **Directions:** South end of Main Street, near Talbot Hotel.

Wexford

B&B

McMenamin's Townhouse

3 Auburn Terrace Redmond Road Wexford Co Wexford
Tel: 053 46442 Fax: 053 46442
Email: mcmem@indigo.ie Web: www.wexford-bedandbreakfast.com

Seamus and Kay McMenamin's redbrick end-of-terrace Victorian house is within walking distance of the town centre and has been one of the most highly-regarded places to stay in this area for some years. It is useful for first or last night overnight stops for travellers on the Rosslare ferry, as a base for the Wexford Opera or for a short break in this undervalued corner of Ireland. Bedrooms have neat shower rooms and they take pride in providing top quality beds and everything that could be required, including TV and tea/coffee-making facilities. The McMenamins' extensive local knowledge is generously passed on to guests and this, together with a really good breakfast - quite extensive menus include a range of fruits and juices, old-fashioned treats like kippers and lambs' kidneys in sherry sauce, served with freshly baked breads and home-made preserves - gets you off to a good start and helps to make the most of every day. Children welcome (under 2s free in parents' room, cots available without charge). No pets. **Rooms 5** (all shower only). B&B about €40 pps; ss about €10. Closed 20-29 Dec. Visa, MasterCard. **Directions:** Central near bus/rail station opposite cineplex.

Wexford

RESTAURANT / PUB

The Sky & The Ground

112 Main Street Wexford Co Wexford
Tel: 053 21273 Fax: 053 21832

Candle light, framed old advertisements, basic tables and chairs and a worn wooden floor create the atmospheric drinking space at The Sky & The Ground, a genuine old-style pub that frequently features traditional Irish music sessions. The "Heavens Above" restaurant upstairs also has lots of character- and the wine shop next door is under the same management; it stocks over 250 wines and beers from all over the world: choose your wine there and they will open in Heavens Above with no corkage charge. **Seats 65.** Open daily 5-10 (Sun 4-9). Set D from €20; also à la carte. Closed 25 Dec, Good Fri. MasterCard, Visa, Laser. **Directions:** On the south end of Wexford's Main Street.

Wexford

HOTEL

Talbot Hotel

Trinity St Wexford Co Wexford **Tel: 053 22566** Fax: 053 23377
Email: talbotwx@eircom.net Web: talbothotel.ie

Sister to the Stillorgan Park Hotel in Dublin, this 1960s hotel actually dates back to 1905 and has undergone massive renovation during the last few years. It is well-located on the harbour-front location and also convenient to the town centre - indeed, so many activities revolve around it that many would say the Talbot is the town centre. A warm welcome from friendly staff, plus the contented crowd that always seems to be milling around the foyer, immediately sets arriving guests at ease - and one is immediately struck by the range and quality of original paintings, which is a feature of great interest throughout the hotel. Bedrooms are inevitably somewhat limited by the age and style of the building, but are pleasant and comfortable, with phone, TV and tea/coffee trays as standard. The basement leisure centre is an unexpectedly characterful area, confirming the feeling that the Talbot will always spring a few surprises. Short breaks offered. Conference/banqueting facilities. Leisure centre, indoor swimming pool. Children welcome. Wheelchair access. Own parking. No pets. **Rooms 99** (all en-suite, 2 for disabled) Lift. B&B about €70 pps, ss about €20. Open all year except Christmas. Amex, Diners, MasterCard, Visa. **Directions:** On harbour front. ◇

Wexford

HOTEL

White's Hotel

Georges Street Wexford Co Wexford **Tel: 053 22311** Fax: 053 45000
Email: info@whiteshotel.iol.ie Web: www.whiteshotel.ie

From the outside this famous hotel looks relatively modern, certainly when approached from the car park, but the reality is that there was a hostelry on this site in the late 18th century, which is more apparent when viewed from George Street. Older bedrooms have been modernised and there's a health and fitness club (but no swimming pool) in the basement. Major reconstruction is due shortly, when the hotel is to be completely redesigned to build 80 new bedrooms , conference centre, swimming pool - and much else besides. Conference/banqueting (500/380). Secretarial services. Parking. Children welcome (under 3s free in parents' room, cots available). Pets by arrangement. Lift. **Rooms 82** (all en-suite). B&B €67.50 pps; ss €22. Open all year. Amex, Diners, MasterCard, Visa, Laser. **Directions:** Follow signs when leaving N25 or N11.

COUNTY WICKLOW

Wicklow is a miracle. Although the booming presence of Dublin is right next door, this spectacularly lovely county is very much its own place, an away-from-it-all world of moorland and mountain, farmland and garden, forest and lake, seashore and river. It's all right there, just over the nearest hill, yet it all seems so gloriously different.

In times past, much of Wicklow was recorded (by those who kept the official histories) as a mountain stronghold where rebels and hermits alike could keep their distance from the capital. But modern Wicklow has no need to be in a state of rebellion, for it is an invigorating and inspiring place which captivates everyone who lives there, so much so that while many of its citizens inevitably work in Dublin, they're Wicklow people first, and associate Dubs - if at all - an extremely long way down the line.

Their attitude is easily understood, for even with today's traffic, in 2004 it is only a short drive on notably handsome roads to transform your world from the crowded city streets right into the heart of some of the most beautiful scenery in all Ireland. Such scenery generates its own strong loyalties and sense of identity, and Wicklow folk are rightly and proudly a race apart. Drawing strength from their wonderful environment, they have a vigorous local life which keeps metropolitan blandness well at bay.

While being in a place so beautiful is almost sufficient reason for existence in itself, they're busy people too, with sheep farming and forestry and all sorts of light industries, while down in the workaday harbour of Arklow in the south of the county - a port with a long and splendid maritime history - they've been so successful in organising their own seagoing fleet of freighters that there are now more ships registered in Arklow than any other Irish port.

The richly varied quality of life extends inland from Arklow, as it does along the entire Wicklow coast. In the southeast of the county, the attractive village of Aughrim scored best in all Wicklow in the latest Tidy Town Awards (announced 8th September 2003) with a rating of 266 (88.7%). Up in the hills nearby, the fascinatingly re-created village of Macreddin, setting for the Brook Lodge Hotel complex, has a lively Organic Market on the first Sunday of each month, a mecca for foodies.

Local Attractions and Information

Arklow, Tourism Information 0402 32484
Ashford, Mount Usher Gardens 0404 40116
Avoca, Tourism Information 0402 35788
Blessington, Russborough House & Gardens 045 865239
Bray, Kilruddery House & Gardens 01 286 3405
Bray, National Sealife Centre 01 286 6939
Derrynamuck, Dwyer McAllister Traditional Cottage 0404 45325
Enniskerry, Powerscourt House & Gardens 01 204 6000
Glendalough Farm Market (second Suns) 0404 43885

Glendalough, Tourism Information	0404 45688
Glendalough, Visitor Centre	0404 45325
Kilmacanogue, Avoca Handweavers Garden	01 286 7466
Kilquade, National Garden Exhibition Centre	01 281 9890
Macreddin Organic Market (first Suns month)	0402 36444
Rathdrum, Avondale House	0404 46111
Rathdrum, Kilmacurragh Arboretum	01 647 3000
Wicklow County, Gardens Festival (May-July)	0404 20100
Wicklow Mountains, National Park	0404 45425
Wicklow Town, Wicklow Historic Gaol	0404 61599
Wicklow Town, Tourism Information	0404 69117

Arklow

Kitty's of Arklow

féile bia **PUB / RESTAURANT**

56 Main Street Arklow Co Wicklow
Tel: 0402 31669 Fax: 0402 31553
Email: conor@kittysofarklow.com Web: www.kittysofarklow.com

A big blue double-fronted building in the centre of town, Kitty's is something of an institution in Arklow. Large and airy ground floor bar areas are decorated in retro '50s style (with big comfortable chairs and old-fashioned radiators) and there's a lofty first floor restaurant with a slightly olde-world feel (open fireplaces and lots of wood). It's very popular with locals ranging from young commuters to large family groups, who like the informal atmosphere and modern food at affordable prices - the early evening menu is especially good value. Menus include a wide range of seafood and descriptions aren't too fussy: typical starters include a goats cheese & spinach tartlet with tomato relish, while main courses might include several fish dishes. Vegetarians are well looked after and coeliac options are also available on request. Good quality ingredients are used and it's a place you could find yourself going back to, not least because notably friendly, efficient and professional staff make sure everyone's happy. Children welcome. **Seats 110** (private room 24). Air conditioning. D daily 6-10. Early D from €20 (6-7pm). Set D €35, also à la carte. House wine €17. Bar food daily, 12-5 (Sun from 12.30). Closed 25 Dec & Good Fri. Amex, Diners, MasterCard, Visa, Laser. **Directions:** Centre of town, beside car park.

Arklow

Plattenstown House

COUNTRY HOUSE

Coolgreaney Road Arklow Co Wicklow **Tel: 0402 37822** Fax: 0402 37822
Email: mcdpr@indigo.ie Web: www.wicklow.ie/farm/f-plattn.htm

About halfway between Dublin and Rosslare (each about an hour's drive away) and overlooking parkland, this quiet, peaceful place is set in 50 acres of land amidst its own lovely gardens close to the sea - and Margaret McDowell describes her period farmhouse well as having "the soft charm typical of the mid-19th century houses built in scenic Wicklow". There is plenty to do in the area, with golf, riding stables and forest walks all nearby, as well as the sea. There's a traditional drawing room furnished with family antiques overlooking the front garden, a TV lounge available for guests' use and a lovely dining room where breakfast is served - and evening meals are also offered by arrangement. Bedrooms vary in size and outlook according to their position in the house and have interestingly different characters, but all are comfortably furnished. Children welcome (under 3s free in parents' room). No pets. **Rooms 4** (3 en-suite with shower only, 1 with private bathroom). B&B €38pps, ss €7. Weekend short breaks - 2 B&B and one dinner €85-95; 3 B&B midweek €90-102. Closed at Christmas. MasterCard, Visa. **Directions:** Top of Arklow town, small roundabout, straight on to Coolgreaney Road. 5 km on left.

Ashford

Ashford House

PUB

Ashford Co Wicklow **Tel: 0404 40481** Fax: 0404 40990
Email: tom@ashfordhouse.ie Web: www.ashfordhouse.ie

This well-maintained large pub in the centre of Ashford village presents a neat face to the world and has cheering open fires, plenty of natural materials and friendly staff to create a warm and welcoming tone. A high-ceilinged bistro behind the bar area also has an open fire; daytime food can be served in either area - a useful place for an informal bite. Bar menu all day, 12.30-closing. L&D daily (12.30-3, 6-9.30) Toilets wheelchair accessible. Amex, MasterCard, Visa, Diners, Laser. **Directions:** Dublin-Wexford road (N11); off roundabout on Main St. ◇

Ashford

Ballyknocken House

FARM GUESTHOUSE

Gleanealy Ashford Co Wicklow
Tel: 0404 44627 Fax: 0404 44696
Email: cfulvio@ballyknocken.com Web: www.ballyknocken.com

FARMHOUSE OF THE YEAR

Perfectly placed for walking holidays in the Wicklow Hills, playing golf, or simply for touring the area, Catherine Fulvio's charming Victorian farmhouse provides comfort, cosiness, good food and hospitality. After a period working at nearby Tinakilly House, Catherine took over this family business in 1999 - the farm has been in the Byrne family for three generations and they have welcomed guests for over thirty years - and she has since refurbished it throughout in old country style. A gently Victorian theme prevails throughout (not too fussy): bedrooms have been charmingly done up, with antique furniture and very good beds - and pretty bathrooms, five of which have Victorian baths. The dining room, parlour and sitting room have also had the makeover and her energetic quest for perfection also extends to the garden, where new fruit tree, roses and herbs are now settling in. Comfort and style aside, Catherine cooks splendid dinners based on local produce, including vegetables and herbs from the Ballyknocken farm (with wine list including some specially imported wines); the cooking style is modern and (influenced by her Italian husband Claudio) there's a Mediterranean flavour. All this plus extensive breakfasts and a relaxing atmosphere ensure guests keep coming back for more: the obvious winner for our Farmhouse of the Year Award! * NB: Catherine is opening Ballyknocken Cookery School in April 2004. **Rooms 7** (all en-suite) B&B €55 pps, ss €30. Residents D Tue-Sat, Set D €35, houses wines €20. No D on Sun. Non-resident group (8+) lunches catered for, by arrangement. Closed Dec-Jan. MasterCard, Visa. **Directions:** From Dublin turn right after Texaco Petrol Station in Ashford. Continue for 3 miles.House on right.

Aughrim

Clone House

COUNTRY HOUSE

Aughrim Co Wicklow **Tel: 0402 36121** Fax: 0402 36029
Email: stay@clonehouse.com Web: www.clonehouse.com

The oldest part of Jeff and Carla Watson's rambling country house in the lovely unspoilt south Wicklow countryside goes back to the 1600s, although it was largely rebuilt in 1805 after burning in the 1798 Rebellion. Today this elegantly furnished and hospitable house is full of comfort, providing a quiet and relaxing haven, away from the stresses of modern life. Open fires in every room are a particularly attractive feature - and thoughtful little touches abound, including fresh fruit and chocolates in each bedroom (some with four posters), as well as tea and coffee making facilities - and no television to intrude into this tranquil retreat. Carla cooks a 5-course dinner by arrangement - and non-resident parties of any size can be accommodated if there is room. Children under 3 free in parents' room (cot available). No pets. Gym, weight room, sauna; table tennis; garden. **Rooms 7** (5 en-suite, 2 private bathrooms, 5 shower only, all no smoking) B&B €75pps, ss €40. Dinner at 8pm by arrangement, €55. Wines about €18 (BYO corkage €8). 10% SC on dinners. Open all year. MasterCard, Visa. **Directions:** Follow brown house signs from Aughrim or Woodenbridge.

Aughrim

Lawless Hotel

RESTAURANT / HOTEL

Aughrim Co Wicklow **Tel: 0402 36146** Fax: 0402 36384
Email: reservations@lawlesshotel.com Web: www.lawlesshotel.com

Picturesquely situated beside the river in the lovely village of Aughrim, the O'Toole family's historic hotel dates back to 1787; it was a popular meeting place during the 1798 uprising and, with the arrival of the railway in the 1800s, began a new lease of life as the Railway Hotel. Renovations and extensions have, on the whole, been undertaken with respect for the character of the original building; the adjacent holiday homes tend to dominate the village, but have now blended in a little. Recently refurbished bedrooms tend to be on the small side, but are attractively furnished. There's a lovely dining room overlooking the river beside the bridge and a paved riverside area at the back is used for informal summer food - and makes a romantic spot for wedding photographs. A man-made angling park beside the hotel offers all year angling, with special disabled facilities. Conference/banqueting (250/250). Secretarial services. Fishing. Garden. Parking. Children welcome. No pets. **Rooms 14** (all en-suite). B&B €77.50 pps, ss €25. Food available 12.30-2.30 & 5.30-8.30 daily. Wheelchair access (ground floor only). Closed 24-26 Dec. MasterCard, Visa, Laser. **Directions:** Take N747 from Arklow town via Woodenbridge.

Avoca

Avoca Handweavers

féile bia CAFÉ

Avoca Village Co Wicklow **Tel: 0402 35105** Fax: 0402 35446
Email: info@avoca.ie Web: www.avoca.ie

Avoca handweavers, established in 1723, is Ireland's oldest business. It's a family owned craft design company which now has half a dozen branches throughout Ireland (most of which feature in this Guide) and the business originated here, at Avoca village, where you can watch the hand weavers who produce the lovely woven woollen rugs and fabrics which became the hallmark of the company. Today, the appeal of Avoca shops is threefold: the high standard of crafts sold, their beautiful locations, and restaurants that have built up a well-deserved reputation for imaginative, wholesome home-cooked food. Garden. Parking. Children welcome. Pets allowed in some areas. **Seats 75.** Open all day (10-5) Mon-Sun. House wine about €12.50. No service charge. Wheelchair access. Closed 25-26 Dec. Amex, Diners, MasterCard, Visa, Laser. **Directions:** Leave N11 at Rathnew and follow signs for Avoca.

Blessington

Downshire House Hotel

féile bia HOTEL

Blessington Co Wicklow **Tel: 045 865 199** Fax: 045 865 335
Email: info@downshirehouse.com Web: www.downshirehouse.com

Situated just 18 miles from Dublin on the N81, in the tree-lined main street of Blessington, this friendly village hotel offers unpretentious comfort which is very winning. Blessington is an attractive village in an area of great natural beauty and archaeological interest – and it's also very close to Ireland's great Palladian mansion, Russborough House, home of the world-famous Beit art collection. The present owners have run the hotel since 1959 and instigated many improvements, including conference facilities for up to 100 and refurbishment of public areas. Simply furnished bedrooms, which include two single rooms, all have en-suite bathrooms with full bath and shower. This is a place that people feel comfortable with, because it exudes that indefinable sense of being well-run and genuinely hospitable that goes with caring management. You will also eat well here - not the competitive cutting-edge food of young chefs in the city, but wholesome, satisfying country fare served by friendly and professional staff with a real desire to please: a soothing and restorative place to take a break. Conference/banqueting (100). Garden, walking. Children welcome; cots available (€8). **Rooms 25** (all with full en-suite bathrooms). B&B €84pps; ss €9. Closed 21 Dec-7 Jan. MasterCard, Visa, Laser, Switch. **Directions:** 18 miles from Dublin on the N81.

Bray

The Tree of Idleness Restaurant

RESTAURANT

Seafront Bray Co Wicklow **Tel: 01 282 8183** Fax: 01 282 8183
Email: treeofidleness@eircom.net

This much-loved seafront restaurant opened in 1979 when the owners, Akis and Susan Courtellas, arrived from Cyprus bringing with them the name of their previous restaurant (now in Turkish-held north Cyprus). A collection of photographs of old Cyprus in the reception area establishes the traditional Mediterranean atmosphere of the restaurant – and the menu cover bears a drawing of the original Tree of Idleness. Since Akis' death some years ago, Susan has run the restaurant herself with the help of Tom Monaghan, restaurant manager since 1980 and, since 2002, Mark McGillicuddy, the head chef. It is he who now offers modern Greek Cypriot/Mediterranean menus based on the style which has made this restaurant famous - and the most remarkable feature of the Tree of Idleness is its consistency, in maintaining both high standards and the unique house style. Alongside the classics – tzatziki, humus, taramasalata, Greek salad, dolmades, moussaka (including a vegetarian variation), souvlaki – there are some specialities which have had the world beating a path to the door for over 20 years. Then there is the dessert trolley, which is nothing less than temptation on wheels: it always carries a range of fresh and exotic fruits, baklava, home-made ice creams, several chocolate desserts, Greek yoghurt mousse and much else besides. Service is invariably excellent and the wine list includes a wide selection of house wines (some Greek) and some rare vintages, including wines from the Russian Massandra Collection, which go back to 1923. No children under 10 after 8 pm. **Seats 50.** D Tue-Sun, 7.30-10.30 (Sun to 10). Set D €45, à la carte also available. House wines from €20. 10% SC. Closed Mon, Christmas & 2 weeks Aug. Amex, MasterCard, Visa, Laser, Switch. **Directions:** On seafront towards Bray Head.

Delgany

Glenview Hotel

Hotel / Restaurant

Glen O' The Downs Delgany Co Wicklow
Tel: 01 287 3399 Fax: 01 287 7511
Email: sales@glenview.com Web: www.glenviewhotel.com

Famous for its views over the luxuriantly green and leafy Glen O'The Downs, this well-located hotel has all the advantages of a beautiful rural location, yet is just a half hour's drive from Dublin. State-of-the-art facilities are offered in the conference centre, there's an excellent Health and Leisure Club (now including beauty treatment and therapy rooms) and the bedrooms are all attractively furnished in warm colours and a gently modern style. Public areas include a very pleasant, comfortably furnished conservatory bar, which is a good place for an informal meal (Conservatory Bistro menu, international cooking, 12.30-9). All this, together with special breaks (golf, health and fitness, riding) offering good value, make the hotel a valuable asset to the area. Conference/banqueting (250/180). Secretarial services, ISDN lines, video conferencing. Leisure centre (indoor swimming pool). Snooker room (adults only). Garden, woodland walks. Children welcome (under 2s free in parents' room, cots available without charge, play room). No pets. **Rooms 70** (all en-suite, 1 suite, 12 executive rooms). Lift. B&B €115, ss € 38. Hotel closed 25 Dec.

Woodlands Restaurant: The restaurant has a great natural asset in forest views over the Glen-O'-the Downs although it can otherwise be somewhat short on atmosphere. The presence of head chef Derek Dunne, a well-known successful competitor in the Irish Culinary Team, puts the food on a more ambitious level than most hotel dining rooms. He presents interesting table d'hôte and à la carte menus based on local ingredients - quite a lot of seafood, Wicklow lamb, venison - and mainly classical French in style. Cooking is competent but may not always live up to the promise of the menu. Restaurant not suitable for children after 7.30pm. **Seats 90.** Air conditioning. Pianist some evenings. D daily, 6.30-9.30; L Sun only, 12.30-2.30. Set D €45, à la carte also available; Set Sun L €25. House wines from €20. No SC. Closed 25 Dec, bank hols. Amex, Diners, MasterCard, Visa, Laser. **Directions:** On N11, turn left 2 miles southbound of Kilmacanogue.

Dunlavin

Rathsallagh House, Golf & Country Club

féile bia COUNTRY HOUSE

Dunlavin Co Wicklow
Tel: 045 403 112 Fax: 045 403 343
Email: info@rathsallagh.com Web: www.rathsallagh.com

This large, rambling country house is just an hour from Dublin, but it could be in a different world. Although it's very professionally operated, the O'Flynn family insist it is not an hotel and - despite the addition of an 18-hole golf course with clubhouse in the grounds - the gentle rhythms of life around the country house and gardens ensure that the atmosphere is kept decidedly low-key. Day rooms are elegantly furnished in country house style, with lots of comfortable seating areas and open fires. Accommodation includes beautiful big rooms with luxurious bathrooms in a new block, built discreetly behind the main courtyard in materials which will age gracefully to match the older buildings while, as in all old houses, the original rooms do vary; some are very spacious with lovely country views while other smaller, simpler rooms in the stable yard have a special cottagey charm. Rathsallagh is renowned for its magnificent Edwardian breakfast buffet, which was recognised in 2001 through selection as National winner of the Guide's Irish Breakfast Awards. Breakfast at Rathsallagh offers every conceivable good thing: including silver chafing dishes, full of reminders of yesteryear. Good food, warm hospitality and surroundings that are quiet or romantic to suit the mood of the day make Rathsallagh an ideal venue for conferences and small weddings. Conference/banqueting 150. Golf (18), gardens, tennis, cycling, walking. Pool table. Beauty salon. Pets allowed by arrangement. **Rooms 29** (2 suites, 2 for disabled). B&B €125, ss €65. Closed 6-12 Jan.

Restaurant: Head chef John Luke creates interesting menus based on local produce, much of it from Rathsallagh's own farm and walled garden. A drink in the old kitchen bar is recommended while reading the 4-course menu - country house with world influences - then guests can settle down in the graciously furnished dining room overlooking the gardens and the golf course. Menus are not over-complicated but offer a well-balanced selection of about five dishes on each course, changed daily. John Luke sources his ingredients with care and there is a welcome directness and simplicity of style on the menu that is carried through in confident cooking of dishes that are well-conceived and visually tempting but especially memorable for flavour. Leave room for some Irish farmhouse cheese served from a traditional trolley, or delicious desserts which are often based on fruit from the garden. **Seats 120** (private room, 48) D Daily, 7-9. Set D €60-65; house wine €18-20; SC discretionary. * Not suitable for children under 12. Lunch is available only for residents, but food is served at Rathsallagh Golf Club, 11-8.45 daily. Non-residents welcome for dinner, by reservation. Amex, Diners, MasterCard, Visa, Laser. Helipad. **Directions:** 15 miles south of Naas off Carlow Road, take Kilcullen Bypass (M9), turn left 2 miles south of Priory Inn, follow signposts.

Enniskerry

féile bia CAFÉ

Powerscourt Terrace Café

Powerscourt House Enniskerry Co Wicklow
Tel: 01 204 6070 Fax: 01 204 6072
Email: simon@avoca.ie Web: www.avoca.ie

Situated in a stunning location overlooking the famous gardens and fountains of Powerscourt House, the Pratt family of Avoca Handweavers opened this self-service restaurant in the summer of 1997. It is a delightfully relaxed space, with a large outdoor eating area as well as the 160-seater café, and the style and standard of food is similar to the original Avoca restaurant at Kilmacanogue. So head chef Catherine Davey ensures that everything is freshly made, using as many local ingredients as possible – including organic herbs and vegetables – with lots of healthy food. Avoca cafés are renowned for interesting salads, home-bakes and good pastries, and also excellent vegetarian dishes many of which, such as oven-roasted vegetable and goat's cheese tart, have become specialities. Parking (some distance from the house). Children welcome. **Seats 160** (indoors; additional 140 outside terrace; private room 20-90). No-smoking area. Toilets wheelchair accessible. Open daily 10 -5 (Sun to 5.30). House wine about €13. Closed 25-26 Dec. Amex, Diners, MasterCard, Visa, Laser. **Directions:** 2 miles from Enniskerry Village.

Glendalough

B&B

Derrymore House

Lake Road Glendalough Co Wicklow **Tel: 0404 45493** Fax: 0404 45517
Email: patkelleher@eircom.net Web: http://homepage.eircom.net/~derrymore/

Very close to Glendalough, on a six-acre site of natural mountain woodland, Pat and Penny Kelleher's friendly B&B is in an unique position in the valley of Glendalough, overlooking the Lower Lake. It makes a quiet base for the outdoor pursuits which can be so enjoyable in the area - notably walking, fishing and horse riding - and seems like an oasis of calm when there are too many visitors around for comfort. Bedrooms are appropriately furnished in a fresh country style with antique furniture, TV/VCR and neat en-suite shower rooms. A guests' sitting room has multi-channel TV/VCR and a library of videos and, in fine weather, it is very pleasant to have a private garden to sit in. Home-baked bread for breakfast. Not suitable for children under 5. No pets. **Rooms 5** (all en-suite). B&B €35 pps; ss €15. Closed Nov-Feb. **Directions:** Follow signs tor Glendalough - on the right as you approach.

Glendalough Area

N B&B

Derrybawn Mountain Lodge

Derrybawn Laragh Glendalough Co Wicklow
Tel: 0404 45644 Fax: 0404 45645
Email: derrybawnlodge@eircom.net Web: www.derrybawnlodge.com

On Derrybawn Mountain, close to Glendalough, Aidan and Teresa Kavanagh's purpose-built guesthouse offers spacious hotel standard accommodation in a secluded location, at very moderate prices. Bedrooms are furnished in a straightforward, practical style with everything you could need - double and single bed, TV, phone, tea/coffee making and hair dryer), bathroom with full bath and overbath shower - and there's a comfortably furnished residents' lounge (where smoking is allowed). Both Teresa and Aidan are members of the local mountain rescue team and can advise on activities in the area; maps and books are also available for reference in the lounge. Children welcome (under 5 free in parents' room, cot available free of charge, baby sitting arranged). Dogs allowed outside (facilities provided). Wheelchair access. Garden. Golf, fishing, equestrian, walking nearby. Off season/short breaks and group rates offered. **Rooms 8** (all en-suite, all no smoking). B&B €45, ss €13. Evening meals available for groups, by arrangement. Closed 24-27 Dec. Amex, Diners, MasterCard, Visa, Laser. **Directions:** Signed from main road.

Grangecon

CAFÉ

Grangecon Café

Grangecon Co Wicklow **Tel: 045 403 982**
Fax: 045 403 982 Email: grangeconcafe@eircom.net

Wholesome aromas at Jenny and Richard Street's smashing little place in the charming village of Grangecon bode well for the hungry traveller, also the sight of contented locals relaxing, books in hand, over a post-prandial coffee. It really is little, with just two simple wooden communal tables, a display area for their lovely cold meats, salads, home-bakes and farmhouse cheeses, a larder freezer stocked with home-cooked ready meals to take home and a few shelves displaying speciality products not usually found in country villages, many of them organic - pasta, rice, orzo, olive oils, mustards, teas, coffees, home-made preserves. Their stated aim is "to provide you with a really good food stop": this they do in spades. The menu is understandably brief but the quiche is a little classic and comes with a scrumptious salad; similarly moist, freshly-baked brown bread arrives with cooked ham (Rudd's), cheese (Sheridan's) and chutney (home-made), also garnished with salad: simple and excellent - why aren't there more places like this? No wine but you can opt for delicious chilled Crinnaughton apple juice, which comes from Cappoquin, and B-Y-O is fine (the pub across the road can supply wine if required). Luscious Illy coffee to finish and maybe a slice of wholesome dried apricot cake - just don't leave without a packet of their absolutely delectably light and crispy home-baked crackers for cheese. Seats 12. Open all day Tue-Sat, 10am-5pm. Closed Sun, Mon. and all Jan. **No Credit Cards. Directions:** 3 miles north of Baltinglass on road to Dunlavin.

Greystones

Bel's Bistro

Ⓝ **RESTAURANT** Church Road Greystones Co Wicklow **Tel: 01 201 6990**

Everything about Bel's is modern, from the striking building in Greystones' main street it is housed in, to the large, high ceilinged dining area on two levels at the front (with a lower level at the rear). It's strictly bistro style, so no table cloths, but everything else is high quality and the ambience created is impressive. Early bird menu is short and good value, as is the well-conceived children's menu, while the a la carte selection is much more extensive. Open Mon-Sat 5.00-12.00 (last orders 10.30pm) and Sun. Bank Holidays 12.00-10.00pm. A la carte. House wines from €17. Amex, MasterCard, Visa.

Greystones

The Hungry Monk

féile bia **RESTAURANT** Church Road Greystones Co Wicklow **Tel: 01 287 5759**
Fax: 01 287 7183 Email: hungrymonk@eircom.net

Well-known wine buff Pat Keown has run this hospitable first floor restaurant on the main street since 1988. Pat is a great and enthusiastic host; his love of wine is infectious and the place is spick and span – and the monk-related decor is a bit of fun. A combination of hospitality and interesting good quality food at affordable prices are at the heart of this restaurant's success – sheer generosity of spirit ensures value for money as well as a good meal. Seasonal menus offered include a well-priced all-day Sunday lunch and an evening à la carte menu. Menus are well-balanced to include traditional dishes as well as more unusual ones such as chicken El Greco and several vegetarian dishes with an international flavour. Blackboard specials include the day's seafood dishes and also any special wine offers; the outstanding wine list includes a wide range of half bottles and wines by the glass. *Downstairs, The Hungry Monk Wine Bar offers a short well-chosen menu of about eight varied dishes and a carefully selected short wine list. Children welcome. Restaurant **seats 50.** Air conditioning. D Tue -Sat 7-11; L Sun only, 12.30-8. D à la carte; Set Sun L about €22. House wines from €17, SC 10%. *Wine Bar open Tue-Sat, 5-12, Sun 4-10 Closed Mon, 24-26 Dec. Amex, MasterCard, Visa, Laser. **Directions:** Centre of Greystones village beside DART. ◇

Greystones

Vino Pasta

RESTAURANT Church Road Greystones Co Wicklow **Tel: 01 287 4007** Fax: 01 287 4827

Attractive awnings and clear signage make a good impression at Bill and Avril Tyrrell's popular neighbourhood restaurant and, once past the tiny bar/reception area, terracotta walls, ethnic bric-à-brac and a crowd of happy diners create a warm atmosphere. Table settings are bistro-style - paper cloths & napkins - and Avril's menu is moderately priced, majoring in pastas and pizzas, with daily fish specials on a blackboard menu. Prompt, friendly service, sound cooking and generous portions add up to a good deal, making this the kind of place that locals pop into frequently. Limited wine list. **Seats 60.** Air conditioning. Children welcome up to 7pm. D Tue-Sun 5-11 daily (Sun 3-9). A la carte. House wine €16.50. 10% sc on parties of 6+. Closed Mon, 25 Dec, 2 wks July. MasterCard, Visa, Laser. **Directions:** End of Main Street beside DART station.

Kilmacanogue

Avoca Handweavers - Kilmacanogue

féile bia **CAFÉ** Kilmacanogue Co Wicklow **Tel: 01 286 7466**
Fax: 01 286 2367 Web: www.avoca.ie

Avoca Handweavers is one of the country's most famous craft shops but it is also well worth allowing time for a meal when you visit. People come here from miles around to tuck into the famously wholesome home-cooked food at Avoca Handweavers Restaurant, where head chef Eimer Rainsford supervises the production of home-cooked food which is as healthy as it is delicious. The importance of sourcing only the very best ingredients has always been recognised at Avoca, where food is based as much as possible on local and artisan produce, and there is a commitment to using products from recognised Quality Assurance Schemes. (In recognition of this commitment, Avoca Cafés were the 2003 recipients of the prestigious Féile Bia Award). The style at Avoca is eclectic and, although they are perhaps especially well-known for great baking and wholesome traditional dishes like beef and Guinness casserole, their salads and vegetables are also legendary - and their repertoire also includes a lot of dishes influenced by other cultures, notably Mediterranean and middle-eastern. There is also a wide range of excellent delicatessen fare for sale in the shop - and you can make many of their dishes at home too, using recipes given in the two handsome Avoca Café Cookbooks. * Also at: Avoca, Powerscourt, & Suffolk Street, Dublin 2 (see entries). Children welcome. **Seats 200.** Air conditioning. Open daily, 10-5. House wine about €12.50. No s.c. Closed 25-26 Dec. Amex, Diners, MasterCard, Visa, Laser. **Directions:** On N11 sign posted before Kilmacanogue Village.

Kiltegan

COUNTRY HOUSE

Barraderry Country House

Barraderry Kiltegan Co Wicklow
Tel: 059 6473209 Fax: 059 647 3209
Email: jo.hobson@oceanfree.net Web: www.barraderrycountryhouse.com

Olive and John Hobson's delightful Georgian house is in a quiet rural area close to the Wicklow Mountains and, once their family had grown up, the whole house was extensively refurbished and altered for the comfort of guests. Big bedrooms with country views are beautifully furnished with old family furniture and have well-finished bathrooms, and there's a spacious sitting room for guests' use too. Barraderry would make a good base for touring the lovely counties of Wicklow, Kildare, Carlow and Wexford and there's plenty to do nearby, with six golf courses within a half hour drive, several hunts and equestrian centres within easy reach and also Punchestown, Curragh and Naas racecourses - and, of course, walking in the lovely Wicklow Mountains. Garden. Children welcome (under 3s free in parents room). Pets allowed in some areas. Rooms 4 (all en-suite). B&B €45 pps; ss €5. Closed 15 Dec-15 Jan. MasterCard. **Directions:** 7 km from Baltinglass on R747, 1 km Kiltegan.

Kiltegan

HOTEL / COUNTRY HOUSE

Humewood Castle

Kiltegan Co Wicklow
Tel: 059 647 3215 Fax: 059 647 3382
Email: humewood@iol.ie Web: www.humewood.com

It's impossible to imagine anywhere more romantic to stay than Humewood Castle. A fairytale 19th-century Gothic Revival castle in private ownership set in beautiful parkland in the Wicklow Hills, it has been extensively renovated and stunningly decorated. While the castle is very large by any standards, many of the rooms are of surprisingly human proportions. Thus, for example, while the main dining room provides a fine setting for some two dozen guests, there are more intimate rooms suitable for smaller numbers. Similarly, the luxuriously appointed bedrooms and bathrooms, while indisputably grand, are also very comfortable. Recent additions include two bedroom lodges on the grounds with own sitting rooms and self-catering kitchens. Country pursuits are an important part of life at Humewood too - horseriding, fishing, shooting, deer stalking, hunting and falconry can all be arranged - but even if you do nothing more energetic than just relaxing beside the fire, this is a really special place for a break. It's also a wonderful location for a wedding and conferences, product launches and corporate entertaining packages can be tailored to meet specific requirement. Conference/banqueting (100/100). Business centre, secretarial services. Snooker. Garden, tennis, walking, cycling. Parking. Children welcome. Pets by arrangement. **Rooms 13** (all en-suite, 3 suites, all no smoking). Room rate with breakfast, from €480 high season. Residents' L €30, D €65; house wine about €23; s.c.15%. Amex, MasterCard, Visa. **Directions:** Dublin - N81- Baltinglass - R747 Hacketstown Road.

Macreddin

HOTEL

The BrookLodge Hotel

Macreddin Village Co Wicklow **Tel: 0402 36444** Fax: 0402 36580
Email: brooklodge@macreddin.ie Web: www.brooklodge.com

Built on the site of a deserted village in a Wicklow valley, this extraordinary food, drink and leisure complex exists thanks to the vision of three brothers, Evan, Eoin and Bernard Doyle. The driving force is Evan, a pioneer of the new organic movement when he ran The Strawberry Tree restaurant in Killarney. Now their new "village" has taken root and is thriving, with an hotel and restaurant already receiving national recognition for their strong position on organic food (BrookLodge won the Euro-Toques Natural Food Award in association with the Guide, in 2003), and a little "street" with an olde-worlde pub (Actons), a micro-brewery and gift shops selling home-made produce and related quality products. Organic food markets, held on the first Sunday of the month (first and third in summer) have proved a great success. The hotel is spacious and welcoming, with elegant country house furnishings, open fires and plenty of places to sit quietly or meet for a sociable drink. A new spa centre - called The Wells - and additional bedrooms are due for completion by early 2004; it will include a indoor-to-outdoor swimming pool, gym, juice bar and a wide variety of exclusive beauty and health treatments. Midweek, weekend and low season special offers are good value. Conference/banqueting (150). Secretarial services, video conferencing. Equestrian centre. Garden, walking. Snooker. Children welcome (cots available). Pets allowed in some areas by arrangement. **Rooms 54** (all en-suite, 12 suites). Lift. B&B from €105 pps; ss €40. Open all year.

The Strawberry Tree: The Strawberry Tree restaurant is in an unusual room, with a mirrored ceiling - quite unlike the rest of the hotel - a little strange in the daytime, but very romantic when candlelit at night. The original philosophy prevails here and the most interesting aspect of the menu is the page headed 'Organic, Free Range and Wild Food' which both lists the suppliers and sets out the BrookLodge philosophy of sourcing from producers using slow organic methods and harvesting in their correct season. Thus, for example, farmhouse cheeses are from Sheridan's Cheesemongers, meat from Hugh Robson's organic farm in Co Clare and organic vegetables from Denis Healy - plus, of course, their own produce grown just outside the kitchen, when available. Chef Frederick Souty's background is classical French - as good a base as there is when it comes to sourcing the best and cooking with finesse - and, given the quality of ingredients used and the standard of cooking, meals at Macreddin represent very good value. **Seats 120** (private room, 45). Air conditioning. Toilets wheelchair accessible. D Mon-Sat 7-10, L Sun only 1-7. Set D €48, Set Sun L €30. House wines €21. SC discretionary. Closed D Sun. *William Actons Pub - Bar food daily, 12.30-9; The Orchard Café, light meals 12.30-7 (to 9 in summer). Amex, Diners, MasterCard, Visa, Laser. **Directions:** Signed from Aughrim.

Newtownmountkennedy

Druids Glen Marriott Hotel & Country Club

HOTEL

Newtownmountkennedy Co Wicklow
Tel: 01 287 0800 Fax: 01 287 0501
Email: events.druids@marriotthotels.com Web: www.marriott.ie

Just 20 miles south of Dublin, in a stunning location between the sea and the mountains and adjacent to the famous Druids Glen Golf Club, the hotel has general appeal but is particularly attractive for the business guest and for conferences and corporate events. Convenient to the capital and easy to reach, there's a feeling of space throughout which is increasingly difficult to achieve in the city - and an away-from-it-all atmosphere that can be conducive to productive meetings. Public areas are impressive - the tone is set in the large marbled foyer with its dramatic feature fireplace and seating areas, bars and dining areas lead off it in an open plan arrangement. Bedrooms, many of them "double/doubles" (with two queen sized beds), are all very spacious and have excellent facilities - and all bathrooms have separate bath and walk-in shower. In addition to golf, there's a wide range of recreational facilities on site, while those nearby include horse riding, archery, quad biking, orienteering and team building - and, of course, gentler attractions like the Wicklow Mountains National Park and Powerscourt Gardens are on the doorstep. A place to relax and unwind as well as do business. Conference/banqueting 250/220; business centre, secretarial services. Golf (18); hotel spa and health club, swimming pool; walking, garden. **Rooms 148** (all en-suite, 11 suites, 137 executive, 6 disabled). Lift. Children welcome (under 12s free in parents' room, cots available without charge; playroom). 24 hr. room service, laundry/valet service. B&B €105, ss €80.

Flynns Steakhouse: Quite small and intimate, with an open log fire and candlelight, Flynn's has more atmosphere than the bigger daytime Druids Restaurant (where breakfast, carvery lunch and dinner are served). American style steaks and grills are the speciality but, demonstrating a welcome commitment to using Irish produce, a supply of Certified Irish Angus has been contracted for the hotel; just remember that American-style means big - 24oz porterhouse and ribeye, for example...Rack of Wicklow lamb is another speciality and there's a sprinkling of other dishes with an Irish flavour which might not be expected in an international hotel, like Dingle crab cakes, Guinness braised mussels - and an Irish cheese platter. **Seats 55** (private room 15). Not suitable for children under 12. D Thu-Sat, 7-10. Set Sun L € 25, Set D from €30, also à la carte. House wine, from €22; SC discretionary. Closed Sun D-Wed. *The larger Druid's Restaurant serves breakfast, lunch & dinner daily; L carvery, Set D from €40, Druids Irish Menu à la carte. Bar meals also available in 'The Thirteenth' bar or, in fine weather, on a sheltered deck outside the two restaurants. Amex, Diners, MasterCard, Visa, Laser. **Directions:** 20 miles south of Dublin on N11 at Newtownmountkennedy.

Rathdrum

Avonbrae Guesthouse

GUESTHOUSE

Rathdrum Co Wicklow **Tel: 0404 46198** Fax: 0404 46198
Email: info@avonbrae.com Web: www.avonbrae.com

Lovers of the outdoor life will find that Paddy Geoghegan's hospitable guesthouse makes a comfortable and relaxed base - walking, cycling, riding, pony-trekking, golf and fishing are major attractions to this beautiful area, but it's also ideal just for a quiet break. (Paddy offers weekly and weekend rates and off-season breaks which are very reasonable.) Simply furnished bedrooms vary in size and outlook but all have tea and coffee trays and en-suite facilities (only the smallest room has a bath). There are open fires as well as central heating and a comfortable guest sitting room. For fine weather, there's a tennis court in the well-kept garden, and although this perhaps sounds grander than it is, there is even a nice little indoor swimming pool. Children welcome (under 2s free in parent's room, cot available). Pets permitted by arrangement. **Rooms 7** (all en-suite, 1 with private bathroom). B&B €35 pps; ss €10. Evening meals €22 at 6.30pm. House wine €13.35. Packed lunches available by arrangement (€6). Closed 1 Dec-1 Mar. MasterCard, Visa. **Directions:** About 500 yards outside Rathdrum on Glendalough Road.

Rathnew

Hunter's Hotel

HOTEL / RESTAURANT

Newrath Bridge Rathnew Co Wicklow
Tel: 0404 40106 Fax: 0404 40338
Email: reception@hunters.ie Web: indigo.ie/~hunters

A rambling old coaching inn set in lovely gardens alongside the River Vartry, this much-loved hotel has a long and fascinating history – it's one of Ireland's oldest coaching inns, with records indicating that it was built around 1720. In the same family now for five generations, the colourful Mrs Maureen Gelletlie takes pride in running the place on traditional lines with her son Richard, who is the manager. This means old-fashioned comfort and food based on local and home-grown produce – with the emphasis very much on 'old fashioned' – which is where its charm and character lie. There's a proper little bar, with chintzy loose-covered furniture and an open fire, a traditional dining room with fresh flowers – from the riverside garden where their famous afternoon tea is served in summer - and comfortable country bedrooms. Conference (30). Garden. Parking. Children welcome. No pets. **Rooms 16** (1 junior suite, 1 shower only, 1 disabled). Wheelchair access. B&B from €95 pps, ss about €20.

Restaurant: In tune with the spirit of the hotel, the style is traditional country house cooking: simple food with a real home-made feeling about it - no mean achievement in a restaurant and much to be applauded. Seasonal lunch and dinner menus change daily, but you can expect classics such as chicken liver pâté with melba toast, soups based on fish or garden produce, traditional roasts – rib beef, with Yorkshire pudding or old-fashioned roast stuffed chicken with bacon – and probably several fish dishes, possibly including poached salmon with hollandaise and chive sauce. Desserts are often based on what the garden has to offer, and baking is good, so fresh raspberries and cream or baked apple and rhubarb tart could be wise choices. **Seats 50.** Non-smoking restaurant. Toilets wheelchair accessible. L daily, 1-2.30 (Sun 2 sittings: 12.45 & 2.30). D daily 7.30-9. Set D about €35. Set L about €24. No s.c. House wine about €16. Closed 3 days at Christmas. Amex, Diners, MasterCard, Visa. **Directions:** Off N11 at Ashford or Rathnew. ◇

Rathnew

Tinakilly Country House & Restaurant

HOTEL / RESTAURANT

Rathnew Co Wicklow **Tel: 0404 69274** Fax: 0404 67806
Email: reservations@tinakilly.ie Web: www.tinakilly.ie

Josephine and Raymond Power have been running this fine hotel since January 2000 and they have retained those things which Raymond's parents, William and Bee Power, achieved to earn its reputation, while also bringing a youthful enthusiasm and energy which has contributed a new liveliness of atmosphere, making it a favourite destination for both business and leisure. It's a place of great local significance, having been built in the 1870s for Captain Robert Halpin, a local man who became Commander of The Great Eastern, which laid the first telegraph cable linking Europe and America. Tinakilly is one of the country's top business and corporate venues, but there is also a romantic side to its nature as all bedrooms have views across a bird sanctuary to the sea, and there are also period rooms, some with four-posters. To all this, add personal supervision by caring owners, friendly, well-trained staff, lovely grounds and a very fine kitchen and the recipe for success is complete. Conference/banqueting (65). Secretarial services. Fitness suite. Garden, walking, tennis. Children welcome (under 2s free in parents' room, cots available without charge). No pets. **Rooms 51** (all en-suite, 6 suites, 33 junior suites, 12 executive, 1 suitable for disabled). Lift. B&B €128 pps; ss €61. Closed 24-26 Dec.

Brunel Dining Room: This panelled split level restaurant is in the west wing of the house, which catches the evening sunlight, and it has a relaxed, intimate atmosphere. Local meats - notably Wicklow lamb and venison - and seafood, provide the basis for the cooking, plus herbs from the kitchen garden. Signature dishes include fillet of veal with noilly prat, pink grapefruit and asparagus, and foie gras with roast mango, spinach, pine kernels and raisins. **Seats 80** (private room, 30). Air conditioning. D Mon-Sat 7.30-9, Sun 6.30-8.30. Set D €46. House wine from €21. SC discretionary. Closed 24-26 Dec. Amex, Diners, MasterCard, Visa, Laser. **Directions:** From N11/M11 main Dublin - Wexford Road to Rathnew Village, Tinakilly is 500 metres from village on R750 to Wicklow Town.

Roundwood

Roundwood Inn

RESTAURANT / PUB

Roundwood Co Wicklow **Tel: 01 281 8107**

Jurgen and Aine Schwalm have owned this 17th century inn in the highest village in the Wicklow Hills since 1980. There's a public bar at one end, with a snug and an open fire, and in the middle of the building the main bar food area, furnished in traditional style with wooden floors and big sturdy tables. The style that the Schwalms and head chef Paul Taube have developed over the years is their own unique blend of Irish and German influences. Excellent bar food includes Hungarian goulash, fresh crab bisque, Galway oysters, smoked Wicklow trout, smoked salmon and hearty hot meals, notably the excellent house variation on Irish stew. The food at Roundwood has always had a special character, which together with the place itself and a consistently high standard of hospitality, has earned it an enviable reputation with hillwalkers, Dubliners out for the day and visitors alike. Bar meals 12-9.30 daily. Bar closed 25 Dec, Good Fri.

The restaurant is in the same style and only slightly more formal than the main bar, with fires at each end of the room (now converted to gas, alas) and is available by reservation. Substantial dishes such as rack of Wicklow lamb, roast wild Wicklow venison, venison ragout, pheasant and other game in season are perennial favourites. German influences are again evident in long-established specialities such as smoked Westphalian ham and wiener schnitzel, but there are also classics which cross all the usual boundaries: roast stuffed goose often appears on winter menus, especially around Christmas time, for example - and the roast suckling pig is not to be missed. An interesting mainly European wine list has many special bottles from Germany unlikely to be found elsewhere. Not suitable for children after 6.30. **Seats 45** (private room, 25). D Fri & Sat, 7.30-9; à la carte. L Sun only, 1-2. (Children welcome for lunch). House wine about €16; SC discretionary; reservations advised. No SC. Restaurant closed L Mon-Sat, D Sun-Thu. Amex, MasterCard, Visa, Laser. **Directions:** N11, follow sign for Glendalough.

Wicklow

WICKLOW

Wicklow town has character and is well-placed as a base when exploring the area. **The Grand Hotel (Tel: 0404 67337 www.grandhotel.ie)** does not quite live up to its name, perhaps, but is a relaxed, friendly and comfortable place nonetheless and there are developments afoot which should see big changes during the 2004 season; (bar meals served daily 12.30-9.) Restaurants to check out include **The Bakery (Tel 0404 66770),** an interesting old place in Church Street which still has the original ovens in situ, and **Rungantino's River Café (Tel 0404 61900),** which is on the river in the centre of the town and specialises in seafood.

Woodenbridge

Woodenbridge Hotel

HOTEL

Vale of Avoca Arklow Co Wicklow **Tel: 0402 35146** Fax: 0402 35573
Email: wbhotel@iol.ie Web: www.woodenbridgehotel.com

This pleasant country hotel lays claim to the title of Ireland's oldest hotel, with a history going back to 1608, when it was first licensed as a coaching inn on the old Dublin-Wexford highway - and later came to great prominence when gold and copper were mined in the locality. Today, it is very popular for weddings and makes a friendly and relaxing base for a visit to this beautiful part of County Wicklow. The many other historical associations in the area include the home of Charles Stewart Parnell, nearby at Avondale. Bedrooms - many of them overlooking Woodenbridge golf course - are comfortably furnished, with phone, TV and tea/coffee trays. As well as a more formal restaurant, food is available in the lively bar (traditional Irish music in summer). Children welcome (under 4s free in parents' room; cots available without charge). No pets. **Rooms 23.** B&B about €70pps, ss about €12. Food available 12.30-9. Closed 25 Dec. Amex, MasterCard, Visa. **Directions:** N11 to Arklow turn off 7 km.

NORTHERN IRELAND

BELFAST

The origins of the cities of Ireland are usually found in 5th Century monastic centres which were overrun by the Vikings some four hundred or so years later to become trading settlements that later "had manners put on them" by the Normans. But Belfast is much newer than that. When the Vikings in the 9th century raided what is now known as Belfast Lough, their target was the wealthy monastery at Bangor, and thus their beach-heads were at Ballyholme and Groomsport further east. Then, when the Normans held sway in the 13th Century, their main stronghold was at Carrickfergus on the northern shore of the commodious inlet which was known for several centuries as Carrickfergus Bay.

At the head of that inlet beside the shallow River Lagan, the tiny settlement of beal feirste - the 'town at the mouth of the Farset or the sandspit' - wasn't named on maps at all until the late 15th Century. But Belfast proved to be the perfect greenfield site for rapid development as the Industrial Revolution got under way. Its rocketing growth began with linen manufacture in the 17th Century, and this was accelerated by the arrival of skilled Huguenot refugees after 1685.

There was also scope for ship-building on the shorelines in the valleymouth between the high peaks crowding in on the Antrim side on the northwest, and the Holywood Hills to the southeast, though the first shipyard of any significant size wasn't in being until 1791, when William and Hugh Ritchie opened for business. The Lagan Valley gave convenient access to the rest of Ireland for the increase of trade and commerce to encourage development of the port, while the prosperous farms of Down and Antrim fed a rapidly expanding population.

So, at the head of what was becoming known as Belfast Lough, Belfast took off in a big way, a focus for industrial ingenuity and manufacturing inventiveness, and a magnet for entrepreneurs and innovators from all of the north of Ireland, and the world beyond. Its population in 1600 had been less than 500, yet by 1700 it was 2,000, and by 1800 it was 25,000. The city's growth was prodigious, such that by the end of the 19th Century it had the largest shipyard in the world, the largest ropeworks, the largest linen mills, the largest tobacco factory, and the largest heavy engineering works, all served by a greater mileage of quays than anywhere comparable. And it was an essentially Victorian expansion - the population in 1851 was 87,062, but by 1901 it was 349,180 - the largest city in Ireland.

Growth had become so rapid in the latter half of the 19th Century that it tended to obliterate the influence of the gentler intellectual and philosophical legacies inspired by the Huguenots and other earlier developers, a case in point being the gloriously flamboyant and baroque Renaissance-style City Hall, which was completed in 1906. It was the perfect expression of that late-Victorian energy and confidence in which Belfast shared with conspicuous enthusiasm. But its site had only become available because the City Fathers authorised the demolition of the quietly elegant White Linen Hall, which had been a symbol of Belfast's less strident period of development in the 18th Century.

However, Belfast Corporation was only fulfilling the spirit of the times. And in such a busy city, there was always a strongly human dimension to everyday life. Thus the City Hall may be on the grand scale, but it was nevertheless right at the heart of town. Equally, while the gantries of the shipyard may have loomed overheead, they did so near the houses of the workers in a manner which somehow softened their sheer size. Admittedly this theme of giving great projects a human dimension seems to have been forgotten in the later design and location of the Government Building (completed 1932) at Stormont, east of the city. But back in the vibrant heart of Belfast, there is continuing entertainment and accessible interest in buildings as various as the Grand Opera House, St Anne's Cathedral, the Crown Liquor Saloon, Sinclair Seamen's Church, the Linenhall Library, and Smithfield Market, not to mention some of the impressive Victorian banking halls, while McHugh's pub on Queen's Square, and Tedford's Restaurant just round the corner on Donegall Quay, provide thoughtful reminders of the earlier more restrained style.

Today, modern technologies and advanced engineering have displaced the old smokestack industries in the forefront of the city's work patterns, with the shipyard ceasing to build ships in March 2003. Shorts aerospace factories are now the city's biggest employer, while parts of the former shipyard are being redeveloped as the Titanic Quarter in memory of the most famous ship built in Belfast. The energy of former times has been channeled into impressive urban regeneration along the River Lagan. Here, the flagship building is the Waterfront Hall, a large state-of-the-art concert venue which has won international praise, complemented by the Odyssey Centre on the other side of the river. In the southern part of the city, Queen's University (founded 1845) is a beautifully balanced 1849 Lanyon building at the heart of a pleasant university district which includes the city's noted Lyric Theatre as well as the respected Ulster Museum & Art Gallery, while the university itself is particularly noted for its pioneering work in medicine and engineering.

Thus there's a buzz to Belfast which is reflected in its own cultural and warmly sociable life, which includes the innovative energy of its young chefs. Yet in some ways it is still has marked elements of a country town and port strongly rooted in land and sea. The hills of Antrim can be glimpsed from most streets, and the farmland of Down makes its presence felt. They are quickly reached by a somewhat ruthlessly implemented motorway system, relished by those in a hurry who also find the increasingly busy and very accessible Belfast City Airport a convenient boon. Belfast is also very much part of the country around it - and in the final analysis, is uniquely itself.

Local Attractions and Information

Arts Council of Northern Ireland 028 90 385200
Belfast Castle & Zoo 028 90 776277
Belfast Festival at Queens (late Oct-early Nov) 028 90 665577
Belfast Welcome Centre 028 90 246609
City Airport 028 90 457745
Citybus Tours 028 90 458484
Fernhill House: The People's Museum 028 90 715599
Grand Opera House 028 90 241919
International Airport 028 94 484848
Kings Hall (exhibitions, concerts, trade shows) 028 90 665225
Lagan Valley Regional Park 028 90 491922
Linenhall Library 028 90 321707
Lyric Theatre 028 90 381081
National Trust Regional Office 028 97 510721
Northern Ireland Railways 028 90 899411
Odyssey (entertainment & sports complex) 028 90 451055
Sir Thomas & Lady Dixon Park (Rose Gardens) 028 90 320202
Tourism Information 028 90 246609
Ulster Historical Foundation (genealogical res.) 028 90 332288
Ulster Museum & Art Gallery 028 90 383000
Waterfront Hall (concert venue) 028 90 334455
West Belfast Festivals 028 90 313440

Belfast

★ **RESTAURANT**

Aldens Restaurant

229 Upper Newtownards Road Belfast BT4 3JF
Tel: 028 9065 0079 Fax: 028 9065 0032
Email: info@aldensrestaurant.com Web: www.aldensrestaurant.com

A canopy in the restaurant's new aubergine-toned livery highlights the discreetly distinctive public face of this fine contemporary restaurant, leading diners to the warmth and elegance that lie within. It is greatly to proprietor Jonathan Davis's credit that he had the courage and foresight to introduce this shaft of bright light to an area previously bereft of good eating places - it was one of Belfast's wave of chic, uncluttered modern restaurants (the second wave is now taking the city by storm) and has always been immaculately maintained; the new exterior colour scheme was the first phase of a complete re-vamp and has now been applied to the interior also. A welcoming bar/reception area has comfortable seating and pleasing details - fresh flowers, choice of olives, newspapers and food guides to browse over a drink - while tables are smartly set up with quality linen, tapenade, olive oil and butter, along with three types of bread; opaque glass windows soften the light and give a sense of privacy, with strips of mirror adding reflections on painted walls - an interesting, subtle background for food which shares a sense of contemporary simplicity. Head chef Cath Gradwell has been here since the restaurant opened in 1998, (bringing a raft of cosmopolitan experience at Roux restaurants and others), and her lively international menus change daily and make the most of local and seasonal ingredients in a cooking style that is now well established, with strong emphasis on flavour combinations, fish and local produce: dishes that combine classic and contemporary influences and employ a wide range of ingredients are well-conceived and executed with flair. Menus are admirably simple, with no pretentious or over-complicated explanation of dishes and, while not overlong, there is plenty of choice. The simplest of choices - charentais melon, with melon sorbet - takes its place alongside luxurious dishes like carpaccio of beef with seared foie gras with strawberries, black pepper & balsamic vinegar, and affordable classics, perhaps with an update, chicken liver paté with hot toast & red onion marmalade. Main courses offer a similarly wide range and prime dishes like grilled halibut steak with tomato & herb cream sit happily beside humbler everyday foods like mushroom curry with rice pilaf: vegetarian dishes are always offered and display the same combination of down to earth qualities and creativity - two or three options on each course are usually vegetarian, perhaps including a tempting twice-baked spinach soufflé with wild mushrooms - and side dishes are imaginative. Consistently excellent food and and professional service from smartly-uniformed staff make this one of Northern Ireland's finest restaurants and it offers extremely good value, notably the lunch specials and a short dinner menu. An interesting, well-priced wine list mixing the old and new world, includes an extensive house wine selection and a fair number of half bottles. **Seats 70.** Children welcome. No smoking area; air conditioning. L Mon-Fri,12-2.30; D Mon-Thu 6-10, Fri & Sat 6-11; Set D £16.95 (Mon-Thu), Lunch special (main course & coffee) £6-9; à la carte also available. House wines from £13.95; sc discretionary. Closed L Sat, all Sun, public hols, 2 weeks July. Amex, Diners, MasterCard, Visa, Switch. **Directions:** On the Upper Newtownards Road at junction with Sandown road.

Belfast

An Old Rectory

GUESTHOUSE

148 Malone Road Belfast BT9 5LH
Tel: 028 90 66 7882 Fax: 028 90 68 3759
Email: info@anoldrectory.co.uk Web: www.info@anoldrectory.co.uk

Conveniently located near the King's Hall, Public Records Office, Lisburn Road and Queen's University, Mary Callan's lovely late Victorian house is set well back from the road in mature trees, with private parking. A former Church of Ireland rectory, it had the benefit of being in the Malone conservation area and retains many original features, including stained glass windows. There's a lovely drawing room with books, sofas, comfortable armchairs with cosy rugs over the arms - and a very hospitable habit of serving hot whiskey in the drawing room at 9 o'clock each night. Accommodation is on two storeys, every room individually decorated (and named) and each has both a desk and a sofa, magazines to browse, also beverage trays with hot chocolate and soup sachets as well as the usual tea and coffee; better still there's a fridge on each landing with iced water and fresh milk, helpful advice on eating out locally is available (including menus) and, although they don't do evening meals, breakfast is an event. Children welcome (under 7 free in parents' room, cot available without charge, baby sitting arranged). Garden, walking. No pets. Rooms 5 (3 en-suite, 2 with private bathrooms - 2 shower only, 3 with bath & shower). B&B £25.30 pps, ss £12. Closed 1 week Christmas, 1 week Easter, all July. **No Credit Cards. Directions:** Between Balmoral Avenue and Stranmillis Road.

Belfast

The Bank Gallery

Ⓝ **RESTAURANT**

The Edge May's Meadow Belfast **Tel: 028 9032 2000**

Donal Keane is a fine chef who may be remembered from a number of good restaurants in Northern Ireland, where he brought something special to the kitchen - and especially in fish cookery, at which he excels. Now proprietor-chef in his own Laganside kitchen, he should have the opportunity to develop in his own way - one to watch! L Mon-Fri 12.30-2; D Mon-Sat: Mon-Wed 5.30-9.30; Thu-Sat 5.30-10. MasterCard, Visa. **Directions:** Laganside.

Belfast

Beatrice Kennedy

RESTAURANT

22 University Road Belfast BT7 1NJ
Tel: 028 9020 2290 Fax: 028 9020 2291
Email: reservations@beatrice.kennedy.co.uk Web: www.beatrice.kennedy.co.uk

Named after the lady whose home it once was, the dining area of this unusual restaurant begins in what would have been her front room and extends into adjoining areas towards the back, retaining something of the authentic lived-in feeling of a private period residence; although now furnished with white-damasked tables, it has a Victorian atmosphere with a small open fireplace and mantelpiece and a few books and leftover personal effects: softly-lit, atmospheric, intimate, it exudes an atmosphere of calm in which to enjoy proprietor-chef Jim McCarthy's accomplished cooking. Ingredients are carefully sourced, dishes are smoked on the premises and breads, desserts and ice creams are all home-made. The style is modern, with Thai and Chinese influences seen in dishes like red braised pork (with spiced aubergine salad) and Thai smoked duck, but also flavours closer to home in roast cod with crushed potato and sauce vierge. Presentation is very special, especially the desserts - which are minor works of art; desserts come with a BK signature in cocoa on the rim of each plate, then the motif is repeated on little home-made chocolate medallions served with coffee - a nice touch. **Seats 80** (private room 25). D Sun-Sat, 5-10.30 (Sun to 8.30); L Sun only 12.30-2.30. Early D about £10 (5-7), Set Sun L about £15. Closed Mon, 24-26 Dec, 11-14 Jul. Amex, MasterCard, Visa, Switch. **Directions:** Adjacent to Queen's University. ◇

Belfast — **Bourbon**

Ⓝ RESTAURANT

60 Great Victoria Street Belfast BT2 7BB **Tel: 028 9033 2121**
Fax: 028 9089 099 Web: www.bourbonrestaurant.com

Behind an unassuming entrance lies an amazingly theatrical interior: totally at home alongside neighbouring buildings like the Crown Liquor Saloon and the Grand Opera House, it features pillars, palms, ornate plaster work and wrought iron, chandeliers and statues - everything, in short, to convey sumptuousness. Not to everybody's taste, to be sure, but it works - and provides the perfect antidote for diners who've had an overdose of minimalism. But there a bit of that here too - don't expect pristine white linen, silver and crystal: what you actually get is bare table tops and, oddly, the ubiquitous black rubber place mats - and paper napkins! So it should come as no surprise that menus are modern too, offering international contemporary classics - a main course of pan fried seabass, with basil mash & sauce vierge was singled out for favourable comment on a recent visit. Helpful staff, competent cooking and - most of all - amazing atmosphere make this a place worth visiting. Definitely different! Open: D Mon-Sat, 5-11; L Mon-Fri, 12-3. Set 2-course L, £11.50. Also à la carte. Closed Sun. **Directions:** City centre.

Belfast — **Café Clementine**

RESTAURANT

245 Lisburn Road Belfast BT9 7EN **Tel: 028 9038 2211**
Fax: 028 9038 2547 Email: theclemclem@aol.ie

In a red-painted mid-terrace house, this attractive addition to the busy Lisburn Road food scene is an all-day restaurant on three levels. Food service begins with breakfast in the bright contemporary ground floor area, merging into lunch (including a soup & gourmet sandwich deal - baguette or ciabatta with a range of luscious fillings like chargrilled vegetables or salmon gravadlax) and a more serious evening menu (tapas plate, confit of crispy duck, assiette of seafood, local venison in season) begins at 5 o'clock and may be served upstairs in a smaller room with a little bar. Interesting quality food, great staff - including a dedicated chef committed to sourcing quality ingredients - customer-friendly hours and fair prices make this a great find. Finishing with a frappuchino (iced cappuccino) will send you off with a spring in your step on a hot day. **Seats 100.** (Private rooms 40/16). Smoking unrestricted; air conditioning. Open all day: breakfast 9.30-10.30, L 11.30-3, D from 5 (except Sun & Mon, closes 4.30pm). Set D £17.50. House wine from £10.50, also BYO. Closed 12 Jul week, 3 days Christmas. MasterCard, Visa, Switch. **Directions:** 1 mile out of City Centre passing City Hospital, bright red building on right hand side.

Belfast — **Café Paul Rankin**

CAFÉ

27-29 Fountain Street Belfast BT1
Tel: 028 9031 5090 Fax: 028 9032 8340

A little sister of Paul and Jeanne Rankin's acclaimed restaurant, Cayenne, Café Paul Rankin offers informal quality food (notably their speciality baking) throughout the day - be it for a quick cup of coffee or a more leisurely bite with a glass of wine, this is the in place for a shopping break. The breakfast menu includes Jeanne's toasted muesli & yoghurt while hot food on offer after 11.00am includes BBQ chicken panini. Smart pavement tables for fine weather too - and food to go. *Also at 12-14 Arthur Street. Open Mon-Sat 7.30am-6pm (Thu to 9pm) and Castle Court Shopping centre on Royal Avenue. Open Mon-Sat 8.00am-6.00pm (Thu to 9pm) and Sun 1-6pm. MasterCard, Visa, Switch. **Directions:** Town centre, near City Hall.

Belfast — **Café Renoir**

CAFÉ

95 Botanic Avenue Belfast BT9 **Tel: 028 9031 1300**

This is an in -place for discerning types in the university area, who can start the day off well with a fine breakfast or drop in at any time during the day to choose from menus that offer sassy contemporary food for every mood. Open Mon-Thu 0am-9.30/10pm, Fri & Sat 11am-10.30pm. MasterCard, Visa. **Directions:** University area.

Belfast

Café Zinc

RESTAURANT

12 Stranmillis Road Belfast BT9 5AA
Tel: 028 90 682266 Fax: 028 90 663189 Web: www.cafezinc.com

Chameleon-like, this smart modern wine bar in the Malone area - cool marble floors, glass and chrome, monochrome paintings, luxurious seating - changes character as the day progresses. Opening with a sassy breakfast menu (bagels, croissants, traditional fry - including vegetarian - and delicious Lily coffees), open sandwiches and some temptingly down to earth specialities like Guinness pie, home-made Lincolnshire sausages come on stream at lunch time. The evening brings another change of tempo, with fresh pasta, tapas and a rather more formal arrangement of starters, main courses etc. that takes in some of the lunchtime specialities plus a few more heavyweight dishes. Cooking is good and it's the cool place to be - all this and cocktails too. (Cocktails £3.50, shooters £2.50). **Seats 60** (private room 20). Children welcome. Toilets wheelchair accessible, air conditioning. Breakfast daily: Mon-Sat 10-12, Sun to 2. L from 12, D daily 5-9 (Thu-Sat to 10). Closed 25-26 Dec. Amex, Diners, MasterCard, Visa, Switch. **Directions:** Located beside Botanic Gardens. ◇

Belfast

Cargoes Café

CAFÉ

613 Lisburn Road Belfast BT9 7GT **Tel: 02890 665451**

This is a special little place run by partners Radha Patterson and Mary Maw, who take a lot of trouble sourcing fine produce for the delicatessen side of the business and apply the same philosophy to the food served in the café. Modern European, Thai and Indian influences work well together here; simple preparation and good seasonal ingredients dictate menus - where you might find dishes like smokey bacon & potato soup, Moroccan chicken with couscous, vegetarian dishes such as goat's cheese & tarragon tart or wild mushroom risotto. There are classic desserts like lemon tart or apple flan, and a range of stylish sandwiches. Children welcome. Seats 30. No smoking restaurant. Open Mon-Sat 9 am-5 pm, L 12-3. A la carte; sc discretionary. Toilets wheelchair accessible. MasterCard, Visa. ◇

Belfast

Cayenne Restaurant

★ RESTAURANT

7 Ascot House Shaftesbury Square Belfast BT2 7DB
Tel: 02890 331 532 Fax: 02890 261 575
Email: reservations@cayennerestaurant.com Web: www.cayennerestaurant.com

Paul and Jeanne Rankin continue to offer exciting quality food without frills at accessible prices at Cayenne - and regular diners will notice a new extension to the restaurant, which provides an extended bar area with a lounge for pre- and post-dinner drinks and quick dining. The Rankins always been ahead of the trends - and recognise that it's not just what people want to eat that changes, but how they want to eat as well. So, fine dining this is not: eating is very definitely fun at Cayenne and it's the quality of Paul Rankin's quick fire cooking that draws the crowds - and it is a credit to the legendary teamwork of this kitchen that the food is equally good when he cannot be here himself. The accent is now firmly on accessibility, but it is never at the expense of quality: the decor may be minimalist, but furnishings and table appointments are very good - and the new extension also allows for private dining and conference rooms. Many dishes have equal appeal on Cayenne menus, and they are constructed to allow flexibility, with soups, salads, rice and noodle dishes offered separately between the appetisers and main courses. The quality of ingredients is excellent, as always, and flavours remain global - mainly oriental with some Mediterranean touches: potato and paremsan ravioli and green coconut crusted cod with mango rice, pak choi and roast sweet peppers, for example. These tantalising tastes and textures from around the world are served with charm and friendliness by smart, well-trained young staff - bringing accessible excellence to contemporary diners who enjoy an animated environment and don't mind rubbing shoulders with neighbouring diners in the café atmosphere of this warmly decorated dining room. Fine wine list; an extensive drinks menu also includes cocktails, shooters, mocktails (non-alcoholic) and an after dinner range. Seats 90. No smoking area; air conditioning, L Mon-Fri 12-2.15 and Sun 1-3, Set L from £12. D Mon-Sun 6-10.15 (to 11.15 Fri & Sat, to 9 Sun)). A la carte. House wine from £14.95. sc discretionary (except 10% on parties of 6+). Closed L Sat, 12 July, 25-26 Dec. Amex, Diners, MasterCard, Visa, Switch. **Directions:** 5 mins from Europa Hotel.

Belfast

Conor Café Bar

CAFÉ

11A Stranmillis Road Belfast BT9 5AF **Tel: 028 9066 3266** Fax: 028 9020 0233

Just across the road from the Ulster Museum, Manus McConn's unusual high-ceilinged room is bright with natural light from a lantern roof and was originally the William Conor studio (1944-1959). The art theme is carried through to having original work always on show - there's a permanent exhibition of Neill Shawcross's bold and colourful work. Open for breakfast and brunch, through coffee, lunch, afternoon tea and eventually dinner, this is a casual place with a distinctive style - light wood booths along the walls and a long refectory-style table down the centre. Good coffee, home-baked scones, informal food such as warm chicken salad, hot paninis with mozzarella, modern European dishes including lots of pastas, comfort food (like fish & chips with mushy peas) and classic dishes such as moules mariniere and steak & Guinness pie. Popular with locals - this place is a real find for those visiting the Museum (especially on Sundays). **Seats 50.** Open daily 9am-11pm. A la carte. Licensed. Closed July fortnight. MasterCard, Visa, Switch. **Directions:** Opposite Ulster Museum.

Belfast

The Crescent Townhouse

HOTEL / RESTAURANT

13 Lower Crescent Belfast BT71NR
Tel: 028 9032 3349 Fax: 028 9032 0646
Email: info@crescenttownhouse.com Web: www.crescenttownhouse.com

This is an elegant building on the corner of Botanic Avenue, just a short stroll from the city centre. The ground floor is taken up by the Metro Brasserie and Bar/Twelve, a stylish club-like bar with oak panelling and snugs, particularly lively and popular at night (necessitating 'greeters' for the entrance). The reception lounge is on the first floor. Spacious bedrooms, which have phones with data points, TV and trouser press, are furnished in country house style, with practical furniture, colourful fabrics and good tiled bathrooms. In addition, there are two superior rooms, decorated more elaborately in a period style with canopied beds and luxurious bathrooms with roll-top baths and separate showers. Fax, photocopying and secretarial services are available through reception. Breakfast is taken in the contemporary split-level Metro Brasserie, which is also open for dinner; lunch is available at Bar/Twelve: Mon-Sat 12-3. The wine list includes quite an extensive cocktail menu and a number of wines by the glass. Children welcome before 7pm (under 12s free in parents' room, cots available without charge). No pets.* Weekend breaks offer very good value. **Rooms 11** (2 superior, 3 no smoking) 24 hour room service. B&B £50 pps, ss £30. Metro Brasserie Seats 70. D Mon-Sat 6-10; D £10.95-13.50, otherwise à la carte. House wine £12. sc discretionary. Closed Sun. Amex, MasterCard, Visa, Switch. **Directions:** Opposite Botanic Railway Station.

Belfast

Crown Liquor Saloon

ATMOSPHERIC PUB

46 Great Victoria Street Belfast BT2 7BA
Tel: 028 9027 9901 Fax: 028 9027 9902

Belfast's most famous pub, The Crown Liquor Saloon, was perhaps the greatest of all the Victorian gin palaces which once flourished in Britain's industrial cities. Remarkably, considering its central location close to the Europa Hotel, it survived The Troubles virtually unscathed. Although now owned by the National Trust (and run by Bass Leisure Retail) the Crown is far from being a museum piece and attracts a wide clientele of locals and visitors. A visit to one of its famous snugs for a pint and half a dozen oysters served on crushed ice, or a bowl of Irish Stew, is a must. The upstairs restaurant section, "Flannigans Eaterie & Bar", is built with original timbers from the SS Britannic, sister ship to the Titanic. **Crown:** bar food served Mon-Sat 12-3. **Flannigans:** 11-9. Closed 25-16 Dec. Diners, MasterCard, Visa. **Directions:** City centre, opposite Europa Hotel. ◇

Belfast

Deanes Brasserie

RESTAURANT

34-40 Howard Street Belfast BT1 6PF
Tel: 028 9056 0000 Fax: 028 9065 0001
Email: liz@deanesbelfast.com Web: www.deanesbelfast.com

On the ground floor under Restaurant Michael Deane, this much larger restaurant is all buzz and offers an eclectic contemporary menu, with something for everybody. Risotto of bacon, mushroom & parmesan, and braised sausage with white bean chilli & tomato are both typical, also modish fish & chips - there's a separate vegetarian menu, prices are moderate, service slick and efficient and everything on the wine list is under £20 (except champagne). **Seats 100.** Air conditioning. Children welcome. L Mon-Sat 12-2.30, D Mon-Sat 5.30-10.30 (post theatre menus, last orders 11 pm). A la carte; sc charge discretionary (10% on parties of 6+). Closed Sun, Christmas, New Year, Easter Mon, 12-13 July. * A new Pan-Asian sister restaurant - Chokdee - has recently opened around the corner at 44 Bedford Street. Amex, MasterCard, Visa, Switch. **Directions:** 200 metres from back of City Hall on left.

Belfast

Feasts

Ⓝ CAFÉ

39 Dubln Road Belfast BT2 7HD **Tel: 028 9033 2787**
Email: craignash@compuserve.com

A small but interesting deli and coffee shop on a busy city centre street, and easily identified by an eye-catching blue canopy, Feasts has been run for the past five years by food-lovers Penny and Craig Nash, who concentrate on offering simple food prepared with top quality ingredients. Space inside is limited but there are tables on the pavement to accommodate more patrons, when weather allows. Big on pasta dishes - pasta is made freshly on the premises daily - they also offer a wide selection of sandwiches and pastries, an excellent choice in farmhouse cheeses and good coffee. They also provide an office phone-in menu for neighbouring businesses. Open all day 9.00am-6.00pm. MasterCard, Visa, Switch. **Directions:** opposite cinema on Dublin road.

Belfast

Giraffe

Ⓝ CAFÉ

54-56 Stranmillis Road Belfast BT9 5AD
Tel: 028 9050 9820 Fax: 028 9050 9428

Located on a pleasant road close to the University, Giraffes is a buzzy cafe with a mix of tables, chairs and sofas, complete with newspapers, the eponymous giraffe statue and other jazzy African-style themes in the decor. Colourful table settings and china add to the ambience that attracts a regular clientele, and the food quality is obviously to the standard that keeps bringing them back -that plus the excellent value for money, particularly the breakfasts which also include a vegetarian option. It's a lively place for a casual meal and no one to interrupt you while you sit and read or just watch the world go by. Open: Mon-Thu 12noon-10pm, Fri & Sat 9am-11pm, Sun 9am-10pm. Also at: 537 Lisburn Road, Belfast BT9 7GQ. MasterCard, Visa. **Directions:** Near QUB.

Belfast

Hastings Europa Hotel

HOTEL

Great Victoria Street Belfast BT2 7AP **Tel: 028 9027 1066** Fax: 028 9032 7800
Email: res@eur.hastingshotels.com Web: www.hastingshotels.com

This landmark 1970s city centre building is the largest hotel in Northern Ireland and particularly striking when illuminated at night. The location is exceptionally convenient, both to the business and commercial districts and the city's entertainment and shopping areas. It has undergone many changes since first opening in the '70s and has been renovated and refurbished to a high standard, including the addition of executive rooms, with air conditioning, ISDN lines and safe as well as usual facilities expected of a top hotel. The location is exceptionally convenient, both to the business and commercial districts and the city's entertainment and shopping areas. Off the impressive tall-columned entrance foyer is an all-day brasserie (6am-midnight) and the lobby bar, featuring Saturday afternoon jazz and other live musical entertainment. Upstairs on the first floor you'll find the Gallery lounge (afternoon teas served here to the accompaniment of a pianist) and a cocktail bar with circular marble-topped counter. But perhaps the hotel's greatest assets are the function suites, ranging from the Grand Ballroom to the twelfth floor Edinburgh Suite with its panoramic views of the city. Nearby parking (special rates apply) can be added to your account. Staff are excellent (porters offer valet parking), and standards of housekeeping and maintenance are high. Children welcome (under 14s free in parents' room; cots available without charge). Conference/banqueting (750/600); business centre; secretarial services. Pets by arrangement. **Rooms 240** (1 presidential suite, 4 junior suites, 56 executive rooms, 115 no smoking, 2 for disabled). Lifts. B&B from £50 pps, ss about £20; Room rate from £160. Closed 24-25 Dec. Amex, Diners, MasterCard, Visa, Switch. **Directions:** Located in the heart of Belfast.

Belfast

Hastings Stormont Hotel

HOTEL

Upper Newtonards Road Belfast BT4 3LP
Tel: 028 9065 1066 Fax: 028 9048 0240
Email: res@stor.hastingshotels.com Web: www.hastingshotels.com

Four miles east of the city centre, the hotel is directly opposite the imposing gates leading to Stormont Castle and Parliament Buildings. There's a huge entrance lounge, with stairs up to a more intimate mezzanine area overlooking the castle grounds. The main restaurant and informal modern bistro are pleasantly located. Spacious, practical bedrooms have good worktops and offer the usual facilities; several rooms are designated for female executives. The hotel also has eight self-catering apartments with their own car parking area, featuring a twin bedroom, lounge and kitchen/dinette, available for short stays or long periods. The self-contained Confex Centre, comprising ten trade rooms, complements the function suites in the main building. Weekend rates and short breaks are good value. Conference/banqueting 500/300. Own parking. Wheelchair accessible. No pets. **Rooms 109** (2 suites, 34 executive rooms, 23 no-smoking, 1 for disabled). Lift. B&B £58 pps, ss £20. Closed 25 Dec. Amex, Diners, MasterCard, Visa, Switch. **Directions:** 4 miles East of Belfast city centre, directly opposite Stormont Parliament Buildings.

Belfast

Hawthorne Coffee Shop

CAFÉ / RESTAURANT

Fulton's Fine Furnishings Boucher Crescent Belfast BT2 6HU
Tel: 028 90 384705 Fax: 028 384701

If you're shopping or have business in the area, this stylish contemporary café in a well known furniture store is a great place to know about, as they specialise in real home cooking and the art of scone making is alive and well here. There's nothing flashy about the food: expect lovely flavoursome dishes like home-made soup with wheaten bread, quiches - asparagus & salmon, vegetable - seafood pie and steak & mushroom hot-pot and several casseroles daily. There's always a large selection of salads and home-made desserts like banoffee and lemon meringue pie and there's free refills of coffee. An added attraction between 12 and 2 is to listen to the resident pianist play on the Steinway baby grand in the corner. **Seats 127.** Mon-Sat: morning coffee, lunch, afternoon tea. A la carte. MasterCard, Visa, Switch. **Directions:** Off M1, take Stockmans Lane exit off roundabout, left into Boucher Road, left again into Boucher Crescent (at Fultons Fine Furnishings Store).

Belfast

Hilton Belfast

HOTEL

4 Lanyon Place Belfast BT1 3LP **Tel: 028 90 277 000**
Fax: 028 90 277 277 Email: hilton_belfast@hilton.com

Occupying a prominent position on a rise beside the Waterfront Hall, the interior of this landmark hotel is impressive: the scale is grand, the style throughout is of contemporary clean-lined elegance - the best of modern materials have been used and the colour palette selected is delicious - and, best of all, it makes the best possible use of its superb waterside site, with the Sonoma Restaurant and several suites commanding exceptional views. Outstanding conference and business facilities include the state-of-the-art Hilton Meeting service tailored to individual requirements and three executive floors with a Clubroom. All rooms have air-conditioning, satellite TV, in-room movies, and no-stop check-out in addition to the usual facilities. Recreational facilities are also excellent. The absence of private parking could be a problem, as the multi-storey carpark next door is not owned by the hotel. Conference/banqueting (400/260); secretarial services; business centre; video conferencing; ISDN lines. Leisure centre; indoor swimming pool; beauty salon. Children welcome (cots available). **Rooms 195** (6 suites, 7 junior suites, 38 executive rooms, 68 no-smoking, 10 for disabled). Lifts. Room rate (max. 2 guests) from £98. Open all year. Amex, Diners, MasterCard, Visa, Switch. **Directions:** Belfast city centre, beside Waterfront Hall. ◇

Belfast

Holiday Inn Belfast

HOTEL

22 - 26 Ormeau Avenue Belfast BT2 8HS
Tel: 028 903 28511 Fax: 028 906 2 6546
Email: belfast@ichotelsgroup.com Web: www.belfast.holiday-inn.com

Conveniently located less than half a mile from most of the main city centre attractions, this contemporary hotel offers luxurious modern accommodation, with excellent business and health and leisure facilities. The style is classy and spacious bedrooms are designed particularly with the business guest in mind - the decor is unfussy and warm, with comfort and relaxation to match its use as a workbase; superior rooms all have modem points, fridge, interactive TV with on-screen checkout facility and Sky Sports, trouser press, power shower, cotton bathrobe and quality toiletries, while suites have a hallway as well as a separate sitting/dining room. 'The Academy' offers state-of-the-art conference and training facilities, and business support. Conference/banqueting (120/100); business centre, secretarial services, video-conferencing. Children welcome (under 16s free in parents' room, cot available without charge). Leisure centre; swimming pool; beauty salon. **Rooms 170** (2 suites, 36 executive, 102 no smoking, 10 for disabled). Lift. 24 hour room service. B&B 83.95pps (Room only £140, max. 2 adults & 2 children). Special weekend rates available. Open all year. Amex, Diners, MasterCard, Visa, Switch. **Directions:** Opposite BBC, 2 minutes walk from City Hall via Bedford Street.

Belfast

The John Hewitt

Ⓝ BAR / RESTAURANT

Donegall Street Belfast BT1 **Tel: 028 9023 3768**

The in-place pub for discerning Belfast people, who like the combination of traditional interior and good quality sassy modern food. High-ceilinged, with a marble bar and an open fire, there's a pleasing preference for conversation and civilised relaxation. Open daily; food served 12-3 (Fri 12-6).

Belfast

HOTEL

Jurys Inn Belfast

Fisherwick Place Great Victoria St Belfast BT2 7AP
Tel: 028 9053 3500 Fax: 028 9053 3511
Email: bookings@jurys.com Web: www.jurysdoyle.com

Located in the heart of the city, close to the Grand Opera House and City Hall and just a couple of minutes walk from the major shopping areas of Donegall Place and the Castlecourt Centre, Jurys Belfast Inn set new standards for the city's budget accommodation when it opened in 1997. The high standards and good value of all Jurys Inns applies here too: all rooms are en-suite (with bath and shower) and spacious enough to accommodate two adults and two children (or three adults) at a fixed price. Rooms are well-designed and recently refurbished, with good amenities for a hotel in the budget class. **Rooms 190.** Room rate £73, (max. 3 guests w/o b'fst). Closed 24-26 Dec. Amex, Diners, MasterCard, Visa. **Directions:** City centre, close to Opera House.

Belfast

RESTAURANT

Manor House

43/47 Donegall Pass Belfast BT71DQ
Tel: 028 90 238 755 Fax: 028 90 238 755

Easily found just off Shaftesbury Square, this long-established Cantonese restaurant has been in the Wong family since 1982; it has since expanded to meet demand with various renovations and refurbishment although the style remains traditional. In common with many other Chinese restaurants, the menu is long, but Joe Wong's menu - which is given in Chinese as well as English - offers more unusual choices in addition to the many well-known popular dishes. There is, for example, a wide range of soups - and specialities include Cantonese-style crispy chicken and seafood dishes like steamed whole seafish with ginger and scallions. Children welcome. Parking in nearby carpark. **Seats 80** (private room, 40). Air conditioning. L 12.30-2.15 Mon-Fri, D 5.30-11 daily, Set L about £5.95, Set D about £12.95-£20; also à la carte. House wine about £9.95. SC discretionary. Closed 25-26 Dec, 12 Jul. MasterCard, Visa, Switch. **Directions:** Off Shaftesbury Square,within town centre. ◇

Belfast

HOTEL

McCausland Hotel

34–38 Victoria Street Belfast BT1 3GH
Tel: 028 9022 0200 Fax: 028 9022 0200
Email: info@mccauslandhotel.com Web: www.mccauslandhotel.com

Well-located close to the Waterfront Hall, this sister establishment to The Hibernian Hotel in Dublin is in a magnificent landmark building designed by William Hastings in the 1850s in Italianate style - its ornate four storey facade has carvings depicting the five continents and looks particularly impressive when floodlit at night. Classic modern design and high quality materials combine to create an exclusive venue for business and leisure guests. Individually appointed bedrooms - decorated in a contemporary country house style, all with some items of antique furniture - include wheelchair-friendly and lady executive rooms (with thoughtful little emergency overnight kits in the bathroom for unplanned visits). Rooms also have fax/modem points and entertainment systems which include TV/CD/radio and VCR. Conference/banqueting (60/64); secretarial services. Children welcome (under 2s free in parents' room; cots available without charge). No pets. **Rooms 60** (9 junior suites, 30 no smoking, 3 for disabled). Lift. 24 hour room service. Parking in nearby carpark (Mon-Sat only). B&B about £70 pps. Merchants Brasserie: L Mon-Fri 12.30-2.30; D daily. 7-9.30. Bar meals served in Café Marco Polo, 12-9.30 daily. Closed Christmas. Amex, Diners, MasterCard, Visa, Laser, Switch. **Directions:** On Victoria Street in central Belfast, between Anne Street and Albert Clock. ◇

Belfast

RESTAURANT / PUB

McHugh's Bar & Restaurant

29-31 Queen's Square Belfast BT1 3FG
Tel: 028 9050 9999 Fax: 028 9050 9998
Email: info@mchughsbar.com Web: www.mchughsbar.com

This remarkable pub is in one of Belfast's few remaining 18th century buildings. It has been extensively and carefully renovated allowing the original bar (which has many interesting maps, photographs and other memorabilia of old Belfast) to retain its character while blending in a new café-bar and restaurant. Good modern food includes an interesting lunch menu (chicken and tiger tail prawns with noodles and ketchap manis - 'open flame' wok cooking is a speciality), a slightly more formal evening menu and light food through the day. **Seats 100** (private room, 35). Air conditioning. L Sun-Fri,12-3; D daily 5-10.30 (Sun to 9); Set D £18, also à la carte. Bar food 12-10.30 daily. House wine from £11.45. Toilets wheelchair accessible. Parking in nearby carpark. Closed 25 Dec, 1 Jan, 12/13 Jul. Amex, MasterCard, Visa, Switch. **Directions:** Turn right at Albert Clock.

Belfast

The Morning Star

PUB / RESTAURANT

17-19 Pottinger's Entry Belfast BT1 4DT
Tel: 028 9023 5986 Fax: 028 9032 9311

Situated in a laneway in the middle of the city, The Morning Star is a listed building and has been trading as a public house since about 1840. The Morning Star always had a good name for food and Corinne and Seamus McAlister, who have been running the business since 1979, have built on that and earned a reputation for carefully sourced 'real' food, much of it local, including salmon smoked by Charles Mulholland of Belfast and pork sausages made on the premises - and The Morning Star does not knowingly serve any Genetically Modified Foods. With due respect for the special character of the pub, the McAlisters have made changes that now allow an impressive range of menus through the day, offering a wide range of food, including traditional specialities like Irish stew, champ and sausage, local Strangford mussels, roast Antrim pork and aged Quality Assured Northern Ireland beef. Daily chef's specials, blackboard specials, there seems no end to the choices offered each day. There's also a restaurant upstairs where more ambitious meals are served, including themed dinners and special wine evenings. It is worth remembering that this can be a very busy pub, especially at weekends. **Seats 120** (private room 18). No smoking area; air conditioning. Toilets wheelchair accessible. Food served Mon-Sat 11.45-9. Sun L 12-6. Set D £18.95 otherwise à la carte. Pub closed 25 Dec, 12 Jul. Diners, MasterCard, Visa, Switch. **Directions:** Beside HI Park. Between Ann Street and High Street.

Belfast

Nick's Warehouse

RESTAURANT / PUB

35-39 Hill St Belfast BT1 2LB
Tel: 02890 439 690 Fax: 02890 230 514
Email: nicks@warehouse.net.co.uk Web: www.nickswarehouse.co.uk

Nick's Warehouse is a clever conversion on two floors, with particularly interesting lighting and efficient aluminium duct air-conditioning. It's a lively spot, notable for attentive, friendly service and good food, in both the wine bar (where informal light meals and some hot dishes are served) and the restaurant (slightly more formal with structured à la carte menus). A network of trusted suppliers provide the superb ingredients that are the basis for lively contemporary menus offering a wide range of dishes which are consistently interesting and often offer unusual items including game in season. There's always an imaginative selection of vegetarian dishes and menus are considerately marked with symbols indicating dishes containing nuts or oils and also shellfish. The cheese selection is interesting too - you can choose between house cheeses (St Amie, Brie, & Bellingham Blue) or Irish cheeses (Cashel Blue, smoked Gubbeen & Cooleeney). Wide choice of teas of coffees and an informative, well-priced wine list that makes good reading - and includes a small selection of fine wines, a special Spanish listing and about eight keenly priced house wines. Children welcome before 9 pm. Air conditioning. **Seats 135** downstairs(+ 45 upstairs, available as private room at night). L Mon-Fri 12-3, D Tue-Sat 6-10. House wines from £11.50. Closed Sat L, all Sun, D Mon, 25-26 Dec, 15 Jan, Easter Mon/Tue, 12 July. Amex, MasterCard, Visa, Diners, Switch. **Directions:** Near St.Anne's Cathedral, off Waring St. ◇

Belfast

Northern Whig

BAR

2 Bridge Street Belfast BT1 1LU
Tel: 028 9050 9888 Fax: 028 9050 9880
Email: info@thenorthernwhig.com Web: www.thenorthernwhig.com

Located in the former offices of the Northern Whig newspaper and convenient to the city's now fashionable Cathedral Quarter, this is an impressive bar venue of grand proportions. The high ceilings of the old press hall have been retained - and now look down on several gigantic statues that have been salvaged from Eastern Europe and are in keeping with the scale of the building. A long bar has comfortable contemporary seating in coffee and cream, where Belfast's trend-setters meet for drinks or a bite to eat - or you can take a pavement table on a sunny afternoon and watch the world go by, sipping cocktails or sampling something from the reasonably priced menu. Very popular with the local business fraternity for lunch and for a relaxing drink after work - and many stay on for a bite to eat. Expect upmarket bar food - pasta, risotto, tandoori chicken with wild rice - and good service from black-clad young staff. **Seats 160** (private room 40). No smoking area; air conditioning. Toilets wheelchair accessible. Children welcome. Open 10am-1am; bar food 12-9. MasterCard, Visa, Switch. **Directions:** From front of City Hall: walk to 2nd set of traffic lights, turn right, left at next lights; cross road - Northern Whig is on the corner.

Belfast

The Olive Tree Company

CAFÉ

353 Ormeau Road Belfast BT7 3GL **Tel: 028 90 648898**
Fax: 028 90 648898 Web: www.olivetreecompany.com

This unique delicatessen/café specialises in freshly marinated olives, handmade cheeses and salamis - and also sells an exclusive range of French specialities, notably from Provence. The café offers authentic French patisserie and food with a Mediterranean flavour, mainly based on the best of local Irish produce. Think sandwiches with tapenade (olive paté with vine-ripened tomatoes & spring onions, or dolmades (vine leaves) salad with organic natural yoghurt and ciabatta bread and you'll get the flavour. Hot dishes include specialities like 'brodetto' a traditional Italian fish stew, or contemporary dishes such as warm duck salad with chilli & lime dressing. **Seats 26.** No smoking restaurant. Shop open daily: Mon-Sat 9am-6pm (café to 5), Sun 11-5. (No wine but BYO allowed.) Closed 8-15 July, 24 Dec-2 Jan. **No Credit Cards. Directions:** From Belfast City Centre, take the direction for Newcastle/Downpatrick, cross the Ormeau Bridge - spot the Ormeau Bakery landmark and The Olive Tree Company is on the right.

Belfast

Opium

Ⓝ BAR

3 Skipper Street Belfast BTI 2DZ **Tel: 028 90 232 448**
Email: justin@opiumbar.co.uk Web: www.opiumbar.co.uk

In a back street in the Cathedral quarter, you'll find Belfast's newest kid on the block, Opium, a rather smartly packaged den of Asian fusion, an unusual place which has the distinction of having well-known Belfast chef Simon (Ginger) McCance involved. It's a tall narrow building with two floors of sleek, themed rooms: black bamboo-lined mirrored walls, Chinese red shot silk curtains, hardwood furniture and hand-carved screens downstairs; plush red carpeting and silk-lined walls in a glitzy cushion-strewn lounge upstairs. The menu caters for all appetites or diets, starting with Asian-style tapas - salt and chilli pork ribs, sweet soy chicken wings or potato wedges with sweet chilli and sour cream. For something more filling, you can choose between sandwiches, warm salads, crispy spiced chicken wrap with sweet chilli drizzle. Main courses have an international feel to them, such as roast fillet of salmon with potato rosti and coriander salsa or rib-eye steak with Asian spiced butter. It's all substantial bowl food straight from the wok and it's all very tempting. If there's a quarrel, it's not with the food but rather the seating arrangements - low tables leave no room for knees! Open Mon-Sat L 12-4pm, D 5-9pm. Set D £20. Also à la carte. House wines from £13.50. sc discretionary. Closed Sun; 12-15 July.

Belfast

Oxford Exchange

RESTAURANT

1st floor St George's Market Oxford Street Belfast BT1 3NQ
Tel: 028 90 240014 Fax: 028 90 235675
Email: oxfordexchange@mountcharles.com

Dining in an historically interesting building has a certain cachet at any time, but this stylish venue over the recently renovated glass-roofed St. George's Market is particularly fascinating. The market is a redbrick listed Victorian building and Paul Horshcroft's successful conversion has created a pleasing restaurant with views of either the daytime market scene below or, at night, the attractively lit Laganside area. There's a small bar area, with comfortable seating, and a large restaurant with many striking features (including a designer gas fire) where interesting good-value lunches are served and, later, a fine dining dinner menu takes over. Head chef Sean Jones came here from London's Canteen which explains ambitious dinner menus that offer chargrills and traditional food with a modern twist: try a Wot soup (!) with fresh-baked bread or warm smoked salmon to start, then follow with roast loin of wild boar with celeriac and mushroom puree with creamed onions; desserts are updated classics: steamed lemon pudding, perhaps, with raspberry sorbet and exotic fruit coulis. Stylish food, attractively presented, with professional service and (especially at lunch time) good value - no wonder this place is popular with a broad range of discerning diners, from visitors to the market to barristers from the nearby law courts. Quite convenient to Waterfront Hall for pre-theatre meals. Interesting wine list. **Seats 110.** Open Mon-Sat 12-10. A la carte. House wine from £10.95. SC discretionary (except 10% on parties of 8+). Closed Sun; 25 Dec, 1 Jan, public holidays. MasterCard, Visa, Laser, Switch. **Directions:** Opposite Waterfront Hall.

Belfast

Rain City

Ⓝ RESTAURANT

33-35 Malone Road Belfast BT9 6RU **Tel: 028 9068 2929**
Fax: 028 9068 2060 Web: www.raincitybelfast.com

Another Paul Rankin enterprise, Rain City is found on the Malone Road on the corner with Eglantine Avenue and has the look of two terrace houses knocked into one, with attractive seating in the two bay windows. Walls stripped back to the original Belfast red brick alternating with walls done in cream paint are the main features of the decor and with wooden floors, pine tables laid out in a cafe style and colourful artworks, it has a lively yet relaxed atmosphere. Open all day, it offers breakfast, brunch, lunch, kiddie's menu while the evening menu includes a wide selection of appetisers, pastas, pizzas, entrees and desserts. Presentation is attractive without any great frills, the portions are sizeable, the cooking is good and it represents good value too, so it's no surprise to find it a busy place. The family restaurant par excellence. **Seats 110.** Open daily 8am-10.30pm. sc discretionary but 10% added on parties of 6+. Closed Christmas Day. Amex, Diners, MasterCard, Visa, Switch. **Directions:** Near Queen's University.

Belfast

Ramada Hotel Belfast

HOTEL

117 Milltown Road Shaws Bridge Belfast BT8 7XP
Tel: 028 9092 3500 Fax: 028 9092 3600
Email: mail@ramadabelfast.com Web: www.ramadabelfast.com

This modern hotel near Shaws Bridge in Belfast, enjoys a beautiful setting in the Lagan Valley Regional Park, overlooking the River Lagan. Bedrooms are decorated in a fairly neutral modern style and have all the facilities expected of a new hotel, including in-room safes, TV with satellite and movie channels, telephone with voicemail and either a king-size bed or two singles. There are also executive suites available, intended mainly for business guests. Conference and banqueting facilities include 12 meeting rooms of various sizes, with up-to-date technology, and there is a ballroom suitable for weddings, conferences and exhibitions. On-site leisure facilities include sauna, steam room, spa and fitness suite as well as an indoor swimming pool and there's free parking for 300 cars. Conference/banqueting 900/550. Garden, walking. No pets. Children welcome, (under 5s free in parents' room, cot available without charge). **Rooms 120** (4 suites, 116 executive, 83 no smoking, 6 for disabled). Lift. 24 hour room service. B&B £45 pps, ss £15; room-only rate £80 (max. 2 guests). Open all year.

Belfast Bar & Grill: Cream walls display prints of Belfast by the noted Irish photographer Christopher Hill and this Belfast theme is carried through to the menu where the food is distinctly Irish traditional with inspiration from land sea and shore. **Seats 90.** Open for lunch & dinner daily. L &D daily. Set L £14.50, Set D from £16.50. House wine from £13.95. Amex, Diners, MasterCard, Visa, Switch. **Directions:** In Lagan Valley Regional Park, near Shaws Bridge.

Belfast

Ravenhill House

B&B

690 Ravenhill Road Belfast BT6 0BZ
Tel: 028 9020 7444 Fax: 028 9028 2590
Email: olive@ravenhillhouse.com Web: www.ravenhillhouse.com

IRISH BREAKFAST AWARD - ULSTER

Although it is beside a busy road, the Nicholson family home is a late Victorian redbrick house and has some sense of seclusion, with mature trees, private parking and a quiet tree-lined street alongside. A comfortable ground floor lounge has an open fireplace, a comfortable big sofa, lots of books and a PC for guests who want to use the Internet, at a modest charge. Breakfast is served in a bay-windowed dining room with white-damasked tables and the breakfast buffet is displayed on the sideboard in a collection of Nicholas Mosse serving bowls - a feel for craft objects that is reflected elsewhere, including the fact that beds and other furniture has been specially commissioned from an Islandmagee craftsman - bedrooms, which are a mixture of single, twin and double rooms, are comfortably furnished with style, are all en-suite with tea/coffee making facilities and TV. A printed breakfast menu reflects a commitment to using local produce of quality and includes a vegetarian cooked breakfast; the Nicholsons use the St George's Farmers' Market and support the concept behind it. They also make what they can on the premises, including marmalade and wheaten bread for breakfasts. All these good things, plus a particularly helpful attitude to guests, make this an excellent and value for money base for a stay in Belfast. **Rooms 5** (all en-suite, 3 shower only, 2 with bath).B&B £30. ss £10. Closed Christmas & New Year. MasterCard, Visa, Switch. **Directions:** Follow signs for A24 to Newcastle. Located on corner of Ravenhill Road and Rosetta Park.

Belfast

★★ RESTAURANT

Restaurant Michael Deane

36-40 Howard St Belfast BT1 6PF
Tel: 028 9033 1134 Fax: 028 9056 0001
Email: liz@deanesbelfast.com Web: www.deanesbelfast.com

Michael Deane's reputation for offering meticulously prepared dishes, served with old world efficiency and charm in an elegant ambience remains unchallenged This is exceptional food, based on great classic cooking, and the difference is on the plate: it is on a different level to anything else in Belfast, and equal to the best in Ireland. Perhaps the contrast is all the more striking as, to reach the oasis of the restaurant, diners walk through the bustling ground floor brasserie, climb the broad staircase and are admitted to the inner sanctum. Here all is comfort; the fin de siècle sitting room, the elegant dining room, the smart, attentive and knowledgeable staff and that open kitchen with the ever-present Deane meticulously controlling the pace of events and timing food to perfection. To experience the sheer breadth and refinement of Michael Deane's cooking, the eight course Menu Prestige (£58) is the yardstick against which all serious cooking in Ireland should be judged: 'Amuse Bouche' (a delectable prawn bisque with four fantastic fresh prawns, perhaps); 'potato & foie gras soup'; 'study of lobster'; scallop, cauliflower & asparagus; foie gras, sticky rice, cucumber & curry, carpaccio of monkfish, shiitake & cabbage, roast squab, carrot confit, foie gras croquette & vanilla, chariot de fromage; dessert du chef; coffee & chocolate. Simple on the page - simply superb on the plate. Like his Dublin counterpart, Kevin Thornton, Michael Deane is short on words and generous with the foie gras in dishes that never fail to amaze and delight. The main menu offers two courses for £33 and dishes tasted on a recent visit which reflect the richness and deftness of the cooking confirmed the exceptional talent and skill of this great chef ; there is also a thoughtfully crafted Vegetarian Menu (two courses from a choice of about ten, £27.50). Michael Deane was one of the first chefs in Ireland to cook fusion food - something in he succeeded brilliantly although it has failed in so many other hands - and, although it now for his classic skills that he is (rightly) receiving recognition, he also blends fusion themes into classic menus. The wine list is grand but not overawing, and the discreet advice given to match wines with the meal is outstanding. There isn't a chef in Ireland who can surpass Michael Deane and this small restaurant offers an alternative to the fashion for informality that is becoming increasingly rare. A meal here will be remembered long after the price has been forgotten - but it is, in any case, extremely good value for money. **Seats 30.** Air conditioning D Wed-Sat 7-9.30; L Fri only, 12.15-2. D £33-£58; sc discretionary (10% added to bills of 6+). Closed Sun-Tue, Christmas & New Year, Easter, 1 week July, bank hols. Amex, MasterCard, Visa, Switch. **Directions:** 200 metres from rear of City Hall on left.

Belfast

RESTAURANT

Shu

253 Lisburn Road Belfast BT9 7EN
Tel: 028 9038 1655 Fax: 028 9068 1632
Email: eat@shu-restaurant.com Web: www.shu-restaurant.com

The smartly painted Victorian frontage and traditional arched windows provide a vivid contrast to the stainless steel efficiency of the bar and de rigeur 'on view' kitchen of this fashionable restaurant. After a courteous welcome, guests are led into a large L shaped room which is light and airy, with shiny metal muted by terracotta pillars and discreet covers. This is a smoothly run operation, with many regulars of all age groups. Belfast born head chef, Paul Catterson (ex Quaglino's and Zinc in London, and La Stampa in Dublin) runs a slick engine room and his classical and brasserie fare is complemented by restaurant manager Julian Henry's marshalling of a tip top waiting staff. And the food should not disappoint. Paul provides a menu founded on his classical training but with wider world influences: roast salmon with asparagus, smoked parma ham and herb risotto is typical; well-executed starters and main courses like caesar salad and crisped confit pork choucroute with spiced prawns, onions and avocado creme fraiche are in the same vein, allowing choice equally for the adventurous and more conservative diner. Upbeat classical desserts to finish, or Irish farmhouse cheese. Downstairs in the basement cocktail bar "Simply Shu", a simpler, more casual menu is offered with dishes like salt & chilli squid, Thai green curry with chicken and ribeye steak with peppered sauce, all in the £4-£8 range (also available for private hire with buffet food or canapés from £5 per person.) Not suitable for children under 10 after 7 pm. **Seats 76** (private room 22). L Mon-Sat, 12-2.30, D Mon-Sat 6-10. 2-course menu £11.50; otherwise à la carte (average main course £14). House wines £11.50-13.50; s.c. discretionary (10% on parties of 6+). Closed Sun, 24-26 Dec, 11-13 Jul. Amex, MasterCard, Visa, Laser, Switch. **Directions:** Half mile south on Lisburn Road.

Belfast

Sun Kee Restaurant

RESTAURANT

38 Donegall Pass Belfast BT7 1BS
Tel: 02890 312016 Fax: 028 9024 2849

The Lo family's little place just off Shaftesbury Square has earned widespread recognition as the city's most authentic Chinese restaurant. What you get here is a combination of the classic Chinese dishes which are already familiar - but created in uncompromising Chinese style, without the usual "blanding down" typical of most oriental restaurants. They also offer more unusual dishes, which offer a genuine challenge to the jaded western palate: be prepared to be adventurous. It is unlicensed (but you may bring your own). The main difficulty is getting a reservation, as it's an extremely popular spot. Children welcome. **Seats 60.** D daily 5-10.30; range of 'banquet' menus for varying numbers (from £22 per person), also à la carte. Closed Jul. **No Credit Cards. Directions:** Beside Police Station.

Belfast

Ta Tu

RESTAURANT / BAR

701 Lisburn Road Belfast BT9 7GU
Tel: 028 9038 0818 Fax: 028 9038 0828
Email: info@ta-tu.com Web: ta-tu.com

When publican/restaurateur Bill Wolsey opened Ta Tu, in the late spring of 2000, it immediately became one of 'the' places and both bar and restaurant have always been packed at weekends. The design incorporates an ultra-modern high-roofed 'warehouse' with a long bar where the bright young things meet and greet and, at the rear, a more intimate restaurant area reminiscent of photographs depicting pre-war airship lounges. Menus change monthly and the food is, as one might expect, adventurous and beautifully presented; an all-day menu offers a wide range of dishes in various practical combinations; vegetarian dishes are highlighted with a V and a number of dishes, including a vegetarian starter and main course, are picked out as 'express' for extra-fast service; evening à la carte menus are longer and more relaxed. Excellent waiting staff really know the menus; the wine list offers a wide range of carefully chosen wines at reasonable prices and there's a long list of wines by the glass. No children after 7pm. * The very trendy Bar Bacca in Franklin Street is in the same ownership. Restaurant **Seats 90.** Air conditioning. L 12-6, D 6-9.30 (Sun to 8.30). A la carte. House wines from about £9.95. Bar food served 12-9.30 daily. Closed 25 Dec. MasterCard, Visa. **Directions:** From the city centre, take Lisburn Road - about 1 mile on the right. ◇

Belfast

Tedfords Restaurant

RESTAURANT

5 Donegall Quay Belfast BT1 3EF
Tel: 028 9043 4000 Fax: 028 9024 8889

Sailing folk may remember Tedfords as a ship's chandlers - you can almost smell the sisal even now, especially as there are reminders a-plenty of this listed building's venerable maritime past. An informal ground floor restaurant is pleasantly arranged on two levels with a railing around the upper one, which makes the small area seem more spacious and allows staff to move around the tables without disturbing diners too much, although many prefer the more sophisticated dining room upstairs, which lends a sense of occasion to a meal here. There's an appropriate emphasis on things from the sea and good fish cookery is the strength of this restaurant: New England seafood chowder, smoked salmon in various combinations (with crab mayonnaise, wheaten bread & lemon salad perhaps) and Thai steamed mussels are typical light dishes that might appear on lunch or evening menus, while main courses vary more in style: fish & chips at lunchtime, perhaps, turbot with celeriac dauphinoise, wild mushroom jus & straw potatoes for dinner. Should you prefer non-fishy fare, there are plenty of other choices including a vegetarian dish of the day. Service can be a little slow. Informative, fairly priced wine list. **Seats 45.** No smoking area. L Tues-Fri 12-3.00; D Tues-Sat 6-10pm. Pre-theatre D Tues-Sat, 5-6.30, £14.95-£16.95. Otherwise à la carte. House wine from £9.95; sc discretionary. Toilets wheelchair accessible. Children welcome. Parking in multi-storey carpark next door. Closed Sun/Mon, July fortnight, Christmas & bank hols. Amex, MasterCard, Visa, Switch. **Directions:** 3 minute walk from Waterfront Hall, next to multi storey car park.

Belfast

TENsq

HOTEL / RESTAURANT

10 Donegall Square South Belfast BT1 5JD
Tel: 028 9024 1001 Fax: 028 9024 3210
Email: mail@ten-sq.com Web: www.ten-sq.com

This delightful boutique hotel opened has established a special niche for discerning visitors to Belfast. It is situated in a particularly attractive listed Victorian building and the location - just opposite the City Hall and within walking distance of the whole city centre area - is superb. Renovation throughout the

building has been completed to an exceptionally high standard and, although the end result is refreshingly contemporary, it has been achieved with great sensitivity to the the original building: a striking feature, for example, is the lovely old stained glass in many of the original windows, which is now subtly echoed in the interior design. Accommodation - in generous high-windowed rooms, theatrically decorated in an uncompromisingly modern style - is both simple and very luxurious; even the most dyed-in-the-wool traditionalist would be won over by the sheer style of these rooms and they have wonderful bathrooms to match. Features include well-planned lighting, state-of-the-art entertainment systems and - going a stage further than the usual mini-bar - a collection of drinks, nibbles and bits and pieces that would be worthy of a small corner shop, all neatly tucked away out of sight. The restaurant and bar attract discerning non-residents and it is a bonus for residential guests to have amenities of this standard on-site. Staff are warm, welcoming and generally efficient, with none of the stuffiness sometimes encountered in exclusive hotels. All round, this stylish and increasingly accomplished hotel is a tremendous asset to Belfast. Conference/banqueting 70/160. **Rooms 23** (3 deluxe, 20 superior, 2 for disabled). Air conditioning, safe, ISDN, TV/DVD/video channel, tea/coffee-making facilities, iron & trouser press. Lift. B&B room rate about £99-200 (max 2 guests). Closed 25 Dec.

Porcelain: In discreetly oriental surroundings on the first floor, with well spaced tables, this elegant restaurant may seem a little impersonal at a quiet lunch time but comes to life at night when the grand piano is played and the restaurant is busy. Black lacquer tables are stylishly set with tall glasses, fresh flowers, linen napkins and staff welcome arriving guests warmly. Japanese cuisine dominates menus but there are European dishes too - and, should you decide to go Japanese, there should be plenty of assistance in selecting dishes, if required. Cooking is based on the best quality ingredients and is, for the most part, skilfully executed, although a recent visit suggested that it can be inconsistent - even in a sushi & tempura mixed plate, some components were more successful than others - and service, also, can sometimes be friendly and helpful rather than professional and efficient. Stylish presentation is a plus point, however, and delicious desserts might include a wonderful orange pannacotta with yogurt ice cream; a cheese selection is also offered 'continental' unfortunately, which seems a shame when Irish farmhouse cheeses can match the best in Europe. **Seats 165.** L Mon-Sat 12.30-3; D Mon-Sat 6-11. Set L about £16; Porcelain Express 2/3 course menu 12-3 & 6-10.30 (Fri & Sat available 6-7.30pm only), about £12.95/£14.95. Set D from about £17.95. Also à la carte. House wine about £12.50. SC discretionary. Closed 25 Dec. Amex, MasterCard, Visa, Switch. **Directions:** Corner of Linenhall Street at rear of City Hall. ◇

Belfast

RESTAURANT

The Water Margin

159-161 Donegall Pass Belfast BT7 1DP
Tel: 028 90 326888 Fax: 028 90 327333

This big, brassy 200-seater in a converted church at the bottom of the Ormeau Road is the biggest Chinese restaurant in Ireland. Inside, East meets West - a comfortable reception lounge with red leather sofas leads into the large open dining space with round tables of various sizes, lots of artificial plants and garish stained glass windows, all bright reds and greens and mythical beasts. An open bar runs the length of the inside wall and the dining area is divided between the ground floor and a gallery with a purple painted vaulted ceiling and an adjoining opaque glass walled function room. The menu is massive and it pays to either know Chinese food really well or have inside information to find your way about. An extensive Dim Sum menu offers uncompromising authentic Chinese dishes such as steamed ox tripe and steamed fish head (in black bean sauce), a reminder that there is a large Chinese community in Belfast. Finally you arrive at the safe haven of the set banquets, and the familiar territory of Western favourites: aromatic duck, sesame toast, sweet and sours, sizzlings and fried rice are all here - also desserts like chocolate gateau, mango pudding with cream and the fresh orange segments. At this level, the food is pretty average (and by no means cheap), but there is plenty of noisy atmosphere and the Water Margin is somewhere to experience on a busy night for that alone. [There is also a sister restaurant in Coleraine, Co. Londonderry.] **Seats 200.** Open 7 daily, 12-11.30. Set menus from about £20 per person. House wine about £20. Open all year. MasterCard, Visa, Laser. **Directions:** Bottom of Ormeau Road. ◇

Belfast

The Wellington Park Hotel

HOTEL

2 Malone Road Belfast BT9 6RU **Tel: 028 9038 1111** Fax: 028 9066 5410
Email: reservations@mooneyhotelgroup.com Web: www.mooneyhotelgroup.com

Located in the fashionable Malone Road area close to the University, just five minutes from the city centre, this friendly, family-owned and managed hotel is quite a Belfast institution. Many regard it as the only place to stay when in the city and it is certainly near most of the city's cultural attractions - Ulster Museum, Botanic Gardens, Odyssey Arena, Waterfront Hall, the Grand Opera House and St George's Market are all within walking distance on a fine day, or just a short taxi ride. It is also a popular conference venue and has all the most up to date audio-visual equipment and conference facilities, but private guests need not worry about being overrun by conference delegates, since one of the bars is exclusively for their use. The spacious foyer and public areas are comfortably furnished, as are the refurbished bedrooms, featuring the usual facilities, some with modem points and voice-mail. Guests have free use of Queen's University sports centre, a few minutes from the hotel. The Dunadry Hotel & Country Club, a fifteen minute drive from the city, is in the same ownership, also the new Armagh City Hotel (see entries). Conference/banqueting (400/250); secretarial services. Own parking. Wheelchair accessible. Children welcome (under 12 free in parents' room; cots available without charge). No pets. **Rooms 75** (all en-suite, 2 for disabled). Lift. 24 hour room service. B&B £65 pps, ss £40. Closed 24-26 Dec. Amex, Diners, MasterCard, Visa, Switch. **Directions:** From Queen's University, head south up Malone Road, hotel is on the right hand side.

COUNTY ANTRIM

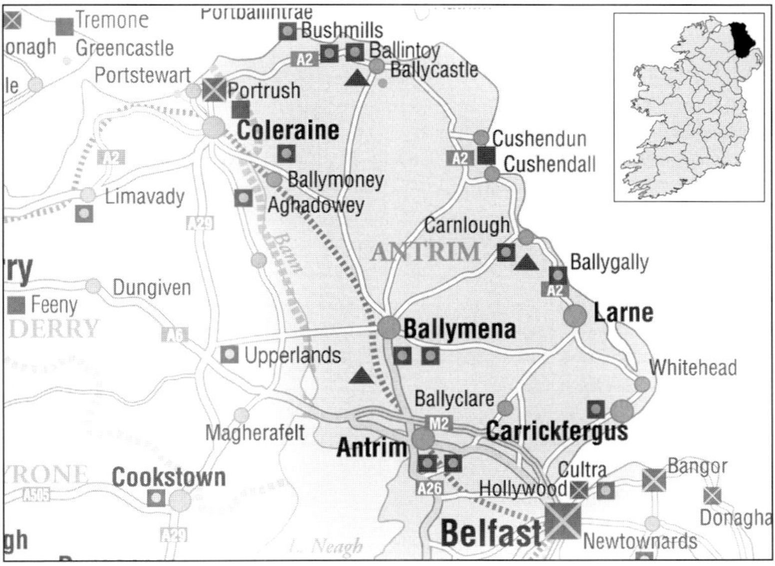

The Antrim Coast may be timeless in its beauty, but today its picturesque ports are enjoying the fruits of restoration and development at places as various as Ballycastle, Glenarm and Carrickfergus. With the Giant's Causeway – the legendary coastline's most famous feature – designated for nearly twenty years now as a World Heritage Site, the announcement in 2003 of Government planning towards an overall strategy for the improvement and protection of the entire coastal area was welcome.

With its boundaries naturally defined by the sea, the River Bann, the extensive lake of Lough Neagh, and the River Lagan, County Antrim has always had a strong sense of its own clearcut geographical identity. This is further emphasised by the extensive uplands of the Antrim Plateau, wonderful for the sense of space with the moorland rising to heights such as Trostan (551m) and the distinctive Slemish (438m), famed for its association with St Patrick.

The plateau eases down to fertile valleys and bustling inland towns such as Ballymena, Antrim and Ballymoney, while the coastal towns ring the changes between the traditional resort of Portrush in the far north, the ferryport of Larne in the east, and Carrickfergus in the south.

In the spectacularly beautiful northeast of the county, the most rugged heights of the Plateau are softened by the nine Glens of Antrim, havens of beauty descending gently from the moorland down through small farms to hospitable villages clustered at the shoreline and connected by the renowned Antrim Coast Road. Between these sheltered bays at the foot of the Glens, the sea cliffs of the headlands soar with remarkable rock formations which, on the North Coast, provide the setting for the Carrick-a-Rede rope bridge and the Giant's Causeway. From the charming town of Ballycastle, Northern Ireland's only inhabited offshore island of Rathlin is within easy reach by ferry, a mecca for ornithologists and perfect for days away from the pressures of mainstream life.

Local Attractions and Information

Antrim town, Lough Neagh cruises 028 94 481312
Antrim town, Shanes Castle 028 94 428216
Antrim town, Tourism Information 028 94 428331
Ballycastle, Carrick-a-Rede Rope Bridge 028 20 731582
Ballymena, Tourism Information 028 25 660300
Ballymoney (Dervock), Benvarden Garden 028 20 741331
Ballymoney, Leslie Hill Open Farm 028 27 666803
Bushmills, Antrim Coast and Glens 028 20 731582
Bushmills Irish Whiskey-World's Oldest Distillery 028 20 731521
Carnlough, Always Ireland Activity Holidays 028 28 885995

Carrickfergus Castle 028 93 351273
Carrickfergus Waterfront 028 93 366455
Carrickfergus, Andrew Jackson Centre 028 93 366455
Dunluce Castle Visitor Centre 028 20 731938
Giants Causeway 028 20 731855
Giants Causeway & Bushmills Railway 028 20 741157
Glenariff Forest Park 028 21 758232
Larne, Carnfunnock Country Park 028 28 270451
Larne Ferryport 028 28 872100
Larne, Tourism Information 028 28 260088
Lisburn, Irish Linen Centre & Lisburn Museum 028 92 663377
Lisburn, Tourism Information 028 92 660038
Portrush, Tourism Information 028 70 823333
Rathlin Island Ferries 028 20 769299
Rathlin Island Visitor Centre 028 20 763951
Templepatrick, Patterson's Spade Mill 028 94 433619

Ballintoy

Whitepark House

Ⓝ COUNTRY HOUSE / B&B

Whitepark Bay Ballintoy Co Antrim
Tel: 028 207 31482
Email: bob@whiteparkhouse.com Web: www.whiteparkhouse.com

A warm welcome from chatty and well-informed hosts Bob and Siobhan Isles awaits visitors to Whitepark House which enjoys stunning views of the Bay, with a path down to the beach straight across the road. As a vegetarian, Bob also prepares a great vegetarian breakfast in addition to the traditional Ulster Fry. Only three bedrooms but all have distinctive colour themes and lots of exotic touches. **Rooms 3** (one bathroom for all) B&B £55 for two sharing, £30 for single occupancy. 5% surcharge on credit card payments. MasterCard, Visa. **Directions:** From Ballintoy, 2km on A2 to Bushmills on east side of Whitepark Bay.

Ballycastle

The House of McDonnell

ATMOSPHERIC PUB

71 Castle Street Ballycastle Co Antrim BT54 6RN
Tel: 028 2076 2975 Fax: 028 2076 2586
Email: toms1744@aol.com Web: www.houseofmcdonnell.com

The House of McDonnell has been in the caring hands of Tom and Eileen O'Neill since 1979 and in Tom's mother's family for generations before that – they can even tell you not just the year, but the month the pub first opened (April 1766). Tom and Eileen delight in sharing the history of their long, narrow premises with its tiled floor and mahogany bar: it was once a traditional grocery-bar, and is now a listed building. The only change in the last hundred years or so, says Tom, has been the addition of a toilet block "but outside the premises you understand" and, most recently, some old photographs which have come to light have now been put on display. Music is important too – they have a good traditional music session every Friday and love to see musicians coming along and joining in. They're usually open from 11 am until "late" in summer, but only in the evenings in winter, although it's worth checking out at weekends anyway, all year. **Directions:** Near the Diamond.

Ballygally

Hastings Ballygally Castle Hotel

HOTEL

Coast Road Ballygally Co Antrim BT40 2QZ
Tel: 028 2858 1066 Fax: 028 9074 8152
Email: gm@bgc.hastingshotels.com Web: hastingshotels.com

This coastal hotel really has got a (very) old castle at the heart of it - and they've even got a ghost. (You can visit her room at the top of the castle). The whole thing is quite unlike any of the other Hastings hotels and, although on-going investment is dramatically improving standards, the hotel still has character and some rooms are quite romantic. The beach is just a stone's throw away, across the road. Conference/banqueting (200/130). Children welcome; (under 14 free in parents' room; cots available). Wheelchair accessible. Parking. Children welcome. Pets by arrangement. **Rooms 44** (2 suites, 8 executive rooms, 6 shower only) B&B £47.50pps, ss £20; no sc. Toilets wheelchair accessible. Open all year. Amex, Diners, MasterCard, Visa, Switch. **Directions:** Situated on the coast road between Larne and Glenarm.

Ballygally

RESTAURANT

Lynden Heights Restaurant

97 Drumnagreagh Rd Ballygally Co Antrim BT40 2RR
Tel: 028 2858 3560 Fax: 028 2858 3560

On a clear day, the Doran family's restaurant high up above the coast road has the most amazing views - and the dining room is in a conservatory, to make the most of it. There's a cosy bar, where orders are taken by friendly, neatly uniformed waiting staff. Well-balanced menus offer a wide choice of dishes on every course, with seafood the main strength, and also game in season - although this is less obvious on the set menus where the choice is more limited. On the carte, three of the seven starters and three main courses are seafood dishes, cooked in a fairly classic style and given the occasional contemporary twist. Steaks get a predictably good showing too, and also Ballymoney ham, with traditional parsley cream sauce; vegetarian dishes are not much in evidence, but a separate menu is available on request. Good ingredients, sound cooking, hearty portions and efficient service all complement this restaurant's natural appeal. An interesting, informative and well-priced wine list is changed monthly. Parking. **Seats 60.** D Thu-Sat, 6-9 (from 5pm in summer), Sun 5-7.30; L Sun only, 12.30-3. Set D about £16.50, also à la carte; Set Sun L about £15. Children welcome. Toilets wheelchair accessible. Closed Mon-Wed. Amex, MasterCard, Visa, Switch. **Directions:** Situated between Larne and Glenarm - signed off the coast road.

Ballymena

HOTEL

Adair Arms Hotel

Ballymoney Road Ballymena Co Antrim BT43 5BS
Tel: 028 2565 3674 Fax: 028 2564 0436
Email: reservations@adair.com Web: adairarms.com

Located in the centre of Ballymena town, this attractive creeper-covered hotel has been owned and managed by the McLarnon family since 1995. Very much the centre of local activities – the bar and lounge make handy meeting places, and there are good conference and banqueting facilities (250/230) – it's also a popular base for visitors touring the Glens of Antrim and the coastal beauty spots. Bedrooms are not especially big, but they are comfortably furnished and well-maintained, with all the usual amenities. Children welcome (under 4s free in parents' room. Pets by arrangement. **Rooms 44** (all en-suite) B&B £45 pps, ss about £15. Weekend specials available. Closed 25-26 Dec. Amex, MasterCard, Visa, Diners. **Directions:** In the town centre. ◇

Ballymena

HOTEL

Galgorm Manor Hotel

136 Fenaghy Rd Ballymena Co Antrim BT42 1EA
Tel: 028 2588 1001 Fax: 028 2588 0080
Email: mail@galgorm.com Web: galgorm.com

Set amidst beautiful scenery, with the River Maine running through the grounds, this converted gentleman's residence was completely refurbished before opening under the present management in 1993 and it is now one of Ireland's leading country house hotels. Approaching through well-tended parkland, one passes the separate banqueting and conference facilities to arrive at the front door of the original house, (which is a mere 100 yards from the river). An impressive reception area with antiques and a welcoming log fire sets the tone of the hotel, which is quite grand but also friendly and relaxed. Day rooms include an elegant drawing room and a traditional bar, as well as the more informal Ghillies Bar in a characterful converted buildings at the back of the hotel (where light meals are also served). Accommodation includes three suites; two rooms have four-posters. All rooms are very comfortably furnished with good bathrooms, and most have views over the river. The latest phase of development adds 48 new bedrooms, a new conference suite and a leisure centre with swimming pool, jacuzzi and fitness suite. Conference/banqueting (500/500) golf (9/18), fishing, horse-riding,walking & garden. Wheelchair accessible. **Rooms 24** (3 suites, 3 executive rooms,8 for disabled) B&B about £55 pps, ss about £40. Dinner Tue-Sat 7-9.30pm in Dining Room. Lunch in Ghillies Bar Mon-Sat 12-2.30pm/Dinner Mon-Sun 6-9.30pm. Open all year.

Restaurant: Galgorm Manor has had a good reputation for its food since opening. Table d'hôte menus with an emphasis on local produce are offered at lunch and dinner. Menus are changed monthly and always include vegetarian dishes. The panelled Board Room has an antique dining table seating 12, for private parties. **Seats 73** (private room, 16). L &D daily. Toilets wheelchair accessible Children welcome. Parking. Amex, Diners, MasterCard, Visa. **Directions:** From the Galgorm roundabout, take the third exit for Cullybackey (Fenaghy road). About 2 miles, on the left. ◇

Ballymena

Marlagh Lodge

COUNTRY HOUSE

Ballymena Co Antrim **Tel: 028 2563 1505**

Robert and Rachel Thompson are moving to this address from their well-known country house The Moat Inn at Templepatrick (see entry) and expect to re-open at Ballymena late autumn 2003.

Ballymoney

Harmony Hill Country House

RESTAURANT / GUESTHOUSE

Balnamore Ballymoney Co Antrim BT53 7PS
Tel: 028 2766 3459 Fax: 028 2766 3740
Email: webmaster@harmonyhill.net Web: www.harmonyhill.net

Trish and Richard Wilson's lovely country house is very peacefully situated in a 5-acre woodland garden, with a mill race bordering and lots of birdlife in the old mill building. The house itself is something of an enigma, with an interesting and rather grand eighteenth century section - including a beautiful light-filled drawing room - on the left as you go in, while accommodation across the hall is in a very different style: generous, rather low-key rooms have steps up to optional sleeping platforms (not necessarily used - hence the possibility of accommodating a family of five in one room) and, at the end of a mysterious plant-filled passage towards the back of the house, there is quite a substantial restaurant which, again, divides into two areas of very different character. One section is divided into booths, providing a homely spot for solitary guests dining in the company of a good book or for times when the restaurant is not busy enough to use all the tables; the other section is more open, with traditional dining tables but the whole set-up is very appealing. The menu, incidentally, is also most unusual: instead of simply naming the dishes, head chef Cora Maxwell presents them as little recipes, hence 'Soused Trout: Gently poach the freshest trout fillets in white wine vinegar & court bouillon peppered with star anise & pickling spice, chill well then serve with a light salad of mixed leaves, radish and quail's eggs'. Ingenious. Open fires play a major part in the life of this house - an open peat fire can be lit in every bedroom (so romantic!), there's a big fire in the drawing room and one in the restaurant too - the logistics of running so many fires must be quite a challenge, but they give the house great atmosphere. Garden. **Rooms 6** (4 en-suite, 2 shower only, 2 with private bathrooms). Limited room service. children welcome (under 2s free in parents' room; cot £5). B&B36 pps, ss £6. (Restaurant: **Seats 50.** Non-residenst welcome by reservation. D Wed-Sat, 6.30-9.30; Set D £25. L Sun, 12.30-2. House wine £10.95. Restaurant closed Mon, Tue, 25-26 Dec.) House open all year. MasterCard, Visa, Switch. **Directions:** Off A26, 1.5 miles outside Ballymoney.

Bushmills

Bushmills Inn

HOTEL

9 Dunluce Rd Bushmills Co Antrim BT57 8QG
Tel: 028 2073 3000 Fax: 028 2073 2048
Email: mail@bushmillsinn.com Web: www.bushmillsinn.com

Only a couple of miles from the Giant's Causeway, Bushmills is home to the world's oldest distillery – a tour of the immaculately maintained distillery is highly recommended. The Bushmills Inn is one of Ireland's best-loved hotels. It has grown since its establishment as a 19th-century coaching inn, but its development under the current ownership – including complete restoration before re-opening in 1987 – has been thoughtful and a recently added wing was so skilfully designed that it is hard to work out where the old ends and the new begins. Inside, it's the same story: all the features which made the old Inn special have been carried through and blended with new amenities. The tone is set by the turf fire and country seating in the hall and public rooms – bars, the famous circular library, the restaurant, even the Pine Room conference room – carry on the same theme. Bedrooms are individually furnished in a comfortable cottage style and even have "antiqued" bathrooms – but it's all very well done and avoids a theme park feel. It's hard to think of a better base for a holiday playing the famous golf courses of the area (Royal Portrush is just four miles away) - or simply exploring this beautiful coastline and its hinterland; since the Magilligan-Greencastle ferry opened in 2002, day trips can comfortably include a visit to the beautiful Inishowen peninsula in Co. Donegal. The inn is also a popular venue for small conferences, held in an oak-beamed loft. Wheelchair accessible. Garden. Fishing. Children welcome. Pets permitted by arrangement. **Rooms 32:** 22 in Mill House,10 in Coaching Inn; (4 superior, 7 shower only, 22 no smoking, 1 for disabled) B&B £49 pps in Coaching Inn, £79 pps in Mill House (£99pps in superior rooms), ss £10-20. Restaurant: **Seats 110** (private room, 40) D daily 7-9.30 (Sun 6-9.30), L Day menu 12-7; (Sun: carvery from 12.30-2.30pm and day menu 3-6pm). House wines from £10; SC discretionary. Open all year. MasterCard, Visa, Switch. **Directions:** On the A2 Antrim coast road, in Bushmills village, as it crosses the river.

Bushmills

The Distillers Arms

BAR / RESTAURANT

140 Main Street Bushmills Co Antrim BT57 8QE
Tel: 028 2073 1044 Fax: 028 2073 2843
Email: simon@distillersarms.com Web: www.distillersarms.com

Housed in an 18th century building which was once the home of the distillery owners, Simon Clarke's stylish modern bar and restaurant underwent major renovations before re-opening late in 2001 - and the results are impressive. The bar - which leads into the restaurant at the far end - is clean-lined but not hard-edged: smart modern lightwood bar stools have comfortable curved backs and fresh flowers on the bar, the use of different woods and using table lamps to soften the lighting all help to create a warm atmosphere, emphasised by comfortably domestic seating groups and sofas inside the door. The restaurant is more rustic by comparison, with open stonework and a fireplace giving it an old-world character. As much as half of the menu could be seafood, including imports like tiger prawns and sea bass as well as local catches, including lobster and crab from Rathlin Island. Starters include seared king scallops, confit of duck leg with wilted chicory and Bushmills whiskey and onion marmalade; a wide selection of other equally interesting dishes ranges from warm duck liver salad to imaginative vegetarian choices like crisp golden choux fritters with Cashel Blue and parmesan on salad. Main courses are in the same vein, with seafood and mainstream vegetarian dishes especially appealing although there is plenty to choose from (steaks, various, pork cutlets with Lakeshore grain mustard & thyme cream, braised lamb shank). A dynamic young team with genuine enthusiasm for the industry is clearly at work here and their achievement so far is impressive. They are tackling the wine list imaginatively, with many wines sourced directly from auction and sold with only a small mark up, so the value offered is excellent.Toilets wheelchair accessible. Children welcome. **Seats 76.** L 12.15-3.15, D 5.15-9 (weekends to 9.30). Sun L £13, Set D £25, otherwise à la carte. House wines from £10. Probably closed Mon off-season (Oct-Mar), but winter times not confirmed at time of going to press. MasterCard, Visa, Switch. **Directions:** 300 yards from Old Bushmills Distillery.

Carnlough

Londonderry Arms Hotel

HOTEL

20 Harbour Road Carnlough Co Antrim BT44 0EU
Tel: 028 2888 5255 Fax: 028 2888 5263
Email: ida@glensofantrim.com Web: glensofantrim.com

Carnlough, with its charming little harbour and genuinely old-fashioned atmosphere (they still sell things like candyfloss in the little shops) is one of the most delightful places in Northern Ireland. The Londonderry Arms Hotel, built by the Marchioness of Londonderry in 1848 as a coaching inn, was inherited by her great grandson, Sir Winston Churchill, in 1921. Since 1948 it has been in the caring hands of the O'Neill family. The original building and interior remain intact, giving the hotel great character. They do good home-made bar meals or afternoon tea which you can have in the bar or beside the fire in a comfortably old fashioned lounge. Bedrooms - which are all en-suite and include 14 newer ones added at the back of the hotel - are comfortable and well-furnished in keeping with the character of the building. Many of the older rooms have sea views, and it is worthwhile discussing the type and location of your room when booking as one or two are badly positioned for a restful night's sleep. The hotel is a good conference venue and makes a very pleasant base for a short break exploring the Glens of Antrim. Conferences/banqueting (100/140). Parking. Wheelchair accessible. Children under 4 free in parents' room; cots available. No pets. Walking, cycling. **Rooms 35** (all en-suite, 8 no smoking, 1 for disabled). Lift. B&B £42.50 pps. Children welcome. D daily, L Sun only. Barfood served daily. Amex, Diners, MasterCard, Visa, Switch. **Directions:** On the A2 Antrim coast road.

Carrickfergus

Quality Hotel Carrickfergus

HOTEL

75 Belfast Road Carrickfergus Co Antrim BT38 8BX
Tel: 028 9336 4556 Fax: 028 9335 1620
Email: info@qualityinncarrickco.uk

Conveniently located to Belfast airport (10 miles) and the scenic attractions of the Antrim coast, this modern hotel makes a comfortable base for business and leisure visitors. It has good conference facilities (600), meeting rooms (max. 60) and in-room amenities (desk, fax/modem line) for business guests. Bedrooms include three suitable for disabled guests, two suites, two junior suites and 20 non-smoking rooms; all are furnished to a high standard with well-finished en-suite bathrooms (all with bath and shower). B&B about £45 pps, ss about £30. Restaurant open daily 5.30-10; food available in Mac's Pub Mon-Sat 12-3, Mon-Sun 5.30-9.30. Open all year. Amex, Diners, MasterCard, Visa, Switch. **Directions:** Main Coast Road exit Belfast North (8 miles). ◇

Cushendall

Cullentra House

Ⓝ B&B

16 Cloughs Road Cushendall Co Antrim
Tel: 028 2177 1762 Fax: 028 2177 1762 Email: cullentra@hotmail.com

Olive and James McAuley are charming people who go out of their way to ensure their guests are happy. Although there is nothing remarkable about the house itself, it is very well located for touring this beautiful area and they are extremely hospitable hosts - and their success in various tourism award schemes over the years underlines the fact that their guests are very happy with the service provided. Three rooms are well appointed with all the necessary facilities, breakfast is as good as you would expect from such caring hosts, and they will also prepare an evening meal if ordered in advance. **Rooms 3.** B&B £18pp. Closed Christmas Day. MasterCard, Visa.

Dunadry

Dunadry Hotel & Country Club

HOTEL

2 Islandreagh Drive Dunadry Co Antrim BT41 2HA
Tel: 028 9443 4343 Fax: 028 9443 3389
Email: reservations@mooneyhotelgroup.com Web: www.mooneyhotelgroup.com

This attractive riverside hotel is well-located close to Belfast International Airport and only about 15 minutes from the city centre. It was formerly a mill and it succeeds very well in combining the character of the old buildings with the comfort and efficiency of an international hotel. It has excellent facilities and is surrounded by ten acres of grounds, making it a good choice as a business and conference venue - and, equally, as a weekend retreat. Stylish, spacious bedrooms include three suites and eleven executive rooms – all have good amenities, including satellite TV, and executive rooms have computer points and fax machines. The most desirable rooms have French windows opening on to the gardens or the inner courtyard and a new informal restaurant makes the most of its situation overlooking the river. Leisure facilities within the grounds include a professional croquet lawn, fun bowling, trout fishing and cycling, as well as a leisure centre with the most up to date fitness equipment, indoor swimming pool and professional beauty therapist. *Sister hotel to the Wellington Park Hotel in Belfast city and the new Armagh City Hotel (see entries). **Rooms 83** (all en-suite, 2 for disabled). B&B £77pps, ss £42.50; room-only rate also available, £67.50 (max. 2 adults & 2 children).* Short breaks offered. Restaurant: D Tue-Sat, L Sun; Bistro: 7.30am-10pm daily; Bar snacks: 11-11. Closed 24-26 Dec. Amex, Diners, MasterCard, Visa, Switch. **Directions:** Near Belfast airport; look for signs to Antrim/Dunadry.

Portballintrae

Sweeney's Public House & Wine Bar

RESTAURANT / WINE BAR

Seaport Avenue Portballintrae Co Antrim BT57 8SB
Tel: 028 2073 2405 Fax: 028 2073 1850 Email: seaport@freeuk.com

This attractive stone building is on the sea side of the road as you drive into Portballintrae and is very handy to both the Royal Portrush Golf Club and the Giant's Causeway. It's a pleasant place, with a welcoming open fire in the bar and a choice of places to drink or have a bite to eat. Unpretentious food is in the modern international café/bar style; seafood, including lobster, wild salmon and locally caught white fish, is a speciality. Although likely to suit all age groups during the day, it can get very busy during the evening, especially on live music nights (folk & country; there is a late licence to 1 am on Friday and Saturday). A useful place to break a day exploring the area, Sweeney's is reassuringly consistents. Children welcome. **Seats 120** (private room, 32) No smoking area; air conditioning. Food available every day (12-9.30pm), à la carte; house wines from about £7.50; sc discretionary. Toilets wheelchair accessible. Own parking. No reservations. Closed 25 Dec. Amex, Diners, MasterCard, Visa, Switch. **Directions:** Centre of village overlooking bay & harbour. ◇

Portrush

Academy Restaurant

RESTAURANT

University Of Ulster Ballywillan Road Portrush Co Antrim BT56 8JL
Tel: 028 7032 3970 Fax: 028 7032 3997
Email: m.caldwell@ulster.ac.uk Web: www.ulster.ac.uk/portrush/

It is not widely known beyond the immediate area that the Portrush's School of Hotel, Leisure & Tourism at the University of Ulster (previously the the renowned NI Hotel & Catering College) is also open to the public as a normal commercially-operated restaurant. Lunch in the Academy offers a brasserie style menu with quick, professional service, while dinner offers fine dining and a more formal style of service including plated dishes, silver service and guéridon preparation and flambé work. The kitchen and restaurant are staffed by students following higher education programmes in hospitality and the culinary arts under the guidance of professional restaurant manager, Martin Caldwell, and head chef, Martin Devaney. Menus and wine lists are bang up to date, the food is excellent and beautifully presented and service is friendly, attentive - and highly efficient. The quality and value offered are both outstanding. They also do theme evenings, wedding receptions/banqueting and conferences - and even have accommodation. **Seats 80** (private room available on request). No smoking restaurant. L Mon-Fri 12.30-1 (also Sun in Jun-Jul); D Wed-Sat, 7-8. Set L £11.50, Set Sun L £13.99. Set D £15.95; à la carte L&D also available. House wine £9.25. Closed Sun (except Jun-Jul), Easter, Christmas. MasterCard, Visa, Switch. **Directions:** M2 from Belfast, A26 to Portrush - Ballywillan Road.

Portrush

FARMHOUSE / B&B

Maddybenny Farmhouse

18 Maddybenny Pk Portrush Coleraine Co Antrim BT52 2PT
Tel: 028 7082 3394
Email: accommodation@maddybenny22.freeserve.co.uk
Web: www.maddybenny.freeserve.co.uk

Just two miles from Portrush, Rosemary White's Plantation Period farmhouse was built before 1650. Since extended, and now modernised, it makes a very comfortable and exceptionally hospitable place to stay, with a family-run equestrian centre nearby (including stabling for guests' own horses). There is also snooker, a games' room and quiet sitting places, as well as a a garden and an area for outdoor children's games. The accommodation is just as thoughtful. The bedrooms are all en-suite and there are all sorts of useful extras – electric blankets, a comfortable armchair, hospitality tray complete with teacosy, a torch and alarm clock beside the bed, trouser press, hair dryer – and, on the landing, an ironing board, fridge and pay phone for guest use. Across the yard there are also six self-catering cottages, open all year (one wheelchair friendly). No evening meals, but Rosemary guides guests to the local eating places that will suit them best - and her breakfasts are legendary, so make sure you allow plenty of time to start the day with a feast the like of which you are unlikely to encounter again. Maddybenny was the Guide's Farmhouse of the Year in 2000. Golf, fishing, tennis and pitch & putt nearby. Children welcome (cot available without charge, children's playground). Garden. **Rooms 3** (all en-suite) B&B £25pps (children £10), ss £5. Closed Christmas. MasterCard, Visa. **Directions:** Signposted off A29 Portrush/Coleraine road.

Portrush

RESTAURANT

Ramore Wine Bar

The Harbour Portrush Co Antrim BT56 8BN
Tel: 028 7082 4313 Fax: 028 7082 3194

An upmarket fast food operation is all that remains of the wonderful Ramore Restaurant, which was once the leading light of cosmopolitan fine dining in Northern Ireland. However, the informal style of this large restaurant overlooking the harbour is clearly popular with the holiday market and is a real hit with the young - teenagers, families with young children - who appreciate the fun & friendly atmosphere, the speed and prices which are reasonable for the quality of food. Menus are much the same as the old wine bar - a wide selection of contemporary dishes ranging from tortilla chips with dips, through bang bang chicken with oriental salad, peanut & garlic dips, chilli steak in pitta with salad & garlic mayo or lamb steaks with red pepper & cherry tomato salsa on bruschetta to jumbo prawn salad or vegetarian options like cheese & spinach flan. Prices are very accessible - almost everything is still around £10 - but the downside is noise, discomfort and scanty service.* The nearby Harbour Bar is in the same ownership; the old front retains its original character. **Seats 170.** L&D daily: L12.15-2.15, D 5-10 (Sun,12.15-3 & 5-9). A la carte; house wine about £7.50. sc discretionary. Toilets wheelchair accessible. Closed 25 Dec. MasterCard, Visa, Switch. **Directions:** At the harbour in Portrush. ◇

Portrush

HOTEL

Royal Court Hotel

233 Ballybogey Rd Portrush Co Antrim BT56 8NF
Tel: 028 7082 2236 Fax: 028 7082 3176
Email: royalcourthotel@aol.com Web: www.royalcourthotel.co.uk

Set in a spectacular clifftop location just outside Portrush, and a 10 minute drive from the Giant's Causeway, the Royal Court offers the most desirable hotel accommodation in the area. Public areas are spacious and comfortable – the dining room has the sea view. Bedrooms are all well-furnished with good bathrooms, but vary considerably in size and outlook – the best are on the sea side and have little private balconies. Very handy to a number of golf links including the Royal Portrush and an excellent base for touring this lovely area. Conference/banqueting (300/240). Wheelchair accessible. Children under 4 free in parents' room; cots available. No pets. **Rooms 18** (all en-suite, 5 suites, 3 executive rooms) B&B £47.50pps, ss £12.50. Closed 26 Dec. Amex, MasterCard, Visa, Switch. **Directions:** From Ballymena head north on M2, at Ballymoney roundabout take 3rd exit to Portrush (B62). Hotel at end on right hand side.

Templepatrick

HOTEL

Hilton Templepatrick

Castle Upton Estate Templepatrick Co Antrim BT39 ODD
Tel: 028 9443 500 Fax: 028 9443 5511
Web: www.templepatrickhilton.com

This purpose-built hotel and resort is very close to Belfast International Airport, yet it is located in 220 acres of parkland in the Castle Upton Estate, on the banks of Six Mile Water. Business and leisure facilities are very good, especially for golf, and bedrooms have views over the golf course and estate, making it an attractive weekend retreat and a good venue for conference/team-building events. Conference/banqueting (500). Business centre; secretarial services; video conferencing. Health Club, swimming pool. Golf (18), pitch & putt, fishing, equestrian, tennis. Garden, walking. Children under 15 free in parents' room; cots available. Pets permitted by arrangement. **Rooms 130** (1 suite, 56 executive rooms, 65 no-smoking, 7 for disabled). Lift. B&B from about £75 pps, ss about £20; no sc. Open all year. Amex, Diners, MasterCard, Visa, Switch. **Directions:** M2 from Belfast; Templepatrick roundabout, 3rd exit. ◇

Templepatrick

COUNTRY HOUSE

The Moat Inn

12 Donegore Hill Templepatrick Co Antrim BT41 2 HW
Tel: 028 9443 3659 Fax: 028 9443 3726
Email: info@themoatinn.com Web: www.themoatinn.com

Robert and Rachel Thompson's pretty blue-painted house dates from about 1740 and it now makes a home of character, with unusual guest accommodation. The Thompsons undertook daunting renovation work with equanimity before opening for guests in 2000 and the house - which is packed with antiques, books and musical memorabilia (Robert's special interest) - feels as if their family has lived here for generations. Bedrooms are individually furnished as if in a private house - the Red Room, the Print Room and the Blue Room (with original Victorian four-poster bed) - with immaculately arranged tea/coffee trays and lots of interesting collectibles on display. Guests assemble for dinner in front of the drawing room fire, and you dine by candlelight at fine old mahogany dining tables. ***NB: Just as the guide was going to press, we heard that Robert and Rachel Thompson are moving to Marlagh Lodge, Ballymena, Co Antrim (Tel 028 2563 1505), where they will be operating a business similar to The Moat Inn, from about November 2003.** MasterCard, Visa, Switch. **Directions:** Follow Donegore signs from Templepatrick (M2 Junction 5).

COUNTY ARMAGH

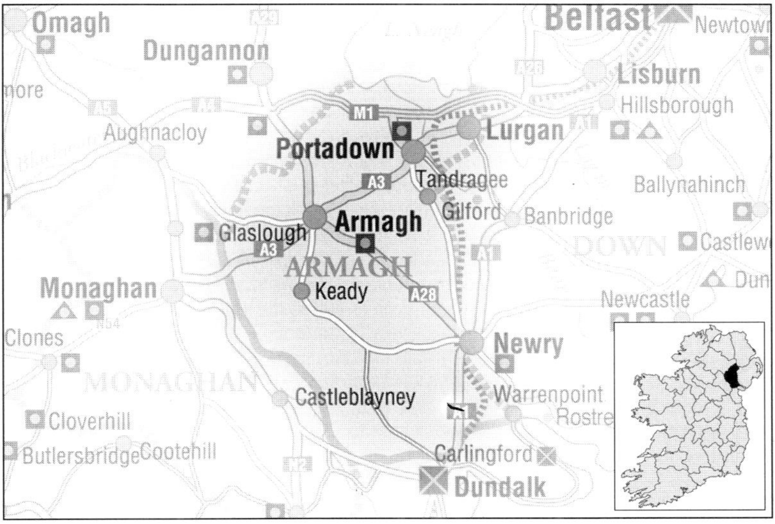

Mention Armagh, and most people will think of apples and archbishops. In the more fertile northern part of the county, orchards are traditionally important in the local economy, with the lore of apple growing and their use a part of County Armagh life. And the pleasant cathedral city of Armagh itself is of course the ecclesiastical capital of all Ireland, and many a mitre is seen about it.

But in fact Armagh city's significance long pre-dates Christian times. Emhain Macha - Navan Fort- to the west of the town, was a royal stronghold and centre of civilisation more than 4,000 years ago. Marking the county's northern coastline, the inland freshwater sea of Lough Neagh provides sand for the construction industry, eels for gourmets, and recreational boating of all sorts. In times past, it was part of the route which brought coal to Dublin from the mines in Coalisland in Tyrone, the main link to the seaport of Newry being the canal from Portadown which, when opened in 1742, was in the forefront of canal technology.

That County Armagh was a leader in canal technology is only one of its many surprises. The discerning traveller will find much of interest, whether it be in the undulating farmland and orchards, the pretty villages, or the handsome uplands rising to Carrigatuke above Newtownhamilton, and on towards the fine peak of Slieve Gullion in the south of the county, down to Forkhill and Crossmaglen and the Gaelic football heartlands, where they were disappointed to lose to neighbouring Tyrone in the first ever all-Ulster all-Ireland final in Croke Park in Dublin on September 28th 2003, but a new season with its fresh opportunities beckons.

Local Information and Attractions

Annaghmore (nr Portadown) Ardress (NT house) 028 38 851236
Armagh, County Museum 028 37 523070
Armagh, Planetarium 028 37 523689
Armagh, Astronomical Observatory 028 37 522928
Armagh, Palace Stables Heritage Centre 028 37 529629
Armagh, St Patrick's Trian Visitor Centre 028 37 521801
Bessbrook, Derrymore House 028 30 830353
Forkhill (Slieve Gullion)Ti chulainn Cultural Centre 028 30 888828
Loughgall, Loughgall Country Park 028 38 892900
Lough Neagh, Discovery Centre, Oxford Island 028 38 322205
Markethill, Gosford Forest Park 028 37 551277
Moy, The Argory (NT Mansion) 028 87 784753
Newry, Derrymore House 028 30 830353
Portadown, Moneypenny's Lock (Newry Canal) 028 37 521800
Scarva, Newry Canal Visitor Centre 028 38 832163
Slieve Gullion Forest Park 028 30 848226

Armagh

Armagh City Hotel

HOTEL 2 Friary Road Armagh Co Armagh BT60 4FR **Tel: 028 3751 8888** Fax: 028 3751 2777 Email: reservations@mooneyhotelgroup.com Web: www.mooneyhotelgroup.com

Located at the heart of the "orchard county" of Armagh, this hotel is a sister establishment to the Dunadry Inn, Co. Antrim and Wellington Park Hotel, Belfast (see entries). While its uncompromisingly blocky design and modern materials may disappoint those who had hoped for an hotel that would have empathy with the traditional style of Ireland's historic ecclesiastical capital, it has brought welcome facilities to the area, including Northern Ireland's largest hotel conference facility. An events entrance with its own parking area separates delegates from other guests and has an impressive foyer, with separate check-in facilities. The main hotel entrance may seem disappointing by comparison - a cafeteria style 'Deli' and informal dining area located in the foyer give a poor impression on arrival - but the bar and more formal restaurant areas are at the back of the hotel, looking out on to pleasant landscaped gardens. Clean-lined contemporary bedrooms are practical - and well-equipped for business guests, with air conditioning, ISDN lines, safe and TV with video as well as the usual phones, tea/coffee making facilities and trouser press. Conference/banqueting (1,200/600); back up business services; leisure centre with swimming pool. Telephone for details, including information on special breaks. **Rooms 82** (10 executive, 30 no smoking, 4 disabled, 2 shower only). B&B from £40 pps. Room-only rate about £60 (max. 2 adults & 2 children). Amex, Diners, MasterCard, Visa, Switch. **Directions:** From Dublin take A28 to Armagh City, when the police station is in sight, follow the road round to the left to the hotel.From Belfast take M1 to Junction 11, then M12 on to A3 , hotel is situated just before Palace Stables.

Armagh

Manor Park Restaurant

Ⓝ RESTAURANT 2 College Hill The Mall Armagh Co Armagh BT61 **Tel: 028 3751 5353**

Pascale Brissaud, who is originally from Perpignan, has moved his popular restaurant, Chez Pascale, from Newtownbutler to this listed building on The Mall in Armagh city. Specialities that have travelled with him include dishes like a gratin of Dublin Bay prawns with fresh garlic & nut butter - and classic Burgundy snail timbale in an almond butter. Wide-ranging menus offer luxurious dishes like fresh lobster and foie gras, also game in season - and plenty of more familiar local produce too. This is great news for Armagh and should do very well. D Tue-Sun, 5-11, L Sun only 12-3.30. Set L £12.95, Set D from £14.50 (early, 5-7; or late 10-11.30) Also à la carte. House wine £9.95. Closed Mon, 2 weeks Jan. MasterCard, Visa, Laser, Switch.

Lurgan

The Brindle Beam Tea Rooms

RESTAURANT House of Brindle 20 Windsor Avenue Lurgan Co Armagh BT67 9BG **Tel: 028 3832 1721**

This in-store self-service restaurant is a real one-off. Nothing is bought in and Alannah Gilpin, who has been head chef for ten years, puts the emphasis firmly on real home cooking. There are two freshly-made soups each day and hot dishes like beef stew, made with well trimmed fat-free chump steak - with no onions. None of the pies or casseroles contain onions as some customers don't like them, but they're still full of flavour. Their salad cart is a special attraction, with anything up to 30 different salads served each day, and several different hot dishes including baked or grilled chicken breasts, salmon and always some vegetarian dishes too. There's also a huge variety of tray bakes and desserts - and only real fresh cream is used. Scrupulously clean, with reasonable prices (not cheap, but good value for the quality) and real home cooking, this place is a gem. **Seats 110** (private room 50). No smoking restaurant, Open Mon-Sat, 10-5, L 12-2, Aft Tea 2-4.30 (Sat to 4.45). A la carte self-service except special set menus, e.g. Christmas. Unlicensed. Closed Sun, 25-26 Dec, Easter, 12-13 Jul. **Directions:** Town centre; located inThe House of Brindle Store. ◇

Portadown

Café Paul Rankin

Ⓝ CAFÉ High Street Mall Portadown Co Armagh BT63 **Tel: 028 3839 8818** Fax: 028 3839 8808

More good news for Portadown, now that Café Paul Rankin - until recently very much a Belfast thing - has opened here. Anyone familiar with the cafés will make a beeline here for a tasty daytime bite: Caesar salad, penne a la romana, chunky chicken chowder are the kind of dishes to expect, along with gourmet sandwiches like ham & cheese toasties, and roast Mediterranean vegetable & goats' cheese panini. Children welcome. Wheelchair accessible. Seats 40. No smoking area. Open all day, 7 days. Closed 25 Dec, 1 Jan. MasterCard, Visa, Switch. **Directions:** Town centre.

Portadown

Seagoe Hotel

HOTEL

Upper Church Lane Portadown Co Armagh BT63 5JE
Tel: 028 3833 3076 Fax: 028 3835 0210
Email: info@seagoehotel.com Web: www.seagoehotel.com

Attractively situated in its own grounds on the edge of Portadown, this fine hotel has been in the same ownership for many years but underwent a complete makeover a few years ago. The design is innovative and exceptionally easy on the eye and, once inside, the tone of the whole development is set by stylish public areas which are outstanding not only for grace and scale of design, but also the use of extremely high quality materials in construction, furnishing and decor. Easy wheelchair access throughout the building has been thought through in detail (the pay phone in the lobby is wheelchair accessible, for example). Bedrooms have contemporary simplicity teamed with warm, rich fabrics and good work space for business guests; executive rooms also have modem and fax facilities. Business/conference facilities are equally special - but it's not all work, as there's a separate function entrance (popular for weddings as well as conferences), with its own dramatic lobby/reception area - and there are two superb honeymoon suites. Bar and restaurant areas are designed with equal care, looking on to a delightful courtyard garden in the centre of the building. Own parking. Garden. **Rooms 34** (all en-suite, 2 disabled with shower only). Room only Mon-Thurs £70 single, £96 double, Fri/Sat/Sun all rooms £50. Lift. Restaurant open for lunch and dinner daily. 12-2.30 & 5-9.30 (Sun to 9) and bar meals (paninis, ciabatta, steak etc.) are available at the same times. Closed 25 Dec. Amex, Diners, MasterCard, Visa, Switch. **Directions:** Off A27 (Old Lurgan Road). ◇

Portadown

Yellow Door Ruggers Bistro

Ⓝ **RESTAURANT**

Portadown RFC Chambers Park Portadown Co Armagh BT62
Tel: 028 3839 4860

Housed within Portadown Rugby Club's clubhouse at Chambers Park, the aptly named Ruggers Bistro looks just like a sports centre from the outside but once up the steps it's a smart and inviting eatery. It features two rooms, with the dining room bright and modern and the bar - with a balcony overlooking the rugby grounds - a little more conventional. There's nothing conventional about the food or the service, though, and there's also great attention paid to the decor, the china and the presentation. Food is simply superb: delicious breads (from their deli), a perfectly dressed Caesar salad (with pancetta & fresh anchovies), pasta with salmon, fresh pesto and fresh peas - and a generous vegetarian chilli with aubergines & mozzarella were among the dishes attracting praise on a recent visit. Charming service, and great value too: lunch menus are well priced, under £10, and although dinner is more expensive, it still represents good value. There's a junior menu and brunch is available on the last Sunday of the month between 11am and 3pm. Open: Wed-Sat L 12.00-2.30pm and D 6.30-9.30pm and Sun L 12.00-2.30. House wine £8.50. *A sister establishment, The Yellow Door Deli, has an 80-seater restaurant as part of a delicatessen at 74 Woodhouse Street, Portadown. (Tel: 028-38353528). ◇

COUNTY DOWN

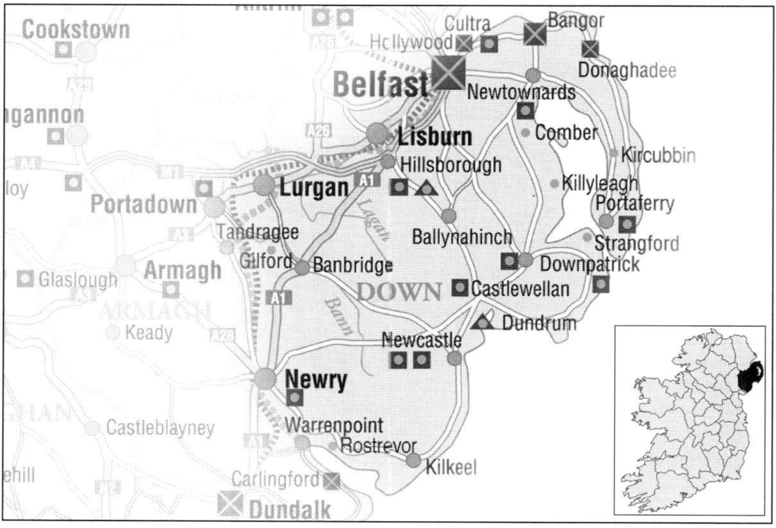

County Down rings the changes in elegant style, from its affluent shoreline along Belfast Lough - the "Gold Coast" - through the rolling drumlin country which provides Strangford Lough's many islands, and on then past the uplands around Slieve Croob, with the view southward being increasingly dominated by the purple slopes of the Mountains of Mourne.

The Mournes soar to Northern Ireland's highest peak of Slieve Donard (850m), and provide excellent hill-walking and challenging climbing. When seen across Down's patchwork of prosperous farmland, however, they have a gentleness which is in keeping with the county's well-groomed style. In the same vein, Down is home to some of Ireland's finest gardens, notably Mount Stewart on the eastern shore of Strangford Lough, and Rowallane at Saintfield, while the selection of forest and country parks is also exceptional.

Within the contemporary landscape, history is much in evidence. St Patrick's grave is in Downpatrick, while the Ulster Folk and Transport Museum at Cultra near Holywood provides an unrivalled overview of the region's past. The coastline is much-indented, so much so that, when measured in detail, County Down provides more than half of Northern Ireland's entire shoreline. Within it, the jewel of Strangford Lough is an unmatched attraction for naturalists and boat enthusiasts, while Portaferry has one of Ireland's longest-established saltwater aquariums in Exploris.

In the south of the county, the increasingly prosperous town of Newry on the river inland from Carlingford Lough is – with Lisburn in County Antrim – one of Ireland's two new cities under a re-designation of 2003. Newry is responding with enthusiasm to its new status, and the urban regeneration of this interesting canalside centre is intriguing to watch.

Local Attractions and Information

Bangor, Events Office	028 91 278051
Bangor, Tourism Information	028 91 270069
Bangor, North Down Heritage Centre	028 91 271200
Castle Espie Wildfowl and Wetlands Centre	028 91 874146
Cultra, Ulster Folk & Transport Museum	028 90 428428
Downpatrick, Down Cathedral	028 44 614922
Downpatrick, St Patrick Centre	028 44 619000
Dromore, Kinallen Craft Centre	028 97 533733
Dundrum, Murlough National Nature Reserve	028 43 751467
Greyabbey, Mount Stewart House	028 42 788387
Hillsborough, Hillsborough Castle Gardens	028 92 681300
Kilkeel, Nautilus Centre	028 41 765555

Millisle, Ballycopeland Windmill 028 91 861413
Mourne Mountains, Guided Wildlife Walks 028 43 751467
Newcastle, Tollymore Forest Park 028 43 722428
Newtownards, Kingdoms of Down Tourism 028 91 822881
Portaferry, Exploris Aquarium 028 42 728062
Rathfriland, Bronte Interpretive Centre 028 40 631152
Saintfield, Rowallane Gardens 028 97 510131
Strangford, Castle Ward 028 44 881204
Strangford Lough, Wildlife Centre 028 44 881411

Bangor

HOTEL

Clandeboye Lodge Hotel

10 Estate Road Clandeboye Bangor Co Down BT19 1UR
Tel: 028 9185 2500 Fax: 028 9185 2772
Email: info@clandeboyelodge.com Web: www.clandeboyelodge.com

Set in woodland on the edge of the Clandeboye estate, this comfortable modern hotel fits in well with its rural surroundings. The stylish foyer creates a good impression, with a welcoming fire and plentiful seating areas. Off it is the Lodge Restaurant with gothic-style windows and furnishings (where breakfast is also served). Good-sized bedrooms have neat, well-planned bathrooms (suites have whirlpool baths); standard amenities include phones with voicemail and fax/modem points. A country-style pub, The Poacher's Arms, is in an original Victorian building beside the hotel. Conference/banqueting (300/300) Golf (18/9), walking & garden available. Children under 4 free in parents' room; cots available). Wheelchair accessible. No Pets. Credit card numbers are taken when booking - and the deduction may be made before your arrival. Children welcome. Parking. Weekend specials. **Rooms 43** (all en-suite) Lift. B&B from £40 pps, ss £20. 24 hour room service. Closed 24-26 Dec. Amex, Diners, MasterCard, Visa, Switch. **Directions:** 15 minutes from Belfast, on outskirts of Bangor.

Bangor

HOTEL

Marine Court Hotel

The Marina Bangor Co Down BT20 5ED
Tel: 028 9145 1100 Fax: 028 9145 1200
Email: admin@marinecourt.tsnet.co.uk Web: www.marinecourthotel.com

Excellent leisure facilities at the Marine Court's Oceanis Health & Fitness Club are this hotel's greatest asset – these include an 18 metre pool, steam room, whirlpool and sunbeds, plus a well-equipped, professionally-staffed gym. The hotel overlooks the marina (beyond a public carpark) but the first-floor Lord Nelson's Bistro restaurant is the only public room with a real view and only a few bedrooms are on the front – most overlook (tidy) service areas. While the decor is very neutral, furnishings are good quality, with plenty of worktop and tea/coffee tray, hair dryer and trouser press standard in all rooms. Conference/banqueting (300/260). Leisure centre; swimming pool. Children welcome (cots available without charge). Private parking. No Pets. **Rooms 52** (3 junior suites, 18 executive rooms, 16 no smoking, 1 for disabled). Lift. 24 hour rooms service. B&B £40pps, ss £20. Closed 25 Dec Amex, MasterCard, Visa, Switch. **Directions:** 14 miles from Belfast/10 miles Belfast City Airport, A2.

Bangor

HOTEL

Royal Hotel

26/28 Quay Street Bangor Co Down BT20 5ED
Tel: 028 9127 1866 Fax: 028 9146 7810
Email: royalhotelbangor@cs.com Web: www.the-royal-hptel.com

This old hotel near the marina came into new ownership a few years ago but has lost none of its friendliness or old-fashioned charm. There's a warm personal welcome, a clear willingness to help guests in any way possible and the building has some endearing idiosyncracies - although, alas, the early 20th century lift with folding grille doors and a mind of its own, has been replaced by a sleek new early 21st century one. Rooms vary - the best are the new ones on the front, overlooking the marina. Small conferences (40); Children welcome (under 5s free in parents' room; cots available). No Pets. **Rooms 50** (7 executive rooms, 8 shower only, 1 for disabled). Lift. B&B about £45pps, ss £15. Special offers sometimes available. Nearby parking. Closed 25-26 Dec. Amex, Diners, MasterCard, Visa. **Directions:** A2 from Belfast, at bottom of Main Street turn right (keeping in left lane). Hotel is 300 yards on right facing marina. ◇

Bangor

☆ RESTAURANT

Shanks Restaurant

Blackwood Golf Centre 150 Crawfordsburn Road
Bangor Co Down BT19 1GB
Tel: 028 9185 3313 Fax: 028 9185 2493
Web: www.shanksrestaurant.com

The setting is unusual for Robbie and Shirley Millar's restaurant, which was designed by Sir Terence Conran's company. On two floors (the first floor is mostly taken up by the bar and reception area, with some tables in use for extra-busy sittings, and a balcony for al fresco eating), the main restaurant is downstairs. The interior is attractive, in soft mauves and greys upstairs with plush leather and suede furniture, and warm blue and dove grey walls downstairs with deep red leather banquette seating, lightwood chairs and smart table settings. The windowed kitchen at one end allows you to watch chef-patron Robbie Millar and his team of chefs at work, while Shirley supervises the front-of-house team with quietly attentive efficiency. At its best, Robbie's contemporary cooking brings together the best local ingredients in really creative combinations, often demonstrating Mediterranean influences and some from Asia. The 3-course dinner menu is good value, although some dishes carry a supplement (mostly £3). Menus are wide-ranging but not over-elaborate, offering a choice of six or seven dishes on each course at dinner, about three for lunch, with dinner menus including the luxurious ingredients expected at this level: prawn and monkfish bouillabaisse with white beans, chorizo, roast peppers and saffron rouille; starters sometimes read like main courses, making choices more difficult - for example, lobster with a potato ravioli. Accomplished fish cooking is a strength, and also local meats - as in a speciality dish of spring lamb with Jersey royals, grilled manchego peppers, asparagus & salsa verde. Desserts and petits fours are good but not exceptional - cheese is probably a better choice (although it also attracts a supplement). Shanks remains one of the country's finest restaurants - food here is based on the highest quality ingredients, ambience and service are excellent; also, for the quality, Shanks generally offers outstandingly good value, particularly on set menus - although this is compromised somewhat by the number of supplements. Very good wine list. Children welcome; vegetarian menu available. **Seats 60** (private room, 36) L & D Tue-Fri, L 12.30-2.30, D 7-10. Set 2/3 course L, £17/21. Set D £33/38 (vegetarian £33). House wine from £15; SC discretionary. Closed L Sat all Sun & Mon; Christmas; Easter & July 12th period. Amex, MasterCard, Visa, Switch. **Directions:** 2km off A2 dual carriageway from Belfast to Bangor.

Comber

RESTAURANT WITH ROOMS

The Old Schoolhouse Inn

100 Ballydrain Road Castle Espie Comber Co Down BT23 6EA
Tel: 028 9754 1182 Fax: 028 9754 2583
Email: info@theoldschoolhouseinn.com Web: www.theoldschoolhouseinn.com

Almost next door to Castle Espie, The Old Schoolhouse is run by Avril (chef) and Terry (the host) Brown. The restaurant has old-world charm and character and has always been a magnet for returning regulars, who enjoy the straightforward and traditional cooking (with a hint of modernism). Local produce is used as much as possible in, for example, a speciality of seared clams with locally smoked bacon & crispy mangetout; oysters come from a local oyster farm and other fresh produce like bacon and fresh vegetables and herbs also come from local suppliers. The separate bedroom block is self-contained with its own breakfast room and honesty bar/lounge. Bedrooms, which are comfortably furnished in hotel style, are named after American Presidents of Ulster descent. Conference/banqueting (60/85). Children welcome (under 2s free in parents' room, cots available without charge). Garden. **Seats 85** (private room, 45). No smoking area. D Mon-Sat, 7-10; L Sun Sun only (except for parties, by arrangement),12-3. Set D from £16.95; Set Sun L £14.95. House wine £12.50. SC discretionary. Closed D Sun. Open all year. Rooms 12 (all en-suite, 2 for disabled) B&B £65 pps. MasterCard, Visa, Amex, Switch. **Directions:** A22 from Belfast to Comber 3 miles out of town. 1 mile past Castle Espie on left.

Crawfordsburn

HOTEL

The Old Inn

11-15 Main Street Crawfordsburn Co Down BT19 1JH
Tel: 028 9185 3255 Fax: 028 9185 2775
Email: info@theoldinn.com Web: www.theoldinn.com

The pretty village setting of this famous 16th century inn – the oldest in continuous use in all Ireland – belies its convenient location close to Belfast and its City Airport. Oak beams, antiques and gas lighting emphasise the natural character of the building, an attractive venue for business people and private guests alike. Individually decorated bedrooms vary in size and style, most have antiques, some have four-posters and a few have private sitting rooms. The conference and banqueting suite has been extended so weddings of up to 125 guests can now be accommodated and there's a delightful little garden that is popular for photographs. The hotel's restaurant '1614' has undergone a total upgrading recently as have all the front of house areas while a new garden terrace and outdoor dining area are planned in time for 2004. The Ulster Folk and Transport Museum and the Royal Belfast Golf Club are also nearby. There are several eating areas in the hotel - food is served in the olde worlde bar during afternoon and early evening and Restaurant 1614 is open for dinner and Sunday lunch; the Churn Bistro serves informal evening meals daily (7-9.30). Conference/banqueting (120/125) Ample parking. Garden, walking. Children welcome. Pets allowed by arrangement. **Rooms 32** (all en-suite) B&B £37.50pps, ss £17. Closed Christmas. Amex, MasterCard, Visa, Switch. **Directions:** Off A2 Belfast-Bangor, 6 miles after Holywood.

Donaghadee

Grace Neill's

PUB / RESTAURANT

33 High Street Donaghadee Co Down BT21 0AH
Tel: 028 9188 4595 Fax: 028 9188 2553
Email: stephen@graceneills.freserve.co.uk Web: www.graceneills.co.uk

Dating back to 1611, Grace Neill's lays a fair claim to be one of the oldest inns in all Ireland; Grace Neill herself was born when the pub was more than two hundred years old and died in 1916 at the age of 98. Extensions and improvements under the present ownership have been completed with due sensitivity to the age and character of the original front bar, which has been left simple and unspoilt. The back of the building has been imaginatively developed in contemporary style, creating a bright, high-ceilinged restaurant area, which has recently been refurbished on an elegant nautically-inspired theme. Delicious easy-going food that keeps people going back might include a risotto of crab with saffron & spring onion, a starter portion salad of rare beef, blue cheese, walnuts & mustard mayonnaise and (a great favourite this) homemade pork & leek sausage with champ & red onion marmalade; quite a few dishes are available as starter or main course portions. Good desserts include an unmissable chocolate & Guinness flavoured brownie cake and there might be Cashel Blue cheese, with grapes & oat biscuits. Consistently good, imaginative food, efficient service and (fairly) reasonable prices make this a place people keep coming back to. Sunday Brunch is a speciality, with live jazz. Children welcome before 7 pm. Own parking. No smoking area. Toilets wheelchair accessible. Seats 72.L Tue-Sat,12-2.30 (Sun to 3.30); D Tue-Sat, 6-9.30; Set D about £21,50, also à la carte; sc discretionary. Closed D Sun, all Mon; 25-26 Dec, 1 Jan & 12-13 July. (Please phone to check times.) MasterCard, Visa. **Directions:** A2 from Belfast, located at junction in New Street heading back around one way system. Through an arch, off the main High Street. ◇

Donaghadee

Pier 36

PUB / RESTAURANT

36 The Parade Donaghadee Co Down BT21 0HE
Tel: 028 9188 4466 Fax: 028 9188 46 36
Email: info@pier36.co.uk Web: www.pier36.co.uk

Good food, especially seafood, is attracting the crowds to Denis and Margaret Waterworth's harbourside pub. Denis is the front of house part of the team, while Margaret oversees the kitchen - and the food is excellent for pub cooking, with some traditional dishes and also plenty of choice for palates hungry for flavours from all around the world. Menus change through the day, but fresh home baked breads are a point of pride and simply grilled local lobster is a speciality - but global influences show in dishes like Thai fishcakes with a sweet chilli dressing and orange & cardamom duck breast on a lentil dhansak with poppadom crisps, pear & apple chutney. Aside from a good selection of seafood, there is plenty else to choose from - wild boar comes from Moyallen foods, there's organic free range chicken; menus offered include a dedicated salad menu and an unusually extensive separate vegetarian menu too, with three starters and six main courses to choose from. Desserts, listed on a blackboard, tempt with lots of old favourites, like lemon tart, sticky walnut tart, profiteroles and rice pudding brulée, all served with ice cream, fresh cream or custard - and there's also a nice little coffee menu. Prices are keen, with most evening main courses around £10-12, and you'd better book early at weekends as plenty of people seem to like the idea of a stroll on the pier before supper here. Children welcome. **Seats 130.** No smoking area. Toilets wheelchair accessible. L daily 12-2.30, D Mon-Sat 6.30-9.30 (Sun 12-8.30). Early D menu available 5-6.30pm. A la carte; house wine about £8.25. Bar food served daily, 12-8.30 (Sun to 8.30) Closed 25 Dec. . MasterCard, Visa, Switch. **Directions:** At the pier, Donaghdee. ◇

Downpatrick

Denvirs

ATMOSPHERIC PUB

14 English Street Downpatrick Co Down BT30 6AB
Tel: 028 4461 2012

What a gem this ancient place is. It's a wonderful pub with two old bars and an interesting informal restaurant, genuinely olde-worlde with an amazing original fireplace and chimney discovered during renovations. There's also delightful accommodation in sympathetically updated rooms. And there's a first floor room, with some remarkable original features, suitable for meetings or private parties. Go and see it - there can't be another place in Ireland quite like it. Private room available for conferences/meetings etc. (70). Wheelchair accessible. Children welcome. Pets permitted. Rooms 6 (all en-suite) B&B about £30pps, ss £5. Bar/Restaurant: Food served from 12-2.30pm daily & 6-8pm Mon-Fri (6-9pm Sat). Closed 25 Dec. Amex, Diners, MasterCard, Visa. **Directions:** On same street as Cathedral and Courthouse in Downpatrick. ◇

Downpatrick

The Mill At Ballydugan

HOTEL / RESTAURANT

Drumcullen Road Ballydugan Downpatrick Co Down BT30 8HZ
Tel: 028 4461 3654 Fax: 028 4483 9754
Email: nkillen@internet.com Web: www.ballyduganmill.com

Hidden away in rolling County Down countryside just outside Downpatrick the site of this 18th century flour mill is very atmospheric: looking out onto ruined stone outbuildings, it is almost like being in a medieval castle courtyard. The Mill would be worth a visit if only to see the magnificent restoration undertaken by the owner, Noel Killen, over more than a decade - but, since opening for business in 2000, there is much more to it than that. The building now houses a bistro/coffee shop on the ground floor, a more formal restaurant on the first floor and, above it, function rooms and accommodation. Bedrooms are appropriately furnished in traditional country style, with exposed beams and brass-and-iron beds, but have also the convenience of phones, TV with video channel, tea/coffee-making facilities and safe. Just a few hundred yards away, Ballydugan Lake is stocked with fish - all round, this is an ideal base for fishing, golfing. Downpatrick races and touring holidays in this lovely area. The restaurant is open to non-residents, and also available for private functions, such as weddings. Conference/banqueting (120/86); secretarial service. Garden. Children welcome, under 5s free in parents' room (cots available free of charge). **Rooms 10** (1 shower only, 6 no smoking, 1 for disabled) Restaurant **seats 50.** MasterCard, Visa, Switch. **Directions:** Downpatrick enroute to Newcastle past race course take first right hand turn and follow road to the Mill. ◇

Downpatrick

Pheasants Hill Country House

COUNTRY HOUSE

37 Killyleagh Road Downpatrick Co Down BT30 9BL
Tel: 028 44617246 / 838707 Fax: 028 44 617246
Email: info@pheasantshill.com Web: www.pheasantshill.com

In 'St Patrick's country', Pheasants' Hill was a small Ulster farmstead for over 165 years until it was rebuilt in the mid-'90s - and is now a comfortable country house on a seven-acre organic small-holding within sight of the Mourne Mountains, 12 miles away. It is in an area of outstanding natural beauty and abundant wildlife bordering the Quoile Pondage (a wetland wildlife reserve and favoured fishing spot) and the property is right on the Ulster Way walking trail. It is an idyllic spot, as guests soon discover when they are welcomed with tea in front of the fire, or in the orchard on fine summer afternoons. The bedrooms, which are named after flowers and herbs, differ in character and outlook but are all comfortably furnished with generous beds and the advantages of modern facilities, including television, radio alarm clock, tea/coffee making facilities, quality toiletries, hair dryer and books and magazines to read; rooms away from the road at the back are quieter. Breakfast is a major event and worth factoring in as a main meal in your day - the extensive menu even includes a vegetarian cooked breakfast mini-menu within it, although anyone who is not a dedicated vegetarian will find it hard to resist dry-cured bacon and home-made sausages made with their own free range Tamworth pork and many other serious temptations. Perhaps the wisest action is to stay for several nights to allow the opportunity of trying as many variations as possible - it can be difficult to make the best choices on a one-night stay anyway, as you will be asked to make a selection the night before, when you haven't had a chance to get the measure of it. *Farm shop: rare breed free range pork, bacon, lamb, beef & organic poultry sold. Delivery service available. Children welcome (babies under 1 free in parents'; room; cots available, £5). Internet access available (£5 per 10 minutes). Garden, fishing, walking. **Rooms 4** (3 en-suite, 2 shower-only,1 with private bathroom). B&B about £29, ss £10. Closed 20 Dec-2 Jan. Amex, Diners, MasterCard, Visa, Switch. **Directions:** On A22, 3 miles north of Downpatrick, 3 miles south of Killyleagh. ◇

Dundrum

The Buck's Head Inn

RESTAURANT

77 Main Street Dundrum Co Down BT33 OLU
Tel: 028 4375 1868 Fax: 028 4481 1033
Email: buksheadi@aol.com Web: www.thebucksheadinn.co.uk

Michael and Alison Crothers have developed this attractive, welcoming place from a pub with bar food and a restaurant, to its present position as a restaurant with bar. Alison is in charge of the kitchen and sources local produce, especially seafood, including oysters from Dundrum Bay, which might be baked with a garlic & cheddar crust and Kilkeel cod, with mushy peas and chips. Well-balanced and interesting menus have a pleasing sense of place - aside from the seafood, county Down beef is used for the Sunday roast sirloin and steaks on the dinner menu, lamb is from the Mournes, the famous butchers McCartneys of Moira supply sausages for the traditional bangers & champ; many tempting dishes are offered and, although there has been a move towards more global dishes, the range of styles ensures there is something to please all tastes. desserts are tempting and a short but imaginative vegetarian menu is also offered. At lunch time there's a shortish à la carte and daily blackboard specials - and they are open for high tea as well as dinner. Regular visits here confirm that the cooking is consistently good (and, indeed, always becoming more interesting) and service under the direction of the proprietor Michael Crothers, is friendly and efficient. The atmosphere is always pleasant - and, since the conservatory at the back was replaced with a more contemporary dining room (overlooking a walled garden), it is larger and more comfortable for all-year dining. This is a fine restaurant, providing an admirably comprehensive service: well worth planning a journey around. Interesting wines are supplied by the highly respected wine merchant James Nicholson. Children welcome. *Ask about accommodation - a previous owner, Maureen Griffith, offers B&B nearby. **Seats 80** (private room, 50) No smoking area L 12-2.30, High Tea 5-6.45, D7-9.30 (Sun to 8.30). Set Sun L from £13; Set D from £17.50, otherwise à la carte. House wine from £11; sc discretionary. Closed Mon off-season (Oct-Apr); 25 Dec. Amex, MasterCard, Visa, Switch. **Directions:** On the main Belfast-Newcastle road, approx 3 miles from Newcastle. ◇

Gilford

Oriel of Gilford

RESTAURANT

2 Bridge Street Gilford Co Down BT63 6EN
Tel: 028 3883 1543 Fax: 028 3883 1180
Email: orielrestaurant@aol.com Web: www.orielrestauran.com

Tucked away in a corner of County Down, alongside the River Bann, Barry and Louise Smyth's charming country restaurant is in a series of rooms with a cottage-like atmosphere. A cosy, relaxing bar/reception room has a welcoming open fire (and newspapers and magazines to browse over an aperitif or coffee) mixed furniture which combines character with comfort - and the restaurant areas alongside are well-lit with a pleasantly contemporary feeling. The decor in the back room has a slightly 'café' atmosphere despite quality table settings, but all are well set up and the round tables, especially, are both sociable and pleasing on the eye, with beautiful crisp white linen and fine porcelain - and the combination of a warm welcome and caring, professional service gets a visit off to a good start. Cooking is in the hands of head chef Damian Tumilty (formerly of Peacock Alley in Dublin) and the menus are characterised by lively, colourful dishes that aren't afraid to be bold with flavours: imaginative starters might include terrines, risottos and unusual soups (a light velouté of creamed local cauliflower with sauté wild mushrooms, for example) while a speciality main course that those with a hearty appetite should try is cannon of Irish lamb with confit shoulder, braised salsify, caramelised onions & rosemary jus - or there might be a luxurious alternative from the sea, such as braised fillet of halibut with cos lettuce, fennel purée & garden peas; this is imaginative, sophisticated cooking - and people are willing to travel a long way for it. Delicious desserts range from traditional hot 'club' puddings (irresistible in winter) to refreshing offerings including a range of home-made ice-creams and sorbets - and the niceties are observed to the end, when home-made petits fours served with cafetière coffee (or any other from a coffee menu) sends guests off with a smile on their faces. A well-priced wine list includes some unusual bottles and all the menus offered represent good value. **Seats 50** (private room, 16). No smoking restaurant; air conditioning. D Tue-Sat, 5.30-9.30; L Sun only 12.30-2.30. Set L £16; early D £11.95 (Tue-Fri, 5-7); Set D £29.95, also à la carte. House wine from £11.95; sc discretionary. Closed D Sun, all Mon, Christmas, 1 week Jan.& Jul. Amex, MasterCard, Visa, Switch. **Directions:** 4 miles from Banbridge on Tandragee Road.

Hillsborough

PUB / RESTAURANT

The Plough Inn

3 The Square Hillsborough Co Down BT26 6AG
Tel: 028 9268 2985 Fax: 028 9268 2472
Email: derekpatterson@theploughn.ifreserve.co.uk

PUB OF THE YEAR

Established in 1752, this former coaching inn enjoys a fine position at the top of the hill. Since 1984, it has been owned by the Patterson family who have built up a national reputation for hospitality and good food, especially seafood. Somehow they manage to run three separate food operations each day, so pleasing customers looking for a casual daytime meal and more serious evening diners. The evening restaurant is in the old stables at the back of the pub and booking is required; although renowned for seafood, a sprinkling of meat and poultry dishes will always include fine Angus steaks - a fillet with cracked peppercorn crust and Bushmills whiskey cream perhaps - and there's a vegetarian menu available. A major redevelopment programme, completed in 2002, has mercifully left the characterful old bar intact (fairly traditional bar food is still available there) and also the original Plough Restaurant, which has a separate entrance between the back of the pub and the carpark. However the rest of the pub, including the adjacent building on the opposite side of the entrance (left, as you approach through the arch) has been given a seriously stylish contemporary makeover and now rejoices in the name Barretro-Café-Bar-Grill. If that sounds confusing on paper, it is much the same on site; the café, which specialises in pastries, savouries and coffees, is open most of the day and can be accessed directly from the street (look out for the dashing blue canopy), while the grill is above the old bar and offers bistro fare, which can be roughly translated as more substantial dishes from all over the world; bookings are taken there for business lunches but not in the evening. Lots of cool leather seating, interesting lighting, incorporating existing features like the old mahogany bar into a design which is uncompromisingly modern, yet warm and welcoming, are just some of the attractions. While there is obvious youth appeal, people of all ages feel comfortable here and the staff, who are clearly very proud of it, are friendly and helpful. It is very extensive, so allow yourself time to have a good look around and get your bearings before settling down to eat; if the weather is fine, you might find a seat on the new sun terrace, which is away from the road at the back of the building, off the new bar. Children welcome in the café, but the bar is unsuitable for children. Parking. **Seats 150** (private room, 40) No smoking area. Air conditioning. L daily, 12-2.30 (Sun to 3) D 6-9.30 daily. Closed 25 Dec (no food 26 Dec). *The Pheasant Inn at Annahilt. is a sister establishment. Amex, Diners, MasterCard, Visa, Switch. **Directions:** Off the main Dublin-Belfast Road, turn off at Hillsborough in village square.

Holywood

CAFÉ

Bay Tree Coffee House & Restaurant

118 High Street Holywood Co Down BT18 9HW
Tel: 028 9042 1419 Email: suefarmer@utvinternet.com

Since 1988, The Bay Tree has been attracting people from miles around to its delightful craft shop and coffee house on the main street. The craft shop, which sells exclusively Irish wares, is a busy, colourful place specialising in pottery, with over two dozen Irish potters represented. There is also a gallery exhibiting the work of Irish artists and - perhaps best of all - Sue Farmer's delicious food. Baking is a strength, especially the cinnamon scones which are a house speciality. There's quite a strong emphasis on vegetarian dishes and organic salads, especially in summer, when you can also eat out on a patio in fine weather. No reservations for lunch, but they are required on Friday evenings, when the Bay Tree is open for dinner. Children welcome. Parking. Wheelchair accessible. No smoking restaurant. **Seats 55.** Open all day Mon-Sat, 8am-4.30 (re-opening on Fri only, D 7-9.30).L 12-2.30 Mon-Sat. Set D Fri only £17.50. sc discretionary. Closed Sun, Christmas, Easter, May Day & July 12th week. **No Credit Cards. Directions:** Opposite the police station.

Holywood

RESTAURANT

Fontana Restaurant

61A High Street Holywood Co Down BT18 9AE
Tel: 028 9080 9908 Fax: 028 9080 9912
Email: colleen@btopenworld.com Web: www.fontanasrestaurant.co.uk

A first floor restaurant over a classy kitchen shop ("down the alley & up the stairs"), Fontana is fresh and bright, with clear yellow walls which work well with lightwood chairs and vinyl banquette seating.

Proprietor-chef Colleen Bennett was one of the first of the new wave of chefs who have taken Northern Ireland by storm in recent years and she offers lovely zesty, loosely structured menus that suit the atmosphere of the room. Starters and main courses overlap to a great extent, with small and large portions of many dishes offered. A dish like Caesar salad with parmesan oil, broccoli, asparagus, green beans, red chilli & fresh herbs might come in two sizes, for example, and appear on both the lunch and dinner menus. Vegetables and salads are used with great panache and seafood is usually strongly represented - accomplished cooking, stylishly simple presentation and clear flavours make an appealing combination. Imaginative use of fresh produce (locally sourced where possible) is a striking characteristic of the food at Fontana - and there's an unusually extensive vegetarian choice offered separately. Outside eating area. Toilets wheelchair accessible. On street parking. Children welcome. **Seats 54.** L Tue-Sat 12.30-2.30 (Sun brunch 11-3), D Tue-Sat 5-9.30. Set 2/3 course D £13.50/£16.50, otherwise à la carte (average meal about £25); house wine £12.50; SC discretionary, except 10% added on tables of 6+. Closed D Sun, all Mon, 25-26 Dec & 1 Jan. MasterCard, Visa, Switch. **Directions:** Three doors from Maypole flag pole.

Holywood

HOTEL

Hastings Culloden Hotel

Bangor Road Holywood Co Down BT18 0EX
Tel: 028 9042 1066 Fax: 028 9042 6777
Email: res@cull.hastingshotels.com Web: www.hastingshotels.com

Hasting Hotels' flagship property, on the main Belfast to Bangor road, is set in 12 acres of beautifully secluded gardens and woodland overlooking Belfast Lough and the County Antrim coastline. The building was originally the official palace for the Bishops of Down, and is a fine example of 19th-century Scottish Baronial architecture. The elegant and luxurious surroundings include fine paintings, antiques, chandeliers, plasterwork ceilings, stained glass windows and an imposing staircase. The spacious bedrooms include a large proportion of suites and the Presidential Suite, with the best views; all are lavishly furnished and decorated and offer the usual facilities, plus additional details such as bathrobes and fine toiletries in the splendidly equipped bathrooms, a welcoming bowl of fruit and nice touches like ground coffee and a cafetière on the hospitality tray. Business and conference facilities have been further improved in the recent past, making the Culloden an even more attractive venue. The hotel also has a fine health club, the 'Cultra Inn' (an informal bar and restaurant in the grounds), and an association with The Royal Belfast Golf Club, four minutes away by car (book the complimentary hospitality limousine). Conference/banqueting (500); business centre, secretarial services. Leisure centre; swimming pool. Hairdresser. Garden. Children welcome (under 12s free in parents' room; cots available). No pets. **Rooms 79** (16 suites, 21 executive rooms, 29 no-smoking). Lift. B&B about £80 pps, ss £48. Room-only rate also available, £140 (2 guests). Open all year. Amex, Diners, MasterCard, Visa, Switch. Helipad. **Directions:** 6 miles from Belfast city centre on A2 towards Bangor.

Holywood

COUNTRY HOUSE

Rayanne Country House

60 Demesne Road Holywood Co Down B18 9EX
Tel: 028 9042 5859 Fax: 028 9042 5859
Email: rayannehouse@hotmail.com Web: www.rayannehouse.co.uk

Situated almost next to the Holywood Golf Club and Redburn Country Park, and with views across Belfast Lough, the McClellands' family-run country house is a tranquil spot in which to unwind, and a fine alternative to impersonal hotels. Bedrooms, some with views of Belfast Lough, are individually decorated to a high standard with phones and television - and little extras like fresh fruit, spring water, sewing kit, stationery and a hospitality tray with bedtime drinks and home-made shortbread as well as the usual tea & coffee facilities. Numerous other facilities available in the house on request include fax/photocopying, trouser press. It's a relaxing place, with friendly staff and a great breakfast, offering a wide range, including unusual dishes such as prune soufflé, French toast topped with black and white pudding & served with a spiced apple compôte, grilled kippers and a 'healthy house grill' (with nothing fried). Friendly staff are helpful and make families with children most welcome (cot available free of charge); beach, shops and restaurants are all just a few minutes' walk away - and evening meals are also offered at Rayanne, in a restaurant which is open to non-residents. Garden, walking, cycling. Parking. Wheelchair accessible. Pets by arrangement. **Rooms 8** (all en-suite and no smoking) B&B £35pps. ss £20. Open all year. MasterCard, Visa, Switch. **Directions:** Take A2 out of Belfast towards Holywood (6 miles).

Holywood **Sullivans Restaurant**

RESTAURANT

2 Sullivan Place Holywood Co Down BT18 9JF **Tel: 028 9042 1000**
Fax: 028 9042 6664 Web: www.sullivansrestaurant.co.uk

Chef-proprietor Simon Shaw's bright, friendly and informal bar, restaurant & café celebrated a decade in business in 2003 - and excellent food, varied menus, a lively atmosphere and fair prices are the secret of his success. He offers lively lunch and sandwich menus ranging from a choice of home-made soups served with crusty bread to pork & leek sausages & mash or salmon skewer with stir-fried rice. Quality ingredients have always been the building blocks of his cooking and he seeks out interesting produce from trusted suppliers like La Rousse Foods and Helen's Bay Organics; vegetarians do well here, with interesting choices on the regular menus as well as a separate vegetarian menu offering about half a dozen dishes that can be mixed and matched as starters or main courses. Generosity is a key feature as well as good cooking - seen in portion sizes, and also special offers: the early dinner menu is a steal and there's also a great short dinner menu for two, including a bottle of wine, at £32.50. **Seats 65.** Air conditioning. Open for L&D daily: L daily 12-2.30 (Sun from 11), D Tue-Thu 6-9, Fri & Sat 5-10, Sun 5-9. Early D £12.50 (5-7pm, 2-course), also à la carte; house wine £10-12; sc 10% on parties of 6+. Closed D Mon, 2 days Christmas,1 week Jul. MasterCard, Visa, Switch. **Directions:** Just off main Belfast-Bangor dual carriageway.

Killyleagh **Picnic**

Ⓝ **CAFÉ**

Killyleagh Co Down

Just beside the castle in Killyleagh, this smashing little deli and café is well worth knowing about: lovely simple daytime food to enjoy while you're there - and a great range of carefully sourced goodies to take home. Open daily from late morning in summer, closed Sun off season.

Kircubbin **Paul Arthurs Restaurant**

Ⓝ **RESTAURANT**

66 Main Street Kircubbin Newtownards Co Down BT22 2SP
Tel: 028 4273 8192 Web: www.paul-arthurs.co.uk

On the first floor opposite the supermarket - where you could buy a bottle of wine to go with your meal - Paul Arthurs' restaurant is a simple modern room with an open kitchen where you can watch the great man at work. Very simply laid tables give one or two hints that this place might not be quite what it first seems - linen napkins, for example. Modern menus are interesting and the cooking is good: a lunchtime chunky seafood chowder, for example, is just that, with really big pieces of fish, and home-made pork and leek sausages with champ are worth travelling for. Evening menus are not over-extensive but offer a god range of dishes, including more meat and poultry than fish - although there is always a catch of the day. Vegetarian options are listed separately (goats cheese risotto with sunblush tomatoes and rocket, perhaps) and there's even a vegan choice. This great little place is a great asset to the area, and it should do well. There are plans for a license soon, also landscaping of gardens. Air conditioning. Toilets accessible by wheelchair. **Seats 45.** L&D Tue-Sat,L 12-2.30pm; D 5-9pm and L Sun, 12.00-2.30pm. A la carte. BYO wine. Closed D Sun, all Mon, & Christmas. MasterCard, Visa, Switch. **Directions:** On main street, 1st floor, opposite supermarket.

Newcastle **Burrendale Hotel & Country Club**

HOTEL

51 Castlewellan Road Newcastle Co Down BT33 0JY
Tel: 028 4372 2599 Fax: 028 4372 2328
Email: reservations@burrendale.com Web: www.burrendale.com

Just outside the traditional seaside holiday town of Newcastle, and close to the championship links of the Royal County Down golf course, this area on the edge of the Mourne mountains has a remote atmosphere yet it is just an hour's drive from Belfast. Public areas in this friendly hotel are spacious and include the Cottage Bar with an open log fire, welcome on chilly days. Well-appointed accommodation includes family rooms and all rooms are well-equipped with phone, writing desk, TV with video, tea/coffee making facilities and trouser press; new superior rooms are furnished to a higher standard, and have air conditioning. Golf is a major attraction to the area but a varied programme of other special breaks is also offered throughout the year and it is a popular conference venue. Conference/banqueting (250 /200); business centre, secretarial services; video conferencing available. Leisure centre, swimming pool; beauty salon. Snooker, pool table. Children welcome (under 4s free in parents' room; cots available without charge; playroom, crèche). Garden, walking, cycling. **Rooms 68** (3 suites, 18 executive rooms, 20 no smoking, 10 for disabled, 4 shower only). Lift. 24 hour room service. B&B about £55 pps, ss about £20. Bar and restaurant meals available L&D daily. Open all year. Amex, Diners, MasterCard, Visa, Switch. **Directions:** On A50 Castlewellan Road. ◇

Newcastle — Hastings Slieve Donard Hotel

HOTEL

Downs Road Newcastle Co Down BT33 0AH
Tel: 028 4372 1066 Fax: 028 4372 4830
Email: res@sdh.hastingshotel.com Web: www.hastingshotels.com

This famous hotel stands beneath the Mournes in six acres of public grounds, adjacent to the beach and the Royal County Down Golf Links. The Victorian holiday hotel par excellence, the Slieve Donard first opened in 1897 and has been the leading place to stay in Newcastle ever since. Recent years have seen great improvements in both the public rooms and accommodation. Bedrooms are finished to a high standard and all the bathrooms sport one of the famous yellow Hastings' ducks. The nearby Tollymore Forest Park provides excellent walking on clearly marked trails, just one of the many outdoor pursuits that attract guests; should the weather be unsuitable, the Elysium health club has enough facilities to keep the over-energetic occupied for weeks - and is soon to be extended. The hotel also offers a wide range of special breaks. Conference/banqueting (825/400). Business centre; secretarial services. Leisure centre. (18), Leisure centre, swimming pool, beauty salon. Pitch & putt. Own parking. Children welcome (under 14s free in parents' room; cots available without charge). No pets. **Rooms 124** (2 suites, 10 junior suites, 112 executive rooms,1 for disabled). 2 Lifts. B&B about £95 pps, ss £25. Open all year. Amex, Diners, MasterCard, Visa, Switch. Helipad. **Directions:** Situated 32 miles south east of Belfast.

Newcastle — Sea Salt Bistro

CAFÉ / RESTAURANT

51 Central Promenade Newcastle Co Down BT33 0HH
Tel: 028 4372 5027 Email: seasalt@euphony.net

A good meal will add greatly to your enjoyment of a visit to this traditional holiday town on the sea edge of the Mountains of Mourne, so make a point of seeking out Caroline (front of house) and Andrew (the chef) Fitzpatrick's restaurant in a seafront terrace, wedged between an ice-cream parlour and a chemist's shop. Sea Salt opened in 1997 as a delicatessen and café, seating only a dozen or so at lunch time - now, having re-designed the interior in a classy contemporary style inspired by the sea, they have re-opened with renewed energy and a commitment to using local produce creatively in global cooking. Daytime snack menus feature gourmet sandwiches - wraps, baguettes, ciabatta with salads - and an extensive hot and cold drinks menu that includes a choice of coffees, teas and refreshing juices like organic lemonade and pure fruit smoothies. Lunch and dinner menus are more substantial, but the ethos is carried through. Seafood stars in popular dishes like Dundrum Bay mussels Thai style with chilli, garlic, coriander & ginger and seafood chowder with Ardglass crab, salmon & prawns but you'll also find all-time favourites like chicken liver paté with brandy and rosemary (served with crisp ciabatta slices and green salad) and duck confit with caramelised red onion heading up main courses as diverse as Co. Down sirloin steak with creamy Ulster champ & brandy peppercorn sauce and a vegetarian dish of aubergine & buffalo mozzarella galette with red pepper pesto & salad. With no drinks licence and a modest £1 corkage, everyone brings their own and part of the charm of the evening is to see what diners on adjoining tables have brought in their carrier bags. Booking is essential. **Seats 30.** No smoking area; air conditioning. Open daily in summer from 9am: L 12-4 daily, D Wed-Sun D 7-9. Set D £19.50, D Wed-Sun. Closed Mon in winter. MasterCard, Visa, Switch. **Directions:** Seafront Newcastle, foot of Mournes. ◇

Newry — The Bank

RESTAURANT / BAR

2 Trevor Hill Newry Co Down BT3 1DN **Tel: 028 3083 5501**

A fine old old banking hall near the bridge makes an impressive setting for this smart contemporary restaurant and bar. Tables in a raised area near the window, where smoking is allowed, are conventionally set up while other dining spaces are provided at high tables with tall stools in the body of the hall, and raised booths along the wall. It fills up quickly at lunch time, when fashionable fare like tortilla rolls, stuffed pitta bread and panini competes with regular sandwiches and old favourites such as pork & spring onion sausages with champ & shallot gravy. Evening menus begin straight after lunch and offer larger portions of slightly more formal dishes. Clearly a hit with the locals, The Bank is just the kind of stylish place that the new city of Newry needs. Not suitable for children after 7pm. Open Mon-Fri 11.30-12.15, Sat 12-2. Food served 12-9 , L 12-3, D 3-9. Closed 25 Dec, Good Fri. MasterCard, Visa, Laser, Switch. **Directions:** Town centre. ◇

Newry

Canal Court Hotel

HOTEL

Merchants Quay Newry Co Down BT35 8HF
Tel: 028 3025 1234 Fax: 028 3025 1177
Email: manager@canalcourthotel.com Web: www.canalcourthotel.com

This canalside hotel serves Newry well with badly needed facilities, including business/conference services as well as a health & leisure complex and spacious, comfortable accommodation. Conferences(300). Leisure centre (gym, swimming pools, jacuzzi, sauna, steam room). **Rooms 51.** B&B from about £55 pps. Open all year. Amex, Diners, MasterCard, Visa. ◇

Newtownards Area

Beech Hill

Ⓝ **B&B**

23 Ballymoney Road Craigantlet Newtownards Co Down BT23 4TG
Tel: 028 9042 5892 Fax: 028 9042 5892
Email: info@beech-hill.net Web: www.beech-hill.net

Victoria Brann's attractive Georgian style house is set in the peaceful Holywood Hills and is handily placed in relation to the city, airports and ferry port. It has great style - and the benefit of an exceptionally hospitable hostess, who does everything possible to ensure that guests have everything they need. Ground floor bedrooms have panoramic views over the North Down countryside and are furnished with antique furniture - and, believe it or not, the beds are made up with fine Irish linen; all also have en-suite bathrooms with lots of special little extras. Breakfast is a meal worth allowing time to enjoy - and it is served in a spacious conservatory overlooking a croquet lawn. **Rooms 3** (all en-suite). B&B £33pps. ss £10. Open all year. MasterCard, Visa. **Directions:** A2 from Belfast. Right up Ballymoney Road. 1.75 Miles on left.

Newtownards

Edenvale House

COUNTRY HOUSE / B&B

130 Portaferry Road Newtownards Co Down BT22 2AH
Tel: 028 9181 4881 Fax: 028 9182 6192
Email: edenvalehouse@hotmail.com Web: www.edenvalehouse.com

Diane Whyte's charming Georgian house is set peacefully in seven acres of garden and paddock, with views over Strangford Lough to the Mourne mountains and a National Trust wildfowl reserve. The house has been sensitively restored and modernised, providing a high standard of accommodation and hospitality. Guests are warmly welcomed and well fed, with excellent traditional breakfasts and afternoon tea with homemade scones. For evening meals, Diane directs guests to one of the local restaurants. Edenvale is close to the National Trust properties Mount Stewart and Castle Ward. Children welcome (under-10s free in parents' room; cots available without charge). Pets permitted. Garden. **Rooms 3** (all en-suite and no-smoking). B&B £30pps, ss £5. Closed Christmas. MasterCard, Visa. **Directions:** 2 miles from Newtownards on A20 going towards Portaferry.

Portaferry

The Narrows

ACCOMMODATION / RESTAURANT

8 Shore Road Portaferry Co Down BT22 1JY
Tel: 028 4272 8148 Fax: 028 4272 8105
Email: info@narrowhouse.co.uk Web: www.narrows.co.uk

On the Portaferry waterfront, an archway in the middle of a primrose yellow facade attracts attention to the inspired 18th century courtyard development that is central to Will and James Browns' unusual guesthouse and conference facilities. The ground floor includes a cosy sitting room with an open fire and a spacious restaurant; the style throughout is light and bright, with lots of natural materials and local art. Uncluttered modern bedrooms are all different and have a serene, almost oriental atmosphere; all are en-suite but only three have baths. For guests with special needs, all the shower rooms are wheelchair-friendly, eight are specially designed and there is a lift. There are two interconnecting rooms and two family rooms; children's tea is available at 5 pm. A fine room over the archway, opening onto a private balcony, provides banqueting/conference facilities for 50. The restaurant is open for lunch and dinner every day and can be most a enjoyable place for an outing. Children welcome. Own parking. Children under 2 free in parents' room; cots available. Pets by arrangement. **Rooms 13** (all no-smoking, 8 for disabled). Lift. B&B from £39-45pps. Dinner B&B £59pp per night. Meals: L daily 12-2.30 (Sun to 3.30); D daily 7-9.30 (Sun 5.30-8.30). Set D £15-20. A la carte. Open all year. Amex, MasterCard, Visa, Switch. **Directions:** A20 to Portaferry, on shore front. ◇

Portaferry

Portaferry Hotel

HOTEL

The Strand Portaferry Co Down BT22 1EP **Tel: 028 4272 8231**
Fax: 028 4272 8999 Email: info@portaferryhotel.com

This 18th-century waterfront terrace presents a neat, traditional exterior overlooking the Lough towards the attractive village of Strangford and the National Trust property, Castleward, home to an opera festival each June. Extensions and refurbishment undertaken by John and Marie Herlihy, who have owned the hotel since 1980, have been sensitively done and the inn is now one of the most popular destinations in Northern Ireland – not least for its food. There's an excellent lunchtime bar menu (including 'Children's Choice') available every day except Sunday. Accommodation is comfortable and most of the individually decorated en-suite bedrooms have views of the water. Small conference/private parties (14/85); Own parking. Children (Under 2s free in parents' room; cots available). No pets. **Rooms 14** (4 no-smoking) B&B £45.00-£52.50 pps, ss £10.

Restaurant: A slightly cottagey style provides the perfect background for good unpretentious food. Local produce features prominently in prime Ulster beef, Mourne lamb and game from neighbouring estates – but it is, of course, the seafood from daily landings at the nearby fishing villages of Ardglass and Portavogie that take pride of place. Well-balanced table d'hôte lunch and dinner menus are offered, plus a short carte, providing plenty of choice although majoring on local seafood. An excellent breakfast is also served in the restaurant. **Seats 80.** Not suitable for children under 12 after 8 pm. L&D daily: 12.30-2.30, 5.30-7, 7-9 (Sat to 10). Set menus & à la carte L available; house wine from about £11.50; sc discretionary. Toilets wheelchair accessible. Open all year. Amex, Diners, MasterCard, Visa. **Directions:** On Portaferry seafront. ◇

Rostrevor

Celtic Fjord

RESTAURANT

8 Mary Street Rostrevor Co Down BT34 3AY **Tel: 028 4173 8005**

In an attractive house on the main street, Cathy (front of house) and Michael (the chef) Keenan run this pleasing restaurant: arriving guests are promptly welcomed and offered an aperitif in the reception, then shown into one of the interesting, warmly decorated dining rooms where Michael's set menus offer plenty of choice - nine or ten dishes on each course at dinner, and are keenly priced. The style ranges from the traditional - first courses like soup of the day with freshly-baked bread or chicken liver paté with Cumberland sauce and main courses such as crisp fried haddock with tartare sauce - to more contemporary fare typically including chunky fish cakes with pimento & cucumber relish and tangy mayonnaise and garlic pork tossed with crunchy vegetables, soy, spices and pasta. There is also a separate, individually priced steak menu offering variations on all the popular steak dishes - and a Japanese style sirloin with honey soy and crispy garlic beansprouts. Desserts tend to be classic - French apple flan with crème patissière is typical. This is not cutting edge food but good cooking, pleasantly efficient service and reasonable prices make for a very pleasant dining experience. **Seats 75** (private rooms, 32, 20, 22). L Wed-Sat 12-3, Sun: 12.30-8.30. D Wed-Sun 6-9.30 (Sun to 8.30). 2/3 course Set D about £16.95/£21.95. Also a à la carte. Closed Mon, Tue, 25 Dec. MasterCard, Visa, Switch. **Directions:** On Main Street,halfway up the Hill. ◇

Strangford Village

The Cuan

PUB / GUESTHOUSE

6-10 The Square Strangford Village Co Down BT30 7ND
Tel: 028 4488 1222 Fax: 028 4488 1770
Email: info@thecuan.com Web: www.thecuan.com

On the square, just up from the car ferry that goes over to Portaferry, Peter and Caroline McErleann's village inn presents a neat, inviting face to the world and would make a comfortable base for a short break, when exploring this beautiful area. Over a century old, it has character with open fires, cosy lounges and a homely bar, where good food is available every day - local seafood is the main speciality, notably speciality dishes like seafood crêpe and scampi - also excellent steaks and hearty traditional food like beef & Guinness casserole and venison sausages with champ & onion gravy. There's a good choice for vegetarians too, also a short children's menu. Bedrooms, including two family rooms, are comfortably furnished with good bathrooms (nearly all with bath and shower), television and tea/coffee making facilities. There's also a sitting room for residents, with television and video. Small conferences/banqueting (15/80). Children welcome (under 2s free in parents' room, cots available without charge). **Rooms 9** (2 shower only, all no smoking, 1 for disabled). Limited room service (on request). B&B £39.95. Special breaks offered, eg 2 nights & 1 dinner £89; SC discretionary. Food served 12-9 daily. Closed 25 Dec. MasterCard, Visa, Switch. **Directions:** 7 miles from Downpatrick on the A25; on the square, near the ferry.

Warrenpoint

RESTAURANT

The Duke Restaurant

7 Duke Street Warrenpoint Co Down BT34 3JY **Tel: 028 4175 2084**
Fax: 028 4175 2084 Web: www.thedukerestaurant.com

Seafood straight from Kilkeel harbour and most other produce sourced with a ten mile radius is the foundation for Ciaran Gallagher's success at his popular restaurant, which occupies the whole of the first floor over pleasantly traditional pub, The Duke. Arriving up the (rather steep) stairs, guests are met promptly and efficiently, seated at tables laid with the familiar black rubber place mats, good contemporary cutlery, heavy paper napkins and plain white plates. A comfortable mixture of traditional and modern styles, divisions that lend some intimacy, the busy atmosphere and friendly service all add up to a relaxed ambience. Like the surroundings, menus are balanced and well-tailored to the clientele; the midweek set menu is exceptionally good value and goes down a blinder, keeping the restaurant full all week - and there will be four or five daily fish specials at more realistic prices. Crowd pleasers like surf'n'turf and chicken kiev take their regular places alongside some more ambitious dishes for discerning diners, like hake fillet grilled with lemon butter, steamed courgette flower with prawn mousseline & lobster cream sauce - or roast venison with roast vegetables and shallots & cranberry jus. Desserts are not a strong point but, on the whole, the cooking is as accomplished as it is generous, the staff cheerful and attentive and the value is terrific: who could ask for more? Ciaran Gallagher has recently bought the entire premises and the adjoining property, so expansion is on the cards in the future. **Seats 65.** Air conditioning. D Tue-Sat, 6-10, (Sun 5.30-9.30). Midweek Special Set D £12.95, also à la carte. House wine from £8.95. No SC. Closed Mon. Amex, MasterCard, Visa, Switch. **Directions:** Just off town square.

COUNTY FERMANAGH

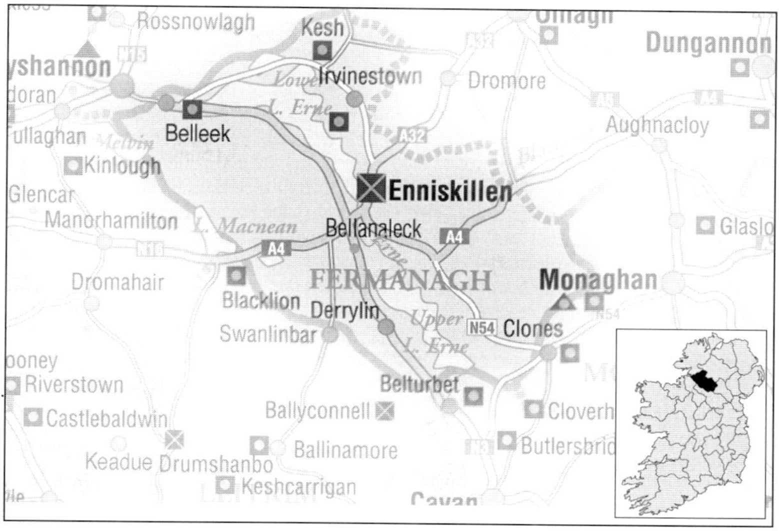

Ireland is a watery place of many lakes, rivers and canals. So it's quite an achievement to be the most watery county of all. Yet this is is but one of Fermanagh's many claims to distinction. It is the only county in Ireland in which you can travel the complete distance between its furthest extremities within the heart of its territory entirely by boat. Elsewhere, rivers often divide one county from another, but Fermanagh is divided - or linked if you prefer - throughout its length by the handsome waters of the River Erne, both river and lake.

Southeast of the county town of Enniskillen, Upper Lough Erne is a maze of small waterways. Northwest of the historic and characterful town, the riverway opens out into the broad spread of Lower Lough Erne, a magnificent inland sea set off against the spectacular heights of the Cliffs of Magho. It's a stunningly beautiful county with much else of interest, including the Marble Arch caves, and the great houses of Castle Coole and Florence Court, the latter with its own forest park nestling under the rising heights of Cuilcagh (667m).

And if you think lakes are for fishing rather than floating over, then in western Fermanagh the village of Garrison gives access to Lough Melvin, an angler's heaven. You just can't escape from water in this county. So much so, in fact, that Fermanagh folk will tell you that during the more summery nine months of the year, the lakes are in Fermanagh, but in the damper three months of winter, Fermanagh is in the lakes..........

Local Attractions and Information

Belleek, Porcelain and Explore Erne Exhibition 028 68 659300
Bellanaleck, Sheelin Lace Museum 028 66 348052
Enniskillen, Ardhowen Lakeside Theatre 028 66 325440
Enniskillen, Castle Coole House & Parkland 028 66 322690
Enniskillen, Enniskillen Castle 028 66 325000
Enniskillen, Florence Court 028 66 348249
Enniskillen, Lakelands Tourism 028 66 346736
Enniskillen, Lough Erne Cruises 028 66 322882
Enniskillen, Tourism Information 028 66 323110
Enniskillen, Waterways Ireland 028 66 323004
Florence Court, House and garden 028 66 348249
Florencecourt, Marble Arch Caves 028 66 348855
Garrison, Lough Melvin Activity Holiday Centre 028 68 658142
Kesh, Ardess Craft Centre 028 68 631267
Kesh, Castle Archdale Country Park 028 68 621588
Newtownbutler, Crom Castle 028 67 738174

Bellanaleck

The Sheelin

RESTAURANT

Main Street Bellanaleck Co Fermanagh BT92 2BA
Tel: 028 6634 8232 Fax: 028 6634 8232
Email: a.donnelly@web.de Web: www.thesheelin.com

John and Annett Donnelly's delightful thatched cottage restaurant has been making serious waves in the area since they took over here in 2001: while it always seems as if nothing could change here, their philosophy of food and wine has brought about a quiet revolution in what was already a good little restaurant. It is a simple enough concept on the face of it: over 300 bins in the wine cellars, menus completely changed every six to eight weeks, never more than six choices on any course. Their motto should be music to the ears of discerning diners everywhere: large wine list, small menu, only fresh produce. That produce includes local specialities such as home-smoked kassler (the matured black bacon used is an Enniskillen speciality) and Lough Erne crawfish (a house speciality, grilled in white wine & garlic, and served on salad with lemon crème fraîche). The style is basically fairly classical, but contemporary influences show in some dishes. Everything is home-made, including accompaniments like spätzle and noodles and a range of usual desserts. There's a warm welcome here, too, and a characterful bar alongside the restaurant. Children welcome. **Seats 44** (private room 16). No smoking area. Open high season Tue-Sun, 12.30-10pm; low season Wed-Sat 5-10pm and Sun 12.30-10pm. D Set L £12; Set D £15.90-£22.90. House wines (20), from £10. SC discretionary. Closed Mon, all Jan. Diners, MasterCard, Visa, Laser, Switch. **Directions:** Main Enniskillen - Dublin road 3 miles outside of Enniskillen, direction Cavan. ◇

Belleek

The Thatch

CAFÉ

Belleek Co Fermanagh BT93 **Tel: 028 6865 8181**

This coffee shop is really special: a listed building dating back to the late 18th century, it's the only originally thatched building remaining in County Fermanagh. Home-made food has been served here since the early 1900s and the tradition is being well-maintained today, with home-made soups, a range of freshly made sandwiches and toasted sandwiches all made to order, hot specials like stuffed baked potatoes and (best of all) delicious bakes like chocolate squares, carrot cake and muffins. Drinks include a coffee menu and, more unusually, you can also buy fishing tackle, hire a bike - or even a holiday cottage here. Open Mon-Sat. 9-5 (from 10 off-season). Closed Sun. **Directions:** On the main street.

Enniskillen

Blakes of the Hollow

PUB / RESTAURANT

6 Church Street Enniskillen Co Fermanagh BT74 6JE
Tel: 028 6632 2143 Fax: 028 6774 8491
Email: blakep@btconnect.com

One of the great classic pubs of Ireland, Blakes has been in the same family since 1887 and, up to now, has always been one of the few places that could be relied upon to be unchanged. Not a food place, a pub. Maybe a sandwich, but mainly somewhere to have a pint and put the world to rights. It is a great relief to Blakes' many fans all over the world that the building is listed both inside and out because major changes have recently been taking place at this historic establishment. The good news is that the original Victorian bar still remains untouched after 115 years while several new features have been developed on the rest of the site, including Café Merlot (serving informal, bistro-style food) on the lower ground floor, The Atrium - a gothic style bar spread over two floors and Tonic, a brash, buzzy bar with youth appeal. The most exciting development promises to be Restaurant No.6 @ Blakes of 'The Hollow' although it hasn't quite reached its potential yet. Open all year. Diners, MasterCard, Visa, Switch. **Directions:** Town centre. ◇

Enniskillen

Francos Restaurant

RESTAURANT

Queen Elizabeth Road Enniskillen Co Fermanagh BT74
Tel: 028 6632 4183

This large, strikingly decorated restaurant was one of Enniskillen's first contemporary eating places and remains one of the most popular. Informal food, including pizzas, pastas and barbecues, are the order of the day - and it's all done with great style. The range is impressive and really does offer something to everyone, with pasta dishes offered for as little as £6 - and lobster at £29. Seafood from Donegal and Sligo is a speciality (fresh grilled lobster on a bed of colcannon, perhaps), also new age pizzas with Mediterranean style toppings like goat's cheese, spinach & pesto. **Seats 140** (private room, 60). Toilets wheelchair accessible. Children welcome. Open Mon-Sat, 12.30-11 (Sun to 10.30 pm). A la carte. Houses wines from about £10. Closed 25 Dec. Amex, MasterCard, Visa, Switch. ◇

Enniskillen

Gallery Restaurant

RESTAURANT / GUESTHOUSE / COUNTRY HOUSE

139 Irvinestown Road Enniskillen
Co Fermanagh BT74 4RN
Tel: 028 6632 8374 Fax: 028 6632 8263

A large Georgian style countryhouse in a secluded situation with mature trees, the interior - all marble floors and murals of vistas and vines - comes as a surprise, although the accommodation is more in keeping with the countryhouse feel: two of the bedrooms have four-posters and all are comfortably appointed. Since taking over the restaurant in late 2001, chef Gerry Russell has built up a following for accomplished cooking that reflects his experience in Belfast, London and Perth - the latter especially evident in fusion and Thai-influenced dishes (for example, hot and sour broth with pak choi, chestnut mushrooms and a sweet chilli sambal). Good, freshly-made breads are served with dipping oils while your select from short but well-judged menus which are frequently altered to include seasonal produce and typically will include fresh fish, home smoked bacon and dry aged steak as well as a vegetarian option - flavours tend to be complex and interesting side orders are priced separately. A brief dessert menu offers some little gems, like a lemon & lime blur with coconut and white chocolate ice cream, which could well be the highlight of your meal. Occasional wine dinners are offered at a set price, with wines matched to each course. Sunday lunches are priced for two or three courses (although side orders charged separately); there's a nice little children's menu and plenty of room for them to let off steam outside. Seats 40. No smoking restaurant. L 12-2.30, D 6-9.30 (Sun 5-8). Set Sun L about£11.95/13.95; otherwise à la carte. House wines from £9.95. Closed Mon, Tue. Accommodation: **Rooms 5** (all no smoking). B&B about £28 pps, ss £5. MasterCard, Visa, Switch. **Directions:** On the edge of town, signed on main Enniskillen-Irvinestown road. ◇

Enniskillen

Killyhevlin Hotel

HOTEL / RESTAURANT

Dublin Road Enniskillen Co Fermanagh BT74 6RW
Tel: 028 6632 3481 Fax: 028 6632 4726
Email: info@killyhevlin.com Web: www.killyhevlin.com

Just south of Enniskillen, on the A4, this spacious, well-run modern hotel on the banks of the Erne has much to offer, including a warm welcome; it is a popular choice for business guests and would make a relaxing base from which to explore this fascinating and unspoilt area - and it's also a pleasant place to break a journey as there is food available all day and the soothing river views from the Boathouse Grill Bar are lovely. Outdoor activities such as golf and horse-riding are available nearby but, given the location, fishing and river cruising are particular attractions and the hotel gardens reach down to the riverbank and their own pontoon, where visiting cruisers can berth. Conference/banqueting facilities (600/400); business centre, secretarial services, video-conferencing. There are also some holiday chalets in the grounds, with private jetties. Ample parking. Children welcome (under 4s free in parents' room; cots available, £10; playground). Wheelchair accessible. Pets permitted by arrangement. Garden, cycling. **Rooms 43** (1 suite, 2 executive rooms, 1 for disabled, 11 no smoking). B&B £60 pps, ss £20; SC incl. Closed 24-25 Dec. Amex, Diners, MasterCard, Visa, Switch. **Directions:** On the A4 just south of Enniskillen.

Enniskillen

Rossahilly House

COUNTRY HOUSE

Rossahilly Enniskillen Co Fermanagh BT94 2FP
Tel: 028 6632 2352
Email: enquires@rossahilly.com Web: www.rossahilly.com

Just three miles from Enniskillen, the approach to Monica Poole and Eric Bell's beautifully located 1930s guesthouse may take you past an unsightly disused farmyard but, once you get there, it's definitely worth it. It's on an elevated site with panoramic views overlooking Lower Lough Erne: "A little bit of heaven" is what one guest called it and it's easy to see why. The entrance is through a neat conservatory style entrance with comfortable seating overlooking manicured lawns towards the lough - and there's a lovely traditionally tiled hallway too, setting the tone for a house that has been furnished with character. Accommodation in individually decorated bedrooms has been thoughtfully organised for the maximum comfort and security of guests - not only with phone, TV with video, tea/coffee making and pressing facilities, but also a safe and fax available on request. There is a lot to do in the area - they're specialists in fly-fishing holidays - and there is a tennis court on site. The dining room is only open to residents (and parties by arrangement), offering good home cooking (notably excellent baking). Everything is meticulously sourced and well cooked - presentation is attractive and service, by local waiting staff, both efficient and friendly. Licensed. Children welcome (under 4s free in parents' room). **Rooms 3** (1 suite, 2 junior suites, all no smoking). Room service all day. No smoking dining room, seats 20 (private room 10). Residents D 7-8.30. Set D £30. House wine from £12. MasterCard, Visa, Switch. **Directions:** 3 miles from Enniskillen on Kesh Road.

Enniskillen

Scoffs Restaurant & Wine Bar

RESTAURANT / WINE BAR

17 Belmore Street Enniskillen Co Fermanagh BT74 6AA
Tel: 028 6634 2622 Fax: 028 6634 2622 Email: scoffsrest@aol.com

Just a few minutes walk from the town centre, this popular bistro-style restaurant and wine bar has been pleasing a wide range of customers for the last four years - and clearly doing it very successfully as they have expanded from 60 seats to 140. Early evening opening and a wide-ranging menu - offering everything from inexpensive pastas to more serious (but still moderately priced) 'dinner' dishes - partly explain the wide appeal, but friendly, attentive staff and an atmosphere of relaxed informality are equally attractive. Large laminated menus include some fascinating choices and interesting vegetarian options - which, like those with nuts or flour, are considerately highlighted. Modern classics like slow cooked lamb shank with brunoise of vegetables & creamy mash are well cooked and stylishly presented, and the only down side is that dishes charged extra at £2.80 can add significantly to the costs of a meal. *A contemporary daytime sister establishment, Café Cellini, has riverside views - and they serve a good (Illy) coffee. **Seats 140** (private room, 14). No smoking area. Toilets wheelchair accessible. Children welcome. D daily, 5-11. L Sun only 12-3pm. D from £20. A la carte. House wine from £9.50. Closed 25 Dec. Diners, MasterCard, Visa, Switch. **Directions:** Access from main shopping centre.

Kesh

Lough Erne Hotel

HOTEL

Main Street Kesh Co Fermanagh BT93 1TF **Tel: 028 6863 1275** Fax: 028 6863 1921
Email: info@loughernehotel.com Web: www.loughernehotel.com

In a very attractive location on the banks of the Glendurragh River, this friendly town centre hotel has twelve comfortable rooms with en-suite bath/shower rooms, TV and tea/coffee facilities. The hotel is understandably popular for weddings, as the bar and function rooms overlook the river and have access to a paved riverside walkway and garden. Popular for fishing holidays, it would also make a good base for a family break; there is plenty to do in this lovely and unspoilt area, including golf, watersports and horse-riding. Conference/banqueting(200/180). Fishing, cycling, walking. Off-season breaks and self-catering accommodation in one and two bedroom cottages (from £250pw) also on offer. Garden. Limited wheelchair access. Own parking. Children welcome. Pets permitted in some areas. Rooms 12 (all en-suite) B&B £35pps, ss £5; sc discretionary. Closed 25 Dec. Amex, Diners, MasterCard, Visa, Switch. **Directions:** From Dublin N3 to Belturbet, A509 to Enniskillen, A35 to Kesh.

Killadeas

Manor House Country Hotel

HOTEL / RESTAURANT

Killadeas Co Fermanagh BT94 1NY
Tel: 028 6862 2211 Fax: 028 6862 1545
Email: info@manor-house-hotel.com Web: www.manor-house-hotel.com

This impressive lakeside period house makes a fine hotel. The scale of the architecture and the style of furnishings and decor lean very much towards the luxurious in both public areas and accommodation. Spacious bedrooms range from interconnecting family rooms to deluxe doubles and romantic suites with canopied four-poster beds, and front rooms have stunning views. Recent changes have included extensive refurbishments and the addition of an impressive new conference and banqueting area with its own separate entrance, which has been discreetly added to the side and rear of the original building and, despite its large size and more contemporary approach, in no way detracts from the appeal of the old house. Leisure centre, indoor swimming pool. Children under 3 free in parents' room. No pets. **Rooms 81** (all en-suite, 6 suites) B&B about £55pps, ss about £30. The Belleek Restaurant is also well positioned to make the most of the lovely view, especially at breakfast and lunchtime. Dominic Almond, who has been head chef "for years" is doing a good job and both food and service match the grand surroundings. Bar meals available 12.30-9 pm daily, 12.30-3.30 and 6.30-9.30. Restaurant **seats 65** (private room 30). Non-smoking restaurant. Air Conditioning. L&D daily. [*Information on the nearby Inishclare restaurant, bar & marina complex is available from the hotel, which is in common ownership.] Open all year. Amex, MasterCard, Visa. **Directions:** 6 miles from Enniskillen on the B82. ◇

Killadeas

The Waterfront Restaurant

RESTAURANT

Rosigh Bay Killadeas Co Fermanagh BT94 **Tel: 028 686 21938**

This beautifully located restaurant has an attractive bar, decorated to a fairly nautical theme with antiques and memorabilia, and a sunny waterside seating area for fine weather. The menu - a fairly extensive à la carte - offers a balanced choice of quite upscale dishes, notably seafood but plenty else besides, including vegetarian dishes and strong on meats and poultry. Cooking is sound, portions are hearty and it's good value. Opening times after Easter: Weds-Sat, 6-9 pm & Sun 12.30-3, followed by teas until 5.30, then the evening a la carte menu. Open daily in July & August. Off season, open Fri, Sat & Sun only, 6-9 pm. L Sun only 12.30-3.30pm. MasterCard, Visa, Switch. Directions: 2.5 miles beyond Manor House Hotel, on Enniskillen-Kesh road.

COUNTY LONDONDERRY

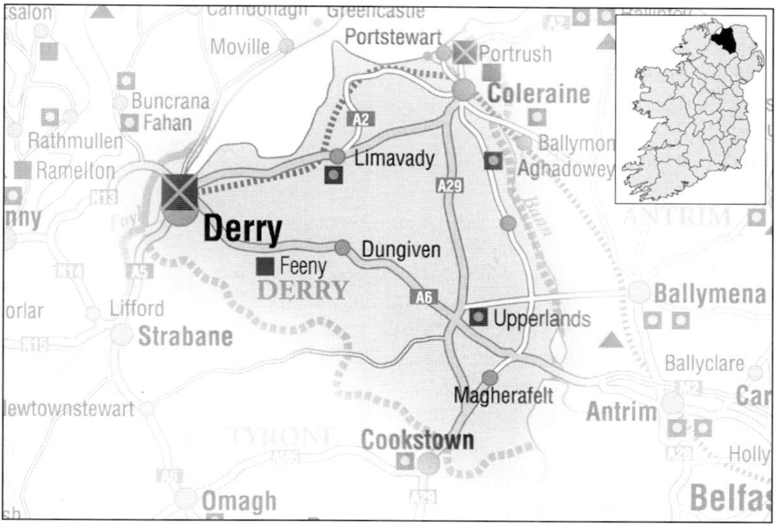

When its boundaries were first defined for "modern" times, this was known as the County of Coleraine, named for the busy little port on the River Bann a few miles inland from the Atlantic coast. It was an area long favoured by settlers, for Mountsandel - on the salmon-rich Bann a mile south of Coleraine - is where the 9,000 year old traces of the site of some of the oldest-known houses in Ireland have been found.

Today, Coleraine is the main campus of the University of Ulster, with the vitality of student life spreading to the nearby coastal resorts of Portstewart and Portrush in the area known as the "Golden Triangle", appropriately fringed to the north by the two golden miles of Portstewart Strand. Southwestward from Coleraine, the county - which was re-named after the City of Derry became Londonderry in 1613 - offers a fascinating variety of places and scenery, with large areas of fine farmland being punctuated by ranges of hills, while the rising slopes of the Sperrin Mountains dominate the County's southern boundary.

The road from Belfast to Derry sweeps through the Sperrins by way of the stirringly-named Glenshane Pass, and from its heights you begin to get the first glimpses westward of the mountains of Donegal. This is an appropriate hint of the new atmosphere in the City of Derry itself. This lively place could reasonably claim to be the most senior of all Ireland's contemporary cities, as it can trace its origins directly back to a monastery of St Colmcille, otherwise Columba, founded in 546AD. Today, the historic city, its ancient walls matched by up-dated port facilities on the River Foyle and a cheerfully restored urban heart, is moving into a vibrant future in which it thrives on the energy drawn from its natural position as the focal point of a larger catchment area which takes in much of Donegal County to the west in addition to County Londonderry to the east.

The area eastward of Lough Foyle is increasingly popular among discerning visitors, the Roe Valley through Dungiven and Limavady being particularly attractive. The re-establishment of the ferry between Magilligan Point and Greencastle in Donegal across the narrow entrance to Lough Foyle has added a new dimension to the region's infrastructure, as does the up-grading of the increasingly busy City of Derry Airport at Eglinton.

Local Attractions and Information

Bellaghy, Bellaghy Bawn (Seamus Heaney centre)	028 79 386812
Castlerock, Hezlett House	028 70 848567
City of Derry Airport,	028 71 810784
Coleraine, Guy L Wilson Daffodil Garden	028 70 344141
Coleraine, Tourism Information	028 70 344723
Derry City, The Fifth Province - Celtic culture	028 71 373177
Derry City, Foyle Arts Centre	028 71 266657

Derry City, Foyle Cruises (year round) 028 71 362857
Derry City, Foyle Valley Railway Centre 028 71 265234
Derry City, The Guildhall 028 71 377335
Derry City, Harbour Museum 028 71 377331
Derry City, Millennium Forum Theatre 028 71 264426
Derry City, Orchard Gallery 028 71 269675
Derry City, The Playhouse 028 71 268027
Derry City, St Columb's Cathedral 028 71 267313
Derry City, Tourism Information 028 71 267284
Derry City, Tower Museum 028 71 372411
Downhill, Mussenden Temple & Gardens 028 70 848728
Draperstown, Plantation of Ulster Visitor Centre 028 79 627800
Garvagh, Museum & Heritage Centre 028 29 558216
Limavady, Roe Valley & Ness Wood Country Parks 028 77 722074
Limavady, Tourism Information 028 77 760307
Magherafelt, Tourism Information 028 79 631510
Magilligan, Lough Foyle Ferry (to Donegal) (ROI t.n.) 077 81901
Moneymore, Springhill (NT house) 028 86 748210
Sperrin Mountains, Sperrins Tourism 028 79 634570

Aghadowey

Greenhill House

GUESTHOUSE

24 Greenhill Road Aghadowey Coleraine Co Londonderry BT51 4EU
Tel: 028 7086 8241 Fax: 028 7086 8365
Email: greenhill.house@btinternet.com Web: www.greenhill.house.btinternet.co.uk/

Framed by trees with lovely country views, the Hegarty family's Georgian farmhouse is at the centre of a large working farm. In true Northern tradition, Elizabeth Hegarty is a great baker and greets guests in the drawing room with an afternoon tea which includes a vast array of home-made teabreads, cakes and biscuits. There are two large family rooms and, although not luxurious, the thoughtfulness that has gone into furnishing bedrooms makes them exceptionally comfortable – everything is in just the right place to be convenient - and Elizabeth is constantly maintaining and improving the decor and facilities. Little touches like fresh flowers, a fruit basket, After Eights, tea & coffee making facilities, hair dryer, bathrobe, good quality clothes hangers and even a torch are way above the standard expected of farmhouse accommodation. There's also a safe, fax machine, iron and trouser press available for guests' use on request. Elizabeth provides a home-cooked residents' dinner based on local ingredients by arrangement, served at 6.30pm – please book by noon. (No wine). Guests have been welcomed to Greenhill House since 1980 and, wonderfully comforting and hospitable as it is, Elizabeth constantly seeks ways of improvement, big and small: this lovely house and the way it is run demonstrate rural Irish hospitality at its best: a very worthy recipient of our Farmhouse of the Year Award for 2003. Children welcome, cot available. No pets. Garden. **Rooms 6** (all en-suite, 2 shower only, 3 no smoking). B&B £27.50 pps, ss £7.50. Closed Nov-Feb. MasterCard, Visa. **Directions:** On B66 Greenhill Road off A29 7 miles south of Coleraine, 3 miles north of Garvagh.

Aghadowey

The Brown Trout Golf & Country Inn

HOTEL / RESTAURANT

209 Agivey Road Aghadowey Co Londonderry BT51 4AD
Tel: 028 7086 8209 Fax: 028 7086 8878
Email: bill@browntroutinn.com Web: www.browntroutinn.com

Golf is one of the major attraction at this lively country inn, both on-site and in the locality. Newcomers will soon find friends in the convivial bar, where food is served from noon to 10 pm every day. Spacious en-suite rooms with plenty of space for golfing gear are all on the ground floor, arranged around the main courtyard. New cottage suites overlooking the golf course (just 100 yards from the main building) are the first of this standard to be completed in Northern Ireland. Restaurant: Up a steep staircase (with chair lift for the less able), the restaurant overlooks the garden end of the golf course. The kitchen team aims to produce good home cooking with local fresh ingredients - fresh salmon with a chive and dill sauce, toasted muffins with cream cheese and hot garlic Aghadowey mushrooms or sirloin steak with a Bushmills whiskey sauce. Small conference/private parties (40/50); Tennis, horse-riding, golf (9/18), fishing, walking, garden & children's playground available. Children under 4 free in parents' room; cots available). Pets permitted. **Rooms 15** (all en-suite) B&B £42.50pps, ss £15. Stair lift. Restaurant **seats**

40 (private room, 40). Toilets wheelchair accessible. No smoking restaurant. Open all day (7am-10pm) L 12-3 daily, Set menus from £12.50; also à la carte; house wine about £8.95; sc discretionary. Bar meals: 12-9.30. Open all year. Amex, Diners, MasterCard, Visa, Laser, Switch. **Directions:** Intersection of A54/B66 7 miles south of Coleraine.

Coleraine

Charly's Restaurant

RESTAURANT

34 Newbridge Road Coleraine Co Londonderry BT52 1TP
Tel: 028 7035 2020 Fax: 028 7035 5299
Email: chatroom@charlys.com Web: www.charlysrestaurant.com

This big, bright roadside restaurant is inviting, like an American diner, and a great fun place for all age groups, especially the kids, and it has been recently renovated in the bar and waiting area. What you get here is good quality fashionable food for all the family - "Charly's Special", a fillet steak with champ, bacon, & garlic mash, is the most expensive dish on the menu at £14.50 - served with speed, efficiency and charm. It has heaps of atmosphere and a huge seating capacity but, although tables are turned around quite rapidly, there's no sense that you're being hurried. Most main courses are under about £10; it's great quality for the price and service is terrific - no wonder it's always busy. **Seats 120.** No smoking area; air conditioning. Children welcome. Open daily high season: 12-10pm; (open low season: L&D Tue-Fri, all day Sat & Sun). A la carte except Set Sun L £11.50 (12-2.30, also main menu, 12-9.30). House wine from £9. Closed Mon in low season, also Tue-Fri afternoons, 3-5pm; open most bank hol Mondays; closed 25-26 Dec. Amex, MasterCard, Visa, Switch. **Directions:** Belfast-Ballymoney; 1 mile from new hospital.

Feeny

Drumcovitt House

COUNTRY HOUSE

704 Feeny Road Feeny Co Londonderry BT47 4SU
Tel: 028 7778 1224 Fax: 028 7778 1224
Email: drimcovitt.feeny@btinternet.com Web: www.drumcovitt.com

Drumcovitt is an intriguing house with an impressive Georgian front dating from 1796 - and, behind it a much older farmhouse, built about 1680. It is a listed building and many of the windows and wonderful interior features have been retained but, however interesting its history, today's creature comforts are very much in evidence - central heating extends throughout the house and an adjacent converted barn, and there are big log fires to relax beside while enjoying a fine collection of books, or making a jigsaw. Outdoor pursuits aplenty too: this unspoilt area is perfect for walking, bird-watching, visiting archaeological sites in the Sperrins and much else besides - horse riding, golf and angling are all available nearby and the Giants Causeway, beaches, Bushmills, Derry city and much of Donegal are within easy striking distance. The three guest rooms are the two main front bedrooms (both with a double/ king-size bed and single) and a twin in the older part; in true country house fashion bathrooms are not en-suite, but two good modern showers (one over bath) are shared by the three rooms; all are spacious and comfortably furnished with tea/coffee-making, television and phone. Florence and Frank Sloan are solicitous but relaxed hosts, who enjoy sharing their unique home and the area around it with guests; Florence also cooks for guests - not just a very fine breakfast menu but a surprisingly extensive dinner menu (from which you can choose before noon for that evening). This is a delightful place, but not one to rush through so allow more than one night if you can. Fax, safe and ironing facilities available for guests' use. Family celebrations/reunions up to about 20 can be catered for in house and three barn cottages, which are available for self-catering. **Rooms 3.** Children welcome (cot available without charge; games room). B&B £26, no ss. Closed Christmas. Amex, Diners, MasterCard, Visa, Switch. **Directions:** 0.5 mile east of Feeny Village on B74 off A6.

Kilrea

Arbutus

Ⓝ **RESTAURANT**

13 Bridge Street Kilrea Co Londonderry
Tel: 028 2954 0140 Fax: 028 2954 0140

Food is serious business at Arbutus, with a simple but interesting menu cooked to perfection using high quality ingredients - and a huge amount of flair and skill. Each dish tastes wonderful, and is artistically and appropriately garnished - and the service is friendly and relaxed. Incredibly delicious home-made bread; perfect seafood in filo pastry; succulent crisp-coated duck confit served on a bed of pretty pink freshly-stewed cinnamon-flavoured peach & pear; perfectly cooked seabass fillets beautifully garnished with fresh summer herbs; fantastic ice creams served on a bed of coarsely crushed praline - these are just some of the dishes singled out for special praise this year. If there is a fault it is only that the chintzy style and downbeat ambience of the restaurant doesn't quite match the food - but the staff are lovely and food like this is a real treat by any standards. **Seats 50.** Open Wed-Sat D 5.00-9.30pm Set D £18.50-£21.50 Gourmet D £35. House wines from £8.95. MasterCard, Visa. **Directions:** Diamond Centre - follow signs for Ballymena.

Limavady — Streeve Hill

B&B / COUNTRY HOUSE

25 Dowland Road Limavady Co Londonderry BT49 6HP
Tel: 028 7776 6563 Fax: 028 7776 8285
Email: pandjwelsh@yahoo.co.uk

Peter and June Welsh have welcomed guests to their lovely 18th century home since they moved here in 1996. It is a very charming house, with a Palladian facade of rose brick and fine views over parkland towards the Sperrin Mountains – but there is also beauty closer to home, in and around the house itself and in the nearby gardens of their former home, Drenagh. The stylish country house accommodation at Streeve Hill is extremely comfortable and the food and hospitality exceptional. Although the maximum number they can accommodate is six, they are happy for guests to bring friends to dine (provided 24 hours notice is given). They also cater for private dinner parties. Breakfast is another high point and, in the event of fine summer weather, it can be even more enjoyable if served on the terrace outside the drawing room. Horse-riding, walking, fishing, garden available. Children welcome (under 3s free in parents' room; cots available without charge). No Pets. **Rooms 3** (all en-suite & no-smoking,1 shower only). B&B £45pps, ss £10; sc discretionary. Closed Christmas/New Year. Amex, MasterCard, Visa. **Directions:** Exit Limavady take B021 for Castlerock, follow Estate wall on right. 200 yards past lodge turn right at end of wall.

Limavady — The Lime Tree

RESTAURANT

60 Catherine Street Limavady Co Londonderry BT49 9DB
Tel: 028 7776 4300
Email: info@limetreerest.com Web: www.limetreerest.com

Stanley and Maria Matthews' restaurant is on a main street of this handsome, wide-streeted town in a beautiful and prosperous part of the country. There is a great sense of contentment about The Lime Tree; the room is pleasant but quite modest, Stanley is a fine chef and Maria a welcoming and solicitous hostess. Ingredients are carefully sourced, many of them local; menus are generous, with a classical base that Stanley works on to give popular dishes a new twist, in starters like three cheeses tartlette with sun-dried tomatoes & roasted garlic and crab cakes with a chilli jam, for example, while perennial main course favourites include Hunters sirloins steak with a crushed black peppercorn sauce and hake goujons rolled in chopped nuts, with tartare sauce or a lemon mayonnaise dip. Menus are not over-extensive, but change frequently to suit different occasions - there's a keenly-priced set business lunch and a short à la carte lunch menu, for example, then an attractive early dinner menu which is exceptionally good value, followed by a dressier set dinner for the main evening menu, which also has an accompanying (and more adventurous) à la carte. Sunday lunch brings yet another variation, offering a balanced choice between traditional and more unusual dishes. Stanley's cooking is refreshingly down-to-earth - new dishes are often introduced, but if it's on the menu it's because it works: there are no gimmicks. Good cooking and good value go hand in hand with warm hospitality here and it is always a pleasure to visit The Lime Tree - indeed, some discerning guests enjoy it so much that they travel up from Belfast for lunch at least once a month. Children welcome. A concise, interesting wine list also offers predictably good value. * Advisable to phone ahead about lunch times as these can vary. **Seats 30.** No smoking area. L Wed-Sun, 12-2; D Wed-Sun, 6-9 (Sat to 9.30; Sun to 8.30). Set L £6.95/8.50; Set Sun L £13.95. Early D £9.95/£12.95 (6-7pm only, excl Sat). Set D £19.95; also à la carte; house wine £10.75; sc discretionary. Toilets wheelchair accessible. Closed Mon &Tue (Sat. lunch booking only), 25-26 Dec, 1 week Feb/Mar, 12th Jul & 1 week Oct. Amex, MasterCard, Visa, Switch. **Directions:** On the outskirts of town, main Derry-Limavady road.

Londonderry — Beech Hill Country House Hotel

HOTEL

32 Ardmore Road Londonderry Co Londonderry BT47 3QP
Tel: 028 7134 9279 Fax: 028 7134 5366
Email: info@beech-hill.com Web: www.beech-hill.com

Beech Hill is just a couple of miles south of Londonderry, in a lovely setting of 42 acres of peaceful woodland, waterfalls and gardens. Built in 1729, the house has retained many of its original details and proprietor Patsy O'Kane makes an hospitable and caring hostess. Comfortable bedrooms vary in size and outlook – many overlook the gardens – but all are thoughtfully and attractively furnished with Mrs O'Kane's ever-growing collection of antiques. Public rooms include a good-sized bar, a fine restaurant (in what was originally the snooker room, now extended into a conservatory overlooking the gardens) and, unusually, a private chapel, now used for meetings, private parties or small weddings. Facilities include picnic areas in the grounds for fine weather and a fitness suite with sauna, steam room, jacuzzi and weight room. The US Marines had their headquarters here in World War II and an informative small museum of the US Marine Friendship Association is housed within the hotel. Conference/banqueting (100/106); secretarial services. Fitness centre. Tennis, garden, fishing, walking. Children welcome (under 2 free in parents' room; cot £10). **Rooms 27** (4 suites, 2 junior suites, 8 executive rooms, 1 for disabled). Lift. B&B £45pps, ss £15; SC discretionary. Closed 24/25 Dec.

Ardmore Restaurant: The restaurant has always been a particularly attractive feature of Beech Hill: it is elegantly appointed in traditional style and well-positioned overlooking gardens - and, although the head chef has changed from time to time, a consistently high standard of cooking and service has ensured a loyal local following. The present incumbent, Hugh MacNamee, maintains the tradition of classical French cuisine. Various combinations of menus are offered, including specials which tend to be very luxurious - a starter of sautéed duck foie gras with vanilla and cardamom sauce, for example - and there's a separate vegetarian listing of five or six interesting dishes which can be served as a starter or main course. The wine list offers good value - and a number of famous New World wines with Northern Irish connections. **Seats 90.** No smoking restaurant. Children welcome. L daily, 12-2.30; D daily 6-9.45. Set L £17.95, Set Sun L £17.95. Set 2/3 course D, £21.95. Full D menu £27.95. A la carte also available. House wines (6), £12.95. SC discretionary. Amex, MasterCard, Visa, Switch. **Directions:** Main Londonderry road A6.

Londonderry

RESTAURANT

Browns Restaurant, Bar & Brasserie

1-2 Bond Hill Londonderry Co Londonderry BT47 6DW
Tel: 028 7134 5180 Fax: 028 7134 5180
Email: eat@brownsrestaurant.com Web: www.brownsrestaurant.com

The city's leading contemporary restaurant has a devoted local following and no wonder - the welcome (and service) may be a little on the cool side, but the cooking's cool too and it's the food that keeps them coming back for more. Recent refurbishment has resulted in a relaxed space with subtle blends of natural colours, textures and finishes - and a new addition is a private dining facility called The Back Room, featuring a bespoke menu service that allows menus to be created to match specific budgets, themes etc. Proprietor-chef Ivan Taylor's approach to food never stands still, and his cooking is consistently terrific. Wide-ranging menus offer a wide range of fresh-flavoured dishes, including delicious starters like an inspired combination of fine beans, Roquefort & walnuts with grilled pancetta & duck 'crackling', and a perfectly judged main dish of mustard glazed tenderloin of pork with roast apples, mushrooms & sauce charcutière - a good example of how to modernise classics without forgetting the basics. Desserts ring some changes with the classics - or espresso, vin santo & home-made biscotti might make a pleasing alternative. All round, there's imagination, a certain amount of style, dedication and consistency - not bad after more than 15 years in business. Tue-Sat: L12-2.15; D 5.30-10.30. Early Set D £10.95 Tues-Fri. 5.30-7.30pm. House wine £12.50. Closed Sun, Mon, 1st 2 weeks Aug. Amex, MasterCard, Visa, Laser, Switch. **Directions:** Opposite the old Waterside railway station.

Londonderry

HOTEL

City Hotel

Queens Quay Londonderry Co Londonderry BT48 7AS
Tel: 028 7136 5800 Fax: 028 7136 5801
Email: res@derry-gsh.com Web: www.gshotels.com

Centrally located on a quayside site overlooking the River Foyle, Derry's newest hotel is also the latest from what is currently one of Ireland's most vibrant and quality-conscious hotel groups, Great Southern Hotels. Bright and contemporary, it is fashioned in a similar mould to other new hotels in the group, such as the highly successful one at Dublin Airport, and would make an equally attractive base for a leisure visit or for business - all rooms have a workstation with modem/PC connections, voice mail, interactive TV systems and mini-bar and there's a business centre providing secretarial services for guests. Well-located close to the old city, business districts and main shopping areas, it also has free private parking for guests and on-site leisure facilities. Conference/banqueting (450/350). **Rooms 145** (1 suite, 4 junior suites). Lift. 24 hour room service. Children welcome (under 2s free in parents' room, cot available without charge). Leisure centre: swimming pool, Jacuzzi, steam room, sauna, dance suite, gym, hydrotherapy). B&B £50pps. Room rate: £100 (max 3 guests).

Thompson's on the River Restaurant: Smart table settings, a pleasant open plan layout, a value for money menu and very professional service are the hallmarks of this 140-seater restaurant within the hotel, which is earning a reputation for accomplished cooking. An early bird menu at £12.95 offers plenty of choice for a great price, while the à la carte - that includes main courses such as pan seared fillet of beef and roast monktail - is also reasonably priced. Open daily for D 7-9pm and Sun 6.30-9.15pm. Set D £24. Also Sun L 1-3pm. Amex, Diners, MasterCard, Visa, Laser. **Directions:** In Derry city centre, overlooking River Foyle.

Londonderry

Exchange Restaurant & Wine Bar

RESTAURANT

Queens Quay Londonderry Co Londonderry BT48 7AY
Tel: 028 7127 3990 Fax: 028 7127 3991

A great addition to this thriving waterfront area, The Exchange is just outside the walled city and its cool contemporary design makes a great contrast to the age of nearby landmarks. Although seriously modern, this is a friendly and welcoming place that appeals to all age groups and their colourful, fresh-flavoured food suits the mood perfectly. They seem to have a winning formula here as prices are reasonable, ingredients are sourced locally as far as possible and head chef Sean Noonan's cooking fits the bill very well. At first glance the menu seems very international but close examination reveals plenty to please traditionalists too and blackboard specials reflect the same desire to please a wide range of customers. The Exchange has got off to a good start and it should do very well. Seats 120. Toilets wheelchair accessible. Children welcome. Air conditioning. L Mon-Sat, 12-2.30; D daily 5.30-10 (Sun to 9.30). A la carte. House wine £9.75. SC discretionary. Closed L Sun, 25 Dec. Amex, MasterCard, Visa, Laser, Switch. **Directions:** Opposite City Hotel.

Londonderry

Fitzroys Restaurant

RESTAURANT

2-4 Bridge Street 3 Carlisle Road Londonderry Co Londonderry BT55 7EF
Tel: 028 7126 5821 Fax: 028 7126 5821 Email: fitzroys@lineone.net

This large modern restaurant beside the Foyle Shopping Centre is on two floors and very handy for shoppers, visitors or pre- and post-theatre meals. Menus change through the day and offer a wide range of food in the current international fashion - rack of lamb with herb crust, black pudding mash, pea and baby onion jus indicates the evening style while a large daytime menu ranges from hot breakfasts and designer sandwiches to a range of substantial 'chef's specialities'. A useful one to know about. **Seats 80.** Food served all day from 9.30 am -10.30pm. (Breakfast to 12.30, lunch to 6, D 6-10, à la carte; Sun brasserie menus all day (12-8). Wed & Thurs 7-10pm 4-course D for £10. Early closing Mon/Tue (7pm). House wine from £7. Closed 25-26 Dec. MasterCard, Visa, Laser, Switch. **Directions:** Beside Foyleside Shopping Centre.

Londonderry

Hastings Everglades Hotel

HOTEL

Prehen Road Londonderry Co Londonderry BT47 2NH
Tel: 028 7132 1066 Fax: 028 7134 9200
Email: res@egh.hastingshotels.com Web: www.hastingshotels.com

Situated on the banks of the River Foyle, close to City of Derry airport and just a mile from the city centre, this modern hotel is well located for business and pleasure in a quieter situation than city centre alternatives. Like all the Hastings Hotels, Everglades Hotel undergoes an on-going system of refurbishment and upgrading, a policy which pays off in comfortable well-maintained bedrooms and public areas which never feel dated. Accommodation is all of a high standard, with good amenities including air conditioning and a spacious desk area, although beds are only standard size which is now unusual in a hotel of this class (and unnecessary as rooms are generally spacious). The hotel is well located for golf, with the City of Derry course just a couple of minutes away and six other courses, including Royal Portrush, within easy driving distance. Conference/banqueting (400/300); secretarial services; video conferencing (on request). Wheelchair accessible. Own parking. Children under 14 free in parents' room; cots available. No pets. **Rooms 64** (2 suites, 1 junior suite, 4 executive, 24 no-smoking, 1 for disabled). Lift. B&B £48.50pps, ss £15; no sc. Closed 24-25 Dec. Amex, Diners, MasterCard, Visa, Switch. **Directions:** From Belfast follow M2. Hotel is on A5 approx 5 miles from City.

Londonderry

Mange 2

Ⓝ **RESTAURANT**

2 Clarendon Street Londonderry Co Londonderry
Tel: 028 7136 1222

A new addition to the Derry food scene, Mange 2 is off the Strand Road and offers an unpretentious menu of good food served in generous portions and with style. If anything, the cafe-like interior does not do it justice, as you are greeted by a charming, keen and knowledgeable staff and the chef is doing a good job creating interesting combinations. Chicken in various ways, fish, duck, pork and beef all feature strongly on the evening menu which, like other menus offered, is laminated; but there are at least nine starters to choose from and there's also a vegetarian menu priced at £9.95. The wine list is limited but well priced. Open: Mon-Sat D 6-9pm and Sun L 11.30-3.30pm. A la carte. House wines £9.95. **Directions:** Off Strand Road

Londonderry

HOTEL

Tower Hotel Derry

Off The Diamond Londonderry Co Londonderry BT48 6HL
Tel: 028 7137 1000 Fax: 028 7137 1234
Email: reservations@thd.ie Web: wwwtowerhotelderry.com

This attractive new hotel has the distinction of being the only one to have been built inside the city walls and, while this does have its disadvantages (the constraints of the site restricted the amount of parking provided, for example), these are offset by wonderful views over the river and a real sense of being at the real heart of the city. Accommodation and facilities have obvious appeal for both leisure and business visitors - the style throughout is bright and sassy, and rooms are pleasingly decorated, with all the necessary modern facilities, including phones/ISDN, hospitality trays, TV, trouser press etc. (also a safe in suites). There is a fitness suite with gym and sauna - and a great view. An attractive bistro restaurant off the lobby has the potential to appeal to non-residents as well as hotel guests. Conference/banqueting 250/180). **Rooms 93** (3 suites, 4 disabled). Lift. Room service (limited hours). Children welcome (cot available without charge). B&B about £30pps, ss about £20. Closed 24-27 Dec. Amex, Diners, MasterCard, Visa, Laser. **Directions:** City centre - old town. ◇

Portstewart

GUESTHOUSE / RESTAURANT

Cromore Halt Inn

158 Station Road Portstewart Co Londonderry BT55 7PU
Tel: 028 7083 6888 Fax: 028 7083 1910
Email: info@cromore.com Web: www.cromore.com

This friendly, family-owned guesthouse and restaurant has been managed by Niall O'Boyle and his wife Kate since it opened in 1994 and it feels like a small hotel. It would make an equally good base for a business or leisure visit as the rooms are furnished to hotel standard in an uncluttered modern style and have all the expected facilities, including satellite television, direct dial phone with computer line, tea & coffee making, trouser press, keycard & safety deposit box - and there's a quiet first floor residents' lounge. The restaurant, in a large, pleasant room furnished in a relaxed informal style, is open for lunch and dinner every day, and has earned a great reputation in the locality for quality, value and good service. Conference/banqueting (80); secretarial service. **Rooms 12** (all en-suite & no smoking, 1 disabled). Lift. Children welcome; cot available free of charge. B&B £35. ss £5. Closed 24-26 Dec. MasterCard, Visa, Switch. **Directions:** From Coleraine direction, follow signs for Portstewart. Take B185, Cromore Halt on left as you enter Portstewart.

Portstewart

RESTAURANT

Smyths Restaurant

2 - 4 Lever Road Portstewart Co Londonderry BT55 7EF
Tel: 028 7083 3564 Fax: 028 7083 5551
Email: smithsrestaurant@utvinternet.com

Alison and Robert Smyth's smart little restaurant is on the ground floor and, up a steep staircase that is a reminder of the home it once was, has a pleasant bar and bistro overlooking The Diamond, used for daytime meals and some evenings (there's live music here two nights a week). The arrival of the talented and energetic team at Smyth's has proved a great asset to the area - chefs Alison Smyth and Brian McGuinness direct the kitchen, offering a range of menus tailored to different times of day and days of the week: a shortish 'brasserie menu' suggests lots of delicious dishes for lunch or informal evening meals and more extensive evening menus share the same characteristics: sound flavour combinations are used in colourful, clear-flavoured seasonal food which is attractively presented without gimmicks; vegetarian dishes are imaginative (as in roasted vegetable tarte tatin with a pesto sauce) but creative use of vegetables is an integral part of most dishes (as in pork medallions with braised fennel, caramelised apple ring & baked beetroot, for example). Gorgeous puds too (poached peaches in white wine syrup with panna cotta, perhaps) or Irish farmhouse cheeses to finish. Special evenings are often held (e.g. an Italian night, or an Irish/French one for the Beaujolais Nouveau). All this and good service too. **Seats 40** (private room, 20). No smoking area. Music in bar 2 nights a week (traditional/acoustic sets) while a new entertainment is acoustic jazz after dinner on Thursdays. L Tue-Sun, 12-3, (bar snacks 3-5.30) Set L £14; D Tue-Sun, 5.30-10 (Sun to 8.30), Set D £14-17 Sun only, otherwise à la carte. House wine £8.99. Closed all Mon (except some bank hols), 25-26 Dec, 1 Jan. MasterCard, Visa, Switch. **Directions:** At the Diamond, opposite Agherton Church.

Upperlands

COUNTRY HOUSE

Ardtara Country House

8 Gorteade Road Upperlands
Maghera Co Londonderry BT46 5SA
Tel: 028 7964 4490 Fax: 028 7964 5080
Email: valerie_ferson@ardtara.com Web: www.ardtara.com

Former home to the Clark linen milling family, Ardtara is now an attractive, elegantly decorated Victorian country house with a genuinely hospitable atmosphere. Well-proportioned rooms have antique furnishings and fresh flowers. All the large, luxuriously furnished bedrooms enjoy views of the garden and surrounding countryside and have king size beds and original fireplaces, while bathrooms combine practicality with period details, some including free-standing baths and fireplaces. Breakfast is a high point, so allow time to enjoy it. Tennis, woodland walk, golf practice tee. No pets. Conferences/Banqueting (40/50). Rooms 8 (3 suites) B&B about £75pps, no ss.

Restaurant: In a dining room converted from its previous use as a snooker room – still with full Victorian skylight and original hunting frieze – the philosophy of head chef Martin Nelson is to use seasonal and local ingredients and offer a balanced choice on the menus, with game well represented in season. **Seats 35** (private room, 10). No smoking restaurant. D daily in summer(Tue-Sun off season),7-9 (Sun 6-8). L Sun only, 12.30-2.30. Set Sun L £14.50. Set D £25. House wines from £11.15. Ring to check opening times off-season; closed 25-26 Dec. Amex, MasterCard, Visa, Laser, Switch. **Directions:** M2 from from Belfast to A6. A29 to Maghera. B75 to Kilrea.

COUNTY TYRONE

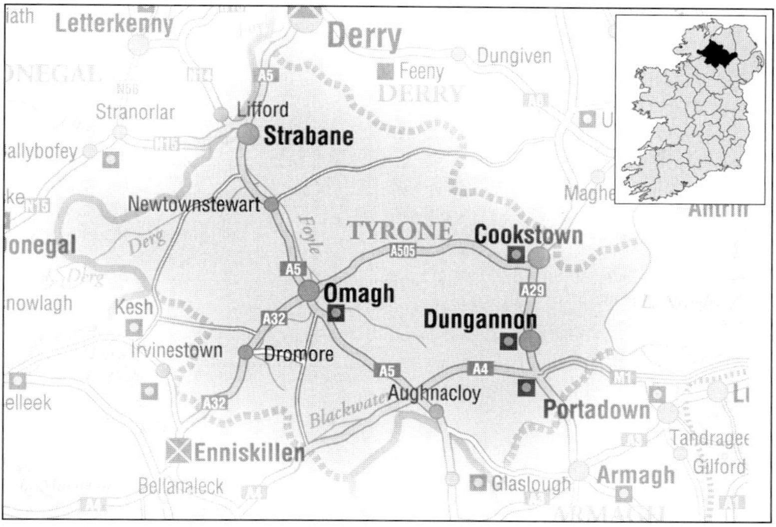

In Ireland, history is everywhere, and the timescales can stretch to infinity. But even so, 99 years can seem a very long time to be in unsuccessful pursuit of a sporting trophy. Yet this had been Tyrone's experience with the Sam Maguire Cup, the coveted trophy for the All-Ireland Gaelic Football Championship. The long quest finally ended on September 28th 2003 in the spectacular setting of Croke Park stadium in Dublin, when Tyrone defeated neighbours Armagh in a hard-fought final.

People in Ireland identify strongly with their counties. This is as it should be. The county boundaries may have evolved in many ways over a very long period, often in obscure ways. But in the 21st Century, Irish counties – for all that they vary enormously in size – seem to provide their people with a sense of place and pride which survives modern efforts to create newer administrative structures.

Tyrone is not Ireland's most glamorous county in terms of scenery, location or climate. But this Guide goes to press at the end of September 2003 with all of Ireland enthralled by the story of Tyrone's great victory, and enthused by the thought of what it will do for the spirit of a place which has been downtrodden by history. Tyrone will enjoy a new confidence, which will in turn invigorate its hospitality industry.

Tyrone is Northern Ireland's largest county, so it is something of a surprise for the traveller to discover that its geography appears to be dominated by a range of mountains of modest height, and nearly half of these peaks seem to be in the neighbouring county of Londonderry.

Yet such is the case with Tyrone and the Sperrins. The village of Sperrin itself towards the head of Glenelly may be in Tyrone, but the highest peak of Sawel (678 m), which looms over it, is actually right on the county boundary. But much of the county is upland territory and moorland, giving the impression that the Sperrins are even more extensive than is really the case.

In such a land, the lower country and the fertile valleys gleam like jewels, and there's often a vivid impression of a living - and indeed prosperity - being wrested from a demanding environment. It's a character-forming sort of place, so it's perhaps understandable that it was the ancestral homeland of a remarkable number of early American Presidents, and this connection is commemorated in the Ulster American Folk Park a few miles north of the county town of Omagh.

Forest parks abound, while attractive towns like Castlederg and Dungannon, as well as villages in the uplands and along the charming Clogher Valley, provide entertainment and hospitality for visitors refreshed by the wide open spaces of the moorlands and the mountains.

Local Attractions and Information

Ardboe, Kinturk (Lough Neagh) Cultural Centre 028 86 736512
Benburb, Benburb Castle and Valley Park 028 37 548241
Castlederg, Visitor Centre (Davy Crockett links) 028 81 670795
Clogher, Clogher Valley Rural Centre 028 85 548872

Coagh, Kinturk Cultural Centre 028 86 736512
Cookstown, Drum Manor Forest Park 028 86 762774
Cookstown, Wellbrook Beetling Mill (Corkhill) 028 86 748210
Cranagh (Glenelly), Sperrin Heritage Centre 028 81 648142
Creggan (nr Carrickmore), Visitor Centre 028 80 761112
Dungannon, Heritage Centre 028 87 724187
Dungannon, Tourism Information 028 87 767259
Dungannon, Tyrone Crystal 028 87 725335
Dungannon, Ulysses S Grant Ancestral Homestead 028 85 557133
Fivemiletown, Clogher Valley Railway Exhibition 028 89 521409
Gortin, Ulster History Park 028 81 648188
Newtownstewart, Baronscourt Forest Park 028 81 661683
Newtownstewart, Gateway Centre & Museum 028 81 662414
Omagh, Ulster-American Folk Park 028 82 243292
Omagh, Tourism Information 028 82 247831
Strabane, Gray's Printing Press (US Independence) 028 71 884094
Strabane, Tourism Information 028 71 883735
Strabane, President Wilson Ancestral Home 028 71 3844

Dungannon

COUNTRY HOUSE

Grange Lodge

7 Grange Road Dungannon Co Tyrone BT71 7EJ
Tel: 028 8778 4212 Fax: 028 8778 4313
Email: grangelodge@nireland.com

Norah and Ralph Brown's renowned Georgian retreat offers comfort, true family hospitality and extremely good food. The house is on an elevated site just outside Dungannon, with about 20 acres of grounds; mature woodland and gardens (producing food for the table and flowers for the house) with views over lush countryside. Improvements over the years have been made with great sensitivity and the feeling is of gentle organic growth, culminating in the present warm and welcoming atmosphere. Grange Lodge is furnished unselfconsciously, with antiques and family pieces throughout. Bedrooms (and bathrooms) are exceptionally comfortable and thoughtful in detail. Norah's home cooking is superb and, although they no longer accept bookings from non-residents for dinner, they will cater for groups of 10-30. Grange Lodge is fully licensed and dinner menus change daily (in consultation with guests). Resident dinner (from £24) must be pre-booked, especially if you want to dine on the day of arrival. Breakfasts are also outstanding, so allow time to indulge: a sumptuous buffet beautifully set out on a polished dining table might typically include a large selection of juices, fruit and cereals and porridge is a speciality, served with a tot of Bushmills whiskey, brown sugar and cream - and that's before you've even reached the cooked breakfast menu, served with lovely fresh breads and toast and home-made preserves. Conferences/banqueting (30) Fishing, walking, garden, snooker. Not suitable for children under-12. Pets allowed in some areas. **Rooms 5** (3 shower only, all no smoking) B&B £39 pps, ss £16. Room service (limited hours) Closed Christmas. MasterCard, Visa. **Directions:** 1 mile from M1 junction 15. A29 Armagh, follow "Grange Lodge" signs.

Moygashel

CAFÉ

The Loft @ The Linen Green

Moygashel Co Tyrone BT71 7HB **Tel: 028 8775 3761**

A long space with high ceilings, attractive windows and painted metal beams - all vaguely reminiscent of an industrial past - with a gallery area overlooking the gift shop below, this is a good place to have a bite when shopping, or to break a journey. Good baking - fresh scones, tray bakes - salads (curried chicken, sweetcorn, tomatoes), sandwiches and desserts like lemon meringue pie and apple tart. Cosmopolitan paninis too and a good selection of hot drinks. Open Mon-Sat, 10am-5pm.

Omagh

GUESTHOUSE / RESTAURANT / BAR

Hawthorn House

72 Old Mountfield Road Omagh Co Tyrone BT79 7JX
Tel: 028 8225 2005 Fax: 028 8225 2005
Email: information@hawthornhouse.co.uk Web: www.hawthornhouse.co.uk

On the edge of the town, in a lovely part of the country at the foot of the Sperrin Mountains, Hawthorn House is run by owner-chef Michael Gaine - who is from Kenmare, Co. Kerry and has many years in the hotel industry under his belt - and his wife, Mary. Public areas, which include a small bar, are furnished to a high standard and bedrooms are large and comfortable, with all the usual amenities; further bedrooms, a bistro bar and conference facilities were under construction at the time of the Guide's most recent visit and are due for completion for the 2004 season. The restaurant, which is open for both lunch and dinner every day, has earned a reputation for fine contemporary cooking, although there has been a change of style since it was extended in 2002 and a carvery lunch has been introduced. Conference/banqueting (40/100). Garden, walking. Children welcome (under 6s free in parents' room; cots available without charge). Special breaks offered. No Pets. **Rooms 5** (1 shower only). B&B £30pps, ss £10. Restaurant **seats 140** (private room, 60). L 12-2.30 daily, D 7-9.30 daily. Open all year. Amex, MasterCard, Visa, Switch. **Directions:** 5 minutes from Omagh Town Centre.